THE TRANSFER OF POWER
1942-47

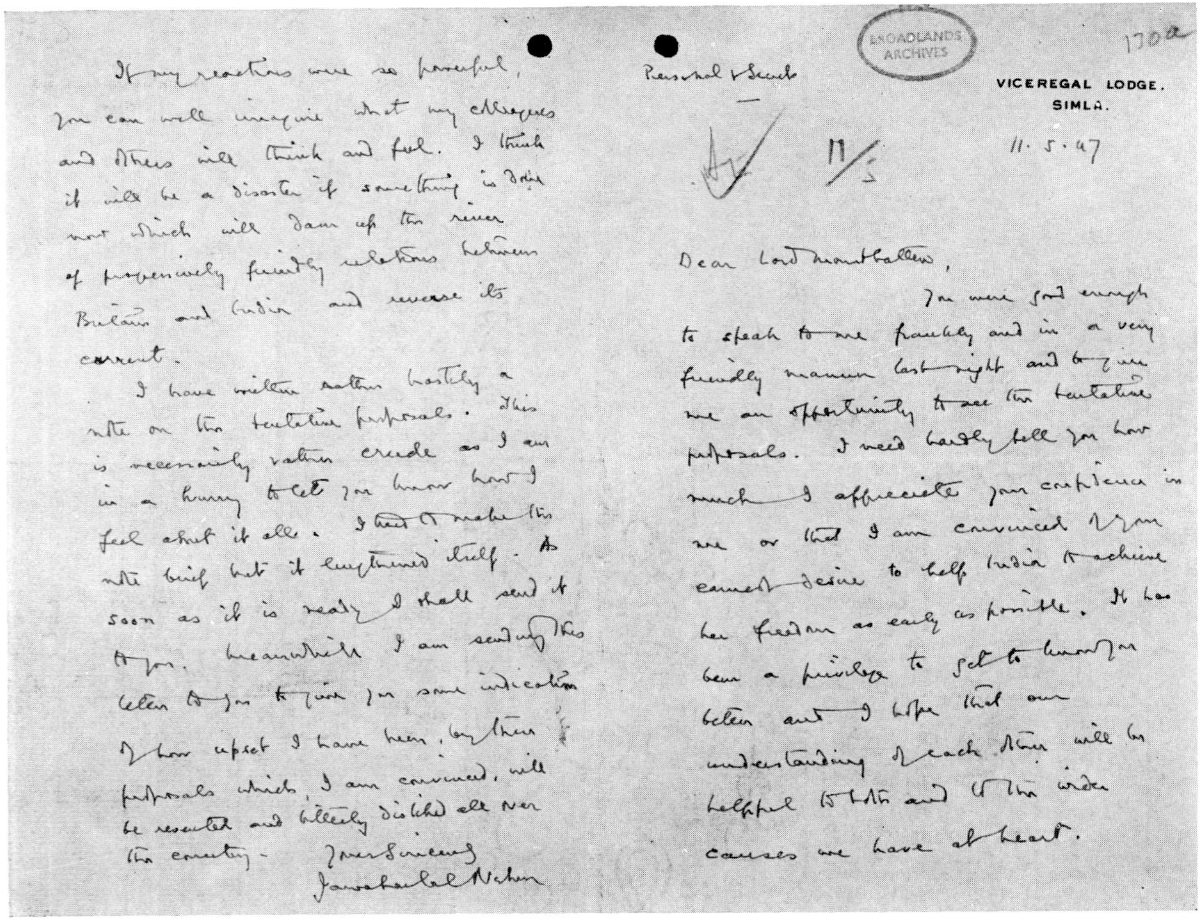
170a

BROADLANDS ARCHIVES

Personal & Secret

VICEREGAL LODGE.
SIMLA.

11.5.47

Dear Lord Mountbatten,

You were good enough to speak to me frankly and in a very friendly manner last night and to give me an opportunity to see the tentative proposals. I need hardly tell you how much I appreciate your confidence in me or that I am convinced of your earnest desire to help India to achieve her freedom as early as possible. It has been a privilege to get to know you better and I hope that our understanding of each other will be helpful to both and to the wider causes we have at heart.

If my reactions were so powerful, you can well imagine what my colleagues and others will think and feel. I think it will be a disaster if something is done now which will dam up the river of progressively friendly relations between Britain and India and reverse its current.

I have written rather hastily a note on the tentative proposals. This is necessarily rather crude as I am in a hurry to let you know how I feel about it all. I tried to make this note brief but it lengthened itself. As soon as it is ready I shall send it to you. Meanwhile I am sending this letter to you to give you some indication of how upset I have been by these proposals which, I am convinced, will be resented and bitterly disliked all over the country.

Yours sincerely
Jawaharlal Nehru

Pandit Nehru to Lord Mountbatten. Facsimile of the first and last pages of his letter of 11 May 1947. Document 402.

CONSTITUTIONAL RELATIONS
BETWEEN BRITAIN AND INDIA

THE TRANSFER OF POWER
1942-47

Volume X The Mountbatten Viceroyalty
Formulation of a Plan
22 March—30 May 1947

Editor-in-Chief
NICHOLAS MANSERGH, Litt.D., F.B.A.
Fellow of St. John's College, Cambridge

Editor
PENDEREL MOON, M.A.

Assisted by
DAVID M. BLAKE, M.A., M.Litt. *and* LIONEL CARTER, M.Sc., Ph.D.

LONDON
HER MAJESTY'S STATIONERY OFFICE

© Crown Copyright 1981
First published 1981

ISBN 0 11 580085 9*

Printed in England for Her Majesty's Stationery Office
by Eyre & Spottiswoode Ltd, Thanet Press, Margate, Kent

CONTENTS

ILLUSTRATIONS

Frontispiece
Pandit Nehru to Lord Mountbatten. Facsimile of the first and last pages of his letter of 11 May 1947. Document 402. (*Trustees of the Broadlands Archives Settlement*)

Between pages 546 and 547
The Swearing-in Ceremony, 24 March 1947. (*Photo Division, Ministry of Information and Broadcasting, Government of India*)

Mr Gandhi and Lord Mountbatten, 1 April 1947. (*Rear-Admiral P.N. Howes*)

Mr Jinnah with Lord and Lady Mountbatten on his arrival for his first interview with the Viceroy, 5 April 1947. (*Photo Division, Ministry of Information and Broadcasting, Government of India*)

The *jirga* at Landi Kotal, 29 April 1947. (*Times Newspapers Ltd*)

CONTENTS

ILLUSTRATIONS

Foreword

On 9 March 1966 the Prime Minister, Mr Harold Wilson, announced in the House of Commons that the closed period for official records was to be reduced from fifty to thirty years. He stated that the Government also proposed that the range of Official Histories, which had hitherto been confined to the two great wars, should be extended to include selected periods or episodes of peacetime history and considered that there was scope for extending to other Oversea Departments the Foreign Office practice of publishing selected documents relating to external relations. The Prime Minister hoped that both of these subsidiary proposals, supplementing the reduction in the closed period to thirty years, would be acceptable in principle to the Opposition parties, who would be associated with their implementation.[1]

On 10 August 1966 the Prime Minister announced that a standing inter-party group of Privy Counsellors was to be appointed to consider all such proposals[2] and on 8 June 1967 that its members were, for the Government and to act as Chairman, the Right Hon. Patrick Gordon Walker, Minister without Portfolio; for the Official Opposition, the Right Hon. Sir Alec Douglas-Home; and for the Liberal Party, Lord Ogmore.[3]

A project to publish documents from the India Office Records had been under discussion for some years and on 30 June 1967 the Prime Minister, in replying to a written question in the House of Commons, announced that the first of the new series of selected documents to be published was to relate to the Transfer of Power in India. His statement was as follows:

As I informed the House on the 9th of March 1966, the Government have decided to extend to other Oversea Departments the Foreign Office practice of publishing selected documents concerned with our external relations, subject to inter-party agreement through the Group of Privy Counsellors whose composition I announced on the 8th of June. I am happy to inform the House that the Group have agreed that in view of the great interest now being shown in historical circles in the last days of British rule in India the first selection of documents to be published under the new arrangements should be documents from the India Office records on the Transfer of Power and the events leading up to it.

The scheme will follow closely the lines of the Foreign Office series of *Documents on British Foreign Policy* from 1919 to 1939, and, as in that series, the editors will be independent historians who will be given unrestricted access to the records and freedom to select and edit documents for publication. Professor P. N. S. Mansergh, Smuts Professor of the History of the British Commonwealth at Cambridge, has expressed willingness to accept

---

[1] *Parl. Debs.*, 5th ser., H. of C., vol. 725, Written Answers to Questions, cols. 561–3.
[2] *Ibid*, vol. 733, cols. 1706–7.   [3] *Ibid.*, vol. 747, col. 1291.

appointment as Editor-in-Chief, and the scheme will be in full operation by the end of the year.[4]

Mr E. W. R. Lumby was appointed Assistant Editor and fulfilled the duties of that office until his death on 23 January 1972, by which time the first three volumes in the Series had been published and the fourth was in an advanced stage of preparation.

Sir Penderel Moon, O.B.E., sometime Fellow of All Souls College, Oxford, was appointed Assistant Editor in September 1972 when Volume IV was about to go to press and the editing of Volume V to begin.

Mr D. M. Blake, who joined the Historical Section in March 1968, and Dr L. J. Carter, who came in August 1970, have assisted since appointment in the assembly, selection, preparation and indexing of documents for publication.

The Editors would like to record their thanks to Miss Lois Atkin who has undertaken the typing necessary for the production of the Volume.

The series will cover the period 1 January 1942 to 15 August 1947. The Volumes so far published with their subtitles and dates of publication are as follows:

Volume I	The Cripps Mission January–April 1942	(1970)
Volume II	'Quit India' 30 April–21 September 1942	(1971)
Volume III	Reassertion of authority, Gandhi's fast and the succession to the Viceroyalty 21 September 1942–12 June 1943	(1971)
Volume IV	The Bengal Famine and the New Viceroyalty 15 June 1943–31 August 1944	(1973)
Volume V	The Simla Conference: Background and Proceedings 1 September 1944–28 July 1945	(1975)
Volume VI	The post-war phase: new moves by the Labour Government 1 August 1945–22 March 1946	(1976)
Volume VII	The Cabinet Mission 23 March–29 June 1946	(1977)
Volume VIII	The Interim Government 3 July–1 November 1946	(1979)
Volume IX	The fixing of a time limit 4 November 1946–22 March 1947	(1980)

The principles of selection, the arrangement of documents—which is in chronological order throughout in so far as that has been ascertainable—together with other details of presentation were explained in the Foreword to the first Volume (pp. vi-x) with some further comments on particular points added in the Foreword to Volume III (pp. viii-xii). There is no need, therefore, to recapitulate what has been written on these matters here. It may, however, be worth while restating the purpose of the Series. It is to make

---

[4] *Parl Debs.*, 5th ser., H. of C., vol. 749, Written Answers to Questions, cols. 147–8.

available to scholars in convenient printed form the more important British historical records relating to the Transfer of Power in India.

N. MANSERGH

Historical Section
India Office Records
February 1980

Introduction to Volume X

'This is not a normal Viceroyalty on which I am embarking', commented Lord Mountbatten in an address, itself a departure from precedent, at his swearing-in ceremony in New Delhi on 24 March [No. 8; see also No. 26]. It was not normal because the Viceroyalty was to be the last, the incoming Viceroy being specifically charged with responsibility for transferring power into Indian hands by June 1948 in accordance with the terms of H.M.G.'s statement of 20 February 1947 [Vol. IX, No. 438] and of the directive in letter-form which had been sent to him on 18 March [Vol. IX, Enclosure to No. 543]. Furthermore because of the new constitutional arrangements that would need to be made and the many complex questions of administration that would need to be resolved before such transfer could be effected a solution of the fundamental issue, unity or division, in the Viceroy's view 'must be reached within the next few months'. The fixing of a time-table had thus introduced, as Cabinet and Viceroy intended, its own imperative. The more closely the implications of that imperative were studied the greater appeared to be the urgency, both in London and in Delhi, on administrative, legislative and political grounds, for decisions on substantive issues, the Secretary of State pointing out on 27 March that the date of 1 October 1947 (to which the Prime Minister had alluded as that by which the Viceroy should report to H.M.G. on the steps to be taken for the transfer of power if it proved impossible to proceed on a unitary basis) might not allow of sufficient time for the preparation of the necessary legislation to be put through Parliament [No. 26], while at a Staff Meeting in New Delhi on 29 March the Viceroy emphasised that the psychological effect of coming to the right decision very quickly would be great, including the possibility of establishing some form of dominion status for India 'which could run experimentally until June 1948' [Addendum to No. 33].

The Viceroy's sense of the importance of the time-table in association with mounting Indian, and more especially Congress, pressure for an early transfer introduced a new momentum, the outcome of which was the effecting of transfer in August 1947, some ten months before the scheduled June 1948 date. Yet though so much was thus compressed in so short a time, there would seem to have been no consequential loss in the fullness of the documentary record as this and the two succeeding volumes when published may be thought to testify: indeed, if anything, rather the contrary. But there were departures in administrative arrangements and procedures, some arising generally from the nature of the Viceroyalty and personality of the Viceroy, others more particularly from the staffing and other arrangements, devised to provide the resources thought needful for the quick and effective discharge of the Viceroy's task. It may be helpful to mention these since by necessary consequence they were reflected in the documentary record and awareness of them enables one the more easily to follow the sequence of events in a complex and crowded narrative.

The Prime Minister had told Lord Mountbatten that he could count on his assistance in getting what staff he might need and in February Lord Mountbatten made his principal recommendations. They were that General Ismay should be appointed 'Chief of the Viceroy's Staff' with the duties of a *Chef de Cabinet* and Sir Eric Mieville 'Principal Secretary', Mr George Abell remaining in the traditional office of Private Secretary to the Viceroy and Captain Brockman RN coming out as Deputy Private Secretary[1] [Vol. IX, No. 377]. All these appointments were duly made. In addition Alan Campbell-Johnson joined the staff as Press Attaché—an appointment that was in itself an innovation and afforded evidence of Lord Mountbatten's concern to establish good relations with the Press and, through the Press, to reach out to a wider public [cf. Nos. 20, 33, 34]. Three Indian *Aides de Camp* were attached to the Viceroy and the Viceroy invited the co-operation of the Governors in the sharpest possible discouragement of any expression of anti-Indian bias or prejudice [Nos. 24 and 165, para. 36]. The Viceroy himself took advantage of the 'happy coincidence' of 'the great Asian Relations Conference' with his arrival in Delhi to hold a reception for Conference delegates, the great majority of Indian guests at which had apparently never before received an invitation to the Viceroy's House [No. 59; see also No. 33 and Vol. IX, No. 515].

Overall the expanded Viceregal staff by bringing about, as it did, a widening of the range of activity in the Viceregal office and of contacts between members of the staff and the Indian leadership correspondingly added to the number and variety of the sources of historical material deserving of study. This came about in a number of ways. The Viceroy would have an interview with one of the Indian political leaders or a Provincial Premier but when this was concluded the exchange of views might be continued, frequently in more detail, by Lord Ismay. An interesting example of phase two of this procedure is to be found in Gandhi's protracted exchanges with Ismay on the detail of Gandhi's plan, already outlined to the Viceroy, which led on to unusual complexities [Nos. 73, 83, 85, 86 and 88]. Generally a record of both the Viceroy's and Lord Ismay's interview appears to have been made and in the present volumes the note of the first interview is almost always included while that of the follow-up talk is included according to the Editors' assessment of its intrinsic interest or importance. A variant of such procedure may be seen when Lord Ismay, Sir Eric Mieville, Mr Abell or Mr Christie visited provinces or persons to follow up enquiries or to elicit further views, e.g. Nos. 108, para. 3 and 242.

Altogether more important was the despatch of Ismay, with Abell, to

---

[1] In the event Captain Brockman was given the title 'Personal Secretary' as Mr I. D. Scott continued as Deputy Private Secretary to the Viceroy.

London on 2 May, Ismay acting both as spokesman for the Viceroy and pur-veyor to the Viceroy of the views of the Secretary of State or of the India and Burma Committee of the Cabinet, meetings of which Ismay and Abell were invited to attend [e.g. Nos. 320, 341, 355]. There was a period before Lord Mountbatten joined them in London on 19 May in which this role was central to the London–Delhi consultative process [cf. Nos. 137, 223, 312, 317, 320, 323, 327] no fewer than ten telegrams passing between them on 10 May. When later on the Viceroy was in London the rôle was filled in reverse by Sir Eric Mieville who remained in Delhi and served as a link with the Indian leaders [cf. Nos. 489, 490, 492, 497]. Exchanges between them were also on a very considerable scale.

Two other innovations deserve mention. On 25 March the Viceroy held the first [No. 14] of a series of Staff Meetings with the second, third and fourth [Nos. 20, 24, 29] following on succeeding days. Such meetings continued down to the actual transfer of power and thirty-three had taken place by 18 May when the Viceroy's departure for London occasioned a temporary interlude. At the Meetings the Viceroy might consider memoranda in a special Viceroy's Conference Paper series, report on discussions he had had, outline still tentative political moves, seek to elicit comment upon them or give instructions on enquiries to be made or action to be taken. The records of those meetings are reprinted selectively, principally because a number of the items, e.g. reports on discussions or outlines of policy, may already have been more fully recorded or expounded. Additionally there were meetings to which Lord Mountbatten invited selected members of his staff, political leaders, Governors and others. Some were clearly of great moment, two on 11 May, at which Nehru was present and outlined his objections to the draft proposals the Viceroy had shown him the evening before, outstandingly so [Nos. 404 and 405]. Such gatherings were recorded under the heading 'Miscellaneous Meetings'; good examples of the range of subjects considered at them being recorded in Nos. 162, 194 and 203. Fifteen were held before the Viceroy's departure for London.

Distinctive in character but more familar in style are the Personal Reports which, following upon an expression of interest by the King-Emperor, the Viceroy decided to send weekly for circulation to the King, the Prime Minister, the Secretary of State, Cripps and Alexander, the last two in their capacity as former Members of the Cabinet Mission [No. 58]. Later the circulation was widened to include all members of the India and Burma Committee [Nos. 210 and 220]. The first such Report was dated 2 April [No. 59] and others followed at weekly intervals except when the Viceroy was in London. The traditional channels of communication, including the exchange of weekly letters between the Secretary of State and the Viceroy, as also the fortnightly letters of Governors to the Viceroy, continued but more momentous matters tended increasingly to be dealt with in the Viceroy's Personal Reports or, as between Viceroy and the Governors, especially of key Provinces, directly as they arose and claimed attention.

The early developments in the Viceroyalty may be viewed in the perspective of the letter already alluded to sent to Lord Mountbatten by the Prime Minister on 18 March [Vol. IX, Enclosure to No. 543] setting out the views of the Cabinet on the policy which the Viceroy should pursue. That letter, which served by way of directive (the reasons for proceeding by this means were explained to the Governors at a Conference on 15 April [No. 147]) recorded that it was the definite objective of H.M.G. to obtain a unitary government for British India and the Indian States, if possible within the Commonwealth, through the medium of a Constituent Assembly set up in accordance with the Cabinet Mission Plan. Since, however, there was no question of compulsion on parties or States, the Viceroy was further advised that, should he conclude that there was no prospect of reaching a unitary government for British India, either with or without the States, he was, as already mentioned, to report by 1 October 1947 on the steps he thought should be taken for the handing over of power by June 1948, it being essential that there should be the fullest co-operation with the Indian leaders in all steps taken as to the withdrawal of British power, such cooperation being envisaged as the keynote of the administration. None the less, whereas the Cabinet Mission had been sent out to secure Indian agreement on how power might be transferred, Lord Mountbatten was commissioned to form his own conclusions and report. The difference was vital, Lord Mountbatten himself remarking on 28 March that he did not believe the Indian political leaders yet realised the extent of his powers [No. 29].

Lord Mountbatten lost no time in having a series of meetings with Indian leaders at which he sought to get to know them and to elicit their views on major issues. The records of them constitute one of the more remarkable examples in modern times of history in the making, conveying, as they do, something of the immediacy of moments when the fulfilment of purpose was conditioned by the resolution of complex problems and over-shadowed by uncertain and dangerous prospects, civil war, to which there were not infrequent allusions, the most menacing among them.

The meetings began on 24 March, the day of the swearing-in, when the Viceroy saw the Nawab of Bhopal, Chancellor of the Chamber of Princes for $1\frac{1}{4}$ hours, the Maharaja of Bikaner, Liaquat Ali Khan, Pandit Nehru, who 'struck me as most sincere', and to the last two he spoke of his intention to approach the discharge of his 'appalling responsibility ... in an atmosphere of stark realism' [Nos. 9, 10, 11, 12]. On the next day, as already noted in another context, the Viceroy held the first of his Staff Meetings at which he reported *inter alia* on Nehru's views on the possible partition of the Punjab [No. 14]. Later that day the Viceroy resumed his soundings of Indian leaders seeing first Dr Matthai and then Sardar Patel [Nos. 15 and 16]. On succeeding days there were further Staff Meetings, at the fourth of which on 28 March the Viceroy indicated that he had it in mind to invite certain important Indian leaders including Gandhi, Jinnah, Nehru and Liaquat and Patel to stay with him at Simla at an appropriate time probably late April [No. 29], and at the sixth of which on 31 March, the Viceroy outlined in strictest confidence a veiled partition plan for the interim period but for possible application only should the Cabinet Mission proposals appear finally unacceptable [Addendum to No. 34]. But in his discussions unity or some form of union on the lines of the Cabinet Mission Plan was set out as the first aim and desired goal.

Interviews with Dr Rajendra Prasad and Maulana Azad [Nos. 22 and 27] on 26 and 27 March were followed between 31 March and 4 April by five meetings with Mahatma Gandhi [Nos. 37, 47, 53, 66 and 73] of much human as well as political interest. At the second of them Gandhi, to the astonishment of the Viceroy, proposed that Jinnah be invited forthwith to form the Central Interim Government—a proposal which Mountbatten noted later in the day, after discussion with Nehru, was 'even less realistic' than when Gandhi had laid it before the Cabinet Mission [No. 48; see also No. 55]. At the fourth meeting on 3 April, Gandhi allowed that if the Muslim League were completely intransigent partition might have to come [No. 66]. On 5–6–7 April came the first three interviews with Jinnah [see Nos. 84 and 92] the tenor of which became widely known but a full account of which has not hitherto been published. No little forethought had been given to them by the Viceroy and his staff [Nos. 64 and 76]. Jinnah claimed, as Bhopal had forecast, there was no chance of union and only one solution—'a "surgical operation" on India, otherwise India would perish altogether' [No. 84, see also No. 28], the Viceroy responding with the observation first that he had not made up his mind and second that an "anaesthetic" should precede any surgical operation. At a Staff Meeting on the morning of 7 April, following his first two meetings with Jinnah, the Viceroy said he felt certain that the only way to obtain Jinnah's cooperation would be to tell him that the British accepted Pakistan as the ultimate goal from the Muslim point of view but that he did not intend to create chaos by turning it over to him 'more quickly than was possible', hoping that in the meantime he would be able to strengthen the centre by including Jinnah in the Government with a truncated Pakistan as an ultimate aim. But in this, as in other, cases, it was his intention to tell the Indian leaders of his decision but not in the meanwhile abandon his strong position deriving from the fact that he alone could make it [No. 87]. At the meeting with the Viceroy later that day Jinnah, insistent that no compromise plan could work, called for the handing over of power, preferably province by province [No. 92]. He had, he said, come to the conclusion also that the Defence forces must be separated since that was the only basis on which it would be possible to have any form of central organisation on terms of parity, on which the Viceroy commented that in discussing these proposals he was 'very far from agreeing' with Jinnah.

There followed further meetings of much historical interest between the Viceroy and Nehru on 8 April [No. 96] and the Viceroy and Jinnah on 8 and 9 April [Nos. 101 and 105], the Viceroy explaining to the two leaders that he was still gathering background information and that he was going to make his recommendation to H.M.G. without necessarily obtaining the agreement of the Indian parties but after hearing their views. He invited Nehru and Jinnah separately to indicate what his solution would be. Nehru responded that if power were to be demitted Province by Province, each should be free to decide whether to join a Hindustan Group or a Pakistan Group or possibly remain independent. Before that happened the Punjab and Bengal would have to be divided whilst a fresh election would be needed to obtain the real views of the people of the N.W.F.P. A strong centre would be essential, certainly to begin with [No. 96]. Jinnah's answer to the Viceroy's question was that as the Cabinet Mission's Plan was beyond possibility of resurrection, Pakistan, with the splitting of the Defence Forces, was an essential basis for any plan. After he had heard Jinnah's arguments for Pakistan, the Viceroy pointed out that they applied 'also to the partition of the Punjab and Bengal, and that by sheer logic if I accepted his arguments in the case of India as a whole, I had also to apply them in the case of these two Provinces . . . he expressed himself most upset at my trying to give him a "moth-eaten" Pakistan'. But the Viceroy was insistent that if the whole were to be partitioned there would be no alternative to a consequential partition of these two communally divided provinces [No. 101]. In a letter on 9 April to Liaquat on the Armed Forces the Viceroy recorded that the Cabinet Mission's Plan still held the field and that so long as Parliament remained responsible, the Indian Army could not be divided [No. 106, for Liaquat's views see Nos. 94 and 135].

The Viceroy's meetings with Jinnah may be thought to mark the end of a phase in which a principal preoccupation was the eliciting of the views of the political leaders of British India and the Princely States. During that phase the ordinary responsibilities of government and law and order continued, the Viceroy at the end of it, 9 April, reporting that 'the whole country continues in a dangerously unsettled state' [No. 108] with the situation in the Punjab [see Nos. 32 and 40] and the N.W.F.P., where over and above local tension there was a demand from the Congress for the removal of the Governor [Nos. 70, 73 and 114], sources of particular concern.

At his meeting with Nehru on 8 April the Viceroy had asked him [No. 96] whether the Congress High Command would be prepared to issue a joint appeal for a truce until the Viceroy had finalised his plan. On receiving an affirmative answer the Viceroy approached Jinnah who also assented [No. 101] but the issue of the appeal was delayed till 15 April because of differences of opinion about who should sign it [Nos. 125, 136, 140, 151 and 152].

There were two particular problems carried over from the previous Vice-royalty to be disposed of. The first was the question of compensation for the members of the Secretary of State's Services, a question complicated by the different interests and prospects of Indian and British members after transfer [see Nehru's comments in No. 18]. However on 14 April, following the Viceroy's strong representations [see Nos. 59 and 118], the Cabinet finally agreed that while compensation should be granted on a scale already proposed to British members, it should not be payable to Indian members 'save in a limited number of cases' [No. 144]. The Governors were later reported as being 'delighted' with the terms of the settlement [No. 165]. The second problem related to the I.N.A. prisoners and acquired renewed urgency by reason of an Assembly motion, due for debate on 3 April, calling for their general release. The situation was reviewed by Pandit Nehru and the Viceroy on 1 April, then considered by the Viceroy with the C.-in-C. [Nos. 48 and 50] before a meeting, the second in the 'Miscellaneous' category, at which Nehru, Liaquat, Baldev Singh and Auchinleck were present [No. 52]. After further deliberation it was agreed that the Government would oppose the request for the prisoners' release but that judges of the Federal Court would review the individual cases and report [see Nos. 60, 61, 62, 63, 69]. The episode, which concluded with withdrawal of the resolution on 3 April [No. 69], provided an instance of concerted action by Viceroy and members of the Interim Government. For the most part, however, despite reported advances in the conduct of business [Nos. 74 and 105], relations between Congress and League members of that Government remained strained to openly antagonistic [cf. Nos. 65 and 95].

The phase of enquiry and elucidation of opinions was followed by one of provisional planning with the Viceroy using Staff Meetings, held on 10, 11 and 12 April, as sounding boards for still tentative ideas. At the first, on 10 April the Viceroy said the cardinal principles of the plan uppermost in his mind were (i) that no mention of Pakistan as such should be made though Jinnah was determined to have it and Congress, Gandhi excepted, prepared to let him, (ii) that there would be demission of power to Provinces who would be free to join together in one or more groups with the States free to join groups if and as they wished, (iii) that the Interim Government would remain in being until at least June 1948, possibly strengthened by adding Mr Jinnah to it, with the Provinces, however, free in the meantime to take over certain subjects, (iv) that the Punjab and Bengal would be partitioned and (v) there would be a general election in the N.W.F.P. Some doubts were expressed in the discussion that followed on the practicability of partial and varied demission of powers to Provinces before the date of final transfer by reason of the constitutional difficulties that would be raised. The Viceroy also reflected upon a possible future Commonwealth rôle indicating his belief that (despite the seemingly insuperable barrier for the Congress of the republican commitment in the Objectives Resolution) the Indian leaders 'would have to ask that India should remain within the British Commonwealth', Nehru himself having given an impression of 'groping for a formula' [No. 110 and see also No. 11]. The Viceroy thought this might be provided on the pretext of 'bowing to the wishes of the majority'—by which allusion was evidently intended to enquiries about the possibility of dominion status for India, or parts of it, which had been made by, among others, the Chancellor of the Chamber of Princes, the Nawab of Bhopal, on behalf of States individually or in groups [No. 9], the Dewan of Travancore through Mieville [No. 6] and Jinnah obliquely through Bhopal [No. 28]. To all these enquiries Mountbatten had responded in terms tersely restated to Liaquat on 11 April when he said he was 'not prepared even to discuss the suggestion of any part of India remaining within the Empire unless the suggestion came from all parties together, and even then I could not say what the policy of H.M.G. would be' [No. 126]. The issue had, however, acquired a particular, over and above its general, interest by reason of the impending nationalisation of the armed forces. On 5 April the C.-in-C. had advised the Viceroy that neither members of the British army nor British officers in the Indian Army could serve in an India outside the Commonwealth without resigning their commissions [No. 80]. Accordingly one consequence of secession appeared to be the withdrawal forthwith of all British personnel from the armed forces—a possibility that was to cause concern not least to the Defence Member, Baldev Singh, who discussed it with the Viceroy on 16 and 22 April [Nos. 161 and 198].

At the second of the three Staff Meetings, held on 11 April, the Viceroy said it had been his desire to hand over power to a unified India with a strong centre, a united India with a weak centre being his second best. But Jinnah was intent on Pakistan and it was clear to him that if any attempt to impose the Cabinet Mission Plan were made the Muslim League would resort to arms [No. 119]. The same day V.P. Menon was directed to put flesh on the draft of a plan, framed on the assumption that it had been impossible to reach agreement on the Cabinet Mission Plan for a unified India [No. 120], which in its skeletal form involved demission of authority to Provinces, the partition of the Punjab, Bengal and Assam together with a general election in the N.W.F.P. [See also No. 125 for Nehru's views on partition of Assam and No. 127 for Burrows' report on gathering strength of the movement to partition Bengal].

At the Staff Meeting on 12 April the Viceroy summarised the position reached in saying that of the many possible plans two were receiving most thought—'Plan "Union"' which was the Cabinet Mission's plan, possibly modified, and 'Plan "Balkan"' which 'contemplated leaving to each Province the choice of its own future and would almost certainly result in a form of truncated Pakistan and the eventual abolition of a Centre' [No. 129].

The next stage was the laying of an outline of a 'programme of action' before the Governors at their conference on 15–16 April. The programme [No. 139] contemplated first a strengthening of the Interim Government by attempting to persuade Jinnah to join it. Secondly, Nehru was to be asked to postpone the session of the Constituent Assembly fixed for late April. As a third step the Indian leaders were to be invited to talks at Simla where a determined effort was to be made to secure compromise on the basis of the Mission's Plan. If these talks failed an announcement of partition would be made on the lines of the plan under consideration and details given of arrangements for ascertaining the wishes of the provinces and for demission of power to them or groups of them. Finally, the 'programme of action' contemplated the maintenance of the existing Central government until June 1948 with an attempt to form coalitions in the provinces. The reactions to this programme by the Governors of Provinces most deeply affected by partition or otherwise are recorded in Nos. 147 and 158. They may usefully be studied with other exchanges of view taking place at that time on the Punjab and the N.W.F.P. in No. 141; on the N.W.F.P. and elections there in Nos. 143, 167 and 171; on the Punjab in No. 156; on Sikh attitudes in No. 173; and on Bengal in Nos. 154 and 163. The last two references bear on the possibility of preserving an autonomous, or quasi-autonomous, united Bengal with No. 174 recording Jinnah's view that coalition government in the Province was premature.

In his third Report dated 17 April the Viceroy wrote that after 'three weeks of incessant talks with all the leaders' he was convinced that 'we have got to make up our minds one way or the other in the very near future if we are to avert civil war'; that he had only 'very slender hopes of getting acceptance of the Cabinet Mission plan'; and that partition 'may prove to be the only possible alternative'. Though a first draft of a plan had been discussed with the Governors he would defer sending it to London 'as it is all so tentative' but he had it in mind that Ismay should take it home with him in person. The Governors, who had expressed unanimous support for the line he had taken with Indian leaders, urged 'the greatest possible speed' in making a decision 'for even the quieter Provinces feel that we are sitting on the edge of a volcano and that an eruption might take place through any of the three main craters— Bengal, Punjab and N.W.F.P.—at any moment'. He also indicated his concern that the Central Government 'should be as strong as possible till we hand over' [No. 165].

On 17 April the Prime Minister sent the Viceroy news of Lord Pethick-Lawrence's impending resignation and the appointment of Lord Listowel as his successor [No. 166].

Arrangements proceeded almost immediately for the projected Simla Conference. There was further consideration of the terms of a draft announcement [Nos. 181 and 214] with a backward glance at a possible intermediate scheme between the Cabinet Mission and Pakistan plans [No. 190] and suggestions of a possible Commonwealth rôle in two talks which the Viceroy had with Krishna Menon on 17 and 22 April [Nos. 169 and 200]. Subsequent to the first of these talks the Viceroy asked that the idea of granting 'some form' of dominion status as early as possible be urgently investigated with a view to keeping India within the British Commonwealth [No. 177] while on 23 April he discussed with Bhabha how the Congress might circumvent the obstacle in the way of their acceptance of Commonwealth Membership [No. 202]. At a staff meeting on 25 April the Viceroy briefed Ismay on this question, further advising him that he should warn the Secretary of State when he reached London that there was 'a move afoot' for an application by Pakistan to remain within the Commonwealth and point out 'the difficulties which would result' [No. 214]. On 25 April Ismay laid before the Viceroy the "V.P. Menon Plan" an essential feature of which was a transfer of power on the basis of a dominion constitution which, *inter alia*, would have the advantage of making an earlier transfer possible [No. 222]. On 1 May a Conference Paper was circulated proposing for consideration a method of transferring power to successor authorities which would result in a dominion status form of transitional government, it being noted that this would be in accord with expressed wishes of the Congress as regards the transitional period [see Vol. IX, No. 511, Enclosure, Item 1, para. 2] and not inconsistent with the desire of the League that Pakistan should remain a part of the Commonwealth [No. 273; see No. 272 for Staff Meeting discussion on a related aspect of the dominion status issue].

Meanwhile in the Provinces and the States there were developments that had a bearing upon particular features of the plan as well as influencing Indian leaders' reactions to it either as a whole or in part. In the former category fell the question of how best to ascertain the wishes of the people of the N.W.F.P. On 16 April, at the Viceroy's third Miscellaneous Meeting, at which both Nehru and Liaquat as well as the Governor were present, there was discussion of the suggestion that the situation would be eased by an announcement that an election would be held in the Province, no date being specified [No. 162]. On 17 April Nehru wrote advising that no such announcement be made at present since it would be interpreted as an affront to the Ministry and an encouragement to Muslim League violence [No. 167]. Against a background of continuing disorder in the Province [Nos. 114, 186, 203, 211, 287 and 310] and of Congress demands in person and in the Press for the resignation of the Governor [Nos. 171, 325, 328 and 343], the means to be adopted for ascertaining the people's will remained crucial with a plebiscite, or referendum, held independently and apart from an election, coming into consideration as an alternative to an election, though Jinnah was insistent that there must also be an election should the vote in the referendum go in favour of Pakistan [Nos. 185, 190, 250, 275, 283, 297, 307, 310, 312, 314, 317, 322, 327]. The Viceroy's response to the developing crisis in the Province which he described as 'the greatest danger spot in India and the bone of contention between Congress and the Muslim League' [No. 276] was to seek first hand information by a visit there on 28–29 April, an account of which will be found in Nos. 209, 238, 241, 247, 259, 265 together with a graphic overall summary in the Viceroy's fifth Personal Report of 1 May [No. 276]. On 7 May Jinnah issued a statement repudiating the suggestion that the League had ever decided to resort to direct action in the Province, complaining of the intolerable situation that had developed because of the Provincial Congress Government's 'ruthless policy of crushing the Muslims' and appealing to Muslims 'to do all in their power to remain peaceful' [No. 354, appendix]—an appeal which Nehru, the following day at a Miscellaneous Meeting, said he did not consider 'for non-violence at all'. Nehru stated that he was 'intellectually in favour of a referendum' but 'in a calmer atmosphere'. Agreement was reached on it, the Viceroy informing Ismay that he recommended that a referendum should be held 'as soon as the whole picture for the rest of India has emerged' [Nos. 350, 358 and 359]. This procedure was subsequently embodied in the draft Statement and approved by the Cabinet [Nos. 476, 516 and 521].

There were also critical questions relating to the determination of the future of the other two Provinces with 'volcanic' properties, the Punjab and Bengal. When Acharya Kripalani, the President of the Congress, saw the Viceroy on 17 April he noted that the point had been reached 'at which the Congress must reluctantly accept the fact that the Muslim League will never voluntarily come into a Union of India' and that being so, 'rather than have a battle we shall let them have their Pakistan, provided you will allow the Punjab and Bengal to be partitioned in a fair manner' [No. 168]. This might be thought of as tanta-mount to an expression of acquiescence in practice on the part of the Congress in the League insistence on partition of India in principle; but the prospect of the partitioning of the two provinces prompted, in Bengal, suggestions for an alternative solution and, in the Punjab, representations from the Sikh leadership on the actual demarcation of the boundary.

With regard to Bengal, the Chief Minister, Suhrawardy, contemplated a future for the Province as a united and independent state, assuring the Viceroy that he could get Jinnah to agree that on that basis it need not join Pakistan [Nos. 227 and 228]. K.S. Roy, leader of the opposition in the Bengal Legis-lative Assembly, had told the Governor, however, that it was inconceivable that Bengal should stand by itself as an independent state but he was ready to meet the Chief Minister more than half way in respect of a Coalition govern-ment to ensure a peaceful transfer [No. 5]. The Hindu Mahasabha lent their support to partition and the constitution of a Hindu dominated West Bengal

[No. 201]. The alternative possibilities, partition or independence, to which should be added, by way of further refinement in the event of partition, a plebiscite in Calcutta or some form of joint administration for that city, were much canvassed by the Governor and party leaders national and provincial [Nos. 199, 208, which contains a note by the Governor on the working out of partition, 214, 216, 231, 233, 242, 243 and 264]. In the Punjab practical problems of provincial partition were aggravated by the presence of a third party, the Sikhs. Their leadership demanded that, in the event of partition, any boundary whether final or merely 'notional' (i.e. provisional) should be so drawn that the greatest possible proportion of the Sikh people would come within the Eastern (i.e. non-Muslim) part of the Province. To achieve this result they argued that the demarcation should be based not just on a simple calculation of the relative numbers of Muslims and non-Muslims in contiguous districts, but on other factors such as the ownership of property, the relative population strengths of the two communities in the Punjab as a whole, and the location of Sikh shrines, and should be accompanied by a transfer of populations [Nos. 198, 240, 258, 269, 298 enclosure, 324, 333, 336, 338, 340]. The Governor, however, reached the conclusion that an agreed partition of the Punjab appeared virtually impossible or, as he later put it, 'manifestly not acceptable' to all parties [Nos. 263, 298, 305 and 333].

In the meantime Jinnah maintained his stance in respect of Bengal as well as the Punjab, namely that while India should be partitioned, any partition of the provinces was a most dangerous proposition and would 'loose terrible forces' [No. 203]. But the Viceroy, by contrast with the Governor who judged the situation had been radically changed by Jinnah's public statement on 30 April that Pakistan must include the whole of the Punjab [Nos. 298 and 276, Annex I], did not feel from what Jinnah had said to him personally that he 'would in the end absolutely refuse to acquiesce in the partition of the Punjab' [No. 314].

Constituting a further particular element in the situation were the Princely States. On 9 April Nehru had explained to the Viceroy that he was deeply interested in the future of the States, and regretted the secrecy in which he alleged the Political Department worked and also their encouragement of reaction in the States [No. 102], the last a judgement repudiated by the Viceroy who said that if officers of the Department were giving such encouragement they are acting entirely contrary to the policy of the Crown Representative [No. 218]. On 18 April Nehru was reported to have told the All-India States' People's Conference at Gwalior that any State which did not 'come into the Constituent Assembly now will be regarded as hostile, and will have to bear the consequences of being so regarded' [No. 181, note 2]. In the face of such seemingly threatening pressure, it was apparent that some of the Princes at any rate felt vulnerable, the Maharaja of Patiala complaining to the Viceroy on 20 April that it had been unfair of the British to weaken the Princes in recent years, instead of strengthening them before they were left to stand on their own legs [No. 184], and other Rulers seeking the Crown Representative's advice [Nos. 187 and 188] on what action they should take. The matter was discussed at the Viceroy's Nineteenth Staff Meeting on 21 April when the Viceroy noted that the Cabinet Mission had advised that the States should join the Constituent Assembly at a certain stage which had not yet been reached, and on 28 April instructions were issued to Residents to the effect that Rulers who consulted them should be advised that they were not obliged to send representatives to the Constituent Assembly until a new plan was announced or the Cabinet Mission Plan fully accepted [Nos. 188 and 245; for the Viceroy's meeting with Nehru on his Gwalior speech see Nos. 193 and 211, paras. 25–30, and for his discussion with Bhopal on 26 April see No. 225]. At the same time Residents were told [No. 245] that as soon as the forthcoming announcement on the transfer of power had been made, Rulers would be well advised to act promptly in consulting public opinion and in announcing whatever decision they might reach about joining the Constituent Assembly. The Viceroy informed Nehru of the nature of the instructions that had been issued [No. 303]. On 5 May Sardar Panikkar explained why the Maharaja of Bikaner as head of the group of States which had joined the Constituent Assembly had acted as he did, the chief reason being a conviction that a strong centre was essential for the States [No. 319].

The shaping of the new plan remained the dominant consideration. On 24 April the Viceroy reported that he had formed a special Committee consisting of Ismay, Mieville and Abell under his own general direction on the production of the plan and the announcement to be associated with it [No. 211, para. 23]. The Committee had held meetings with Liaquat [No. 190]; with Nehru [No. 194]; with Jinnah [No. 203] and was to do so on 25 April with Patel [No. 206], all on an individual basis. The premise from which discussion started was in each case the failure of the Cabinet Mission Plan and as a result the search for a settlement on the basis of partition with the provinces (or parts of them) making their own choice. These discussions were followed by further soundings of the principal leaders with Mieville on 30 April—the Viceroy being on his visit to N.W.F.P. and the Punjab [No. 276]—showing the statement to Jinnah who did not react favourably, Bengal being 'the main bone of contention' [No. 256], and going through it with Nehru who contented himself with observations on particular points, chief among them elections in the N.W.F.P. which he deemed 'unnecessary and dangerous' [No. 257]. On 1 May Nehru wrote to the Viceroy to convey the reactions of the Congress Working Committee 'to recent developments and the new proposals, in so far as we know them'. He mentioned that Gandhi had also been present, and reported that the Committee was 'prepared to accept the principle of partition based on self-determination as applied to definitely ascertained areas. This involves the partition of Bengal and Punjab' [No. 267]. Meanwhile, also on 1 May, the Viceroy had had a lengthy meeting with the Governor of Bengal regarding the particular problems posed for that Province by the prospect of partition [see pp. xx and xxi above]. As a result the Viceroy decided to have the plan 'slightly redrafted' by introducing a modification in the procedure whereby Bengal and the Punjab were to vote on the various options before them [Nos. 264 and 276, para. 30; the nature of the modification may be studied by comparing Nos. 260 and 279]. Reporting on these developments to the Secretary of State the Viceroy dwelt on the problems of partition in Bengal and the Punjab, but stressed that the essence of the plan was to make it apparent to India and the world that so far as possible Indians themselves were being allowed to choose how they wished to transfer power [No. 276].

The full text of the draft announcement embodying the plan was sent to the Secretary of State on 1 May [Nos. 278 and 279] and, as the Viceroy had advised the Prime Minister on 25 April [No. 223], Ismay left for London on 2 May for discussion of it with the Cabinet India and Burma Committee [No. 276]. With these discussions a third phase may be deemed to have opened—a phase in which consideration was given at the London end to the draft plan and how it was to be presented, while in India the Viceroy received further views and representations on the outline or detail of the forthcoming transfer—a feature of it being an extensive exchange of communications between the Viceroy and Ismay, the former reporting on developments in India and the continuing conversations he was having there with Indian leaders, the latter on discussions at the India and Burma Committee on the draft proposals, the background to which he had filled in at the Committee's Meeting on 5 May [Nos. 320 and 323]. After exchanges of view, a revised draft of the Announcement was circulated to the Committee on 6 May [No. 331] with further meetings on the following days [Nos. 341 and 355].

In Delhi on 4 May the Viceroy had occasion to thank Gandhi for 'the strong and courageous statement' he had made rebuking the Press in general and 'his own in particular' for unauthorised disclosures and criticisms of the Viceroy [Nos. 306 and 309] but when the Viceroy outlined the plan he had sent to London Gandhi maintained that it was a case of the British 'practically imposing partition'—a theme which he further developed in a letter on 8 May alleging that 'it would be a blunder of first magnitude for the British to be party in any way whatsoever to the division of India' [No. 348]. On the same day, at the Viceroy's Tenth Miscellaneous Meeting [No. 350], Pandit Nehru outlined a plan which he considered preferable to that in the draft Announcement, and which he called 'The Cabinet Mission's plan with modifications'. This involved the demission of power to the Central Government in June 1947 with any suggestion that Pakistan should be created straight away ruled out. Provinces should, however, be given the option of forming Groups and later would be able to secede; only then would the question of partitioning Provinces arise. The Viceroy thought that H.M.G. were most unlikely to consent to this, but said that he considered it essential to meet Nehru's views as far as possible. Accordingly he sent a telegram, dated 8 May, to Ismay in which he stated that Nehru hoped that, in the wording of the plan, sufficient emphasis would be laid 'on the "Union of India", which was core of the Cabinet Mission plan' with Provinces not adhering being referred to as 'contracting out of the Union of India' [No. 357]. The same evening the Viceroy telegraphed asking Ismay to distribute copies of the Viceroy's Conference Paper [No. 273] drafted on the basis of the 'V.P. Menon Plan' and already alluded to [above p. xix], to the India and Burma Committee, and to let its members know that 'Patel and Nehru have now themselves indicated through V.P. Menon a desire for a form of early Dominion Status ... at least until a new Constitution has been fully framed'. This the Viceroy described as 'the greatest opportunity ever offered to the Empire and we must not let administrative or other difficulties stand in the way' [No. 360; and Nos. 388 and 390 for memoranda circulated by the Secretary of State to the India and Burma Committee commenting on these developments]. The issues involved were further considered at the Viceroy's Staff Meeting on 9 May [No. 366]. With regard to the League the Viceroy had reported on 8 May that 'in recent conversations ... with Jinnah ... [he] did not appear seriously to contest the idea of a truncated Pakistan' [No. 351]. Yet the Viceroy felt that the possibility that Jinnah might reject the draft plan could not be altogether excluded despite such indications to the contrary and since, in such circumstances, it would be 'out of the question to carry on' he proposed to tell Jinnah that the only alternative was demission on the basis of the Government of India Act which would probably prove even less acceptable [Nos. 345, 346 and 351]. This course, however, did not commend itself to the Secretary of State [No. 389] and was regarded by the India and Burma Committee as being in breach of pledges to minorities [No. 449] when later the suggestion came before them. At an India and Burma Committee Meeting on 8 May members had concluded that should Pakistan ask to remain within the Commonwealth while India became independent and should the question be raised in Parliament the reply should be that no answer could be given to a still hypothetical question [No. 355] but the point was later made that the Dominion Prime Ministers, who had been informed of the draft proposals and the background to them [No. 352; and No. 420 for Smuts's critical reaction], should also be informed of this possibility as was later done [Nos. 368, 369 and 452].

On 9 May Ismay sent the Viceroy the text of the draft announcement as revised up to that date [No. 379]. On the same day Patel strongly urged an immediate transfer of power to the Central Government 'as it now stands' with 'the Viceroy standing out' [No. 375] while on 10 May at the Eleventh Viceroy's Miscellaneous Meeting at which Nehru was present the Viceroy explained that V.P. Menon had been working for some time past on a scheme for an early transfer of power on a dominion status basis [No. 382]. The Viceroy noted, after V.P. Menon had expounded his scheme, that under it the transfer of power would take place much earlier than June 1948, Pandit Nehru observing that he considered it very desirable that 'there should be a transfer of power as soon as possible on a Dominion status basis' [No. 382; see also No. 381 for a report by the Viceroy of Krishna Menon's views on this].

Still on 10 May—a day of intense activity as the documentary record indicates—the Viceroy now in Simla with Nehru staying with him as his guest let Lord Ismay know of his proposed time-table [No. 396] and also an outline of the Statement [No. 397] he proposed to make when he told the Indian leaders of the agreed, revised plan on 17 May. But the next day the Viceroy cabled to the Prime Minister to say he had had to postpone his invitation to the Indian leaders from 17 May to 2 June [No. 407]. The reason for this abrupt and, to London, disconcerting change is best given by the Viceroy who telegraphed Ismay to say that on evening of 10 May he had 'an absolute hunch that the redraft from London might not be accepted by Congress' and that accordingly he had asked Nehru who was staying with him to have a look at it [No. 410]. The next morning Nehru told the Viceroy that the draft had 'produced a devastating effect upon me' and that the 'relatively simple proposals that we had previously discussed now appeared, in the garb that H.M.G. had provided for them, in an entirely new context which gave them an ominous meaning'. The whole approach was 'completely different': a new picture 'of fragmentation and conflict and disorder' emerged [No. 402]. 'You can imagine the bombshell this has been', Mountbatten cabled Ismay [No. 410] while Mieville reported 'We are naturally a bit rattled' by what he described as 'Nehru's *volte-face*' [No. 413], Ismay rejoining 'So are we' [No. 421]. Some indication of the impact in London may be gathered from a draft telegram (not actually sent) stating that 'we [i.e. the India and Burma Committee] have made no alterations of substance' except as regards the referendum in the N.W.F.P., and that they could not, therefore, understand Nehru's objections [No. 428]. Nehru, however, continued to hold to his view of a substantial shift in the London revised draft remarking 'things that emerge from London are so peculiar' [No. 419].

Discussion on the draft was resumed on 11 May with V.P. Menon now called in [No. 405], Nehru elaborating his objections to the plan as revised in London [No. 406] and consideration being given to a redrafting which Mountbatten advised London 'will mean a very considerable recast both in principle and detail' [No. 412]. The points at issue and the amendments proposed are set out in a number of documents [See e.g. Nos. 405, 406 and 414]

in the period between the Nehru 'bombshell' early on 11 May and the despatch
of a revised draft announcement to London on the evening of 13 May [No.
429; for text see No. 430]. The revised draft was laid before the India and Burma
Committee on 14 May when the Prime Minister noted that there appeared to
have been a substantial change in the attitude of the Indian leaders, that in
particular the possibility of early attainment of dominion status by India, or
part of it, seemed to have produced a radical change in the situation and he
doubted whether it would be profitable to consider the revised draft in detail
until they had further explanation of the changes in it from the Viceroy
[No. 437]. On 14 May the Prime Minister telegraphed the Viceroy indicating
that he felt it impossible to decide 'the very important issues' raised other than
in discussion and he invited Mountbatten to return for consultations [Nos. 438,
439 and 440]. A review of these and associated developments in the North-
West Frontier Province and Bengal will be found in the Viceroy's Personal
Report (No. 7) of 15 May [No. 451]. A reflection of the progressive focusing
of attention on a dominion solution may be noted in the Prime Minister's
proposal on 14 May for a review of existing Commonwealth and Imperial
relationships [No. 436; see also Nos. 392 and 418].

The Viceroy had earlier stated that he intended to clear the revised draft
with Nehru and Jinnah [No. 429]. Congress reactions were conveyed to the
Viceroy on 16 May. The Congress accepted the plan 'generally' but their
acceptance was strictly subject to 'the other parties agreeing to it as a final
settlement' [Nos. 464 and 471; see also No. 472 for Nehru's view stressed very
vehemently that once the Announcement was made the Interim Government
should be treated by convention as a Dominion government, together with
the Viceroy's reservations about this]. Jinnah and Liaquat, however, declined
to express agreement in writing [No. 454] and were not to be persuaded
otherwise though Jinnah submitted a detailed commentary on the draft [No.
463].

The text of the draft announcement amended in the light of League and
Congress comments may be studied in No. 465. At an interview with Jinnah
and Liaquat on 17 May the Viceroy said he intended to advise H.M.G. that the
transfer of power should take place as soon as possible and preferably by 1
October and also, that having received requests both from the Congress and
the League that India and Pakistan should remain within the British Commonwealth, he intended to pass both requests to H.M.G., the outstanding question
being whether Jinnah would prefer Pakistan to have its own Governor General
or to share a common Governor General with Hindustan [No. 473]. The
revised Draft Announcement, as taken to London by the Viceroy, is reproduced
in No. 476. Associated with it were proposals to cover the interim period also
shown to the Indian leaders [Nos. 466, 477, 482 and 489].

On 17 May, which may be taken as the opening date of the concluding

phase covered in this volume, the Secretary of State circulated to the India and
Burma Committee a revised version of the Viceroy's revised draft which he
felt, subject to consideration of one major point might be an acceptable
compromise between the Viceroy's draft and that earlier agreed by the Committee [No. 475]. On 19 May the Viceroy joined the Committee in its deliberations, outlining the course of developments in India and commenting on
Nehru's criticisms of the earlier draft statement on the grounds first that it
obscured the position of the Constituent Assembly as set out in the Cabinet
Mission plan and second that it would result in the Balkanisation of India. The
Viceroy told the Committee that the latest draft statement which he had
prepared had been accepted generally by the political leaders in India and
'represented the maximum degree of agreement that could be secured' [No.
485]. There was a further meeting of the Committee on 20 May [No. 494]
when questions of timing and dominion status were considered while on
21 May the Secretary of State circulated a note from the Viceroy on Dominion
status and some of the unsettled questions relating to its application and the
ways in which it might be presented and implemented [No. 504]. The Secretary of State for his part submitted a paper considering how the proposed
offer of dominion status should be linked with the announcement of partition
[No. 505] and contending that it was desirable not to make a statement on
dominion status until partition had been proposed and accepted by both sides.
These papers were considered by the India and Burma Committee on 22 May
[No. 517, Minute 3], but the exact wording of that part of the Announcement
which related to Dominion Status was not decided until the Committee's
final meeting with the Viceroy on 28 May. The Viceroy also secured the
concurrence of the Committee to the substitution of 'one or two successor
authorities' in the text for 'such successor authorities' with a view to lessening
apprehensions lest India be further divided, such amendment being subject to
the decision on the future of Bengal [No. 553, Minute 3].

On 22 May the Prime Minister circulated a memorandum on Indian policy
to the Cabinet which recited the sequence of events and discussions and noted
that the Viceroy had convened a conference of Indian leaders for 2 June at
which he would make a final effort to obtain a compromise on the basis of the
Cabinet Mission Plan, but failing which the Viceroy proposed to lay before
them the Statement, which he had brought with him from India, and which
had now been considered and (subject to minor amendments) approved by the
India and Burma Committee in consultation with him [No. 516]. Both
memorandum and draft announcement were considered by the Cabinet on
23 May and the draft announcement was approved in principle, the Cabinet
noting with satisfaction the proposal for the early attainment of dominion
status for the parts of a partitioned India (including Bengal should it decide to
remain united) and agreeing that the Viceroy should have a wide measure of

discretion to modify details of the plan [No. 521]. The opposition had been told of it, Mountbatten seeing its leader, Mr Churchill [Nos. 517, Minute 1, and 513], and Dominion Governments were informed, the revised statement being welcomed by them [Nos. 527, 528, 538, 539, 544 and 555] as was reported by the Secretary of State for Dominion Affairs to the India and Burma Committee on 28 May [No. 553, Minute 3].

A number of contentious issues, potentially prejudicial to acceptance of the plan embodied in the draft Announcement, were before the India and Burma Committee at the meeting on 28 May, which was the last the Viceroy attended [No. 553]. First among them were representations by Nehru [No. 540] that in view, as he saw it, of Jinnah's non-acceptance of the plan as a final settlement the proposals set out in the draft should be abandoned and the Cabinet Mission's plan imposed—a proposal the Committee deemed impossible of acceptance. The statement of view by Jinnah to which Nehru referred was contained in a letter sent by Jinnah to Sir E. Mieville on 21 May in which he (Jinnah) had argued that Congress were seeking to impose a new condition by demanding that the interim Government should function as a dominion Government by convention, and had also protested at no change having been made in respect of the proposed partition of Bengal and the Punjab despite his 'very strong objections' [No. 514]. Note was also taken of Nehru's reported statement that the Congress could agree to Bengal remaining united only if it remained in the Union of India—(on 18 May the Viceroy had told the Governor of Bengal that his talks with Nehru had led him to believe that it was extremely unlikely that the Congress High Command would accept an independent Bengal, the province in their view having no future except in Hindustan [No. 478; see also No. 525])—which, in the Viceroy's judgment, diminished the prospects of saving the unity of Bengal and opened the possibility of a non-viable Eastern Bengal submitting a claim for recognition as a separate dominion. This the Committee were not prepared to entertain concluding that, in the eventuality of partition, Eastern Bengal would have to unite with one or other of the successor dominions. There was also discussion of, *inter alia*, the drafting of the Indian Independence Bill; arrangements for carrying on the Interim Government in the interim period between the announcement of the plan and the actual transfer of power—a problem which the Viceroy felt it would only be possible to solve by detailed negotiations in Delhi; the division of the Indian Armed Forces; and the withdrawal of British troops from India.

A draft of a broadcast to be made by the Viceroy at the time of the announcement was circulated and commented upon [Nos. 507, 532 (Prime Minister), 529 and 557 (Secretary of State)].

The stage accordingly was set for the meeting with the Indian leaders now fixed for 2 June.

By far the greater part of the hitherto unpublished documents reproduced in this volume are drawn from the official archives of the India Office in the custody of the India Office Records or from the Mountbatten Papers.

The documents reproduced from the India Office Records are from the following series of which the three most important are asterisked:

L/E/8	Economic Department Files (including Communications and Overseas Department)
L/F/7	Financial Department Collections
L/I/1	Information Department Files
*L/PO	Private Office Papers
L/P &J/5	Political Department Miscellaneous (including Governors' Reports)
L/P &J/7	Political Department Files
L/P &J/8	Political Department Collections
*L/P &J/10	Political Department Transfer of Power Papers
L/P &S/12	External Department Collections
L/P &S/13	Political 'Internal' Department Collections
L/S &G/7	Services and General Department Collections
L/WS/1	War Staff Files
R/1	Crown Representative's Records
*R/3/1	Papers of the Office of the Private Secretary to the Viceroy[2]

Every document in these series is referred to in the text by the appropriate series notation followed by the number assigned to the particular file, collection, or volume in which the document is filed or bound. Thus the notation L/P &J/ 10/40 refers to the fortieth file in the series called Political Department Transfer of Power Papers. Each document in a file, collection, or volume is identified by a folio reference.

The Editors are indebted to the Trustees of the Broadlands Archives Settlement for the loan of their microfilms of those official and demi-official Indian Papers of the Earl Mountbatten of Burma which are in their custody and for permission to make copies of documents from those microfilms. Documents from this source are cited in the present Volume as the 'Mountbatten Papers'.

Some documents, not in any of these archives, have been obtained from elsewhere, notably the Cabinet Office and the Prime Minister's Office.[3] The Editors have also consulted those papers of Sir Stafford Cripps which are now in the keeping of the Public Record Office and a few documents from this source have been included in the present Volume.

The most important categories of telegraphic communications between the

---

[2] This series includes three files (R/3/1/176–8) from the Office of the Secretary to the Governor of the Punjab.

[3] A file (R/30/1/10) containing copies of these documents can be consulted in the India Office Records.

Secretary of State and the Viceroy were classified in the following ways. One category of telegrams from the Viceroy to the Secretary of State carried the letter 'S', or 'S.C.' if the Viceroy was at Simla or in Camp i.e. on tour. Another category consisted of 'U' telegrams, which were reserved for the most secret and personal matters, the letter 'U' indicating the nature of the telegram, irrespective of whether it did, or did not, carry a 'Secret' or 'Private' prefix. 'U' telegrams could be enciphered or deciphered only in the Private Offices of the Secretary of State or the Viceroy. Some 'S' or 'S.C.' telegrams were marked 'Superintendent Series' which indicated to Superintendents of Telegraph branches that especial care should be taken to safeguard their security. Certain changes in the channels of communication between the Viceroy and the Secretary of State, made at the beginning of Lord Wavell's Viceroyalty, may be studied in the Appendix to Volume IV, and a small alteration in these arrangements—made with regard to the likely wishes of members of an Interim Government—is recorded in the Appendix to Volume VIII.

It may also be helpful to mention that of the Papers and Minutes of the India and Burma Committee of the Cabinet those relating solely to Burma are excluded as treating of matters outside the scope of this Series.

In conclusion the Editors desire to acknowledge once again the friendly assistance and advice they have received from the officials at the India Office Library and Records, among whom they would like to mention the Director, Mr B. C. Bloomfield, and the Deputy Archivist, Mr Martin I. Moir.

N. MANSERGH
PENDEREL MOON

Abbreviations

A.D.C.	Aide-de-Camp
A.F.(I)	Auxiliary Force (India)
A.F.P.F.L.	Anti-Fascist People's Freedom League (Burma)
A.G.G.	Agent to the Governor-General
A.H.Q.	Army Headquarters
A.L.F.S.E.A.	Allied Land Forces, South-East Asia
A.P.A.	Associated Press of America
A.P.I.	Associated Press of India
B.B.C.	British Broadcasting Corporation
B.E.S.T.	Bombay Electric Supply and Tramways Co.
C.A.	Constituent Assembly
C.-in-C.	Commander-in-Chief
C.I.D.	Criminal Investigation Department
C.I.O.	Central Intelligence Officer
C.O.	Commanding Officer
C.O.H.Q.	Combined Operations Headquarters
C.O.S.	Chiefs of Staff
C.P.	Central Provinces
C.S.P.	Congress Socialist Party
C.S.V.	Conference Secretary to the Viceroy
C.V.S.	Chief of the Viceroy's Staff
D.B.S.T.	Double British Summer Time
D.C.I.	Defence Committee India
D.I.B.	Director of the Intelligence Bureau
D.I.G.	Deputy Inspector-General
D.I.K.	Dera Ismail Khan
D.P.S.V.	Deputy Private Secretary to the Viceroy
E.A.	External Affairs
F.A.	Foreign Affairs
G.G.	Governor-General
G.M.T.	Greenwich Mean Time
G.S.	Governor's Secretary
H.E.	His Excellency
H.E.H.	His Exalted Highness

H.H.	His Highness
H.M.	His Majesty *or* Honourable Member
H.M.G.	His Majesty's Government
H.Q.	Headquarters
I.A.	Indian Army
I.C.S.	Indian Civil Service
I.G.	Inspector-General
I.N.A.	Indian National Army
I.P.	Indian Police
J.P.S.V.	Joint Private Secretary to the Viceroy
M.C.S.	Member of the Council of State
M.L.A.	Member of the Legislative Assembly
M.S.V.	Military Secretary to the Viceroy
N.H.Q.	Naval Headquarters
N.W.F.P.	North-West Frontier Province
P.A.	Political Adviser
P.L.A.	Provincial Legislative Assembly
P.M.	Prime Minister
P.S.V.	Private Secretary to the Viceroy
R.I.A.F.	Royal Indian Air Force
R.I.N.	Royal Indian Navy
S.A.	*Sturmabteilungen* (Brown Shirts)
SACSEA	Supreme Allied Commander South-East Asia
SEAC	South-East Asia Command
S.S.	*Schutzstaffeln* (Black Shirts)
S. of S. *or* S/S	Secretary of State
U.K.	United Kingdom
U.K.H.C.	United Kingdom High Commissioner
U.N.O.	United Nations Organisation
U.P.	United Provinces
U.S.	United States (of America)
U.S.S.R.	Union of Soviet Socialist Republics
V.C.P.	Viceroy's Conference Paper
Y.E.	Your Excellency

Principal Holders of Office

UNITED KINGDOM

CABINET

Members of the India and Burma Committee are italicised.[1]

Prime Minister and First Lord of the Treasury	*Mr Clement Attlee*
Lord President of the Council and Leader of the House of Commons	Mr Herbert Morrison
Secretary of State for Foreign Affairs	Mr Ernest Bevin
Lord Privy Seal	Mr Arthur Greenwood Lord Inman (from 17 April 1947)
Minister without Portfolio	Mr Arthur Greenwood (from 17 April 1947)
Chancellor of the Exchequer	*Mr Hugh Dalton*
President of the Board of Trade	*Sir Stafford Cripps*
Minister of Defence	*Mr A. V. Alexander*
Lord Chancellor	Viscount Jowitt
Secretary of State for the Home Department	Mr J. Chuter Ede
Secretary of State for Dominion Affairs	*Viscount Addison*
Secretary of State for India and Burma	*Lord Pethick-Lawrence* *Earl of Listowel* (from 23 April 1947)
Secretary of State for Scotland	Mr J. Westwood
Secretary of State for the Colonies	Mr A. Creech Jones
Minister of Labour and National Service	Mr G. A. Isaacs
Minister of Fuel and Power	Mr E. Shinwell
Minister of Health	Mr Aneurin Bevan
Minister of Agriculture and Fisheries	Mr T. Williams
Minister of Education	Mr George Tomlinson

OTHER MINISTERS MENTIONED IN THIS VOLUME

Minister of Food	Mr John Strachey
Postmaster-General	*Earl of Listowel* (until 23 April 1947)

[1] Lord Chorley, Mr C. P. Mayhew and Mr A. G. Bottomley joined the India and Burma Committee in the period covered by this Volume and Mr A. Henderson became a full member; see No. 301. Their names appear in a list of the revised composition of the Committee circulated on 6 May 1947 under the reference I.B.(47) 58. Public Record Office, CAB 134/345.

INDIA OFFICE

Secretary of State	Lord Pethick-Lawrence
	Earl of Listowel (from 23 April 1947)
Permanent Under-Secretary	Sir David Monteath
Parliamentary Under-Secretary	Mr Arthur Henderson
Deputy Under-Secretary	Sir William Croft
Assistant Under-Secretaries	Sir Paul Patrick
	Mr G. H. Baxter
Private Secretary to the Secretary of State	Mr R. M. J. Harris

INDIA

Viceroy, Governor-General and Crown Representative	Rear-Admiral Viscount Mountbatten of Burma
	Sir John Colville (acting from 19–30 May 1947)
Chief of the Viceroy's Staff	Lord Ismay
Principal Secretary [to the Viceroy]	Sir Eric Mieville
Private Secretary to the Viceroy	Mr G. E. B. Abell
	Captain R. V. Brockman R. N. (acting from 2–30 May 1947)
Reforms Commissioner	Mr V. P. Menon

INTERIM GOVERNMENT (EXECUTIVE COUNCIL)

External Affairs and Commonwealth Relations	Pandit Jawaharlal Nehru
Defence	Sardar Baldev Singh
Home, including Information and Broadcasting	Sardar Vallabhbhai Patel
Finance	Mr Liaquat Ali Khan
Posts and Air	Mr Abdur Rab Nishtar
Food and Agriculture	Dr Rajendra Prasad
Labour	Mr Jagjivan Ram
Transport and Railways	Dr John Matthai
Industries and Supplies	Mr C. Rajagopalachari
Education and Arts	Maulana Abul Kalam Azad
Works, Mines and Power	Mr G. H. Bhabha
Commerce	Mr I. I. Chundrigar
Law	Mr Jogendra Nath Mandal
Health	Mr Ghazanfar Ali Khan

GOVERNORS OF PROVINCES

Madras	Lieutenant-General Sir Archibald Nye
Bombay	Sir John Colville
	Sir S. V. Ramamurti I.C.S. (acting 19–30 May 1947)
Bengal	Sir Frederick Burrows
United Provinces	Sir Francis Wylie I.C.S.
Punjab	Sir Evan Jenkins I.C.S.
Central Provinces and Berar	Sir Frederick Bourne I.C.S.
Assam	Sir Andrew Clow I.C.S.
	Sir M. S. A. Hydari I.C.S. (from 4 May 1947)
Bihar	Sir Hugh Dow I.C.S.
North-West Frontier Province	Sir Olaf Caroe I.C.S.
Orissa	Sir Chandulal Trivedi I.C.S.
Sind	Sir Francis Mudie I.C.S.

PRIME MINISTERS (PREMIERS) OF PROVINCES

Madras	Mr O.P. Ramaswamy Reddiar
Bombay	Mr B. G. Kher
Bengal	Mr H. S. Suhrawardy
United Provinces	Pandit G. B. Pant
Central Provinces and Berar	Pandit R. S. Shukla
Assam	Mr Gopinath Bardoloi
Bihar	Mr Sri Krishna Sinha
North-West Frontier Province	Dr Khan Sahib
Orissa	Mr Harekrishna Mahtab
Sind	Sir Ghulam Hussain Hidayatullah

The Punjab was administered by the Governor under Section 93 of the Government of India Act 1935.

Chronological Table of Principal Events

1947

23 March– 2 April	Asian Relations Conference held at Delhi

March

24	Mountbatten sworn in as Viceroy and Governor-General
25	Agreement for a United States of Indonesia and Netherlands-Indonesian Union signed in Batavia Viceroy's First Staff Meeting
29	Withdrawal of British troops from Cairo and the Delta to the Canal Zone completed
31	Viceroy holds first of five interviews with Gandhi

April

5	Viceroy holds **first** of six interviews with Jinnah
15–16	Conference of Governors; approval for draft proposals for transfer of power
15	Issue of joint Gandhi-Jinnah appeal for abstention from acts of violence and disorder
23	Earl of Listowel succeeds Lord Pethick-Lawrence as Secretary of State for India
25	V. P. Menon's draft plan for transfer of power as an interim arrangement based on a Dominion Constitution submitted to Viceroy
28–29	Mountbatten visits N.W.F.P.
30	Announcement in Parliament of compensation terms for members of Indian Services

May

1	Nehru acquaints Mountbatten with Congress Working Committee's reactions to recent developments and 'the new proposals' in so far as known to them
2	Ismay leaves for London for discussion of draft plan for Transfer of Power
11	Nehru writes of 'devastating effect' on him of draft proposals as reformulated by H.M.G.
12	Royal Family return to U.K. from South Africa
13	Revised draft plan despatched to London
18	Mountbatten leaves for London for talks with Cabinet

Summary of Documents

CHAPTER I

Ascertaining the views of Indian leaders: 22 March to 9 April 1947

CHAPTER 2

The first formulation of a plan: 10 April to 5 May 1947

CHAPTER 3

Consideration of the plan in London and India: 5 to 10 May 1947

CHAPTER 4

The Nehru 'bombshell' and the revision of the plan: 11 to 17 May 1947

CHAPTER 5

The Viceroy's visit to London and Cabinet approval of revised plan: 17 to 30 May 1947

CHAPTER 6

The States

I

Sir O. Caroe (North-West Frontier Province) to Rear-Admiral Viscount Mountbatten of Burma (Extract)

L/P&J/5/224: ff 68–9

CONFIDENTIAL
D.O. No. GH–34

GOVERNMENT HOUSE, PESHAWAR,
22 March 1947

2. Here are we between the storm-ridden Punjab on one side and the tribes on the other, and in the strange position of having a Congress Government which has—or had—a considerable Moslem backing. But the influence of the North-Western Punjab to the East and the tribes to the West—all declaiming against Hindu-Sikh domination—is, I think, certain to squeeze Congress out before long, for Congress is not natural here. The shifting of the balance might have happened before if the League had had any leaders to compare with the Khan Brothers. The tribal attitude is beginning to crystallize under the leadership of the Afridis, and I wrote to Abell a few days ago to explain how this was working out. Here I will only say that the attitude of the longer-headed tribesmen and of the League also, in so far as they have thought at all, is to keep the tribes in reserve until the time comes when we have to hand over, and not to get them embroiled while we are still here. Meanwhile I think the elements that count in the tribes will refuse to deal either with Congress or with the League separately, and that there will be a more or less effective tribal boycott of any attempt by the present Constituent Assembly to send up an Advisory Committee.

3. Our disorders here have not approached the Punjab rages in fury. But there has been butchery of defenceless minorities in villages of Peshawar and Hazara and some forcible conversions. The Ministry have survived the first shock, and with the aid of troops (who had to fire on a protest demonstration) have managed to carry through the budget session of the Assembly with the Opposition in jail. So much for democratic processes. I shortened the session, which finishes, I am glad to say, to-day. The only new feature is the bringing into Peshawar City of Red Shirts. For the moment this has sent Congress stock up, but it was a totalitarian move and as such will bring its revenges, more particularly as it has been undertaken by a party whose power is by no means consolidated on this frontier.

4. As I see my job during the next year it is to prevent the disintegration of

the North-West Frontier. The more I think of it the more I am struck by the refusal of the Cabinet Mission to face up squarely to this question. Their statements scarcely mentioned the land frontier or the tribes, who also fail to figure in the Prime Minister's statement of 20th February. Yet they are just as vital to India as the States. The various forces acting on this frontier, particularly since the 20th February statement, may produce a resultant [?disturbance] which will even cause this part of India to fly off into space, and I think all our efforts in these parts during the next year should be directed to ensure that there is an orderly handing over of India's land frontier in a state of stability. For this is one of the most essential needs of the new India, and a considerable amount of force up to the end will be needed to secure it. But not one word have we ever been able to get out of His Majesty's Government on this subject. If the Punjab can return to constitutional courses, that will make a difference. The tribes in their hearts even now won't recognise that power will be handed over. (They regard themselves as realists, and what is more they are so). They are certainly anxious about their position, and would much rather go on with an orderly balance which secures them the considerable benefits they enjoy at present than have to face the chaos which at one time was supposed to suit the Pathan outlook. One thing is certain, and that is that they will in no sense submit to any local control which could remotely be represented as exercised by a Hindu-dominated Government.

2

Cabinet

India and Burma Committee. Paper I.B. (47) 39

L/P&J/10/78: ff 18–19

FUTURE RELATIONS BETWEEN INDIA AND ADJACENT COUNTRIES

MEMORANDUM BY THE SECRETARY OF STATE FOR INDIA

INDIA OFFICE, *22 March 1947*

At the informal meeting of Ministers held on 14th March,[1] there was some discussion about future relations between India and adjacent countries, particularly Afghanistan and Nepal. Following this discussion I think my colleagues may be interested in the annexed factual note[2] in regard to British and Indian representation in those two countries.

2. During the course of discussion the question was also raised whether it was not desirable that Afghanistan and other States on the borders of India,

such as Nepal and Tibet (Bhutan, though an independent State (not under suzerainty) in treaty relations with H.M.G., has no recognised international status and may be regarded as a British-protected State) should be formally acquainted with the policy of H.M.G. in regard to India as announced on 20th February, and the India Office was, therefore, invited to consider the question in consultation with the Foreign Office. The matter has been considered accordingly and it is felt that there are serious objections to any such proposal.

3. In the first place, the Prime Minister's statement of 20th February was made *urbi et orbi* and there is no occasion to communicate a copy of it to foreign Governments unless there is any particular aspect of it to which H.M.G. desire to draw attention. If it were communicated to the Afghan and other Governments, it would surely be necessary to point out the implications of the statement as it affects the foreign Governments concerned and to say that, as H.M.G.'s control in India will be withdrawn not later than June, 1948, it will be necessary for the foreign Governments to prepare to deal in future with the Indian Government alone.

4. Secondly, it would presumably also be necessary to give some indication of H.M.G.'s view as to the future, in international law, of the Treaty obligations which at present govern relations between Afghanistan in particular and H.M.G. This would evidently be a delicate matter unless we are in a position to say here and now upon what authorities in India the Treaty obligations now undertaken by H.M.G. will, after June 1948, devolve.

5. Thirdly, the Afghan Government have recently raised with us, both in Kabul and in London, very difficult questions about the future of the tribal areas between Afghanistan and British India to which evasive replies have necessarily had to be returned since we were advised by Lord Wavell that these matters would necessarily have to be examined in consultation with the Interim Government and that the present was a most inopportune time for consultations on such a topic. If a communication were now to be made to the Afghan Government, they would be encouraged to re-open this awkward question and to press for a definite reply which we are in no position to give.

6. On the whole I feel that there would be grave disadvantages in making any statement on our own initiative to the Governments of adjacent countries until we are in a position to specify with a good deal more precision than we are at present with what authorities in India they will have to deal in international matters after the transfer of power. If we could be certain that when that time comes there would be a single Indian Government responsible for all India's foreign relations there would be some advantage in putting foreign

[1] See Vol. IX, No. 530, Item 3. The meeting was in fact held on 13 March 1947.
[2] Not printed.

Governments on notice that these were the authorities with whom they would have to deal in the future; but so long as there is a possibility that the frontiers of India will be under the control of more than one authority it would, I suggest, be highly dangerous to make any statement which would provoke questions to which we could give no positive answer at this stage.

7. In anticipation of the approval of my colleagues to this course, I am taking steps to inform Lord Mountbatten in the sense indicated above.

P.-L.

3

Mr Alexander to Lord Pethick-Lawrence

L/WS/1/993: f 25

OFFICE OF THE MINISTER OF DEFENCE,
GREAT GEORGE STREET, S.W.I,
22 March 1947

Dear Pethick-Lawrence,

You wrote on 11th March[1] to ask me to obtain the views of the Chiefs of Staff on a memorandum about the advisability of withdrawing our invitation to India to send two representatives to the Commonwealth Advisory Committee on Defence Science.

The Chiefs of Staff feel that this invitation should be withdrawn since the representation of India on this Commonwealth Advisory Committee, like the attendance of Indian students at Service Staff Colleges, is open to the grave objection that it precludes the discussion of Top Secret subjects or of information derived from U.S. sources and thus imposes a serious handicap on the usefulness of the proceedings. I agree with this view.

Since the Government of India have taken the initiative by asking whether "the invitation should be modified by the recent announcement of H.M.G."[2] it looks as though they rather expect us to withdraw it. At any rate they can hardly complain if we do. And, of course, you would make it clear that our decision would at once be reconsidered if India should decide to remain within the Commonwealth.

I am sending a copy of this letter to the Prime Minister.

Yours sincerely,
A. V. ALEXANDER

[1] Not printed: see L/WS/1/993: ff 39–43.   [2] Tel. 931 of 5 March. *Ibid:* f 48.

4

Government of India, Defence Department to Secretary of State

Telegram, L/WS/1/1013: f 82

IMMEDIATE   NEW DELHI, *22 March 1947, 6.30 pm*
TOP SECRET   *Received: 23 March, 4.10 pm*

No. 1164. In view of constitutional changes which will be put into effect by
1st June 1948 and consequent reorganisation within Indian Army, Government
of India now wish to withdraw all Indian troops serving overseas by the end of
1947. This is in addition to early withdrawal from Iraq which H.M.G. have
suggested and [in] which Government of India have concurred. Request your
approval and formal acceptance by H.M.G. of notice of this intention
with following programme.

Japan Withdrawal by 15th September 1947 in accordance with prescribed
six months notice. Government of India would, however, be grateful if
H.M.G. would agree to an earlier date.

Malaya Complete withdrawal by 31st December 1947.

Mideast, Egypt and Palestine Withdrawal forthwith.

Burma Complete withdrawal by 31st December 1947. (This date is also being
communicated to the Government of Burma).[1]

---

[1] In tel. 7138 of 3 June the Secretary of State informed the Government of India, Defence Department,
that H.M.G. accepted these proposals in principle but requested the retention until 1 June 1948 of
certain skilled Indian administrative units in Malaya and Singapore, and the retention 'for a period'
of three Indian Infantry Battalions in Burma together with the administrative troops necessary to
support both them and the Burma Army. In tel. 2663 of 31 July 1947 the Government of India,
Defence Department, agreed to the retention until 31 March 1948 of certain of these units though it
was not able to meet H.M.G.'s requirements in full. Its agreement was subject to the proviso that
Indian troops 'will in no case be used to suppress any national movement and to sufficient officers
being forthcoming for the future armies of India and Pakistan'. L/WS/1/1013 and 1014.

5

Record of Interview between Mr Kiran Shankar Roy and
Sir F. Burrows[1]

Mountbatten Papers. Official Correspondence Files: Interviews

22 March 1947

After some desultory talk, the conversation was steered by Mr Roy to the
present political situation in Bengal and its relation to the political situation
elsewhere in India. He said it was inconceivable that Bengal should stand by
itself as an independent State and that there was no possibility of the Hindus
co-operating if the dominant Muslim majority made that an issue. What the
Hindus would probably do in such circumstances would be immediately to
launch a passive resistance movement (if it remained at that), refuse to pay any
taxes to the existing Government of Bengal and set up a parallel Government of
their own to which they would pay taxes. He expressed great appreciation of
the Chief Minister's (Mr Suhrawardy's) recent speeches but felt that they were
the expressions mainly of his own individual opinion and had but slight
backing from the Muslim League Party.

H.E. said that in his view Pakistan, envisaged as enjoying sovereign and
independent status, would be difficult to apply to Bengal divided as it is from
the nearest potential Pakistan unit, the Punjab, by over 700 miles of territory
comprising two Hindu Provinces and with three Hindu Provinces as its
neighbours. He suggested that the proper course for Mr Roy and his Party to
adopt was to be reasonable and to meet the Chief Minister more than half way
so that a Coalition Government could be set up in Bengal irrespective of what
happened in the rest of India to enable a peaceful transfer of power to be made.

Mr K.S. Roy replied that if that could be accomplished he and those for
whom he spoke would be more than satisfied and he added that they would be
content to leave the issues of the number and distribution of portfolios in
such a Coalition Government in the hands of the Governor.

---

[1] Mr Tyson sent Mr Abell a copy of this note on 24 March and said that Mr K.S. Roy had, at his own
request, asked to see Sir F. Burrows 'probably to try to find out what H.E. was thinking about the
present move to set up a separate (Hindu) Province of West Bengal'.

  Mr Tyson added:

  'As you probably know, the proposal for a separate West Bengal is at present primarily a Hindu
Mahasabha idea and though it has had a guarded blessing from some high ranking Congress
leaders at Delhi, the Congress Party is not yet committed to it and opinion among Hindus in
Bengal is still very divided. So far as we know, K.S. Roy himself has not publicly committed
himself to any scheme of the kind, though it is obvious from his visit to H.E. that he sees and is
ready to exploit the bargaining value of the movement vis-à-vis Suhrawardy's pleas for an independent Bengal in which the 45 % Hindu element will have their fair share.'

  Mountbatten Papers, Official Correspondence Files: Bengal, Partition of, Part I(a).

6

Note by Sir E. Mieville

Mountbatten Papers. Official Correspondence Files: States, Relations with the, Part I(a)

23 March 1947

NOTE OF A TALK WITH SIR C.P. RAMASWAMI IYER

Sir C.P., who is a Hindu and Dewan of Travancore, came to see me this afternoon. He started by talking about Travancore and saying how fortunately they were placed as regards British India, having a long seaboard on one side and mountains on the other, with only a narrow strip at the top which could easily be defended by state forces. He said that he had already made a definite statement to the effect that Travancore had no intention of taking part in the Constituent Assembly and that unless a strong central government was formed she would remain an independent state. He asked me if I thought there was any chance when things settled down of a new treaty with Great Britain. I asked what sort of treaty he had in mind and he said what he would like most would be for Travancore to become a Dominion on the grounds that its population was greater than that of the whole of Australia, to say nothing of New Zealand, but failing that he hoped it would be possible to enter into a trade treaty. As to the former, I gave him no encouragement. As to the latter, I said that I did not foresee that there would be any great difficulty.

2. He went on to say that the Princes must individually decide for themselves as to their future, and he did very much hope that we would not suggest to them that they should make peace with Congress. There was a feeling that Congress were going to bluff us and if they did it would create the worst possible impression with the Muslim League and further that it would not be like the British to let down the Princes who had stood by us all these years. He finally added that when His Highness of Bhopal was given an audience with the Viceroy, he had every reason to believe that His Highness was the bearer of a letter from Jinnah saying that the Muslim League would not enter the Constituent Assembly.

7

Mr Abell to all Governors' Secretaries (except U.P. and Madras)[1]

R/3/1/149: f 65

SECRET   THE VICEROY'S HOUSE, NEW DELHI, *23 March 1947*
No. 1299/2
My dear —

H.E. the Governor may already have given some orders about the examination of the records in the Governor's Secretariat. If not, perhaps the matter could be considered now, in view of the transfer of power next year.

2. For this purpose, papers can probably be broadly classified as follows:
(1) Papers of no permanent interest which should be destroyed;
(2) Papers of an embarrassing nature;
(3) Papers of interest to the new Provincial Government, e.g. about conventions in regard to the Public Service Commission, which do not come in category (2).

3. Papers in category (3) can clearly be handed over. Papers in category (2) should be destroyed unless they are likely to be of permanent interest to H.M.G., in which case the matter should please be reported to me, and I will consult the India Office if necessary.[2]

4. No confidential papers emanating from H.M.G. should be handed over without a reference to this office.

Yours sincerely,

G. E. B. ABELL

[1] The Governor's Secretary (Madras) had himself raised this question with Mr Abell who thereupon wrote to the Governor's Secretary (U.P.) for advice, and therefore Mr Abell's letters to these two Governors' Secretaries, though to the same effect, were cast in slightly different terms. R/3/1/149: ff 49–50, 58, 64, 71.

[2] So far as is known files from only two Governors' Secretariats were transferred to London: three from the Punjab (now available for consultation in the India Office Records as R/3/1/176–8) and eighty-six from Bengal (now available as R/3/2/1–86).

8

Government of India, External Affairs Department to Secretary of State

Telegram, L/P&J/10/78: f 26

IMMEDIATE   NEW DELHI, *24 March 1947, 5.40am*
Received: 24 March, 6.20am

No. 2326. Circular. Following from Principal Information Officer.

Following is not repeat not for publication before 05.00 hours repeat 05.00 hours G.M.T. on 24th March 1947. Following is text of brief address by H.E. Lord Mountbatten at swearing-in ceremony to-day.

Begins: Although I believe it is not usual for a speech to be made at the swearing-in ceremony I should like to say a few words to you and to India.

This is not a normal Viceroyalty on which I am embarking. H.M. Government are resolved to transfer power by June 1948; and since new constitutional arrangements must be made and many complicated questions of administration resolved—all of which will take time to put into effect—this means that a solution must be reached within the next few months.

I believe that every political leader in India feels as I do the urgency of the task before us. I hope soon to be in close consultation with them and I will give them all the help I can.

In the meantime every one of us must do what he can to avoid any word or action which might lead to further bitterness or add to the toll of innocent victims. I know how very many there are who are determined to work to that end and I shall do everything I can to support them. I have many Indian friends. Some were made when I was out here twenty-five years ago—it was here in Delhi that my wife and I became engaged. In the three years that I was with South East Asia Command I made many more among the Indian fighting forces with whom I am so proud to have been associated.

It will be no easy matter to succeed Lord Wavell who has done so much to take India along the path to self-government. I have always had a great admiration for him and I shall devote myself to finishing the work which he began.

I am under no illusion about the difficulty of my task. I shall need greatest goodwill of the greatest possible number and I am asking India today for that goodwill. *Ends.*

Important caution: please look out for immediately succeeding telegram which will include last minute alterations, if any.[1]

Text not to be released before stipulated time.

For Joyce, Information Department. (Please copy to Sudhir Ghose).

[1] No changes were made to the text.

9

*Record of Interview between Rear-Admiral Viscount Mountbatten
of Burma and the Nawab of Bhopal*

Mountbatten Papers. Viceroy's Interview No. 1

TOP SECRET   *24 March 1947*

This interview lasted $1\frac{1}{4}$ hours. The Nawab of Bhopal, who is Chancellor of
The Chamber of Princes, offered me personally all possible assistance. He
implied that he had turned the scales in persuading Mr Jinnah to accept the
Cabinet Mission's plan at Simla. He felt that nothing had yet happened which
made the situation irrevocable, but that it was daily becoming more difficult.
He passed, as third party and for what it was worth, a message to me from Mr
Jinnah declaring that nothing would induce the latter to accept any form of
unified government. But he did not personally feel that this declaration was
necessarily irrevocable.[1] He said that Mr Jinnah had purposely refrained from
issuing any statement which might be embarrassing to me—and this point was
repeated later by Mr Liaquat Ali Khan.[2]

The Nawab raised the question of future political relations between the
States and the United Kingdom. He mentioned the possibility of States, or
groups of States, being granted Dominion status—or perhaps similar re-
lationship with other countries, for example the United States of America.
He spoke of the question of buying arms from the United Kingdom or the
United States.

He showed himself bitterly regretful of the recent split among the Princes.
He talked of a group of States "flirting with Congress". The present, he felt
was the wrong moment for such realignments. He considered that it would not
be possible for him to retain the position of Chancellor much longer; he
might well have to resign. He would perhaps be succeeded by the Maharajah
of Patiala—whom he described as "a Sikh in the Congress pocket".

The Nawab of Bhopal denied any accusation that he was throwing in his
lot with the Muslim League. He asked me whether there was any possibility
of British authority being extended beyond the time limit of June 1948. I
replied that I envisaged no such possibility; but if all the Indian parties together
asked for such an extension, I would recommend their request to His Majesty's
Government.

[1] [Note in original:] This point of view was retracted [3] days later when he telegraphed me from
Bombay [No. 28] saying that there was now no hope of persuading Mr Jinnah to agree to an unified
Government.

[2] See No. 12.

10

Record of Interview between Rear-Admiral Viscount Mountbatten of Burma and the Maharaja of Bikaner

Mountbatten Papers. Viceroy's Interview No. 2

TOP SECRET   *24 March 1947*

The Maharajah of Bikaner began with tremendous protestation of personal friendship for me. He expressed himself most gratified that his forecast that I would return to India as Viceroy had proved correct. He gave his explanation of the difficulties in the Chamber of Princes, and put forward the point of view of the "dissidents". He then spoke in great confidence of this split. He claimed that he had been primarily responsible for the appointment of the Nawab of Bhopal as Chancellor and that he had a great admiration for him. The "dissidents" were inclining to Congress not along communal lines but because they felt that Congress was the one central party which possessed the potential to extend itself beyond communities. Bikaner, Jaipur, Jodhpur, Patiala, Baroda and Gwalior were now proposing to go ahead and join the Constituent Assembly, and generally to drift towards the centre. He felt quite sincerely that this would make my own job easier.

The Maharajah also gave an account of the lines along which it was planned that the States should develop. It was proposed, within the next 3 to 5 years, to introduce democratic government and constitutional sovereignty—though the right of the ruler directly to control the armed forces would be retained.

I gave Bikaner the same answer as I had given to Bhopal[1] concerning the extension of British authority after June, 1948. He said that for personal reasons he would love the British to stay—but he would have to follow the Congress lead and did not believe that Congress would "eat their words".

[1] See No. 9.

11

Record of Interview between Rear-Admiral Viscount Mountbatten of Burma and Pandit Nehru

Mountbatten Papers. Viceroy's Interview No. 3

TOP SECRET   *24 March 1947*

Pandit Nehru struck me as most sincere.

I started off by asking him what, in his opinion, was the greatest problem confronting India at the present time. He surprised me by replying that the economic problem was the the most serious. This was not being really gripped. The Forward Planning Department had been abolished 18 months ago, and he greatly regretted this. He felt it essential to have an impartial man in charge, as the Muslim League were opposed to all forward planning as it meant planning for an unified India.

We then discussed the history of the Cripps Offer and the Cabinet Mission. Nehru seemed 95 % in agreement with the Mission's statement and with Lord Wavell. I challenged him on the disagreements and reservations which he expressed, and he produced convincing arguments.

I asked him about Mr Jinnah. He gave me a remarkable word-picture of Jinnah's character. He described him as one of the most extraordinary men in history. A financially successful though mediocre lawyer, Jinnah had found success late in life. He had not been politically successful until after the age of 60. Nehru explained Jinnah's creed, which he admitted had scored enormous success, as always to avoid taking any positive action which might split his followers; to refuse to hold meetings or to answer questions; never to make a progressive statement because it might lead to internal Muslim dissensions. These negative qualities were ones which had a direct appeal to the Muslims— therefore it was not to be hoped that logic would prevail.

I said that it was not a question of logic but of the time limit. What if I were to say to Jinnah that he would be granted his Pakistan? Nehru agreed that it might be possible to frighten Jinnah into co-operation on the basis of the short length of time available.

I next asked Nehru what he felt about the Coalition Government. He gave his opinion that it had been a most tragic act to force the Muslim League in, as they would anyhow have joined voluntarily before very long. He now, indeed, knew that Jinnah had actually decided that the Muslims would have had to enter the Government after a few more weeks.

Pandit Nehru agreed that he was not accepted by the Muslims as the leader of the Interim Government. The Muslim League did not intend that the Government should have its own powers and stand on its own feet. They deliberately intended that responsibility should continue to rest on the Viceroy under The Act of 1935. He understood the British object to transfer power by stages. But how was this to be achieved if the Muslim League did not recognise him?

We then spoke of the Three resolutions passed by the Congress party on 5th March[1] (discussion of partition in the Punjab is recorded elsewhere[2]); and of Compensation for members of the Services.[3]

I told Nehru, in the same way as I told Liaquat in my interview with him today, that I considered that I had an appalling responsibility to make up my mind what to recommend to His Majesty's Government. I drew attention to the remarkable position in which His Majesty's Government had placed me. I said that I intended to approach the problem in an atmosphere of stark realism.

In connection with the time factor, I pointed out that it took two years to separate Burma. I was less interested that India should be handed over on lines which might ultimately prove correct than that mechanism should be set up to avoid bloodshed after the departure of the British. I asked Nehru if he agreed that the Army was the final guarantor of law and order, and that the morale and discipline of the Army was of the highest importance. He agreed. I pointed out the problems which arose in trying to get the Army nationalized within the time limit.

Nehru said that he did not consider it possible, with the forces which were at work, that India could remain within The Commonwealth. But basically, he said, they did not want to break any threads, and he suggested "some form of common nationality" (I feel that they are beginning to see that they cannot go out of the Commonwealth; but they cannot afford to say that they will stay in; they are groping for a formula). Nehru gave a direct implication that they wanted to stay in; but a categorical statement that they intended to go out.

Addendum to No. 11

I think that it was evidence of Nehru's fairness of mind that he said he would look for someone other than his previous nominee to be Trade Agent in Malaya, since Lord Wavell had objected to him on the ground that he took part in an anti-British movement during the war.

¹ Vol. IX, Enclosure to No. 511.   ² No. 14.   ³ See No. 18.

12

Record of Interview between Rear-Admiral Viscount Mountbatten of Burma and Mr Liaquat Ali Khan

Mountbatten Papers. Viceroy's Interview No. 4

TOP SECRET   *24 March 1947*

The first half hour of this interview was spent in discussion of the Finance Bill. Then Liaquat gave me his impressions of the Cabinet Mission meetings and of Mr Jinnah. He emphasized that Jinnah was most anxious not to embarrass me in any way. He gave me his version of how the Coalition Government has been formed—a totally different version to that rendered by Nehru—and quite untrue. I told him that it was my object that the Cabinet should function more and more as a Coalition Government—at present it was the only body representing every shade of opinion in India, and I set great store by it—but only if it could be made to function properly. Liaquat said that he was opposed to Cabinet Committees but I persuaded him into suggesting that they should be set up. (He made this suggestion at a Cabinet meeting later in the day but it was turned down by Congress.)

Liaquat then proposed that decisions of the Cabinet should have to be voted by a majority of each party as well as by a majority of the Cabinet itself. (This suggestion is being investigated apart.)[1]

I told Liaquat, in the same way as I told Nehru in my interview with him today, that I considered that I had an appalling responsibility to make up my mind what to recommend to His Majesty's Government. I drew attention to the remarkable position in which His Majesty's Government had placed me. I said that I intended to approach the problem in an atmosphere of stark realism. In connection with the time factor, I pointed out that it took two years to separate Burma. I was less interested that India should be handed over on lines which might ultimately prove correct than that mechanism should be set up to avoid bloodshed after the departure of the British. I asked Liaquat if he agreed that the Army was the final guarantor of law and order, and that the morale and discipline of the Army was of the highest importance. He agreed. I pointed out the problems which arose in trying to get the Army nationalized within the time limit.

[1] On 25 March Mr Abell prepared a note on 'System of Voting within the Cabinet' in which he pointed out that Mr Liaquat Ali Khan's proposal 'would mean that the Muslim League had a complete right of veto in every case that came up'. He did not believe for a moment that the Congress would even look at it nor that Mr Liaquat Ali Khan could seriously have thought that his request would be granted. Mr Abell therefore suggested that nothing further need be said about it unless Liaquat raised it again. Mountbatten Papers, V.C.P.8.

13

Sir E. Jenkins (Punjab) to Rear-Admiral Viscount Mountbatten of Burma

Telegram, L/P &J/8/663: f 177

IMMEDIATE   LAHORE, *24 March 1947, 11.15 pm*
CONFIDENTIAL   *Received in India Office: 24 March, 11.30 pm*
No. 70–G. Punjab situation. My immediately preceding telegram.[1] Khizar, Firoz and Giani Kartar Singh saw me at different times today. Khizar has resisted pressure to join League and has advised Mamdot strongly in favour of settlement with minorities. He thinks some of League leaders realise extreme danger of present Moslem position but none of them is anxious to face Jinnah. Firoz was complacent and tried to develop latest Moslem theory that Hindus and Sikhs, particularly latter, were aggressors everywhere. I asked him how he

accounted for the non-Moslem corpses. Kartar Singh asked that Sikhs might be invited to any consultations which are held by the Viceroy at New Delhi. He added that in (?absence) of agreement acceptable to Sikhs between Congress and League, Sikhs must insist on partition of the Punjab and that Sikhs would resist with all their resources any endeavour to set up Moslem Ministry in the meantime. Failing agreement as above partition must be effective and working before June 30th 1948. In view of importance of Sikhs in the Punjab Kartar Singh's request deserves most serious consideration.[2]

Repeated to Secretary of State.

[1] In tel. 69–G of 24 March Sir E. Jenkins reported that communal rioting was reported from Hodal, Gurgaon District and that a communal riot had also occurred on 22 March at Kartarpur, Jullundur District. L/P &J/8/663: f 178.

[2] Lord Mountbatten replied in tel. 630–S of 25 March as follows: 'I will certainly keep in mind the importance of consulting Sikhs.' R/3/1/176: f 58.

14

Minutes of Viceroy's First Staff Meeting, Item 4

Mountbatten Papers

TOP SECRET

Those present during discussion of Item 4 of this meeting held at The Viceroy's House, New Delhi on 25 March 1947 at 10.30 am were: Rear-Admiral Viscount Mountbatten of Burma, Lord Ismay, Sir E. Mieville, Mr Abell, Captain Brockman, Mr Campbell-Johnson, Lieutenant-Colonel Erskine Crum

RE-DRAWING OF PROVINCIAL BOUNDARIES

HIS EXCELLENCY THE VICEROY stated that during his conversation with Pandit Nehru the previous day,[1] the latter had admitted the entity [unity] of the Punjab and confessed that he would regret partition. Pandit Nehru had suggested a temporary partition (primarily in order to avoid Section 93) into three areas—the first predominantly Muslim, the second predominantly Hindu and the third a mixed area. There might be separate Ministers for each area all under the one Governor. They might meet together and advise the Governor each on their own area matters. The arrangement would be strictly temporary, to last only as long as the British retained responsibility. Pandit Nehru had pointed out that Mr Jinnah was much opposed to partition. HIS EXCELLENCY THE VICEROY said that he had asked Pandit Nehru to send him full proposals together with the opinion[2] of the Constitutional Adviser. He added that he would take no further steps without consulting Mr Jinnah.

[1] See No. 11.   [2] Not printed. See Mountbatten Papers, V.C.P.7.

MR ABELL gave his opinion that the partition of Bengal was almost bound to follow any partition in the Punjab. He drew attention to the many objections against partition on a short term basis.

LORD ISMAY cast doubt upon the possibility of ever re-uniting the Punjab once a partition, however temporary, was made. HIS EXCELLENCY THE VICEROY said that he doubted that it would be possible to form a Government in the Punjab on any basis other than temporary partition.

SIR ERIC MIEVILLE drew attention to a telegram[3] from the Governor of the Punjab saying that Kartar Singh had stated that, in the absence of an agreement acceptable to the Sikhs between Congress and the League, the Sikhs must insist on the partition of the Punjab and would resist with all their resources any endeavour to set up a Muslim Ministry in the meantime. The Governor of the Punjab had stressed that, in view of the importance of the Sikhs in the Punjab, Kartar Singh's request deserved the most serious consideration.

HIS EXCELLENCY THE VICEROY:

decided to defer further discussion of this matter to a later date.

[3] No. 13.

15

Record of Interview between Rear-Admiral Viscount Mountbatten of Burma and Dr John Matthai

Mountbatten Papers. Viceroy's Interview No. 5

TOP SECRET   *25 March 1947*

Dr Matthai struck me as an absolutely first class man, balanced, reasonable and with a sense of humour. He pointed out the most difficult situation of those who, in the present non-cooperative mood of the Coalition Government, tried to steer an independent and honourable course. These persons, among whose number he counted himself, became more and more disliked by both sides. Dr Matthai said that he had done everything in his power to back up Mr Liaquat Ali Khan in the latter's Budget proposals, and the only result was a bitter attack on him in the Muslim organ *Dawn*. He suggested that all who tried to steer a straight, unbiased course would find themselves becoming increasingly unpopular from both sides.

Dr. Matthai confessed that everyone was most pessimistic about the future. But he, like the other political leaders I have met, agreed that the British Government's policy of sending me out with "carte blanche" was the only possible way of dealing with the situation. He also said that no one in this country had so far got into Jinnah's mind, but thought that I might have a chance of doing so, and breaking down his façade. He agreed that Jinnah had been holding out for a long time on the basis of a negative nuisance value, but he described Jinnah as much more of a realist than he made out.

Matthai gave his opinion that, but for Congress, there was no body in India which would not move Heaven and Earth to keep the British.

16

Record of Interview between Rear-Admiral Viscount Mountbatten of Burma and Sardar Patel

Mountbatten Papers. Viceroy's Interview No. 7

TOP SECRET   *25 March 1947*

SARDAR PATEL was most charming for the first hour of this interview, evincing a considerable sense of humour. He is apparently very fond of Sir Stafford Cripps.

He said that the reason why the Cabinet meeting the previous day had gone so smoothly was that all the members had previously decided not to make it stormy for me first time. He told me that he thought I ought to dismiss the Muslim League members of the Cabinet because they represented an organisation which, as a result of their "direct action" resolution, had the avowed intention of attacking the central organisation. His opinion was that the Muslims were proud of what had happened recently in Assam, the Punjab and the North-West Frontier Province.

I pointed out that the Coalition Government was the only means I had of dealing with responsible leaders of both parties. If I did away with that, Congress would be the first to suffer.

The rest of this interview was on the subjects of Control of the Secretary of States Services and Compensation for the Services, which are recorded elsewhere.[1]

[1] See No. 20, Items 5 and 6.

17

Sir H. Dow (Bihar) to Rear-Admiral Viscount Mountbatten of Burma (Extract)

L/P&J/5/182: ff 83–4

D.O. No. 80–G.B.   *25 March 1947*

2. Reactions to H.M.G.'s statement of the 20th February are still rather indeterminate in this province, where there are few politicians who have an all-India reputation, or are sufficiently capable of independent thought to deserve one. The Hindu press does not quite know how to take the Congress suggestion that the Punjab should be divided, and is also doubtful about the partition of Bengal, which seems implicit in the Congress proposal and has certainly been given an added impetus by it. I should say that local Hindu opinion is still very strongly in favour of "Akhund Hindustan", and that those who give hesitant support to ideas of partition do so rather in the belief that it will show the complete unworkability of Pakistan than because they are prepared to contemplate the division of India into two independent states.

★   ★   ★

4. Mr. Gandhi has been here since 5th March and is doing a certain amount of mild touring in the areas which suffered most from the riots. The public press have given sufficient publicity to his tours and discourses to make it unnecessary for me to say much about them. I was on tour in the south of the province when he arrived, but got in touch with him on my return to Patna and asked him to come and see me. We had a very frank talk for an hour, and he was in a most friendly mood. I told of the way public feeling in this province had been worked on during the last six months, and how even those who proposed to work for communal harmony had no love of peace in their hearts but had mainly tried merely to divert hatred into other channels. We discussed the Ministry's attitude towards reparations and rehabilitation and he asked my permission to take up what I had said with the Ministry. To this I raised no objection, as I had only told him what I had told the Ministers themselves a dozen times. Mr. Gandhi seems to have put my criticisms to the Ministry so bluntly that I am not surprised that they have reacted strongly, and I have since written to Mr. Gandhi, for their benefit, putting my criticism in my own words rather than his. I don't think he intends to make trouble between me and the Ministry: in any case this is an aspect of the matter which I feel competent to deal with. On the whole, Gandhi's visit to Bihar seems to be doing good, and he has been downright in his condemnation of those responsible for the riots. It is generally supposed that he came here at the earnest solicitation of Dr. Syed Mahmud, and that the other Ministers resent not having been con-

sulted by their colleague, but it seems likely that criticism of the Bihar Ministry which he received from Suhrawardy and from "Colonel" Gill had something to do with it. The Ministers, however, dare not show any open resentment, and Dr. Mahmud, who is a hopeless administrator and whom his colleagues were alleged to be plotting to edge out of the Ministry, is now Gandhi's host and for the time being invulnerable to attack. Undoubtedly the presence of Gandhi in Bihar is doing much to reassure local Muslims, who feel that they cannot be subjected to further mass attacks while he is here. But I do not think that either Gandhi himself or the general body of Muslims feel that there has been anything like the change of heart in the Hindus that his discourses lay insistence on.

5. I did not discuss with Gandhi his insistence on an official inquiry into the Bihar riots. Nothing about this has come up to me officially, but the Press has announced that it is to be a one man Commission, and that Mr. Justice Reuben of the Patna High Court has been selected: he is an ICS man, being a Jew from the Bombay Presidency. The Chief Secretary informs me that Mr. Reuben has been approached but has made various conditions that Government have not yet accepted, and that he is now very annoyed at the premature publicity which the proposal has been given. I still do not think that the inquiry can possibly do any good. While there are widespread communal disorders still raging and possibly spreading in other parts of India, there is no likelihood that an official report on Bihar will have more than an academic interest by the time it is completed, and in the meantime any publicity given to its proceedings can do nothing but harm. Events are now moving fast. Everybody, apparently including the members themselves, has lost interest in the work of the Calcutta Enquiry Commission, and one is tempted to think that these matters might be left over for future examination by the pundits of the Historical Records Commission.

18

Rear-Admiral Viscount Mountbatten of Burma to Lord Pethick-Lawrence

Telegram, R/3/1/183: ff 93–4

MOST IMMEDIATE   NEW DELHI, *25 March 1947, 6 pm*
SECRET   *Received: 25 March, 4.30 pm*
No. 625–S. COMPENSATION

1. I had a preliminary talk with Nehru yesterday 24th March, and explained H.M.G's decision. He was frankly astounded. His attitude was that the Indian Government wish members of the Secretary of State's Services to continue in employment after June 1948 and the new Government would be prepared to offer them continuous employment on the same conditions as heretofore. In

particular he objected to the compensation terms which H.M.G. intended to pay, which were in effect an encouragement to leave the Service.

2. I pointed out that from the British Officers' point of view the transfer to service in the new Indian Government would in fact be the termination of a definite contract and might well be regarded by them as being in the nature of a gamble. If, however, British Officers had already been compensated I thought there was a far better chance that they would accept such a gamble and that they would be more likely to continue to serve with the new Indian Government.

3. Nehru appreciated that H.M.G. must do what they liked in regard to British Officers but he thought that to offer similar terms to Indian Officers in the Secretary of State's Services was quite unnecessary and in any case the compensation proposed was too large. He was confident that this action would be bitterly resented. I pointed out that in no circumstances would H.M.G. consider any discrimination between British and Indian Officers of the same Service. I added that had H.M.G. proposed such discriminations I was sure that the Interim Government would have been the first to protest at such treatment.

4. With reference to your telegram 3899 of 24th March[1] I am seeing Patel today 25th March and in my immediately succeeding telegram[2] I give the draft of the announcement which I propose to put to my Cabinet on Wednesday the 26th March, and to make public in the newspapers of Friday the 28th March. I should be grateful if you would arrange for the necessary question to be asked in Parliament on Thursday afternoon. As soon as this has been mentioned in Cabinet, I will send your two despatches[3] to the Home Department and the Defence Department. I do not think that I should delay any longer once Patel has been informed.

5. I have included in the announcement mention of the fact that members of the Services will be entitled to the leave due to them after the date on which they are permitted to retire with compensation. This follows from paragraph 9 of your despatch Services No. 1. Moreover, the effect of the announcement will be completely spoiled if the point about leave is not covered.

6. The last paragraph provides for releases being spread out over a period of time. This has been mentioned in regard to officers of Defence Services in paragraph 10 of despatch Military No. 1 but is not covered by the despatch relating to civilians. I am advised that in some Provinces and to some extent at the Centre, it would be desirable to spread out the releases as substitutes become available, and not to keep all British officers till the final date of transfer.

[1] In this telegram Lord Pethick-Lawrence asked Lord Mountbatten to let him know, as long as possible in advance, of the date when he proposed to broach the matter of compensation with his Council. L/S &G/7/913: f 5.   [2] R/3/1/183: ff 95–6.

[3] These despatches conveyed officially to the Governor-General in Council the decisions on compensation reached before Lord Mountbatten's departure for India (see Vol. IX, Nos. 502, 518 and 529). *Ibid:* ff 56–88.

19

Cabinet

India and Burma Committee. I.B. (47) 15th Meeting

R/30/1/10: ff 2–4

Those present at this Meeting held at 10 Downing Street, S.W.1, on 25 March 1947 at 9.45 pm were: Mr Attlee (in the Chair), Sir S. Cripps, Mr Alexander, Viscount Addison, Lord Pethick-Lawrence, the Earl of Listowel

Also present were: Mr Henderson, Sir E. Bridges, Sir D. Monteath, Sir W. Croft, Sir G. Laithwaite; Mr S.E.V. Luke (Secretary)

Compensation terms for Members of the Indian Services Appointed by the Secretary of State and for Officers of the Indian Fighting Services
(Previous Reference: I.B.(47)14th Meeting, Minute 3)[1]

The Committee had before them telegrams Nos. 625–S[2] and 626–S[3] of 25th March from the Viceroy to the Secretary of State for India regarding the terms of the announcement on compensation which he proposed to communicate to the Interim Government on 26th March and to publish on 28th March.

THE SECRETARY OF STATE FOR INDIA asked the Committee to consider, first, the procedure proposed by the Viceroy for handling this matter and, secondly, the actual terms of the draft announcement. On the first point, he thought that the Viceroy's proposal to communicate only the proposed text of his announcement to the Interim Government and then to proceed with publi-·cation immediately was open to certain disadvantages. It seemed desirable that the Interim Government should consider the question in the light of the Secretary of State's two recent despatches as well as of the draft announcement, since the matter was now being laid for the first time before the Government of India as such. As His Majesty's Government were now reverting to a scheme which had been formally withdrawn at an earlier stage, the Government of India would have particular reason for feeling that they were being treated unceremoniously if they were not given an opportunity of considering the matter in the light of the full exposition set out in those despatches, and this might make an unfavourable impression at the outset of the new Viceroy's relations with his Cabinet. Moreover, the timetable proposed would afford the Interim Government insufficient opportunity to record their views, and for their reactions to be communicated to His Majesty's Government. They might, therefore, have ground for complaint that no attention had been given

---

[1] Vol. IX, No. 529.   [2] No. 18.
[3] This telegram conveyed the text of the draft announcement on compensation. R/3/1/183: ff 95–6.

to their views, and this might have an unfavourable effect upon the subsequent discussion of the question of ultimate financial liability. There was the further consideration that the proposed timetable would make it impossible for the Governor of Burma to give his Executive Council any opportunity to consider the corresponding problem of the payment of compensation to the Burma Services. The Governor would not receive the compensation tables until mid-day on 28th March at the earliest, and it would be most unfortunate if the Government of Burma and the Burma Services first heard of the matter through the repetition of Press messages from India. On the other hand, the Committee would recall that the Viceroy was particularly anxious to make an announcement on compensation on his arrival in India in order to put heart into the Services concerned. There was also a strong risk of leakage once the matter had been placed before the Interim Government.

The Committee felt that there were strong grounds for asking the Viceroy to delay publication of his announcement for a few days. They had particularly in mind the consideration that the statement to be made in Parliament would almost certainly provoke questions whether the British Government was to meet the cost of compensation and what action had been taken to reach agreement on this aspect of the matter with the Government of India. If it could only be said that a general proposition about compensation, such as that contained in the Viceroy's draft announcement, had been put to them and that they had no more than one day to consider their position, there was bound to be criticism. The Committee felt that a delay of a few days should not materially affect the Viceroy's objective, with which they were in full sympathy, of restoring the morale of the Services.

The Committee then considered the text of the Viceroy's draft announcement contained in his telegram No. 626–S. They were informed that this was based on a tentative draft which had been handed to the Viceroy before he left England. The Committee considered that the modifications introduced into the original draft, though no doubt intended for the sake of brevity, had resulted in some undesirable omissions and some obscurities, and that the Viceroy should be asked to make certain amendments in the text.

The Committee considered that, in communicating the terms of the Viceroy's announcement to Parliament, it would be necessary to preface the statement by a short historical introduction referring in particular to the pledge made in 1945 by the then Secretary of State for India.

The Committee—

(1) Invited the Secretary of State for India to inform the Viceroy that His Majesty's Government would strongly prefer that the announcement on compensation terms should be deferred for a few days; and that in the meantime he should communicate to the Interim Government the Secretary of State's two despatches on the subject.

(2) Invited the Secretary of State for India to reconsider the draft of the announcement in the light of their discussion, and to suggest any necessary amendments to the Viceroy.

(3) Invited the Secretary of State for India to arrange for the terms of the Viceroy's announcement, prefaced by a short historical introduction, to be communicated simultaneously to Parliament, and for the details of the compensation scheme to be made public in a White Paper.

(4) Invited the Secretary of State for Burma to inform the Governor of Burma of the developments in India on the compensation question.

20

Minutes of Viceroy's Second Staff Meeting

Mountbatten Papers

TOP SECRET

Those present at this Meeting held at The Viceroy's House, New Delhi on 26 March 1947 at 10 am were: Rear-Admiral Viscount Mountbatten of Burma, Lord Ismay, Sir E. Mieville, Mr Abell, Captain Brockman, Mr C. P. Scott, Mr Campbell-Johnson, Lieutenant-Colonel Erskine Crum

Item 3

THE BREAK-UP OF COMMUNAL PARTIES ON POLITICAL LINES

HIS EXCELLENCY THE VICEROY said that, during the conversation he had had with Nehru two days previously,[1] the latter had agreed that the Congress Party was likely eventually to break up on political lines. The present co-operation between different shades of political feeling within Congress was based on nationalistic aspirations, and a split on party rather than communal lines was probable after those aspirations had been achieved.

HIS EXCELLENCY THE VICEROY gave his opinion that the whole political system in India was likely to change after the withdrawal of the British. If Mr. Jinnah could be made to realise this, and that he might become an ever more powerful political figure after the re-alignment, it might be a way of breaking down his present negative attitude.

MR. ABELL pointed out that the recent Budget negotiations had caused dissension among the ranks of the Congress Party. The compromise eventually reached had inclined considerably towards capitalism, and caused considerable dissatisfaction among the adherents to the Left. However the system of separate electorates, which had been first introduced in the Act of 1919 owing to the

[1] No. 11.

pressure of communal feeling, stood in the way of any split into political rather than communal parties.

HIS EXCELLENCY THE VICEROY emphasized that public opinion in the United Kingdom would welcome a break-up of the communal parties and a re-alignment into parties corresponding to the Conservatives, Liberals and Socialists.

Item 5
CONTROL OF THE SECRETARY OF STATE'S SERVICES

HIS EXCELLENCY THE VICEROY said that, during his interview with Sardar Patel the previous day,[2] the latter had broached the subject of control of the Secretary of State's services, and claimed that this had been the main subject of his talks with Mr. Henderson. HIS EXCELLENCY THE VICEROY pointed out that this fact had never been disclosed to him in London nor to any member of his Staff. Sardar Patel wanted to secure that the Secretary of State's control should be transferred forthwith to the Government of India or, failing that, to the Governor General. He had quoted an instance of it taking three months to remove a Commissioner of Police from Bombay.

MR. ABELL stated that the latest proposal was that those members of the Services who wanted to leave after June 1948, would be retained under the control of the Secretary of State; the remainder would be gradually passed over to local control.

HIS EXCELLENCY THE VICEROY said that the main objection to this proposal was that it was still hoped to find a formula for retaining a connection between India and the Commonwealth; one of the main bargaining points with Pandit Nehru would be that India could not do without all the British personnel.

MR. ABELL pointed out that the transfer of control to the Governor General would leave the latter in an embarrassing position as the final arbiter; moreover, any such move would require amendment in Parliament of the 1935 Act.

HIS EXCELLENCY THE VICEROY directed P.S.V. to discuss the matter further with Sardar Patel and in particular to point out:

(a) That this subject had not been discussed in London before his departure;
(b) That any change in control would require amendment of the 1935 Act in Parliament.

Item 6
COMPENSATION FOR MEMBERS OF THE SERVICES

HIS EXCELLENCY THE VICEROY stated that, during his interview with Sardar Patel the previous day, he had raised the question of compensation for members of the Services. Sardar Patel had expressed himself as horrified with His Majesty's Government's intention; and stated that nobody, either Indian or

British, would be kept on by the Central Government after June 1948 if he accepted compensation. Sardar Patel's main point was that the Government of India had categorically stated that they wanted everybody to stay on and had offered the same conditions of service as at present. HIS EXCELLENCY THE VICEROY had explained to Sardar Patel that the reason for the inclusion of Indians in the compensation offer was to avoid discrimination. Sardar Patel had then spoken at length on the subject of discrimination and had given instances. He (His Excellency) had replied that it was not denied that there had been, in the past, cases of discrimination, but these had gradually decreased.

Attention was drawn to the two telegrams[3] of 26th March which had been received from the Secretary of State in reply to those[4] which had been despatched the previous day. The Secretary of State had requested that more time should elapse before the issue of any announcement and that His Excellency's Cabinet should consider the matter on the basis of the Secretary of State's two despatches rather than solely on the draft announcement. HIS EXCELLENCY THE VICEROY decided that these despatches should be issued to members of the Government and that the issue of an announcement should be postponed.

HIS EXCELLENCY THE VICEROY pointed out that the decisions of His Majesty's Government contained in the despatches would not have to be amended in view of the position taken up by Sardar Patel. No alteration would be necessary because any question of the Indian Government refusing to re-employ those who received compensation was a separate decision and did not affect His Majesty's Government's offer. He emphasised that the position of Indian officers who decided to stay on must be clarified. Would they get compensation if they changed their minds and wanted to leave after a period? In his own opinion such persons would have no claim on the British Government.

HIS EXCELLENCY THE VICEROY added that he considered that Sardar Patel was still open to some negotiations on this matter.

HIS EXCELLENCY THE VICEROY:

(i) directed P.S.V. to arrange for the issue of the Secretary of State's two despatches to members of the Cabinet;

(ii) decided to ask the members of the Cabinet at the meeting the following day to treat this matter as confidential pending issue of an announcement.

[2] No. 16.

[3] These telegrams reported the outcome of the discussion in No. 19 and explained why the India and Burma Committee wished Lord Mountbatten to defer the announcement on compensation. L/S &G/ 7/914: ff 447b–9.

[4] See No. 18.

Item 7
COURT CIRCULAR
HIS EXCELLENCY THE VICEROY:
directed M.S.V.
(a) to include in future editions of the Court Circular mention of all interviews
he held, except those with "unofficial contacts";
(b) to issue an amendment to the Court Circular of the previous day to include
the interviews he had then held;
(c) to ensure that all issues of the Court Circular were in future rendered to him,
through Pers. Sec., for approval.

Item 10
HIS EXCELLENCY'S LETTERS TO MR JINNAH AND MR GANDHI
HIS EXCELLENCY THE VICEROY:—
directed the Press Adviser to issue background information to the effect that
he had written to Mr Jinnah and Mr Gandhi on the day of his arrival asking
them to come to see him.

21

Note by Mr Abell

Mountbatten Papers. Official Correspondence Files: Interviews

26 March 1947

MR. V.P. MENON, Reforms Commissioner, has had a remarkable career. He
comes from a land-owning family in Malabar, Madras Presidency, but started
his Government service as a lowly paid clerk on, I think, about £2 per month.
Subsequently he became a petty Revenue official in Madras, then resigned and
got employment as a clerk in the Reforms Office of the Government of
India.

He has been in the Reforms Office, which deals with Constitutional matters,
since 1914, and has been head of the office since 1942.

He is a member of the Government [Governor] General Secretariat, and has
been in the close confidence of Lord Linlithgow and Lord Wavell. He has more
than once been to London for discussions with the Viceroy.

He has an encyclopaedic knowledge of everything to do with the Indian
Constitution, and his knowledge and judgment are often more [?most] valuable.

Up to recently he knew everything in connection with high policy that was
going on between the Viceroy and the India Office. Lately he has been rather

less closely in confidence because he is a Hindu, and is inevitably under pressure from Congress to tell them what is going on. Often he can be most valuable with his information of Congress reactions and intentions, but there is a danger that for such information he may pay a price in revealing some of the secrets of the Viceroy, though I do not think he would do this consciously. At any rate, one finds that Indian officials now are in an extremely difficult position. The feelings between the communities are much the same as though a civil war was going on. An official, if he tries to be impartial, is merely suspected on both sides, so he tends to take shelter with one side or the other, according to his community. Mr. Menon now is genuinely convinced of the rightness of the Congress view on the general political position.

Thus, though he is an old friend of mine, and one of the people I like best in Delhi, I am convinced that it is not possible to take him into confidence as fully as has been done in the past.

G. E. B. ABELL

22

Record of Interview between Rear-Admiral Viscount Mountbatten of Burma and Dr Rajendra Prasad

Mountbatten Papers. Viceroy's Interview No. 10

TOP SECRET   *26 March 1947*

Dr. Prasad struck me as a most delightful man. He gave me an interesting account of why the murders in Bihar followed those in Calcutta—saying that this was largely the result of letters written by relatives who had suffered.

He gave a reasonable picture of the whole present situation, particularly about food. He felt that, whatever other arrangements might be made, there would have to be a central food organisation. India could not do without this—and he believed that the Muslims realised it.

23

Sir F. Mudie (Sind) to Rear-Admiral Viscount Mountbatten of Burma (Extract)

L/P&J/5/263: ff 54-5

D.O. No. 165/FR   GOVERNMENT HOUSE, KARACHI, *26 March 1947*

2. As I told Your Excellency when I saw you in Karachi, my Ministers have

suddenly woken up to the political situation. The reason is the report that they
received from a Muslim ICS officer who had gone to the Punjab on Government business. He reported that there was no sign of compromise between the
Muslims and the Sikhs and that both sides were talking as if the real civil war
had yet to come. This would happen as soon as the troops were removed. In
the meantime both sides were trying to make the best use of the lull to prepare
themselves for what was to come. The Muslims, according to him, were afraid
as the Sikhs were better organised than they were for civil war and would
also have the help of the armies of the Sikh States in the Eastern Punjab. The
result was a hurried meeting of the Sind Muslim League Party at which they
appointed a committee of their own members with power "to co-opt six
persons of the Province who must be members of the Muslim League (if
Mussulmans)" to draft a constitution for Sind to enable it to receive power
transferred to it by the British Government. They also called upon the Government of Sind (1) to establish Home Guards immediately and equip them with
the requisite arms, (2) to increase the Sind Police Rangers (a quasi military body
of police raised to deal with the Hurs) to enable them to perform the duties
of the Military in case the British army left the Province of Sind and (3) to
organise village security.

3. I think that these resolutions were meant to be secret, but one of the
Ministers gave them out to the press the same evening. Next day one or two of
my Ministers discussed them with me. They were not quite happy about them.
I agreed that they could not afford to ignore either the possibility that, in
accordance with H.M.G.'s latest statement and the Cripps' offer, power might
be handed over to Sind or the possibility that we would in the next year have
to take special measures to maintain the peace. But I suggested that, following
the precedent of the Constituent Assembly, it would be better if the committee
contemplated were elected by the Sind Assembly rather than by the League
Party. The Ministers agreed, with the result that a resolution to be moved in
the Sind Assembly was drafted.

4. I also suggested that before any action was taken Jinnah should be consulted and that you should be informed of what was contemplated. They agreed
to both. Jinnah over the telephone approved of the idea, but said that he would
not like to say anything final till he had consulted his Working Committee
and I gave a copy both of the Muslim League Party's resolution and of the
draft resolution to be moved in the Sind Assembly to Mieville. That is how the
matter stands at present. For the time being the committee appointed by the
Muslim League Party, which consisted of the Ministers, the Speaker and one
or two Muslim MLAs, is dead.

24

Minutes of Viceroy's Third Staff Meeting, Item 4

Mountbatten Papers

TOP SECRET

Those present for Item 4 of this Meeting held at The Viceroy's House, New Delhi on 27 March 1947 at 10 am were: Rear-Admiral Viscount Mountbatten of Burma, Lord Ismay, Sir E. 'Mieville, Mr Abell, Colonel Currie, Captain Brockman, Mr Campbell-Johnson, Lieutenant-Colonel Erskine Crum

AIDES DE CAMP

HIS EXCELLENCY THE VICEROY stated that Sardar Baldev Singh, when he had seen him the previous day, had welcomed the idea that HIS EXCELLENCY should have two Indian Aides de Camp, and said that their attachment from the Indian Army could easily be arranged.

HIS EXCELLENCY THE VICEROY:

directed M.S.V. to inform C.-in-C. India of this, with a view to the early provision of two Indian Aides de Camp

25

Sir C. Corfield to Mr Abell

R/3/1/136: ff 32–4

SECRET   POLITICAL DEPARTMENT, INDIA,
                                              NEW DELHI, *27 March 1947*

My dear Abell,

His Excellency asked me for a note about the alternative machinery which would carry out the duties now performed by the Political Department as that Department contracts. I enclose it herewith.

As you know, the Secretary of State has agreed that we should aim at closing down Political Agencies and Residencies by the end of 1947.

Yours sincerely,

C. CORFIELD

Enclosure to No. 25

SECRET

Prior to 1937, when paramountcy was exercised by the Governor General in Council, the Political Department was a department of the Central Govern-

ment with the Viceroy as Member in charge. When the Government of India
Act of 1935 came into force from the 1st April 1937 paramountcy became
vested in the Crown Representative as a separate constitutional entity under the
special control of the Secretary of State for India.

This constitutional change made little difference in practice, until persons
came into power in the Central Government who were hostile to Indian States
and pledged to eliminate or neutralise the Rulers.

The practice *before the 1st April 1937* was for the Political Department to act
as the channel through which any matters of common concern to British
India and the Indian States were administered by both parties in the interests of
India as a whole. The Political Department had no technical experts and relied
on the other Departments of the then Government of India to give technical
advice on such matters as customs and excise, railways, posts and telegraphs
etc.

After the 1st April 1937 it was suggested that the Political Department,
which then became the Secretariat of the Crown Representative, should have
its own technical experts. This suggestion was negatived on grounds of expense
and needless duplication, and it was agreed that previous practice should
continue. The Political Department continued therefore in regard to matters
of common concern to be the channel with the same watching brief as before
i.e. to ensure that on the one hand States rights and interests were protected and
on the other that all-India interests were not prejudiced.

There is another sphere of the Political Department's duties which is no concern
of the Central Government, i.e. the sphere of undiluted paramountcy relating
to such questions as succession, minority administrations, and prevention of
gross misgovernment. Their duties in this sphere must on the lapse of paramountcy be undertaken by the States themselves and will be dealt with by
Succession Acts, Regency arrangements and internal constitutionalisation.

For matters of common concern new arrangements are required in view of
the prospective lapse of paramountcy involving the gradual disappearance of
the Political Agents, Residents, the Political Department and eventually the
Crown Representative. These new arrangements can only be made by establishing direct contact between individual States or groups of States and the
Central Government.

If this contact were to be established with a new 'Political Department' of
the Central Government, the States would be gravely concerned even if the
Department was known by a different name and would interpret its establishment as an attempt of the Central Government to grasp paramountcy. Moreover, there is no need for such a new department of the Central Government
at any rate during the interim period. All the necessary experts on matters of
common concern exist in each Department of the Central Government to
deal with the subjects with which that Department is concerned, e.g. Food,

Commerce, Agriculture etc. as these Departments already do in the case of the Provinces. And if a State eventually decides to remain independent there is the External Affairs Department available to deal with it, as with any other independent administration.

Whether this direct contact with Central Government Departments will lead to those Departments obtaining some new control over States corresponding to the past control of paramountcy is a question with which we are not concerned. We cannot alter the economic and geographical unity of India. But this control will be different in character from paramountcy control, and will develop on mutually agreed lines based on common interests. For instance, if a State remains independent, the External Affairs Department may negotiate for a diplomatic representative to reside in the State: or if a State adheres to a Union which does not include commerce as a union subject, the Commerce Department would arrange to have a Trade Agent in the State in the same way as they might do in the case of a Province. In some cases States or groups of States may nominate their own representative to reside at the Union Centre for purposes of liaison and the protection of their own interests.

It was hoped that these new arrangements would be made by negotiation during the interim period (see para. 4 of Memo. on States' Treaties and Paramountcy),[1] but no forum for such negotiations has yet been settled, except for those States which have decided to join the Constituent Assembly and on the assumption that the truncated Constituent Assembly continues to function in order to frame a constitution for those parts of India which are prepared to form a union under its aegis.

All that the Political Department can do now is to relieve itself of its duties as swiftly as possible and

(a) in the sphere of undiluted paramountcy encourage States to set up alternative arrangements;

(b) in the sphere of matters of common concern place the States in direct contact with the appropriate Department of the Central Government or with the Provincial Government concerned with these matters.

Any other course would be interpreted as a breach of faith and would not lead to satisfactory conclusions, in so far as such conclusions can be reached in the time available.[2]

[1] See Vol. VII, No. 262.
[2] This note was circulated as Viceroy's Conference Paper V.C.P. 11.

26

Lord Pethick-Lawrence to Rear-Admiral Viscount Mountbatten of Burma

Mountbatten Papers. Letters to and from the Secretary of State

INDIA OFFICE, *27 March 1947*

My dear Mountbatten,

I hope that you had a comfortable journey out and that you and the members of your staff are already beginning to feel settled in Delhi. I also hope that the time you had in Delhi with Wavell proved sufficient to enable you to have fruitful discussion with him and to "feel the pulse" of the Indian situation before his departure. The Prime Minister has arranged for Wavell to have a talk tomorrow with the members of the India and Burma Committee at which we shall, no doubt, hear not only his parting impressions of the Indian situation but also the upshot of his talks with you in Delhi.

2. May I say here how much I welcomed your decision to make a short speech[1] at the swearing-in ceremony on the 24th March, and how well chosen [your] words appeared to me to be. I am, of course, eagerly awaiting full accounts of your first exchanges of view with Indian leaders.

3. As we were at pains to make clear in our replies to your telegrams 625–S and 626–S,[2] about compensation my colleagues and I entirely appreciated your motives in trying to make an announcement on this matter during the present week and our advocacy of the case for postponing an announcement arose from the belief that the advantages to be gained, from the point of view of the members of the Services, from an immediate announcement might well be outweighed by an even greater measure of resentment on the part of your Council and Indian political opinion generally than that which we seem likely to have to meet in any case. I am sorry that the replies to your two telegrams were not a model of neatness but they were produced under great pressure—we carried on until 2 a.m.—and the questions involved are so complex that it is hardly surprising that one or two points were missed the first time round.

4. One of the principal matters engaging my attention at the present time is, of course, the time-table for the whole operation of transferring power in June 1948. The only fixed point so far, apart from June 1948 itself, is the date of October 1st mentioned in the Prime Minister's letter to you of 18th March[3] as the date by which you are to report to His Majesty's Government on the steps which you consider should be taken for the handing over of power, if by that time there is no prospect of reaching a settlement on the basis of a unitary government for British India. I am not[at] all sure that from the point of view of the time required to prepare and to get through Parliament the legislation

which will be required, it will not be necessary to reach conclusions as to what we are going to do before October. After we have had your views, decisions by the Cabinet will be required before the drafting of legislation can be put in hand, and I think it must be introduced before or at any rate immediately after Christmas. I am having this subject considered in greater detail and will let you know the outcome later, but I should like you to have it in mind that it may be necessary to take a definite view as to what we are going to do earlier than 1st October.

5. Attention is also being given here to the Punjab problem in the light of Jenkins' letter to Wavell of 7th March (No. 653)[4] and his telegram No. 70–G of 24th March.[5] It is a relief that the Punjab situation appears to be steadying and I think the improvement can to a large extent be attributed to the energy and resource with which affairs have been handled by Jenkins as evidenced, for example, by his letter to Wavell No. 657 of 17th March.[6]

6. You will remember that at the informal meeting of Ministers held after dinner on 14th March[7] there was some discussion about future relations between India and adjacent countries, particularly Afghanistan and Nepal, and that the India Office was invited to consider, in consultation with the Foreign Office, the question which you raised, namely, whether it was not desirable that such countries should be formally acquainted with the policy of His Majesty's Government in regard to India as announced on 20th February. I now send you a copy of a memorandum[8] on this subject which I circulated to my colleagues a few days ago.

[Paras. 7 and 8, on the supply of two excavators for the Mor irrigation project in Bengal, omitted.]

[1] See No. 8.　　　　　[2] See No. 18 and its note 2.　　　　[3] Vol. IX, Enclosure to No. 543.
[4] Vol. IX, No. 501.　　　[5] No. 13.　　　　　　　　　　　[6] Vol. IX, No. 540.
[7] See Vol. IX, No. 530, Item 3. The meeting was in fact held on 13 March 1947.
[8] No. 2.

27

Record of Interview between Rear-Admiral Viscount Mountbatten of Burma and Maulana Azad

Mountbatten Papers. Viceroy's Interview No. 14

TOP SECRET   *27 March 1947*

Maulana Azad is a charming old gentleman who, though he understands English, spoke through an interpreter. He told me first that if he had not been due at that particular moment to leave the presidency of Congress, that party would have accepted the Cabinet Mission's plan. He said that blame in the first place must be laid on Congress, although it was the Muslim League which was now intransigeant. He considered that there was a good chance that I would succeed in 'deflating' Mr. Jinnah; partly by flattering him and partly because he really has nothing to stand on. One of his great objects was to have ministers in the Central Government, and he had no intention of allowing them to leave it.

For points covered in the rest of this interview, see Minutes of 4th Staff Meeting, Item 11.[1]

[1] No. 29.

28

The Nawab of Bhopal to Rear-Admiral Viscount Mountbatten of Burma
(via Governor's Secretary, Bombay)

Telegram, Mountbatten Papers. Official Correspondence Files:
Transfer of Power, Part I (a)

IMMEDIATE   *27 March 1947, 10.40 pm*
SECRET   *Received: 28 March, 1.30 am*

No. 141–C. I had a four hours' talk with Mr Jinnah. He will be going to Delhi in four or five days. There is no chance of the Muslims now agreeing to any form of Union Government. If H.M.G. agrees to division and concedes Pakistan, I was agreeably surprised to find that Jinnah can be persuaded to remain within the Commonwealth.

He will agree to this when the time comes, but is not naturally prepared to make any public announcement or mention of this at this stage. He said any such declaration would be premature.

When the Viceroy meets him His Excellency would not of course allow Jinnah to suspect that I had passed on this information to H.E.

29

Minutes of Viceroy's Fourth Staff Meeting

Mountbatten Papers

TOP SECRET

Those present at this Meeting held at The Viceroy's House, New Delhi on 28 March 1947 at 10 am were: Rear-Admiral Viscount Mountbatten of Burma, Lord Ismay, Sir E. Mieville, Mr Abell, Mr Christie, Colonel Currie, Captain Brockman, Mr Campbell-Johnson, Lieutenant-Colonel Erskine Crum

Item 7

THE INDIAN ARMED FORCES

HIS EXCELLENCY THE VICEROY said that he had given a dinner party the previous evening to the Commander-in-Chief in India and the Army Commanders. Field Marshal Auchinleck had expressed the view that it would take from five to ten years satisfactorily to divide the Indian Army. The Muslim League's declared policy was that they did not want an unified Army. But surely the result of splitting the Army communally would be that the non-Muslim parties would be much the stronger. They would be able to take over General Headquarters, the main supply dumps and a large majority of the officers. The Muslims would be left with a greatly inferior share. He intended to point this out to Mr. Jinnah.

LORD ISMAY added the point that there was not, in the Indian Army, a single wholly Muslim unit, whereas there were numbers of units which consisted wholly of personnel of other communities.

HIS EXCELLENCY THE VICEROY emphasized that whoever controlled an unified Army, or the most efficient divided Army, controlled India. The Armed Forces—for the Indian Navy and Air Force were to be reckoned with also—were the biggest bargaining point there was. It seemed to him that one possible weakness of the Cabinet Mission's plan was that, if the Army was used to quell riots and disturbances, the Central Government would have a stranglehold over the minority party. Some solution must be found to ensure that this did not happen. Perhaps the Army might be used internally only on the majority vote of both major parties. The Central Government would be able to wield great influence by the positioning of troops, although locally troops would be under the orders of provincial governments. There might be a pre-agreed positioning of forces, or some such safeguard.

LORD ISMAY pointed out that fundamentally no safeguards were of value if the two major parties were not going to co-operate. If they did co-operate, the rules and safeguards did not matter. HIS EXCELLENCY THE VICEROY said that, although this was to a large extent true, he still wanted study of possible safeguards to be made so that he would be able to put them forward to Mr. Jinnah.

HIS EXCELLENCY THE VICEROY:—

(i) invited C.V.S. to consider what modifications might be made to the Cabinet Mission's plan in connection with the internal use of the armed forces;

(ii) invited C.V.S. further to study the likely result of a division of the Indian Armed Forces on communal lines, and to render him a brief on the subject;

(iii) directed Pers. Sec. to initiate the preparation of a loose-leaf note book, similar to that which he had had in S.E.A.C., and in which might be kept information on subjects such as this.

Item 11

MR JINNAH

HIS EXCELLENCY THE VICEROY drew attention to a telegram[1] which he had received from the Nawab of Bhopal, containing the latter's account of a four hours' talk he had had with Mr. Jinnah the previous day. Reference was also made to a speech which Mr. Jinnah had made and which was reported in the newspapers. This contained a call for a truce on the basis of Pakistan.

MR. ABELL said that the report in the Nawab of Bhopal's telegram that Mr. Jinnah could be persuaded, if granted Pakistan, "to remain within the Commonwealth" was probably a "pre-conference" offer and a typical counterbalance to offset the uncompromising attitude displayed in his speech.

HIS EXCELLENCY THE VICEROY reiterated his policy that he was not prepared to discuss with the representatives of different parts of India the question of whether or not they might remain in the Commonwealth. However, it would be of course a different matter if Mr. Jinnah and the Princes agreed to accept the Cabinet Mission's plan on the condition of continued close contact with the Commonwealth.

HIS EXCELLENCY THE VICEROY said that, in his first interview with Mr. Jinnah (who had accepted his invitation to an interview not by letter but through the newspapers), he intended to remain completely open-minded and to ask Mr. Jinnah for his views. He would inform Mr. Jinnah that the grant of Pakistan would involve, by application of the same principle, the partition of the Punjab and Bengal.

SIR ERIC MIEVILLE gave his view that Pakistan would definitely be unworkable without Calcutta. HIS EXCELLENCY THE VICEROY said that Chittagong might suffice as the port of Eastern Pakistan instead.

MR. ABELL said that one of the best summaries of the reasons for the impracticability of Pakistan was contained in Mr. Coupland's book on "The Indian Problem".[2]

HIS EXCELLENCY THE VICEROY said that he understood from Maulana Azad that Lord Wavell had laid down the condition of acceptance of the Cabinet Mission's long-term plan in his offer to Mr. Jinnah of Muslim League participation in the Interim Government. Although Mr. Jinnah had not replied directly, his appointment of members to the Interim Government implied acceptance of this condition. Maulana Azad had therefore suggested that His Excellency could give Mr. Jinnah the choice of either working the Cabinet Mission's plan or else of removing his representatives from the Interim Government. These alternatives should be propounded to Mr. Jinnah at what was judged to be the most awkward time for him to consider them. HIS EXCELLENCY THE VICEROY said that, if handled carefully, this appeared a most engaging proposition. HIS EXCELLENCY THE VICEROY said that in this connection Maulana Azad had told him that in his opinion the Congress Party might come the small step forward to accept the Cabinet Mission's plan unreservedly provided the Muslim League first made a similar declaration.

MR. ABELL said that it was in a way true that the Muslim League were in the Government under false pretences. On the other hand, they had always said that they would accept the Cabinet Mission's proposals if Congress accepted them unreservedly.

HIS EXCELLENCY THE VICEROY:—

(i) directed P.S.V. to show him the relevant chapter of "The Indian Problem" by Mr. Coupland.
(ii) invited C.V.S. to keep under consideration the question of *approaches* to a solution of the future of India.

Item 12

SIMLA HOUSE PARTY

HIS EXCELLENCY THE VICEROY said that he had it in mind to invite, at the appropriate moment, certain important Indian leaders to stay with him at Simla. These would be:—

Mr. Gandhi
Mr. Jinnah
Pandit Nehru
Mr. Liaquat Ali Khan
Sardar Patel and
The Nawab of Bhopal.

[1] No. 28.
[2] Professor Sir R. Coupland, *A Report on the Constitutional Problem in India*, 3 Parts (London, Oxford University Press, 1942–3).

This represented the minimum number. There would be no representatives of minorities.

There would be no formal meetings, no agenda, no secretariat in evidence—just an informal exchange of ideas. It was possible, in such an atmosphere, that a measure of agreement would be obtained. There would be no press statements, and he would ask his guests to give an undertaking not to issue information to the press. He would also ask them to refrain from making bitter remarks on this occasion. He agreed with Lord Ismay's suggestion that no advisers, only those with executive responsibility, should be present at these informal meetings.

After discussion, HIS EXCELLENCY THE VICEROY decided provisionally on the week beginning 21st April as the best time for this house-party. He said that he considered it of great importance that the Nawab of Bhopal should be persuaded not to resign meanwhile.

MR. ABELL expressed the opinion that there was a risk that the Congress representatives would refuse to attend. HIS EXCELLENCY THE VICEROY said that he hoped very much to be able to persuade Pandit Nehru. He added that he did not believe that the Indian political leaders yet realised the full extent of his powers.

HIS EXCELLENCY THE VICEROY:—

directed P.S.V. to ask Sir Conrad Corfield to do all in his power to persuade the Nawab of Bhopal not to resign from the Chancellorship of the Chamber of Princes until after these meetings.

Item 13

INDIAN OPINION OF HIS MAJESTY'S GOVERNMENT'S POLICY

HIS EXCELLENCY THE VICEROY asked whether it was considered that he was right in thinking that the majority of people in India believed that the British were being compelled to hand over by *force majeure*. MR. ABELL gave his opinion that the majority of the Congress Party, at any rate, gave the Labour Government the credit for a voluntary hand-over.

30

Cabinet

India and Burma Committee. I.B.(47)16th Meeting

L/P&J/10/78: ff 4–10

Those present at this Meeting held at 10 Downing Street, S.W.1, on 28 March 1947 at 11.15 am were: Mr Attlee (in the Chair), Sir S. Cripps, Mr Alexander, Viscount Addison, Lord Pethick-Lawrence, the Earl of Listowel

Also present were: Field Marshal Viscount Wavell, Mr Henderson, Sir D. Monteath, Sir W. Croft, Mr J.A. Simpson, Mr R.E. Field; Mr S.E.V. Luke, Mr E.W.R. Lumby (Secretariat)

Minute 1

Discussion with Field Marshal Viscount Wavell

THE PRIME MINISTER welcomed Field Marshal Viscount Wavell on behalf of the Committee.

In reply to questions, FIELD MARSHAL VISCOUNT WAVELL gave the following appreciation of the present situation in India:—

(a) *Situation in the Provinces*

The situation in the Punjab was now in hand; the Governor had handled it well but he was greatly concerned about the future. Beneath the surface there was a strong undercurrent of unrest and the Sikhs, in particular, were much disturbed. It was impossible to see at present any prospect of an alternative to administration by the Governor under Section 93; the Muslim League had failed to form a Government and the prospects of establishing a coalition administration were negligible. Pandit Nehru was advocating partition of the Province; this would involve great difficulties, but the Governor did not regard this in some form as an impossible solution. In that event, however, he thought that division of the Province into three parts would be necessary. Apart from two isolated cases, the loyalty of the Police and troops in the Province had been entirely satisfactory; they were, however, under great strain and under constant criticism from Congress. The Commander-in-Chief was anxious about the reactions on the Indian Army of the situation in the Punjab, which supplied so large a proportion of the Indian troops. The Governor was also concerned about the position of the British community; he might have to ask for the evacuation of British families in view of the risk that any future disturbances might be directed against the British. As regards the other Provinces, he had been surprised that a more serious situation had not developed in the North West Frontier Province where the existence of a Congress Ministry increased the risks of trouble. Pandit Nehru had proposed, after his recent visit to the Punjab, to go to Peshawar; in response to a personal appeal from the Viceroy, he had abandoned the plan. The United Provinces were quiet, though the Governor was greatly concerned at the progressive lowering of the standard of administration. In Bihar, the Police had been on the verge of disintegration for sometime, and no efforts were being made by the Ministry to tighten discipline. The situation in Bengal was quieter than it had been for some time past. The Prime Minister, though unreliable, was far-sighted enough to recognise the need for a coalition, and had genuinely been attempting to achieve this. This proposal had not, however, been acceptable to Mr. Jinnah, and the Congress demands had been excessive. In the circumstances, the prospects of securing an effective coalition were remote. In general, Lord Wavell's policy had been to try to secure the formation of coalition ministries in all the Provinces for the interim period before the transfer of power took place.

(b) *The Princes*

There were signs that serious cleavage was emerging between the Princes, who might no longer be able to maintain a united front in their negotiations with the Constituent Assembly. There were already indications that some of the Princes were prepared to negotiate direct with Congress and to send representatives to the Assembly without reference to the general decision of the Chamber of Princes. An important meeting of the Chamber was due to be held on 2nd April for further discussion of the position.

FIELD MARSHAL VISCOUNT WAVELL reminded the Committee that there was a legal obligation to return Berar to the Nizam of Hyderabad when power was transferred in India; this would not, in fact, be practicable, but the Nizam intended to press his legal rights as a bargaining counter e.g. to secure a suitable port for his State.

(c) *The Interim Government*

Proceedings in the Cabinet had been conducted in a friendly, good-humoured and practical manner. This, however, had not drawn the Congress and Muslim League representatives closer together. Attempts to persuade them to work through Cabinet Committees had been unsuccessful as the Congress attitude was that this would involve some derogation from Pandit Nehru's position, which they regarded as that of Prime Minister. The Muslim League, on the other hand, would have been ready to work through committees, if they could have been assured of adequate representation. The result was that many more matters came up to the Cabinet itself than was really essential.

Indian Ministers had accepted without bitterness the Viceroy's ruling on the question of the release of members of the Indian Nationalist Army.[1] Pandit Nehru had pointed out that the Viceroy's decision placed them in a very difficult position in view of the resolution which was shortly to be moved in the Assembly. There were some hopes, however, that Ministers would be successful in securing the withdrawal of the resolution. As regards the Budget, Nawabzada Liaqat had made certain concessions to meet Congress views, including the reduction of the rate of the proposed Profits Tax to $16\frac{1}{3}$ per cent. He had, however, made it clear to the Viceroy that no further concessions were possible. The Congress representatives in the Assembly might be restrained from voting against the Budget by recognition of the bad impression that this might create among that section of their supporters who were apprehensive of the influence exerted by big business on the policy of the party. Liaqat himself was a man of great ability and good sense; on a number of occasions he had been successful within the Interim Government in securing concessions to the Muslim point of view without the need for challenging a vote.

(d) *The Food Situation*

This would be a cause of continuing anxiety to the Government of India. During recent years the margin of safety had been a very narrow one. In the Punjab, the 1947 crop would be very moderate; throughout Central India the wheat crops had been attacked by rust and were not worth harvesting even for cattle food. In Bengal the rice crop was good, but prices were rising, possibly owing to hoarding. In Southern India the rice crop was good. There seemed little possibility of securing substantial imports of rice from the Far East in the immediate future.

(e) *The European Community*

For the present there were no signs of undue nervousness, but there was always the risk of anti-British feeling rising to a dangerous point; it was most important that there should be adequate shipping facilities for the return of civilians from India and that no excessive backlog should be accumulated.

(f) *Position of the Viceroy*

FIELD MARSHAL VISCOUNT WAVELL said that it was likely that Congress might put forward a proposal that the Viceroy, during the interim period, should occupy a constitutional position similar to the Governor General of a Dominion, and that it should be agreed that he should not use his powers of veto.

Ministers agreed that, if this proposal was made, it could not be accepted; it would be wholly unacceptable to Parliament.

(g) *Future Developments and Policy*

FIELD MARSHAL VISCOUNT WAVELL said that it was very difficult to foresee the future development of events. All sensible Indians were anxious for a pacific settlement but none were prepared to make concessions. There were internal stresses within Congress itself. Sardar Patel would himself probably be willing to leave the exclusively Muslim areas under the control of the Muslim League in the expectation that economic straits would compel them to seek reunion within a few years. Pandit Nehru would probably be prepared to work the Cabinet Mission plan. Mr. Jinnah, on the other hand, had no intention of allowing the Muslim League to participate in the Constituent

[1] See Vol. IX, No. 553.

Assembly and continued to press for Pakistan in the widest sense; although he no doubt recognised that there was no chance of securing this, it was impossible for him to go back on his public statement on the subject. There was, however, some hope that both sides, when faced with the practical difficulties of partition might achieve agreement on a federal scheme.

Before the statement of 20th February, he had thought that the right policy would be to press Congress to unconditional acceptance of the Cabinet Mission plan. In the light of that statement, however, there was little prospect that the Muslim League would agree to participate in the Constituent Assembly. He thought that a last effort should be made to secure their participation and that, if that failed, a start should be made with discussions on the implications and details of partition; an attempt should be made to establish federal arrangements for the Army, and for defence and foreign affairs. The important point was to avoid the development of a situation, like that in Palestine, in which the British Government might be left with responsibility without the power of effective control.

THE PRIME MINISTER thanked Field Marshal Viscount Wavell, who then withdrew.

Minute 2
Message of appreciation to Field Marshal Viscount Wavell
The Committee considered that an expression of appreciation should be conveyed to Field Marshal Viscount Wavell on behalf of the Cabinet, for his distinguished services as Viceroy and Governor General of India.
The Committee:—
> Invited the Secretary of State for India to prepare the draft of a letter of appreciation to Field Marshal Viscount Wavell for consideration by the Cabinet at their next meeting.[2]

Minute 3
Compensation terms for Members of the Indian Services appointed
by the Secretary of State and for Officers
of the Indian Fighting Services
(Previous Reference: I.B.(47)15th Meeting)[3]
THE SECRETARY OF STATE FOR INDIA recalled that at the last meeting of the India and Burma Committee (I.B.(47)15th Meeting) it had been decided to inform the Viceroy that His Majesty's Government would strongly prefer that the announcement of compensation terms should be deferred for a few days; and that in the meantime he should communicate to the Interim Government the Secretary of State's two despatches on the subject. He had now been informed that the Viceroy had sent these despatches to the Departments concerned and would take the case in his Cabinet, or in a committee of the

Cabinet, early next week. The last day on which the announcement could be made in Parliament before the Easter Recess was 3rd April; he could therefore see little prospect that the interval of time between the consideration of the question by the Interim Government and that date would be sufficient for His Majesty's Government to consider the reactions of the Interim Government and for making the necessary administrative arrangements, including final determination of the terms of the announcement. It was, in his view, most desirable that we should at any rate avoid a time-table which made it obvious that we had not allowed adequate time for weighing the Interim Government's counter proposals, and it was clearly most important that we should also have adequate time for considering the text of an announcement which might impose substantial financial obligations on His Majesty's Government. He therefore proposed that the Viceroy should be asked to postpone his announcement until after the Easter Recess.

In discussion, the point was made that the Interim Government might attempt to repudiate the obligation to meet from Indian revenues the pension charges for the officers concerned. No indication had so far been given of such an intention, but it would be important to ensure that nothing in the announcement afforded any suggestion that His Majesty's Government would in any circumstances be prepared to assume this obligation. A further reason for adequate time to examine the terms of the announcement was that, in the case of officers of the Indian Army, the proposals involved the introduction of a scheme of proportionate pension on premature retirement.

THE SECRETARY OF STATE FOR INDIA raised the question of the content of the statement to be made in both Houses of Parliament and of the White Paper which would be published on the same day. It was agreed that the statement should, in the course of a short historical introduction, make particular reference to the pledge given to the civilian Services in 1945 by the then Secretary of State for India. It should be said that His Majesty's Government considered that this pledge should be fully honoured; that they regarded the officers of the Indian Fighting Services as having an equally valid claim; and that accordingly they had authorized the Viceroy to make an announcement. The White Paper should contain the text of the statement made in Parliament, the Viceroy's announcement and the tables of compensation. A separate White Paper should be issued about compensation for the Burma Services, and the statement in Parliament should contain a reference to this.

The Committee:—

(1) Invited the Secretary of State for India to inform the Viceroy that His

[2] On 3 April 1947 Mr Attlee sent Lord Wavell a letter in which he conveyed the Cabinet's appreciation of the services he had rendered as Viceroy. R/3/1/8a: ff 2–3.

[3] No. 19.

Majesty's Government hoped that he would postpone his announcement on compensation terms until after the Easter Recess.

(2) Invited the Secretary of State for India to circulate, for the information of the Committee, the text of the proposed announcement[4] embodying the amendments suggested in his Telegram No. 4006[5] to the Viceroy.

[Minute 4, on Governor's Proclamation of 17 October 1945 in Burma, and Minute 5, on recruitment of Gurkhas, omitted.]

[4] This was done in India and Burma Committee Paper I.B.(47)44 of 1 April 1947. R/30/1/10: ff 5–15.
[5] L/S&G/7/914: ff 445–447(a).

31

Mr Menon to Mr Abell

R/3/1/130: f 203

SECRET   SECRETARIAT OF THE GOVERNOR-GENERAL (REFORMS),
NEW DELHI, *29 March 1947*

My dear Abell,

Please refer to your Secret D.O. letter No. 592/58 of yesterday's date regarding the importance to the Congress of the Sikhs and Assam.[1] This point was touched upon at the interview which I had with H.E. yesterday.[2]

The support of the Sikhs is a matter of paramount importance to the Congress. The Sikhs are a very virile community and the Congress counts a considerable section of them in its fold. Apart from other considerations, if the Congress loses the support of the Sikh community, Hindus in the Punjab will by themselves not be able to stand up to the Muslims, much less to a possible combination of Sikhs and Muslims. It will be of interest to recall in this connection that as early as 1929 the Congress passed a resolution declaring that no solution of the communal question would be acceptable that did not give full satisfaction to the Sikhs, Muslims and other minorities; and that this pledge was recently invoked by the Sikhs in the discussions which led to their participation in the Constituent Assembly.

The position in Assam is that, apart from Sylhet district, it is predominantly a Hindu province. In the province as a whole, out of a total population of 10.2 millions, Hindus number 4.21 millions and Muslims 3.44 millions. If we exclude Sylhet district, the figures are—total population 7.10 millions, Hindus 3.06 millions, Muslims 1.55 millions, Tribes 2.41 millions. Congress naturally cannot be expected willingly to surrender a Hindu majority province to Group 'C'.

The position has inevitably been very much affected by the recent communal disturbances in the country, and in present circumstances the Congress cannot be expected to advise Assam and the Sikhs in the Punjab to accept grouping unreservedly; and in fact, even if they did, the minorities and the Hindus in Assam will certainly not yield to Congress pressure.

Yours sincerely,

V. P. MENON

[1] In this letter Mr Abell informed Mr Menon that Lord Mountbatten had asked for an appreciation of the importance to the Congress of the Sikhs and Assam, with particular reference to the attitude of the Congress about unqualified acceptance of the Cabinet Mission plan. R/3/1/130: f 201.
[2] No record of this interview has been traced.

32

Note by Sir E. Jenkins (Extract)

R/3/1/176: ff 63-5

29 March 1947

Khan Iftikhar Husain Khan of Mamdot and Mian Mumtaz Muhammad Khan Daultana came to see me by appointment at 2.30 pm today. They made the following points:

★   ★   ★

(7) The Muslim League are anxious to assist the administration in every possible way, and would like a settlement of the political and constitutional problem. They did not, however, know how to proceed. In particular, they cannot understand what the Sikhs want or what action can be taken to improve Muslim-Sikh relations.

I said that the Sikhs were not always easy to understand. A few weeks ago some of them seemed to be ready for an alliance with the Muslims; but the situation had been radically changed by the events in the Rawalpindi Division. The Sikhs were now demanding a partition. It might be true that they were preparing for further trouble, but I thought myself that their attitude was defensive and that they did not intend any immediate attack upon the Muslims. I believed that the whole of the Muslim League policy had been mistaken, and I was by conviction a unionist in the sense that I thought a partition would be disastrous and that the Punjab could prosper only if it retained its present boundaries. I thought it would be most difficult to force the Punjab with its present boundaries into any preconceived Central plan. It would be better to find a solution acceptable to the majority of Punjabis, and then to adopt the

Central plan which would suit this solution. If on Sir Sikander Hyat Khan's death Mr. Jinnah had acted differently and had supported the Unionist idea, the Punjab would now be a stable unit capable of taking its place in Group B or even in a separated Pakistan State. As things had turned out, the Sikhs were labouring under a terrible sense of wrong and oppression. Sardar Swaran Singh, a very sensible and temperate man, had been much upset by what he had seen in Rawalpindi, and I could hardly blame him. If the Muslims seriously wanted a reconciliation with the Sikhs, they must act as it is necessary to act after a serious personal quarrel. They must go to the Sikhs preferably in the first instance to some one like S. Swaran Singh—admit the blame for events in the Rawalpindi Division and ask what they can now do to put things right. Hair-splitting about the degree of blame attributable to the different communities would get the Muslims nowhere.

Daultana seemed to think that there was some sense in this, but he said comparatively little.

33

Minutes of Viceroy's Fifth Staff Meeting, Item 1

Mountbatten Papers

TOP SECRET

Those present during discussion of Item 1 of this Meeting held at The Viceroy's House, New Delhi on 29 March 1947 at 10 am were: Rear-Admiral Viscount Mountbatten of Burma, Lord Ismay, Sir E. Mieville, Mr Abell, Mr Christie, Colonel Currie, Captain Brockman, Mr Campbell-Johnson, Lieutenant-Colonel Erskine Crum

THE PRESS

HIS EXCELLENCY THE VICEROY:

(i) directed the Press Adviser to find out and inform him whether the complete lack of publicity given by *The Statesman* that morning to the party he had given the previous day for delegates to the Asian Relations Conference was deliberate; and whether an account of this event had been sent to London;

(ii) directed the Press Adviser to render to him a brief on the subject of Press Conferences, including the point that he would ask editors whether they would attend such conferences personally or whether they could send sufficiently high class representatives;

(iii) directed M.S.V. to arrange for the Editor of *The Statesman* to be invited to luncheon with him on a suitable day.

Addendum to No. 33

Uncirculated Record of Discussion No. 1

Mountbatten Papers

TOP SECRET   *29 March 1947*

The following discussion on policy took place at the Viceroy's Staff Meeting on Saturday 29th March. In view of the secrecy of the subject-matter it is recorded here instead of with the issued minutes of the meeting.

SIR ERIC MIEVILLE said that many of the people whom he had seen during the previous few days had harped on the necessity for a quick decision on India's future. He had, in reply, pointed out that against the desirability for speed must be weighed the fact of the importance and permanence of the decision reached.

HIS EXCELLENCY THE VICEROY emphasized that the psychological effort of coming to the right decision very quickly will be very great: but it must be the right decision. He considered that it might be worthwhile, until the decision was reached, to ask the Party leaders to keep their adherents quiet in order to achieve the minimum of ill-feeling during this vital period. He would (and he intended so to inform the Party leaders) subconsciously at any rate count it against either side that they made trouble. He would watch which side appeared capable of government.

HIS EXCELLENCY THE VICEROY pointed out that, if a decision could be made quickly, it might well be possible to establish some form of Dominion status in India, which could run experimentally until June 1948. This might consist of a "Dominion" of Pakistan; a "Dominion" or "Dominions" of the Indian States (it was known that the Muslims and the majority of the Princes would be willing to remain within the Commonwealth); and a "Dominion" of the rest of British India. All these would be autonomous units, but with certain subjects, such as Defence, Foreign Affairs, Finance, Food and Communications, reserved to some form of central Government. HIS EXCELLENCY THE VICEROY said that in such circumstances he would reserve the right to decide in about April 1948 whether to recommend handing over power after June 1948 to a Central Government or whether to let the union of the autonomous units lapse.

HIS EXCELLENCY THE VICEROY said that, after he had decided what solution to recommend to His Majesty's Government, he would return to London to see that solution put through. He felt that he had great powers to speed the processes of legislation.

34

Minutes of Viceroy's Sixth Staff Meeting

Mountbatten Papers

TOP SECRET

Those present at this Meeting held at The Viceroy's House, New Delhi on 31 March 1947 at 10 am were: Rear-Admiral Viscount Mountbatten of Burma, Lord Ismay, Sir E. Mieville, Sir C. Corfield, Mr Abell, Colonel Currie (for items 1 and 3), Captain Brockman, Mr Campbell-Johnson, Lieutenant-Colonel Erskine Crum

Item 1

ASIAN ART EXHIBITION

HIS EXCELLENCY THE VICEROY:

(i) directed M.S.V. to arrange for himself (if free at the time) and Her Excellency to attend the Asian Art Exhibition that evening;

(ii) directed Press Adviser to inform the Press that they (or Her Excellency alone) would be attending.

Item 3

MR GANDHI

HIS EXCELLENCY THE VICEROY:

(i) directed P.S.V. to invite Mr Gandhi to come and see him at 5 pm that day;

(ii) directed Press Adviser to arrange for photographers to be present to photograph the meeting.

Item 6

THE ALTERNATIVE MACHINERY WHICH WOULD CARRY OUT THE DUTIES NOW PERFORMED BY THE POLITICAL DEPARTMENT AS THAT DEPARTMENT CONTRACTS (V.C.P. 11)[1]

The Meeting considered a paper on this subject which had been prepared by the Political Adviser. SIR CONRAD CORFIELD emphasised the difficulties of persuading the States to form composite units until they had firmly grasped the fact that the British were going to withdraw in June, 1948. Only by physical removal of representatives and the delegation of duties could the States be made to face the facts and take the necessary steps. He added that he considered that the States might be willing, on the withdrawal of the present system whereby paramountcy was exercised, to continue to be represented on a Committee under the Crown Representative.

HIS EXCELLENCY THE VICEROY:—
approved V.C.P. 11 subject to the addition at the end of Para. 4 of the words
"by recalcitrance on the part of individual States".

Item 7

THE NAWAB OF BHOPAL

SIR CONRAD CORFIELD recalled that he had been asked[2] to do all in his
power to persuade the Nawab of Bhopal not to resign from the Chancellorship
of the Chamber of Princes until after the projected Simla house party. He gave
his opinion that it would in fact be more difficult to use the good offices of the
Nawab of Bhopal on that occasion if he was still Chancellor. He could be
more suitably invited and used in his capacity of Chairman of the Major
States Committee.

HIS EXCELLENCY THE VICEROY:—
withdrew his previous direction that the Nawab of Bhopal should be asked not
to resign from the Chancellorship of the Chamber of Princes until after the
Simla House Party.

Addendum to No. 34

Uncirculated Record of Discussion No. 2

Mountbatten Papers

TOP SECRET   *31 March 1947*
AN ALTERNATIVE TO THE CABINET MISSION'S PLAN

HIS EXCELLENCY THE VICEROY said that it was, and would remain, his
primary object to persuade the Indian political leaders fully to accept the
Cabinet Mission's plan for the future of India. He was convinced that that plan
represented the ideal solution. However, in case of continued non-acceptance
of it, other possible plans must be devised. He was at present thinking on the
lines of the following alternative:—

1. The essence of the plan would be a form of Partition with a central
   authority for reserved subjects; this to be an experimental arrangement
   and to come into being in the near future.
2. The three units which would be the result of this Partition would be:—
   (a) Hindustan, to include the predominantly Hindu provinces.
   (b) Pakistan, to include the predominantly Muslim provinces.
   (c) The States.
3. Each of these units would be offered a form of Dominion status. In the
   case of the States, the larger would be offered this status by themselves;
   the smaller would have to combine into units of suitable size.

---

[1] Enclosure to No. 25.   [2] See No. 29, Item 12.

4. In view of the grant of Pakistan, and on the same principles which justi-fied that grant, there would be partition of the Punjab and Bengal.
5. The plan would be brought into force in about May 1947, and would run experimentally until June 1948.
6. The Central authority, which might be called "Central Government" or "Central Council", would deal only with the reserved subjects of Defence; Foreign Affairs; Communications; Food; and Finance to cover these.
7. The Central Authority, as well as the Hindustan Government, would be situated in Delhi.
8. Each of the reserved subjects would be dealt with by a Council or Board, containing representatives from Hindustan, Pakistan and the States.
9. The Viceroy would continue to have the right of veto on these reserved subjects.
10. About three months before June 1948, a decision would be made as to whether or not the Central authority would remain in being after that date.

HIS EXCELLENCY THE VICEROY said that the main advantages of this plan were that it involved the almost complete transfer of power at a much earlier moment than was at present envisaged; that all parties would have something to gain from it; that the help of the British would still be available in the interim period, working solely for the good of India; and that it would mean that India would at least have temporary experience of the benefits of a form of Dominion status. He wished to be assured, before going further, of the practicability of the plan.

SIR CONRAD CORFIELD said that he agreed with the basic idea as far as the States were concerned; it was practicable.

MR. ABELL drew attention to the difficulties of setting up any form of Pakistan government in the time allowed. SIR CONRAD CORFIELD agreed with this, making the point that there was no power to which to demit in Pakistan except individual provinces.

SIR ERIC MIEVILLE said that he did not consider that the formula "Dom-inion status" was altogether satisfactory. HIS EXCELLENCY THE VICEROY agreed with this point of view, and said that some other formula would have to be devised.

LORD ISMAY considered that the main difficulty would be the formation of the Central Authority. MR. ABELL pointed out that it would not be possible to compel the Muslim League to take an interest in the central subjects. He added that the boundary question in the partitioned Provinces would take much time to resolve.

HIS EXCELLENCY THE VICEROY said that in his view the most difficult part would be the eventual decision whether or not to keep the Central authority in existence after June 1948. In this connection, he made reference to the reports in Hansard of the speeches in the India debate of Mr. Zilliacus and Mr. Churchill, both of whom had suggested some sort of organisation under U.N.O.[3]

HIS EXCELLENCY THE VICEROY said that there were three possible prototypes on which to model the future constitution of India—the United States of America; the Australian Commonwealth, where federal rights had only recently been handed over to the Central Government by the States; and the Union of Soviet Socialist Republics, where the Ukraine, for example, had sovereign rights but at the same time was represented at the centre.

HIS EXCELLENCY THE VICEROY:—

invited the senior members of his staff further to consider the plan outlined above, together with the difficulties therein involved.

[3] See *Parl. Debs.*, 5th ser, H. of C., Vol. 434, 5 and 6 March 1947, cols. 546–9, 676–8.

35

Lord Pethick-Lawrence to Mr Attlee

L/WS/1/1070: ff 221–5

INDIA OFFICE, *31 March 1947*
Secretary of State's Minute: Serial No. 56/47

Prime Minister.

You will no doubt have seen a copy of the letter from the Minister of Defence to me, dated 22nd March,[1] about the advisability of withdrawing our invitation to India to send two representatives to the Commonwealth Advisory Committee on Defence Science.

For the reasons given in his letter, the Minister of Defence agrees with the views of the Chiefs of Staff that the invitation should be withdrawn.

I also agree, and recommend that the invitation should be withdrawn.

I feel, however, that, in our reply to the Government of India, it is necessary to give a reason for our decision and I think that, though it may be politic to take advantage of the opening afforded by their reference to it, it is as well to make it clear that it is not solely the announcement of the 20th February which causes this change of policy on our part, but the uncertainty as to whether India will remain in the Commonwealth. This, the governing consideration, will operate in similar contexts to which the Minister of Defence alludes—

[1] No. 3.

unless and until India definitely opts to stay in the Commonwealth as a fully co-operating member.

I therefore suggest, in regard to the Advisory Committee on Defence Science, that the following reply should be sent to the Government of India's telegram (copy annexed for ready reference):[2]

"It is now unlikely that the Advisory Committee on Defence Science will meet before September if as early as that. Apart from this consideration the situation is, as you suggest, altered by the decision announced by H.M.G. on 20th February that power in India will be finally transferred not later than June 1948, and in view of the uncertainty that prevails as to the precise relationship of India to the British Commonwealth thereafter, I think the Government of India will share our view that it would be inappropriate for India to become, for possibly so short a period, a member of the Common-wealth Advisory Committee on Defence Science. We, therefore, think it would be advisable that further action should be deferred for the time being on the Recommendations of the preliminary Informal Commonwealth Conference on Defence Science held in June 1946".

I think it is not necessary to say specifically, as suggested by the Minister of Defence, that our decision would at once be reconsidered if India should decide to remain within the Commonwealth.

2. I now learn from the Ministry of Defence (letter of 28th March C.O.S. 359/7)[3] that you have approved a recommendation that for the same governing reason no further invitations should be extended for the attendance of Indian students at the Imperial Defence College, the Joint Services Staff College and other similar establishments which have access to top secret information or information from U.S. sources.

Though it would be desirable to deal with such cases merely by refraining from offering invitations it is not unlikely that the Government of India will, without waiting for a specific invitation, nominate successors to the Indian officers who are now doing courses at such establishments; and indeed there is an outstanding case of an Indian R.I.N. officer already nominated and about to leave India (on 7th April) for a course at the Naval Staff College where top secret information is divulged. I propose, therefore, to add to the above draft telegram a paragraph in the following terms:—

"The same uncertainty affects the question of the attendance of Indian officers, during the transition period at any rate, at the Imperial Defence College, the Joint Services Staff College and the three Service Staff Colleges; and the Government of India will no doubt agree that embarrassment will be avoided if vacancies already offered are not filled and if no further invita-tions are issued till the future situation is more clear. This will apply to the case of Commander (S) Srinivasan who I understand is due to leave on or about 7th April to attend Naval Staff College (N.H.Q. signal 270901 refers).

I will let you know whether there are any other courses at other establishments than those mentioned above which also are affected".

3. I am sending a copy of this minute to the Minister of Defence.[4]

PETHICK-LAWRENCE

[2] See No. 3, note 2.
[3] Not printed: see L/WS/1/1070: f 228.
[4] On 3 April Mr Simpson noted that Mr Attlee had ticked Lord Pethick-Lawrence's Minute. The G. of I., Defence Dept was accordingly informed of the decisions, in the terms proposed by Lord Pethick-Lawrence, in tel. 4461 of 4 April. L/WS/1/993: ff 10–12. See also No. 71.

36

Minutes by Mr Abell, Mr Scott and Captain Brockman

R/3/1/136: f 38

31 March–4 April 1947

D.P.S.V.

We should consider whether we should send the Secretary of State Sir Conrad Corfield's paper[1] on the alternative machinery which will carry out the duties now performed by the Political Department. If you have not got a copy of the paper it is available as VCP 11 in the Conference Secretariat.

G. E. B. ABELL
31.3.1947

P.S.V.

I do not know the lines on which discussion developed in yesterday's conference.[2] Subject to that, my views are as follows.

2. The Political Department has hitherto performed a dual function: it has provided liaison (in both directions) between British India and the States; and it has been the machinery for the exercise of the Crown's suzerainty. This latter function covered dynastic etc. questions and will cease next year. Some machinery will clearly have to take the place of the former.

3. I do not fully understand why Political Adviser is averse from the Government of India having relations with the States through a special Department; and prefers that the various separate Departments of the Government of India should deal direct. It seems to me that his plan will lead to a great overlapping of functions, as each of the main Departments concerned would inevitably have to set up a division to deal with States; and there would have

[1] Enclosure to No. 25.   [2] See No. 34, Item 6.

to be a great deal of inter-departmental co-operation. It seems, on the other hand, logical that the future Government of India should maintain a Political Department of some kind for dealing with the States, in the same way as it will maintain an E.A. Department for dealing with foreign countries. It seems to me inevitable that as the present Political Department contracts, some similar organisation will have to step in and take its place: there cannot be a vacuum in the handling of day-to-day administrative problems which arise between British India and the States, and for which the present Political Department provides the nexus. I do not think that Political Adviser's note should be sent to the Secretary of State, as he might have wished to write it somewhat differently if he had known that it was going to London. At any rate, he should be consulted before it is sent. The Secretary of State will in fact become fully in the picture when he receives the minutes of the forthcoming Residents' Conference.

I. D. SCOTT
1.4.1947

I agree with D.P.S.V. The parallel case seems to be the British Colonies and Dominions, which deal in London with the Colonial and Dominion Offices rather than direct with the other Departments of State.

R. V. BROCKMAN
2.4.47

I had had the same doubts myself, but don't usually horn in on P.A.'s business. —Please find out if he wants the paper to go home.—There is no need to encourage him to say 'Yes', but he did mention the matter to me.

G. A.
2/4

He does not want the paper to go home.

I. D. S.
4/4

37

Record of Interview between Rear-Admiral Viscount Mountbatten of Burma and Mr Gandhi

Mountbatten Papers. Viceroy's Interview No. 14

TOP SECRET   *31 March 1947*

Mr. Gandhi arrived, accompanied by Miss Patel, at 5 p.m.

Miss Patel was shown to the waiting room, and unfortunately we only discovered she was here on Mr. Gandhi's departure. Her Excellency apologised, and invited her to come and sit with her next time she came.

Mr. Gandhi, Her Excellency and myself first of all faced up to a barrage of cameras, and then we started purely social, friendly talks in which, at Mr. Gandhi's suggestion, Her Excellency took part for the first hour. She then made an excuse to leave, so that we could get down to business. But as Mr. Gandhi showed no inclination for getting down to business, and as he promised to give me two hours every day for the rest of the week, I felt there was no hurry and deemed it advisable to let him talk along any lines that entered his mind.

Thus he talked of his life in England, of his life in South Africa, his recent tour of Bihar, his discussions with former Viceroys and Members of the Cabinet. He expressed a high regard for Lord Halifax as a Viceroy, but regretted his subsequent record in the Cabinet and in America, which he felt was to some extent retrieved by his statesmanlike speech in the House of Lords this February.[1]

We parted at 7.15, both of us, I am sure, feeling that we had progressed along the path of friendship.

[1] See Vol. IX, Nos. 468 and 473, para. 2.

38

Rear-Admiral Viscount Mountbatten of Burma to Lord Pethick-Lawrence

R/3/1/81: f 115

31 March 1947

Dear Secretary of State,

I should be grateful if I may be given the instructions of His Majesty's Government as to the the principles which should govern the withdrawal of British forces from this country on the transfer of power.

At a Staff Conference held in London before I left for India (see COS(47)36th Meeting)[1] opinion was, I believe, unanimous that there should be no withdrawal of British Forces below the agreed ceiling until power had been actually transferred i.e. until June 1948. With this opinion I am in agreement, although I should of course expect to be given discretion to send off, in advance of the actual date of transfer, such details as I considered expedient.

Would you be so good as to let me know whether His Majesty's Government approve this policy in order that the necessary planning may be put in hand at once. This would, of course, be on the basis that the final withdrawal, after June '48, should be completed with the utmost possible speed.

Yours sincerely,

MOUNTBATTEN

[1] Vol. IX, No. 487.

39

Lord Pethick-Lawrence to Rear-Admiral Viscount Mountbatten of Burma

R/3/1/142: ff 69–71A

INDIA OFFICE, *31 March 1947*

My dear Mountbatten,

In paragraph 3 of my letter of 21st March[1] I briefly referred to the future of Berar as being one of those matters of common concern to which, in the view of the Cabinet Mission, the State concerned and "those likely to control the succession Government or Governments" should be giving attention during the interim period with a view to arriving at an understanding about the terms of settlement after Paramountcy has been withdrawn. I promised to write separately on this issue.

2. Since then I have seen your [predecessor's] telegram No. 580–P of 21st March[2] and my anticipation is confirmed that there has so far been little progress towards discussion of the future of Berar between the interested parties; and I imagine that neither you nor Corfield will be too sanguine about Nehru's reaction to Rau's renewed approach. Nor, in view of H.E.H.'s well-known personal views on the subject of Berar and of Hyderabad's present attitude towards an Indian Union, does it appear likely that H.E.H's Government will agree to participate in any such negotiations, even if Nehru does set up the necessary Assembly machinery for consultation, unless it has good reason to think that there will be substantial advantage to the State in a settlement now. But if we let matters take their course, there may well be a dangerous hiatus after we depart. The results might be grave; if the Indian Army lost its unity, Hyderabad forces might even step in and take forcible possession of Berar, with incalculable consequences. It seems clear, therefore, that we have really no alternative but to do our utmost to induce agreement during the next few months.

3. There are, however, certain limitations inherent in the statutory position. Section 47 of the Government of India Act 1935 declares that Berar is under sovereignty of the Nizam, but provides for its administration with the Central Provinces by agreement between the Crown and the Nizam. The Agreement now current includes concessions to H.E.H., notably the provision of certain military assistance in the event of subversive troubles in Hyderabad, and an annual payment of Rs. 25 lakhs, and this Agreement would, it is clear, be voided by any failure on our part to observe the concessions, in particular the military arrangement, or by any statutory amendment inconsistent with the provisions of the 1935 Act. It is true, however, that the Crown did reserve the right, failing a fresh agreement, to make suitable administrative arrangements

for Berar—though not on a basis essentially different from the present—while claiming full and exclusive jurisdiction and authority. But this was subject to recognition of the Nizam's sovereignty and the other concessions, and it remains clear, in light of the statutory position, that there is in fact no opportunity for adjustment between the Crown and Hyderabad during the interim period.

4. It seems therefore that the only solution is for H.M.G. to promote an arrangement between Hyderabad and the Interim Government, which seems, as indicated in paragraph 2 of your predecessor's telegram of 21st March, the most appropriate authority in British India in present circumstances to handle a negotiation of this kind. For I note that Nehru has taken the lead in the discussions with the States Negotiating Committee, and his political influence with the Congress Ministry in the Central Provinces and Berar is no doubt sufficient to overcome local opposition to what may seem from the all-India standpoint a satisfactory settlement. Moreover, in view of the announced intention of numbers of important Hindu States to enter the Constituent Assembly (which I gather may be the result of the promise to them of certain concessions) Nehru may feel that it would now be no indication of weakness on the part of British India but rather a recognition of Hyderabad's increasingly isolated position, if the Interim Government were to initiate discussions with its Government. I recognise of course that an arrangement between the Interim Government, in association with the Central Provinces and Berar Government, and Hyderabad would be in the nature of a "Gentleman's Agreement" as regards future action; it could have no present validity. Further, it would be necessary for you as Crown Representative to be kept fully informed of what transpires. But from Nehru's point of view it would surely be of value to show that Congress was not disposed to be intransigent with so important an element of the future India, while the Nizam, influenced by Sir Mirza Ismail, might see the advantages of coming to terms in good time with the party likely to be predominant in the territory surrounding his dominions.

5. Our own interests would appear to be served by the promotion of an agreement which would secure, *inter alia*, the following objectives:—

    (*a*) that a partition issue in the province of C.P. and Berar is avoided as long as we remain in India;

    (*b*) that in view of the agreement to provide specified troops to support the

---

[1] Vol. IX, No. 557.

[2] In this telegram the Crown Representative reported that there had so far been no discussion between Hyderabad and British India regarding the future of Berar. Sir B.N. Rau, in discussion with Sir C. Corfield, had taken the view that in present circumstances the Interim Government was the most appropriate British India authority to conduct negotiations with Hyderabad. Rau would, therefore, approach Pandit Nehru again and suggest that the Central Government should give early consideration to the question of setting up negotiating machinery. R/3/1/142: f 68.

Nizam in case of subversive movements in the State (which in existing circumstances might easily arise) a clash with the Interim Government over the movement of the troops in question might be avoided; and

(c) that the future position as regards Berar might be so regulated as to prevent it remaining a leading case for the dismemberment of British India when Paramountcy obligations cease. The claim of Kalat to recover Quetta and the leased territory now embodied in British Baluchistan is in many respects similar, but in the event of an agreement over Berar would be considerably compromised.

6. Would it not be possible for you to bring Nehru and the Prime Minister of the C.P. into informal negotiations with Sir M. Ismail and others of H.E.H.'s Government if a possible basis of agreement can be devised? And might the basis of agreement be somewhat on the following lines?

(a) during the interim period the terms of the Berar Agreement including the military clause will be respected by the Interim Government and the Central Provinces and Berar Government, that is to say, in particular if (under the terms of S.286(I) of the Act) the Crown Representative requests the assistance of armed forces to uphold the Nizam in his dominions, the Interim Government will not demur to the Governor-General requiring the despatch of such forces; and

(b) it shall be a "gentleman's agreement" that after the transfer of power

(i) the Central Government on which the Province of Central Provinces and Berar depends will continue to acknowledge the Nizam's sovereignty in Berar (and possibly will associate him, as we know he wishes, with the grant to that Province in respect of Berar of its new Constitution)

(ii) the Central Government will secure to Hyderabad unrestricted import from overseas of the material necessary to its economic development and, by agreement with the Defence authorities, of such war material as Hyderabad needs for its internal security.

(c) In return the Nizam will undertake to relinquish any claim to special localised protection, will undertake to disinterest himself in the question of Berar reverting to his effective sovereignty, and will cease to expect an annual payment of Rs. 25 lakhs as quit rent.

7. It may be somewhat optimistic to hope for agreement on this or similar lines, but it does seem worth the Interim Government's while to try to secure such an agreement and, if successful, to ensure its acceptance by the Constituent Assembly. Something at least would be gained if an offer were made to Hyderabad from Congress quarters which was sufficiently generous to make its rejection impolitic. As I have said above, the statutory position seems to rule out any direct adjustment between Hyderabad and the Crown at this stage, but this does not preclude an understanding between British India and Hydera-

bad which would come into operation only after the statutory provision for Berar and the Berar Agreement had become dead letters.

8. These are the best suggestions I can offer. I shall be interested to hear whether you and Corfield think that something can be made of them.

Yours sincerely,

PETHICK–LAWRENCE

40

Sir E. Jenkins (Punjab) to Rear-Admiral Viscount Mountbatten of Burma (Extract)

L/P&J/5/250: ff 62–3, 65–6

SECRET   GOVERNMENT HOUSE, LAHORE,
No. 662.   *31 March 1947*

3. The situation is at present under control everywhere. There is an uneasy peace in the Rawalpindi, Attock, Jhelum and Multan districts, and also in the cities elsewhere which were involved in the rioting. There has been one new disturbance at a village in the Hamirpur Tahsil of the Kangra District, and another of a more serious character at Hodal—a small town at the southern end of the Gurgaon district. I have just heard that certain villages in Gurgaon are also affected and that additional troops have been called in from Delhi. A recent disturbance at Kartarpur in the Jullundur district does not seem to have been communal in origin, and was quickly suppressed.

4. There are various rumblings below the surface, and there may be a recrudescence of serious trouble at any time. The Muslims are fatuously complacent. They say that they were not the aggressors; that Master Tara Singh set things off with his violent statements; and that even now the Sikhs are making a great parade of their *Kirpans*, in respect of which they have an exemption on religious grounds. Some bad speeches are being made in mosques, and Intelligence reports suggest that some members at least of the Muslim League would be glad of further trouble.

The Hindus and Sikhs are for the time being acting together. They realise, I think, that their speeches on 3rd March were injudicious; but they hold quite rightly that there was no justification for the general massacre in the Rawalpindi Division. They are intent on a partition of the Punjab, and are not inclined for any reconciliation with the Muslims.

★   ★   ★

6. Politically there have been no moves of any importance. I have been in touch during the fortnight with Ghazanfar Ali Khan, Khizar (twice), Giani

Kartar Singh, Firoz, Swaran Singh, Mamdot, Daultana, and Muhammad Ibrahim Barq, the former Education Minister; also with sundry Hindu leaders. The Muslim League seem to be divided into two schools of thought. Ghazanfar and others like him still think that a purely Muslim Ministry would be able to run the Punjab. They believe that if a general election were held, they would win all the Muslim seats and would have a clear majority of Muslims only. Mamdot and Daultana do not apparently share this view. They recognise that the non-Muslims, and particularly the Sikhs, could make it quite impossible for a Muslim Government to carry on at all. They are therefore concentrating on Muslim grievances—particularly the alleged repressive action of Police and troops in the Rawalpindi Division, the aggressive tactics of Master Tara Singh, and the carrying of *Kirpans* by Sikhs. Barq, who is an ingenuous young man and had previously been approached by the Muslim League, said that many members of the League would like to take office in order to stop all proceedings in Rawalpindi. Khizar is convinced that a Muslim Ministry must fail. He has returned to his estate at Kalra in the Shahpur district, and has asked me to let him know if there is any change in the situation.

The non-Muslims have made it clear that they will not tolerate any Muslim Ministry, and although Mamdot and Daultana would, I think, like to approach the Sikhs again, it is most improbable that the Sikhs will co-operate with them in any way.

We can, I think, only wait and see what happens. The cleaning up process in the Rawalpindi Division and elsewhere will be very difficult and tiresome, and we must expect criticism and opposition. For the time being there is no alternative to a Section 93 administration.

41

Sir O. Caroe (North-West Frontier Province) to Rear-Admiral Viscount Mountbatten of Burma

Telegram, Mountbatten Papers. Official Correspondence Files: North-West Frontier, Situation in, Part I(a)

IMMEDIATE   *31 March 1947, 5.25 pm*
CONFIDENTIAL   *Received: 31 March, 10 pm*
No. CA/43. N.W.F.P. situation.

Large processions are daily parading all cities in defiance of ban and have begun invading cantonments. Jails are over-crowded and further arrests will compel release of ordinary criminals. Police are tired and inadequate and aid by troops may well lead to firing on demonstrations. Tribes are restive and further firing incidents may cause them to raid. News from here is being distorted and neither radio nor press give true picture.

2. I urged Premier again today not to confine himself to repressive measures but to attempt conciliation or aim at coalition, but have met with blank refusal. Main danger is with tribes—a feature which makes conduct of provincial affairs here different to that in other provinces. Possible courses are (a) for Governor-General to take tribal affairs into his own portfolio until future of tribes is settled. This would undoubtedly have pacifying effect. (b) For Governor to issue direction under section 57 Government of India Act assuming control at least of law and order. This however might shortly place me in section 93. (c) Leave Ministry to pursue present courses into greater difficulties and deal with symptoms as best we can.

3. I realise present circumstances may necessitate following course (c) to sub-serve larger all-India interests. But if so I must point out real danger to peace of frontier and ask to be clearly informed in order that I may give reason to officers who are working under great strain.

4. I will discuss these matters with Ismay on Wednesday.[1]

This telegram has not repeat not been repeated to Secretary of State for India.

[1] On 1 April Mr Abell informed the Governor's Secretary that Lord Mountbatten did not propose to reply to this telegram until Lord Ismay returned, but that it looked as though it would be difficult to adopt any other than course (c) of those mentioned by the Governor. Mountbatten Papers, Letters to and from Provincial Governors: N.W.F.P.

42

Sir H. Dow (Bihar) to Rear-Admiral Viscount Mountbatten of Burma

Telegram, R/3/1/148: f 37

IMMEDIATE
CONFIDENTIAL

31 March 1947, 7 pm
Received: 31 March, 11 pm

No. 37/S. My Revenue Minister[1] and also Dr. Mahmud Shah Development Minister are on way to Delhi, apparently with view of discussing Bihar riots Enquiry Commission with Interim Government or Congress High Command. Matter has not yet come before me officially, but I understand that Gandhi is pressing for open public enquiry, and my ministers who hate the idea of an

[1] Mr K.B. Sahay.

enquiry at all but have been over-borne will probably give way on this point also. I am quite sure that an open enquiry would involve recrudescence of communal trouble, but Gandhi is probably so confident that he has effected change of heart in Bihar Hindus that he may try to insist on putting this to the proof. I am sending this telegram in case you should be seeing Gandhi almost immediately, and should be grateful for any influence you can exert to turn him from this dangerous experiment.[2]

[2] Mr Abell minuted on this telegram: 'The League have demanded an enquiry into the Bihar riots and the Congress have supported the proposal in a lukewarm way because they cannot afford to reject it. An enquiry into the Calcutta riots is going on now.

  The Governor and the Ministry have always been against it, and Lord Wavell took the view that it could do no good now and might do much harm.

  I agree with the Governor. We should avoid an enquiry.'

43

Note by Field Marshal Sir C. Auchinleck[1] on communal affiliation of Officers in the Indian Army[2]

Mountbatten Papers. Official Correspondence Files: Armed Forces, Indian, Vol. I, Part I

COMMANDER IN CHIEF IN INDIA, NEW DELHI, *undated*

Indian *Officers* are mixed throughout the Army in *every* unit, whatever its "class composition", entirely irrespective of class or religion.

A "Hindu" Army

Very broadly:

Armoured Regts	1 (Madrassis) in process of formation
Artillery Regts	24 (including Sikh and Madrassi Regiments)
Engineer Coys	28 *all* Madrassis
Infantry Battalions	31 including Sikh and Madras battalions but not Gurkha battalions
Gurkha Battalions	30 (ten for early disbandment)
Transport companies (MT)	31 (includes Sikhs, Madrassis and Christians)
Transport companies (AT)	10 (includes Sikhs)

Signals, Supply, Medical, Ordnance, E & M E units all mixed composition would require complete organisation and rebuilding.

  The same applies to the mixed Armoured, Artillery, Engineer and Infantry units of the Army.

C. J. A.

A "Muslim" Army

Armoured Regts	NIL (all mixed regiments)
Artillery Regts	12
Engineer Coys	12
Infantry Battalions	1 (all others are mixed battalions)
M.T. Coys RIASC	22
A.T. Coys RIASC	10

Signals, Supply, Medical, Ordnance, E.M.E. all of mixed classes from all over India.

Would need to be completely broken down and reorganised before separate "class" units could be formed.

Large proportion of Muslims in the mixed Armoured Regiments come from "non-Pakistan" areas like Rajputana, Eastern Punjab and U.P.

Some Muslim M.T. Coys are from Bengal.

[1] The Editors asked Brigadier P.E. Mansergh who was military assistant to General Sir Arthur Smith at the relevant time, if he could identify the initialled signature at the end of the section on 'A "Hindu" Army' and the handwriting in this note. Brigadier Mansergh was satisfied from internal and other comparative evidence that the initials and the handwriting were those of Field Marshal Auchinleck. He added that his recollection of General Sir Arthur Smith, 'a British Service Officer, is that, on receipt of such a request from Viceregal Lodge, he would at the first opportunity, have sought audience with General Auchinleck, the undoubted Indian Army expert—and to whom such queries "were meat and drink"—and the "Auk" would have taken on drafting the answer to such a query personally, (you couldn't stop him!).'

In the light of further comparative evidence now before them the Editors see no reason to doubt the correctness of the above attribution of authorship.

[2] Presumably this note was written in response to the Viceregal request in No. 29, Item 7.

44

The Nawab of Bhopal to Pandit Nehru

R/1/30/40: ff 62–3

TAJ MAHAL HOTEL, BOMBAY,
1 April 1947

My dear Panditji,

I propose to place before the General Conference of Rulers and Representatives for ratification, as contemplated, the general understanding reached between the two Negotiating Committees in regard to the allocation of States' quota of seats and the method of selection of their representatives in the Constituent Assembly and the fundamental points discussed at the meet-

ings held on the 8th and 9th February and 1st and 2nd March, 1947.[1] I am
desired by the Standing Committee of Princes to request that you may kindly
intimate to me as early as convenient the acceptance by the Constituent
Assembly of the aforesaid general understanding reached between the two
Negotiating Committees on all these three matters.

A list of the Princes present at the meeting of the Standing Committee is
appended.

Yours sincerely,
HAMIDULLAH

Enclosure to No. 44

1. His Highness the Chancellor (in the Chair).
2. His Highness the Maharaja Scindia of GWALIOR.
3. His Highness the Maharaja (Holkar) of INDORE.
4. His Highness the Maharaja Saheb of BIKANER.
5. His Highness the Maharao Raja Saheb of BUNDI.
6. His Highness the Maharaja Saheb of REWA.
7. His Highness the Maharaja Saheb of ALWAR.
8. His Highness the Maharaja Saheb of DEWAS JUNIOR.
9. His Highness the Maharaj-Rana Saheb of DHOLPUR.
10. His Highness the Maharawal Saheb of DUNGARPUR.
11. His Highness the Maharaja Saheb of NABHA.
12. His Highness the Maharaja Saheb of NAWANAGAR.
13. His Highness the Maharaja Saheb of TEHRI-GARHWAL.
14. His Highness the Raja Saheb of KHILCHIPUR.
15. His Highness the Raja Saheb of MAIHAR.
16. His Highness the Maharaja Saheb of PATNA.
17. His Highness the Raja Saheb of KHAIRAGARH.
18. His Highness the Raja Saheb of BAGHAT.

OBSERVERS

19. His Highness the Maharaja Saheb of BHARATPUR; and
20. His Highness the Raja Saheb of BHOR
    attended by special invitation.

[1] See Vol. IX, Nos. 374–5, 389, 406, 477, 485–6.

45

Cabinet

India and Burma Committee. Paper I.B.(47)42 (Extract)

L/P&J/10/90: ff 12–13

PROPOSED TREATY WITH INDIA TO PROVIDE FOR MATTERS ARISING
OUT OF THE TRANSFER OF POWER

MEMORANDUM BY THE SECRETARY OF STATE FOR INDIA

INDIA OFFICE, *1 April 1947*

1. This paper is confined to the Treaty which is to deal with "matters arising out of the transfer of power." It is assumed in this paper that India will not remain within the Commonwealth. Though some modifications would be necessary, the content of the Treaty now under discussion will be substantially the same if India remains in the Commonwealth, though in that event it will be styled an Agreement. This memorandum deals only with the content of the Treaty. The question of the method of negotiating it or of negotiating Treaties with more than one authority (if that proves necessary) will have to be considered but the first necessity is to decide what we wish to secure.

2. The matters arising out of the transfer of power which we have to consider for inclusion in the Treaty appear to me to fall into two classes viz:—

A. *Matters in respect of which permanent provision is required.*

(i) Recognition by H.M.G. of the status of the authority with whom the Treaty is being concluded.

(ii) Exchange of diplomatic representatives.

(iii) An agreement as to the persons who will become Indian subjects and the persons who will remain British subjects.

(iv) Acceptance by the new Indian authorities of certain international obligations.

(v) The acceptance by the new Indian authorities and the allocation among them of existing obligations to individuals and corporations.

B. *Matters in respect of which it is desirable that transitional arrangements should be made.*

(i) The continuance temporarily of diplomatic and consular representation of India by British diplomatic and consular officials where India has no representation.

(ii) The continuance, pending the conclusion of discussions on defence questions, of certain defence arrangements.

(iii) Facilities for the withdrawal of the remaining British personnel after the transfer of power.

I deal with these items in turn.

[The remainder of the India and Burma Committee Paper, dealing with the items in detail, omitted.]

46

Cabinet

India and Burma Committee.   Paper I.B.(47)45

L/P&J/10/92: ff 105–7

PROCEDURE FOR NEGOTIATION OF THE TREATY RELATING TO MATTERS ARISING OUT OF THE TRANSFER OF POWER

MEMORANDUM BY THE SECRETARY OF STATE FOR INDIA

INDIA OFFICE,*1 April 1947*

1. In I.B.(47)41[1] and 42[2] I have put forward proposals as to the content of the Treaty relating to matters arising out of the transfer of power.

2. It was contemplated in the Statements of the Cabinet Mission of May 16th (paragraph 22) and May 25th (paragraph 4), that the Treaty would be negotiated with representatives appointed by the Constituent Assembly. On the assumption that the transfer of power would be to a government set up under the new Constitution framed by the Constituent Assembly the Law Officers gave an Opinion on the procedure for the transfer of power, which also contemplated negotiation with representatives of the Constituent Assembly. A copy of this Opinion is annexed for reference.[3] On the other hand in paragraph 13 of the Statement of 20th February we stated that negotiations in regard to matters arising out of the transfer of power would be undertaken with the representatives of those to whom we proposed to transfer power.

3. The Constituent Assembly meets again on the 28th April. If it proceeds in accordance with the Cabinet Mission's plan it should shortly thereafter divide up into Sections. If it does so there may be a considerable interval before the next full session. The question therefore arises whether we should at this stage invite the Constituent Assembly to nominate representatives for Treaty negotiations at a later date.

4. If the Constituent Assembly should become fully representative before it divides into Sections I think that we should invite it to nominate representatives for negotiating the Treaty. If it does not become representative it would, of course, be possible to do this if the invitation were coupled with a request that places should be left vacant for the Muslim League. I do not, however, think

that it would be desirable to do this. So far we have ourselves taken no step which recognises the Constituent Assembly in its present unrepresentative state as the equivalent of the Constituent Assembly set up by the Cabinet Mission. If we were now to take a step which appeared to recognise it as the body with whom we ought to negotiate the Treaty that would be interpreted as recognition by us that the Constituent Assembly, whether or not it becomes fully representative, represents the successor authority to whom power will be transferred and this would be inconsistent with paragraph 13 of the Statement of 20th February.

5. Unless, therefore, the Constituent Assembly becomes fully representative I do not think that we should take any steps to secure the nomination of representatives to negotiate the Treaty until we have decided to what authorities we propose to transfer power. As, however, the substance of the Treaty will have to be negotiated before the second reading of the legislation and as its content will affect some provisions of the Bill, the necessity for having authorities with whom Treaty negotiations can be undertaken emphasises the need which would arise in any case for a decision in the late summer or early autumn on the question to what authorities power is to be transferred.

6. This does not, however, mean that no progress can be made with these matters in the meantime. My colleagues will see that I have proposed that the most important matters, namely the obligations of the Secretary of State and Secretary of State in Council referred to as Category I[4] in my memorandum I.B.(47)42 should be dealt with in the sterling balances negotiations with representatives of the Interim Government which are due to be resumed in late April or in May and which we hope will take place in London. If this proposal is agreed to we should be able to deal with the most important category of obligations before the autumn.

7. Because of the importance of getting a settlement in regard to the obligations in Category I in the sterling balances negotiations I think it is desirable that a representative of the Congress should be joined with the

[1] This paper, dated 1 April 1947, was entitled 'Question of Nationality in relation to the proposed Treaty with India providing for matters arising out of the Transfer of Power.' At the beginning of the paper it was explained that: 'on the assumption that India secedes from the Commonwealth, one of the questions which has to be settled is that of nationality.' L/P &J/10/95: ff 70–84.

[2] No. 45.

[3] Not printed. The Annexure reproduced Nos. 246 and 450 in Vol. VII.

[4] Paper I.B.(47)42 divided H.M.G.'s responsibility for outstanding Indian obligations into four categories. Category I, which was the highest category of responsibility, was defined as covering 'persons whose contracts are with the Secretary of State or Secretary of State in Council *and were concluded in circumstances which laid a special moral obligation on H.M.G.*, beyond that arising from their general control of Indian affairs, and who, also, will remain British subjects'. It was suggested that members of the Secretary of State's Services, European Officers of the Indian Army and holders of Sterling Indian Securities fell into this category. L/P &J/10/90: ff 17–20.

Finance Member in the further negotiations on the sterling balances and there would be great advantage if we could secure that Sardar Patel was a member of the Delegation. If he and Liaqat come to London for that purpose we might be able to use the occasion for informal preliminary consultations with Liaqat and Patel on the matters to be dealt with in the Treaty.

8. I think there would also be great advantage if we could arrange as was recently suggested by the President of the Board of Trade for Pandit Nehru to come to London ostensibly for discussions on foreign affairs. We could then seek to have preliminary conversations with him on the question of a Treaty of Friendship and Alliance and if his visit could be arranged to fall towards the end of the sterling balances negotiations he could be joined with the other representatives in the discussions on the Treaty relating to matters arising out of the transfer of power.

9. I think it would be appropriate for the negotiations in India on the Treaty arising out of the transfer of power to be conducted by the High Commissioner with officials sent from here, including a legal adviser, but on this we need to secure the Viceroy's views.

10. I therefore propose:—

(1) That if the Constituent Assembly becomes fully representative we should request it, through the High Commissioner, to set up a body with which negotiations can be conducted as to the Treaty. It will be desirable to ensure that this body is appointed before the Constituent Assembly divides into Sections.

(2) That if the Constituent Assembly does not become fully representative we should take no formal steps to secure the appointment of a negotiating body by the Indians but should pursue the more important matters in connection with the sterling balances negotiations and should aim at linking with them informal discussions as to the content of the Treaty.

(3) That our proposals as to the content of the Treaty should be sent to the Viceroy for consideration and comment, and that we should consult him also as to whether the High Commissioner should conduct the negotiations.

(4) That we should consult the Viceroy as to the desirability of trying to secure that Sardar Patel comes to London for the sterling balances discussions with the Finance Member and as to the possibility of arranging a visit by Pandit Nehru towards the end of those negotiations or during the summer in which the question of the Treaty of Friendship and Alliance could be ventilated in a preliminary way.

P.–L.

47

Record of Interview between Rear-Admiral Viscount Mountbatten of Burma and Mr Gandhi

Mountbatten Papers. Viceroy's Interview No. 19

TOP SECRET   *1 April 1947*

Mr. Gandhi asked if he might take a walk round the Viceroy's garden at 9 o'clock, which he did accompanied by Rajkumari Amrit Kaur. Her Excellency went to meet him and accompanied him for part of the walk.

I met him at 9.30 as arranged, and we drew up chairs in the garden and continued our conversations.

He gave me his views on the origin of Hindu-Muslim animosity, and though he did not hold the British responsible for its origin, he said their policy of "Divide and Rule" had kept the tension very much alive, and that I should now reap what my predecessors had deliberately sown.

He urged me whatever happened to have the courage to see the truth and act by it, even though the correct solution might mean grievous loss of life on our departure on an unprecedented scale.

Finally, he gave me the first brief summary of the solution which he wishes me to adopt:

Mr. Jinnah should forthwith be invited to form the Central Interim Government with members of the Muslim League. This Government to operate under the Viceroy in the way the present Interim Government is operating.

Any difficulty experienced through Congress having a majority in the Assembly to be overcome by their able advocacy of the measures they wished to introduce.

I need not say that this solution coming at this time staggered me. I asked "What would Mr. Jinnah say to such a proposal"? The reply was "If you tell him I am the author he will reply 'Wily Gandhi'." I then remarked "And I presume Mr. Jinnah will be right"? To which he replied with great fervour "No, I am entirely sincere in my suggestion."

At this moment the A.D.C. reported that the Tibetan Mission had arrived, and our conversation therefore had to be terminated until the following day.

I did however obtain Mr. Gandhi's permission to discuss the matter with Pandit Nehru and Maulana Azad, in strict confidence, the next time they came to see me.

Addendum

During the course of the discussion Mr. Gandhi gave it as his considered opinion as a student of history and of world politics that never before, in any case of history he had read about in recent or past times, had so difficult or responsible a task been imposed on any one man as that which now faced me. I thanked him sincerely for realising the position in which I was placed.

48

Record of Interview between Rear-Admiral Viscount Mountbatten of Burma and Pandit Nehru

Mountbatten Papers.   Viceroy's Interview No. 20

TOP SECRET   *1 April 1947*

The interview lasted from 3 to 4.20 p.m.

I began by giving him an account of my talk with Mr. Gandhi,[1] which the latter had agreed I should do. Pandit Nehru was not surprised to hear of the solution which had been suggested, since this was the same solution that Mr. Gandhi had put up to the Cabinet Mission. It was turned down then as being quite impracticable; and the policy of Direct action by the Muslim League, and the bloodshed and bitterness in which it had resulted, made the solution even less realistic now than a year ago.

He said he was anxious for Mr. Gandhi to stay a few days longer in Delhi, as he had been away for four months and was rapidly getting out of touch with events at the Centre.

We next discussed the partition of the Punjab and Ghazanfar Ali Khan's suggestion for fresh elections. Pandit Nehru pointed out that the atmosphere engendered by fresh elections at this time could not fail to lead to a recrudescence of communal strife and bloodshed; and that at the end of the elections there was absolutely no guarantee that a Muslim League Government could be formed. And even if they had a small paper majority, the districts in which the Sikhs and Hindus predominated would now in no circumstances willingly accept the rule of an unrepresentative Government.

He linked the question of partition of Bengal with that of the Punjab. He had not yet had the opportunity of discussing with Mr. Gandhi his reasons for opposing the Congress resolution[2] on partition; but he realised that Mr. Gandhi was immensely keen on a unified India, at any immediate cost, for the benefit of the long term future.

I told Pandit Nehru that I recognised that there were long term and short term considerations which must affect the decision I had to make, and that although the long term ones should theoretically predominate, I hoped he would agree that I could not base my decision solely on them if the consequences were to be greatly increased chances of heavy bloodshed in the immediate future. He said that no reasonable man would argue with these premises.

We discussed the position between Bengal and Assam, where the Governor of Bengal had been unable to persuade his Government to take the necessary steps to stop the Muslim League activity across the borders of Bengal into Assam; and Pandit Nehru drew my attention to the fact that a Member of my Central Government, Mr. Nishtar, had recently been associating himself with the Direct Action policy of the Muslim League.

We next discussed the work which Mr. Gandhi is now carrying out in Bihar. We both recognised the high purpose which impelled him to carry out this very difficult task in the hopes of healing the sore spot in Bihar. But, as Pandit Nehru so aptly pointed out, Mr. Gandhi was going round with ointment trying to heal one sore spot after another on the body of India, instead of diagnosing the cause of this eruption of sores and participating in the treatment of the body as a whole. I entirely agreed, and said that it appeared that I would have to be the principal doctor in producing the treatment for the body as a whole, and that my prescription (which would in fact be my decision) would have to be very carefully made out if a cure was to be effected even temporarily.

Finally, he agreed that although an early decision would not necessarily affect the ultimate and basic causes of communal strife, a decision which was acceptable to most Indians and communities would undoubtedly remove the immediate cause of continued communal strife.

In conclusion he asked me if Lord Wavell had told me about the I.N.A. matter, to which I replied he had put me fully in the picture and that I had also discussed it with the Commander-in-Chief, and with the Cabinet in London.[3] He informed me that the matter was coming up in the Legislative Assembly the day after tomorrow, and that it would be impossible to have it postponed again since it had been postponed so often and for such long periods. The motion was bound to be carried and thereafter the Government would be faced with the dilemma that my predecessor had exercised his veto and over-ruled the Cabinet, and had since departed. He therefore had to take my directions in the matter, much as he regretted embarrassing me so early in my term of office.

His view appeared to be most reasonable, but he pointed out that a popular Government could not remain in office in the face of complete disregard of, or opposition to, the expression of popular will in the Legislative Assembly.

He also saw that my position would be irretrievably damaged with one side or the other according to any complete and absolute decision I might take; that is to say, if I supported Lord Wavell's veto, I should damage my position with all Indian politicians at the beginning of the negotiations, since I should be

[1] No. 47.　　[2] Vol. IX, Enclosure to No. 511, Item 3.
[3] See Vol. IX, Nos. 488, 507, 516, 530 and 553.

commencing my period of office with the unconstitutional act of reverting to the use of the veto. On the other hand, if I reversed Lord Wavell's veto, after it had been supported by the British Cabinet, immediately on his departure, and if as a consequence the Commander-in-Chief resigned (with the risk of many other resignations to follow in his train), I should have precipitated a crisis which could not fail to jeopardise my position in the United Kingdom where for the sake of India I obviously required at this time the strongest support from H.M.G.

Pandit Nehru and I agreed that we were both placed in an impossible position by this resolution, and that some form of workable compromise must be found.

I suggested that we should declare an amnesty for political offences, since all the I.N.A. were in on both the political charge of waging war against the King and the criminal charge of brutality. Would it not satisfy the Legislative Assembly if an amnesty on the political offence caused an immediate review by the High Court of the sentences and reduced them proportionately?

Pandit Nehru felt that he had a better compromise to offer, in the suggestion that the Commander-in-Chief should be stated to have himself undertaken that the sentences should be reviewed on a certain date, either by himself or by the High Court, with a view to a reduction which would result in the immediate release of the least serious offenders, whilst leaving the others still in prison.

I refused to give any opinion except in the presence of the Commander-in-Chief, and arranged for him and his Defence Member, and both of us to meet together for a discussion after the Cabinet meeting tomorrow.

49

Record of Interview between Rear-Admiral Viscount Mountbatten of Burma and Sardar Patel

Mountbatten Papers.   Viceroy's Interview No. 21

TOP SECRET   *1 April 1947*

The interview lasted from 7 to 7.30 p.m.

After the Cabinet Committee meeting on the subject of compensation, Sardar Patel remained back for his weekly interview. He gave me a cutting from *Dawn* dated 1st April which showed that two Members of my Interim Government, Nishtar and Ghazanfar Ali Khan, had attended a meeting of the Committee of Action of the All-India Muslim League. Detailed proceedings of the Committee were published, which although they ostensibly referred to civil disobedience movements, were, according to Sardar Patel, ill-concealed movements of violence. He asked me how much longer were Members of the Government to be allowed to dabble in active subversive organisations plotting against the existing Provincial Governments. I admitted the difficulty of the situation and said that I would probably speak to Mr. Jinnah at a suitable moment during our interviews: but that I was not prepared to take any precipitate action on this report. I pointed out that although I was glad to note there was no sign of any of the Congress Members of Government being associated in the same way, the Hindus were not free of the charge of themselves making trouble.

I informed him that I had brought out Mr. Alan Campbell-Johnson as my Press Liaison Officer, and that he had been on my staff for the best part of five years in C.O. HQ., and H.Q. SACSEA. He replied that he had already met him and was very glad I had a Press Liaison Officer which he thought would be helpful.

I told him that he could send for Mr. Campbell-Johnson at any time he liked, and that I would instruct him to be as helpful as possible with the Information Department of the Government.

Sardar Patel then raised the question of the proposed enquiry into the Eastern Bengal and Bihar riots and massacres. He told me that he was strongly opposed to any further inquiries, and that the inquiry into the Calcutta riots, which had been going on for some six months and had cost a great sum of money and which could not reach the public for another six months, had proved that such inquiries were quite valueless.

The trouble was that the Bengal Prime Minister, Mr. Suhrawardy, had pressed for an inquiry into the Bihar massacres, and that Mr. Gandhi had felt it incumbent on him to support this request. The latter had in fact brought pressure to bear on the Bihar Government to get them to agree, albeit very reluctantly.

I told him that the Governor of Bihar was against these inquiries and that I shared the Governor's view. Sardar Patel promised to speak strongly to Mr. Gandhi on this subject.

He urged me to send a telegram to the Governor of Bengal.

50

Record of Interview between Rear-Admiral Viscount Mountbatten of Burma and Field Marshal Sir C. Auchinleck

Mountbatten Papers.   Viceroy's Interview No. 22

TOP SECRET   *1 April 1947*

The talk lasted from 10.15 till midnight.

I spoke to the Commander-in-Chief on the telephone as soon as Pandit Nehru had given notice of the impending motion on the I.N.A.,[1] and asked him to be ready to come to a small meeting in my room with Pandit Nehru, Mr. Liaquat Ali Khan and Sardar Baldev Singh.

Later in the evening the C.-in-C., having held a meeting with the senior officers of his Staff, asked if he could come and see me before the Cabinet meeting the next morning, and as this was to take place at 9.15 a.m., I arranged for him to come and see me at 10.15 p.m. on 1st April.

We went through the whole history of the I.N.A. case, and although he was his usual friendly self and spoke with the utmost frankness, I detected a frame of mind which made him more difficult to deal with than I can remember at any time since October 1943. It was clear to me that he had in mind that any retreat from the position he had taken up on the advice of his staff and senior commanders would be impossible, since he would lose the confidence of the Army. He made it quite clear that once his utility had gone he would not feel justified in staying.

When I pressed him about what was likely to happen with the rest of his staff and commanders, he replied that he knew that most of them would resign, because they had raised the matter with him. He had given them instructions that they were on no account to do so, or act in any precipitate manner that could be held as a threat, but that they were to indicate their desire, if necessary, for release in due course.

It was only with the utmost difficulty that I got him to see that it might be necessary to take at least one pace forward from this position if I was not to be faced with two entirely inacceptable alternatives at the next morning's meeting.

[1] See No. 48.

51

Rear-Admiral Viscount Mountbatten of Burma to Sir F. Burrows (Bengal)

Telegram, R/3/1/148: f 39

SECRET   *1 April 1947*

No. 674–S. Dow telegraphs strongly opposing inquiry into Bihar riots.[1] Home Member Patel agrees. He will speak to Gandhi on this line.

I understand Suhrawardy has been pressing for inquiry into Bihar riots but does not wish to accept simultaneous inquiry into the East Bengal riots at Noahkali and Tippera.

My own view is that there should either be inquiries into both areas simultaneously or none at all. Personally I think there should be none at all since it is sufficiently established that the Muslims are responsible for the East Bengal riots and the Hindus responsible for the Bihar riots.

Not only will inquiries take much time and cost much money, but so far from doing good they are merely likely to arouse further communal feelings. I therefore trust you will do your best to get Suhrawardy to drop request, which in any case could not be granted unilaterally.

Repeated to Governor of Bihar.

[1] No. 42.

52

Minutes of Viceroy's Second Miscellaneous Meeting

Mountbatten Papers

TOP SECRET

Those present at this Meeting held at The Viceroy's House, New Delhi on 2 April 1947 at 11.15 am were: Rear-Admiral Viscount Mountbatten of Burma, Pandit Nehru, Mr Liaquat Ali Khan, Sardar Baldev Singh, Field Marshal Sir C. Auchinleck, Mr Campbell-Johnson

THE INDIAN NATIONAL ARMY

HIS EXCELLENCY THE VICEROY explained that this was an informal meeting. The situation of which Lord Wavell had informed him had now come to a head. Pandit Nehru explained the position to him yesterday[1] after which he had sent for the C.in.C. and seen him the previous night.[2] He proposed to

[1] No. 48.   [2] No. 50

begin with a dispassionate summary of the situation. Briefly the history of the matter was that some 60,000 Indians had been captured by the Japanese after the fall of Singapore. Two-thirds of these prisoners of war had decided not to change sides, but the remaining third had done so. He was anxious to impute no motive but simply to set out the facts. The problem after the war was what to do with the I.N.A. In accordance with law they could all have been arrested and tried; in fact three officers were first tried and cashiered after which only those men who had criminal charges against them were tried. We were now left with a dozen men serving sentences and there was a non-party motion up before the Legislative Assembly the following day calling for their release, which was likely to be passed unanimously.

HIS EXCELLENCY said that he entirely understood and appreciated the position of the present Government. When members of the Legislative Assembly expressed a unanimous point of view, normally a Coalition Government would have to bow before it but there was in this case the point of view of the C.in.C. to be considered. He had never come across an officer more devoted to India than Field Marshal Auchinleck and it was largely because of Field Marshal Auchinleck's liberal and understanding attitude that this matter of the I.N.A. had assumed such small proportions. The dozen men in question were in jail only on brutality charges and it was brutality against their own kind. It was the C.in.C.'s view that if these men were released and the last vestige of discipline flouted, he could not hold himself responsible for the discipline of the Army as at present constituted. The C.in.C. was making no threat and it would be only with the utmost regret that he would feel his usefulness to the Army would lapse. The C.in.C. promised that he would do his utmost to keep his senior staff and Commanders at their posts but if he were to go on this issue he was sure they would only stay on as a matter of duty, until reliefs could be found.

From his Excellency's point of view it was a peculiar situation. He was endeavouring to act as the constitutional head of a constitutional government and the last thing he wanted to do was to exercise a veto. It was a paradoxical position. He was statutorily responsible for law and order in India. When he was in England he had asked whether he could divest himself of this responsibility. The matter had been investigated and the answer had been that, without legislation in both Houses, the British Cabinet could not give the authority for him to be divested. He had been warned that he was responsible for law and order and in any case the present situation throughout the country was so serious that only the possession of such a fine instrument as the Indian Army could enable him to carry out the responsibility. He was "in a cleft stick". Politically he desired to be a constitutional head but he had to face the consequences of the unconditional release of these men which would involve the loss of the C.in.C. who would be going because the last prospects of the coherence and discipline within the Army would have disappeared. He said that he hoped that this was a fair statement of the position.

PANDIT NEHRU said that it was a fair statement. The matter was now coming before the new Viceroy for the first time. Lord Wavell had cabled London before taking the serious step of exercising the veto.[3] He felt there was nothing in these cases which need impair the discipline of the Army, but they valued the opinion of the C.in.C. It had been known to them that his term might expire early this year but they had wished him to continue. The fact that the C.in.C. felt strongly on this matter was a big consideration with the Government. Otherwise they were ready to have gone on regardless of the consequences. Speaking as a politician he did not see that there would be serious consequences. This issue had been before the Assembly for over a year. Mr. Liaquat Ali Khan had himself been on the point of accepting a similar resolution when he (Pandit Nehru) was absent abroad but had postponed doing so. The resolution was coming up again tomorrow. There was now no possibility of postponing it once more and no excuse for doing so. There was no doubt about the feeling in the House or in the country. This was not due to any liking on the part of the people for brutality. The whole question was considered in its political aspect and in no other. The people's view was that violence was in the air and that these men had been acting under their own code.

THE VICEROY stressed that free prisoners of war had been coerced to come over to the I.N.A. PANDIT NEHRU said that he would like to appeal to the C.in.C. He knew the Government's difficulty, the Government knew his. Let them try to find some way out. The Government did not want to put the C.in.C. in a false position or he to put the Government in one.

MR. LIAQUAT ALI KHAN said that his view was very much the same as Pandit Nehru's. He fully appreciated the position of the Commander-in-Chief. He was the best judge of what the effect would be on the Army. Some disagreed with his view but the C.in.C. knew more than outsiders and the majority accepted what he said. But in the country opinion was practically unanimous. It was very difficult for people to understand why no action had been taken against 20,000 and only against 12. THE VICEROY intervened to explain that it was very largely due to the C.in.C.'s efforts that there were only 12 left and that 20,000 had been released. There were no politics involved and the position seemed to be very widely misunderstood. These people were not in prison for "waging war against the King". They were in for brutality against fellow Indians. If possible, it should be stated categorically that there were no political offences left to be tried. The 20,000 I.N.A. men had been dismissed. Although the additional charge of "waging war against the King" had been laid by the lawyers, he stressed once again that these men were

---

[3] See Vol. IX, Nos. 516 and 553.

in only for brutality. They had committed a form of crime which would make any form of discipline impossible in any Army in the world if it went unpunished. If the civilised world really knew what they had done, it would be horrified. If they were in fact in prison for political offences, HIS EXCELLENCY said he would certainly be on the Government's side in the matter, but these were disciplinary offences of the worst type and could not possibly be condoned. HIS EXCELLENCY said that he had served as the Field Marshal's colleague and that he himself had had to fight against the I.N.A; thus he was fully able to appreciate his position. PANDIT NEHRU had instanced the parallel case of the Burma National Army. They had fought against us too, but there was no recorded case of brutality among the Burmese, against members of the regular Burma Army. He felt they should say "we accept the motion only on political lines, but we cannot release men on pure brutality charges when we are informed that the discipline of the Army will be affected." He recognised there was the feeling among Indians that "the British were keeping our brothers in a prison", but this was a misunderstanding which the Government should remove. They had all the resources of a modern Government, All-India Radio, etc., with which to put the case. In any case the men could have their sentences reviewed, but each must be reviewed on the merits of the case.

HIS EXCELLENCY said at this point that he had a special message to give from Mr. Attlee in Cabinet which he had asked him to give to Pandit Nehru in person.

The British Cabinet wished in a spirit of good will, speaking as a legislative body with perhaps greater administrative experience than their Indian colleagues, to warn them of the danger of undermining the loyalty and strength of their own armed forces in this crisis. This serious warning they had given in a body and had asked him to convey personally. It applied not simply to the period during which the British would remain in India, but thereafter as well.

Lord Wavell had also asked him to say that he had been into this problem for many months and had particularly wanted to clear it in Cabinet before the new Viceroy came in. His decision to enforce the veto was so that he could take the responsibility with all his experience of the case. His Excellency did not wish to take shelter behind his predecessor but this had been Lord Wavell's motive in exercising his veto a week before his departure.

PANDIT NEHRU said that the list of the 12 men seemed to indicate that they should be regarded as a group. Did the C.in.C. distinguish between any of them? Field Marshal AUCHINLECK said that each case had been taken on its merits. He had reviewed them a month ago. They had been considered by his Legal Department, which was a good one, then by the Adjutant General and then by himself. If there was any reason for remission it would be taken into account. The list actually included 15 names. This comprised 10 men guilty of brutality and 5 who had deserted with arms in their hands who were not in the same category. Altogether 3 were already released having served their sentence, which left 12.

PANDIT NEHRU agreed that the 5 were not in the same category although they had probably come under I.N.A. influence. HIS EXCELLENCY THE VICEROY pointed out that if a soldier deserted at any time or in any way, he was tried and usually shot. Here they had not been. These need not be called I.N.A. cases. On the other hand he felt it was quite impossible for anyone to condone a man who organised a public flogging of a fellow Indian to death. FIELD MARSHAL AUCHINLECK said he had just concluded a trial on a similar charge. If there was the slightest failure on his part to take a firm line in such cases and if he then had to stay on, he could not answer for the discipline of the Army.

HIS EXCELLENCY felt that, if only publicity could be given to the fact that no political offences were now involved and that the political and military offences could be separated in the public mind, the Government's difficulty would be largely solved. PANDIT NEHRU observed that no-one in the Government sympathised with brutality. The difficulty was the size of the I.N.A. issue and the fact that these men were identified with the I.N.A. Some of the I.N.A. men were good, some bad. The issue was dying but these things kept it alive. It was not a question of condoning a crime. These men had undergone some punishment already. He felt that Burhan-ud-Din and Rashid were the two most important. He had met Burhan-ud-Din who was an attractive fellow and had misbehaved from folly or fear or whatever it was.

HIS EXCELLENCY asked whether that was not the way all crimes were committed, but PANDIT NEHRU suggested that there was a difference. PANDIT NEHRU then asked the C.in.C. whether he could refer the matter to some special committee, apart from his usual action, for review. FIELD MARSHAL AUCHINLECK asked what this committee should do. Was it to review the validity of the evidence? They had been defended by eminent counsel. Sapru himself had expressed astonishment at the fairness of the court-martial procedure. The difficulty here was that a precedent would be set for any case of this nature to be subject to review by somebody else and the whole competence of his judicial authority would be undermined.

MR. LIAQUAT ALI KHAN then asserted that these offences had not been committed within the Indian Army. FIELD MARSHAL AUCHINLECK vigorously denied this and then briefly recapitulated the position. The numbers involved in the I.N.A. had been very large. Although theoretically everyone who had joined the I.N.A. should have been tried, it would have been both unwise and impolitic to do so, and the trials would have taken many years to clear. It had been important to establish that a crime had been committed against the State. To this end Shah Nawaz had been tried. MR. LIAQUAT ALI KHAN observed that he had then been let off. FIELD MARSHAL AUCHINLECK explained that this was not so and that he had been cashiered which was, as THE VICEROY pointed out, and PANDIT NEHRU agreed, a disgrace. PANDIT NEHRU asked why was it that everyone felt so strongly about the I.N.A. The people were not all mad. The truth was that the normal rules did not apply. The punishment of cashiering these men would have usually ruined a man's career but it had not ruined these men. It all depended on what motive was imputed by public sentiment.

HIS EXCELLENCY said that he hoped the C.in.C. would take a step forward towards a compromise, provided the morale of the Army was not affected. Not all the men were of equal importance. A Havildar clerk and a Sepoy, for instance, were involved. MR. LIAQUAT ALI KHAN then returned to the case of Shah Nawaz and elaborated a legal point. He had been found guilty of waging war against the King and of abetment of murder. This was more serious than the charge of grievous hurt. What people did not understand was that if you remitted Shah Nawaz, what justification was there for carrying on with these cases? HIS EXCELLENCY said that he understood that, in the case to which MR. LIAQUAT ALI KHAN was referring, the order had been given for a man to be shot without trial. An order in a battle was one thing, but to give an order in cold blood involving brutality, was another. On purely legal grounds Mr. Liaquat Ali Khan was probably right, but this was a moral issue. Mr. LIAQUAT ALI KHAN said that the popular view was that it had been a mistake to start the trials at all but that then the pressure of public opinion had caused them to be called off. THE VICEROY intervened to ask whether MR. LIAQUAT ALI KHAN was in fact suggesting that the C.in.C. had been mistaken in showing clemency. MR. LIAQUAT ALI KHAN said this was so and FIELD MARSHAL AUCHINLECK observed that many had said the same thing at the time. PANDIT NEHRU said that he had emerged after 20 years' retirement from the Bar to plead in these cases and that there had been technical evidence of murder as far as Shah Nawaz was concerned but no responsibility. Shah Nawaz was, in his view, a fine man. THE VICEROY pointed out that all the cases were reviewed by the correct reviewing authority, but one case had been so technical that clemency had been shown. There followed an argument as to whether the release of Shah Nawaz was due to the pressure of opinion. HIS EXCELLENCY drew attention to the fact that Pandit Nehru had said that the release was on the merits of the case. HIS EXCELLENCY said that on the face of it he could not believe that public opinion could not make a distinction when the charge was of stringing a man up and arranging for a whole company to flog him to death. PANDIT NEHRU asked whether this was not regular court-martial procedure and both HIS EXCELLENCY and FIELD MARSHAL AUCHINLECK pointed out that it most certainly was not.

PANDIT NEHRU then said he wanted help in the Assembly. He would like to ask that a High Court Judge should review the evidence. The political element would be removed, only the brutality examined. THE VICEROY reiterated that the political issue was not involved in the sentences and stressed that what Pandit Nehru was asking was that the brutality only should be examined. FIELD MARSHAL AUCHINLECK asked again what was the object? Was it to cast doubt on the fairness of the procedure that had taken place under his command? Where would his authority be if this were done? PANDIT NEHRU explained that the only way to meet the House was to be frank. He did not wish to have Lord Wavell's over-ruling veto mentioned. He suggested saying something along the lines that they appreciated public feeling but at the same time realised the importance of the C.in.C.'s opinion and were not anxious to do anything without his approval. The C.in.C. had considered the problem, not from a political angle, but in terms of brutality. Other cases should be cited and the effect on Army discipline stressed. He would add that there had been regular reviews of the cases but in this instance he was prepared to ask the High Court Judge to review not the whole case, not whether justice or injustice had been done, but just to review the position in an advisory capacity. MR. LIAQUAT ALI KHAN thought that that would not be effective. The justice and the evidence would have to be reviewed. Defending Counsel had thought the men were innocent. HIS EXCELLENCY said that that was not unusual and added that if they were to grip the matter firmly now it would come to an end, but if they temporised it would arise again. PANDIT NEHRU felt that it was not a question of gripping things. They had gone too far, but if the civilian element was introduced it might provide an honourable way out. HIS EXCELLENCY agreed that this might be so.

FIELD MARSHAL AUCHINLECK said that as they had now left principle and were discussing the matter in terms of expediency, what result were they expecting at that level? From the form taken by the discussion today it would seem that no half measures would be effective. What would happen if the judges recommended that there should be no change in the decision already reached? He asked quite frankly whether, if the Government was not strong enough to resist the I.N.A., they could withstand the recent mutinies of the Royal Indian Navy or the claims to release anyone else guilty of flouting military discipline?

FIELD MARSHAL AUCHINLECK stressed that he had no wish to be awkward but the facts must be faced and the VICEROY also added that he and the C.in.C. were not trying to be selfish but to take the long term view. PANDIT NEHRU explained once again that they were passing through a period of transition when it was difficult to apply rigid rules. The matter probably did not apply to the Royal Indian Navy. It applied simply to certain people who were now in prison. Looking at it from the viewpoint of the Armed Forces without, of course, the inside knowledge or experience of the C.in.C., it seemed to him that the I.N.A. issue was itself disturbing Army morale. Many people within the Indian Army welcomed the leniency being shown. The matter was constantly being argued out and the best thing was to put an end to it now. HIS EXCELLENCY felt that the discussion had now reached a stage where they should make up their minds and he asked the C.in.C. whether he could see his way to meeting the Government's problem by means of calling in a High Court Judge in this special case. FIELD MARSHAL AUCHINLECK again asked what was the object of asking him to invite a judge? Was it to be simply a sop to his own dignity? If that was the case it would be quite unacceptable. He said that his conscience was at stake and he was not prepared to condone anything which might be said to cast doubt upon the integrity of himself or of the officers under his command who had handled these cases.

PANDIT NEHRU observed that the dignity of the Legislative Assembly was also involved and pointed out what his own position was in relation to the Assembly. If he was compelled to go against the wishes of the Assembly, he would have to resign. His request to the C.in.C. was that a judge should be appointed by him who would report to him. This proposal was unacceptable to the C.in.C. HIS EXCELLENCY then suggested that the Chief Justice might be appointed to conduct the enquiry by the Government. Would that be acceptable? FIELD MARSHAL AUCHINLECK said he was in no position to refuse it, but would not like to give his own personal view without taking legal advice.

At this point, SARDAR BALDEV SINGH declared that there was no question of asking for any further remittances beyond the ones in question. FIELD MARSHAL AUCHINLECK said that, if they thought they could make any such limitation, well and good, but he warned them that there would be more pressure to follow; but all three Ministers agreed that there was no question of asking for any further remittances.

HIS EXCELLENCY stressed the need for trying to reach an accommodation and asked once again about the Chief Justice. FIELD MARSHAL AUCHINLECK said that he was not prepared to ask him himself but could not stop the Government asking him and wished to reserve his position. MR. LIAQUAT ALI KHAN thought the C.in.C. would be in a better position if he in fact called for the enquiry rather than the Government, but FIELD MARSHAL AUCHINLECK repeated that this concept was not acceptable to him. HIS EXCELLENCY felt that the Ministers were obviously anxious to do all they could to help, having regard to their position *vis à vis* Legislative Assembly, and he asked that an effort should be made now to find a formula. FIELD MARSHAL AUCHINLECK therefore wrote out a first draft of the formula which was subsequently amended and approved by His Excellency and the Ministers. Before the meeting adjourned PANDIT NEHRU stressed that he wanted to bring out in his speech tomorrow the distinction between political and military offences and expressed uncertainty as to whether the charge of waging war against the King was still on the charge sheet. HIS EXCELLENCY THE VICEROY stressed again that there was no question whatever of these men being in gaol on that charge. They were included among the 20,000 who had been "dismissed". They were in gaol now simply on grounds of brutality.

53

Record of Interview between Rear-Admiral Viscount Mountbatten of Burma and Mr Gandhi

Mountbatten Papers. Viceroy's Interview No. 23

TOP SECRET   *2 April 1947*
The meeting lasted from 2.30 to 4.30 p.m.

To begin with we discussed the question of holding enquiries in Bihar and Bengal. I told him the views of the Governor of Bihar, of Sardar Patel and of myself, that enquiries were a waste of time and money, as well as a potential source of further communal strife.

He flatly disagreed, and said that it was, in his opinion, essential that the Congress Government in Bihar should in all events show good faith by holding an enquiry which would reveal the appalling excesses committed by the Hindus in Bihar.

We both agreed, however, that this was really a matter for the Provincial Government to settle, and I suggested that he should discuss the matter in the meanwhile with the Home Member, Sardar Patel.

After this Mr. Gandhi came down firmly for his great plan, which he had revealed to me originally on Tuesday. I will repeat it here in greater detail.

He wants me to invite Mr. Jinnah to form a new Central Government for India, which will be the Government to which I am to turn over power. He suggests I should leave it to Mr. Jinnah to select the Ministers, if necessary entirely from the Muslim League, but if he feels so inclined he can of course then make it a coalition Government by including Nehru and other Congress Ministers as well as representatives of Minorities. In fact he suggests that Jinnah would be well advised to try and get the highest class team together and one likely to enjoy the greatest confidence of the Assembly.

He assured me that the Muslim League had many men of greater calibre than, for example, Nishtar and Ghazanfar Ali Khan.

The essence of the scheme was that it should be put through quickly in order that I might have as many months as possible as Viceroy and President of the Cabinet, and, by retaining the right of veto, continue to exercise complete control in the interests of fair play. The fact that I should be there to see fair play for the first few months would ensure Mr. Jinnah's Government no doing anything foolish which would prejudice its reputation in the Assembly or in the country; and he felt that I could guide them along in a manner which would ensure their continuing along the straight and narrow path after I left in June 1948.

If Mr. Jinnah refused this offer, then, Mr. Gandhi pointed out, the offer would have to be made to the only other great party in India—Congress. He hoped that Congress would invite Ministers from all shades of opinion including the Muslim League to participate in a Coalition Government.

I twitted him that he really desired me to form a Central Government run by Congress, to whom I would turn over power, and that the preliminary offer to Jinnah was merely a manoeuvre.

He assured me with burning sincerity that this was so far from being the case that he then and there volunteered to place his whole services at my disposal in trying to get the Jinnah Government through first by exercising his influence with Congress to accept it, and secondly by touring the length and breadth of the country getting all the peoples of India to accept the decision. He convinced me of his sincerity, and I told him so.

He agreed that I should discuss this plan with Maulana Azad and Nehru.

Finally, he said that he proposed also to discuss it with those two and with Mr. Kripalani. He agreed as to the supreme importance of complete secrecy, particularly as far as the Press were concerned.

He asked if he might quote me as being in favour of this plan, to which I replied that the most he could say was that I was very interested by it, but that I would require an assurance from some of the other leaders that they considered it capable of being implemented before I would commit myself to its support.

We discussed alternatives, and I told him I favoured the Cabinet Mission plan most of all, and he replied that he too would be in favour of it if it could be revived.

Finally I discussed the possibility of turning over power to the areas of India in accordance with the wishes of the majority of the residents in those areas. Broadly speaking this would make a Hindu India with a Congress Government in Delhi, a truncated Pakistan, and the large States like Mysore, Travancore, Hyderabad, Kashmir, and groups of States, each having separate power turned over to them, owing allegiance to a Central authority for Defence, External Affairs, Communications, and possibly food.

He agreed that whatever the decision, it should be taken soon and implemented as early as possible, and that meanwhile it would be an excellent thing if I remained in charge of the Central Government with the power of veto until June 1948.

54

Cabinet

India and Burma Committee.   I.B.(47)17th Meeting, Minute 2

L/P&J/10/92:   ff 101, 103–4

Those present at this Meeting held at 10 Downing Street, S.W.1, on 2 April 1947 at 11.45 am were: Mr Attlee (in the Chair), Mr Hugh Dalton, Sir S. Cripps, Mr Alexander, Lord Pethick-Lawrence, Viscount Addison, the Earl of Listowel

Also present during discussion of Item 2 were: Mr Henderson, Sir D. Monteath, Sir W. Croft; Mr S.E.V. Luke, Mr G.M. Wilson, Mr R.E. Field, Mr E.W.R. Lumby (Secretariat)

Procedure for negotiation of the Treaty relating to matters arising out of the Transfer of Power
(Previous Reference: I.B.(47)14th Meeting, Minute 5)[1]

The Committee had before them a memorandum by the Secretary of State for India (I.B.(47) 45)[2] regarding the initiation of negotiations for the treaty to be concluded on the transfer of power, together with two further memoranda (I.B. (47) 41[3] and 42)[4] relating to its content.

THE SECRETARY OF STATE FOR INDIA pointed out that the only bodies in India with whom negotiations might at this stage be started were:—
(a) the Constituent Assembly;
(b) the Interim Government; or
(c) the Central Legislature.
Communal differences rendered it difficult to conduct even preliminary conversations with any of these three bodies, and it might therefore be preferable to start conversations in this country in connection with the forthcoming talks about the Indian sterling balances.

The Committee did not feel able to reach any definite conclusions until they had had the opportunity to examine the papers more fully. The following provisional views were, however, expressed:—
(i) Preliminary negotiations on the treaty should not be linked to the talks on sterling balances.
(ii) Informal discussions might be started with representatives of the Interim Government and could, if necessary, be transferred later to some other body; the Interim Government might be prepared to nominate a small Committee consisting of, say, Pandit Nehru, Nawabzada Liaqat and Sardar Baldev Singh, for this purpose.

[1] Vol. IX, No. 529.   [2] No. 46.   [3] See No. 46, note 1.   [4] No. 45.

(iii) Neither the Viceroy nor the High Commissioner for the United Kingdom in India could undertake the negotiations on behalf of His Majesty's Government and it would be necessary to send out a special team for this purpose, which should include a fully qualified lawyer to deal with the question of nationality.

The Committee:—

Decided to consider the matter further at another meeting.

55

Record of Interview between Rear-Admiral Viscount Mountbatten of Burma and Maulana Azad

Mountbatten Papers.   Viceroy's Interview No. 23

TOP SECRET   *2 April 1947*

The meeting lasted from 5 to 5.45 p.m. I introduced him to Mr. Campbell-Johnson.

I told him straight away of Gandhi's plan, of which he already knew from Gandhi that morning.

He staggered me by saying that in his opinion it was perfectly feasible of being carried out, since Gandhi could unquestionably influence the whole of Congress to accept it and work it loyally. He further thought that there was a chance I might get Jinnah to accept it, and he thought that such a plan would be the quickest way to stop bloodshed, and the simplest way of turning over power.

When questioned categorically whether he preferred Gandhi's plan to the Cabinet Mission plan, he had to admit that if a whole-hearted acceptance by all parties of the Cabinet Mission plan came about, this would be preferable to the Gandhi plan.

I mentioned the other alternative which I had put to Mr. Gandhi an hour before, and he thought this also a very good alternative.

In fact Maulana Azad said that the sooner a decision could be taken and implemented, and the longer I could remain at the Centre to get things straightened out and running smoothly before I left, the better for the future of India.

I invited him to criticize my method of handling the Cabinet, and he was so complimentary that I had to accuse him of gross flattery and begged him to give me sincere constructive criticism. He replied he was absolutely sincere, and that he was certain that that view was shared by every Member of the Cabinet.

(*Note.* I realise that every Member of the Cabinet is probably out to ingratiate himself and his party, and that this form of flattery is to be expected at this stage.)

56

Sir J. Colville (Bombay) to Rear-Admiral Viscount Mountbatten of Burma
(Extract)

L/P&J/5/168: f 84

CONFIDENTIAL   *2 April 1947*
Report No. 81

7. On the general political situation here I can add little to what I said in my last two letters to Wavell. My Ministry is trying its best and except for certain rather idealistic notions,—such as prohibition and nationalisation, (which I may not personally be enthusiastic about, but which are essentially for the majority to decide)—it is fairly practical. In their attitude towards the Muslims it is difficult for Ministers to avoid unconscious bias but I think they are honestly trying to be fair, and the Prime Minister is particularly anxious to preserve this feeling. Politically they are beginning to feel that their real opponents are the Congress Socialists and the Communists. In conversation with me some of them show signs of anxiety as to standing alone after June 1948, but what the ties with Britain may be they hesitate to suggest. It might interest you to know that the telegram which I sent welcoming Your Excellencies in the name of the Government and people of Bombay was really from the Government and was framed in consultation with the Prime Minister. This is an indication of good feeling which was not evident before in Congress circles.

57

Certain Members of the Indian Central Legislature from the Punjab to Pandit Nehru

R/3/1/157: f 213

Sir,   *2 April 1947*

We, the undersigned Members of the Central Legislature from the Punjab, beg to submit the following for favour of forwarding the same with your endorsement to H.E. the Viceroy and to H.M.G. for their urgent consideration and immediate action thereon:

Unfortunately, the relations between the Muslims and Non-Muslims in the Punjab were already much strained due to the agitation carried on by the Muslim League for Pakistan, but the recent tragic happenings in North-Western Punjab have very rudely shaken the confidence of the Hindu and the Sikh minorities in the belief that there will be any fair deal for them at the hands of the Muslims in future.

The Muslims and Non-Muslims are almost equally balanced and no Government can carry on without the support of the three communities. Fortunately the population of the Province is so divided that there are distinct and contiguous areas where Muslims and Non-Muslims predominate. We have given our anxious and deep thought to this problem after considering all its pros and cons. We have come to the conclusion that the only way out of the present dead-lock is to partition the Punjab into two Provinces. That and that alone, in our view, can ease the tension in the Province which may increase at any moment. We further venture to add that it is no longer a long term constitutional issue, but an urgent and immediate administrative problem which should have first priority. Effective steps may, therefore, be taken forthwith to constitute two Provinces out of the present Punjab by passing an *Order-in-Council* or by any other way which may be found suitable. We are fully convinced that Partition is the only solution of this vexed problem.

We are, Sir,

Your most obedient servants,

(1) PANDIT THAKUR DAS BHARGAVA M.L.A.
(2) RAIZADA HANS RAJ M.L.A.
(3) DIWAN CHAMAN LALL M.L.A.
(4) SARDAR MANGAL SINGH M.L.A.
(5) SARDAR SAMPURAN SINGH M.L.A.
(6) SARDAR SURJIT SINGH MAJITHIA M.L.A.
(7) S.B.CAPT. HARINDRA SINGH M.L.A.
(8) S.B.SIR SOBHA SINGH M.C.S.
(9) CH.SRI CHAND M.L.A.
(10) SIR BUTA SINGH M.C.S.
(11) FT.LT. RUP CHAND M.C.S.

58

Rear-Admiral Viscount Mountbatten of Burma to Lord Pethick-Lawrence

L/P&J/10/79: ff 520–1

PRIVATE AND SECRET   *2 April 1947*

Dear Secretary of State,

Thank you for your letter of the 27th March,[1] which I received after I had drafted the attached report.

Since my last talk with you on the subject of sending separate letters to the Prime Minister and Members of the Cabinet Mission, I have reconsidered the matter and feel that the best solution will be for me to prepare a weekly report which I will include with my letter to you and which I would be grateful if you would circulate to the Prime Minister and the members of the Cabinet Mission.

When I said goodbye to the King on board HMS Vanguard, he asked me to write him regular informative letters about India, and here again I feel that this request will most easily be met if you would be so kind as to send one copy of the weekly report each week to His Majesty.

With this letter therefore I am enclosing five copies of my first Personal Report, for distribution as follows: (1) H.M. the King, (2) the Prime Minister, (3) yourself, (4) President of the Board of Trade, (5) Minister of Defence.

I was interested to read your views about the time-table for the whole operation of transferring power in June 1948. I had already come to the conclusion here that a decision about what we are going to do would have to be taken at a considerably earlier date than we envisaged during our talks in London. I quite understand the point you make about the time required to prepare and get through Parliament the necessary legislation, but I hope whatever is decided that it will be possible to make an announcement of our intentions at an early date before legislation is introduced.

Every British officer or official who has heard about the new compensation is overjoyed, and I am sure that no single better move could have been made by H.M.'s Government at this present moment so far as the British personnel of the Secretary of State's Services are concerned.

Thank you for the two enclosures to your letter which I am having examined, together with the position regarding excavators to which you referred.

I need hardly tell you that both the Wavells were kindness itself to me and my wife, and could not have been more helpful. On the day of my arrival I had a long talk with him alone before dinner, and with Ismay and Mieville and Abell after dinner,[2] which were good value.

---

[1] No. 26.   [2] See Vol. IX, No. 562.

There is little doubt that he leaves a very high reputation here in India.

All the Staff here have rallied round in the most loyal way and all have offered to stay on if I need them or go if I do not need them.

Yours sincerely,

MOUNTBATTEN OF BURMA

59

Viceroy's Personal Report No. 1

L/P&J/10/79: ff 522–5

TOP SECRET   *2 April 1947*

I have now completed my first week in office, during which I have had a series of individual interviews with every Member of the Cabinet, Field Marshal Auchinleck, some of the Princes and their representatives, and leaders of the British community and Scheduled Castes. I have held an informal meeting with the Service Commanders-in-Chief and Army Commanders; next week I shall hold a meeting with the Residents, and the week after with the Governors.

I should like to be able to paint an encouraging picture of my first impressions, but fear it would be misleading if I did so. The scene here is one of unrelieved gloom, and even that inveterate optimist Field Marshal Auchinleck has given up hope of any reasonable settlement, but begged me not to be infected by his gloom. At this early stage I can see little common ground on which to build any agreed solution for the future of India. The Cabinet is fiercely divided on communal lines; each party has its own solution and does not at present show any sign of being prepared to consider any other.

In addition, the whole country is in a most unsettled state. There are communal riots and troubles in the Punjab, N.W.F.P., Bihar, Calcutta, Bombay, U.P., and even here in Delhi. In the Punjab all parties are seriously preparing for civil war, and of these by far the most businesslike and serious are the Sikhs, who already have a plan to seize the main irrigation centres in order to exercise physical control over the whole of the Punjab. Although I am anxious to visit the Punjab and N.W.F.P. as soon as possible, there is too much to be done in Delhi to allow me to get away, and I have therefore sent Ismay off to visit Jenkins and Caroe.

In Bengal the Governor has been unable to persuade his Ministry to take action regarding the demonstrations by Muslim immigrants on the Assam border, and it looks as if further disorders may result. There has been a considerable amount of trouble with the Police in Bihar, but the situation is now reported to be under control. The strikers returned to duty, and the chief ringleader in the affair has surrendered on Mr. Gandhi's advice.

The only conclusion that I have been able to come to is that unless I act quickly I may well find the real beginnings of a civil war on my hands. There are many who think I have come out with a pre-conceived plan as to the transfer of power approved by H.M.G., which I am going to produce at the appropriate moment. I have made it quite clear in my conversations that this is not so. But I am convinced that a fairly quick decision would appear to be the only way to convert the Indian minds from their present emotionalism to stark realism and to counter the disastrous spread of strife to which I have referred above.

One of my first actions was to send letters to Mr. Gandhi and Mr. Jinnah, asking them to meet me here in Delhi. The first news I had that they both had accepted was contained in the Indian newspapers, but subsequently I received letters of acceptance from both. I hope to see Mr. Jinnah later on this week. I have had three meetings with Mr. Gandhi this week, all of them of an explora-tory nature, and it would be too early for me to comment on the solution which he has in mind. I am continuing my discussions on Thursday and Friday.

The swearing-in ceremony was carried out on Monday last, the 24th, with full ceremonial. The whole of the Cabinet was present, but only about half a dozen of the Princes. I decided that this was a good opportunity to make a short statement,[1] a copy of which I attach. I am informed that this statement was very favourably received. In this connection it may be of interest to report that Mr. Liaquat Ali Khan asked me, during an interview I had with him the next day, whether this speech was my own idea; and on being told by me that this was the case asked if he might quote me, as he had been told on no less than three occasions that this statement had been made at the request of Congress.

Although it had been understood that the Nawab of Bhopal and the Maharaja of Bikaner would attend the swearing-in ceremony they absented themselves, Bhopal on the grounds of a previous engagement, and Bikaner on the plea of ill health. Both are very old personal friends and came to see me later on the same day.

The Nawab of Bhopal raised with me[2] the question of the future political relations between the States and the United Kingdom, and mentioned the possibility of States or groups of States being granted dominion status. This last aspect was also raised in very definite terms by Sir Ramaswami Aiyer, the Dewan of Travancore, and by H.H. the Khan of Kalat. In all these cases I have been careful to make it quite clear that I have no authority to discuss any project of this nature, and that I could take no steps to encourage it, but that I would carefully note what had been said.

[1] See No. 8.   [2] See No. 9.

In my talks with the Cabinet Ministers I asked each of them whether they agreed that law and order could only be maintained in a country like India if the police force had behind them a non-partisan high class and efficient army. Without exception they all agreed. I next asked if they agreed that the first requirement of any solution I might arrive at for the transfer of power was that it should be done in such a way as to minimise the risk of future strife and bloodshed. To this also they agreed. I asked them if they thought the Indian Army would be sufficiently Indianised to stand on its own legs by June 1948. Varying views were expressed, but all agreed that only a committee of experts could answer the question.

When I asked them whether they thought that the army could be divided along communal lines by June 1948, the Congress Members unhesitatingly said it was out of the question, but the Muslim League Members appeared to think it was possible. All however agreed that this question again could only be answered by experts.

Nehru informed me[3] that he considered that of all India's problems the economic one was the most serious at the present time. It was not being really gripped and it was difficult to see what could be done at present, as the Muslim League were opposed to all forward planning as this entailed planning for a unified India. Nehru added that he did not consider it possible for psychological and emotional reasons that India could remain within the Commonwealth; but basically he said they did not want to break the threads tying our two countries together. He actually went so far as to suggest that future relations between the two countries might best be served by some form of common citizenship. I have the impression that a formula may have to be found.

During the past week I have had three Cabinet meetings on consecutive days, all of which were long and difficult to handle. The Budget proved to be a particularly difficult matter to handle. Mr. Liaquat Ali Khan, by producing a poor man's budget and hitting the capitalists through his capital gains tax and measures against tax evasion, succeeded in putting Pandit Nehru in a difficult position, backed as the Congress Party are by money from the large industrialists and financiers. The other main trouble is that a number of items come before the Cabinet which would certainly not do so in Whitehall, but would be dealt with in the first instance by Cabinet Committees. My predecessor, however, found it impossible to arrange for the setting up of any Cabinet Committee owing to the mutual hostility of the two major parties in the Cabinet. I referred to the desirability of setting up Cabinet Committees in my talks with individual Ministers and again at the Cabinet meeting, with the result that agreement has now been reached on the setting up of three Cabinet Committees. These committees are at present on an *ad hoc* basis, which I am sure is the best answer in present circumstances, as the setting up of permanent Cabinet Committees would be far more difficult in view of the disagreement between the two major parties.

The size of India's post-war armed forces will be discussed in the Cabinet soon, but I shall try to get this matter examined first by the Defence Committee which has never yet met. In view of the financial situation the Muslims will press for a reduction in the size of the defence forces with the intention of reducing the power of the army. The existence of a unified army on a large scale is one to which the Muslims could not subscribe in present circumstances.

We have exchanged telegrams[4] on the subject of the compensation of the Secretary of State's Services. I informed senior British officials and officers of H.M. Government's generous action, and they have all agreed that this would create a profound impression out here and greatly strengthen the morale of the Services, at least so far as British personnel are concerned. I took the case first in a small Committee of Cabinet consisting of myself, Nehru, Liaquat, Patel, and Baldev Singh.[5] In spite of their hostility to the whole idea of compensation they made a real effort to meet me and I got the impression that provided compensation is not paid to Indians, save in very special cases, they might not in the end altogether repudiate liability for compensation paid to British officials. Next morning I took the matter in full Cabinet and they accepted the telegram giving the views of the Government of India which we had drafted in Committee. The upshot is that they want H.M.G. to pay compensation to the British officials and for Indians to get nothing unless they can prove that their prospects have been prejudiced by unpopular action they may have taken before the transfer of power. I have recommended that their view about compensation for Indians should be accepted, especially as they are ready to let H.M.G. take the credit for having wanted to make no discrimination;[6] and I have made it clear that it must be open to H.M.G. to discuss with the Government of India the financial liability for all compensation paid.

[3] See No. 11.

[4] See, in particular, tels. 672-S, 673-S, 700-S and 701-S of 2 April. L/S &G/7/914: ff 384-91.

[5] The Committee also stressed 'the need to transfer control of Secretary of State's Services at once' (tel. 672-S) and in the telegram reporting the discussion in full Cabinet (tel. 700-S) Lord Mountbatten again noted that it was clear that 'my colleagues attach great importance to transfer of control of Services and this was much stressed.' In tel. 4464 of 4 April Lord Pethick-Lawrence replied that it was 'impossible to transfer control of Services between now and date of transfer of power as this would necessitate legislation which we really cannot undertake at this stage'. In tel. 870-S of 24 April Lord Mountbatten reported that Sardar Patel had again pressed this point but in tel. 908-S of 27 April he (Mountbatten) advised that the Secretary of State should raise no hope that the subject would be reconsidered. *Ibid:* ff 390, 386, 371-3, 243, 200.

[6] In tel. 700-S of 2 April Lord Mountbatten reported that the Indian Cabinet had suggested 'that the British Government should announce that though they wished to offer compensation to Indian officers as well as British officers, in view of the increased prospects for Indian members of Service and fact that feelings of patriotism would naturally impel them to serve on, the Government of India have desired that compensation should be payable only in special cases' to Indian officers. *Ibid:* f 389.

The way is at last clear for H.M.G. to make an announcement and I am most relieved that things went as well as they did with the Cabinet.

In view of the seriousness of the shipping situation, which was impressed on me at the Defence Committee meeting held before I left England, I have gone personally into the question of the movement of civilians from India, and taken steps which I hope will ensure that there are no empty berths in ships returning to the U.K. from India. The whole problem is being handled by a member of my Personal Staff, under Ismay, and I hope that the instructions I have issued and the reports I have called for will ensure that there are no further cases of ships sailing from India with empty berths.

It was a happy coincidence that the great Asian Relations Conference have been sitting in Delhi during the first week after my arrival,[7] and we gave a garden party for all the 300 delegates and senior officials and Indian delegates. It appears that the great majority of the Indians present had never before received an invitation to the Viceroy's House; and although it might have been too pointed to have had such a party the first week of our arrival, the fact that they were all associated with the Asian Conference gave me that excuse, and the occasion appears to have produced the most favourable reactions.

My wife has been very busy establishing contact with the leading Indian women, and has already had personal interviews with a dozen of the leading women of all parties, and addressed the women delegates of the Asian Conference, where she received a great reception.

On re-reading the earlier part of this report let me say that I would not like any of the Cabinet to think that I am in any way infected by the gloom which appears to surround me. I feel as optimistic about the future now as I felt in similar gloomy conditions a week after I reached Delhi in October 1943.

[7] Papers on the Asian Relations Conference, held from 23 March–2 April 1947, may be found on L/P &S/12/4637 and a report by Sir T. Shone on the Conference in despatch No. 36 of 25 April is on L/SG/7/1251.

60

Rear-Admiral Viscount Mountbatten of Burma to Pandit Nehru

Mountbatten Papers. Official Correspondence Files: Indian National Army

No. 1141/10   *2 April 1947*

Dear Pandit Nehru,

I asked the Commander-in-Chief to stay for luncheon with me in order that I might prevail upon him in private to agree to the suggestion which you had made,[1] for I could see how strongly he felt that he must stand by his principles if he was to continue to be of any use to India.

I am pleased to say that he promised to meet the proposal you had made, as a sincere tribute to his desire to help the Government in their present difficulty. He asked me for an assurance, however, that his present agreement would not be used as a precedent to have other cases in which he was the reviewing authority referred to any outside jurist, and I replied that since all three Members who had attended the meeting had given me that assurance, I was prepared on the strength of that to add my assurance to yours.

Knowing the Chief as well as I do, this is a greater gesture from him than possibly a similar gesture would have been from anyone else.

I am so glad to have been able to help even in a small way in the very difficult task you have in front of you.

I enclose the final version of the draft formula,[2] which you will note is almost unchanged from the draft we prepared together, except that the Chief has now agreed to accept the available Judges of the Federal Court, which I hope you may feel will adequately meet the case.

My best wishes and sympathetic thoughts will be with you when you stand up in the Assembly tomorrow; for believe me, I fully appreciate all that this means to you.[3]

Yours very sincerely,
[MOUNTBATTEN]

[1] See No. 52.
[2] See No. 62, para. 7.
[3] Lord Mountbatten sent similar letters enclosing the draft formula to Mr Liaquat Ali Khan and Sardar Baldev Singh. Later on 2 April he sent Pandit Nehru a further revision of para. 2 of the formula which had been made at the request of the Chief Justice of the Federal Court (see No. 63 for the revised text of para. 2). Mr Abell also informed Mr Liaquat Ali Khan and Sardar Baldev Singh of this revision. Mountbatten Papers, Official Correspondence Files: Indian National Army.

61

Pandit Nehru to Rear-Admiral Viscount Mountbatten of Burma

Mountbatten Papers. Official Correspondence Files: Indian National Army

17 YORK ROAD, NEW DELHI, *2 April 1947*

Dear Lord Mountbatten,

Thank you for your letter of the 2nd April[1] enclosing a copy of the draft formula as agreed to by the Commander-in-Chief. I appreciate that the Commander-in-Chief has been trying to accommodate himself, in spite of his strong feeling in the matter, to what I suggested to him.

[1] No. 60.

2. This very strong feeling of his, however, in this matter has made me realise, even more than before, the difference in the British and Indian approach to this as well as other problems. I think I can understand fully the outlook of a soldier in matters of army discipline. Few persons will disagree with the proposition that discipline must be maintained in an army and that political considerations should not be allowed to interfere with it. But the army consists of human beings with human feelings. In India the soldier has a dual pull—that of army discipline and what he conceives to be loyalty to his country. If both these act in the same direction, then all is well. If they act in contrary directions, then he is torn between these two loyalties. The obvious way out is to avoid any such conflict by combining the two conceptions, the army standing for the country. Normally this happens in a free country; but that has not been so in India. The result has been, as is well known, that some of the brightest of our youths have kept away from the army. Those who have joined it have had to suffer from this inner conflict.

3. Every Indian, whatever his views may be, can understand this and appreciate it. That is why a very large proportion of Indian officers and men in the regular army have sympathised with the INA regardless of individual merits or demerits. In the present case also there is a cleavage between the general opinion of most Indians in the army and the opinion of British officers.

4. About the assurance that the present proposal would not be used as a precedent, I have already said that I do not intend to do so. Apart from other reasons, I would not like to have to pass through again the ordeal which I have had to face in recent weeks. I have had a feeling, however, that the Commander-in-Chief has shown a lack of faith in me in regard to my handling of this situation. Having told him how I intended doing it, I would, of course, have endeavoured to do so. I have to face and attempt to satisfy not only a large audience in the Assembly but also a vast public outside. Whether I would succeed or not, I do not know. Even if I succeed in a formal sense, it would be of little help if I left a feeling of dis-satisfaction and discontent in the minds of my hearers and others. I have to deal with the situation, therefore, not in a formal, brief and concise manner, but rather in a way so as to bring the whole picture before the members of the Assembly and then gradually to concentrate on the narrower issue. I have not to deal with soldiers whom I can command, but sensitive human beings who resent nothing so much as an order.

5. I have just received your second letter[2] dated 2nd April with which you have sent me the revised formula as approved of by the Chief Justice.

6. I am grateful to you for the trouble you have taken in this matter.

Yours sincerely,
JAWAHARLAL NEHRU

[2] See No. 60, note 3.

62

Rear-Admiral Viscount Mountbatten of Burma to Lord Pethick-Lawrence

Telegram, L/P &J/10/83A: ff 5–6

MOST IMMEDIATE   NEW DELHI, *2 April 1947, 9.40 pm*
TOP SECRET   *Received: 2 April, 5.30 pm*

No. 709–S. On Tuesday evening[1] without any previous warning Nehru informed me that Resolution demanding release of I.N.A. prisoners would be moved in Legislative Assembly on Thursday,[2] and that he was in no doubt it would be carried unanimously since Moslem League had joined forces with Congress on this matter.

2. He informed me that Lord Wavell's veto could no longer be regarded as operative and asked me for my instructions as to how I wished the Government to handle the situation.

3. He pointed out that the Cabinet had agreed among themselves to keep Wavell's use of veto a secret as they feared that a leakage of the fact would have disastrous repercussions in the country and on the position of the Viceroy; since it was widely believed that H.M.G. (? did not) intend Viceroy to use his veto at this stage.

4. He told me that as representatives of popular parties in a Coalition Government neither Congress nor League members could remain in the Government if forced to turn down such unanimous resolution on so important a subject.

5. I explained my position fully and decided to call a special meeting of Nehru, Liaquat Ali Khan, Baldev, Auchinleck and myself to take place after Wednesday morning's Cabinet.

6. On Tuesday night I had a long interview with Auchinleck[3] who regretted that he was unable to depart from position he had taken up with Wavell, since any further capitulation by him would so weaken his position with the Army that it would be useless his staying on, and so weaken Army as to make it in his opinion incapable of being sure of maintaining law and order in the increasingly difficult situation with which we are faced.

7. The meeting after the Cabinet was an extremely difficult one to handle,[4] but I am happy to report that I have prevailed upon the Government to face up to the Legislative Assembly and themselves turn down request for release in consideration for Auchinleck agreeing to following formula. *Begins.* Although Government does not question that in this matter Commander-in-Chief has acted throughout in good faith and according to his lights for the

[1] See No. 48.   [2] 3 April 1947.   [3] See No. 50.   [4] See No. 52.

good of India and armed forces, they are, in view of the special circumstances of the case, prepared to request him to call in as advisers, in this matter only and without creating any precedent whatever, the available Judges of the Federal Court.

What we have in mind is that these advisers should examine proceedings of various courts-martial and give their opinion as to the desirability of reviewing the findings and sentences in each case. Their recommendations would be given most careful consideration by Commander-in-Chief, who would then decide whether any further action is necessary. *Ends.*

8. Auchinleck's agreement was only obtained after main meeting and subsequent to his meeting his Commanders-in-Chief and Senior Staff Officers. Previously I had had a discussion with the Chief Justice, who also agreed.

9. It is too early to say how this will go through Assembly, but I am infinitely gratified that my Government should have been prepared to take my constitutional advice without putting me in the position of having to consider exercising the veto.

10. Please inform Prime Minister that I conveyed his advice to Nehru not to take any action which could lessen the discipline and efficiency of the Indian Army in the future.

63

Rear-Admiral Viscount Mountbatten of Burma to Lord Pethick-Lawrence

Telegram, Mountbatten Papers.   Official Correspondence Files:
Indian National Army

IMMEDIATE   NEW DELHI, *2 April 1947, 11.15 pm*
SECRET   *Received: 2 April, 9.50 pm*
No. 711-S. My telegram No. 709-S dated today.[1] I.N.A. At the request of the Chief Justice and with the agreement of the Commander-in-Chief the second paragraph of the formula has been amended to read as follows:

"What we have in mind is that these advisers should examine the proceedings of the various Courts Martial and give their opinion as to the desirability of reviewing the findings and sentences in each case, and make a report to the Commander-in-Chief whether in their opinion the findings and sentences should be altered or modified in any manner."

[1] No. 62.

64

Minutes of Viceroy's Seventh Staff Meeting

Mountbatten Papers

TOP SECRET

Those present during discussion of Items 10 and 11 of this Meeting held at the Viceroy's House, New Delhi on 3 April 1947 at 10 am were: Rear-Admiral Viscount Mountbatten of Burma, Sir E. Mieville, Captain Brockman, Mr Campbell-Johnson, Lieutenant-Colonel Erskine Crum

Item 10

BREAK-UP OF COMMUNAL PARTIES ON POLITICAL LINES

HIS EXCELLENCY THE VICEROY said that Sardar J. J. Singh, whom he had seen the previous day, had expressed the opinion that, at the moment the last reason for Congress unity, which was based on the desire to get rid of the British, disappeared; and as soon as the Muslim League was no longer threatened by Congress (which threat was the main reason for their unity); there would be a complete upheaval of the present main parties in India. HIS EXCELLENCY THE VICEROY said that, as he had previously indicated, he shared this belief. It was likely, in his opinion, that there would be a repetition of what had occurred in every other country after war. While Congress's main object remained to get rid of the British, all classes would remain united in the face of the common foreign "foe". The moment this "war" was over there would be a break-up into political and economic groups. A new lot of leaders would arise whose names were equally unknown now ʃas those of Lenin, Trotsky, and Stalin had been in Russia in 1916. The present equivalents to Kerensky would be swept from power with the possible exception of a few outstanding men. Sardar Singh had expressed the opinion that an economic revolution, leading possibly to a physical revolution and the emergence of Socialist or Communist ideals, was coming very soon in India and that nothing could stop it. HIS EXCELLENCY THE VICEROY said that Sardar Singh was the first Indian who had expressed such an opinion to him. Sardar Singh had explained this on the simple grounds that he lived outside India, and was therefore able to regard events more objectively.

Item 11

LIST OF "AWKWARD QUESTIONS"

SIE ERIC MIEVILLE handed to His Excellency a list of "A few questions that the Viceroy might consider putting to Mr Jinnah regarding Pakistan."

Addendum to Item 11

Mountbatten Papers. Official Correspondence Files: Transfer of Power, Part I(a)

A FEW QUESTIONS THAT THE VICEROY MIGHT CONSIDER PUTTING TO
MR. JINNAH REGARDING PAKISTAN

Geographical.   If it is decided to hand over responsibilities to entirely separate Governments for Hindustan and Pakistan, what case could be made out which would justify H.M.G. in handing over to Pakistan the areas contiguous to Hindustan in which there is a non-Muslim Majority? These areas amount to thirteen districts in the Punjab and eight districts—including Calcutta—in Bengal. (Lists attached).

Is not the claim for the whole of the Punjab and Bengal simply a claim to non-Muslim territory? The Congress have said that they are ready to concede the Muslim majority districts. On what principle do you base your demand for the addition of Sikh and Hindu territory?

If the whole of the Punjab were included in Pakistan, do you think you can
(a) cope with the Sikhs;
(b) impose your will on the rest of the non-Muslim population;
(c) maintain the necessary good relations with Hindustan in spite of the hostility that your actions would arouse?

The same argument applies *vis-à-vis* the non-Muslim areas in Bengal.

You have frequently said that Muslim feeling is now so strong that a United India is impossible. On the assumption that the Punjab and Bengal are to be divided and that H.M.G. will not be a party to giving the League more than the Muslim majority districts, how would you set about the Partition? Would you suggest a Boundary Commission or a decision by H.M.G.? It must be remembered that time is short.

Defence.   Could you propose
(a) to maintain a separate Army and Air Force;
(b) to build munition factories and other industries necessary to support such forces; and
(c) to be strong enough to face Russia and Hindustan at one and the same time?

Where are the resources in finance, minerals and expert manpower to justify such a course? Surely you can only survive in a defensive Alliance with Hindustan—e.g. a common Defence Council.

Finance.   Would not the financial position in Pakistan be such that it would be difficult to maintain its social services and impossible to make adequate provision for defence?

It will be necessary for Pakistan to pay a proportionate share of the existing Government of India's liabilities including, in particular, defence, National

Debt and pension charges of an All-India Character—What authority would be entrusted with the working out of the division of these liabilities and how would Pakistan be able to meet their obligations?

Would Pakistan feel obliged to set up their own Central Bank and their own Currency? If so, would not this create serious difficulties for them? Would Pakistan have its own Customs Barriers and create a Customs Service of its own?

List of districts

Punjab	Bengal
Hissar	Burdwan
Rohtak	Birbhum
Gurgaon	Bankura
Karnal	Midnapore
Ambala	Howrah
Simla	24-Parganas
Kangra	Jalpaiguri
Hoshiarpur	Darjeeling
Jullundur	
Ludhiana	
Ferozepore	
Amritsar	
Gurdaspur	

65

Record of Interview between Rear-Admiral Viscount Mountbatten of Burma and Mr Liaquat Ali Khan

Mountbatten Papers. Viceroy's Interview No. 26

TOP SECRET   *3 April 1947*

The meeting lasted from 11.10 a.m. to 12.15 p.m.

I took him to task for allowing Members of the Interim Government to take an active part in the Committee of Action of the League, as reported in *Dawn*. He explained that most of the Members of the Interim Government belonged either to the Congress Committee or the Muslim League Working Committee. I accepted this but complained that the League Ministers were actively associated with the Committee of Action, to which he replied that they had been members of the Committee of Action before joining the Interim Government.

I told him that in their own interests they should either resign or refrain from taking an active part in the Committee of Action, and that I should probably take a convenient opportunity of expressing this view to Mr. Jinnah. I ended with the very strong advice to him not to embarrass the position of the League in the Government by allowing these activities to continue.

We discussed the setting up of the Appointments Committee of the Cabinet. He gave me his very strong reasons against this at some length, and I have asked him to let me have these reasons in writing together with his proposal as to how the political difficulty can be overcome.

I asked him whether, in the event of my obtaining complete Congress adherence to the letter and spirit of the Cabinet Mission's statement of the 16th May, he felt there was any chance that Mr. Jinnah would then come back to his original agreement. He replied that the communal strife had become so bitter that he felt there was now no chance.

I then asked him what, if he were in my place, his solution would be for the transfer of power.

He smiled engagingly and said: "Since my dealings with the Congress Members of the Interim Government, I have come to realise that they are utterly impossible people to work with, since there is no spirit of compromise or fair play in them, and the majority are thinking only of ways and means by which they can do down the Muslim League and improve their own position". He continued: "I consider the position now so intolerable that if Your Excellency was only prepared to let the Muslim League have the Sind Desert, I would still prefer to accept that and have a separate Muslim State in those conditions than to continue in bondage to the Congress with apparently more generous concessions."

Finally, he gave me a brief report of progress in his Department, and asked me to include in the Defence Committee, when it was set up, the Member for Communications, Mr. Nishtar, so as to ensure that there would be at least two Muslim League Members on the Committee.

66

Record of Interview between Rear-Admiral Viscount Mountbatten of Burma and Mr Gandhi

Mountbatten Papers. Viceroy's Interview No. 28

TOP SECRET   *3 April 1947*

The interview lasted from 2.30 to 4.30 p.m.

He brought with him Mrs. Aruna Asaf Ali, wife of the Indian Ambassador to Washington, who had been reported as violently anti-British. She had refused to accept Her Excellency's invitation to come and meet her, and Gandhi therefore brought her along to bring them together forcibly, the outcome of which appears to have been very happy.

We continued our talks on Mr. Gandhi's great scheme for the All-India Jinnah Government. He informed me that those of the leaders of the Congress he had spoken to had all agreed that it was feasible and would support him, but that he had not yet had time to talk to Pandit Nehru, which he intended to do that evening.

He was more than ever intense about his scheme as being the best solution. But he agreed that if I was unable to decide on that solution, he would support me in any other solution which I could put before him as being in the best interests of the Indian people.

He agreed that if the Muslim League were completely intransigent, partition might have to come, though he was most anxious to retain as strong a Centre as possible in this case.

He agreed that an early decision was vital to end communal conflict and to give time to implement the decision. And finally he reiterated his desire that whatever happened I should retain firm charge at the Centre till June 1948 at the very earliest, in order to act as an umpire and exercise a guiding hand during the early stages of self-government.

He said that his great friend Badshah Khan was staying with him. I had never heard the name and asked him to elucidate. He referred to him as the Frontier Gandhi, and I then recognised him to be the same person as I knew under the name of Abdul Ghaffar Khan, brother of Dr. Khan Sahib the Premier of the Congress-Muslim Government in the N.W.F.P.

Mr. Gandhi said that Abdul Ghaffar Khan had informed him that the Governor, Sir Olaf Caroe, had demanded the resignation of his brother, Dr. Khan Sahib, and had shown himself to be very partial towards the Muslim League and to influence the British officials in that Province accordingly.

In view of the fact that Lord Ismay had just returned from a visit to the N.W.F.P. I sent for him, and Mr. Gandhi repeated his allegation.

Lord Ismay explained the position as he saw it, and pointed out that there must have been a misunderstanding.

I invited Mr. Gandhi to bring Abdul Ghaffar Khan at 2.30 the following day to meet Lord Ismay and myself.

67

Lord Pethick-Lawrence to Rear-Admiral Viscount Mountbatten of Burma

Mountbatten Papers. Letters to and from the Secretary of State

PRIVATE AND SECRET   INDIA OFFICE, *3 April 1947*
My dear Mountbatten,

From all accounts you must be having a busy time and an exhausting one too, as I know what long discussions with Indian leaders in Delhi in the hot weather can be like! Moreover, you still have the toughest customer to come in Mr. Jinnah, whose Pakistan Day message suggests that even in the new circumstances he does not contemplate a conciliatory move, at any rate in the first instance.

2. As things have worked out you have been faced at the outset with the necessity to deal with your Cabinet on what are perhaps the two most intractable single problems (that is, apart from the general problem of the arrangements for the transfer of power) namely, Compensation and the I.N.A. prisoners. As for the former, the position has, of course, been from the outset one of Scylla and Charybdis in that there has been no satisfactory middle course between, on the one hand, going back upon the June 1945 Statement to a greater or less extent and, on the other hand, forcing through a settlement in the teeth of the Interim Government and one that, consequently, might all too likely have proved unworkable in practice. Looking back, it was, I think, unfortunate that it was decided to withdraw my original Despatch of 26th November[1] with the result that the official reactions of the Government of India have only been received now instead of three months ago. But I am very glad that there should now be agreement between yourself and Ministers here upon a course which seems likely both to reduce your Government's resentment to a minimum and to prove workable in practice. You will by now have received my telegram agreeing to the immediate release of an interim communiqué committing us to make a final announcement not later than the end of the present month. I can quite understand how very anxious you are to make this announcement although the advantages which you hope to derive from its effect upon the European members of the Services now seem likely to be counteracted to some extent by its effect upon the Indian members.

3. As for the I.N.A. prisoners, you have good reason to feel gratified by the readiness of your Cabinet to accept your advice. Though I realise that the settlement involves some weakening of Auchinleck's position, this is undoubtedly less objectionable than your having to repeat the veto and I congratulate you on your handling of the matter.

4. I have recently been reading Jenkins' letter to Wavell of the 7th March No. 653[2] about the political situation in the Punjab and his telegram No. 70–G of the 24th March.[3] I have also seen a statement by Tara Singh in which he supports partition and says that the Sikhs would not join any ministry which is dominated by the Muslim League.

5. The note which Jenkins enclosed with his letter of the 7th March was, of course, with the purpose of indicating the need for negotiations for a Coalition Government and naturally emphasised the very strong objections which exist, from the point of view of the interests of the Punjab as a whole, to any form of partition. I recognise the force of the considerations which Jenkins put

forward and I appreciate that his note was drafted with the intention of bringing them home to political leaders and thus inducing a sense of compromise in
which a Coalition, preferably of all three parties, might be formed. But I think
it is very important that, if and when it is possible to make any further political
move in regard to the Punjab, we should consider carefully in what directions
we ourselves want the situation to move from the point of view of securing a
peaceful transfer of power.

6. If a Coalition of the Muslims and Sikhs or of all three communities were
secured in the Punjab it seems very likely that, if we failed to get an all-India
settlement, and therefore, in the all-India sphere, had to transfer power to more
than one authority, a local coalition Government in the Province could not
hold together and would inevitably break up. This might happen shortly
after we had left, which would be disastrous enough for India, or at the last
minute before the transfer of power, which would be particularly embarrassing
for H.M.G. I think it would be bound to happen sooner or later because the
Punjab Muslim League would want to join with Sind (and the N.W.F.P. if
the trend against the Red-Shirt-Congress Government gathers sufficient force)
in forming a Pakistan while the other elements in the Punjab Government
would be strongly opposed to this and would wish the Punjab to go into the
all-India constitution. Moreover, even if there were an all-India settlement, it
would necessarily be on the basis of minimum powers for the Central Government and autonomy in all other matters for Provinces. It would probably also
have to be on the basis of grouping of Provinces. If so, I should anticipate that
the Punjab Coalition Government would break down for the same reasons in
those circumstances.

7. Therefore, it seems to me that, in spite of its grave practical difficulties
and dangers, the partition of the Punjab to such degree and in such form as will
satisfy the rival nationalisms in the Province is really unavoidable from the
political point of view of the transfer of authority in June 1948. If, however,
we were to go for partition in the Punjab, we should, I think, have to go for it
also in Bengal for broadly similar reasons. But partition of Bengal is more
difficult because it involves putting Calcutta into Hindustan, because there is no
local political deadlock in Bengal existing or in sight to justify taking such a
step and because the Muslim League would, I think, be much more opposed to a
partition of Bengal involving the loss of Calcutta than to a partition of the
Punjab.

8. It seems to me, therefore, that it would be desirable at a fairly early date
for you to confer with Burrows and Jenkins together and discuss the problem
with them from this all-India point of view. Perhaps you could find an op-

¹ Vol. IX, No. 96.   ² Vol. IX, No. 501.   ³ No. 13.

portunity to do this at the Governors' Conference which you have convened for the middle of April.

9. I am not, of course, seeking to lay down any definite view on behalf of H.M.G. in what I have written above. (I have not, as a matter of fact, had any real opportunity of discussing the problem with my colleagues). It is merely an indication of the way my own mind is working on the matter at the moment and I am quite open to conviction. But before any positive step is taken about the Punjab situation I should be glad to have, for consideration with my colleagues, your views on the point of view I have put forward in the light of a discussion with the Governors of these two Provinces.

10. Recent reports from the disturbed Provinces suggest that the law and order position generally is improving, although the police strike in Bihar presents a new and very disturbing feature. As the events of 1942 showed, Bihar is certainly the Achilles' heel and it may well be that the police in Bihar have taken their cue from the police in Burma whom A.F.P.F.L. unwisely used as one of the instruments in their "war of nerves" against H.M.G. before the recent London discussions. Faced as their leaders now are with the responsibilities of office, they realise too late how much longer it takes to build up than to destroy the reliability of a police force.

11. I have read with much interest the description in Mr. Herbert's letter of 13th February to your Political Secretary (D.O. No. 16R)[4] of the political situation in Hyderabad. In the atmosphere of communal and political tension which evidently prevails in the State the path of any outsider who holds the office of President of Council must be one of great difficulty. I imagine that Sir Mirza Ismail, owing to his previous experience of handling Hindus in two States, is an asset to the Nizam at this juncture and more remotely to the prospects of a united India. Possibly this would equally apply to Sir M. Zafrullah Khan, though I judge that there is no immediate prospect of his being asked to replace Sir Mirza.

12. The King's agrément for the appointment of Mr. Henry F. Grady as the first U.S. Ambassador to India has been officially notified to your External Affairs Department, but you may like to know privately the opinions which have been expressed here about the selection. The American Embassy in London have told us that they think the choice a particularly good one since Mr. Grady is not only no stranger to India, but, though a business man, is as near as possible an official. His latest assignment (which, oddly enough, was not mentioned in the list of posts officially supplied) was Head of the American team of officials which collaborated in propounding the Anglo-American plan for Palestine which has become to be known as the Grady-Morrison plan. According to the Foreign Office he is regarded as entirely reliable, i.e. not unduly sensitive to political pressure, well disposed to us, and businesslike. His

prestige and ability are undoubtedly high and it is thought that he will make a conspicuous success of his Mission.

13. The British Ambassador in China has sent us some further details about Dr. Lo Chia-Lun, the first Chinese Ambassador to India. Sir R. Stevenson comments that Dr. Lo is an entertaining person of great intellectual distinction. He twice refused the offer of the Delhi post but was eventually prevailed upon to accept it. He is believed to prefer his academic work and professes his ineptitude for diplomacy but both he and his wife are said to be "congenial and stimulating". I trust that they will be an asset to the Diplomatic Corps in New Delhi.

14. My colleagues and I are hoping to have over Easter a few days of relief from the prolonged strain of recent months although I shall, of course, be keeping in close touch with the Office.

4 L/P &S/13/1203.

68

The Maharaja of Bikaner to Rear-Admiral Viscount Mountbatten of Burma

Mountbatten Papers. Official Correspondence Files: States, Relations
with, Part I(a)

SECRET AND PERSONAL   DEVI BHAWAN,
                                        38 NEPEAN SEA ROAD, BOMBAY,
                                                      3 April 1947

My dear Lord Mountbatten,

I am writing to thank Your Excellency most sincerely for having given me an opportunity of talking to you at such length in Delhi the other day on the present problems confronting the States so soon after your arrival and at a time when you must have been so busy.[1] It is a matter of much gratification to the Princes generally and particularly to me, in view of my having had the privilege of enjoying your friendship ever since our childhood, that in Your Excellency we have a real friend in whose hands the interests of the Princes we feel are safe and who will see that justice is done to us.

2. Although Your Excellency was good enough to give me a considerable portion of your valuable time, yet naturally it was not possible for me fully to mention the various important details in connection with the question of the States' participation in the Constituent Assembly. I therefore take the liberty of writing this letter in continuation of our talk, as I feel that the whole position

1 See No. 10.

in all its aspects should be properly placed before you, particularly, as Your Excellency is no doubt aware, there have been considerable differences of opinion on the subject between two important groups of Princes.

3. From the very outset when it was known that the Muslim League had decided not to participate in the work of the Constituent Assembly His Highness the Chancellor and his Advisers were hesitant to conduct the discussions with the Negotiating Committee set up by the Constituent Assembly, in the ground that the Constituent Assembly was not "fully representative" of all the political parties in British India. Sir Sultan Ahmed who, as Your Excellency is aware, is Constitutional Adviser to the Chancellor in a public statement had some time ago declared that as the Constituent Assembly was not fully representative of British India the Princes could not participate in its work. This was disapproved by the States in general. It also became clear that this attitude had aroused widespread misunderstandings both in British India and in the minds of the people of the States about the *bona fides* of the Princes.

4. When some of us saw the way events were shaping and that we were possibly heading for a deadlock which would not be in the interests of the States, a conference was arranged by me in Bikaner which was attended by the Maharaja of Patiala and the representatives of some important States. It was decided there after full consideration that, while we were anxious to maintain unity in the ranks of the Princes and would normally co-operate and work through the Negotiating Committee set up by the Chamber of Princes, if any attempt were made to postpone or delay action in regard to the States' participation in the Constituent Assembly and its committees, or if the policy enunciated were in our view against the interests of the States, we would intervene and as a last resort if necessary negotiate independently of the States' Negotiating Committee as we felt the matters involved were of too vital a nature seriously affecting the States.

5. Though the principle that the negotiations should take place was accepted by the General Conference of Princes which was held last January, what actually happened was not wholly in conformity with the co-operation promised to the Cabinet Mission. A resolution was passed at that Conference[2] and published widely in the papers laying down certain *sine qua non*, the prior acceptance of which was declared to be essential for negotiation. The British Indian Negotiating Committee on the other hand had been appointed only for the strictly limited purpose of deciding the procedure of the participation of the States and the allocation of seats.

6. An *impasse* was thus threatened, and at my suggestion a week before the date fixed for the two Negotiating Committees to meet we decided to contact immediately the leaders of the Constituent Assembly in order to avert a breakdown. Our group, which consisted of Gwalior, Udaipur, Jaipur, Jodhpur,

Bikaner, Patiala and Rewa met Pandit Jawaharlal Nehru, Maulana Azad and Sir N. Gopalaswami Ayyangar at a dinner given by me at Bikaner House, New Delhi, and discussed all matters informally and a satisfactory agreement was reached on all the points on which the Princes had laid stress. Sardar Patel could not come to that dinner but I saw him separately and he also was in agreement with the line taken.

7. During the discussions, which created a very friendly atmosphere, it was stated on behalf of the British Indian leaders that they welcomed such informal talks which would facilitate agreements being reached, and that friendly approaches for this purpose were made by them to His Highness the Chancellor, but such approaches had unfortunately been turned down as being premature and not serving any useful purpose.

8. This was the position when the two Negotiating Committees met on the 8th and 9th February. On the first day of the discussions, i.e. on the 8th, again the attitude of the Chancellor and his Advisers, I fear, led very nearly to a breakdown as an unconditional acceptance of the resolution passed by the Conference of Princes was insisted upon by the Chancellor as a pre-requisite of any negotiations. But the situation was saved by the discussions being postponed until the next day to see if some kind of a *via media* could be found.

9. On the second day, i.e. on the 9th, when the Negotiating Committees met again the Chancellor, to our surprise, opened the proceedings by saying that since no agreement appeared to be possible the discussions of the Negotiating Committees may be adjourned *sine die*. Thus the previous day's deadlock seemed to come to a head but the difficulty was got over by His Highness of Patiala, as already arranged by our group the previous evening, opposing the Chancellor's suggestion and asking Pandit Nehru to make a statement on the consensus of opinion on the points raised. This he did basing it on the agreement already reached between our group and the British Indian leaders at the dinner party at Bikaner House referred to earlier. Pandit Nehru's statement was found to be acceptable by the represenatives of the States as meeting their point of view. Thus a breakdown of the negotiations was happily prevented. The only points that then remained for the Negotiating Committees to discuss were the allocation of the seats and the method of representation which were postponed to a later meeting, i.e. the 1st March. In the meanwhile the two Secretariats were asked to work out a scheme of allocation of seats which would be considered by the two Negotiating Committees separately and then discussed at the subsequent meeting.

10. It was at this stage that Mr Attlee made his historic statement of February 20. This important declaration was interpreted by some to mean that in the absence of agreement between the political parties India will be split up into

² See Vol. IX, No. 326.

many governments. This idea gave to the reluctant and hesitating section of the States a handle to try and delay matters by stating that a new situation had been created and the entire question had to be considered *de novo*. It was even suggested that there was no purpose in continuing the discussions between the two Negotiating Committees on the two remaining points left for discussion, namely, the allocation of seats to the States and the method of their representation in the Constituent Assembly.

11. In fact, a resolution was actually drafted at a meeting of the Ministers' Committee which recommended to the Princes that the whole question be considered afresh before continuing the discussion of the Negotiating Committee. It may be stated that most of the major States were not represented at this meeting; and the draft resolution had been given wide publicity prematurely. Pandit Nehru, who was most accommodating, came again to dinner at Bikaner House at my invitation the day previous to the resumption of the Negotiating Committee discussions, and met apart from His Highness of Patiala the representatives of the other major States of our group, and a way was found for completing the negotiations already in hand and details in regard to both the allocation of seats and the method of representation were mutually settled and agreed upon.

12. When the resolution referred to above was brought up at the meeting of the Constitutional Advisory Committee, our group opposed it and finally it was decided to remit it to the Ministers' Committee for reconsideration, and to resume the discussions with the Negotiating Committee as orginally fixed. Accordingly the two Negotiating Committees met again on the 1st and 2nd March and completed the work satisfactorily.

13. There is one further point which I would like to emphasise. The group of our States represents the major States in Rajputana, Punjab and Central India, *which will feel the first effects of the absence of a strong central government*. States like Travancore and Mysore, placed as they are far away from the centre of communal tension, can perhaps afford to go slow. *With us in Rajputana, the Punjab and Central India, the matter is immediate and any weakening of the central authority will involve us in chaos*, and I feel that Your Excellency will be the first to appreciate this point. The importance of the great Southern Indian States is not denied, but in this matter their problems are of a less immediate character than those of the important States of Northern India whose existence as powerful units must depend on a stable central government.

14. A definite cleavage of opinion had thus been gradually appearing in the Princes' ranks, one section comprising of our group of States who were desirous of co-operating fully in the work of the Constituent Assembly, while some of the rest favoured a policy of "wait and see".

15. The differences became more pronounced at the recent meetings in

Bombay as Your Excellency is no doubt aware from the reports in the Press. Our group desired that the agreement reached by the two Negotiating Committees be ratified and that the States be urged to enter the Constituent Assembly at the earliest possible stage, whereas the other section wanted the States to join the Constituent Assembly, only at the final stage, i.e., after the group and provincial constitutions have been framed. The acceptance of the latter point of view would have involved a very considerable delay, extending perhaps to some six months or even a year, with the possibility that such a time may not come at all as group constitutions may possibly never be framed if the Muslim League ultimately continued to stand out. Our group therefore considered that thus to delay the formation of a strong centre for any considerable period was fraught with grave dangers to the States and would definitely be against their interests, and particularly in view of June 1948 having been fixed for the transfer of power.

16. During the meeting of the Constitutional Advisory Committee on the 31st March I had tried my best to get the Princes to realise the urgency of the situation and the dangers of a policy of "wait and see", but I found that all my efforts met with unrelenting opposition and matters began to become somewhat personal. I felt that I had done my duty and, knowing that in spite of my endeavours the opposite point of view would strongly continue to be pressed by the large majority of Princes present in the Standing Committee, where none of our group except His Highness of Gwalior and myself were present, I had decided the day before not to attend the meeting of the Standing Committee the following morning. However, the draft of a letter to be sent to Pandit Jawaharlal Nehru had to be approved by the Standing Committee that day and since I had had a good deal to say in regard to that the previous day I found it necessary to attend the Standing Committee meeting for about 10 or 15 minutes until the draft was passed. After that without saying anything I quietly went out of the room and sent in a note to the Chancellor asking him to forgive me if I did not attend that meeting as it would "place me in an awkward position since my views on the present problem, as Your Highness knows, are totally different. Neither can I remain silent nor do I wish to speak any more on my point of view which has so many times been repeated before Your Highnesses. May I request that this may be read out to the Standing Committee?" Another reason which led me to take this step was that the Bikaner State as well as the other States of our group had already announced their intention to particpate in the Constituent Assembly.

17. I further decided that it would be better to explain my point of view in a memorandum,[3] which was circulated to the Princes and Ministers who were present in Bombay before the actual meeting of the General Conference on the

[3] The Maharaja of Bikaner's memorandum is not on the file.

2nd April, and a copy of which I attach for your Excellency's perusal.

18. This action on my part, as it happened, strengthened the hands of His Highness of Gwalior, who was I am glad to say able to persuade the general body of Princes after prolonged discussions to arrive at a compromise. As Your Excellency will notice from the resolution[4] passed by the General Conference, actually it is superfluous for the conference to say that such States as may decide to participate in the Constituent Assembly may do so, for it has no right to prevent any State from taking any action which it may consider necessary. However, a number of points to which our group had attached importance have been partly met; and I am glad that the Princes generally have thus been persuaded to desist from taking a step which would have been entirely misunderstood by the British Indian public as well as the people of the States as being unpatriotic. The resolution is silent as regards the all-important point of the States' participation in the committees appointed by the Constituent Assembly, and the consensus of opinion in the Constitutional Advisory Committee was definitely against participation. Our group however, as already decided some time ago, do not wish to lose the opportunity and will be sending in our representatives to the committees, at an early date.

19. We are also particularly anxious that the Princes, by any step that they took, should not in any way embarrass the discussions that Your Excellency is at present having with the British Indian leaders. On the other hand our group felt that it will be strengthening Your Excellency's hands if nothing was done at this stage by the Princes which would give the impression that they were holding back and not co-operating with the Constituent Assembly and thus create another serious obstacle to get over.

20. In my appeal to the Princes Your Excellency will notice that I have alluded to the point which I had already mentioned to you during our conversation in Delhi as being one to which great importance must be attached, i.e. *regarding constitutional reforms in the States*. Both in the Constitutional Advisory Committee and in previous meetings of the Standing Committee I pressed for a declaration on this question without delay, and I have laid special stress on this point in the appeal which I made to the Princes—in fact, I have been pressing for a clear declaration for the last three years.

21. I trust what I have stated in this letter and the enclosed appeal will make clear to Your Excellency the very weighty reasons which have led our group to take a different attitude from the rest of the States. We hope that better advice may eventually prevail and the other States may also come to our way of thinking and act accordingly before it is too late.

22. May I therefore beg Your Excellency to be good enough to bear in mind these differences, and in any future discussions that may take place I hope you will be pleased not only to invite the Chancellor as representing the views of

the Princes and States as a whole or others of his way of thinking but also someone from our group of States, so that both the viewpoints may be placed before Your Excellency.

23. I believe Your Excellency already knows my Prime Minister, Mr K. M. Panikkar. May I request Your Excellency to be good enough at your convenience to spare a few moments and give him an interview? As you may be aware, he is one of the most experienced Ministers of the States who has been acquainted with all constitutional discussions ever since the appointment of the Butler Committee in 1927, and it is no exaggeration to say that there are not many Ministers who have got such a grasp of the States' problems or who are in possession of such a complete knowledge about the States and their affairs. He has made a particular study of problems connected with India and South-East Asia and has written several books. He is also a member of the States Negotiating Committee. I have complete confidence in him.

24. Since Your Excellency is desirous of ascertaining all points of view and since I am writing this letter in connection with our group of States I feel Your Excellency will permit me to mention another name from amongst our foremost Ministers, namely, Sir V.T. Krishnamachari, Prime Minister of Jaipur, who is also a member of the States Negotiating Committee. He too is one of our most experienced and capable Ministers and was Dewan of the progressive State of Baroda for well over 15 years. He is a very sound statesman who can be depended upon for his judgment, tact and spirit of compromise, and who is ever ready to appreciate the other man's standpoint. He has also represented the States at various international conferences and was Chairman of the Ministers' Committee for a term.

25. May I be permitted to suggest that Your Excellency may be pleased to give him also an interview at your convenience, if you have not already done so, for I feel that by seeing both these Ministers Your Excellency will have a further clear picture of the various questions relating to the States, and since they will both be in Delhi in connection with the work of the Constituent Assembly they will always be available to submit to your Excellency whenever required the point of view of our group of States. Apart from this, both of them have wide contacts and wield considerable influence.

26. I sincerely hope and pray that it may be vouchsafed to Your Excellency during your Viceroyalty to see to the satisfactory solution of the Indian problem, including the States. No one knows better than myself that you, with your well known and declared goodwill for India and her people, will leave no stone unturned in achieving this great aim.

27. I trust Your Excellency will forgive me for the length to which this

⁴ See No. 91, note 3.

letter has run, but the urgency of the matter and the importance of the issues involved are my only excuses.

With kindest regards and all good wishes to both Your Excellencies and hoping this finds you all in the enjoyment of excellent health.[5]

Yours very sincerely,
SADUL SINGH

[5] In a letter dated 14/16 April 1947 Lord Mountbatten thanked the Maharaja for expressing so forcibly the different points of view held by the members of the Standing Committee of the Chamber of Princes, and assured him that he would bear these varying views fully in mind in so far as they affected questions on which he had to reach decisions in the near future. Mountbatten Papers, Official Correspondence Files: States, Relations with Part I(a).

69

Rear-Admiral Viscount Mountbatten of Burma to Lord Pethick-Lawrence

Telegram, L/P&J/10/83A: f 3

IMMEDIATE   NEW DELHI, *3 April 1947, 11.55 pm*
CONFIDENTIAL   *Received: 3 April, 10.30 pm*

723–S. The I.N.A. resolution was taken in Central Assembly today. Nehru made an excellent speech in which he backed up Commander-in-Chief very strongly and said that the Government would resign if his amendment to resolution was not accepted. The amendment was on lines of formula already telegraphed.[1]

2. Liaquat Ali Khan promised me only this morning to give Nehru his full support if things became difficult in Assembly. This unified action by Government in face of a politically inflamed house which was unanimous for first time, was extremely courageous particularly on the part of Nehru.

3. The final result was that the resolution was withdrawn.

4. Please inform Prime Minister.

[1] See Nos. 62 and 63.

In a letter to Field Marshal Auchinleck on 3 April, Lord Mountbatten explained that Sir P. Spens came to The Viceroy's House about an hour before the I.N.A. resolution was discussed in the Assembly. It transpired that the Chief Justice and his colleagues did not want it to appear from the Statement that they had been requested to advise by the Commander-in-Chief or were to report to him. The references to Field Marshal Auchinleck in these two respects were therefore deleted from the text of the formula. Mountbatten Papers. Official Correspondence Files: Indian National Army.

70

Minutes of Viceroy's Eighth Staff Meeting, Item 12

Mountbatten Papers

TOP SECRET

Those present during discussion of Item 12 of this Meeting held at The Viceroy's House, New Delhi on 4 April 1947 at 10 am were: Rear-Admiral Viscount Mountbatten of Burma, Lord Ismay, Sir E. Mieville, Mr Abell, Captain Brockman, Mr Campbell-Johnson, Lieutenant-Colonel Erskine Crum

NOTE OF AN INTERVIEW BETWEEN THE GOVERNOR OF
THE N.W.F.P. AND LORD ISMAY ON 2ND APRIL,
1947

The Meeting considered a Note[1] which Lord Ismay had prepared on an interview which he had had with the Governor of the N.W.F.P. on 2nd April.

HIS EXCELLENCY THE VICEROY made reference to a letter written by Pandit Nehru to Sir Olaf Caroe. In this Pandit Nehru told Sir Olaf that he had suggested to Lord Wavell that Sir Olaf should resign.[2] HIS EXCELLENCY THE VICEROY said that he gave Pandit Nehru considerable credit for having been honest enough to repeat to the Governor's face what he had said to the Viceroy. Lord Wavell had explained to him the circumstances which led up to this state of affairs. Sir Olaf Caroe had advised Pandit Nehru in strong terms not to visit the Frontier as he could not be responsible for his safety. In fact it had been Lord Wavell who had stopped Pandit Nehru from going,[3] but the latter had attributed the refusal to Sir Olaf Caroe and had rather naturally felt it very strongly that he was not allowed to visit a Province where there was a Congress Government nor those regions which were his responsibility as Member for External Affairs.

MR. ABELL then gave a brief explanation of the circumstances which had led up to an enquiry into the behaviour of the local Commissioner at the time of Pandit Nehru's visit, and his eventual exoneration by a Madras High Court Judge. Lord Wavell had written to the Governor of the N.W.F.P. asking that arrangements should be made for this official to go on leave until his retirement, but no answer had yet been received.

HIS EXCELLENCY THE VICEROY said that, in this particular issue, as in all others, it was necessary to face up to realities. The object, which must be continually borne in mind, was to hand over power in the most peaceful and dignified manner possible. To that end Pandit Nehru was indispensable. It had

---

[1] Not printed. See, however, No. 108, para. 6 for an account of the interview between Lord Ismay and Sir O. Caroe on 2 April.

[2] See Vol. IX, No. 549; Pandit Nehru's letter to Sir O. Caroe has not been traced.

[3] See Vol. IX, No. 550.

also be be realised that, unless the British members of the Services played their part to the last, there would be a loss of prestige and honour; therefore it was equally essential that there should be no victimisation of British officials. These two essentials were practically impossible to reconcile. One way out might be to bring all those concerned face to face after having seen them individually. There were doubtless other possibilities, which he wished Lord Ismay to look into. He himself might have to point out to Pandit Nehru the immensely injurious results which would follow from the latter getting killed on the Frontier. It was apparent that Pandit Nehru desired much closer control than he at present exercised. HIS EXCELLENCY THE VICEROY said that he wanted a brief on the precise legal and political situation.

HIS EXCELLENCY THE VICEROY added that he had great faith that, if Pandit Nehru could be caught at the right moment, there was no man more quickly able to shed all traces of emotionalism. It was, however, necessary to choose the right moment—as was shown by an incident at the previous day's Cabinet Meeting. A report had come forward that Travancore had made an agreement with a "foreign" power (which was presumably Great Britain) over the disposal of her uranium deposits.[4] Pandit Nehru had been by no means dispassionate over this issue, and had in the end declared that he would, in the extreme, send the Indian Air Force to bomb Travancore.

LORD ISMAY stressed the unnaturalness of the present situation in the N.F.W.P. and gave his opinion that the tribesmen were most unlikely to tolerate it indefinitely.

HIS EXCELLENCY THE VICEROY:—

directed C.V.S. to prepare for him a brief on the situation in the N.W.F.P., with particular reference to methods of solving the issue between Sir Olaf Caroe and Pandit Nehru.[5]

[4] See Vol. IX, No. 469, note 6.
[5] No brief by Lord Ismay has been traced. However on 11 April 1947 Mr Abell submitted a note by Mr Scott on the N.W.F.P. and the Tribal Areas adjoining. The note did not discuss methods of solving the issue between Sir O. Caroe and Pandit Nehru. Mountbatten Papers, Official Correspondence Files: N.W.F.P., Situation in, Part I(a).

71

Lord Pethick-Lawrence to Rear-Admiral Viscount Mountbatten of Burma

Telegram, L/WS/1/1070: f 219

PRIVATE   INDIA OFFICE, *4 April 1947*
No. 43. 1. In view of the uncertainty as to the relationship of India to the Commonwealth after June, 1948, the question of the desirability of allowing

India to have access to top secret information has been under review by the Chiefs of Staff and Minister of Defence.

2. On their recommendation which I supported the Prime Minister has agreed:—

(a) that the invitation to India to become a member of the Commonwealth Advisory Committee on Defence Science should be withdrawn. This Committee is due to hold its first meeting about September next and if India had agreed to become a member she would have sent two representatives to attend.

(b) that no further invitations should be extended for the attendance of Indian students at the Imperial Defence College, the Joint Services Staff College, the three Service Staff Colleges and other establishments which have access to top secret information and information from United States sources.

3. The above decisions have been conveyed officially to the Defence Department in my telegram No. 4461, dated 4th April.[1] The matter will, of course, be reconsidered at once should India decide to remain in the Commonwealth as a fully co-operating member though I have thought it best not to say so in the official telegram.

4. I appreciate that these decisions are likely to be unpalatable to your Government and I regret that it has been necessary to make them but I think you will agree that there was really no option. They may have the effect of making them face definitely a question with which they have been toying in a rather indefinite way.

[1] This telegram was in the terms proposed in No. 35. L/WS/1/993: ff 10–11.

72

Mr Abbott to Mr Abell

R/3/1/89: ff 165–6

D.O. No. G.S. 197   GOVERNMENT HOUSE, LAHORE,
4 April 1947

My dear Abell,

Will you kindly refer to your D.O. letter No. 90/13 of the 1st April 1947,[1] which, for some unknown reason, was only delivered here this afternoon?

[1] In this letter Mr Abell noted that Mr Ghazanfar Ali Khan kept saying in public and private that if there was a general election in the Punjab it would be possible for the Muslim League to obtain a stable majority. Mr Abell wondered what was the maximum number of seats that the League could win in the Punjab, including all Muslim constituencies and any Miscellaneous Seats that might go to Muslims. R/3/1/89: f 158.

The formal distribution of seats in the Punjab Assembly is given in the table
in the Fifth Schedule to the Government of India Act. I enclose a detailed
analysis of them which I have prepared, to which some general remarks on the
position have been added by H.E. You have not asked for the actual strength
of parties at the present moment, and I would not care to have to be definite
about the allegiance of certain of the Muslim Unionists.

Yours sincerely,

S. E. ABBOTT

Enclosure to No. 72

A. *Definitely Muslim* (1) Men   84
                 (2) Women   2

Total: 86   86

B. *Definitely non-Muslim*

Hindus: Men	42
Women	1
Sikhs: Men	31
Women	1
Anglo-Indian	1
Indian Christians	2
European	1

79   79

C. *Non-communal electorates:*—

(1) Held by Muslims and likely to be retained
by them: 4
     (a) Tumandars
     (b) North Punjab Landholders
     (c) West Punjab Landholders
     (d) Non-Union Labour—North

(2) Held by non-Muslims and likely to be retained   3
by them:
     (a) East Punjab Landholders
     (b) Central Punjab Landholders
     (c) University

(3) Doubtful seats: 3
     (a) Trade Union Labour (present—Hindu)
     (b) Non-Union Labour East (present—Muslim)

(c) Commerce and Industry (present—Hindu)

(a) will probably remain Hindu owing to the power of the purse among the voters.

(b) This will be likely to go Hindu. The present Muslim succeeded by Congress support, but he joined the League, and Congress would not try this experiment again.

(c) Voters mainly Hindu business. Seat would stay Hindu, unless the convention, at present in force, is retained by which it is held in rotation by the various communities.

Total: 175 Muslim certainties	90
Non-Muslim certainties	82
Non-Muslim probabilities	3
	175

Note by Sir E. Jenkins

There is little doubt that if a General Election were held now, the Muslim League would win 90 seats or thereabouts, and would thus have a clear (though hardly stable) majority. But in the present situation this result would have no significance. The Hindus and Sikhs would positively refuse to let a Muslim Ministry (with or without Christian or Scheduled Caste support) function at all. The Sikhs in particular would rebel and would use force; and the Ministry would be unable to hold a Session of the Assembly. The Muslim League could not logically object to direct action, since they themselves considered it justified against the Coalition Ministry; their line (according to Khizar and other observers) would be to use their power to suppress the Hindus and Sikhs without regard to logic or constitutional considerations. The Constitution has broken down in the Punjab because the Muslims on the one hand and the non-Muslims on the other desire to rule alone, and their ambition cannot be achieved by peaceful means. A Muslim Ministry now would mean instant civil war.[2]

E. M. JENKINS

4.4.47

[2] Mr Abbott's note and Sir E. Jenkins' additional comments were circulated as V.C.P. 21 dated 8 April. Mountbatten Papers.

73

*Record of Interview between Rear-Admiral Viscount Mountbatten of Burma
and Mr Gandhi and Khan Abdul Ghaffar Khan*

Mountbatten Papers. Viceroy's Interview No. 30

TOP SECRET   *4 April 1947*

The meeting lasted from 2.30 to 4.30 p.m.

Mr. Gandhi brought with him as promised Abdul Ghaffar Khan. Lord Ismay
attended the meeting.

Abdul Ghaffar Khan gave a very forthright denunciation of the Governor
of the N.W.F.P. and all his officials, particularly the political officers dealing
with the tribes.

He accused the Governor of being pro-Muslim League and of trying to
make the task of the Government under his brother, Dr. Khan Sahib, as
difficult as possible. He said that the subordinate British officials of the I.C.S.
followed his example.

He stated that the tribes were completely under the control of the British
political officers and invariably did what they said.

When challenged on this point by Lord Ismay, he quoted the case of the
war. Once the political officers told the tribes that the British Empire was
engaged in a life and death struggle, the tribes gave no more trouble whatsoever
until they were informed that the British had won the war.

C.V.S. and I did our best to refute this theory. I reminded Abdul Ghaffar
Khan of the tribes' descent into Peshawar in 1930, which no amount of appeals
by the political officers could prevent.

The fact remains that this remarkable old man is firmly convinced that Sir
Olaf Caroe and all his officers are intensely pro-League and are doing their
best to undermine the position of the Congress on the Frontier.

I asked Mr. Gandhi for his views. He said he feared that there were many
British members of the I.C.S., particularly among the highly placed ones, who
could not bear to see the British leave India, and who had clung all along to the
theory that if they could only support the Muslim League actively, to the
point at which it could be held that the British could not leave India to civil
war, then the British would be compelled to stay.

He pointed out that the views held by Mr. Winston Churchill were so well
known that had he been in power or had there been any chance of his returning
to power, the line taken by all those I.C.S. officials would have achieved its
object.

Lord Ismay said that great as his affection was for his late chief, it was his
opinion that if Mr. Churchill now by some miracle returned to power, the
pressure of public opinion in England would preclude his being able to reverse

the present decision. Indeed, all the rest of the Conservative party agreed with the Labour Party's policy, except for mention of the earlier date.

I asked Mr. Gandhi for some more examples of biassed officials. He said that although he did not know Sir Francis Mudie personally, all his friends in Sind told him that he was extremely pro-Muslim League and much too friendly with his Government.

I pointed out that he had previously agreed with Abdul Ghaffar Khan that Sir Olaf Caroe was insufficiently friendly with his Congress Government in the N.W.F.P., and now he accused Sir Francis Mudie of being too friendly with the Muslim League Government in Sind.

Mr. Gandhi replied that he did not wish Governors to be biassed one way or the other; their friendliness with their Governments should be the impartial friendliness which a constitutional monarch should bestow upon any Government which came to power.

He advised me most strongly to get rid of any officials who could not be brought to see that they must remain impartial and helpful during the final stages.

After this Mr. Gandhi spoke about the Princes. He said that the Princes were really the creation of the British; that many of them had been gradually created up from small chieftains to the position they now held, because the British realised that they would become strong allies of the British under the system of paramountcy.

In fact, he maintained that the British had, from imperialistic points of view, acted very correctly in backing the Princes and the Muslim League, since between these two, had we played our cards really well, we could have claimed it was impossible for us ever to leave India. He appreciated that my task was rendered all the more difficult by the line taken by my predecessors.

He considered it wicked of Sir Stafford Cripps not to have recommended the turning over of paramountcy to the Central Government representing the sovereignty of the Indian nation.

I replied that although I could see the argument for turning over paramountcy to a really strong Central Government representing the whole of the Indian nation, I had not yet seen any workable scheme for producing a really strong Central Government, and in fact the chances of there being any body to whom paramountcy could be turned over seemed to me to be remote.

Only one scheme would achieve this, and that was the famous Gandhi scheme. I therefore asked him to explain this once more for Lord Ismay's benefit. On conclusion I asked Abdul Ghaffar Khan if he really thought that Congress would accept this scheme, and that it would be workable. To this he gave a very definitely affirmative reply.

I then invited Lord Ismay to take Mr. Gandhi to his room and put his scheme in writing.[1]

[1] See Enclosure to No. 85 for Lord Ismay's revised note on Mr Gandhi's scheme.

74

*Record of Interview between Rear-Admiral Viscount Mountbatten of Burma
and Dr John Matthai*

Mountbatten Papers. *Viceroy's Interview No. 31*

TOP SECRET   *4 April 1947*
The meeting lasted from 5 to 6 p.m.

We first discussed the conduct of Cabinet business. Dr. Matthai said that the strides taken in the last ten days would have seemed impossible to him a fortnight ago. Cabinet committees which had been so violently opposed up to that moment were now working with the utmost success. Matters such as the budget controversy over which he feared the Government would finally break up had been surmounted by the process of reasonable compromise in Cabinet Committee.

He said that the whole Cabinet liked the way I handled business and that I was getting them more and more on my side, and he now felt for the first time that there was some slight hope that if I could make the present Coalition Government into a workable proposition this might prove a Centre to which I could ultimately turn over power.

He too agreed that a decision must be made very early, and implemented as soon as possible, and he admitted the great advantage of my being present to see the initial stages up to June 1948 through.

He considered Mr. Jinnah to be the main difficulty since he believed Mr. Liaquat Ali Khan and Mr. Nehru could work together as a team.

75

Note by Mr V. P. Menon

Mountbatten Papers. *Official Correspondence Files: Plans,
Alternative (For Transfer of Power), Part 1*

undated
Criticism of the scheme for the Interim Govt. proposed by Gandhi.

Gandhi is not being quite fair to H.E. when he puts forward his proposal that the selection of the Cabinet for an Interim Government should be left entirely to Jinnah. He knows full well that similar offers have been made by him in the past and that Jinnah never took them seriously.

2. In August 1940, on the concluding day of the Congress Working Committee's session, in which they rejected Lord Linlithgow's offer for the reformation of the Central Government, Rajagopalachari in a statement to the *Daily Herald* made a "sporting offer" intended to dissipate "Mr. Amery's difficulty as to minorities". He said that if H.M.G. would agree to a Provisional National Government being formed at once, he would persuade his colleagues in the Congress to agree to the Muslim League being invited to nominate the Prime Minister who would form a National Government as he might consider best.

3. Subsequently, Gandhi issued a statement to the effect that Congress had no desire to mount to power at the expense of a single national interest and that Lord Linlithglow would therefore have no opposition from Congress if he formed a Cabinet composed of representatives of different parties. He however qualified this statement by a very important proviso, namely, that Congress would be content to remain in opposition so far as the war effort was concerned and so long as the Government machinery had to subserve imperialistic ends.

No one—least of all the Muslim League—took this offer seriously; the joke, if joke it was, failed to amuse the Congress world; and it thoroughly annoyed the Hindu Mahasabha.

4. This question of participation in the Central Government on the basis of Lord Linlithgow's offer of August 1940 was considered by the Working Committee of the Muslim League. A minority of about 5 were against co-operation with the Government and Jinnah himself stood with this group. The late Sir Sikandar Hayat Khan opposed further haggling and said that the offer should be accepted in principle, details being settled personally. Jinnah said that he was prepared to abide by the advice of the majority but warned the members of the consequences of full co-operation; the entire burden of responsibility for protecting the Indian Empire, crushing the Congress, suppressing internal strife, supplying men and money, and running the administration, would fall on the League; and at the same time, they would have to work under the constant fear that Congress might decide to co-operate, and that Government might refuse to consider the Pakistan scheme. Jinnah's adroitness was proved by the sequel. Though in this meeting he was in a minority on the main question, he prevented any outright decision in favour of accepting the Government's offer, and subsequently obtained a verdict of rejection.

5. There is no reason to suppose that Jinnah will now accept an offer which he has rejected previously. If he forms a Government composed entirely of Muslim League nominees, that Government will find itself facing a predominant Congress majority in the Central Legislature from which Jinnah has to get his essential legislation and supply. On the other hand, if there is a coalition,

it will have to be formed on conditions more acceptable to the Congress than to the League. In either event, the assurance of co-operation by the Congress is more a wishful thinking and would certainly place Jinnah in the position of having to adjust his views to those of the Congress. This is perhaps not un-intended by Gandhi. In a Legislature where the Congress has got predominant representation, the question whether a "particular proposal is in the interests of the Indian people" will in practice be decided by that party. The fact that H.E. as the arbitrator has decided on a particular course of action will not help Jinnah either with the Legislature or with the public.

6. The position of H.E. will become under the proposed arrangement one of very great difficulty and embarrassment. At no time is it desirable that the Governor-General should be brought into the vortex of party politics. This is to be particularly avoided at the present juncture when we are engaged in the process of transfer of power and our primary duty should therefore be to concentrate on devising an arrangement under which the parties themselves will have to face up to their tasks and responsibilities. Further, such a develop-ment might well cast doubts on H.E.'s *bona fides* and might do irreparable damage to good relations between India and Great Britain.

7. According to Gandhi's proposal, Jinnah is at liberty to plan for Pakistan and even to put his plans into effect provided that he is successful in appealing to reason and does not use force. This is asking for the impossible. If Jinnah could persuade the Sikhs and Hindus of the Punjab and Hindus of Bengal to join Pakistan, he would automatically get his Pakistan without joining the Interim Government on dubious terms. On the other hand, if Jinnah still persists in his scheme of separation, he will be giving his case away by entering the Central Government. This was the main motive which induced him to keep out of the Central Government in the past: and, as a matter of fact, he has never attached any importance to effective participation on the side of the Muslim League in the present Interim Government.

8. It is Gandhi's habit to make propositions, leaving many of their impli-cations unsaid, and this method of negotiation has put him and the Congress in difficult positions in the past. For example, there is no reference here to the Muslim League participation in the Constituent Assembly. If Jinnah were to accept his proposal, Gandhi probably takes it for granted that the Muslim League would enter the Constituent Assembly. It seems to me clear therefore that the present proposals do not expose his full mind.

9. Since the Cabinet Delegation's visit last year, Gandhi is out of accord with the policy of the Congress Working Committee as well as the members of the Interim Government on several questions of major importance. It should not therefore be taken for granted that his present proposals will carry the support of either the Congress Working Committee or of Nehru and Patel.

10. It is suggested that if Jinnah rejects the offer the same offer is to be made *mutatis mutandis* to the Congress. It should be borne in mind that all the factors which have been mentioned as working to the disadvantage of Jinnah will for the same reason work to the advantage of the Congress. H.E.'s main task is to find a solution to the present deadlock between the League and the Congress. It is no solution to suggest that power should be transferred to the Congress to the exclusion of the Muslim League. If the proposition were as simple as that, it would have been solved long ago.

76

Viceroy's Staff Meetings
Uncirculated Record of Discussion No. 3

Mountbatten Papers

TOP SECRET

Those present during this discussion which took place at the end of The Viceroy's Ninth Staff Meeting held at The Viceroy's House, New Delhi on 5 April 1947 at 10 am were: Rear-Admiral Viscount Mountbatten of Burma, Lord Ismay, Sir E. Mieville, Mr Abell, Captain Brockman, Mr Campbell-Johnson, Lieutenant-Colonel Erskine Crum

LORD ISMAY said that he had spent an hour with Mr. Gandhi the previous day after the latter's interview with the Viceroy. He had reduced to writing an outline of Mr. Gandhi's scheme for an Interim Government pending the transfer of power.[1] The salient features of this scheme were that Mr. Jinnah was to be given the option of forming a Cabinet of his own selection; and that if he rejected this offer, the same offer should be made *mutatis mutandis* to Congress. LORD ISMAY said that he had sent copies of this outline to Sir Eric Mieville, Mr. Abell and Rao Bahadur Menon, and after a meeting with them on the subject, Rao Bahadur Menon had rendered a note[2] containing criticism of the scheme. It was clear that Mr. Gandhi's plan was not a new one. HIS EXCELLENCY THE VICEROY pointed out that Mr. Gandhi had made no attempt to disguise this fact.

LORD ISMAY said that, after their talk the previous evening, he, Sir Eric Mieville, Mr. Abell and Rao Bahadur Menon had come to the unanimous conclusion that Mr. Gandhi's scheme was not workable. It would put the Viceroy in an impossible position; Mr. Jinnah's Government would be completely at the mercy of the Congress majority; every single legislative or political

[1] See Enclosure to No. 85, for Lord Ismay's revised note on Mr Gandhi's scheme.   [2] No. 75.

measure would be brought up to the Viceroy for decision and every action the Viceroy took after the initial stages would be misrepresented. LORD ISMAY pointed out in support of this belief that Mr. Gandhi the previous day had accused Sir Evan Jenkins of responsibility for the present situation in the Punjab; Sir Olaf Caroe of responsibility for the present North-West Frontier troubles; Sir Francis Mudie of excessive support of the Muslim League Government in Sind; and the whole Civil Service and Indian Political Service of all manner of sins, including corruption.

SIR ERIC MIEVILLE agreed that under Mr. Gandhi's scheme the position of the Viceroy would become one of the greatest difficulty and embarrassment and read an extract from Rao Bahadur Menon's note to support this opinion. He asked what influence Mr. Gandhi had with the rank and file of the Congress party. Could he, for example, sway the Congress majority in the Assembly to his wishes?

MR. ABELL replied that Mr. Gandhi's influence with the rank and file of the Congress party was very considerable but he had more difficulty with the leaders, particularly Sardar Patel. Moreover, Mr. Gandhi could not stay in Delhi and thus in control of the situation all the time.

LORD ISMAY said that Mr. Gandhi's proposition had already been put up to Mr. Jinnah who had rejected it and would do so again. He wondered whether Mr. Gandhi would now take any further steps on the scheme outside.

HIS EXCELLENCY THE VICEROY said that Mr. Gandhi's scheme was undoubtedly wild except for the fact of Mr. Gandhi's amazing personal influence which might induce Congress to accept it. A main danger in his opinion was that Mr. Gandhi might die—then the scheme would completely break down. He had made it quite clear to Mr. Gandhi, during one of their talks, that he was not going to be a party to any manoeuvre whereby he would make an offer to Mr. Jinnah which the latter was likely to refuse. Mr. Gandhi had quite sincerely stated that he would prefer Mr. Jinnah to form a Government, but had insisted on the inclusion of the clause that if Mr. Jinnah rejected the offer it must thereafter be made to Congress.

HIS EXCELLENCY THE VICEROY said that he had told Mr. Gandhi that he intended to formulate all conceivable workable alternative plans for the future of India, talk over them all with the different Indian leaders and finally discuss them at the projected meeting at Simla. He intended to inform Mr. Jinnah of Mr. Gandhi's scheme, and all the other alternatives, at an early stage so that he could discuss it with the other leading Muslim League personalities before the Simla house party. He felt that Mr. Jinnah should be told all the possible plans and that there should be no manoeuvring.

HIS EXCELLENCY THE VICEROY said that he was sure that the only way for him to handle the situation was to make it quite clear that there was a completely new element in the way in which negotiations were to be conducted. Unlike the Cabinet Mission, which had to obtain the agreement of all major parties, his task was only to recommend to His Majesty's Government what, in his opinion, was the best solution. He would clearly not choose any solution which was completely unacceptable to either side, but on the other hand he would not ask either side for their acceptance. This would have to be made quite clear. He would make up his own mind. If either party raised vociferous objections to the solution he recommended, that would go against them.

LORD ISMAY, SIR ERIC MIEVILLE and MR. ABELL all agreed that it was desirable that the Indian leaders should not be asked to give their written acceptance of the selected plan. MR. ABELL pointed out that, if Mr. Gandhi went to Congress with his offer, it would put the Muslim League in a very awkward position. Therefore, he did not consider that Mr. Gandhi's scheme should be ranked as a possible solution.

HIS EXCELLENCY THE VICEROY said that, nevertheless, it would serve to remain as a frightening alternative to Mr. Jinnah. It would not be very easy for Mr. Jinnah to refuse Mr. Gandhi's offer. Basically, Mr. Gandhi's object was to retain the unity of India and basically he was right in this. Mr. Gandhi honestly considered that the only hope of unity came from a Coalition Government. He thought that the present Coalition Government was functioning very creakily. He felt that the Muslims' fear must be removed before it could be made to work better. Once the British had handed over to a unified India, Mr. Gandhi doubtless thought that the Indians themselves would be able to adjust matters and set up some sort of Pakistan, if necessary. Mr. Gandhi's viewpoint was that, since it was impossible to get Mr. Jinnah to agree to Congress running the Interim Government, the only way was to get Mr. Jinnah to run it himself and for him (Mr. Gandhi) to use his great influence to induce Congress to accept that.

HIS EXCELLENCY THE VICEROY said that he had asked Dr. Matthai whether he considered that there was any hope of turning over to a unified India. Dr. Matthai had expressed the opinion that the Indians attached great importance to words. They were most unlikely to accept such a term as "federation" although they might accept an "alliance" which would produce identical results. It was the same thing with the word "Commonwealth". Dr. Matthai had also emphasised that no single person in India had really addressed themselves yet to the problem of the handover in June 1948. When that time came the Indian leaders would be in absolute despair. HIS EXCELLENCY THE VICEROY said that he had reiterated to Dr. Matthai His Majesty's Government's determination to withdraw in June 1948, but Dr. Matthai had asked him whether the British would stay on if all parties asked them. MR. ABELL recalled that Mr. Gandhi had told the Viceroy that he expected, when the time came, to be the only person who then still wanted the British to leave.

HIS EXCELLENCY THE VICEROY then summarised the several ideas which were at present in his mind. Firstly, everybody was agreed that the decision must be made as soon as there was enough data to go on—possibly in two months' time. Secondly, the form of decision would not be an agreement which the Indian leaders would publicly accept, but a unilateral decision from which there would be no appeal. Thirdly, efforts would have to be made to get His Majesty's Government to approve it at once. He hoped that it would be legally possible for him to make an announcement of the decision in India while the legislation to put it into force was still being passed through Parliament. Fourthly, the earliest possible legislation and implementation was essential. The new organisation, whatever it was, should be working by the end of 1947. He would remain until June 1948 in the role of an umpire and adviser. HIS EXCELLENCY THE VICEROY emphasised that this gave the best prospects of British withdrawal by June 1948 and was therefore the most honest approach. However, His Majesty's Government would have kept their pledge when the handover took place at the end of 1947, so it might be necessary for him to ask the Indian Cabinet whether they wanted him to stay until June 1948.

MR. ABELL cast doubt on the possibility of the Viceroy staying on as envisaged in the guise of an umpire and adviser. This he considered would be impossible if the Indian parties were fighting each other.

HIS EXCELLENCY THE VICEROY emphasised that whatever solution he eventually came to, he could not imagine himself agreeing to one which completely abolished the centre. If this abolition was the only possible solution, it could not be brought into effect before June 1948. Whatever the eventual answer was, it must be one that put a stop to communal strife.

SIR ERIC MIEVILLE reverted to the point that there was a possibility of Mr. Gandhi putting up his scheme prematurely to Congress and possibly passing a resolution on it through the Congress Working Committee. HIS EXCELLENCY THE VICEROY said that he would talk about this with Pandit Nehru that day. HIS EXCELLENCY THE VICEROY:—

(i) invited C.V.S. and Pers. Sec. to prepare an appreciation on the various possible solutions;

(ii) directed Pers. Sec. to include in his next letter to the Secretary of State an outline of his present thoughts on the future timetable;

(iii) decided to talk to Pandit Nehru that afternoon about Mr. Gandhi's scheme.

77

Mr V.P. Menon to Sir E. Mieville

Mountbatten Papers. Official Correspondence Files:
Interim Government of India, Part 1

NEW DELHI, *5 April 1947*

My dear Mieville,

I enclose four copies each of two notes—(1) Tactics to be adopted with Gandhi as regards his scheme, and (2) Transfer of power—possible alternatives. I am sending copies to Abell.

2. I shall be glad to come for discussion tomorrow evening if you will kindly let me know the time.

Yours sincerely,
V. P. MENON

Enclosure 1 to No. 77

Tactics to be adopted with Gandhi as regards his scheme

(1) H.E. will no doubt put the proposals of Gandhi to Jinnah. In view of past history Jinnah may be expected to reject them.

(2) H.E. should postpone further meetings with Gandhi till he has had a full discussion with Jinnah on this question.

(3) If Jinnah rejects the proposal, H.E. should inform Gandhi of the attitude of Jinnah to the scheme and also explain why it is not possible for him to make a similar offer to the Congress.

(4) Here H.E. could mention that his chief purpose in interviewing the leaders is to seek an agreement between the parties so that peace could be restored and an acceptable basis for the transfer of power be worked out.

(5) If H.E. were to decide to go ahead with the Congress, neither of these objects would be secured.

(6) The question then arises how best the parties could be brought together on some other basis. This will require further consideration which will inevitably take a little time.

In other words, we must, while keeping Gandhi in good humour, play for time.

Enclosure 2 to No. 77

Transfer of Power—Possible alternatives

(1) The first alternative is to see whether the Cabinet Delegation's Plan could be worked by agreement between the two parties. If this is possible, it would be the ideal solution: even if a Constitution is not produced before June 1948,

H.M.G. could transfer power to a Coalition Government which is agreed on the long-term constitutional plan.

Note: The chief obstacle in the way of the League coming into the Constituent Assembly is the Congress objection to Grouping. Jinnah wants compulsory grouping whereas Congress would leave it to the Provinces to come in or not. Congress has gone some way to meet the Muslim League, but not enough to induce the latter to come in. In the present state of communal bitterness it is unlikely that we will be able to persuade the Congress to go any further. Gandhi's idea of "appealing to reason" will certainly not be accepted by Jinnah, since he knows very well that neither of the minorities in 'B' and 'C' Groups will play up to the Muslim League.

(2) If all our efforts to induce the parties to work together on the basis of the Cabinet Delegation Plan fail, it seems inevitable that we shall have to consider some form of Pakistan. The Muslim League spokesmen have consistently insisted that the Pakistan which they envisage will comprise the existing Provinces of Bengal, Assam, the Punjab, the N.W.F.P., Sind and British Baluchistan. On the other hand, the minorities in Bengal and in the Punjab and the Hindus in Assam are violently opposed to such a scheme for the division of India. This scheme also failed to find favour with the Cabinet Delegation who in para. 6 of the Statement of May 16 made it clear that it would be unjustifiable to include in Pakistan substantial blocs of Hindu majority areas contiguous to the rest of India. The Cabinet Delegation accordingly suggested that if a separate Muslim State was to be set up in India, it would entail the exclusion of (a) the whole of the Ambala and Jullundur Divisions of the Punjab; (b) the whole of Assam except the Sylhet district; and (c) a large part of Western Bengal including Calcutta. It seems therefore that this is roughly the picture of Pakistan which we can give to the Muslim League in the event of the parties not agreeing on a common basis to work the Cabinet Delegation Plan.

(3) If Pakistan on these lines is acceptable to Jinnah, he must be told that boundaries will have to be delimited and that a Central Government could be set up for these areas as early as possible. Having regard to the pronouncements made in Parliament, I do not think we can force the N.W.F.P. to join Pakistan. It will therefore be necessary to test public opinion in the Province on this issue by holding immediate general elections.

(4) The next question is whether it is possible to bring this Pakistan area (which will draft its own Constitutions, provincial as well as group) in relations with the Union Centre in respect of the three common subjects, namely, Defence, External Affairs and Communications. There are two methods. The first one is for Pakistan to join the Constituent Assembly, like the Indian States, at the stage at which the Union Constitution is drafted. If we fail to bring the League into the Assembly on the basis of a Union Constitution

for both Pakistan and Hindustan on these three subjects, the relationship between these two States could be regulated by treaty.

(5) Assuming Jinnah neither agrees to come into the Union Constituent Assembly nor accepts the smaller Pakistan, what are we to do? This is a very difficult question to answer. We may then be faced with the necessity of parting with power, irrespective of the consequences, to whatever Central Government is functioning at the time.

(6) There is a proposal by Sir B.N. Rau for a composite Central Cabinet in which portfolios will be allocated on a territorial basis, certain subjects being dealt with by the whole Cabinet.[1] I am personally not attracted by this idea at all and this scheme has more foes than friends.

[1] See No. 262, note 2.

78

Rear-Admiral Viscount Mountbatten of Burma to Lord Pethick-Lawrence

L/P&S/13/1831: ff 123–4

No. F.592/89   THE VICEROY'S HOUSE, NEW DELHI,
                                                        5 April 1947

My dear Secretary of State,
Thank you for your letter of the 21st March.[1]

I hope to be able to provide you with an indication of the programme for the contraction of paramountcy in the form of the proceedings of the Residents' Conference, which has been called for 9th and 10th April and over the opening of which I intend to preside.

It will, of course, be possible to keep you informed of the progress in implementing that programme, as progress occurs, but I doubt whether for the present it will be of advantage to cast these into periodical and routine reports.

Since part of the programme for the contraction of paramountcy will be the placing of States in direct contact with the Central Government and Provincial Governments, reports of progress along the lines laid down at the Residents' Conference will cover the problem of integration with British India, para. 2 (b) of your letter.

But as regards internal integration, para. 2 (a) of your letter, progress reports would require the continuation of Political Officers. In para. 1 of your letter you appear to contemplate continuation and even intervention "possibly up to the date of our departure". I fear that any tendency to delay withdrawal

[1] Vol. IX, No. 557.

will defeat the very object at which we are aiming, namely to make States stand on their own legs. As Political Officers disengage themselves we shall progressively cease to have the machinery capable of furnishing the information suggested under (a), and it is only by their withdrawal that we shall maintain the pressure behind the shock, administered by the announcement of 20th February. This shock has already made many of the small States, notably in Western India and the Punjab Hills, realise their individual weakness and begin to get together actively, but there are still areas where only physical withdrawal will lead to action.

I propose therefore to furnish you first with the proceedings of the Residents' Conference and then with information, as it accrues, of the progress achieved in implementing their conclusions. If this can readily be cast in the form of periodic reports, so much the better. I hope you will agree.

2. As regards matters of common concern to the States and British India (para. 4 of the Memorandum on States Treaties and Paramountcy),[2] you will have seen from my predecessor's telegram, No. 580–P of 21st March[3] that Rau is suggesting to Nehru that the Interim Government should set up negotiating machinery. I have not yet received Nehru's reactions to the suggestion.

Meanwhile as you will have seen from my predecessor's telegram No. 552–P dated 19th March 1947[4] my Political Department is already taking up departmentally with the Central Government various questions, relating to administrative arrangements, consequent on the lapse of Paramountcy, and the nature of the problem will thus be brought forcibly to the notice of the various members of the Interim Government.

3. In the last sentence of your letter you remark that the Interim Government and States constitutionally "have no contact with one another", and remind me that the Crown Representative will have to be aware of what is going on between them. This seems hardly consistent with the last sentence of para. 4 of the Memorandum of 12th May 1946, in which the words "should it be so desired" seem to me to contemplate the possibility of negotiations between States and "those likely to control the Succession Government" being undertaken without my assistance as Crown Representative. I do not however anticipate that much will happen without my Political Department being well in the picture.

Yours sincerely,
MOUNTBATTEN OF BURMA

[2] Vol. VII, No. 262.   [3] See No. 39, note 2.   [4] Vol. IX, No. 548.

79

*Record of Interview between Rear-Admiral Viscount Mountbatten of Burma
and Mr Krishna Menon*

Mountbatten Papers. Viceroy's Interview No. 33

TOP SECRET   *5 April 1947*

Mr. Menon, whom I saw twice in London before coming out, came to see me at 12.15 and stayed to lunch at 1.15.

I asked him categorically whether Mr. Gandhi's scheme of turning over the Central Government to Mr. Jinnah could be made to work.

Mr. Menon replied emphatically, but with due consideration for Mr. Gandhi, that he was afraid that not even Mr. Gandhi could put this particular scheme through; even if Mr. Jinnah could be made to accept it.

80

*Record of Interview between Rear-Admiral Viscount Mountbatten of Burma
and Field Marshal Auchinleck[1]*

Mountbatten Papers. Viceroy's Interview No. 34

5 April 1947

I told the C-in-C that I had been absolutely amazed at the receipt of the Secretary of State's telegram No. 43 of 4th April,[2] telling me that an official telegram had already been despatched to the Defence Department of the Government of India cancelling the invitation to India to become a member of the Commonwealth Advisory Committee and informing them that in future no more Indian students would be admitted to the Imperial Defence College, the Joint Services Staff College, etc. It was unbelievable that this sort of telegram should be despatched without any prior consultation with me and even without my knowledge. It had come at a most unfortunate time in the middle of the Gurkha negotiations. I said that I proposed to make the strongest possible protest direct to the Prime Minister.

The C-in-C did not think that the telegram would do much harm. He had, in fact, been expecting it for some time. From the purely local point of view it was a relief since Indian officers with the necessary qualifications for these courses were few and far between and were urgently required in India at the moment.

[1] Lord Ismay was present for the first part of the Meeting.   [2] No. 71.

I then gave the C-in-C a rough outline of one of the many alternative schemes for the future set-up in India that were revolving in my mind. A feature of this scheme was the almost immediate offer of Dominion or Commonwealth status to India.

The C-in-C pointed out that the British Army, and indeed the Indian Army with its complement of British officers, could not serve in any India that was neither under the Crown nor a British Dominion, since the oath of allegiance taken by the officers was to the King.

In the course of further discussion, the C-in-C suggested that one of the things that would please Indian opinion more than anything else was the abolition of the India Office. I asked Lord Ismay to mention this possibility to the Reforms Commissioner and get his views.[3]

[3] During discussion of Item 8 at the Viceroy's Twelfth Staff Meeting on 10 April 1947, Lord Ismay reported that he had consulted Mr Menon on the constitutional implications of abolishing the India Office. Mr Menon had replied that he did not consider that opinion either in Congress or Muslim League circles was now seriously interested in the abolition of the India Office before power was transferred. Furthermore, he had pointed out that abolition would involve piecemeal legislation and had produced arguments against abolition which Lord Ismay considered unanswerable. Mountbatten Papers.

81

Sir F. Burrows (Bengal) to Rear-Admiral Viscount Mountbatten of Burma

Telegram, R/3/1/148: f 42

IMMEDIATE   5 April 1947, 3.45 pm
SECRET   Received: 5 April, 7.45 pm
No. 78–S. Your telegram 674–S of April 1st.[1] I have spoken to Suhrawardy who assured me that he has never pressed for an enquiry in Bihar and would not consider himself justified as Premier of another Province for doing so. He has shown me some correspondence in which Mr Gandhi on December 5th suggested a Joint Enquiry into occurrences in Bihar and Noakhali: this was in reply to suggestions by Suhrawardy that Gandhi's place was in Bihar rather than in Noakhali. Gandhi said that he could not accept at their face value allegations regarding occurrences in Bihar passed on to him by Suhrawardy and went on to make suggestion for a Joint Enquiry. Gandhi referred to this again in a letter of December 22nd. Pandit Nehru endorsed suggestion in a postscript to a long private letter of December 29th to Suhrawardy and made a brief passing reference to it in a further private letter of January 1st. To none of these suggestions did Suhrawardy make any reply.

2. There has been no public demand by influential quarters in Bengal for an

enquiry into Noakhali incident and as I mentioned in my telegram 329 of December 7th to Secretary of State repeated Viceroy[2] we have no intention of setting up any such enquiry.

Repeated Governor of Bihar.

[1] No. 51.   [2] R/3/1/148: f 9.

82

Sir G. Squire to Mr Weightman

L/P&S/12/1811: f 191

SECRET   BRITISH LEGATION, KABUL,

D.O. No. 706/44/NGO   *5 April 1947*

Dear Weightman,

Will you please refer to the India Office memorandum No. EXT. 6036/46 of the 6th September 1946 and previous correspondence on the subject of Anglo-Afghan relations?[1]

2. As your are aware Afghan anxiety regarding developments on the North-West Frontier has been increasing of late. Since my return from Delhi I have had interviews both with the Foreign Minister and the Prime Minister at which the subject was raised. The view taken by the Afghan Government is that the tribesmen in tribal territory are more closely connected with the Afghan Government than with the Interim Government of India and the Afghans have, as you know, already asked that the tribes should be given the option of securing their complete independence or of joining themselves to Afghanistan if they wish to do so rather than continue as part of India. The Afghan Government feel however that Afghanistan's political position as a separate country precludes them from putting this point of view across to their kinsmen east of the Durand Line whereas they have received information that missions from both of the Congress party and the Muslim League from India are constantly visiting the tribes in order to try and secure their adherence.

3. I endeavoured to counter this argument by saying that their present difficulties were inherent in the international position and asked for concrete suggestions, adding that I was sure that the Government of India would not wish to put any obstacles in the way of a reasonable presentation of the Afghan case. I pointed out however that the tribal areas, and in fact the whole of the North-West Frontier Province, were economically dependent on India, and that, whatever the sentiments of the inhabitants might be towards Afghanistan they could hardly afford to forego the more substantial benefits which at present accrue to them from their association with India.

[1] L/P &S/12/1811.

4. Both the Prime Minister and Foreign Minister assured me that they had hitherto refrained from all efforts to influence tribal opinion but they felt now that in fairness to themselves they can no longer hold aloof. Not only was considerable pressure being put on them by their own subjects but some of the tribes were also complaining that the Afghan Government were giving them no lead or advice in the matter of their political future.

5. It is obvious that the Afghans could, if they wish, either invite tribal leaders privately to visit Kabul or could themselves send secret emissaries to the tribes to advise them and to put forward the Afghan point of view. The Prime Minister said however that they did not want to take action behind the backs of the Government of India; nor indeed had he decided which of these two courses would be open to the fewer objections, though he added that if they invited the leading maliks to Kabul each of them would bring at least a hundred other maliks with him and this would cause undue publicity and great embarrassment. It therefore seems as if they would prefer to send emissaries to visit the tribes, though privately and in such a way as to avoid publicity. We can hardly prevent them from doing this and it is obviously better that such emissaries should come with our knowledge and consent than that they should be sent without it. I am awaiting definite proposals from the Afghan Government. Meanwhile I am sending this report for your information and should be glad of instructions as to the attitude I should adopt towards the more definite proposals which I expect shortly to receive.

6. I am also sending copies of this letter to Baxter, Donaldson and Caroe.

Yours sincerely,

G. F. SQUIRE

83

Mr Gandhi to Lord Ismay

*Mountbatten Papers. Official Correspondence Files: Interim
Government of India, Part 1*

PERSONAL   BHANGI COLONY, READING ROAD,
                                            NEW DELHI, *5 April 1947*

Dear Lord Ismay,

Pandit Nehru gave me what you have described as an outline of a scheme.[1] What I read is merely a copy of the points I hurriedly dictated whereas, as I understood from H.E. The Viceroy, you were to prepare a draft agreement after

[1] See Enclosure to No. 85 for Lord Ismay's revised note on Mr Gandhi's scheme.

the line of the points I had dictated. Of course, you were at liberty to amend them, add to them and omit what you wished to omit.

I had a chat with Pandit Nehru twice during the day, the second time when he handed a copy of the outline at 5 p.m.

The 7th point should read thus:—

"Within the framework hereof Mr Jinnah will be perfectly free to present for acceptance a scheme of Pakistan, even before the transfer of power, provided however, that he is successful in his appeal to reason and not to the force of arms which he abjures for all time for this purpose. Thus, there will be no compulsion in this matter over a Province or part thereof."

What I could not recall yesterday I now recall.

The 8th will read as follows:—

"In the Assembly the Congress has a decisive majority. But the Congress shall never use that majority against the League policy simply because of its identification with the League but will give its hearty support to every measure brought forward by the League Government, provided that it is in the interest of the whole of India. Whether it is in such interest or not shall be decided by Lord Mountbatten as man and not in his representative capacity."

I have finished dictating this at 8.45 p.m. I am anxious that it reaches you tonight. Therefore, I have only made manifest correction and addition. The outline is by no means complete. When a draft agreement is prepared, many other points which should occur to any draftsman will have to be covered.

I must add that Pandit Nehru has at least one vital objection to the outline. But I will not tax you with its mention here. If the outline appears workable to H.E. I would like to wait on him once more and discuss Pandit Nehru's objections. Before putting it before Q.A. Jinnah I would like to show it to a few friends.

Yours sincerely,
M. K. GANDHI

84

Record of Interviews between Rear-Admiral Viscount Mountbatten of Burma and Mr Jinnah

Mountbatten Papers. Viceroy's Interview No. 35

TOP SECRET   *5 and 6 April 1947*

When Mr. Jinnah first arrived on Saturday 5th April, he was in a most frigid, haughty and disdainful frame of mind. A number of photographs was taken of him standing between myself and Her Excellency. He was recorded in the newspapers as describing himself on this occasion as "a thorn between two roses". (Later I challenged him on this, and told him I thought he had said "A rose between two thorns". He said "Yes, but in my mind I was expecting Her Excellency to be between you and me".)

After having acted for some time in a gracious tea-party hostess manner, he eventually said that he had come to tell me exactly what he was prepared to accept. I said that I did not want to hear that at this stage—the object of this first interview was that we should make each other's acquaintance. For half an hour more he made monosyllabic replies to my attempts at conversation—but one and a half hours after the interview started he was joking, and by the end of our talk last night (6th April, when he came to dinner and stayed until half an hour past midnight) the ice was really broken.

Our talks covered all subjects. I made it clear to him that I had not yet made up my mind what solution to recommend to His Majesty's Government, and that at the present I was utterly impartial. But I explained that it was my policy to make a decision as soon as possible after seeing all concerned. He agreed not to force the pace, assenting that, whereas the whole of India was awaiting a quick decision, that decision must be the right one. I added that the problem, as I saw it at the moment, was not so much what to do, but how to do it in the time.

Mr. Jinnah claimed that there was only one solution—a "surgical operation" on India, otherwise India would perish altogether. I replied by reiterating that I had not yet made up my mind, and pointed out that an "anaesthetic" must precede any "surgical operation".

He gave me an account (which worries me a great deal) about his previous negotiations with Mr. Gandhi, including his version of the Gandhi/Jinnah correspondence in September 1944. He emphasized, and tried to prove from this account, that on the Muslim side there was only one man to deal with, namely himself. If he took a decision it would be enforced—or, if the Muslim League refused to ratify it, he would resign and that would be the end of the Muslim League. But the same was not true of the representatives of Congress—there was no one man to deal with on their side. Mr. Gandhi had openly confessed that he represented nobody—he only agreed to "endeavour to use his influence" —he had enormous authority with no responsibility. Nehru and Patel represented different points of view within Congress—neither could give a categorical answer on behalf of the party as a whole. Mr. Jinnah related that, when the impasse in the formation of the Interim Government occurred, he had refused to let the Muslim League join if Congress insisted on including a Congress Muslim. He claimed that Congress's only object in this insistence was to show that the Muslims were not united. After he had had 48 hours' negotiations with Gandhi, a formula had been devised whereby Congress would agree publicly that the vast majority of Indian Muslims were represented by the

Muslim League, and he (Jinnah) would then agree to them nominating a Congress Muslim to the Government. Gandhi had definitely agreed to this formula, but the Congress party had rejected it. Gandhi had thereupon withdrawn his agreement and stated that he had made "a Himalayan mistake". This went to show, as Mr. Jinnah emphasised, that not only Gandhi's word but also his signatures were valueless. And he took the opportunity further to compare the position between the two parties—only the Muslim League had a leader whose word could be relied upon.

He also spoke of the emotionalism of the Congress leaders, pointing out that they had every reason for this when it was a question of getting rid of the British, but this reason no longer held good.

He accused Congress leaders of constantly shifting their front. They were determined, he said, to inherit to the full all the powers now exercised by the British in India. They would stoop to anything to gain this object—even to acceptance of Dominion status—rather than that any part of India should be handed over to the Muslims.

At the end of our interview, after he had told me a succession of long stories about how appallingly the Muslims had been treated, I informed him that what fascinated me was the way that all the Indian leaders spoke with such conviction.

He said that in his view the members of the Cabinet Mission had been imbued with the wrong attitude—they had come out pleading for agreement instead of laying down a solution. I pointed out to him that I was in a very favourable position compared with the Cabinet Mission and others who had been sent out to find a solution to India's future, as I did not have to obtain prior acceptance from the Indian parties to the course I intended to recommend to His Majesty's Government. I said that I would of course not recommend any solution which was patently unacceptable. He seemed pleased with these remarks.

(Note: For the discussion of policy which [took place] following on H.E.'s account of this interview see Uncirculated Record of Discussion No. 4)[1]

[1] No. 87.

85

Lord Ismay to Mr Gandhi

Mountbatten Papers. Official Correspondence Files: Interim
Government of India, Part 1

PERSONAL   *6 April 1947*

Dear Mr Gandhi,

Thank you for your letter of 5th April.[1] It was very kind of you to dictate
it at such a late hour in order that it might reach me last night.

I think that there has been some misunderstanding about the form of the
short note which I prepared last Friday. As I understood it, Lord Mountbatten,
on the conclusion of his talk with you, asked if you would be so good as to
spare a little more time for a talk with me about your plan, in order that I
might prepare a short note summarising its salient features in general terms. He
had no intention, so far as I knew, that I should attempt anything formal or
elaborate. I have now shown him your letter and he confirms that my interpretation of his wishes was correct.

I have prepared a revised copy of my note substituting your version of point
7 for the original and including your point 8. This covers much the same ground
as my original points 3 and 4, which therefore now become redundant.

Lord Mountbatten has asked me to say that he much looks forward to having
another talk with you about your plan before you leave.

May I conclude with an expression of my personal thanks for having spared
me so much of your time last Friday.

Yours sincerely,

ISMAY

P.S. The Viceroy assures you that he will not mention your plan to Mr Jinnah
    until he has had a further talk about it with you.

Enclosure to No. 85

OUTLINE OF A SCHEME FOR AN INTERIM GOVERNMENT PENDING
TRANSFER OF POWER

1. Mr Jinnah to be given the option of forming a Cabinet.

2. The selection of the Cabinet is left entirely to Mr Jinnah. The members
may be all Moslems, or all non-Moslems, or they may be representatives of
all classes and creeds of the Indian people.

3. If Mr Jinnah accepted this offer, the Congress would guarantee to co-operate freely and sincerely, so long as all the measures that Mr Jinnah's Cabinet bring forward are in the interests of the Indian people as a whole.

4. The sole referee of what is or is not in the interests of India as a whole will be Lord Mountbatten, in his personal capacity.

These are now redundant owing to new para. 8.

5. Mr Jinnah must stipulate, on behalf of the League or of any other parties represented in the Cabinet formed by him that, so far as he or they are concerned, they will do their utmost to preserve peace throughout India.

6. There shall be no National Guards or any other form of private army.

7. Within the framework hereof Mr Jinnah will be perfectly free to present for acceptance a scheme of Pakistan, even before the transfer of power, provided, however, that he is successful in his appeal to reason and not to the force of arms which he abjures for all time for this purpose. Thus, there will be no compulsion in this matter over a Province or part thereof.

8. In the Assembly the Congress has a decisive majority. But the Congress shall never use that majority against the League policy simply because of its identification with the League, but will give its hearty support to every measure brought forward by the League Government, provided that it is in the interest of the whole of India. Whether it is in such interest or not shall be decided by Lord Mountbatten as a man and not in his representative capacity.

Mr. Gandhi's draft.

9. If Mr Jinnah rejects this offer, the same offer to be made *mutatis mutandis* to Congress.

[1] No. 83.

86

Mr Gandhi to Lord Ismay

Mountbatten Papers. Official Correspondence Files: Interim Government of India, Part 1

PERSONAL
BHANGI COLONY, NEW DELHI,
6 April 1947

Dear Lord Ismay,

Many thanks for your letter of even date.[1]

The very thought that at the threshold of my friendship with Lord Mountbatten and you, there can be any misunderstanding at all fills me with grave doubt about my ability to shoulder the burden I have taken upon my weak self. It is impossible, at every stage, to reduce to writing conversations and that would be, in my opinion, a bar to friendship. I can only say that there must be some

[1] No. 85.

defect in my understanding or my attentiveness if I misunderstand very simple things. I do not feel inclined to reproduce the talk about this topic except to mention one thing, viz: that H.E. mentioned Menon to you and said you should prepare something in conjunction with him and I was to give you the points which were to become the basis of the draft you were to prepare.

So far as you are concerned you correctly took down what you heard from me. But as it did not answer what I wanted to say, I have given you[2] my considered view about point 7.

Now that I have reread Nos. 3 and 4 I must differ from you in your view that with the new version of No. 7 and filling in of No. 8, Nos 3 and 4 become redundant. But of this later, if we ever reach the consideration stage of the "outline".

Yours sincerely,

M. K. GANDHI

P.S. Since writing this, Badshah Khan came into my room and I find that he confirms the gist of the conversation with Lord Mountbatten as described by me and adds that when we went to your office I told you that I had only to give the points as I hastily thought of them in order to enable you and your draftsman to prepare a draft agreement.

M. K. G.

[2] No. 83.

87

Viceroy's Staff Meetings
Uncirculated Record of Discussion No. 4

Mountbatten Papers

TOP SECRET

Those present during this discussion which took place during The Viceroy's Tenth Staff Meeting held at The Viceroy's House, New Delhi on 7 April 1947 at 10 am were: Rear-Admiral Viscount Mountbatten of Burma, Lord Ismay, Sir E. Mieville, Mr Abell, Captain Brockman, Mr Campbell-Johnson, Lieutenant-Colonel Erskine Crum

After he had given his account of his interviews with Mr. Jinnah on the previous two days,[1] HIS EXCELLENCY THE VICEROY said that he felt positively certain that the only way to obtain Mr. Jinnah's co-operation would be to tell him that the British accepted Pakistan (a truncated version if necessary) as the ultimate goal from the Muslim point of view; but that we did not intend to create chaos by turning it over to him more quickly than was possible; nor was it for us to tell the Indians exactly how to set it up. In the meanwhile, it was to be hoped that it would be possible to strengthen the centre by the inclusion of Mr. Jinnah in the Government, by providing in the absence of "parity" such safeguards as might be agreeable to the Muslims and to make use of Mr. Gandhi to put through a solution with the aim and object eventually of creating a truncated Pakistan.

HIS EXCELLENCY THE VICEROY said that he did not believe that Mr. Jinnah had thought of the most elementary mechanics whereby Pakistan was to be run. All the Indian leaders whom he had met were very ignorant of the mechanics of administration and under-estimated the difficulties. They were likely to devise a much shorter programme than events would prove it possible to adhere to. Things would take much longer to settle than was anticipated.

HIS EXCELLENCY THE VICEROY stated that he did not believe that Mr. Jinnah was opposed to the idea of an Interim Government working under a British Viceroy. Perhaps the Muslims could be given some form of parity in the Interim Government. The British might lay down the broad principles on which the transfer of power was to take place, together with a series of conditions and a programme to work to.

MR. ABELL said that it was not in his opinion likely that Congress would agree to the Muslim League being given parity in the Interim Government. There was no justification on census figures for such parity. Congress had never agreed to it and he thought they never would.

LORD ISMAY suggested that a Committee might be established from members of the Interim Government to consider the practical working of the ultimate solution. There might be parity in this Committee, which would sit under the Chairmanship of the Viceroy. Mr. Jinnah might be induced to co-operate on the condition that it would be the first object of a new Government to set up such a Committee. LORD ISMAY suggested that His Excellency might tell Mr. Jinnah that he wanted him in the Government because, as things stood, he could only get his (Mr. Jinnah's) views at second hand; that he himself would be prepared to hear Mr. Jinnah in a continuous series of Committee conferences; H.E. might add that this seemed to him by far the best chance of getting through the Cabinet Mission's plan in its entirety.

HIS EXCELLENCY THE VICEROY gave his view that, although Mr. Jinnah might be induced to start work on such a basis, he would not in the end agree to the Cabinet Mission's plan as the final solution. He foresaw that eventually a truncated Pakistan would emerge but while he (His Excellency) remained in India, he felt sure that Mr. Jinnah would accept any Central Government of which he was the head.

MR. ABELL expressed doubt as to whether Mr. Jinnah would in fact agree

¹ See No. 84.

to join the Central Government on such terms.

SIR ERIC MIEVILLE suggested that, whether or not Mr. Jinnah joined the Government, a small committee consisting of two Congress representatives, two Muslims, one Sikh and perhaps the Nawab of Bhopal should be set up under the Viceroy to hammer out the final plan.

HIS EXCELLENCY THE VICEROY said that he was opposed to any suggestion which would involve his throwing away his present strong position whereby he alone would make the decision. His idea was that he should tell the Indian leaders of his decision—there would be no written agreement nor would he ask for their acceptance. But they would have to be made to believe in the impartiality, competence and firmness of the decision. He was in the position of a testator on behalf of His Majesty's Government. His ideas at the present were that, to attain the earliest possible transfer of power, India should be offered Commonwealth status as soon as possible. He would remain as constitutional head of the Government until June 1948. The British would remain at the beck and call of India for any assistance required during the period for which India chose to remain a member of the Commonwealth. After June 1948 it would be up to the Indian leaders to decide whether to break up the Central Government or not. It would be their full responsibility. In this way he believed that honour would be satisfied. This course ought to put an end to the present chaos and bloodshed.

LORD ISMAY asked whether His Excellency intended to obtain the covering sanction of His Majesty's Government before he told Indian leaders of his decision. He pointed out that His Excellency's directive was to recommend the plan to H.M.G. He also said that he was much concerned over the question of the early introduction of Dominion or Commonwealth status. If power was transferred before June 1948 what would happen to the British Army in India— and indeed to the Indian Army with British officers owing allegiance to the King? He advised that it would be wisest to avoid any premature grant of Dominion status.

SIR ERIC MIEVILLE pointed out that, if Dominion status was granted in, say, June 1947, the Viceroy would remain in an advisory capacity only. If the Indian Government did not wish to take his advice there was no necessity for them to do so. The Viceroy would not attend meetings of the Cabinet. He would have no powers of any sort.

HIS EXCELLENCY THE VICEROY said that he fully understood these objections to the grant of Dominion status as such. Some formula whereby powers would be reserved would have to be devised. He was still nebulous in his own mind as to the details of the outline which he had propounded. There was only one new element in this outline and that was that a decision in principle should be taken right away and the Indians themselves should be left to work it out in detail.

LORD ISMAY said that he had received two letters[2] in the last two days from Mr. Gandhi who referred to the preparation of a "draft agreement" between himself and the Viceroy. LORD ISMAY said that it was important to get out of Mr. Gandhi's mind any idea that the note which he had prepared giving the outline of Mr. Gandhi's scheme in any way constituted a preparation for a draft agreement. Possibly he had mentioned his scheme to Pandit Nehru who may have expressed disagreement with it?

HIS EXCELLENCY THE VICEROY said that Mr. Gandhi should be reminded that he (His Excellency) had always insisted that it would be necessary to talk over Mr. Gandhi's scheme with Pandit Nehru. Before taking any such steps he must first be convinced that Pandit Nehru agreed with it.

LORD ISMAY read out the draft of a letter to be sent by the Viceroy to Mr. Gandhi in reply.[3] HIS EXCELLENCY THE VICEROY generally approved this draft subject to minor amendments.

HIS EXCELLENCY THE VICEROY:—

(i) directed the senior members of his staff to think over the outline plan which he had expounded above;

(ii) invited C.V.S. to re-draft and render to him the letter which he was to send to Mr. Gandhi.

[2] Nos. 83 and 86.   [3] See No. 88 for the letter as sent.

88

Rear-Admiral Viscount Mountbatten of Burma to Mr Gandhi

*Mountbatten Papers. Official Correspondence Files: Interim
Government of India, Part 1*

7 April 1947

Ismay has shown me your letter to him of 6th April,[1] and we both are most upset to think that any act, or omission, on our part should in any way increase the great burden you are bearing. I therefore think it right to send you the following personal explanation.

As we were parting last Friday afternoon, I said that your plan had many attractions for me and I asked you if you would be so good as to explain it to Ismay, who had not been present when you first propounded it. On your agreeing to do so, I asked Ismay to make a note of its salient features, and I authorised him to talk it over in confidence with the Reforms Commissioner. I am extremely sorry if by these observations I gave you the impression that I wished your plan reduced to the terms of a formal agreement.

[1] No. 86.

As I explained to you during the many talks that we have enjoyed, my aim has been and is to keep a perfectly open mind until I have had the advantages of discussions with important Indian political leaders with the object of seeking an agreement between all parties so that peace can be restored in the country and an acceptable basis for the transfer of power be worked out. When these preliminary conversations have been completed, I shall then have to make up my mind as to what I am going to recommend to His Majesty's Government and, before I do so, I shall most certainly take advantage of your kind offer of further discussion with you.

89

Mr Gandhi to Rear-Admiral Viscount Mountbatten of Burma

Mountbatten Papers. Papers of Special Interest, File (2) of 1947

BHANGI COLONY, READING ROAD, NEW DELHI,
7 April 1947

Dear Friend,

I have pressing letters from friends in the Punjab asking me to go there, even if for a few days. Pandit Nehru agrees. Nevertheless I would like you to guide me too.

Then Noakhali calls. If the wires received by me during the last two days are to be relied upon, there is increasing lawlessness in Noakhali. Attempts at roasting people alive have been traced twice, and looting etc. is going on. You will see my public statement in the Press.[1]

This outbreak of violence is not a mere detail. If it cannot be dealt with now, it won't be fourteen month hence.

Yours sincerely,
M. K. GANDHI

[1] The *Statesman* of 7 April 1947 reported remarks made by Mr Gandhi at his prayer meeting on 5 April in the course of which he reminded his audience of the folly of looking upon one religion as better than the other. He said he was sure that recent happenings were due to the atmosphere of hate that pervaded the land and he called on his audience to join him in fasting during a 'National Week' to begin the following day.

90

Rear-Admiral Viscount Mountbatten of Burma to Mr Gandhi

Mountbatten Papers. Papers of Special Interest, File (2) of 1947

7 *April 1947*

Dear Mr Gandhi,

Many thanks for your letter of today.[1] I find it difficult to advise you. Though the root causes of the disturbances in the Punjab still exist there has been a considerable measure of success in dealing with immediate disturbances, and I doubt whether you ought to exhaust yourself by undertaking any tour in the Punjab at this time of the year.

I quite agree that these outbreaks of violence are not a mere detail. What we have to secure is a settlement between the parties at the centre and, if possible, a combined front against violence. It is the effort to find a solution which will occupy all my efforts in the near future, and I know I can rely on help from you wherever you may be.

I enjoyed meeting you so much and found all you had to say of the greatest interest.

Yours sincerely,
MOUNTBATTEN OF BURMA

[1] No. 89.

91

Rear-Admiral Viscount Mountbatten of Burma to Lord Pethick-Lawrence

Telegram, R/1/30/40: f 58

SECRET 7 *April 1947, 4 pm*

No. 751–P. Reference my telegrams 412–P March 5th[1] and 550–P March 18th.[2]

[1] Vol. IX, No. 486.   [2] Vol. IX, No. 541.

2. You will have seen text of Resolution passed by General Conference of Rulers at Bombay on April 2nd.[3]

3. At meeting on April 1st Standing Committee recommended strict adherence to Cabinet Mission Plan involving participation of States representatives in Constituent Assembly only at final stage when Assembly meets to settle Union constitution. This recommendation was strongly opposed by representatives of certain States which have already declared intention of joining Constituent Assembly as soon as possible. To preserve appearance of unity among States Chancellor secured unanimous assent of General Conference of Rulers to formula that acceptance by Constituent Assembly of understandings reached in earlier negotiations must precede "participation of the representatives of such States as may decide to do so in the work of the Constituent Assembly at the appropriate stage".

4. Omission to define meaning of words "appropriate stage" leaves unresolved fundamental difference between States. Consequences of this difference will immediately become apparent if Constituent Assembly endorses the "understandings" said to have been arrived at between the two negotiating Committees. These understandings, it will be recalled, were not explicit, and Constituent Assembly was not in any way committed (para. 4 of my telegram 272–P February 11th).[4] The next move now appears to lie with the Constituent Assembly.

[3] This Resolution ratified the general understanding reached between the States' Negotiating Committee and the corresponding Committee of the Constituent Assembly at their meetings on 8 and 9 February and 1 and 2 March 1947 subject 'to the acceptance of the aforesaid understanding by the Constituent Assembly provided that this acceptance must precede the participation of the representatives of such States as may decide to do so in the work of the Constituent Assembly at the appropriate stage'.

The Resolution also noted with approval the confirmation in the Statement of 20 February 1947 that Paramountcy would cease at the end of the interim period and it authorised the Chancellor and Standing Committee of the Chamber of Princes to conduct negotiations with the Crown Representative and Interim Government subject to certain provisos. R/1/30/40.

[4] Vol. IX, No. 375.

92

Record of Interview between Rear-Admiral Viscount Mountbatten of Burma and Mr Jinnah

Mountbatten Papers. Viceroy's Interview No. 38

TOP SECRET   7 April 1947

The meeting lasted from 4 to 6.30 p.m.

I introduced Mr. Jinnah to Lord Ismay.

Mr. Jinnah continued to give me the background of the negotiations with Mr. Gandhi and the Cabinet Mission. I tried by every means to bring him up to the point of saying that he would accept the Cabinet Mission plan and enter the Constituent Assembly.

I warned him that Congress had made an unsatisfied request that the Muslim League should either enter the Constituent Assembly or be expelled from the Interim Government, and I told him that Lord Wavell had indicated that he had only offered him seats in the Interim Government on the understanding that he would enter the Constituent Assembly.

He hotly denied the latter, and said that if I searched the files I would find that he had carefully preserved his position in this matter, and he had nothing to add to what was stated in the letters.

He pointed out at great length that it was quite valueless entering the Constituent Assembly or even trying to go back to the Cabinet Mission plan, since the whole bases of the Cabinet Mission plan were that it had to be worked in a spirit of co-operation and mutual trust. In May 1946 there had been some prospect that this atmosphere could be created. Now, nearly a year later, the atmosphere so far from improving had taken a serious turn for the worse, and it was clear that in no circumstances did Congress intend to work the Plan either in accordance with the spirit or the letter.

He said that India had now passed beyond the stage at which any such compromise solution could possibly work; and he categorically called upon me to hand over power as soon as possible, preferably Province by Province, and let the Provinces themselves choose how they formed into groups. Alternatively, if I preferred it, I could name the groups myself.

On the question of defence he said he had come to the conclusion that the Defence forces must be separated and that Pakistan and Hindustan must be responsible separately for their own defence. On no other basis would it be possible to have any form of central organization on terms of parity.

I pointed out that in discussing his proposals I was very far from agreeing with him, but I naturally had to consider every proposal put to me.

I said that even if his proposals proved to be the correct solution, they could only be satisfactorily implemented if I had the necessary time at my disposal for each step to be satisfactorily carried out.

I drew his attention to Brigadier Cariappa's recent statement, supported by four or five other senior Indian officers, that it would be a minimum of five years before the present Indian Army could expect to be efficient and stand on its own legs, without the help of British officers.

If this period were cut down to June 1948 and on top of that we were asked to perform the miracle of cutting the Army into half, did he seriously consider that this could be implemented by the time I had to leave in June 1948?

He smiled in a cryptic way and said "How then do you propose to leave in June 1948; is it then your intention to turn this country over to chaos and bloodshed and civil war?"

To this I replied that there was one thing of which I was quite certain, and that was that I was going in June 1948, and withdrawing all British personnel unless by some miraculous event all Indian parties united together to beg us not to go in the interests of the Indian people as a whole. Such a request I would be prepared to consider laying before His Majesty's Government, though I could not guarantee what their answer would be.

On the conclusion of the interview I introduced him to Mr. Campbell-Johnson.

93

Rear-Admiral Viscount Mountbatten of Burma to Lord Pethick-Lawrence

Telegram, L/PO/10/18: f 300

PRIVATE   *7 April 1947*

756–S. At our last talk we agreed that in certain circumstances I should pass messages through you to Prime Minister. In view of his having authorised decisions on future participation of Indians at College and Conferences in U.K. without any reference to me, I would be grateful if you would pass the following message to him. *Begins:* I am sorry to add to your burdens, but you told me that I might communicate direct with you whenever I wished.

2. I have received a telegram from Secretary of State for India, No. 43 of April 4th,[1] telling me that an official notification has *already* been sent to Government of India to the effect that (a) the invitation to India to become a member of Commonwealth Advisory Committee has been withdrawn: and (b) no further invitations are to be extended to Indian students at Imperial Defence College, etc.

3. Frankly, I am astonished that a telegram on a question of high policy

like this should have been despatched without my having been consulted or even informed in advance. I do not suggest that I could have influenced decision, and I am relieved to have C.-in-C.'s assurance that little harm is likely to be done.[2] But prior notification would at least have enabled me to advise, in the light of conditions this end, as to timing and form of communication. It would also have enabled me to pave the way for its receipt. Its arrival in the middle of Gurkha negotiations is unlikely to help matters.

4. I most earnestly beg that you will issue specific instructions that I am to be consulted on matters of this kind in future. *Ends.*

[1] No. 71.   [2] See No. 80.

94

Mr Liaquat Ali Khan to Rear-Admiral Viscount Mountbatten of Burma

L/P&J/10/79: ff 498–9

P.S.F. 2093/47   NEW DELHI, *7 April 1947*

Dear Lord Mountbatten,

During my last interview with you I touched briefly on the inadequate representation of Muslims in the Armed Forces. I am writing now to state my views more fully and to raise a question vitally affecting the future of the country.

2. The Indian Armed Forces (Army, Navy and Air Force) are now in the process of reorganisation and nationalisation. The object of reorganisation is to produce a wholly Indian balanced force of all arms and services. The object of nationalisation is to replace all British officers and men in the Indian Armed Forces by Indians as soon as possible and in any case before June 1948. Nationalisation affects mainly the officer cadre. Selection of Indian officers for the appointments of Commanders-in-Chief of the Army, Navy and Air Force, Army Commanders, Principal Staff Officers and other senior posts in all three Services is, I understand, already in hand under the control of the Defence Member.

3. Both these processes—reorganisation and nationalisation—are proceeding on the basis of a United India, having a single Army, Navy and Air Force. The fundamental constitutional issue of a United or Divided India is thus being prejudiced on a most vital point to the grave detriment of the Muslims. Because of the overwhelming preponderance of Hindus in the officer cadre and particularly in the senior ranks, the Indian Armed Forces organised as a single force for the whole of India will necessarily fall under the complete

control of non-Muslims. The proportion of Muslims in the Other Ranks of the Army is being brought down from the pre-war ratio of 40% to less than 30% and no steps are being taken to see that they are represented in each arm and service. Their representation in the Air Force (officers and men), and in the Navy (officers) is in the neighbourhood of 15% and in the technical services of the Army is much lower. Such strength as they have is dispersed all over and not organised into Muslim units. Indeed there are no wholly Muslim units even in Infantry, although there are a number of wholly Hindu units.

4. The division of India implies the division of the Armed Forces to serve Pakistan and Hindustan. Without its own Armed Force Pakistan would be like a house of cards. But a division of the Armed Forces is a delicate and difficult operation which cannot be carried out in a day. The present stage when the Armed Forces are in the process of reorganisation and have not taken final shape is the really critical stage. Once this process is completed, the pattern will be set and it will require a major upheaval again to reorganise them on a different pattern so as to produce two separate balanced forces. Other obstacles apart, time alone will not permit this second operation before June 1948. It is imperative, therefore, that the Armed Forces should now be reorganised in such a manner that they can be readily split up at the proper time. It is also essential to secure the adequate representation of Muslim officers and men in each branch of the Army, Navy and Air Force by conversion of units and training of personnel. There would then be a self-contained and balanced force to serve Pakistan and another to serve Hindustan and these two forces would be held together in a single command till the constitutional issue is decided.

5. Unless this is done, the Armed Forces which are the ultimate sanction and support for any State will become predominantly Hindu in character and will be completely under the control of the Hindus.

6. A decision on this fundamental question is immediately necessary before any steps in the reorganisation and nationalisation of the Armed Forces are taken. It affects so vitally the future constitution of the country that the execution of the decision cannot, for obvious reasons, be entrusted to a Member belonging or affiliated to one political party. I suggest therefore that in the implementation of the proposal in paragraph 4 above the Commander-in-Chief should be directly responsible to you and not to the Defence Member.

Yours sincerely,
LIAQUAT ALI KHAN

95

Mr Liaquat Ali Khan to Rear-Admiral Viscount Mountbatten of Burma

Mountbatten Papers. Official Correspondence Files:
Cabinet (Indian)

NEW DELHI, *7 April 1947*

Dear Lord Mountbatten,

You asked me for my proposals regarding appointments which are at present made with the approval of the Governor General. My proposal is that the present procedure under which the Member in charge of the Department concerned with the appointment makes recommendation to the Governor General should continue. The recommendation of the Member is made after reference to the Establishment Committee or the Selection Board as the case may be, thus ensuring consideration of the case from the point of view of the overall manpower position in the Government of India and of the suitability of the various officers for the particular post which is to be filled.

The proposal to have a Committee of the Cabinet, consisting of Pandit Nehru or Sardar Patel, Dr Matthai and myself to deal with such appointments is impracticable in the present circumstances. All appointments which would be referred to such a Committee are bound to be discussed in the context of differences between the Congress and the Muslim League parties in the Government with the result that there would always be two votes against one. Bringing the matter before the whole Cabinet, thereafter, would be fruitless for the same reason and if references were to be made to the Governor General in cases of difference of opinion the Governor General would find it embarrassing to deal with them.

I need hardly emphasise how important it is from the point of view of sound administration that the officers who have to advise upon and implement policies are suitable for the job that they have to perform and are acceptable to the Member under whom they have to work. On both these points it is the Member in charge of the Department who is best qualified to decide. The working of a Department could be made impossible by forcing upon it officers who would not be suited for the work intended for them. The same officers would perhaps do well elsewhere.

Yours sincerely,

LIAQUAT ALI KHAN

96

Record of Interview between Rear-Admiral Viscount Mountbatten of Burma and Pandit Nehru

Mountbatten Papers. Viceroy's Interview No. 39

TOP SECRET   *8 April 1947*

The meeting lasted from 11 a.m. to 1 p.m.

Lord Ismay showed him his correspondence with Mr Gandhi and explained the present position about the Gandhi plan.[1] I asked Pandit Nehru to convey to Mr Gandhi a message explaining that I could not yet say anything further about the Plan since I was still busy getting background information.

We then discussed with Pandit Nehru what his solution would be for the transfer of power. He thought that it would not be right to impose any form of constitutional conditions on any community that had a majority in any specific area. Thus, if we were to demit Province by Province, he felt they should have the right to decide whether to join a Hindustan Group, a Pakistan Group, or possibly even remain completely independent. He added that of course before such a thing were done the Punjab and Bengal would have to be split into separate Provinces.

In reply to a question about how to obtain the real views of the people of the N.W.F.P. on which Group they wished to join he suggested that a fresh election should be held after a statement had been made.

The whole thing revolved round having a strong Centre, certainly to begin with, and for that reason Pandit Nehru would favour making a statement soon and transferring power to Provinces while there was still time for me to be in charge at the Centre to help in the early stages of negotiations at the Centre.

He agreed that a formula would have to be found which would prevent the Congress Party from being able to impose their will upon the Army by majority vote, if the Army were kept as a single Service under the Centre.

We also discussed the question of the States, and came to the provisional conclusion that Pakistan should be encouraged to set up their own Constituent Assembly, and the States should choose into which Constituent Assembly they would come.

Lord Ismay is working out further details of the result of these proposals.

After Lord Ismay left, we discussed the question of the Appointments Committee. I read to him the letter dated .... from Liaquat Ali Khan,[2] and we agreed on the form of answer which I gave to Mr Abell, who joined the meeting for a short period.

In particular, Pandit Nehru would like me to find out from the Governor-General and Governor in Malaya (Mr Malcolm Macdonald and Sir Edward

Gent) whether the appointment of Mr J Thivye to be the Agent of the Government of India in Malaya would be acceptable to them. I gather he is quite popular out there and knows a lot about Labour. But in view of the fact that he was closely associated with the Indian Independence League, there might be some local objections which would have to be cleared.

He also discussed the appointment in Ceylon, and said he would be putting up a new proposal about this shortly.

Nehru thought that the only way the Gandhi plan could be made use of was by offering the premiership of the Interim Government to Jinnah, with the object of strengthening the central authority until the handing over of power in June 1948.

Addition to note on Interview with Pandit Nehru

I asked Pandit Nehru whether the Congress High Command would be prepared to issue an appeal for the cessation of all hostilities or provocative acts, in fact for a truce until I had given my decision. He said that he was sure there would be no difficulty to get them to agree to this. I said I would mention the matter also to Mr Jinnah.

[1] See Nos. 83, 85, 86 and 88.   [2] No. 95.

97

Mr Gandhi to Rear-Admiral Viscount Mountbatten of Burma

Mountbatten Papers. Official Correspondence Files: Interim Government of India, Part 1

I AURANGZEB ROAD, NEW DELHI,
8 April 1947

Dear Friend,

Many thanks for your two letters of the 7th inst.

As to the first,[1] I am glad that as I read it, whatever misunderstanding, if there was any, was of no consequence.

As to the second letter,[2] the weather would not stand in the way of my going to the Punjab. I must ask the voice within for the final guidance. If I do go, I shall let you know the date.

Of course, you can rely upon my help no matter wherever I happen to be at the time.

Yours sincerely,
M. K. GANDHI

[1] No. 88.   [2] No. 90.

98

Rear-Admiral Viscount Mountbatten of Burma to Sir H. Dow (Bihar) (Extract)

R/3/1/148: f 45

No. 40/6.   *8 April 1947*

2. You will have seen my telegram No. 674–S dated 1st April,[1] from which
you will see that I have been doing my best to discourage an enquiry, but I
must report that I had no luck with Mr Gandhi, who was most insistent that
an enquiry was necessary to re-establish confidence. He pointed out that this
was really a matter for the the provincial governments concerned, and begged
me not to interfere. I told him I had already expressed my views against the
need for such an enquiry, as this conversation[2] took place just about the time
the telegram was being despatched.

[1] No. 51.   [2] No. 47.

99

Mr Fry to Mr Hopkinson[1]

L/P&S/12/4210: f 14

TOP SECRET   NEW DELHI, *8 April 1947*
No. F.7–NEF/46
Sir,

I am directed to refer to the correspondence resting with your letter
No. 4(4)–P/47, of the 5th February 1947,[2] and to say that the Government of
India have now reviewed their attitude towards the political relationship between China, Tibet and India. As a result, it has been decided to adopt for the
present the following line of policy, which I am to request you to make known
to the Mission in Lhasa for their guidance.

2. The conditions in which India's well-being may be assured and the full
evolution be achieved of her inherent capacity to emerge as a potent but
benevolent force in world affairs—particularly in Asia—demand not merely
the development of internal unity and strength but also the maintenance of
friendly relations with her neighbours. To prejudice her relations with so
important a Power as China by aggressive support of unqualified Tibetan independence (for which, whatever may have been the situation earlier, there has
in the past year or two been little positive sign of ardour in Lhasa) is therefore
a policy with few attractions. It follows that while the Government of India

are glad to recognise and wish to see Tibetan autonomy maintained, they are not prepared to do more than encourage this in a friendly manner and are certainly not disposed to take any initiative which might bring India into conflict with China on this issue. The attitude which they propose to adopt may best be described as that of a benevolent spectator, ready at all times—should opportunity occur—to use their good offices to further a mutually satisfactory settlement between China and Tibet. It should be added, recollecting in particular the participation of the Tibetan Goodwill Mission in the recent session of the Chinese National Assembly, that the Government of India would not for a moment consider objection to or interference with any arrangement that Tibet might come to directly with China.

3. In regard to the Indo-Tibetan boundary, the Government of India stand by the McMahon Line and will not tolerate incursions into India such as that which recently occurred in the Siang valley. They would however at all times be prepared to discuss in a friendly way with China and Tibet any rectification of the frontier that might be urged on reasonable grounds by any of the parties to the abortive Simla Conference of 1914.

> I have the honour to be,
> Sir,
> Your most obedient servant,
> L. A. C. FRY
> Deputy Secretary to the
> Government of India

¹ Political Officer in Sikkim.   ² Not on L/P &S/12/4210.

100

Rear-Admiral Viscount Mountbatten of Burma to Mr Liaquat Ali Khan

Mountbatten Papers. Official Correspondence Files: Cabinet (Indian)

8 April 1947

Dear Mr Liaquat Ali Khan,

Thank you for your letter of the 7th April¹ about appointments.

It seems to me that it would be better from every point of view to have important appointments considered by a Committee of the Cabinet. Even from the Party angle I do not see that the Muslim League gains by allowing all external appointments to be settled by the Hon. Member, External Affairs in consultation with me.

I believe that if Committees are set up they will work by the usual process of

¹ No. 95.

agreement and compromise, and I have already said in Cabinet there is nothing to prevent a Member who finds himself in a minority in a Committee from forcing the issue, in the last resort, to the whole Cabinet, though I should deprecate this happening often.

There are several important selections which have to be made soon and I think we should set up an Appointments Committee without further delay. Unless you tell me you have any further points you wish to take up privately I will raise this at tomorrow's Cabinet.

In regard to the appointment of the High Commissioner in London, I enclose a copy of a letter[2] I have sent to the Commerce Member.

Yours sincerely,
MOUNTBATTEN OF BURMA

[2] This letter is not on the file.

IOI

Record of Interview between Rear-Admiral Viscount Mountbatten of Burma and Mr Jinnah

Mountbatten Papers. Viceroy's Interview No. 41

TOP SECRET   *8 April 1947*

The meeting lasted from 6 to 8 p.m.

I asked Mr. Jinnah whether he would be willing to join with the other high commands in issuing an appeal for no further provocative acts which could lead to bloodshed. He asked me if I had seen in the newspapers an account of his speech in Bombay.[1] I admitted I had, and acknowledged that he had already appealed for a truce; but I pointed out that a unilateral appeal appeared to me to be almost valueless, since the other side could always force bloodshed by their actions. He agreed and said that if I wished him to join in an appeal for a truce against provocative action and bloodshed, he would be prepared to do so. (As both Pandit Nehru and Sardar Baldev Singh had told me that their own high commands would be prepared to do the same, this is a hopeful sign.)

Mr. Jinnah explained the origin of "Direct action", and said that until he had resorted to "direct action" the League position was becoming more and more insecure, but he denied that they had ever instigated bloodshed anywhere, though it could perhaps be said that they had created the situation in which Congress had started bloodshed (not Mr. Jinnah's exact words, but he said something to that general effect).

I told Mr. Jinnah that I was going to make my decision on what to recommend to H.M.G. without necessarily obtaining the agreement of the major parties, but merely after hearing their views. In this respect my approach was different from that of the Cabinet Mission, since it would be for the major parties to try and get round me to make a decision which would suit them, rather than for me to try and get them to come to some agreement. He quite saw the point. I also reiterated that come what might, I would leave India in June 1948 unless a simultaneous invitation from all parties in India to stay were forthcoming, and even then I could only transmit such an invitation to H.M.G. without however knowing whether they would be prepared to agree. In other words he must count on British officials being out of India by June 1948. He said it had been a shock, but he quite understood the position.

I then asked him what, if he were in my place, his solution would be; and he repeated once more the demand for Pakistan, together with a splitting of the Defence Forces.

I tried once more to bring him back to the Cabinet Mission plan, but he was absolutely adamant that it was useless to resurrect a plan which could only have been tried if the utmost goodwill had prevailed between all parties in 1946, and which now was foredoomed to failure.

I invited Mr. Jinnah to put forward his arguments for partition. He recited the classic ones.

I then pointed out that his remarks applied also to the partition of the Punjab and Bengal, and that by sheer logic if I accepted his arguments in the case of India as a whole, I had also to apply them in the case of these two Provinces.

Whilst admitting my logic, he expressed himself most upset at my trying to give him a "moth eaten" Pakistan. He said that this demand for partitioning the Punjab and Bengal was a bluff on the part of Congress to try and frighten him off Pakistan. He was not to be frightened off so easily; and he would be sorry if I were taken in by the Congress bluff.

I replied "I would not be taken in; because if I agreed to such partition, it would be on your able advocacy; but I could not of course allow your theories to stop short at the Provinces."

He was most distressed, and said that it would greatly weaken his Pakistan, and appealed to me not to destroy the unity of Bengal and the Punjab, which had national characteristics in common: common history, common ways of life; and where the Hindus have stronger feelings as Bengalis or Punjabis than they have as members of the Congress.

I said I was impressed by his arguments; and was therefore beginning to

---

[1] In a speech in Bombay on 27 March 1947 Mr Jinnah appealed for a truce on the basis of Pakistan, the elimination of the British in India and India for Indians. 'I am fighting for Pakistan', Mr Jinnah said, 'which means I am fighting for the freedom of India. . . . I appeal to Muslims and Hindus and others to examine the position. Do not be carried away by dreams. Let us be practical. Let us agree to divide. . . .'

revise my ideas about any partition anywhere in India; since any argument that he produced for not agreeing to partition within the Punjab and Bengal applied with even greater force to India as a whole. For if he was to insist on the partition of India, he would be breaking up a great sub-continent of numerous nations, which *could* live together in peace and harmony; who could, united, play a great role in the world; but who, divided, would not even rank as a second-class Power. The more so since he evidently intended to destroy even the mere vestiges that remained of the Indian Army, after the passing of this morning's budget proposals for the armed forces and the likelihood of the withdrawal of all British officers by June 1948.

I am afraid I drove the old gentleman quite mad, because whichever way his argument went I always pursued it to a stage beyond which he did not wish it to go.

As regards the splitting of the Defence Forces, I referred to Mr. Liaquat Ali Khan's letter,[2] and I told him that I entirely saw the justice of his claim to split the armed forces of India, and he would be at liberty to do so after I had ceased to be responsible for law and order in India. Furthermore, after I had made my decision and H.M.G. had approved it, if this decision should be in favour of partition I would be prepared to set up committees forthwith to work out how the defence forces could be split up, and also how in the meanwhile a central authority controlling the Army could itself be controlled in such a manner that the majority could not use it against the minority in any way whatsoever.

[2] No. 94.

102

Pandit Nehru to Rear-Admiral Viscount Mountbatten of Burma

R/3/1/142: f 73

17 YORK ROAD, NEW DELHI,
9 April 1947

Dear Lord Mountbatten,

As you know I am deeply interested in the future of the Indian States, more specially from the point of view of the people of the States. Unfortunately the Political Department works in secret and no one knows what it does. Even the Members of the Interim Government remain in ignorance of the activities of the Political Department although these activities are often of vital significance to the future of India. My own experience has been that representatives of the Political Department encourage reaction in the States and frown upon progressive tendencies. Because of these activities, the gap between what is called British India and the Indian States widens.

2. During the past few months I have often addressed Lord Wavell about the Political Department and have requested him for information. Sometimes some little information has been supplied; but this has seldom been adequate. I have addressed him particularly in regard to Bastar State. This State is large in area but sparse in population. It is full of very valuable mineral deposits. At present the Ruler is a minor and the Government is completely controlled by the Political Department. For some time past there have been rumours of all manner of concessions to Hyderabad State in Bastar. These include mining rights and control over railway lines. In effect Bastar becomes an economic vassal of Hyderabad. Hyderabad itself is one of the most backward and feudal States in India and it is odd that it should be entrusted with the development of Bastar. The Central Provinces Government, which adjoins Bastar, will be affected by any such concessions to Hyderabad. It seems particularly un- fortunate that vital agreements should be entered into by the Political Depart- ment when the Ruler of the State is a minor. I beg of you to prevent any such developments which might have serious consequences. At a time when the whole future of India, including the States, is being fashioned any binding agreements of this type may well come in the way of other arrangements. I understand that some steps are contemplated also in regard to Berar and that this Province will be handed over to Hyderabad State. How far this is true I do not know. But if there is any truth in this statement, it will be bitterly resented by the people of Berar.

3. My difficulty is that we function completely in the dark in regard to these very important developments affecting the States. I doubt if there is any one in India, whether among the Rulers of the States or the people of the States, who has any faith in the present set-up of the Political Department. Innumerable complaints reach me and there is no way to find out the truth. I suggest that some arrangement should be made so that far greater publicity could be given to all activities connected with the States, and for this purpose the present set-up should be changed.

Yours sincerely,

JAWAHARLAL NEHRU

103

Lord Pethick-Lawrence to Rear-Admiral Viscount Mountbatten of Burma

Telegram, L/S &G/7/914: f 356

MOST IMMEDIATE   *9 April 1947*
PRIVATE

45. I gather from your telegram 742–S[1] that you have not so far informed your Cabinet of our decision to accept their proposal that we should not pay compensation to Indians. As a result of attempts to draft necessary announcements I am impressed by great if not insuperable difficulties of justifying proposed departure from June 1945 pledge. Prime Minister has therefore agreed that matter should be reconsidered by Ministers as a matter of urgency and that meanwhile you should be asked not to report our decision to members of your Cabinet. I will of course telegraph again as soon as I possibly can.

[1] In tel. 742–S of 5 April Lord Mountbatten had expressed unwillingness to refer to the Indian Cabinet further points of detail which Lord Pethick-Lawrence had raised, saying that he would rather wait until he put the draft of the proposed announcement on compensation to his colleagues. L/S&G/7/914: f 364.

104

Mr Attlee to Rear-Admiral Viscount Mountbatten of Burma (via India Office)

Telegram, L/PO/10/18: f 301

PRIVATE   *9 April 1947*
No. 46. Following personal from Prime Minister.

Your telegram No. 756–S, dated 7th April.[1]

I am sorry that you were not informed of these decisions in advance. I will see that this is done in future.

I was much interested in your report[2] of your first week's work, which is very encouraging. Your success over the I.N.A. and Service Pensions has been most gratifying.

[1] No. 93.   [2] No. 59.

105

Record of Interview between Rear-Admiral Viscount Mountbatten of Burma and Mr Jinnah

Mountbatten Papers. Viceroy's Interview No. 42

TOP SECRET   *9 April 1947*

The meeting lasted from 4 to 5.30 p.m.

I invited him to give me his views on the way I should give my decision, together with his reasons. He did so at some length, pointing out that no other solution except full Pakistan could possibly bring peace to India, since anything less would be sure to produce further strife and bloodshed. He even promised peace on the Frontier, where he said the tribes would beyond any question accept Pakistan with great relief. He gave as an example the Islamia College, which though 15 miles from Peshawar, in the jungle, and full of valuables and so, one would have thought, a natural target for tribal raiders, had never been attacked in 30 years, simply because it was a Muslim college.

He said that the "Begin all and end all" of Pakistan was to have their own army, and nothing short of this could possibly satisfy them.

I told him that I had insufficient expert knowledge to say how long would be required to implement any decision for a partition of the armed forces; but pointed out that the complete nationalisation of the three Services by June 1948 would so greatly weaken them that I did not see how they could possibly stand partition on top of nationalisation. He agreed he also was no expert and said that the views of experts would be required as to when partition could be implemented in the Services. I further pointed out that I remained statutorily responsible for law and order in India until June 1948, and that I had absolutely no intention of taking any steps that would weaken the efficiency or even the morale of the Army during that period.

I suggested that the difficulty could be overcome (if indeed I were finally to decide on some form of partition) by setting up a committee of experts to work out the steps that were needed, together with a time-table for carrying them out, and that in the meanwhile the Indian Army, Navy and Air Force should remain under the control of some central body which should be presided over by me while I was here, and subsequently would have to be so constituted that no single party could control the army and use it to impose their will on other parties.

To all of this he agreed as being reasonable. Once more he appealed to me not to give him a moth-eaten Pakistan; and once more I pointed out that although I had not made up my mind in any way whether to agree to partition or not, I simply could not visualise being so inconsistent as to agree to the partition of India without also agreeing to partition within any Provinces in which the same problem arose. He was most distressed at the way my mind was working.

I told him that I regarded it as a very great tragedy that he should be trying to force me to give up the idea of a united India. I painted a picture of the greatness that India could achieve—four hundred million people of different races and creeds, all bound together by a central Union Government, with all the economic strength that would accrue to them from increased industrialisation, playing a great part in world affairs as the most progressive single entity in the Far East.

I finally said that I found that the present Interim Coalition Government was every day working better and in a more co-operative spirit; and that it was a day-dream of mine to be able to put the Central Government under the Prime Ministership of Mr. Jinnah himself.

He said that nothing would have given him greater pleasure than to have seen such unity, and he entirely agreed that it was indeed tragic that the behaviour of the Hindus had made it impossible for the Muslims to share in this.

Some 35 minutes later, Mr. Jinnah, who had not referred previously to my personal remark about him, suddenly made a reference out of the blue to the fact that I had wanted him to be the Prime Minister. There is no doubt that it had greatly tickled his vanity, and that he had kept turning over the proposition in his mind.

Mr. Gandhi's famous scheme may yet go through on the pure vanity of Mr. Jinnah!

Nevertheless he gives me the impression of a man who has not thought out one single piece of the mechanics of his own great scheme, and he will have the shock of his life when he really has to come down to earth and try and make his vague idealistic proposals work on a concrete basis.

At 5.30 Lord Ismay came in with Cabinet papers which had not previously been circulated, and as the Cabinet was to meet at 6 o'clock I asked Mr. Jinnah to go along with Lord Ismay so that they could reduce to writing Mr. Jinnah's proposals.[1]

[1] The record of Lord Ismay's subsequent discussion with Mr Jinnah is in Mountbatten Papers, Viceroy's Interview No. 43.

106

Rear-Admiral Viscount Mountbatten of Burma to Mr Liaquat Ali Khan

L/P&J/10/79: f 500

No. 38   *9 April 1947*

Dear Mr. Liaquat Ali Khan,

Thank you for your letter, P.S.F. 2093/47, of the 7th April,[1] about the Armed Forces and the inadequate representation of Muslims in them.

I think that part of what you say prejudges an issue which has yet to be decided. The policy that holds the field is the Cabinet Mission's plan and unless that is finally abandoned there can be no question of a complete partition of India.

In any case, so long as I am Viceroy, I consider it my duty to ensure that no steps are taken which will weaken the Indian Army as the ultimate resource on which the country depends for maintaining internal security as well as external defence. I could not agree to splitting up the Army while Parliament is responsible for India.

If any form of partition were decided on I should, of course, be prepared to agree to an investigation as to the need for, and if proved, the method of, implementing a partition of the Armed Forces.

I will speak to the Commander-in-Chief about the points you make about the inadequate number of Muslim Officers in the Armed Forces.

Yours sincerely,

MOUNTBATTEN OF BURMA

P.S. I have just received your letter[2] about the appointments Committee and will therefore not raise it in Cabinet.[3]

[1] No. 94.   [2] No. 95.

[3] Lord Pethick-Lawrence circulated the text of this letter and No. 94 to members of the India and Burma Committee under the reference I.B.(47)48 of 17 April 1947. L/P &J/10/79: f 497.

107

Rear-Admiral Viscount Mountbatten of Burma to Lord Pethick-Lawrence

Mountbatten Papers. Letters to and from the Secretary of State

PRIVATE AND SECRET   *9 April 1947*

Dear Secretary of State,

I am forwarding herewith my second personal report, but have no letter this week from you to answer.

2. As I said in my last letter[1] I am meeting the Residents from the States during the present week, and next week the Governors are coming to Delhi for a conference. Unfortunately Burrows is still on the sick list, but I am glad to say he is making steady progress, and his doctors assure him that a short spell in the hills when he can get there will complete the cure. He is, of course, carrying on with business from Government House, but it is unfortunate at the present time that he is prevented from moving about.

3. The trouble on the Assam border, to which I referred in my last report,[2] now appears less formidable than might have been expected. It seems that the proposal to cross the border into Assam from Bengal is being dropped, and that sabotage and other trouble making in the district will be left to local Muslims. If this turns out to be the case it may be due to the difficulty of financing the Muslims from Bengal, and also the effect of Suhrawardy's influence on local Bengal Muslims. Suhrawardy's replies to Burrows' original approach about this matter were, you will remember, very unsatisfactory, but he may have been able to do privately rather better than he intimated.

4. I was very perturbed to receive your telegram No. 43 of the 4th April[3] about the withdrawal of the invitation to India to become a member of the Commonwealth Advisory Committee on the Defence of the Commonwealth, and that no further invitations should be extended to Indian students at the Imperial Defence College and the joint Services staff colleges. You will of course have seen my reply, No. 756–S of the 7th April,[4] and I hope you will appreciate that in view of the position in which I am placed at present, and the difficult negotiations on which I am engaged, that action such as the Government took without first consulting me has put me in a most awkward position. I do hope that I shall be consulted on all matters of this kind in the future.

5. You will have seen the telegrams from Caroe about the situation in the N.W.F.P. and in Peshawar City.[5] The twenty four hour curfew imposed on Peshawar City and the military action taken seems to have resulted in little if any improvement and the situation still remains very tense. I have referred to Ismay's visit to Caroe, and the possible future course of events, in my report attached.

6. I have been looking at the correspondence about the activities of the British Council in India.[6] Patrick wrote to Abell on the 15th February, forwarding copies of Sir Angus Gillan's report of his visit in January, and in his reply of 28th February Abell gave Lord Wavell's views on the recommendations in the report. My wife and I have discussed the matter since our arrival with Shone, and we consider it most important that there should be plenty of

money for financing the work of the British Council in India. I should be so glad if you could let me know how the matter is progressing.

Yours sincerely,
MOUNTBATTEN OF BURMA

¹ No. 78.   ² No. 59.   ³ No. 71.   ⁴ No. 93.   ⁵ See L/P &J/8/660.
⁶ Papers on this subject are on L/I/1/79.

108

Viceroy's Personal Report No. 2

L/PO/6/123: ff 23–30

TOP SECRET   *9 April 1947*

During this week I have continued my series of individual meetings with members of the Cabinet, leaders of the British community and minorities, and at great length with Mr. Gandhi and Mr. Jinnah.

2. The whole country continues in a dangerously unsettled state, although communal riots and troubles appear less obvious than they did last week. The situation in Bihar and Assam is on the whole slightly better, and Calcutta and Bombay are quieter; but the N.W.F.P. and the Punjab are still most unsettled, and there has been trouble at Gurgaon, within 20 miles of Delhi, which necessitated Jenkins flying down to the area for a day's visit.

3. Ismay is back from his visits to Jenkins and Caroe, and has reported on the situation in the Punjab and the N.W.F.P. Jenkins has no hope of getting out of Section 93 at present, certainly not this month and probably not next. The trouble is that a general election will solve nothing. The League would probably get a majority of up to 5 out of 175 seats, and would then proceed to form a government with a bare Muslim majority, without Sikh or Hindu representation; and then I am told there might be real trouble. The only hope of a peaceful unified Punjab lies in a Union or Coalition Government, but there seems no real hope of this, anyway at present.

4. The only alternative to a Union Government is partition of the Punjab; this is recommended by Congress but could in Jenkins' view probably only be imposed by force, which would require a lot of troops, and spell economic ruin for the Province. I referred in my last report¹ to the Sikhs' preparations for serious civil war, and I am anxious to avoid any chance of hot headed action on their part. On Jenkins' recommendation I have decided to call them into consultation, and have asked Baldev Singh to invite Tara Singh and Gyani Kartar Singh to come and see me in Delhi.

¹ No. 59.

5. In the N.W.F.P. the problem, unlike the Punjab, is not a communal one, the clash being between Congress financed Muslims and the Muslim League. It is complicated by the tribes, who broadly speaking are in sympathy with the League. The present Congress Government have clapped the opposition into jail, and feelings are running high; meanwhile the tribes may flare up at any moment. The Governor thinks that if things are allowed to continue as at present there must be a progressive worsening of the situation and a dis-integrating frontier.

6. Caroe told Ismay that he recommends forcing a general election on the Government on the grounds that it is necessary to ascertain, beyond any shadow of doubt, to whom power should be transferred after we leave. The best way to do this would probably be to dismiss the Ministry, dissolve the House, and for the Governor to take powers under Section 93. Only thus would a clean election be assured, but it is clearly a big and difficult move which might infuriate Congress.[2]

7. I shall be discussing the matter fully with Caroe during the forthcoming Governors' Conference. The situation is not made easier by the fact that Nehru on the 19th March[3] asked my predecessor that Caroe should be asked to retire, and Nehru informed Caroe of this in a letter dated the 26th March,[4] copies of which were sent me by both Caroe and Nehru. Nehru has kept this matter secret, and it is not generally known.

[Paras. 8–10, summarising Lord Mountbatten's five meetings with Mr. Gandhi (see Nos. 37, 47, 53, 66 and 73), omitted.]

11. After my last interview with him on the 4th April I arranged for him to spend an hour with Ismay in order that the salient features of his scheme might be reduced to writing. This was done, (see Annex 1),[5] but in two letters to Ismay, Mr. Gandhi[6] has affected to be most disappointed and has taken the line that the object of these talks was to produce a formal *draft agreement* and not a mere summary. In other words he was hoping for a Mountbatten-Gandhi pact! I have written to him[7] making it clear that at the present stage I have no intention of making up my mind on the solution I propose to recommend for His Majesty's Government's consideration, and that it would be premature to prepare any cut and dried plan even in draft form. He has accepted my rebuff very gracefully.

[Paras. 12–20, on Lord Mountbatten's first meetings with Mr Jinnah (see Nos. 84, 92 and 101), omitted.]

21. The *Statesman* of the 6th April reported my invitation to Mr. Jinnah and his sister thus:—

"Lord Mountbatten then invited Mr.
Jinnah and Miss Jinnah for dinner.
(Other riot news on page 4.)"

22. Perhaps this has some connection with a report from the Governor of Bihar to the effect that, in one jail there, prisoners who have long been on hunger strike and are being forcibly fed are now going on a further strike against not getting enough food when they are forcibly fed, and against only being forcibly fed once instead of twice a day.

23. I have also seen Dr. Ambedkar, the Scheduled Caste leader, who informed me that in his opinion the Cabinet Mission and His Majesty's Government had betrayed the Scheduled Castes. He said that they had been exploited and oppressed in the past and the same would happen to them in the future. Even now, he added, they were treated in the most monstrous way and he quoted a case from the United Provinces where, he said, four Scheduled Caste men had recently been burnt alive by Caste Hindus. I am making enquiries about this matter.

24. I have reported separately by telegram[8] the result of the meeting of the Princes during the past week at Bombay. A face-saving formula has been found, but it is quite clear that certain States, led by the Maharajah of Bikaner, who have already thrown in their lot with Congress, will now be able to join in the Constituent Assembly immediately, instead of the States joining as a body after Sections A, B and C have completed their work, as had been envisaged originally. The Maharajah of Bikaner has sent me a sixteen page letter of explanation.[9]

25. There have been two Cabinet meetings during the past week, which have proceeded rather more smoothly than the week before. There was a long and acrimonious discussion on the request from Caroe for discretion to use air power in the event of large scale tribal incursions into the settled districts. The Cabinet decision was that the Governor of the N.W.F.P. should be informed that they would regard as regrettable the necessity for taking air action, but would not, if it became absolutely essential, be opposed to such action being taken. The power to determine the use of air power in such circumstances has been retained by the Central Government, but in times of great urgency I am empowered to issue the necessary orders, in consultation with Nehru, Liaquat Ali Khan and Baldev Singh if time permits. Nehru's attitude was very helpful in this case, particularly since he disapproves in principle of proscriptive bombing. Curiously enough in the Cabinet meeting the next day he stated that it could not be tolerated that Travancore should sell the rights of India's principal resources of uranium.[10] When provoked by Muslim members he

[2] Lord Ismay's notes on his interview with Sir O. Caroe on 2 April 1947 were circulated as V.C.P. 17 of 3 April. Mountbatten Papers.
[3] Vol. IX, No. 549   [4] Not traced.
[5] Not printed; this was the same as Enclosure to No. 85.   [6] Nos. 83 and 86.
[7] No. 88.   [8] No. 91.   [9] No. 68.   [10] See Vol. IX, No. 469, note 6.

admitted that he would certainly approve the use of air power against Travancore if necessary to bring them to heel. This, however, was said in a moment of real anger.

26. I had a particularly difficult time during the past week over the I.N.A. The long foreseen all-party motion came before the Legislative Assembly calling for the release of the 12 I.N.A. men at present in jail, and both Nehru and Liaquat assured me that this was certain to be passed unanimously. Nehru told me that Wavell's veto in the Cabinet had been kept a secret and that since he had left I would either have to reimpose the veto or bow to the will of the Assembly. If I forced the Government to resist an all-party unanimous motion the entire Government would be forced to resign.

27. These 12 men remaining in jail were sentenced on charges of desertion and for brutality against their own kind. Auchinleck's view was that if these men were released he could not hold himself responsible for the discipline of the Army as at present constituted, and did not see how his services could be of any further use. Nehru informed me that there was no doubt about the feelings in the House, or in the country which he shared, that these men should be released. This was not due to any liking on the part of the people for brutality, but the whole question was considered in its political aspect, and in no other.

28. After a preliminary meeting first alone with Nehru[11] and then with Auchinleck,[12] I called a special meeting[13] consisting of Nehru, Liaquat Ali Khan, Baldev Singh and Auchinleck. This was long and very tense. Eventually we found a formula[14] whereby, without creating a precedent, the available Justices of the Federal Court were to be asked to review the case of these men, and to recommend whether there should be any alterations to the sentences. Auchinleck said he must have time to consider this proposal. However I got him and the Chief Justice to lunch, and we managed to produce an acceptable formula. Nehru accepted the compromise and, as a result of his most statesman-like and courageous speech in the Legislative Assembly, the motion was eventually withdrawn.

29. You can imagine what a relief it was to me not to have to use the veto within a fortnight of my arrival and to have been spared resignations on one side or the other.

30. I am doing my best to keep my end of the bargain about civilian passages. I am most grateful for the extra ships provided, not so much in the interests of passengers' convenience, but because of the real importance of reducing our commitment in the case of serious trouble, however remote that may be. I have asked Ismay to get a grip of the problem for me, and my Joint Private Secretary, who is engaged almost entirely on this emergency planning, has already visited most of the provinces, to link up with the Governors and Army Commanders.

31. However great the demand may be, the problem of getting bodies into berths is not so simple as it looks from a distance, especially when some of the berths are steerage, or for men only. There has been a complete run down of the civil passage control organisation since the war, and the only control now is exercised by a non-official committee of shipping agents. The Commander-in-Chief is not at all anxious to undertake military control over civilian passengers at this stage, and I think he is right. However, I shall have the advice of his experts and I hope also their assistance in strengthening the present machinery. Not unnaturally civilians, given a free choice, normally only travel homewards in the spring. Many had already given up hope this year: hence the numerous cancellations. It takes time to call down the next on the list, say from Assam or Madras, and you cannot force civilians and their families into a reserve pool at a Transit Camp. In fact, short of a full blooded evacuation, compulsion will get us nowhere. We have not got the legal sanction for it, nor would my government be interested in providing themselves with the powers.

32. However, I shall do the best I can with persuasion, and hope that, without causing any alarm, I can arrange not only to space out applications but to fill accommodation. But please ask the Ministry of Transport to be as reasonable as they can about spacing the allocations. Say 24,000 people may wish to leave India in the 12 months ending 30 June 1948 (this is only a guess) the allotment should be approximately 1,500 a month from July to February, and 3,000 a month from March to June.

33. I shall be telegraphing to you about the Poles in Kolhapur and other refugees. It is most important that they should be out of India before February 1948 so that they do not compete for shipping with other civilians next spring. As there are over 9,000 Poles, they would provide a useful cushion for filling space which might otherwise be difficult during the slack season. This calls for a very early decision by His Majesty's Government about the destinations of these people, whether final or intermediate.

34. I referred in my previous letter to the setting up of Cabinet Committees and this week has seen the first meeting of the Defence Committee, although it has existed on paper for some years. The Committee considered a paper on the size of India's postwar forces with the result that an agreed recommendation is going forward to the Cabinet for the adoption of a contract budget for the armed forces for the next five years of Rs.102.5 crores. This is a satisfactory achievement which should save much time in Cabinet, when the matter is discussed there. I had my leg pulled by Liaquat about my love of Cabinet Committees the other day and the whole Cabinet joined in a good humoured laugh at my expense.

35. My wife has continued her contacts with Indian women and their

[11] No. 48.   [12] No. 50.   [13] No. 52.   [14] See Nos. 62 and 63.

organisations, and has up to date had interviews with approximately twenty-
five leading women of all religious denominations and political views, and
engaged over a wide field of activities, particularly in medical, nursing, educational and welfare work. Mrs. Aruna Asaf Ali, the wife of the Indian Ambassador to Washington, who was reported as violently anti-British, was
reluctant to accept my wife's invitation to come and meet her, but Mr. Gandhi
fortunately heard of this and persuaded her to come along with him one day,
as he did not approve of her attitude. As a result of this she had a long talk with
my wife, and the outcome of this appears to have been very happy, and they
made real friends. On Monday 7th April the Muslim League women gave a
tea party for her.

M. OF B.

109

*Sir E. Jenkins (Punjab) to Rear-Admiral Viscount Mountbatten
of Burma*

R/3/1/176: ff 100–7

SECRET   *9 April 1947*
No. 663

Dear Lord Mountbatten,
There is now little doubt that some at least of the Sikh leaders are preparing
for a violent agitation against the Muslims in the Punjab. I append for Your
Excellency's information translations of two Gurmukhi documents:

(1) an unsigned pamphlet giving a grossly exaggerated account of events in
the Rawalpindi Division; and

(2) an appeal purporting to be signed by 18 Sikhs, including Sardar Baldev
Singh, for what appears to be a "war fund" of Rs 50 lakhs.

Document (1) was distributed some days ago by Giani Kartar Singh to
Akali Jathedars and Secretaries from all over the Punjab and the Punjab States.
Document (2) came into our hands in print by accident; it was sent to the *Ajit*
(a Lahore newspaper) by the Shiromani Akali Dal for publication. The editor
did not publish it in full, but misdirected a copy to our Press Branch apparently
in place of a document on which he wanted Press advice.

2. Both documents can be read as legitimate appeals for help in cash or kind;
but they can also be read as preliminary indications of violent action against the
Muslims. Document (2) in particular mentions a date equivalent to 15th June
as specially significant for the Sikhs. The more unpleasant interpretation is
supported by intelligence reports of the activities of Master Tara Singh and
Kartar Singh. Both have advocated retaliation against the Muslims and both
have been in touch with the Rulers of Sikh States. General Messervy told me

on his return from Delhi that General Savory had been informed by the Raja of Faridkot that Tara Singh had invited him to take part in what would amount to military operations in his part of the Punjab. The Raja of Faridkot saw me today and was not quite so specific; but he told me that Tara Singh and Kartar Singh were dissatisfied with the attitude of the Maharaja of Patiala and had therefore asked him to take a political lead. He wanted my advice, and I said that I thought the violent talk of Tara Singh and Kartar Singh might do very great harm; that we could get no solution in the Punjab without at least the acquiescence of Muslims, Hindus and Sikhs; and that while I thought he should keep on good terms with the Akali leaders, he should certainly not lend himself to extreme propaganda of any kind. On the contrary he should do his best to guide the Akali leaders into more moderate courses. I thought Tara Singh sincere and Kartar Singh a clever party manager; but it was their habit to take precipitate action when no action was really needed, and it seemed to me futile for the Sikhs to settle any policy until they knew the result of the conversations now taking place in Delhi. The Raja confirmed my information about the violence of the views of Tara Singh and Kartar Singh. He said that they had borrowed a Jeep from him and had driven about in the Ferozepore district telling people that the time was coming when they would have to settle with the Muslims. He had been at some pains to counteract this propaganda. He said he was grateful for my advice and would follow it. The Raja is a very light weight and will not count much one way or the other. He is on bad terms with the Maharaja of Patiala, and at the moment on friendly terms with the Maharaja of Nabha, who does not count at all. I have no information as to the attitude of the Maharajas of Kapurthala and Jind; neither of them has any of the qualities of a leader.

3. I do not suggest any special action at present, since the Sikhs have good reason for resentment against the Muslims, and an immediate attack upon them by Government would be injudicious. I have seen Sardar Swaran Singh, the former Development Minister, today and have asked him to do his best to stop the more extreme forms of propaganda, which will only be turned against the Sikhs by the Muslims. Your Excellency may perhaps think it proper to let Sardar Baldev Singh know that you are aware of what is going on and consider it wrong for a Member of the Executive Council to take part in extreme communal activity. He may deny that he really signed document (2), but he is nominated in it as a treasurer of the fund which the Sikhs are raising.

Yours sincerely,

E. M. JENKINS

Enclosure 1 to No. 109

Translation of Gurmukhi Pamphlet (five sheets).
"Thousands of innocent Sikhs murdered in cold blood."
"Loot and Arson in Attock and Jhelum Districts. Villages after villages destroyed and razed to the ground."

"Sikhs! Read Patiently and Ponder over it."
"In order to establish Pakistan, the atrocities committed on Sikhs in the Punjab since 5th March 1947 have not come to light because of censorship on news. Although the Sikh population is small in the Districts of Attock, Rawalpindi and Jhelum, they own valuable property in these places. All the Sikh residents of these districts, excepting only a few, have been done to death, their properties looted, houses burnt, women outraged and many young girls forcibly converted to Islam. Their woeful tale is worth your patient hearing. But all this has been done according to a pre-arranged plan. At first, the Muslims took the Sikhs into their confidence on the pretext of providing them shelter from being attacked. Later, they were forced to part with their money in order to pay to the goondas who threatened to attack them. Even so, they were attacked and looted. Besides spears and swords, guns and bombs were also used. Lambardars were the ring-leaders of the goondas. Only the lives of those Sikh women were saved who agreed to their forcible conversion to Islam. The others either committed suicide or were burnt alive. The souls of all these innocent women are crying for help. The goondas had brought camels and bullock-carts to take away the booty. About thirty thousand Sikh lives have been saved by the Military, and all of them are now in Relief Camps. Those who owned lacs of rupees are today longing for a piece of bread".
Herewith are details of incidents village by village:
[*This section omitted.*]
There are thousands of Sikhs in Relief Camps, including women and children. They stand in need of everything. Thousands of young girls need clothing.
Oh Sikhs! Read this and think yourself. What have you to do under the circumstances? In your veins, there is yet the blood of your beloved Guru Gobind Singhji. Do your duty.

Enclosure 2 to No. 109

Translation of a pamphlet printed by the *Ajit* of Lahore (5-4-47):—
"O, Khalsaji! A critical condition has arisen for the Panth which arose after the last great Ghallughara (general massacre of Sikhs). The Ghallughara which has occurred specially in Pothohar and the Frontier is too painful for us to describe. It is not yet known what the future will bring. The time is extremely grave and situation is extremely critical. Now for us matters have gone to the extent of "throne or the coffin". In order to maintain the existence of the Panth

at this juncture, every Sikh should do his duty to the Guru's Panth. In obedience to the Panth, lies the life of a Sikh. By dint of their strength the Muslims want to thrust Pakistan on Sikhs, Hindus and Christians and they have already shown to us a specimen of Pakistan storm. In their majority zones they have perpetrated such tyrannies as cannot be described. Thousands of Sikh and Hindu women and children have been murdered; Keshas and beards of hundreds have been chopped off and an effort has been made to convert them to Islam; hundreds of women have been abducted; whole villages have been burnt up. Hundreds of chaste women jumped into wells and have sacrificed their lives in many other ways in order to preserve their honour. The Panth which plumed itself on rescuing others' girls, finds its own daughters in the hands of tyrants. Rest assured, as it is only a small specimen of Pakistan and more terrible incidents are yet to come. But Khalsaji, we are the Sikhs of that Guru who having had his four children slaughtered said: "what if four have fallen. Thousands still survive." We have to fight this tyrannical Pakistan and have to keep the Panth in high airs. This Panth has been prospering all the more after every Ghallughara and rest assured that even now the Panth will prosper. Be alert; you should recover yourself.

Fifty lakhs of rupees are required at this time for fighting the Pakistan in which lies our death. Although our community is poor, it has been winning every morcha by dint of sacrifice in the name of Tenth Guru. It is our vigorous appeal that money should be collected from every house, every mohalla, every village and every city for achieving victory in the forthcoming clash. Collect one rupee per head. If poor Sikhs are unable to pay rupee one per head, it is the religious duty of the Sikhs of that village or town to make up the deficiency. In this way 50 lakh rupees should be collected very soon. This sum should be collected up to the 15th Baisakh.

This Baisakh should prove a re-birth of the Khalsa and should always serve to give encouragement to the Sikhs in history. Besides, entire Sikh public is requested to offer prayers every day for "Victory to the Panth". Such a terrible conflict is approaching that even the sum of Rs. 50 lakhs collected once cannot be sufficient. Hence all Sikhs are requested to give one-tenth of their income for this task. And in every house one handful of flour should be set apart for the Guru's Fund at the time of kneading flour.

Note: For purposes of receiving this money, S. Baldev Singh Defence Member, Government of India, Delhi and Sardar Bhag Singh (of Gurdaspur) Advocate, Teja Singh Hall, Amritsar have been appointed treasurers. Collected money should be sent to one of these two persons by hand or by money order."
Sd/-Tara Singh (Master)
      Harkishan Singh (Bawa)
      Bagh Singh (Advocate)
      Jogindar Singh Mann, M.L.A.

Gurbachan Singh, M.L.A.
Indar Singh, M.L.A., Cawnpore.
Mohan Singh Jathedar Sri Akal Takht Sahib.
Buta Singh (Sir).
Udham Singh Nagoke.
Jagjit Singh Mann, M.L.A.
Pritam Singh Gujran, Pardhan, Shrimoni Riasti Akali Dal.
Santokh Singh, ex-M.L.A.
Kartar Singh Giani, M.L.A., Pardhan, Shrimoni Akali Dal.
Baldev Singh (Hon'ble) Delhi.
Jaswant Singh Duggal, M.L.A.
Ujjal Singh, M.L.A.
Narotam Singh, Advocate, Hissar.
Hukam Singh, Advocate, Montgomery.

110

Viceroy's Staff Meetings
Uncirculated Record of Discussion No. 5

Mountbatten Papers

TOP SECRET

Those present during this discussion which took place at the end of The Viceroy's
Twelfth Staff Meeting held at The Viceroy's House, New Delhi on 10 April 1947 at
10 am were: Rear-Admiral Viscount Mountbatten of Burma, Lord Ismay, Sir. E.
Mieville, Mr Abell, Captain Brockman, Mr Campbell-Johnson, Lieutenant-Colonel
Erskine Crum

An Outline Plan

HIS EXCELLENCY THE VICEROY said that the cardinal principles of the
plan at present uppermost in his mind were as follows:—

(i) Although Mr. Jinnah was determined to have Pakistan, and Congress,
with the exception of Mr. Gandhi, appeared to be prepared to let him
have it, no mention of Pakistan as such should be made in the announcement giving the plan for India's future.

(ii) There would be demission of power to Provinces, who would be free
at their own discretion to join together into one or more groups. These
groups would be free to form their own Constituent Assemblies. States
would be free to join groups if and as they desired.

(iii) The Interim Government, possibly strengthened by the inclusion of

Mr. Jinnah, would remain in being until at least June 1948; Provinces would, however, be at liberty to withdraw to themselves such subjects excluding certain reserved subjects, as they wished.

(iv) The Punjab and Bengal would be partitioned.

(v) There would be a general election in the N.W.F.P. and possibly in other Provinces also.

(vi) Apart from the plan proper, which would simply be announced and not subject to agreement, advice in the form of a charter would be tendered to the Indian leaders on how certain points might be dealt with after the departure of the British. Their agreement to these would have to be obtained. An example would be a standstill order on the disposition of troops which would be laid down by the Commander-in-Chief before we left.

HIS EXCELLENCY THE VICEROY emphasized the necessity in reaching a solution, which not only would do justice, but would also make it clear to the eyes of the world that justice was being done. The plan which he had outlined above fulfilled this proviso by giving the greatest measure of self determination. It was also important that the Indian people should take the onus of making a decision. Thus Britain could not then be blamed after the event. Arbitrary imposition of grouping, which was a weakness of the Cabinet Mission's plan, was to be avoided. Another point in favour of this outline plan was that advantage could be taken of that great principle of Indian procedure—the slow pace at which events moved.

SIR ERIC MIEVILLE expressed the opinion that points (ii) and (iii) above of the Viceroy's plan would be difficult to combine. If demission to Provinces was intended, all subjects without exception should, it seemed, be handed over. MR ABELL agreed that this would raise constitutional difficulties. But, in any case, it was generally agreed by all authorities that it would be impossible to bring in new Constitutions before June 1948. In effect, the *de facto* authorities in each Province would have to rule by decree.

LORD ISMAY emphasized that Provinces would not get full power until after June 1948. They would only be warned, in the announcement of the plan, to prepare themselves to assume full power after that date.

Mr. Jinnah

On the question of the inclusion of Mr. Jinnah in the Cabinet, HIS EXCELLENCY THE VICEROY related that he had made a tentative suggestion to Mr. Jinnah that he might become Prime Minister. This suggestion had had a far greater effect on Mr. Jinnah than he would have thought possible. HIS EXCELLENCY THE VICEROY said that he believed that Pandit Nehru was a big enough man to stand down in Mr. Jinnah's favour from his position of Vice-President of the Interim Government. The question arose whether Mr. Jinnah should be offered this post alone or a portfolio.

MR ABELL said that the Muslim League would probably want the portfolio with the maximum patronage. LORD ISMAY suggested the possibility of Mr. Jinnah being made Defence Member, but MR ABELL said that this suggestion had been tried before without success. The Commander-in-Chief was very much opposed to it. MR ABELL added that he considered it very doubtful whether Mr. Jinnah would co-operate at all before he knew the chosen plan.

HIS EXCELLENCY THE VICEROY said that he intended to take the following line with Mr. Jinnah when he saw him that afternoon:—

(i) He had not yet made up his mind on the issue of Partition.

(ii) He had made up his mind that if he became convinced that Partition was in the best interests of India and decided on it, the same principle would have to apply to the "doubtful" Provinces—the Punjab and Bengal.

Thus nothing would shake him in the decision that the solution would have to be either a "moth-eaten" Pakistan or united India.

(iii) If he did eventually decide on a form of Pakistan it would not be for him to say whether it would be necessary for the Indian Armed Forces to be divided or not. The mechanics of the division would have to be worked out by representatives of the parties concerned. Moreover, there would be no question of division until after June, 1948, because it would compromise his mandate to ensure maintenance of law and order.

THE PROGRAMME OF EVENTS

LORD ISMAY said that, in a rough forecast of events which he had made out, he had suggested that the Viceroy's Simla house party should take place on 1–8 May and that His Excellency should return to England with firm proposals on 8–15 May. HIS EXCELLENCY THE VICEROY said that these dates appeared highly optimistic to him.

During discussion of the future programme,

(1) It was agreed that the first preliminary step should probably be the partition of the Punjab.

(2) MR ABELL expressed doubts as to the advisability of holding the Simla house party at all. He thought that it might only make matters more difficult, as there was so little chance of reaching agreement between the parties. HIS EXCELLENCY THE VICEROY said that at least a fortnight's notice of the Simla house-party would be necessary, if it were to take place.

(3) HIS EXCELLENCY THE VICEROY said that he was beginning to weaken on the desirability of his returning to London with the plan for H.M.G.'s approval. It might be better to telegraph the outline plan home and ask permission to tell the Indian leaders of it. He intended to show how his mind was working in his next letter to the Secretary of State.

(4) LORD ISMAY said that he saw no necessity for immediate Parliamentary

legislation for approval of the plan. It could surely be announced by H.M.G. in the same way as the announcement of 20 February. Parliamentary legislation for the details could follow in due course.

INDIA AND THE COMMONWEALTH

HIS EXCELLENCY THE VICEROY said that it was his belief that the Indian leaders would have to ask that India should remain within the British Commonwealth, and that a Viceroy should stay on with constitutional powers and the right of veto, accorded voluntarily, over the control of the armed forces. He recalled that Pandit Nehru, the first time he had seen him, had made it apparent that he was groping for a formula—possibly "dual nationality"—whereby India would retain a close link with the United Kingdom. One possibility was that all the other parts of India would wish to stay on in the Commonwealth, and the Congress-dominated area or areas would be able to "save their face" on the pretext of "bowing to the wishes of the majority". Anyhow, no pressure would be brought to bear—it was a matter for decision by the Indians alone.

III

Record of Interview between Rear-Admiral Viscount Mountbatten of Burma and Dr Rajendra Prasad

Mountbatten Papers. Viceroy's Interview No. 44

TOP SECRET   *10 April 1947*

The meeting lasted from 12 noon to 12.45 p.m.

Dr. Rajendra Prasad gave me a brief account of his visit to the projected Kosi Dam area, and he spoke enthusiastically of the scheme.

I asked him what he would do if he were in my place about the transfer of power. He said he found it impossible to divest himself momentarily from his association with being a Hindu and a member of Congress, and asked me what my ideas were.

I said that I still had a completely open mind, but that it had become clear to me that Mr. Jinnah was thinking only along the line of partition.

Dr. Rajendra Prasad enlarged on the disastrous consequences of the break-up of Indian unity; and I expressed agreement with his sentiments and his reasoning. I then asked him whether he considered that those reasons were strong enough to override the objection that there would almost certainly be a civil war if I were to enforce it against the wishes of the Muslim League.

He agreed that the position now reached made civil war very likely if I were to try and enforce a decision against the wishes of any large section of the people.

I then asked him if he thought that Congress would accept voluntarily a decision which virtually abandoned the idea of Indian unity if that were the only way that I could transfer power without a risk of civil war. He said that if that were the position, he was inclined to agree that it might be accepted; since he did not see how I had any alternative but to transfer power in any manner which would not involve civil war.

We both eventually agreed that if it were possible to introduce a time element into the stages by which partition was implemented, that this would give some prospect of reason prevailing over communal emotional sentiments.

I asked him about the food situation in India, and he replied that although stocks were far shorter than he would like to see them, and although there were the added difficulties that wheat eaters had to be given rice and rice eaters had to be given wheat, according to locality, time of year and stocks available, he nevertheless did not fear any famine, and thought that we should get through the next year—short but not disastrously short of food.

112

Record of Interview between Rear-Admiral Viscount Mountbatten of Burma and Mr Kripalani

Mountbatten Papers. Viceroy's Interview No. 45

TOP SECRET   *10 April 1947*

Mr. Kripalani came to see me at 12.45 prior to staying on to luncheon with his wife.

He asked me whether I proposed to give a decision on the transfer of power myself or whether I had considered seriously calling in an outside authority to arbitrate. I asked what he had in mind, and he said he had no special ideas, beyond possibly United Nations arbitrators.

I asked him whether he thought that a committee of arbitrators would be likely to come to any different conclusion to myself; and he admitted that it was unlikely. I asked him also whether he would be prepared to accept the long additional delay needed to set up such a body and for them to complete their work, and whether the country would not deteriorate irreparably in that interval. He was inclined to share my doubts.

He then asked in what way Congress could place their services at my disposal to help me in my difficult task. He pointed out that it was a democratic institution, of which he was the elected President only for a term of office, and that he would have no authority to speak except to a brief supplied by the Working Committee; nor could he give any undertakings unless ratified by the Working Committee.

I pointed out the impracticability of my dealing with 15 men, and said I really must ask for the minimum number who could be responsible to answer for Congress. I asked him whether he as President, Pandit Nehru as leader of Congress in Government, and Mr. Gandhi as the spiritual factor behind Congress, would be sufficient for me to negotiate with when it came to proclaiming the Congress view. He was inclined to agree, without being very specific.

I told him that I would not go far towards taking a final decision without keeping at least as much in touch with Congress as with the Muslim League.

I pointed out, however, how much easier it was to deal with the Muslim League, since Mr. Jinnah had maintained that he could speak practically firmly on their behalf and did not anticipate that his Working Committee would repudiate any agreement that he made. Mr. Kripalani replied: "If you will not take it amiss, may I say that that is the way that all organisations built up on a Hitlerite principle work".

During lunch, I arranged for him to have a word with Lord Ismay about getting an agreed appeal for a truce between all parties.

He left it to Lord Ismay to work out the formula.

113

Pandit Nehru to the Nawab of Bhopal

R/1/30/40: f 64

No. CA31/ASF/47.   COUNCIL HOUSE, NEW DELHI,
                                                        10 April 1947

My dear Nawab Saheb,
Will you please refer to your letter dated the 1st April[1] asking me to intimate to you the acceptance by the Constituent Assembly of the "general understanding reached between the two Negotiating Committees in regard to the allocation of States' quota of seats and the method of selection of their representatives in the Constituent Assembly and the fundamental points discussed at the meetings held on the 8th and 9th February and 1st and 2nd March, 1947"?

2. In the course of the discussions between the two committees, I made it clear that a formal ratification by the Constituent Assembly was unnecessary and that our committee was only required to report the result of its negotiations with your committee to the Assembly. This report, giving an account of what happened at our discussions, will be made to the Constituent Assembly on the 28th April.

[1] No. 44.

3. At our discussions we exchanged views on what you regarded as fundamental points; and, on the basis of the general understanding arrived at as a
result of that exchange, the two committees proceeded to consider the question
of the allocation of seats amongst the States and the method of selection and
reached an agreement thereon. The general understanding and the agreement
will be included in the report to be made to the Assembly.

4. The entry of the States' representatives into the Constituent Assembly
has now become a matter of urgency, especially in view of the Prime Minister's
Statement of February 20th. I would, therefore, request you to be so good as to
invite the States, which have not already done so, to choose, without delay,
their representatives in accordance with the agreement arrived at, so that they
may take their seats in the constituent Assembly from the next session onwards.

Yours sincerely,
JAWAHARLAL NEHRU

114

Rear-Admiral Viscount Mountbatten of Burma to Pandit Nehru

*Mountbatten Papers. Official Correspondence Files: North-West Frontier
Province, Situation in, Part I(a)*

TOP SECRET   *10 April 1947*
No. 1420.
My dear Pandit Nehru,
It was good of you to send me copies of the correspondence with Sir Olaf
Caroe.[1]

There are many difficulties about the position on the Frontier and I am
trying to familiarise myself with the position as quickly as I can. I think you will
recognise, however, that as I do not yet know Caroe I can hardly be expected
to judge immediately on his suitability for the post, and on the way he is
discharging the duties of his office. To remove a Governor is a serious matter,
and I do not think I can possibly come to an immediate decision. Meanwhile I
must, of course, give the Governor my support.

I think you should know that Lord Wavell told me of your letter to him,[2]
and strongly advised me not to take any early action in this matter.

Yours sincerely,
MOUNTBATTEN OF BURMA

[1]This correspondence has not been traced.   [2] Vol. IX, No. 549.

115

Note by Sir E. Jenkins

R/3/1/176: ff 130–4

10 April 1947

Giani Kartar Singh came to see me at his request at 4 p.m. today. I gave him a letter from P.S.V., which had just arrived, and also a letter from P.S.V. to Master Tara Singh, which he promised to deliver immediately. I said that I understood that the letters contained invitations to an interview with H.E. the Viceroy.

2. Giani Kartar Singh said that it was in anticipation of such an invitation that he had come to see me. He wished me to plead the Sikh cause with H.E. I asked him what the Sikhs really wanted. He replied that H.M.G. might endeavour to settle with the Muslim League and the Congress (a) on the basis of the Statement of 16th May 1946, or (b) on some other basis. It would be grossly unfair for the British to leave India without making proper provision for the Sikhs.

I suggested that we assume (a) in the first instance. If Mr. Jinnah and the Congress leaders decided to co-operate in the Constitutent Assembly, would the Sikhs co-operate also or would they stand out?

The Giani replied that the Sikhs were still dissatisfied with the Statement of 16th May 1946. They would go into the Constituent Assembly if they were guaranteed in Section B the same right of communal veto as had been granted to the Muslims in the full Assembly.

Moreover, the Sikhs were now convinced that there must be an immediate partition of the Punjab. The two new Provinces could both be in Section B, but both must have the right to contract out of the new constitution.

I pointed out here that partition would be extraordinarily difficult and that I personally was convinced that unionism was the best thing for Punjabis. If partition were sanctioned, I doubted if the Hindu Jats of the Ambala Division would wish to be included in the Sikh State. Their idea was to form a separate Jat State, including the whole or part of the Meerut Division of the United Provinces and a large part of the Ambala Division of the Punjab.

The Giani said that the Sikhs had no intention of coercing the Hindu Jats and that if the Hindu Jats wanted a separate Province of their own, he would raise no objection. The Sikh conception was of a non-Muslim State, including nearly the whole of the Sikh country. Such a State would be amalgamated or federated with the Phulkian States, and should be free to join Hindustan or Pakistan, or to remain completely independent and to make a separate treaty with H.M.G.

I questioned the Giani as to his ideas about boundaries. He said that the Sikhs would let the Hindu Jats have Rohtak, Gurgaon, about half the Karnal district, and about half the Hissar district. They would expect the remainder of Karnal and Hissar, the whole or the greater part of Ambala and the whole of Simla to be included in the Sikh State. They thought the Ravi the most suitable boundary between the Sikh State and the Muslim State; but he personally would not insist upon the Sikhs taking over Lahore City. He made it clear that he would wish Montgomery to be included in the Sikh State, and that Nankana Sahib in the Sheikhupura district and its neighbouring villages should be a "free city". He thought once the partition had been effected, there would be voluntary movements of population and that the Sikhs now living in the Lyallpur district would exchange with Muslims living in Montgomery.

I repeated my arguments against partition. I said that I thought it would mean economic and political ruin, and asked whether the Giani's ideas excluded some sort of a Punjab Federation. He replied that he would have no objection to a Federation of a limited kind, e.g. for such subjects as Irrigation and Electric Power; but it would have to be a voluntary Federation between equals, and there could be no question of Muslim domination over the Sikhs.

3. I asked him if he thought the Muslims would accept a partition. He said that he really did not know, but that it was the only solution of the present communal problem, which could not be solved in any other way. I said that if the Muslims did not agree to partition and if partition were ordered, a very considerable force would be needed to effect it. The Giani said cheerfully that we had only to put the two Governments into office and they would see to the rest. The British had taken the Punjab from the Sikhs, and it would be logical enough to return it to them.

4. I then took the discussion to (b) in paragraph 2 above—the possibility of an agreement between H.M.G., the Muslim League and the Congress on some new basis—and to the possibility of a complete breakdown. I asked the Giani if he thought any settlement likely. He said that the Sikhs did not particularly want a settlement, and would accept no settlement which did not provide for them. The British could not fairly disregard the Sikhs who during the last century had supported them in many ways. If they liked, they could leave the Punjab without a Government, and the communities would then fight it out; but the Sikhs would not tolerate any arrangement which placed them under the domination of another community. He realised that my advice would be taken by H.E. the Viceroy and he trusted that I would do nothing to injure the Sikh case or to suggest the feasibility of any arrangement that did not satisfy the Sikhs. I said that I had always done my best to help the Sikh community, since I was well aware of their importance in the Punjab. I doubted if India could be peaceful if the Punjab were in a state of chaos; and the Punjab

could hardly be peaceful if the Sikhs were not reasonably satisfied with their political condition. I had as great an affection for the Punjab as for my own country, since I had spent the greater part of my life here, and my only object was to leave the Punjab in the best possible state from the point of view of Punjabis. For the reasons I had given I was against partition; but if the Punjabis would be satisfied with nothing else, they would presumably get their own way in the end. But the difficulties of partition were enormous, and I hoped that the Sikhs would not rule out the possibility of some local settlement with the Muslim League.

The Giani then said that the Muslim League had shown no real signs of wanting a settlement. They had talked about it constantly, but their whole attitude had been that they were a separate nation and must dominate the entire Punjab. They could only do that by force and the Sikhs would not let them do so. He quite appreciated my sentimental dislike of partition—the British had done a great deal for the Punjab during the last century and naturally hated to destroy their own handiwork. Whatever H.M.G. decided to do now he hoped that the decision would be fair to all.

5. I took the opportunity of mentioning to the Giani the undesirable character of his propaganda—particularly two recent Gurmukhi pamphlets about events in the Rawalpindi Division and about the need for a "war fund" of Rs 50 lakhs.[1] The Giani said that he had not read the first of these pamphlets (as I think he distributed it himself, I doubt if this statement was true), but would correct any inaccuracies which it contained. I pointed out that whatever his intentions might be, propaganda of this kind gave the impression that the Sikhs were about to attack the Muslims. The Giani laughed heartily at this, and said that the Sikhs would do no such thing until after the British left India. They had no intention of fighting a war on two fronts, nor would it be in their interest to annoy the British unnecessarily at the present stage.

6. The Giani ended our interview by detailing a number of grievances and suggestions of the usual kind, on which I have made a separate note.

E.M.J.

[1] See No. 109.

116

Record of Interview between Rear-Admiral Viscount Mountbatten of Burma and Mr Jinnah

Mountbatten Papers. Viceroy's Interview No. 46

TOP SECRET   *10 April 1947*

Mr. Jinnah came at 4 o'clock, but I arranged to leave the field clear for Lord

Ismay to talk to him until 4.45 and go through the points he had written down after his last meeting. From 4.45 to 6.30 I was present at the discussions.

Mr. Jinnah could not possibly have been more clear that he would have nothing to do with the Cabinet Mission plan; and so we went ahead and followed up his desire for partition logically. He said that what he wanted was a surgical operation cutting off the 5 Provinces in the 'B' and 'C' areas, and turning them over to Pakistan, leaving the other six Provinces to Hindustan. He stressed that time did not permit any negotiations or details, and urged that I should give an over-all decision as soon as possible and allow the details to be worked out subsequently.

Lord Ismay and I were at pains to point out to him that unless we could get some indication of what mechanics were required to implement any decision, it would be impossible for us to consider such a decision.

I then explained to Mr. Jinnah that although I still retained a fully open mind, the only way in which I could follow his advice was to pursue it to its logical conclusion. I said to him as regards the questions of a united India: "You claim the right of a large minority people to partition on a big scale. If I grant you this how can I refuse Congress, who will press for exactly the same right for the large Hindu minorities in the Punjab and Bengal to be partitioned?"

We argued these points back and forth, Mr. Jinnah's main point being that I must make his Pakistan "viable". He quoted the partition of Poland as not having been made on the basis of counting heads or taking into account the will of the people.

I told him I was not prepared to proceed on this basis, and that I must follow a course that would be generally acceptable, so far as it was mechanically possible in present conditions to ascertain the will of the people. For this purpose I had in mind an immediate announcement that I would demit power to Provinces in June 1948, and that Provinces would have the right forthwith to decide whether they wished to join any other group of Provinces or remain entirely autonomous. I presumed in fact that Sind, half of Punjab and probably the N.W.F.P. would form one Group, part of Bengal another Group, which together would form Pakistan. The remaining Provinces I assumed would wish to join Hindustan.

I pointed out that Pakistan and Hindustan would then have to set up their constitution-making machinery and that the Indian States would have the opportunity of joining up with one or the other of these two Constituent Assemblies, or of making separate negotiations, though how this should be done would require working out.

Mr. Jinnah became more and more distressed and displeased at the turn the conversation was taking, claiming that Congress were deliberately drawing a red herring across my path, and threatening that in that case he would demand the partition of the Province of Assam. I replied that certainly I would grant him the same rights of course as Congress, and if he wished to put the Muslim majority areas of Assam in with Bengal he must let me have his proposals.

I continued to stress that this scheme was very tentative: until I could see what mechanics were involved I could neither tell whether the scheme was in fact practical or how long it would take to implement it.

Since he denied that the scheme I had just outlined was in any way what he wanted, he said he could not possibly contribute anything useful to working out the mechanics. Lord Ismay accepted that he should work out the mechanics, which would be submitted to Mr. Jinnah for his views.

I pointed out that if it became evident in the course of investigation that the scheme could not be implemented in full by June 1948, then we would endeavour to work out a proposal by which the Indians could continue negotiations on a programme of implementation after our departure.

We next discussed the procedure to be adopted in following through whatever proposal I finally decided to make to H.M.G. Mr. Jinnah urged me not to write any letters on the subject, and we agreed that it would be a good thing to put the proposals to the Prime Minister before I announced the proposed decision formally to the leaders.

Mr. Jinnah said he had wanted to call his Working Committee but had now decided not to do so for the present.

He asked to be allowed to see what the Congress proposals were for carving up the Punjab and Bengal, so that he could submit counter proposals.

I decided that I would ask Pandit Nehru to come and see me and ask him for the proposed boundaries for the partition of the Punjab and Bengal, and to discuss with him the solution on which I had been working with Mr. Jinnah.

I also said that I would suggest to Pandit Nehru that the Constituent Assembly should not meet on the 28th April, but should have its meeting postponed until after the decision had been announced.

Lord Ismay submitted the draft he had prepared for the joint call by the leaders of both parties for a truce to provocative action and violence. Mr. Jinnah took it away with him to consider the wording carefully, it being arranged that Sir Eric Mieville should see him about getting the final wording agreed by him before it was submitted to Pandit Nehru.

Finally, I should like to record that in the course of this conversation I took the opportunity of Mr. Jinnah's bitter complaints about my ruining his Pakistan by cutting out half of the Punjab and Bengal including Calcutta and by making it economically very difficult if not impossible to function, to try and bring him back to the Cabinet Mission plan. I told him that I entirely agreed with him that the moth-eaten Pakistan which was all I could possibly offer him was almost unworkable, and I strongly expressed my inability to see why he was not prepared to accept the Cabinet Mission plan, which gave him the whole of the Punjab, the whole of Bengal including Calcutta and the whole of Sind, with complete autonomy, and in fact accorded to him a really worth-while and workable Pakistan.

I pointed out that so far as I could see the only difference between the scheme I was prepared to give him and that which he could get under the Cabinet Mission plan was that under the Cabinet Mission plan he was obliged to accept a small weak Centre at Delhi controlling Defence, Communications, and External Affairs. I pointed out that these three might really be lumped together under the heading of General Defence, and that I did not see how under the new scheme he could possibly avoid joining some organisation at the Centre to take care of General Defence. In fact I prophesied that he would find that he had thrown away the substance for the shadow, and that he was going to get an almost unworkable truncated Pakistan which would still be obliged to share a common organisation at the Centre to arrange over-all defence. Whereas if only he would come back to the Cabinet Mission plan, he could have the whole of the Pakistan he wanted, without really having any tighter organisation over him at the Centre than he would sooner or later be bound to accept under the truncated scheme; added to which, I pointed out, he was ruining the position of India as a great Power, and forever pulling her down to something below a second class Power.

117

Pandit Nehru to the Nawab of Bhopal

R/1/30/40: f 65

No. CAII-Com-47   COUNCIL HOUSE, NEW DELHI,
                                                              10 April 1947

My dear Nawab Saheb,

I have seen Sir Sultan Ahmed's letter of the 7th April[1] addressed to Iengar on the subject of States' representatives on the Committees of the Constituent Assembly, particularly on the Advisory Committee on Fundamental Rights etc. and the Union Powers Committee. Both these committees are meeting from the 14th April onwards and their reports have to be presented to the Constituent Assembly at the session commencing on the 28th April.

2. You will agree that it is very important that these committees should have the advantage of considering the States' points of view on the matters referred to them before they submit their reports. I hope, therefore, that you will now send your recommendations to the President for nominations to these com-mittees. In the meanwhile, I understand that the President is nominating Sir B. L. Mitter and Sir V. T. Krishnamachari on the Union Powers Committee

and Sardar K. M. Panikkar on the Advisory Committee on Fundamental Rights etc.

3. I have, in a separate letter,[2] explained to you that the ratification of the Constituent Assembly to the agreement reached between the two committees is not required and that it is, therefore, not necessary to hold up your recommendations for nominations to the committees.

Yours sincerely,
JAWAHARLAL NEHRU

[1] Not on R/1/30/40.   [2] No. 113.

118

Rear-Admiral Viscount Mountbatten of Burma to Lord Pethick-Lawrence

Telegram, L/S&G/7/914: f 347

IMMEDIATE   *11 April 1947*
PRIVATE

787–S. Your private telegram No. 45 dated April 9th.[1] I have not yet informed Cabinet of H.M.G.'s decision to accept proposal that compensation should not be paid to Indians. As I told you in my telegram No. 742–S of April 5th,[2] I had greatest difficulty in persuading my Cabinet to go as far as they did and I most seriously deprecate reopening question. They are quite determined on the subject and have gone a long way to meet us in agreeing that H.M. Government should announce that they were prepared to include Indians in compensation scheme.

2. Those Indians who think their future will be prejudiced as a result of their actions, can state a case for compensation, and for all the rest, the prospects are good and existing terms will, I am sure, be guaranteed. Though the pay and number of appointments above time scale may possibly be reduced the elimination of most [of the] British element in the services gives Indians a much better chance of promotion than before.

3. I earnestly submit that there can be no question of change of decision in this matter. My relations with Cabinet will be seriously affected if H.M.G. insist on a course which will be regarded as an unfriendly act by all my colleagues and one likely to cause a break-up of what remains of the services.

[1] No. 103.   [2] See No. 103, note 1.

119

Viceroy's Staff Meetings
Uncirculated Record of Discussion No. 6

Mountbatten Papers

TOP SECRET

Those present during this discussion which took place at the end of The Viceroy's Thirteenth Staff Meeting held at The Viceroy's House, New Delhi on 11 April 1947 at 10 am were: Rear-Admiral Viscount Mountbatten of Burma, Lord Ismay, Sir E. Mieville, Mr Abell, Captain Brockman, Mr I. D. Scott, Mr Campbell-Johnson, Lieutenant-Colonel Erskine Crum

HIS EXCELLENCY THE VICEROY said that it had always been and would remain his main desire to hand over power to an unified India with a strong centre. The next best to this would be to hand over to an unified India with a weak centre—such as was envisaged in the Cabinet Mission plan. He had now had six meetings with Mr Jinnah. The one the previous day had lasted for three hours.[1] He had brought all possible arguments to bear on Mr Jinnah but it seemed that appeals to his reason did not prevail. He had pointed out to Mr Jinnah the enormous advantages of retaining an unified India—as one, India could be immensely powerful and in the front rank of world powers. He had asked Mr Jinnah why he could possibly wish to throw away such advantages. Mr Jinnah had not been able in his presence to adduce one single feasible argument in favour of Pakistan. In fact he had offered no counter arguments. He gave the impression that he was not listening. He was impossible to argue with. They had covered the whole ground time and again on every conceivable basis with no progress whatever. He had assured Mr Jinnah that he regarded himself as more or less the first head of the Indian state and that it was his sole intention to do whatever was best in the interests of the Indian people. Mr Jinnah was a psychopathic case. He was, whatever was said, intent on his Pakistan—which could surely only result in doing the Muslims irreparable damage. HIS EXCELLENCY THE VICEROY said that it was, however, quite clear to him that, if any effort was made to try and impose the Cabinet Mission plan, the Muslim League would resort to arms. He added that until he had met Mr Jinnah he had not thought it possible that a man with such a complete lack of sense of responsibility could hold the power which he did.

LORD ISMAY said that he believed that the dominating feature in Mr Jinnah's mental structure was his loathing and contempt of the Hindus. He apparently thought that all Hindus were sub-human creatures with whom it was impossible for the Muslims to live. HIS EXCELLENCY THE VICEROY pointed out that, in any case, the Muslims and Hindus would have to live together. He had told Mr Jinnah that he believed that Congress were so keen on keeping an unified India that he might be capable of persuading them to pay the price of giving over the whole of Bengal, the Punjab, Assam, and the North West Frontier Province on the condition that a weak centre should be retained. He had also told Mr Jinnah that he believed that it would be possible so to work out the Constitution of the Centre that neither party could move the Armed Forces without the consent of the other, but again Mr Jinnah had not listened.

LORD ISMAY said that he had got the impression that, for the last half hour of the previous day's meeting with Mr Jinnah, there had been some change of atmosphere. Mr Jinnah had made some effort to be helpful. He had said that, whatever the Viceroy decided, whether he agreed with it or not, he would never doubt His Excellency's sincerity or good faith. He had also proffered helpful advice on two or three points.

HIS EXCELLENCY said that there had come a moment in his interview with Mr Jinnah two days previously when the latter, with a smile on his face, had hesitantly mentioned that, although he did not suggest that it might affect the decision, the first act of the Pakistan Government would probably be to apply for admission to the British Commonwealth on Dominion status. HIS EXCELLENCY THE VICEROY said that he had informed Mr Jinnah that his instructions were to do nothing which would in any way help towards the splitting-up of India. It was the desire of His Majesty's Government, he had said, that there should be a strong unified India free to choose herself whether she wished to remain in the British Commonwealth or not. He had explained that he could not possibly be a party to any suggestion that Pakistan should enter the Commonwealth, nor could he give any indication of what His Majesty's Government's attitude might be. HIS EXCELLENCY THE VICEROY said that he believed that this had been a very rude shock to Mr Jinnah, who had apparently thought that His Majesty's Government would jump at his suggestion.

SIR ERIC MIEVILLE said that he did not believe that Pakistan was an economic possibility. MR ABELL said that the political objections to Pakistan were in his opinion much greater. Economically it could be made to work, weak though it would be. A paper on the economic viability of Pakistan had been sent in by Mr Zinkin and Commander Nicholls was at the moment preparing a criticism of this paper.[2]

HIS EXCELLENCY THE VICEROY said that in his opinion the time factor was of over-riding importance. Mr Jinnah had no idea of the broad outline of the mechanics and time-table of establishing Pakistan. Everyone must bear in mind that the sheer logic of events and mechanical difficulties were likely to wield the greatest influence.

[1] See No. 116.
[2] Mr Zinkin's paper, and Commander Nicholls' critique, are on R/3/1/141.

LORD ISMAY said that it was fast becoming apparent that it would be impossible to hand over complete power to the Provinces by June 1948. They would not be ready to receive it. Some sort of a central organisation would have to remain for a few years. There always remained the possibility that Mr Jinnah might be invited to be Prime Minister of the Central Government. HIS EXCELLENCY THE VICEROY said that, from what he had seen of Mr Jinnah, he doubted that if he was brought into the Government any measure would thereafter be passed on its merits. LORD ISMAY pointed out that there was always a tendency for responsibility to improve people in such cases out of all recognition. MR ABELL said that he did not think that Mr Jinnah would accept an invitation to join the Central Government. HIS EXCELLENCY THE VICEROY said that he believed that he might do so on the grounds that it was the best way of getting his own policy through, but he would probably ask for a portfolio. MR ABELL considered that there might be great difficulty in persuading Congress to grant the Muslim League another seat.

HIS EXCELLENCY THE VICEROY said that he was seeing Pandit Nehru that afternoon and he intended to take him fully into his confidence, which he had not yet done. He had not yet in fact asked the Congress leaders, with the exception of Mr Gandhi, for their proposals.

HIS EXCELLENCY THE VICEROY emphasised that he still retained a completely open mind. He wanted, however, Lord Ismay to start to work out the details of the plan at present primarily under consideration. When and if the time came for this plan to be announced, he wanted a most careful preamble to be written making it clear that his view had all along been completely impartial; that it was only when it became apparent that the retention of any form of an united India would start civil war that he had regretfully been obliged to give up this ideal; and that he had therefore chosen a means which gave the choice of their future, as well as the somewhat primitive democratic machinery could allow, to the Indian people themselves.

HIS EXCELLENCY THE VICEROY finally emphasised that the chosen plan would of course be put up for approval to H.M.G. before Indian party leaders were informed of the decision. He visualised that a simultaneous announcement might be made in Parliament by the Prime Minister and by himself over the wireless in India. He decided that he would make this announcement only in English and not also in Urdu.

120

Lord Ismay to Mr V. P. Menon

Mountbatten Papers. Official Correspondence Files: Plans, Alternative
(For Transfer of Power), Part (1)

TOP SECRET   *11 April 1947*

My dear Menon,

I send you herewith the bare bones of a possible plan for the transfer of power. The Viceroy would be glad if [you] would:—

(a) Amend the draft in any way you think right and put some flesh upon it.

(b) Consider what the procedure would be immediately after H.M.G. have made their announcement. For example, will a general election throughout India be necessary? How will we set about the partition of the Punjab, Bengal and Assam? Presumably the decision will rest with H.E. and will not be open to argument. What will be the machinery for those groups who wish to confederate to get together and to frame their constitution? and so on and so forth.

(c) Work out a rough timetable.

I ought to explain that nothing very precise is required at this stage. The object is to give H.E. a general line on how this plan would be implemented *if* it were adopted, and approximately how long the various processes would take.

Yours sincerely,

ISMAY

PS. Would it be convenient for you to come to a Staff Conference on the above at my office at 3.0 p.m. tomorrow, 12th April? I much hope so.[1]

Enclosure to No. 120

ONE OF THE POSSIBLE PLANS FOR THE TRANSFER OF POWER WHICH ARE RECEIVING EXAMINATION.

Since it has been impossible to reach agreement on the Cabinet Mission plan for a unified India, H.M.G. have decided, with effect from June 1948, to demit authority to Provinces, or to such confederations of Provinces as may decide to group themselves together in the intervening period.

2. The Indian States will become independent from the date of the transfer of power and are, of course, at liberty to negotiate with any confederation to join them [?it].

[1] See No. 139 for the Paper prepared as a result of deliberation by the Viceroy's Staff.

3. In order to create Provinces to which authority can be demitted, it will be necessary, unless stable Ministries can otherwise be established by a certain date, to—

(a) Partition the Punjab:

(b) Partition Bengal and Assam: and

(c) Arrange for a general election in the N.W.F.P.

4. In order that Provinces or such groups of Provinces and States as may be formed may be in a position to receive authority on the due date—

(a) Those Provinces and States which wish to be grouped together should arrange forthwith to work out their respective constitutions: and

(b) Provinces may from hence forward take over from the centre all subjects, except the union subjects, for which they can make suitable administrative arrangements. This take over will clearly be progressive as time passes.

5. Ultimately, therefore, the Central Government will be left only with the union subjects, and such other subjects as the Provinces themselves desire them to retain, e.g. perhaps food.

6. When the date for transfer arrives, the Central Government, as it at present exists, will disappear. Consequently in the period between now and then it will be necessary to create machinery to co-ordinate the policy governing the union subjects for all India, or alternatively to arrange for a standstill period during which the existing machinery functions, pending the completion of arrangements to take its place.

121

Record of Interview between Rear-Admiral Viscount Mountbatten of Burma and Mr Rajagopalachari

Mountbatten Papers. Viceroy's Interview No. 48

TOP SECRET   *11 April 1947*

The meeting lasted from 12 noon to 12.45 p.m.

I told Mr. Rajagopalachari in strict confidence the general drift of my conversations with Mr. Jinnah, and he admitted with great expressions of regret that the ideal of a unified India could not be imposed by force, and if in fact the decision to hand over to a unified India were to lead to civil war that would indeed be a tragic paradox. He accepted entirely that I must be guided by what was practicable and what would produce a peaceful solution; but begged me not to make such binding decisions that the Indian people could not work out their own salvation as time went on.

He pointed out that most of the leaders took a long time to obtain sufficient influence to become leaders, and once this had happened they were usually embittered old men who had become obstinate and not open to reason.

I suggested to him that if such leaders could be brought into the Government (for example Mr. Jinnah) the added responsibility might modify their views and make them take a far more balanced and responsible outlook.

He said that this might be true in a few cases and was admittedly true in the case of Pandit Nehru, but he would be very surprised if it were to come true in the case of Mr. Jinnah. He said that his great reputation had been made in the legal profession, and his knowledge of administration was nil.

We then discussed the question of the fighting forces being completely Indianised by June 1948 and the effect on their efficiency. Mr. Rajagopalachari stated that he had never shared the general view that politicians held, that Indianisation could be completed in so short a time without the gravest effect on efficiency, and he was of the opinion that five to ten years must elapse before it would be sound to withdraw British officers.

I told him that Brigadier Cariappa, the most senior Indian officer, had given a most courageous lead in his statement to the Indian Press in London that it would take five years before they could do without British officers; and that I had been interested to find that all other senior Indian officers I had seen shared his views, except Commander Choudhury, the most senior R.I.N. officer, who considered it would take at least ten years in the case of the Navy. Mr. Rajagopalachari was glad to think that Brigadier Cariappa had had the courage to make this statement, particularly since he said that it was due to the senior Indian officers themselves that the politicians had been misled; for, as far as he knew, all Indian officers had combined together to give the impression that the sooner the British were pushed out the better (since he presumed that they were looking forward to rapid promotion in consequence).

Mr. Rajagopalachari asked whether I did not think that a respectable contract could be drawn up which would allow British officers to continue serving for five years with the Indian Army after the transfer of power.

I told him that the British might not wear their hearts on their sleeves, but that they were all the more emotional for repressing their emotions, and I could not imagine any officer of the calibre that they would wish to keep who would be prepared to resign his Commission in order to take on a five-year contract with a foreign power.

Mr. Rajagopalachari then asked me if I could think of any formula or device by which the services of British officers could be retained; and I replied that that was entirely up to the Indians themselves; but that the most obvious one of course was for India not to leave the Commonwealth.

He thought that they were pretty well committed to do this, and could see no way out. To this I replied that if they chose not to make any statement about severing their connection with the Crown at all, I thought there would probably be no difficulty in finding a formula for the officers to serve, since they would not have to resign their commissions.

Mr. Rajagopalachari thought that there might be difficulty even about this if it came to be realised generally.

I then suggested that if that were the case, they had only to counter it by saying that this continuation of the link with the Crown would be reviewed after five years or any other period they thought desirable.

Mr. Rajagopalachari thought that this might be a solution, and he would give the matter further consideration. I pointed out that if he quoted me to anybody else it would not help in his pursuing the matter, and he entirely agreed, and said he did not intend to mention the fact that we had discussed it.

We talked of course of the analogy of Ireland; and finally he asked whether it would not be possible to have some UNO organisation through which the loan of British officers would be possible; but I came back to my original suggestion as being the only one I could see by which they could have our officers.

I ended by saying "In any case it is absolutely no concern of mine what happens to your Services after June 1948, and the only people who would gain by not severing their connection with the Crown would be the Indians; and I therefore do not intend to say anything more about it."

122

Record of Interview between Rear-Admiral Viscount Mountbatten of Burma and Lieutenant-Colonel de la Fargue

Mountbatten Papers. Viceroy's Interview No. 49

TOP SECRET   *11 April 1947*
HIGHLY RESTRICTED CIRCULATION
The meeting lasted from 12.45 to 1.45 p.m.

Lt-Col. de la Fargue is Chief Secretary, N.W.F.P. Government. He stated that in his opinion a free clean election in the Frontier Province would be more likely to return Congress to power than the League. He said it would be necessary to go into Section 93, because if the party in power arranged the elections they would almost always be rigged unfairly. But even with a Section 93 Government, he thought that an election would return Congress to power.

He said that Abdul Ghaffar Khan was the most unpopular man on the Frontier, but that on the other hand his brother Dr. Khan Sahib was absolutely first class, and all stories about his being neurotic and unbalanced were nonsense, and arose from his outbursts of ungovernable temper. He himself had even had to strike him once to bring him to his senses, after which they had been better friends than before.

I told him that though in normal times I would consider it highly reprehensible to discuss his Governor with him, I was sure Lord Ismay would agree that in this time of absolute crisis I must obtain a British opinion on Pandit Nehru's shocking report on the Governor. Pandit Nehru had in fact asked for his removal and had spoken to me about it in no unmeasured terms.

Colonel de la Fargue very courageously replied that although the Governor was a man with great knowledge of the Frontier, he was in fact biassed against his Congress Government, and had lost the confidence of all fair-minded people in the Province. He said that his continuation in office was in fact a menace to British prestige.

123

Mr Gandhi to Rear-Admiral Viscount Mountbatten of Burma

Mountbatten Papers. Papers of Special Interest, File (2) of 1947

BHANGI COLONY, READING ROAD,
NEW DELHI, *11 April 1947*

Dear Friend,

I had several short talks with Pandit Nehru and an hour's talk with him alone, and then with several members of the Congress Working Committee last night, about the formula I had sketched before you and which I had filled in for them with all the implications. I am sorry to say that I failed to carry any of them with me except Badshah Khan.

I do not know that, having failed to carry both the head and heart of Pandit Nehru with me, I would have wanted to carry the matter further. But Panditji was so good that he would not be satisfied until the whole plan was discussed with the few members of the Congress Working Committee who were present. I felt sorry that I could not convince them of the correctness of my plan from every point of view. Nor could they dislodge me from my position although I had not closed my mind against every argument. Thus, I have to ask you to omit me from your consideration. Congressmen, who are in the Interim Government are stalwarts, seasoned servants of the nation and, therefore so far as the Congress point of view is concerned, they will be complete advisers.

I would still love you to take the place that the late C. F. Andrews took. He represented no one but himself. And, if you ever need my service on its merits, it will be always at your disposal.

In the circumstances above mentioned, subject to your consent, I propose, if possible, to leave tomorrow for Patna.

I have not forgotten the book about tribal expeditions. I have not yet been able to lay my hands on it, for I cannot recall the name of the author nor the year in which I read the book. As I told you, it was years ago in South Africa that I came across it. My search will continue wherever I am and as soon as I trace the book, it shall be sent to you.

I must confess a slip of memory I am answerable for in the course of our talks. I was wrong in connecting Sir Francis Mudie with the late Pandit Nehru. The incident I referred to was in connection with 'Muddiman', not 'Mudie'. The charge, almost universally believed by Congressmen against the present Governor of Sind, remains unaltered, in spite of my slip of memory.[1]

I hope these constant interviews are not proving an unbearable strain.

Yours sincerely,
M. K GANDHI

[1] See No. 73 for the record of Mr Gandhi's observations on Sir F. Mudie.

124

Sir E. Mieville to Rear-Admiral Viscount Mountbatten of Burma

Mountbatten Papers. Official Correspondence Files: Interviews

11 April 1947

Your Excellency,

I saw Mr Jinnah for half an hour this afternoon. He was at his very best. He started by recalling the luncheon party at which we were both present at Buckingham Palace last December and told me how much he had enjoyed it. He said that his enjoyment was enhanced by the fact that on talking to the King he found that His Majesty was pro Pakistan. On talking to the Queen after luncheon he found that Her Majesty was even more pro Pakistan, and finally when he had a conversation with Queen Mary he found that Her Majesty was 100% Pakistan! I replied that I was sorry that Their Majesties had acted in such an unconstitutional way as to express their opinions on political matters connected with their Indian Empire, at which he laughed quite a lot.

After a few remarks on Pakistan we got down to the draft statement which Your Excellency handed to him yesterday deploring the bloodshed and acts of violence throughout the country. He started by saying that in many of his speeches he had condemned such violence in far stronger terms than set out in the draft. I then pointed out to him that the whole object of the draft was that it should be signed both by him on behalf of the Muslim League and by Mr Kripalani as President of Congress. He replied that he did not think Mr Kripalani's name would carry any weight with the masses and in fact the only name that would do so in addition to himself was Mr Gandhi's. He then said that I could tell Your Excellency that if Mr Gandhi would put his signature to such a statement, as to the exact terms of which he was not particular (he quite liked the draft statement as set out but thought perhaps some amendments would be necessary) he would be perfectly ready to sign it himself.

He finally said that he must be frank and tell me that such a suggestion had been made by Lord Wavell on the occasion of the Calcutta riots and on that occasion Mr Gandhi had refused to sign on the grounds that he was no longer an active member of the Congress Working Party and that he held no official position at all. He did not know what Mr Gandhi's reactions would be in this case but repeated that so far as the masses were concerned he thought that from the Congress angle Mr Gandhi's was the only name that would carry the necessary weight.

E. MIEVILLE

125

Record of Interview between Rear-Admiral Viscount Mountbatten of Burma and Pandit Nehru

Mountbatten Papers. Viceroy's Interview No. 51

TOP SECRET   *11 April 1947*

The meeting lasted from 4 to 5.30 p.m.

I began by giving him an account of my negotiations up to date with Mr. Jinnah. Pandit Nehru did not express any surprise, and said he thought that they had gone pretty well exactly as he feared they would.

I pointed out to Pandit Nehru that I had been able to tell Mr. Jinnah in all honesty that I had not discussed any solution with any member of the Congress other than Mr. Gandhi, and that his was a plan that I had said I would not consider unless it was clear that influential members of Congress were prepared to back it.

Pandit Nehru was obviously pleased to find that my independent and impartial conclusions were very much on the same lines as he would like to have seen them adopted, namely a unified India with a strong Centre.

At this stage Sir Eric Mieville came in with the draft of the joint truce message, which had been submitted to Mr. Jinnah. Pandit Nehru expressed great surprise that Mr. Jinnah was prepared to sign a statement renouncing the use of force for political purposes; but he agreed that it would be an excellent thing if he would do so.

Sir Eric said that Mr. Jinnah wanted Mr. Gandhi to be the co-signatory and not Mr. Kripalani. He had further warned Sir Eric that Mr. Gandhi had refused to sign a document in similar circumstances after the Bengal massacres. Pandit Nehru pointed out that this was not exactly true and he thought that it might be possible to get Mr. Gandhi to sign.

At this stage a letter was brought in from Mr. Gandhi[1] saying that he had been unable to get leading members of Congress to support his plan, and proposed to leave for Patna on the next day. I sent a message asking him to come and see me at 11.45 on the following morning to discuss the statement and report progress.

Pandit Nehru undertook to talk the matter over with Mr. Gandhi before I saw him.

After this I asked Lord Ismay to join the meeting and he explained the position about producing a programme for the implementation of Pakistan.

The discussion was however cut short by the arrival of Mr. Liaquat Ali Khan, and I asked that Pandit Nehru and Lord Ismay should continue their conversations over the weekend.

Unfortunately time did not permit me to ask Pandit Nehru for the exact Congress proposals for the boundary revisions in the Punjab and Bengal; and this is information which Lord Ismay will have to obtain from him when next he sees him.

Meanwhile I warned Pandit Nehru that Mr. Jinnah was going to counter with a request for the partition of Assam. Pandit Nehru said that this was a perfectly reasonable request and could easily be agreed to.

[1] No. 123.

126

Record of Interview between Rear-Admiral Viscount Mountbatten of Burma and Mr Liaquat Ali Khan

Mountbatten Papers. Viceroy's Interview No. 52

TOP SECRET   *11 April 1947*
The meeting lasted from 5.30 to 6.40 p.m.

First of all I gave Mr. Liaquat Ali Khan a rough outline of my conversations with Mr. Jinnah, and reiterated the present position as regards working out a Pakistan plan. I was most impressed by the way he took my statement that

I would in no circumstances prevent Provinces from being partitioned if I accepted the principle of Pakistan.

He quite saw all the mechanical difficulties and the delays that there must be, and asked me what I would do to ensure continuity after I left in June 1948.

I told him that I contemplated making a public statement giving the programme which I thought ought to be followed and the principles on which negotiations should be conducted. His reply was "Ah, but supposing they do not adhere to what you have laid down?" I replied "That would be just too bad; that is one of the penalties you have to pay for being free." To which he replied "But do you not recognise that your responsibilities extend beyond June 1948? If your Government fix a date which cannot be adhered to, are you going to imperil the implementation of your decision?" To this I replied: "Most certainly; it has nothing to do with us after June 1948."

He then discussed the partition of the Army, about which he wrote to me on [7 April].[1] I pointed out to him that so long as I was statutorily responsible for law and order in India nothing would induce me to take one step that would imperil the efficiency of the Army. He fully accepted this.

I said I would put up proposals for setting up the necessary machinery to produce plans and finally implement a split; but that it would be along the lines that the Indian parties themselves would have to work out the final details.

He said "After June 1948, who will see that the Centre uses the Army correctly and not unfairly?" I said "Presumably you will have two Defence Ministers meeting on equal terms and giving joint agreed instructions to a single Commander-in-Chief".

He then asked me whether there was any chance of this Commander-in-Chief being British, and I replied that that was entirely dependent on the Congress and the Muslim League getting together and saying they wished to retain sufficient connection with the Commonwealth to enable them to have the services of a British Commander-in-Chief.

On this he said "But there is no doubt that Pakistan wants to remain a dominion, we want to have your officers." I replied that I was not prepared even to discuss the suggestion of any part of India remaining within the Empire unless the suggestion came from all parties together, and even then I could not say what the policy of H.M.G. would be. I said that if he discussed the matter during his visit to London,[2] would he please bear in mind that this had been my answer to him, and that this was in accordance with the policy of H.M.G. He said he quite understood and would respect my attitude.

[1] No. 94.

[2] It had been intended that Mr Liaquat Ali Khan, with two other Members of the Interim Cabinet, should lead the Indian delegation to the Sterling Balances negotiations to be held in London during May 1947. In the event these discussions did not take place and a party of Indian officials visited London in July to discuss interim arrangements.

I mentioned to him very briefly that the Orissa Government wanted some money; but unfortunately at this moment we were interrupted, and I never got down to receiving his reactions.

After the interruption he raised the question of the Appointments Committee. He pointed out that it was Sardar Vallabhbhai Patel who had put this up and that his object in doing so had been to ensure that in even those five portfolios which Muslim League Members held the Congress could put in whomever they liked, since the matter would ultimately be settled by a majority vote in the Cabinet. For that reason the League would sooner have the appointments of only five out of the 17 Departments, than be defeated even in these five by Cabinet vote.

I said I could not share his view. I was there as a trustee for the Government of India as a whole and not for any one particular party. I considered he should accept the External Appointments Committee consisting of Pandit Nehru, himself and Sardar Baldev Singh, and an Internal Appointments Committee consisting of Sardar Patel, himself and Dr. Matthai.

He said he would agree on two conditions: (a) that the Member whose Departments were being considered should be co-opted as a Member of the Committee for this item, thus ensuring that in League Departments they would be at least "two—two"; (b) that the Appointments Committees should make their recommendations direct to me and not to the Cabinet, since he pointed out that the present procedure was that the Member concerned sent his proposal to the Viceroy and with the Viceroy's concurrence the appointment was made. The procedure now would be that the Committee could send their recommendations to the Viceroy who would make the appointments; in the event of disagreement between the members of the Committee, the Committee would meet the Viceroy who would give a decision on merit.

He pointed out that I would be put in an intolerable position if the matter had to come to the whole Cabinet; personalities would be discussed, and finally a vote would be taken which I would find it almost impossible to overrule.

I promised to go into this and communicate with him further.[3]

(P.S.V. Please see me *re* this point.)

Finally, he asked me whether I would see Mr. Jinnah's Deputy Leader of the Muslim League in the Legislative Assembly. I said I would be glad to do so when I could fit him in, and would in any case ask to see him at the Garden Party.

[3] In the event Lord Mountbatten decided not to proceed with the proposal for Appointments Committees and on 28 April he sent Mr Liaquat Ali Khan a letter in similar terms to the one to Pandit Nehru which is summarised in No. 145, note 1. Mountbatten Papers, Official Correspondence Files: Cabinet (Indian).

127

Sir F. Burrows (Bengal) to Rear-Admiral Viscount Mountbatten of Burma
(Extract)

L/P&J/5/154: f 56

SECRET   GOVERNMENT HOUSE, CALCUTTA, *11 April 1947*
F.J.B. 22

3. The movement for partitioning Bengal, to which I referred in my 'general' letter of March 19th,[1] continues to gather strength. A conference convened by the Hindu Mahasabha at Tarakeswar (Hooghly district) during the Easter holidays was attended by a very large and enthusiastic audience. A resolution was passed authorizing Dr Syama Prasad Mookerjee to constitute a council of action to establish a separate homeland for the Hindus of Bengal; 100,000 volunteers are to be enrolled by the end of June, the Constituent Assembly are to be asked to appoint a Boundary Commission; and as soon as the area of the new Province has been settled, the Hindu members of the Legislative Assembly in this area are to demand that it should be constituted into a Province, if necessary leaving the Bengal Assembly and forming themselves into a separate legislative body. It was emphasized that the new Province should be constituted before the British Government transferred power. Another resolution demanded the formation of two regional Ministries as an immediate step to restore peace and order in the Province. On the same day as the Tarakeswar Conference the Executive Committee of the Bengal Provincial Congress Committee also urged the immediate setting up of two regional Ministries, and resolved that if His Majesty's Government contemplated handing over its power to the existing Government of Bengal, such portions of Bengal as wished to remain within the Union of India should be formed into a separate Province. The attitude of the Hindu Mahasabha has surprised nobody, but the Muslims have been quick to criticize the manner in which the local Congress leaders have subordinated nationalism to communalism. The Communists continue to oppose partition, as does Sarat Bose's Forward Bloc, but the weight of Hindu opinion has definitely swung against them. The Muslim leaders are trying to laugh the movement off as a political stunt to kill Pakistan, but I think they now realise that the partitionists mean business. In all the discussions about partition, I have yet to see any reference to section 290 of the 1935 Act, which is the only constitutional method of altering the boundaries of a Province—though I appreciate that some departures from the Act may be necessary between now and June 1948.

[1] Vol. IX, No. 546.

128

Cabinet

India and Burma Committee. Paper I.B.(47)47

L/P&J/10/79: ff 513–17

CONSTITUTIONAL DEVELOPMENTS—ATTITUDE OF AFRIDIS
LETTER FROM GOVERNOR OF THE NORTH-WEST FRONTIER
PROVINCE TO THE PRIVATE SECRETARY TO THE VICEROY

NOTE BY THE SECRETARY OF STATE FOR INDIA

INDIA OFFICE, *11 April 1947*

I circulate herewith, for the information of my colleagues, a copy of a demi-official letter from the Governor of the North West Frontier Province to the Private Secretary to the Viceroy on the subject of the attitude of the Afridis to the present constitutional developments.

P.-L.

Sir O. Caroe to Mr Abell

CONFIDENTIAL   GOVERNMENT HOUSE, PESHAWAR,
D.O. No. GH–33   *17 March 1947*
Dear Abell,
I forward, for the information of His Excellency the Viceroy, a copy of a note and covering letter which I have addressed to the External Affairs Department after an interview with all the Maliks and some leading Elders of the Khyber tribes. Apart from anything which is done to bring this to the notice of the Constituent Assembly I think it important that what the Khyber tribes say should be brought to the notice of His Majesty's Government. What the Afridis say today the rest of the tribes will probably say tomorrow, or something very like it.

2. These matters of course raise directly my special responsibility, referred to in paragraph XV(a) of my Instrument of Instructions, by which I am categorically commanded to have no hesitation in exercising this special responsibility when danger arises such as is likely to affect the discharge of my functions *vis-à-vis* the tribes. I would think it right that I should be clearly informed on the authority of His Majesty's Government whether they desire that this responsibility, in present circumstances, should be discharged to the full or not. Such an assurance may conceivably arise over a visit by the Advisory Committee of the Constituent Assembly to this Province. But it would of course be necessary to decide on the basis of developments which arose how far the special responsibility was attracted by any particular circumstances. The

substantial necessity is that sufficient action should be taken to prevent any disintegration of the North-West Frontier during the period between now and handing over charge.

Yours sincerely,

O.K CAROE

Sir O. Caroe to Mr Weightman

D.O. No. GH–32   PESHAWAR, 17 March 1947
Dear Weightman,
I forward, for the information of the Government of India, a copy of a note which I have recorded after seeing a *Jirga* of the Khyber Maliks and certain leading Elders. I consider it to be a matter of great importance that the Afridi attitude in these matters should be conveyed to the proper quarters.

2. It is perhaps unnecessary for me to correct an impression which has gained ground that the Maliks and Elders are appointed by authority, and are therefore official nominees, who voice some sort of officially inspired policy. They are in reality, and not only in theory, selected by the people themselves and are the people's representatives. They cannot therefore say or do anything which they feel would be against the interest or general wishes of the tribe and for which the tribe would hold them responsible. They therefore take great care to say only those things in which they know their tribe would support them. There are many instances in which Sections have punished Maliks and Elders for action even in minor matters to which the Sections did not agree: in major matters of policy the leaders voice the majority tribal opinion of the time. There are of course dissentients in every body politic, but the leaders take the measure of them before they embark on a public statement of the wishes of the tribe.

3. The Afridi attitude will without doubt influence the decisions of other tribes.

Yours sincerely,

O. K. CAROE

PESHAWAR, 15 March 1947

I had my annual interview with all the leading Maliks and Elders of the Khyber Afridis and the Shinwaris to-day. Speaking with solemnity, they said they wished to give me advance information of what the bigger *Jirga* of the Afridi tribe had to say on the present situation, and it was as follows. There was a message which they desired should be communicated to the Government of India, and through them to H.M.G. They were the leading tribe on the North-West Frontier, and they thought they did not speak with too much pride in believing that their lead would be generally followed by the other tribes. They asked that their decision should be conveyed to Government, and it was this. On no account were they prepared to deal in any way with the Advisory Committee of the present Constituent Assembly, which they regard as purely a Hindu body. Neither were they prepared to deal with any separate body which might seek to approach them on behalf of the Muslim League. On this point they wished it to be understood that they regarded the Muslim League as mainly representative of Muslim India only, and if they wanted to join up with any exclusively Moslem organisation they were much closer to Afghanistan. H.M.G., the Government of India, the Constituent Assembly itself, and India as a whole should understand that, until the Hindus and Moslems had come together, the Afridi tribe would not deal with any Committee which was sent up to the Frontier. They added that if any member of a partial Committee were to seek entrance to their territory they would refuse it and would not accept responsibility for his safety. They also particularly asked that it should be conveyed in the proper quarter that they would not accept Moslems who had adopted the Congress party ticket as true representatives of Moslem India. They further added that they would not agree as a tribe to deal with the Constituent Assembly in Peshawar: the meeting if any must be on their own ground. If any people went to a Peshawar meeting, they would be persons of no consequence and would be repudiated by the tribe.

2. They then said that they had been surprised that the North-West Frontier tribes had not been mentioned in the announcement made by the Prime Minister in Parliament on February 20th. As they saw the position the security of India's land frontiers must depend on the friendship of the North-West Frontier tribes, and they were potentially as important to India as the Indian States. They thought it strange that nothing had been said regarding their own position, and they wished it to be conveyed to H.M.G. that when the time came for handing over power they would expect transfer of the Khyber Pass to be made to themselves, and not to the Hindu Congress or the Muslim League. They had of course certain benefits which they would desire to secure for themselves in return for the free use of the Khyber Pass, and they were prepared to negotiate these.

3. I told the Maliks that what they had said would be conveyed to the proper quarter. I reminded them at the same time that there were two sides to every agreement, and they must not forget that their economic future, and their benefits in the way of service and so on, were bound up with India in a very particular way. I also observed to them that now that the Brigade had been withdrawn from the Khyber and the Khyber Rifles substituted for troops, the security of the Pass was entirely in the hands of the Khyber Rifles and the Khassadars, all of whom were local tribesmen, so that in effect the guardianship of the Khyber had already been returned to them.

4. There is no doubt that the Maliks meant what they said, and that what they said represents the present feeling of the tribe as a whole.

O. K. CAROE

Governor and A.G.G., N.W.F.P.

129

Viceroy's Staff Meetings
Uncirculated Record of Discussion No. 7

Mountbatten Papers

TOP SECRET

Those present during this discussion which took place at the end of The Viceroy's Fourteenth Staff Meeting held at The Viceroy's House, New Delhi on 12 April 1947 at 10 am were: Rear-Admiral Viscount Mountbatten of Burma, Lord Ismay, Sir E. Mieville, Mr Abell, Captain Brockman, Mr I. D. Scott, Mr Campbell-Johnson, Lieutenant-Colonel Erskine Crum

HIS EXCELLENCY THE VICEROY said that of the many possible plans which were still under consideration, the two receiving most thought at the moment were:—

(a) Plan "Union", which was the Cabinet Mission's plan possibly modified in some respects; and

(b) Plan "Balkan", which contemplated leaving to each Province the choice of its own future and would almost certainly result in a form of truncated Pakistan and the eventual abolition of a Centre, although it would be necessary to retain a Centre for some time after June, 1948, at least to deal with Defence until the Armed Forces were divided.

Plan "Union"

MR. ABELL said that Mr. Jinnah had always proclaimed that he would accept the Cabinet Mission plan if Congress did so unreservedly. He gave his opinion that there was now no chance of Congress doing this. LORD ISMAY said that he did not believe that it was impossible that Congress would do so, though it would indeed mean a complete change of heart.

HIS EXCELLENCY THE VICEROY said that he believed that there was a chance that, if the alternatives were clearly stated to them, the Congress leaders would take the step forward required to denote unequivocal acceptance. He had got the impression that the Congress leaders desired a united India above all and might well, if they were told the alternative, decide to accept Plan "Union" so as to achieve this end. The next step must clearly be to try and obtain Congress's agreement.

HIS EXCELLENCY THE VICEROY said that he had learnt the previous day that Mr. Gandhi's plan, which involved offering the premiership of the Interim Government and the selection of a new Cabinet to Mr. Jinnah, had been turned down by the Congress leaders. He was going to see Mr. Gandhi that morning and would try and work round to the possibility of getting his influence to bear on the unreserved acceptance by Congress of the Cabinet Mission's plan. Not until after that acceptance would it be possible to approach Mr. Jinnah again.

MR. SCOTT suggested that the Viceroy might then appeal to a representative Muslim body before accepting Mr. Jinnah's opinion as final. There were three such bodies in existence—the All-India Muslim League Council, the All-India Muslim League Committee and the Muslim members of the Constituent Assembly who had been elected although they had never taken their seats. HIS EXCELLENCY THE VICEROY said that this was indeed a suggestion worthy of consideration, although he would obviously not be able to address the chosen body in person. Perhaps a member of his staff might read an address from him, or such an address might be recorded. It would be valueless to leave it to Mr. Jinnah to put his (His Excellency's) point of view forward. MR SCOTT emphasized that, if this appeal to a Muslim body was made, the maximum publicity for it would be necessary, the issue must be put before the whole world. In a private meeting, not open to the glare of world publicity, Mr. Jinnah would, without doubt, have his own way.

HIS EXCELLENCY THE VICEROY said that a possible alternative would be to call a Press Conference and, through that, tell the world in concise and irrevocable language exactly what the situation was. He pointed out that he had got the Prime Minister's permission to convene a Press Conference whenever he thought it necessary.

MR SCOTT pointed out that the Muslim League's main fear was what was going to happen to them after June, 1948. HIS EXCELLENCY THE VICEROY said that this was confirmed by points raised in an interview which he had had the previous day with Mr. Liaquat Ali Khan.[1] The latter had suggested that after June, 1948, an impartial British head of the State should remain. HIS EXCELLENCY THE VICEROY said that such a person would be in a most difficult position as impartial decisions were always apt to annoy both sides. LORD ISMAY and SIR ERIC MIEVILLE agreed that such a person would be in an impossible position, having responsibility with no authority.

Plan "Balkan"

HIS EXCELLENCY THE VICEROY said that, if plan "Balkan" was eventually chosen, he intended, when the announcement of the decision was made, to broadcast a preamble showing how negotiations had progressed since his arrival. He would make clear that he had tried throughout to look at the

whole problem objectively. He would say that he had always believed that an
united India was the ideal answer, preferably with a Central Government
similar to that at present in power, and with safeguards for the minorities. He
would point out that he had devoted a long time to trying to obtain acceptance
of a plan for an united India but that in the end he had found that it would be
impossible to impose such a plan without a recrudescence of bloodshed,
leading perhaps to civil war. He had therefore decided that the only answer
was to leave the decision in the hands of the people themselves and to give the
Provinces freedom to decide on their own future with the option of joining
one or more groups.

SIR ERIC MIEVILLE asked how the Provinces would make their decisions.
HIS EXCELLENCY THE VICEROY pointed out that in most cases there was no
doubt of what each Province desired. In the North-West Frontier, however, it
would probably be necessary to have an election; and in the Punjab and
Bengal partition might have to come. He went on to say that he would, in this
preamble, make clear the choices which had been put before Mr. Jinnah—
acceptance of Plan "Union" with a small centre and what would, in fact, be an
untruncated Pakistan; or a truncated Pakistan with some central organisation
to begin with at any rate, as the Army was certainly going to remain united
until June, 1948. The preamble would have to contain a review of the sincere
attempts on the part of the British to find a peaceful solution. It would require
most careful presentation.

MR. ABELL said that during his conversation with Rao Bahadur Menon the
previous day, the latter had at first insisted on the desirability for granting
Dominion status to India immediately if Plan "Balkan" was brought into
operation. He had pointed out the disadvantages of this and had given his
opinion that the Governor General must keep the power in his own hands
until June, 1948. Rao Bahadur Menon had eventually withdrawn from this
position.

Finally, LORD ISMAY threw out the suggestion that the possibility of
making use of the United Nations Organisation should not be ruled out.

[1] See No. 126.

130

*Record of Interview between Rear-Admiral Viscount Mountbatten of Burma
and Mr Hossain Imam*

Mountbatten Papers. Viceroy's Interview No. 53

TOP SECRET   *12 April 1947*

The meeting lasted from 11.10 to 11.40 a.m.

Mr. Hossain Imam told me the usual tale of woe about Congress perfidy
against the Muslim League, and explained how it was that Congress had

wrecked the chance of the Cabinet Mission plan being adhered to. I asked him what he suggested I should do, and of course he came out with "Pakistan". I pointed out that the Pakistan principle could be applied also to the extent of partitioning the Punjab and Bengal; with the logic of which he agreed, but appealed to me to "temper logic with mercy"!

I then said that although my mind was still completely open, two alternatives were beginning to take shape in my mind: (a) that we should do everything in our power to try and get a Union of India in the interests of her future greatness and prosperity, and that the Cabinet Mission plan appeared to be the best solution. I asked him whether he thought the Muslim League would accept the Cabinet Mission plan if Congress unreservedly accepted H.M.G.'s declaration of the 6th December last, and also agreed that the Centre should be operated in such a way as not to impose the will of the majority on the minority on questions of defence, etc.

He replied that so long as Congress couldn't impose direct taxation to raise the finance needed for defence, but could only call upon Hindustan and Pakistan to pay the appropriate contribution proportionate to their population and wealth, and provided they couldn't misuse the Army to their own advantage, he himself thought that the Cabinet Mission plan might prove acceptable. He pointed out, however, with considerable truth, that unless there were an agreement which both sides intended to honour in the spirit as well as in the letter, with real goodwill and mutual trust, he failed to see how any form of union could function; and if it could not function then it was better to split, however unfairly the partition might work out for the Muslims.

This brought me to my second alternative; and I said that if partition had to come, it would have to be applied not only for India as a whole but in such Provinces as wished to partition themselves. In other words my alternative (b) was a completely moth-eaten Pakistan, without even the port of Calcutta.

Mr. Hossain Imam was horrified at my suggestion that there should be a Pakistan without the port of Calcutta, and once more appealed to me to give Pakistan some chance of survival.

At the end he expressed the hope that I would not come to any decision until I had seen how the Constituent Assembly was working on the 28th April, since I should then see the Congress aim of domination over the Muslims. I invited him to keep me or Sir Eric Mieville informed of such proceedings in the Constituent Assembly as he thought bore out his contention.

Mr. Hossain Imam appears to me to be a much more moderate-minded Muslim than I have recently come across, and his arguments appear to be reasonably unprejudiced.

131

Record of Interview between Rear-Admiral Viscount Mountbatten of Burma and Mr Gandhi

Mountbatten Papers. Viceroy's Interview No. 54

TOP SECRET   *12 April 1947*

The meeting lasted from 11.45 a.m. to 1.45 p.m.

I thanked him for the letter[1] he had sent me the previous day saying that he had been unable to get his great plan for a Jinnah government through responsible members of Congress, and had therefore had to withdraw it. He regretted his failure very much, but said he thought I could still go ahead on the plan myself if I ardently believed in it.

I told him that however much I believed in it I couldn't possibly go ahead with success in a matter in which he had already failed himself with the Congress.

I then told him I wanted to report to him in strict confidence all my conversations with Mr. Jinnah, to put him in the picture.

I then said that although my mind was still open I was now particularly studying two alternative solutions: (a) the Cabinet Mission plan; (b) a truncated Pakistan. I asked him how much he personally favoured a united India, and of course he said he was extremely anxious for it. I asked him how far he thought Congress would go towards accepting the Cabinet Mission plan, and warned him that Mr. Jinnah was bitterly opposed to the Cabinet Mission plan and therefore Congress would have to go at least as far as Mr. Jinnah wanted before he would even consider it.

Mr. Gandhi said that the whole bone of contention was the interpretation of the meaning of the Cabinet Mission plan, and he suggested that I should call in the High Court to interpret it. I told him that the differences of opinion had already been resolved by the statement of the Cabinet of the 6th December; but he held that the people who drafted the statement were not the people who had to interpret it, and gave as an analogy Acts of Parliament. He said that if a difference of opinion arose as to the meaning of a particular clause in law, it was the judge who settled the meaning and who interpreted the law and not the people who framed the law. He seemed convinced that Congress would accept any interpretation the High Court gave.

I told him I did not see how we could possibly have a different interpretation put on the meaning of the Cabinet Mission plan to that which the Cabinet Mission themselves had announced on December the 6th after taking legal advice.

No. 123.

I then discussed the joint statement calling for a truce and a denunciation of the use of force to obtain political ends. He said he would gladly sign the statement shown to him or any similar statement if Mr. Jinnah and I wished him to do so; though he must point out that the statement, to have any value, should be signed by Mr. Kripalani on behalf of the Congress as a whole.

He said he had told Pandit Nehru that if indeed I could get Mr. Jinnah to sign and abide by this statement, I should have taken the greatest step politically in the recent history of India, and one which he hoped he had been instrumental in putting into my head.

Although I have absolutely no recollection of Mr. Gandhi making any such suggestion, I felt it would be politic not to point this out. For although I believed it to have been my own idea I am only too delighted that he should take the credit.

In the meanwhile Lord Ismay came down at my request with the Cabinet Mission plan and the Statement of December the 6th. Mr. Gandhi appeared never to have read this statement although he knew of its existence. He thought he was at Noakhali at the time and did not have time to read it. After reading it very carefully he came back to his original point of view that the Cabinet Mission statement should be submitted to the High Court for interpretation, and he felt sure the Congress would abide by their decision.

Lord Ismay pointed out that it was less a matter of finding out what the actual legal interpretation was than of ascertaining what common interpretation would be acceptable both to the Muslim League and Congress; and to this Mr. Gandhi unreservedly agreed.

Meanwhile he called upon me to renounce the use of the British Army, and said that he included the British officers of the Indian Army in that term; in other words any of the armed forces under my orders.

I pointed out that except for the Punjab, which is under a Section 93 Government, in all other Provinces it was the local Government that called out the troops, and that if he wanted that practice to stop, why didn't he make a start by talking to the Congress Government in Bihar where he was off to that evening. He said sadly he had already spoken to them, and that if they had had a strong conviction of non-violence they would offer themselves as sacrifices rather than allow these massacres to continue or trying to stop them by the use of troops.

I did not altogether follow his argument here, and may have misquoted him. But since it appeared to be purely academic, and a matter he was going to put before the local Congress Govt. in Bihar, I did not pursue it.

He then said that he advised me to go on strengthening the Interim Government, and making them function correctly for the next 14 months; after which he considered I should hand over power to the Interim Government. This staggered Lord Ismay and myself, and we both pointed out that that meant handing over power to one party, namely Congress, to the grave disadvantage of the other party, the Muslim League, which would not fail to produce strife, possibly leading to civil war.

Mr. Gandhi, with a wily smile, pointed out that if Mr. Jinnah indeed signed the paper we were sending round to him he could not again use force for political purposes.

I must say I was speechless to find that he proposed, if Mr. Jinnah indeed meant to both sign and stick to the statement, to take advantage of this to impose a Congress Government over the Muslims. Here again I find it hard to believe that I correctly understood Mr. Gandhi.

Finally, after substituting the word "communities" instead of "peoples" and having the declaration of truce retyped, Mr. Gandhi appended his signature in all three scripts: English, Urdu and Gujerati; and Lord Ismay took the paper for Sir Eric Mieville to take round to Mr. Jinnah.

132

Record of Interview between Rear-Admiral Viscount Mountbatten of Burma and Sardar Patel

Mountbatten Papers. Viceroy's Interview No. 55

TOP SECRET   12 April 1947

The interview lasted from 3 to 4.15 p.m.

I first of all gave Patel an account of my negotiations with Mr. Jinnah, and an explanation of why I have never consulted him, or any member of Congress, before as to the solution that they suggested should be followed for the transfer of power. I pointed out that this had meant that I could truthfully tell Mr. Jinnah of my own views for the best future of India without having got my ideas from any member of Congress. I told him that my own views were that the very best for the future of India would be a firm Union with a strong Central Government, and that I would like to see the present Interim Government operating by itself, with the possible addition of Mr. Jinnah with an important portfolio, and to transfer power to that Central Government when I leave in June 1948.

I told him that my next best solution was the Cabinet Mission plan, and that the one solution that I did not wish to be forced into was Pakistan, but that if it were Pakistan it would have to be a truncated Pakistan.

I then asked Sardar Patel if he felt that Congress could be made to accept the Cabinet Mission plan without any reservations. He asked me if I meant by that that they should accept H.M.G.'s statement of the 6th or 7th December.

pointed out that what I meant was that if Mr. Jinnah could be made to accept the Cabinet Mission plan, then that Congress and he should accept the same interpretation, or at least agree upon an interpretation to be accepted. Sardar Patel informed me that it was he who finally got Congress to agree to accept the Cabinet Mission plan at the last moment, and that he remained the strongest protagonist in the Congress Party of the Cabinet Mission plan. (In passing it may be of interest to record that Lord Wavell informed me on the 22nd March that it was Sir Stafford Cripps who went to Sardar Patel and persuaded him that Congress' best interests lay in accepting the Cabinet Mission plan, since otherwise it left the field clear to the Muslim League. He implied that the motive was to obtain an apparent success for the Cabinet Mission and conceal for as long as possible their failure.)

Sardar Patel told me that the mistake that all the British had permanently made with Mr. Jinnah was always to give way to him, as a means of saving his face. He said that Mr. Jinnah would only accept the Cabinet Mission plan when the force of circumstances gave him no alternative. He told me that as soon as I announced the partition of Bengal, the Muslims of Bengal would secede from the League in order to preserve the entity of Bengal. He thought that this might possibly follow in the Punjab, and it would not be unlikely that there would be a revolt of the League against Mr. Jinnah if he had nothing better than the Sind, and possibly half of the Punjab to offer them for Pakistan, if Congress still retained their hold on the N.W.F.P.

Thus he thought that there was a real chance that either Mr. Jinnah would be forced to come to my terms, or be overthrown by the League. In either case Sardar Patel promised me his support in getting Congress to support the Cabinet Mission plan at such a moment. He promised to send me information as to the exact present position of Congress with regard to the acceptance of the Cabinet Mission plan.

He complained very bitterly at the decision he had only recently learnt that H.M.G. would not turn over the Secretary of State's Services until June 1948.[1] He asked me how I imagined it was going to be possible for the Interim Government to govern, if they had no control over their Services, and how he could get rid of disloyal members who are harming the Central Government.

I told him that if he reported to me any cases of disloyalty, and supported it by good evidence, I would take any necessary steps myself.

I pointed out to him that since it was now highly doubtful that there would be a unified India, and since, in fact, Pakistan was looming up before us, I did not see to whom the Secretary of State's services could be turned over, since it was not even clear who would be in Pakistan and who would be in Hindustan.

Finally he made a long dispassionate and reasoned indictment against Lord Wavell in his system of government. He said that until the formation of the Interim Government, Lord Wavell had governed with a strong Centre, and had kept law and order in the Provinces. Since the formation of the Interim Government Lord Wavell had allowed such power to go to the Provinces that they could defy the Central Government, and by the introduction of the Muslim League members, against the advice of Congress, had so weakened the Centre that India was rapidly disintegrating into a lawless state.

He called upon me to strengthen and support the Central Government to keep unruly Provinces in order, and show that I meant to maintain proper law and order, and stop further bloodshed.

I replied that my first preoccupation must be to find, as soon as possible, the correct solution and announce it, which I felt would do more than anything else to remove the causes of the strife. In the meanwhile I intended to put out a truce, to be signed by Mr. Gandhi and Mr. Jinnah.

¹ See No. 59, note 5.

133

Record of Interview between Rear-Admiral Viscount Mountbatten of Burma and Maulana Azad

Mountbatten Papers. Viceroy's Interview No. 56

TOP SECRET   *12 April 1947*

The interview lasted from 4.15 until 5.15 p.m.

I gave Maulana Azad the broad outline of my conversations with Mr. Jinnah. In conclusion he told me that whereas the full Pakistan, such as proposed by the Cabinet Mission, could be made to work, a truncated Pakistan would spell disaster for the Mussulmans, and that if Mr. Jinnah were now prepared to accept such a decision he would be committing suicide.

He failed to see why Mr. Jinnah could not accept the Cabinet Mission plan, since after all it gave them the right to secede from the rest of India at the end of ten years if they wished.

He said that I had handled the negotiations on absolutely correct lines, but advised me to find out the precise points on which Mr. Jinnah had decided to withdraw his acceptance of the Cabinet Mission plan, and that I should then try and meet these points.

He understood that Mr. Jinnah's objections were two-fold:—

(1) The way that the Sections would function in Group C. The main worry was Bengal and Assam, but this appeared to have been solved by H.M.G.'s statement of the 6th or 7th December.

(2) This was a minor point about the constitution of the Cabinet. Mr. Jinnah had been most insistent that if any vacancy among the minority

seats in the Cabinet occured, he should have a voice in filling the vacancy. Maulana Azad felt that the Congress could well agree to this League request if it were put up for action.

He went on to tell me that if I were to announce the partition of Bengal, he thought it highly likely that the Muslims of Bengal would separate from the League, and he thought that it was possible, but slightly less likely, that this would also happen in the Punjab. At least he said that if it became known that Mr. Jinnah had agreed to a partition, there would probably be a violent reaction from the Muslims of these Provinces, which might lead to revolt.

Maulana Azad volunteered to go to any length to support me in trying to get the Cabinet Mission plan accepted by both Congress and the League. He told me that whatever anybody else told me, it was his conviction that if Mr. Jinnah really accepted the Cabinet Mission plan, at almost any stage within the next few months, the chances of Congress co-operating were really very fair.

He next raised the question of the frontier. He pointed out that in the N.W.F.P. there had always been a system of diarchy, and that the Government [Governor] had a responsibility both for the Provincial Government, and for the Political Department for the tribes. In 1938 the Congress Ministry felt the difficulty of this position, and had complained bitterly. Last year after the elections Maulana Azad went to Peshawar, and found that the Congress members, who had won the election, did not want to form a Ministry until they could be assured of the attitude of the new Governor, and the Political Department. He therefore went to see Lord Wavell, who said that Dr. Khan Sahib need have no apprehensions for Lord Wavell intended to give the new Governor instructions which would ensure his working in well with the Congress Ministry. Lord Wavell, at Maulana Azad's request, went so far as to write him a letter giving him this assurance, a copy of which Maulana Azad says he will send me.[1] Maulana Azad then went to Peshawar and recommended Dr. Khan Sahib to form a Ministry.

No sooner had Sir Olaf Caroe arrived than he made it quite clear that he was violently anti-Congress and pro-League. It was not only a question that he failed to give the full co-operation that Lord Wavell promised, but that he did not bother to conceal his deliberate hostility. Maulana Azad said that he had come to the painful conclusion that it was difficult, if not impossible, for the Congress Ministry to continue to co-operate with the Governor.

I told him that I had had similar reports from Pandit Nehru, Mr. Gandhi and Abdul Ghaffar Khan, and that I recognised that this was now acknowledged to be the Congress point of view. I had only been here three weeks and one hour, during which time I have been fully occupied on what I regarded as my first priority, an over-all solution for India. I should continue to treat that as my first priority, and I could not guarantee to devote any time to the Frontier at present. Furthermore, as soon as a decision could be announced, I considered that it would probably be necessary to go into Section 93 in the N.W.F.P., and to hold a new election. After that I would be quite prepared to consider whether the present Governor should continue. I pointed out that Lord Wavell had warned me of these attacks against the Governor, and had recommended me to take no precipitate action. Maulana Azad regretted that I felt it necessary to order fresh elections in the N.W.F.P., since he pointed out that very fair elections had been held only a year ago, and that beyond some propaganda by the League in the urban areas, nothing had happened to change the situation. In fact he thought that Congress would be re-elected.

I told him that Pandit Nehru had thought that Congress might not be re-elected, since the frontier people were always "against the Government". Maulana Azad asked me whether I would be prepared to hold elections in other Provinces, and I replied "No, not unless it could be proved to me that they were necessary". He then asked me why I considered an election necessary in the N.W.F.P., and I replied that in all other Provinces the separate electorates enable one to forecast, with considerable accuracy, the results of elections as between the League and Congress, since all Muslims voted for the League. In the N.W.F.P., however, the election was largely an issue between the Congress Muslims and the League Muslims, and of course there was no separate electorate in this case. I said that the results would clearly show whether the inhabitants wanted a League or a Congress Government.

Maulana Azad said that if I was detemined to hold an election, he presumed it would only be if I gave a decision in favour of Pakistan, since if the Cabinet Mission plan were accepted he assumed a Coalition Government would be formed in most Provinces, including the N.W.F.P.

[1] The letter referred to by Maulana Azad has not been traced.

134

Lord Pethick-Lawrence to Rear-Admiral Viscount Mountbatten of Burma

Mountbatten Papers. Letters to and from the Secretary of State

PRIVATE AND SECRET   INDIA OFFICE, *12 April 1947*

My dear Mountbatten,

Thank you for your letter of 2nd April,[1] enclosing the first of your series of personal reports, which, I need hardly say, I have read with the keenest interest. I quite agree that it will be the best plan that you should send me copies of these weekly reports for distribution to the Prime Minister and my colleagues

[1] No. 58.

of the Cabinet Mission and I at once passed on to them the copies of your first report which you sent me. The copy for His Majesty The King was also sent on immediately to South Africa.

2. It is clear from your first report and from subsequent Press messages that your exploratory talks have covered an immense amount of ground and the only cause for regret is that they should have disclosed a scene of such unrelieved gloom. However, it is heartening to know that you yourself have remained unaffected by the atmosphere prevailing around you.

3. I was interested to learn that the impressions you have formed so far go to confirm the view expressed in my letter of 27th March[2] that we are likely to have to reach conclusions before October as to how power is to be transferred in June of next year.

4. I must offer you my congratulations upon securing the agreement of the members of your Cabinet to the setting up of Cabinet Committees, which should do much to facilitate the transaction of business. I can quite understand that, to begin with, it is better that the Committees should be on an *ad hoc* basis but, once established, they should be capable of consolidation and development.

5. I am afraid that you will have found my private telegram No. 45 of 9th April[3] about compensation rather disconcerting. I have this morning received your private telegram 787–S,[4] urging that our previous decision to accept the recommendation of the Government of India in regard to the compensation of Indians should not be reversed. As you know, I have all along felt great difficulty over what I would regard as failure to carry out the undertaking given by Amery in June, 1945 and confirmed by myself at my meeting with members of the I.C.S. and Indian Police Associations in Delhi on 13th April, 1946.[5] The difficulty was brought home to me more forcibly than ever when we came to prepare revised drafts of the announcement to be made by yourself and of the statement to be made in Parliament and, after long and anxious personal consideration, I felt compelled to lay the full facts of the situation once again before my colleagues in order that there might be no question of their having taken a decision likely to land them in Parliamentary and other difficulties without full realisation of the facts. The matter was considered again by the India and Burma Committee yesterday evening and the Committee took a decision for which the Prime Minister will be seeking the approval of the full Cabinet at a meeting to be held on Monday afternoon, after which it will be possible to go ahead with the arrangements for an announcement before the end of the month on the basis of the Cabinet's decision.

6. I have received your letter No. 38/11 of 31st March,[6] seeking the in-

structions of His Majesty's Government as to the principles which should govern the withdrawal of British Forces from this country on the transfer of power. I am having the problem examined at once and will reply to your letter immediately a decision has been reached.

7. As regards other matters, you may like to know that Ernest Bevin, when he had a talk with Stalin in Moscow on the 24th March, brought up the subject of India, saying that we were trying to settle this difficult problem in the interests of world peace in such a way as not to prevent India from having friendly relations with us and our allies. He said that he foresaw dangers when the Indians attain their independence unless all of us acted with great care. Stalin apparently agreed that India is a difficult question and said that Russia was not interfering but wished success to Great Britain in her enterprise. It would clearly be imprudent to take Stalin's profession of non-interference at its face value, particularly having regard to certain recent signs to the contrary of which you will doubtless be aware, but it would be interesting to hear in due course any views you may have formed on this matter during the course of your preliminary *tour d'horizon*.

8. Wavell sent me on 4th March a copy of a memorandum by the Naga National Council which he had received, setting out the case of the Naga people. I have shown this to Sir Henry Knight, who agrees that we need not at this stage take the memorandum very seriously. His impression is that the Naga National Council is a self-constituted body of the more conservative educated Nagas, mainly Government officials and school-masters, living round Kohima, and represents little, if at all, the more distant tribal leaders and traditional "elders" of the villages. I should, however, be glad to hear from you at your convenience whether you attach any importance to the memorandum and, if so, what your views upon it are.[7]

9. Knight suggests that the real problem underlying the memorandum is the preservation of the Naga Hills' economic equilibrium until the bulk of the Nagas are educated enough to compete with the free and independent Indian voter. It is difficult to see how this is to be attained; some form of interim

[2] No. 26.   [3] No. 103.   [4] No. 118.   [5] See Vol. VII, No. 104.
[6] No. 38.
[7] It may be noted that on 29 March 1947 the Naga National Council sent a copy of this memorandum to the Prime Minister together with copies of letters dated 27 and 28 March 1947 to Lord Simon and Mr Churchill both of whom had also been sent copies of the memorandum. The memorandum sought, in its own words, 'to present the case of the Naga people for self-determination, for the realisation of which an appeal is made to H.M.G. and the Government of India to set up for the Naga people an Interim Government for a period of ten years, at the end of which the Naga people will be left to choose any form of Government under which they will live'. The India Office did not acknowledge the Memorandum either on the Prime Minister's behalf or the Secretary of State's, presumably because of the doubt (indicated in para. 8 above) whether the Council was fully representative of the Naga people as a whole. L/P &J/7/10635.

self-government with some control by the Central Indian Government seems inevitable. Mere incorporation into Assam might lead either to the collapse of the Naga economy and to famine or to the relapse of the Nagas into head-hunting isolation.

10. I note from Abell's letter to Harris No. 1005 of 22nd March[8] that the Constituent Assembly Sub-Committee on tribal and excluded areas is to visit Assam this month, and I shall be interested to hear how they get on. I also look forward to seeing Sir Andrew Clow's note[9] on the future of the Assam Hill areas to which reference is made in Abell's letter.

[Para. 11, on the undesirability of adding to the number of permanent European Judges, omitted.]

[8] and [9] *Ibid.*

135

Mr Liaquat Ali Khan to Rear-Admiral Viscount Mountbatten of Burma

L/PO/4/24: f 91

No. 26–P.S.F.R./47   NEW DELHI, *13 April 1947*
Dear Lord Mountbatten,

I thank you for your letter No. 38/11 of the 9th April 1947[1] which, as I pointed out in my last interview with you, shows some misunderstanding of the proposals in my letter No. PSF 2093/47 of the 7th April 1947.[2]

2. I made two suggestions:—

    (i) to secure an adequate representation of the Muslims in each branch of the Army, Navy and Air Force,

and (ii) to reorganise the Armed Forces so that they can be split up when a decision on the partition of the country is taken.

3. I did not ask and still do not ask for a partition of the Armed Forces at this stage. That would be as much prejudging the constitutional issue as the present plans which presuppose a United India. I suggested a middle course which would not be to the advantage or prejudice of either Party. This neutral position would be obtained by reorganising the forces in such a manner that they can be readily split up at the proper time.

4. As I explained in my earlier letter the present plans for the re-organisation and nationalisation of the Armed Forces assume that they are to continue as a single entity. No regard is, therefore, paid either to the creation of Muslim units or to the representation of Muslims in suitable numbers and ranks in all the arms and services. If this process continues unaltered the unique opportunity

which has presented itself for the re-organisation of the forces through de-mobilisation and the withdrawal of the British element will have been lost. A year later the Armed Forces will be down to their peace-time size. The Muslim officers and men will be distributed pell-mell over them. The control of the forces will be in Hindu hands. It would be futile to hope that in those circumstances, a re-organisation of the Armed Forces so as to provide a balanced force for Pakistan would ever be achieved.

5. The very least that should be done immediately is the preparation of a Plan for the partition of the Armed Forces. The preparation of such a plan by the Commander-in-Chief and his staff is an essential preliminary in any case and cannot possibly be held to prejudge the issue or to affect the Armed Forces in any way. It will necessarily take some weeks to prepare and if taken in hand at once should be ready by about the time that the decision on the main constitutional issue is reached. The time limit set by H.M.G. demands that no time should be lost. I hope, therefore, that you will agree to issue a directive to the Commander-in-Chief to prepare a Plan for the partition of the Armed Forces.

6. I shall be glad to know the outcome of your reference to the Commander-in-Chief about the inadequate representation of the Muslims in the Armed Forces and the steps which he proposes to take to rectify it.[3]

Yours sincerely,
LIAQUAT ALI KHAN

[1] No. 106.   [2] No. 94.

[3] Lord Mountbatten acknowledged this letter on 14 April. He said he felt it right that Mr Liaquat Ali Khan's proposals should now be considered by the Defence Committee and he suggested that Liaquat circulate a short paper containing his views before its next meeting. L/PO/4/24: f 90.

136

Mr Abell to Sir H. Dow (Bihar)

Telegram, Mountbatten Papers. Official Correspondence Files:
Political Situation in India and Constitutional Position of Viceroy,
Part 1

MOST IMMEDIATE   *13 April 1947, 8pm*
CONFIDENTIAL

795-S. Please see that following Private and Personal message from Viceroy is given to Gandhi on his arrival in Patna tonight:—

I so much enjoyed our talks during the past ten days and hope you have had a good journey.

Mr Jinnah is perfectly ready to sign statement deploring acts of violence etc. which you signed before you left Delhi provided that your and his signatures are the only ones that appear on the document. As you mentioned that you thought Mr Kripalani's signature might also be added, though I gathered that you did not make this a stipulation, I am not issuing statement until I hear from you. Pandit Nehru is agreeable to leaving matter to my discretion, but I feel I must have your views. Unless statement bears your signature alone Mr Jinnah will not sign. May I therefore appeal to you to agree. Please reply urgently.

137

Viceroy's Staff Meetings
Uncirculated Record of Discussion No. 8

Mountbatten Papers

TOP SECRET

Those present during this discussion which took place at the end of The Viceroy's Fifteenth Staff Meeting held at The Viceroy's House, New Delhi on 14 April 1947 at 10 am were: Rear–Admiral Viscount Mountbatten of Burma, Lord Ismay, Sir E. Mieville, Mr Abell, Captain Brockman, Mr I. D. Scott, Mr Campbell-Johnson, Lieutenant-Colonel Erskine Crum

LORD ISMAY said that, in consultation with Principal Sec., P.S.V. and Mr Menon, he had just completed the drafts of (i) a statement to be issued in the event of the choice of Plan 'Balkan'; (ii) a time-table of events; and (iii) a note outlining the salient features of the above papers for consideration at the Governors' Conference the following day.

HIS EXCELLENCY THE VICEROY said that he visualized first writing to Acharya Kripalani to ask whether the Congress Party was prepared to adhere to the Cabinet Mission's Plan as clarified by the statement of 6th December; or to inform him of exactly what reservations to this Plan they held. He would then try to arrange that the Congress Party should in fact have no reservations; and that they should include in this renunciation their support for the Sikhs, in so far as this affected unqualified acceptance of the plan. He would then transmit Congress's acceptance to Mr. Jinnah, and put before him the choice of

(a) accepting the Cabinet Mission's plan, which would in practice result in an untruncated Pakistan with a weak centre or

(b) insisting on the imposition of Plan 'Balkan', which would in practice result in a truncated Pakistan with a centre existing for some time to deal with the division of the Armed Forces, which would in no circumstances be split up before June 1948; and with some sort of a central organisation (even if it were only a Joint Chiefs of Staff organisation or a series of conferences) existing even after the division for the co-ordination of Defence.

LORD ISMAY suggested that it might be necessary, if it became apparent that Plan 'Balkan' would have to be decided upon, for His Excellency to fly to London in order to hasten a decision on the part of H.M.G. This would presumably take place before the Simla House-Party. MR ABELL said that he did not believe that H.M.G. were convinced of the urgency of the situation.

HIS EXCELLENCY THE VICEROY said that he would in all probability desire Lord Ismay to go to London on his behalf. In his next Personal Report, he intended to stress the urgency of reaching a quick decision, and to warn the Government of the likelihood of Lord Ismay's visit. He might also attach the draft statement itself. He hoped to have, by next Wednesday, the support of the Governors added to that of the Residents on the necessity for a very early decision. H.M.G. would have to be plainly told that failure to make a quick decision would be tantamount to failure to take the responsibility for civil war off the Viceroy's shoulders. The only alternative he could recommend, it should be made clear, was immediate evacuation. Permission would also have to be obtained for him to make a personal explanation of the events leading to the decision.

138

Record of Interview between Rear-Admiral Viscount Mountbatten of Burma and Field Marshal Auchinleck (Extract)

Mountbatten Papers. Viceroy's Interview No. 64

TOP SECRET   *14 April 1947*

(Note:—Lord Ismay and Sir Eric Mieville were present throughout this interview).

I showed the C-in-C. a copy of the letter[1] which I had received from Mr. Liaquat Ali Khan that morning, asking that steps should be taken:—

(*a*) to ensure adequate representation of the Muslims in each branch of the Armed Forces, and

(*b*) to re-organize the Armed Forces so that they could be split when a decision on partition was taken.

Field Marshal Auchinleck said that Mr. Liaquat Ali Khan's first claim, that there was inadequate representation of Muslims, was in the main unfounded, fortuitous though this was. The proportion of Muslims in the Army was 29%.

[1] No. 135.

Though this figure had dropped in comparison with the situation of 37% before the war, it still represented a larger percentage than the total Muslim population of India. The drop was largely caused by the fact that Madrassis before the war constituted only 3% and now constituted 20% of the Army. Anyhow, Pakistan if created, would not be able to afford a bigger Army than the total represented by 29% of the Indian Army now. Nevertheless, Mr. Liaquat Ali Khan was correct in his belief that the Hindus dominated the Armed Forces from behind the scenes. Most of the senior officers were Hindus, as the Muslim senior officers had, for one reason or another, faded out.

On Mr. Liaquat Ali Khan's second request, that the Armed Forces should be re-organized on a communal basis, Field Marshal Auchinleck stated that such re-organization would be a very complicated and difficult process, taking many months if not years. He said that he was not prepared to undertake responsibility for planning such re-organization. That would require a large new staff. I told him that I had it in mind that a Committee of Indians should be responsible for preparing the plans—possibly a sub-Committee of the Defence Committee—because, if we did decide on Pakistan, we should at least give the semblance of fair play. I suggested, and he agreed, that he and other senior British officers should be prepared to appear before such a Committee as expert witnesses. He agreed with this procedure and said that he would brief the Defence Member and be ready to produce the requisite information. He said that he had already discussed the matter with the C. in. C's Committee and come to the conclusion that it was impossible to proceed with planning on any other terms of reference but that there would be an unified India. He quoted examples to prove this. However, he added that a plan for re-organization on communal lines was in fact already in existence, although it had been prepared some time previously and for a different purpose. It was estimated that units in course of re-organization would be out of action for at least a year. I told him that I fully understood the nigh impossibility of splitting up the Army—but one of my objects was to prove that it was impracticable.

Field Marshal Auchinleck then pointed out that by no means all the Muslims in the Armed Forces had their homes in what might become Pakistan and could not therefore be expected to join the Pakistan Army. This was also true, but by no means to the same extent, of Hindus from areas inside Pakistan. He also emphasized that it would not be possible to affect the communal balance by varying the order of demobilization, and said that it was not a question of keeping on volunteers—the vast majority of serving soldiers were only too keen to be demobilized (although they might want to come back later). None were being released against their will. It was also essential to keep the flow of recruits going.

I then told the C.in.C. of my last interview[2] (recorded separately) with Mr Liaquat Ali Khan, in which he had sounded me on the possibility of Pakistan remaining in the Commonwealth and retaining the services of British officers. I had told Liaquat that he was talking to the wrong person, and should approach the High Commissioner, and had emphasized that, to the best of my belief, H.M.G. would not be prepared to sacrifice the unity of India by considering side-offers of this nature.

Sir Eric Mieville asked what the effects on the Army of a decision in favour of Pakistan would be, and Field Marshal Auchinleck replied that they would be very serious. There would, he said, be any amount of trouble. The Muslims would not take orders from Hindu officers, and vice versa. Any indication that the Army would be split would have appalling effects. It would produce less difficulties if it was made clear that existing arrangements would continue until June 1948—an announcement to that effect would give a hope of holding the forces together.

I said that I would indeed make this clear, and might well make a personal appeal to the Armed Forces, when and if an announcement proclaiming our intention to create Pakistan was made, to the Armed forces to hold together.

*   *   *

I then told the C.-in-C. the outline of Plan "Balkan", and mentioned that I thought that both parties would accept it (although I would not ask for specified acceptance). He, on the other hand, thought that Congress would do their best to wreck it as soon as it was put into operation.

I pointed out that, although I thought that Jinnah was so obdurate that he would get all he wanted without making me resort to Plan "Balkan", it was his great fear of being swallowed by Congress unless he had his own Army that would lead him to such a step; and that nothing that I could do would cast this fear aside. Field Marshal Auchinleck agreed that this fear was genuine, but felt that it was largely self-induced. He felt that there was no real other solution and that nothing else would really convince the Muslims other than that both sides should agree to a change of heart and be generous, acknowledging that they had both been wrong in the past.

I asked him what he thought was likely to happen next. He replied that if matters went on as they were now doing with no settlement, no agreement, the general situation was bound to deteriorate and the Army was bound to be affected (the Muslim League would ensure this if they did not get their way); no improvement could be expected. If the Punjab were split there would be trouble with the Muslim minority in the Eastern Punjab who would have nothing to look forward to. If the Sikhs took action against them they were likely to appeal immediately to the Muslim majority in the Western Punjab— and that indeed would lead to civil war. It was doubtful whether the Muslim troops would stand steady again on this issue but there was always a hope that any large scale defection would be stopped so long as there were British officers.

[2] No. 126.

I asked whether he thought it would be advisable for us to take a firm line and demand that instead of a certain number of British officers being repatriated each month, the whole lot should wait until June, 1948. He pointed out that the large number of those due to go home were emergency-commissioned officers whom it was impossible to retain; also we were bound not to bring in any more British officers. Nevertheless there would be a considerable number left until June, 1948, although those with the closest influence on the troops—the Platoon, Company and Battalion Commanders —would be mainly Indian. It would, of course, be necessary to get financial permission for any double banking resultant from the retention of British officers and there was likely to be extra opposition to this politically, backed by the Indian officers themselves. He went on to say that the British officers' hold was already loosening and would continue to do so as the Indian soldiers came to the point of fully realising that the British were leaving in June, 1948. Pandit Kunzru was already being told by Indian officers that British officers were going round their men painting gloomy pictures of what would happen after the British left.

Lord Ismay pointed out that, despite the objections to the retention of British officers, the alternative appeared to be carnage on a grand scale. On this Field Marshal Auchinleck promised to look into the matter more deeply. He pointed out that a number of British officers from Gurkha regiments which were being handed over to the Indian Army might be used during the interim period. He added that the Army was on the whole loyal at the moment. So was the Navy but any trouble in the Army was bound to spread there. The situation in the R.I.A.F. was better than a year previously, although the officers were very politically minded. Overall he would say that the situation had deteriorated rapidly over the last three months.

On the question of State forces Field Marshal Auchinleck expressed the opinion that these should be incorporated in the Regular Army after June, 1948. He felt that the States should not be allowed to have their own private armies.

Finally he pointed out that he would be in England from the 1st May and would therefore be available to be called in by Lord Ismay if required.

139

Viceroy's Conference Paper V.C.P. 28

Mountbatten Papers

TOP SECRET   THE VICEROY'S HOUSE, NEW DELHI, *14 April 1947*

ONE OF THE POSSIBLE PLANS UNDER EXAMINATION

1. The attached paper will be considered at the Governors' Conference on Tuesday 15th April, 1947, under Item 2 of the Agenda.

2. This paper consists of

(A) a covering note for the Governors' Conference;

(B) an outline of the programme of action as drafted by the Viceroy's staff, and

(C) a draft announcement giving the details of one of the possible plans under examination.

V. F. ERSKINE CRUM
Conference Secretary

A.

COVERING NOTE FOR GOVERNORS' CONFERENCE

1. The programme of action and the draft announcement attached are a formulation of one scheme which has been put forward for resolving the deadlock.

2. Important points for discussion are:—

(1) The advisability of trying to get Jinnah into the Cabinet.

(2) The tactics that should be adopted to secure acceptance by both sides of the Cabinet Mission Plan.

(3) The partition of the Punjab.

(4) The partition of Bengal.

(5) The problem of Sylhet.

(6) Whether in Section A power should be formally demitted to executives appointed by the Provinces or to an executive appointed by Section A of the existing Constituent Assembly.

(7) The detailed proposals for setting up the Constituent Assemblies in Sections B and C.

(8) Obviously it would be best if the parties came to terms on the basis of at any rate some sort of Central authority. Is it necessary to make it clear that the Plan can be changed by agreement of both parties? Or would this destroy the decisive effect of the announcement?

228 THE TRANSFER OF POWER

B.

OUTLINE OF PROGRAMME OF ACTION AS DRAFTED BY THE STAFF

14TH APRIL, 1947

(to be telegraphed with the statement to H.M.G.)

PART I. *Action prior to the Announcement.*

STEP ONE. *Strengthening of the Cabinet.*

1. H.E. to approach Congress and ask them to agree that the Muslim League should have one more seat in the Cabinet, provided this is taken by Mr. Jinnah himself.

2. If the Congress agree, H.E. to speak to Mr. Jinnah. Mr. Jinnah should be told that if no agreement is reached in a very short time H.M.G. will announce a decision on the basis of the small Pakistan. It will be a great advantage to be able to discuss plans for the transfer of power in a small committee *inside the Government* fully representative of the major parties.

STEP II. *Postponement of the Constituent Assembly.*

3. Nehru should be asked to postpone the session of the Constituent Assembly fixed for the 28th April.

STEP III. *Simla Talks.*

4. Whether Mr. Jinnah agrees or not, he and the other principal leaders (Nehru, Patel, Liaquat, Baldev Singh and possibly Bhopal) should be invited to Simla for discussions starting on the 7th May. Nehru and Jinnah should be asked to arrange that the Working Committee of the Congress and the Muslim League are in Simla. A determined effort should be made to secure compromise on the basis of the Cabinet Mission Plan.

5. If the Simla talks fail an announcement should be made on the lines of the attached draft.

PART II. *Action after the announcement.*

STEP IV. *Partition.*

6. Subject to discussion with the parties which should begin immediately after the announcement the detailed arrangements for the demission of authority should be as follows:—

(a) *Provinces in Section A.* (i.e. Madras, Bombay, U.P., Bihar, the C.P. and Orissa).

Authority will be demitted to an executive appointed by Section A of the Constituent Assembly.

(b) *Sections B and C.* (i.e. Section B—Punjab, N.W.F.P. and Sind; Section C—Bengal and Assam).

(1) Any Province in these sections may either

(i) accede to Section A or

   (ii) form a group with other Provinces, or

   (iii) stand out independently.

(2) The members of each of the existing Legislative Assemblies in the Punjab and Bengal will be invited to sit in two separate bodies representing the new Provinces. These bodies will be the Constituent Assemblies for their respective Provinces, and it will be their duty to frame the Provincial constitutions.

(3) It will be for these Constituent Assemblies to decide whether to join Groups.

(4) The Constituent Assemblies so formed will set up Committees which will deal with all matters arising out of the partition including especially the planning and the reorganisation of the administrative departments in the Provinces on a partition basis and the preparations for taking over Central subjects.

(5) Similarly in Assam members in the existing Legislature representing Sylhet will be invited to sit separately and decide whether to accede to the new Muslim Province in Bengal or to remain in Assam.

(6) The Provincial Constituent Assembly for the rest of Assam, for Sind and for the N.W.F.P. will be either the Legislature (excluding the Sylhet representatives in the case of Assam) or the members from these Provinces already elected to the existing Constituent Assembly, as may be decided after consultation with the parties.

(7) In 1948 H.M.G. will demit authority to executives appointed by the Group Constituent Assemblies, by Provincial Constituent Assemblies if there are any Provinces which do not join groups.

(8) In Sections B and C especially in the Punjab and Bengal a great deal of detailed work will have to be done if administrative machinery is to be set up which will enable power to be taken over in an efficient manner. It is essential that this work should begin with the least possible delay.

(9) The boundaries between the new Provinces in the Punjab and Bengal will be subject to minor adjustments either by negotiation or, in the event of disagreement, by reference to a Boundary Commission appointed by the Governor General whose decision will be final.

STEP V.

7. From the date of the announcement until June, 1948, we should:—

(a) maintain the present Central Government and support its authority. The Congress will expect a freer hand for the Central Government in the Congress Provinces, e.g. in regard to law and order;

(b) try to secure coalition governments in the provinces;

(c) give every help to prospective successor authorities to prepare themselves to receive power on the due date. It will be necessary to set up separate administrative machinery in the new Groups and Provinces, and for those concerned to examine in consultation together the innumerable administrative, financial and defence problems arising out of the partition, including particularly those that arise out of the need to establish workable relations with the tribes on the North Western and North Eastern Frontiers of India.

C.

ONE OF THE POSSIBLE PLANS UNDER EXAMINATION

Revised draft announcement prepared by the Staff—14th April 1947.

1. H.E. the Viceroy's attempt to obtain agreement to any plan for a united India has proved unsuccessful. H.M.G. have, therefore, decided with profound regret that partition is the only alternative that is consistent with their pledge that there shall be no compulsion of unwilling parts of the country.

2. The constitutional, adminstrative, financial, geographical and defence problems which will in these circumstances confront successor authorities both individually and collectively are of almost infinite variety and bewildering complexity. It is essential that these authorities should be determined as soon as possible if the demission of authority to them by June, 1948, is to be peaceful, methodical and effective.

3. Accordingly H.M.G. have reached the following decision:—

1) The general principle will be that Provinces will have the right to decide their own future.

2) As the Cabinet Mission pointed out every argument that can be used in favour of Pakistan can equally be used in favour of the exclusion of the non-Muslim areas from Pakistan. Certain readjustments of Provincial boundaries will, therefore, be an indispensable preliminary.

3) Arrangements will be made for Bengal to be partitioned into two Provinces, one comprising Muslim majority districts and the other comprising the rest of the Province.

4) The Sylhet district of Assam will be given the option of joining the new Muslim Province to be created in Bengal.

5) Arrangements will be made for the Punjab to be partitioned on the same principle as Bengal.

6) In order to ascertain the wishes of the people in the N.W.F.P., where there is a very confused political situation, a general election will be held as soon as possible.

4. Very early steps will be taken to implement this decision and announcements will be made by H.E. the Viceroy from time to time, after consultation with the Party leaders. One of the first points to be dealt with will be the grouping of the Provinces in accordance with the wishes of the people.

5. H.M.G. hopes that as soon as the intentions of the Provinces about the grouping become known it will be possible for arrangements to be negotiated by which the Indian States can take their appropriate place in the new India.

6. The problems arising out of the need to establish workable relations with the Tribes on the North Western and North Eastern Frontiers of India will also require urgent examination as soon as the Grouping is known.

140

Mr Crofton[1] to Mr Abell

Telegram,[2] Mountbatten Papers. Official Correspondence Files: Political Situation in India and Constitutional Position of Viceroy, Part 1

MOST IMMEDIATE

CONFIDENTIAL

Received: 14 April, 2.30 pm

14 April 1947, 11.30 am

Your telegram No. 795–S of April 13th.[3] Following from Gandhi to His Excellency the Viceroy. *Begins* "Just received message. Many thanks I had comparatively quiet journey. Am of opinion President of Congress should also sign. You should know reason for exclusion of the President of Congress. However I leave final decision to you and Panditji". *Ends.*

[1] Secretary to the Governor of Bihar.   [2] The telegram number is illegible.
[3] No. 136.

141

Record of Meeting between Lord Ismay and Sir O. Caroe, Sir E. Jenkins, Sir E. Mieville, Mr Weightman, Mr Abell, and Captain Lascelles on 14 April 1947

Mountbatten Papers. Viceroy's Miscellaneous Meetings[1]

Lord Ismay suggested that each Governor should begin by giving his views on the general proposition which they had just read (i.e. Plan Balkan).

Sir Evan Jenkins said that as he understood it, there was to be complete partition, with separate Constituent Assemblies, and a boundary commission to settle boundaries where necessary. He then gave details and figures of Muslim and non-Muslim majorities in the Province, showing that no demarcation could prevent there being serious minority problems in each of the provinces. The Muslim aim, vehemently pursued, was to dominate the whole

[1] Though included in the numbered series of Minutes of Miscellaneous Meetings in the Mountbatten Papers, this particular meeting is not numbered.

Punjab within its present boundaries. The Sikh aim, even more vehemently pursued, was to frustrate the Muslims. The Jats wished to separate and join with the U.P., but their claim was not being very strongly voiced. He doubted whether there was any possibility of an announcement of partition without it being followed by an immediate blow-up. There was therefore a military problem of considerable magnitude. His military commander had told him that he would need four operational divisions with an army headquarters to deal with the situation; Punjab troops would not carry out the task. He himself thought that if partition was to be the plan, non-essential British civilians should be evacuated and extra troops be brought into the area before any announcement of partition was made. He added that even if such an announcement had the backing of Mr. Jinnah, there might still be a blow-up.

Sir Eric Mieville asked what were the alternatives to plan of partition. Sir Evan Jenkins replied that there were three alternatives, namely: (a) reversion to unionism: (b) partition: or (c) civil war. If we were unable to get (a) or (b), then there was little option but to withdraw and leave both sides to fight it out. He had no doubt that the Sikhs would fight at some stage, but would rather wait until we were out of the way.

Lord Ismay said that it was not much use talking about 'four divisions of troops', since they did not exist. We should have to do the best we could with whatever troops were available. Sir Evan Jenkins replied that this further pointed to evacuation and reduction of commitments. At present the British-controlled official machine kept the two sides apart, and so at any moment one side might set upon it. The Sikhs had planned such an attack in 1942. The opposing parties were not well armed, but had a certain quantity of firearms. Lord Ismay thought that there could be no serious harm to the bulk of British personnel in the Province provided that Indian troops remained under control and did their duty, and British persons were collected in the key points; but widespread murder and pillage in the villages was possible. We were entirely dependent on the loyalty and integrity of the Indian Army. But there was nothing new in this.

Sir Evan Jenkins said that the leaders of the various parties would be prepared to come and talk with him if he asked them, but added that the Sikhs, being a purely Punjab party, were free agents in any such talks, and were not disposed to enter into negotiations with local Muslim leaders, who had to refer everything back to Mr. Jinnah. There followed some discussion on means of bringing about any form of agreement between Muslims and Sikhs, in which Sir Evan said that the Muslim policy was one of 'daring us to leave', by threatening us with the bogy of the conditions which would be the result of our departure: and that the Sikhs were almost certain to ask for partition on their own terms and would be content to have the Hindus in with them.[2]

It was finally agreed that an attempt should be made to get Mr. Jinnah to co-operate on the basis of the May 16th statement. If that failed, the Viceroy should ask the High Commands of all parties to call off the whips, and instruct their respective followers in the Punjab to get together, and try to reach an agreement on partition in the best interests of the Province. Should the various parties come to an agreement at these talks, the further processes would be fairly easy, since the politicians would then be pledged to a policy and would have to bring their respective communities into line. But if these talks failed, enforced partition only, with all its military problems, would remain.

Lord Ismay asked Sir Olaf Caroe to put forward his views.

Sir Olaf said that however bad the situation in the Punjab might be, disintegration on the frontier would make it worse. The situation in the N.W.F.P. was already most serious and might get worse. Though the tribes were not yet very troublesome, the situation was delicate; for the first time since 1897 they were achieving a real tribal unity and would consequently have a big influence. He agreed that it was right to have an election, but thought that the mechanics were a matter for further consideration. It was difficult for a Governor to take over under section 93 when the existing government had a majority. The only constitutional justification for such action was when the administration had completely broken down.

Lord Ismay said there was reason for an election because of the doubt as to which group the Province would join. Sir Olaf agreed to this but asked how an election could be forced when there was a government majority. Sir Evan Jenkins said that the legislature could be dissolved without dismissing the ministry. Mr. Abell suggested that as a matter of law section 93 could probably be invoked, in view of the Governor's special responsibility relating to the tribes, though if this was done, it would be resented by the Congress and he did not advise it.

A discussion followed in which it was agreed that the process of Indianising the administration in the southern provinces should go ahead as fast as possible, though the British officials and troops thus released would not be made available for employment in the north.

Sir Olaf stated that an official approach had been made by the Afghan Government to the Government of India, with a request to negotiate with the tribes: this was welcomed by the tribes, and was, in his opinion, a further sign of disintegration on the frontier. He thought that the maintenance of the *status quo* on the frontier until June 1948 should be one of our main objects and that future adjustments should be left to future governments. Mr. Weightman thought that we must allow planning for the frontier in fairness to the successor government.

2 Later on 14 April, Sir E. Jenkins had an interview with Lord Mountbatten at which he went over the points that he had made at the present meeting. Mountbatten Papers, Viceroy's Interview No. 59.

Other points raised by Sir Olaf Caroe concerning the visit of the Advisory Committee to the frontier, the control of the tribes and officers for the Frontier Corps were disposed of in further discussion.

142

Maulana Azad to Rear-Admiral Viscount Mountbatten of Burma

Mountbatten Papers. Official Correspondence Files: Azad, Maulana

22 PRITHVIRAJ ROAD,
NEW DELHI, *14 April 1947*

Dear Lord Mountbatten,

There is one point I forgot to discuss with Your Excellency when I met you last Saturday.[1]

You will remember I pressed that the League should accept the Cabinet Mission plan and the interpretation of December 6th. The Congress has accepted both. If, however, the League should argue that the Congress accept-ance of the interpretation of 6th December does not meet the League's ob-jections, I would suggest the following way out. Let both the Congress and the League agree that they will accept your reading of the 6th of December inter-pretation, not in your capacity as the Viceroy but in your personal capacity. I hope you will put this to Mr Jinnah when you meet him again, and if he is prepared to accept this solution, I am confident that I can persuade the Congress to do the same.

Yours sincerely,
A. K. AZAD

[1] No. 133.

143

Record of Interview between Rear-Admiral Viscount Mountbatten of Burma and Sir O. Caroe

Mountbatten Papers. Viceroy's Interview No. 60

14 April 1947

I saw Sir Olaf Caroe from 6 to 7 p.m. He gave me a picture of the situation in the N.W.F.P. We discussed at length his dealings with the Congress Govern-ment under Dr. Khan Sahib. We also discussed at length the tribes, and I was glad to hear that he thought that the tribes would not give any trouble for some time as they were busy organising themselves to meet the situation when the British would leave.

I informed the Governor that Lord Wavell had told me that he was widely suspected of pro-Muslim sympathies, that I was bound to have a lot of trouble with the Interim Government on this account and told him that he was indirectly accused of this and of unsatisfactory dealings with the tribes by Pandit Nehru, Mr. Gandhi, Abdul Ghaffar Khan and other Congress Ministers.

He assured me that although he had many friends of long standing who were now in the Muslim League camp he also had other Muslim friends who were not. He liked Dr. Khan Sahib and was doing his best to help him run the Government, and to try and stop him from using totalitarian methods in dealing with opponents.

I told the Governor that it was only fair to warn him now, before any possible question of personal knowledge came in, that the situation with the Interim Government might make my position impossible unless their attitude towards him changed. I pointed out that so long as he was Governor he could count on my full and unquestioned support, but when I became more familiar with the situation I might have to discuss his position with him.

Sir Olaf asked me straight out if I wanted him to resign, to which I replied "No, I don't want you to do anything until I have had time to go into the matter and I shall do nothing further without sending for you and discussing the question in a friendly and frank manner with you. I am sure we can reach a satisfactory solution, bearing in mind that my principal duty is to arrange for the peaceful and happy transfer of power to Indian hands, and that I cannot let anything or anybody stand in the way of this being achieved."

I told him that if we had to part he could count on my doing it in as friendly spirit as possible and that the fact that I was considering introducing Indian Governors into some Provinces of the same type might facilitate any change if it became necessary.

Finally I sympathised with him in his troubles and reiterated my promise of full support, subject to Congress Ministers not making the position untenable.

144

Cabinet. C.M.(47) 36th Conclusions, Minute 2

R/30/1/10: ff 51–3

Those present during discussion of Item 2 of this Meeting held at 10 Downing Street, S.W.1 on 14 April 1947 at 3 pm were: Mr Attlee (in the Chair), Mr Arthur Greenwood, Mr Hugh Dalton, Sir S. Cripps, Mr Alexander, Viscount Jowitt, Mr. J.

Chuter Ede, Viscount Addison, Lord Pethick-Lawrence, Mr J. Westwood, Mr A. Creech Jones, Mr G. A. Isaacs, Mr E. Shinwell, Mr T. Williams, Mr George Tomlinson
    Also present were: Mr John Strachey, Sir Edward Bridges

INDIA AND BURMA
Compensation for Members of Indian and Burma Services
(Previous Reference: C.M.(46)98th Conclusions, Minute 6.)[1]

The Cabinet had before them a memorandum by the Prime Minister (C.P. (47) 127)[2] regarding the compensation for loss of career and prospects to be paid to members of the civilian Services in India and Burma, when their appointments under the Secretary of State were terminated as a result of constitutional changes in India and Burma, and to officers of the Indian and Burma Armed Forces.

THE PRIME MINISTER said that, since this matter had last been considered by the Cabinet on 19th November, 1946, it had been the subject of discussions with the Government of India and of prolonged consideration by the India and Burma Committee.[3] The position now reached was that the Government of India would raise no objection to the payment of compensation on the scales proposed to European members of the Services, though they still contended that the cost should be borne by His Majesty's Government; but they were strongly opposed to the payment of any compensation to Indian officers, whether by themselves or by His Majesty's Government, save in a limited number of cases where it could be shown that an individual would actually be damnified as a result of the constitutional changes. The Viceroy strongly recommended that the views of the Government of India on this point should be accepted; and his recommendation was endorsed by the India and Burma Committee. The Secretary of State for India dissented, however, from this recommendation; and favoured the adoption of a scheme whereby Indian members of the Services would receive compensation on a lower scale than that proposed for the European members.

THE SECRETARY OF STATE FOR INDIA AND FOR BURMA said that in his view the proposals recommended by the India and Burma Committee could not be reconciled with the pledge given by his predecessor on 1st June, 1945, in connection with the announcement of a scheme for recruiting war-service candidates to the Indian and Burma Services at the end of the war in Europe. Under this scheme war-service recruits to the Services were to have been entitled to compensation for loss of career and prospects as a result of constitutional changes; and, in a communiqué issued at the time of the announcement of this scheme, it was stated that existing members of the Services would be given terms which would be not less favourable, considered as a whole, than those applicable to the new entrants. This scheme of recruitment was open to

Indians as well as Europeans; and some Indians were in fact in process of being recruited under it when it was abandoned. In his view, therefore, the Government were pledged to give existing members of the Services, whether Indian or European, compensation on the termination of their appointments under the Secretary of State which was not less favourable than that promised to war-service recruits under the scheme announced in June 1945.

In discussion, it was pointed out that the basis of the proposed compensation was the loss of career and prospects due to the termination of service under His Majesty's Government. The bulk of the Indian members of the Services would not in fact suffer such loss. Indeed, it was likely that their prospects would be improved by the withdrawal of the European members of the Services. Special provision was proposed for the minority who were not retained in the service of the Government of India after the transfer of power or could prove that their actions taken in the course of their duty before the transfer of power had created a prejudice against them and damaged their prospects. It was reasonable to assume that, apart from these, the Indian members of the Services would be willing to continue in service under an Indian Government: indeed, it was known that many of them were ardent nationalists who would welcome the opportunity of serving an Indian Government.

Apart from the merits, there were strong arguments of expediency on the side of accepting the view of the Government of India. They had good grounds for objecting to a proposal that Indians should receive financial compensation for becoming the servants of an Indian, instead of a British, Government; they would certainly decline to pay such compensation from Indian funds; and, in view of their attitude, it would be inexpedient that His Majesty's Government should insist, against their wishes, in paying this compensation from the British Exchequer. The Government of India had gone a long way to meet our views on this question of compensation generally; and it would be unwise for us to insist on this particular proposal, which would have to be justified on the basis of the statement of 1st June, 1945, rather than the merits. It was a relevant consideration that, while that statement had promised to existing members of the Services treatment not less favourable than that to be accorded to officers recruited under the war-service scheme, that scheme had in fact been abandoned.

The point was also made that the alternative proposed by the Secretary of State for India, while it would have the disadvantage of discriminating between Indian and European members of the Services, would not in any way meet the views of the Government of India.

THE CHANCELLOR OF THE EXCHEQUER stressed the fact that acceptance of the scheme recommended in C.P. (47) 127 did not necessarily imply that the cost of the proposed compensation would be borne by His Majesty's Govern-

[1] Vol. IX, No. 55.   [2] R/30/1/10: ff 34–50.   [3] See Vol. IX, Chapter 6.

ment: the source from which the money was to be found still remained a matter for negotiation with the Government of India.

The Cabinet—

(1) Approved the scales of compensation recommended by the India and Burma Committee, as set out in C.P. (47) 127, to be paid to members of the civilian Services in India when their appointments under the Secretary State were terminated as a result of constitutional changes, and to officers of the Indian Armed Forces;

(2) Invited the Secretary of State for India to communicate to the Viceroy the draft statements contained in Annexes II and III to C.P. (47) 127; and took note that, subject to any comments by the Viceroy, the Government's decision would be announced in both Houses of Parliament in the terms of the draft contained in Annex III;[4]

(3) Agreed that compensation on the same scales should be paid to members of the Burma Services and to officers of the Burma Armed Forces; and invited the Secretary of State for Burma to authorise the Governor of Burma to submit these proposals to his Council.

[4] The text of the statement made on 30 April 1947 by the Prime Minister in the House of Commons and by the Secretary of State for India in the House of Lords, and the text of the announcement made the same day by the Viceroy in New Delhi, will be found in Cmd. 7116.

145

Pandit Nehru to Rear-Admiral Viscount Mountbatten of Burma (Extract)

Mountbatten Papers. Official Correspondence Files: Cabinet (Indian)

SECRET   17 YORK ROAD, NEW DELHI,
                                                    14 April 1947

Dear Lord Mountbatten,

Some days ago you mentioned to me the desirability of having an Appointments Committee for considering appointments abroad. I agreed with the proposal as indeed I had done previously when Lord Wavell was here. I think some such procedure would be desirable.

2. As a matter of fact, when the Interim Government came to office in September last year, the procedure we followed was for all the Members of the then Cabinet to meet informally almost every day to consider matters of common interest. At these meetings such appointments were considered and it was only afterwards that official action was taken.

3. When the Muslim League members came in, I suggested a continuation

of this procedure to them; but they were not agreeable to joining these informal meetings. It became difficult to consult them on such issues.

4. If it is still possible, I shall welcome the formation of an Appointments Committee as suggested. Indeed there should be two such committees, one dealing with external appointments and the other with internal appointments. The former might consist of Mr. Liaquat Ali Khan, Dr. John Matthai and myself. The other committee, i.e., the one for internal appointments, might consist of the Home Member, Sardar Patel, Mr. Liaquat Ali Khan, and Sardar Baldev Singh. I think it would be desirable to have Sardar Baldev Singh in this second committee both because the Defence Member is interested in some appointments and because it is better to have another representative of a minor community associated.[1]

5. Meanwhile many appointments are pending and some are of an urgent character. We shall have to consider in the near future the choice of Ambassadors for France and the USSR. This, however, is not an immediate issue. Before we send Ambassadors we intend sending Counsellors to make the necessary arrangements. These Counsellors should be chosen within two or three weeks.

6. I have asked the External Affairs Department to send you the report which Krishna Menon has made on his European tour.[2] This will also have to be taken into consideration. Several countries of Europe have expressed a desire to exchange diplomatic representatives with India. I have recently also received a letter from the Prime Minister of Nepal making the same suggestion. To all of these we have replied that we shall gladly exchange diplomatic representatives with them. We shall have to work out some system of priority or some other arrangement. Krishna Menon has made a suggestion in regard to this in his report.

7. All these matters are not urgent although they cannot be delayed long. As you are fully occupied with very important consultations and decisions, I should not like to add to your burdens at present. But I wanted to keep you informed of the position.

[1] In the event no agreement was reached on the composition of the proposed Committee(s) and on 28 April Lord Mountbatten wrote to Pandit Nehru stating that 'as there is likely to be a new statement of policy soon, I think we had better drop these proposals for the moment, and carry on as at present'. Mountbatten Papers, Official Correspondence Files: Cabinet (Indian).

[2] A copy of Mr Krishna Menon's report is on L/P &S/12/4633.

146

Sir V. T. Krishnamachari to the Nawab of Bhopal[1]

*Mountbatten Papers. Official Correspondence Files: States, Relations
with, Part I(a)*

JAIPUR, *14 April 1947*

Your Highness,

I thank Your Highness for your telegram. I certainly understand your
attitude.[2] My object in sending the telegram was to acquaint you with the fact
that I accepted the invitation to serve on the Committee in my personal
capacity.[3]

2. There can be no difference of opinion as regards the fundamental propositions. I accept every one of them and I may mention that it was partly at
my instance that Mr Jawaharlal Nehru made his statement on the 9th of March[4]
which the Princes and Ministers considered satisfactory.

3. As regards the manner of "implementation" of the general propositions,
I find considerable difficulty in arriving at a decision. The Chamber's resolution[5] suggests that these should be accepted by the Constituent Assembly. To
this I see serious objection. In regard to the States, the Constituent Assembly has
to decide only the "central" constitution—namely the content of the three
union subjects. Take the most important "fundamental proposition"—hereditary succession. This is entirely a "domestic concern" of the States and to ask
the Constituent Assembly to accept the principle is to invest it with jurisdiction
and authority which it does not possess. This, I think, is objectionable. Pursuing this point further, I presume it is not the intention to ask the Central
Government, in the new Constitution, to "guarantee" hereditary succession
etc. The "paramountcy" claimed by the Crown at present is the direct result
of such a guarantee and the States cannot escape paramountcy in the Centre if
they ask for such a guarantee. The same remarks apply with stronger force, to
"territorial integrity". As regards the other general propositions, Clause (iv) of
paragraph 15 of the Cabinet Mission makes it clear for example that the States
will retain all subjects and powers other than those ceded to the Union. The
principle is of course not open to challenge. The crux of the matter is in giving
effect to it when the details are shaped. It is for the States' representatives to see
that this is carried into effect in the Constitution as framed. In other words the
"acceptance" of the general proposition by the Constituent Assembly does not
carry us far.

4. Would it not be the best course for the States (i) to make it clear by a
public declaration that their entry into the Assembly is subject to the Cabinet

Mission's proposals and the "understandings" reached on the 9th March and (ii) having made the declaration, enter the Assembly and shape the provisions regarding the Centre, instead of asking for ratification?[6] There is always the protection available to the States—that is for each State to decide, after seeing the final picture, whether it will join a federal union or establish another form of relationship with the Centre.

5. Or possibly we may ask that the Congress Working Committee should endorse the "understandings" of the 9th March in which case the States will participate in the work of the Assembly. It is of course understood that such participation does not commit any State to acceptance of the Constitution as framed.[7]

6. There is one consideration which is most dominant in my mind. Time is pressing and the delay in settling the constitution is strengthening the elements in the Country—Communists and others—who are determined that there should be disorder. It is high time that the constructive elements in the country came together to fight these forces. In fact it is already late.

7. I hope that Lord Mountbatten's talks with the leaders in British India will bring all parties together in the Assembly on an agreed plan.

8. I am afraid I have written indefinitely. The reason is that I have not yet come to a definite conclusion as regards the method of implementation of the fundamental propositions. I am now discussing this with some of my friends and shall write further.

9. The Chamber Constitution gives discretion to individual States in regard to matters of method etc. and in this lies the strength of the Chamber. All of us are anxious only to serve the interests of the States to the utmost and I am sure Your Highness will like me to tell you freely in what way I feel on these important questions.

Yours sincerely,
V. T. KRISHNAMACHARI

[1] Copies of this and a subsequent letter of 17 April were sent to Lord Mountbatten by the Maharaja of Bikaner who added that he was 'in entire agreement with all that he [Krishnamachari] says'. Mountbatten Papers, Official Correspondence Files: States, Relations with, Part I(a).
[2] Neither the Nawab of Bhopal's telegram, nor that of Sir V.T. Krishnamachari, are on the file.
[3] On 10 April 1947 Sir B. L. Mitter and Sir V. T. Krishnamachari had been nominated to the Union Powers Committee of the Constituent Assembly; see No. 117, para. 2.
[4] This, and the references in paras. 4 and 5, relate to the meeting of the Constituent Assembly Committee and the States' Negotiating Committee on 9 February 1947; see Vol. IX, Nos. 374-5, 389 and 406.
[5] This appears to refer to Vol. IX, No. 326.
[6] cf. No. 44.
[7] In his subsequent letter of 17 April Sir V. T. Krishnamachari reiterated that: 'If after seeing the final constitution, we find that our fundamentals are not satisfied it is open to us to refuse to accept it. This safeguard meets our case adequately'. Mountbatten Papers, ibid.

147

Minutes of First Day of First Governors' Conference

L/PO/6/123: ff 372–4, 381–92

TOP SECRET

Those present at this Meeting held on 15 April 1947 at 10.30 am were: Rear-Admiral Viscount Mountbatten of Burma, Sir J. Colville, Lieutenant-General Sir A. Nye, Sir F. Wylie, Sir E. Jenkins, Sir H. Dow, Sir F. Bourne, Sir A. Clow, Sir F. Mudie, Sir O. Caroe, Sir C. Trivedi, Sir A. Hydari, Mr Tyson (representing Sir F. Burrows); Lord Ismay, Sir E. Mieville, Sir C. Corfield, Mr Abell, Mr Christie (for Items 1 and 2 only), Captain Brockman, Mr Campbell-Johnson, Lieutenant-Colonel Erskine Crum

ITEM I HIS EXCELLENCY THE VICEROY'S OPENING REMARKS

HIS EXCELLENCY THE VICEROY extended a welcome to the Governors and said that he felt much honoured and privileged in joining a team which was bearing the burden of the day in India. No one whom he had met in the United Kingdom had any idea of the difficulties under which they were labouring and the burden which they were bearing. If he could do anything to make H.M.G. realise this he would do so.

HIS EXCELLENCY THE VICEROY thanked the Governors for the letters which they had written to him since his arrival and apologised that he had not yet been able to answer them all. He hoped to be able to reply personally in future.

He said that when it became apparent that he was to be not only Viceroy, but also a form of Cabinet Mission in himself, he had asked the Prime Minister whether he might bring out two high-level advisers, Lord Ismay and Sir Eric Mieville, and an additional staff. Their position was entirely outside the normal staff machinery and one of the main reasons for having brought the two advisers was that they should not only be able to travel round on his behalf in India, but also to visit London when necessary. He paid a compliment to Lord Wavell's staff who had remained on and accepted the new party in a magnificent, open-armed manner.

HIS EXCELLENCY THE VICEROY said that the dominating impression which he had gathered since his arrival was the necessity for a very early decision on how power was to be transferred. This need had not been fully appreciated before he left London. He said that he had not yet met any responsible Indian leader who seemed fully to realise the implications of the hand-over of power by June 1948. One or two, for example Pandit Nehru, admitted that it was a terrifying problem but none had yet got to the stage of suggesting how it should be dealt with. One factor on which he was relying was an increasing realisation on the part of the Indian leaders of what they were taking on. He emphasized that the British must do everything in their power to assist as the different problems of the transfer became apparent.

HIS EXCELLENCY THE VICEROY said that he had been told both by the Prime Minister and by the members of the Cabinet Mission that he was not to attempt to devote himself to looking after British interests during his Vice-royalty. He was, in fact, to regard himself less as the last British Viceroy than as the first head of the new Indian State. With this end in view, he was for example asking an ever growing proportion of Indians to the parties in Vice-roy's House.

HIS EXCELLENCY THE VICEROY stated that he had gained the impression, both from what he had been told and from what he had read in the newspapers, that there was a feeling among the Indian leaders that some British officials might be incapable of adjusting themselves to the new policy. He fully under-stood that those who had devoted their lives to India must find it very hard to adapt themselves to the new circumstances. The only way in which he person-ally could fully appreciate their difficulty was to compare in his own mind what his feelings would be if the Royal Navy was handed over to another country. Therefore, those officials who were incapable of adjusting themselves should be given an opportunity of early release with full honours. He gave two examples of reports which had been made to him by members of the Interim Government. First, it had been reported that a British official, when told on the telephone that some houses in an outlying district were on fire, had replied "We are leaving anyhow. What do we care?" Secondly, a senior British official was reported to have said on 21st February "That bloody fool Attlee must be mad". These reports might well not be true but it was regretful that they were being circulated.

HIS EXCELLENCY THE VICEROY pointed out that the principle of trans-ferring power to the Indians was one on which all political parties in the United Kingdom had been agreed on for many years. The present divergence of opinion at home was on the question of the date of transfer, which many true lovers of India sincerely felt to be wrong. He explained that this date had been fixed on the best available advice and was the latest date which could be accepted if any breakdown in the Secretary of State's Services and the ad-ministrative machine was to be avoided and if the British were not to be left in that most deplorable of all positions—responsibility without power.

HIS EXCELLENCY THE VICEROY said that he had already been asked by many people whether the British really intended to leave in June 1948, and had always confirmed that this was so—that they would leave in any circumstances. He had been asked whether such circumstances included civil war, and had replied that was so, although the whole object of the final months must be to avoid leaving the country to civil war. He had been asked whether there were any means whatsoever which would cause a delay; to this he had said that he had no authority to answer; but if by any chance all Indian Parties put forward a request for the British to stay, he would forward it for the consideration of H.M.G. He had given no encouragement to lead to the supposition that H.M.G.'s reply would be favourable.

HIS EXCELLENCY THE VICEROY concluded by saying that he felt that the present was a most exciting time to be in India. There had been many cases of Empires being acquired but none of Empires being given up in circumstances which were so very difficult and which required such very careful handling.

[Item 2, on the movement of civilians to and from India, omitted.]

ITEM 3 RELEASE OF THE SERVICES

The paper[1] before the meeting contained a resumé of the present situation in regard to the release of the Services, and a recommendation to the effect that in the programme for release, the public interest must come first; the policy might have to vary from Province to Province; but, subject to this, officers who had been offered employment should be favourably considered for release.

(a) Compensation

HIS EXCELLENCY THE VICEROY gave a brief explanation of past events in connection with the question of compensation.[2] He said that, on November 26th, H.M.G. had agreed to a scale of compensation which included Indian members of the Services. Despatches had been sent out. Sardar Patel had reacted violently against these proposals and said that the Indian Government would in no case pay compensation, although they would be willing to pay proportionate pensions. Deadlock had ensued and the visit of Mr Arthur Henderson had produced no results. The Indian Government had then asked that all the Secretary of State's Services should be turned over to them. The question had dragged on for some weeks without decision.

HIS EXCELLENCY THE VICEROY said that, after his appointment had been announced, Lord Wavell had telegraphed him[3] to the effect that no single factor was having so great an effect on morale as the lack of a decision on the Secretary of State's Services, the members of which were uncertain as to their future and the treatment which they would receive. H.M.G. had eventually decided to underwrite the compensation without in any way prejudicing what the Government of India might finally decide to contribute. He had come out with a draft statement and two days after his arrival spoken to Sardar Patel about it. Sardar Patel, and in fact the whole Indian Interim Government, were violently opposed to H.M.G. giving any form of compensation whatever. They said that they wished all of the Secretary of State's Services to remain. He had pointed out that they were not really in a position to renew contracts as the future situation could not be foreseen. Sardar Patel had declared that the Indian Government would not offer future employment to anyone accepting compensation. He had succeeded in getting that point of view modified to the extent that persons staying on would not get compensation while they stayed on, but would get it from H.M.G. if they left before their usual time of retirement. Exceptions to this rule would be for those who were dismissed for disgraceful conduct and such cases would have to be proved before an independent tribunal. However, in the case of Indian members of the Secretary of State's Services, the situation was very difficult. The Indian Government had pointed out that H.M.G. were offering the most generous terms to Indians to leave the Services at the time when they were most needed. They had called this an unfriendly act towards India. HIS EXCELLENCY THE VICEROY said that he did not think that this attitude was altogether unreasonable. The Indian Government had drawn a parallel with the way in which the Administrative Services of South Africa and Ireland had been dealt with. He had said that he was sure that the vast majority of Indians would wish to continue serving, as their prospects would in fact be improved; and that the compensation proposals would in fact only cater for those who had incurred, possibly through good service to the British, the displeasure of Provincial Governments. The Indian Government had agreed provisonally that the Public Services Commission should investigate such cases and that they would pay the compensation in such cases themselves. On SIR FRANCIS WYLIE'S suggestion, HIS EXCELLENCY THE VICEROY said that he would consider whether such cases should not come before the Governor General instead.

HIS EXCELLENCY THE VICEROY said that the total cost of compensation had been computed to be approximately ten million pounds for the British members of the Services, and the same for the Indian members. H.M.G. were still unwilling to go back on their pledge of no discrimination. The Indian Government, however, stood firm on their ground. SIR JOHN COLVILLE confirmed that not only Congress but all the Indian parties were unanimous on this issue. HIS EXCELLENCY THE VICEROY then asked what the reactions of Indian members of the Services were likely to be when they heard that they were not to receive compensation.

SIR CHANDULAL TRIVEDI said that he thought that the initial reaction would be one of great disappointment but that this would change when the Indian members came fully to appreciate the position.

SIR AKBAR HYDARI said that he believed that only a very small minority of the Indian members really wanted compensation. Most would want to stay on as their chances had indeed improved.

MR TYSON said that he did not believe that that would apply to his Hindu colleagues in Bengal. They felt that there was no hope of fair treatment in the Services in future under a Muslim League ministry. SIR AKBAR HYDARI

[1] V.C.P. 25 of 14 April 1947.   [2] See Vol. IX, Chapter 6.   [3] See Vol. IX, No. 500.

pointed out that many of these Bengali officials would be willing to serve if they got transfers. The aim, therefore, should be to adjust the situation between provinces.

SIR HUGH DOW said that the question of compensation for Indian members of the Services had been discussed at a general meeting of the Indian Civil Service in Bihar and the decision was that all Indian members unanimously did not wish to press for compensation, although all the Europeans would support their claims. It was possible, of course, that this attitude was influenced by the fear of victimization. SIR CONRAD CORFIELD said that at a similar meeting in Delhi there had been a division of opinion, although there was a majority for not wanting compensation.

SIR FRANCIS WYLIE said that the Indian officials in his Province on the whole wanted compensation. However, the vast majority would doubtless go on serving.

SIR JOHN COLVILLE said that he thought that the general situation would be accepted by both sides. SIR FRANCIS MUDIE said that certain Muslims serving in Sind but who came from outside the Province were not too happy about their future. SIR EVAN JENKINS said that he believed that the Indian members of the Services in the Punjab were hoping for compensation. This was probably true of all provinces in which there was an acute communal problem. Inter-provincial transfer would not in his opinion be easy. Nevertheless, he felt that the majority would eventually get employment, though it was impossible to get away from the fact that not to pay constituted a breach of faith.

HIS EXCELLENCY THE VICEROY pointed out that the demand for Indian officials was likely greatly to exceed the supply. He reiterated that His Majesty's Government had been prepared to underwrite the offer of compensation but that the Indian Government had unanimously said that it would be regarded as an unfriendly act designed to sabotage the future successful administration of India. Sardar Patel had given the opinion that many Indian officials on receipt of compensation would leave the Services and go instead into business.

SIR FRANCIS MUDIE said that another view was that there would be a greater chance of retaining them in the Services if compensation was given.

SIR CHANDULAL TRIVEDI said that he firmly believed that the opinion of the great majority of Indian officials was that they should not press for compensation and would not mind not receiving it. This was largely influenced by a feeling of patriotism. He did not think that an announcement that H.M.G. had decided, at the insistence of the Indian Government, not to grant compensation to Indian officials would be regarded as a breach of faith.

SIR AKBAR HYDARI suggested that, in lieu of offering compensation, H.M.G. should guarantee Pensions, the Provident Fund and the Family Pensions. HIS EXCELLENCY THE VICEROY said that, although it might be taken by the Indian Government as an imputation of bad faith, this suggestion should be looked into.

HIS EXCELLENCY THE VICEROY summed up by saying that, although it was highly desirable that H.M.G. should honour their pledge, this was not really possible in view of the position taken up by the Indian Government.

Discussion then turned to compensation for British members of the Services. SIR HUGH DOW said that he believed that many of them would wish to stay on as long as the situation was tolerable, provided that the offer of compensation remained open: what they needed was to feel that they had a way of escape.

MR. ABELL confirmed that the offer of compensation held good for all the different branches of the Secretary of State's Services.

HIS EXCELLENCY THE VICEROY said that evidence was most conflicting as to the number of British officials the Indian Government was actually likely to request to stay on.

HIS EXCELLENCY THE VICEROY:—

(i) invited Their Excellencies the Governors to make it clear to the British members of the Services, when the announcement on compensation was issued, that it was more than just a cash offer, although it represented £10 millions; it was a gesture on behalf of H.M.G. of genuine goodwill towards the members of the Services and H.M.G. fully realised the difficulties under which they were working.

(ii) invited Their Excellencies the Governors also to make the position clear to Indian members of the Services;

(iii) directed P.S.V. to look into the possibility of appeals for compensation by Indian members of the Services, who felt that they were being, or would be, victimised because of previous good service to the British, being sent for consideration to him rather than to the Public Services Commission;

(iv) directed P.S.V. to examine what measures could be taken to protect officers retained until a late stage from losing their chance of alternative employment.

(v) directed P.S.V. to look into the suggestion that H.M.G. should guarantee the Pensions, Provident Fund and Family Pensions of members of the Services.

(b) *Staggering of release*

HIS EXCELLENCY THE VICEROY said that he felt that the question of timing the release of members of the Secretary of State's Services was a matter of national much more than of personal interests. Governors should unhesitatingly retain those who were most needed over this last difficult period. Those who were not required, or who were not trusted for one reason or another, might have to go first. Only Governors could decide the rate of release in the different Provinces.

SIR JOHN COLVILLE said that the numbers affected in Bombay were very small. There were only 22 executive I.C.S. officers left there. He said that he would stagger releases in the manner outlined by the Viceroy.

SIR ARCHIBALD NYE said that the great majority of those in Madras had applied for entrance into the Foreign, Home or Colonial Services. Some older men would prefer to stay on. The release could be satisfactorily staggered.

SIR EVAN JENKINS said that the position in the Punjab was rather more difficult. The general attitude was that most wanted to retire, mainly on account of the false accusations made against them, which were part of a propaganda campaign. Apart from the immediate troubles in the Punjab, which would involve some replacements, all the younger and most useful members had applied to join other Services. He had had to refuse some permission to fly home for interviews. The general feeling was that those allowed to go now had a better chance of future employment than those who, because of their efficiency, had to stay on. He felt that every effort should be made to change the method of selection, and had already forwarded a memorandum to this effect supported by the Governor of Bengal.

MR ABELL said that Lord Wavell had tried, without success, to persuade H.M.G. to send a selection committee out to India. H.M.G. had declared that they were committed to the present arrangements.

LORD ISMAY said that he believed that the reason for this was the British Civil Service was desperately short itself.

SIR HUGH DOW asked what the criterion was for deciding whether or not officials should be retained. He explained that his Ministry would probably not want to retain any. Was he justified in over-ruling them?

SIR CHANDULAL TRIVEDI said that the Orissa Ministry would take a different view. As the two Provinces shared a Services' cadre, he suggested that they should co-operate closely—perhaps by talks on ministerial level. HIS EXCELLENCY THE VICEROY agreed that this would be a good idea.

SIR FREDERICK BOURNE said that he presumed that all members of the Services would be free to leave as soon as the terms of compensation were announced. HIS EXCELLENCY THE VICEROY made it clear that this was not so—Governors could keep whom they wished until June, 1948, (although there was nothing to stop men retiring on proportionate pension without compensation meanwhile). Governors had complete rights to hold individuals back from interviews.

In answer to other queries, HIS EXCELLENCY THE VICEROY stated that those who entered other Services would not be qualified to draw full compensation; that an offer and refusal of a post in another Service did not disqualify a man from compensation; that European officers who stayed on for a period after June, 1948 would get compensation (unless dismissed for disgraceful behaviour) and pension, which latter would be payable by the Government of India and not guaranteeed by H.M.G. and that officers who accepted compensation and then tried to stay on would not be able to as the Indian Government would not have them. He also said that the Government of India had declared themselves prepared to renew the contracts, on the same terms as before, of those who wanted to stay.

SIR JOHN COLVILLE said that he considered that a clause binding India to continue to pay pension should be included in any treaty signed by the two Governments. HIS EXCELLENCY THE VICEROY said that he presumed that this was being covered in the sterling balance negotiations, but would have the matter looked into.

SIR OLAF CAROE said that there was a larger ratio of British officials in the N.W.F.P. than elsewhere—although most were I.P.S. rather than I.C.S. Owing to the peculiar position of the tribes it would probably be necessary to hold on to these men longer than elsewhere. He had been informed that they could count on no military officers after 1st January. This would leave the political officers in the Agencies in a difficult situation. He felt thatthere should be co-ordination of the dates of non-availability of military and political officers. HIS EXCELLENCY THE VICEROY said that he would certainly have this point taken up.

SIR CHANDULAL TRIVEDI agreed that the release of members of the Secretary of State's Services should be staggered. He made the point that the real security for Indian officials' pensions must surely be settled conditions in India.

SIR CONRAD CORFIELD said that the position was not very difficult as regards the Crown Representative's cadre. He hoped that Provincial Governments would not be alarmed when they were told that they would have to deal direct with States.

MR TYSON pointed out that all those summoned to the United Kingdom for interview had been told to pack up and sell their possessions in India before they left, although only 25 out of 60 of them were likely to be accepted for appointments. HIS EXCELLENCY THE VICEROY said that he would take up this matter personally with H.M.G.

MR TYSON added that Sir Frederick Burrows felt that it was wrong to retain officers against their will.

HIS EXCELLENCY THE VICEROY summed up by saying that he felt that Governors should do what they felt right on the question of release. In principle, however, it would be best to send men home in the reverse order of efficiency. Every effort should be made to hold on until the end to those best capable of maintaining British prestige.

HIS EXCELLENCY THE VICEROY:—

    (i) approved V.C.P. 25;

    (ii) directed P.S.V. to find out and inform him whether the question of the

Indian Government continuing to pay pensions to Europeans was being covered in the sterling balance negotiations;

(iii) directed C.V.S. to look into the possibility of co-ordinating the dates of non-availability of military and political officers in the N.W.F.P.;

(iv) directed P.S.V. to draft, for his approval, a telegram to the Secretary of State for India asking for amendment of the regulation that all members of the Services called to the United Kingdom for interview should first pack up and sell all their possessions in India.

ITEM 4 THE GENERAL POLITICAL SITUATION

(a) *The Prime Minister's Letter*

A paper[4] containing copies of a letter written by the Prime Minister to The Viceroy was handed round.

HIS EXCELLENCY THE VICEROY explained that this letter had been given to him at his request. He had originally asked the Prime Minister for a directive, but it had transpired that the Governor General's Instrument of Instructions could only be amended by both Houses of Parliament. Therefore a letter has had to do instead—there was a precedent for this, as Mr. Churchill had written a letter[5] to Lord Wavell on his appointment.

HIS EXCELLENCY THE VICEROY drew particular attention to the paragraphs in this letter which read:—

"The date fixed for the transfer of power is a flexible one to within one month; but you should aim at June 1, 1948, as the effective date for the transfer of power." and

"You will no doubt inform Provincial Governors of the substance of this letter."

(b) *His Excellency The Viceroy's Talks with Indian Leaders*

HIS EXCELLENCY THE VICEROY gave a short account of the talks which he had had to date with Indian leaders. He also spoke of the working, since his arrival, of the Interim Government.

(c) *One of the possible plans under examination*

A further paper[6] was then placed before the meeting. This contained:—

(i) a covering note for the Governors' Conference;

(ii) an outline of the programme of action as drafted by The Viceroy's Staff; and

(iii) a draft announcement giving the details of one of the possible plans under examination. This was called, for ease of reference, Plan "Balkan".

HIS EXCELLENCY THE VICEROY stressed that this was only one of the many plans which were at present being considered. He also emphasized that, if it was not possible to obtain an united India, it was of the utmost importance that, in the eyes of the world, it should be Indian opinion rather than a British decision which made the choice as to the future.

HIS EXCELLENCY THE VICEROY gave his opinion that partition of India would be a most serious potential source of war.

SIR CONRAD CORFIELD said that it was also surely true that, the earlier partition was carried out, if it had to be done, the greater was the chance of building up the machinery to organize an unified defence.

With this there was general agreement.

HIS EXCELLENCY THE VICEROY pointed out that a quick decision would also give Pakistan a greater chance to fail on its demerits. The great problem was to reveal the limits of Pakistan so that the Muslim League could revert to an unified India with honour. THEIR EXCELLENCIES THE GOVERNORS all agreed that the necessity for an early decision was paramount.

SIR FRANCIS MUDIE added the view that the demand for Pakistan was largely psychological. Once granted, even on paper, he thought that the two parties would be ready to talk about unity again.

SIR EVAN JENKINS said that he thought that the Muslims' demand for Pakistan was potentially much less dangerous than the possible subsequent pressure which might come from non-Muslim parties to ensure that they got it.

(d) *The Cabinet Mission Plan*

SIR CONRAD CORFIELD asked whether it would not be right to assume that the Cabinet Mission's plan was now dead.

HIS EXCELLENCY THE VICEROY said that he would not lightly abandon any plan for an unified India. He wanted it to be proved before the world that the British had made every possible effort to achieve this object.

MR. TYSON said that Sir Frederick Burrows felt that the Cabinet Mission's plan represented the only possible peaceful solution for Bengal.

SIR JOHN COLVILLE felt that a last effort to get the Cabinet Mission's plan through should be made if only in order to throw the alternative into relief. There was general agreement with this point of view.

(e) *Mr. Jinnah*

It was generally agreed, during discussion of this paper, that it would be most advisable to make every effort to get Mr. Jinnah into the Cabinet.

SIR AKBAR HYDARI reported a conversation which he had had the previous night, and at which he had been given a description of the talks between The Viceroy and Mr. Jinnah. HIS EXCELLENCY THE VICEROY said that this description was absolutely false.

(f) *The Constituent Assembly*

HIS EXCELLENCY THE VICEROY stated that Pandit Nehru had informed him that it would be constitutionally impossible to postpone the session of the Constituent Assembly fixed for 28th April. This Assembly would therefore have to meet on that date, although it might then adjourn itself for a period.

4 Vol. IX, Enclosure to No. 543.   5 cf Vol. IV, Enclosure to No. 172.   6 No. 139.

(g) The North-West Frontier Province

Among the recommendations in the paper before the Meeting was one that a general election should be held in the N.W.F.P. as soon as possible after the issue of an announcement on H.M.G.'s policy. HIS EXCELLENCY THE VICEROY said that it was hoped that such an announcement might be made within a month.

SIR OLAF CAROE said that it seemed to him that the N.W.F.P. and the tribes might be used as a very strong lever in obtaining some sort of compromise on the lines of the Cabinet Mission's plan. Hitherto there had been an almost complete absence of recognition of the important place the tribes and the North-West Frontier generally must take in the India of the future. As an example, the Prime Minister's letter had spoken of the desirability of continued collaboration with India in the Indian Ocean area, but had made no mention of India's land frontiers, as though these were not vital. Without a solid Frontier neither one India nor two Indias could emerge. Apart from the general aspect of the Frontier's importance to the defence of all India, the ruling point was that neither the North-West Frontier tribes nor the Province itself (which depended on heavy subventions) could possibly subsist economically under a real Pakistan partition scheme. The tribes at present cost the Centre about $2\frac{1}{2}$ crores a year, and the Province already cost the Centre 1 crore and was asking for more. Any Government in the N.W.F.P.—Congress, League, or otherwise, would be forced to demand continuance of the present subventions, and would certainly even ask for more, as indeed the last League Government did. A recognition of this fact by all parties, and particularly by the League Command, would do a great deal to put All-India questions between Congress and the League in a proper perspective, and SIR OLAF CAROE suggested this should be done before all hope of securing a compromise on the basis of the Cabinet Mission's Plan was abandoned.

SIR OLAF CAROE went on to say that the state of tension in the N.W.F.P. under the present regime was extreme. While recognition of the basic factor which he had mentioned by the League and the tribes and everyone concerned was essential, that recognition would not come under the present state of tension. The only way, as he saw it, of curing this state of tension was to announce a general election straight away rather than at a later stage. There would be more hope, he felt, of the proposed Simla negotiations succeeding when the air had been cleared in the N.W.F.P. in this manner. If Congress got in again, their position would be strengthened by the recognition that the Frontier was an All-India question in any case. If the League got in, recognition of this essential feature would make them more moderate and less inclined to push for a partition plan.

SIR OLAF CAROE said that, if it were decided that a general election would be held forthwith, he would dissolve the Assembly and ask the present Ministry to remain in power over the period of the election, the mere announcement of which would do a great deal to ease the tension. Such an announcement might draw the two different aspects together—first envisaging the All-India importance of the Frontier and its dependence on India's purse; and then stating that continuance of the present situation of extreme tension and confusion was impossible. It would also state that it was essential that civil liberties should be restored without loss of time, thus resulting in the release of the Opposition.

SIR OLAF CAROE emphasized that the problem in the N.W.F.P. was a very immediate one. The whole place was liable to "drop to bits" at any moment. He felt that whatever party got in after early elections would have to face up to realities. He would rather risk any disturbances the elections themselves might bring than a continuation of the large emotional processions which were taking place at the moment, organized by the Muslim League in an effort to overthrow the Government. He believed that passions would be cooled by elections.

SIR AKBAR HYDARI said that Congress would surely take it as an unfriendly act on the Governor's part to order elections.

HIS EXCELLENCY THE VICEROY said that he had asked Pandit Nehru to dinner the following night and would arrange a talk with him and Sir Olaf Caroe. He pointed out that the great objection to having elections in the N.W.F.P. now, only a month before it was hoped to reach a general decision, was that they would be liable to fog the main issue and incur the annoyance of Congress. He would, however, consider the matter further.

SIR OLAF CAROE said that the Afghanistan Government had written to the Indian Government asking for permission to negotiate direct with the tribes. He hoped that the answer to this request would be in the negative. He also suggested that a Cabinet Committee should be set up to deal with N.W.F.P. affairs.

HIS EXCELLENCY THE VICEROY:—

(i) directed P.S.V. to ensure that the Government of India's answer to the Afghan Government on the latter's request for permission to negotiate direct with the tribes was not despatched without his prior approval;

(ii) decided to consider further the desirability of holding elections forthwith in the N.W.F.P., and to discuss this question further with Sir Olaf Caroe and with Pandit Nehru;

(iii) decided to consider further the question of setting up a Cabinet Committee to deal with N.W.F. affairs.

(h) *Partition of the Punjab*

SIR EVAN JENKINS gave a full explanation of the difficulties inherent in the partitioning of the Punjab, describing particularly the demands of the Sikhs and the Jats. He said that, if, in the present situation, attempts at partition were made without having obtained the prior agreement of all interested parties, there would be fighting on a large scale. Partition could then only be imposed by force, and a large number of troops would be required.

HIS EXCELLENCY THE VICEROY
invited C.V.S. and H.E. The Governor of the Punjab to consider together in detail the procedure for partitioning the Punjab.
(j) *Partition of Bengal*

MR. TYSON said that, when the Cabinet Mission's plan had first been published, it would be true to say that there was a feeling of relief in all the parties in Bengal that that Province was not to be partitioned. When H.M.G.'s statement of 20th February had been shown to the Chief Minister, the latter had declared that it looked as if his Government would inherit Bengal. He had evidently been thinking of an independent Bengal, preferably as a Dominion within the British Commonwealth. The Hindus had also evidently read into the statement of 20th February a danger that Bengal would be handed over to what was, in effect, a Muslim League Government.

MR. TYSON explained that there was no alternative Ministry to that at present in power. Bengal (unlike the Punjab) was only really concerned with two communities—33 million Muslims, and 25 million Hindus of whom 9 million were members of the scheduled castes. It was very difficult to say whether the scheduled castes representatives in the Assembly really did represent the opinions of the scheduled castes. But it could be taken that, in general, all the Hindus were opposed to the idea of Pakistan.

MR. TYSON went on to explain in detail the distribution of Muslims and Hindus in the different divisions and districts of Bengal. He said that a partition of Bengal on the basis of majorities in districts could be carried out. He believed that the Hindus would prefer that to an independent Bengal. And he believed that Western Bengal would be economically possible—so long as it included Calcutta. All the heavy industries were in Western Bengal. In Eastern Bengal jute was grown and baled but not manufactured. In Northern Bengal tea was grown and manufactured—but there was very little tea in the predominantly Muslim areas. Eastern Bengal alone was not a going concern and never would be. It could not feed itself and never would be able to do so even if the jute-growing there was stopped in favour of crops. It would become, in Sir Frederick Burrows' words, a "rural slum". MR. TYSON said that the Muslims knew all this as well as the Hindus—so they felt that the object of the cry to partition Bengal was to "torpedo" Pakistan. He could not think of any way in which it would be possible to "sell" Eastern Bengal as a feasible proposition.

HIS EXCELLENCY THE VICEROY said that there was no question of trying to "sell" it. Mr. Jinnah had already virtually accepted the proposition. Anything that resulted in "torpedoing" Pakistan was of advantage in that it led the way back to a more common-sense solution. He asked what the Bengal Chief

Minister's reactions were likely to be when he heard that Mr. Jinnah had accepted a truncated Pakistan.

MR. TYSON said that he thought that the Chief Minister would be very frightened and would go a long way to keep Bengal a separate unit. He was not, he believed, very keen to link up with the North-West Muslim Provinces. He wanted to run Bengal as an independent Province with a Muslim majority.

HIS EXCELLENCY THE VICEROY

directed P.S.V. to arrange for him to see the Chief Minister of the Bengal Government when the latter next came to Delhi.

(k) Bihar

In connection with the question of the withdrawal by Provincial Governments of what were at present Central Government subjects, SIR HUGH DOW said that a very large proportion of the total mineral resources in India were situated in Bihar. If full responsibility for mining these was given to the Provincial Ministry they were likely to hold the rest of India up to ransom.

(l) Sind

SIR FRANCIS MUDIE said that Sind, as an independent Province with possibly parts of the Punjab added, would be in a fairly strong economic position and probably, with a few more industries, fairly self-sufficient.

SIR EVAN JENKINS expressed doubt as to whether Punjabis would ever join up with Sind.

HIS EXCELLENCY THE VICEROY concluded by saying that, from the afternoon's meeting, it appeared possible that the Muslims in Bengal would not follow Mr. Jinnah's lead; that there was a chance of a Congress Ministry being returned again in the N.W.F.P.; and that Mr. Jinnah's Pakistan would, in the end, consist only of Sind and part of the Punjab. He finally added that he wished to make it quite clear that he was in no way opposed to the Muslim League and pro-Congress. His one object was to hand over India in the best interests of her people.

148

Mr Liaquat Ali Khan to Rear-Admiral Viscount Mountbatten of Burma

R/3/1/90: ff 5–10

No. 29-P.S.F.R./47   NEW DELHI, *15 April 1947*

Dear Lord Mountbatten,

I believe that during the consultation that you are holding with provincial Governors, provincial administrations and the conditions prevailing in the various provinces are likely to come under review. It is a matter of vital concern to the Muslim League that the situation in the Punjab should be understood in its true perspective, and that you should bear in mind our deep resentment of the present partial and unjustified attitude that is being adopted by Sir Evan Jenkins, the Governor of the Punjab.

You are doubtless aware of the background of events which led to the promulgation of Section 93 administration in the Punjab.

Malik Sir Khizr Hayat Tiwana, the leader of the Unionist Party of 15 members, resigned from the Premiership of the province on the ground that in view of H.M.G.'s statement of February 20th, he did not any longer want to be an obstacle in the way of the self-realisation of the Muslims of the Punjab, and that by relinquishing office he wished to leave the way clear for an understanding between the genuine representatives of the majority and minority communities in the Punjab. After Sir Khizr Hayat's resignation, the Governor of the Punjab called upon the leader of the largest party in the House, viz., the Khan of Mamdot, leader of the Muslim League Party, to form a Government. Simultaneously with this announcement, the Hindu and Sikh leaders started an avowedly violent agitation to prevent the formation of a ministry by the representatives of 57% of the population of the province. On the 3rd and 4th of March extremely provocative speeches were made by the Hindu and Sikh leaders, armed processions were organised in almost every important city and district of the province, and the Muslim people and their national organisation, the Muslim League were intimidated, insulted and humiliated in an unbearable manner. This led to general disturbances all over the province, despite the genuine and now widely recognised efforts of the Muslim League to maintain peace and later on to restore order and confidence when the riots had actually broken out. It is true that during the disturbances in many places the non-Muslims suffered more heavily than the Muslims. This, however, is often the case with aggressors as has recently been so well illustrated by the very heavy losses of the German people during the last Great War. In the case of the Punjab, it was inevitable when chaotic conditions had been brought about in a predominantly Muslim province. The responsibility of this lies with the Hindu and Sikh leaders.

The disturbed state of the Punjab was made an excuse by the Governor for the imposition of Section 93 in the province, despite the fact that the leader of the Muslim League Party claimed his constitutional right of facing the House after the Governor had invited him to form a Government.

Events in the Punjab since the imposition of Section 93 have made it clear that the present administration has made it a matter of policy to suppress, intimidate and coerce the Muslims and it appears as if the Governor considers it his personal concern to do all that he possibly can to prevent the majority community in the Punjab from having its proper share in the administration of the province.

Everywhere in the riot affected or threatened areas—which cover nearly the whole of the province, the administration is adopting an attitude of hostility towards Muslims. In all districts vast numbers of Muslims have been indiscriminately arrested and even in places like Amritsar where the Muslims have suffered the heaviest losses, many more Muslims than non-Muslims are in jail. Throughout the province an overwhelming percentage of responsible officials are non-Muslims. Out of 29 District Magistrates[1] only 9 are Muslims whilst there is not a single Muslim Commissioner or D.I.G. of Police in the Punjab. Similarly, the special investigation staff set up to enquire into the recent disturbances is preponderantly non-Muslim, so much so that in Rawalpindi only 5 out of 26 officials of this are Muslim, and this at a time when justice by any except a mixed staff is out of the question.

The general behaviour of the administrators is one of open hostility towards the Muslims. Responsible officials, who are expected to have no political affiliations, openly declare their hostility to the Muslim ideal of Pakistan, and the D.I.G. of Rawalpindi Division recently issued a press statement couched in unrestrained terms threatening direct vengeance on the Muslims. High ranking leaders of the Muslim League are treated with contempt and intimidated by the officials, who openly threaten them with reprisals by Sikhs. To all sections of the Muslims, the officials make no secret of their partiality for and sympathy with the Sikhs, and paint in lurid colours the prospects of Sikh retaliation. Muslims are complacently informed that the Sikhs are arming aggressively, as if it were the duty of Government to encourage such preparations rather than to prevent them.

Even in a technical matter like the censorship of news, the most provocative and aggressive speeches and statements of Sikh and Hindu leaders are allowed to pass, whilst even the mildest utterances by the Muslim leaders are withheld from publication.

The Sikhs and Hindus are at the same time being encouraged in every way to adopt an aggressive attitude. Despite reports of large-scale arming by the Sikhs, and of smuggling of arms from the adjoining Sikh States who have publicly declared their resolve to support the Akali Party and its policy in every way—reports which the officials themselves confess to be well-founded—nothing is being done in the matter. In the present state of high tension the Sikhs are being allowed to display large swords under the name of Kirpans, whilst the Muslims are being deprived everywhere of even pen-knives. The Sikhs do not claim their religious sacrament of carrying a Kirpan in the army, or the police, in the law courts, the legislatures or in jail, but they are allowed to carry Kirpans when doing so imperils the peace of the land. On the other hand when the Muslims claim the right to wear a sword, it is argued that whilst the weapon in the possession of a Sikh is an emblem of spirituality in the

[1] Sir E. Jenkins minuted: '14 are British I think.'; see however No. 160, para. (5).

hands of a Muslim it becomes a menace to others, although it is freely admitted that the chief present danger to the Punjab comes from the temper of the Sikhs.

Any impartial assessment of the position in the Punjab leads one to the inescapable conclusion that the Governor and his subordinates want to foster chaos in the province. The minorities are being deliberately encouraged to oppose any reasonable settlement with the majority, and are being led to believe that if they are able to create further disturbances in the province, it would be a political argument in their favour and against the Muslims in the final disposition of power in India.

I have placed these facts before you, because I feel that unless the Governor of the Punjab is persuaded to alter his present attitude very serious consequences may follow, which might have effects that cannot be limited to the boundaries of the Punjab.

I also feel that the time has come when a final decision must be taken to replace Section 93 in the Punjab by a popular Government. The Muslim League is in a position to form a ministry and to command a majority in the provincial Legislature, and I cannot see how the Governor can continue to resist the normal application of constitutional methods. The refusal of the Governor to allow the Muslim League to form a ministry directly helps the other parties to maintain their intransigent attitude. The argument is sometimes advanced that as the formation of a ministry by majority party is not likely to accord with the wishes of the minorities who will create disturbances, the majority party should not be allowed to form a ministry at all. You will appreciate that such an argument, if applied generally, will place a decisive weapon in the hands of minorities all over the country, who will thus be able to prevent the majority parties effectively from forming a Government in any Province by threatening a disturbance of the peace. This, you will agree, would be an impossible proposition.

I shall be glad to see you at any time convenient if any of the points raised in this letter require further elucidation or discussion.

Yours sincerely,
LIAQUAT ALI KHAN

149

Record of Interview between Rear-Admiral Viscount Mountbatten of Burma and Sir F. Mudie

Mountbatten Papers. Viceroy's Interview No. 65

TOP SECRET   *15 April 1947, 6–6.45 pm*

After Sir Francis Mudie had given me an account of how his Government was working, I took him into the garden and informed him categorically that he was accused of being violently pro-Muslim League and of failing in his constitutional duties to look after the interests of the minorities in Sind. I told him that Mr Gandhi had made this accusation[1] as well as other Congress leaders, and that an article by Jai Prakash Narain which Mr. Gandhi had sent me, called upon me to dismiss Sir Francis from the post of Governor for failing in his duty.

Sir Francis assured me that the accusations were completely without foundation; that he constantly pulled up his Government and did his best to look after the interest of the minorities; but that he naturally did his best to get on well with his Government, because that, he presumed, was the correct attitude for a constitutional Governor to take.

He informed me that the real grounds for Congress dissatisfaction with him lay in the 1942 period, when he was Chief Secretary to the Government of the U.P., under Sir Maurice Hallett, and when together they had had to round up and imprison Congress leaders, for which he thought they would never forgive him.

I then told him that Mr. Godbole had warned me that two Bills were coming up for my assent, concerning the alienation of land and impersonation at elections, which were causing the most violent feeling among the Hindus who regarded both Bills as directed against them. I invited the Governor to give me a very full brief if he really wished me to give my assent.

He gave me a verbal explanation of what was behind these two Bills, but promised to let me have it in writing as well.

I finally told him that I accepted his explanation in regard to the Congress accusations; that I realised that political capital was being made the whole time out of the attitude of high British officials; and that he could count on my support. I did warn him, however, to be ever careful not to give Congress the least excuse for accusing him of partiality.

In conclusion we discussed the prospects of Pakistan consisting only of Sind and the western half of the Punjab, and he expressed the view that this would be a perfectly feasible economic proposition, and since the total population of

[1] See Nos. 73 and 123.

the two areas would only be in the neighbourhood of 15 millions, i.e. less than 4 per cent of the total population of India, nobody could really say that this Pakistan was seriously destroying the unity of India. In fact it might be regarded as a fairly large Indian State which had decided not to join the Constituent Assembly.

This opens up a new vista, since now we could go ahead giving Mr. Jinnah his truncated Pakistan, whilst keeping a strong Centre for the rest of India at Delhi; all this on the assumption that the N.W.F.P. retains a Congress Government and that the Muslim League will not want the expense of trying to run a Province which needs $3\frac{1}{2}$ crores spent on it over and above its income (mostly for the tribes), and that Suhrawardy will not agree to the partition of Bengal and will throw in his lot with Congress.

Anyhow, here is a new plan which we will consider tomorrow at the Governors' Conference.

150

Record of Interview between Rear–Admiral Viscount Mountbatten of Burma and Sir C. Trivedi

Mountbatten Papers. Viceroy's Interview No. 66

TOP SECRET   *15 April 1947, 6.45–7.30 pm*

We began by gossiping over old times when I was in S–E Asia Command and he was Secretary to the Defence Department. He told me he had been astounded to find how few Indians had even a glimmering of defence, and to the best of his knowledge no political leaders had even a glimmering.

I told him that I supposed that of all notable Indian civilians he must have an absolutely unrivalled knowledge of defence from his job during the war.

Sir Chandulal admitted that this was so.

I then asked him what he was going to do about it, since I pointed out that he owed quite a particular responsibility to the future of his nation. He shrugged his shoulders and said "What can I do about it; I have got a small Province that gives no trouble, and none of the leaders ever come to see me, and I of course have no reason ever to come to Delhi". I replied "Well you are here now, and will be seeing Pandit Nehru tomorrow night. Why don't you arrange a conversation with him and discuss defence." He thought this was an admirable idea, but he also wanted to see Mr. Liaquat Ali Khan to press him for the money to build his new capital, which had been promised in 1936 and had never materialised.

We discussed the pros and cons of India remaining within the Commonwealth, and Sir Chandulal Trivedi told me how completely sunk he had been on reading the resolution in the Constituent Assembly about an Independent Sovereign Republic.[1]

I talked to him generally along the lines of Sir Archibald Nye's arguments,[2] and told him that Lord Ismay had informed me that a Committee had been sitting at Whitehall at the time that I had left, to decide whether it was worth while the British accepting India as a partner in the Commonwealth if she asked to be allowed to remain in.[3] I told him that I greatly feared the answer would be no, since India had everything to gain by remaining in, and we had nothing whatever to lose by her going out. I pointed out that our commercial interests were adequately safeguarded by the sterling balances which tied India to us for years to come.

I admitted to him that I was one of the very few responsible Englishmen who appeared to be in favour of India remaining within the Commonwealth, and this I realised was largely a hangover from my sentimental association with the Indian Army in S.E.A.C. during the Burma campaign.

He asked me whether no-one else felt as I did, and I told him in strict confidence that the King had a tremendous sentimental attachment towards India, and in so far as was constitutionally proper I was sure he would recommend accepting any request India made to remain connected with the Commonwealth, or at all events be pleased with any decision by India not to sever her connection with the Crown.

I suggested to him that he should not quote our conversation to anyone, not that I minded particularly, but that it would certainly not help him in his arguments, and it would be a slight embarrassment to me if people thought I was in favour of India remaining within the Commonwealth.

He appreciated my attitude, and asked if I would arrange for him to have an interview with Pandit Nehru after dinner the following night, as he said he wanted to get to work right away.

Perhaps something may come of this.

[1] See Vol. IX, No. 190.

[2] In his record of his interview with Lieutenant-General Sir A. Nye on 14 April 1947, Lord Mountbatten recorded:

> We discussed the desirability of India remaining in or leaving the Commonwealth. He put forward the point of view that India was militarily about the weakest country in the world in proportion to her population; and since her industrial development would be slow and the nationalisation of the armed forces would set her back still further, she would be so weak a member of the Commonwealth and such a liability to defend in view of her land frontiers and the threat of Russia, that he did not think, or doubted very much whether, it would be wise to include India in the Commonwealth.
>
> From a commercial point of view the sterling balances tied India to us for many years to come, and although we might have found it hard to resist a sincere request to remain within the Commonwealth, and indeed he felt it would be a very ungracious act to refuse to keep India within the Commonwealth, he thought it would be a mistake to do any propaganda that might tend to make the Indians ask to stay in.

Mountbatten Papers. Viceroy's Interview No. 63.   [3] See Vol. IX, Nos. 338 and 522.

151

Rear-Admiral Viscount Mountbatten of Burma to Lord Pethick-Lawrence

Telegram, L/P&J/10/79: f 504

MOST IMMEDIATE   NEW DELHI, *15 April 1947, 7.15 pm*
                                         Received: 15 April, 6.40 pm

806–S. Personal. After a fairly stormy passage I obtained the signature of Jinnah and Gandhi to a public statement deploring recent acts of violence among all communities and denouncing for all time use of force to achieve political ends.

Full text of release to Press today, Tuesday, follows [in] my immediately succeeding telegram.

Please inform Prime Minister.[1]

[1] In tel. 4988 of 17 April Lord Pethick-Lawrence heartily congratulated Lord Mountbatten on having obtained the joint statement which he had great hope would lead to an improvement in communal relations. L/P &J/10/79: f 502.

152

Rear-Admiral Viscount Mountbatten of Burma to Lord Pethick-Lawrence

Telegram, L/P&J/10/79: f 503

MOST IMMEDIATE   NEW DELHI, *15 April 1947, 7.15 pm*
                                         Received: 15 April, 4.45 pm

807–S. Personal. My 806-S of today. Text of release as follows.

Begins. On His Excellency the Viceroy's initiative and at his specific request Mr Gandhi and Mr Jinnah signed the following declaration and authorised its publication.

"We deeply deplore the recent acts of lawlessness and violence that have brought the utmost disgrace on the fair name of India and the greatest misery to innocent people, irrespective of who were the aggressors and who were the victims.

We denounce for all time the use of force to achieve political ends, and we call upon all the communities of India, to whatever persuasion they may belong, not only to refrain from all acts of violence and disorder; but also to avoid both in speech and writing, any words which might be construed as an incitement to such acts".

(Signed) M.A. Jinnah; M.K. Gandhi April 15th 1947.
Ends.

153

Rear-Admiral Viscount Mountbatten of Burma to Mr Mozumdar[1]

Telegram, Mountbatten Papers. Official Correspondence
Files: Political situation in India and Constitutional Position of Viceroy, Part 1

IMMEDIATE   *15 April 1947, 10.30 pm*
812-S. Please pass following to Mr Gandhi from Viceroy. *Begins.*

I am glad to inform you that Pandit Nehru also agreed to leave the decision
to me.[2] I consider it so vital that the appeal should issue that I thought it best
that it should go out over the signatures only of yourself and Mr Jinnah.

2. Mr Jinnah has now signed and a communiqué is being immediately
released. *Ends.*

[1] Chief Secretary to the Government of Bihar.
[2] See No. 140.

154

Record of Interview between Rear-Admiral Viscount Mountbatten of Burma
and Mr Tyson

Mountbatten Papers. Viceroy's Interview No. 69

TOP SECRET   *15 April 1947, 11.10–11.40 pm*
In the absence of Sir Frederick Burrows at the Governors' Conference, I saw
Mr. Tyson. He gave me many messages from Sir Frederick Burrows, and told
me that he was not as ill as had been at first feared, and he was confident that
he would pull through. He said that Sir Frederick wished to come and see me
as soon as he was fit enough to do so.

Mr. Tyson enlarged on the state of affairs in Bengal, which he had described
at the Governors' meeting; and he gave me a full account of the deplorable
police situation. It appears that Calcutta had some 1200 policemen, mainly
Gurkhas, as they had never recruited from the plains. When the I.G. asked for
an increase of 50 per cent, Mr. Suhrawardy, the Chief Minister, insisted that
they must all be Muslims. To speed up training it was decided that they must
be ex-soldiers; there were none suitable in the Province, so they sent to the
Punjab for 600 Punjabi Mussalmans. These were given preferential treatment
by the Muslim Government, and went round saying they had been enrolled
for a special purpose which would be revealed later. The Gurkhas now referred
to them as Suhrawardy's private army. Mr. Tyson prophesied that it was only

a matter of days before the two police forces got into armed conflict. Within ten minutes of his leaving me, my Personal Secretary brought in the attached Intelligence Report,[1] showing how accurate Mr. Tyson's forecast was.

We discussed partition, and Mr. Tyson was most emphatic that [sic] despite the views which had been expressed to the contrary at the Governors' Conference, chiefly by Sir Akbar Hydari, in his conviction that the Muslim part of Bengal could not stand by itself economically; nor even in alliance with the rest of a truncated Pakistan. It was clear that Suhrawardy was frightened, otherwise he would never have offered the Hindus a joint electorate. It is true that he hoped to have an entirely independent Bengal (which must be guarded against), but if that was not allowed and they had to choose between Pakistan and Hindustan, Mr. Tyson's own view was that they would choose Hindustan rather than accept partition. He thought that Sir B. N. Rau's scheme for partition was in no way feasible.[2] On the other hand, he thought the proposals put forward in the Staff Paper[3] under Item 2 might be worked.

He gave me his views on Assam, which coincided with what I had already heard.

[1] Not printed. The report gave details of an incident in Calcutta on 10 April when Gurkha constables fired on a lorry carrying Punjabi Muslim constables.
[2] See No. 262, note 2.   [3] No. 139.

155

Mr V. P. Menon to Mr Abell

Mountbatten Papers. Official Correspondence Files: Azad, Maulana

SECRET
No. 526/AS   NEW DELHI, 16 April 1947
My dear Abell,
Please refer to your letter No. 592/94 of yesterday's date forwarding a copy of Abul Kalam Azad's letter[1] to H.E. In making his proposal that Jinnah should form the Central Cabinet, you will remember that Gandhi had added a clause that "the sole referee of what is or is not in the interests of India as a whole will be Lord Mountbatten in his personal capacity".[2] The present proposal of Azad is in principle not very different from this clause.

2. With my letter of the 12th April[3] I had sent you a note in which I had examined the differences between the Congress and the League on the Cabinet Delegation's plan and suggested some possible bases of compromise. Jinnah's extreme position is that in Sections B and C he should be able to use his Muslim

League majority in order to secure Group Constitutions as well as to frame Provincial Constitutions.

3. It seems to me to be clear that the role suggested by Azad is one which H.E. cannot properly take up. If H.E. were to decide for example that all decisions in Sections B and C should be taken by simple majority vote, I do not believe that the Congress will acquiesce in it; on the other hand, Jinnah would not accept an award from H.E. which would modify his position in regard to the procedure in the Sections.

4. As you know, I am by no means of the view that compromises on the Cabinet Delegation's plan are impossible; but such compromises must be the result of discussion among the parties themselves. A judicial tribunal could properly adjudicate on all disputed points but to throw this burden on H.E. is bound to place him in a very embarrassing and invidious position: sooner or later one party or the other is bound to raise the criticism that he takes a partisan view at the instance of H.M.G. The most that H.E. can do is to bring the parties together and suggest for their consideration possible lines on which they could implement the Cabinet Delegation's plan. (Some of these have already been indicated in my note referred to above).

5. Further, even if Jinnah accepted this proposal, which is a very remote possibility, I have myself no doubt that Azad will find it difficult to get the Congress to accept it. My definite view is that we cannot seriously entertain a proposal of this nature.[4]

Yours sincerely,

V. P. MENON

[1] No. 142.   [2] See No. 83.

[3] Mountbatten Papers, Official Correspondence Files: Azad, Maulana.

[4] Mr Abell submitted Mr Menon's letter to Lord Mountbatten on 17 April saying that he agreed with the comments in it. Mr Abell added:

'Though Maulana Azad's suggestion is an encouraging indication that at any rate some Congressmen would like to get back to the Cabinet Mission Plan, I am sure that nothing is likely to come of the proposal. Incidentally, Mr Menon has it on very good authority

(a) that the Muslim League have entirely abandoned the Cabinet Mission Plan, and

(b) that the Congress would not accept Maulana Azad's proposal.'

Ibid.

156

Note by Sir E. Jenkins[1]

Mountbatten Papers. Official Correspondence Files: Punjab, Situation in, Part I(a)

TOP SECRET   *16 April 1947*

The Partition Problem

Should the partition of the Punjab become unavoidable, the following steps should be taken to effect it:—

(1) It should be announced that the Punjab will be divided into two parts—one consisting of districts with a Muslim majority and the other consisting of districts with a non-Muslim majority. Adjustments may be made by agreement in respect of *tahsils* contiguous to the Muslim or non-Muslim portion and having Muslim or non-Muslim majorities.

(2) A Boundary Commission will be set up—

    (a) to effect the adjustments permissible under (1), and

    (b) to determine what portion, if any, of the new non-Muslim Province should be released to form a separate Jat Province.

N.B. (b) will only arise if it is clear in the discussions leading up to the announcement that there is to be a separate Jat Province.

(3) The Boundary Commission should consist of two Muslims and two non-Muslims elected by Members of the Punjab Assembly with a neutral Chairman agreed upon by them.

(4) When the Boundary Commission has taken its decisions, the Punjab Assembly will be divided into two, or if necessary into three, parts. The members sitting for territorial constituencies will be allotted to the Provinces to which their constituencies belong (that is to say to the Muslim Province, the non-Muslim Province, and the Jat Province, if any). Members for special constituencies will be allotted to the Province in which most of their constituents reside.

(5) The Members for the Muslim and non-Muslim Provinces will be responsible for all measures necessary to give effect to the partition. They will negotiate between themselves and with whatever body may be representing the new Jat Province as a whole. The main matters to be decided will be—

    (i) distribution of finances, assets, and public debt;

    (ii) distribution of the services;

    (iii) future of the High Court;

    (iv) relations between the Provinces in such matters as the use of the Central Canal Workshops, the Lyallpur Agricultural College, etc.

(6) Having dealt with the matters discussed in (5) and other matters of the

same kind, the members for each Province will have to set about framing the Provincial constitution. They will have to decide in the first instance what Group, if any, to join. If a Province joins a Group, its constitution will presumably be made for it along with the constitutions of the other Provinces in the Group. If it stands out, it will have to act independently.

(7) It is most important that all proceedings relating to the partition and to the new constitutions should be carried out by non-officials. They will need expert official advice, which will have to be provided by a special staff located at the Centre.

2. It is most improbable that any partition of the Punjab will go through smoothly; the best we can do is to provide a machinery by which the Punjabis can decide matters for themselves.

[1] The authorship of this note has been established from the references to it on the file. Copies were sent by the Viceroy's Private Office to the Governors of Bengal and Assam with a request that they should prepare similar notes on the partition of their Provinces for the information of the Viceroy. Mountbatten Papers, Official Correspondence Files: Punjab, Situation in, Part I(a).

157

Sardar Patel to Mr Henderson

L/PO/12/16: ff 6–7

CAMP, SURAT, GUJARAT, *16 April 1947*

My dear Henderson,

Many thanks for your letter of the 27th March.[1]

2. I was thinking of writing to you a personal letter but the business of the Assembly and preoccupations with important administrative and constitutional matters have not left me the necessary leisure. I had, therefore, to content myself with what you call a "letter of a strictly business character", hoping to make up for it some time later.

3. Without in any way indulging in mutual admiration I feel I should state that I greatly welcomed the opportunity of meeting you personally. An exchange of ideas on personal basis serves to further a mutual understanding of respective points of view and promotes good will. Had such methods rather than stand-offishness governed the procedure between the administrators and the politicians in India in the past, I have no doubt that both would have mutually

[1] In this letter Mr Henderson had acknowledged one from Sardar Patel in which the latter had pressed for action by H.M.G. regarding the future of the Services. Mr Henderson had added that he would like 'to take this opportunity of stating how glad I was to have your letter, even though it was of a strictly business character'. L/PO/12/16: f 9.

benefited. I am glad that ever since the Labour Government has come into power these personal discussions rather than correspondence have been adopted as the channel of discussions over important matters.

4. I was rather disappointed to find that, contrary to my expectations, after receiving your telegram that the previous proposals had been withdrawn with a view to being replaced by the revised ones, we received a despatch on the services containing almost precisely the same proposals. In these circumstances, I had no alternative but to reiterate my previous opposition to the old scheme of compensation. I expect by now you have been apprised of the stand we have taken upon that issue and I do hope that His Majesty's Government will reach a decision in accord with the unanimous Indian opinion.[2] To flout that opinion at this stage of political development, and now that the relations between the two countries are on such a friendly basis, is likely to retard the good work that has recently been done in restoring feelings of amity and goodwill between the two countries.

5. We are all watching with admiration the keen struggle which all of you are putting up both against the elements and your own domestic difficulties. I made it a point to refer in my public speeches at Ahmedabad and Bombay to the calmness, courage and fortitude with which your people are facing up to these difficult and complicated problems. I wish every success to the efforts of your Government in grappling with these difficulties and hope that our people will emulate the fine example set by yours.

6. You must be following closely the political developments in this country ever since the declaration of 20th February. I do not think that even our worst critic can say that we have not responded to that declaration in the spirit in which it was made or we were expected to. But unfortunately others have not reacted to the declaration in the proper spirit. It appears that the League has stiffened rather than relaxed its attitude to Pakistan. Their mood is hardly one of compromise or conciliation. It is not a question of 'give and take' on both sides but the demand for 'give' on one side and 'take' on the other. Conciliation and compromise can only be achieved when the desire is mutual but if there is only one-way traffic, only either surrender or firm stand can bring about the close of this sorry episode. Even otherwise, in view of the happenings in the Punjab and the North West Frontier Province and the direct action launched in the Frontier and Assam, opinion is fast crystallising that the days of concessions have passed. I hope His Majesty's Government will understand this attitude and will not ask for any further concessions. To quote the saying which Sir Stafford Cripps mentioned in the House of Commons, 'appetite comes with eating', and so far every concession given has been made a ground for asking for more. This process cannot go on indefinitely and we must cry a halt some time. That moment has now come and if there could be no further agreement to a united

India owing to League's intransigence, there is no alternative but to divide. But such division can only be brought about if, in accordance with the same principle, the so-called majority Provinces are divided into predominantly Hindu and Muslim areas. I am mentioning all this to provide you with a background to our resolution[3] on the declaration of 20th February.

7. We hope and expect a great deal from the new Viceroy who, I must say, has approached his new responsibilities with vigour and determination. He has a quick grasp and a great sense of urgency. The problem of transfer of power is bristling with difficulties and complications and we have no time to lose. I hope both here and in London the machinery of Government will move quickly otherwise we may be in more trouble than we have bargained for.[4]

With best wishes,

Yours sincerely,

VALLABHBHAI PATEL

[2] See No. 144.   [3] See Vol. IX, Enclosure to No. 511, Item 1.

[4] Mr Henderson showed this letter to Lord Listowel who commented: 'Thank you. An interesting letter, and a very nice tribute to the Party and yourself.' It was also shown to the Prime Minister.

158

Minutes of Second Day of First Governors' Conference

L/PO/6/123: ff 398–408

TOP SECRET

Those present at this Meeting held on 16 April 1947 at 10.30 am were: Rear-Admiral Viscount Mountbatten of Burma, Sir J. Colville, Lieutenant-General Sir A. Nye, Sir F. Wylie, Sir E. Jenkins, Sir H. Dow, Sir F. Bourne, Sir A. Clow, Sir F. Mudie, Sir O. Caroe, Sir C. Trivedi, Sir A. Hydari, Mr Tyson (representing Sir F. Burrows); Lord Ismay, Sir E. Mieville, Sir C. Corfield (Items 1–3), Mr Abell, Mr Christie (Items 1–2), Captain Brockman, Mr Campbell-Johnson, Lieutenant-Colonel Erskine Crum

[Item 1, on release of the Services; and Item 2, on movement of civilians to and from India, omitted.]

ITEM 3   THE GENERAL POLITICAL SITUATION

HIS EXCELLENCY THE VICEROY began by reiterating his honest assurance that he maintained complete impartiality towards both the Muslim League and Congress. He felt that as a matter of principle it would be preferable to hand over to an unified India, but that equally it would be wrong to force the Muslims to give up Pakistan if sufficient safeguards for their minority position in an united India could not be provided. He reiterated that, if a form of Pakistan was eventually decided on, he would in no circumstances agree to a split in the Indian Armed Forces before June 1948.

Copies of the paper[1] containing "one of the possible plans under examination" which had been handed round at the meeting the previous day, were then reconsidered.

HIS EXCELLENCY THE VICEROY said that, from the discussion the previous day, it appeared that this plan might require amendment in certain respects. It had transpired that Bengal was quite likely to choose to stay united and independent. In the North West Frontier Province, quite apart from the political and sentimental desires of the people, the great cost of running the Province might make the Muslim League less keen to take it on. The total population of the Frontier Province was $3\frac{1}{2}$ million with $2\frac{1}{2}$ million tribesmen. The population of Sind was 4 million and the Muslim part of a partitioned Punjab would be 15 million. Therefore there was a total of about 24 million people who might be in Pakistan if Bengal and Assam were excluded. This figure represented 6% of the total population of India, and a Pakistan set up to include these areas only might be a compact little entity capable of maintaining itself economically and unlikely to interfere with the rest of India. Such a solution might make everybody happy—Mr. Jinnah would have a viable Pakistan with the choice of not taking over the N.W.F.P., which could be regarded as a liability; and Congress would have the rest of India.

LORD ISMAY said that, whereas Mr. Jinnah's avowed object was to have a Pakistan consisting of Sind, the whole of the Punjab, the North West Frontier Province, Assam and the whole of Bengal, he believed that he would sooner take whatever was given to him, however much reduced, rather than join up with the rest of India.

HIS EXCELLENCY THE VICEROY asked whether it was agreed that, in the cases of those Provinces which had been in Section A of the Cabinet Mission's Plan, authority should be demitted to an executive appointed by Section A of the present Constitutional Assembly. SIR JOHN COLVILLE, SIR ARCHIBALD NYE and SIR FRANCIS WYLIE agreed with this procedure.

SIR OLAF CAROE suggested that separate words should be used when talking of the "partition" of India as a whole and the "partition" of the Provinces. HIS EXCELLENCY THE VICEROY said that, although this was confusing, it was intentional on his part to use the same word as he wanted to give the Muslim League the impression that the same principle must be applied throughout. A statement to this effect might be made.

HIS EXCELLENCY THE VICEROY said that he would, before sending out the invitations for the Simla house party, ask Sir Conrad Corfield's advice as to which Princes to invite. He said that he thought that the date of 7th May was optimistic for this party. Mid-May would be nearer the mark.

SIR EVAN JENKINS said that, as he saw it, the Simla talks were likely to be a turning point. The Congress and the Muslim League would either agree to revert to the Cabinet Mission's statement or refuse to do so. If they agreed, the position of the Sikhs still constituted a difficulty as the Sikhs were demanding partition in any event. The Muslim League would not agree to such partition as they would say that they had accepted the Cabinet Mission's Plan on the basis of an unified Punjab. SIR EVAN JENKINS said that he considered that it was therefore very important that, before the Simla meeting, His Excellency the Viceroy should emphasize to the Sikhs that their position in the Punjab was closely analogous to the position of the Muslims throughout India and that they must expect similar treatment. If the Muslims insisted on the partition of India, the same principle would have to apply to The Punjab. If, on the other hand, the Muslims agreed to an unified India, the Punjab would not be split. In the latter case safeguards for the Sikhs would have to be devised— for example The Punjab might be divided into two zones of which the Sikh one would have the option of secession after ten years. SIR EVAN JENKINS said that he considered that great pressure would be necessary to induce the Sikhs to accept this.

SIR CONRAD CORFIELD said that the Maharajah of Patiala could probably help in this matter and suggested that he should be invited to attend the Simla talks in his capacity as pro-Chancellor.

SIR EVAN JENKINS went on to say that the danger from the local point of view was that the Sikhs might try to upset any efforts at orderly settlement. If there was no agreement on the basis of the Cabinet Mission's Plan, and Plan "Balkan" had to be brought into operation, the Punjab could be partitioned satisfactorily only by agreement. He did not think that it would be possible to go further at the Simla talks than to agree to the principle of partition and that the details should be worked out separately. He emphasized that it was most desirable to avoid any discussion of such details at Simla.

HIS EXCELLENCY THE VICEROY said that it might be necessary to ask Sir Evan Jenkins to attend the Simla house party. SIR EVAN JENKINS said that he would be readily available if required.

SIR CONRAD CORFIELD said that if the Working Committee of the Congress and the Muslim League were asked to be in attendance he felt that the leading Dewans of States should also be invited. HIS EXCELLENCY THE VICEROY approved this suggestion.

SIR EVAN JENKINS said that he considered that a decision on partition of the Punjab should come first in the programme and that a boundary commission, possibly under a British Judge of the High Court should be set up to lay down the new boundary line. A time limit for this, possibly a month, would have to be fixed and agreement by the different parties to the suggested boundary would have to be obtained. It would have to be made clear in the statement

¹ No. 139.

how partition was to be brought about before the choice of their future was given to the different parts of the Province.

HIS EXCELLENCY THE VICEROY said that it was quite clear to him that any form of enforced partition would involve the use of troops on a big scale and create very considerable difficulties. SIR HUGH DOW said that he believed that there would also be serious repercussions in other Provinces. SIR ANDREW CLOW said that he could not conceive a partition in The Punjab by agreement. He thought that it should be laid down first and left open to modification. SIR EVAN JENKINS agreed that it was unlikely that agreement would be obtained. HIS EXCELLENCY THE VICEROY asked whether an announcement of a partition plan, without prior consultation of the parties concerned, would not be an invitation to the use of force?

HIS EXCELLENCY THE VICEROY then said that it was for consideration whether Provinces should, instead of being given the choice of remaining independent, only be allowed to choose which of two Constituent Assemblies they wished to join. It might be better to name two Constituent Assemblies to which the Provinces would have the choice of adhering—the Hindustan and Pakistan Constituent Assemblies. He thought that it was essential to introduce these two new words into the Plan. He felt that it would be most undesirable in many ways to give Bengal the opportunity of standing out independently. Although it was obviously in many ways desirable to adhere to the principle that Provinces should choose their own future, it would be necessary to be very cautious and not to encourage too many independent nations. He had, when first formulating the principle, not clearly realised this danger. Nevertheless, nothing should be included in the plan which would conflict with the policy of H.M.G. He suggested that Provinces might be asked in the first instance to join one or other Constituent Assembly. However, it would be impossible to exercise compulsion if this meant the use of force. Final choice would have to be left to the Provinces.

LORD ISMAY said that he doubted whether any formula other than to give the Provinces absolutely free choice as to their future would be accepted by His Majesty's Government. Such freedom of choice was inherent in the Prime Minister's statement.

HIS EXCELLENCY THE VICEROY then asked the Governors for their views as to whether complete freedom of choice to remain independent should be given to Provinces.

SIR JOHN COLVILLE said that he considered it important to avoid splitting India into more units than was absolutely necessary. Therefore, all should be given the choice of joining only two Constituent Assemblies with the option of contracting out at a later date. SIR ARCHIBALD NYE and SIR FRANCIS WYLIE agreed with this view.

SIR EVAN JENKINS said that a Sikh Province in a partitioned Punjab might insist on standing out independently. What could then be done? Could force be used to persuade them to adhere to one or other side? He thought that Provinces should be left to choose complete independence if they really wanted it, and that we should not commit ourselves into forcing a Province into any particular group. SIR HUGH DOW and SIR FREDERICK BOURNE said that they considered that Provinces must be left the option to contract out.

SIR ANDREW CLOW thought it was essential to keep the Provinces together in, at the most, two separate units until after June 1948. To divide the Army into more than two parts, for example, would be almost an impossibility. SIR AKBAR HYDARI said that he agreed with SIR ANDREW CLOW. It was the people who mattered, not only the political parties. If India was "Balkanised" more than was proposed by Mr. Jinnah, it was the people who would suffer.

SIR FRANCIS MUDIE said that he would be in favour of setting up two or preferably three Constituent Assemblies. All Provinces should be made to join one or the other with the option of contracting out.

SIR OLAF CAROE said that he would be in favour of leaving out all possibility of allowing Provinces to stand out independently.

SIR CHANDULAL TRIVEDI said that his views were identical with those of Sir John Colville.

SIR CONRAD CORFIELD said that, as freedom of choice had already been given to one-third of India by the lapse of paramountcy over the States, he did not see why the rest of India should not be allowed equal freedom.

MR. TYSON said that Bengal as an independent unit would be economically viable as it would receive jute and tea export duties as well as customs duties and income tax. He thought that the Muslim League Ministry would go a long way towards bringing in the Hindus on the basis that Bengal was to remain independent. If Bengal was not to be independent the Muslim League Ministry would prefer to link themselves with Pakistan rather than with Hindustan. The Hindustan minority in Bengal would of course prefer to go to Hindustan.

SIR CHANDULAL TRIVEDI said that he did not believe that the Hindus in Bengal really wanted an independent Bengal. With this MR. TYSON agreed.

MR. TYSON said that he believed that Sir Frederick Burrows would prefer an independent Bengal to a divided Bengal. MR. ABELL said that, if Bengal was given a free choice, it might negotiate with the Hindu Centre although it would not join it.

MR. TYSON said that if Bengal remained united it was most unlikely that it would join either Constituent Assembly.

SIR CHANDULAL TRIVEDI asked whether the Bengali Hindus were likely to upset the Cabinet Mission Plan by insisting on partition. MR. TYSON said that this was most unlikely. They would certainly prefer the Cabinet Mission Plan to partition.

MR. ABELL pointed out that, once Provinces had joined a Constituent Assembly, it would in practice be extremely difficult for them to get out again.

HIS EXCELLENCY THE VICEROY pointed out that they would be given the choice of which Constituent Assembly they wished to join. If Provinces were invited to remain independent they would probably choose to do so. It would be necessary to include a safeguard that they could secede after the British had left. He felt it essential that we should not turn over to more separate units than was absolutely necessary. The crux of the matter was whether it was in the best interests of India to insist on the partition of Bengal or to allow it to be an independent nation. If Bengal was allowed the choice to remain independent, that would be helping towards the "Balkanisation" of India and going against everything that Congress stood for, and their sacrifice in agreeing to Pakistan. Mr. Jinnah would also object to an independent Bengal. Therefore, this proposal was likely to have much opposition. The only way in which Bengal could opt to remain united would be by a majority vote of both communities. If this happened, then both Congress and Mr. Jinnah would have very great difficulty in opposing the suggestion that it should remain independent.

SIR ANDREW CLOW said that Sylhet contained 60% Muslims. He was not sure how this district would vote but it would probably be in favour of Pakistan. The whole of the rest of Assam would be very pleased if Sylhet left, as it was a deficit district and a liability. HIS EXCELLENCY THE VICEROY said that he would take an early opportunity of informing Mr. Jinnah of this as he was sure that he did not realise it.

SIR ANDREW CLOW went on to say that if there was an Eastern Pakistan, Assam would be cut off from the rest of India. There were no rail connections. He pointed out that the Goalpara district of Assam had a 46% Muslim population at the last census. This might have turned into a majority by now. He stressed that an hostile Bengal could throttle Assam, which was entirely dependent on it. HIS EXCELLENCY THE VICEROY suggested that it would probably be a question of negotiating transit rights through Bengal.

SIR ANDREW CLOW said that it should be made clear that those who were to decide the future of Sylhet were the representatives of territorial constituencies within Sylhet itself. The total of these representatives would be 25. HIS EXCELLENCY THE VICEROY agreed that this should be made clear.

HIS EXCELLENCY THE VICEROY also said that it should be made clear in the draft time-table that the choice of the N.W.F.P. would take place after an election.

SIR OLAF CAROE said that if Congress won the next elections in the

N.W.F.P. the Province would become a part of Hindustan. It was the object of holding the elections to find out whether the Province wished to join Pakistan or Hindustan. However, he thought that it was extremely unlikely that Congress would win. He had very little doubt that the N.W.F.P. would in fact come in on the Pakistan side. If they had become part of Hindustan, they would be completely cut off from the remainder.

The Meeting then considered the draft announcement to be made if Plan "Balkan" was decided on.

A paragraph in this announcement referred to the problems of almost infinite variety and bewildering complexity which would confront the successor authorities. SIR EVAN JENKINS said that he did not know how sufficient highly-trained staff could be produced to deal with these problems.

SIR CONRAD CORFIELD said that he thought that existing arrangements would have to continue for a certain period until the new arrangements could be brought into force.

HIS EXCELLENCY THE VICEROY said that he thought it probable that the British would have to put forward a plan on which the successor Governments would be able to work. He did not believe that there were sufficient highly-trained Indians to make such a plan. It would have to be done by the British.

LORD ISMAY said that a special staff would be required to deal with this. HIS EXCELLENCY THE VICEROY suggested that some of the members of the Secretary of State's Services might be made available for this purpose as they became redundant from other jobs. SIR EVAN JENKINS said that he had no highly-enough qualified men available.

HIS EXCELLENCY THE VICEROY said that he considered it essential that all possible help should be given by the British in order that he should fulfil his directive to ensure as far as possible the future prosperity and happiness of the people in India.

SIR OLAF CAROE said that the type of British official required would be those who had spent most of their time with the Central Government.

HIS EXCELLENCY THE VICEROY:—
(i) invited C.V.S. to redraft V.C.P. 28[2] in the light of the discussion;
(ii) directed P.S.V. to arrange for copies of V.C.P. 28, as redrafted, to be sent to Governors;
(iii) invited Governors to treat this document as a highly secret and personal paper;
(iv) invited C.V.S. to consider the organisation of a special staff to formulate plans on which the successor Governments would be able to work.

ITEM 4 COMMUNAL STRIFE

HIS EXCELLENCY THE VICEROY said that he had been interested to see the

[2] No. 139.

different reactions in the Delhi newspapers to the joint appeal by Mr. Gandhi and Mr. Jinnah calling on all to refrain from the use of force for political ends. Mr. Nishtar, who had come to luncheon, had pointed out how deplorable it was that the *Hindustan Times* had coupled the announcement of this appeal with reports of communal riots in the N.W.F.P. and criticism of Mr. Jinnah for not having personally visited scenes of disorder as Mr. Gandhi had. HIS EXCELLENCY THE VICEROY said that he felt that this was a most ungracious spirit in which to greet the appeal and wished this point of view to be conveyed to the Editor of the *Hindustan Times*. The complete absence of comment in the Muslim League newspaper *Dawn* was perhaps to be preferred.

SIR OLAF CAROE drew attention to the embarrassment which was caused to Governors by members of the Interim Government visiting Provinces without giving prior notice. He quoted examples.

SIR EVAN JENKINS stated that the ex-Prime Minister of the Punjab had intimated to him that one of the main reasons for his resignation was the embarrassment caused by such visits. Members of the Interim Government had in certain cases actively stimulated communal ill-feeling.

THEIR EXCELLENCIES THE GOVERNORS all felt that it would be most desirable if they were in future given notice of visits by members of the Interim Government.

HIS EXCELLENCY THE VICEROY:—

(i) decided to discuss the question of visits by members of the Interim Government to Provinces at a Cabinet Meeting and to attempt to persuade the Members to give prior warning of such visits to the Governors or Governments concerned;

(ii) invited Their Excellencies the Governors to inform him if any Inflammatory speeches were made in Provinces by members of the interim Government in future;

(iii) directed the Press Attaché to convey to the Editor of the *Hindustan Times* his disappointment at the way in which the joint appeal by Mr. Gandhi and Mr. Jinnah had been, in that morning's issue of the paper, coupled with stories of communal strife and attacks on Mr. Jinnah.

ITEM 5 COMMUNISTS

MR. TYSON said that Sir Frederick Burrows would much like to see the Central Government declare Communists illegal.

SIR ARCHIBALD NYE said that in Madras it had been found possible to imprison a number of Communists, not because they were Communists, but because they had broken the law in one way or another. This, however, was only a temporary measure. He gave his opinion that there was no evidence to support the belief that money for Communist organisations in India was supplied by Russia.

HIS EXCELLENCY THE VICEROY said that he agreed with Sir Archibald Nye both in the way in which he treated Communists, and that Russia was not providing funds for their activities. He felt it would be most dangerous to declare the Communists illegal. This would have all the aspects of a Fascist action. He did not believe that it was ethically sound in time of peace to ban a political party which was not openly engaged in subversive activities.

LORD ISMAY pointed out that the Communist Party had not been banned in the United Kingdom, even during the period in the war before Russia entered.

HIS EXCELLENCY THE VICEROY:—

(i) decided to take no action on the suggestion that Communists should be declared illegal;

(ii) invited Their Excellencies the Governors to include in their fortnightly letters information of Communist activities in their Provinces.

ITEM 6   PRIVATE ARMIES

HIS EXCELLENCY THE VICEROY said that he had been amazed to find what a very large number of "private armies" there were in India. Altogether it was estimated that there were approximately 413,000 persons in such organisations. These were divided between 12 different private armies, of which the Communists had a strength of only 1,000 and one Hindu Mahasabha organisation of over 100,000.

SIR EVAN JENKINS said that the troubles in the Punjab had really begun with an attempt to ban private armies. The Prime Minister had decided to take this course rather than to try to maintain a balance of power between them. The Hindu private army in the Punjab had taken the ban very quietly and so had the Muslims except in Lahore. There there had been trouble which was the immediate *casus belli* in the Province. The ban had then been quickly withdrawn and now the Sikhs had started up a private army of their own. He had decided that he could not now consider the question of reintroducing the ban in view of the general situation.

SIR OLAF CAROE said that the Red Shirts, a Congress organisation in the N.W.F.P., were one of the best known of all the private armies. They had been started 15 years ago. Since the Congress Ministry had been in power, they had not been much in evidence until recently; but then, without any warning, the Ministry had brought in between 6 and 7,000 Red Shirts in uniform to Peshawar City on the pretext that they were to protect the Hindus there. The military had refused to work in conjunction with the Red Shirts and had withdrawn from Peshawar. The presence of the Red Shirts had stimulated enormous processions on the part of the Muslims, whose organisation in the N.W.F.P. was called Green Shirts. Then the Red Shirts had been withdrawn by the Ministry—again without him being informed—and a large unofficial fine had been levied to pay for their stay. The presence of the Red Shirts in Peshawar had caused a very dangerous situation which might have become even worse as the Ministry wished to make them into special police and arm them with official rifles.

HIS EXCELLENCY THE VICEROY asked whether the Central Government could issue an ordinance banning private armies. MR. ABELL said that this would not be constitutionally possible. Such legislation would have to be introduced by Provinces.

MR. TYSON suggested that the two main parties might order a ban from the Centre. He felt that this would be obeyed. HIS EXCELLENCY THE VICEROY said that he would take this suggestion up during the forthcoming meeting at Simla. He would call upon the Party Leaders to have these private armies suppressed and also try and persuade the Central Government to co-ordinate action to this end by Provincial Governments.

SIR FRANCIS WYLIE said that, in the United Provinces, District Magistrates had been authorised to ban the wearing of uniform if the situation required it. He added that he was doubtful of the prospects of persuasion by Party Leaders proving successful. SIR EVAN JENKINS pointed out that Congress did not have to control the Mahasabha if it did not want to.

SIR OLAF CAROE said that he was very doubtful that an appeal not backed up by forcible measures would be successful. With this SIR EVAN JENKINS agreed.

SIR FREDERICK BOURNE pointed out that many of these volunteer organisations regarded themselves more in the nature of athletic clubs. It would not be possible to ban them. HIS EXCELLENCY THE VICEROY said that he had no objection to athletic clubs as such. The criterion would be that they must not parade through the streets in coloured shirts, nor carry arms. SIR HUGH DOW said that, in one training camp, members of one of these clubs were taught, among other subjects, how to throw acid.

SIR CHANDULAL TRIVEDI said that there were no private armies in Orissa. His Prime Minister had been able to persuade the local Muslim leaders not to form one.

HIS EXCELLENCY THE VICEROY:—
(i) decided to raise the question of the banning of private armies with the Indian leaders at the Simla conference;
(ii) invited Their Excellencies the Governors to keep him informed concerning the activities of private armies and of any ideas they might have to abolish them.

ITEM 7   DISBANDMENT OF THE AUXILIARY FORCE (INDIA)
SIR JOHN COLVILLE stated that he understood that there was a proposal that the Auxiliary Force (India) should be disbanded in the near future. He felt that it would be preferable, if possible, to keep it in being during the interim

period until June 1948. It might prove useful in support of the police in the maintenance of law and order.

THEIR EXCELLENCIES THE GOVERNORS expressed general agreement that the Auxiliary Force (India) should not be disbanded before June 1948. MR. TYSON said that Sir Frederick Burrows attached great importance to this. SIR ARCHIBALD NYE emphasised that it might be most useful in the unlikely event of an "awkward withdrawal".

LORD ISMAY pointed out that it had been decided that there should be no move of British troops until after the transfer of power. Why could not the Auxiliary Force (India) be treated on the same basis?

HIS EXCELLENCY THE VICEROY:—

invited C.V.S. to inform the Commander-in-Chief that it was the general view of the Governors' Conference that the A.F.(I) should be retained until the transfer of power, and to ask him for a note on the present position of this question for the information of His Excellency The Viceroy.

[Item 8, on future policy regarding honours; Item 9, on future of High Courts and compensation for High Court Judges; Item 10, on Forestry and Police Officers; Item 11, on private servants on Governors' estates; Item 12, on Special Responsibilities of the Governors; and Item 13, inviting Governors to inform Lord Mountbatten when their Prime Ministers were visiting Delhi so he could see them, omitted.]

159

Note by Sir T. Shone

L/S &G/7/1251: ff 109–10

16 April 1947

As I had not yet met Mr. Jinnah (he had not been in Delhi since my arrival), and as I had called on Mr. Gandhi last week, I arranged to see Mr. Jinnah at his house this morning. I was with him for nearly an hour, during which he treated me to a discourse on the necessity and inevitability of Pakistan, using all the well-worn arguments for regarding the Muslims as a different people from the Hindus. I need not set out these arguments here. Mr. Jinnah appeared to be quite unbending in his insistence on Pakistan which, indeed, savoured of the psychopathic. He maintained Pakistan provided the only means by which India could achieve the political and governmental stability which was in her own and the general interest.

2. Mr. Jinnah argued that an unified India was an artificial creation; India had never really been one, even under the Hindu and Muslim emperors; in so

far as unity had existed in ancient days, it had been maintained by the sword. This had also been the case under British rule. In these days unity could only be based on the will of the people; the hundred million Muslims did not want it; they wanted Pakistan. Mr. Jinnah sought to draw a comparison between the Indian Empire and the former Austro-Hungarian Empire which had broken up because the various peoples comprised in it wanted their independence.

3. Speaking as if he were certain of achieving his goal, he said Pakistan would be in great need of outside assistance to develop its resources which were potentially immense. Moreover, no country could stand alone these days or cut itself off from the outside world. Even the greatest powers must have friends and allies. He saw only three great powers to whom Pakistan could turn for assistance—the Soviet Union, the United States, and the United Kingdom. France was now out of the picture. He did not know the Russians nor did he intend to learn the Russian language at his age; while the Americans were better known in India, they were still comparative strangers. He felt that the best chance for Pakistan lay in dealing with the British, between whom and Indians there was more of a basis for mutual understanding, despite all their differences, than with either of the other powers he had mentioned. He did not subscribe to all that other people said about the exploitation of India by the British; in any case it was the future that mattered now; as to that, to put it bluntly, "better the devil you know".

4. Asked about the Indian Army, Mr. Jinnah said Pakistan must have its own armed forces and he professed to see no difficulty in this.

5. Asked about the suggested division of Bengal, Mr. Jinnah described this suggestion—like the proposed division of the Punjab—as a red herring. The idea behind both was to convince the Muslims that they could only get a truncated and "moth-eaten" Pakistan which would not be worth-while. He maintained that the Muslim population of Bengal was 60% of the whole and that of the Hindu population of 40% only half were Caste Hindus. The Scheduled Castes, he argued, would rather be with the Muslims. As regards the Punjab, the Sikhs were making a great mistake. There were $3\frac{1}{2}$ millions of them and if the province were divided, there would be 2 million or so in one part and $1\frac{1}{2}$ million in the other. It would be far better that they should all stay together in Pakistan, where they could expect to be well treated. He had tried to get the Sikhs to state what they wanted and had promised to consider their demands with all sympathy. They were in many ways admirable people; but unfortunately they lacked leadership of a high order and while they were often very successful in small ways of business, they seldom produced outstanding men in law, science and politics. If they were divided, they could not play the part they might hope to do or ought to do if they stayed together—in Pakistan.

160

Note by Sir E. Jenkins

R/3/1/90: ff 12–16

16 April 1947

This letter[1] from Mr. Liaquat Ali Khan to H.E. tells only part of the story and that inaccurately. For convenience I have numbered the points in the letter to which I refer in this note.

(1) On 24th January the Muslim League started an intensive agitation against the Coalition Ministry.[2] The *casus belli* was the imposition of a ban on the Muslim League National Guards simultaneously with a similar ban on the Rashtriya Swayam Sewak Sangh. On 26th January the Premier decided to withdraw the bans, and it at once became apparent that the Muslim League intended to continue their agitation. On 27th morning I sent for Mamdot, the League leader, and warned him that if the agitation continued, he would probably reduce the Punjab to chaos and might even force the Ministry out of office. I knew that the agitation could not be kept non-communal. If the Ministry resigned, it would be my duty to call upon him to form a Government, and I thought it most unlikely that he would be able to do so. The basis of the agitation had been changed to a demand for "civil liberties", and I told him that I was very ready to discuss this demand with my Ministers if he would put the position to his colleagues in the League and see me again. Mamdot was quite reasonable, but at 3 p.m. a big meeting was held by the League at which the resignation of the Coalition Ministry was demanded. The Premier would not at that stage consider resignation, and the agitation continued. The League claimed that it was non-communal. It was inevitably communal, since the Ministry was supported not only by the Unionist Muslims, but by the Congress and the Sikhs.

The agitation shook the Coalition Ministry very badly, and before 20th February the Premier had decided on a compromise. H.M.G.'s Statement of 20th February shook the Premier still further, and he decided on 2nd March, just after the compromise had been concluded, to resign. He gave me only 8 hours' notice of this decision, and his colleagues only about 4 hours' notice.

On 2nd March, after seeing the Finance Minister and the Development Minister, the leaders respectively of the Congress and Panthic parties, I sent for Mamdot and called upon him to form a Government. I reminded him of our conversation of 27th January (of which I have a record) and said that in my

[1] No. 148.
[2] See Vol. IX, Chapter 5 for documentation on the Punjab situation between 25 January and 22 March 1947.

opinion only a coalition Government could succeed. He said that he would do his best to make terms with the other parties.

On the night of 3rd March a very large non-Muslim meeting was held at Lahore, at which violent speeches were made. At this point the non-Muslims were undoubtedly to blame; but they had put up with 34 days of League agitation and were in a hysterical state.

On 4th March rioting broke out in Lahore. On that evening the Coalition Ministers, who had been asked to carry on pending the formation of a new Ministry, told me that they must resign at once, as they could take no further responsibility for the situation. On 5th and 6th March rioting broke out in Multan, Rawalpindi, Amritsar and Jullundur. The non-Muslims were not specially armed at any of these places, with the possible exception of Rawal-pindi, though they undoubtedly gave considerable provocation. At Multan the trouble was started by a procession of students, and within three hours the Muslims killed about 120 Hindus. Casualties were heavy in the other cities also, and except in Amritsar the non-Muslims suffered much more heavily than the Muslims.

By 6th–7th March the trouble was spreading to the rural areas of the Rawal-pindi Division and the Multan district. In the Rawalpindi and Attock districts and later in part of the Jhelum district there was an absolute butchery of non-Muslims. In many villages they were herded into houses and burnt alive. Many Sikhs had their hair and beards cut, and there were cases of forcible circumcision. Many Sikh women who escaped slaughter were abducted.

The Muslim League made no efforts to maintain peace and Mamdot made no serious attempt at forming a Ministry. At the time he had no majority and he gave me the impression that he was not anxious to take responsibility for quelling a very serious outbreak of violence.

(2) The total number of dead is not yet known. The latest figure is just under 3,000, and I believe that the final figure may be 3,500. The communal propor-tions have not been accurately reported, but I should say that among the dead there are 6 non-Muslims for every Muslim. Mr. Liaquat Ali Khan can hardly realise the terrible nature of the rural massacre. One of my troubles has been the extreme complacency of the League leaders in the Punjab, who say in effect that "boys will be boys". I have no doubt that the non-Muslims were pro-vocative in the cities, but the Muslims had been equally provocative during their agitation and had in particular murdered a Sikh constable in Amritsar.

(3) I was forced into Section 93 in circumstances which were fully reported at the time, and my reasons for getting into this extremely unsatisfactory position were known to Lord Wavell and the Secretary of State. Mamdot had failed to produce a majority, and it was obvious that he could not begin to control the situation.

(4)[3] We are dealing with the aftermath of very serious disturbances. In one

Police Station alone of the Rawalpindi district the Police tell me that they are investigating 500 murders. It is quite impossible for me to declare an amnesty, nor can I permit people to retain looted property, abducted women, and so on. In one village of the Attock district the Police found 30 lorry loads of loot.

(5) The cadres of the Punjab services are mixed, and it is impossible to guarantee that the Muslims will have their full share of senior appointments. I cannot pass over senior British and non-Muslim officials to make room for Muslims. Of the 29 districts, 10 are held by British officers, 9 by Muslims and 10 by Hindus or Sikhs. There is one Muslim Commissioner, who is on leave. He happens to be quite incompetent. The Chief Secretary is a Muslim. The investigation staff is an improvisation. We asked all suitable retired officers to join it, but the Muslims have mostly refused. The I.G. of Police has his eye on this, since the staff is not yet complete.

(6) It is untrue that the officials are hostile to the Muslims. They have been deeply shocked both by the atrocities committed in the rural areas and by the complacency of the League. Scott, DIG Rawalpindi, a good fighter but no politician, gave an interview to some journalists at which he unwisely expressed his disgust.

(7) It is untrue that our censorship is worked with intentional partiality. We are frequently defeated by clever journalists.

(8) Everything possible is being done to keep the Sikhs and Hindus quiet. The Kirpan question has already been explained to H.E. Briefly, the Sikhs have had the legal right to carry swords since 1924, and it would be most unwise to take them on on this issue immediately. The only possibility would be to allow the Muslims to carry swords. H.E. has already told me that he does not *prima facie* favour this and has instructed me to refer the matter to him if it is proposed to give any concession to the Muslims.

(9) For what object the British officials in the Punjab, including myself, are "fostering chaos" I do not know. Every British official in the I.C.S. and I.P. in the Punjab, including myself, would be very glad to leave it tomorrow. With two or three possible exceptions no British official intends to remain in the Punjab after the transfer of power. Six months ago the position was quite different; but we feel now that we are dealing with people who are out to destroy themselves, and that in the absence of some reasonable agreement between them the average official will have to spend his life in a communal civil war.

(10)[4] The Punjab is not now in a constitutional, but in a revolutionary situation. If a Muslim League Government were formed tomorrow, it would be attacked by the non-Muslims, and particularly the Sikhs, with a violence which might prove uncontrollable and would certainly involve frightful

[3] This relates to para. 5 of No. 148.   [4] This relates to para. 12 of No. 148.

slaughter by Police and troops. If Mr. Liaquat Ali Khan means to start an agitation against authority in the Punjab, he will produce very much the same result. He might be reminded that it was the Muslim League, and not the non-Muslims, who first attempted to dislodge a Ministry by force.

E. M. J.

161

Record of Interview between Rear-Admiral Viscount Mountbatten of Burma and Sardar Baldev Singh

Mountbatten Papers. Viceroy's Interview No. 70

TOP SECRET   *16 April 1947*

Sardar Baldev Singh came to see me at 6.30. I asked the Governor of Sind to come and explain to him the object of the Sind Landholders' Mortgages Bill, 1947, about which Sardar Baldev Singh had written to me on the 14th April, inviting me to intervene. Sir Francis Mudie was able to convince Sardar Baldev Singh that this measure was not one to which assent could justifiably be withheld.

After the Governor of Sind had left I invited the Governor of the Punjab to discuss the translation of the pamphlet by the *Ajit* of Lahore dated the 5th April,[1] in which it stated that Sardar Baldev Singh was prepared to receive money on behalf of the Sikhs' fund, which was obviously designed to support a civil war.

He categorically denied in the presence of Sir Evan Jenkins that he had ever signed this appeal, or had agreed to be Treasurer. Sir Evan Jenkins accepted his assurance. Sir Evan Jenkins then left Sardar Baldev Singh and myself alone.

He told me he had asked to see me urgently in order to seek my advice; could I tell him whether it was the definite intention of H.M.G. to withdraw every British officer and man from the Indian armed forces by the end of June 1948, or was there any prospect of retaining the services of any of them after that date. He explained that on my answer depended an immediate decision he had to make whether to start implementing the full speed nationalisation scheme.

My reply was that until India disclosed her intentions about remaining within the Commonwealth or severing her connection with us, it was a question I could not answer.

In my personal opinion if India were to say she would like to remain within the Commonwealth as a free nation (the word "Dominion" need never be used) H.M.G. would be most likely to agree, and I certainly would use my best offices to obtain agreement.

If the resolution passed by the Constituent Assembly that India was to become an independent sovereign republic[2] made it difficult for the political leaders now to eat their words, I reminded him that a face saving formula could easily be found; all they had to point out was that there had been no date put to this resolution, which had been passed before H.M.G.'s statement of the 20th February. They could now say that a date had to be settled, and suggest that it should not be put into effect for five years, and then the position could be reviewed, and if necessary a plebiscite taken.

On such an arrangement I felt confident that H.M.G. would agree to leave British officers, and that that was the best chance of getting British officers to volunteer to stay.

Sardar Baldev Singh told me he had spoken to Mr. Bhabha since he had last seen me, and had found him enthusiastically in favour of this idea, but he had not yet had time to contact Dr. Matthai, but intended to do so.

I urged him to continue lobbying, and said "Why did you not see Nehru?". He said, "I have seen him, and he is very interested but cannot give a quick decision, and wants at least another month or six weeks to think it over."

I informed him that I was thinking of inviting the principal leaders, including himself, to Simla in about a month's time, to discuss the final decision that I shall have to take on the course to recommend to H.M.G. for the transference of power.

I pointed out that if he was prepared to delay the decision until then, that that would be the psychological moment for him to put it to the leaders of all parties at Simla, though I would advise him to continue lobbying individual members of the Cabinet and Congress beforehand.

I told him that the decision at Simla would be taken in accordance with what appeared to be the will of the people; although I hoped it would be for a strong India, or at least the Cabinet Mission plan, we had to face the likelihood of it being partition. He himself said he thought partition was now the only acceptable solution. I pointed out that in that event Mr. Jinnah had insisted on partitioning the armed forces, and indeed Mr. Liaquat Ali Khan had already put up a paper for circulation,[3] which would be taken at the Defence Committee Meeting next week, in which he proposed preparations for partitioning the armed forces.

I pointed out that if indeed partition had to be put through soon after our departure in June 1948, and soon after complete nationalisation had taken place, the armed forces, already greatly weakened by a far too quick nationalisation, would surely expire under the strain of partition. He was quite excited and worried, and vehemently agreed.

I told him that although I had had no direct request for British assistance, I had had sufficient hints from both Mr. Jinnah and Mr. Liaquat Ali Khan to show

[1] See Enclosure 2 to No. 109.   [2] See Vol. IX, No. 190.   [3] See No. 215.

that Pakistan would want to remain in the British Empire, and receive assistance
from British officers. Although I personally could be no party to holding out
any hope that the part of India which wanted to break away, was going to
receive British help, I did feel that this was a very strong lever for Sardar
Baldev Singh to use in his discussions with Congress, since if all the Muslim
League members were already in favour of remaining within the Commonwealth, and receiving British assistance, Congress would be ill-advised not to
accept the same advantages.

In fact if he was in general agreement that partition had to take place, then
the only chance of the armed forces surviving was strong British help, which in
turn depended on both Hindustan and Pakistan agreeing to remain within the
British Commonwealth at least for a limited period.

Sardar Baldev Singh said that he had decided not to start implementing
complete nationalisation until after the Simla meetings, at which he hoped to
obtain a favourable decision on the question of retaining the link with the
Commonwealth. I reminded him that although he was at liberty to quote me,
to do so would be to defeat his own ends. He entirely agreed.

162

Minutes of Viceroy's Third Miscellaneous Meeting

Mountbatten Papers

*Those present at this Meeting held at The Viceroy's House, New Delhi on 16 April
1947 at 11 pm were: Rear-Admiral Viscount Mountbatten of Burma, Pandit Nehru,
Mr Liaquat Ali Khan, Sardar Baldev Singh, Field Marshal Sir C. Auchinleck, Sir
O. Caroe, Lord Ismay, Sir E. Mieville, Mr Abell; Captain Brockman (Secretariat)*

SITUATION IN THE N.W.F.P.

HIS EXCELLENCY THE VICEROY read out a telegram[1] which had been received over the telephone during dinner, reporting rioting, looting and arson in
Dera Ismail Khan. He said that he thought it would be a good opportunity,
while all those present were in the house for a dinner party that they should
discuss whether there was anything which could be done to ease the situation in
the Province.

SIR OLAF CAROE said that he intended to see General Messervy at Rawalpindi on his way back the next day. He thought that the report might perhaps
be rather alarmist, but if troubles spread to the rural areas then it would be a
serious affair. A telegram on the previous day[2] had said that half the city was
burnt and this was very unfortunate, as it was the wealthiest city in the Frontier

Province, a big centre of trade and had suffered very little from communal trouble in recent years. The last occasion was 1939 and previous to that in 1931, and on each occasion part of the bazaar had been burnt. He added that the population of the city was roughly 50-50 Muslim-Hindu, but that it was swollen during the winter months by tribesmen up to a number of say, 150,000 who came down to trade from as far as Afghanistan.

HIS EXCELLENCY THE VICEROY asked if Sir Olaf Caroe would give a brief description of the situation in the N.W.F.P. He said he felt sure that everyone would agree that at the present time, just before he hoped to make a recommendation to H.M.G. about the final hand-over of power, it would be particularly unfortunate if the N.W.F.P. went the same way as the Punjab and became reft with communal trouble.

SIR OLAF CAROE explained that the trouble was caused by a Muslim League movement against the Government in the Province. He thought there was no substance at all in their complaints, but a number of excuses had been found to start trouble. The recent disturbances have, for example, been caused largely by the enforced conversion of a young woman and her transfer from one village to another. After her husband and father had been murdered, she was remarried to a Muslim and forced to embrace Islam. Finally she was brought to Peshawar City for protective custody where it was clear from the statement she made before a District Magistrate and in the presence of her new husband, that she wished to return to her relations from whom she had been removed by force.

This case had been made into a bitter outcry against the Provincial Government and an excuse for civil disobedience on a large scale. More trouble had been caused after the burning of villages and collective fines which had been introduced in the Hazara district. Other excuses have been found to cause trouble and civil disobedience with the result that nearly all the Opposition Party in the Government [sic] and a large number of their supporters, have been arrested and were in jail.

SIR OLAF CAROE said that at the last election the votes between the two sections of Muslims in the Province had been almost equal but in his opinion there had been a swing against the present Government in the last twelve months. The movement against the Government now had, he felt, much behind it and although the tribes had been quiet up to the present they were busy organizing themselves on a scale which he had not seen in all his experience in the Frontier.

The tribes were taking a keen interest in the N.W.F.P. and were saying that the present set-up there was unsatisfactory and should cease, but SIR OLAF CAROE said that he had told them that that was no business of theirs. They were undoubtedly excited by the happenings in the various districts, but

¹ Not traced.
² Tel. 117–CB from the Chief Secretary to the Govt of the N.W.F.P. L/P &J/8/660: f 173.

although they opposed the present set-up, they did not wish to join in trouble on a communal basis. In fact, the Afridis made it quite clear at a recent Jirga that they would not have the Advisory Committee of the Constituent Assembly visiting them until Congress and the Muslim League had considered their differences and the Committee was fully representative of an united India.

HIS EXCELLENCY THE VICEROY asked whether these were their own genuine opinions, or whether these thoughts had been put into the heads of the tribes by others.

SIR OLAF CAROE said he was sure that tribes held these opinions honestly and he had told them he would forward them to the proper quarter. PANDIT NEHRU said that the Advisory Committee referred to was dealing with widely different subjects and there was no question of the Committee going to the N.W.F.P. at present as it was obviously undesirable in the present state of affairs.

MR. LIAQUAT ALI KHAN said that he felt that the trouble in the N.W.F.P. and elsewhere was due to the fact that H.M.G. had announced that they would hand over power in June 1948 without making a definite decision to whom power was to be handed over: the result was there was bound to be discord between the parties and that each would do their utmost to be in power in the Province when the terminal date was reached.

HIS EXCELLENCY THE VICEROY said this endorsed his view that there was not a moment to lose and that an early recommendation to H.M.G. about the final turn-over of power was essential. He hoped that the decision would be acceptable to all parties and would prevent bloodshed in the future. In the meantime it was essential to avoid any further trouble in India. He felt that Sir Olaf Caroe had the most difficult job of all the Governors at the present time and he was anxious to send him back to his Province with some constructive advice and a firm policy which might be carried out during the crucial period of the next 6 to 8 weeks.

SIR OLAF CAROE said that he had considered recently whether it would be possible to hold elections in the N.W.F.P. at an early date. He was of the opinion that they could be held under the control of the present Government with the idea of giving it a fresh mandate or of finding an alternative Government. HIS EXCELLENCY THE VICEROY said that elections could not take place immediately, but would have to wait until after he had made his recommendations to H.M.G.

PANDIT NEHRU agreed that the elections would probably cause some disturbances if they were held now, but it was desirable to obtain the views of the people before the final turn-over of power was effected. HIS EXCELLENCY THE VICEROY thought that it might be helpful if the Governor issued a statement of such sort on his return to the Province. SIR OLAF CAROE agreed but thought it would be unnecessary to mention when the elections would take place or to say anything about the mechanics of carrying out the elections; he thought that the mere fact of announcing that elections would take place would be sufficient to ease the tension.

MR. LIAQUAT ALI KHAN thought that when elections were held, the authority in power at the time must be completely neutral. He thought it most undesirable that there should be one single party in power at the time of the elections. Possibly the Governor, who of course was completely impartial, could have the responsibility.

PANDIT NEHRU thought that impartial elections could be conducted by the permanent officials rather than by the Governor. He said that the proposal by Mr. Liaquat Ali Khan meant in fact that the Government should be dismissed and that the Governor should take over control under Section 93. He thought that this was not helpful, would not result in impartial elections and would undoubtedly be bitterly resented.

SIR OLAF CAROE thought it was by no means necessary to go into Section 93 and drew attention to the Punjab elections early in 1946 when a Unionist Government was in power and were in effect practically swept out of existence. He thought, however, there were certain things which must undoubtedly be put right before elections were held and he added that one of the Governor's special responsibilities was to see that the elections were conducted in a perfectly fair manner.

HIS EXCELLENCY THE VICEROY said that he did not think it was necessary to decide now the mechanics of carrying out the elections. He was much opposed to the Governor going into Section 93 and he suggested it might be possible to ensure fair elections by additional officials and observers being drafted to the Province. He asked whether the leaders present would be in agreement with him if the Governor was authorised to say on his return, that after the recommendation had been made to H.M.G. about the transfer of power and before the transfer of power had been effected, elections would be held in the N.W.F.P.

MR. LIAQUAT ALI KHAN said that all that he wanted to make clear was that it must be fully understood that the machinery for the elections would be such that they would be held without any interference from anyone else. HIS EXCELLENCY THE VICEROY said that he agreed but he was most anxious to avoid bringing in Section 93. PANDIT NEHRU said that he did not think, in view of the present situation in the N.W.F.P. that it should be announced at the present time that elections would be held. It would appear if such an announcement were made that the Provincial Government's hand had been forced by the agitations that were taking place.

HIS EXCELLENCY THE VICEROY thought that a statement might be linked not only with the Governors' Conference, but with the statement which had just been issued denouncing violence. It might take the form of saying that at a suitable moment fresh elections would be held. MR. LIAQUAT ALI KHAN said that before elections were held it was essential to give an indication of the authorities to whom power would finally be transferred. Then would be the time to hold impartial and fair elections to ascertain the views of the electorate on their future. SIR OLAF CAROE thought that it would be possible to hold elections this summer, but that a start should be made now on the revision of the Electoral Rolls.

Some discussion then took place on the Pir of Manki. SIR OLAF CAROE said that he had advised his Chief Minister against his arrest and the Prime Minister had agreed. The Pir of Manki was undoubtedly the most sincere and the best leader of the Opposition. For a time he had confined his activities to normal Opposition tactics but when he announced he would hold a procession in Peshawar and demonstrate outside the jail he (Sir Olaf Caroe) had told the Prime Minister that he should consider carefully whether the time had now come for his arrest, in which case he would not stand in his way; and so he was arrested.

HIS EXCELLENCY THE VICEROY suggested that the Pir of Manki might be released if it was agreed that a statement of the type which they had been discussing was issued. PANDIT NEHRU, however, thought this would have a bad effect and that he should not be released until the Opposition movement which he controlled had entirely ceased their activities.

SIR OLAF CAROE pointed out that the arrest of the Pir of Manki had had a great effect among the tribes who had been holding Jirgas and calling for his release. In fact, there was remarkable tribal unity being shown against the Government in this respect. He did not think that the Pir of Manki had been stirring up trouble or violence although since his arrest his followers had undoubtedly been doing so, but this was because he was not there to guide them. PANDIT NEHRU did not entirely agree with this and said that they had had evidence that the Pir of Manki had advocated methods other than peaceful ones, and had been inciting his followers to violence. SIR OLAF CAROE said that the Pir of Manki preachings had been directed almost entirely to the tribes and although they had been organising to an unprecedented extent and holding Jirgas, they had so far not committed themselves to hostilities. In all his 25 years at the Frontier, he never remembered such feeling being displayed by the tribes. He considered that the Pir of Manki was an organiser and not an agitator and that any suggestion to the contrary was unfair to him. In fact, before he was arrested he had said that the movement would fail if it indulged in violence. He had very little doubt that if the Pir of Manki was released he would bring influence to bear to promote communal harmony.

HIS EXCELLENCY THE VICEROY said that nothing which had been said by Sir Olaf Caroe had given the impression that the latter wanted to do anything but ensure peaceful conditions in the Province. In fact, he thought that the object at present must be not to hold elections, but to ensure a return to settled conditions, with a view to turning over the N.W.F.P. as peacefully as possible. He thought that the Government had failed in allowing such a state of turmoil to develop in the Province. It made the holding of elections in present circumstances unfair to either side. In fact, SIR OLAF CAROE said that he would not be prepared to forecast which side would win the elections at the present time.

PANDIT NEHRU said that he was sure that people who had come to see him from the N.W.F.P. were arrested on their return. The Governor expressed disbelief of this and said it would be unwise to listen to stories of this type. PANDIT NEHRU agreed that it was impossible to rely entirely on telegrams and letters, but they did give an indication of feeling in the Province. HIS EXCEL-LENCY THE VICEROY said that his own personal opinion was that the Pir of Manki should be released and that possibly he might be bound over to keep the peace, but he realised that the Provincial Government must decide the question of his release.

SIR OLAF CAROE said that administration in the N.W.F.P. was nearing the breaking point. The jails were all full at present and it was very difficult to retain control. He was attempting to deal with processions by using the minimum of force and great restraint had been exercised by the troops. The procedure was to arrest say 5 or 6 from each procession and persuade the remainder to disperse. Outside the cities there had not been much trouble except in the Hazara district where there was long standing communal antagon-ism which had lasted for the past 100 years. SIR OLAF CAROE said that he thought the solution might be to call off all processions although there could be no ban on meetings. But he felt that the greatest anodyne would be the proposed announcement that elections would be held, and that this must be coupled with a renewal of constitutional processes.

LORD ISMAY said that, as there seemed to be general agreement that some sort of statement should be issued, he had attempted to draft something and he read out what he had in mind. It was generally agreed that this would form a basis for further action.

After a discussion on the military situation in the N.W.F.P., H.E. the Commander-in-Chief left the meeting.

HIS EXCELLENCY THE VICEROY read out a further telegram No. 120–CB of 16th April[3] which had just been received about the situation in D.I.K. He said that he thought that a statement on the lines proposed was essential. PANDIT NEHRU thought that any statement about fresh elections which was issued now would obviously be linked with the disturbances at D.I.K. and would be interpreted as a success for the Opposition movement. HIS EX-CELLENCY THE VICEROY said that he quite saw Pandit Nehru's point, but

Ibid: f 172.

thought that the statement might be linked with the recent Governors' Conference and with his assumption of the Viceroyalty three weeks ago. It might be possible to lay the emphasis on these two points and to take care not to associate the statement with the present situation. In fact he thought that now was the ideal time to issue such a statement. He thought Sir Olaf Caroe should go back to his Province and send for his Chief Minister at once. He should describe the talks he had had here and say that the Viceroy told him that no elections could be held while there were the present disturbances and the situation would have to quieten down first. He said that he did not think that he could send Sir Olaf Caroe back without any instructions and sit here himself doing nothing.

After further discussion it was agreed that Lord Ismay should draft a statement on the lines of the discussion during the meeting and that it should be considered by His Excellency the Viceroy in consultation with Pandit Nehru, Mr. Liaquat Ali Khan and Sardar Baldev Singh at a short meeting before the Defence Committee Meeting on the next day.

(It was subsequently decided that Sir Olaf Caroe should not return at once to the N.W.F.P. but that Dr. Khan Sahib should be flown to Delhi on 17th April for discussions with His Excellency the Viceroy, Pandit Nehru and the Governor).

163

Note by Sir T. Shone

L/S&G/7/1251: ff 106–8

17 April 1947

Mr. Suhrawardy, Chief Minister of Bengal, called on me on the 15th April and stayed for over an hour, during which he did most of the talking. The following are the main points he made—often in the bantering and even flippant way which he affects, but which does not necessarily mean that his remarks are not to be taken seriously.

He said Mr. Jinnah was adamant about Pakistan and that the Constituent Assembly was "dead". He threw out the idea that H.M.G. might transfer power to the Provinces and the States. An united India, if it were possible at all, could only be built up from below—not imposed or arranged from above. He said more than once "Divided we stand; united we fall". He seemed to think it inevitable that India would split up into a considerable number of separate portions; even the Hindu Provinces, e.g. Madras, might divide. There might have to be plebiscites to decide how such divisions should be effected.

But under whose authority could they take place? Was there time for plebiscites before June 1948? And if not, who would supervise them after that?

When I took Mr. Suhrawardy up on his remark that the Constituent
Assembly was dead, he agreed that it was not so dead that it would discontinue
its labours, and might produce a constitution which would serve to bring
together some portions of the country. Some of the States had already joined
it and more would probably follow suit, mainly from fear of the trouble which
the Congress Party could stir up in the States. But many other States would
seek salvation in independence or in banding together.

He did not think that India would grow together again, if it ever did, for a
long time, during which there would certainly be strife and very probably
fighting. It might be that various portions of India would try to negotiate
treaties with each other but he feared that some of them would scrap with
others sooner or later. Eventually U.N.O. might have to intervene and the
Indian question would occupy U.N.O. for years.

Mr. Suhrawardy expressed the utmost distaste for a divided Bengal. The
Province, as now constituted, could become an independent State of wealth
and importance, with its 65 million inhabitants. He wanted foreign capital
and the assistance of British enterprise to develop Bengal; American capital
was also "waiting on the door-step". But how could one know now whether
Bengal would be divided or not? And Calcutta was vital to Bengal. At a later
stage in the conversation Mr. Suhrawardy said he supposed the Hindus might
have Howrah while the Muslims kept Calcutta. But he repeated that he did
not want to have anything to do with dividing Bengal; and he certainly did
not want to have to fall back on Chittagong as the port of a mere Eastern
Bengal under Muslim control

Asked what would happen to the Indian Army in the event of Pakistan,
Mr. Suhrawardy said it would have to be divided. Asked if it would not be
tragic to break up such a magnificent force, Mr. Suhrawardy replied "You
British made it what it is; but if it is not split up, it will only come to fighting
amongst itself". He went on to complain that he had no army of his own in
Bengal—(as he did when I saw him in Calcutta last February). After all, one
day Mr. Nehru, on a big black horse, might lead a Hindu army against Muslim
Bengal. Mr. Nehru would not get the Punjabis to join it, anyway. When it
was suggested that Mr. Nehru hardly seemed to be cast for this role,
Mr. Suhrawardy said that as an alternative Mr. Nehru might try to induce
the Nepalese to move against a Muslim Bengal.

Asked about the Communists, Mr. Suhrawardy affected to regard their
influences in Bengal as relatively unimportant. But they had been clever in
remaining non-violent; he sometimes wished they had gone in for violence,
as it would then have been easier to deal with them.

Asked about the Socialists, Mr. Suhrawardy said "Aren't we all Socialists now?". He had some things he wanted to say to Mr. Liaquat Ali Khan on this score. In so far as Bengal was concerned, he did not want budgets that would cripple industrial development in which lay the hope of salvation.

As regards the Socialist Party, Mr. Suhrawardy opined that they had lost the main plank in their platform, now that the British had made up their minds to quit India. The Socialist Party's main appeal to popular opinion had always been to "get the British out". Mr. Suhrawardy then said "I suppose Nehru won't offer to accept Dominion Status"—and after a pause went on to express the opinion that Nehru would not dare to do so.

Throughout Mr. Suhrawardy's conversation, there was a strong implication that he wished Bengal at least to maintain a close connexion with Great Britain; indeed, at one point he said "I suppose I could offer Bengal to England on a platter, but that the offer might be refused". He again dropped a remark— not untinged with sarcasm, as when he first made it to me in Calcutta—about the High Commission becoming an Embassy.

When speaking about the division of Bengal, Mr. Suhrawardy asked where in the world could one go nowadays, to settle down in peace. Was England a good place,—or Ireland? Or perhaps the Balearic Islands? One must have work of some kind; he believed hall porters at hotels in New York did very well. Several of his remarks in this context gave the impression that however much he dislikes the prospect of a divided Bengal, he fears it may come about.

As Mr. Suhrawardy was leaving, I mentioned that I was going to meet Mr. Jinnah for the first time next day.[1] He said "I hope you will be able to talk—if you want to. Generally, Mr. Jinnah will listen to someone for two minutes or so and then get impatient".

[1] See No. 159.

164

Rear-Admiral Viscount Mountbatten of Burma to Lord Pethick-Lawrence

Mountbatten Papers. Letters to and from the Secretary of State

PRIVATE AND TOP SECRET   *17 April 1947*

Thank you so much for your letter of the 3rd April,[1] which arrived a day after I despatched my letter of the 9th April[2] covering my Personal Report No. 2.[3]

2. I was interested to read your views on the partition of the Punjab and Bengal. We have been thinking on very much the same lines here, and have come to the conclusion that, in the unfortunate circumstances of the Cabinet Mission plan proving unacceptable to all parties, partition is probably inevitable. I refer to this matter rather more fully in the enclosed Report.

3. Your letter of the 31st March[4] about the future of Berar has been sent to the Resident at Hyderabad for his comments. The Political Adviser has already consulted the Resident informally during the latter's visit to Delhi last week. Their first thoughts on the problem are that it would be valueless to suggest negotiation until the situation in British India is crystallised, and that in any case the basis of agreement which you suggested would probably be unacceptable to the Nizam. However, the matter is being gone into fully, and I will let you have a considered reply in due course.

4. Sir Mirza Ismail came to luncheon on the 14th April, but I did not have a chance of more than a few minutes talk with him. He is seeing Ismay and Mieville later in the week to discuss a solution of his own to the political situation. I was, however, able to arrange for him to have a meeting with Bourne, who had just arrived for the Governors' Conference, to discuss Berar.

5. Thank you for the information you gave me about the new American and Chinese Ambassadors. Mr Grady's advice on the economic and industrial future of India has already caused some press comment out here; and his remarks on Indian unity have, I see, already brought him into conflict with *Dawn*. I imagine that he is now wishing he had not been so outspoken at his first press conference.

6. You will recall that before we left London the future of the Andamans and Nicobar islands was discussed.[5] I have had this looked into since my arrival, and Ismay has sent a short paper to Monteath[6] which I expect you will see in due course.

7. I have had two letters[7] during the past week from Liaquat Ali Khan concerning the alleged inadequate representation of Muslims in the Indian armed forces; and asking that the armed forces should be reorganised in such a manner that they could readily be split up between Hindustan and Pakistan at the proper time. He also suggested that in the implementation of this proposal the Commander-in-Chief should be directly responsible to me and not to the Defence Member.

8. I have replied[8] pointing out that he is attempting to prejudge an issue which has not yet been decided, and that until the Cabinet Mission plan is finally abandoned there is no question of a complete partition of India. I added that I considered it my duty to ensure that no steps were taken which would weaken the Indian Army as the ultimate resource on which the country depended for maintaining internal security as well as external defence.

9. I have since told Liaquat Ali Khan that I consider that the whole subject

[1] No. 67.   [2] No. 107.   [3] No. 108.   [4] No. 39.
[5] See Vol. IX, No. 530.
[6] Mountbatten Papers, Official Correspondence Files: Andaman and Nicobar islands.
[7] Nos. 94 and 135.   [8] No. 106

should be dealt with by the Defence Committee, and that a detailed examination of the problem might be handled by a sub-committee in the first instance. In any case, I do not think that these investigations should be the responsibility of the Commander-in-Chief, although of course there would be no objection to the Commander-in-Chief and other British officers appearing before a committee of Indians as expert assessors to help them to arrive at a decision.

10. I have already sent a reply to your telegram 4393 of the 2nd April,[9] about the amendment to the Premature Retirement Rules. I am most anxious to avoid further acrimonious discussion in Cabinet, but the fact that your telegram was addressed to the Home Department has made things difficult; for if Patel chooses to raise the matter, I shall be in no position to say that it should not be discussed. I would ask that any controversial matters of this nature should be referred to me in the first instance so that we can decide on a line of action, and I hope in this case you will feel able to withdraw your original telegram.

11. I had a very successful meeting with the Residents last week, but the minutes of the meeting are not yet ready. I will send them to you as soon as they are completed.[10] I have just finished my series of meetings with the Governors, but this letter will be despatched too early for me to comment in full on the talks, which I hope to do next week.

12. I will also reply next week to the points raised in your letter of the 12th April,[11] which has just arrived.

[9] L/S &G/7/776: ff 157–8.
[10] The minutes of the Residents' Conference held on 9 and 10 April 1947 are on L/P &S/13/1831.
[11] No. 134.

165

Viceroy's Personal Report No. 3

L/PO/6/123: ff 42–9

During this week I have continued my series of individual meetings with Members of the Cabinet, the British Residents from the Indian States, and at great length with Jinnah.[1] I referred in my last report[2] to the fact that I had invited Tara Singh and Gyani Kartar Singh to come and see me in Delhi. I have now had a reply, and hope to meet them next Friday, the 18th April.

2. The dangerously unsettled state of the whole country continues, and communal riots and troubles are on about the same scale as they were last week. In the Punjab the Gurgaon area is quieter, but there have been riots in Amritsar which have necessitated a 24-hour curfew. In the N.W.F.P., rioting, looting and arson have been reported from Dera Ismail Khan. Half the city is in

flames and there is severe communal fighting. Peshawar is quieter on the whole; but there has been trouble again in the Hazara district, where the District and Assistant Commissioners' cars were stoned. The tribes are still very restless, but they are acting with restraint. But the tension both in the Punjab and the N.W.F.P. is still very high. I have retained here the Governor of the N.W.F.P., (Caroe) and sent for his Prime Minister, Dr. Khan Sahib, so as to have a meeting to-night with Nehru, as the situation is so explosive.

3. In Bengal, there were more incidents in Calcutta on Sunday the 13th April. In Bombay a curfew at night has been imposed; and similarly at Benares, where in addition the District Magistrate has fined the city a sum totalling nearly four lakhs of rupees for the disturbances and damage there.

4. I wish I could paint a more optimistic picture of the state of the country, but it would be wrong of me to do so, and the Governors' Conference (which I refer to at the end of this report) agrees entirely with this picture.

5. Although I am convinced, as indeed are all the Governors and leaders with whom I have discussed the matter, that the only step which is likely to clear the air of communal strife is an early and generally accepted decision on how power is to be transferred in June 1948, I felt that there was one step I could take at once to reduce the tension. I accordingly asked Mr. Jinnah when he came to see me if he would sign a joint appeal with Congress to renounce the use of force for political ends. He tried to evade a firm answer for about 20 minutes, by drawing my attention to his various speeches deploring massacres, etc. When he had finished I said "Of course if you would find it in any way embarrassing to renounce the use of force and if I would be putting you at a disadvantage with Congress by suggesting you should settle your differences by negotiations instead of direct action, please consider the matter closed". There was an awkward pause, and he then said "I should be proud to give a lead in this matter and am grateful to you for giving me the opportunity."

6. The next time I saw Jinnah I gave him a copy of the draft statement to take away and study. He warned me that Gandhi had refused to sign a similar appeal for Lord Wavell after the Calcutta massacres, and he did not think I would suceed in getting Gandhi to sign this time. No decision was reached, however, as to who the precise signatories on the Congress side would be; but Ismay tells me that as Jinnah said goodbye to him he said "Who will sign for Congress, Gandhi or Kripalani?". Ismay replied that this would probably have to be settled by Congress themselves.

7. The next day Jinnah agreed to sign if Gandhi would also sign. I therefore got hold of Gandhi who after amending the wording slightly, then and there signed the declaration in three scripts. Mieville then took the declaration to Jinnah to sign, and said that Kripalani, as President of the Congress, had agreed to sign after him.[3] Jinnah thereupon refused to sign and said he would not sign

[1] See Nos. 84, 92, 101, 105 and 116.   [2] No. 108.   [3] See No. 124.

if an unknown nobody like Kripalani was to sign on the same sheet of paper. Mieville was unable to move him or get him to accept any other signatories. On my instructions Mieville then got in touch with Nehru, who was furious but finally said he would leave it to me. Then Kripalani said that he had been instructed by Gandhi to sign and could not agree to having his name left off unless Gandhi agreed. By this time Gandhi had left by train for Patna, so I sent him a telegram,[4] in reply to which Gandhi passed the ball back to Nehru and myself.[5] Nehru wrote two pages of protest but finally left it to me, and so I issued the statement, of which a copy is attached.

8. I have related this incident at some length to give an idea of the fantastic difficulties with which the simplest negotiations are hedged. It took us four days to get this statement through, and much time on it has been unnecessarily wasted by myself, my staff, and the most important political leaders in India. I only hope that both sides will abide by this declaration, but I fear that they may very well get out of it by accusing the other side of breaking the truce first.

9. In the annex to my last report[6] I gave the outline of Gandhi's scheme for the Interim Government pending transfer of power, by which Jinnah was to be given the option of forming a Cabinet. You will remember I refused to be drawn into expressing my views on this curious scheme until he had obtained the fullest backing of Nehru and other responsible Congress leaders. On the 11th April[7] I received a letter from Mr. Gandhi saying that he had been unable to get his plan through responsible members of Congress and with the greatest regret he therefore had to withdraw it. In my final meeting with him[8] I asked him what he would advise me to do, and he said that in my position he would go on strengthening the Interim Government and making it function properly for the next 14 months, after which he considered I should hand over power to the Interim Government. I pointed out to him that that meant virtually handing over power to the majority party, to the grave disadvantage of the Muslim League, which could not fail to produce strife possibly leading to civil war.

10. Gandhi, with a wily smile, pointed out that if Jinnah indeed signed the appeal, to which I have just referred, for a political truce, and the renunciation of force, then he could not again use force for political purposes. I must say that I was speechless at this immoral suggestion, and shook my finger at him. But he only blinked and smiled.

11. I have had six meetings during the past week with Jinnah, averaging between two to three hours each, and the conversations continued on the lines which I reported last week. He has made it abundantly clear that the Muslim League will not in any circumstances reconsider the Cabinet Mission

plan, and he is intent on having Pakistan. I got him to see Ismay and give him his ideas on Pakistan, but when Ismay produced the notes he had made, Mr. Jinnah said "That is your scheme not mine". When pressed for details of his scheme and how it was to be carried out, he said "You must carry out a surgical operation; cut India and its army firmly in half and give me the half that belongs to the Muslim League". I told him that if I accepted his arguments on the need for partition of India, then I could not resist the arguments that Congress were putting forward for the partition of the Punjab and Bengal. He was quite horrified and argued at great length on the need to preserve the unity of the Punjab and Bengal, pointing out that the Punjabis and Bengalis regarded their Provinces as unified territories which they would hate to see split up.

12. I told him that I had been so impressed by his arguments that I was prepared to accept them. He was delighted, but only until I pointed out that his arguments had also convinced me that the partition of India itself would be criminal. Then we started going round the Mulberry bush again.

13. Finally I told him that I had deliberately refrained from discussing the scheme for the transfer of power with any member of Congress except Gandhi, and that I was not adopting the scheme the latter had put up. I said no one had done any propaganda with me; but that I had come to the conclusion myself that what would be best for India would be a complete Union with the strongest possible Central Government. In fact I would like to see the present Interim Government strengthened by his joining it himself, so that I could turn over to the Interim Government in toto in June 1948. If I had invited the Pope to take part in the Black Mass he could not have been more horrified. I hastened to assure him that I should not allow my personal feelings on what was good for India to interfere with working out a solution which would be acceptable to the people of India in their present frame of mind. But I warned him categorically that if I finally decided to recommend to His Majesty's Government that there should be partition, then that principle would be applied right through to the Provinces and that partition would follow the boundaries of the communal majorities; since I was convinced that the non-Muslim communities in the Punjab and Bengal would be just as likely to fight if put under Muslim domination as Muslim Leaguers would be likely to fight under Congress domination.

14. I told him that while I remained statutorily responsible, through the Secretary of State, to His Majesty's Government and Parliament for the preservation of law and order in India, I would not agree to the partition of the

4 See No. 136.   5 See No. 140.
6 This was the same as Enclosure to No. 85.
7 No. 123.   8 See No. 131.

armed forces, which had already been so weakened by nationalisation that they could not possibly stand partition as well. I did however tell him that I would be prepared to have the matter investigated by the Defence Committee if a decision on partition were finally taken.

15. Although Jinnah did not lose his friendly attitude, his arguments became more and more futile, and he ended by saying "If you persist in chasing me with your ruthless logic we shall get nowhere".

16. I regard Jinnah as a psychopathic case; in fact until I had met him I would not have thought it possible that a man with such a complete lack of administrative knowledge or sense of responsibility could achieve or hold down so a powerful a position.

17. Finally I pointed out that the most he could hope for from me was to allow Provinces, and where applicable halves of Provinces, to decide whether they wished to join Pakistan. I pointed out that at this rate it looked as though he would get Sind and western Punjab for certain; the N.W.F.P. would be a doubtful starter (and if he got it would cost him $3\frac{1}{2}$ crores a year to keep the tribes quiet.) In the east I pointed out that he would get the most useless part of Bengal, without Calcutta, and if he wished it he could have Sylhet back from Assam.

18. Since I was not prepared to split the armed forces until we had left, it would be necessary to keep a central organisation to control the army for the over-all defence and internal security requirements of India; and this central organisation would have to continue to act for a long while, while the armed forces were being split.

19. I summed up by pointing out that the choice before him was likely to be:—
 (i) The Cabinet Mission plan which gave him all five Provinces of Pakistan with complete autonomy and with only a very weak Centre to which they would owe allegiance for three subjects which might be covered by the general term Defence;
    or
 (ii) A very moth-eaten Pakistan, the eastern and north-west frontier parts of which were unlikely to be economic propositions, and which would still have to come to some Centre for general defence subjects for a long while after we had left.

20. He said "I do not care how little you give me as long as you give it to me completely. I do not wish to make any improper suggestion to you, but you must realise that the new Pakistan is almost certain to ask for dominion status within the Empire". I advised him to address himself to Sir Terence

Shone on this matter, since I could not possibly recommend to His Majesty's Government that they should take on such a severe liability as the moth-eaten Pakistan was bound to be.

21. He ended up in a rather more reasonable frame of mind, regretting his inability to re-consider the Cabinet Mission plan. He said it could only have been worked in a spirit of the utmost co-operation and mutual trust which might have been possible a year ago; but that the atmosphere now so far from improving was continuously worsening, and it was clear that in no circumstances did Congress intend to work the plan either in accordance with the spirit or the letter.

22. It seems quite clear that if any attempt is made to impose the Cabinet Mission plan on the Muslim League, they will resort to arms to resist it.

23. Having had nearly three weeks of incessant talks with all the leaders, I think I ought to let you know the lines on which my mind is working.

24. In the first place, I am convinced that we have got to make up our minds one way or the other in the very near future if we are to avert civil war and the risk of a complete breakdown of the administration. On this there is complete unanimity of opinion, both European and Indian, in this country. The Governors have not a shadow of doubt about it. My first conclusion, therefore, is that our decision must be announced before the end of May at latest.

25. Secondly, I have very slender hopes of getting acceptance of the Cabinet Mission plan, and I am very much afraid that partition may prove to be the only possible alternative.

26. Thirdly, I feel strongly that the scheme of partition should be such as will not debar the two sides from getting together, even before we transfer power, if saner counsels prevail when the bewildering complications of partition are more clearly realised.

27. I will not send you even a first draft of the plan at this stage, as it is all so tentative, but I have discussed it with the Governors and hope to let you have a further report next week. The chances are that I will send Ismay home with the draft announcement towards the end of this month to discuss it with you, and try to reach the earliest possible agreement on the precise terms.

28. Once this is done, I plan to try to get Jinnah, Nehru, Patel, Liaquat, Baldev Singh and possibly Bhopal and Patiala, to come and stay with me in Simla. The date at which I am aiming is the 15th May. Alternatively I might aim at a rather bigger "round table conference". I will then make one final determined effort to secure some compromise on the basis of the Cabinet Mission plan. If I fail, I shall have to fire my last shot in the shape of our announcement of partition. I shall ask both Nehru and Jinnah to have their

working committees in Simla, so that they may refer to them before pronouncing a definite view.

29. I ought to add that whatever the decision may be, I feel that the central Government should be as strong as possible until we hand over. In this connection I am thinking of trying to get Jinnah to join the Cabinet. One of the difficulties would be the question of an appropriate and acceptable portfolio. I doubt whether Congress would surrender either External Affairs or Home Affairs, and I doubt whether Jinnah would look at anything else. Perhaps he might be Leader of the House? The talks in Simla would then be in the nature of a discussion of a Cabinet Committee, which would, I think, be all to the good.

30. The Governors' Conference concluded yesterday afternoon, and in the evening we gave a dinner party of a hundred for the Governors, at which Members of the Interim Government headed by Nehru and Liaquat, the Ambassadors, Commanders-in-Chief, and other British and Indian notables in Delhi were present. Many remarked on the excellent spirit that prevailed.

31. I think everyone is agreed that the Governors' Conference was of great value, and I certainly learnt a lot about the different situations in different Provinces. I am sure that this exchange of information does everybody good. The Governors are unanimous that to ask the Interim Government to legislate against British subjects entering India except by permit would be about the worst psychological blunder which we could commit at this moment, and I am reporting this separately.[9] They are delighted at the way compensation has come out, and the Indian Governors—Sir Chandulal Trivedi and Sir Akbar Hydari—not only thought that it was quite fair to the Indian members of the Civil Services that those who could continue their career without diminished prospects should not be offered compensation, but they both pointed out that any who did take compensation for no better reason than to line their pockets and take a commercial job would cause real ill-feeling in India, not only against themselves personally but against the British Government for wrecking the prospects of independent India's administration being continued in an efficient manner.

32. I am glad to say that the Governors have expressed their unanimous support of the line I have taken with the various Indian leaders; and all of them urge the greatest possible speed in making a decision and an announcement; for even the quieter Provinces feel that we are sitting on the edge of a volcano and that an eruption might take place through any of the three main craters—Bengal, Punjab and N.W.F.P.—at any moment; with the risk of sporadic eruptions in Assam, Bombay and Bihar.

33. I have had separate interviews with the 10 Governors, and with the Secretary to the Governor of Bengal as Burrows was unfortunately not fit

enough to come up in person. I was glad to hear however that he is beginning to recover and should be all right as soon as he has had a spell in Darjeeling.

34. The Congress have been at pains to attack the Governors of the Punjab, N.W.F.P., and Sind (Jenkins, Caroe and Mudie), as being violently and unfairly pro-Muslim League. I was amused to receive in the middle of yesterday's meeting a five page indictment from Liaquat Ali Khan[10] accusing Jenkins of being violently pro-Congress and anti-Muslim. This makes me sure Jenkins must be doing well. I also believe that Mudie is doing his best to look after the minorities in spite of Congress's accusations. I am also convinced of Caroe's essential straightforwardness and desire to handle the very difficult situation on the Frontier in the most impartial and statesmanlike manner. But I think that at the moment he is suffering badly from nerves. I have warned him[11] that I may be confronted with a situation in which it would be difficult to retain him, but that I will give him my full support until such a situation arises. I shall try and keep in touch with him and his Province in case the position gets worse. I do not envy him his job which I should say is the most difficult out here.

35. My wife has visited both Indian and British Military and Civilian Hospitals, educational establishments, the College of Nursing, and welfare centres; and has had discussions with eminent Indian personalities, including Mrs. Kripalani, wife of the Congress President. This week she has had conferences with the Governors' wives, together with representatives of the various Departments and Headquarters of National Organisations and Associations concerned with medical, nursing and general welfare services of the Provinces.

36. We have had two garden parties and have about three luncheon parties of 30, and larger dinners each week, at which I have made it a rule that not less than 50 per cent of those present must be Indians. There has been the greatest spate of Indian names in the Visitors' Book ever known at Viceroy's House, and the atmosphere appears to be remarkably friendly. I now have three full time Indian A.D.C.s, a sailor, soldier and airman from the major communities. Unfortunately I feel I must record that my young daughter sitting with two English ladies to whom she had not been introduced heard one say to the other "It makes me absolutely sick to see this house full of dirty Indians". I recounted this story to the Governors, and have invited their co-operation in sending home anybody who expresses sentiments of this type.

[9] See tel. 815-S of 17 April 1947. L/S &G/7/753: f 131.   [10] No. 148.
[11] See No. 143.

166

Mr Attlee to Rear-Admiral Viscount Mountbatten of Burma
(via India Office)

Telegram, L/PO/10/35: f 79

MOST IMMEDIATE   *17 April 1947*
PRIVATE AND TOP SECRET

U.–7 Following personal from Prime Minister.

We shall in the very near future be announcing the resignation of Lord
Pethick-Lawrence and the appointment of Lord Listowel as Secretary of
State for India. I thought you would like to have this information, which is of
course for yourself alone, in advance.

2. I have read your weekly reports with the greatest of interest. They are
both encouraging and invaluable. All good wishes.

167

Pandit Nehru to Rear-Admiral Viscount Mountbatten of Burma

*Mountbatten Papers. Official Correspondence Files: North-West Frontier
Province, Situation in, Part I(a)*

SECRET AND PERSONAL   17 YORK ROAD, NEW DELHI,
                                                        17 April 1947

My dear Lord Mountbatten,
In the hope of meeting Dr Khan Sahib I have postponed my departure for
Gwalior and I am now leaving at 1 p.m. tomorrow, 18th April. I am afraid it
is not possible to postpone it still further without upsetting numerous rather
important engagements and disappointing a large number of people. I had
hoped that Dr Khan Sahib would arrive this evening; but I am told that some
engine trouble has delayed his departure from Peshawar. He is now due
tomorrow some time in the morning. I hope I shall meet him, but I am not
sure.

2. Because of all this uncertainty I am writing this letter to you so that I
might let you know how I feel about this question which we have discussed at
length. I have given a great deal of thought to it since last night.[1] I did so not
only because it was an important matter in itself but also because of its significance. Indeed my mind has been so full of this subject that I have not been able
to do anything else effectively. I feel I must write to you and let you know

what my reactions are after this full consideration. I might add that I have consulted four of my colleagues also.

3. I think I realise fully how anxious you are to stop the rioting and blood-shed that are going on in various parts of India; also your particular anxiety to prevent worse developments in the Frontier areas. May I say that I agree with you entirely in both these matters? I hate violence, more especially of the brutal and vulgar type that we have seen lately in India and I would go very far indeed to stop it. The question is how best this can be done. We have seen in the past steps being taken, ostensibly with a good object, but leading to wrong results and greater trouble. My fear has been that the proposal made last night might, instead of leading to peace, result in an encouragement to violence. The more I thought of it the more this conviction has grown and my colleagues share this conviction.

4. It is a little difficult to isolate any one question or part of the country from another. Obviously what is happening is part of a pattern and every single thing that takes place produces its reactions elsewhere. At the present moment the principal affected areas are Bengal, Punjab, the Assam frontier, and the North-West Frontier Province. From all accounts the situation in the first three of these places, though under control, is tense and explosive. Anything that happens in the Frontier will immediately produce its effect in the other three regions.

5. It does little good to blame others for the mis-deeds of large numbers of people of all groups and communities. Nevertheless I think it is perfectly true to say that the violence and brutality that we have seen in India during the last eight months are the resultants of the deliberate policy of the Muslim League called "Direct Action". That violence has bred violence in others also. Essentially the tactics of the Muslim League have been remarkably similar to those of the Nazis in their early days with their Brown Shirts and Black Shirts. Insofar as a belief grows that these tactics succeed, the method is pursued with greater vigour. In the Punjab they succeeded in bringing about the fall of the Ministry and immediately after horrible consequences followed. That kind of thing may very well be repeated in the Frontier on a worse scale. It seems to me essential that it should be demonstrated beyond doubt that these methods cannot be allowed to succeed. A policy of appeasement results in encouragement of these methods and in inflaming people who are opposed to these methods and suffer from them. As soon as they think that Government is partial, they despair and take the law into their own hands.

6. It is no good merely following a negative policy of repression. But a positive policy, whatever it may be, should in no way be linked up to what appears to be a surrender to violent methods. That positive policy must be to

¹ See No. 162.

create a feeling that no group will be dominated over by another. It was with this object in view that we suggested divisions of the Punjab and of Bengal, much as we dislike them.

7. In the Frontier Province a proposal of the Governor for fresh elections has in effect been a proposal of the Muslim League and has been stoutly resisted by the present Ministry who were elected only a year ago and have a substantial majority in the Legislature. That, of course, is not enough reason to avoid elections and I entirely agree with you that power should be transferred after making sure that the recipients represent the majority of the people in that area. For this purpose, if an election is necessary, it should take place. But to announce now that a general election will be held would undoubtedly be looked upon as a triumph for the policy pursued by the Muslim League and as an open rebuff to the present Ministry. In the Frontier it might well result in the resignation of the Ministry. This would create a difficult situation for us in the Centre and, I think, would certainly lead to a revival of the violent agitation in the Punjab and the Assam border. It would also make large numbers of people in Eastern Punjab feel that the Muslim League is being supported and encouraged. Exactly what the consequences might be I do not know. But I am sure they would be far reaching. In attempting to solve one problem we might well have to face a number of graver problems and even that one problem may not be solved at all.

8. I know the Frontier sufficiently to realise the dangers inherent in the situation. All my instinct tells me that those dangers will increase if anything is done which makes people believe that Government are siding with the Muslim League in that Province. Already there is, rightly or wrongly, an amazing lack of faith in the *bona fides* of the Governor and many other officials. If this new step is taken and the Governor is the mouth-piece of the proposal, the conviction would grow that there is no hope in any constitutional activity and people would cease to think in terms of elections and prepare for other methods.

9. I have little doubt that however the statement may be phrased it would be interpreted as an affront to and a letting down of the present Ministry and an encouragement to the Muslim League. The Congress organisation and all those who sympathise with it would view it as such, as well as vast numbers of people who have no particular political affiliations. It would thus be a blow to the various constitutional processes that are going on and might even powerfully affect the reception to such proposals as you may make in the course of the next few weeks. Large numbers of people will feel as if they were disillusioned and cease to take interest in these proposals. They would revert to a mentality of distrust and hostility which is always there somewhere at the back of their minds.

10. I am writing to you frankly because I think I owe it to you and myself to do so. Dr Khan Sahib will, of course, be able to tell you his own reactions and his own appraisement of the situation in the Frontier. He is, as I am sure you will find, a frank straight-forward man of exceeding courage. He is popular even with his opponents because of these qualities. His judgment is not always right but his instincts are very sound. In his virtues and his failings he is the best type of Pathan. He is very unlike his brother whom you have met, though he is very closely attached to him.

11. If I may say so, no statement of the kind suggested, that is with any reference to general elections, should be made at this stage. The very first thing that should be done is for the appeal made by Mr Gandhi and Mr Jinnah to be backed up by those in the Frontier and for the Muslim League to cry halt to their methods. It would naturally follow that most of the people in prison should be released. At present the happenings at D.I. Khan and other places are too near to be dissociated with any new proposal. I appreciate what you said that a proposal might naturally follow the Governors' Conference. But I do not think this has very much importance in the public mind and there will be far better opportunities I hope in the near future. No proposal should be such as to make people think that it is a surrender to the violent methods and encouragement of the Muslim League. Fortunately you are looked upon as impartial in this matter. I do not wish people to think otherwise, though I am quite sure that they would be wrong in thinking so.

12. I am myself inclined to think, though this is largely conjecture, that the situation in the Frontier Province will not deteriorate now. The only chance of its deteriorating is the belief that further violence will bring dividends. Such a belief has to be scotched and there will be a rapid improvement. Later will be the time for making any announcement, and whatever the announcement may be, it should come from Dr Khan Sahib. This may take any appropriate form.

13. Please forgive me for this long letter. About the Frontier Dr Khan Sahib will be able to give you a better picture than I can; but about reactions in other places I am in a somewhat better position to know than he is. I only hope that, though the situation is full of urgency, nothing may be done in a hurry which might have evil results.

Yours sincerely,
JAWAHARLAL NEHRU

168

Record of Interview between Rear-Admiral Viscount Mountbatten of Burma and Mr Kripalani

Mountbatten Papers. Viceroy's Interview No. 73

TOP SECRET   *17 April 1947, 5.15–6.15 pm*

To begin with I expressed my regret to Mr. Kripalani that after having obtained his agreement to sign the joint truce, I had been unable to get Mr. Jinnah to agree. He was very nice about it, and said that while he did not blame me, he must point out that the result had been most unfortunate from every point of view; particularly since there had been this most unfortunate leakage in the papers that he was to have signed, and since it was well known that Mr. Jinnah's chief complaint about Mr. Gandhi was that he did not in any way represent Congress. He said "Let us face it, you have been heavily defeated by Mr. Jinnah in your first round with him".

I replied "If Mr. Jinnah had succeeded in evading signature of the document altogether, that would have been defeat; but much as I should like to have had your signature on it, I am afraid that I cannot regard the absence of your signature as a defeat, though I apologise for the discourtesy".

He then brought out copies of the *Hindustan Times* and *Dawn*, and pointed out the different ways the declaration had been treated in the two papers—played up magnificently in the *Hindustan Times*; played down to zero in *Dawn*. Alongside the brief announcement, he pointed out, was a shockingly provocative distorted news account of 300 Muslims killed on the Frontier. I sent for a copy of today's *Dawn*, and showed him that *Dawn* had made full amends in giving the declaration a great splash today. This, he said, was only because they had been unable to resist the popular outcry against the bad handling of this item the day before. I then drew his attention to the fact that the *Hindustan Times*, in the very article announcing the truce, attacked Mr. Jinnah for not having visited the riot areas; and I asked him if he thought that this was the right spirit in which to start a truce. He replied that *Dawn* was a Muslim League organ, and the *Hindustan Times* independently run. I replied "You suggest that Mr. Gandhi's son doesn't try to toe the party line or follow his father's wishes?"

I next asked him whether he had made up his mind as to what advice he would like to give me for the transfer of power. He replied "The point has now been reached at which the Congress must reluctantly accept the fact that the Muslim League will never voluntarily come into a Union of India. Rather than have a battle we shall let them have their Pakistan, provided you will allow the Punjab and Bengal to be partitioned in a fair manner".

I asked him whether Congress unequivocally accepted the Cabinet Mission plan, as clarified by the statement of December the 6th. His reply was "H.M.G. themselves admit that we have accepted it". I invited him to write me a letter setting forth the details of the acceptance. He said it was all quite clear in the various resolutions, but that if I wished it he would look them up.

I told him that when I have the final meeting with the leaders, which I hoped would be in a month's time, I should undoubtedly ask the question straight-out whether they accepted the Cabinet Mission plan, and that it would be to the advantage of Congress to be able to say "Yes", even if it were only for the sake of history.

We then discussed what could be done to maintain law and order. He said "The only thing we ask of the British is to maintain law and order and be fair and impartial during their last 14 months out here." I assured him that this was our policy; and he replied "There are many officers of all seniorities who have been out here too long to be able to change their outlook. I do not believe they can be impartial; they are so strongly imbued with anti-Congress ideas or pro-Muslim ideas. On the Frontier, even Indian members of the ICS have been affected; the whole of the Frontier administration is now anti-Congress; that's what makes the situation there so difficult."

He told me that he had been brought up under British rule, and although he did not like the rule he had to admire the complete efficiency with which the British could keep law and order if they wanted to. I replied that conditions had changed: Governors were the constitutional Heads of Provinces and had to do what their Governments told them to do. He said that to this day the prestige of a British Governor stood so high that he was convinced that any man worth his salt could make his Government keep law and order. I quoted the case of Bihar, and told him of the difficulties Sir Hugh Dow was experiencing. He said I do not wish to speak against any man by name. I invited him to say what he thought, and he very reluctantly said "Sir Hugh Dow is one of the most notorious anti-Congress men in India. No wonder his Government cannot co-operate with him."

I told him that I had no knowledge of Sir Hugh Dow's politics, but that it was the policy of H.M.G. to be impartial and I was quite certain that Sir Hugh Dow would follow that policy.

Note: Before he left Mr. Kripalani handed me the attached correspondence[1] to show how impossible it was for Congress ever to deal with the Muslim League, who evidently were prepared to resort to any device to avoid getting together for any discussion.

[1] No correspondence is attached to this note on the file.

169

*Record of Interview between Rear-Admiral Viscount Mountbatten of Burma
and Mr Krishna Menon*

Mountbatten Papers. Viceroy's Interview No. 74

TOP SECRET   *17 April 1947, 6.40–7.40 pm*
SPECIALLY RESTRICTED CIRCULATION

Mr. Krishna Menon reminded me that he was staying out here specially in the
hope of being of use to me personally as a friend (or acquaintance) of some four
years standing, to help to give me the background of what was going on in
Congress circles, and to help me put over any points that I found too delicate
to handle directly myself. He offered to stay as long as he was of use, and I have
asked him to stay at all events till next week.

He gave me an encouraging report of the reactions of the Congress party
generally in Delhi, both to Her Excellency's and to my own activities.

He hoped that through the pressure of events and seeing so many people
every day, I would not be led into the fault which he felt had obscured the mind
of so many English people in recent times out here, of not being able to see the
wood for the trees.

He confirmed that Congress viewed with the gravest suspicion the Governors of the N.W.F.P., Punjab, Bihar, and Sind. He said they were all notorious
imperialists who in the old days have worked on the "Divide and Rule"
principle. He said that Mudie was widely held to have joined forces with the
Muslim League to get them into power, and that Dow's reputation was so
notorious that it made it very difficult for the Ministry (which he admitted
was weak) to work with him. He thought Jenkins was doing his best in the
Punjab, but held him in part to blame for allowing the critical situation to
develop which had resulted in government under section 93.

He said that Caroe and all his political officers, British and Indian, had been
preaching the anti-Congress doctrine for so long to the tribes that even if some
of them wanted to they would find it difficult to sing a different tune with
success.

He asked me how I had got on with Jinnah, and I told him that I might have
to yield to a truncated Pakistan. Krishna Menon said that although Congress
would regret this, he did not think they would resist it any longer if I made a
point of it; and he offered to help me put this idea over with Nehru if required.
I told him of the demand to split the army, and how over-rapid nationalisation
would render it so weak that it could not be split until well after June 1948. I
told him that as a serving officer I regretted very much to see the magnificent
Indian Army grossly weakened, and the potentially fine R.I.N. and R.I.A.F.

possibly strangled altogether through failure to start Indianisation several years earlier or alternatively through our inability to continue the process for several years longer.

He asked "Would you be prepared to keep British officers with our three Services for as long as we wished, and would you turn them over officially to us?" I replied: "That depends on you". He asked "How"? I explained that it was my considered opinion that no British officer worth his salt would willingly resign his commission to become an adventurer in the Indian Services. The only way he could serve India and retain his commission would be by a Treaty and Mission, which everyone who had any experience thought was next to useless; or alternatively by India deciding not to quit the Empire and not to sever the link with the Crown, so that officers while still holding the King's Commission could continue to serve India. I said that men like Field Marshal Auchinleck and General Slim could not possibly be expected to stay in any different circumstances, and I did not see how anyone else could either.

After some discussion about the origin of India wishing to shake the dust of the British Empire off her feet, he admitted that he himself had been responsible for inventing the term "Independent Sovereign Republic" for the Resolution[1] in the Constituent Assembly; and he said that he now regretted choosing such drastic terminology so early on in the final stage. He asked what he could do to try and make amends.

I suggested:

(a) That he should postpone the implementation of this resolution for five years in the first instance, to be reconsidered by plebiscite at the end of that time. He could quite openly give the reason that this was to enable British officers to remain and assist a gradual hand-over throughout the Army, since June 1948 was too precipitate a date.

(b) He should avoid the expression "Dominion Status" and use a term like "Free Nation of the Commonwealth" or "Free India" or, as he himself put it, "Union of India".

(c) That on no account must they renounce the link with the Crown, since even Ireland had that link, and India needed it at least to that extent if officers were to retain the King's commission while serving in a Free India.

I pointed out that it would not be necessary for Indian officers to retain the King's commission, since even now the majority of Indian officers only held a Viceroy's commission.

Mr. Menon said that the Congress difficulty would be to retain a link with the Crown, because he said for purely political warfare motives Congress had been attacking the Crown as a symbol of oppression, and it would be difficult to explain to the people such a fundamental change in political outlook.

I told him that that was his headache; he could not have his cake and eat it;

[1] Vol. IX, No. 190.

and that unless Congress could find some way of accepting the link with the Crown and of putting it over to the people, I was not prepared to play.

He asked me whether a scheme of dual nationality could not be worked out to get round this. I told him I did not see how he could ever get round the link with the Crown which was necessary to obtain British officers; though he could avoid publicity on it by not drawing attention to it. All he had to do was not to sever the link.

I told him that it was up to Congress to make the first move if they wanted a move to be made. I had no intention of making one, because I had received the strictest instructions[2] not to make any attempt to keep India within the Commonwealth; indeed, I was not sure if H.M.G. would even approve any move at all, since a meeting which was taking place at Whitehall at the time of my departure had come to the conclusion that we could get all the commercial benefits we wanted out of India through the sterling balances and a friendly treaty, without having to go to the extent of including such a very weak nation in our defence organisation.

He asked what my own views were and I told him in strict confidence that I was one of those sentimental fools who would always try to help any nation that wanted to be within the Commonwealth; but this was merely my private view, and I might quite well be shot down by the Powers that be for expressing it.

I also told him that I was not prepared to negotiate with the various parts of India, e.g. the States, Pakistan &c who in any case wished to be within the Commonwealth. And I pointed out that in any union the Congress would be the only people trying to keep out of the Commonwealth; if they persisted, then so far as I was concerned I would not support anybody else coming [?in].

Finally he said to me: "Unless you take the first step and approach us, nothing will be done". I replied: "Then nothing will be done, because it is entirely your loss, and I am not going to allow any sentimental reasons make me pull your chestnuts out of the fire. If you do not take the first step, you will have a rotten army; you will lose all the benefits of the Commonwealth; and you will save the other nations of the Commonwealth the expense, anxiety and responsibility of your defence".

He then said that he did not mean there could not be private off-the-record discussions; he meant that the first step could not be taken publicly by the leaders without reversing everything that they had preached to their people.

I then asked him what he proposed. He said: "If the British were voluntarily to give us now Dominion Status, well ahead of June 1948, we should be so grateful that not a voice would be heard in June 1948 suggesting any change, except possibly to the word dominion if that had been actually used up to that date."

I said that I was in favour of taking steps if it was a feasible proposition; if the

Muslims were to stay in a Union of India, I would certainly recommend Dominion Status next month; but since I knew they were not, I could not possibly recommend the present Interim Government being given dominion powers; the Muslim League would violently object to being placed in a position of a permanent minority in the Cabinet.

He asked me whether I could not propose equal dominion status to Hindustan and Pakistan, and the States that joined those two confederations. I said: "Certainly provided I could retain full powers over defence, since I would have to coordinate the use of the single army for both Indian dominions."

He said that Dominion Status without control over the Army would be laughable and would never be accepted by the Indians.

I told him to go away and think of any solution by which dual dominion status could be granted; with a machinery that would satisfy the Muslim League that the army was being fairly administered and operated. He said he would think about the problem.

I told him that he had no authority to quote me, that he could discuss the tenor of the discussions with Nehru as long as he made it clear that I would never take the first step; and that I did not know whether I should receive any backing at all in a desire to help from H.M.G.

[2] [Note in original:] This remark was made in the way of "tactics". It was based on the fact that I knew that a Committee had been sitting in London to consider the advantages and disadvantages of keeping India within the Commonwealth; and that the direction that I should make efforts to keep an united India within the Commonwealth was not included in the original draft of my directive, and was in fact put in on my own suggestion.

170

Viceroy's Staff Meeting
Uncirculated Record of Discussion No. 9

Mountbatten Papers

TOP SECRET
Those present during this discussion which took place at the end of The Viceroy's Sixteenth Staff Meeting held at The Viceroy's House, New Delhi on 18 April 1947 at 10 am were: Rear-Admiral Viscount Mountbatten of Burma, Lord Ismay, Sir E. Mieville, Mr Abell, Captain Brockman, Mr I. D. Scott, Mr Campbell-Johnson, Lieutenant-Colonel Erskine Crum

HIS EXCELLENCY THE VICEROY said that the germ of a new plan had come into his mind as a result of a conversation which he had had the previous day. This concerned the question of India remaining, in some way, within the

British Commonwealth. The main points of the plan, which he wished the senior members of his staff to think over, were as follows:—

1. There was difficulty over who should take, or who should appear to take, the first step. If the responsible Indian leaders (who appeared to him to be unanimous about the desirability of the object) did so, they would without doubt be forced to resign in the face of the irresponsible and self-seeking outlook of certain of their followers. If H.M.G. did so, they would be accused of imperialism, and the chances of a successful outcome would doubtless be prejudiced.

2. This difficulty could be overcome by taking advantage of the resolution which had already been passed by Congress asking for immediate Dominion status, and granting it.

3. The grant would have to take place this year; or the objects would not be achieved.

4. Some workable solution must be found to prevent the grant of Dominion status resulting in the complete control by Congress of the Muslim League. Perhaps Dominion status would have to be granted to Hindustan and Pakistan separately.

5. The control of the Indian Armed Forces would have to remain in the hands of the Viceroy. If there was a separate grant to Hindustan and Pakistan, a committee of a representative from each might be set up to control the Armed Forces with The Viceroy having the casting vote (preferably at the invitation of both parties). Alternatively, a board of the High Commissioners of the other Dominions and some members of the Council of State might be set up for this purpose.

6. British troops might either
(a) be under the control of such a board;
(b) be under the Viceroy's personal command;
(c) go.

7. The words "Dominion status" had an unfortunate association in the eyes of the Indians, and were almost universally misunderstood. Some other formula, some new words, must therefore be devised.

171

Minutes of Viceroy's Fourth Miscellaneous Meeting
Mountbatten Papers

Those present at this Meeting held at The Viceroy's House, New Delhi on 18 April 1947 at 11.30 am were: Rear-Admiral Viscount Mountbatten of Burma, Sir O. Caroe (not present for first two paras. of the record), Pandit Nehru, Dr Khan Sahib, Lord Ismay, Sir E. Mieville; Lieutenant-Colonel Erskine Crum (Secretariat)

THE SITUATION IN THE N.W.F.P.

HIS EXCELLENCY THE VICEROY opened the Meeting by thanking Pandit Nehru for the letter[1] which he had sent him that morning. He went on to say that he had hoped to be able at the present time to give all his attention to efforts to find a solution for the future of India as a whole and to avoid details which only concerned individual Provinces. However, he felt that the situation in the N.W.F.P. was, if not dealt with now, likely to prejudice the wider problem. His immediate object, therefore, was to find a temporary expedient which would restore that situation and maintain peace until an over-all solution for the whole of India had been decided. He hoped that that solution when found, would be acceptable to all parties, and would result in the prevention of bloodshed. From the latest reports it appeared that the situation at the Frontier was deteriorating both in those areas which were the direct responsibility of Dr. Khan Sahib and in the tribal areas.

HIS EXCELLENCY THE VICEROY said that Sir Olaf Caroe had explained to him that the main difficulty at the moment was that the Muslim League had started agitations which were gravely embarrassing the Government of the Province. In dealing with these agitations, the Government was gradually getting itself into a position, not by any means wholly intentionally, whereby most of the Opposition were in jail. He pointed out that it was very difficult to carry on constitutional government in such a state of affairs. In the United Kingdom during the war, only one member of Parliament had been imprisoned under the special Defence Regulation No. 18b. HIS EXCELLENCY THE VICEROY said that Sir Olaf Caroe was fully aware that he was considered by many to be pro-Muslim League but he had denied this in what had impressed him (His Excellency) as being a most sincere way. If the intention of the British had been to remain in India, it was conceivable that they might have tried for a "divide and rule" policy. But as the British were going in June 1948—and his instructions on this point were inflexible—and as all were agreed that it was of the utmost importance to leave the country as peaceful as possible, it was not rationally conceivable that any Governor should violently take sides with one or other political party at this stage.

[1] No. 167.

Sir Olaf Caroe then entered the room.

DR. KHAN SAHIB complained that on many occasions Sir Olaf Caroe had not taken his advice.

SIR OLAF CAROE said that he had the greatest admiration for Dr. Khan Sahib, whom he considered to be an outstanding and most courageous man. They had had many differences of opinion in the past for various reasons. He agreed that he had on occasions not accepted Dr. Khan Sahib's advice—because to have done so would have made the position of his Ministry more difficult. As a specific point he had disagreed with Dr. Khan Sahib over the question of interference—though from the highest motives—by the Executive in the discretion of magistrates, particularly in their judicial functions.

PANDIT NEHRU said that he fully upheld the principle that there should be no such interference. DR. KHAN SAHIB said that it was Sir Olaf Caroe who interfered with him. HIS EXCELLENCY THE VICEROY said that he would be quite ready to send an independent judge to look into this question if both Sir Olaf Caroe and Dr. Khan Sahib wished it.

SIR OLAF CAROE said that another matter on which he had not always taken Dr. Khan Sahib's advice was that of the posting of officials. The reason for this was because he considered that much caution should be exercised before transferring officials just because there had been trouble in their districts.

DR. KHAN SAHIB remarked that if he was to be trusted to run the Province, he should not be accused of favouritism.

HIS EXCELLENCY THE VICEROY said that at the Governors' Conference two days previously, this question of posting had been discussed. The Governors had felt that there was a distinct tendency on the part of many Ministries to ask for the immediate transfer of officials whenever there was any trouble. In the Governors' unanimous opinion such impulsive transfers were likely to cause breakdown of the administration.

DR. KHAN SAHIB interpolated the remark that many of his recommendations for transfer had been changed unilaterally by the Governor without him being consulted.

SIR OLAF CAROE denied this, saying that he always discussed appointments with Dr. Khan Sahib and there was no question of varying them without consulting him. HIS EXCELLENCY THE VICEROY suggested that if in any case personal discussion between the two proved impossible, the Governor and the Prime Minister should exchange personal and confidential notes.

HIS EXCELLENCY THE VICEROY said that it was a clear principle that Governors should not interfere with postings except when Ministries tried to transfer officials hurriedly after trouble. It was also an obvious principle that Ministries should avoid such actions.

DR. KHAN SAHIB'S next complaint was that Sir Olaf Caroe interfered too much with day-to-day work, saw many files before him, and thereby stultified his opinions. He stated that he had always seen the files before Sir George Cunningham, when the latter had been Governor. SIR OLAF CAROE admitted that when he had first been appointed he had possibly, on occasions, expressed his own views too freely on files—but he said that that procedure had come to an end some time ago.

Then DR. KHAN SAHIB said that Sir Olaf Caroe was wont to call conferences without inviting him. He quoted particular cases of this. SIR OLAF CAROE explained why this had been done. HIS EXCELLENCY THE VICEROY said that it was agreed in principle that this was an incorrect procedure.

HIS EXCELLENCY THE VICEROY then said that he considered that the hour had come to cease recrimination. He asked Dr. Khan Sahib what policy he would best like to follow.

DR. KHAN SAHIB said that he believed that every outbreak of disorder should be treated at once and firmly. Leniency, in his view, only led to further outbreaks.

SIR OLAF CAROE said that this was surely a very large question—how far a popular Government could go in time of trouble to order the suppression of a movement which was directed against it. Whenever there had been serious violence he had done his best in every possible way to assist his Ministry to enforce law and order. He had had most helpful backing from Pandit Nehru, for which he was thankful, in dealing with tribal inroads. The question of whether or not to ban processions and demonstrations under Section 144 was a very difficult one. He had been trying to persuade his Ministry on the one hand to enforce law and order, and on the other hand so to act that a return to normal conditions would follow as soon as possible. In dealing with a procession which was getting out of hand, one could either use the police in lathi charges and perhaps tear gas, or one might bring in troops—which was likely to result in heavy loss of life. The Military had informed him that they considered that District Officers had, on the whole, particularly in Peshawar, dealt with crowds very well without calling troops in.

HIS EXCELLENCY THE VICEROY said that he was sure that Dr. Khan Sahib would agree to the principle that it was wrong to call in a single soldier unnecessarily. DR. KHAN SAHIB agreed.

SIR OLAF CAROE stated that, after troops had been called in to deal with the situation at Peshawar and had had to open fire, feeling had been aroused more than ever before and there had been a large number of assaults in the city that night. He had been unable on this occasion to consult Dr Khan Sahib so he had given orders that the city should be occupied by troops. The situation now was that the present administration was being held in position by the use of troops.

HIS EXCELLENCY THE VICEROY asked Pandit Nehru whether he agreed that a popular Government should never have to be held in power by the use of troops if this was in any way avoidable. PANDIT NEHRU agreed thoroughly.

DR. KHAN SAHIB then said that Sir Olaf Caroe imagined things. He also said that, if he were given a free hand, he would promise that there would be no rioting, no processions, no murders.

HIS EXCELLENCY THE VICEROY then asked Dr. Khan Sahib whether he could continue government if all troops were withdrawn. DR. KHAN SAHIB said that indeed he could, provided that all officials were withdrawn also.

PANDIT NEHRU asked Dr. Khan Sahib whether he was complaining against being restricted. DR. KHAN SAHIB said that he was.

HIS EXCELLENCY THE VICEROY asked Dr. Khan Sahib what he would do if he had a completely free hand. DR. KHAN SAHIB said that he would deal severely with anybody who broke the law.

HIS EXCELLENCY THE VICEROY then told Dr. Khan Sahib that it was widely held that the Pir of Manki had on many occasions publicly preached non-violence. DR. KHAN SAHIB said that this was only true of the immediate past. Six months ago the Pir of Manki said that he would shoot the Governor if he were told to do so. DR. KHAN SAHIB added his opinion that the Pir of Manki had been behind all the recent murder and looting.

HIS EXCELLENCY THE VICEROY said that he wanted now to start discussing positive action and a draft statement was handed round, which, it was suggested, should be issued by Sir Olaf Caroe after his return, announcing that elections would be held in the N.W.F.P. in due course. DR. KHAN SAHIB said that he would be prepared for an election at any time. He would not stay in power for one moment longer than he was wanted. He was fully in favour of this principle. HIS EXCELLENCY THE VICEROY related that, when Mr. Liaquat Ali Khan had suggested that the Province should be put under Section 93 pending elections, Sir Olaf Caroe had declared himself quite ready that the present Ministry should continue in power until after the elections were held. He went on to say that the last thing that he wanted to do was, by trying to help, to make matters worse. The essential thing was to establish a truce in accordance with the appeal signed by Mr. Gandhi and Mr. Jinnah and to keep the Province quiet until the main decision was made. He was wondering what steps could be taken to stop the present disturbances. First it was, of course, desirable that the Muslim League should call off their direct action campaign— and that was surely what Mr. Jinnah's signature on the appeal implied. Secondly, could the Government of the Province make any gesture? Might it perhaps be possible to issue a fresh statement saying that, as an act of clemency, all political offenders would be released on the condition they did not take advantage of the truce. If they did, they would be put back in jail. Perhaps processions might be prohibited—but not political meetings and the freedom of speech. He was not suggesting that those who had committed criminal acts should be released.

DR. KHAN SAHIB agreed thoroughly with this line of action. He added that he did not think that any condition should be made in the release of political prisoners. PANDIT NEHRU also agreed that such a statement should be issued, and made suggestions as to the wording of it. SIR OLAF CAROE agreed that a statement on the lines suggested by The Viceroy would be helpful. He gave his view that the important thing was that processions must stop. He suggested that political leaders accused of violence should not be released and this was agreed. It was also agreed that those guilty of the technical crime of breaking the ban to take part in processions should be released.

There was then a short discussion of and agreement on a draft note to be issued to the Press concerning the results of this meeting.

HIS EXCELLENCY, THE VICEROY asked whether it was considered that it was very important not to arm the rival factions in the N.W.F.P. DR. KHAN SAHIB and PANDIT NEHRU agreed that it was.

SIR OLAF CAROE said that it was Dr. Khan Sahib's policy to let everybody who was likely to vote for him have a gun. DR. KHAN SAHIB said that this was not the case. He had been issuing permits for fire-arms recently, but solely for record purposes. Nevertheless, he felt that the villagers must have something to protect themselves with. The trouble was that the good villagers had no arms and the "undesirables" had arms without licences. PANDIT NEHRU pointed out that there were and always had been a large number of guns on the Frontier.

PANDIT NEHRU said that the rough dividing line between Congress and Muslim League supporters in the N.W.F.P. was on class lines. SIR OLAF CAROE did not agree with this. He thought that the present division was largely a reproduction on the political stage of old factions.

HIS EXCELLENCY THE VICEROY said that Dr. Khan Sahib had been accused of holding up Press telegrams and SIR OLAF CAROE said that there had been some unwise censorship by the Government. DR. KHAN SAHIB said that there had been only one case of censorship. He said that he would repeat the orders that had been issued that there should be none.

HIS EXCELLENCY THE VICEROY said that he would much like to visit the N.W.F.P. as soon as occasion permitted.

DR. KHAN SAHIB said that he would be very pleased if His Excellency would come; he felt sure that such a visit would be most helpful. SIR OLAF CAROE and PANDIT NEHRU agreed with this.

HIS EXCELLENCY THE VICEROY:—
(i) invited C.V.S. to prepare a draft of the statement to be issued by the Government of the N.W.F.P.;
(ii) approved the draft, suggested by C.V.S., of a note to be issued to the Press on the results of the Meeting.

172

Record of Interview between Rear-Admiral Viscount Mountbatten of Burma and Mr Weightman

Mountbatten Papers. Viceroy's Interview No. 75

TOP SECRET   *18 April 1947, 3.40–4 pm*

I saw Mr Weightman to say goodbye to him on his going on leave; and to ask him how he was getting on with Nehru.

He told me that he liked working with Nehru very much; that he was very straight, and was more and more prepared to listen to reason on every subject except the Frontier, which was a complete blind spot with him. He insisted on listening to the Khan brothers who knew practically nothing of the Frontier, as was proved by the fact that the first time they went up to visit in the Waziristan direction the visit nearly ended in the loss of Nehru's and their own lives. He was convinced that Nehru's explanation that this had been engineered was the wrong one; on the contrary it was the lack of calmness and confidence of the Khan brothers which had nearly led to disaster.

He thought that it would be months before Nehru could be made to see any sense about the Frontier, although he was making great strides in every other direction and was beginning to show quite a keen interest in the possibility of India remaining somehow in the Commonwealth. He was sure he had begun to see how much India would lose by secession; but that he was at a loss to know how to reverse their propaganda policy of "complete independence".

I gave him a very brief outline of my talk with Krishna Menon[1] on condition that he did not mention it.

[1] No. 169.

173

Record of Interview between Rear-Admiral Viscount Mountbatten of Burma and Master Tara Singh, Giani Kartar Singh and Sardar Baldev Singh

Mountbatten Papers. Viceroy's Interview No. 76

TOP SECRET   *18 April 1947*

The meeting lasted from 4.10 to 5.50 p.m.

I welcomed the Sikhs and told them what a warm place they had in my heart, since the Sikh units had fought with such magnificent gallantry in S.E. Asia.

I told them I had seen the Maharaja of Faridkot who had told me something of his ideas (but bearing in mind his request not to refer to their letter to him in front of Sardar Baldev Singh, I did not mention this).[1]

I asked them about the situation in the Punjab, and immediately they began a long tale of woe of how the Sikhs had been gratuitously attacked and beset by the Muslims; how peaceful the Sikhs were, and how they would never again be able to live in peace and harmony with Muslims, and would accept nothing that would put them under their domination.

To begin with, they complained about the police: instead of the police being enlisted on a basis proportionate to the population, the situation at present was that 73 per cent of the police were Muslims and only 27 per cent were Sikhs and Hindus combined. They freely admitted that it was incidental that it had grown up like this, and that in normal conditions it did not matter. But now they wanted the principle regulated as soon as possible. There were at present 32,000 policemen, they said. But they understood the Governor was re-cruiting another 6,000 shortly; and they felt that all the 6,000 should be non-Muslims in order to bring the final proportion up to as near 50% Muslims, 20 Sikhs 30 Hindu as possible. They wanted special machinery set up to achieve this, since they said if it was left to the present organisation it would be certain that the majority of the new 6,000 would be Muslims; and even if I should issue instructions that non-Muslims would be given a special chance, they would most certainly be rejected on the plea of being unsuitable by the existing Muslim officers.

I undertook to write to the Governor about this.[2]

Next they complained that in the absence of martial law (which they would prefer) the special ordinances issued by the Governor would have been satis-factory but for the fact that they were not observed in all areas. In particular soldiers had been prevented from going to the assistance of the Civil Power in certain districts. I invited the Defence Member to go into the position on his own, since it affected his department.

[1] In this Interview, which took place on 17 April 1947, the Raja of Faridkot handed Lord Mountbatten a letter, dated 19 March 1947, which he had received from Master Tara Singh, Giani Kartar Singh and Sardar Ishar Singh Majhail. In this it was stated that the Panth felt the Raja of Faridkot was 'in a position to help and consolidate the Sikh ideals of life, living and brotherhood and we, therefore, approach you to take over the entire policy, organisation and safety of life and property regarding the districts of Ludhiana, Ferozepore and portions of Lahore and its administration'.

In the Interview the Raja added that he had the personal assurance of League leaders in the Punjab towards certain areas being included in a new Sikh State. Lord Mountbatten noted that 'these were the very areas that Sir Evan Jenkins had pointed out at the Governors' Conference as likely to be the most hotly disputed between Muslims and Sikhs; and I regard the fact that here are the beginnings of mutual agreement on a division as a very hopeful sign'. Mountbatten Papers, Viceroy's Interview No. 71.

[2] Lord Mountbatten's correspondence with Sir E. Jenkins on this subject has not been traced.

They then handed me the attached paper entitled "Notes for the talk with H.E., 18–4–1947".³ I discussed their two suggestions:

(a) That there should be an early announcement of the creation of two separate ministries for the Eastern and Western parts of the Punjab to carry on with the Interim Period.

(b) The question of police recruitment.

As regards (b) I repeated that I would write to the Governor.

With regard to (a), Sardar Baldev Singh stated that Mr Jinnah had informed him that he accepted the principle of the transfer of populations in the Punjab (I invited him to put this point to me in writing); and he told me that 20,000 Sikhs had already fled from various predominantly Muslim areas in which riots had taken place, and were now taking refuge in Patiala.

I said that I would go into this, but pointed out the appalling difficulties involved in such a form of partition.

They countered by pointing out that if indeed Pakistan were granted by me this would be even more difficult to effect.

I replied that if I was reluctantly driven to accept Pakistan I certainly would agree to the partition of the Punjab however difficult it might be; but I would resist this if the Cabinet Mission plan or any comparable plan were accepted.

They were of the opinion that it should not be impossible on this basis to obtain an agreed partition, but if it could not be granted they insisted I should arbitrate. I told them that nothing would induce me to give a decision which would require military enforcement.

I warned them that the Jats were pretty certain to ask for the south-eastern parts of the Punjab, to join up with the Jat areas of the U.P. They said that they knew the Jats wanted a separate province, consisting of the Jat parts of the Punjab and U.P., and that they were not opposed to this.

They admitted that they (the Sikhs) would not be in a majority in any part of the Punjab, but said that they were now so bitterly anti-Muslim that they would not mind forming a Hindu-Sikh Province.

I asked them what their views were about the Sikh States, and they told me that matters were now being negotiated to bring Patiala, Kapurthala, Faridkot, Nabha, Jind & Khalsia definitely into a Sikh States Confederation, and hoped that Malerkotla which they claimed to be a Sikh State in spite of it being ruled by a Muslim Nawab, would come into the Confederation. They also hoped that the Raja of Nalagarh might join the Confederation, for although it was a predominantly Hindu State, he was the brother-in-law of the Maharaja of Patiala!

They said they recognised and fully accepted that no parts of British India could join up with an Indian State, since I had to transfer power for British India, and could not transfer parts of British India to States, to whom I would be returning Paramountcy. (I thought it wiser not to draw their attention to the fact that this was at variance with what the Maharaja of Faridkot had told me at my interview with him yesterday, when he claimed that Tara Singh and Kartar Singh had written to him asking him to take over parts of British India—or perhaps they only meant him to take over the political leadership.)

They then proceeded to shower me with leaflets and publications. These two unkempt, jungly-looking old men were immensely learned in their knowledge of every part of the Cabinet Mission's negotiations and the subsequent debates in the House. They told me that the Sikhs had definitely rejected the Cabinet Mission plan in the first place, but that under persuasion from Major Billy Short and Sir Stafford Cripps, followed by discussions with Lord Pethick-Lawrence and Lord Wavell, and in face of verbal assurances given by the last two, they reluctantly yielded. They pointed out that the late Secretary of State and Viceroy had promised them adequate safeguards which had never materialised. They drew my attention to a letter dated 1st June 1946[4] from the Secretary of State, which Master Tara Singh had received in reply to his letter of the 25th May;[5] and to the remarks which Sir Stafford Cripps made in the House on the 18th July 1946,[6] and supplied me with printed copies of both. They pointed out that paragraph 19 (vii) of the Cabinet Mission plan stated that "In the Union Constituent Assembly resolutions varying the provisions of paragraph 15 or raising any major communal issue shall require a majority of the representatives present and voting of each of the two major communities".

They pointed out that since the Sikhs had been given the status of the third and only other major community, they had been expressly excluded from this advantage, and that whereas a Muslim or even a Christian (since he belonged to the "General" communities) may raise an issue and vote on communal questions, and that the presence of even four Muslims of which three voted against a communal issue would prevent its being carried, the Sikhs were debarred from this since they were not one of the two major communities.

They were generous enough to say that they were sure that this must be an error in drafting, but that they had been unable to get it changed and had been advised to try and obtain safeguards in the Constituent Assembly. These they were trying to obtain, but Congress were averse from granting them, since if they varied the Cabinet Mission plan in any way they felt it would give Mr Jinnah an excuse for not joining the Constituent Assembly.

The Sikhs invited me to inform Congress that I recommended the Congress to give them these safeguards.

I said I did not wish to do anything of the sort until I was getting down to the final considerations.

They warned me that if they were not granted the communal veto, to which

[3] Not on the file.   [4] Vol. VII, No. 424.
[5] Vol. VII, No. 380.   [6] *Parl. Debs.*, 5th ser., H. of C., vol. 425, cols. 1394–1416.

they considered themselves entitled, they would be obliged to leave the Constituent Assembly. I asked them not to do this until I was having my final discussion with leaders before recommending a solution to H.M.G.

Finally I asked them if they would accept the Cabinet Mission plan if these safeguards were put in. They said that they would only give up their insistence on partition if I could ensure that they obtained adequate safeguards from being dominated by the Muslims. They suggested an allocation of 40 per cent of the seats to the Muslims, 30 to the Sikhs and 30 to the Hindus. I told them I did not think anybody else would accept such an allocation, but that I agreed that the question of safeguards would want very careful investigation.

They held that even if the Muslim League joined the Constituent Assembly, negotiations would be bound to break down on the question of the proportion of seats, offices and appointments, which the Muslims would demand and the Congress would not grant.

Finally they asked that, if I did decide on Pakistan and on a partition of the Punjab, I should publicly give them the choice of joining either Pakistan or Hindustan, so that they might have some bargaining power to gain the best terms. This I agreed was entirely fair.

Just before they left I pulled their leg about their kirpans, for these scholarly old gentlemen came in with the most enormous swords. I told them that the Muslims wanted the right to carry swords as they did. They said they would not mind in the least; although I pointed out if both sides were to wear swords civil war would be more than ever likely to come about.

At the end of the interview I arranged for them to meet Sir Eric Mieville, and to put their case to him, since it was difficult for me to remember everything they had told me, and since I had wanted the interview to be informal I had had no member of my Staff present.

174

Sir F. Burrows (Bengal) to Rear-Admiral Viscount Mountbatten of Burma

Telegram, R/3/1/130: f 211

IMPORTANT   *18 April 1947, 8.5 pm*
SECRET   *Received: 19 April, 8.45 am*
No. 95–S. My Chief Minister informed me at interview today that while in Delhi this week he had put to Jinnah the strong pleas I had made to him that either the Cabinet plan should be accepted and the League should enter the Constituent Assembly or that a very strong Coalition government should be set up immediately in Bengal. (I had made it clear to Suhrawardy that I re-

garded the adoption of one or other of these courses as only method of avoiding civil strife and paving the way in peaceful transfer of power in Bengal.)

Jinnah told Suhrawardy that he regarded the Cabinet plan as dead: that he is not accepting the Congress invitation to discuss it and that he has no intention of entering Constituent Assembly.

As regards forming a Coalition Cabinet in Bengal Jinnah's view was that the proposal was premature.

175

Sir F. Bourne (Central Provinces and Berar) to Rear-Admiral Viscount Mountbatten of Burma

R/3/1/142: ff 78–80

D.O. No. 7/G.C.P.   GOVERNOR'S CAMP, CENTRAL PROVINCES
                                           AND BERAR, *18 April 1947*

Dear Lord Mountbatten,

My wife is writing to Lady Mountbatten to thank Your Excellencies for your very kind hospitality for which we both are most grateful.

2. I did not find an opportunity of giving Your Excellency an account of my interview with Sir Mirza Ismail which I rather think you wished me to do. I mentioned it briefly to Corfield, but something more in detail may be of use. The points discussed were as follows:—

(*a*) We both agreed that H.E.H.'s sovereignty in Berar could not be doubted and that in the absence of a fresh treaty Berar must revert to H.E.H. on the termination of paramountcy.

(*b*) Sir Mirza wanted His Majesty's Government to come out with a public statement in regard to this state of affairs. I said that I saw no object in this when the position was clearly stated in the various treaties. On the other hand, it would be undesirable for His Majesty's Government to go out of their way to stress the matter.

(*c*) He said that H.E.H. regarded the return of Berar to his Dominions as a highly important point of sentiment and prestige. But he had no intention of merely incorporating Berar in Hyderabad: he proposed to set it up as a province under his suzerainty. I asked what advantage the people of Berar would get from this and he said that they would in this manner cease to be chained to the Central Provinces. I said that their union with the Central Provinces had conferred many benefits upon them. Approximately as much money was spent on Berar as they contributed to the common stock and they had the advantage of participating in large cadres of Government servants. I suggested that the only people who would benefit in Berar were the opportunist politicians, with whom Sir Mirza Ismail had been in communication, who look forward to holding posts in the ministry or in a separate Legislative Assembly. He made it clear that Hyderabad expected no financial advantage and indeed would be prepared to spend money in helping Berar, though I do not myself see how members of the Hyderabad Services could be used extensively in Berar so long as Berar remained a semi-independent province. I think Sir Mirza is influenced on the one side by H.E.H. who, I know, has a very strong sentimental feeling in favour of recovering Berar, while on the other side, he is influenced by politicians of the non-Brahmin faction in Berar who have always felt that their political future was obscured by the leading part taken by the Central Provinces Brahmin in the conduct of provincial affairs.

(d) Finally, I tried to make the point that with so many inevitable fundamental changes due to take place in India, it would be better, at least for the time being, to avoid additional causes of irritation. I agreed that matters could not be left to slide and that with the termination of paramountcy some new arrangements would have to be made. I suggested that for all parties the best arrangement might be a new short-term treaty, say for 10 years, maintaining existing arrangements, renewable or terminable at the end of that period by negotiation between the parties. I understand that Corfield would prefer something of this sort and I think Sir Mirza himself saw the point, though whether he can make H.E.H. see it is another matter.

Yours sincerely,
F. C. BOURNE

176

Lord Pethick-Lawrence to Rear-Admiral Viscount Mountbatten of Burma

Mountbatten Papers. Letters to and from the Secretary of State

PRIVATE AND SECRET   INDIA OFFICE, *18 April 1947*
My dear Mountbatten,
Thank you for your letter of 9th April,[1] enclosing your "personal report No. 2",[2] the copies of which have been distributed on the lines agreed between us.

2 I was very glad to learn that, although Burrows was unable to get to Delhi for the Governors' Conference, he is making good progress and can look forward to complete recovery.

3. Three has not yet been time for Mr Gandhi's outline for a scheme for an interim Government pending the transfer of power to be fully examined and,

in any case, I would not at this stage wish to anticipate my successor's views upon it, but I cannot help saying that, on a first reading, it appears to be remarkably detached from the realities of the situation.

4. As I rather anticipated, the road you had to tread with Jinnah appears to have been up-hill all the way, but I consider that it was a great personal triumph for you that you succeeded in persuading him to put his name to a joint statement with Mr Gandhi for publication.

5. I am leaving it to my successor to deal with certain matters referred to in your second personal report, for example, civilian passages and the activities of the British Council.

6. In paragraph 9 of your first personal report of the 2nd April[3] you mentioned that the Nawab of Bhopal and others have raised with you the question of the future political relations between the States and the United Kingdom, mentioning the possibility of States or groups of States being granted Dominion status. This particular idea seems rather fanciful since, of course, the States are not at present British territory at all and they could hardly be incorporated (apart from some organic relationship with the rest of India if that elects for Dominion status) as part of the British Empire; the most presumably that we could consider would be a special Treaty relationship. It is, however, quite clear that the only possible policy for H.M.G. to pursue at this stage is to stick to the lines of the Cabinet Mission's Memorandum on States' Treaties and Paramountcy[4] which in paragraph 3 noted the desire of the Indian States to contribute to the framing of the structure of the new India and take their due place in it when it is completed. It is out of the question for us at present to do anything to encourage States to stand out completely.

7. In my letter to you of 21st March[5] about the effect of H.M.G.'s Statement of 20th February on the question of the relaxation of Paramountcy in Indian India I mentioned that we might at any time find ourselves in the difficulty that the Central Government might put effective obstacles in the way of our using force to support our intervention in a particular State. In regard to Hyderabad I developed this point further in my letter to you of 31st March[6] about Berar. In this connection my attention has been drawn to paragraph 6 of the top secret letter of the 15th March[7] from the Resident at Hyderabad to your Political Secretary about steps to be taken on the death of the present Nizam. The Resident suggests that he should make arrangements with the military authorities to send troops as reinforcements to the State troops if the Hyderabad Government so request and the circumstances seem to require it. This seems to me to be precisely the type of case in which you might possibly encounter

[1] No. 107.   [2] No. 108.   [3] No. 59.
[4] Vol. VII, No. 262.   [5] Vol. IX, No. 557.   [6] No. 39.
[7] L/P &S/13/1210: ff 25–6.

difficulties with the Central Government and I have no doubt that when plans are being made in Hyderabad and elsewhere, this danger will be borne in mind.

8. I was interested in Mudie's fortnightly letter to you of 26th March (DO.No.165/FR).[8] So far as I am aware, no other Province has taken steps to prepare itself in any way for the additional powers and responsibilities which may descend upon it as a result of H.M.G.'s Statement of 20th February. Congress Provinces may, I suppose, be excused to some extent since they can comfort themselves with the thought that the Congress Committee, the Constituent Assembly or Section "A" thereof will do the job for them.

Yours sincerely,
PETHICK-LAWRENCE

[8] No. 23.

177

Viceroy's Staff Meeting
Uncirculated Record of Discussion No. 10

Mountbatten Papers

TOP SECRET

Those present during this discussion which took place at the end of The Viceroy's Seventeenth Staff Meeting held at The Viceroy's House, New Delhi on 19 April 1947 at 10 am were: Rear-Admiral Viscount Mountbatten of Burma, Lord Ismay, Sir E. Mieville, Mr Abell, Captain Brockman, Mr I. D. Scott, Mr Campbell-Johnson, Lieutenant-Colonel Erskine Crum

LORD ISMAY said that a Meeting was to be held that afternoon to revise the draft programme and the draft of Plan "Balkan"[1] which had been discussed at the Governors' Conference, in the light of the decisions then reached. He hoped to let the Viceroy have a copy of the amended programme and plan on Monday 21st April.

SIR ERIC MIEVILLE said that Sir Mirza Ismail had suggested that a round-table conference should be held to devise the future constitution of India. In his (Sir Eric Mieville's) opinion, the numbers to be invited to such a conference should be reduced considerably from those suggested by Sir Mirza Ismail, and the object of the conference should rather be to arrange the demission of power. He suggested that a limited time, say three days, should be devoted to this conference. He felt that it might not have any very great results but might serve to put matters right in the eyes of the world. It would be the Viceroy's personal choice as to who was to attend the conference.

LORD ISMAY said that he agreed with these ideas. He pointed out that the Viceroy had now seen the Indian leaders individually and the time was approaching for him to see them collectively. He also pointed out that the Viceroy had seen most of the leaders holding extreme points of view—the "whites" and the "blacks". He felt that the time had now come to see the "greys" all together. In view of the historic nature of the decision to be taken, he considered that it would be worth while to get together such representatives on the Viceroy's own personal invitation, so that one last effort should be made and that the Viceroy should hear from all sides together how they proposed that power should be demitted.

MR ABELL said that he was also in favour of this suggestion but he felt that those invited might have to include the whole Cabinet. In fact the conference would represent the Cabinet Meeting with some outside representatives. LORD ISMAY emphasized that the invitations must be personal. He added that this conference would in no way take the place of the Simla house party.

HIS EXCELLENCY THE VICEROY approved the idea in principle. He felt that the first stage should be to fill in the names of those to be invited. He pointed out that there could be no question of this conference failing because all that he would be doing would be asking for advice to help him to decide what solution to recommend to His Majesty's Government.

HIS EXCELLENCY THE VICEROY said that he felt that the time was now coming when he should stop having a large number of personal interviews and the whole staff should get down to digesting all that had been said and heard. The first essential was to tabulate the objectives. These perhaps were:—

(i) To devise ways and means of demitting authority by June, 1948.

(ii) To demit power in such a way as to cause least risk of strife and bloodshed after the decision had been made—i.e. no compulsion of minorities.

(iii) To aim at the greatest retention of unity and at a strong Centre as could be got through.

(iv) To take care that there was universal application of principles—i.e. there would be no partition of India on communal lines without partition of Provinces on communal lines.

(v) To keep, if possible, India within the British Commonwealth and, in order to achieve this, to grant some sort of Dominion status as early as possible. HIS EXCELLENCY THE VICEROY said that he felt that this was the most important single problem facing the staff at the moment.

(vi) If it was impossible to retain India within the Commonwealth, to maintain between her and the United Kingdom the closest possible friendship.

MR ABELL said that he felt that the Muslim League was in a weak position

[1] See No. 139.

and susceptible to "squeeze". HIS EXCELLENCY THE VICEROY said that he had got this same impression. He felt, however, that there was at the back of Mr Jinnah's and Mr Liaquat Ali Khan's mind a lack of realisation that the British were indeed going in June 1948. Could they not be made fully to realise this and could they not be presented with an outline of the full horrors of working out Pakistan? Perhaps he might write a letter to Mr Jinnah pointing out that the latter had said that it was for him to devise the mechanics of establishing Pakistan and giving an outline programme which would show the full difficulties. MR ABELL stressed the necessity for having an alternative to offer to Mr Jinnah. Therefore, in his view, the first move should be to go to Congress and make every effort to persuade them to agree to the Cabinet Mission Plan. MR CAMPBELL-JOHNSON said that Mr Colin Reid of the *Daily Telegraph*, who knew Mr Jinnah well, was of this same view—that Mr Jinnah could be "squeezed" if there was an alternative to offer.

HIS EXCELLENCY THE VICEROY asked whether Dominion status could be granted if the Cabinet Mission Plan was agreed upon. MR ABELL said that authority could be demitted straight away to the Constituent Assembly. HIS EXCELLENCY THE VICEROY finally re-iterated that the most urgent question now requiring investigation was how to grant some form of Dominion status during 1947 if the Cabinet Mission Plan was not accepted, and it was decided that there would have to be some form of Pakistan.

178

Record of Interview between Rear-Admiral Viscount Mountbatten of Burma and Mr Liaquat Ali Khan

Mountbatten Papers. Viceroy's Interview No. 77

TOP SECRET   *10 April 1947, 4.10–6.10 pm*

I first of all went through his long letter[1] to me of April the 15th paragraph by paragraph; and I read out, paragraph by paragraph, Sir Evan Jenkins' answers[2] to the Muslim League charges against him. We had a general talk, in which I convinced Liaquat of Sir Evan Jenkins' sincerity. I told him that the ridiculous situation had come about that when I had seen the Governor of the Punjab on the first day of the Governors' Conference I had told him that Mr. Gandhi and other Congress leaders had complained to me of his anti-Congress/pro-Muslim bias; and that after he had finished defending himself against that charge on the first day, on the second day he was called upon to defend himself against Mr. Liaquat Ali Khan's charge of his being pro-Congress and anti-Muslim League. I said that the matter would be laughable if it were not so tragic.

I explained to Mr. Liaquat Ali Khan exactly why I could in no circumstances consider allowing the Nawab of Mamdot to try and form a Ministry; for even if he was given all the Muslim seats and thus a majority of five in a house of 175, I now knew from the Sikh leaders themselves that they would resist with all the power at their command any attempt at being governed by the Muslims after the massacres that they had suffered at their hands.

I told him that unless all parties agreed to a sensible solution at my hands for the transfer of power, the only possible future for the Punjab was partition, and in the meanwhile I had absolutely no intention whatever of allowing the Muslim League to try its hand at governing.

He accepted this remarkably well.

He strongly protested when I told him that I was against allowing non-Sikhs to carry swords to defend themselves against the kirpans carried by the Sikhs in the Punjab. He quite saw that on religious grounds I could not ban the kirpan, and he therefore urged that other inhabitants of the Punjab should be allowed to carry swords which they already had in their houses, so as to be able to defend themselves against sudden attacks by the Sikhs.

I told him that I considered it was wrong that the Sikhs had been given permission to carry these big swords, but since this wrong could not now be undone, I did not see how a second wrong could put it right. I said that if we allowed all parties to go armed in the Punjab, it was an invitation to civil war.

Liaquat protested bitterly at this discrimination in favour of the Sikhs, and asked me to reconsider the matter. I promised to do this, but held out no particular hope that I would change my view.

I then told Liaquat that I was now in a position to give him some idea of how my mind was beginning to work towards a solution. Provided he would give me his word of honour not to disclose anything I told him without obtaining my prior permission I would give him a brief outline of my views. He very readily agreed to this, but asked if I would eventually allow him to consult Mr. Jinnah. I said "I will of course agree to this later on but not in the present form or at this stage."

I then took him through practically all the alternative plans which we have been discussing. I started off with Pakistan and complete partition of the Punjab and Bengal and Assam. I told him that I had no doubt that the Indian leaders and their peoples were in such an hysterical condition that they would all gladly agree to my arranging their suicide in this way. He nodded his head, and said "I am afraid everybody will agree to such a plan; we are all in such a state".

I told him that the worst service I could do to India, if I were her enemy or completely indifferent to her fate, would be to take advantage of this extraordinary mental condition to force the completest partition possible upon them,

[1] No. 148.   [2] No. 160.

before going off in June 1948 and leaving the whole country in the most hopeless chaos.

I then returned to the Cabinet Mission plan, and he said at once it was quite useless discussing the Cabinet Mission plan; the League had a phobia against the mere words "Cabinet Mission". I asked him if I produced a "Mountbatten Plan" that was very nearly the same in form and substance, whether this would have a better chance. He said that psychologically he was sure that on both sides it would stand an incomparably better chance of being accepted than anything with the name "Cabinet Mission" attached to it.

I asked him whether he thought the League would accept Groups B & C as allotted to them under the Cabinet Mission plan, with safeguards for the Sikhs, and two separate Indian Armies under their own Army Headquarters which would be run by an overall Defence Headquarters, in the same way that H.Q. SACSEA and H.Q. ALFSEA ran the 12th and 14th Armies in Burma and Malaya. To this he replied: "Now you are beginning to talk; but with power resting with the Central authority to raise taxes for defence finances the majority community would be given a crippling hold over the economy of the whole country."

I suggested to him that the various groups might be assessed according to their populations and the size of the armies they maintained, and pay a contribution towards a Central Defence Fund for the running of the Centre, and for keeping centralised technical schools for the Services. He jumped at this and said he thought it would be a very good plan.

I told him that I had in mind the idea of a preliminary round-table talk with representatives of all the Minorities. He seemed to think that this would be an excellent thing.

I then told him how completely impractical we thought his Leader was, and how we had been unable to get Mr. Jinnah down to earth at all.

Liaquat surprised me by saying "If your Staff will work out exactly what partition means and then if you present the full difficulties to Mr. Jinnah, he will of course understand them even though he has not worked them out for himself".

We talked about Pakistan remaining in the Empire, as both Jinnah and Liaquat had suggested, and I said that I was quite certain that neither the British nor the Americans (who were now together for defence purposes) would dream of backing one part of India against another, or even getting themselves involved with the loan of officers, equipment, etc.

He agreed that there were only two Powers in the world to-day that counted: the British Commonwealth Group linked with the United States on the one hand, and Russia on the other hand. I asked him whether he was prepared to join hands with Russia and all that that implied, and he shook his head and said "No, never". I then said "So you see, the only hope of your being able to remain within the Commonwealth is if the rest of India wants to do so, and that can only happen if there is some overall agreed plan under which the Muslim League with the Indian States and Congress *all* want to remain within the Commonwealth for a period of at least five years." He agreed absolutely that this was the goal to aim at.

I asked him whether he thought such a plan had any prospect of being put through, and he said that the recent massacres and riots had frightened everybody, and now people had had a fore-taste of civil war, they realised what would happen if they could not find an acceptable solution. He said "Although we are all being most intransigent now, you may find that you can bring considerable pressure on every group you meet if you are able to show them a plan which will get them out of their present impasse."

Finally, I told him that I wished to have one high class member of the Muslim League and one from the Congress to work with my Staff and start examining the various alternative plans. I asked him if he would be the Muslim representative and if he would act quite unofficially as my adviser from the Muslim League angle, and that I proposed to ask Pandit Nehru to act in a similar capacity for Congress.

Liaquat gladly accepted and said I could count on his complete support, and that he would put aside all other work and place himself at the disposal of myself and my staff. I said I would make an appointment on Monday or Tuesday for him to come for a meeting with Lord Ismay, Sir Eric Mieville and Mr. Abell, and myself.

Meanwhile he promised to go away and ruminate over everything I had told him, and start thinking out possible future lines of approach.

I have an impression that Mr. Liaquat Ali Khan intends to help me find a more reasonable solution than this mad Pakistan.

In conclusion, I asked him if he could talk to the Editor of *Dawn* and invite him to take a more helpful line than his present unco-operative attitude. Liaquat promised to speak to him.

179

Rear-Admiral Viscount Mountbatten of Burma to Lord Pethick-Lawrence

Telegram, Mountbatten Papers. Official Correspondence Files: North-West Frontier Province, Situation in, Part I(a)

IMMEDIATE   NEW DELHI, *19 April 1947, 10 pm*
EN CLAIR   *Received: 19 April, 8.30 pm*

No. 830–S. Following is text of announcement by N-W.F.P. Government. *Begins.* The Provincial Government associate themselves wholeheartedly with the Gandhi-Jinnah appeal and they call on all the people in the Province to respond to it in all sincerity. They invite special attention to the injunction that all should "not only refrain from acts of violence and disorder, but should also avoid both in speech and writing any incitement to such acts".

The Government have, for their part, decided in the spirit of that appeal unconditionally to release *as soon as* conditions permit, all political prisoners who are not charged with offences of violence.

The Government have no intention of interfering with the freedom of expression of political opinions or with peaceful meetings, but they must impress upon all in the Province that processions and picketing have, in the past, proved an incitement to acts of lawlessness and violence, and that they cannot be permitted until normal conditions return. *Ends.*

180

Rear-Admiral Viscount Mountbatten of Burma to Lord Pethick-Lawrence

Telegram, Mountbatten Papers. Official Correspondence Files: North-West Frontier Province, Situation in, Part I(a)

IMMEDIATE   NEW DELHI, *19 April 1947, 8 pm*
SECRET   *Received: 19 April, 8 pm*

No. 831–S. My immediately preceding telegram.

I kept Caroe here for an extra day after the Governors' Conference and Khan Sahib flew down at Nehru's invitation. I had discussions with all three of them[1] and as a result a statement is being put out this evening of which the text will be [has been] sent you in clear.

The background is that I had proposed to Nehru that a general election should be held on the Frontier very soon as the only available means of easing the tension. Nehru was not against elections in principle but objected to making an announcement to this effect at the present moment.[2] He thought that it would be taken as a surrender to the forces of disorder. However the result of the threat was that our discussions with Khan Sahib enabled us to get agreement on the statement which I hope may help to quieten things down.

As you know their jails are full to overflowing with political prisoners and I consider that their release should prove the first step to ease the tension and avoid trouble spreading throughout the Frontier.

[1] See No. 171.   [2] See No. 167.

181

Viceroy's Conference Paper V.C.P. 32

Mountbatten Papers

SECRET   THE VICEROY'S HOUSE, NEW DELHI, *20 April 1947*
PROPOSALS FOR A MEETING WITH INDIAN LEADERS

1. The attached paper will be considered at The Viceroy's Staff Meeting at 10.00 hours on Monday, 21st April, 1947.

2. This is the only paper for that meeting. No agenda is being issued.

V. F. ERSKINE CRUM
Conference Secretary

Proposals for a Meeting with Indian Leaders
Copy of a Minute from C.V.S. to H.E.

Your Excellency

1. As a result of a series of meetings which I have had with Principal Secretary, P.S.V., Rao Bahadur Menon and J.P.S.V., we commend the following proposals to Your Excellency. The time factor is extremely important and we submit that we should have a preliminary discussion on them at tomorrow morning's Staff Meeting and that we should continue discussion after lunch. This would entail cancellation of your present afternoon engagements, which presents no difficulty.

2. We think that a final conference with the Indian Leaders should be held as soon as possible. The draft invitation at Appendix 'A' shows what we have in mind as regards rendez-vous, date, composition and purpose of the conference.

(a) *Rendez-vous*
    We think that Delhi would be preferable to Simla which has unfortunate associations. Delhi is also probably more convenient to all concerned.

(b) *Date*
    We have worked to the 5th May on the following basis:—
    (i) We hope that your telegram to H.M.G. (see Appendix 'B') will be despatched on Tuesday 22nd April.
    (ii) There is then bound to be a considerable interchange of telegrams whether I go home or not on the subject not only of the plan, but more particularly of the draft announcement. It would be unsafe to make arrangements on the assumption that full agreement could be reached between yourself and H.M.G. in less than a fortnight.
    (iii) It would be a pity to let H.M.G. think that they were being rushed.
    (iv) We are hard at work preparing material for your use at the

conference and we would not like to guarantee that this would be approved by you in under ten days or so.

It is on that reasoning that we have suggested in our draft invitation that the Conference should assemble on or about 5th May.

(c) *Composition*

You will see that we have reverted to the original idea of a *small* conference and that we have rejected the "Mirza" plan. Our reason is that, once you start to extend the circle, you run the risk of either producing unwieldy numbers or of missing out someone who has as good a claim as the next man. We are also convinced that it would be a mistake to include any representatives of the States in a conference which relates to British India.

(d) *Purpose*

The purpose of the Conference would be

(i) to explore every possibility of reaching agreement on the basis of the Cabinet Mission's Plan; and

(ii) if it looks as though no such agreement can be reached, for you to say that the only possible alternative is Partition and that in that event it will be a truncated Pakistan.

This would be the climax of the Conference.

Note: Rao Bahadur Menon is preparing a note which shows how India might be kept within the British Commonwealth, whether unified or divided. This is *not* an alternative plan. There are only two alternative plans—Union or Partition.

3. The appendices to this paper are:—

Appendix 'A'—draft invitation.

Appendix 'B'—draft telegram to H.M.G.

Appendix 'C'—draft announcement.

Appendix 'D'—draft time-table of events.

It should be noted that Appendix 'D' has not yet been subjected to detailed staff discussions.

Appendix 'A'
Draft Invitation to the Indian Leaders

I have spent very many hours during the last month in talking over the problems which confront us with the leaders of opinion in India, and you yourself have been good enough to spare me a great deal of your time.

Convinced as I am that an announcement ought be be made at the earliest possible moment as to how H.M.G. propose to transfer authority to Indian hands by June, 1948, I am most reluctant to postpone the submission of my final advice on this matter to London for even a day longer than is necessary. On the other hand, the issues are of such overwhelming importance that I am

anxious to have a final check-up on the various alternative solutions which
have been suggested to me. I am therefore inviting the following in addition
to yourself, to meet me round the table in Delhi for a final series of talks
beginning about 5th May—

> Pandit Nehru
> Sardar Patel
> Mr. Jinnah
> Mr. Liaquat Ali Khan and
> Sardar Baldev Singh

I earnestly trust that you may see your way to accepting this invitation.

I must emphasise that I shall not ask the Conference for advice as to the
future constitution of India since that is clearly a matter for the Indian people to
settle among themselves. My sole purpose is to arrive at final conclusions as to
how authority should be transferred.

It is my hope that the talks should not take more than three or four days.

Appendix 'B'
Draft telegram to the Secretary of State

1. You will have gathered from my Personal Report No. 3[1] that I consider
that a decision as to whom we are to demit power must be taken within a very
short time. My reasons for this belief are contained in that Report and they
have been reinforced by Nehru's recent speech in Gwalior[2] and by my interviews with the Sikh leaders.[3]

2. I propose to hold a final conference commencing on or about 5th May in
Delhi. The draft invitation (see my immediately succeeding telegram) shows
what I have in mind as regards composition and purpose.

3. My determination is that this should bring things to a head. If I can get no
sort of compromise on the basis of the Cabinet Mission's plan I propose to
confront the Conference with the statement that Partition is the only alternative; that in that event, a truncated Pakistan is all that I can offer to the Muslim
League; that there is no room for further discussion of the Muslim claim for
larger territories; and that H.M.G. have approved this policy.

4. I am also sending you the following telegrams at once:—
(i) the draft announcement which in the last resort I should propose to hand

---

[1] No. 165.
[2] In an address on 18 April 1947 to the All-India States' People's Conference which was meeting at
Gwalior, Pandit Nehru was reported to have said: 'Any Indian State which does not come into the
Constituent Assembly now will be regarded as hostile, and will have to bear the consequences of
being so regarded. Our aim is to liberate as much of India as we can, and then to deal with the question of independence for the rest. India's march toward freedom would brook no more obstruction.'
Elsewhere Pandit Nehru said: 'The Punjab and Bengal will be partitioned; I am making this statement with all the responsibility I possess.'
[3] See No. 173.

to the conference as representing the decision of H.M.G. The question of synchronising the announcement in Parliament with the statement at this end can be considered later;

(ii) a plan of action subsequent to the issue of the announcement. This will not come up for discussion at the conference.

5. May I have your immediate approval to the issue of the draft invitations to the Conference and may I have as soon as you can possibly manage it, your approval of the draft announcement. It is imperative that we should be agreed on the form and substance of this paper before I embark on my discussions here. The plan of subsequent action can be discussed at greater leisure.

6. The issues are to me clear cut but if it would be of any assistance to you I would be prepared to send Ismay, who knows my mind and the general background here, home at once. Please let me know your wishes as soon as possible.

Appendix 'C'
REVISED DRAFT ANNOUNCEMENT—19.4.47.

1. On the 20th February, 1947, H.M.G. announced their intention of transferring power to Indian hands by June, 1948. Had it been possible to obtain agreement on any plan for a Union of India, the process of transfer would have been comparatively simple. Unfortunately, however, despite the efforts of His Excellency the Viceroy, the Congress and the Muslim League have so far been unable to agree and in the Punjab the Sikhs remain very anxious about their position. H.M.G. have, therefore, decided with profound regret that the only course consistent with their pledge that there shall be no compulsion on unwilling parts of the country is to demit power to more than one authority.

2. The constitutional, administrative, financial, geographical and defence problems which will in these circumstances confront successor authorities, both individually and collectively, are of almost infinite variety and bewildering complexity. Time is short and if there is to be any chance of an orderly transfer next year, it is essential that the successor authorities should be determined at the earliest possible date and that they should prepare themselves, to receive power by the due date.

3. It is not for H.M.G. to attempt to lay down the ultimate constitution of India. This is a matter for the Indians themselves to determine. But it is essential for H.M.G. to make such temporary arrangements as will enable power to be demitted by the due date.

4. Accordingly H.M.G. have reached the following decisions:
    (i) If any Provinces do not wish to join the existing Constituent Assembly they will have the right to set up their own Constituent Assemblies or to join together in a Group Constituent Assembly;
    (ii) As the Cabinet Mission pointed out, every argument that can be used

in favour of Pakistan can equally be used in favour of the exclusion of the non-Muslim areas from Pakistan. Certain readjustments of Provincial boundaries will, therefore, be an indispensable preliminary;

(iii) Arrangements will be made for Bengal to be partitioned into two Provinces, one comprising Muslim majority districts and the other comprising the rest of the Province;

(iv) The Sylhet district of Assam will be given the option of joining the new Muslim Province to be created in Bengal;

(v) Arrangements will be made for the Punjab to be partitioned on the same principle as Bengal;

(vi) In every case the 1941 census will be taken as authoritative;

(vii) If necessary a Boundary Commission will be set up in one or more of the Provinces to be partitioned. The members will be two Muslims and two non-Muslims, elected by the Provincial Legislature, with a neutral chairman to be agreed upon, but if there is no agreement upon a Chairman one will be appointed by the Viceroy;

(viii) Minor adjustments of the new boundaries will be permissible, either by agreement or as the result of the findings of a Boundary Commission. Such adjustments will not extend beyond boundary tahsils or subdivisions. The decision of the Boundary Commission, in each case, will be final;

(ix) There will be a general election in the N.W.F.P. as soon as possible. A fresh and clear mandate in this Province is necessary.

5. Very early steps will be taken to implement these decisions and announcements will be made by H.E. the Viceroy from time to time, after consultation with the Party leaders.

6. H.M.G. hope that as soon as the intentions of the Provinces in this matter are known it will be possible for the Indian States to take their proper place in the new India.

7. The problem arising out of the need to establish satisfactory relations with the tribes on the North Western and North Eastern Frontiers of India will also require urgent examination as soon as the Grouping is known.

Appendix 'D'

REVISED PROGRAMME OF ACTION
(To be telegraphed with the statement to H.M.G.)

N.B. This will be subject to alteration after discussion with the parties.

PART I ACTION PRIOR TO THE ANNOUNCEMENT
STEP I *Strengthening of the Cabinet*

1. H.E. to approach Congress and ask them to agree that the Muslim League should have one more seat in the Cabinet, provided this is taken by MR. JINNAH himself.

2. If the Congress agree, H.E. to speak to MR. JINNAH. MR. JINNAH should be told that if no agreement *on the basis of the Cabinet Mission's Plan* is reached in a very short time H.M.G. will announce a decision on the basis of the small PAKISTAN. It will be a great advantage to be able to discuss plans for the transfer of power in a small committee *inside the Government* fully representative of the major parties.

STEP II *Simla Talks*

3. Whether MR. JINNAH agrees or not he and the other principal leaders (NEHRU, PATEL, LIAQUAT, and BALDEV SINGH) should be invited to take part in discussions at DELHI starting on about the 5th May. NEHRU and JIN-NAH should arrange that their Working Committees are in DELHI. A determined effort should be made to secure compromise on the basis of the Cabinet Mission Plan.

4. If it is impossible to obtain agreement on the basis of the Cabinet Mission Plan the announcement (telegram No.   dated   ) should be made at once.

PART II ACTION AFTER THE ANNOUNCEMENT
STEP III *Partition*

5. Subject to discussion with the parties which should begin immediately after the announcement the arrangements for Partition should be as follows:—

(*a*) *Section A.*, i.e. the provinces of MADRAS, BOMBAY, U.P., BIHAR, C.P. and ORISSA.
    The Constituent Assembly will consist of the members of the existing Constituent Assembly representing these Provinces, and any other Provinces that may accede.

(*b*) *Other Provinces*, i.e. the PUNJAB, N.W.F.P., SIND, BENGAL and ASSAM.
    (1) The PUNJAB, BENGAL and ASSAM will have been split up as indicated in the draft announcement.
    (2) The Provinces, including the new Provinces formed by Partition, may either:—
        (i)   accede to Section A., or
        (ii) form a joint Constituent Assembly with other Provinces, or
        (iii) stand out independently.
    (3) The members of each of the existing Legislative Assemblies in the PUNJAB and BENGAL will be invited to sit in two separate bodies representing the new Provinces. These bodies will be the Constituent Assemblies for their respective Provinces, and it will be their duty to frame the Provincial constitutions.
    (4) The Constituent Assemblies so formed will set up Committees which will deal with all matters arising out of the partition including

especially the planning and the reorganisation of the administrative departments in the Provinces on a partition basis and the preparations for taking over Central subjects.

(5) Similarly in ASSAM members of the existing Legislature representing territorial constituencies in SYLHET will be invited to sit separately and decide whether to accede to the new Muslim Province in BENGAL or to remain in ASSAM.

(6) For the rest of ASSAM and for the N.W.F.P. and for SIND, the Provincial Constituent Assemblies will be either the existing Legislature (after the elections in the case of the N.W.F.P. and excluding the SYLHET representatives in the case of ASSAM) or the Members from these Provinces already elected to the existing Constituent Assembly. The alternatives will be a matter for discussion with the Parties.

(7) It will be for these Constituent Assemblies to decide whether to exercise the option stated in sub-para. (*b*)(2) above.

(c) *Baluchistan*

The constituent assembly for British BALUCHISTAN will be the members of the SHAHI JIRGA and the non-official elected members of the QUETTA Municipality. The constituent assembly so formed will exercise the option stated in sub-para. (*b*)(2) above.

STEP IV

6. From the date of the announcement until June, 1948, we should:—

(a) maintain the present Central Government and support its authority, especially in the Congress Provinces;

(b) try to secure coalition governments in the Provinces;

(c) give every help to prospective successor authorities to prepare themselves to receive power on the due date. It will be necessary to set up separate administrative machinery in the new Groups and Provinces, and for those concerned to examine in consultation together the innumerable administrative, financial and defence problems arising out of the Partition, including those that arise out of the need to establish workable relations with the tribes on the North Western and North Eastern Frontiers of India;

(d) continue the efforts to secure by treaty or constitutional provision some form of central authority to cover at least the minimum subjects.

STEP V *Demission of Power*

7. If when the time comes in 1948 no central authority of any kind has been set up power will be demitted to executives set up by the section or provincial Constituent Assemblies, as the case may be.

182

Sardar Patel to Rear-Admiral Viscount Mountbatten of Burma

Mountbatten Papers. Official Correspondence Files: Press and Publicity,
Part I(a)

NEW DELHI, *20 April 1947*

My dear Lord Mountbatten,

I received your letter No. 1427 dated the 19th April[1] yesterday afternoon on my return from Bombay after my Gujerat tour.

2. In the message which I sent to the All India Newspaper Editors' Conference, I had already appealed to the Editors to assist Government in dealing with the difficult times through which we are passing. When I was at Surat, I received a suggestion from my Secretary that I should send another message to the Conference to take action regarding the appeal issued by Gandhiji and Jinnah. Since the League Press is not represented in the Conference, I thought it futile to make a suggestion to one side only to follow up the appeal. I am, therefore, issuing another message to all newspapers asking them to print the Gandhi-Jinnah appeal repeatedly in a prominent position, and particularly at any time when local tension or similar circumstances require it. A copy of my message is enclosed for your perusal.[2]

3. The All India Radio are being instructed similarly to use the appeal at frequent intervals, and in particular in their rural programmes which reach listeners who may not be able to read the newspapers. A letter is also going to all Associations of Film Exhibitors urging them to ask of their members to use the appeal on a cinema slide in various languages to be shown in intervals or at other appropriate times in their programmes. Finally, an Express letter is going to all Provincial Governments informing them of the action taken by us and suggesting that they should produce posters and leaflets in the languages of the provinces and give them the widest and most prominent distribution possible.

4. If you consider that my Department can be useful in any other way in this direction, please let me know, and I shall see that the needful is done.

5. But I feel I should be failing in my duty and be untrue to myself, if I concealed my innermost conviction that unless and until the Muslim League is compelled to withdraw its "Direct Action" Resolution and this step is followed up by active attempts to keep its followers in check and under control, the necessary psychological atmosphere in which the appeal could strike a responsive chord would be completely lacking, and the appeal itself would not serve much useful purpose. It is futile to expect an ordinary man in the street to exercise restraint or to make any positive contribution to the restoration of

feelings of amity if incidents are happening which outrage and inflame public opinion. After reading an account of the wholesale murders, looting, arson and forced conversions of non-Muslims in Dera Ismail Khan, there would indeed be few among them who would be able to pay any attention to an appeal to eschew violence. I am enclosing a typical example of the letters[3] which I receive from different corners of India together with the cutting to which the writer refers. I am also sending you another cutting which gives the allegations in greater detail. Such are the events on which the mass mind is being fed and such is the reaction which is being produced! While untold sufferings and outrages are being perpetrated on non-Muslims and minorities are being systematically eliminated in the Muslim majority areas and organised whole-sale preparations are being made to "capture" the Province of Assam, without any corresponding effort on the part of the League leaders to deal with their followers on the spot, in contrast Gandhiji is buried in the midst of his self-imposed mission in Bihar calculated to assuage the feelings of Muslims in regard to a tragedy which overtook them six months ago and which was quelled under the active intervention of Congress Members of the Interim Government within a week. The signature of Mr Jinnah on the appeal is a mockery if he does not himself feel the urge to visit the areas such as Dera Ismail Khan, Rawalpindi and Multan which are, or have been, the scenes of orgies of murder, arson and loot. If he is sincere in his appeal, his place is quite clearly in the Frontier to restrain his followers and not in Delhi.

5. Ever since you assumed office and I had my first interview with you, I have been pressing upon you the need for urgent action. While I do not deny that the signature of Mr Jinnah on the truce would be a creditable achievement, if sincerely followed up, I feel that the time which we are letting slip and every day that these tragedies are being perpetrated without securing positive action such as I have suggested above, would make the success of your mission more remote than ever. You have already acquired a reputation for being a man of quick decision and action and a person possessed of a great sense of urgency. India has also been impressed by the earnestness of purpose and the message of goodwill underlying your first speech on the assumption of office, but the sands of time are running out and I hope you will believe me when I say that the man in the street is already commenting that a month has elapsed, while bestiality still prevails in the N.W.F.P. and parts of Punjab and Bengal. I shall appeal to you with all the earnestness at my command to create, by securing a

[1] In this letter Lord Mountbatten informed Sardar Patel that Dr John Matthai had suggested that he initiate a move to secure a proper follow-up by the Press of all parties to the Gandhi-Jinnah appeal. Lord Mountbatten asked Sardar Patel, as Member for Information and Broadcasting, to let him know what plans he had for inducing the Press to implement the appeal in a realistic way. Mountbatten Papers, Official Correspondence Files: Press and Publicity, Part I(a).
[2] Not printed.   [3] Not printed.

firm and positive action from the League such as I have stressed above, a psychological atmosphere in which the excellent appeal issued by both the leaders will touch the hearts of the people. Therein lies the only chance of putting an end to the tension and the insecurity, which the poisoned atmosphere, ever since the passage of the "Direct Action" Resolution in July and the first sample of its enforcement on 16th August 1946, has created and continued to promote, and which the attempts of the League, after the declaration of the 20th February, to "capture" the Provinces of Assam, N.W.F.P. and the Punjab have accentuated, and to the resultant tragedies which have overtaken thousands of men, women and children.

Yours sincerely,

VALLABHBHAI PATEL

183

Sir A. Clow (Assam) to Rear-Admiral Viscount Mountbatten of Burma

R/3/1/130: ff 213–15

No. 254.   GOVERNMENT HOUSE, SHILLONG,
20 April 1947

Dear Lord Mountbatten,

When I was in Delhi Your Excellency asked me for a note on the relation between the Assamese Hindus' objection to grouping with Bengal and the arrangement of constituencies. The enclosed note will, I hope, explain the position.[1]

Yours sincerely,

A. G. CLOW

Enclosure to No. 183

ASSAM AND GROUPING

The population of Assam, at the 1941 census, consisted of (in lakhs):—

Caste Hindus	35
Scheduled Castes	7
Muslims	34
Tribals & Christians	26

Muslims, owing to the Bengal famine and other causes, have gained ground since then, and some tribals were recorded as Hindus. But ignoring this, the position broadly is that the Caste Hindus, the Muslims and the others form three almost equal groups. In the legislature however, out of 99 Indian members, the unreserved general seats are 40 and thanks to the Poona Pact no

Scheduled Caste candidate opposed to them has much chance in the 7 reserved seats. The general constituencies contain such a large majority of Caste Hindus that, at the cost of putting in some 'stooges', they can command 47 seats plus the 3 Indian planting and commercial seats, making 50. Muslims have 34 seats. There are only 15 other seats, of which only 9 are exclusively tribal or Christian. Thus, ignoring the European seats, the Caste Hindus can expect to start with a full half of a house of 99 and in present circumstances have the resources to capture a proportion of the remainder.

2. But on an outright system of separate electorates the Caste Hindus would start with no more than the Muslims, and the intermediate groups, consisting mainly of tribals and Christians, would hold the balance. With the Pakistan issue out of the way, most of these would be as likely to side with the Muslims as with the Hindus. This would be no unnatural alliance for all these groups are under-privileged, and so are the Muslims. Between the introduction of the reforms in 1937, when about a third of the seats went to candidates associated neither with Congress nor the Muslims, and 1945, we had Hindu-dominated ministries for about 18 months, a 93 Administration for 8 months and Muslim-dominated ministries for nearly 6 years. So that, even if there was strictly proportionate representation, the Caste Hindus could no longer rely on dominating the situation. It is, however, conceivable that in Group C, which would have a Muslim majority, the distribution would not be on the strictly proportionate basis indicated by the 1941 census. Muslims might be increased to allow for the substantial fresh immigration, backward peoples might be given weightage, the excluded areas would come in, and further castes might be cut out of the Caste Hindu total and treated separately.

3. Thus the Caste Hindus are apprehensive, and not without cause, that a constitution framed for Assam in Section C would put them in a far weaker position than they hold at present, and perhaps an even weaker position than they deserve. And they would have a poor chance of getting secession approved at the next ensuing election, for the enfranchised groups might well feel content with a situation which gave them so much power. This is not the only objection the Assamese Hindus have to grouping: they dislike the Bengalis even when they are not Muslims. But it is, and has always been, the main objection. At the fight in the All-India Congress Committee in January, one of our ministers openly avowed it, saying

"There were so many groups in Assam—hill tribes, people from the plains, Ahoms and so on—and if they all got separate electorates, there would be no hope for the people of Assam to achieve unity in future and opting out of the group would be out of the question."

[1] Lord Mountbatten thanked Sir A. Clow for his letter and note in a letter of 25 April 1947. R/3/1/130: f 216.

This was almost an admission of Saadulla's claim that a plebiscite in Assam would vote for grouping. I do not feel so sure as my Hindu ministers seem to be that, under a wide franchise and without separate electorates, Caste Hindu rule will last a very long time. But it will have a far bigger chance of lasting under a constitution framed by the present Assam legislature or the present Constituent Assembly than under one framed by Section C.

4. If it had been arranged that the Section would frame only the constitution for the Bengal cum Assam group and would accept the wishes of the Assam representatives regarding their own provincial constitution, the opposition to grouping here would have been small. It is not easy to be sure about the position now, but a convention to this effect might diminish opposition sufficiently to permit Assam to enter and co-operate in the Section, if it becomes a reality. There is substance in the plea that it is unfair to Assam that its constitution should be framed by a body in which 5 out of 6 members are Bengalis. Bardoloi's claim that Assam should not have its constitution framed by Bengal has consequently had some appeal. But I believe that what he fears is that Assam would get a constitution framed by the Muslims of Bengal and Assam, with the aid of Scheduled Caste men in Bengal.

184

Record of Interview between Rear-Admiral Viscount Mountbatten of Burma and the Maharaja of Patiala

Mountbatten Papers. Viceroy's Interview No. 78

TOP SECRET   *20 April 1947*

His Highness dined with me, and I had a talk with him from 2100 to 2145 hours.

After referring to my last visit to Patiala, His Highness took the usual line of expressing his intense grief that the British were deserting their allies and friends of long standing by their departure from India. He also said that if we were proposing to do that, he thought it had been very unfair of us to weaken the States in the way we had done over the last few years instead of strengthening them so that they could stand on their own legs when we went.

He told me that he had a large number (I think 20,000) of Sikh refugees from the massacre areas of the Punjab, who were constituting a great problem for him.

He said he was trying to keep Tara Singh and Kartar Singh in order, but they were of course apt to be inflammatory; and he told me that he thought that they and the Raja of Faridkot were being extremely foolish in the plans they were trying to hatch (and about which the Raja of Faridkot had told me). He had warned the Raja of Faridkot that any idea that the departure of the British could be made the occasion of a 19th Century grabbing match was out of the question and could not fail to have the most disastrous repercussions ultimately on the grabbers.

H.H. of Patiala said that although he would do all in his power to preserve peace and avoid strife, he could not but be worried at the prospect of our departure, since he believed that chaos and riot were the least that could be expected after we had gone, and that they would be lucky if they escaped civil war.

As usual, he asked me whether we would not reconsider our decision to go, and I gave him the usual answer.

185

Minutes of Viceroy's Eighteenth Staff Meeting

Mountbatten Papers

TOP SECRET

Those present at this Meeting held at The Viceroy's House, New Delhi on 21 April 1947 at 10 am were: Rear-Admiral Viscount Mountbatten of Burma, Lord Ismay, Sir E. Mieville, Mr Abell, Mr I. D. Scott, Captain Brockman, Mr Campbell-Johnson, Lieutenant-Colonel Erskine Crum

Item 2

SITUATION IN THE N.W.F.P.

HIS EXCELLENCY THE VICEROY said that he intended to speak to Mr. Liaquat Ali Khan that afternoon concerning the possibility of holding fresh elections in the N.W.F.P. He would point out that Pandit Nehru had stated that he would not stand in the Viceroy's way if he insisted on fresh elections; but would emphasize that his decision on this matter would be taken on the basis of whether or not he considered that the Muslim League was responsible enough to be given the chance to form a Ministry. He would add that he saw fully Pandit Nehru's reasoning that to order fresh elections at the present moment would appear to be surrendering to force; and that his decision would be enormously influenced by the ability of the Muslim League to display political discipline and to show a potential responsibility to govern. He would make it clear that he could not possibly support attempts to overthrow Constitutional Governments by violence, and would in fact use force against such attempts. He would say that a first gesture on the part of the Muslim League might be to tone down the attitude of *Dawn* and other Muslim League newspapers in this matter.

MR. SCOTT said that he was not sure that the Muslim League leaders had full control over their followers in the N.W.F.P. If it was locally decided there to carry on the agitations against the ban on processions, he doubted whether Mr. Jinnah and Mr. Liaquat Ali Khan would be able to stop it.

HIS EXCELLENCY THE VICEROY:—

decided to take the line which he had indicated above with Mr. Liaquat Ali Khan when he saw him that afternoon.

Addendum to No. 185

Uncirculated Record of Discussion No. 11

Mountbatten Papers

TOP SECRET

HIS EXCELLENCY THE VICEROY drew particular attention to the Record[1] of the interview which he had had with Mr. Liaquat Ali Khan on Saturday 19th April.

HIS EXCELLENCY THE VICEROY said that he felt that, in deciding on a solution, he was torn between two opposite requirements. First it was essential not to lose an hour in reaching a decision. Secondly, it would be wrong to reach any decision without the Indian Leaders knowing what it implied and involved. At the present time the Indian leaders had no conception of what Partition of India, resulting in a truncated Pakistan, would involve. If only they could be given a year's education and experience to find this out they might gain a very different outlook. Therefore he felt that some saving clause must be introduced into the announcement containing the decision. This was a principle which required examination. Perhaps the decision now taken should be made subject to ratification at a future date in about a year's time.

LORD ISMAY said that he felt that the inclusion of any definite escape clause which gave the impression of avoiding finality in the decision would be wrong. The climax should come on the announcement of the decision. He felt also that it would be perhaps unnecessary to include an escape clause as the bewildering complexity of what they were faced with might make the Indian Leaders change their minds after trying to work things out.

MR. ABELL suggested that the opening paragraph of the draft announcement, which was contained in the paper[2] before the meeting, could be suitably amended to get over this difficulty by inclusion of some reference to the fact that efforts would continue in the interim period to persuade the Indian Leaders to come to agreement.

HIS EXCELLENCY THE VICEROY said that he intended to prepare a personal statement which he would probably broadcast immediately after the announcement containing the decision. He would give an account of what had happened during the previous two months and paint a picture of the conditions to which he felt that a decision in favour of Partition would lead. It was essential that the world as well as India should know that India was choosing her own future.

HIS EXCELLENCY THE VICEROY said that the opening paragraphs of the draft announcement should also be amended to make this point clear. There should be no hint that the British were deciding on India's future. Their one object was to demit power as the Indians themselves wanted. The world must be informed that the choice was in the hands of the people of India. HIS EXCELLENCY THE VICEROY added that he believed that both Pandit Nehru and Mr. Jinnah were most susceptible to world opinion.

During discussion of the draft letter at Appendix 'B' to the paper before the meeting which contained an invitation to Indian leaders to attend a conference, HIS EXCELLENCY THE VICEROY decided that he would not ask Mr. Gandhi to attend but would rather write to tell him that the meeting would be held and that he would be kept in close touch with events.

MR. ABELL stated that he had been told by a newspaper correspondent who had seen Mr. Jinnah two days previously that the latter was in a most disturbed state of mind. It was possible that Mr. Jinnah was ill but more probable that he was bewildered by the impact of events. MR. SCOTT said that he had also got the impression that Mr. Jinnah was indeed becoming seriously troubled by the prospect opening out before him. He felt that this process should be allowed to take its course; there would be a psychological moment at which to take advantage of it.

[1] No. 178.   [2] No. 181.

186

Record of Interview between Rear-Admiral Viscount Mountbatten of Burma and Mr Abdur Rab Nishtar

Mountbatten Papers. Viceroy's Interview No. 80

TOP SECRET   *21 April 1947, 12 noon–1 pm*

I gave Mr. Nishtar the same sort of general description of the present state of planning for the transfer of power as I had given to Mr. Ghazanfar Ali Khan just previously.[1] He protested violently against my adopting the same rule with Provinces as with India as a whole about partition, pointing out that in the case of Pakistan there was a very good reason which was absent in the case for the partition of Provinces. He said that the Hindus had a Central Government already, or were about to set one up as a result of the Constituent Assembly, whereas the Muslims were never going to have a Central Government of their own, and would be in a permanent minority in the Hindu Central Govern-

[1] See Viceroy's Interview No. 79. Mountbatten Papers.

ment. For that reason it was necessary to have completely sovereign States so that they could negotiate on the same level, irrespective of numbers. This in his opinion did not apply to the Provinces; in any case vast numbers of the Hindus and Muslims were geographically bound to remain within opposite areas, and it seemed a crime to break up the economic unity of the Punjab or Bengal merely because some of these provinces had majority areas of the opposite community.

I said that I would not contest his argument, since it was quite impossible for me to use such a weak argument to differentiate between the demand for Pakistan and the demand for partition within Provinces.

The second point which he wanted to raise was that of getting out of Section 93 in the Punjab. He talked at great length about this, but his arguments were immaterial, since I told him that having seen the Sikh delegation I knew that any attempt to hold fresh elections and to have a Muslim League Government would result in the Sikhs rising and fighting, which I was determined to avoid at all costs. In fact I asked him to use his influence to stop further strife in the Punjab.

Finally, I called upon him to use his exceptional influence in the Frontier with the Muslim League to call off their further activities. I gave him a brief history of the discussions with Dr. Khan Sahib, and told him that the offer to release 5,000 political prisoners was definitely the first gesture towards a real truce. He denied this, since he said they had so hedged about their amnesty that they would be able to keep anybody they liked in prison, and that those leaders whom they could not afford to let out had already been charged with violence, even though they had only taken part in peaceful processions. He further said that he doubted whether any one of the 5,000 prisoners would take advantage of the release offer; he thought they would insist on remaining in prison. He told me that so long as Dr. Khan Sahib and his Government were in command they would continue to make provocative trouble, which would be hard for the Muslim League to sit down to.

I then told him that the situation was quite clear. If he and his friends could not control the Muslim League on the Frontier, and would not insist upon their taking their release from prison when it was offered, and on their not taking part in any further provocative demonstrations, then they would be playing straight into the hands of the Congress Government, who would declare that they were being subjected to the use of force to try and overthrow the Government, and would in the result call upon me to give them additional support which I should have no choice but to provide. In fact I had every intention of providing it, and would draft in the necessary additional troops without hesitation. The one way, in fact, which would prevent me from giving an impartial decision as to whether fresh elections were necessary, would be for the Muslim League to continue to use force and to make trouble on the Frontier.

He said it would be very difficult to carry out my wishes unless he could make a statement to his people up there to the effect that I was now considering the question of whether to order fresh elections; in fact, he said, unless he might repeat what I had told him publicly, he did not see how he could exercise any restraining influence.

I told him that I could not agree to his repeating what I had said to him; that he must use it merely as personal advice of his own. But I told him that there would shortly be an announcement that I was going to the Frontier next week, and that it stood to reason that when I went there I should want to see the leaders of both sides; that I would give a decision on the N.W.F.P. question at the same time as on the wider position of India as a whole—within the next month; and that this was the line I suggested would be the best to pursue.

I left him finally with an exhortation to do his best to stop his people, in their own interests, from continuing to make trouble.

187

Record of Interview between Rear-Admiral Viscount Mountbatten of Burma and the Maharaj-Rana of Dholpur

Mountbatten Papers. Viceroy's Interview No. 81

TOP SECRET   *21 April 1947, 1.50–2.10 pm*

His Highness expressed grave concern at the challenge which had been thrown down by Pandit Nehru, at the States' People's Congress Conference at Gwalior,[1] to the Rulers of Indian States; by which he endeavoured to force them to choose between abandoning the arrangements made by the Cabinet Mission for their joining the Constituent Assembly or incurring the hostility of Congress. He said they had no option but to take up the challenge, since it appeared to be grossly unfair to try and blackmail them in this way, when they had done nothing wrong, other than to be one of the few sections in India which were falling in with the Cabinet Mission's wishes.

He was convinced that no solution could be implemented by June 1948, and that we should have to stay. He was further convinced that no part of India could stand outside the British Commonwealth, and he asked my views on this.

I replied that I would in no circumstances stay after June 1948, or consider

[1] See No. 181, note 2.

acting on any request by a single section of India to be allowed to remain within the Commonwealth; it would have to be backed respectively by a demand from *all* the parties in India.

He said he had a mutual friend who was working on Sardar Vallabhbhai Patel to try and induce him to see the impossibility of India leaving the Empire. I asked him to write and let me know if anything transpired from this which he felt it might be of use to me to know. I pointed out that I could obviously be no party to any discussions on these lines, or even express any opinion.

188

Minutes of Viceroy's Nineteenth Staff Meeting, Item 1

Mountbatten Papers

Those present at this Meeting held at The Viceroy's House, New Delhi on 21 April 1947 at 3.30 pm were: Rear-Admiral Viscount Mountbatten of Burma, Lord Ismay, Sir E. Mieville, Sir C. Corfield, Mr Abell, Mr Christie, Captain Brockman, Mr I. D. Scott, Mr Campbell-Johnson, Lieutenant-Colonel Erskine Crum

THE STATES

HIS EXCELLENCY THE VICEROY said that the Maharaj-Rana of Dholpur and The Nawab of Rampur, who had come to lunch with him that day, had asked his advice on what line to take in the situation created by Pandit Nehru's recent speech at Gwalior, at which he had given the States what amounted to an ultimatum either to join the Constituent Assembly or be treated as hostile. He expected similar questioning from the Nawab of Bhopal and Sir C. P. Ramaswami Aiyer. As he saw the position, the Cabinet Mission had laid it down that the States should join the Constituent Assembly at a certain stage, which had in fact not yet been reached because the Muslim League had not joined it. Could it, though, be argued that this stage would ever be reached if the Muslim League continued not to come in?

SIR CONRAD CORFIELD said that it had been the Cabinet Mission's intention that the States should be given appropriate representation in the final Constituent Assembly. In the preliminary stage—which had already taken place—the States were represented by a Negotiating Committee. The final stage would come when representatives of Sections and States were to "reassemble to settle the Union Constitution". He added that he had advised the Maharaj-Rana of Dholpur to wait until a new plan was announced or full acceptance by both major parties of the Cabinet Mission's plan was obtained.

HIS EXCELLENCY THE VICEROY:—
   (i) decided to tender this same advice to representatives of States who might ask his guidance in future;
   (ii) invited the Political Adviser to inform him in a letter of the exact legal position, and show why he was in his rights in tendering such advice;
   (iii) decided to speak to Pandit Nehru on the basis of this letter; and to ask him not to take any steps to put his "ultimatum" into force until the issue of an announcement giving the over-all decision.

189

Sir C. Corfield to Mr Abell

R/1/30/40: ff 66–8

NEW DELHI, *21 April 1947*

Dear Abell,

Pandit Nehru has threatened the Rulers of Indian States that, if they do not forthwith send their representatives to the Constituent Assembly, they will be regarded as hostile and will have to bear the consequences of being so regarded. Some Rulers have already enquired what action they should take in view of this threat.

2. The Cabinet Mission plan provided for three stages in the work of the Constituent Assembly—a preliminary stage, for the purposes specified in paragraph 19(iv); an intermediate stage for the settling of Provincial and Group constitutions (paragraph 19(v)); and a final stage for settling the Union constitution (paragraph 19(vi)). At the preliminary stage the States were to be represented by a Negotiating Committee, and at the final stage by representatives not exceeding 93 in number (paragraph 19(ii)). The States were not concerned with the intermediate stage.

3. That the States were only expected to send representatives to the final Constituent Assembly is perfectly clear from paragraph 19(ii). Arguments that States should send representatives to the Constituent Assembly at an earlier stage have been based on the use of the word "reassemble" in paragraph 19(vi); but such arguments are very far fetched, and ignore the plain meaning of the Cabinet Mission as expressed in paragraph 19(ii) with its reference to States' representation in "the final Constituent Assembly".

4. Though the only reasonable interpretation of the Cabinet Mission plan is that the States were expected to send their representatives to the Constituent

Assembly at the final stage i.e. when representatives of the Sections reassemble to settle the Union constitution, the parties concerned are at liberty to make any changes by agreement, and some States have agreed to earlier participation. But the fact is that the Constituent Assembly as now constituted is not the fully representative Assembly which "it is of the essence of the plan" that it should be (paragraph 6 of H.M.G.'s Statement of February 20th); and in my view Rulers would be fully justified in deferring any decision about joining it until it is known whether it will become the fully representative body envisaged by the Cabinet Mission or whether negotiations will have to be conducted with another Assembly or an Assembly in a different form. The decision to be made by Rulers need not be deferred for long, since the new form, if any, must clearly be determined in the very near future.

5. I therefore propose to advise any Rulers who consult me that they are justified in deferring a decision about joining the Constituent Assembly until H.M.G. have decided to what authorities they propose to transfer power in British India. I shall be glad to know whether this advice has the Crown Representative's approval

Yours sincerely,
C. L. CORFIELD

190

Minutes of Viceroy's Fifth Miscellaneous Meeting

Mountbatten Papers

TOP SECRET

Those present at this Meeting held at The Viceroy's House, New Delhi on 21 April 1947 at 4.30 pm were: Rear–Admiral Viscount Mountbatten of Burma, Mr Liaquat Ali Khan, Lord Ismay, Sir E. Mieville, Mr Abell; Lieutenant-Colonel Erskine Crum

Item 1

THE NORTH WEST FRONTIER PROVINCE

HIS EXCELLENCY THE VICEROY said that he intended to visit the North West Frontier Province the following week. He pointed out to Mr Liaquat Ali Khan that, though he had a certain sympathy with the Muslim League problem in the North West Frontier Province, he could not be a party to surrendering to any form of violence. He would be gravely embarrassed in giving a decision in favour of elections if this violence continued—particularly if it should so be that the present Government there called upon him to use force to suppress this violence.

HIS EXCELLENCY THE VICEROY said that anything which Mr Liaquat Ali Khan could do in this matter to help induce a more peaceful atmosphere, particularly by influence on *Dawn* and the rest of the Muslim League press, would be of great assistance.

MR LIAQUAT ALI KHAN gave his opinion that the statement[1] which had lately been put out by the Government of the North West Frontier Province saying that political prisoners would be released would not have any effect. He went on to make allegations of oppression by that Government, but finally said that he would do all he could to help in the way requested by His Excellency.

Item 2

THE CHOICE BY PROVINCES OF THEIR OWN FUTURE

HIS EXCELLENCY THE VICEROY told Mr Liaquat Ali Khan that one of the proposals now under examination was that Provinces should be left to choose their own future. This method of reaching a decision would give the greatest measure of choice to the Indian people themselves, and would involve a higher degree of democracy than making a decision after consulting only the leaders.

There was then a discussion on what means could best be employed in the different Provinces most accurately to ascertain the will of the people. Among the suggestions discussed were the following: Sub-paragraphs (a), (b), (c), (d) & (e)

(a) *Madras, Bombay, U.P., Bihar, C.P., Orissa and Sind*
The elected members of the Constituent Assembly for these Provinces should take the decision.

(b) *N.W.F.P.*
It was agreed that
(i) The number of elected members of the Constituent Assembly for this Province was too small to leave the decision in their hands;
(ii) to leave the vote to them, or any other smaller body chosen on a population basis by the Legislative Assembly, might also well result in a Congress Government getting voted into Pakistan, which would be a farcical situation;
(iii) it was therefore probably best to leave the decision to the Legislative Assembly itself, after new elections.

(c) *The Punjab*
It was agreed that the decision here should be taken by the elected members of the Constituent Assembly, (possibly re-elected by the Legislative Assembly on a territorial basis). A decision not to partition the Punjab would, to be valid, have to be taken by a majority vote both of the Muslim League members and of the non-Muslim League members.

[1] See No. 179.

356 THE TRANSFER OF POWER

There would have to be an arbitrary demarcation of the partition line first, which would be subject to compromise later.

(d) *Bengal*

It was agreed that the procedure should be as follows:

(i) whether or not to partition would first be decided by the elected representatives to the Constituent Assembly; the Muslim League members and the non-Muslim League members voting separately; a two-thirds majority of each of these bodies in favour of partition being required in order to carry that issue;

(ii) a boundary commission would then make an arbitrary partition, subject to compromise later;

(iii) the issue would then be referred, for confirmation by the people of Western Bengal, to those on the electoral roll for secondary elections— provided that, on investigation, the scheduled castes were adequately represented. This procedure would not, MR LIAQUAT ALI KHAN felt, take more than a month;

(e) *Assam*

It was agreed that the elected members of the Assembly for Sylhet should make the decision as to that district's future. For the remainder of the Province, the procedure would be as in (a) above.

Plebiscites

HIS EXCELLENCY THE VICEROY gave his opinion that the ideal method of ascertaining the will of the people, particularly in Western Bengal, would be by means of plebiscites. However he considered, and MR LIAQUAT ALI KHAN fully agreed, that the time factor put all possibility of plebiscites out of the question.

Weightage

HIS EXCELLENCY THE VICEROY felt that the psychological disadvantage of abolishing the weightage system in Legislative Assemblies for the purpose of ascertaining the will of the people would cause an outcry and would outweigh any advantages.

The North West Frontier Province

MR LIAQUAT ALI KHAN declared that he would prefer the North West Frontier Province to be part of Pakistan, though it might cost $3\frac{1}{2}$ crores, rather than it should be part of Hindustan (which would result in Pakistan having Hindustan armies on both sides).

The Framing of Constitutions

MR LIAQUAT ALI KHAN astounded the meeting by saying that he thought it should be possible to frame a Constitution for Pakistan within six months.

The Scheduled Castes

HIS EXCELLENCY THE VICEROY asked Mr Liaquat Ali Khan whether he thought that the scheduled castes in Western Bengal would have the least idea what they were voting about. MR LIAQUAT ALI KHAN replied that the issue would be quite clear to them—the choice between oppression under the caste Hindus and freedom under the Muslims. He added that he considered the Viceroy's responsibility to give them every chance to escape from the domination of the caste Hindus was very great. He also pointed out that the scheduled castes and the Muslims together had a majority in Western Bengal.

Item 3

THE RETENTION OF INDIA WITHIN THE COMMONWEALTH

During discussion of this subject, MR LIAQUAT ALI KHAN made the following points:

(a) In his opinion India would not be able to stand on her own legs by June 1948, whether united or divided.

(b) He could not answer for India as a whole, the question whether or not she would ask to remain in the British Commonwealth after June 1948. He felt it possible that the Hindus would prefer to stew in their own juice rather than ask. But Pakistan would certainly ask to be allowed to remain in.

(c) He would have preferred a decision by the British, instead of to leave in June 1948, to stay for 5 years and gradually transfer, as liquidator, the Central subjects to the successor authorities.

(d) He would not trust the Hindus to observe any provisions or safeguards in connection with defence after the British had left.

(e) He had definite information that there was already a movement among some Hindu officers to establish a military dictatorship after the British had left.

(f) He, as a politician, considered himself incapable of making plans to split the Armed Forces. He felt that the British should make such plans, starting forthwith. He had put up a note[2] to the Defence Committee to this effect. If Pakistan got their own Army before the British left, there might be a chance of success for a Combined Chiefs of Staff organization with Hindustan.

Item 4

AN INTERMEDIATE PLAN

HIS EXCELLENCY THE VICEROY asked Mr Liaquat Ali Khan whether he could suggest any alternative plan, short of the Cabinet Mission's plan, which would not result in complete Pakistan and all the great disadvantages, which absolute partition would entail.

MR LIAQUAT ALI KHAN was very difficult at first, and said that he could think of nothing; he foresaw a worse fate for the Muslims in any form of

[2] See No. 215.

united India than even in a truncated Pakistan. But eventually he suggested that a possible alternative would be for two independent sovereign states to be set up and the Constituent Assemblies of the two to devise machinery for running those matters, connected with Defence, which were of common interest.

MR LIAQUAT ALI KHAN said that the only hope, in a meeting of the Indian leaders, was to put two clear-cut alternatives before them, both showing full implications. He did not think that such a meeting would be so likely to succeed as individual conversation between His Excellency and party leaders.

He also asked that, in such a meeting, the Cabinet Mission's plan should not even be mentioned—because Congress would doubtless intimate immediate acceptance of it, and the Muslim League would then be put in an impossible position. HIS EXCELLENCY THE VICEROY said that he would have to offer the Cabinet Mission's plan again at such a meeting—if only for form's sake.

191

Rear-Admiral Viscount Mountbatten of Burma to Sardar Patel

Mountbatten Papers. Official Correspondence Files: Press and Publicity, Part I(a)

No. 1427   NEW DELHI, *22 April 1947*
Dear Sardar Patel,
Thank you for your letter of 20 April.[1] I note what you are doing about the Press and I am glad you have made an appeal to support the one by Mr Gandhi and Mr Jinnah.

I sympathise with much that you say in paragraphs 4 and 5 but you know the difficulties. I have talked to Mr Liaquat Ali Khan, Mr Ghazanfar Ali Khan and Mr Nishtar and asked them to do whatever they can to reduce the tension on the Frontier and to ensure that *Dawn* takes a more reasonable line. I am going to the Frontier myself in a week's time.

Yours sincerely,
MOUNTBATTEN OF BURMA

[1] No. 182.

192

Minutes of Viceroy's Twentieth Staff Meeting

Mountbatten Papers

TOP SECRET

Those present at this Meeting held at The Viceroy's House, New Delhi, on 22 April 1947 at 10 am were: Rear-Admiral Viscount Mountbatten of Burma, Lord Ismay, Sir E. Mieville, Mr Abell, Mr Christie, Captain Brockman, Mr Campbell-Johnson, Lieutenant-Colonel Erskine Crum

Item 2

THE RETENTION OF INDIA WITHIN THE BRITISH COMMONWEALTH

HIS EXCELLENCY THE VICEROY pointed out that representatives of approximately half the inhabitants of India had already asked to be allowed to remain within the British Commonwealth. These included the Muslim League, the Scheduled Castes and the States—although all the States' subjects might not be of the same opinion as their rulers. All these applicants seemed to think that they were doing Great Britain a favour by asking to stay in. HIS EXCELLENCY THE VICEROY asked whether it was considered that there was any possibility of granting some form of Dominion status to India as a whole or, more probably, to the separate parts of India in the near future. In such an arrangement the Governor General might perhaps be chairman with a casting vote, preferably voluntarily accorded, in a Defence Council containing also one representative of both Hindus and Pakistan. British troops would probably have to be retained under the personal orders of the Governor General.

MR. ABELL said that the main difficulty in such a suggestion was that it was likely to take at least a year to set up a Pakistan Government.

LORD ISMAY said that he did not think that it should be categorically stated that His Majesty's Government would not accept a unilateral application on the part of Pakistan to remain within the Commonwealth. If forced into a position whereby only one part of India wanted to remain in the Commonwealth, he felt that H.M.G. might consider accepting such an application. In his opinion that would be more likely to prevent a war than not to allow either side to remain in.

HIS EXCELLENCY THE VICEROY said that he was considering informing Pandit Nehru, possibly through Krishna Menon, that both Pakistan and the States had expressed a desire to remain within the Commonwealth; that he could not suppress such requests; and that he was of the belief that popular sentiment within the rest of the British Commonwealth would not allow them to go unanswered. HIS EXCELLENCY THE VICEROY went on to say that planning for the grant before June 1948—possibly by January 1948—of Dominion status to India, whether united or divided, should continue concurrently with the plans now being prepared in connection with the main decision.

LORD ISMAY said that he felt it possible that Hindustan and Pakistan, if set up, would ask for a British Governor General to stay on after June 1948 in any event.

HIS EXCELLENCY THE VICEROY said that the incumbent of such a post would have a most difficult task as he would be the apparent focus of authority without possessing any factual power. On the credit side, however, it would be a great advantage before the eyes of the world to receive such a request from all the Indian parties.

Item 3
AN INTERMEDIATE PLAN

HIS EXCELLENCY THE VICEROY said that he was convinced that the Cabinet Mission's plan could somehow be resurrected under a new name and form. The problem at the moment was that the Muslims could not face the prospect of domination by the Hindus. If they were allowed a separate State, they would have the chance to negotiate for a Centre to be set up after having gained initial independence. They were apparently prepared to give up the full Pakistan with a small Centre which they would have had in Sections B and C of the Cabinet Mission's plan and opt instead for a truncated Pakistan with full initial independence. This gave an idea what store they set by it.

Item 4
THE CHOICE BY PROVINCES OF THEIR OWN FUTURE

MR ABELL said that, as a result of the meeting[1] with Mr Liaquat Ali Khan the previous day, the system of ascertaining the will of the people at present under consideration was that:

(a) each Province, the majority of whose elected members to the Constituent Assembly had already taken their seats, would make a new declaration of adherence to that Assembly through those representatives;

(b) in all other Provinces the Legislative Assemblies would sit and elect a new set of representatives under the Cabinet Mission system. In the case of the N.W.F.P. this would be done after new general elections. In the case of the Punjab, Bengal and Assam the choice of the new representatives would be made on a territorial basis, each half of the Legislative Assembly in each Province voting separately. These representatives would then decide the future for their Provinces.

[1] No. 190.

193

Record of Interview between Rear-Admiral Viscount Mountbatten of Burma and Pandit Nehru

Mountbatten Papers. Viceroy's Interview No. 84

TOP SECRET   *22 April 1947, 11–11.30 am*

I had half an hour's talk with Pandit Nehru, and he then stayed on for a Staff Meeting, which lasted from 11.30 to 1.15 and the minutes of which have been recorded by the Conference Secretary.[1]

First of all I discussed with him telegram No. 5058-S of the 18th April,[2] from the Secretary of State, asking me to influence Nehru to accept an invitation to send a representative to London for Commonwealth consultations, to discuss the Japanese question. He told me that he had heard of this proposed conference, but had not seen any direct invitation as yet. He personally was quite prepared to accept if the Cabinet would agree and if the invitation came but was afraid he could not spare the time to go himself, particularly in the near future with the problems of the decision about the transfer of power coming to the boil. He even said that it was unlikely that any Congress Member of the Cabinet could be spared to go to London on the Sterling Balances Mission.

I told him that Mr. Liaquat Ali Khan had already spoken to me complaining at this attitude, and that I really couldn't recommend him to go on such a vital mission without a Congress representative. Nehru suggested Dr. Matthai and Mr. Bhabha; but I said they were Minority representatives and could not take the weight of a Congress decision, and that I should personally advise Mr. Liaquat Ali Khan against going to London without a Congress representative; for however busy Congress representatives were going to be as a result of my present discussions and H.M.G.'s announcement, it was certain that the Muslim League would be equally busy if not more so.

He then asked me whether I could get the Chancellor of the Exchequer to come to India, and I told him definitely "No"; that he was far too busy.

I next attacked Pandit Nehru on the subject of the Political Adviser's letter to P.S.V. of the 21st April;[3] and expressed my great disappointment that a man whom I had regarded as a statesman and as a friend should have descended once more to the level of a demagogue in making inflammatory speeches at the States' People's Conference in Gwalior.[4] I put the arguments in Sir Conrad Corfield's letter very forcibly to him; and, to my surprise, he admitted their validity. He informed me that he had been wrongly reported in the Press. So far from being a demagogue and a hot-headed leader, he was keeping the

[1] No. 194.   [2] L/P &S/12/2944.   [3] No. 189.   [4] See No. 181, note 2.

extreme elements in order. He was, he considered, on the side of monarchy; but he was also trying to prevent Rulers from making unilateral decisions without consulting the wishes of their own people, for this could only end in disaster. He was not speaking as a member of Congress, and certainly not as a Member of the Interim Government, but as President of the States' People's Organisation.

He said his statement had been misquoted in the Press. He had not threatened to treat those Indian States that did not forthwith send representatives to the Constituent Assembly as hostile; but said that failure to send representatives to the Constituent Assembly was behaving in a hostile manner to the Constituent Assembly and to their own people, and would produce reactions accordingly. He agreed that it was not essential for States to send their representatives to the C.A. prior to the new decision provided it were not long delayed; but the main advice he would give to the Rulers was that they should consult the wishes of their people and make them feel that they were coming in together into whichever Constituent Assembly they finally decided to join.

I must confess that he seemed most reasonable about the whole thing.

Next, I discussed the information from the Governor of the N.W.F.P. saying that the political prisoners whom the Congress Government were prepared to release were refusing to leave the jail. I told him that I had talked to all the Muslim League Members of the Cabinet and had urged them to use their influence to call off any form of aggressive political movement that could lead to violence; but that I felt that, when I got up there on my visit next week and saw both the Government and the leaders of the Opposition, I must be allowed to make it clear that if I considered it necessary I should order new elections.

Pandit Nehru raised no objection to this, provided, he said, I undertook to connect it entirely with the question of ascertaining the will of the people in connection with the transfer of power and made it quite clear that any idea of an election could in no way be connected with the present situation, and further that I should warn them that, so far from their activities helping the situation, it would be the one thing which might prevent the election taking place, at all events for some time.

I undertook to abide by this.

194

Minutes of Viceroy's Sixth Miscellaneous Meeting

Mountbatten Papers

TOP SECRET

Those present at this Meeting held at The Viceroy's House, New Delhi on 22 April 1947 at 11.30 am were: Rear-Admiral Viscount Mountbatten of Burma, Pandit Nehru, Lord Ismay, Sir E. Mieville, Mr Abell; Lieutenant-Colonel Erskine Crum (Secretariat)

Item 1

THE CHOICE BY PROVINCES OF THEIR OWN FUTURE

HIS EXCELLENCY THE VICEROY explained the plan which was under consideration at the present time for convening a meeting with Indian leaders before the final decision on what to recommend to H.M.G. was made. He said that he intended at that meeting to begin by making one more attempt to persuade both parties to accept the Cabinet Mission's plan; but he felt that the attempt was bound to fail owing to Mr. Jinnah's conviction that the Cabinet Mission's plan could only be worked if there was the utmost goodwill on the part of both parties—an element which was not present now.

HIS EXCELLENCY said that the alternative to the acceptance of the Cabinet Mission's Plan (or another similar plan for an united India) would be the Partition of India. He felt, however, that a decision to divide the country could not be taken by the British. It would surely be better for the Provinces to make their own choice.

MR. ABELL then gave a description of the procedure envisaged for ascertaining the desires of the Provinces.[1]

During the discussion which followed, PANDIT NEHRU made the following points:—

(a) He generally agreed with the procedure envisaged;

(b) he pointed out that the questions to be asked of the voters in the Punjab and Bengal (i.e. first whether they wished the Provinces to be partitioned; and, secondly, whether they wished the whole or parts of the Provinces to remain independent, to adhere to Hindustan or to adhere to Pakistan) were most closely interconnected and would require to be most carefully phrased;

(c) the 1941 census figures were not very accurate in parts of India, especially parts of Bengal, where there were almost equal numbers of Muslims and non-Muslims. An investigation by the Statistical Survey subsequent to the census had divulged enormous divergencies. Separate electorates

[1] See No. 192, Item 4.

gave a great temptation to "cook" numbers, particularly of women in purdah;

(d) there was no doubt that, until recently, there had been a very strong sense of union in Bengal—but this had lately been overcome among non-Muslims. Any decision to make Bengal an independent unit would mean in the eyes of the majority of non-Muslims a continuation of the present structure. They would imagine that, although the Province was called independent, a way would be found to associate it with Pakistan later;

(e) if the N.W.F.P. decided to adhere to Hindustan, it would be completely cut off territorially. PANDIT NEHRU agreed that it was right and fair that elections should be held in the N.W.F.P. before the transfer of power but said that he was opposed to them being held too hurriedly;

(f) there were considerable difficulties inherent in any suggestion that two independent Sovereign States should share the same External Affairs organisation. External Affairs, he considered, were not wholly connected with Defence, as had been suggested. PANDIT NEHRU claimed that any persons put forward by Pakistan for diplomatic appointments would be completely Muslim League-minded, whereas Hindustan would appoint people from a wide and largely non-political field. Difficulties would be created if, for example, an Indian ambassador somewhere represented the point of view of an united India, whilst his counsellor appointed by Pakistan was concerned only with the affairs of Pakistan; but he felt that a joint Consular service might perhaps be workable;

(g) under any plan which created a centre to begin with, the Muslim League Provinces would always have the option of breaking away whenever they wanted to. This, PANDIT NEHRU considered, would be a considerable threat which should not be dealt with simply by the fact that Congress would have a permanent majority;

(h) the process of separation was bound to take a long time. During the interim period representatives of the Constituent Assemblies of Hindustan and Pakistan could meet together to consider common subjects. Eventually power might be handed over to these Constituent Assemblies. Meanwhile the Interim Government should continue in operaton, gradually transferring its power;

(i) the Constituent Assembly was due to end its preliminary session soon. Then it was supposed to break up into sections. He would look into the possibility of extending the preliminary session to avoid this happening before the overall decision was announced. There were matters like the drafting of Constitutional principles which could be got on with meanwhile.

(j) he agreed that there was no necessity for the choice by other Provinces of their future to wait upon the readiness of the N.W.F.P. to make its decision;

(k) in drawing up a time-table for the Constituent Assembly the previous day, the conclusion had been reached that a Constitution would be drafted by 31st October 1947.

HIS EXCELLENCY THE VICEROY emphasised the following points:—

(i) In deciding the Partition issue, a $\frac{2}{3}$rds majority of either party or an overall majority of each party would be required in those halves of Provinces where this issue was voted on;

(ii) he would ask the Muslim League to allow their members elected to the Constituent Assembly for Provinces a majority of whose representatives had joined the Assembly, to attend the meeting at which the vote would be taken as to whether they wished to continue in the present Constituent Assembly;

(iii) he visualised a Defence Headquarters being taken "into trust" during the interim period so that it should not be used to the advantage of one or other of the parties;

(iv) if the Cabinet Mission's plan was not accepted the new Constituent Assemblies would have complete freedom to decide Constitutions outside the bounds inherent in that plan, but no steps should be taken in this direction by the present Constituent Assembly until a decision was announced;

(v) he would see Dr. Prasad before the end of the present session of the Constituent Assembly in order to explain the situation to him.

Item 2
THE STATES

HIS EXCELLENCY THE VICEROY emphasised that States would have complete freedom of choice as to which Constituent Assembly they should join, independent of geographical considerations. Their representatives would be chosen on the lines laid down in the Cabinet Mission's plan.

PANDIT NEHRU said he thought that the future of Kashmir might produce a difficult problem.

195

Note by Lieutenant-Colonel Erskine Crum[1]

Mountbatten Papers. Provinces and their future, Part I(a)

undated

The 2/3rds Majority

1. This question arose over the partition of Bengal, and is, I think, applicable only to that.

2. The number of voters in Bengal is:

	General	Muslims	Total
West Bengal	14	8	22
East Bengal	12	26	38

3. It was originally suggested that a simple majority in either Community (counting "General", of course as a Community) in either half of the Province should suffice to carry the Partition issue.

4. Almost certainly there will not be a majority of either community in favour of Partition. Equally probably there will not be a majority of *Muslims* in *West* Bengal in favour of Partition. The only community likely to vote in favour of Partition are the *General* in *West* Bengal.

5. Say, for example, only 8 of the 14 General in West Bengal (a simple majority) voted in favour of Partition, and all the other voters in both halves of the Province voted against Partition. This would result in a total of

8 in favour of Partition

52 against Partition

but, on the procedure in paragraph 2 [3] above, would suffice to carry the issue.

6. It was in view of this that it was suggested that a majority of at least 2/3rds of the 14 General in West Bengal (i.e. a vote of 10 or over) should be required to carry the issue.[2]

---

[1] This note relates to No. 194, Item 1, Conclusion (i).

[2] At his Twenty Second Staff Meeting on 25 April 1947, Lord Mountbatten decided to drop the suggestion that a two-thirds majority would be required in the voting procedure. Item 7, Conclusion (iii). Mountbatten Papers.

196

Rear-Admiral Viscount Mountbatten of Burma to Sir C. Corfield

R/1/30/40: f 69

SECRET   THE VICEROY'S HOUSE, NEW DELHI,

No. 592/45   *22 April 1947*

My dear Corfield,

Abell has shown me your letter of the 21st April.[1]

I spoke exactly along these lines to Pandit Nehru when I saw him today.[2] He said he wished to make it clear that he had been misquoted in the newspapers, since the tenor of his remarks was to the effect not that he threatened Rulers that they would be regarded as hostile if they failed to send representatives forthwith to the Constituent Assembly, but that the failure of Rulers to take part in the Constituent Assembly would be behaving in a hostile manner. He added that failure to consult the will of their people in any way would also be behaving in a hostile manner.

He quite agreed that in view of the impending statement which we hope H.M.G. will make soon, Rulers could quite well wait until this statement was made before deciding to send representatives; but he wished to point out that the best way to avoid being regarded as hostile by the States' People's Conference was to ensure some measure of consultation with their own people about their future.

He stressed that he was not speaking as a Member of Congress, and still less as a Member of the Cabinet, but purely as President of the States' People's Organisation.

I should like to add that in my own view Rulers would be well advised to consult the will of their people, and then make a quick decision and announcement about joining the Constituent Assembly as soon as the statement by H.M.G. has been made.

Yours sincerely,

MOUNTBATTEN OF BURMA

[1] No. 189.   [2] See No. 193.

197

Sir F. Mudie (Sind) to Rear-Admiral Viscount Mountbatten of Burma

Mountbatten Papers. Official Correspondence Files: Sind,
Situation in

D.O. No. 240   GOVERNMENT HOUSE, KARACHI,
                                                          22 April 1947

Dear Lord Mountbatten,

I promised to let you have some ammunition with which to meet the Congress attack on me that I am unfair to the minorities in Sind. This is not very easy to do as I am constantly doing what I can to prevent their being unfairly treated but I may mention the following cases as being of some importance:

(1) The ministry unanimously, at a Cabinet Meeting, wished to supersede a Hindu, who had been certified by the Chief Court as fit to hold the post of District and Sessions Judge. I appointed him to the post by an order made in my individual judgement.

(2) All the ministers, except possibly the Premier, wished to make the rules regarding the communal ratio in the Services applicable to promotions. At present they apply only to new appointments. I refused to agree. So they got a member of their party in the Assembly to move a resolution to that effect. This was carried, all the Muslims voting for it and all the Hindus against, but, as the result of what I had said the day before to the Ministers, they all remained neutral, incurring a certain amount of obloquy thereby.

(3) The Hindus here give me credit for the maintenance of the peace. This has involved, on some occasions, action contrary to my ministers' real wishes or over their heads. Last August I threatened two with dismissal for issuing an inflammatory statement.

(4) I have also, on occasions when I thought Hindu members of the Services were being unfairly treated, referred the matter to the Public Service Commission under the concluding provisions of section 266(3) of the Government of India Act, 1935.

2. I hope that these instances will be sufficient for your purpose but I would like to mention certain general matters which are of importance in this connexion. The first is, as I told you in Delhi, that the real gravamen of the Congress charge against me is that I was Chief Secretary of the U.P. in 1942 when the Congress rebellion was suppressed. Before that the Congress and I got on fairly well. I am not accused of anything excepting defeating them, but that is a serious charge.

3. The other reason for the attack on me is that I have always considered

it important not to presume too much on the friendliness of my ministry. Admittedly, I get away with a good deal that I could not get away with if I had a Congress ministry, but any suggestion that a Muslim League ministry should be treated with less respect than a Congress ministry would be greatly resented. The League is, at present, suffering from an extreme inferiority complex which makes them, at times, difficult to deal with. But what the Congress want me to do is to treat my ministry in a way that would produce a constitutional crisis in a Congress province. If I did, it would be a snub to the League which would be just what the Congress want. It would also weaken the Sind Government, by setting the Governor against the ministers, which also from the Congress point of view is desirable.

4. This question arose very acutely last July, when on the advice of the Premier, I prorogued the meeting of the Assembly that had been called to elect representatives of Sind to the Constituent Assembly immediately after that election was over. The Congress were opposed to this, as they had suborned the single vote on which the ministry's majority depended by a promise of cheap land and so thought that they could defeat the ministry and gain power. It seemed to me that if advice is tendered by both the Premier and the Leader of the Oposition on a purely political matter, the Governor should act on the advice of the Premier. If a Congress Governor were to depart from that rule there would be trouble.

5. My real reason, however, apart from the constitutional one, was that I was sure that if the opposition, which consisted of the Congress plus a number of Muslim stooges, all but one of whom lost their seats at the last election, got power then there would be widespread communal rioting, in which, of course, the Hindus would have lost very heavily. I would have got the Province into the position now existing in the N.W.F.P. and previously existing in the Punjab. I would have had a ministry with a small majority in the Assembly, but violently opposed outside it. It was as a result of my action on this occasion that, as I told you, Nehru, in a public statement, said that both I and my Premier should be dismissed. My action has been justified by the result of the recent election and by the ensuing communal peace when nearly every other Province was disturbed. Many of the Hindus in Sind see it now and are grateful. But a strong Government in Sind does not suit the All-India Congress book, and I daresay the leaders at the Centre do not realise the local situation. Unfortunately Governors cannot explain these things!

6. I am afraid that this is rather a long letter but I thought it worthwhile to set forth the case fairly fully.

Yours sincerely,

F. MUDIE

198

*Record of Interview between Rear-Admiral Viscount Mountbatten of Burma
and Sardar Baldev Singh*

Mountbatten Papers. Viceroy's Interview No. 85

TOP SECRET   *22 April 1947, 3.30–4 pm*

Baldev Singh was in a very depressed frame of mind. He had been into the
question of the splitting of the Army with the Chief, and was convinced that
nothing useful could be done before June 1948 if the Army were also to be
nationalised by that time. He said he entirely shared the Commander-in-Chief's
view that any leakage of the intention to divide the army would have serious
repercussions on the morale of the troops. He agreed with me that it would
not only be difficult to avoid such a leakage, but that if in fact an announcement were made which involved Pakistan, the army could not fail to look
over their communal shoulders. Altogether he was very worried about it, and
said the C.-in-C. was equally worried. He still remained convinced that the
answer was for Congress to remain within the Commonwealth and use
British officers; but he did not appear to have progressed very far with the
Congress leaders along these lines, although he said he had written to Pandit
Nehru.

I asked him what he thought would happen if the report in the newspapers was
proved true, that Pakistan intended to ask to be allowed to remain within the
Commonwealth. I pointed out that although I would do nothing whatever to
encourage any part of India to remain within the Commonwealth, this appeal
might go over my head direct to the peoples of the Commonwealth, and
might prove irresistible. I warned him that then the Pakistan army might have
all the best British officers and equipment at the expense of the Hindustan
army. He realised that this introduced a new element which would have to
be carefully considered.

I then gave him a brief description of how our plans were progressing, and
he told me that he was convinced that if sufficient pressure were brought on
Mr Jinnah, the Muslim League would give up their idea of Pakistan; and one
way of doing this was to threaten to divide the Punjab, not only according to
population but also on the basis of actual property, as this would rob the
Muslims of some valuable parts of the Punjab. I told him that on principle I
was opposed to dividing a Province by ownership of big land estates rather
than on the basis of populations.

As Mr Chundrigar was announced at this time, I arranged for Sardar
Baldev Singh to see Lord Ismay's Committee and give his evidence to them.

199

*Record of Interview between Rear-Admiral Viscount Mountbatten of Burma
and Mr Chundrigar (Extract)*

Mountbatten Papers. Viceroy's Interview No. 86

TOP SECRET   *22 April 1947, 4–4.45 pm*

After this[1] I gave Mr. Chundrigar a brief description of the general state of
planning, and he told me that in the case of the partition of Bengal, if it ever
took place, one thing was quite certain and that was that Calcutta, if given a
proper chance, would opt to remain with the rest of Bengal in Pakistan:
because, he said, although the population of Muslims was only about one
third of that of the whole, 40% of the Hindus in Calcutta were Scheduled
Castes, the bulk of whom he thought would definitely vote against partition.

I told him I could give no undertaking to carry out any form of plebiscite,
which appeared to me to be too complicated to be got through in the time
available.

I also talked to him about the N-W Frontier, and invited him to use his
influence with the Muslim League leaders up there to call off their campaign.
I told him that I considered that the Direct Action policy of the Muslim League
was the cause of the start of all the bloodshed and trouble. He pointed out
that Direct Action had never actually been implemented; the notorious 16th
August was called "Direct Action Day" merely because that was the day on
which Muslim League Members were to meet together to discuss the desirability of Direct Action; in fact this had never been implemented.

I somewhat drily pointed out that it was hardly necessary to implement it
observing that it had started as a direct result of this date. I told him that I
would probably discuss this matter with Mr. Jinnah, and get him to issue an
explanatory statement pointing out that Direct Action was not part of the
Muslim League policy, since the view was widely held that it was.

[1] Mr Chundrigar had protested at the procedure adopted over the proposed appointment of the
Joint Secretary of the Commerce Department.

200

*Record of Interview between Rear-Admiral Viscount Mountbatten of Burma
and Mr V. K. Krishna Menon*

Mountbatten Papers. Viceroy's Interview No. 87

TOP SECRET   *22 April 1947, 4.50–6.50 pm*

I had a long and friendly talk with Mr. Menon over a cup of tea. We properly
let down our hair together and discussed every aspect of the plan now being

worked on, and in particular of its relation to the world situation. I found that
he had very shrewd views on the future trend of governments in the U.K. and
America, and on world-wide politics.

He expressed his fear to me of American absorption from every point of
view. He thought that Mr. Grady had been shooting off his mouth in a manner
which revealed only too well and clearly what the Americans' object in India
was: they wished to capture all the markets, to step in and take the place of
the British, and finally he did not exclude the possibility that their aim might
even be to get bases in India for ultimate use against Russia.

I discussed with him the announcement in the Press that if Pakistan were
formed it would undoubtedly wish to remain within the British Commonwealth. I told him that I had made clear to those Muslim Leaders who had
spoken to me about it that I had no authority whatever to deal with the
question of Pakistan remaining within the British Empire, and that in fact I
should probably advise against it, since we could not wish to back one side of
India against another if it came to civil war. The only way of avoiding the
risk of this would, of course, be not to concede the Pakistan demand to remain
within the Empire. But I pointed out that if the demand went over our heads
to the peoples of the British Commonwealth, the demand might be too
strong to be resisted, and that in fact he must now reckon with the extreme
likelihood of Pakistan being a British dominion.

If that happened they would of course have a complete call on British
officers, and all the Services, who wished to remain in India, since they could
so remain whilst retaining the King's Commission. Not only would they be
able to get the same equipment as Hindustan, but could do a great deal better,
since they could obviously get secret equipment not available to anybody not
within the Commonwealth, and they could go to our schools and make use
of our experimental establishments, and keep up-to-date. In fact, backed by
British and American arms and technique, Pakistan would in no while have
armed forces immensely superior to those of Hindustan, and in spite of the
obvious disadvantages from which they would at first suffer, there was no
reason why they should not be able to rise above these with British and
American help; and I presumed that places like Karachi would become big
naval and air bases within the British Commonwealth.

I asked him how he would like to see that happen; and he absolutely shuddered, and said "How can we prevent it"? I said "By the simple expedient of
being in the Commonwealth yourselves; then there can be no question of
Pakistan getting ahead of you, nor could there be any question of the unilateral
use of bases without full consultation."

He said "I see that, but how in the world can it be achieved?" (He pointed
out that they had pretty well burnt their boats by the statements about leaving
the Empire and that it would be extremely difficult for him to get it over,

even with Nehru, who would be the only person who would immediately understand it, and even more difficult with Patel; and that even if the three of them got together, he did not see how they could get it across to Congress or to the peoples of Hindustan).

I pointed out that this was entirely a matter for themselves to decide. But I suggested to him a solution along the lines he himself had raised last time, namely Dominion Status before June 1948, so as to avoid the necessity of having to make any declaration when we left, and thus leave India within the Commonwealth. My proposal was that if we could possibly get the scheme working in time, Pakistan and Hindustan should be declared independent dominions, with a Central Defence Council, a single army (pending partition) and with myself at the head of the Central Defence Council and as Governor-General of both dominions on a constitutional basis. I pointed out that the British Army would come directly under my command, and that that would be my personal contribution to the Defence Council. I suggested that in order not to imperil the sovereignty of dominion status, each dominion could voluntarily accord me the right of a casting vote as Chairman of the Defence Council.

He seemed rather smitten with this idea, but said immediately, that it would be far better to declare India a single dominion which would consist of two parts—Pakistan and Hindustan, since he still harped on the fact that to give each side dominion status was advertising the complete separation of Pakistan.

I urged him to open his eyes and see things clearly. If Pakistan were given independent status, then they were cutting themselves adrift from the British Commonwealth.

He said that the furthest he thought it would be possible to go would be to call themselves an Independent Nation in relation with the British Commonwealth.

I reminded him that the crux of the matter was that they should not sever their connection with the Crown, since on this depended the ability of British officers holding the King's Commission to serve in India. Once more I said to him "You cannot have your cake and eat it; make up your mind which you want to do."

Finally he told me that Pandit Nehru was over-working to the point of a breakdown; that he had relays of shorthand typists in and out all during the day and night. Not only was he dealing with the big problems, but he was always going down and attending to every little item; personally attending small meetings, and even trying to interfere in street scenes. He asked me if I could not take him away for two or three days on a holiday; and said laughingly "to avoid both of you breaking down from over work". I said "Where shall I take him, Simla?" He said "No, that is too official; you would neither of you stop working". I said "Where else"? He said "Why not try Kashmir"?

I said "What would happen? I thought he wanted to make the Maharaja lick his boots, or alternatively that the Maharaja was likely to throw him into jail." He said that that was all nonsense; it would be an opportunity for the Maharaja and Nehru to get together again, and he believed that I might possibly heal the breach.

He asked me if I could persuade the Maharaja to release political prisoners from the jails in Kashmir in the same way as I had persuaded Dr. Khan Sahib to release his; after this the way would be open to restore friendly relations between Nehru and the Maharaja. I said I thought this was a bit difficult to arrange at long distance, and I should probably have to go and see the Maharaja personally at first. He admitted that this was a more reasonable way of setting about it.

But he still wished me to take Nehru away for two or three days, anywhere restful, so that we could get to know each other—"For", he said, "between you, you can solve all the problems of India".

He told me that Nehru was becoming unpopular with the Hindus through his international and unbiassed outlook.

I told him I was expecting to see the President of the Hindu Mahasabha soon; and he then urged me, in that case, to see the Secretary of the Shia Conference, Mr. Ali Zaheer, who had been in the first Interim Government and had made way when Mr. Liaquat Ali Khan joined. He said he was at Lucknow, but would come up if sent for. He claimed that the Shias were a fairly numerous section of the Muslim community, all of whom were opposed to the Muslim League.

201

Record of Interview between Rear-Admiral Viscount Mountbatten of Burma and Dr Shyama Prasad Mukherji

Mountbatten Papers. Viceroy's Interview No. 88

TOP SECRET   *23 April 1947, 12.30–1.20 pm*

Mr S. P. Mukherji explained to me the difference between the Hindu Mahasabha and Congress, stressing that Congress by no means represented Hindus only, since they embraced all other creeds who wished to join the Congress which was purely a political party. Indeed, he said, Congress frequently did not look after the interests of the Hindus sufficiently.

He then said that the main object of his visit was to convince me of the necessity for partitioning Bengal if the Cabinet Mission plan were to fail. He produced plans and papers, and went into matters at great length.

I arranged for him to see Lord Ismay and leave with him the plans and papers, since this was all useful technical information to be used in the working out of the plan for the transfer of power.

202

Record of Interview between Rear-Admiral Viscount Mountbatten of Burma and Mr C. H. Bhabha

Mountbatten Papers. Viceroy's Interview No. 89

TOP SECRET   *23 April 1947, 3.30–4.15 pm*

He congratulated me on getting the Cabinet Meeting finished in one hour and one minute this morning, and said this was an all-time record since the Interim Government was formed. In the past, he said, literally hours had been wasted arguing backwards and forwards *ad nauseam*. I asked him whether he felt I was being too quick in closing down discussions. He replied "You cannot be too quick for my liking". I then asked him whether he thought it was to the liking of the politicians, since he himself was a business man. He said there was plenty of evidence that Cabinet were fully satisfied that they were getting enough opportunity for discussion, and very pleased with the quick disposal of business now taking place.[1]

I gave him a very brief review of the progress of the Plan, and mentioned the great stumbling block of splitting the army if we had to accept Pakistan. I pointed out that if nationalisation was to take place by June 1948, the Indian Army would not be worth much for several years to come, and if it had to be split on top of that, both parts would be virtually valueless. I also pointed out that the Navy and Air Force would in any case be of very little value if they were nationalised in under ten years, and even then, unless India joined either the British Commonwealth-U.S. power group or the Russians, they could not expect to get the latest type of secret aircraft, ships and equipment. I further pointed out that at the present moment as a result of the late war the British Commonwealth and the United States used the same technique, weapons and equipment as the Indian Services themselves; but that if they severed their connection with the British Commonwealth, then they would

---

[1] In his record of his interview with Mr Bhabha on 28 March 1947 Lord Mountbatten recorded:
'Mr Bhabha belies his appearance in that he is exceedingly astute. I talked mainly about procedure with him. He said that he was no politician, but would not give a seat on the board of his least important Company (and he controls very many) to any of the members of the Interim Government. They did not know how to set about their business. He congratulated me on introducing the system of Cabinet Committees, and said that, whatever my views and final decision might be, anybody who speeded up procedure would be respected.'
Mountbatten Papers, Viceroy's Interview No. 13.

have to make up their mind whether to join forces with Russia or accept a completely secondary role, with no prospect of modern equipment, particularly in the Air Force.

He became most enthusiastic and said he not only agreed with every word I had said, but that he and Baldev Singh had been having long and earnest discussions on this matter. Already Baldev Singh had written to Pandit Nehru pointing out the situation if they allowed British officers to go, and had received the reply that whatever the cost they must be allowed to go. He (Bhabha) and Baldev Singh had no intention of sitting down under this, and Bhabha had now offered to enter the ring. I asked him how he proposed to set about this, and he said he thought that he would now write to Nehru. I suggested to him that he was wasting his time, since if the Defence Member failed, how could another Member succeed. He then asked me what my advice would be, which was exactly what I hoped he would do. Before giving it I asked him if I could rely on his not quoting me or even mentioning that he had been discussing this subject with me. He readily promised this, pointing out that if it was known that he had been discussing the matter with me it would be fatal to the success of his own efforts.

I gave him the following advice:

"Discuss the whole question with Matthai. If you can get him to see your point of view, then I would suggest the three of you signing a joint letter and calling yourselves the Minority Representatives of the Interim Government. I would suggest sending this letter only to the five Congress Members, and that having set out in black and white the seriousness of the position, you should invite them to meet in the near future privately at some house where you can discuss matters with them without my being present or the Muslim League Members.

"Properly worded this invitation is bound to be accepted.

"At this meeting you should point out how very worried you three Members are, who are allied to but not members of Congress, since it seems quite clear to you that if Pakistan is about to emerge—as seems quite possible from all indications—then it also seems quite clear that Pakistan will ask to be allowed to remain within the British Commonwealth. Whatever the views of the Viceroy or H.M.G. may be, a public appeal from the people of Pakistan to the people of the British Commonwealth not to desert them in their hour of need and not to throw them out of the Empire to which they have belonged for so long, may well produce a popular reaction to accept them into the fold and hold out a helping hand. Thus Pakistan would remain on the secret list of equipment and technique and, with our matériel and personnel, could rapidly forge ahead with their armed forces, thus constituting a very grave threat to Hindustan.

"Unless Hindustan chose to link up its fate with Russia (and accept the inevitability of coming under the consequent Communist influence), they would either have to remain out in the cold, with an entirely negligible Navy and Air Force and an out-of-date relatively inefficient Army, or throw in their lot with the British Commonwealth. By doing the latter they would prevent Pakistan from stealing a march on them, they would improve their position in the world, and they would have a closer link with Pakistan than could be provided by any other means; since they would both be members of the British Commonwealth of Nations and could even call in representatives from the other nations of the Commonwealth to take part in their discussions if they so wished rather than advertise their differences by having to go to U.N.O."

Mr. Bhabha seemed to like this idea more and more and got quite excited. He said "Of course, this makes absolute sense, and I am realist enough to see it; but the Congress have done so much propaganda and tub-thumping in the past that I do not see how they can possibly swallow all their words now however much they might want to if they could be made to see the point."

I said that there were the following alternative methods at Congress's disposal, any one or more of which could be used to save their face and not cut their link with the British Empire:

(a) The notorious Independent Sovereign Republic resolution in the Constituent Assembly was passed *sine die* before the announcement of our departure in June 1948. All they had to do was not to link up this resolution with the date of our departure; in other words, take no action to implement it. If any question was raised they could answer that this was still the ultimate goal for Hindustan to aim at, but they certainly were not going to throw out all British officers while any of them were still prepared to stay and help; and that the matter would be reconsidered in five years' time.

(b) No action should be taken to sever the connection with the Crown or to ask the King to drop his title "Emperor of India". Here again, this method had the advantage that no positive action was required. If anybody were to ask what the situation was, the reply could be that the link with the Crown would not be severed until the matter had been considered again in five years' time.

(c) That I should receive a suggestion from Congress to act on their resolution to turn India over to dominion status as soon as possible *before* June 1948. In this case the only feasible solution appeared to be to make two dominions— Pakistan and Hindustan—and remit everything to them, except Defence including control of the Army which would be run jointly by a Commonwealth Defence Council at the Centre. I would be Governor-General of the two dominions, and Chairman of the Commonwealth Defence Council, with a casting vote, and directly responsible for the British Army still in India. When June 1948 came I should of course resign my position and go, and give place to an Indian Governor-General or rather to two Indian Governor-Generals who could sit together on the Defence Council.

Mr. Bhabha liked this latter scheme particularly, because this would mean that it would be a running concern when June 1948 came, and it would be the easiest of all for remaining within the Empire. He saw that the difficulty was to make the arrangements in time. But he really seemed dead set on going all out to achieve some results. He begged me not to speak to any member of Congress, particularly to Nehru. He promised to keep me in touch with progress, and I told him if he rang up at any time I would see him immediately.

Finally, I impressed on him that India stood to gain so much from remaining within the Commonwealth in comparison with what the other Commonwealth nations might gain, that there was in any case no object in my trying to press the suggestion. I personally admitted that I was keen to be of service to India and help in this respect, but I could not guarantee how pleased the other Empire countries would be to have India in, though I thought that from Dr. Evatt's recent remarks Australia would welcome her; and from what the Prime Minister mentioned to me before I left I thought H.M.G. would also accept them, but on the other hand would not mind if they did not join.

203

Minutes of Viceroy's Seventh Miscellaneous Meeting

Mountbatten Papers

TOP SECRET

Those present at this Meeting held at The Viceroy's House, New Delhi on 23 April 1947 at 4.15 pm were: Rear-Admiral Viscount Mountbatten of Burma, Mr Jinnah, Lord Ismay, Sir E. Mieville, Mr Abell; Lieutenant-Colonel Erskine Crum (Secretariat)

Item 1
THE NORTH-WEST FRONTIER PROVINCE

HIS EXCELLENCY THE VICEROY said that, before the Meeting began, Mr Jinnah had pointed out to him that, whereas in other countries there were many ways, for example bye-elections, in which it could be shown that Governments had lost the confidence of the people, in India the only way to show this was by means of demonstrations. He had told Mr Jinnah that he had seen enough of demonstrations in the North-West Frontier Province to take note of them and their significance. If they continued, it would become a question of yielding to force.

MR JINNAH stated that there had been a bye-election in the North-West Frontier Province recently, which the Congress party had lost.

HIS EXCELLENCY THE VICEROY went on to say that Mr Jinnah had asked him whether he would order a general election in the North-West Frontier Province, but he had replied that he would not do so until violence there had ceased. Mr Jinnah had, however, pointed out that, if Congress appreciated that elections would be held if all was quiet, they would themselves start agitations and provocation of the Muslim League.

MR JINNAH stated that Congress had what he called "trained, paid agents" in the Red Shirts. He said that he had no similar organisation in the North-West Frontier Province because he could not afford it.

HIS EXCELLENCY THE VICEROY stated that he reserved the right to make up his mind about the desirability of ordering a general election. He had already warned[1] Pandit Nehru to that effect in the presence of Mr Liaquat Ali Khan. He made it clear that his decision would be influenced by the behaviour of the Muslim League in the Province. This was not a threat, but a statement of the inevitable.

There followed a discussion as to whether Mr Jinnah should visit the North-West Frontier Province to ask his supporters there to refrain from violence. HIS EXCELLENCY THE VICEROY offered to lend him an aircraft for this purpose. The alternative of the Muslim League leaders from the North-West Frontier Province being sent for to come to Delhi to see Mr Jinnah was also considered. But it was eventually decided that Mr Jinnah should instead issue an appeal from Delhi by press and radio to his supporters in the North-West Frontier Province to refrain from violence. The lines upon which this appeal should be drafted were agreed.

Item 2
THE PRESS

HIS EXCELLENCY THE VICEROY drew Mr Jinnah's attention to an advertisement in *Dawn* concerning a secret broadcasting station, and MR JINNAH promised to give the editor of *Dawn* instructions not to publish such advertisements in future.

Item 3
THE CHOICE BY PROVINCES OF THEIR OWN FUTURE

HIS EXCELLENCY THE VICEROY explained to Mr Jinnah the outlines of a plan then under consideration, whereby Provinces would be given the choice of their own future.

MR JINNAH asked for this plan in writing, and HIS EXCELLENCY THE VICEROY said that a copy would be sent to him as soon as possible. MR JINNAH gave his word of honour not to show the document to anybody except Mr Liaquat Ali Khan. MR JINNAH also said that he would be prepared to

[1] See Nos. 171 and 193. Mr Liaquat Ali Khan, however, was not present on these occasions.

consider any plan which Congress might let him have for the partition of Bengal and the Punjab.

HIS EXCELLENCY THE VICEROY:

invited Prin. Sec. to take a copy of the plan at present under consideration to Mr Jinnah when practicable.

Item 4
PARTITION OF PROVINCES

MR JINNAH said that Muslims were more virile than Hindus. Therefore there had been an enormous increase in the proportion of Muslims, particularly in Bengal and Assam, since the 1941 census. An "unknown person" had applied his mind to the problem of the proportionate increase, and prepared, on the data of increases between previous censi, a rough estimate of the present proportions.

HIS EXCELLENCY THE VICEROY said that he doubted that it would be practical to take such claims into consideration when deciding on demarcation of boundaries, in view of the time factor.

MR JINNAH said that he had not accepted the partition of Bengal and the Punjab, as reported in certain Hindu newspapers; but had not considered it worthwhile to issue denials. MR JINNAH said that the partition of Provinces was a most dangerous proposition and bound to lead to trouble, as it was not based on "wisdom and foresight", but born of "bitterness and spitefulness". It would "loose terrible forces" and was "suicidal". It was a "most dangerous thing when an angry man lost his judgement".

HIS EXCELLENCY THE VICEROY pointed out that all these "arguments" in favour of non-partition of Provinces applied equally to the non-partition of India.

MR JINNAH said that in Western Bengal the caste Hindus were only 37% of the total Hindu population. The 63% scheduled castes Hindus would be ruined if they were cut off from those in Eastern Bengal. The idea made them shudder. "Any average man" should be asked.

HIS EXCELLENCY THE VICEROY pointed out that these views were very different to those which had been expressed to him by Dr Mukherjee earlier that day.[2]

Item 5
THE DIVISION OF THE INDIAN ARMED FORCES

MR JINNAH gave his opinion that, if India was divided into Hindustan and Pakistan, Pakistan would be able to work out its own constitution within six months, and arrangements could also be made within that period to divide between the two nations all subjects except Defence. He would, he said, like to see the Armed Forces divided before June 1948. But, if that was impossible, (and he could not judge till he had been informed of all the facts), he felt that the British should lay down the principles of division. He very much hoped that, after a decision had been made, all inter-communal feeling would subside and Hindustan and Pakistan would be able to come together and work out the details. But he considered that, if they continued to quarrel, the Governor-General should remain as the representative of H.M.G. to ensure that the principles were carried out.

HIS EXCELLENCY THE VICEROY pointed out that the Governor-General in such circumstances would be in an impossible position—with responsibility and no authority.

LORD ISMAY gave his opinion that it would be physically impossible, especially in view of the concurrent process of nationalization, to split the Army by June 1948 without wrecking one magnificent Army and producing two valueless ones.

MR JINNAH said that some men who were about to be demobilized had told him that it was impossible for Muslim officers to remain in the present Army except "under torture". Life for them was intolerable. After full, deliberate consideration, he had come to the conclusion that Congress wanted to seize power by a coup d'état. This could only be prevented by a quick decision to split the Army. The longer the Army was kept unified, the more was the position endangered. A few days previously the General Secretary of the Congress Party had stated publicly that he and Mr Liaquat Ali Khan would be the first to be taken prisoner.

LORD ISMAY pointed out that a coup d'état by Congress was hardly likely to succeed quickly. It would result in a long-drawn-out civil war. He added that to split the Army quickly would be to let loose all over India a very dangerous band of men.

MR JINNAH stated that he was of the opinion that Pakistan and Hindustan, though they might eventually come together—and he hoped and believed that they would—, would not be able to stand alone against a powerful aggressor. For his part, if, in Pakistan, he found the need—and he thought there would be such need—he would ask for others to help him.

HIS EXCELLENCY THE VICEROY pointed out that the suggestion to split the Army had already been put up to the Defence Committee by Mr Liaquat Ali Khan. It would be considered there, and Mr Jinnah would be kept fully informed and be given every facility to investigate the difficulties. He went on to warn Mr Jinnah that he could not take any step which, in the opinion of his military advisers, was likely to compromise the maintenance of law and order so long as the responsibility therefor remained statutorily his. He then explained how a kind of "Combined Chiefs of Staff" organisation could work in India, and showed how safeguards could be devised in favour of the Muslims

2 No. 201.

if it proved impossible to split the Army before June 1948. He added that the speed at which events would move depended mainly on the Indian leaders themselves.

Item 6
THE CABINET MISSION PLAN

MR JINNAH said that it was impossible for the Cabinet Mission's plan ever to be accepted, and gave a long account of the negotiations which had taken place in the autumn of 1946.

204

Sir T. Shone to Sir N. Brook (Extract)

L/S&G/7/1251: ff 67-8

DESPATCH NO. 31   OFFICE OF THE HIGH COMMISSIONER FOR
THE UNITED KINGDOM, 6 ALBUQUERQUE
ROAD, NEW DELHI, *23 April 1947*

4. For many years past, the Budgets presented in the Legislative Assembly by British officials have, as a gesture of its disapproval of foreign rule, been invariably opposed and thrown out by the nationalist opposition and had consequently to be sent to the Viceroy for certification. It was therefore to be expected that the first Budget of the Interim Indian Government, presented by an Indian Finance Minister, would be spared the fate of its predecessors and would be passed with acclamation. In actual fact, all the demands for grants were passed without a single cut-motion being carried, and the Finance Bill, which included the contentious issue of the lowering of the Super Tax rates, was passed without a division of the House. The same, however, cannot be said for the Finance Minister's taxation proposals (contained in the two Bills dealt with in some detail in Annexures "A" and "B" to this Despatch)[1] which aroused a storm of criticism and caused the editor of *Capital* to refer to it as "the most controversial budget ever presented to an Indian Legislature .... the storm of criticism about which will persist for many months and years to come".

5. The burden of the criticism (which has been repeated *ad nauseam* in practically every quarter) was that the cumulative effects of the taxation proposals (the Business Profits Tax, the Capital Gains Tax, the Corporation Tax, and the lowering of the super tax levels) would be to inflict a crippling blow on Indian industry at a time when industry required to be encouraged in order to increase the production of consumer goods, the lack of which was one of the chief causes of present inflationary trends in India. It was argued that the enterprise of industrialists would be enfeebled because the state would take the profits which would otherwise have been devoted to schemes of

expansion and replacement. The lowering of the super tax levels would mean that many people who ordinarily invested their surplus income in industrial concerns would no longer have surplus income to invest, with the result that capital for new ventures would be lacking.

6. There can be little doubt that the original proposal for a 25% tax on Business Profits (with abatement of Rs.1 lakh only) would have been a heavy burden on and a real deterrent to industrial enterprise, as it would probably have, in most cases, reduced the level of return on shares to below that allowed as "standard profit" under the Excess Profits Tax. It is probably true that the tax as finally accepted by the Finance Member (with abatement of 6% on capital and a $16\frac{2}{3}\%$ tax on residue profits) represents a reasonable levy on industry at a time when profits are still high and when money continues to be plentiful, and should make available to the investing public a reasonable supply of funds for further investment. On the other hand there is little doubt that industry is still concerned at this new burden and an early result has been the decision of some leading firms to abandon proposals for fresh developments which were under consideration, whilst prices on the Stock Exchanges continue at the low levels to which they fell on first announcement of the Budget proposals.

7. In announcing his original proposals, the Finance Member stressed that he had certain "social objectives" in mind, to even out the glaring disparities between the income levels of the small wealthy class and the poverty-stricken masses. Whilst denying at the time that the methods he proposed would have prejudicial repercussions on Indian industry, he was finally compelled, by the weight of criticism both within and without the Legislative Assembly, to accept drastic modifications to his proposals which reduced the anticipated yield of the new taxes by over 50%. Since the Finance Member's original proposals had commanded the support of all Muslim League representatives and of a large proportion of the Congress backbenchers—and since his proposals must in theory have been approved by the Cabinet of the Interim Government—it is a little difficult to understand why the Finance Member was obliged to yield to the protestations of a minority.

8. It was revealed in the debate that the Cabinet of the Interim Government had not all been privy to the Budget taxation proposals, and that these were discussed only with Pandit Nehru and Mr. John Matthai. Whilst the Muslim League Ministers and Mr. Rajendra Prasad (Food Minister) approved the original taxation proposals, Mr. Vallabhbhai Patel (Home Minister) and Mr. Baldev Singh (Defence Minister) were opposed to them, the latter for personal reasons and the former as the representative and spokesman for the wealthy Hindu industrialists, who for the past twenty-five years have supplied funds to the Congress Party.

[1] Not printed.

205

Sir C. Corfield to Mr Abell

R/1/29/3217: ff 13-14

SECRET   NEW DELHI, *23 April 1947*

My dear Abell,

Please refer to your d.o. letter No. 529/38 dated the 12th April 1947[1] enclosing for advice a copy of a letter[2] from Pandit Jawaharlal Nehru concerning the Political Department.

I enclose for His Excellency's consideration a draft reply,[3] but would like to add some comments in case His Excellency thinks the reply should be amplified.

In the correspondence regarding Datia affairs[4] Lord Wavell authorised me to write to Pandit Nehru as follows:—

21st Novr '46.

"I have placed your letter of the 17th November about Datia State before His Excellency, who has asked me to discuss the question with you at your convenience."

Pandit Nehru did not even acknowledge this letter but instead wrote to Lord Wavell eight days later saying that he had not seen me yet and perhaps I had gone out of Delhi. My office is on the same floor of the Secretariat and in the same block as his. I had been in Delhi the whole time. Lord Wavell replied to Pandit Nehru informing him that I had been here all the time, and saying that I was about to visit Datia but that I should be glad to go and see him on my return. There was no response to this. On this occasion at least Pandit Nehru had the opportunity, of which he failed to take advantage, to penetrate the mysteries of the Political Department!

We have been pressing the States for years to associate their people more closely with their administrations. The progress made has been largely due to our influence. But we have not advised Rulers to abdicate to self-appointed urban malcontents at the dictation of British Indian political organisations or to introduce forms of government which have not always been particularly successful in British India. In fact we are precluded by the Secretary of State's orders from interfering in any way with the *form of government* in States, though we now may, and in fact do, encourage liberalisation in every way open to us.

I do not know why Pandit Nehru should consider that Bastar's interests are more likely to be sacrificed by an agreement with its neighbour, Hyderabad, than its other neighbour, the Central Provinces. And the Crown Representative would expose himself to no less criticism if he made for Bastar, during the minority of its Ruler, agreements with industrial firms as suggested by Pandit Nehru in his letter of 21st November 1946 to Lord Wavell.[5]

APRIL 1947 385

As I explained to His Excellency no negotiations regarding Berar can begin until it is clear with whom the negotiations can usefully be held. If only the Nizam could bring himself to exchange his rights in Berar for a port, these negotiations might be successful. But ever since Lord Curzon in 1902 secured agreement for Berar to be administered with the Central Provinces instead of by the Resident, the Nizam has nursed a grievance which clouds his common sense on this issue.

It is entirely incorrect that the Central Government functions completely in the dark in regard to the activities of the Political Department. There is continual day to day contact between this Department and Departments of the Central Government. Inter-departmental conferences are a common occurrence, and we arrange frequent joint conferences with representatives of Indian States. I have often discussed cases with individual members of the Interim Government, principally Dr Matthai, Sardar Baldev Singh, Mr Bhabha and Mr Liaquat Ali Khan. I have only had one occasion for similar discussion with Pandit Nehru himself and that was on general questions when I called on him shortly after his assumption of office. The reason is that major questions of common interest to the States and British India requiring discussion have not yet arisen in the sphere of External Affairs and Commonwealth Relations.

In any case the Political Department is now closing down, and this alone would seem to rule out making any change in its set up. Nor would it be permissible to allow Pandit Nehru to secure control over the Political Department, since this would insensibly lead to handing over the powers and obligations of paramountcy to a successor Government contrary to the promises given to the States.

Yours sincerely,

C.L. CORFIELD

[1] A brief note asking for Sir C. Corfield's advice on No. 102.   [2] No. 102.
[3] Not printed; this was similar to No. 218.   [4] See L/P &S/13/1830 for this correspondence.
[5] Not traced.

206

Sir H. Dow (Bihar) to Rear-Admiral Viscount Mountbatten of Burma

Mountbatten Papers. Official Correspondence Files: Bihar,
Situation in

D.O. No. 102–G.B.   GOVERNOR'S CAMP, BIHAR,
23 April 1947

Dear Lord Mountbatten,

I was very glad of the opportunity to meet so many members of Your Excellency's Government during the recent Governors' Conference, but at the same time was very disappointed not to be able to meet Sirdar Patel, with whom I had hoped to have a frank talk about law and order matters in Bihar.

2. The recent police mutiny was a very serious affair.[1] The Area Commander had only just enough troops to deal with it. The leader of the rebellion, an ex-constable, Ramanand Tewari, and some 400 police are now in custody awaiting trial. Mahatma Gandhi's ill-judged intervention increased our difficulties, and my ministry were very apprehensive that he would continue to interest himself in the question after return to Bihar. I am very pleased to be able to report that, on the intercession of my Premier, Mahatma Gandhi has agreed not to intervene further in this matter.

3. So far so good, but there is no doubt that the majority of the Bihar Police Force, though they have returned to duty, are still disaffected and cannot be relied on in an emergency. We have appointed an Indian Police Officer to go systematically into police grievances and make a report to Government: police pay has been improved lately but their housing conditions are still bad. But there is no doubt that the main trouble is not economic but political. The known attitude of the ministry to many senior police officers has encouraged indiscipline and more serious still, their failure to curb in time the seditious activities of Ramanand Tewari among the rank and file of the police has had deplorable results. Ramanand Tewari has been backed by Jai Prakash Narain and the C.S.P., who are still supporting the cause of the rebel constables and I should estimate that something between sixty and eighty per cent of the Bihar Police Force would, in the case of a show down between the Congress and the C.S.P., range themselves on the side of the latter rather than act on the ministry's orders.

4. An added anxiety is the existence of our Anti-Smuggling Force, which consists almost entirely of ex-I.N.A. men, armed with Italian rifles and under no effective discipline. I had some difficulty in persuading the ministry to follow the example of other Congress Governments in not admitting ex-I.N.A. men into the police force, but this decision was almost neutralised by the creation of this armed Anti-Smuggling Force, which is not under police control. Your Home Department (see Porter's letter No. 1997/47–P11(I) dated 8th March 1947)[2] have expressed some anxiety about this force, and I have recently objected to the bald and evasive reply which my Government proposed to send on this subject, and have suggested emendations in the draft which I do not yet know whether the Minister has accepted. My Government proposed to say that the force consisted mainly of ex-Army men under the control of the Additional Secretary, Political Department. The fact is that the head of the force is a retired Deputy Collector (and, in my opinion, a very shifty and tactless one) who has been given the status of an Additional Secretary to Government, and that out of the 333 men who had been recruited up to the

8th instant, no less than 297 were ex-I.N.A. men, of whom 246 were non-Beharis recruited from outside the province. They are very undisciplined and act independently of the district officers, many of whom have complained about their arbitrary actions. They are all armed with captured Italian rifles, though many of them were recruited from non-combatant units such as labour battalions and have never handled a rifle before. Naturally there have been several incidents the latest of which was the murder of Abdul Bari, which has pulled the Ministry up with a bit of a jerk.

I believe your Defence Member is also anxious to see the liquidation of this force. In any crisis they would certainly be found on the side of disorder, and are an added responsibility to the Local Area Commander, who has naturally made his view known to A.H.Q.

5. My Prime Minister has now realised his mistake and has ordered some re-organisation and disarmament of this force, but I have been unable to find out how far this has been carried out. He is, I think, handicapped by the presence here, in Mahatma Gandhi's entourage, of "Major-General" Shah Nawaz of the I.N.A. who actually went so far as to ask for Government rifles to arm some of his followers engaged in "reconstruction work": the Prime Minister wished to comply with this demand, but I disallowed it.

6. My Prime Minister is now aware of the seriousness of the state into which law and order in this province has been allowed to drift, and is genuinely anxious to improve matters. His personal relations with me are now quite good, and I think he knows that I have no desire but to be helpful. But it's not very easy for him to break with his past, and he will need all the support and encouragement that Sirdar Patel can give him. It is certainly very difficult for him to take a strong line against prominent members of the C.S.P. who are still encouraging police insubordination unless he is assured of the firm support of the Central Government.

7. My Prime Minister expects to be in Delhi for the Constituent Assembly from the 28th instant. He intends to see Sirdar Patel and to discuss with him particularly the question of the appointment of a Commission to enquire into the Bihar riots. Although my ministry have been overborne in this matter by Mahatma Gandhi, they are at heart dead against the holding of any such

---

[1] On 24 March 1947 the Gaya police went on strike because a police havildar had been fined for contempt of court. Next day the Patna police joined the strike in sympathy and over the following two days police mutinied in a number of towns in Bihar and took charge of police armouries. After the mutineers in Gaya surrendered to the Army on 27 March the situation in the Province progressively improved. On 29 March Mr Gandhi saw Ramanand Tewari who eventually surrendered the following morning. L/P &J/5/182. At his prayer meeting on 27 March Mr Gandhi said the police should never go on strike and he hoped they would call their strike off unconditionally and request the Bihar Ministry to appoint an impartial arbitrator. He expressed regret that the Bihar Government had employed British soldiers to deal with the strikers.

[2] Not traced.

enquiry. They know that it means a grave risk of the recrudescence of communal repercussions in other provinces. I know that too, and should have to consider over-ruling my ministry if, under Mahatma Gandhi's influence, they persist in making a recommendation against their better judgment. In that event I suppose Mahatma Gandhi might persuade my ministry that they ought to resign, which is the last thing which they want to do, or which I want them to do. I don't know what Sirdar Patel's view of this matter is, but I hope he is on the side of the angels and not of the Mahatma. I don't suppose you will think this a suitable letter to show to Sirdar Patel, but you will perhaps speak to him and I shall be most grateful for anything that can be done to stiffen and encourage my Prime Minister to take a firm line in these matters.[3]

Yours sincerely,

H. DOW

[3] Lord Mountbatten replied on 27 April stating that he would do all he could to persuade Sardar Patel to support the Ministry and in particular the Premier, and that he (Mountbatten) intended to show Patel Sir H. Dow's letter at the earliest possible moment. Mountbatten Papers, Official Correspondence Files: Bihar, Situation in.

207

Viscountess Mountbatten of Burma to Rear-Admiral Viscount Mountbatten of Burma (Extract)

Mountbatten Papers. Official Correspondence Files: Interviews

CONFIDENTIAL   *24 April 1947*

Miss Jinnah spent an hour and a quarter with me yesterday afternoon, and, as previously, was most friendly to me, personally.

It was difficult, however, to stop her from talking politics almost continuously, although I tried to steer the conversation quite often on to other subjects. Nevertheless, she somehow always managed to return to political topics, and made violent attacks on Congress and the Hindu community as a whole. She seemed almost fanatical at times in her attitude.

I was interested to note in our conversation that she made frequent references to the fact that "the Muslims would fight for separation and their rights if these were not agreed to", whilst the next moment she would stress the way her brother was supporting in every way the Non-violence Declaration, and at the same time made continuous references to the fact that Pandit Nehru and others in Congress were doing just the opposite.

Like Mr. Jinnah, she has, of course a persecution mania, and is obviously convinced that the Hindu intends to subjugate and dominate the Muslim completely.

She gave me a number of concrete examples of persecution and discrimination by the Hindus, and asserted that the police and Government officials, even here in Delhi, were also discriminating in favour of the Hindu. As an example she stated that Muslims in the Delhi area were searched much more drastically than anyone else to see if they were carrying fire-arms or other unauthorised objects, and said that she had had complaints on this score that very day, (the other side of the picture is, of course, given equally forcibly by Congress Members, and by Raj Kumari Amrit Kaur, a paper on which is attached[1] regarding the North West Frontier Province).

When I tried to be sympathetic regarding the Muslim demand for Pakistan, but at the same time asked for information as to how Pakistan in its original form or in a modified one would really work, Miss Jinnah refused to give any definite answer, saying all the time that the problems involved would be quite easy once Muslim demands had been agreed to.

As far as Bengal and the Punjab were concerned she admitted that the non-Muslim communities might not wish to remain permanently within Pakistan, but that they would, of course, be allowed to make their own choice. This, on the other hand, she stated, would have to be made possible for the Muslim minority in the Hindu areas.

[The remaining four paras. of Lady Mountbatten's note omitted. See, however, No. 276, para. 35 for one of the points covered.]

[1] Not on the file.

208

Mr Tyson to Mr Abell

Mountbatten Papers. Official Correspondence Files: Bengal Partition of, Part I(a)

TOP SECRET   GOVERNMENT HOUSE, CALCUTTA,
D.O. No. 40 CR   *24 April 1947*

My dear Abell,

Please refer to your top secret letter No. 592/92 of the 18th April[1] and enclosure. As requested I enclose a Note on the steps that would have to be taken if Bengal has to be partitioned. His Excellency the Governor has asked me to make the point that he is putting up a scheme of partition because he has been asked to do so and not because he believes in it! He has in fact no reason to believe that he could get it translated into action here without a revolt in

[1] This letter enclosed a copy of No. 156 and asked Sir F. Burrows for a similar note on the partition of Bengal/Assam. Mountbatten Papers, Official Correspondence Files: Bengal, Partition of, Part I(a).

East Bengal and furious rioting in Calcutta unless, of course, Jinnah accepts, and persuades the existing Bengal Ministry to accept, partition. What differentiates us here from the Punjab is that we have a Ministry in "occupation" of both East and West Bengal and they are in no mood to let in a Ministry derived from the Opposition, to run half the Province. The present Ministry in Bengal command a clear majority over all other parties in the Assembly and a comfortable working majority over the official Opposition in the Council.

His Excellency's scheme of partition is outlined in the top secret Note headed "Partition of Bengal". You will see that an important foot-note has been added to the scheme regarding the future position of Calcutta. Under the formula of partition which His Excellency has felt obliged to recommend, Calcutta must be allocated to West Bengal: but there can be no doubt that a fairer arrangement would be one under which both Provinces could enjoy the benefits to be derived from access to the wealth of Calcutta. Such an arrangement would also be more fair to Calcutta itself. The disposition of Calcutta might well prove an important bargaining point in inducing the League to accept a truncated Pakistan in Bengal.

In another respect His Excellency's scheme differs from that of the Governor of the Punjab in that Sir Frederick would, if possible, avoid actual partition until the date when power is handed over generally in India, in the middle of 1948. It will take us all the intervening time to effect a partition but in the meantime, under Sir Frederick's scheme, the two halves of the Province would have a foretaste of what partition involves and there might be some hope of their agreeing to a united Bengal under a Coalition Ministry at the time we go.

Yours sincerely,

J. D. TYSON

Note by Sir F. Burrows

TOP SECRET

PARTITION OF BENGAL

The programme, if partition were to be decided upon, should be as follows.

2. The first step must be to set up a constituent assembly for each of the proposed new provinces—

(i) to work out, by means of mutual discussions, on a basis of equality, (by joint committees, arbitration and the like) the details of the partition;

(ii) to draft the provincial constitution; and

(iii) within the limits of the general scheme, to decide, each for its own province, what links, if any, the new province will have with other authorities.

3. The members of these two constituent assemblies should be the sitting

members, Indian and Anglo-Indian only, of the Bengal Legislative Assembly. For the purpose of constituting the two constituent assemblies, it will be necessary to have a provisional partition of the Province forthwith. This partition will be variable by mutual consent, but will hold good until so varied, either on the advice of a Joint Boundary Commission or by agreement otherwise arrived at.

4. The provisional partition will be made according to the following formula, viz:—

On the basis of the 1941 Census, districts with a Muslim majority will be allocated to the new province of East Bengal: districts with a non-Muslim majority, including the city and suburbs of Calcutta,[2] will be allocated to the new province of West Bengal.

5. The Indian and Anglo-Indian members of the existing Legislative Assembly will be invited to sit in two separate constituent bodies representing the new provinces, for the purposes listed in para. 2 above. To determine membership of each constituent assembly, it will be necessary to allocate the sitting members of the Assembly to East or West Bengal according as the majority of their constituents are in East or West Bengal. This process will be carried out immediately by Chief Whips of parties in the Legislative Assembly sitting as a Committee, the decision of the Governor being final in case of disagreement.

6. Partition will take effect in Bengal from the date on which H.M.G. decide to make over power in India. The object to be aimed at by the constituent assemblies must be to arrive by that date at agreements covering all points arising out of the partition and of the assumption of certain powers at present administered by the Centre.

7. In the meantime the administration of Bengal will be carried on under the

[2] [Note in original:] The criterion of partition adopted precludes the allocation of Calcutta otherwise than to West Bengal as Muslims are in a comparatively small minority in the city and suburbs (Census 1941: *Hindus*—1,531,512; *Muslims*—497,535; *Others*—63,844). At the same time it must be recognized that the prosperity of both halves of the Province is bound up with accessibility to Calcutta, and that much of the prosperity of Calcutta itself is derived from East Bengal. Both communities in Bengal are looking to Calcutta—its income tax and customs receipts, jute export duty and other sources of revenue at present allocated wholly or partly to the Centre—as the most promising source of funds to redress Bengal's chronic impecuniosity and to finance future development. If a means could be found, within the formula of partition, to preserve for the future province of East Bengal an equal right with West Bengal to facilities in, to revenues accruing from and to unrestricted access to, the city and suburbs of Calcutta, it would be unquestionably for the benefit both of Calcutta and of the two Provinces and would really be the fair solution. The constitution of Calcutta as a kind of condominium might go a long way in the last resort to reconcile the Muslim League to the partitioning of Bengal. Without a share of Calcutta's prosperity, the League in Bengal know that there is no future for a province of East Bengal. (By Calcutta here is meant the city of Calcutta and so much of the suburbs as fall under the police jurisdiction of the Commissioner of Police. Howrah is not included.)

existing Government of India Act 1935 by means of a coalition ministry working, as regards the details of administration, in two parts as regional ministries for East and West Bengal respectively. The Legislature of the Province as at present constituted will remain in being till the date from which partition is to take effect, but a convention will be established that for the Province as a whole only legislation agreed to by the coalition ministry as a whole will be introduced or promoted in the Legislature: as regards legislation promoted by either regional ministry for its own area, only the members of the Legislature representing the constituencies allocated to the area concerned will speak or vote. For this purpose it will be necessary to allocate the European members of the Bengal Legislative Assembly and all the members of the Bengal Legislative Council to either East or West Bengal. This will be done on the same basis as, and by a process similar to, that described in paragraph 5, the decision of the Governor being final.

Explanatory Note (Extract)

SECRET

Objects of Partition

It is probably desirable that the minimum of "partition" should be settled under the aegis of the British,—that in fact we should only "decide" enough (and that, as far as possible, variable by agreement) to secure the very early setting up of two provisional authorities with whom we can then proceed to negotiate for the handover in 1948 and who can themselves negotiate with each other on equal terms for the final solution of the very complicated series of mutual problems involved in partition, such as the distribution of finance, the services, existing provincial institutions and other Bengal Government assets and liabilities. As far as possible the temporary adjustments of these matters that must be covered by a British "award" should be of the nature of a "stand-fast order", coupled with a distribution on the basis of the *per capita* strength of the two provisional Provinces where this is appropriate, though we should also aim at putting the two parties in the way of attaining a final settlement over the whole field of partition by mutual consultation, joint committees, arbitration and the like. If we try to work out these things by ourselves before we go—and it must be remembered that we have never expressed our belief in partition on its merits—we could hardly hope to secure agreement and we would risk not having anyone in power to whom we could hand over in 1948. We should as soon as possible put the responsibility for settling the problems of partition squarely on Indian shoulders. The final settlement of the boundary between the two new Provinces, for example, should be the work of a regular Joint Boundary Commission whose terms of reference (and criteria of decision), involving possibly a number of local plebiscites, should be settled by mutual negotiation between the two Constituent Assemblies or their representatives. Meanwhile, however, to make a start at all, there must be some provisional territorial partition by us—the Viceroy and H.M.G.—(agreed to by the party leaders, if possible, in any settlement which the Viceroy may shortly try to bring about). It is this provisional,—perhaps temporary and certainly (by agreement) variable,—partition that this Note is intended to deal with.

Controlling conditions

There being no time now specifically to consult public opinion on the basis of adult franchise, we must make a partition which will conform to what is believed on present evidence to be the wish of the majority community in any particular area, as evidenced at the General Election of 1945–6 and by the current "partition" agitation. Except for some uncertainty as to the effect of the Scheduled Caste vote—(the various "scheduled castes" aggregated some nine millions of Bengal's twenty–five million Hindus in the 1941 census, apart from a large number of Hindus who did not specify their caste (or lack of it))—the Hindus at the General Election may be said to have voted for Congress ideals and against Pakistan. The present "Partition" agitation is in fact an anti-Pakistan movement,—those who support it would rather face the division of Bengal, in order to retain a connection with a Hindu-controlled Central Government, than remain in an independent Bengal (whether Muslim-controlled or under joint Hindu-Muslim control) or a Bengal linked with some form of Pakistan. On the other hand, more than 90% of the Muslim voters of Bengal at the General Election supported the Muslim League's Pakistan programme. This, rather than considerations of viability, a good strategic boundary or equality of opportunity for future development, is the fundamental consideration that must be reflected in any division of Bengal made in present circumstances under British auspices. This means that in existing circumstances the only safe guide is to assume that all Muslims favour some form of Pakistan and most Hindus (there are no other significant non-Muslim communities in Bengal) oppose coming into any form of Pakistan and would prefer a partitioned Bengal with the Hindu part linked with a Central Government at New Delhi. Fortunately the population distribution in Bengal renders a rough and ready partition on these lines possible,—though it could be much improved, no doubt, by a Boundary Commission, with suitable terms of reference, that could visit the areas affected and if necessary take plebiscites. The essential thing for present purposes, therefore, is to find a formula for a provisional partition which, while *prima facie* fair to both Hindus and Muslims, on the basis stated above, will be simple in application and quick and certain in operation, so as to permit of the earliest possible establishment of the respective constituent bodies whose task it will be to set up executive authorities to take over from us in 1948 and to settle the problems of partition and, within the limits permitted, their own future connections (if any) with a Central authority, and to draw up their own future constitutions.

The Formula of Provisional Partition
The formula suggested is that partition at this stage should be on a district basis, Muslim majority districts falling to the new East Bengal and non-Muslim majority districts to the new West Bengal. The basis of calculation will be the 1941 Census.

209

Record of Interview between Rear-Admiral Viscount Mountbatten of Burma and Sardar Patel

Mountbatten Papers. Viceroy's Interview No. 90

TOP SECRET   *24 April 1947, 11 am–12.55 pm*

To begin with I thanked him for his suggestion that I should visit the riot affected areas of Rawalpindi, Multan, Dera Ismail Khan, and Bannu districts. I told him that time did not permit my visiting them all, but that I was proposing to stop off at Rawalpindi on the way back from Peshawar. He said that conditions were absolutely tragic up there and that I would reap a rich harvest by taking an interest in the refugees and making the country feel that an interest was being taken. He regretted that I could not get into the midst of these areas in the time available.

I then had a brainwave and took him along to see Her Excellency, and we agreed that she should stay on at Rawalpindi when I came back, and do a separate tour of all the badly affected riot areas. He was delighted with this proposal and said it would do untold good.

I then told him that the next two items which I proposed to discuss with him were ones that he would not like much, since I proposed to talk to him pretty straight.

I asked him if he had read my minute of the 23rd April, about the appointment of Mr. Banerji.[1] He replied that he had. He asked me in what way the tone of his minute had offended me. I read out to him: "I regard a reference to the Selection Board as both pointless and inappropriate". I pointed out that this was the most direct criticism of myself, that it was discourteous and disloyal to the President of the Cabinet that he should receive from a colleague a minute of this kind; it could not be tolerated by anybody and least of all by me, since I did not take behaviour of this sort kindly.

He said he had meant no offence, but that he himself had been put in an embarrassing position by my ordering his own recommendation to be reviewed by a Committee of Secretaries which included his own Secretary. I told him that if in the first place he had consulted the Establishment Committee, he would not have put himself in this position. He then drew my attention to a written ruling saying that the Establishment Committee were not to have appointments of Secretaries referred to them. I got P.S.V. along, who confirmed that this was a written ruling of Lord Linlithgow's which Lord Wavell, by convention, had reversed and in fact had always insisted that appointments of Secretaries should go through the Establishment Committee.

The Home Member disclaimed all knowledge of this; for (as he explained) had he known about this convention, he would of course have abided by it. He pointed out that in the circumstances he had only been carrying out the written orders, and had felt greatly embarrassed at having his nomination referred by me to the Establishment Committee.

I freely admitted the misunderstanding about Lord Linlithgow's written rule and Lord Wavell's unwritten convention, and said that I would take steps to clear this up when the Appointments Committee was discussed in Cabinet. I told him, however, that nothing could possibly excuse the tone of his minute to me, and I asked him what he proposed to do about it. He said "What would you like me to do about it"? I replied "I would like you to take back the minute, tear it up and incidentally mine as well, and send me a perfectly straightforward simple minute to say that in view of the Establishment Committee's remarks you wished to re-submit the proposal that Mr. Banerji should be appointed". I added that in these circumstances I would agree; but I reiterated that I would not stand for any further treatment from him on these lines.

He took it all in very good part.

I then discussed the position of Mr. Williams. I said "Do you wish me to get rid of Mr. Williams; in fact are you trying to get rid of all Englishmen?" He indignantly denied this; said that he had a high opinion of Williams; that the fact that he had chosen an officer who was senior to him and whose post was becoming redundant on the amalgamation of External Affairs and Commonwealth Relations Departments did not show any lack of confidence; and that if Williams wished to stay on he (Sardar Patel) would be delighted to keep him.

I said I had not met Williams, but I was glad to have good reports of him from Sardar Patel, because I would like to offer him the job of Secretary to the Governor-General (Public) in succession to Mr. Godbole who was leaving under arrangements made by Lord Wavell. Sardar Patel said that Lord Wavell was giving him up as there was not enough work for both him and V.P. Menon. I replied that I would guarantee to find more than enough work for

[1] See No. 210, paras. 3–6 for the background to this incident and transcripts from the minutes referred to.

both of them in view of the pressure at which we were now working; and I said that I certainly wanted a high class officer to take the place of Godbole, and if he was able to spare Williams I should be grateful if he would sound him with a view to my offering him this job.

He said he would talk to Williams.

We next discussed the case of the Chief Commissioner of Delhi.[2] I told him that unless he could explain the two criticisms that he had made of him, I was not prepared to consider them, because as they stood I did not agree with Mr. Patel's conclusions.

The first case concerned the Muslims wishing to prosecute the Editor of the *Hindustan Times* for allowing a cartoon to be published entitled "Mahomed goes to the Mount", which showed Mr. Mohamed Ali Jinnah walking to a mountain which had the likeness of my own face on the top of it. In regard to this, he pointed out that he had a fortnight previously submitted the relevant proceedings of the Press Advisory Committee, and explained that it had been agreed that prosecutions would not be made unless the Press Advisory Committee in general said that there was a case. Since they had already said that there was no case, Mr. Patel complained that a man with the Chief Commissioner's authority had no right to try and make out that it was for the Home Member to take a decision; and that in fact all he had to do was to quote the ruling of the Press Advisory Committee. He considered that in doing this the Chief Commissioner was endeavouring to imply to the Muslims that the matter rested with the Home Member, to the detriment of communal relations.

I had to admit that I saw the force of this argument, which was not at all clear from his minute, and to that extent I thought that the Chief Commissioner appeared to have acted incorrectly.

The second case concerned Mr. Christie's failure to inform the Home Member that Mr. Ghazanfar Ali Khan, the Health Member was going to tour the riot areas in Delhi, in order to see for himself what the police were doing. He complained that since it was quite clear that he was only going for communal propaganda purposes to look into a department which was not the Health Department but the Police Department, he (Patel) should have been informed.

I told him that I could not see that the Chief Commissioner had committed any great crime in this error of judgment, and it certainly did not merit the last paragraph of the Home Member's minute.

I then asked him straight out "Do you want to get rid of the British Chief Commissioner, because if so you have only to say so and then we shall know where we stand." He replied that he did not specially want to get rid of a British Chief Commissioner, though he did not think that Mr. Christie was able to shake off his pro-Muslim League feelings, and did not think he was a particularly suitable Chief Commissioner.

I then said that I would send for Mr. Christie; show him the Home Member's minute; discuss the matter candidly with him; and then I would discuss the matter with Sardar Patel again. I said that I must, however, know who he proposed to replace Mr. Christie by. Mr. Patel said that there were four vital posts in Delhi (the Chief Commissioner—British; the Deputy Commissioner—a Sikh; the Judge—a Hindu; and the Superintendent of Police—an Indian Christian). Mr. Christie had made a great point that the Muslims had been inadequately represented, and Sardar Patel therefore proposed to find a Muslim to replace Mr. Christie if he went. I agreed with the idea in principle but said I would reserve judgment.

Sardar Patel had one final sting. He pointed out that the Delhi Police Force had ten European officers, four Muslims, and only one Hindu. For seven months he had been trying to get Mr. Christie to change the proportions of the Hindu and Muslims police officers without success.

I said that I would speak to Mr. Christie about this also.[3]

I then took the opportunity to discuss the Home Member's request to see all mercy petitions. I apologised for the delay in answering, which had been due to my not having had a meeting with him for nearly a month. I told him that I thought it would be a waste of his time to see all mercy petitions, and that it would be better if he only saw those petitions which were not to be rejected. He accepted this with good grace.

I then discussed with him the line I was going to take in the North-West Frontier. I told him I proposed first of all to see the Government and hear their troubles; then I proposed to see the Muslim League leaders (and I had arranged with Mr. Jinnah to appeal to them to cease their agitation and come out of prison). I proposed to tell the League leaders that so long as this agitation continued, leading to provocative demonstrations, riots and bloodshed, I would support the elected Government with all the strength at my disposal, drafting in additional troops if necessary. On the other hand, after peaceful conditions were restored I would give careful consideration to the question of whether there should be fresh elections before the transfer of power. I told him that this general line had been agreed to by Pandit Nehru, Dr. Khan Sahib and Mr. Liaquat Ali Khan at the various discussions we had had. Sardar Patel signified his agreement by nodding his head.

I invited him to come at 3 o'clock on Friday for discussions with the senior members of my Staff about the plan for the transfer of power, and he accepted gladly.

[2] Mr W. Christie.
[3] Lord Mountbatten's record of his interview with Mr Christie on 26 April 1947 is in Mountbatten Papers, Viceroy's Interview No. 95.

Finally he said "Since you have come out here things have got much worse. There is a civil war on and you are doing nothing to stop it. You won't govern yourself and you won't let the Central Government govern. You cannot escape responsibility for this bloodshed". Asked to elucidate a little more, he explained that he was not trying to link my arrival with the bloodshed since the bloodshed had been occasioned by HMG's statement of the 20th February, and the desire of the Muslim League to seize power wherever they could, hoping that I would transfer power to them.

He concluded by saying: "If you will not act yourself, then turn over full authority to the Central Government and let us stop the Muslim League war in the Punjab and N–W. Frontier; let us stop the Muslim League being mobilised in Bengal to attack Assam; let us govern."

Addendum to No. 209[4]

Record of Viceroy's Interview No. 90 with Sardar Vallabhbhai
Patel, 24. 4. 47.

I deliberately suppressed an ugly scene with Patel to avoid inflaming British Staff opinion against him when they read this record.

The existing record says in para. 4:— "I asked him if he had read my Minute for the 23rd April about the appointment of Mr. Banerji. He replied that he had. He asked me in what way the tone of his Minute had offended me. I read out to him: 'I regard a reference to the Selection Board as both pointless and inappropriate.' I pointed out that this was the most direct criticism of myself, that it was discourteous and disloyal to the President of the Cabinet, that he should receive from a colleague a Minute of this kind; it could not be tolerated by anybody, least of all by me, since I did not take behaviour of this sort kindly".

At this point a scene occurred. Patel became very angry at being ticked off. I then ordered him to withdraw his Minute and tear it up in which case I would tear up my own. He categorically refused. I then told him in that case I would see Nehru and inform him that I was flying home to resign my appointment unless Patel left the Interim Government. I would make it a straight issue that one of us would resign. He questioned whether I would throw up the Viceroyalty after only a month in the job. I replied that he evidently did not know me. I could be tougher than him and unless he withdrew his Minute then and there I would send for his Prime Minister and announce my resignation to him.

Patel suddenly realised that I meant business and completely collapsed, and gave in.

The interview was still difficult but his whole approach had changed and he was respectful and helpful. I reciprocated and this was the beginning of a firm friendship.

My victory over Patel made such a deep impression on me at the time that I actually noted in my personal, very brief diary, "ticked off Patel".

M. of B.

⁴ This note was evidently prepared at a later date.

210

Rear-Admiral Viscount Mountbatten of Burma to the Earl of Listowel

Mountbatten Papers. Letters to and from the Secretary of State

PRIVATE AND TOP SECRET   *24 April 1947*

In my letter of the 17th April[1] I said that your predecessor's letter of the 12th April[2] had just arrived; his letter of the 18th April[3] has just reached me, and so in this letter I am replying to the points mentioned in both these communications.

2. I followed up the publication of the joint statement by writing to Patel[4] and asking him to take steps to ensure that the press took an objective line in reporting events in the country at the present time, and did not add to our difficulties by tendentious and one sided reports. I have just had a reply from Patel[5] giving me a copy of the instructions which have been sent out to the press, but like all party leaders he found it impossible to complete his letter without a violent attack on the attitude of Jinnah and the Muslim League. I am, however, satisfied that we have made a step forward, and the statement by Gandhi and Jinnah and the favourable press it has received in India, should be a great help to us in the coming weeks.

3. Patel has also figured in another incident which I feel I must report this week. He has always been one of the Congress leaders who have stated publicly that he is anxious to keep British officials after the transfer of power in June 1948. He has, however, never shown any practical signs to support these statements, and his attitude has been made particularly clear in the case of the appointment of a relief for Mr. Porter, Secretary of the Home Department, who is going home on seven months leave.

4. The obvious person to succeed Mr. Porter is Mr. Williams, the joint Secretary of the Home Department, who is a competent official with Home Department experience and 24 years service in the I.C.S. Patel however proposed that Mr. Banerji, who is now Secretary of the Commonwealth

¹ No. 164.   ² No. 134.   ³ No. 176.
⁴ See No. 182, note 1.   ⁵ No. 182.

Relations Department, should be appointed in Mr. Porter's vacancy, and this can hardly be resisted as Mr. Banerji is senior to Mr. Williams.

5. Mr. Banerji is not however a particularly competent official, and Mr. Williams having heard of the recommendation has asked to be allowed to go home on leave. Mr. Williams, as Joint Secretary of the Home Department, is concerned with Service questions, compensation, proportionate pension, terms of repatriation and so on. He is thus a key man at the present time, and with the greatest regret I have had to turn down his application for leave; though in the circumstances it would be too much to expect that we can get the best out of him. I feel very sorry for him.

6. Meanwhile I think you should know that since Patel had not referred the question of Mr. Porter's relief to the Selection Board I asked that this should be done. As a result the Home Member wrote on a minute[6] the following remarks:

"I am not surprised that the Selection Board felt embarrassed at the indication of my preference. I myself feel equally embarrassed in having to deal with this matter once again in the light of the Selection Board's comments. In the very nature of things, the Selection Board cannot appreciate the requirements of the Department in the same way as I can. I regard a reference to the Selection Board as both pointless and inappropriate.

The appointment of a Joint Secretary to act in a leave vacancy is by no means an invariable rule. There are instances in which a Joint Secretary has not stepped into the place of Secretary in a leave vacancy. Apart from this, I regard the next six months, or even more, as most crucial from the point of view of the work which is entrusted to the Secretary of the Home Department. A more experienced and senior man is clearly necessary, and I am glad that the Selection Board have agreed on Mr. Banerji's complete suitability for the post, and in view of this their further remarks regarding the officiating appointment of the Joint Secretary in the Department seem quite out of place and uncalled for."

I could not overlook this insubordination, and have replied[7] on the same minute sheet:—

"I agree to the appointment of Banerji. There are some points about the tone and substance of the Home Member's minute which I think should probably be taken in Cabinet. I should like to discuss the matter with the Home Member at our next interview."

7. I saw him today on this subject and have recorded a condensed version of the interview in paragraph 31 of my Personal Report No. 4.

[Para. 8, on the appointment of a European barrister to a permanent vacancy in the Oudh Chief Court, omitted.]

9. In his letter of the 12th April, Pethick-Lawrence referred to the case of

the Nagas. I discussed the matter with Clow, when he was here for the Governors' Conference, and he said that the Naga National Council is self-constituted, but is as representative a body as can be found of the more educated Nagas, particularly of the Angami and Aos tribes.

10. In the copy of the memorandum which my predecessor sent you on the 4th March,[8] the Naga National Council in their reference to an interim government meant an interim form of British rule. The placing of the hill tribes under a Central Indian Government would mean that they would be subject to politicians at Delhi, who would be even more unaware of their needs than the politicians in Assam, and to whom they would have no access. If they can be brought with suitable safeguards within the framework of the Assam constitution, they can themselves expect some share in the Government there and will have access to and influence over the Government.

11. The question is not one which merely affects the Nagas. It affects in the same or only a slightly less degree all the excluded and partially excluded areas of Assam. The real problem is not preservation of the economic equilibrium. The excluded areas are all deficit districts and will have, as at present, to be supported by some other part of India. But the main problem is the protection of these people from exploitation, and the preservation of their way of living.

12. Clow has set out his views on the subject briefly in a pamphlet entitled "The Excluded and Partially Excluded Areas of Assam",[9] of which I attach an uncorrected copy. It is being reprinted, and copies will be sent to you, but I thought it might be useful for you [to] have this copy in advance.

13. Your predecessor in his letter of the 12th April referred to Bevin's discussion with Stalin on the subject of India, and I was interested to read the account of what they said. I took the opportunity during the Governors' Conference of discussing with them the Communist Party in India. and the possibility of financial aid being supplied by Soviet Russia.[10] The Governors' were all very doubtful whether such financial aid was being given, although Burrows' Secretary referred to a report that the Russian Representative on the World Youth Delegation, which visited India early in the year, had handed over a sum of half a lakh of rupees, and had promised further payments for the Party's work in future. This was the subject of your Private Secretary's letter of the 17th April, to my Private Secretary,[11] and is under further investigation in the light of the Foreign office remarks. We were unanimously opposed to any attempt at declaring the Communist party illegal; a step which even in the height of the war was never attempted by H.M.G.

[6] Sardar Patel's minute was dated 21 April 1947. Mountbatten Papers, Demi-Official Correspondence Files: Patel.

[7] Lord Mountbatten's reply was dated 23 April. *Ibid.*   [8] See No. 134, note 7.

[9] L/P &J/7/10635.   [10] See No. 158, Item 5.   [11] L/P &J(S)/File 1057 of 1946.

14. I have referred paragraphs 6 and 7 of your predecessor's letter of the 18th April to my Political Adviser, and will let you have comments in due course. I quite agree with the remarks that a special treaty relationship with the U.K., rather than Dominion status, is the only possible future for the Indian States, unless British India elects for Dominion status and they join the Union of India.

15. I am forwarding herewith for your personal information the record[12] of my meetings with the Governors: additional copies are also being sent separately for circulation as may be required. As I said in my last report,[13] it was a very successful conference, and I am sure we all got very good value out of it.

16. The Governors also unanimously recommended that everything possible should be done to assist British officers of the Indian Police to obtain employment when they retire from India. There are fairly good prospects for I.C.S. officers and for most members of the technical services, but police officers are badly placed because they seldom have University degrees, and their experience does not at first sight qualify them for appointments elsewhere under the Crown, except possibly in the Colonial Police forces, where there seem to be few vacancies.

17. Many of the British police officers are men of considerable ability with adequate secretarial training and experience. The Governors and I feel that they should not be automatically excluded from consideration for the Home Civil Service. After the last war several were taken into the I.C.S.; one became Chief Commissioner of Delhi, and another is now an invaluable member of the Central Board of Revenue. I should say that a policeman with a really first class record would be a better choice for some Departments in Whitehall than an I.C.S. officer with a less good record.

18. I think special efforts should also be made to secure vacancies for police officers in business through the organisation that has been set up for the purpose, and I should be grateful if you would draw the attention of those concerned to this request by the Governors and myself.

19. Finally, I should like if possible to help British members of the Provincial Services, some of whom are likely to retire. Could it be arranged that the Re-employment Bureau which you have started should accept enquiries from Provincial Service officers and assist them in finding appointments?

20. I am forwarding herewith two copies of each of my first three Personal Reports in response to the telegram from your Private Secretary. I am sorry that we have no more spare copies but I will send 8 copies of the Report in future.

MOUNTBATTEN

[12] Nos. 147 and 158.   [13] No. 165.

211

Viceroy's Personal Report No. 4

L/PO/6/123: ff 51–9

TOP SECRET   *24 April 1947*

During this week I have continued my series of meetings with members of the Cabinet and I have also concluded my meetings with the Provincial Governors. I am now cutting down my interviews to enable me to devote more time to the preparation of the plan for transferring power.

2. The unsettled state of the country still continues, although on the surface things may appear quieter, but the N.W.F.P. has been in a particularly unsettled state during the past week. The situation in Dera Ismail Khan and the surrounding districts is still not completely under control and I refer later on in this report to the steps I have taken which I hope will effect an improvement.

3. Eastern India is quieter, but the Army authorities there consider that the situation is worse than in July 1946 and far more ominous of grave and widespread disturbance. The Provincial Ministries, other than Orissa, are certainly leaning more and more heavily on the army, while the latter's resources are, with disbandment, daily decreasing.

4. The police situation in Bengal is particularly deplorable. In Calcutta there were recently 1200 policemen, mainly Gurkhas, as recruitment from the plains had never been resorted to. When the Inspector General asked for an increase of 50 per cent, Mr. Suhrawardy, the Chief Minister, insisted that they must all be Muslims. To speed up training it was decided that they must be ex-soldiers and as there were none suitable in the Province, 600 Punjabi Musulmans were secured from the Punjab. The latter were given preferential treatment by the Muslim Government, with the result that they have now come into armed conflict with the Gurkha policemen and I am afraid that the police situation may deteriorate. The Muslim Government of Bengal has just imposed a pre-censorship on news comments criticising the activities of the police force in Bengal.

5. The Governor takes the view, and has told Suhrawardy, that the Bengal Ministry, by unfair treatment and taking a communal line, is fast ruining the one reliable police force that Calcutta possesses which has taken the Government through all the Calcutta troubles of the past two years, in spite of being abused by both Hindu and Muslim papers just as it suited their politics from time to time.

6. In Bihar the Governor, Dow, tells me that his Congress Government is both incompetent and weak. In his opinion less than half his Ministry

would qualify even for a seat on a parish council in England. There is now virtually no reliable police force in Bihar, so that the situation is that there is no buffer between lawlessness and the Army and the latter are called out at each slight disturbance.

7. The Bihar Government has recently employed nearly 300 ex-I.N.A. men, against the advice of the Governor, as an anti-corruption force. Dow prophesied that they would end up by killing innocent people through lack of any sort of discipline and training and the next day they accidentally killed an important member of the local Congress party, Abdul Bari.

8. The Chief Minister was so shaken by this that he agreed to disarm and disband the entire outfit. But unfortunately "Major-General" Shah Nawaz, late of the I.N.A., was able, according to the Governor, to exercise his influence with Miss Mridula Sarabhai, one of Mr. Gandhi's entourage, so that the matter has not yet been satisfactorily settled.

9. Just as the Governors' Conference finished last week the telegrams about the situation in Dera Ismail Khan started to come in. I therefore took advantage of Caroe's presence to hold a small meeting with him, Nehru, Liaquat Ali Khan and Baldev Singh after the official dinner for the Governors in order to see whether there was any thing which could be done to ease the situation in the Province.[1] This was a most difficult meeting, which turned largely about the desirability of issuing a statement regarding future elections in the Province. I suggested that Caroe should be authorised to say on his return that after a recommendation had been made to His Majesty's Government about the transfer of power, and before the transfer of power had been effected, elections would be held in the N.W.F.P. to ascertain whether the Province would be a Congress or a Muslim League Province. Nehru was however of the opinion that such an announcement should not be made in existing circumstances as he thought it would appear that the Provincial Government's hand had been forced by the agitations which were taking place. I then suggested linking the proposed announcement not only with the Governors' Conference and the fact that I had only recently taken over, but also with the Gandhi-Jinnah statement denouncing violence. However it was not possible to arrive at an agreed solution.

10. I therefore held back Caroe for another day, and Nehru invited Dr. Khan Sahib, the Chief Minister, to come down by air to Delhi. After another difficult meeting[2] at which Khan Sahib accused Caroe of non-cooperation, which the latter refuted, it was eventually agreed that the Government of the N.W.F.P. would issue an immediate announcement, based on the Gandhi-Jinnah appeal, to the effect that all political prisoners, who were not charged with offences of violence, should be released as soon as conditions permitted, it being understood that processions and picketing would not be allowed

until normal conditions returned. The announcement was drafted on the spot and it looked as though we had made a step forward.

11. Recent telegrams however show that most of the 5000 political prisoners now refuse to leave the jail. I have spoken strongly to all four Muslim League members of my Cabinet inviting them to use their influence and have also decided to visit the N.W.F.P. next Monday and Tuesday, the 28th and 29th April. I have pointed out separately to Jinnah and all four of the Muslim League members that I could not be a party to surrendering to any form of violence and that the Muslim League will make it impossible for me to give a decision in favour of fresh elections while the programme of agitation (usually leading to violence) in the Province is allowed to continue, particularly if the present Government there finds it necessary to call upon the use of force to suppress these demonstrations. I have no doubt that fresh elections will be necessary in due course, but the Province must settle down before these can be held, as it would be fatal to let it appear that the Provincial Government had given way to threats of violence.

12. A striking commentary on the state of the country is provided by the proposal which came before the Cabinet this week that the Government should sponsor a compulsory scheme of insurance against loss of banking and business communities on account of civil disturbances. I think the pressure behind this proposal comes from the Congress industrialists and bankers, as the insurance companies are at present suffering severe losses, for example at Dera Ismail Khan. Such a scheme may help to focus attention on the true state of affairs here when in peacetime the Governments have so little control over internal affairs that it is necessary to establish a scheme of compulsory insurance on the same lines as operated throughout the war.

13. I had my interview last Friday with the Sikhs represented by Master Tara Singh, Gyani Kartar Singh and Sardar Baldev Singh.[3] Any hopes that I still entertained of being able to avoid the partition of the Punjab if Pakistan is forced on us were shattered at this meeting; all three Sikhs made it quite clear that they would fight to the last man if put under Muslim domination. They considered that the Cabinet Mission had let them down badly, and presented me with a book called *The Betrayal of the Sikhs* on this subject, written by Landen Sarsfield. They have an encyclopaedic knowledge of every letter that passed with the Secretary of State and of all statements made on the subject in the House of Commons and brought with them copies of *Hansard* and all the correspondence.

14. In particular they were very bitter about paragraph 19 (vii) of the Cabinet Mission plan, which stated that "In the Union Constituent Assembly resolutions varying the provisions of paragraph 15 or raising any major

[1] No. 162.   [2] No. 171.   [3] No. 173.

communal issue shall require a majority of the representatives present and voting of each of the two major communities". They pointed out that although they had been given the status of the only other major community, they had been expressly excluded from this paragraph, since they were not one of the two major communities. They pointed out that a Christian or Anglo-Indian, who came under the heading of "General", could in fact vote on such issues from which the Sikhs were excluded. They particularly wanted the same right of communal veto as the other two major communities on questions affecting their interests. I advised them to raise this matter in the Constituent Assembly.

15. The previous day the Raja of Faridkot had handed me a letter he had received from Tara Singh and Kartar Singh, in which they invited him to "take over the entire policy, organisation and safety of life and property regarding the districts of Ludhiana, Ferozepore and portions of Lahore and its administration".[4] I was warned by the Raja that if Sardar Baldev Singh accompanied the other two Sikhs they would not speak freely on this and this proved to be the case. Later I saw the Maharaja of Patiala,[5] who told me he had made it very clear to the Raja of Faridkot that any attempt on the part of small Rulers to play a game of grab at this time would, in his opinion, be disastrous and that he would do everything he could to prevent it. He offered his services to try and keep the peace among the Sikhs to the best of his ability. But he said he feared the situation had so deteriorated that he simply did not know how the Sikhs could be prevented from fighting, unless they were completely separated from the Punjab and guaranteed against any attacks. Even then, the preparations for civil war now going on showed what was brewing. In this connection I have seen an appeal issued by the Sikhs' leaders, calling for a "War Fund" of Rs 50 lakhs, which sounds very ominous.[6]

16. Liaquat Ali Khan has appealed to me to allow the Muslims to carry swords, since the Sikhs are legally allowed for religious reasons to carry kirpans, which puts them at a great advantage whenever street fighting starts. For the present I have told him that two wrongs do not make a right, and two men with swords are more likely to start a fight than two men with only one sword![7]

17. I referred in my report last week[8] to the lines on which my mind was working, and to the hope that I might be able to let you have a report this week. We have been hard at work since the Governors' Conference, but I am afraid that matters have not yet reached the stage at which I can let you have a firm recommendation.

18. I am naturally still doing everything in my power to get the Cabinet Mission plan accepted. But although Congress have nominally accepted both the plan and statement of the 6th December, Jinnah and the Muslim League leaders I have spoken to are convinced that Congress have no intention whatever

of complying with the spirit of the plan. They consider that Congress would merely use their permanent majority at the Centre to manipulate the army, to bring pressure to bear on Groups B and C where necessary and to manipulate the right to raise finance for the Centre to the detriment of the internal economy of Groups B and C. In evidence of this they draw attention to the Constituent Assembly decision that Customs must be dealt with by the Centre in view of their implications on external affairs.

19. Liaquat went so far as to say that it was providential that Congress had refused the Cabinet Mission plan during the time that the League had accepted it, since it was now clear that they intended to use the Cabinet Mission plan to obtain a permanent stranglehold over the predominantly Muslim groups.

20. I have already pointed out to Jinnah and the League leaders that there must be some form of Centre or Supreme Defence Council even if Pakistan comes about, and that this Centre will have to deal with practically the same subjects as the Centre envisaged in the Cabinet Mission plan; that is to say, over-all defence. So we come to the ridiculous situation where Jinnah in his insistence on Pakistan is likely to get a very truncated edition of it and still have to go to some form of Centre, instead of accepting complete autonomy over Groups B and C with a somewhat similar Centre. The real difference of course lies in the fact that in the former case there would be parity at the Centre and the League could not be outvoted. But it shows what value the League sets on this parity, since to obtain it they are prepared to sacrifice the richest plums of Pakistan.

21. This is the one bargaining counter I have left, for it is just possible that when faced with the full stupidity of what they are doing, the League might make some gesture to accept a compromise Cabinet Mission scheme and Congress in their desire to retain some form of unity might also be more forthcoming. But I am afraid this is a very pious hope and there are no signs that I shall succeed.

22. At the moment I favour a final meeting to consist only of Nehru, Patel, Jinnah, Liaquat Ali Khan and Baldev Singh (with Gandhi hovering about in the background as usual) and with the Working Committees at their disposal. I aim at getting this meeting together about the middle of next month and may hold it at Delhi rather than Simla.

23. I have formed a special Committee consisting of Ismay, Mieville and Abell, who are working on the production of a plan under my general direction. This would of course include the draft of an announcement by His Majesty's Government how they intend to transfer power on the due date. We four have met one of the principal leaders each day this week—Liaquat on Monday,[9]

4 See No. 173, note 1.   5 No. 184.   6 See No. 109.
7 See No. 178.   8 No. 165.   9 No. 190.

Nehru Tuesday,[10] Jinnah Wednesday[11] and Patel on Friday.[12] I have found that if one gets a single leader to give evidence before a small committee they are more reasonable and go out of their way to be helpful not only in pointing out difficulties which would be encountered from their own party, but also frequently drawing attention to the difficulties which would be raised by the other party.

24. With the additional staff which His Majesty's Government kindly authorised me to take out, I have more than doubled the high level staff which Wavell had, and both staffs are very happily integrated and pulling very well together. Ismay and the ex-C.O.H.Q./S.E.A.C. members of my staff all agree with me that none of us had to work so hard or on such complicated problems during the war. But there is a sense of exhiliration about tackling this task and we are all impressed with a sense of vital urgency.

25. I have been asked by two of the Princes[13] what line to take in the new situation created by Nehru's speech at Gwalior last Saturday,[14] at which he was reported to have given the States what amounted to an ultimatum, either to join the Constituent Assembly or be treated as hostile. The Nawab of Bhopal and Sir C.P. Ramaswami Aiyer have since asked me for interviews, and I understand they will be raising the same question.

26. I saw Nehru on the 22nd,[15] and hauled him over the coals for his inflammatory speech at Gwalior, and said I was disappointed to find that a man who could be so statesmanlike in Cabinet, could be such a demagogue when let loose in public. I also told him that for Members of the Interim Government to make statements of this type without prior reference to the Cabinet was highly reprehensible.

27. He took my 'ticking off' in good part, and was at pains to explain that he was speaking only in his personal capacity as President of the States' People's Conference, and was not speaking on behalf of either the Cabinet or even Congress. He further claimed that he had been misquoted, since he had only intended to convey that failure on the part of Rulers to send representatives to the Constituent Assembly was behaving in a hostile manner towards the Constituent Assembly and to their own people, and would produce reactions accordingly.

28. I told him that I considered that the intention of the Cabinet Mission had been that the representatives of States were only to come into the Constituent Assembly in the third and final stage which had not yet been reached. I further pointed out that in view of further possible developments in regard to Pakistan of which he was well aware, some of the States would more properly be joining a Pakistan Constituent Assembly. I told him I regarded his speech as mistimed and unfortunate, and that I was authorising the Political Adviser to tell Rulers who sought his advice that my personal view was that

I could not see how failure to join the existing Constituent Assembly before the time laid down by the Cabinet Mission or before it was decided whether it was to be the only Constituent Assembly, could be regarded as hostile; although of course I was in no position to speak on behalf of the existing Constituent Assembly.

29. Nehru said he quite agreed that in view of the impending statement which I hoped His Majesty's Government would make soon, Rulers could quite well wait until that statement was made before deciding to send up their representatives; but that he wished to point out that the best way to avoid being regarded as hostile by the States' People's Conference was to ensure some measure of consultation with their own people about their future.

30. I have informed Corfield[16] that in my own view Rulers would in fact be well advised to consult the will of their people, and then make a quick announcement about joining the Constituent Assembly (or Assemblies) as soon as the statement by His Majesty's Government has been made.

31. Nehru is not the only Minister I have had to deal with this week. A few days ago I received a discourteous minute from Patel.[17] So I sent for him and told him "They tell me you are a tough guy. Well so am I. Now will you take back your minute or do you want me to bring it up in Cabinet?" He took it back.

32. Liaquat Ali Khan's paper[18] demanding the partition of the armed forces between Pakistan and Hindustan comes before the Defence Committee on Friday. Although I am insisting that so long as I am statutorily responsible for law and order in India I will not agree to the actual partition taking place, Auchinleck and Baldev Singh have both expressed themselves as very worried at the effect that the mere planning of partition would have on the morale and loyalty of the army. On the other hand, if Pakistan is finally decided on the news could in any case not be kept secret and we should be faced with the difficulty of an army subject to communal calls with the one restraining influence, the British officer, in process of gradual removal.

33. The item about Gurkhas had a stormy passage both in the Defence Committee and Cabinet. The Government of India's decision to continue to employ Gurkhas with the Indian Army was taken three days before the Muslim League joined the Interim Government.[19] The League now to a man, are opposed to the employment of "foreigners" in the Indian Army, pointing out that unlike the British who could plead genuine manpower shortage,

[10] No. 194.   [11] No. 203.
[12] No. 216; this meeting took place on Friday, 25 April 1947, i.e. a day after the date of this report.
[13] See Nos. 187 and 188.   [14] See No. 181, note 2.
[15] No. 193.   [16] No. 196.
[17] See No. 209 and No. 210, paras. 3–6.   [18] See No. 215.
[19] See Vol. VIII, No. 534, para. 9 and Vol. IX, No. 16.

India had more than a million unemployed demobilised soldiers. A long and heated discussion was provoked, at which I finally had to give a ruling in favour of the majority, that the Indian Army should continue to employ Gurkhas.

34. It required extremely tactful handling to avoid the Cabinet then and there turning down His Majesty's Government's request for Gurkhas on the grounds that if they continued in the Indian Army, it would be very difficult in the eyes of the world to separate Gurkhas employed by the Indian Government from those employed by the British Government. I had to ask them finally how they proposed to stop Nepal sending Gurkhas to join the British army; did they intend to deny the inhabitants of an independent Kingdom the right to buy a ticket to go across India to join the British Army, and if so had they thought out the full repercussions?

35. Meanwhile as you will have heard by telegram, Lyne had a friendly interview yesterday with Nehru, and with the latter's full consent, is going to Katmandu at the end of this week.[20]

36. My wife had two full days with the Governors' wives last week; the first being the occasion of a formal Conference covering their various problems regarding medical, educational and welfare work; the second being spent in informal discussion with them together with representatives of various Government Departments and organisations with whose work the Governors' wives are concerned. These talks helped considerably towards the clarification of many mutual problems, and showed directions in which assistance might be given to future development.

37. My wife has also continued her tours of hospitals and welfare centres, and has had talks with further leading personalities, including Mrs. Sarojini Naidu, and Mr. Frank Anthony, leader of the Anglo-Indian community. She also saw Miss Jinnah alone who shocked her with her threats of civil war if Pakistan were turned down.[21]

38. Auchinleck arrives home on the 1st May; he knows my latest views and can give a first hand account of the lamentable state of the country. I sincerely hope that the Prime Minister and Cabinet Ministers concerned will send for him on his arrival.

[20] See tel. IRKU 267 of 23 April 1947. L/WS/1/1024. Major-General L.O. Lyne headed a War Office deputation which was visiting Delhi and Katmandu to hold preliminary discussions on the Gurkha question.
[21] See No. 207.

212

Sir E. Jenkins (Punjab) to Rear-Admiral Viscount Mountbatten of Burma

Telegram, R/3/1/177: ff 4–5

IMMEDIATE

24 April 1947, 11 pm
Received: 25 April, 3 am

No. 82-G. In letter dated today 24th April Mamdot demands formation of Ministry which would evidently consist of Muslims only or of Muslims supported by a few Christian or Scheduled Caste Members. He asks for early interview so that he may submit his proposals.

2. Formation of such a Ministry would unquestionably precipitate non-Muslim rebellion of extreme violence in Central and Eastern Punjab. Conditions have changed radically since Ministry making was suspended on 5th March and we are now in revolutionary situation with all communities preparing for final struggle. Non-Muslims would believe with reason that Mamdot would endeavour to use police and troops to suppress them, and would withdraw criminal proceedings against Muslim Offenders in Rawalpindi Division and Multan. Mamdot would find himself involved immediately in something like Civil War and would in my judgement be unable even to hold obligatory Budget Session of Assembly. Civil Services would be split from top to bottom and task of British Officers would become quite impossible. Some of them including several Senior Police Officers would probably ask to be relieved at once. Your Excellency can judge better than I can probable effect of upheaval on this scale in your discussions with party leaders.

3. I doubt if Mamdot has majority in Assembly but if I resist him on this ground alone I commit myself to acceptance of communal Ministry as soon as majority is proved. I propose therefore to tell Mamdot frankly *first* that a communal Ministry cannot in my judgment carry on the Government of the Punjab in accordance with the provisions of the Government of India Act and *secondly* that no move to form a Ministry will be made until Your Excellency's discussions with the leaders are concluded, when the future of the Punjab will presumably be clearer. In dealing with *first* I would rub in League's assertion of right of direct action in January and February. Decision on these lines may lead to agitation by Muslims but it appears to me the only possible decision. If Your Excellency could prevail upon Jinnah to accept it the effect would be good. Local leaders are fatuously complacent and if I were in their place I would not dream of forming a Ministry.

4. I cannot defer seeing Mamdot beyond Monday 28th April and shall be

grateful for orders by then.[1] In view of importance of this telegram and to save ciphering I am repeating to Secretary of State for information.

[1] In tel. 885–S of 25 April Lord Mountbatten said he entirely agreed with Sir E. Jenkins and was sending Mr Abell to see him the next day. R/3/1/89: f 170.

213

Major Crichton to Sir G. Squire

L/P&S/12/1811: f 185

SECRET
D.O. No. D.3140–NWA/47.   NEW DELHI, *24 April 1947*
Dear Squire,
Please refer to your D.O.No.706/44/NGO of the 5th April[1] on the subject of Anglo-Afghan relations.

2. We cannot possibly accept the Afghan view that the tribesmen in tribal territory (if by this they mean tribal territory on the Indian side of the Durand Line) are more closely connected with the Afghan Government than with the Government of India. Ever since the Durand Agreement of 1899 (page 256 of Aitchison's Treaties Volume XIII) it has been recognised that all territory including the tribal areas on the Indian side of the Durand Line forms part of India. The fact that there is an interim Government in India does not alter that position in the slightest and it follows that any overt attempt by the Afghan Government to exercise influence in these areas would be open to the same strong objection as in the past. You will see from Chapter XI of the last Afghan Précis (compiled by Dundas)[2] that this matter has a long history and that Afghan attempts to interfere in our tribal areas have always been strenuously resisted. That attitude, we consider, must be maintained so long as the Afghans continue to recognise the Durand Line as the boundary between India and Afghanistan, and we take it that there is no intention on their part of denouncing it. The attitude of H.M.G. and the Government of India in this matter has in fact already been made clear to the Afghan Government in the course of the recent discussions held with the Foreign Minister on Afghan Frontier Policy—vide para. 4 of the record forwarded with my demi-official letter (written as Chargé d'Affaires) No. F.706/44 of the 22nd December 1945.[3]

3. As for the other aspects of the matter, it is of course quite irrelevant whether or not the Afghan Government are under pressure from their own subjects; but we are frankly sceptical of the Prime Minister's statement that our tribes are looking to the Afghan Government for a lead. Our own inform-

ation is that the tribes, at present, are indifferent to Afghan interest in the problem of their future and intend to rely on themselves when it comes to determining the question of their association with an independent Indian Government. This question, as the Afghan Government are doubtless aware, is one for negotiation between the tribes and the Constituent Assembly and Pandit Nehru has made it amply clear in his public declarations that there is no intention whatever of depriving the tribes of their existing freedom or of attempting to impose any scheme on them against their will. Afghan anxiety is therefore misplaced and the Prime Minister need have no apprehension that tribal sentiment and wishes will be ignored.

4. We should be glad if you would speak in this sense if the Foreign Minister or Prime Minister should revert to the subject again and make it quite clear that the Government of India could not possibly countenance any interference in their tribal areas by emissaries of the Afghan Government.[4] This does not imply that the Government of India do not recognise that the Afghan Government has a natural and lively interest in seeing a satisfactory arrangement emerge from the discussions with the tribes and the Government of India will at all times keep that fact in mind.

5. I am sending copies of this letter to Baxter, Donaldson and Caroe.

Yours sincerely,

G.C.L. CRICHTON

[1] No. 82.

[2] *Précis on Afghan Affairs—Vol. II from the middle of 1927 to the end of 1936. Compiled by Mr A.D.F. Dundas* (New Delhi, Government of India, Foreign and Political Department, 1938). L/P &S/20/B. 305.

[3] L/P &S/12/1811: ff 316–23.

[4] In his letter D.O. No. F.706/44/N.G.O. of 9 May, Sir G. Squire reported that he had conveyed to the Afghan Foreign Minister the views of the Government of India as contained in No. 213. Ali Muhammad was 'disappointed and said so frankly. He admitted that the Government of India's contention was unanswerable but reiterated what he had often said before that as long as the British Government remained responsible for the control of the Frontier the Afghans had nothing to say. He thought it however somewhat hard that when we had announced that the British Government would be relinquishing that control in June next year we should still expect the Afghan Government to refrain from all attempts to clarify a potentially dangerous situation until the British had actually left India. He expressed the fear that the new Indian Government would attempt to coerce the tribes to come under Indian administration and that this would lead to a conflagration in which Afghanistan would inevitably be involved, with results that no-one could foresee.' L/P &S/12/1811: f 147.

214

Minutes of Viceroy's Twenty Second Staff Meeting

Mountbatten Papers

TOP SECRET

Those present during discussion of Items 5–7 of this Meeting held at The Viceroy's House, New Delhi on 25 April 1947 at 10 am were: Rear-Admiral Viscount Mountbatten of Burma, Lord Ismay, Sir E. Mieville, Mr Abell, Captain Brockman, Mr I. D. Scott, Mr. Campbell-Johnson, Lieutenant-Colonel Erskine Crum

Item 5

THE RETENTION OF INDIA WITHIN THE COMMONWEALTH[1]

HIS EXCELLENCY THE VICEROY recalled that he had always made it absolutely clear in his discussions with Indian leaders that there would be no question of the British remaining in India after June, 1948, unless they were specifically asked to do so by an united request from all Indian parties. If such a request was made, he would forward it for the consideration of H.M.G. He said that he was personally of the opinion that such a request should be refused if it was possible to refuse it with honour. He felt that, whereas all possible assistance must obviously be given to India, on request and if she remained within the Commonwealth, by the provision of officers to assist her Armed Forces, the task facing a British Governor-General, as a high level umpire, with a small team of advisers, would be fraught with frightful difficulties. He said that he wanted Lord Ismay to discuss this question when he went to London and to point out that there was hardly one responsible person of every Indian party who had not thrown out some hints that they wanted the British to stay after 1948. He felt that there was a distinct possibility that, if an united request was made, His Majesty's Government might decide to accede to it and leave a British Governor-General (possibly himself), in India after June 1948. He also felt that there was a possibility that His Majesty's Government might accept an unilateral application by Pakistan to remain within the Commonwealth. Lord Ismay should warn the Secretary of State that there was a move afoot towards such a request being made and point out the difficulties which would result.

LORD ISMAY said that he considered that the greatest care should be exercised over this question in conversations in India also. The Indian leaders were very suspicious and any verbal statements made might easily be misunderstood.

SIR ERIC MIEVILLE said that he believed that any move to grant India Dominion status before June 1948 would be interpreted by the Indians as an effort to keep them in the Commonwealth after that date.

HIS EXCELLENCY THE VICEROY:—
invited C.V.S. to speak to members of His Majesty's Government in London
on the lines which he had indicated above.

Item 6
THE NORTH WEST FRONTIER PROVINCE

HIS EXCELLENCY THE VICEROY drew attention to the reports in that
morning's papers of a statement[2] by Mr Jinnah to his followers in the North
West Frontier Province. He pointed out that this statement was on the lines
that had been agreed at the meeting[3] with Mr Jinnah two days previously.

Item 7 (*Extract*)
PROPOSALS FOR A MEETING WITH INDIAN LEADERS

LORD ISMAY explained that the draft invitation to the Indian Leaders and
the draft announcement, contained in this paper,[4] had been redrafted from the
previous issue, as a result of a series of meetings which he had held over the
previous few days with Sir Eric Mieville, Rao Bahadur Menon, Mr Abell and
Mr Christie.

The meeting then considered in detail the revised draft announcement at
Appendix "C" to this paper.

HIS EXCELLENCY THE VICEROY asked whether there was any question
but that the Sylhet District was the only predominantly Muslim district in
Assam. This point should be checked.

HIS EXCELLENCY THE VICEROY said that he considered it highly
probable that the Muslims would demand a plebiscite for Calcutta and the
areas immediately surrounding that city. He understood that the population
thereof was composed of a quarter Muslim, a quarter Caste Hindus and the
remaining half Scheduled Caste Hindus and other minorities. He believed that
both Mr Jinnah and Mr Liaquat Ali Khan thought that the Muslim League
would win a plebiscite in the Calcutta area. He foresaw that, at the meeting
which it was proposed to hold, there would be much argument over the
future of Calcutta. It was, after all, the second largest city in the Empire and
its fate was bound to be a major issue. He pointed out that the avowed intention
of referring the choice of their future to the Indian people themselves was that
a completely fair answer should be obtained. It would be most undesirable to
lay down a procedure of self-determination which would give the wrong
answer. There were several possible lines to take. For example:—

(a) Should it be stated that there was not time for a plebiscite anywhere
    and that it was essential that there was consistency in the procedure
    adopted throughout India? Or

---

[1] Previous Reference: No. 192, Item 2.   [2] See Appendix to these Minutes.
[3] No. 203.   [4] The meeting was considering a revised version (V.C.P. 33) of No. 181.

(*b*) should it be decided on that there should be a plebiscite in Calcutta and the immediately surrounding areas? Theoretically was it the only fair way, to hold a plebiscite? Or

(*c*) would such a plebiscite lead to bloodshed and excessive delay? Or

(*d*) should a plebiscite perhaps be held at a later date? Or

(*e*) should Calcutta be declared a free city?

LORD ISMAY gave his opinion that, once any exceptions to the general procedure were allowed, there would be pressure for other exceptions to be made—for example in Lahore. MR SCOTT agreed with this and said that the same was true of Assam. MR ABELL pointed out that Calcutta was a creation of the British and the Hindus as far as capital investment was concerned. MR CHRISTIE stated that Mr Tyson had been quite clear that Calcutta should be part of Western Bengal. He felt that a plebiscite would be a sure way of inviting a blood-bath.

LORD ISMAY suggested that Mr Christie should fly to Calcutta to discuss the draft announcement with the Governor of Bengal and that Mr Abell should go and discuss it with the Governor of the Punjab. HIS EXCELLENCY THE VICEROY approved this suggestion. He also said that Sir Akbar Hydari, who (it was believed) was still in Delhi, should be called in for consultation.

HIS EXCELLENCY THE VICEROY also asked Sir Eric Mieville to discuss the outlines of the plan contained in the draft announcement with Mr Jinnah.

Discussion then turned to the timetable which it was hoped that events should take. In the course of this discussion, MR SCOTT suggested that a period of about a fortnight should be given to the Working Committees of the respective parties to consider the alternative plans in the light of full publicity and with the implications of each choice fully before them. He felt that, once the machinery of Partition was set in train, it would be very difficult to arrest and reverse it. If the Working Committees were given full time to discuss the alternatives, the Left and Right Wings of each party might come into opposition. There was already a strong element in each, he believed, in favour of accepting a compromise on the lines of the Cabinet Mission Plan. Some Congress members were probably ready to make concessions in order to obtain an unified India. On the other hand, Mr Jinnah and Mr Liaquat Ali Khan were, he felt, beginning to realise the full implications of a truncated Pakistan.

MR ABELL said that he considered that there would be plenty of opportunity after the issue of the announcement to obtain public opinion in the full limelight of publicity. He believed that, in any case, there would be a pause after the issue of the announcement. The Parties would have any amount of time to join up again.

HIS EXCELLENCY THE VICEROY said that it was most important that, with the issue of the announcement, the impression should not be created that

Partition was a foregone conclusion, but that the question had been referred for decision to the will of the people. The programme would really have to be decided on what the results of the expression of the people's will, through their representatives, were likely to be. He would like to see a decision reached as quickly as possible in order to stop recrimination and strife. He felt that there was bound to be a spate of venom during the period between the issue of the announcement and the time when the votes were cast. However, to improve the chances for returning to an united India, he felt that an escape clause should be included in the announcement.

HIS EXCELLENCY THE VICEROY said that he would consider as counting as a form of Union of India any plan in which the Centre dealt with the same subjects as in the Cabinet Mission's Plan. The crux of the matter seemed to him to be that, in the Cabinet Mission's plan, the Hindu majority at the Centre would be able permanently to out-vote the Muslim minority and use the reserved subjects to subdue them. The alternative was that the representatives of Pakistan and Hindustan should come together to a common Centre on the basis of parity. If this form of an united India could be obtained, it might be possible for the Punjab, Bengal and Assam to remain united.

MR ABELL pointed out that, if Pakistan and Hindustan were two Sovereign States, their representatives would not really meet on the basis of true parity. That would be dependent on the relative strength of the two. HIS EXCELLENCY THE VICEROY said that he realised this point. His object was to create the effect of two Sovereign States, or separate blocs, negotiating at the Centre rather than having a system of majority voting.

HIS EXCELLENCY THE VICEROY asked whether there was likely to be sufficient intelligent Muslim officials to administer Pakistan. MR ABELL said that they would probably hire Hindus for some of the more difficult administrative appointments.

MR CHRISTIE said that, in his belief, Pakistan would be able to starve Hindustan within the course of a year or two. All the surplus food in India was in Pakistan and it could not be argued that they would not [sic] have to export this surplus for economic reasons because they would be able to grow jute and cotton instead for export.

HIS EXCELLENCY THE VICEROY said that he wished a brief to be prepared from which he would speak at the meeting with the Indian Leaders. Perhaps at this meeting he would spend the first day in making every effort to secure acceptance of the Cabinet Mission's plan. The first day's meeting might perhaps be a short one, and the leaders might be asked to consult their Working Committees in the afternoon, and return with an answer the following day. If that answer was unfavourable, he might next bring forward the possibility of complete Partition on the basis of the draft announcement before the meeting, making it clear that he would not be prepared to alter the details of this except by agreement with all parties. He might then revert to the possibility of some form of Centre. The meeting would have to be handled very carefully, step by step.

MR SCOTT said that he believed that the leaders of both the major parties in India were seriously worried. They did not know what was in the Viceroy's mind. He added that he did not consider that the present disturbances in India should be taken too much account of. He personally did not believe that there was likely to be a civil war within a month, although he agreed that the present state of affairs could not go on indefinitely. LORD ISMAY pointed out that lawlessness was on the increase in a most frightening way.

[The conclusions of this minute, which included detailed amendments to the draft announcement in No. 181, omitted.]

Appendix to No. 214
MR JINNAH'S SPEECH OF THURSDAY 24th APRIL

"I have had talks with His Excellency the Viceroy more than once and, as a result therefore, the first step has been taken by the Frontier Government in announcing:

(1) Their decision to release unconditionally all political prisoners as soon as conditions permit; and

(2) that they have no intention of interfering with the freedom of expression of political opinion or with peaceful meetings, but processions and picketing cannot be permitted until normal conditions return.

Since then, the Viceroy last evening discussed with me specially the grave situation that has arisen in the North-West Frontier Province; and, notwithstanding his preoccupations, he has interrupted the important business with which he is so immediately concerned and has decided to go to the Frontier on Monday next.

The fact that His Excellency is going to the Frontier is undoubtedly a clear indication of his earnestness to examine the situation personally and to establish contact with the leaders in the Province, and his determination to remove the root-cause of the serious trouble and situation that has arisen in the Province.

As a result of my talk, I feel that the Viceroy is determined to play fair. And in view of these circumstances, I appeal to the Muslims generally and the Muslim Leaguers in particular, to maintain peace, law and order so as to give the Viceroy every opportunity to fully understand the situation.

I am glad that Mr Nishtar is already there and I feel confident that he will guide and help our people in every way he can."

215

Note by Indian Cabinet Secretariat

*Mountbatten Papers. Official Correspondence Files: Armed Forces,
Indian, Volume I, Part I*

IMMEDIATE   NEW DELHI, *25 April 1947*
TOP SECRET AND PERSONAL
No. DCI/I–161/47
The undersigned is directed to forward papers in connection with item 5 on
the agenda of the meeting of the Defence Committee India to be held this
evening at 6 pm.

In view of paragraph 8 of the Defence Member's paper members of the
DCI are requested to treat all these papers as *very specially secret*.

J. G. ELLIOTT
Deputy Secretary (Military)

Paper 1

TOP SECRET
Preparation of plan for the partition of the Indian Armed Forces.

Paper by H.M. Finance

The Indian Armed Forces, Army, Navy and Air Force, are now in the process
of reorganization and nationalisation. The object of reorganization is to
produce out of the war-time forces now undergoing demobilization a balanced
force of all arms and services. The object of nationalisation is to replace all
British officers and men in the Indian Armed Forces by Indians as soon as
possible. Nationalisation affects mainly the officer cadre including the Higher
Command. The question of selecting Indian officers for the appointments of
Commanders-in-Chief of the Army, Navy and Air Force, Army Commanders,
Principal Staff Officers and other senior posts in all the three Services is, I
understand, already under consideration.

2. After H.M.G.'s statement of 20th February 1947, a United India with a
single Army, Navy and Air Force can no longer be taken for granted. In spite
of this, the reorganisation and nationalisation of the Armed Forces are proceeding on the assumption that they are to continue as a single entity. The fundamental constitutional issue of a United or Divided India is thus being prejudged
on a most vital point to the grave detriment of Muslims. The division of
India implies the division of the Armed Forces for no State can exist without
its own Armed Forces on whom rests the ultimate responsibility for internal
security as well as external defence.

3. Another serious consequence of treating the Armed Forces as a single entity is that no regard is paid either to the organization of Muslim units or to the representation of Muslims in suitable number and ranks in all the arms and services. From such figures as I have been able to obtain from the Defence Member so far, I find that the representation of Muslims in the Armed Forces is grossly inadequate particularly in the officer cadre of all the three Services but more markedly in the Navy and the Air Force. I am trying to obtain more information on the subject and shall raise the issue at a later stage. I touch on it here to indicate that Armed Forces which do not have an adequate representation of Muslims in numbers and ranks will not have the confidence of the Muslims—a situation fraught with the utmost danger to the security of the country and of the Armed Forces themselves.

4. In order that the constitutional issue should not be prejudged it is necessary to devise a course of action which should not be to the advantage or prejudice of either political Party. This neutral position would be obtained by reorganising the Armed Forces in such a manner that they can be split up when a decision on the partition of the country is taken. An essential preliminary is the preparation of a plan by the Commander-in-Chief and his staff for the partition of the Armed Forces. This will necessarily take some weeks and if taken in hand immediately should be ready by about the time that a decision on the main constitutional issue is reached. The time limit set by H.M.G. demands that no time should be lost in preparing such a Plan which will in no way interfere either with the present political negotiations on the present status of the Armed Forces.

5. I suggest therefore that—
(i) the Commander-in-Chief should be asked to prepare a plan for the partition of the Armed Forces, and
(ii) action on the present plans for the reorganization and nationalisation of the Forces on the basis of a United India should be suspended until the constitutional issue has been settled. This is of the utmost importance because if present plans are persisted in, their reversal at a subsequent stage will mean a major upheaval which may have most serious effects upon the efficiency of the Armed Forces.

Paper 2

TOP SECRET

Remarks by H.M. Defence

23 April 1947

I have very carefully considered the note by H.M., Finance on the "Preparation of Plan for the Partition of Indian Armed Forces".

2. It is true that the Indian Armed Forces are now in the process of reorganisa-

tion and nationalisation and that this is proceeding broadly as indicated in the note. The need for reorganisation arose due to the imperative urgency of return to post-war conditions within the limited funds available with which is also intermixed the inescapable technical and scientific changes brought about by developments during and experience gained in war. The scheme of national-isation has been drawn up as a result of the overwhelming pressure of public opinion and changes inherent in the present situation which no one can ignore. Both reorganisation and nationalisation could only proceed on an all-India basis. No other course was either possible or practical for the simple reason that the major issue of the defence of India as a whole could not be prejudiced in any way until the larger political issue of Division—if it is indeed to take place—is finally and fully settled in all its bearings and implications. To say that the reorganisation and nationalisation of Armed Forces prejudges the issue of Division, is to subordinate the larger interests of Defence to sectional or Group interests—a proposition which nobody will accept.

3. In para 3 of his Note, H.M. Finance has made reference to "Muslim Units" and "representation of Muslims" in all arms and services of the Armed Forces, in the light of the figures I gave him in reply to his enquiry in this respect. I do not understand the reference to "units". As regards the statement that "representation of Muslims in Armed Forces is grossly inadequate" I must take the strongest objection to the statement as well as the insinuation which incidentally has found place lately in the Muslim League Press as well. I note that H.M., Finance will raise this question later. Meanwhile I will state that neither in the process of reorganisation nor that of nationalisation has any discrimination been made against Muslims or any other community per se. The Armed Forces as now emerging after the war, are being organised on a set-up built on standards of the past with modification to suit the needs of the times and based on the experience of Army Commanders over a long period of time. The entire scheme of this organisation is being drawn up by specialists in various technical branches and services under the direct authority of the C-in-C, and I can say with authority that nothing has happened in this planning to the detriment of any community in any way. If therefore the demand for a plan of the division of the Armed Forces, here and now, is based on the sug-gestion that Muslims are being discriminated against, it is wholly wide out of the mark, to say the least.

4. I have had the implications of the proposal of H.M., Finance examined by the C-in-C. His note is attached. In the short time available to him, he has analysed it in some detail with reference to the administrative, technical and financial implications involved. It is his firm view that the division of the Armed Forces into two on the basis of Hindustan and Pakistan is not possible before June 1948 and indeed for quite a long period thereafter with due

regard to the requirements of Defence and that is if enough funds are found. Of far greater consequence are such factors as the territorial boundaries of the two States and whether Muslims now in the Forces and residing in non-Muslim regions—defined or to be defined—are to be drafted in the scheme of "Pakistan Forces" and if so whether with or without any reference to the Officers and Men concerned.

5. The Armed Forces as a whole have been built up on non-communal basis. They have, fortunately for India, remained free from communal complications up till now. Various factors have contributed to this and among these the chief one is the general belief that whatever the political future of the country, any attempt at the division of the Armed Forces will leave both the Muslim and non-Muslim parts not only weak in numbers but technically and strategically at considerable disadvantage against even the weakest neighbours. The discipline inculcated by association with British Officers has been a cementing force of no small value. In the event of a Division of the country, the division of the Forces will of course have to be faced. In that event and while the process is on, the potency and striking power of the Forces will, I have no hesitation in saying, remain seriously impaired for a considerable time. That issue too will have to be faced when the time comes. What I must lay the greatest emphasis on is that if even the mere indication of splitting the Armed Forces is allowed to gain ground at this stage, it will result in creating chaotic conditions in the ranks and disintegration will set in almost immediately. In the communally surcharged atmosphere in which we find ourselves today—to say nothing of the international situation—such a contingency would be too disastrous to contemplate.

6. Nor can I ignore how the prevailing communal disturbances have affected the administration in certain areas and the repercussions thereof on internal security. Respect for law and order is rapidly waning. In certain parts, large sections of population have lost confidence in the ability of the police to protect life and property. The only relieving factor in this dark picture is that the integrity of the Armed Forces is still unsullied. Their aid is sought after and welcomed by all everywhere irrespective of group or communal considerations. They, on their part, have fully measured up to the expectations of the Government and the people. It would indeed be an irreparable disaster if a Force such as this was exposed to risks that would not only weaken but ultimately destroy its worth.

7. For these reasons—

(a) I am strongly of the view that the time is not opportune to discuss the proposal of H.M., Finance in the Defence Committee of India in terms as stated by him.

(b) I cannot agree to suspend the present plans for the reorganisation and nationalisation of the Armed Forces which, on the other hand, must proceed in view of the urgency of many complex issues that cannot be shelved without serious loss of time and money, and risk of endangering the efficiency of the Forces.

8. In view of the difficulties I have stated and inherent in this problem at this stage, I would suggest instead that H.E. might informally discuss the issues involved personally with H.M. Finance or any other Hon'ble Members as he may deem fit.

BALDEV SINGH

Paper 3 (Extract)

TOP SECRET

Remarks by H.E. the Commander-in-Chief

GENERAL

1. The Armed Forces of India, as they now stand, cannot be split up into two parts each of which will form a self-contained Armed Force.

Any such proposal would involve the rebuilding of two new Armed Forces of which many essential components do not at present exist in duplicate, or are not located suitably to serve two separate sovereign States.

2. "PAKISTAN" includes all the important land frontiers of India, and the Army and Air Forces required to defend "PAKISTAN" from external aggression would be virtually the same as those now required to defend India as a whole.

3. If "PAKISTAN" and "HINDUSTAN" are to have separate Defence Forces, it would seem certain that the combined total of these forces must be greater than that of the Defence Forces designed to serve a United India, since the administrative overheads must be duplicated and there would be a great loss of flexibility.

[The remainder of Field Marshal Auchinleck's paper, explaining in detail the difficulties of dividing the Army, omitted.]

216

Minutes of Viceroy's Eighth Miscellaneous Meeting, Item 2

Mountbatten Papers

TOP SECRET

Those present at this Meeting held at The Viceroy's House, New Delhi on 25 April 1947 at 3 pm were: Rear-Admiral Viscount Mountbatten of Burma, Sardar Patel, Lord Ismay, Sir E. Mieville, Mr Abell; Lieutenant-Colonel Erskine Crum (Secretariat)

THE CHOICE BY PROVINCES OF THEIR OWN FUTURE

HIS EXCELLENCY THE VICEROY said that nobody was a more ardent subscriber to the theory that India should remain completely united than he. If a full Central Government could not remain in power after the British had gone, he would like to see the Cabinet Mission's plan accepted. The last thing he wanted was any form of partition. However, Pandit Nehru and the other Congress leaders whom he had consulted had declared that they did not wish to embody any unwilling provinces (or parts of provinces), which, in the present state of affairs, might go to war rather than accept an united India.

SARDAR PATEL stated that it was a fundamental policy of Congress that there should be no coercion. But it was equally fundamental that they should not themselves be coercion [coerced].

HIS EXCELLENCY THE VICEROY then gave an outline of one of the plans then under consideration, whereby provinces would be given the choice of their own future. In discussion of this plan, SARDAR PATEL made the point that, in the Punjab, Bengal and Assam, the answer to be given to the question of provincial partition would depend on the answers given elsewhere on the partition of India as a whole. For example, people would vote differently if they knew that there was going to be a Pakistan or if they knew that there was not.

HIS EXCELLENCY THE VICEROY said that this difficulty could perhaps be got over by making those Provinces in which there was no question of partition vote first. Then those which might be partitioned would be able to see more clearly on what issues they were voting.

MR. ABELL expressed the view that voting in every Province would depend on decisions in others, and that it would therefore be difficult to lay down an absolutely fair system of priorities.

HIS EXCELLENCY THE VICEROY said that he had got the impression from several sources that Bengal, for economic reasons, wanted to remain as an entity. The Hindus' fear in this, however, was that they might be voted into Pakistan by a slight majority. SARDAR PATEL said that he believed that the feeling in Bengal among non-Muslims was that, whether there was Pakistan or not, they could not remain united unless joint electorates were introduced.

HIS EXCELLENCY THE VICEROY asked what the attitude of the Muslim League to joint electorates was likely to be. For instance, Muslims were 57% of the total population of Bengal. Surely they would welcome joint electorates? If not, why not? MR. ABELL said that the Muslim League feared that Congress would put up Muslim candidates if joint electorates were introduced. SARDAR PATEL gave his opinion that the main objection of the Muslim League to joint electorates was because the Hindus were so much better organised. However, joint electorates could be easily arranged and an additional safeguard could be provided by the reservation of seats according to population.

HIS EXCELLENCY THE THE VICEROY asked what would happen if joint electorates were introduced in the Punjab. SARDAR PATEL said that it was quite possible that a Coalition Government would be set up. HIS EXCELLENCY THE VICEROY remarked that the Muslims would jump at the idea of joint electorates if they had faith in them.

HIS EXCELLENCY THE VICEROY said that, if the Working Committees of the Muslm League and Congress agreed that joint electorates should be set up, this fact might be included in the announcement.

SARDAR PATEL said that the people in Eastern Bengal were very poor. The only industry there was the growing of jute. Both Hindus and British had exploited them. There were no Muslim factories in that part and the people would either have to build jute factories or deal with Calcutta. They could not afford to wait.

HIS EXCELLENCY THE VICEROY said that he had received several reports that the Sikhs intended to fight a war of revenge as soon as the British left India.

SARDAR PATEL said that there were 100 Sikh girls in the possession of the Muslims in Western Punjab. HIS EXCELLENCY THE VICEROY said that he would speak to the Governor of the Punjab about this. He asked what was the object of forcible conversions. SARDAR PATEL said that it was impossible for him to answer this because he had no idea of the Muslim mentality. They might be the result of religious fanaticism or, partly, of efforts to increase the Muslim population. He said that 95% of the Muslims in India were converts from Hinduism and 80% were forcible converts—although they had in some cases been enforced by the old rules of Hindu society. There was no question of forcing or trying to persuade people to convert to the Hindu religion.

SARDAR PATEL said that he thought that His Majesty's Government had got the idea that Mr. Jinnah could still be induced to accept the Cabinet Mission's plan. He gave his opinion that the main result of the statement of 20th February had been a race to capture the different Provinces. He said that in attacking the economic cohesion of India the Muslim League were in fact only attacking themselves.

HIS EXCELLENCY THE VICEROY said that Mr. Jinnah had explained to him his reasons for not accepting the Cabinet Mission's plan. He had said that it could only be worked in a state of mutual trust and co-operation, which was impossible at the moment.

SARDAR PATEL then went through the whole history, at very considerable length, from his own point of view, of the refusals to accept, the acceptances of, and the withdrawals of acceptances of the Cabinet Mission plan. He said that Congress were ready to accept the Cabinet Mission Plan even now with no reservations, including the statement of 6th December. However, on this point he insisted that Sir Stafford Cripps and Lord Pethick-Lawrence had stated in the Houses of Parliament that the Muslim League could not deliberately frame a Constitution in Group 'C', which would make it impossible for Assam to opt out. HIS EXCELLENCY THE VICEROY pointed out that this was not clear in the statement of 6th December. He said that he would look up the record of the Parliamentary Debates concerned.

During his description of negotiations the previous year, SARDAR PATEL implied accusations against Mr. Abell of being biased in favour of the Muslim League. He said that he had called Mr. Abell to his face "the Secretary of the Muslim League". Later he unreservedly withdrew these accusations, and expressed the view that the desire to be fair-minded was apt to result in pressure on both Congress and the Muslim League, both of which were apt to resent it.

SARDAR PATEL said that he understood that the Viceroy had offered Mr. Jinnah a greater degree of parity in the Interim Government if he accepted the Cabinet Mission's statement.

HIS EXCELLENCY THE VICEROY said that this was not the case. He had made no such offers to Mr. Jinnah. However, the latter had told him that the basic reason for his non-acceptance of the Cabinet Mission's plan was his fear of Congress domination, by majority vote, on the reserved subjects. HIS EXCELLENCY THE VICEROY suggested that a possible compromise might be that all major questions in the Cabinet should be settled by a majority of each party, voting separately.

SARDAR PATEL said that this procedure would be impossible to work if, as at present, every honest act suggested by the Hindus was taken by the Muslims as directed against them.

He further pointed out that it could, however, be introduced by legislation of the existing Constituent Assembly if the Muslim League would join it. HIS EXCELLENCY THE VICEROY said that he intended to point out this to Mr. Jinnah.

SARDAR PATEL then made the following statements:—

(a) Congress would not accept any suggestion for a further degree of parity in the present Central Government.

(b) If the Muslim League did not accept the Cabinet Mission's plan, Congress desired partition.

(c) Congress had reached the maximum limit of their concessions.

HIS EXCELLENCY THE VICEROY said that Mr. Jinnah had requested him not, at the proposed meeting of Indian Leaders, to ask him to accept the Cabinet Mission's plan. SARDAR PATEL said, "All right, don't ask him." HIS EXCELLENCY THE VICEROY pointed out that history would judge very harshly of him if he did not. SARDAR PATEL said that history had already exonerated the British, since their statement of 20th February. HIS

EXCELLENCY THE VICEROY said that he would consider asking the question of Mr. Jinnah and Mr. Liaquat Ali Khan separately, and not before the full meeting.

HIS EXCELLENCY THE VICEROY:—

(i) invited C.V.S. to consider introducing into the time-table of events a provision whereby those Provinces in which provincial partition was an issue should vote after those in which it was not;

(ii) decided to speak to the Governor of the Punjab about the report that there were 100 Sikh girls in the possession of the Muslims in Western Punjab;

(iii) decided to look up the records of the Parliamentary debates in which Sir Stafford Cripps and Lord Pethick-Lawrence were alleged to have stated that the Muslim League could not deliberately frame a Constitution in Group 'C' which would make it impossible for Assam to opt out;

(iv) decided to point out to Mr. Jinnah that, if the Muslim League were to join the Constituent Assembly, legislation could be introduced whereby all major questions in the Central Government should be settled by a majority of each party voting separately.

217

Record of Interview between Rear-Admiral Viscount Mountbatten of Burma and Sardar Patel

Mountbatten Papers. Viceroy's Interview No. 93

TOP SECRET   *23 April 1947, 5.10–5.20 pm*

Sardar Patel stayed back after the meeting which he had been attending at Viceroy's House, and saw me alone for ten minutes. He was in a very diffident and chastened mood. He brought out the Banerji/Williams file and said "Will you please allow me to withdraw the minute which you did not like and to substitute this in its place?" (The new minute was merely to the effect that he had seen me personally and had obtained my approval to the appointment of Mr Banerji.) I replied "I accept the withdrawal of this minute"; and I personally removed the offending minute sheet, and pinned on the new one. I then kept the offending minute sheet myself, and told him I considered the incident closed.

He pointed out that P.S.V. must have been misinformed if he thought Lord Wavell had introduced a firm convention that appointments of Secretaries should go before the Establishments Committee, for he could produce half a dozen cases in Lord Wavell's time where this had not been the case. I told him that so far as I was concerned the incident was closed now, and that I was glad to note that he had not been acting in any way in bad faith, and that in fact I was sorry if I had misunderstood the position. "But", I ended up, "I hope you really do understand that I won't have minutes of this sort from you in the future, and I hope you will not try it on again". He made a graceful little gesture of assent, and rose to go.

On his way out, he said that if Her Excellency required any financial assistance from the Central Government to help in looking after the refugees in D.I.K. and other places, [he] would be very glad to do what he could to obtain this for her.

218

Rear-Admiral Viscount Mountbatten of Burma to Pandit Nehru

R/3/1/142: ff 93-4

No. 589/38   25 April 1947
Dear Pandit Nehru,
I have looked up your previous correspondence with my predecessor about the activities of the Political Department, and find that most of the points you raise in your letter[1] have already been dealt with.

If it is true that officers of the Political Department encourage reaction in the States and frown upon progressive tendencies, they are acting entirely contrary to the policy of the Crown Representative: and if you can produce any evidence to substantiate this allegation I will not hesitate to take suitable disciplinary action.

As regards Bastar, I think that my predecessor's letter No. 529/38–C dated November 21, 1946,[2] makes it sufficiently clear that there is no intention of *entrusting* the development of Bastar to the Hyderabad State, or of making Bastar an economic vassal of Hyderabad. Draft agreements are now in preparation, after the most careful study and investigation, to cover the grant by the Bastar Darbar to the Hyderabad Government of a prospecting licence and mining lease in respect of iron ore and for the construction in the Bastar State by the Hyderabad Government of a railway from the Hyderabad border up to Bailadila, where the Bastar iron deposits are situated. The agreements will not be concluded without my approval and before they are approved they will, as my predecessor indicated in his letter, be referred to the Departments concerned of the Central Government for technical advice so that we may be as certain as is possible that the interests of the Bastar State are fully secured. I have no intention of allowing the interests of Bastar to be sacrificed. Your letter goes on to suggest that, when the Ruler of a State is a minor, important agreements should not be entered into on its behalf by the Political Department, or rather the Crown Representative. If the Crown Representative were to accept this suggestion it would mean that a State under minority administration would be condemned to stagnation. I hardly think that you can seriously subscribe to such a proposition even at this stage of our relationship with India.

In regard to Berar I have ascertained that no steps have yet been taken, but it is hoped to arrange as soon as practicable for negotiations between Hyderabad and British India on the lines contemplated in paragraph 4 of the Memorandum on States Treaties and Paramountcy presented by the Cabinet Mission to the Chancellor of the Chamber of Princes on 12th May 1946.

The constitutional position of the Political Department was explained in my predecessor's letter of the 25th November 1946,[3] and I repeat his offer to let you have any information you wish regarding the principles which govern the activities of that Department. I have, however, decided that, in view of the prospective lapse of paramountcy, these activities should be curtailed as rapidly as possible. Thus the Political Department will die a natural death, and be replaced by such direct arrangements as may be found most convenient and acceptable.

However, since I am most anxious to be as open and frank with you as possible I propose to hold an informal meeting in the near future with you and my Political Adviser, at which I shall be glad to give you all information that I properly can.[4]

Yours sincerely,
MOUNTBATTEN OF BURMA

[1] No. 102.   [2] Not traced.   [3] L/P &S/13/1830: f 25.
[4] Pandit Nehru acknowledged this letter on 26 April 1947. R/1/29/3217: f 11.

219

Government of India, External Affairs Department to Secretary of State

Express Letter, L/P &S/12/4197: f 63

SECRET   NEW DELHI 3, 25 *April 1947*
No. F.10(14)–NEF/47
Subject: *British Mission, Lhasa*

British Mission has continued in Lhasa since 1936 on a temporary basis, budget provision for its maintenance having been provided *ad hoc* year by year and not as a matter of course.

2. Government of India now wish to be represented in Tibet (at the start, at all events, on the same temporary basis) and would be grateful to know whether His Majesty's Government desire to retain separate Mission there in future.

If they do not, it would seem feasible to arrange transition from "British Mission" to "Indian Mission" without publicity and without drawing too much attention to change, to avoid if possible any constitutional issue being raised by China.

3. If His Majesty's Government are agreeable, transition might take place in, say, six month's time. Meanwhile the Mission might be authorised to make known informally, and in strict confidence, to Tibetan Government that it will continue in being; Government of India believe that, reluctant though Tibetans might be to see end of British representation in Lhasa, they would welcome assurance of continuance of Mission and, by implication, of India's friendly interest in Tibet.

The issue of the above has been authorised.

L.A.C. FRY
for Secretary to the Government of India

220

The Earl of Listowel to Rear-Admiral Viscount Mountbatten of Burma

Mountbatten Papers. Letters to and from the Secretary of State

PRIVATE AND SECRET   INDIA OFFICE, *25 April 1947*

My dear Viceroy,

I would like to tell you with what tremendous interest I have read your first three Personal Reports;[1] I had not seen the first two at the time of their receipt. I hope you will agree with the suggestion which has, I understand, already been made to you that you should in future send sufficient copies of these reports to be circulated to all the Members of the India and Burma Committee, since they will clearly form an essential part of the background to the decisions which the Committee will be called upon to take during the next few months.

2. To turn to your third report. Pethick-Lawrence has already sent you a message of congratulation[2] upon the achievement of the joint appeal by Mr. Jinnah and Mr. Gandhi for the renunciation of the use of force for political ends. I would like to associate myself with those congratulations and with the hope he expressed that the appeal may have some effect in reducing communal strife. I cannot help noting, however, that in paragraph 22 of the same Report

you draw attention to the likelihood that, if any attempt is made to impose the Cabinet Mission Plan on the Muslim League, they will resort to arms to resist it.

3. It was perhaps hardly surprising that nothing came of Mr. Gandhi's outline for a scheme for an Interim Government pending the transfer of power.

4. Your full and vivid accounts of your prolonged talks with Mr. Jinnah seem to lead remorselessly to the conclusion that there is only the remotest possible chance that the Cabinet Mission's plan can still be implemented. It is clear that this result is not for want of your having impressed upon Mr. Jinnah with "ruthless logic" the probable consequences for the Muslims of insisting on a full-blooded Pakistan, however truncated. It is, of course, only natural that, as a corollary to the Muslim refusal to accept what they represent would be a Hindu Raj on the all-India scale, the non-Muslim elements in those areas which the Muslims regard as naturally destined to become a part of Pakistan are beginning to agitate for partition of provinces. The growing force of this agitation in Bengal, for example, is illustrated by paragraph 3 of Burrows' letter to you of 11th April (No.F.J.B.22).[3]

5. There certainly appears to be an impressive consensus of opinion in official quarters in India as to the need for a very early declaration of H.M.G.'s intentions and I shall, of course, await with keen expectation a more explicit exposition of what you have in mind. I need hardly say, however, that I appreciate all too well the crucial nature of the recommendations which you will be making and you may rest assured that I have complete confidence that you will choose the right moment for making them.

6. It was very encouraging to learn that the Governors are happy about the decision reached in regard to compensation for the Services. In particular, the attitude that appears to have been adopted by Trivedi and Hydari leads one to hope that the decision not to grant compensation to Indian members of the Services except in special cases will not cause resentment on the part of Indian members of the Services.

7. I am sure that the Governors' Conference will have been of the greatest value to the Governors themselves, all of whom are carrying an exceptionally heavy and difficult burden at the present time. The Congress attitude to Jenkins, Caroe and Mudie will only serve to increase the difficulty of their tasks and is greatly to be deprecated. It is also a sad reflection on the states-manship of some Indian political leaders that the best proof of a Governor's success should lie in the equality of the violence with which he is accused of partisanship by either side.

8. The problem raised by Mr. Liaquat Ali Khan in his letters to you of 7th

[1] Nos. 59, 108 and 165.   [2] See No. 151, note 1.   [3] No. 127.

and 13th April[4] about the communal aspect of the reorganisation of the Indian Army is a difficult one and it is to be hoped that your suggestion that the matter should be discussed by the Defence Committee will be acceded to and that the discussion in Committee will be a helpful one. The vital need for avoiding any step which may adversely affect the reliability of the army is well illustrated by one passage in the Governor of Bihar's fortnightly letter to you of 5th April D.O. No. 86/G.B.[5] where he says that, in his Province, a position has already been reached in which the government is only kept in power by the presence and loyalty of the army. This is indeed a significant admission.

9. In paragraph 6 of his letter of 21st April,[6] Pethick-Lawrence referred to our policy in respect of the Indian States, and suggested that our only possible course at this stage is to stick to the lines of the Cabinet Mission's Memorandum on States' Treaties and Paramountcy. You may be interested to know that the American Embassy made an informal approach to the India Office the other day on the basis of reports which have been reaching the State Department from their representative in Delhi. The Embassy asked to be assured that H.M.G. are not contemplating departure from the Mission's plan in so far as the States are concerned, and in particular are not contemplating maintaining direct relations with the States after the transfer of power. The suggestion was that, if this were the case, the U.S. Government might have to consider modifying its present attitude of open support for British Policy towards India.

10. The main ground for this démarche seems to have been an interview in Delhi between Merrell and Nawab Mir Nawaz Jung, the newly-appointed Trade Commissioner for Hyderabad in London, whose status I understand the Hyderabad Government have shown a desire to raise to that of a quasi-diplomatic "Agent General". He apparently told Merrell that Hyderabad intended to remain a separate political entity, independent of any Indian Union, and wished to remain in alliance with the United Kingdom; he added that Bhopal would do the same. He claimed that his own appointment was intended as a covert means of sounding H.M.G. in the matter. He admitted however that Sir Mirza Ismail is clever enough to create the basis of cooperative relations with the Congress successor regime, even if this is not intended to lead to any fusion with an Indian Union.

11. It was suggested to the American Embassy that the reference to Sir Mirza Ismail's disposition to work with Congress indicated that there might not be much in Nawaz Jung's claims: Hyderabad was perhaps chiefly concerned to raise its stock for bargaining purposes with the future leaders of India. In any case, nothing was known in the India Office of any abandonment of the Cabinet Mission's plan in respect of the States, and we did not contemplate continuance with them of special relations outside the Indian Union;

paragraph 12 of the Statement of February 20th in fact implied no change in the Mission's plan. It was of course not beyond the bounds of possibility that before June 1948 the Viceroy might report that there was no possibility of the Mission's hopes as regards the States being realised, and in that event he might propose to H.M.G. some other means of fulfilling our undertakings. But no such proposition was before H.M.G.

12. This conversation was on the Chancery level and it was not apparently desired that the Ambassador should approach me formally on the subject. I am, therefore, passing on the report to you in the same informal manner. I should add that Merrell apparently reported very adversely on the speech made to the States' People's Conference at Gwalior by Nehru,[7] whose lack of statesmanship in this matter he deplored. He also reported that the feeling in Delhi was that the Cabinet Mission's plan in general no longer held the field, that there was no sign of leadership towards an All-India solution among British Indian politicians as a result of your talks, and that while some states had decided to join the Constituent Assembly, the majority showed little intention of doing so. You will of course treat these disclosures of what Merrell has been saying to his Government with all due discretion.

[Paras. 13–18, on Polish refugees in India and the relatives in India of members of the Polish Forces, omitted.]

19. May I, in conclusion, say how particularly pleased I am to learn of your decision to appoint three Indian A.D.C.'s and of the unprecedented extent to which Indians are taking part in official functions. I am sure that changes of this kind, which are long overdue, will have a beneficial effect out of all proportion to their apparent importance.

Yours sincerely,
LISTOWEL

⁴ Nos. 94 and 135.   ⁵ L/P &S/5/182.
⁶ No. 176; the date should be 18 April.   ⁷ See No. 181, note 2.

221

Defence Committee India. Minutes of Third (47) Meeting

*Mountbatten Papers. Official Correspondence Files: Armed Forces,
Indian, Vol. I, Part I*

TOP SECRET
PERSONAL   *25 April 1947*
ITEM V—To consider a paper "Preparation of a plan for the partition of the
Indian Armed Forces" submitted by H.M. Finance.
The committee had before it papers submitted by H.M. Finance, together

with the comments thereon prepared by H.M. Defence and H.E. the Commander-in-Chief.[1] His Excellency in introducing the paper said that he regretted that he had had to over-ride the advice of H.M. Defence and H.E. the Commander-in-Chief in bringing this paper before the committee. They had been so impressed with the need for secrecy, because of the disastrous effect on the armed forces if it was known that this matter was even under consideration, that they had been reluctant to agree to the matter being discussed at all. He too, fully appreciated the great importance of ensuring complete secrecy in this matter. His reasons for bringing the matter to the committee were that he required their views for inclusion in his report to H.M.G. as to the form of government he recommended for India. Pakistan was an issue which must be faced, and the partition of the armed forces was one of its most important implications.

H.M. Defence emphasised all he had written as to the effect on the armed forces of partition. Such division of forces should follow the political decision in favour of Pakistan, assuming that such a decision was taken; if it were to precede such a decision, the consequences might be serious.

H.M. Finance agreed that the decision must obviously follow the political decision, but there must be a plan in readiness to go ahead with separation if Pakistan was accepted. Further nothing must now be done that would in any way complicate what was already a difficult problem.

Points in discussion were:

(a) The technical difficulties of separation were enormous, but if it became politically necessary they would have to be overcome. To delay thinking about them would make it all the more difficult to carry them out should it become necessary. A start must therefore be made now.

(b) It was unfortunate that this issue should have to be considered while the political future was still uncertain. The full implications of Pakistan would require definition to provide a clear basis on which to plan separation of the armed forces. Pakistan would still leave Mohammadans in Hindustan, and vice versa, thus complicating the problems of recruitment. The problem might be further complicated by the theory of two nations whereby Mohammadans resident in Hindustan would be expected to owe loyalty to Pakistan, and vice versa. It was explained, however, that the Hindus and Muslims residing in the two areas would enjoy the full rights of citizenship in those areas, irrespective of their religion.

The political decision will guide but will not settle the armed forces' problem.

(c) If Pakistan is decided upon then each of the two States will require its own forces for internal security, but it can be expected that there will be a treaty between the two to provide for defence against aggression by a common enemy. This would allow of the use of troops by both parties impartially for the common good. There is reason to hope that even if Pakistan is decided upon there will be many interests in common between Pakistan and Hindustan in matters of commerce, finance etc.

(d) It followed that training establishments and ordnance factories could be shared by mutual agreement and that it was by no means essential that the forces of each State should be entirely self-contained. In any event India even when united was not self-contained for war, and was dependent on outside for much of the specialised and technical equipment she needs, as also for research and design.

(e) It was explained that the basis of the paper written by the Commander-in-Chief had been to point out the practical difficulties that would have to be overcome in separating the armed forces. It was in no way intended to influence the decision for or against Pakistan. There were obvious flaws in it, but these resulted from the fact that no clear terms of reference had been given as to the relations between the two States.

(f) It was urged that it was important that the larger military headquarters and staffs, as well as the major units, should be reorganised while British officers were still present. It was therefore essential to delay nationalisation until such reorganisation was complete.

(g) The implications of delaying nationalisation were discussed. It was explained that a plan for nationalisation prepared in armed forces headquarters was ready but that execution of it had been temporarily postponed. There was no intention of delaying preparatory measures, e.g., training of Indian officers required to take over. All that was being held up was the complicated process of cross-posting officers consequent on the withdrawal of the British element. Separation would further complicate these postings as it will be necessary to review afresh the officers suitably qualified and available in both Hindustan and Pakistan. It was explained that the reorganisation taking place in the armed forces was a gradual reduction to the target figure for the new budget, and that the only changes in class-composition of units were those explained in the Commander-in-Chief's paper, which would simplify separation if it ever became necessary. It was explained that a brief delay in executing the nationalisation policy would attract no outside attention, and His Excellency gave an assurance that a political decision on the subject of Pakistan would in all probability be forthcoming by the end of May. The delay, therefore, would not be long.

His Excellency summed up as follows:—

(i) He suggested that the issue should not be put to the Cabinet until the political decision had been taken.

[1] See No. 215.

(ii) He stressed the need for secrecy and suggested that those members of the committee who did not require their papers for subsequent reference should return them to the Cabinet Secretariat at the end of the meeting for safe custody, and reissue when the subject was again put on the agenda.

(iii) He expressed the opinion that the armed forces could probably complete nationalisation by 1st June 1948 without reducing standards to an unacceptably low level. As an alternative he felt that the Armed Forces might complete separation by 1st June, 1948, without undue risk. He emphasised that to attempt both nationalisation and separation by that date was in his opinion running a very dangerous risk. He stressed the unique position of the armed forces and their reputation for impartiality in the existing state of communal tension. He pointed out that he bore personal responsibility for law and order which he must carry until such time as he could hand it over to one or more responsible authorities. While he bore that responsibility he had in the last resort the use of British troops to fall back on. After 1st June 1948 there would be no British troops but the necessity for reliable and impartial armed forces might still exist; and by unduly hastening the process of separation we might defeat our own ends and produce a situation in which the armed forces would be semi-organised and not reliable. Much as he would like to see the separation completed, if it proved to be necessary, he reaffirmed his doubts as to the possibility of doing so in the time available, without a weakening of the Armed Forces which he could not possibly accept whilst responsible for law and order.

(iv) He suggested that it would be wiser to think in terms of pooling the forces of Hindustan and Pakistan, and though each would have its own GHQ, there could remain a Federal GHQ in general control, until such time as separation could be completed without detriment to efficiency.

(v) He agreed that there must be a plan because when Pakistan was announced it would be imperative at once to let the armed forces know where they stood, and to reassure them that preparations for their separation were in hand. He suggested that a personal broadcast by H.E. the Commander-in-Chief might be made indicating how he proposed to proceed.

(vi) The possibility might be examined of setting up a small high level staff to consider, in secret, outline plans for going ahead with separation if it proved to be necessary; and also on the possibility of holding up measures of nationalisation until the political decision was taken.

The Commander-in-Chief said that it had been brought out in discussion that there was really no basis on which he could plan the separation as so many factors were uncertain. He agreed that he could put in hand planning in broad outline only to determine the problems which would have to be tackled and the staff that he would require to undertake the work. He agreed that nationalisation could be temporarily postponed.

The committee:—

(1) decided that the issue should not be put to the Cabinet until the political decision had been made.

(2) directed the Commander-in-Chief to think out (a) the personnel of the small high level committee he should set up, and (b) the broad outline of the problems it will have to tackle if the decision taken involves separation, on the assumption that the terms of reference for the committee would be drawn up in that event by H.E. the Viceroy on the basis of the political decision.

(3) authorised the Commander-in-Chief to hold up nationalisation at his discretion until the political decision was reached, the guiding principle being that no action should be taken which would prejudice or complicate separation should it finally become necessary.

222

Minutes by Lord Ismay and Rear-Admiral Viscount Mountbatten of Burma

Mountbatten Papers. Official Correspondence Files: Plans,
Alternative (For transfer of power), Part (1)

25–28 April 1947

H.E.

In accordance with your instructions, I send you herewith a note on what we generally refer to as the "V.P. Menon Plan".[1]

2. As you will see, it is a long-term plan, which cannot be put into effect until both Hindustan and Pakistan have the necessary machinery to operate it. This is not likely to be until the end of this year, even if everything goes swimmingly.

3. We think it important that, when the time comes, the suggestion for a plan of this kind or anything like it should come from the Indian leaders themselves and should not appear to originate with us.

ISMAY

25th April, 1947

CVS

I should like the plan (amended as desired) to be typed out as an Appendix to

[1] It is presumed that Lord Ismay sent Lord Mountbatten the note appended to these minutes.

the papers you are taking home, so that the Cabinet may be aware of its existence.[2]

Re your para 3—I take it VP can get Congress to put this request forward when the time comes—but if they don't we can still pin it to their existing request for interim dominion status.

M of B

28/4

[2] Mr V.P. Menon's note was subsequently embodied in V.C.P. 40 (No. 273).

Appendix to No. 222

Note by Mr V.P. Menon

TOP SECRET   *undated*

Transfer of power as an interim arrangement

on the basis of a Dominion Constitution

The alternatives before us are (*a*) a United India on the basis of the Cabinet Delegation's plan and, if that is not possible, (*b*) a Divided India. In deciding on this main issue, the question of Dominion Status is not relevant. But in the moves that we may be making the objective of Dominion Status has to be kept in mind as an interim arrangement.

There is now complete frustration in the political field. In the fast moving political scene in India a quick decision is essential. Lawlessness is on the increase. Conflict between capital and labour is constant. Economic instability will add to our political troubles very soon. With the best will in the world British authority in India cannot tackle any of these problems seriously since it is avowedly in the process of liquidation. If then we stick on to the last date and to the last hour, we shall probably find the country in a turmoil, and a measure of responsibility for this state of affairs will be attributed to H.M.G.

The question then is, can a positive contribution be made now?

If H.E.'s efforts succeed in bringing the parties together on the Cabinet Mission plan, there is every advantage in transferring power as early as practicable to an Executive responsible to the Constituent Assembly in which once the League comes in the Princes also will participate. This is the ideal solution.

If we fail on the Cabinet Delegation's plan, the alternative is the division of India. The only reason for us to continue the existing set-up till June 1948 is to see that the arrangements that are necessary to give effect to the partition are implemented. With the best will in the world, we can only set up machinery and cannot, in view of the time factor, be responsible for the ultimate outcome. Is it not then better tactics to confront the parties *as constituted authorities* with the problem from the beginning?

For the transitional period Congress has accepted Dominion Status, and if we accept that proposition immediately, there is a good chance that the interim arrangement may cover a fairly long period during which the question of

Independence *versus* Dominion Status may not come directly in issue so far, at any rate, as the Congress is concerned. On the other hand, if we defer parting with power to the last minute, we may not have any alternative except to hand over on the basis of complete independence.

If the partition issue is settled, it would be difficult for us to resist the Congress claim for freedom to administer their own territories in the manner they like unhampered by an uneasy coalition, and the Muslim League then cannot argue that the whole thing should be deferred till their Pakistan is actually on its feet.

There is the question of the position of the States too. The States get back their freedom when we part with power in British India. There are many matters of common concern which it will be difficult for the existing set-up to settle either on a temporary or a permanent basis. Here again, once a free India (or Indias) knows where it stands, it is up to it to negotiate either a stand-still agreement or a long-term plan.

H.M.G. have already declared that they would like to part with power in an orderly and peaceful manner. If this is to be accomplished, the starting point should be the existing Constitution. On any other basis there will be very great administrative dislocation. There are a considerable number of provisions in the Govt. of India Act and the Orders in Council under it which will have to be kept in being either temporarily or permanently. On the other hand, if power is transferred on the basis of Independence in June 1948, India may have to draft an interim Constitution in addition to a permanent one.

Our starting point for the transfer of power should therefore be the existing Govt. of India Act. It has to be duplicated if there are to be two Indias.

The plan would roughly be on the following lines. If H.E. fails to bring the parties together on the Cabinet Delegation's plan, H.M.G. would then give an award for the partition of India. Some of the partitioned areas (i.e. non-Muslim areas) will probably decide to come into the existing Constituent Assembly. N.W.F.P. may or may not do so. Other partitioned areas will probably have a Constituent Assembly of their own. Each of the Constituent Assemblies will be asked to elect an Executive Council, to which H.M.G. would transfer authority in their respective areas as an interim arrangement till they draft their own Constitutions.

The Act has to be duplicated for these areas with suitable amendments withdrawing the control of the Secretary of State and the special powers of the Governors and the Governor-General. The existing Indian Legislature will be abolished and its place will be taken by the two Constituent Assemblies.

The Governor-General will be common for both Hindustan and Pakistan and will be appointed by His Majesty. The Governors of Provinces will be appointed by the Governor-General on the recommendation of his appropriate Executive Council.

The question then arises what is to happen in regard to matters of common concern e.g. Defence, External Affairs and Communications. For this purpose a Joint Council should be constituted with equal number of representatives selected by both the Hindustan and the Pakistan Executive Councils. This Council would be presided over by the Governor-General and will decide the joint policy on these subjects which will be implemented by the respective Governments. The Commander-in-Chief and other Heads of Services may be called in for advice as occasion arises.

It will be open to the two Governments to appoint Committees to consider the question of common arrangements as regards other joint services in the same way as we shall have to make arrangements with the Indian States. Pending the conclusion of such agreements, the best course would be for the existing services to function in responsibility to the separate Executives in respect of the different areas in which they operate. This arrangement could be superseded by negotiated agreements as they are ready or separate authorities could take over complete control in the two States as soon as they are equipped and ready to do so.

The psychological effect of power having been transferred earlier than 1948 will be an invaluable factor in the long-term view of Indo-British relationship. If there is to be a division of India, it will take not less than 4 or 5 years for both parts of the country to frame their Constitutions, hold elections and come to arrangements about the common matters. Once complete transfer of power is made as an interim measure on Dominion Status basis, the urgency of producing a Constitution immediately will lose its force and the parties will be given time to think things over with leisure and sobriety and proceed meanwhile with the urgent problems of administration and development. Further, the joint arrangement on the Defence side and the part that the Governor-General plays in that sphere will go very far in cementing the good relationship between Great Britain and India. One may also hope that if the two Governments sit together and start drafting agreements they may find that these agreements are required in respect of so many matters that they may ultimately come right round to the view that an impassable barrier cannot be created between the two Indias and that after all a unified Constitution is better for all concerned. Finally it may happen that having realised the importance and usefulness of the presence of a Governor-General appointed by His Majesty, both the parts of India may see the benefit of retaining that link with Great Britain.

223

Rear-Admiral Viscount Mountbatten of Burma to Mr Attlee (via India Office)

Telegram, L/PO/6/120 : f 168

IMPORTANT NEW DELHI, *25 April 1947, 11.55 pm*
Received: 25 April, 10.30 pm

No. 886-S. Please pass following to Prime Minister. As I have reported I have been working hard on a plan and I am sending home Ismay to put it to you and to the Cabinet. He should be able to arrive in London on May 5th.

2. I hope you will be able to arrange that Cabinet Committee keeps time free to discuss proposals with Ismay. I should like him to be back here within ten days at most. Matter is really most urgent.

3. I will telegraph plan as soon as it is ready probably about May 2nd.[1]

[1] In tel. 5564 of 30 April Mr Attlee replied that he was looking forward to seeing Lord Ismay and had arranged for the India and Burma Committee to be available for discussions as soon as he arrived. L/PO/6/120: f 162.

224

Minutes of Viceroy's Twenty Third Staff Meeting, Item 6

Mountbatten Papers

TOP SECRET

Those present at this Meeting held at The Viceroy's House, New Delhi on 26 April 1947 at 10 am were: Rear-Admiral Viscount Mountbatten of Burma, Lord Ismay, Sir E. Mieville, Captain Brockman, Mr I. D. Scott, Mr Campbell-Johnson, Lieutenant Colonel Erskine Crum

THE RETENTION OF INDIA WITHIN THE COMMONWEALTH

LORD ISMAY drew attention to an extract from a leading article in that morning's *The Hindustan Times*. This extract is at Appendix 'A' to these Minutes.

After discussion on what line should be taken by His Excellency the Viceroy and the senior members of his staff in discussing the retention of India within the Commonwealth, His Excellency the Viceroy laid down the following principles:—

(a) The matter should not be raised in conversations with Indian leaders unless they raised it themselves.

(b) The Constituent Assembly had passed a resolution in favour of a sovereign independent republic but, since only Congress were represented in the Constituent Assembly, this did not apply to the rest of British India. Therefore the question of leaving the Commonwealth had not yet arisen.

(c) The Viceroy had received no instructions as to the line that he should take in the event of one or more parts of India expressing a desire to remain within the Commonwealth, but he had been enjoined not to enter into any discussions which might imperil the chances of Indian unity, to attain which had always been and would remain his first ambition and determination. In any case, the question was one of the highest policy and could only be settled by His Majesty's Government, in the light of the situation created by their decision on the question of the demission of power.

(d) If not only Pakistan but some of the larger States (for example Hyderabad, Kashmir and Mysore) asked in a public appeal not to be thrown out of the Commonwealth, it would be difficult to imagine the members of the Commonwealth agreeing to throw them out.

(e) The Viceroy's personal opinion was that the retention of parts of India only in the Commonwealth would be undesirable; but clearly he could not stand in the way of requests to this effect being transmitted to His Majesty's Government.

HIS EXCELLENCY THE VICEROY said that the last thing which he wanted to see, and it would indeed be most disastrous, would be that Hindustan left the Empire irretrievably and Pakistan remained within irretrievably. The solution which must be suggested every time in the most skilful way was that the decision on this matter was in the hands of the Indians themselves.

LORD ISMAY asked whether His Excellency thought that the Chiefs of Staff should be requested to examine the possible retention of parts only of India in the Commonwealth from a purely military point of view. HIS EXCELLENCY THE VICEROY said that he considered that it would be most desirable for the Chiefs of Staff to make such an examination in the strictest secrecy. He pointed out that Field Marshal Auchinleck as well as Lord Ismay would be available in London to attend a Chiefs of Staff Committee Meeting if required.

HIS EXCELLENCY THE VICEROY said that he considered it most important that no Ministers of His Majesty's Government should, at the present time, commit themselves in any way on the question of the retention of parts of India in the Commonwealth and indeed on the whole trend of present events and plans.

LORD ISMAY said that he considered that it should be made quite clear to the Indian leaders that the first principle of His Majesty's Government's policy was co-operation with the Americans. HIS EXCELLENCY THE VICEROY said that this point should indeed be covered in conversations although he believed that the majority of Indian leaders realised the fact already. He said that he had incidentally got the impression that the Americans were beginning to treat the British in the American press in exactly the same way as the Germans had treated the Italians before the war.

HIS EXCELLENCY THE VICEROY:—

(i) directed Pers. Sec. to draft for his approval a telegram to the Secretary of State for India containing an addendum to his Personal Report No.4; this telegram to quote the leading article in that day's *TheHindustan Times* and to say that it was of the utmost importance that the Ministers of His Majesty's Government should remain non-committal at the present time;[1]

(ii) invited C.V.S., on his visit to London, to make a request on his behalf that the Chiefs of Staff should examine, in the greatest secrecy, the possible retention of parts only of India from a purely military point of view;

(iii) invited the attention of the senior members of his staff to the principles laid down under sub-paragraphs (a)—(e) above.

Appendix 'A' to No. 224
Extract from Leading Article, *The Hindustan Times*,
Saturday 26th April, 1947

If there is a settlement between the Congress and the League as a result of which the Muslim majority areas are allowed to constitute themselves into separate sovereign States, we have no doubt that the Union will not stand in the way of Britain establishing contacts with those States. It must be clearly understood, however, that the Indian Union will consider it a hostile act if there is any attempt by Britain to conclude any treaty or alliance involving military or political clauses. As for the Indian States, they cannot be permitted to have any foreign policy or contact apart from the Union. It is inconceivable that the Union will seek British assistance after June 1948 in its relations with those parts of India which stand aloof from it. Therefore, Britain should develop a single integrated foreign policy towards this country with friendship of the Union as its foundation. We have no doubt that the statesmen in control of the present British Government are wise enough to realise these logical implications of the new situation that will emerge after June 1948 and will not do anything calculated to create difficulties in the way of establishment of Indo-British relationship on a basis of lasting friendship.

[1] See No. 232.

225

*Record of Interview between Rear-Admiral Viscount Mountbatten of Burma
and the Nawab of Bhopal*

Mountbatten Papers. Viceroy's Interview No. 96

TOP SECRET   *26 April 1947, 12.30–1.25 pm*

The Nawab said that the principal reason for his visit was to obtain my advice on how the Princes should act under Pandit Nehru's threat of treating them as hostile if they did not immediately join the Constituent Assembly. He also wished to make a complaint against a Member of the Interim Government making such improper threats.

I told him that I had already had a talk with Pandit Nehru,[1] who had explained that this statement was made in his personal capacity as President of the States' People's Conference, and that he had obtained my permission to absent himself from government duties to attend this Conference; thus Pandit Nehru's claim was that his statement could not be regarded as a Government or even a Congress statement, but as that of the President of, and representing the view of, the States' People's Conference.

I further explained that I had pointed out to Pandit Nehru that the Cabinet Mission themselves had laid down that the States should not send representatives to the C.A. until the third phase, which had not yet been reached. Added to this it seemed somewhat foolish that they should send any representatives before the decision on how many Constituent Assemblies there would be had been taken.

The Nawab asked whether he might write me a letter in order that he could have my advice in writing so that he could show it to his brother Princes. I told him that I would certainly write him such a letter, but that I would prefer to show the draft to Pandit Nehru first together with a copy of the letter the Nawab himself was going to write. This arrangement pleased him particularly, since he said it would clear up the misunderstanding with Pandit Nehru, and that he had really come to see him.

H.H. then said to me "I hope you were pleased with the telegram[2] I sent you after my visit to Mr Jinnah, saying that Pakistan was very likely to remain within the British Commonwealth". I told him that this desire on the part of different parts of India to remain within the Commonwealth was an embarrassment unless all of India felt the same way, and I explained the difficulty of the British Commonwealth becoming involved in support of one side against the other in a civil war. H.H. was more insistent even than at his meeting[3] with me on the day I was sworn in; saying that all the Rulers in his group, i.e. the majority of the Rulers, wished to remain within the Commonwealth to a man, and would appeal most strongly if in addition to having Paramountcy returned to them, they were also told that all links with the British Empire must be broken.

I told him that this was not a matter I could usefully discuss until after the decision had been taken on the transfer of power, since I could not be a party to any proposals which would weaken the chance of a unified India.

I gave him a brief survey of the progress of the plan and the lines on which we were working, all of which he thought were good. I told him I was proposing to meet the leaders round about the 15th or 20th May, and was going to ask them to have their working committees in Delhi.

I asked him if he could collect the States' Negotiating Committee in Delhi at the same time. He pointed out that it was defunct having finished its duties, and might be difficult to collect, but that if I invited the 14 members separately he knew they would gladly come. I raised no objection to issuing separate invitations, but I said I could not possibly see each Member for an hour or two, since it would take me several days to get through them. If they came I should have to see them either all together or in two groups of 7. He recognised the force of this. I told him I would be writing to him officially in the course of the next few days telling him whether I wanted the States' Negotiating Committee to come to Delhi, and he could then tell me his official views on how this matter should be handled.

N.B. Bring up at Staff Meeting.[4]

[1] No. 193.　　[2] No. 28.　　[3] See No. 9.
[4] At his Twenty Fourth Staff Meeting on 1 May 1947 Lord Mountbatten drew attention to the record of this interview and directed Mr Scott, in consultation with Political Department, to draft invitations to the members of the States' Negotiating Committee. Item 6. Mountbatten Papers.

226

Sardar Patel to Rear-Admiral Viscount Mountbatten of Burma

R/3/1/130: f 217

HOME MEMBER OF CABINET, NEW DELHI, *26 April 1947*

My dear Lord Mountbatten,
You will recall that during our discussion yesterday[1] the question came up about Provincial constitutions being framed by the Sections in such a manner as to prevent the free and unfettered expression of opinion on the question of grouping by the Provincial electorates and I told you that this was an action which was contrary to the Cabinet Mission Plan.

[1] No. 216.

2. To substantiate my statement I would refer you to the following extract from the letter of Maulana Abul Kalam Azad to the Viceroy dated the 14th June 1946:—[2]

"You are no doubt aware of the strong feeling of resentment which exists among large sections of the people against some of the proposals in the statement, notably the idea of grouping. The Frontier Province and Assam have expressed themselves with considerable force against any compulsory grouping. The Sikhs have felt hurt and isolated by these proposals and are considerably agitated. Being a minority in the Punjab, they become still more helpless as far as numbers go in Section B. We appreciated all these objections especially as we ourselves shared them. Nevertheless, we hoped that according to our interpretation of the clauses related to grouping, which we still hold is the correct interpretation, for any other interpretation would endanger the basic principle of Provincial Autonomy, we might be able to get over some of the obvious difficulties". To this the Viceroy replied in paragraph 3 of his letter dated the 15th June[3] as follows: "The Delegation and I are aware of your objections to the principle of grouping. I would however point out that the statement of 16th May does not make grouping compulsory. It leaves the decision to the elected representatives of the Provinces concerned sitting together in sections. The only provision which is made is that the representatives of certain Provinces should meet in sections so that they can decide whether or not they wish to form groups. Even when this has been done the individual Provinces are still to have the liberty to opt out of the group if they so decide."

3. From this correspondence it is clear that the statement of 16th May, 1946 does not make grouping compulsory. For a constitution to be drawn up in such a way as to prevent a Province from expressing its true will on opting out of grouping would in effect amount to making grouping compulsory.

4. Apart from this, I would invite your attention to the following extract of the speech of Sir Stafford Cripps in the House of Commons on the 18th July 1946 (Page 1404 [Pages 1401-2] of *Hansard Parliamentary Debates* Volume 425, No. 179)—

"There were two main points which the Congress were stressing as to the statement of 16th May. The first was as to whether the provinces were compelled to come into the sections of the Constituent Assembly—sections A, B and C—in the first instance, or whether they could stay out if they wished. We made it quite clear that it was an essential feature of the scheme that the provinces should go into sections, though, if groups were subsequently formed, they could afterwards opt out of those groups. A fear was expressed that, somehow or other, the new Provincial constitutions might be so manoeuvred as to make it impossible for the Provinces afterwards to opt out. I do not myself see how such a thing would be possible, but if anything of that kind were to be attempted, it would be a clear breach of the basic understanding of the scheme. The essence of the constitution-making scheme is that the provincial representatives in sections A, B and C, mentioned in paragraph 19, should have the opportunity of meeting together and deliberating upon the desirability of forming a "group" and upon the nature and extent of the subjects to be dealt with by the group. If, when the pattern of the group ultimately emerges, any Province wishes to withdraw from the group, because it is not satisfied, then it is at liberty to do so after the first election under the new Constitution, when, with no doubt a wider electorate than at present, that matter can be made a straight election issue."

5. Similarly I invite your attention to the following extract of the speech of Lord Pethick-Lawrence in the House of Lords on the 16th December 1946 in which he has dwelt upon the danger of Provincial constitutions being imposed upon a Province contrary to the wishes of its inhabitants or in such manner as to prevent the wishes of the majority of the inhabitants prevailing in the decision whether or not to opt out of the group. (*Hansard Parliamentary Debates* Volume 144, No. 15 of Monday the 16th December 1946)—

"One aspect of this matter is that there is anxiety in certain quarters whether the majority in a Section might not impose a Provincial Constitution upon a Province which would be contrary to the wishes of its inhabitants, and might even be of such a character as to prevent the wishes of the majority of the inhabitants prevailing in the decision whether or not to opt out of the Group. I am sure that neither side have any wish that this should take place. There is no reason why the two major communities should not come to an arrangement between themselves which would avoid any danger of it happening."

6. The All-India Congress Committee resolution of 6th January 1947[4] does no more than stress the necessity of proceeding in the matter of grouping by mutual agreement and not by compulsion or coercion. This is clearly in accord with the intentions of His Majesty's Government as expressed in the above-mentioned extracts of correspondence and Debates. The statement of December 6th implements this intention by making it clear that His Majesty's Government cannot force a constitution on unwilling parts. Government spokesmen in the House of Commons have stressed this on more than one occasion in the debates on India. A typical example is the following extract from Mr. Alexander's speech:—

"We would not contemplate, and Congress itself does not contemplate enforcing upon an unwilling Section of the community anything they do not accept." (p.1555 *Hansard Parliamentary Debates* (House of Commons) Volume 431 No.24). The statement of the 20th February 1947 also lays considerable emphasis on an agreed constitution rather than a constitution settled by majority decisions. The Congress has on its part already stated on a number of occasions that it will adhere to this principle in constitution-building. It is clearly incumbent on the League to work the Sections in a similar spirit. I have no doubt that if this were done, the minorities in the section would react sympathetically and in a cooperative spirit to the reasonable wishes of the majority.

Yours sincerely,

VALLABHBHAI PATEL

227

Record of Interview between Rear-Admiral Viscount Mountbatten of Burma and Mr Suhrawardy

Mountbatten Papers. Viceroy's Interview No. 98

TOP SECRET   *26 April 1947, 3–4 pm*

After telling me what a great friend he was of the late Lord Brabourne and how he had been almost the last person to see him alive, he got down to business.

He told me he had seen Lord Ismay & Sir Eric Mieville and had had a very interesting talk, and was proposing to see them again later on in the day. He told me that they had given him an idea of the general way that our minds were working.

I told him that I was ardently against all forms of partition; I wanted above everything a united India. If I could not have a united India, then I would like the Cabinet Mission plan. If I could not have the Cabinet Mission plan, I would then put it to the Provinces to decide. I had been called upon to partition the Punjab, Bengal and Assam, and I expressed my regret that these Provinces should be partitioned, but said that it was unavoidable.

Mr. Suhrawardy told me that in the case of Bengal, this was far from being the case, and that since my plan included a vote on whether a Province should be partitioned or not, and if not partitioned, whether it was to join Pakistan, Hindustan, or remain independent, he could tell me now that given enough time he was confident that he could get Bengal to remain as a complete entity. He told me that he could get Mr. Jinnah to agree that it need not join Pakistan if it was prepared to remain united.

I told him that this was very good news, for although I was against splitting India up into many units, I considered it far better to keep Bengal as one economic unit than to have it partitioned.

I asked him if he was also going to ask for a separate army, and he said most emphatically; "Yes". I pointed out the appalling difficulties of dividing the army into two as well as nationalising it; those difficulties would be even greater still if the army had to be divided into three, and it would take a minimum of five years, after we had left India in June 1948, for this to come about, and in the meanwhile he would have to accept a Defence Headquarters 'in trust' for India as a whole. He did not like this idea, and seemed to think that the partition of the army could be easily effected. I assured him he was quite wrong, and that in any case I had no intention of allowing the army to be split up while I was still here.

He then mentioned that he hoped British Officers would help in the formation of a Bengal Army; and I replied that I did not see how this could be done, since India was not likely to remain within the Commonwealth. He replied "I beg your pardon; Bengal has every intention of remaining in the Commonwealth". I told him I thought this was undesirable and that I was personally against any part of India being in the Commonwealth if all of India was not in, lest we got mixed up into supporting one side in a civil war. On this, he said: "I do not see how you can kick us out, what have we done to be expelled?". I admitted that that put him in a strong position, but that I still could not recommend it, although when the time came I should have to report it.

Mr. Suhrawardy then said he must have as long as possible to convert Bengal to the idea of being united and independent. I asked him what the minimum time required would be, and he replied that the absolute bare minimum would be two months. I said that I thought that this was in fact the longest time he could count upon, since I hoped to get a decision within one month; voting of the non-partitioned Provinces a week later; and voting of the partitioned Provinces not more that three weeks after that. He asked me not to have a decision on partition until November; and I pointed out that if we left it as late as this, there was practically no prospect of getting partition implemented before we left in June 1948.

I asked Mr. Suhrawardy to give Lord Ismay his ideas on the notional partition of Bengal for voting purposes, and said that I would be available if he wanted to see me again urgently at any time.

228

Minutes by Lord Ismay and Rear-Admiral Viscount Mountbatten of Burma

Mountbatten Papers. Official Correspondence Files: Interviews

26 April 1947

H.E.

We have just seen Mr. Suhrawardy, who came up after his talk with you. We think that he must have very much misunderstood you because, in the course of his opening gambit, he said that you had told him that if Mr. Jinnah was prepared to have Bengal as a separate unit and not as part of a Pakistan state, and that if all were prepared to accept joint electorates, you were going to do your best to keep Bengal as a separate state.

2. We said that he must have misunderstood you since, so far from having any "separate" states, it was your firm intention to get a union of India, and that only if that was absolutely impossible would you consult the wishes of the people, as expressed by their elected representatives, as to the form that partition should take.

3. Mr. Suhrawardy went on to say that you had told him that you must have the answer of the Bengal Constitutent Assemblies within one month of the announcement, i.e. at the end of June. He was much distressed about this on the grounds that it would not give him time to have talks with the opposition and educate them to the advantages of an unpartitioned Bengal.

4. We said that we did not think that your date was an absolutely firm one and that in view of the various processes that had to be gone through before the will of Western Bengal and Eastern Bengal could be expressed, it might well be that the date could be advanced to the 31st July or even to the 31st August.

5. This mention of a date was a new idea to us, and we submit that the latest date by which provinces must reach their decision should be inserted in the announcement.

May I raise this point at the next Staff Conference?

6. After a long talk, we arranged that Mr. Suhrawardy should send us his notes and maps and that we should meet again if necessary.

ISMAY

26th April 1947

I attach a record[1] of my talk with Mr. Suhrawardy, from which you will see how an enthusiast might possibly have been led into the error of thinking that I really preferred to keep Bengal a separate state rather than have a Union of India. It just shows how dangerous these talks are when people do not seem to grasp the full point.

I am absolutely certain that I started off with my usual lecture on a strong union of India, since I say this to everyone whom I am meeting for the first time.

M. of B.
26 April 1947

[1] No. 227.

229

Record of Interview between Rear-Admiral Viscount Mountbatten of Burma and Mr Jinnah

Mountbatten Papers. Viceroy's Interview No. 100

TOP SECRET   *26 April 1947, 5–6.20pm*

I told Mr. Jinnah that I had sent for him to discuss the Nawab of Mamdot's offer to form a Ministry in the Punjab.

Mr. Jinnah explained that Mamdot could now count up to 93 supporters out of the 175 in the Punjab Assembly, since certain minorities had promised him their support. There was thus no question but that he could really form a government and govern; and Mr. Jinnah called upon me to implement my oft-proclaimed desire to get out of Section 93.

I told him that after my talk with Tara Singh and Kartar Singh,[1] I had become convinced that any attempt to impose a mainly one-community government on the Sikhs would produce immediate armed retaliation which might end in civil war. I told him that the Sikhs felt so bitter about the Muslim atrocities that they were only waiting for an excuse for their revenge; and I said that it would be criminal folly to let this occur just before the official discussions and decision on the transfer of power. I pointed out that he knew as well as I did the line that these discussions were likely to take, and the great probability that Pakistan would emerge with a partition of the Punjab. In the light of this, what could be the point of having a brief period of Muslim League government in the Punjab, which could only bring about bloodshed and greatly increase the difficulty of negotiating the boundaries in the partition. I told Mr. Jinnah that nothing would induce me to change my mind and that I was proposing to instruct the Governor accordingly.

I asked him if I might tell the Governor that he (Mr. Jinnah) agreed. He replied "Certainly not, I definitely do not agree."

I then said, "Do you entirely see my point of view and understand my

[1] No. 173.

reasons?" He replied "I entirely see your point of view and I respect your sincerity, though I do not agree with your decision." I replied "One day you will be thankful to me for saving you from getting into this mess that you would like to get into in the Punjab; it is mainly in the interests of the Muslim League that I am making this decision, and I am sorry not to have your agreement."

I told him that I should be seeing the Governor on Wednesday and would discuss the matter at length with him and confirm the decision I had already telegraphed.

Mr. Jinnah said that in that case he would suggest that the Governor should not see Mamdot until after he had seen me. I replied "If you will take the responsibility for this delay I will agree"; whereupon he offered to telephone Mamdot to tell him not to see the Governor until after he had seen me, about Wednesday or Thursday. I promised to telegraph to the Governor accordingly.[2]

He told me that he thought that my talk to the Sikhs must have had a good effect, since he had had a private emissary from Kartar Singh suggesting that they should hold discussions about the Sikh state joining Pakistan after partition. He said he had accepted Kartar Singh's offer to come to Delhi to see him. Mr. Jinnah seemed very gratified by this move, since he said the Sikhs liked him personally and had always trusted him, and that he had publicly stated that he would support the Sikhs against the Muslims any time that any Muslims took unfair action against the Sikhs.

He then asked me how much longer I wished him to remain in Delhi. I replied that he should not leave before the 2nd of May, and should be back by the 15th May, and that I would like him to warn his Working Committee to be ready to meet shortly after the 15th May. I said that if I did not want him and his Working Committee until after the 15th May I would arrange for a message to be sent to him as soon as I knew the date on which he would be wanted, but I did not think it would be later than the 20th May.

I next told him of Mr. Suhrawardy's visit, and said that I had told him that I was strongly opposed to all forms of partition, whether the partition of India itself or the partition of Provinces; and that Mr. Suhrawardy had replied that in the case of Bengal he thought he might be able to keep a united Bengal on condition that it joined neither Pakistan nor Hindustan. I asked Mr. Jinnah straight out what his views were about keeping Bengal united at the price of its remaining out of Pakistan.

He said, without any hesitation; "I should be delighted. What is the use of Bengal without Calcutta; they had much better remain united and independent; I am sure that they would be on friendly terms with us."

I then mentioned that Mr. Suhrawardy had said that if Bengal remained united and independent, they would wish to remain within the Commonwealth. Mr. Jinnah replied "Of course, just as I indicated to you that Pakistan would wish to remain within the Commonwealth". I corrected him and said "No, you told me that if the Pakistan Government was formed, its first act might well be to ask to be admitted to membership of the British Commonwealth." He corrected me, and said I completely misunderstood the position; it was not a question of asking to be admitted, it was a question of not being kicked out. He said that Mr. Churchill had told him: "You have only to stand firm and demand your rights not to be expelled from the British Commonwealth, and you are bound to be accepted. The country would never stand for the expulsion of loyal members of the Empire."

Mr. Jinnah told me that he had asked Sir Stafford Cripps what form legislation on the transfer of power was likely to take; could he count on the fact that it would be in the form that India or parts of India would be granted the same privilege as other members of the British Commonwealth; i.e. the right to secede if they so wished, failing which they would automatically still be in the Empire. Sir Stafford Cripps replied that he was not in a position to answer that question at that time. Mr. Jinnah said "Thus like a true lawyer he evaded the question; but it is quite clear to me that you cannot kick us out; there is no precedent for forcing parts of the Empire to leave against their will."

Finally, I reverted to the Cabinet Mission plan, much to his distaste. I said "You told me that your objection to the Cabinet Mission plan was the fact that the Centre would be controlled by a majority vote of the Congress, and would be able to exert economic and military pressure to the detriment of Groups B & C. Is that your objection to the scheme?" He nodded his head vehemently; and I then said: "I have been looking into this, and there is little doubt that the provision in the Cabinet Mission plan whereby the Constituent Assembly votes on any major communal issue in two parts, and unless there is a majority of the members of both communities present and voting the measure cannot be passed."[3] If that were so, I pointed out, then surely he would have as many safeguards as he would ever get under Pakistan with a Central Defence Council. He replied emphatically "No; it is laid down that a difference of opinion on a major communal question should be decided by the Federal Court. It is clear that the President of the Constituent Assembly is not obliged to take their ruling. I asked the Chief Justice what he would do if his ruling were disregarded, and he replied that the Federal Court would refuse to give any more rulings. That would then leave it open to Congress to impose their will by majority vote.

"In fact the leaders of Congress are so dishonest, so crooked, and so obsessed with the idea of smashing the Muslim League, that there are no lengths to which they will not go to do so; and the only way of giving Pakistan a chance is to make it an independent nation of the British Commonwealth, with its

[2] Lord Mountbatten did this in tel. 902–S of 26 April. R/3/1/89: f 171.
[3] This sentence is evidently not complete.

own army, and the right to argue cases at any Central Council on this basis."

I was quite unable to shake him from this decision; and he begged me not to ask him to reconsider the Cabinet Mission plan again.

230

Sir F. Wylie (United Provinces) to Rear-Admiral Viscount Mountbatten of Burma (Extract)

L/P&J/5/276: ff 71–2

SECRET   GOVERNOR'S CAMP, UNITED PROVINCES,
U.P.–77   *26 April 1947*

7. There is one point arising out of the [Governors'] Conference which I think I should mention. An impression seems to be prevalent that British officers as a class are either opposed to the policy of His Majesty's Government or find themselves unable to adapt themselves to the times. I am sure that this is not true of the U.P. I have myself been a confessed Indian Home Ruler for many years past and there has been no step taken by His Majesty's Government in the last two years which has not had my cordial support. I mention this fact not as a matter of interest but to help my *bona fides* as a witness. I think that I know nearly every European officer now serving in this Province and I can assure Your Excellency that the whole lot of them accept the wisdom of the policy which H.M.G. are following in India and are doing their best loyally to further that policy. I know of no instance where a British officer has spoken foolishly with reference to the present changes and I am certain that those that are left are doing their best to serve the present Government faithfully. There is nothing to be surprised at in this for we have had popular governments before and British officers know well enough from their own country that it is the duty of the civil servant to obey the political minister whom the electorate have set over him. The boot here in fact tends to be on the other foot. Some of our Indian officers take less kindly to the control—and to the inevitable vagaries—of popular ministers than their British colleagues.

231

Mr Christie to Mr Abell

Telegram, Mountbatten Papers. Official Correspondence Files:
Bengal, Partition of, Part I(a)

IMMEDIATE
SECRET

26 April 1947, 9.25 pm
Received: 27 April, 6 am

No. 101–S. Governor Bengal agrees with terms of draft announcement[1] subject to what follows in succeeding paragraph and with procedure for presenting it to leaders.

2. Draft announcement is not inconsistent with proposals in Tyson's D.O. letter No.40–CR of April 24th[2] but Governor considers it most necessary that Viceroy should be satisfied that it is acceptable to Jinnah before it is presented as an award. If Jinnah accepts it is practically certain that East Bengal Muslims will accept. If Jinnah and Bengal Muslims do not accept serious disorders in Bengal are highly probable.

3. Jinnah's attitude is likely to be strongly influenced by arrangement contemplated for Calcutta. On communal majority formula Calcutta should go with West Bengal but East Bengal contributes largely to Calcutta's prosperity, and economy of East Bengal is dependent on access to Calcutta and share of its revenues. Governor therefore considers that interim arrangement for administration of Calcutta should be mandatory in announcement. He suggests insertion of the following paragraph after paragraph 14[3] of draft. *Begins.* "If it is decided to divide the Province of Bengal the present area of Calcutta, as defined in the Calcutta Police Act and the Calcutta Suburban Police Act, will not be included in either of the two half Provinces. Pending the establishment of an executive authority for the administration of Calcutta, by agreement between the two Constituent Assemblies concerned, Calcutta shall be administered by a Council consisting of an equal number of persons elected by each Constituent Assembly, under a Chairman elected by the Council itself". *Ends.*

4. It is not necessary to make any consequential alteration in paragraph 7(a) as M.L.As. representing Calcutta should not be debarred from electing representatives to vote on issue of partition.

5. In paragraphs 7 and 8 Governor suggests that European M.L.As. should be specifically excluded in view of difficulties which arose previously.

[1] See No. 260 for an indication of the text of the draft announcement at this date.
[2] No. 208.
[3] Para. 15 of Appendix C to No. 260 corresponded with para. 14 in the draft announcement shown to Sir F. Burrows.

6. Governor presumes reference to Cabinet Mission's statement in paragraph 8 sufficiently clarifies point that representatives elected need not necessarily be M.L.As.

232

Rear-Admiral Viscount Mountbatten of Burma to the Earl of Listowel

Telegram, L/P&J/10/79: f 458

IMMEDIATE   NEW DELHI, *27 April 1947, 2.25 am*
                                              Received: 27 April, 7.15 am

No. 901–S. Please add following as an addendum to each copy of my personal report No. 4 dated April 24th 1947.[1] *Begins.* Quite apart from speculations about transfer of power there is a good deal of uncertainty here on all sides whether the Indian Union or parts of India will in the future remain with the British Empire.

2. Following is an extract from leading article in *Hindustan Times* for Saturday April 26th which is following up the interest which has been aroused:
[There follows the text of Appendix 'A' to No. 224]

3. In response to many queries I have received during recent interviews from Jinnah, Suhrawardy, Bhopal and others I have said that I can give no consideration to proposals for parts of India to remain within the Empire, as by encouragement of such requests I should imperil the chances of Indian unity. I have added that in any case, the question was one of the highest policy and could only be settled by H.M. Government, in the light of situation created by their decision on the question of demission of power.

4. I think it is of the utmost importance that no one here or at home should commit themselves either privately or publicly on this matter, as situation at present is both delicate and fluid. I think it would greatly help the party leaders to face up to realities if we let it ride for a bit. *Ends.*

[1] No. 211.

233

Note by Mr Christie

*Mountbatten Papers. Official Correspondence Files: Bengal, Partition of,
Part I(a)*

TOP SECRET   *27 April 1947*

1. After sending off telegram 101[1] to PSV on Saturday evening, further discussion took place with H.E. the Governor and the Governor's Secretary. It was decided that the Governor's recommendation in para 3 of the telegram must be modified for the following reasons.

2. The proposed announcement will not involve any immediate change in the administration of Bengal as a whole. The Governor's proposals for the administration of Bengal in the interim period between the announcement and the demission of power are contained in the note attached to Mr Tyson's d.o. of the 24th April.[2]

The draft announcement prescribes a method of allowing the representatives of the peoples to decide whether (*a*) certain provinces (*b*) India as a whole shall be united or divided, and, if the decision should be for partition, the broad, provisional demarcation of areas within which Constituent Assemblies will prepare the respective parts of India to receive power when it is demitted. Because of the exceptional importance of Calcutta to both East and West Bengal, it ought not to be a part of either half province, if partition is decided upon, and its exclusion must be provided for and made mandatory in the provisional demarcation which will be announced. The ultimate machinery for the administration of Calcutta is, however, clearly one of those matters of common concern for which para 14[3] of the draft announcement advises joint consultation between the respective Constituent Assemblies, and should not be the subject of a mandatory provision. But a bare mandatory announcement that Calcutta will be excluded from either half Province of Bengal, might be misinterpreted in the sense that H.M.G. intended to retain some form of control over it. It is therefore desirable to give some definite indication of H.M.G.'s advice in the matter of the joint administration of Calcutta.

3. H.E. the Governor would therefore amend the telegram to PSV as follows, in para 3.

"Governor therefore considers that exclusion of Calcutta from either half province should be mandatory in announcement. He suggests insertion of following paragraph after para 14 of draft.
Begins.
"If it is decided to divide the Province of Bengal, the present area of Calcutta,

---

[1] No. 231.   [2] No. 208.   [3] i.e. para. 15 of the draft of the announcement in No. 260.

as defined in the Calcutta Police Act and the Calcutta Suburban Police Act, will not be included in either of the two half provinces. Pending the demission of power to executive authorities set up for West Bengal and East Bengal respectively, the administration of Calcutta will remain under the executive authority of the Government of Bengal. If at the time of demission of power no other arrangement for the administration of Calcutta has been mutually agreed upon by the Constituent Assemblies concerned, Calcutta should be administered by a Council. . . . .
(etc. as in original telegram).

W.H.J. CHRISTIE

234

Mr Abell to Rear-Admiral Viscount Mountbatten of Burma

R/3/1/130: f 218

27 April 1947

Letter below from the Home Member.[1]

2. The position on this point is perfectly clear. The Cabinet Mission's plan was attractive to Mr Jinnah because it gave him the assurance of being able to control Groups B and C. It was only because of this that he accepted it. As soon as it became clear that the Congress "acceptance" contained reservations which made it doubtful whether he would, in fact, be able to control Groups B and C the Muslim League rejected the Cabinet Mission's plan.

3. Lord Wavell, from the very start, contended that the Congress acceptance was not, in fact, an acceptance because of their reservations, but it was not until December 6th that H.M.G. came out clearly with a firm interpretation. The interpretation of the 6th December which Y.E. read in the meeting last Friday leaves no doubt at all that legally speaking the Bengal-Assam Section can frame a constitution for Assam, and that Assam cannot opt out of the Group until after the new elections. Thus legally speaking the Muslims can rig the constitution of Assam, though if they did so obviously the whole plan for constitution making would break down because, whatever the legal position may be, you cannot frame constitutions by compulsion and without agreement no acceptable constitution will emerge.

4. Sir Stafford Cripps sailed very near the wind in saying what he did ((a) on page 2 of the Home Member's letter).[2] The Secretary of State was more cautious on the 16th December ((b) in Home Member's letter).[3]

5. I think Home Member knows the position perfectly well. It was clear from what he said that even now the Congress would not give any sort of

unequivocal acceptance of the Cabinet Mission's plan which would satisfy Mr Jinnah.

6. Draft acknowledgment for approval.

G.E.B. ABELL

¹ No. 226.
² Mr Abell is referring here to the sentence in No. 226, para. 4 which reads: 'I do not myself see how such a thing would be possible, but if anything of that kind were to be attempted, it would be a clear breach of the basic understanding of the scheme.'
³ Mr Abell is referring here to the sentence in No. 226, para. 5 which reads: 'I am sure that neither side have any wish that this should take place.'

235

Note by Mr Abell

Mountbatten Papers. Official Correspondence Files: Punjab, Situation in, Part I(a)

27 April 1947

P.S.V.'S DISCUSSIONS WITH THE GOVERNOR OF THE PUNJAB
26th April, 1947

Palliatives

I suggested to the Governor that to improve the reception of the announcement by the Sikhs and by minorities in the new Provinces (if the vote is in favour of partition of Provinces) an attempt should be made to secure agreement in advance of the announcement about certain palliatives.

2. We should try to secure that both the major parties accept a policy of coalition ministries now in all Provinces. In the case of the Punjab this would get us out of Section 93 and the coalition ministry might even be representative of the two halves of the Province, and thus include in itself the prospective new governments. A government of this kind would do a great deal to restore confidence both in the immediate situation and in the conduct of the administrative action being taken by way of preparation for Partition.

3. Congress and the Muslim League should promise that if new Provinces are created in the Punjab and Bengal they will see that there will be coalition ministries in the new Provinces *under the new Constitution*. This will ensure representation of minorities in these new Provinces which (if the vote goes that way) will be set up on a communal basis.

4. It is obviously of the greatest importance, and the Governor agreed with this, that the minorities in the two halves of the Punjab and Bengal should receive every possible reassurance. These minorities are formidable in size and are in a very anxious state.

5. There might even be a promise of *statutory* coalition in the new Constitutions.

6. The major parties should promise similarly that the minorities in the new Provinces and in any new groups that may be formed will be given a fair share of representation in the services if there is partition.

7. The minorities should also be assured that after Partition they will receive suitable weightage in the Legislatures of the new groups or Provinces.

8. These are points of real importance which H.E. the Governor thought we should seek to negotiate with the leaders between now and the making of the announcement. There is no real need to wait until the Conference of the "big 5". Any interviews with the Party leaders could be used for this purpose. I have no doubt that the Congress would accept conventions of this kind, but there may be some difficulty with Mr Jinnah, though the time to get an assurance from him is now rather than after the announcement is made. Also, from our point of view, it is at the time of the announcement that one will require these reassurances to the minorities. Otherwise, in the Punjab at any rate, there will be very acute anxiety among the Sikhs and Hindus in the West and among the four million Muslims in the East. Moreover if there is no assurance to minorities the problem of sorting out the administration of the new areas will be doubly difficult because it will be almost impossible to persuade minority members of the Services to continue to serve in the areas where they were recruited and where their homes are. They will all want to go into new areas where their community is in a majority.

V.C.P. 33[1]

A. GENERAL

1. Except for a few drafting points the Governor of the Punjab had no comments on the draft.

2. He agrees that we cannot cope with a full-dress Boundary Commission in the time available, and though it might be necessary at some time after the announcement to accept a proposal to examine minor adjustments (to the extent of boundary tahsils only) he agrees that nothing need be said in the statement.

3. He is anxious about the Sikhs who are in a very dangerous mood and strongly supported certain proposals for palliatives (note attached)[2] which I put to him.

4. In general he is not optimistic about the outcome but has no better proposal to make. He thinks it would be most imprudent not to plan against the possibility that this statement (like the one of February 20th) may only increase the disorder in the Punjab, and will discuss at Rawalpindi with the Army Commander what reinforcements can be provided for Lahore.

5. He emphasised that there must be as much notice as possible to Governors and Army Commanders of the date of the announcement.

B. DRAFTING POINTS (These are minor points and Y.E. need not study them)

[Sir E. Jenkins' detailed drafting suggestions omitted; a number of the points were incorporated in Appendix C to No. 260]

6. I think these drafting amendments can be accepted.

G.E.B. ABELL

¹ Dated 24 April 1947 and circulating further revised versions of the draft invitation to the Indian Leaders and the draft announcement. Mountbatten Papers. See No. 260 for an indication of the text of the draft announcement at this time.
² Presumably Mr Abell's note above.

236

Notes by Sir C. Corfield and Rear-Admiral Viscount Mountbatten of Burma

R/1/29/3217: ff 4–6

SECRET   *22 April 1947*

I had an hour's talk with Pandit Nehru on the 26th instant at his request. I have also received an invitation from Sardar Patel for a talk tomorrow.

2. The main points covered during my talk with Pandit Nehru are as follows:—

Constituent Assembly

I said I had been pleased to see in that morning's paper a statement regarding the report of the Committee of the Constituent Assembly which had held discussions with the States' Negotiating Committee, and that in this report the complete freedom of choice for the States in regard to entering the Assembly had been stressed. Pandit Nehru said that the report would be laid before the Assembly on the 28th, and suggested that in spite of this freedom of choice it would be beneficial not only to the States but also the work of the Constituent Assembly if State representatives were included at once. He said that the inclusion of Sir B.L. Mitter and Sir V.T. Krishnamachari in the Union Powers Committee had been of great value, as they had been able to point out certain errors and omissions which could only be apparent to State representatives.

I then explained to Pandit Nehru the advice which I had given to States about entering the Constituent Assembly, and he did not dispute its propriety. I pointed out that so long as the States were united and neutral they were a stabilising factor, but now that they had ceased to be either they must choose as soon as possible whether to join a Constituent Assembly or be independent: it seemed entirely legitimate however in view of the Statement of 20th February that any State, which did not wish to decide at once, should await His Majesty's Government's decision regarding the authorities to which they proposed to hand over in June 1948. Moreover, there were already a number of State representatives in the Constituent Assembly and they were quite capable of putting forward the State point of view in the meanwhile. An immediate increase in their numbers could hardly affect the results especially in the narrow sphere of Union subjects. It was pointless therefore in my view to harry the States which had not yet decided to send representatives.

Political Department

Pandit Nehru mentioned the alleged reactionary influence of the Political Department. I pointed out that for many years we had been blamed by British India for not interfering in States enough and for not pushing them along the road to democracy. Equally strong criticism (but not so public) had emanated from the States for interfering too much and forcing upon them democratic measures which were contrary to indigenous desires and needs. Before I could point the moral, Pandit Nehru appreciated that these criticisms cancelled out.

I further pointed out that as a semi-diplomatic organisation we were precluded from using publicity to defend ourselves; but our consciences were quite clear. In fact, if it had not been for our influence there would by now have been less association of the people with the administrations in Indian States. I had myself prepared a model constitution act for medium States in 1938, which though now out of date had been used by a number of States as a basis for their political advance.

Pandit Nehru then said that certain Rulers had alleged that though they themselves were anxious to advance they had been advised by the Political Department to go slow. I said this was an 'old story', and we were well used to being the shield behind which some reactionary Rulers were content to conceal their own inclinations. Pandit Nehru did not dispute this, and I thought it politic not to mention that for many years the most advanced constitution in an Indian State (except for Mysore and Travancore) was the one framed by Sir Bertrand Glancy, a previous Political Adviser, for Kashmir.

Future of Indian States

Pandit Nehru asked for my opinion regarding the position of Indian States in the new India. I suggested that their future depended entirely on developments in British India. If British India remained stable in the form of one, two or at the most three Unions, I had no doubt that all the States would adhere in due course and their governments would gradually conform more closely to that of neighbouring Provinces: but if British India disintegrated the future of the States would be entirely different. Much would in my view depend on the extent to which the existing governments in India could provide security of life and limb in their respective areas during the next two years.

As regards the number of State units that would be likely to survive I thought that only about ten or twelve had inherent survival value: composite units would very soon lose their Indian State character: and the only units which could afford temporary independence were those which had or could negotiate an outlet to the sea.

Berar

Pandit Nehru enquired how I thought the question of Berar could be settled. I suggested that if Hyderabad came into the (Hindustan) Constituent Assembly, a sub-committee could be formed therein including representatives of Berar and Hyderabad. If Hyderabad did not come in, the Constituent Assembly might appoint a negotiating Committee of (say) two Berari representatives and a member of the Interim Government who was also a member of the Constituent Assembly. Pandit Nehru enquired how the Hyderabad State subjects could be associated, and I suggested that the Hyderabad Assembly could choose one negotiator on behalf of the State.

Pandit Nehru agreed that the Crown Representative should confine his efforts to providing a forum for negotiation, and that no settlement which was not made direct between Hyderabad and British India would be of the slightest value.

As regards the nature of the settlement Pandit Nehru could not see why Hyderabad should want any outlet to the sea. I suggested that this depended on the scope of Union subjects and whether Hyderabad came into the Union. As a settlement about Berar might have to precede conclusions on both these questions it seemed that Hyderabad would be wise to protect their economic position, until a general agreed settlement had been reached.

Bastar

I raised this question myself and stated that there was nothing sinister in the negotiations with Hyderabad, and that the Central Government departments concerned had been taken into the fullest confidence.

Pandit Nehru appeared to accept this, but suggested that it was dangerous to link Bastar with an inefficient place like Hyderabad. I demurred and said I had good technical opinion to support the view that the Hyderabad Irrigation Department maintained a higher standard than that of even the well-run Province of Madras, that Hyderabad's plan of industrial development was of the highest order, and that its new industrial area had been laid out in accordance with the best technical advice, including town planning and housing of labour. I could not see how Bastar interests would suffer from a railway run by Hyderabad to extract iron ore. Incidentally the Hyderabad State Railways were also an efficient concern.

I found Pandit Nehru very much more receptive than during my last interview with him in October last year, and I am glad that contact has been renewed. Pandit Nehru did not comment on my explanation of the contraction of paramountcy, the gradual withdrawal of local Political Officers and the fade-out of the Political Department.

For H.E.'s information.

C. CORFIELD

27.4.47

Most encouraging. Does Pt. Nehru still wanting [*sic*] a meeting between the three of us?[1]

M. of B.

27/4

[1] In a minute of 1 May Sir C. Corfield suggested it might be suitable if Lord Mountbatten wrote to Pandit Nehru to say he understood the ground had been covered in the talk between Sir C. Corfield and Pandit Nehru but that if he (Nehru) wished a further talk in the Viceroy's presence, this could be arranged. Before this suggestion could be acted on, however, No. 266 was received from Pandit Nehru and Lord Mountbatten replied as in No. 304. R/1/29/3217: f 6.

237

Rear-Admiral Viscount Mountbatten of Burma to Sir F. Mudie (Sind) (Extract)

Mountbatten Papers. Official Correspondence Files: Sind, Situation in

No. 40/4.   *27 April 1947*

My dear Mudie,

Thank you for your letter of the 22nd April.[1] You may well be right in thinking that the main grievance of the Congress against you is the action you took in the United Provinces in 1942, aggravated perhaps by the manner in which fresh elections were held in Sind last year. I agree also that if a Governor of a Congress province treated his ministry in the way in which you are expected to deal with your ministry, there would probably be a series of first class crises. I am grateful too for the peace and tranquillity which at the moment prevails in Sind, in glaring contrast with several other provinces.

2. Whilst I accept, therefore, your statement that you have done your best to secure justice for the minorities, I do want to impress on you that it is necessary to be perhaps over-scrupulous in avoiding even the appearance of partisanship at this particular moment. I know I can rely on you to assist me in this way, and I shall now feel in a better position to deal with any allegations which the Congress may subsequently bring against you.

[Paras. 3–4, on the Sind Landholders Mortgages Bill 1947, omitted.]

[1] No. 197.

238

Rear-Admiral Viscount Mountbatten of Burma to Mr Jinnah

Mountbatten Papers. Official Correspondence Files: North-West Frontier Province, Situation in, Part 1(a)

27 April 1947

Dear Mr Jinnah,

I am anxious, as you know, to talk to League leaders in Peshawar, but the Governor tells me that they will not come to see me unless they are brought as prisoners.[1]

Although I should be exceedingly sorry not to have the opportunity of seeing them I could not possibly see them except as free men, or at least under parole, but I am sure I can rely on you to persuade them not to persist in this unreasonable attitude since you are in a better position to appreciate the consequences.

Yours sincerely,
MOUNTBATTEN OF BURMA

[1] See tel. CA/64 of 26 April 1947. Mountbatten Papers, Official Correspondence Files: N.W.F.P., Situation in, Part I(a).

239

Rear-Admiral Viscount Mountbatten of Burma to Sardar Patel

Mountbatten Papers. Official Correspondence Files: Bihar, Situation In

27 April 1947

I send you a copy of a letter[1] I have received from Sir Hugh Dow the Governor of Bihar.

You will note that he says in the end that he does not suppose I will think his letter a suitable one to show you, but then he does not realise that you and I have agreed to be completely frank with each other, and that I am certain you will appreciate seeing a forthright letter which was not intended for your eyes, but which I feel is a very sincere letter, and one which you would wish to see.

I am asking the Prime Minister of Bihar to come to lunch as soon as I get back from my trip to the N.W.F.P. and the Punjab, and would therefore be grateful if you could let me know what reactions you had in your talks with him. I am sure I need not ask you not to show Dow's actual letter to his own Prime Minister, since this would make my action in sending you the original letter even more irregular!

[1] No. 206.

240

Sardar Baldev Singh to Rear-Admiral Viscount Mountbatten of Burma

Mountbatten Papers. Official Correspondence Files: Punjab,
Part I(b)

I BHAGWAN DAS ROAD, NEW DELHI,
27 April 1947

My dear Lord Mountbatten,

I would like, by Your Excellency's leave, to place before you my considered views with reference to our discussions regarding the constitutional changes now under discussion with particular reference to the division of the Punjab.

2. I would like at the very start to make it clear that though the demand for division is none of our seeking, it is not that we have only now come to the conclusion of its being the only way out of our difficulties. We Sikhs made no secret of our determination not to allow ourselves to be dominated in any communal separatist scheme of the division of India so soon as we became aware of the drift of Muslim League opinion in that direction. This drift came to surface long before the arrival in India of the British Cabinet Mission. In the Memorandum, therefore, which the Panthic Board presented to the Mission, it was made quite clear that Sikhs will in no circumstances agree to remain in Pakistan area and that if Pakistan was to be conceded to the Muslim League, the Punjab must be divided. Later, when the Mission issued its statement of May 16, proposing the Group Plan, so deep-seated were Sikh fears that there was a spontaneous reaction against the absence of any provision for the safeguard of Sikh rights in Group B where Muslim votes enjoyed decisive majority. The Mission's Plan was accepted subsequently only when we were assured both by the highest British authorities and the Congress that no efforts would be spared to secure for the Sikhs in Group B the same privileges that had been given to Muslims in the Constituent Assembly in the matter of securing religious, cultural and other Minority rights. The boycott of the Constituent Assembly by the Muslim League and its refusal to arrive at any settlement with the Sikhs, have confirmed our worst fears.

3. It is noteworthy that throughout this period and before, while the Muslim League under the leadership of Mr. Jinnah regimented Muslim masses behind the demand for Pakistan, every imaginable artifice was employed to rouse Muslim religious fanaticism and to engender hatred of non-Muslims, who because they opposed the League, were dubbed as "enemies of Islam" by Mr Jinnah himself, his accredited colleagues and innumerable Muslim religious sectarian Heads. This was done in spite of everyone of them knowing that religious passions so roused were bound to result in the gravest disorders. No

impartial observer of recent events doubts today that it was these wild and reckless preachments, provoking blood-lust and lauding tyrants and adventurers such as Chingez Khan and Halaku Khan that have led to the abominable atrocities in the Punjab and elsewhere, bringing irreparable grief and ruin to thousands of innocent men, women and children. It is true that there have been some odd affirmations of concern and offers to settle with and protect the Minorities; but in the context of dreadful happenings and in view of the accumulating evidence that these were pre-planned, carefully organised and executed with deliberation, nobody could take the League leaders seriously. It is significant that not until Your Excellency personally intervened, has there been any attempt at restraining the fell actors in this murderous movement aimed against non-Muslims and their few Muslim friends. Bitterness, in fact is still being preached by highly placed League leaders; their accredited Delhi journal is attacking the Punjab Governor's administration because of the arrests of criminals and abettors of crimes.

4. The Muslim League has made no secret of its plan of the Pakistan State. It will be based on Muslim law. The manner in which they have treated non-Muslims even while the authority of British Government still remained clearly shows that later on there will be no room whatever for non-Muslims in the Muslim State. In any event the life and property of Hindus and Sikhs will be wholly insecure. Therefore in order to free the non-Muslims from the fear of an aggressive Muslim domination and to provide adequate protection for them, the Hindus and Sikhs have finally and unalterably come to the conclusion that the only solution is the immediate division of the Punjab. And the Sikhs particularly expect that this division will be so devised as to fulfil the solemn promises given to them by the highest British authorities to fully secure Sikh interests in the scheme of political settlement now under way. These promises were given to us when Master Tara Singh and I met the British Cabinet Mission and your predecessor. We were then assured that Sikh interests will in no circumstances be ignored and I hope now Your Excellency will keep these assurances in view when making your final proposals in regard to the division of the Punjab.

5. It is obvious that the division which implies the drawing up of a line of demarcation will have to be entrusted to a Boundary Commission. Certain broad principles have to be laid down when this commission is constituted. First that the Punjab is the historic Homeland of Sikhs and the line of division should be so aligned as to disturb as little as possible the contiguity and homogeneity of Sikh population. Secondly, that as the division is none of our seeking and has in fact been forced on us by Muslim League's intransigence and organised oppression, it must not inflict on our community inordinate losses—financial, economic or otherwise—as that would put a premium on aggression

or brute force. Thirdly that the line of demarcation should be so drawn up as to reduce to the minimum the risk of future border conflict. Such conflict would be inevitable if the Muslim territory includes a high percentage of Sikh population.

6. It is to be noted that the scheme of division based on population majorities in contiguous districts or tehsils which the British Cabinet Mission also examined, was rejected by the Cabinet Mission itself, among other reasons because it cut the Sikh population into two halves. The non-Muslims particularly the Sikhs, cannot therefore agree to any division merely on the basis of population majorities in contiguous districts or tehsils. The main purpose of division is to avoid conflict. To divide Punjab on the basis of communal majority in the district or tehsil will not solve the real problem. Such a division if made, far from being a solution, will perpetuate conflicts and add to the existing bitterness between Muslims and non-Muslims.

7. We have considered some alternatives which meet the situation far more satisfactorily. These are—

(a) On the basis of landed property held respectively by non-Muslims and Muslims in the Punjab as a whole

(b) On the basis of the population strength of non-Muslims and Muslims respectively according to the latest available statistics in the Punjab as a whole.

8. [(a)] The total area of the British Punjab according to the Census Report of 1941 is 99,089 square miles. The population of non-Muslims in the province as a whole is about 44 per cent. I may state that the latter figure has been challenged time and again by authoritative writers. It is well-known that in winter when the Census enumerations take place there is a large influx of landless floating labour from the Frontier Province and Kashmir into the Punjab. Nearly all these temporary immigrants are Muslims and they have found a place in the total Muslim population of the Punjab in Census figures. The view of writers on the subject has found unexpected support by the analysis of rationing cards in many of the Punjab urban areas which have belied the census figures. The percentage of non-Muslims may in fact well be 47 or even 48.

(b) As for the respective total holdings of landed properties by Muslims and non-Muslims, the position was examined by the Punjab Government in 1931 by the analysis of the incidence of land revenue community-wise. It was then found that of the total sum of Revenue namely Rs. 4,38,13,977, the non-Muslims paid Rs. 2,18,44,913. The revenue figures have since increased but the proportion remains as it was. As to urban property, it is well-known that non-Muslims own as much as 80 per cent of it in the province. The total share of non-Muslims in the immovable property therefore is well over 50 per cent taken as a whole.

(c) It is pertinent here to refer to the scheme of the respective shares in administrative posts of non-Muslims and Muslims which has been in vogue for some years in the Punjab. Although the population of non-Muslims according to Census figures is only 44 per cent, their share in administrative posts was fixed on 50-50 basis, due obviously to the 50 per cent revenue paid by them. Similarly the number of Muslim and non-Muslim Ministers in the Cabinet was also fixed on 50-50 basis.

9. Taking all these factors into consideration we claim that the division of the Punjab should be on the basis of the division of the total area of the Province into half and half, or, 49,544 out of 99,089 square miles. This would be in accordance with the basis as in para 7(a) above viz. the basis of landed property held by non-Muslims and Muslims in the Punjab as a whole. In the event of the division on this basis, the non-Muslim population in Muslim Western region could be transferred to the non-Muslim Eastern region. Mr Jinnah has already accepted the principle of the transfer of population and there should therefore be no objection to the mutual exchange. The advantage of my proposal is that the division based on the respective total land holdings of non-Muslims and Muslims will cause the least amount of economic and financial disturbance to either party.

10. If the division is to be based on population basis, the total non-Muslim population in the province as a whole should be the basis of such a division. The non-Muslim population as I have stated is 44 to 48 per cent. I would propose that 44 to 48 per cent of the total area of the Province should be separated for non-Muslims and the rest for Muslims. This would be in accordance with the basis as in para 7(b) above, viz. the basis of the population strength of non-Muslims and Muslims respectively in the province as a whole.

10.[11.] In any event, I suggest that the claim of non-Muslims on the three Divisions of Ambala, Jullundur and Lahore is incontrovertible. The total area of the three Divisions is 45,945 square miles, and the total population equal to 1,73,52,044. Of these the non-Muslims are 99,56,508, the population of Sikhs being 30,04,707. It will be seen that by dividing the Punjab on this basis, some 80 per cent of the present total Sikh population of the province as well as Nankana Sahib, the birth place of the Founder of Sikh religion would fall within the territory of this area. In this area the total revenue, according to available figures, is Rs. 2,42,28,998. Of this Rs. 1,64,34,704 is paid by non-Muslims the Sikh share being Rs. 83,65,969. Thus both on the basis of population and revenue payments these three Divisions constitute a pre-eminently non-Muslim area and can easily be set apart in the East and South East of the Punjab.

11.[12.] It is impossible to discuss the division of the Punjab without reference to the colony areas. The part that Sikhs have played in the development of the colonies is well-known.

In the words of Sir Edward Maclagan—

"No colony could have had better material, for Ludhiana, Jullundur and Amritsar represent the flower of Indian agriculture. They are the home of Jat Sikhs who have been described as the most desirable of 'Colonists'. . . . In his new environment, (Colony Area) the Jat Sikh has reached a point of development probably beyond anything else of the kind in India. In less than a generation, he has made the wilderness blossom like the rose. It is as if the energy of the virgin soil of the Bar has passed into his veins and made him almost a part of the forces of nature which he has conquered".

Such being the contribution of the Sikhs in the development of the colony areas in the Punjab it would be but their due to claim at least a fair part of it as in return for their labour. As the total area of the three Divisions of Lahore, Jullundur and Ambala (para 10 [11] above) falls short of half the total area of the Punjab, the balance should be made good by assigning either the district of Montgomery or Lyallpur to Sikhs to form part of the non-Muslim part of divided Punjab.

12.[13.] I would emphasise that in any political announcement regarding the division of the Punjab which Your Excellency might have under consideration it would be necessary to give a very clear indication of the lines on which the division is to be based, in the terms of reference to the proposed Boundary Commission. I am clear in my mind that unless this is done, the mere announcement of division or the appointment of a Boundary Commission will create increasing complications and more disastrous disorders both in the Western and Eastern Punjab. It is only fair that the people of the Punjab should now have a clear picture of the division of their province before they are asked to vote on this issue. The non-Muslims have been subjected to unparalleled outbursts of terrorism. The tension in the Province is very great. The only way of easing the situation is to let the people have a clear and unequivocal picture of division and I request Your Excellency most earnestly to see that this is done.[1]

Yours sincerely,
BALDEV SINGH

[1] Lord Mountbatten evidently showed this letter to Sir E. Jenkins and discussed it with him. The latter minuted as follows: 'This shows why the partition of the Punjab would mean civil war. The Sikhs haven't a majority in any one district. They want—on religious grounds like the Muslims—to take over and dominate areas in which they are in a minority. The Bari Doab—the area between the Ravi and the Beas comprising Gurdaspur, Amritsar, Lahore and Montgomery—would become a battle-ground, and Baldev Singh evidently wants to go well west of the Ravi. This won't work. E.M.J. 29.4.47.' Mountbatten Papers, Official Correspondence Files: Punjab, Part I(b).

241

Rear-Admiral Viscount Mountbatten of Burma to Sir O. Caroe
(North-West Frontier Province)

Telegram, Mountbatten Papers. Official Correspondence Files: North-West
Frontier Province, Situation in, Part I(a)

IMMEDIATE   *27 April 1947, 10.35 pm*
CONFIDENTIAL

913–S. I have just had conversation with Jinnah who pressed me to allow Muslim League meeting tomorrow evening followed by procession to Government House which he guaranteed would be orderly. I told him very plainly that whereas there was no objection to a meeting I would have nothing to do with any procession which would be completely contrary to assurance I had given to Khan Sahib. I agreed to see at Government House at the most six delegates from the meeting but I warned him of the answer I would give. Please make arrangements to see that the delegates, if they decide to come, are allowed to proceed to Government House without hindrance.

242

Rear-Admiral Viscount Mountbatten of Burma to Sir F. Burrows (Bengal)

Telegram, Mountbatten Papers. Official Correspondence Files:
Bengal, Partition of, Part I(a)

IMMEDIATE   *28 April 1947, 3 am*
TOP SECRET

914–S. I have considered your views as reported by Christie.[1] At first sight I am very doubtful about amendment you propose[2] but my staff will work on it all tomorrow. Unfortunately I leave in the morning for a short but urgent visit to the Frontier and the Punjab, but I shall give further thought to this before I go.

2. I do not like the idea of a free city. It goes against all the principles on which the rest of the plan is based, it leaves Calcutta cut off from Muslim Bengal, it will not be acceptable to the Hindus, and I do not see how we can enforce it or prevent a fight for the city next year. Besides which it is not for me to make Pakistan into a sensible scheme. I want it to be seen for what it is, while giving the Muslims everything to which they are entitled, and every chance to work out their own salvation.

[1] See No. 231.   [2] See No. 233.

3. Do not forget that my scheme leaves the door open to a united but independent Bengal belonging neither to Pakistan nor Hindustan. Jinnah would raise no objection to this. Do you think Suhrawardy could bring this off?

4. I am very sorry you are unwell. But for that I should certainly have asked you to come to Delhi as I would greatly value your advice and am anxious fully to understand your point of view.

5. Unless on consideration of the points I have made you feel able to change your view about the plan I will send Ismay and Abell on Tuesday morning to discuss matter with you in Calcutta; and if necessary I will fly to Calcutta myself from the Punjab on Wednesday.[3] I am sorry to have to ask you to postpone your visit to Darjeeling but matter is most urgent and important and I must be fully seized of your opinion before Ismay leaves for London on Friday.

6. Your reply should be addressed to Delhi and repeated to Peshawar.

[3] In tel. 102–C of 28 April Sir F. Burrows thanked Lord Mountbatten for offering to come to Calcutta but felt that a visit by the Viceroy just then would be open to misinterpretation. He was proposing, therefore, to go to Delhi himself, arriving on 30 April. Mountbatten Papers, Official Correspondence Files: Bengal, Partition of, Part I(a).

243

Lord Ismay to Sir F. Burrows (Bengal) (by secraphone)

Mountbatten Papers. Official Correspondence Files: Bengal, Partition of, Part I(a)

SECRET   *28 April 1947*

1. The Viceroy, before he left for the Frontier, asked Mieville, Abell and myself to discuss your proposed amendments to the draft announcement with Christie, who has given us a very full report of your views.

2. We have all seen a good deal of Jinnah and I myself was present when the Viceroy told him that if he were to insist on Pakistan, it would mean the partition of the Punjab and Bengal; and that in that event Calcutta would certainly not be in Pakistan. Jinnah made astonishingly little protest and our strong impression is that he is so keen to get the principle of Pakistan settled once and for all, that he will acquiesce in what has come to be known as truncated Pakistan, which excludes Calcutta.

3. There is another point. The principal leaders of all parties have been given fairly full details of the plan by the Viceroy, without of course being told definitely that it is the one to be submitted to H.M.G. None of them has

made any strong protest against it on points of substance. If we now make any major alteration such as you propose, it would mean reopening negotiations with them, with very slender chances of success. In particular, if we were to give Jinnah any indication at all that he had a chance of securing a share in Calcutta, we should never again get him in the mood to accept any plan for Bengal which would also be acceptable to the Hindus.

4. Christie has made your point of view very clear to us and we fully realise the dangers inherent in the situation and the very special position of Calcutta. On the other hand, there are grave risks in any course of action, and we are convinced that from the point of view of India as a whole, and the plan as a whole, we ought not to make any major alterations or any radical departure from our principles.

244

Sir E. Jenkins (Punjab) to Rear-Admiral Viscount Mountbatten of Burma

Telegram, R/3/1/176: f 151

IMMEDIATE   *28 April 1947, 1 pm*
SECRET

No. 84–G Your telegrams 902–S of 26th[1] and 905–S of 27th April.[2] Jinnah's move is intended (a) to increase importance of Muslim League and (b) to transfer direct control of the Punjab from myself to Your Excellency. If Mamdot postpones his interview with me I must make it clear to him in writing that I will not have communal Ministry. I can have no objection to Your Excellency seeing Mamdot independently if you think this wise but there can be no question of joint interview between Your Excellency, Mamdot and myself. Mamdot is only a Provincial Party leader and any procedure adopted with him will have to be available to all Provincial Party leaders. There is absolutely no reason for departing from the normal constitutional procedure in these matters.[3]

Repeated P.S.V., New Delhi

[1] See No. 229, note 2.
[2] In this tel. Mr Abell informed the Governor's Secretary, Punjab, that Mr Jinnah now wanted Lord Mountbatten to see the Nawab of Mamdot with the Governor and Lord Mountbatten was willing to do this. R/3/1/89: f 174.
[3] In tel. 919–S of 28 April Mr Abell reported to Lord Mountbatten in Peshawar that Mr Jinnah took perfectly calmly the news that the Viceroy might not see Mamdot. *Ibid:* f 175.

245

Sir C. Corfield to Rear-Admiral Viscount Mountbatten of Burma

R/1/30/40: ff 70–1; L/P & S/13/1827: f26

SECRET   NEW DELHI, *28 April 1947*
D.O. No. F. 14–R(S)/47
My dear Lord Mountbatten,
I am grateful to Your Excellency for your letter of 22nd April, No. 592/45.[1]

It is perhaps worth recording that, though Pandit Nehru was at one time President of the All-India States' People's Conference, he is now only one of the dozen or more members of the Standing Committee of that organization. Even so, the continued and prominent association with the All-India States' People's Conference of a Member of the Cabinet, and the confusion which this causes when public speeches are made, inevitably increase the difficulties of building up a feeling of mutual confidence between States and responsible authorities in British India.

I enclose herewith a copy of the letter which has been issued to all Residents on the lines which Your Excellency indicated to me yesterday, and of my letter to His Highness the Chancellor forwarding him a copy.

Yours sincerely,

C. L. CORFIELD

[1] No. 196.

Enclosure 1 to No. 245
Mr Wakefield to all Residents

SECRET   NEW DELHI, *28 April 1947*
D.O. No. F. 14–R.(S)/47
My dear . . . . ,
In view of the reports published in the press of the proceedings of the All-India States' People's Conference recently held in Gwalior[2] and the references therein regarding the attitude to be adopted towards Rulers who do not forthwith send their representatives to the Constituent Assembly, His Excellency the Crown Representative's instructions have been taken regarding the advice which should be given to any Ruler who may consult you on the subject.

2. I am to say that, if you are consulted, you should explain that there is no obligation on a Ruler who has accepted the Cabinet Mission Plan to send

[2] See No. 181, note 2.

representatives to the Constituent Assembly until the final stage, when that Assembly reassembles to frame the Union constitution.

3. This stage has not yet been reached; moreover, it is now likely that an announcement will be made by His Majesty's Government before long regarding the authorities to whom the powers of the Central Government in British India will be handed over.

4. As soon as this announcement has been made, His Excellency the Crown Representative considers that Rulers would be well advised to take immediate steps to consult public opinion in their States and thereafter without delay to announce whatever decision they may reach about joining the Constituent Assembly.

5. A copy of this letter has been sent to His Highness the Chancellor of the Chamber of Princes.

Yours sincerely,

E. B. WAKEFIELD

Enclosure 2 to No. 245
Sir C. Corfield to the Nawab of Bhopal

D.O. No. F. 14–R(S)/47   NEW DELHI, *28 April 1947*

My dear Nawab Sahib,

Your Highness mentioned to me on the 26th evening the draft of a letter which was being prepared for Your Highness to address to His Excellency the Crown Representative regarding the attitude reported in the Press of the All-India States' People's Conference to Rulers who failed forthwith to send their representatives to the Constituent Assembly.

I have since discussed the question with His Excellency who has asked me to forward for your information a copy of the instructions which he has authorised for despatch to all Residents.

In view of these instructions the purport of which may, if Your Highness desires, be communicated to any Ruler who is likely to be interested, His Excellency hopes you will agree that no letter from you and reply from him on this subject is now necessary.

Yours sincerely,

C. L. CORFIELD

246

Sir E. Mieville to Sardar Patel

R/3/1/130: f 219

No. 592/58   28 April 1947

Dear Sardar Vallabhbhai,

H.E. has directed me to thank you for your letter of the 26th April[1] about the Cabinet Mission's plan.

H.E. feels that H.M.G.'s statement of the 6th December is perfectly clear about the legal position and that the speeches by Sir Stafford Cripps and Lord Pethick-Lawrence, which you quoted, related to the undoubted fact that without a reasonable measure of agreement you cannot frame a Constitution, and that if any outrageous attempt was made to force an unacceptable Constitution on a Province the Constitution-making machine would break down whatever the legal rights of the parties might be.

Yours sincerely,

E. MIEVILLE

[1] No. 226.

247

Mr Scott to Mr Abell

Telegram, Mountbatten Papers. Official Correspondence Files: North–West Frontier Province, Situation in, Part I(a)

IMMEDIATE   PESHAWAR, *28 April 1947, 7.40 pm*
SECRET   *Received: 28 April, 10 pm*

No. 69–C. On arrival in Peshawar, His Excellency was informed that the meeting that Jinnah had telephoned about last night was taking place.[1] A crowd estimated at 50,000 included large numbers who had walked in from the surrounding district and from tribal territory and Kohat district. Although the leaders of the meeting had undertaken not to break the law by forming a procession, all the authorities agreed that they would insist on seeing the Viceroy even at the risk of breaking the law. Their object in gathering together had been to impress the Viceroy with strength of their cause, and there was a grave risk that meeting would get out of control in their desire to find him, unless he showed himself to them.

2. His Excellency therefore called Chief Minister Dr. Khan Sahib into consultation with himself and Governor; and Dr. Khan Sahib agreed that

[1] See No. 241.

His Excellency should show himself to the crowd for a few minutes from the top of a nearby railway embankment. Dr. Khan Sahib also informed His Excellency that he had called off a simultaneous demonstration of Red Shirts since this could not have failed to lead to bloodshed, for which His Excellency commended him.

3. The crowd was in excellent spirits and greeted His Excellency's appearance with shouts and flag-waving. His Excellency stood for a few minutes in company of Governor and local civil and military officials, and then withdrew after saluting but without making any address.

4. Her Excellency accompanied His Excellency, as it was reported there were many women in the crowd.

(Please pass contents of this message immediately to Pandit Nehru, Sardar Patel and Mr. Jinnah).

Repeated to Secretary of State for India.

248

Sir E. Jenkins (Punjab) to Rear-Admiral Viscount Mountbatten of Burma

Telegram, R/3/1/177: ff 6–8

IMMEDIATE   *28 April 1947, 11.20 pm*
No. 86–G. Mamdot saw me 1530 hours today. He had telephoned during morning to say that he wished to keep the appointment. I asked him whether he had anything to add to his letter.[1] Rather to my surprise he made no reference to any instructions from Jinnah and said that he had nothing to add.

2. He then produced figures for his alleged majority consisting of 84 Muslims, 4 Scheduled Castes and 3 Christians—total 91 in a House of 175 I said I noted the figures, but did not think that a communal Ministry, whether Muslim or non-Muslim, had any chance at all of governing the Punjab in the immediate future under the 1935 constitution. I was convinced that a purely communal Ministry would be dislodged by a violent rebellion and might even be unable to hold its obligatory Budget session. Surely the right course was to await the result of Your Excellency's discussions with the Party leaders. If agreement were reached between the Muslim League and the Congress, we might be able to make a fresh start in a better atmosphere. Agreement might be based on union or on partition, but all parties including the Sikhs would at least know where they stood and might be ready to co-operate with one another immediately so as to bring the agreed solution into force. I thought Muslim League did not realise the extreme danger of the

[1] See No. 212.

present situation and the risk they would be running by attempting to impose their will on the Punjab without some easing of the present tension.

3. Mamdot said that he personally would have accepted my view, but he was under very heavy pressure from his followers, who felt that they were being victimized under section 93 and that no attempt was being made to control the militant Sikhs. He referred particularly to criminal cases in the Rawalpindi district, the procedure for summary trials, the sword-*kirpan* controversy, the liberty allowed to Nihang Sikhs, the circulation of violent Sikh pamphlets, and the suppression of a riot in the Attock jail on 22nd April.

4. I assured Mamdot that I had no desire to frustrate the Muslims, but was so acutely aware of the danger of a communal Ministry that I would be most reluctant to take one on as Governor. All senior British Officers shared my view and were not prepared to take sides in a communal civil war. Events in Rawalpindi had undoubtedly led to many arrests and prosecutions, but in one Police Station alone there had been 500 murders, and I did not see how retribution could be avoided. The Sikhs were in a dangerous mood, but it was no time to stir them up on religious issues. I did not see what the Muslim League would lose by waiting a month or so for a possible easing of the tension.

5. Mamdot then asked whether I was definitely unwilling to accept a Muslim League Ministry and felt that the Muslims must "continue to suffer for another month". I replied that I was unwilling to accept a communal Ministry, whether Muslim or non-Muslim, and that I was sure nothing must be done to impair the possibility of a Central settlement. Mamdot then said that he had already seen Jinnah and might see him again. He asked whether Your Excellency would grant interviews to party leaders during your visit to the Punjab. I said that I thought there would be no time at Rawalpindi but that Your Excellency would probably be glad to see Mamdot at New Delhi. Mamdot then asked whether you would be coming to Lahore and I replied not according to the present programme.

6. Mamdot was rather sulky and hinted at the possibility of a mass Muslim League agitation. I replied that I would sooner deal with this than a fight between a Muslim Ministry and the non-Muslims, but very much hoped that he would accept the need for moderation. Mamdot observed that this was all very well, but the Muslims were not going to accept partition and a civil war seemed almost inevitable. He saw no reason why I should prevent the Muslims from fighting for what they regarded as their rights.[2]

Repeated P.S.V. New Delhi

[2] On 29 April Mr Abell sent a telegram to Mr Scott in which he referred to the last para. of No. 248 and said that Mr Liaquat Ali Khan had taken a very different line about the Punjab in a conversation with Sir E. Mieville the previous evening. He then reported the last sentence of No. 249, second para. Mountbatten Papers, Official Correspondence Files: Punjab, Part I(b).

249

Sir E. Mieville to Rear-Admiral Viscount Mountbatten of Burma

Mountbatten Papers. Official Correspondence Files: Interviews

29 April 1947

Your Excellency,

I dined with Liaquat Ali Khan last night, and after dinner we had about twenty minutes talk. He started on the usual communal lines, saying that whereas the Muslims were being accused of violent methods, people had short memories and had apparently forgotten the iniquities of the Hindus in Bihar. He went on to talk of the proposed plan and said that he was in no way worried about Bengal as he was convinced in his own mind that the province would never divide. He thought that it would remain a separate state, joining neither Hindustan nor Pakistan.

He then went on to the Punjab and said that he could not understand the attitude of the Sikhs to whom the Muslims had offered far better terms than the Hindus. He added that the trouble with the Sikhs was that they were very stupid people and lacked a leader. They talked about Sikhistan, but as a matter of fact there was not a single district in which the Sikhs were in the majority. He had pointed this out to them and told them that it was all a question of counting heads and on that basis the Sikhs had no case. He was not unhopeful of persuading them to join the Muslims, in which case he could see no reason for the division of the Punjab.

He then went on to talk about the North-West Block and said that British help would be needed by the Muslims, particularly to develop their industries. They had been used to dealing with the British who were satisfied with their 5%, whereas if they went to the Marwari Banias, who were the only alternative, barring the Americans, they would want at least 10% on their money and would strangle development, being closely allied to the Hindus.

He finally referred to Dominion status and hoped that we would not drive the Muslims out of the Empire.

E.M.

250

Note by Rear-Admiral Viscount Mountbatten of Burma

Mountbatten Papers. Viceroy's Interview No. 102

29 April 1947

Impressions gained from talks with 16 senior officers and officials of the Services in the N.W.F.P. on the 28th April 1947, at Peshawar.

Without exception everyone, both British and Indian, to whom I spoke was absolutely convinced that fresh elections at the earliest possible moment were absolutely necessary if a great disaster was to be avoided in the N.W.F.P.

They further went on to say that they considered it would be necessary to have section 93 government to ensure fair elections. Some considered this would be necessary for from four to six months, but all agreed that at a pinch two months would be enough, and some went so far as to say that even one month might do.

They pointed out that the black marketeering and the control of rationing and supplying of food and cloth had come into the hands of the Government supporters who could thus exercise unfair pressure on the voters.

The Government were also exercising unconstitutional pressure on the courts, and through the arms licensing. Quite apart from this, they said that if the present Government were in power the actual mechanism of the election would be unfairly worked.

Those who had seen the great Muslim League crowd which had collected at midday today (estimated variously to number between fifty and a hundred thousand) expressed their conviction that if I had not gone and shown myself on the bridge nothing would have been able to prevent the crowd from forcing their way through to Government House to see me, and that this inevitably would have meant troops having to open fire on the crowd, with a terrible loss of life.

General McCay went so far as to tell me at 11 p.m. that night that he considered his troops would still have been firing at that moment if I had not gone to the crowd when I did.

Several drew attention to the fact that it was unprecedented in their experience for such a meeting of Pathans to remain completely orderly, well-disciplined, and good humoured, and that the clapping and cheering with which I had been received was absolutely unknown to the Frontier.

251

Note by Mr Tyson[1]

*Mountbatten Papers. Official Correspondence Files: Bengal,
Partition of, Part I(a)*

29 April 1947

In view of the arguments based on the supposed attitude of the Scheduled Castes to Pakistan and the difficulty of saying how far the present Scheduled Caste Members of the Assembly represent the views of the Scheduled Castes since they were ultimately elected to the Assembly on the vote of Scheduled Caste and Caste Hindus together, H.E. will find the statement below,[2] which I have had run out in office today, extremely interesting and more informative than might have been expected.

It is clear that out of 30 reserved seats no less than 15 were filled without any contest at either the primary or the final elections and that of these 15 no less than 13 went to Congress candidates without contest. (The uncontested seats won by Congress were in Burdwan 2, Birbhum 1, Bankura 1, Midnapore 2, 24-Parganas 2, i.e. 8 out of 10 seats reserved for the Scheduled Castes in West Bengal. In North Bengal Malda 1, Jalpaiguri 1, Rangpur 1, that is to say 3 out of 5 seats in North Bengal went uncontested to the Congress. In East Bengal only one seat (Mymensingh) was uncontested and this went to a Congress candidate. They also obtained one uncontested seat in Murshidabad. The other two uncontested seats were—Mr P. D. Raikut who stood as an Independent for the second seat in Jalpaiguri and the Hon'ble Mr N. N. Roy who won the second seat in Rangpur without a contest).

It would appear therefore that in South West Bengal the Scheduled Castes are Congress-minded and in North Bengal personalities seem to have counted more than politics and the result was divided.

Most of the contests were in Central and East Bengal,—Hooghly, Howrah, Nadia, Jessore, Khulna, Dinajpur, Patna cum Bogra, Dacca, Mymensingh, Faridpur, Bakarganj and Tippera. Of the 15 seats contested all over the Province Congress won 8 and in *each case* was at the top of the Poll at the primary election as well as at the general election. I cannot find a case where an Independent or non-Congress Scheduled Caste candidate headed the list in the primary election and was defeated with the aid of Caste Hindu votes in the final election. In fact there is only one instance in all the 15 seats filled by contest where a candidate who was not the first candidate at the primary

---

[1] Mr Abell minuted on 1 May: 'Handed me by Mr Tyson. This contains interesting information and should remain on record.'

[2] Not printed.

election was returned at the final election: this is the case of the Hon'ble Mr
D. N. Barori who was fourth of 8 candidates in the primary election for two
seats in Faridpur and came up to first or second place in the final election
thereby securing one of the two seats.

J. D. TYSON

252

Note by Mr Christie

Mountbatten Papers. Official Correspondence Files: Bengal,
Partition of, Part I(a)

29 April 1947

There are only two points in which the Bengal proposals[1] differ from our
plan, one, a minor point (method of representation in Constituent Assemblies),
and one of major importance, (Calcutta) which has in fact developed since
Tyson sent his letter.

2. The minor point of difference is that the Governor proposes that the
Members of the Constituent Assemblies for East and West Bengal respectively
will be the sitting Members, (excluding European Members) of the Bengal
Legislative Assembly divided according to the communal majorities in districts,
by a committee of the Chief Whips of parties, the Governor's decision being
final in case of disagreement.

Our plan provides for a division of the Legislative Assembly (by notification which is being drafted) for the purpose of electing representatives on the
one-in-a-million principle laid down by the Cabinet Mission's Statement.

Our method has now been accepted by the Governor, with the proviso
that European M.L.A.s should be specifically debarred from voting and be
ineligible for election to the Constituent Assemblies.

3. On the question of Calcutta, the Governor's original recommendation
was not firm. In his note on the provisional partition of Bengal he recommended
a formula which, in terms, assigned Calcutta and its suburbs to West Bengal.
He added a rider to the effect that a fairer arrangement would be one under
which both Provinces could enjoy the benefits to be derived from access to
the wealth of Calcutta. Such an arrangement would also be more fair to
Calcutta itself. The disposition of Calcutta might well prove an important
bargaining point in inducing the League to accept a truncated Pakistan in
Bengal.

[1] See Nos. 208, 231 and 233.

If this were the only argument of the Government of Bengal it would not be a strong one.

It is no part of our plan to induce the League to accept a truncated Pakistan nor, primarily, to make a fair arrangement. Our attitude is that we do not approve of partition in any form, but if the representatives of the people insist on it, they must accept a rough and ready provisional partition in which those who gain on the swings will lose on the roundabouts.

4. Since Tyson's letter, the Governor's opinion has hardened, and on other grounds. If I interpret his view right, it is that the fairness or unfairness of allotting Calcutta to West Bengal is only a secondary consideration.

The main consideration is that we are about to prescribe a procedure which not only makes the provisional partition of Bengal a cast iron certainty, but removes nearly all chance of Bengal becoming united again. So long as the Bengal Hindus have partition *and* Calcutta, they have all that they want. Reunion with East Bengal would only put them again in a position of numerical inferiority to the Muslims.

But if Calcutta were to be a no-man's land, and the Muslims had a share in it (which need not necessarily be a 50% share of its revenues: that would be a matter for mutual agreement or arbitration), there would be common ground on which the two parts of Bengal might eventually reunite.

The Muslims are likely to fight for Calcutta if they have no share in it at all.

The Hindus are less likely to fight for the absolute control of Calcutta.

The following passage in Mr Suhrawardy's recent statement is significant. "So, in the end, the tussle will rage round Calcutta and its environments built up largely by the resources of foreigners, inhabited largely by people from other provinces who have no roots in the soil and who have come here to earn their livelihood, designated in another context as exploitation."

The effect of our plan would be to set the seal on the partition of Bengal and make Civil War, and paralysis if not destruction of India's greatest commercial centre, almost inevitable. The Governor's proposal lessens the likelihood of Civil War over Calcutta, and provides an important matter of "common concern" as a basis for reunion. The objections to the Governor's proposal that Calcutta should not be allotted to either half province, but should be administered as a condominium, are therefore probably less than the objections to our plan in its effect on Bengal.

5. The question of a corridor has been raised. This would hardly arise, since adjustment of the East Bengal boundaries to include the Muslim majority sub-divisions of the 24 Parganahs District would bring East Bengal right up to the suburbs of Calcutta.

6. The Governor recommends for the interim administration of Bengal, i.e. between the date of the announcement and the demission of power, a

Coalition Ministry, working in two parts as regional ministries for East and West Bengal respectively (and the Legislative business similarly divided by convention). This is the B.N. Rau plan,[2] on which, so far as I know, no decisions have been reached.

The Governor does not refer to the alternative of Section 93, but mentioned to me that he considered it out of the question since his present Muslim Ministry has an absolute majority, and his administrative machine is weak.

W. H. J. CHRISTIE

[2] See No. 262, note 2.

253

Sir H. Dow (Bihar) to Rear-Admiral Viscount Mountbatten of Burma (Extract)

Mountbatten Papers. Official Correspondence Files: Bihar,
Situation in

D.O. No. 113–G.B.   GOVERNOR'S CAMP, BIHAR,
                                                       29 April 1947

3. I had a friendly talk with my Prime Minister on my return from Delhi, very largely about police matters. I feel that the lessons of the recent mutiny have not been lost on him, and that he is now most anxious to make the police force a reliable one and to cut loose from the entanglements in which his encouragement of the I.N.A. have involved him. He is now in Delhi for the meeting of the Constituent Assembly, and I hope it will be possible for you to give him an interview. (I have written to Abell about this).

4. Mr Gandhi is back in Bihar, ostensibly devoting himself to rehabilitation. I am very glad that he has been persuaded not to interfere further in the situation arising out of the police mutiny. There is a general feeling among the Muslim community that there is not likely to be another large scale massacre here so long as Gandhi is in Bihar, but I should hesitate to estimate the benefits of his presence among us much higher than that. He doesn't appear to have much influence in inducing a real change of heart in his own community. The actual work of reconstruction, of rebuilding the houses destroyed in the riots, is, if anything, being impeded by his presence. Houlton, the Relief Commissioner, is getting very fed up with his job, and will soon be leaving it. He finds it difficult to get orders from the Ministers, who send him to discuss matters with Gandhi, who generally goes off at a tangent and makes some quite impracticable suggestion. The latest of these is that the ministry should acquire the lands of all Muslims who wish to leave the province.

254

Rear-Admiral Viscount Mountbatten of Burma to the Earl of Listowel
Telegram, L/P&S/13/1266: f 45

IMPORTANT   NEW DELHI, *29 April 1947, 11.5 pm*
                                        Received: 29 April, 11.40 pm

No. 941–P. Gilgit subdivision is at present administered by H.E. the Crown Representative under 60 years agreement made with Kashmir Government in 1935.

2. Passes to Gilgit are only open during the summer months and Political Department therefore propose that the agreement should be terminated during September 1947 thus enabling the Crown Representative's establishment which includes two Political officers to be removed before termination of paramountcy and giving Kashmir Government opportunity to make suitable alternative arrangements for administration of the area.

3. Department of External Affairs and Defence Departments confirm that premature termination of agreement as proposed will not prejudice All India interests in the sphere of foreign relations and defence. But Nehru has suggested that the question of terminating the agreement be reconsidered next Spring when the nature of Kashmir's relationship to the Union of India will be much clearer.

4. I have given this suggestion careful consideration but do not think it can be accepted for the following reasons. *Firstly*, suggestion directly conflicts with the accepted policy of achieving greatest possible devolution of paramountcy by the end of 1947. *Secondly*, if decision is deferred till Spring 1948 it will be impossible for practical reasons to give effect to it by June 1948. *Thirdly*, *administratively* it will be immensely difficult and complex task to complete final transfer of power throughout India by June 1948 and I cannot think it prudent to complicate the task still further by postponing decisions which can be made now without prejudice to interests of any party. *Fourthly*, postponement would be strongly resented by Kashmir and interpreted as breach of faith.

5. Subject to your approval I propose therefore to terminate the agreement not later than October 1st 1947. Very early reply is requested as the Resident Kashmir should be informed of decision by the end of April.

6. This is a case which falls to be dealt with under final sentence of paragraph No. 12 of Prime Minister's statement of February 20th and I propose merely to inform Nehru personally of decision.[1]

The Secretary of State replied in tel. 5946 of 8 May as follows: 'I agree with the line you take and I ap prove the proposals contained in your para. 5. With reference to your para. 6 I understand that N ehru has now accepted your decision.' L/P &S/13/1266: f 44.

255

The Earl of Listowel to Rear-Admiral Viscount Mountbatten of Burma

R/3/1/81: ff 131–2

INDIA OFFICE, *30 April 1947*

My dear Viceroy,

His Majesty's Government have studied the implications of your letter of 31st March 1947 (No. 38/11)[1] and consider that the following principles should govern the use of British Forces and their withdrawal subsequent to the transfer of power in June 1948:—

1. There can be no question of any withdrawal from India of major British Units of the six Brigade Groups or of essential air forces until June 1948 or the date of transference of power, but you are empowered to withdraw such individuals and details as you may deem necessary before that date.

2. Until June 1948, British Forces can be used in aid of the civil power in India.

3. After June 1948, British Forces in India will be in a country which, whether a Member of the British Commonwealth or not, will be of such status that their presence and activities there will be dependent on the goodwill of its Government. In default of an unsolicited request for aid from the new Government or Governments of India, the tasks of the British Forces remaining in India after June 1948 should, therefore, be confined to:

(*a*) The protection of themselves and such Europeans as may be committed to their charge before June 1948.

(*b*) The movement of themselves to the ports of embarkation.

4. It is important that British troops should leave India as an Armed force. In order to ensure this, it is desired that you should arrange, during the period before June 1948, that British Forces in the country at that date are:

(*a*) provided with arms and equipment, the property of His Majesty's Government and not of the Indian Government. (It is understood that there is at present a sufficient stock of such arms and equipment in the country);

(*b*) organized so as to reduce their reliance on Indian administrative personnel to the minimum.

5. After June 1948, the final withdrawal should be completed with all possible speed. It is important, however, that general agreement be reached

[1] No. 38.

with the Government of India as soon as possible to cover the period after June 1948.

This agreement, which, it is contemplated, will be included in the transitional provisions of any Treaty providing for matters arising out of the transfer of power, should cover acceptance by the Government of India of:

(*a*) the necessity for the retention of certain British Units in India for a period after the date of the transfer of power pending embarkation;

(*b*) responsibility for provision of facilities for the maintenance of such Units in India during the period prior to embarkation;

(*c*) responsibility for provision of facilities for the safe movement of all Units to the selected ports of embarkation;

(*d*) the restriction of the tasks of any British Troops remaining in India waiting for embarkation to those defined in paragraph 3 above.[2]

Yours sincerely,

LISTOWEL

[2] A copy of this letter was circulated to the India and Burma Committee under the reference I.B.(47)54. L/P &J/10/83B: ff 3–5.

256

Sir E. Mieville to Rear-Admiral Viscount Mountbatten of Burma

Mountbatten Papers. Official Correspondence Files: Interviews

TOP SECRET *30 April 1947*

Your Excellency,

In accordance with your instructions, I saw Mr Jinnah this morning and shewed him a draft of the statement.[1] He did not react favourably.

He soon made it clear that Bengal was the main bone of contention, and to a lesser degree Assam. He made the point that if we were sincere in wishing to proceed in accordance with the will of the people, we were certainly not doing so. The Scheduled Castes and the Tribes in the two above-mentioned Provinces were not represented at all in the Legislative Assemblies. Some provision must be made to obtain their views. The only suggestion he made for doing so was that a Plebiscite was absolutely necessary. But later in the conversation he said that the Poona Pact must be abolished. It was obviously an injustice and a wrong that must be righted.

[1] See No. 257, note 1.

Having dealt with Bengal, he then went on to the general plan, which, whilst he did not definitely reject it, he said would lead to terrible complications—to confusion—bitter confusion—and bloodshed.

He said that whilst the justification for Pakistan was that it was impossible to ask two peoples with different religions, habits etc.—in fact two entirely foreign nations—to live together, this did not apply to Provinces, because the minority communities could move to their homelands if they wished to do so—i.e. Hindus to Hindustan and Muslims to Pakistan—though he saw no necessity for doing so, as, so far [as] his Pakistan was concerned, provided that people were loyal to the State, they had nothing to fear. In fact they could have everything they wanted and there would be no discrimination against them.

He finished by saying that he had two definite proposals to make:

1. that the existing Constituent Assembly should be dissolved at once. It was very wrong that it should be continued at the public expense in view of the fact that it is the creation of the very document (i.e. the Cabinet Mission Plan) that is not accepted by either party.

2. that power should be transferred to Provinces as they exist today. They can then group together or remain separate as they wish.

I, of course, refuted many of his arguments but he was quite unmoved.

E.M.

257

Sir E. Mieville to Rear-Admiral Viscount Mountbatten of Burma

Mountbatten Papers. Official Correspondence Files: Interviews

TOP SECRET   *30 April 1947*

Your Excellency,

I saw Pandit Jawaharlal Nehru this afternoon and went through the draft statement[1] with him. He was, of course, well aware of its contents and at the end he only made two comparatively small points. The first was elections in the N.W.F.P. He said that he thought they were both unnecessary and dangerous and if they were connected in people's minds in any way with the terrible things that were happening there now, he was confident that the Congress would have nothing to do with the elections whatsoever. He then went on to

[1] It has not been possible to ascertain whether Sir E. Mieville showed Pandit Nehru and Mr Jinnah Appendix C of V.C.P. 38 dated 30 April 1947, or the preceding draft of the statement namely Appendix C of V.C.P. 36 dated 28 April 1947. However the differences between the two drafts were merely verbal: see No. 260 and its note 1.

tell me of the iniquitous behaviour of the officials in the Province from the Governor downwards and particularly referred to D.I.K. from which he had had many very disturbing reports.

His next point was the representation of British Baluchistan, to which also Mr Jinnah referred in his conversation with me this morning but which I omitted to mention in my report to you. He said that in leaving the decision to the Shahi Jirga we were, in effect, leaving it to a few feudal landlords and we were not consulting the people as a whole. There were three popular organisations in British Baluchistan and he felt that a scheme should be devised for a wider electorate in order to include these organisations which are:

> Anjuman e watan
> Jamiat ul ulema
> Muslim League.

In his opinion they should have a voice in the matter in conjunction with the Shahi Jirga. He admitted that it would take time to organise this but said that really whoever represented Baluchistan would not contribute much and that therefore if their representative were not elected until the end of the year it would make no difference.

He made one further point and that was that the notional partition of Bengal and the Punjab should be by constituencies and not by districts.

He finally talked to me about the Political Department and the winding up of the Residencies. As regards Political Officers, he said that Sir Geoffrey Prior, the A.G.G. in Baluchistan, had been behaving very badly in that he was obviously anti-Congress. So far as the Residencies are concerned, he said that [he had] been given to understand that many important papers were being destroyed by the Residents who were now all winding up their offices, and he suggested that many of the papers might be of great historical interest and that a Committee of non-officials might be appointed to go through them and keep those that they considered suitable.

E. MIEVILLE

258

Lord Ismay to Rear-Admiral Viscount Mountbatten of Burma

Mountbatten Papers. Official Correspondence Files: Punjab, Situation in, Part I(a)

30 April 1947

I had an hour and a half with Giani Kartar Singh, Harnam Singh and Sardar Ujjal Singh this afternoon. They were in a high state of excitement about the partition of the Punjab. They said that this should not be done merely on the basis of counting of heads. Landed property, and particularly ancient shrines, were factors which must be borne in mind.

I said that we had no intention of attempting any permanent demarcation of boundaries, and that all that we contemplated was a provisional arrangement to enable us to transfer authority by June 1948.

My visitors said that they realised this, but protested that the interim arrangements were of vital importance to them, since they would greatly affect the findings of any boundary commission that might be set up. The main burden of their representations was the question of the Lahore Division, and particularly Lahore City. They admitted that the Muslims were in a majority, but that it was a matter of life and death for the Sikhs that the Division should not be handed over to them, even as an interim arrangement. They would far sooner all die fighting.

I took the opportunity at this point to tell them that H.E. was absolutely determined to use all the forces which were at his command to quell any disorders, and that they would be well advised to refrain from violence.

They then reverted to the topic of the Lahore Division, and I asked them what they would do. The only solution that they could think of was as follows. Rawalpindi and Multan Divisions to go the the Muslims; Ambala and Jullundur Divisions to go to non-Muslims; the Lahore Division to be under a joint council until such time as a boundary commission had been able to report on frontiers and transfer of populations.

I asked them in which constituent assembly it was proposed that Lahore should be represented. To this they could provide no solution, beyond the suggestion that it would have to be a special case.

I think that the position of the Sikhs calls for renewed consideration, and I ask Your Excellency's authority to raise this point at the Staff Meeting to-morrow.

ISMAY

259

Rear-Admiral Viscount Mountbatten of Burma to Pandit Nehru

L/PO/6/119: ff 40-4

No. 1427/3.   THE VICEROY'S HOUSE, NEW DELHI,
30 April 1947

Dear Pandit Nehru,

I feel I should like to tell you all about my visit to the Frontier, both because I have had a valuable experience, and because I do not wish you to receive garbled versions of what has occurred.

2. On the first day, I had discussions with the Frontier Ministry, both individually, and collectively with the Governor: and I later talked with twelve of the Muslim League leaders, half of whom were released on parole from the jail in order to see me. The second day I held an Afridi jirga at Landi Kotal, and an informal meeting with about 50 members of the Waziristan tribes in Peshawar. I enclose a copy of the record of these various meetings, and a brief summary of the addresses presented to me by the tribesmen and of my replies.[1] I am sending the Governor copies of these minutes with a request to give to Dr. Khan Sahib a copy of the minutes of the meeting with him and his ministers, and a copy of the minutes of the meeting of the Muslim League to their representatives. I am also giving you a note of my meeting with a deputation representing the Hindu and Sikh minorities. I have already sent you information[2] about the mass meeting which was being held in Peshawar when I arrived on the 28th, and which I visited for a few minutes; and I had an opportunity also of conversations with some 15 of the leading civil and military officials of the District and Province.

3. I need not dilate on the course of my conversations with the Ministry and the Muslim League representatives, as the record is a fairly full one. There are, however, one or two things about Provincial politics which I feel I must say. I think that Dr Khan Sahib is quite wrong in attributing, as he bluntly does, the present agitation in the N.W.F.P. to the machinations of the Governor and his officials. There is quite obviously going on at present in the Province an upsurge of communal feeling, which is finding its vent in agitation against a Ministry which is regarded as being dominated by the essentially Hindu Congress. I have been impressed, both by the mass meeting which I saw, and in conversation with numbers of people with the strength of the movement which is now taking place. However much one may deplore politics which are

---

[1] The various enclosures mentioned in Lord Mountbatten's letter may be found in Mountbatten Papers, Official Correspondence Files: North-West Frontier Province, Part I(a).

[2] See No. 247.

based on pure communalism, the existence of this feeling and its strength must be recognised.

4. A second main impression which I have derived is the strength of feeling which the tribes have about the future of India, and their own place in relation to the future India. They are quite definitely confident of their own strength and position, and are not prepared to contemplate absorption into a State which they regard as likely to be dominated by Hindus. The Afridis went so far as to make it clear that they felt themselves at perfect liberty to come to an accommodation with Afghanistan if they could not reach a satisfactory working arrangement with the successor Government in India.

5. I think it is very important that you should recognise the validity of these impressions, which I am sure represent deeply held convictions.

6. I shall look forward to an early opportunity of discussing my tour further with you.[3]

Yours sincerely,
MOUNTBATTEN OF BURMA

[3] Copies of this letter, the Enclosure reproduced here and Lord Mountbatten's record of his meeting with Muslim League leaders on 28 April, were circulated to the India and Burma Committee under the reference I.B.(47)61 of 8 May. L/P &J/8/660: ff 127-37.

Enclosure to No. 259

MEETING OF H.E. WITH THE GOVERNOR N.W.F.P. AND FOUR
MINISTERS ON 28TH APRIL 1947

H.E. said he was grateful for the opportunity of meeting the Frontier Ministry, and to the Chief Minister in particular for his public spirited advice in regard to the Muslim League mass meeting in the morning.[4] He had only gone to the meeting to avoid the risk of bloodshed if the meeting persisted in forcing their way through to see him. He congratulated the Chief Minister for calling off the Red Shirt demonstration which could only have led to conflict.

2. He explained that his instructions from the British Government were that India should be handed over in accordance with the will of the people in so far as that could be found out. In the Frontier Province, it was not so straight forward as in some other provinces because of the unrest and general pressure on the administration. Further the Muslim League demonstrations indicated further doubt as to whether the Congress would command a majority if fresh elections were held; but he did not wish to order fresh elections in the face of violent agitation which was going on by the opposition. He explained that Mr. Jinnah had been told that violence must first be called off before there could be any question of fresh elections in the frontier, which would determine

[4] See No. 247.

the party to whom power should be handed over. He asked the Council of Ministers for their views.

3. Dr. Khan Sahib said that Jinnah had no influence in the N.W.F.P., and that there was no Muslim League leader in the province other than the Governor and his officials! He gave, in detail, a history of the Hazara troubles, which had started as revenge for the Bihar massacres. The other Ministers agreed that the movement, after Bihar, was entirely communal, and that attempts were now being made to turn it against the Government.

4. H.E. explained that his impression, gained in Delhi, was that the Congress had hitherto stood in the frontier for "quit India". Their objective had been secured as the British were leaving, and this battle-cry could no longer hold the people together. Pandit Nehru's visit and subsequent happenings had impelled the people of the Frontier to view the present Central Government, which was Hindu-controlled, as the inheriting power from the British. This would of course not have mattered if communal feeling had not reached its present intensity, but the Muslim League can now secure support from this anti-Hindu feeling of the Muslims.

5. Yahya Jan said that the last provincial elections had been fought on the Pakistan issue, not the Quit India Resolution; but H.E. pointed out that things were different now because at the time of the provincial elections, the Cabinet Mission had not come out let alone any date being fixed for the departure of the British.

6. The Chief Minister alleged that the Governor and his officials disliked the Congress, for historical reasons, and prophesied that if the present Government were unjustly forced out, terrible consequences would ensue. He added that today's mass meeting had been organised by officials, and stated that officials were showing themselves reluctant to carry out the instructions of the Government.

7. H.E. said that he had that day talked with eight British and Indian officials who had admitted that in years past there had been feeling against Congress, but that now their only objective was to turn over India in as honourable a way as possible.

8. The Chief Minister and Qazi Attaullah stated that the Muslim League was a party of big landowners, and that a coalition between them and the Congress, which stood for the poor was impossible. He also said that the Muslim League party consisted of people who had rendered services to the British Government in the past, and that therefore British officials were now instigating them to seize power.

9. The Governor pointed out that a large number of big Jagirdars and landowners were on the Congress side and that the division was much more

vertical than horizontal. In answer to H.E. they agreed that the Muslim League now included many poor people, but only as a result of fanatical communal agitation.

10. H.E. said that this was the answer to his question: if communal feeling was now the motivating force among the masses of the people, they would turn against a Ministry which was considered to be in alliance with the Hindus. He was sorry if this was so, and was only seeking information.

11. Details of the present agitation were then discussed, in Peshawar, Mardan, Kohat and D.I. Khan districts; and different ministers made allegations that officials were not co-operating with them. Qazi Attaullah, for instance, said that Congress movements had been suppressed in the past, but that officials nowadays did not obey the orders of the Government in dealing with processions, demonstrations, etc.

12. Governor explained how he had constantly to resist victimisation of officials who were invariably blamed whenever any incident occurred in their jurisdiction. There were always demands for their transfer or ousting from office.

The Viceroy drew the Chief Minister's attention to the danger of a breakdown in the administration if this course was persisted in.

13. The Chief Minister then alleged that the Governor interfered with his work, and did not support him. He alleged that the Governor was not acting as a constitutional head.

14. H.E. countered by asking Dr. Khan Sahib if his ministry acted always in a constitutional manner. After some argument, Dr. Khan Sahib admitted that he was "guilty of certain things", but that he did it with the best of intentions.

15. H.E. pointed out that it was not a question of his ordering fresh elections as a result of unconstitutional pressure but that his orders from the British Government were to transfer power in the manner which the Indian peoples themselves wanted. To do this would involve ascertaining whether the existing Government still had a valid mandate, before power was handed over. He asked the ministers if they agreed. Dr. Khan Sahib agreed and the others did not demur.

16. H.E. then pointed out that he would have to go into Section 93 Government for two or three months before this to ensure fair elections and that he felt sure that the present Government would wish the elections to be fair.

17. H.E. asked whether he should invite the Congress and Muslim League high commands to send representatives to observe the elections in the province. The Chief Minister freely agreed to this, although Dr. Khan Sahib reiterated that there was no Muslim League in the N.W.F.P.

18. The Governor admitted that the Congress approach to the frontier problem was a bigger one than the League's, but that in regard to the administration it was a question of trust begetting trust.

19. The Chief Minister said that the solution would be to let those officials go who did not want to stay, and H.E. agreed that this could and should now be done.

20. H.E. ended by restating the policy with which he had come to India, and said that he wished only to find the fairest means of handing over power.

I. D. SCOTT
28.4.47

260

Viceroy's Conference Paper. V.C.P. 38

Mountbatten Papers

30 April 1947

PROPOSALS FOR A MEETING WITH INDIAN LEADERS

1. This paper has again been re-drafted, as a result of a meeting of members of the staff on 30th April.

2. This version and not V.C.P. 36[1] will be considered at the next Viceroy's Staff Meeting.[2]

V. F. ERSKINE CRUM

Appendix A
Draft Invitation to the Indian Leaders

[*Not printed; this was a revised and shortened version of the draft in Appendix A to No.181.*]

Appendix B
Draft telegram to the Secretary of State

[*Not printed; this was a revised and shortened version of the draft in Appendix B to No. 181.*]

[1] Not printed. The differences between Appendix C of V.C.P. 36 and Appendix C of this version were purely verbal.

[2] This Paper was considered in Item 7 of the Viceroy's Twenty-fourth Staff Meeting on 1 May and after some further amendments to the drafts therein, Lord Mountbatten directed that the telegram and draft announcement should be sent to Lord Listowel (see Nos. 278 and 279). Mountbatten Papers.

Appendix C

Note: Amendments since last considered are underlined [italicised].

REVISED DRAFT ANNOUNCEMENT—30.4.47

PART I—INTRODUCTION

1. On 20th February, 1947, His Majesty's Government announced their intention of transferring power in British India to Indian hands by June 1948. They are determined to do their utmost to ensure that this transfer is effected in accordance with the wishes of the Indian people themselves, so far as they can be consulted in the time available, and that it is orderly and peaceful.

2. If it were possible to transfer power to a single Authority, the process would be comparatively simple. His Excellency the Viceroy has, however, reported that the leaders of the main political parties in India have been unable to reach agreement on any form of unified Government. Since His Majesty's Government have given their pledge that there shall be no compulsion on unwilling parts of the country, arrangements must be made to ensure that power can be demitted by the due date to more than one Authority, if that should prove to be the desire of the people of India, as expressed by their elected representatives. *Even if the first decision should indicate that power will have to be demitted to more than one authority, there is nothing in these arrangements to preclude subsequent negotiations for an united India.*

3. The process of transferring power to more than one Authority involves constitutional, administrative, financial and defence problems of formidable variety and bewildering complexity. It is therefore essential that the successor Authorities should be determined at the earliest possible moment, and that they should prepare themselves to receive power by the due date. The arrangements to this end, upon which His Majesty's Government have decided, are set out in Part II below.

4. It is necessary to emphasize that, since little more than a year remains before power is to be transferred, there is not time to ascertain the will of the people *throughout the country* by means of a plebiscite, or to revise the census of 1941, or to attempt any final demarcation of the boundaries of those provinces which have special minority problems. His Majesty's Government are, however, satisfied that the arrangements on which they have decided will ensure a sufficiently accurate indication of the wishes of the people of India to enable the successor Authorities to be equitably determined. His Majesty's Government reiterate that the sole purpose of these arrangements is to ensure a peaceful and orderly transfer of power, and that there is no intention of attempting to frame the ultimate constitution of India, which is a matter entirely for the Indians themselves to determine.

PART II—ARRANGEMENTS FOR THE DEMISSION
OF POWER

5. The procedure for determining the authority or authorities to which power is to be demitted is set out hereunder.

Procedure for Madras, Bombay, U.P., Bihar, C.P., Orissa and the Chief Commissioner's Provinces.

6. The representatives of Madras, Bombay, the U.P., Bihar, the C.P., Orissa and of the Chief Commissioner's Provinces *other than British Baluchistan* in the existing Constituent Assembly will be asked to confirm that it is the wish of their Provinces that the framing of a constitution for those Provinces should proceed in the *existing* Constituent Assembly.

Procedure for Bengal, Punjab, Assam, N.W.F.P. and Sind.

7. For the other Provinces, in some of which there have been insistent demands for Partition, the following preliminary arrangements will be necessary.

Preliminary steps

(a) In Bengal, the Legislative Assembly (*excluding European members*) will be asked to sit in two parts, one representing the Muslim majority districts and the other the rest of the Province.

(b) In the Punjab, where the position of the Sikhs presents particular difficulty, the Legislative Assembly will be divided as in Bengal, *into two parts representing Muslim majority districts and other districts respectively*.

(c) In Assam, the members of the Legislative Assembly, (*excluding European members*), elected from territorial constituencies *included in* the Sylhet District will be asked to sit separately.

(d) In the N.W.F.P. a general election will be held.

In determining the population of districts the 1941 census figures will be taken as authoritative.

Formation of Constituent Assemblies

8. Thereafter the Legislative Assembly of Sind (*excluding the European members*), the newly-elected Legislative Assembly of the N.W.F.P., and the two parts of the Legislative Assemblies of Bengal, the Punjab and Assam will elect representatives on

the principle laid down in the Cabinet Mission's statement of the 16th May 1946.

9. The numbers to be elected would be:—

Province	General	Muslims	Sikhs	Total
Sind	1	3	—	4
N.W.F.P.	—	3	—	3
West Punjab	2	10	1	13
East Punjab	6	6	3	15
West Bengal	15	4	—	19
East Bengal	12	29	—	41
Assam less Sylhet	6	1	—	7
Sylhet District	1	2	—	3

Vote on *partition* of Provinces.

10. The representatives so elected of West Bengal and East Bengal, sitting separately, will vote as to whether or not their Province should be divided. A majority vote of either body in favour of Partition will decide the issue. A similar procedure will be followed in regard to the Punjab and Assam.

Vote on *partition* of India.

11. *Immediately thereafter the representatives of the Provinces or half Provinces (dependent on the decision in paragraph 10 above) of Punjab, Bengal, Assam, Sind and the N.W.F.P. will decide whether, on behalf of the areas which they represent, they wish:—*

(a) to join the existing Constituent Assembly or

(b) to group together *in one or more Constituent Assemblies*, or

(c) to stand out independently and *act as* their own Constituent Assembly.

12. *In order that the successor authority or authorities may have as much time as possible to prepare themselves to receive power, it is essential that all the above processes should be completed without undue delay.*

Baluchistan.

13. In British Baluchistan the members of the Shahi Jirga (other than those members who are nominated as Sardars of Kalat State) and the non-official members of the Quetta Municipality will meet to decide the issues in paragraph 11 above. The meeting will also elect a person to represent

British Baluchistan in further constitutional discussions.

Framing of Constitutions.

14. The Constituent Assembly or Assemblies will then proceed to frame Constitutions for their respective territories.

Joint consultation on common subjects.

15. *The administrative consequences of partition are complex and considerable. Accordingly*, the Constituent Assemblies, if more than one, should also create machinery for joint consultation among themselves on matters of common concern, particularly Defence, and for the negotiation of agreements in respect of these matters.

Tribes of the N.W. Frontier.

16. As soon as the position of the N.W.F.P. is known in the grouping of provinces which will result from the measures described above, the problem arising out of the need to establish satisfactory relations with the tribes on the North-Western Frontiers of India will require urgent examination.

The States

17. His Majesty's Government wish to make it clear that the decisions announced above relate only to British India and that their policy towards the Indian States remains unchanged. A date has been fixed when paramountcy will lapse, and all the rights surrendered by the States to the paramount power will return to the States. They are free to arrange by negotiation with those parts of British India to which power will be demitted whatever measure of association they consider to be in the best interests of their people.

Announcements by the Governor-General.

18. The Governor-General will, from time to time, make such further announcements as may be necessary, in regard to procedure or any other matter, for the carrying out of the above arrangements. *He will for example issue a time-table for the arrangements described above.*

261

Sir E. Jenkins (Punjab) to Rear-Admiral Viscount Mountbatten of Burma

R/3/1/89: ff 182–7

No. 664.   GOVERNMENT HOUSE, LAHORE, *30 April 1947*

Dear Lord Mountbatten,

I promised last night to send Your Excellency a copy of Mamdot's recent letters to me and the draft of the reply[1] which I propose to send him. These papers are enclosed.

Mamdot's first letter was dated 24th April (in his second letter he gives the date wrongly as 23rd). It ended with a request for an early interview. The interview took place on the afternoon of 28th April, and I reported it to Your Excellency in my telegram No. 86–G of the same date.[2] After leaving me I understand that Mamdot had some discussion with his colleagues in the Muslim League, and on 28th April he wrote me his second letter asking for a written summary of my views. This second letter was inadvertently dated 23rd April, but there is no doubt about the date on which it was composed.

2. The Muslim League will presumably publish the correspondence, and my reply therefore needs very careful scrutiny. I think there is no doubt that when an invitation to assist in the formation of a Ministry is followed by a proclamation under Section 93 of the Government of India Act, 1935, the invitation, if it does not actually lapse, is at least suspended. No party leader can *demand* the revocation of a proclamation under Section 93, since the Governor and the Governor-General must be satisfied that conditions justifying revocation exist. I have dealt with this point briefly in paragraph 3(1) of my draft. It is really a very technical point; Mamdot would still be the obvious person to send for if the formation of a Ministry seemed possible.

I was not satisfied about Mamdot's majority, but I did not wish to give him the impression that a few votes one way or the other would affect what is in my opinion the real position. I therefore contented myself with saying that some of his supporters might be unreliable (see paragraph 3(2) of my draft).

The real point is that once any large section of the population declines to recognise a parliamentary majority, a revolutionary situation supervenes and constitutional Government in the ordinary sense becomes impossible. The Muslim League were the first to deny the right of a Ministry to remain in office on the basis of a parliamentary majority alone. The Hindus and Sikhs would now undoubtedly be of the same view. My own opinion is that the Government of India Act, 1935, cannot be worked by a communal Ministry in the Punjab; but I am aware that constitutionally this is rather delicate ground. Abell and V.P. Menon will remember the proposal to introduce

Section 93 in Bengal in 1943-44 and the discussion we then had about the exact scope of the Section.[3] Whether the existence of a revolutionary situation is a sufficient ground for refusing to go out of Section 93 or not, there is the practical point that it would be foolish to permit the formation of a Ministry now when an important announcement about the future of India is imminent. There is perhaps some difference between the justification required for going into Section 93 and the justification required for going out of it. A Section 93 proclamation may be revoked at any time; but it is arguable that the Governor and the Governor-General are entitled to demand something more than a mere capacity to comply with the technical requirements of the Act.

3. I shall be most grateful if Your Excellency can let me have your instructions about the draft within the next day or two. Mamdot was told yesterday that I should require a little time to consider his letter; but he will expect a fairly early reply.

Yours sincerely,

E. M. JENKINS

P.S. Y.E. suggested, and I fully agreed, that I should hand my reply to Mamdot personally, explain it to him, and inform him that Y.E. would be glad to see him in Delhi if he so desired.

E.M.J.

[1] This draft is not printed; see No. 334 for the letter as issued. The only amendment made by Lord Mountbatten was to substitute the words 'in the near future' for 'within a month' in the antepenultimate sentence. R/3/1/89: ff 191 and 194.
[2] No. 248.
[3] See Vol. IV, Chapter 5.

Enclosure 1 to No. 261
The Nawab of Mamdot to Sir E. Jenkins

MAMDOT VILLA, DAVIS ROAD,
LAHORE, *24 April 1947*

Dear Sir Evan,
You will recollect that soon after you had charged me with the responsibility of assisting you in the formation of a Ministry on the 3rd of March, 1947, you were compelled by the sudden resignation of the Caretaker Government to proclaim the application of Section 93 of the Government of India Act to the Province. Immediately following the proclamation, the gravity of the disturbances in the Punjab naturally occupied your attention to the exclusion of all matters, and I also, to the best of my abilities, applied myself to the paramount duty of restoring peace and confidence in the disturbed areas of the Province.

The situation now has, however, returned almost to normal, and I feel that we should permit no further delay in resuming our efforts for the formation of a popular Ministry in the Punjab from the point at which they were left by your letter to me on March 5th, 1947.[4] Moreover, I feel that there is no longer any justification for permitting a suspension of the normal democratic procedure and of depriving a majority of the people of this Province from shouldering the responsibilities of the administration. In particular after H.M.G.'s declaration of February 20th, it would be against the spirit of the times to continue a bureaucratic regime in the Punjab when there is nothing to prevent the formation of a popular and democratic Ministry according to time-honoured constitutional practice.

To facilitate you, therefore, in the choice of your cabinet, I find it my duty to assure you that I possess the support of an absolute majority of the present members of the Punjab Legislative Assembly, and that I am in a position to assist you in the task of appointing a cabinet of Ministers. I am ready to come personally and place the full facts before you, and to give you any further elucidation or assurance that may be required by you.

I may assure Your Excellency that it has always been my keen desire to secure the cooperation of the accredited representatives of the two important minorities—the Sikhs and the Hindus—in the formation of a fully representative Ministry in the Punjab. I shall continue to make these efforts, but the unreasoning refusal of certain minorities to cooperate cannot be permitted to stand permanently in the way of the functioning of normal constitutional and democratic methods. As Your Excellency is very well aware a large number of provincial administrations all over India are composed exclusively of members of one party and community, and it would be illogical to impose an exception contrary to all primary democratic principles only in the case of the Punjab.

In view of the problems which face the Punjab, and of the future for which we must without delay begin to prepare ourselves, I shall be grateful if I am called by Your Excellency at an early date to place the details of my position before you.

Yours sincerely,
IFTIKHAR HUSAIN KHAN

[4] Vol. IX, No. 492.

Enclosure 2 to No. 261
The Nawab of Mamdot to Sir E. Jenkins

MAMDOT VILLA, DAVIS ROAD,
LAHORE, *23[28] April 1947*

My dear Sir Evan,
Following my letter to Your Excellency dated April 23rd, 1947, you were

kind enough to have a long talk with me this afternoon, during which we discussed in detail the points raised in my aforementioned letter. In view of the extreme importance of the matters discussed in our talk, and of the necessity of formulating the conclusions in an authoritative and veracious form, so that they may, if necessary, be fairly placed before the people of the Punjab, I must request Your Excellency to give me a final answer to the questions raised in my letter of April 23rd, 1947. As I am anxious that I should not give an impression that is unfair or incorrect in emphasis or in detail, I hesitate to trust to my recollection of our talk, and am therefore requesting an authoritative answer from you.

It is my impression that during our talk no doubt was cast on my claim that I possess the support of a clear majority of the present members of the Punjab Legislative Assembly. In this respect I would like to emphasise my position that having been invited by you to form a Ministry, it is my constitutional right to prove my majority on the floor of the House. To stress the democratic correctness of my stand I would go further and request that if Your Excellency chooses, previous arrangements may be made so that I can face the Assembly within twenty-four hours of being called upon to take office. I hope Your Excellency will agree that I am at least as anxious as yourself not to undertake responsibilities which I cannot prove and justify by the most immediate and stringent democratic test.

I would also like to assure Your Excellency that I am eager to secure the fullest cooperation of all the minority communities in the formation of a Ministry. It is my claim that I have already the assurance of the support of the representatives of some minority communities. With regard to the Congress with whom we have to deal not only in the Punjab, but in every Province in India, my position is that I am willing to cooperate with them in the Punjab on exactly the same terms as they are prepared to offer to the Muslim League in the Provinces where they represent a majority of the population. An All-India question, by its very definition, cannot be tackled on any other basis. On the other hand, since it is possible to reach a settlement with the Sikhs on a provincial basis, I have already assured them of the fullest satisfaction of all their reasonable demands in the sphere of administration in the Province. I am prepared to pursue efforts in this direction, but I cannot accept their unreasoning veto on the functioning of democracy in the Punjab.

I shall be grateful for an early reply from Your Excellency.

Yours sincerely,

IFTIKHAR HUSAIN KHAN

262

Sir E. Jenkins (Punjab) to Rear-Admiral Viscount Mountbatten of Burma

Mountbatten Papers. Official Correspondence Files: Punjab, Part I(b)

SECRET   GOVERNMENT HOUSE, LAHORE,
No. 665.   *30 April 1947*

Dear Lord Mountbatten,

Your Excellency handed the enclosed papers[1] to me at Rawalpindi and asked for my comments on the statement issued on 21st April by Sardar Swaran Singh and Lala Bhim Sen Sachar.

2. The first four paragraphs of the statement summarize various arguments against any reconciliation between Muslims and non-Muslims in the Punjab. There is nothing new in these arguments and, as usual, the persons advancing them omit to mention that in many places, including the cities of Lahore, Multan and Rawalpindi, the immediate provocation on 3rd March and subsequent days was given by non-Muslims. In Lahore in particular a large meeting, at which inflammatory speeches were made, was attended by Lala Bhim Sen Sachar himself.

3. The fifth and last paragraph of the statement contains, without special explanation, the demand "that as an interim and transitional arrangement His Excellency the Governor-General should instal immediately two or three regional administrations with separate Ministers, under one Governor, for the two or three zones of the existing Province of the Punjab."

This is much the same idea as that put forward recently by Pandit Jawahar Lal Nehru and partly worked out by Sir B.N. Rau.[2] The difficulty in accepting a regional system may be stated as follows.

If the intention is to work the system without an amendment of the Government of India Act, 1935, a high degree of agreement and co-operation between the communities would be necessary. Constitutionally the Punjab would remain as it is now; I would send for the Party leaders and invite one of them (presumably Mamdot) to form a Ministry, including so many representatives from the Rawalpindi and Multan Divisions, so many representatives from the Lahore Division, and so many representatives from the Jullundur and Ambala Divisions; and I would then arrange that business should be so transacted that the three regions were, so far as possible, independent of one another except in certain agreed matters of common concern. Outwardly the Ministry would be an undivided body jointly responsible for the government of the Punjab, but by convention it would work largely in three separate committees. There would have to be a corresponding convention about the working of the Assembly. I feel that if a settlement involving difficult conventions of this kind could be made, there would be little difficulty in going a step further and installing an ordinary Coalition Ministry. In dealing with Sir B.N. Rau's paper, I pointed out some of the difficulties of a regional system, e.g. that in fact it would be virtually impossible for one region to take an independent line in dealing with Education, and that the distribution of our financial resources over the three regions would be a most complicated business.

If on the other hand the intention is that there should be an amendment of the Government of India Act, 1935, or that we should create a new province or new provinces, which would amount to much the same thing, then the demand is simply a demand for partition.

4. I do not think that the authors of the statement have thought out the implications of their demand. Pandit Jawahar Lal Nehru is very well aware of them, and when he discussed the possibility of a regional system with me in March, we agreed that its main use might be to serve as a bridge between Section 93 and some entirely new system of Government. Thus if partition is finally decided upon, the parties might agree to a Coalition Ministry organised by convention on regional lines.

Yours sincerely,

E. M. JENKINS

[1] It would appear from the file that 'the enclosed papers' were the text of the statement by Sardar Swaran Singh and Lala Bhim Sen Sachar. The principal points in the statement are summarised by Sir E. Jenkins. The statement concluded: 'We must make it plain that in the existing circumstances we are not prepared to co-operate with the Muslim League for forming a single Ministry for the whole of the Punjab'. Mountbatten Papers, Official Correspondence Files: Punjab, Part I(b).

[2] See Vol. IX, Nos. 515 and 525. In a lengthy note prepared in late March 1947 Sir B.N. Rau elaborated a scheme for the framing of an interim or provisional constitution. At the Centre the scheme was to be based on the Cabinet Mission's plan. The subjects of Defence, Foreign Affairs and Communications were to come under Ministers responsible for the whole of India. However each of the three Groups would have Ministers who would answer for all remaining subjects within the area of their Group. The Central Ministries for these subjects would, therefore, be divided into three on a regional basis.

With respect to the Provinces Rau proposed that 'where a Province contains distinct regions (whether racial or religious or linguistic), most of the provincial subjects may be dealt with on a regional basis and only the remaining few on a provincial or joint basis'. In such Provinces a Governor 'may within one and the same Cabinet have one set of Ministers exclusively to advise him on the regional subjects of A; another set of Ministers exclusively to advise him on the regional subjects of B; and both sets of Ministers together, in other words, the entire Cabinet, to advise him on joint subjects'. Mountbatten Papers, Official Correspondence Files: Transfer of Power, Part I(a).

Correspondence and noting on Rau's scheme (including a note by Sir E. Jenkins) may be found in the following Mountbatten Papers, Official Correspondence Files: (1) Punjab, Parts I(a) and (b); (2) Punjab, Situation in, Part I(a); (3) Transfer of Power, Part III(a).

263

Sir E. Jenkins (Punjab) to Rear-Admiral Viscount Mountbatten of Burma (Extract)

R/3/1/178: ff 42-3

SECRET   GOVERNMENT HOUSE, LAHORE,
No. 666.   *30 April 1947*

6. The attitude of the political parties is unchanged. The Muslim League are still anxious to form a Ministry, a subject on which I have written separately to Your Excellency.[1] The Muslim leaders are as complacent as ever. Daultana recently toured in the Attock district, and there is credible evidence that he told the people in at least one village that if they could stick it out for a fortnight or three weeks, all proceedings against them would be withdrawn, and the officials who have suppressed the disturbances would be given a hot time. There has been no real attempt to approach the Hindus or Sikhs, the Muslim attitude being that the Muslims are entitled to rule the whole of the Punjab and that when this is admitted they will be good enough to treat the non-Muslims with generosity.

The Sikhs are preparing for an offensive. I believe that the leaders would prefer not to launch it until July 1948 or later; but they will find it difficult to control their followers. There are strong rumours of a retaliatory attack by Sikhs on a suburb of Amritsar or some other place with a strong Muslim element. The Sikhs have committed themselves so deeply to the partition of the Punjab that it will be difficult, and perhaps impossible, for them to take a different line.

The Hindus are still in close alliance with the Sikhs, though there are signs that the Sikhs are not anxious for too close a link with the Congress High Command. Officially the Hindus would like partition, but I am not sure of the attitude of those of them who belong to the Rawalpindi and Multan Divisions.

An agreed partition of the Punjab appears to me virtually impossible. The Sikhs would expect to get the cis-Ravi districts of the Lahore Division and the Montgomery district of the Multan Division, and possibly even the Sheikhupura district across the Ravi. The Muslims on the other hand would not wish to cede the Amritsar district (which has in fact a small non-Muslim majority), and would claim a part of Ferozepore and Jullundur. Indeed most Muslims would be reluctant to part with anything west of the non-Punjabi speaking districts of the Ambala Division. No leader seems yet to have considered the implications and difficulties of partition.

[1] No. 261.

264

Minutes of Viceroy's Ninth Miscellaneous Meeting, Item 1

Mountbatten Papers

TOP SECRET

Those present at this Meeting held at The Viceroy's House, New Delhi on 1 May 1947 at 10 am were: Rear-Admiral Viscount Mountbatten of Burma, Sir F. Burrows, Lord Ismay, Sir E. Mieville, Mr Abell, Mr Tyson; Lieutenant-Colonel Erskine Crum (Secretariat)

THE CHOICE BY PROVINCES OF THEIR OWN FUTURE

HIS EXCELLENCY THE VICEROY said that it was his conviction that the only sensible solution for the future of India was one which would produce the greatest degree of unity that the people could be persuaded to accept. In fact, the Cabinet Mission Plan still "held the field." However, Mr. Jinnah had repeatedly stated that he would not consider accepting it on the grounds that Congress did not intend to carry it out fairly. HIS EXCELLENCY THE VICEROY stated that he was beginning to think that Mr. Jinnah might be right in this belief, especially in view of a statement which Sardar Patel had made to him at a previous meeting[1] in connection with the interpretation by Congress of the procedure for framing the Constitution of Assam, in the light of H.M.G.'s statement of 6th December.

SIR FREDERICK BURROWS asked whether, on the occasion referred to, Sardar Patel had been speaking for the Congress Working Committee or for himself. Sardar Patel, he pointed out, was apt to say many nonsensical things. What authority had he for his statement? HIS EXCELLENCY THE VICEROY explained that he had as yet only brought Pandit Nehru and Sardar Patel into consultation on the present plan as representatives of Congress. The views of the Working Committees would be obtained later; they were due to meet in May. SIR FREDERICK BURROWS asked whether Pandit Nehru subscribed to the view put forward by Sardar Patel. HIS EXCELLENCY THE VICEROY said that this point should be found out.

HIS EXCELLENCY THE VICEROY said that he had explained to Sardar Patel that the thing that most frightened Mr. Jinnah was the prospect of a Centre permanently dominated by the Hindus. He had asked Sardar Patel whether he could think of any way to reduce this fear and the latter had replied that he would never consider parity in the Central Government.[2]

HIS EXCELLENCY THE VICEROY said that, although he considered Mr.

[1] No. 216.

[2] See No. 216 where Sardar Patel is stated to have said that: 'Congress would not accept any suggestion for a further degree of parity in the present Central Government.'

Jinnah about the most difficult and unreasonable man with whom he had ever had to deal, he, and the senior members of his staff, did feel that Mr. Jinnah's fears had some foundation. Therefore, it was to be considered that the Cabinet Mission Plan was 'dead'. SIR FREDERICK BURROWS said that he also considered that there was now no chance of getting the Cabinet Mission's Plan accepted.

HIS EXCELLENCY THE VICEROY went on to explain that, following Mr. Jinnah's demand for Pakistan, Congress had demanded the partition of certain Provinces. Mr. Jinnah had produced arguments against the partition of Provinces, especially in a statement[3] issued to the Press that day. Logically, however, the partition of Provinces should follow the partition of India. Mr. Jinnah had stated that he would insist on the partition of Assam if Bengal was partitioned.

SIR FREDERICK BURROWS said that he would not put the case for the partition of Assam very high. Mr. Jinnah had no more right to assume that the tribal areas wanted Pakistan than Congress had to assume that they did not. If the tribes were excluded and Scheduled Caste Hindus were included with Caste Hindus, there was a total of 4 million Hindus as opposed to 3 million Muslims. SIR FREDERICK BURROWS also stated that he saw no case for the partition of any other Provinces, for example those in which there was a minority community of 15%. With this HIS EXCELLENCY THE VICEROY agreed. He pointed out that it was intended to give only the Sylhet District of Assam the choice of secession.

SIR FREDERICK BURROWS said that he was not sure that there was a general demand among the Bengali Hindus as a whole for the partition of Bengal. The idea, however, was being 'sold' rather well. There was a definite attempt, because of the feeling of frustration among the Hindus in Bengal, to get command of at least part of the Province. Dr. Mukherji was a clever and unscrupulous politician. The Hindu Mahasabha had failed completely to gain representation in the Legislative Assembly, except for Dr. Mukherji's own seat. They were, however, good propagandists.

HIS EXCELLENCY THE VICEROY said that he agreed that Mr. Jinnah was right in claiming that the demands for the partition of Bengal were manoeuvres; nevertheless, these manoeuvres were well founded in logic. SIR FREDERICK BURROWS said that he agreed that the agitation for the partition of Bengal must indeed be taken seriously.

HIS EXCELLENCY THE VICEROY went on to explain the present plan for leaving the choice of their own future to the Provinces themselves. He stated that he was unwilling to put his name to any partition plan on behalf of the British, because the British would then be blamed for the results of partition. He was proposing to make a broadcast explaining this position. He emphasized the point that there was an important loophole in the present plan, in that the Provinces had two different issues on which to vote.

SIR FREDERICK BURROWS said that he had, the previous week end, had a long conversation with Mr. Christie, who had been sent down to see him as the Viceroy's representative. He had considered the draft announcement which was to be put up for the approval of H.M.G. He noticed that in the present form of this announcement it was intended to include Calcutta in Western Bengal. Calcutta, in his opinion, was peculiar and deserved independent consideration. It had grown up simply because of European trade interest and had reached its status dependent on both East and West Bengal. It had been the capital of India for many years. There was no doubt that the Hindus were a majority of the population—approximately 75%. However, for the future prosperity of Calcutta, if it was not to perish, the city should if possible be given the chance to serve both halves of Bengal, if the Province was partitioned. It would be unfair for all the revenues to go to one half of the Province when the other half had done so much for the prosperity of the city. Nearly all the jute was grown in Eastern Bengal and that half should therefore have a share of the excise duties on jute. The same was true to a certain extent on tea.

SIR FREDERICK BURROWS went on to say that he did not believe that Eastern Bengal could live in Partition. It would stagnate to such an extent and become so poor that it would end up as a rural slum. Economically it could not survive. All the coal mines, the minerals and the factories were in Western Bengal. All the jute process mills with two exceptions were in Western Bengal. Eastern Bengal was deficit in food to the extent of 225,000 tons. Although this was only a small percentage of the 6 million tons required to feed the half Province, it was sufficient to cause quite a lot of trouble. It had to be appreciated that the scale of feeding in Eastern Bengal was very low and the population was increasing. If Eastern Bengal was to be properly fed it would be necessary to import 800,000 tons at least. The only money crop in Eastern Bengal was jute. They might turn over from jute to food, although that would kill Calcutta's jute industry. HIS EXCELLENCY THE VICEROY asked whether Eastern Bengal would not use their jute as a bargaining point. SIR FREDERICK BURROWS said that he was not sure about this. He would not put anything beyond them as they were scared of famine. He shuddered to think of the condition in Eastern Bengal in seven years' time. Mr. TYSON agreed with this.

SIR FREDERICK BURROWS said that he had kept off all question of partition in discussion with Mr. Suhrawardy, except on the latter's return from Delhi after an interview with the Viceroy. Mr. Suhrawardy had then declared that he would be prepared to accept Calcutta as an international city. If Calcutta was excluded from Eastern Bengal, the latter would not accept the decision,

[3] See Annex I to No. 276.

but there would be a tremendous row. There would be great difficulty even if Mr.Jinnah accepted it. There would be open revolt and troubles worse than the recent ones in the Punjab.

HIS EXCELLENCY THE VICEROY pointed out that the damage in the Punjab and N.W.F.P. had been inflicted only by the majority community. SIR FREDERICK BURROWS stated that he did not believe that this was always dependent on numbers but also on character and calibre. Many of the Muslims in Bengal were of a very militant nature. He believed that there would be perpetual trouble.

SIR FREDERICK BURROWS explained that he was in favour of a joint control of the city of Calcutta. He had never used the words "free city" in this connection and had never envisaged that Calcutta should be such. The city should, he thought, be administered by five Muslims and five Hindus, elected from each half of Bengal. These persons would form an independent Administrative Council or Cabinet. The Chairman would be elected from amongst them. They could make informative reports to the assemblies of both halves of the Province but would have full control themselves. They would work out the proportions of customs duties, etc. to go to either half of the Province.

HIS EXCELLENCY THE VICEROY asked Mr. Abell to put the case against declaring Calcutta a free city. MR. ABELL explained that the crux of the problem was the question of relationship with the Centre. The Muslims would insist on practically complete freedom but the Hindus would not enter into the administration of any free unit. On this basis it was most difficult to obtain agreement between the communities in the Provinces. A degree of goodwill between communities was surely being assumed that was not likely to exist. Hindus would object to parity on the proposed administrative council. Even if they tolerated this whilst the British remained, they would not do so after June 1948. On the grounds that Hindus represented 76% of the population of the city and owned 90% of the investments, the Hindus were likely to resign—and then a totally Muslim administrative council would have to be put in, in opposition to 76% of the population. It was difficult to see how that situation could last. Furthermore, Congress were acquiescing in the present overall plan. This plan would have to be scrapped if a system of joint control of Calcutta was to be introduced, as Congress would withdraw their support. If efforts were then made to impose another plan on them, Congress might well withdraw from the Interim Government.

MR. ABELL[4] explained that the problem in Calcutta was similar to that in the Lahore Division of the Punjab, which contained both Lahore city and Amritsar, which was the most important Sikh city. There had been suggestions that the Lahore Division would present too great difficulties to division. However, it seemed to him that the present position was that the communities could not share anything. If Calcutta were excluded from the general plan, it would become a bone of contention in the same way as the Lahore Division. The only hope of getting a more reasonable attitude was to let each party—especially the Muslim League—know what they were to get. HIS EXCELLENCY THE VICEROY pointed out that it was evident from Mr. Abell's remarks that anything but a clean partition would produce enmity on the part of Congress. If he fell foul of Congress it would be impossible to continue to run the country.[5] SIR FREDERICK BURROWS said that he fully accepted this. He considered the arguments put forward by Mr. Abell[6] to be most cogent. His greatest object was a peaceful transfer of power.

He clearly understood the Viceroy's difficulties with Calcutta. The Viceroy had to look at the question from an all-India point of view, whereas he looked at it from a provincial point of view. The Viceroy could not jeopardise the safety of all India for the sake of one Province.

HIS EXCELLENCY THE VICEROY said that he also entirely saw Sir Frederick Burrows' reasons for wanting to make Calcutta a free city, and he considered it essential to meet Sir Frederick Burrows' views as far as possible while not compromising his position in India as a whole. He then put forward a suggestion which would increase the chances of Bengal remaining an independent unit. Briefly this suggestion was that members of the Constituent Assembly in Bengal should vote on the future, as between independence or joining Hindustan or Pakistan, of the Province before deciding the issue of partition. They would then clearly know the alternatives when they came to vote for Partition. HIS EXCELLENCY THE VICEROY said that he wanted a clause which would make possible this change of procedure included in the draft announcement.

SIR FREDERICK BURROWS said that he considered that such an amendment to the voting procedure would give only a very limited chance of Bengal remaining unified and independent. He believed that the only hope—and he had told this to Mr. Suhrawardy—was that a strong Coalition Government should be formed immediately. He did not know, however, whether the Hindus would agree to coalition without a link with the Centre. He believed that they would want assurance that there would be some such link. HIS EXCELLENCY THE VICEROY said that Sir Frederick Burrows should renew his efforts to persuade Mr. Suhrawardy to create a Coalition Government, and explain to him the outline of the changes which were being made in the plan. SIR FREDERICK BURROWS agreed to do this.

HIS EXCELLENCY THE VICEROY also suggested that Sir Frederick Burrows should try to persuade Mr. Suhrawardy to make a promise of joint electorates in the future if a decision on a unified independent Bengal was reached. SIR

[4] Mr Abell's name is enclosed within manuscript square brackets in the original.
[5] The preceding two sentences have been crossed through in the original.
[6] The words 'by Mr Abell' have been crossed through in the original.

FREDERICK BURROWS said that Mr. Suhrawardy had already accepted this principle but was opposed to reservation of seats.

SIR FREDERICK BURROWS said that Mr. Suhrawardy's position in the Muslim League was not at all secure. Though clever, he was not popular and would have been got rid of if an alternative leader could have been found. SIR FREDERICK BURROWS said that he discounted a great deal of Mr. Suhrawardy's claim of being able to put across any particular course of action.

HIS EXCELLENCY THE VICEROY pointed out that if Bengal did remain independent, it would want a separate Army. This issue would have to be discussed at the same time as the splitting up of the Army as between Hindustan and Pakistan.

SIR FREDERICK BURROWS said that he did not consider that there was any chance, after a vote in favour of partition, of Eastern Bengal re-joining on the understanding that they would be under a Hindu centre.

There was further discussion on the desirability of introducing a 2/3rds majority system in order to carry the principle of partition. HIS EXCELLENCY THE VICEROY pointed out that [? the] advantages of introducing this system in Bengal and SIR FREDERICK BURROWS said that he was in favour of it. However, after consideration of the figures in the Punjab, which disclosed that the issue would hang on one vote, HIS EXCELLENCY THE VICEROY decided that a simple majority vote would have to prevail.

SIR ERIC MIEVILLE recalled that Mr. Liaquat Ali Khan had expressed the view that the majority of the Scheduled Castes in Bengal would choose independence rather than Partition. SIR FREDERICK BURROWS said that he believed this to be wishful thinking. He did not believe that more than 25% at the most of the Scheduled Castes would go against Caste Hindus. MR. TYSON said that he agreed with this, and quoted figures from the last General Election to substantiate his belief.

HIS EXCELLENCY THE VICEROY said that Sir Evan Jenkins had informed him that Giani Kartar Singh had explained his aversion to joining Hindustan on the grounds that the Sikhs felt that they would be absorbed by the Hindus. In fact, they felt that they would have been absorbed long ago if the Army had not kept them and their religion going.

HIS EXCELLENCY THE VICEROY said that Mr. Suhrawardy had made it very clear that he was in favour of an independent united Bengal. Moreover, Mr. Jinnah had agreed to the concept of an independent Bengal separate from Pakistan.

SIR FREDERICK BURROWS pointed out that Bengal was 700 miles away from the nearest point of the remainder of Pakistan. It could form a link with the Pakistan State but could not effectively be part of Pakistan as such.

LORD ISMAY stated that Mr. Jinnah had told him twice that he contemplated two separate sovereign independent States.

HIS EXCELLENCY THE VICEROY:—

(i) decided to ask Pandit Nehru at his next interview whether he agreed with Sardar Patel's interpretation of H.M.G.'s statement of 6th December;[7]

(ii) invited C.V.S. to amend the draft announcement as indicated above.

(iii) invited the Governor of Bengal to continue his efforts to induce his Chief Minister to form a Coalition Government forthwith; and to explain to him the proposed amendment to the plan.

[Item 2, on an interview between the Governor of Bengal and the Deputy Commander-in-Chief; and Item 3, on the Calcutta Police, omitted.]

[7] See No. 226.

265

Rear-Admiral Viscount Mountbatten of Burma to Mr Jinnah

Mountbatten Papers. Official Correspondence Files: North-West Frontier Province, Situation in, Part I(b)

1 May 1947

Dear Mr Jinnah,

I want to let you know about the results of my visit to the North West Frontier Province. I am sure you will be gratified to hear that the enormous meeting, which you told me was being held, proved to be very orderly and well-behaved, and carried out your instructions not to hold a procession. At the suggestion of the Governor I went with my wife and showed myself to the meeting and had a very friendly reception.

As promised I received a deputation of six from the meeting, and also six of your leaders came out of jail to see me. I also saw members of the Women's Committee and two Muslim Members of the Legislative Assembly.

I enclose a copy of the minutes[1] of the main meeting, from which you will see that I offered selected leaders, which I hope will include Abdul Quayum, parole and full facilities to come down and have a discussion with you. I should like to have a discussion with you before you meet these representatives. I am sure it is essential that they should see you, otherwise I should not be in a position to give an unbiased and unforced decision.[2]

[1] Not printed; see No. 259, notes 1 and 3.

[2] In tel. CA/67 of 1 May Sir O. Caroe reported that the attitude of the League leaders changed on receipt of a telephone message from Mr Jinnah. Previously the leaders had indicated that they would return to detention after seeing Lord Mountbatten but now four or possibly five of them were expected to proceed to Delhi the next day (2 May) to meet Jinnah. Mountbatten Papers, Official Correspondence Files: North-West Frontier Province, Situation in, Part I(b).

I have heard from the Governor of the North West Frontier Province that Kurshid Anwar has been making speeches which openly advocate violence both against the Government and against the minorities. The line he has taken has been directly contrary to your announcement and to the joint appeal that you made with Mr. Gandhi.

I shall be grateful if you could arrange to have Kurshid Anwar withdrawn from the North West Frontier Province since, although he appears to be a League worker, he is clearly operating contrary to the policy of the Party. The Governor also informed me that processions have not yet ceased in some areas.

I had an opportunity of meeting Brigadier Nazir Ahmed at Rawalpindi. As you probably know, he is the third senior Muslim officer in the Indian Army, and I am told he is the outstanding Muslim officer. I told him I was going to mention his name to you, as I considered you should make his acquaintance. In case you wished to see him in the near future I have arranged with his General to give him leave to come to Delhi, should you wish to see him. If you do, I suggest you write to him at 26 Brigade, Rawalpindi.

My wife and I propose to go to Simla for a week and are postponing all engagements. I hope you will not mind therefore if our luncheon party is postponed to the following week.

Yours sincerely,
MOUNTBATTEN OF BURMA

266

Pandit Nehru to Rear-Admiral Viscount Mountbatten of Burma

R/3/1/149: ff 71–4

EXTERNAL AFFAIRS DEPARTMENT, NEW DELHI,
1 May 1947

Dear Lord Mountbatten,

On the 6th March 1947[1] I wrote to Lord Wavell regarding the destruction of records by the Political Department. On the 15th March[2] he was good enough to send a reply to me on this subject. I again wrote to him on the 18th March.[3] To this I had no reply, no doubt because of the change in Viceroyalty soon after. Meanwhile information continues to reach me about the destruction of these records. This information comes to me from various sources, including Ministers of States, and it has been pointed out that many important records are thus being destroyed. I would beg of you to consider this matter, for it would be most unfortunate if any record important from the historical point of view or from the point of view of common subjects between the Government of India and the States is destroyed. I can hardly imagine that the staff of the Residency is competent to judge of the historical value of records. I have suggested, therefore, that this destruction should stop and all the records should be sent to the Imperial Record Department in New Delhi for examination by a group of competent persons, including historians. Delay in weeding out papers will not injure anybody, but if paper is once destroyed, it cannot be replaced.

Further I have pointed out that it is by no means clear to me why any papers from the Political Department or the Residencies should be transferred to the custody of the U.K. High Commissioner in India. The relations of the States in the past for a very large number of years were directly with the Government of India, as constituted then. A change was brought about by the Act of 1935 when the Crown Representative took charge of the Political Department. This did not put an end to the Government of India's concern with these papers or the matters referred to therein.

Indeed the Political Department has been in the past, and is, I believe, even now, financed by the Government of India and all the property of the Political Department or the Residencies necessarily belongs to the Government of India.

An A.P.I. message published in yesterday's papers states that steps are being taken to abolish Residencies and Political Agencies in States. It is said that this is a corrollary to the liquidation of Paramountcy. Further, that the States will correspond directly with the Departments of the Government of India or the provinces. I have also just seen a memorandum[4] issued by the Political Department issuing instructions about certain changes of procedure in regard to direct correspondence of States with the Central Departments.

All these steps that are being taken in the change of procedure vitally affect the Government of India and it is surprising that the Government of India should not be consulted in regard to them before any decisions are taken or orders issued. So far as I know, separate Departments of the Government of India are also not consulted in any way. The relations of the Crown and the Government of India with the Indian States cover a great variety of matters of common concern to States and British India, such as Railways, Posts and Telegraphs, Currency, Customs agreements, supplies of essential commodities, such as food, cloth, etc, etc. Whether or not any State accedes to the Union, some arrangements will have to be made between the State and the Government of India for the continuation of existing arrangements in regard to these

[1] Vol. IX, No. 496.
[2] Vol. IX, No. 535.
[3] Vol. IX, No. 542.
[4] No. F 24–R(S)/47. R/3/1/136: ff 44–73.

matters of common concern until new arrangements are made. At a time when many commodities are in short supply, this is even more necessary and is equally in the interest of both sides.

The Cabinet Mission itself contemplated some such course for the interim period before the coming into operation of the new constitutional structure. The statement of the 20th February 1947 makes it even more imperative that pending the formulation of new relations the existing treaties and agreements should continue in the economic, fiscal and administrative fields. This seems to be inescapable if we are to avoid a break-down in the administration in many spheres affecting the States as well as British India.

The question of Paramountcy does not arise in this connection. We have to distinguish clearly between economic, administrative and fiscal matters which will, in any event, continue to concern both British India and the States and the special rights and obligations of the Crown, such as the right of interference for misrule, deposition or limitation of powers of a Ruler, succession, honours, provision of military aid in support of a State, etc. It is about the former that I am writing to you. I am sure you will agree that the relations between British India and the States have to continue in a properly arranged manner when power is transferred to Indian hands. To break up the existing machinery of the Political Department and the Residencies without anything taking its place, would be to encourage chaotic conditions. The destruction of the records of the Political Department would add to the confusion.

The proposal that there should be direct correspondence between the States and the various Departments of the Government of India will also lead to the encouragement of disruptive tendencies in the economic life and administration of the States and of British India. It seems odd that individual departments of the Government of India should deal directly with a very large number of States in regard to numerous subjects without some machinery for coordination and without the benefit of an agency with local and regional knowledge.

I would, therefore, request you to have the destruction of records now in progress stopped; also, to suspend the present arrangements of the abolition of Political Agencies and the other procedure that has been suggested by the Political Department, in regard to direct correspondence between States and the Government of India Departments. These matters should be fully considered by the Government of India, in consultation with the Political Department before any final decisions are arrived at.

In matters relating to the Political Department we suffer a serious disability. That Department works as a kind of *imperium in imperio*, completely isolated from the Government of India, except in regard to occasional vague contacts. The steps that that Department is now taking are themselves significant of the way it functions without any reference to the Government of India, although it is obvious that the Government of India is vitally interested and will be affected by any changes made. All I can do is from time to time to draw your attention to some particular fact relating to the States or the activities of the Political Department.

Yours sincerely,
JAWAHARLAL NEHRU

267

Pandit Nehru to Rear-Admiral Viscount Mountbatten of Burma

Mountbatten Papers. Official Correspondence Files: Transfer of Power,
Part I(b)

SECRET   17 YORK ROAD, NEW DELHI, 1 *May 1947*

Dear Lord Mountbatten,

The Congress Working Committee met this afternoon and had the benefit of Gandhiji's presence and advice. I thought it desirable to acquaint the Committee with the major developments that had taken place since their last meeting and, in particular, with the steps that you propose to take in the near future. Five of the members of the Committee are members of the Interim Government.

2. Neither I nor my colleagues of the Interim Government, who were present at our meeting, know the full extent of the proposals that Lord Ismay is taking with him to London. But you have been good enough to keep me informed of the broad outlines of these proposals and I placed these before the Committee. I felt that it was important that they should know them and should express their opinion confidentially in regard to them at this stage, in order to avoid any misunderstanding at a later stage. I am writing this letter at the instance of the Committee to convey their reactions to recent developments and the new proposals, in so far as we know them.

3. It has been our Committee's earnest desire that India should achieve her freedom peacefully and in an orderly manner. Our whole policy, even in regard to conflict, has been peaceful. We had accepted the Cabinet Mission's Scheme last year, even though we did not approve of it wholly, in the hope that it might lead to such peaceful and cooperative transfer of power to Indian hands. Subsequently we accepted in its entirety the British Government's interpretation of this Scheme, which they issued on December 6th, 1946, although this was contrary to our own interpretation. In the same hope of achieving results peacefully, we welcomed H.M.G.'s announcement of February 20, 1947. We have tried to adhere faithfully to the Cabinet Mission's

Scheme in our work in the Constituent Assembly and otherwise.

4. We have, however, been faced with a major difficulty. The policy of the Muslim League, started in August last, has deliberately encouraged violence and disorder and has resulted in murder, arson and loot in many parts of India. This has affected the functioning of both the Central Government and several provincial governments. It has indeed been the dominant feature of Indian politics during the past eight months.

5. In view of the fact that we had made it clear at the outset that there should be no compulsion in making or enforcing a constitution for India on any unwilling parts, the necessity for this policy was not obvious, unless it was meant to terrorise and compel others against their will. The announcement of February 20, 1947, led to an intensification of this Muslim League policy and what used to be riots developed into organised large-scale violent attempts to overpower provincial governments. In spite of the most horrible consequences of this policy, it was not stopped or even suspended.

6. Our invitation to the Muslim League to send their representatives to meet ours was not responded to. We reiterated that we were against any compulsion over any part of India, and even indicated our acceptance of the principle of a partition of India in order to avoid conflict.

7. We had hoped that the joint appeal for peace and the declaration that violence must on no account be used for political objectives would lead to the withdrawal of the Muslim League's 'direct action' movement and the cessation of organised violence. This did not happen, and indeed there are indications that there will be an intensification of this policy.

8. Every proposal and every change must be viewed in this context. If policy is to be influenced by the kind of brutal and terroristic methods that have prevailed thus far, then the inevitable result will be civil war on an extensive scale. The continuous appeasement of those who employ such methods and a submission to these tactics is the surest way to encourage them and to produce other dangerous reactions. We can on no account be parties to such a policy.

9. We feel that we must lay stress on this as it is the dominating feature of the situation and other matters are secondary. Unless this is appreciated there can be no common approach to our problems.

10. This applies in particular today to the situation in the Frontier Province. We wish to make it clear that we cannot agree to a surrender to this violence of the Muslim League which has resulted in horrible tragedy and which is still continuing and finding encouragement. We have not seen any condemnation of the events in the Frontier from any Muslim League leader.

11. Any proposal to put an end to a duly constituted provincial government

having a large majority at its command, and to hold elections as a result of terrorism must be considered a surrender and must be resisted.

12. In regard to the proposals which, I presume, Lord Ismay is carrying with him to London, our Committee are prepared to accept the principle of partition based on self-determination as applied to definitely ascertained areas. This involves the partition of Bengal and Punjab. As you know, we are passionately attached to the idea of a United India, but we have accepted the partition of India in order to avoid conflict and compulsion. In order to give effect to this partition every effort should be made to meet the wishes and the interests of the people affected by it.

13. Even before and apart from such partition, recent events have made an administrative division of both Bengal and Punjab an obvious and urgent necessity.

14. In regard to Baluchistan, it would be improper for a few Sardars of the Shahi Jirga or some nominated members of the Quetta municipality to decide the future of the province. An attempt should be made to consult the people of the province. There is still plenty of time to devise some method for this purpose.

15. I have not entered in this letter into any detailed consideration of all your proposals as we have not got them before us in their final form.[1]

Yours sincerely,
JAWAHARLAL NEHRU

[1] On 2 May Lord Mountbatten thanked Pandit Nehru for his letter. He said he had taken note of 'the Committee's acceptance of the principle of Partition based on the will of the Indian people' and hoped to have a further discussion with Pandit Nehru on the whole matter at their next meeting. Mountbatten Papers, Official Correspondence Files: Transfer of Power, Part I(b).

268

Sardar Patel to Rear-Admiral Viscount Mountbatten of Burma

R/3/1/130: f 221

HOME MEMBER OF CABINET, NEW DELHI, 1 *May 1947*

My dear Lord Mountbatten,

In your absence, Sir Eric Mieville replied[1] to my letter of the 26th April 1947[2] about the Cabinet Mission's plan.

2. It seems to me that the main argument of my letter has been missed. The Statement of December 6th is merely clarificatory of a portion of the Cabinet Mission's plan. This clarification came, however, seven months

[1] No. 246.
[2] No. 226.

after the Cabinet Mission issued their Statement. On the other hand, the speech of Sir Stafford Cripps was made only within two months of the Cabinet Mission's Statement of 16th May, and I fail to see how if the Statement of December 6th is regarded as clarificatory of the Cabinet Mission's plan, his speech in the House of Commons cannot be so regarded. The position which I have stated, therefore, does not flow from any general principle, but must be taken as consistent with the intentions of the Cabinet Mission's plan.

Yours sincerely,

VALLABHBHAI PATEL

269

Sardar Baldev Singh to Rear-Admiral Viscount Mountbatten of Burma

R/3/1/178: ff 47–8

I BHAGWAN DAS ROAD, NEW DELHI,
1 May 1947

My dear Lord Mountbatten,

I have in my letter of the 27th April[1] given you my views about the division of the Punjab. In the talks I have had with your Advisers I got an impression that a proposal was under consideration somewhat on the following lines, viz. to make two arbitrary divisions of the province in the first instance and then let the present Members of the Legislature belonging to the respective areas elect one member per million to decide:

i) whether Punjab is to be partitioned,

ii) in case of partition of the Punjab, which Union the area voting will join, when and if India is divided.

The procedure is not quite clear though it looks as if it might be tried. Your Advisers, however, also conveyed the impression that this arbitrary division would include, in the East, the Divisions of Ambala, and Jullundur plus Amritsar District and the rest of the Punjab in the West.

This, I must emphasise, will be most objectionable as it is bound to create an impression that the final division of the Punjab will also be on this basis. Such an impression, as Your Excellency will have seen from my last letter, must be avoided at all costs in the interests of the Province as a whole and particularly the Sikhs. It will also be unjust to the Minorities. I am therefore strongly opposed to this basis of division and would suggest instead that if the plan of your Advisers is to be at all adopted, the Eastern Zone should include in addition to the Divisions of Ambala and Jullundur the districts of Gurdaspur, Amritsar and Lahore as well. Such a division will be approximately as near as the alternatives I suggested in my previous letter and will not create the complications I fear.

I would reiterate with all the emphasis I command that as the division of India is being planned at Mr. Jinnah's insistence, he cannot be allowed to impose his will on the Minorities. The partition of the Punjab is necessitated by Sikh case. The Sikhs cannot and will not be dominated by Muslims and no partition will meet the ends of justice if it does not exclude from Muslim area as large a percentage of Sikh population as possible. I have in my last letter shown how best this can be done.

I am also told that for the Interim period, pending the final division of the Punjab, two Ministries are to be set up each for the area arbitrarily marked out, namely, the Divisions of Ambala and Jullundur plus Amritsar District in the East and the rest of the Punjab in the West. This again will be unjust to the Minorities and I cannot agree to it. Justice and fairplay demand that if an Interim arrangement is to be made the Eastern Zone should include all the three Divisions of Ambala, Jullundur and Lahore. If on the other hand, the Muslim League's intransigence is still to be placated, the Eastern Zone should in no case be less than the Divisions of Ambala and Jullundur plus three out of the six districts of Lahore Division namely Gurdaspur, Amritsar and Lahore. The proposed Interim Ministerial arrangement for the two respective zones I have suggested should continue till the Boundary Commission has given its award for final partition, and machinery is devised to give effect to its decision.

Yours sincerely,

BALDEV SINGH

[1] No. 240.

270

Record of Interview between Rear-Admiral Viscount Mountbatten of Burma and Group Captain S. Mukerjee[1]

Mountbatten Papers. Viceroy's Interview No. 104

TOP SECRET *1 May 1947*

I saw him after luncheon on 1st May.

He is the most senior R.I.A.F. officer, and is the first one to reach Group Captain's rank.

I asked him how long he would wish to keep close connection with the Royal Air Force, if there were no political difficulties in the way. He replied that at the very least five to seven years were required, and that many more

[1] In charge of Training, Air Headquarters, India.

years would be required before India had an aircraft industry and experimental establishments which would enable them to be independent of assistance from England.

I asked him if he had ever met any of the political leaders and had been able to discuss this with them. He said that he had met one or two of them and had endeavoured to impress them with the need for a big air force in India and that at present the R.I.A.F. could not stand on its own legs.

We discussed whether an Advisory British Mission would be of any use to an independent Indian Air Force, and both agreed that though it would be better than nothing, it would fall very far short of continued British integration and assistance.

I pointed out that it was essentially between Indian leaders and senior Indian officers to make up their own minds on this question, since it did not matter much to the British, except for sentimental reasons, whether they remained inside or outside the Commonwealth.

271

Record of Interview between Rear-Admiral Viscount Mountbatten of Burma and Mr Gopinath Bardoloi

Mountbatten Papers. Viceroy's Interview No. 105

TOP SECRET   *1 May 1947*

I sat next to Mr. Bardoloi at luncheon on 1st May. He told me that Assam would make no difficulties about the partition of Sylhet, since the general view was that they belonged to Bengal, and would be no loss to the rest of the Province. The only people who might kick up a fuss would be the 40 per cent non-Muslim minority in the Sylhet district.

I asked him what solution he would prefer for Bengal, from the point of view of Assam. He replied that he would like Bengal to remain unified and join Hindustan, since this would give Assam the very best access to the rest of Hindustan.

If Bengal remained unified and joined Pakistan, it would virtually strangle Assam. If Bengal remained unified and independent they would have to negotiate access through Bengal, but it would not be so difficult as if Bengal had joined Pakistan.

If they had partition he expected to get access to Hindustan through Cooch Behar and Jalpaiguri.

He shared with me the regret that Sir B.N. Rau had failed in his attempt to reach a settlement in Assam recently and attributed this to the shooting that had taken place during his mediation.[1]

[1] In April 1947 Sir B.N. Rau, then on a visit to Assam, negotiated an agreement between Sir Muhammad Saadullah and Mr Bardoloi on the position of certain immigrants who were being evicted from their lands. However the agreement was not endorsed by the Assam Committee of Action of the Muslim League.

272

Minutes of Viceroy's Twenty Fourth Staff Meeting

Mountbatten Papers

TOP SECRET

Those present at this Meeting held at The Viceroy's House, New Delhi on 1 May 1947 at 4.30 pm were: Rear-Admiral Viscount Mountbatten of Burma, Lord Ismay, Sir E. Mieville, Mr Abell, Mr Christie, Mr I. D. Scott, Captain Brockman, Mr Campbell-Johnson, Lieutenant-Colonel Erskine Crum

Item 1

THE RETENTION OF INDIA WITHIN THE COMMONWEALTH

The paper[1] before the meeting contained an extract from a letter from the Secretary of State for India concerning the possibility, which had been mentioned, of States or groups of States being granted Dominion status. It was pointed out that the States were not at present British territory at all and could hardly be incorporated as part of the British Empire.

HIS EXCELLENCY THE VICEROY pointed out that this conclusion did not in any way apply to such separate parts as might be created of British India itself. The question still remained as to what line was to be taken with any such parts as might apply independently to remain within the Commonwealth. The more he thought of it, the more convinced did he become that it would be disastrous to allow only, for example, Pakistan to remain in, and thus back up one part of India against the other, which might involve the United Kingdom in war. He would not personally recommend that such an application should be granted, though his recommendation would doubtless not count for much in a matter of such worldwide importance. On the other hand, he personally was much in favour of British India as a whole being permitted to remain in the Commonwealth, and was using the Pakistan threat to remain in as a lever to help Congress to "take the plunge". He was opposed to a system of alliance as it would not enable the British to help

[1] V.C.P. 37 which circulated the text of No. 176, para. 6.

India in the way they best could—by their presence. In the meanwhile, a completely non-committal attitude on the question should be maintained.

LORD ISMAY said that he entirely agreed that no indication should be given of views held or decisions likely to be reached on this matter. He gave his personal opinion that, when and if the time came, it would be nigh impossible, both on moral, and, he believed, on material grounds, to eject from the Commonwealth any part of India, for example Pakistan, which asked to remain in. Relations with the whole Mussulman bloc, extending from the Middle East, had to be considered. He personally felt that the one way to avoid a civil war would be British backing, if not of the whole, of one part of India. Air power alone would ensure this. There was, also, no doubt that British strategy required harbours and naval bases in India if possible.

MR SCOTT gave his opinion in support of Lord Ismay, so far as moral and material ties and the prevention of civil war in India were concerned.

MR ABELL said that he agreed with His Excellency's views at present. He agreed that the British would have a continuing moral responsibility, but felt that the worst way of fulfilling this might be the unilateral support of Pakistan.

MR CAMPBELL-JOHNSON held similar views. He felt that support by Great Britain of one part of India only would result in India becoming a centre of international tension and intrigue.

SIR ERIC MIEVILLE said that Sir Walter Monckton had been invited by Pandit Nehru to dine with him on 3rd May to discuss "some form of continued allegiance to the Crown". He also stated that Rao Bahadur Menon had informed him that Sardar Patel might well accept an offer of Dominion status for the time being. He also raised the question whether, according to the Statute of Westminster, all members of the British Commonwealth would have to be consulted on the issue of parts or the whole of India remaining in or being ejected.

HIS EXCELLENCY THE VICEROY:—

(i) invited Prin. Sec. to consult Sir Walter Monckton concerning the ruling of the Statute of Westminster on this point;

(ii) invited Prin. Sec. to ensure that he (His Excellency) saw Sir Walter Monckton before the latter dined with Pandit Nehru on 3rd May;

(iii) invited C.V.S. to explain his (His Excellency's) views on this whole subject to H.M.G.

Item 2

THE ANDAMAN AND NICOBAR ISLANDS

HIS EXCELLENCY THE VICEROY said that he wished Lord Ismay to explain to H.M.G. in London that he had taken no further action in connection with the Andaman and Nicobar Islands because, if India was to remain within the Commonwealth, it would be a waste of time to do so; and, if India was not to remain in, very careful handling of the issue would be required at a later stage.

Item 5
LORD ISMAY'S VISIT TO LONDON
HIS EXCELLENCY THE VICEROY said that he much hoped that Lord Ismay's visit to London would not take more than three weeks at the absolute maximum. If it did, he would seriously consider going to London himself, and not returning until clearance was obtained from H.M.G. He emphasized that the need for speed had arisen from the deplorable deterioration in the situation over the last eight months. It was evident that H.M.G., particularly the members of the Cabinet Mission, did not realise the situation produced by this deterioration. For all they knew of the present situation, they might as well have got back to London in 1895.

HIS EXCELLENCY THE VICEROY:—

directed Pers. Sec. to draft, for his approval, a personal telegram from himself to the Prime Minister suggesting that the latter might ask C.V.S. and P.S.V. to dinner alone.

273

Viceroy's Conference Paper V.C.P. 40

L/PO/6/123: ff 444–7

TOP SECRET   THE VICEROY'S HOUSE, NEW DELHI,   *1 May 1947*
A METHOD OF TRANSFERRING POWER TO SUCCESSOR AUTHORITIES
IN INDIA WHICH WOULD RESULT IN A FORM OF TRANSITIONAL
CONSTITUTION ANALOGOUS TO THAT OF A DOMINION
The attached paper prepared by J.P.S.V., on the basis of a paper prepared by Rao Bahadur Menon,[1] is circulated for information. It should be considered in conjunction with and as an Appendix to the plan contained in the draft announcement which is being sent to His Majesty's Government for approval.
                                        V. F. ERSKINE CRUM

This note proposes for consideration a method of transferring power to successor authorities in India which would result in a form of transitional Constitution analogous to that of a Dominion.

[1] See Appendix to No. 222.

2. It is assumed that, initially, partition is inevitable, and that June 1948 is too early a date for the successor authorities to have completed their Constitution-making, and to have set up administrations adequate to discharge their new responsibilities in an orderly manner.

3. The object is, by transferring power immediately, and preserving at the same time the constitutional leadership and arbitral position of the Governor-General, to introduce a measure of gradualness and continuity during the process of transfer, to provide a breathing space for the orderly development of the necessary institutions, and to avoid too sharp a constitutional and administrative break. It is not an alternative to the plan for the exercise of a free choice by the people of India between Union and Partition, but a corollary to that plan.

4. The following are the main features of the proposal. H.M.G. would announce that provinces, and parts of certain provinces, should choose between Union and Partition. If the choice is for partition, one or more Constituent Assemblies, in addition to the existing Constituent Assembly, would be set up.

Each Constituent Assembly would be asked to elect an *Executive Council*, responsible to the Constituent Assembly. To these Executive Councils H.M.G. would transfer authority in their respective areas, pending the adoption of new constitution.

5. This would involve *amendment of the Govt. of India Act*, and its re-enactment, as amended, for as many areas as there are Constituent Assemblies. The amendments should provide for the withdrawal of the control of the Secretary of State for India, and the special powers of the Governors and of the Governor-General. There would be one Governor-General appointed by the Crown. The Governors of Provinces would be appointed by the Governor-General on the recommendation of the appropriate Executive Council. The existing Indian Legislature would be abolished and its place taken by the several Constituent Assemblies, which would have power of future amendment of the Constitution Act, of issuing Orders in Council, etc.

6. For matters of common concern e.g. Defence, External Affairs, Communications, a *Joint Council* would be set up with an equal number of representatives nominated by each Executive Council. This Council would be presided over by the Governor-General and would decide joint policy on those subjects which would be implemented by the respective governments. But the Governor-General would have absolute discretion in all matters affecting British troops in India.

7. Until such time as the executive governments are ready to assume complete control over other subjects and services which are now common, or to negotiate permanent agreements in regard to them, there should be a 'standstill' agreement whereby existing administrative arrangements continued

in each area with responsibility to the executive government of that area.

8. Similar 'standstill' agreements between Indian States and other parts of India for the continuance of existing economic and other relations should be negotiated pending more permanent agreements and definition of the relationship of States *inter se* and with the rest of India.

9. This transitional 'Dominion Status' would continue until and unless brought to an end by the terms of the Treaties to be concluded between Great Britain on the one hand, and the successor governments in India on the other.

10. The proposal has certain clear advantages.

(1) A transfer of actual power well within the time limit, will be a great achievement on its own merits, and will make for lasting goodwill in Indo-British relationships.

(2) It would be in accordance with the expressed wishes of the Congress Party as regards the transitional period, and not inconsistent with the desire of the Muslim League that Pakistan should remain a part of the British Commonwealth.

(3) It will place the responsibility for administration squarely on the successor authorities, before the existing administrative machine has completely run down.

(4) It will remove the main causes of communal and political bitterness, and by lessening the urgency for framing new Constitutions and creating new administrative machinery, will increase the likelihood that these will prove to be workable and sound.

(5) By providing an opportunity for joint consultation on matters of common interest, it will create conditions favourable to an ultimate Union of all the Indias.

(6) If the transitional 'Dominion Status' works well, it may prove to be acceptable as a permanent arrangement.

274

Sir E. Jenkins (Punjab) to Rear-Admiral Viscount Mountbatten of Burma

Mountbatten Papers. Official Correspondence Files: Punjab,
Security Arrangements for Partition of the Punjab

TOP SECRET   GOVERNMENT HOUSE, LAHORE,
No. 667   *1 May 1947*

Dear Lord Mountbatten,

I am discussing the security arrangements for the partition announcement with the Army Commander, the Lahore Area Commander and the Inspector General of Police at 12 noon on Monday May 5th.

2.   I propose to make the following assumptions:—

Central.   (i) Your Excellency will make one further attempt with the party leaders at an arrangement on the lines of the Cabinet Mission's Plan.

(ii) If the party leaders do not accept (i), you will tell them that for the purpose of the transfer of power India must be divided; and that the division involves the partition of the Punjab and Bengal. (The other adjustments will not concern us much here and I need not refer to them). You will attempt to secure the agreement of the party leaders to this arrangement.

(iii) On completion of (ii) Your Excellency will broadcast to India, and H.M.G. will issue a statement on the arrangements for the division. The statement will not *require* a division to be made; so far as we are concerned it will indicate that the Punjab, if partitioned, would have initially to be partitioned into Muslim majority and non-Muslim majority districts; and it will lay down the procedure by which the Punjabis are to decide whether they want this arrangement or not. *This statement will not be issued before May 15th but may be issued at any time after that date.*

Provincial. (iv) I shall receive notice (possibly not more than 48 hours notice) of the date of the statement, and also an advance copy of it.

(v) I shall see the party leaders (Muslim League, Congress, Sikhs) immediately before the statement is released; explain it to them; and urge them to set up a Coalition Ministry—possibly on a regional basis—to carry on while the desirability of partition is examined and the details are being worked out.

There is, of course, much detail, largely technical, which I have omitted; but these broad assumptions should suffice for the discussion on security.

3. My appreciation of the situation will be as follows:—

(a) A peaceful partition of the Punjab is most improbable. The Muslims want virtually the whole of the Punjab; the Sikhs want all districts from the Jumna to the Ravi, and possibly to the Chenab; the Hindus are likely to follow the Sikhs.

(b) The initial boundary will give the non-Muslims the Ambala and Jullundur divisions *plus* Amritsar, and the Muslims the Rawalpindi and Multan divisions and the Lahore division *less* Amritsar.

(c) The statement will excite anger among all Muslims and Sikhs, and fear among those of them, and among Hindus, who will live on the wrong side of the boundary. We can expect no rational examination of the statement; nor any united reaction against partition.

(d) Anger and fear will be general, but may be acutest among non-Muslims in the Lahore, Gurdaspur, Sheikhupura and Montgomery districts; and among Muslims in the Amritsar, Jullundur and Ferozepore districts.

(e) Communal rioting, if it starts, is likely to start in Lahore City, and to spread very rapidly indeed.

(f) We cannot afford to relax our vigilance in the outlying parts of the Punjab, and we shall need in addition to adequate force in the Ambala and Rawalpindi Divisions and in the Multan Division *less* Montgomery, a force strong enough to control quickly and firmly any trouble in the districts mentioned in (d).

(g) This force (the strength and disposition of which will be for the Army Commander to decide) must be in position before the statement is made.

4. I shall be grateful if Your Excellency will let me know whether my assumptions and appreciation are suitable. I am not sure what our line is to be if we have communal trouble so serious as to amount to a general rebellion with no agreed solution in sight. This contingency is by no means impossible. At present it seems that we could only deal with the situation to the best of our ability and await a further decision by H.M.G.

5. Since this was drafted I have seen Jinnah's statement in this morning's newspapers,[1] in which he demands complete Pakistan including the whole of the Punjab. If Jinnah sticks to this, Your Excellency will not secure agreement between the party leaders, and the Punjabi Muslims, with Jinnah's active support, will oppose partition from the first. I have always said that par-

[1] See Annex I to No. 276.

tition requires agreement or at least acquiescence. We cannot impose a partition without forces which I do not believe we possess.[2]

Yours sincerely,

E. M. JENKINS

[2] Lord Mountbatten thanked Sir E. Jenkins for this letter on 3 May. He said he agreed with Sir E. Jenkins' assumptions and appreciation and asked him for his views 'on the possibility and/or desirability of a referendum among the voters, on the question of partition as an alternative to the other machinery which we are considering.' Mountbatten Papers, Official Correspondence Files: Punjab, Security Arrangements for Partition of the Punjab.

275

Rear-Admiral Viscount Mountbatten of Burma to the Earl of Listowel

Mountbatten Papers. Letters to and from the Secretary of State

PRIVATE AND TOP SECRET   *1 May 1947*

Thank you for your letter of the 25th April.[1] I particularly appreciate the kind and encouraging things you say, which are a great help as one is apt to feel rather cut off from Whitehall out here.

2. This letter is being taken home by Ismay and Abell, who will be able to give you a first hand account of the situation, which I am sure will be very helpful. I should like to take this opportunity to tell you how magnificently Abell has played in with our new team and what a grand example he has set to the old staff. He has volunteered to stay on although he has had to give up his magnificent office to Ismay. I could not wish for a more public spirited, competent or delightful P.S.V.

3. While Abell is away my Personal Secretary, Captain R. Brockman, CIE, CBE, R.N., will act as P.S.V.

4. I am forwarding herewith my Personal Report No. 5 for the past week, for distribution as usual. I have aimed at giving you the background of Ismay's mission in this Report.

5. Ismay will give you the background of the difficult situation in the N.W.F.P., and will explain how Nehru will only accept a referendum on the issue of whether the N–W Frontier Province is to join Pakistan or Hindustan, and that if we try to force through an election merely as a result of pressure from the Muslim League civil disobedience movement, Congress will refuse to take part in the election as a strong gesture of their disapproval.

6. I have also charged Ismay with seeing you personally on the subject of Olaf Caroe. I like him immensely and in my opinion he is a very competent, loyal and honest official. But I have had to warn him that Congress are so

bitterly against him that it may not be in the best interests of all concerned to retain him; though whilst he is there I have guaranteed him my fullest support. I still think that he is showing signs of the great strain under which any man in his position must suffer.

7. Thank you for telling me about Merrell's report on his interview with Nawab Mir Nawaz Jung. The line I am taking up here to the question of individual membership of the Commonwealth for parts of India is clearly shown in my Personal Report. I am working a very delicate manoeuvre to give Congress an opportunity of offering to come back into the Commonwealth in some form, which might possibly bear fruit, but it is too delicate a matter to write about at present. Ismay can give you the latest form.

8. The business of the sterling balances has been very difficult. Nehru took the line that neither he nor any of the Congress Members could possibly be spared to go home on the Sterling Balances Mission. On my advice Liaquat Ali Khan brought this to a head at the Cabinet yesterday, when it was agreed that if it was impossible for the British to send a Mission out here, we would send a Mission home about mid-June, which would include Liaquat Ali Khan, Matthai and provisionally Rajagopalachari, though this is not yet firm.

9. I am so glad that the question of compensation for Secretary of State's Services has now been finally settled. The result of the meeting of the Special Cabinet Committee has already been reported by telegram and two copies of the Minutes were sent to the India Office earlier in the week.[2] The statement has been well received by the Indian Press. The statement will, I know, give the greatest satisfaction to all members of the Services out here and will be a great help in improving morale during the difficult months ahead. I shall be glad if you will express my thanks to your colleagues on the I. and B. Committee who have been so helpful in arriving at this satisfactory conclusion.

10. In paragraph 5 of my letter of the 24th April,[3] I referred to the case of Mr Williams and the way that he had been passed over by Patel for the Secretaryship of the Home Department. I asked him for Williams to come as Secretary of the Governor-General's Secretariat (Public) where a vacancy occurs shortly, and where he would be of the greatest help in dealing with the many Service problems which are going to arise during the next year. Somewhat to my surprise, however, Patel at his interview with me this week, suggested that Williams should be appointed as Secretary of the Information and Broadcasting Department where a vacancy occurs shortly. This Department comes, of course, directly under the Home Member and this change of heart on Patel's part is surprising, as I am sure he has no real desire to keep

[1] No. 220.
[2] See L/S &G/7/914.
[3] No. 210.

on any Englishmen. I am however hoping he will release Williams to me, as we really need him, and Williams has no desire to continue serving under Patel.

11. Nehru has recently been taking a keen interest in the future of the Indian States, especially from the point of view of the people of the States, and in a recent letter to me[4] he complained that the Political Department worked in secret and no-one knew what it was doing. In particular, he expressed anxiety regarding the relations of Hyderabad with Bastar and Berar. I think much of the trouble has been due to the fact that although Lord Wavell offered to arrange a meeting between Corfield and Nehru at which the fullest information was exchanged, Nehru never followed this up and has developed a slight sense of grievance, although I think the fault was undoubtedly his. In the last week, however, he has had a very full talk with Corfield,[5] covering such matters as the representation of the States in the Constituent Assembly, the working of the Political Department, the future of the Indian States and the relations of Hyderabad with Bastar and Berar. Corfield reports that the meeting was held in a very pleasant atmosphere and that Nehru had no critical comments to make.

12. I am taking the opportunity of sending Corfield home with Ismay this week for a brief visit which I hope will be helpful both to you and to him. You will, I expect, by now have seen the Minutes of the recent Residents' Conference,[6] which were sent home last week.

[Paras. 13–15, on a report from the C.I.O. Calcutta about aid from Russia to the Communist Party of India; paras. 16–18, on the need to assist British members of the Indian Police to find employment when they retired from India; para. 19, on the need to increase the allotment of honours for India in the 1948 New Year's Honours List; and para. 20, on the reduction in the grant for the British Council in India, omitted.]

21. I am sure Auchinleck, Ismay and Abell will be able to give you a picture which will convince you of the supreme need of speed, and I sincerely trust that you will be able to help forward the pace of the discussion, so as to release Ismay within a week or ten days at the most. The price to pay for any appreciable delay may well be a general communal eruption out here.

22. I was very glad to have Burrows up here; although he still looks to me to be pretty ill, his doctors tell me he is on the mend, and he has promised me that he will go up to Darjeeling on Sunday. In the meanwhile, he is going to suggest to Suhrawardy that he should immediately form a coalition government and offer joint electorates in the future. If he can bring this off, he should be on a good wicket to retain the unity of Bengal as an independent Province.

23. I have been averaging 17 to 18 hours a day for six weeks now, and my doctor wants me to go to Simla to get really rested and fit for the much more

important discussions which will start when Ismay gets back. I think I shall go up after the next Cabinet and come down before the following one. I shall be in just as good touch with you at Simla as in Delhi.

⁴ No. 102.
⁵ See No. 236.
⁶ A copy of these Minutes is on L/P &S/13/1831.

276

Viceroy's Personal Report No. 5

L/PO/6/123: ff 71–89

TOP SECRET *1 May 1947*

During the past week I have still further restricted the number of interviews I have given, and have concentrated chiefly on meetings with Nehru, Patel, Jinnah, Liaquat Ali Khan and Baldev Singh. After having obtained from them various suggestions to be embodied in the plan that we have been working on, I left my Staff to prepare a final draft of the plan whilst I carried out a two day tour to the N.W.F.P. and the Punjab.

2. Ismay (who, like me, has been suffering from a "Delhi tummy") was unable to go round with the plan himself to Jinnah and Nehru as I had arranged. Mieville went, and had a satisfactory interview with Nehru except on the subject of the N.W.F.P.; but he had an unsatisfactory one with Jinnah, who protested strongly against the partition of the Provinces, and demanded that I should immediately dissolve the Constituent Assembly. I attach a copy of the statement he has just issued to the press. Whether this unreasonable attitude is due to fear of his own followers or merely his maddening methods of bargaining remains to be seen. But I do not consider that he is in any position to stop the plan going forward, though his open assent would make it much easier to implement without trouble.

3. I am therefore sending Ismay off as arranged on Friday 2nd May and he will be taking this Report with him. He will have the plan and will be available to explain it to the Cabinet. It is impossible to exaggerate the need for speed. My recent tour has more than confirmed all the reports I have had from outlying parts of India about the shocking deterioration that is taking place in so many Provinces.

4. The essence of the plan is to make it apparent to the people of India and to the world in general that we are allowing, so far as possible, Indians themselves to choose how they wish us to transfer power. Provinces will have the right to decide whether they will all work with the present Constituent

Assembly; whether only some will adhere to it (Hindustan); and whether others will wish to set up a new Constituent Assembly (Pakistan). In the case of the three Provinces, Punjab, Bengal and Assam, in which partition has been asked for if Pakistan takes place, I am proposing machinery to allow the Provinces themselves to decide if they want partition. There is a reluctance to accept any formula, which I believe to be due to the desire of the Indians to force the British to make a decision how they will transfer power, so that we may get the blame if things ultimately go wrong.

5. I am also sending the draft of a broadcast that I feel it is essential I should make, which explains how Indian leaders have refused to agree on anything other than partition, and even that with bad grace.

6. I very much hope that the Cabinet will be able to give me the necessary authority to go ahead and will be able to release Ismay after a week, for we all feel that every day now counts out here if we are to prevent the communal conflict from spreading to unmanageable proportions.

7. Although I can ill afford any time away from Delhi I felt I had to get first hand information of the situation in the N.W.F.P., which at the moment is the greatest danger spot in India and the bone of contention between Congress and the Muslim League.

8. I spent 26 hours at Peshawar and up the Khyber, and except between 2 a.m. and 7 a.m., when I was overcome by sleep and had to retire to bed, I saw an absolute stream of officials and delegations. I had separate talks with 16 British and Indian officials from every part of the Frontier. I met the Governor, the Chief Minister (Dr. Khan Sahib) and his Ministry at what must surely have been one of the craziest meetings ever held with any Ministry. The Chief Minister informed me that he considered Jinnah had no control over the Muslim League on the Frontier whatever; and when I fell into his trap and asked him who ran the League, he replied "His Excellency the Governor and all of his officials with the object of turning my Government out of power". I confess I could not repress my laughter at such a fantastic suggestion.

9. The Ministry of course were violently opposed to my ordering fresh elections, but I warned them that I should require to know whether they had a mandate from their people before I could possibly decide who was to inherit the Province and I think I got them to see this. I also warned them I should probably go into Section 93 for at least two months before-hand to ensure that the elections were fair; since I had had from Nishtar (Communications Member of my Government) three pages of accusations against the way the present Government had arranged the last election. All the British officials had told me that no matter which party was in power the elections would not be fair if they were not held under a Section 93 regime.

10. My mail which is always of large dimensions reached a peak record at Peshawar, where I received 3,129 telegrams, letters and postcards, most of them expressing no confidence in the Congress Government and demanding fresh elections under Section 93.

11. My next meeting was with the Muslim League leaders. Six came from the local jails and six had led a colossal deputation who had gathered in Peshawar to see me. There were also two women and two Muslim Members of the Legislative Assembly. They wanted to come in five groups, and it was only with the greatest difficulty that we persuaded the jailbirds and demonstrators to come in one group, the two Members of the Legislative Assembly in another and the ladies in a third.

12. The Muslim League was a great problem during the visit. The night before I left, I was informed by Jinnah that the leaders who were in jail would insist on coming to Government House under escort as prisoners to see me. I told him that I would not see them under those conditions, and they would lose the opportunity of putting their case before me. Jinnah agreed they should come out on parole. He then told me that he had arranged for a demonstration of one hundred thousand in Peshawar, and wished them to march in procession to Government House to hand in their resolutions. I absolutely forbade this but said I would receive a deputation of six; and he promised to give the necessary orders.

13. In fact the greatest crowd ever seen on the Frontier, variously estimated at between fifty and a hundred thousand, had collected from surrounding areas in Cunningham Park. The Governor told me that the crowd would not disperse until they had seen me, so I sent for the Chief Minister and asked his concurrence to my showing myself to this League demonstration to which he very sensibly assented. I went onto a nearby railway embankment and had a very remarkable reception. I neither spoke nor waved to them, but simply stood there; there were tremendous bursts of clapping, and among the Pakistan cries one could distinctly hear "Mountbatten ki jai". I felt that it was most awkward that the League should look upon me as some sort of saviour, and got my Press Attaché on to toning down the reports of this meeting.

14. Later that night the General Officer Commanding, the Inspector General of Police, the District Commissioner and other officials thanked me for having gone out to the people, as they said that the crowd was determined to break through to Government House and they would have had the biggest killing ever known on the Frontier if I had not shewn myself. Even so, I realised the risk I took in appearing to be partisan, and I sent a full explanation of the incident to Nehru.

15. When I asked the deputation whether they had anything to do with Jinnah they all appeared astounded and said "Of course, he is our leader".

And when I said "Do you obey his orders", they replied "Implicitly; it was on his orders that we did not form a procession to-day". I invited the Governor to repeat these remarks to Dr. Khan Sahib. I urged the leaders to take advantage of the Government's offer of releasing political prisoners and to come out of the jails. I suggested to them that they should call off their civil disobedience movement which had now been in force for two months and had caused so many deaths. They said they would do all this if I could immediately promise them to go into Section 93 and hold fresh elections. I told them that I could not possibly yield to duress and that so long as they were trying to overthrow the present Provincial Government by violence, that Government must have my support. I advised them to follow their leader, who had declared his personal faith in me, and to trust me to see that they got fair play when the transfer of power took place. They said that this would be very difficult to put over to their followers; and I therefore arranged to give the leaders parole to go to Delhi and see Jinnah, where I hope to get this over.

16. The position now is pretty tricky. When Mieville saw Nehru with the plan, he was very upset and said that in no circumstances would Congress agree to yield through violence and pressure to fresh elections being held in the N.W.F.P. When Mieville pointed out that this was entirely for me and the Governor to decide, Nehru said "If you force this issue on us, we shall not contest the elections". This may possibly be quite a good thing, as there are only 7% Hindus in this Province.

17. On the following day, when I went up the Khyber, I held a jirga at Landi Kotal with representatives of the Afridis, Shinwaris, Salmanis and Kullaghoris; and later on return to Government House, I saw representatives of Waziristan tribes, the Mahsuds, Wazirs and Daurs. There is remarkable unanimity among all tribes. They are all disappointed that His Majesty's Government have never taken them into account in their plans and that the Prime Minister omitted any reference to them in his statement. They want an assurance that the Khyber and their respective tribal areas will be returned to them (an assurance which Lord Wavell had already given to them last November). They say they will not deal with the present one party committee if it comes up and in no circumstances will they come under Hindu domina-tion—they would sooner make terms with Afghanistan than do that. The Mahsuds and Wazirs pressed hard for Pakistan and the dismissal of the Congress Government.

18. Subsequently I received a delegation of six Hindus with a horrible tale of woe against the Muslim League, of murder, rape and violence.

19. If I can succeed in getting a truce here, all may be well, but it is not going to be easy with Jinnah in his present mood; and if we do not get a truce, serious trouble may flare up on the Frontier. The British and Indian members

of the I.C.S. are convinced that when we transfer power there will be a great deal of trouble on the Frontier, and that short of retaining the whole Province under Section 93 until the day of our departure there may well be trouble even before we transfer power. I shall watch this Province very carefully.

20. I next flew to Rawalpindi where, joined by the Governor, Jenkins, I and my wife immediately drove out 25 miles to the small town of Kahuta, which had a population of 2,000 Hindus and Sikhs, and 1,500 Muslims. On the night of March the 6th a patrol of the Norfolks found everything peaceful and the inhabitants on the usual friendly terms which they had been on for so many years; on the 7th, the whole town was ablaze.

21. The whole of the Hindu-Sikh part is an absolute wreck, as though it had been subjected to an air raid; but the interesting part is that all the Muslim shops and better class Muslim houses were destroyed along with the Hindu property by the same fire, and only the poorer section of the town, where the Muslims predominated, was saved. The town was burnt largely by Muslims from the rural district round about; and since Kahuta was their sole shopping centre they will now be without many foodstuffs and cloth, and the other essentials they used to buy in Kahuta.

22. The unattractive part of all these massacres is the sadistic violence which distinguishes them. They seem to be very fond of tying whole families together, pouring oil on them and then lighting them as a single torch. Hindu and Sikh women have not been wanting in courage, and many have taken their lives rather than be raped or forcibly converted. Until I went to Kahuta, I had not appreciated the magnitude of the horrors which are still going on.

23. I had a long talk with Jenkins about the partitioning of the Punjab. The bone of contention is going to be the area between the two rivers, Ravi and Sutlej, and it is going to be very difficult to produce a demarcation which will be accepted by both parties. The Sikhs in their endeavours to obtain a real "Sikhistan" are most anxious to take in a large part of the area where most of the land is owned by Sikhs but where the Muslim population predominates. To this I am absolutely opposed. The Sikhs also want their holy places preserved for them, including Lahore itself, the capital-designate of Pakistan! It is significant, however, that when the Sikh delegation saw me they particularly asked that I should not decide whether the Sikhs would join Pakistan or Hindustan, since they had not made up their minds to which side they wanted to go.

24. Jinnah told me that an emissary had come down asking if he would receive Kartar Singh with a view to discussions about the future of "Sikhistan".[1] When Mieville dined with Liaquat Ali Khan, the latter also hinted that there was a chance that "Sikhistan" might join up with Pakistan, and that the

[1] See No. 229.

Muslim League would offer them very generous terms.[2] This would have the effect of avoiding the partition of the Punjab, since both halves would really vote to join up again. And since the principal export of the Punjab is soldiers and the principal imports are the wages and pensions of the soldiers, a split-up of the Punjab would have a very serious effect on the many Muslims living in the "Sikhistan" area as there would be no army really open to them to join.

25. Jenkins is of the opinion that there may be trouble on the announcement of the choice for partition, and I have discussed with him and the General Officer Commanding the necessary troop dispositions to nip such trouble immediately in the bud.

26. Finally, Jenkins gave me an account of his meeting with the Nawab of Mamdot, the leader of the Muslim League party in the Punjab, who on Jinnah's instructions has been to Jenkins with the request to be allowed to form a Government on the grounds that he now commands 84 Muslim seats, and, with 7 minorities, has 91 out of the total 175 seats in the Provincial Assembly. On my instructions Jenkins is going to reject this demand, on two counts. Firstly, that the Sikhs have made it pretty clear that if the Punjab is put under a one-party government they will resist, presumably with violence. Secondly, that a decision about the future of the Punjab will be made within the next month or so, and that that decision may render a one-party government for the whole of the Punjab obsolete.

27. I explained the position personally to Jinnah, who said he quite followed my arguments and saw my point. I then said "May I tell the Governor that he can inform Mamdot that you agree?" whereupon he said in a very mild voice: "I am afraid not; you see I do not agree". It is very difficult to deal with somebody who admits he sees the point and who if he sees the point and has any logic could not possibly fail to agree, yet will not express agreement merely to score a political point.

28. If it were possible to have a worse headache than the N.W.F.P. and the Punjab, then Bengal provides it. Although Burrows had originally agreed, albeit reluctantly, to my plan for voting on the partition of Bengal, by the time I sent my Joint Private Secretary to see him he had changed his mind and wanted Calcutta to be a free city under joint control. I offered to fly down to see Burrows direct from the Punjab, as I knew he was still a pretty sick man, but Burrows replied that he would fly up to Delhi to see me, and he arrived on the evening of Wednesday the 30th April.

29. The next morning we had a long meeting[3] over the question of Calcutta being kept out of any partition and put under joint control. I explained to Burrows that though that might be a solution which would commend itself to his Muslims and possibly to his Congress Bengalis, I was quite certain that the whole scheme would be wrecked if I now introduced this new condi-

tion at this late hour; since Congress would be bound to reject any such suggestion. To force it through against their wishes might cause them to resign from the Government; and from the all-India point of view his proposal was not acceptable. He took my ruling in a very good spirit, saying that although it would make the situation difficult in Bengal and might cause riots in Calcutta, the difficulties of all-India must of course take precedence over any provincial difficulties.

30. We then put our heads together to see what could be done to help over the Calcutta situation, and as a result of our discussions I am having my plan slightly redrafted. Whereas it was my original intention to have one straight vote taken on a single day by all the Bengal members of the Constituent Assembly on the issue of "partition or unity" and that only if unity were decided upon would a further vote be taken on whether they wished to be independent or to go to Pakistan or Hindustan; my new proposal is that there should be provision for a preliminary vote in Bengal (and therefore of course also in the Punjab) by all the Provincial members of the Constituent Assembly to decide whether on the assumption that the Province remains unified, they want to be independent or to join Pakistan or Hindustan. A week or a fortnight later another vote will be taken to decide whether they want partition or not, in the light of this.

31. Burrows' great point is that his Chief Minister, Suhrawardy, is almost certain to be able to fix the first voting in favour of independence, since he has 33 out of 60 seats and Jinnah has given him permission not to join Pakistan. Once the issue is clear before the members that they have to decide between independence or partition and not between going to Pakistan or partition, Burrows thinks there is an outside chance that the Province will remain united. I have no doubt myself that unity is necessary for Bengal; for if the Province is divided, eastern Bengal even with Sylhet will be an uneconomic entity which is bound gradually to fail, and cannot receive any help from the rest of Pakistan. If they wish to ruin Calcutta, it lies within their power to do so by refusing to grow any more jute and growing food instead.

32. I asked him what the situation was like in Bengal. I said: "Are you still sitting on a barrel of gunpowder?" to which he replied "Good Lord no, we got off that a long time ago and are now sitting on a complete magazine which is going to blow up at any time".

33. He told me that the trouble with the police force has now become really serious, and that on Tuesday night some of the Gurkhas went and attacked the Punjabi Musulmans, killing five and wounding five with rifle fire. The Bengal Government have suspended B Company from duty and propose to dismiss

[2] See No. 249.
[3] See No. 264.

all doubtful elements, which he says will prove to be at least 800 of the 1200 Gurkha policemen. They intend to use soldiers temporarily on police duties, which I do not like but suppose is unavoidable, and are going to raise new police as fast as they can.

34. The more I look at the problem in India the more I realise that all this partition business is sheer madness and is going to reduce the economic efficiency of the whole country immeasurably. No-one would ever induce me to agree to it were it not for this fantastic communal madness that has seized everybody and leaves no other course open.

35. To give you one small horrifying example: my wife had Miss Jinnah to tea again last week whilst he was with me. She told Miss Jinnah that she had spent that morning at the Lady Irwin College, and was so delighted to find how happily that institution was working and on what excellent terms the Hindu and Muslim girls were. She quoted the example that in one class of 14 Hindu and 2 Muslim girls, the class had elected one of the two Muslims to be their Head Girl. To this Miss Jinnah replied: "Don't be misled by the apparent contentment of the Muslim girls there; we haven't been able to start our propaganda in that college yet."

36. I might add that the Hindus are nearly as bad, and that the determination, from the highest to the lowest in the land, to make out that the opposite religionists are devils incarnate as well as crooks, makes any sensible solution appear out of the question. The most we can hope to do, as I have said before, is to put the responsibility for any of these mad decisions fairly and squarely on the Indian shoulders in the eyes of the world, for one day they will bitterly regret the decision they are about to make.

37. I feel it my duty to continue to support the Cabinet Mission plan to the last, since I am convinced it is the only reasonable solution for India. Jinnah has repeatedly said that he does not want to discuss it any further since he knows that the Congress do not mean to play fair, and intend to use their permanent majority at the Centre to crush Pakistan. I therefore discussed with Patel[4] a possible compromise whereby there should be a system of voting on communal questions similar to that in vogue for the Constituent Assembly. Patel warned me: "If you raise this question of parity you will incur the everlasting enmity of Congress; that is the one thing we have been fighting against and will never agree to".

38. I then asked him whether Jinnah's accusation that Congress had not even accepted the letter of the statement made by His Majesty's Government on the 6th December was true. Patel denied this. I then read out the actual wording of the statement, and said that it would clear the air if he agreed that Assam would have to have their elections before deciding whether to opt out. Patel said that although they accepted the statement of His Majesty's Govern-

ment, it was quite clear that Assam could opt out whatever the result of the election if they did not like their new constitution, and he quoted Sir Stafford Cripps' statement in the House on the 18th July, 1946 in which he said: "A fear was expressed that somehow or other the new Provincial Constitution[s] might be so manoeuvred as to make it impossible for the Provinces afterwards to opt out. I do not myself see how such a thing would be possible, but if anything of that kind was to be attempted, it would be a clear breach of the basic understanding of the scheme.", to prove his point. I therefore feel that Jinnah has some justification to fear that the Congress do not mean to stick to their acceptance.

39. A new problem has now arisen, in that Jinnah has come into the open and pointed out to me that it is not a question of Pakistan applying for admission to the British Commonwealth, but on the contrary a question of whether the British Commonwealth is in a position to expel Pakistan against her wish. In effect he says "All the Muslims have been loyal to the British from the beginning. We supplied a high proportion of the army which fought in both wars. None of our leaders have ever had to go to prison for disloyalty. Not one member of the Muslim League was present in the Constituent Assembly when the Congress passed the resolution for an Independent Sovereign Republic of India. In fact not one of us has done anything to deserve expulsion from the Empire. And what about the other dominions—Australia and New Zealand—will they accept our being expelled against our will? Is there anything in the Statute of Westminster that allows you to kick out parts of the Commonwealth because a neighbouring State that used to be a member wishes to leave? I asked Mr. Churchill and Sir Stafford Cripps for their views when I was in London. Mr. Churchill assured me that the British people would never stand for our being expelled. Sir Stafford Cripps informed me that he could not answer how the legislation would be framed and whether we should be given an opportunity of deciding whether to stay in on our own."

40. I replied "Emotionally and sentimentally I not only see your point of view but share it. Rationally, I cannot support it; for if one part of India remained within the Commonwealth and you had British officers and British help, and civil war broke out with the other part of India, then the British would be in a quite impossible position and one they would never willingly accept". In fact I warned him to prepare himself for a refusal. He however relied on the power of public appeal over our heads, and expressed confidence in the support that he would get.

41. Although I have never once discussed with any Congress leader the possibility of India remaining within the Commonwealth, all the indications

4 See No. 216.

are that there is violent discussion going on to this effect. My Reforms Commissioner, V.P. Menon, and Nehru's greatest friend, Krishna Menon, and Minority Members such as Baldev Singh and Bhabha, have told me that it is a subject of heated discussion at the moment, particularly as they now realise Jinnah's game and are beginning to be very frightened by its consequences on the rest of India. I presume it was for this reason that the *Hindustan Times* produced their inspired leading article saying that "The Union of India" would regard any such move as a hostile act. I added a paragraph about this to my last report by telegram last week,[5] as I feel certain that Congress should be given no inkling as to what His Majesty's Government's attitude will be, since the main hope of bringing them back into the fold lies in the fact that this is the obvious solution for them over the difficulty of Pakistan. Although I shall keep my own position clear by saying that I shall not personally recommend the retention of Pakistan within the Commonwealth, I shall also point out that Jinnah is of the opinion that he will be able to appeal to the people of the Commonwealth over my head.

42. Auchinleck will be able to give you his views on the partition of the armed forces. Liaquat Ali Khan's paper[6] was taken at the Defence Committee meeting before he left last week. I treated this as a particularly secret matter and only circulated the paper four hours before the meeting and withdrew all copies at the meeting, since I did not wish rumours to get around that we were contemplating such partition. At the meeting the enormous technical difficulties of separation were pointed out in considerable detail, but it was agreed that some form of planning would be essential as soon as a decision had been made.

[Para. 43, outlining the conclusions of the Defence Committee Meeting of 25 April 1947 (No. 221), omitted.]

44. One further complication is that Suhrawardy has told me that if he achieved his great ideal of independence for Bengal, they would also claim the right of remaining within the Commonwealth and expect to be allowed to raise their own armed forces. If they do get their independence they cannot be stopped having their own armed forces, but it would make the need for a Central Defence Council to run a unified armed force until partition could be implemented more necessary than ever.

45. The Constituent Assembly has started its third session this week. The President, Dr. Rajendra Prasad made a statement at the outset in which he said that the Assembly must be prepared not only for a division of India, but also a division of some Provinces, and it might have to draw up a Constitution based on such division. If the proposed union was not to comprise all the Provinces, the Assembly would have to be content with a Constitution for a part of it.

46. The representatives of eight Indian States—Udaipur, Baroda, Cochin, Jaipur, Jodhpur, Bikaner, Rewa and Patiala took their seats in the Constituent Assembly, but one of the representatives of Baroda was accidentally burnt to death in a train on his way to Delhi.

47. Last Sunday my wife held an At Home for the students and staff, numbering about 600 in all, of the women's medical and nursing colleges in Delhi. She has continued her visits to hospitals, medical and welfare centres, dispensaries and canteens and has had discussions here with the heads of these various institutions. She also accompanied me on my tour of the N.W.F.P. and the Punjab, and has stayed for an additional two days to make an extended tour to relief centres, refugee camps and hospitals in the most disturbed areas around Amritsar, Multan, Dera Ismail Khan and Tank.

[5] No. 232.
[6] See No. 215.

Annex I to No. 276
Mr. Jinnah's Statement on Partition
(Reproduced from *Dawn*, dated the 1st May, 1947.)
"I find from the Press reports that the Congress has now started by emphasising that in the event of Pakistan and Hindustan being established, the Punjab will be partitioned; and the Hindu Mahasabha has started a vigorous propaganda that Bengal should be partitioned.

PRINCIPLE OF PARTITION
"I should like to point out that there is a great deal of confusion created on purpose. The question of the division of India, as proposed by the Muslim League, is based on the fundamental fact that there are two nations—Hindus and Muslims and the underlying principle is that we want a National Home and a National State in our homelands which are predominantly Muslim and comprise the 6 units of the Punjab, N.W.F.P., Sind, Baluchistan, Bengal and Assam. This will give the Hindus their national home and national state of Hindustan which means three-fourths of British India.
"Now the question of partitioning Bengal and the Punjab is raised not with a *bona fide* object but as a sinister move actuated by spite and bitterness as they feel that India is going to be divided, firstly, to create more difficulties in the way of the British Government and the Viceroy and secondly to unnerve the Muslims by opening and repeatedly emphasising that the Muslims will get a truncated or mutilated, moth-eaten Pakistan.
"This clamour is not based on any sound principle except that the Hindu minorities in the Punjab and Bengal wish to cut up these provinces and cut up their own people into two in these provinces.

HINDU HOMELANDS

"The Hindus have their homelands. As I said, consisting of six vast provinces. Merely because a portion of the minorities in the Pakistan provinces have taken up this attitude, the British Government should not countenance it because the result of that will be, logically, that all other provinces will have to be cut up in a similar way, which will be dangerous, as to embark on this line will lead to the breaking up of the various provinces and create a far more dangerous situation in the future than at present.

"If such a process were to be adopted, it would strike at the root of the administrative, economic and political life of the provinces which have for nearly a century developed and built up on that basis and have grown and are functioning under the present Constitution as autonomous provinces.

BEWARE OF THE TRAP

"It is a mistake to compare the basic principle of the demand of Pakistan and the demand of cutting up the provinces throughout India into fragmentation. I do hope that neither the Viceroy nor His Majesty's Government will fall into this trap and commit a grave error.

"It is obvious that if the Hindu minorities in Pakistan wish to emigrate and go to their homelands of Hindustan they will be at liberty to do so and *vice versa* those Muslims who wish to emigrate from Hindustan can do so and go to Pakistan; and sooner or later exchange of population will have to take place and the Constituent Assemblies of Pakistan and Hindustan can take up the matter, and subsequently the respective Governments in Pakistan and Hindustan can effectively carry out the exchange of population wherever it may be necessary and feasible.

"The Congress propaganda is intended to disrupt and put obstacles and obstructions and difficulties in the way of an amicable solution. It is quite obvious that they have put up the Hindu Mahasabha in Bengal and the Sikhs in the Punjab, and the Congress Press is inciting the Sikhs and misleading them. The Sikhs do not stand to gain by the partition of the Punjab but they will be split into two halves. More than half of their population will have to remain in Pakistan even if a partition of the Punjab takes place according to their conception, whereas in Pakistan, as proposed by the Muslim League they will play, as one solid minority, a very big part. We have always been very willing to meet them in every reasonable way.

"Besides, the White Paper of February 20 lays down that power will be transferred to authority or authorities which will be made in a manner that will be smooth and create the least amount of difficulties and trouble.

CLEAR-CUT ROAD

"If power is to be transferred to various Governments it can only be done sucessfully to the Pakistan Group and the Hindustan Group which will establblish stable, secure Governments and will be able to run these Governments peacefully and sucessfully.

"The transfer of power to Pakistan and Hindustan Governments must mean a division of the defences as a *sine qua non* of such a transfer and the defence forces should be completely divided—and in my opinion can be divided before June 1948—and the States of Pakistan and Hindustan should be made absolutely free, independent and sovereign. This is a clear-cut road and the only practical solution of India's constitutional problem."[7]

[7] It is evident from papers on L/P &J/7/12245 that Mr Jinnah sent Mr Attlee a copy of this Statement.

Annex II to No. 276

DRAFT OF BROADCAST STATEMENT BY H.E.

A statement will be read to you tonight giving the final decision of His Majesty's Government as to the method by which power will be transferred from British to Indian hands. But before this happens, I want to give a personal message to the people of India, as well as a short account of the discussions which I have held with the Leaders of the political parties and which have led up to the advice I have tendered to H.M. Government.

I spent my first five weeks in India in having daily meetings with all the political leaders—not only of the two major political parties, but with those of all the Minorities—and with many of the Rulers and Dewans of Indian States. I have conferred with all the Governors and Residents; and have had the opportunity of meeting several Provincial Premiers—as well as the Army Commanders and most of the more senior Indian Officers of the Armed Forces. I wish to say this evening how grateful I am for all the helpful advice that has been given to me in the course of these meetings.

I have had the privilege of presiding regularly at the Cabinet Meetings of the Interim Government. I wish to tell you that the members of this Cabinet have carried out their duties in a high-minded and statesmanlike manner; and I take this opportunity of thanking them sincerely for the support and help they have given me.

Nothing I have seen or heard in the past few weeks has shaken my firm opinion that a Unified India is by far the best solution of the problem. Under British administration 400 million people of many races and creeds, living together in a geographically isolated sub-continent, have been welded together into an entity that enjoys the great advantages of unified communications, defence, postal services, and currency; an absence of tariffs and customs barriers; and the basis for an integrated political economy.

My first course, in all my discussions, has been to urge the political leaders to accept the Cabinet Mission plan unreservedly, for in my opinion that plan provides the best arrangement that can be devised to meet the interests of all the communities of India. But to my great regret it has been impossible to obtain agreement between the leaders of the two main parties either on the Cabinet Mission plan, or on any other plan that would preserve the unity of India.

The only alternative is partition. But when the representatives of one community demanded the partition of India, the representatives of another community used the same arguments for demanding the partition of those Provinces which contain large minorities. I am opposed to the partition of those Provinces, just as I am to the partition of India herself, and for the same basic reasons; and I did not feel that I could recommend that His Majesty's Government should take upon themselves the responsibility of deciding on the partition either of India or of any of her provinces. I therefore re-commended to His Majesty's Government that this decision should rest with the people of India; and the statement that will shortly be read out explains how the people of India, through their elected representatives, will decide for themselves whether there is to be a union of India, or whether India is to be divided into two, or possibly more, separate and fully independent sovereign states.

As we are leaving in June 1948, and as the prospect of implementing full partition by then is already very remote, I reluctantly had to abandon the idea of a plebiscite. The next approach has appeared to me to be the use of the Legislatures of the Provinces in conjunction with the representatives that they have elected for the Constituent Assembly; for the latter are based on the Cabinet Mission rule of one per million of population recorded in the 1941 census, whereas in the Provincial Legislatures weightage has been given to the minorities in allotting them additional seats. It therefore appears to me that the fairest compromise between a complete plebiscite and merely taking the views of the leaders and their Working Committees, lies in placing the matter firmly on the Provinces themselves to decide.

The plan may not be perfect; but like all plans, its success will depend on the spirit of goodwill with which it is put into execution. The leaders of the main parties have accepted it, and have given me their assurance that they will do their utmost to make it work. It is up to all of you to help them.

If the transfer of power by June 1948 is to be effected in a peaceful and orderly manner, every single one of us must bend all his efforts to the task. There is no time for bickering, much less for the continuation in any shape or form of the disorders and lawlessness of the past few months. I was shocked on my return here to find the great deterioration in communal relations that had taken place since my last visit to India less than a year ago. So much bitterness, mistrust and hatred appear to have grown up in this short time; and this has been the greatest single disappointing factor that has confronted me. But the inspiring appeal of Mr. Gandhi and Mr. Jinnah has raised fresh hopes in the

The Swearing-in Ceremony, 24 March 1947. Document 8.

Mr Gandhi and Lord Mountbatten, 1 April 1947.   Document 47.

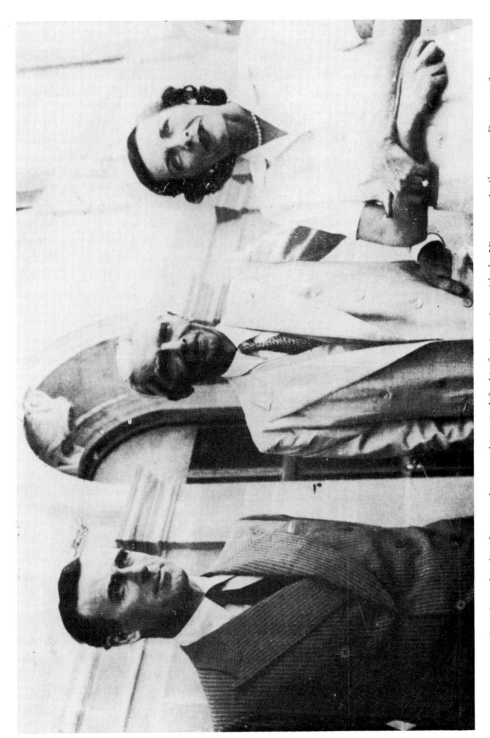

Mr Jinnah with Lord and Lady Mountbatten on his arrival for his first interview with the Viceroy, 5 April 1947. Document 84.

The jirga at Landi Kotal, 29 April 1947. Sir Olaf Caroe is seated on the right of Lord Mountbatten.   Document 276, para. 17.

hearts of all men and women of goodwill. In the meantime, I am determined—and in this determination I am fully supported by the members of my Government—that I will use every means at my command to ensure that the people of this country can go about their daily tasks unmolested.

Depending on how the Provinces vote, the present Armed Forces may have to be divided into two or even more separate entities. This is under investigation by the Defence Committee and the difficulties of replacing the 12,000 British Officers by Indian Officers by the end of June 1948 are such that I do not believe that, on top of this, it will be possible to get very far with any partition of the forces before this date. All parties are therefore agreed on the need to keep the present Armed Forces as a single force until plans for their orderly separation can be put into operation. I have asked the Commander-in-Chief to broadcast tomorrow and to explain the exact position to you; this evening, Pandit Nehru and Mr. Jinnah will say a few words to you when I have finished.

The statement which His Majesty's Government have authorised me to make on their behalf will now be read to you. I promise you that, whichever way the decision of the Indian people may go, I and all my British colleagues, who are due to remain in India until June 1948, will do everything in our power to implement what the Provinces decide. I am confident that every man and woman of goodwill in India will do the same.

277

Sir D. Monteath to Sir T. Shone

L/PO/12/12 ff 56–7

PERSONAL   INDIA OFFICE, *1 May 1947*

My dear Shone,

You were good enough to send me a copy of your confidential letter of the 15th March to Norman Brook[1] about the part played by the India Office in the supply of material to the publicity organisation under your control. I do not think that there is much that I can add to Brook's reply of the 16th April;[2] for it can hardly be letting you into a secret to disclose that that letter was the fruit of close collaboration between us—an inevitable consequence of the present makeshift distribution in Whitehall of the responsibility for conducting business with the High Commissioner in India.

Brook's letter will show you that we in the India Office did our best to resist the perpetration of the breach in the wall of camouflage erected here to

[1] and [2] L/PO/12/12.

conceal the hand of the India Office;[3] for we are very conscious that—as we believe without any justification—the name of the India Office stinks in political Indian nostrils; and, knowing this, the last thing we should wish is, by revealing our part in affairs, to add in any way to the pitfalls through which you have to tread so delicate a way. In all my time in the India Office it has never been possible to convince Indians in India who possess a nationalist and particularly a Congress outlook that the officials in it are other than "die-hard", resisting to the utmost of their ability any step forward by India towards self-government or any relaxation of the control of Indian affairs from White-hall. Possibly influenced by the degree of authority that officials do exercise in India, they fail to recognise that the officials in the India Office can do no more than carry out the policy of the Government of the day and they have always failed to recognise that the role of the Secretary of State for India, and his official satellites, as the heirs at law of the Board of Control set up by Parliament to restrain the freedom enjoyed by the East India Company, has always been that of the protector of India's interests against other claimants. There have been lapses no doubt; but I can in my own experience remember many cases in which the former Secretary of State in Council has successfully resisted proposals by the Foreign Office, the Treasury, the War Office and other Departments and even the whole Government for the expenditure of Indian monies on purposes which he and his Council regarded as unnecessary from the point of view of India's interests. It would be of no use at this time of day to attempt to correct Indian misunderstandings of the past; all that might conceivably be possible, by repetition of the point in casual conversation, is that the India Office as such does not dictate policy but carries out to the best of its ability the policy of H.M.G. towards India, and that, in so far as the present policy of H.M.G. is to release its hold on the reins wholly into India's hands, our endeavours are to effect this in such a way that the reins will not fall and trip India's feet.

In connection with publicity about India—apart from publicity in India about the United Kingdom which is another matter and no concern of the Indian authorities—as in respect of other functions which the India Office has for years past been conducting on behalf of India, our efforts are all directed to making them over to the High Commissioner as rapidly as is possible consistently with the avoidance of confusion. That we are hampered in the performance of this by the inadequacy of staff and other arrangements at India House is our misfortune and not our fault; the cause of the fault we know largely to lie in domestic controversies in India which we cannot remedy; but in regard to publicity in particular, I think that Sudhir Ghosh himself would freely admit that Joyce and his Department are affording, without any reservation, all the facilities required to enable the former to take over full responsibility.

We do fully recognise the delicacy of your position; I am sure that you fully recognise the embarrassments of ours. We are now fairly well hardened and recognise that we shall probably have to continue to suffer under them so long as the India Office exists under that name. It would be unfortunate if as a result of the absorption—as is quite possible—of erstwhile India Office personnel into whatever Department conducts the relations of the U.K. with India, any of the traditional antipathy were to pass with them to it.

If you think for this reason that it would be worth attempting, not as a set task but in an incidental way as opportunity occurs, would it be possible in the improved atmosphere created by the declaration of 20th February and, as I understand, by the personality and personal actions of the present Viceroy to get it across gradually that, anachronism though it may be and *in articulo mortis*, the India Office is not really quite as bad as it is painted? There are, I know, plenty of Indians—those who have penetrated its portals—who do recognise the India Office and its inhabitants as thoroughly friendly to India's advancement; unfortunately these, so to say, enlightened persons have a small place in the ranks of those who at present govern India's destinies.[4]

Yours sincerely,
D. T. MONTEATH

[3] In his letter of 15 March Sir T. Shone drew attention to the repercussions which might follow an answer Mr Henderson had given in Parliament on 10 March about the work of the Public Relations Department of the India Office. In this Mr Henderson said that one function of the Department was to supply the U.K. High Commissioner in India with material regarding developments in the United Kingdom and also to provide guidance on publicity.

In his reply of 16 April Sir Norman Brook agreed that such repercussions would have been avoided had Sir T. Shone's proposal been followed and the cost of the High Commissioner's Publicity Staff been placed on the Treasury Vote. Sir Norman Brook explained the administrative reasons why this course was not followed and acknowledged that the India Office had strongly supported Sir T. Shone's view at the time.

[4] Sir T. Shone sent a lengthy acknowledgement to this letter on 13 May. He said that as regards the India Office they were doing their best to create a better understanding amongst people in India, on the lines suggested in Sir D. Monteath's letter. *Ibid.*

278

Rear-Admiral Viscount Mountbatten of Burma to the Earl of Listowel

Telegram, Mountbatten Papers. Official Correspondence
Files: Transfer of Power, Procedure for determining Authorities to which
Power is to be demitted, Part (1)

MOST IMMEDIATE   NEW DELHI, *1 May 1947, 7.30 pm*
SECRET   *Received: 1 May, 6.50 pm*
954–S.   You will have gathered from my Personal Reports that I consider it imperative that a decision as to whom we are to demit power must be taken within a very short time.

2. I propose to hold a final conference commencing on or about 20th May in Delhi. I should like to be in a position to send out preliminary invitations by 10th May so that Working Committees can be summoned in time.

3. My determination is that this should bring things to a head. If I can get no sort of compromise on the basis of the Cabinet Mission's plan I propose to lay before the Conference the Statement in my immediately succeeding telegram, which Ismay will discuss fully with you on his arrival on 5th May.

279

Rear-Admiral Viscount Mountbatten of Burma to the Earl of Listowel

Telegram, Mountbatten Papers. Official Correspondence
Files: Transfer of Power, Procedure for determining Authorities to which
Power is to be demitted, Part (1)

MOST IMMEDIATE   NEW DELHI, *1 May 1947, 9.15 pm*
SECRET   *Received: 2 May, 2.50 am*
955–S. Following is the text of the announcement referred to in my immediately preceding telegram. *Begins.*

PART I—INTRODUCTION
[There follows the text of paras. 1–4 of No. 260, Appendix C.]

PART II—ARRANGEMENTS FOR THE DEMISSION OF POWER
[There follows the text of paras. 5–6 of No. 260. Appendix C.]

Procedure for Bengal, Punjab, Assam, NWFP, and Sind.

Preliminary steps.

7. For the other Provinces, in some of which there have been insistent demands for Partition, the following preliminary arrangements will be necessary.

(a) In Bengal, the Legislative Assembly (excluding European members) will be asked to sit in two parts, one representing the Muslim majority districts and the other the rest of the Province.

(b) In the Punjab, where the position of the Sikhs presents particular difficulty, the Legislative Assembly (excluding European members) will be divided as in Bengal, into two parts representing Muslim majority districts and other districts respectively.

(c) In Assam, the members of the Legislative Assembly, (excluding European members), elected from territorial constituencies included in the Sylhet District will be asked to sit separately.

(d) In the N.W.F.P. a general election will be held under Section 93 Government.

In determining the population of districts the 1941 census figures will be taken as authoritative.

Formation of Constituent Assemblies.

8. Thereafter the Legislative Assembly of Sind (excluding the European members), the newly-elected Legislative Assembly of the N.W.F.P., and the two parts of the Legislative assemblies of Bengal, the Punjab and Assam will elect representatives on the principle laid down in the Cabinet Mission's statement of the 16th May, 1946.

9. The numbers to be elected would be:—

PROVINCE	GENERAL	MUSLIMS	SIKHS	TOTAL
West Punjab	3	12	2	17
East Punjab	6	4	2	12
West Bengal	15	4	—	19
East Bengal	12	29	—	41
Assam *less* Sylhet	6	1	—	7
Sylhet District	1	2	—	3
Sind	1	3	—	4
N.W.F.P.	—	3	—	3

Vote on partition.

10. The representatives so elected of West Bengal and East Bengal, sitting separately, will vote as to whether or not their Province should be divided. A majority vote of either body in favour of Partition will decide the issue. A similar procedure will be followed in regard to the Punjab and Assam.

Note:—There may be a demand for a preliminary joint meeting of the representatives of both halves of the Punjab or Bengal to consider whether, if the Province remains united, it should enter a joint Constituent Assembly with other Provinces or remain independent. It will be open to either Governor to summon such a joint meeting if he considers it advisable.

11. Immediately thereafter the representatives of the Provinces or half Provinces (dependent on the decision in paragraph 10 above) of the Punjab and Bengal will decide whether, on behalf of the areas which they represent, they wish:—

    (*a*) to join the existing Constituent Assembly or

    (*b*) to group together in one or more Constituent Assemblies, or

    (*c*) to stand out independently and act as their own Constituent Assembly.

12. If, as a result of these votes, Bengal is partitioned, the representatives of Sylhet will sit separately and decide whether

    (*a*) Sylhet should remain part of Assam, or

    (*b*) they should join the Constituent Assembly of East Bengal with a view to Sylhet being incorporated in that half Province.

13. The representatives of Assam (with or without Sylhet, depending on the decision in paragraph 12 above) and of Sind and the N.W.F.P. will decide whether, on behalf of the areas which they represent, they wish

    (*a*) to join the existing Constituent Assembly, or

    (*b*) to join any other group of Provinces, or half Provinces, that may form a new Constituent Assembly, or

    (*c*) to stand out independently and act as their own Constituent Assembly.

14. In order that the successor authority or authorities may have as much time as possible to prepare themselves to receive power, it is essential that all the above processes should be completed without undue delay.

Baluchistan

15. In British Baluchistan the members of the Shahi Jirga (other than those members who are nominated as Sardars of Kalat State) and the non-official members of the Quetta Municipality will meet to decide the issues in paragraph 11 above. The meeting will also elect a representative to attend the Constituent Assembly selected.

Framing of
constitutions

16. The Constituent Assembly or Assemblies will then proceed to frame Constitutions for their respective territories, and will in due course, elect Executives to whom power will be demitted when the time comes.

Joint
consultation on
common subjects.

17. The administrative consequences of partition are complex and considerable. Accordingly, the Constituent Assemblies, if more than one, should also create machinery for joint consultation among themselves on matters of common concern, particularly Defence, and for the negotiation of agreements in respect of these matters.

PART III—THE TRIBES OF THE NORTH WEST FRONTIER

18. As soon as the successor Authorities have been determined, it will be for them to negotiate fresh agreements with the tribes of the North West Frontier of India.

PART IV—THE STATES

19. His Majesty's Government wish to make it clear that the decisions announced above relate only to British India and that their policy towards the Indian States remains unchanged. When paramountcy lapses, all the rights surrendered by the States to the paramount power will return to the States. They are free to arrange by negotiation with those parts of British India to which power will be demitted whatever measure of association they consider to be in the best interests of their people.

PART V—FURTHER ANNOUNCEMENTS BY THE GOVERNOR-GENERAL

20. The Governor-General will, from time to time, make such further announcements as may be necessary, in regard to procedure or any other matter, for the carrying out of the above arrangements. *Ends.*

280

Rear-Admiral Viscount Mountbatten of Burma to Sir F. Burrows (Bengal)

*Mountbatten Papers. Official Correspondence Files: Bengal
Partition of, Part I(b)*

No. 592/92   *2 May 1947*

My dear Burrows,

I feel I must write and tell you how grateful I am to you for having come up to see me in spite of the parlous state of your health, but it made all the difference to me to have the opportunity of a good talk with you, and to feel that we are now working on common ground about the future of Bengal.

You pointed out to me that Eastern Bengal would be in a bad way after Partition because all the jute factories were located in Calcutta in Western Bengal. It has since occurred to me that Calcutta could be completely huffed by Eastern Bengal if approaches were made at once to the various jute factories (most of which are in British hands and, I believe, controlled from Dundee) to transfer their machinery to a suitable location in Eastern Bengal so that the jute and the factories would be in the same half Province.

This would be such a serious matter for Calcutta that if it could be converted into a live threat by preliminary negotiations being started and the news being allowed to "leak" I feel it might well influence the Hindus to accept independent unity rather than Partition.

This is only one of many schemes that could be thought out to frighten off those who wish Partition. Another alternative would be to insist on a general election on the electoral roll, so that the view of the full electorate could be obtained.

I would be grateful for your early remarks on this proposal under the following heads:—

a) desirability
b) feasibility
c) risk of riots during election
d) additional delay likely to be caused before decision is known
e) any other points

I am quite certain in my own mind that if Suhrawardy can be persuaded to form a Coalition Government and offer joint electorates to the non-Muslim communities you will be half-way home in keeping Bengal unified.

I told Jinnah and Liaquat Ali Khan today, in confidence, that you were strongly in favour of a unified Bengal and had agreed that this could only be achieved if they were allowed to be independent. I explained to them my idea of allowing the vote of independence to be taken first, and they both appeared

to be in complete agreement that this was the best course for the future prosperity of Bengal. I somehow feel you will pull this off, and the "outside chance"
will prove a very reasonable bet after all.[1]

Yours sincerely
MOUNTBATTEN OF BURMA

Please telegraph your reply to (a) and (c).

[1] In tel. 972–S of 3 May Lord Mountbatten informed Sir F. Burrows that, since writing this letter, he
had seen K.S. Roy, and transmitted the full text of his interview note (see No. 292). Mountbatten
Papers, Official Correspondence Files: Bengal, Partition of, Part I(b).

281

Mr S. P. Mookerjee to Rear-Admiral Viscount Mountbatten of Burma (Extract)

*Mountbatten Papers. Official Correspondence Files: Bengal, Partition of,
Part I(b)*

c/o DIRECTOR, IMPERIAL AGRICULTURAL
RESEARCH INSTITUTE, NEW DELHI,
2 May 1947

The views I am expressing in this letter are shared by a very large section of
Hindus not only in Bengal but in other parts of India and I hope Your Excellency
will give due consideration to them.

We are definitely opposed to Pakisthan. We say this not merely from the
point of view of Hindus but in the interest of India as a whole. The Constituent
Assembly today represents every province in British India and also a number of
important Indian States. One Moslem majority province namely N.W.F.
Province is represented by a majority of its members. The Muslim members
belonging to Bengal, Sind and the Punjab are no doubt absent and they are
represented only by the Sikh and Hindu members. This obstructionist attitude
on the part of the Moslem League should not weigh with H.M.G. at all.
If H.M.G. can take courage in both hands and announce that it is not going
to depart from the main provisions of the Cabinet Mission scheme, the
situation will at once change. If it is further announced that the Constituent
Assembly will be accepted as the first Provisional Parliament of Free India and
the transfer of power will be made to a Provisional Government to be elected
by the Constituent Assembly on the basis of proportionate representation, the
Moslem League is bound to alter its present attitude of negation and obstruction and take its legitimate part in the administration of the country.

Whether division of India takes place or not, it is essential that the Punjab
and Bengal should be partitioned. I shall not say anything about the Punjab in

my letter as her representatives must have placed full facts before you already. I shall deal with Bengal only.

The reasons why Bengal should be partitioned in any case are as follows:—

1. Bengal's area is about 78,000 square miles and her population is more than 60 millions. Purely from administrative standpoint, creation of two provinces out of the existing boundaries of Bengal is not only possible but eminently desirable. Bengal today is admittedly one of the worst administered provinces in British India.

2. Bengal Hindus have suffered terribly during the last ten years on account of communal misrule and mal-administration. In spite of their immense contribution towards the development of the province, they have no voice in its administration. Protection of Muslim interests is not the only minority problem in India. If ever an impartial survey is made of Bengal's administration during the last ten years, it will appear that Hindus have suffered not only on account of communal riots and disturbances but in every sphere of national activities, educational, economic, political and even religious.

3. Fortunately for Bengal the two major communities live in two compact zones and a separation is rendered easier on this account. Hindu Bengal will have about 35,000 square miles with a population of about 24 millions. This will be equal to, and even larger than, some of the existing provincial units in India and also some States in Europe and America.

4. More than two-thirds of the Hindu population including about 4.5 millions out of 7.6 millions of the scheduled castes will live within Hindu Bengal. This will give an opportunity to both major communities to develop themselves according to their best ability and traditions and the constant ran-cour and strife between one community and another will gradually disappear. Both major communities in the two provinces are soon bound to realise that in their own mutual interest, the minority community in the two respective provinces must be duly protected.

Both the Provinces should remain within the Union of India. If however India is to be divided on communal consideration, partition of Bengal becomes an immediate necessity and the above arguments are strengthened by the following additional ones:—

1. Mr. Jinnah's claim for Pakisthan is based on the theory that Hindus and Muslims are two separate nations and Muslims must have their own homeland and their own State. That being so, Hindus in Bengal who constitute about 26 millions of people may well demand that they must not be compelled to live within the Moslem State and the area where they predominate should be cut off, so that the province thus created may link itself up with the Hindusthan Union. This demand Mr. Jinnah can never resist for, as the Cabinet Mission

pointed out in its scheme of May, 16, the same logic and arguments applicable to Pakisthan apply also to partition of Bengal.

2. If Muslims being 24 percent of India's population constitute themselves into such a formidable minority that their demand for a separate homeland and State becomes irresistible, surely 45 percent of Bengal's Hindu population is a sufficiently large minority which cannot be coerced into living within the Pakisthan State against the will of the people.

3. It is said that if once Bengal and the Punjab are partitioned, the other portions of India have also to be partitioned on similar consideration. This is purely academic. If there are other areas in India which are large enough to be constituted into separate provinces on communal consideration, their claim has to be justified on merits. Surely the existence of small pockets here and there cannot justify the creation of new provinces. Even in Eastern Bengal, there will be numerous towns with majority Hindu population and also several Hindu pockets; but we are not going to claim that each of them is to be converted into a provincial unit. It is only because the Hindu majority areas, contiguous in character, are large enough to form into a separate province that we are justified in putting forward our claim for partition.

4. Mr. Jinnah speaks of transfer of population and property. If an undivided Bengal is thrown into Pakisthan, we have to transfer about 26 millions of Hindus which is next to impossible. On the other hand if Bengal is partitioned, the question of transfer will be comparatively easier. It will affect about nine millions Hindus in Muslim Bengal and six millions Moslems in Hindu Bengal.

5. There is some loose talk of a sovereign undivided Bengal. We do not understand its significance at all nor do we support it in any way. This will give us, Hindus, no relief whatsoever. Sovereign undivided Bengal will be a virtual Pakisthan. Who will frame the constitution of Sovereign Bengal? Obviously, this will be left in the hands of the majority of the Moslem Leaguers who will be guided by fanatical notions of a separate nationhood and we are not prepared to trust our fate to them. Further we do not in any case want to be cut off from the rest of India and we are not prepared to make any compromise on this issue on any consideration whatsoever.

I do hope you will give full consideration to the above points. You have come to India with an open mind and to explore the safest way to transfer power to Indian hands. By being fair to both the major communities in Bengal would it be possible for you to avoid chaos and bloodshed. Our suffering in Bengal today is indescribable. We have ceased to live under a civilized Government and the rule of law has been substituted by the rule of gangsterism. You may either decide the question of partition yourself or set up a machinery which will make it possible for the people of the area concerned to express their views. I would however emphasise, as indeed I did in course of my interview with you,[1] that it is essential that the Bengal ministry must be dissolved as soon as the question of partition is announced. To allow the ministry to continue in office may lead to disastrous consequences from which recovery will become almost impossible.

I have written to Your Excellency with utmost frankness for I honestly believe that it is a life and death question to us. Freedom is about to dawn on India and we, who constitute not a negligible number amongst the people of India and whose contributions to the growth of India's progress have been considerable, have the right to demand that in the Free India to come we must have a territory assigned to us wherein we can live without fear and enjoy the fruits of peace and freedom, without depriving the other majority community of the rightful interests in the area in which it predominates.

[1] See No. 201.

282

Lieutenant-General Sir A. Nye (Madras) to Rear-Admiral Viscount Mountbatten of Burma

R/3/1/152: ff 1B-3

PRIVATE AND SECRET AND PERSONAL   GOVERNOR'S CAMP,
                                                  GUINDY, *2 May 1947*

My dear Dickie,

In the published statements of the British Government we have said that India is at liberty to choose whether she will remain within the British Commonwealth or out of it, but the Prime Minister has usually added that he hopes she will decide to stay in. I notice that Mr. Alexander has made a few speeches recently much on the same lines, and when I was in Delhi in the middle of April I got the general impression that whilst nobody had any intention of proposing to India that she should remain in the Commonwealth, nevertheless if she of her own free will suggested that she should do so, that we would be prepared to say "yes." In short, there seems to be a tacit assumption that it would be, if not in our own interests, at any rate to the mutual benefit of both countries, for India to remain within the Empire.

I have given a good deal of thought to this subject and I have very grave doubts if this tacit assumption is justified. I wonder if anyone has really made a cold, detached, analytical examination of the subject, whether, for example, the Chiefs of Staff have really considered what is involved, whether our own Cabinet has really weighed up the pros and cons? I very much doubt it.

It seems to me that in this changing world strategy is changing, and we must no longer ally ourselves to what in the past may well have been principles, but what today are mere shibboleths. We must align our thought to the changes which are taking place and, in particular, to the shrinking of our Empire, and we must have regard to the realities of the world situation as it confronts us to-day, or rather will confront us to-morrow.

No informed person can dispute that the only real potential danger to world peace in the next few decades comes from Russia. I use the word "potential" because I am no alarmist and I do not think Russia is likely to go to war during, say, the next ten years. If Russia is a threat to the world in general, placed where she is geographically, she is a threat to India in particular, in fact in the foreseeable future, I think it fair to say that the only real threat to India is from Russia.

There has been so much talk about the gallantry of the Indian troops and the leadership which they have shown that there is a danger of people assuming that it follows that, given a little time, the Indian armed forces will be very strong. But the military strength of any country is relative, i.e., relative to the threat which confronts it, and on that basis India (vast though its territory, enormous though its numbers, brave though its people) will be unquestionably the weakest military country in the world. Putting aside its problems of turning captains into majors-general overnight and ignorant coolies into highly qualified technicians, it has no scientific organisation nor the knowledge that goes with it. It has no research organisation nor people qualified to undertake research. I doubt indeed if it will be able to provide the money for such an organisation. It is, therefore, lacking in the very first requirement for any modern war. Secondly, its industrial potential is and will be for a very long time virtually non-existent. It will therefore be quite incapable of maintaining armed forces in action. Indeed, in brief, one may say that of all the numerous requirements which go to make for military efficiency, India will possess but one, i.e., the courage of its people, and this unfortunate country finds itself on the borders of Russia, the strongest military power in the world. If Russia chose to invade India, it would virtually be the process of taking toffee from a child. These poor people would in effect go forth to battle equipped with a loin cloth and a spear.

And if it becomes necessary to introduce some form of Pakistan, the situation of Hindustan is (if indeed that is possible) even more powerless than that of a unified India. Not only would the existing defence forces be truncated, but the natural frontiers of India (whether N.W.F.P. belongs to Hindustan or Pakistan) would be in the hands of a potentially hostile State who could quietly penetrate into the plains of India and place themselves in times of peace in a perfect "jumping off position".

In past wars India has contributed man-power and materials of war, but in a new war where an invader will move with such rapidity, what hope is there of India being able to contribute anything to the common good?

There is one other aspect which merits some consideration. Our strategic interest is not so much that we ourselves as an Empire should possess this, that or the other country, but that we should deny to our potential enemies territory from which they could threaten our sea communications. An enemy in possession of India could undoubtedly threaten our communications, but we have to face cold hard facts. There is nothing that we could do to prevent Russia occupying India if indeed Russia wishes to do so, and India remaining within the Empire will not help one iota.

Surely it follows that if we take India into the British Commonwealth of Nations, we are taking, at least from the defence point of view, an ailing child who has literally nothing whatever to offer but who, on the other hand, constitutes a grave liability. We have seen two major wars in our lifetime. The one thing that our Empire needs is the means to recuperate from these awful losses—peace. How can we contemplate the risk of being involved in another war, by taking on this grave liability for the defence of India?

I have little doubt that amongst the realists in this country, these facts are beginning to be recognised, perhaps not in their stark reality, but sufficiently for the leaders to ponder and ask themselves whether there is a prospect of India achieving independence to-day and losing it to-morrow. I feel quite sure that a man like Jawaharlal Nehru, an interesting combination of a clear-headed realist and a not-so-clear-headed idealist, must be well aware of this menace which is hanging over this country. It must be quite apparent to him that the possibilities ahead of India are simply immense if only she can get security. I have little doubt that despite his published statements, many of which are bitterly anti-British, in fact he has many sentimental, cultural and emotional ties with our country and he realises, indeed he cannot fail to realise, the great benefits which would accrue to India if she can remain in the Commonwealth, and indeed his only problem is how this could be done, consistent with some of the past statements of Congress.

It seems to me that there is, therefore, a distinct possibility in the near future that we may be faced with a request for India not to take its place formally as a member of the British Commonwealth, but for proposals to be put up which in effect would guarantee India all those advantages which accrue to members of the British Commonwealth, whilst at the same time preserving for her some form of independence. In other words, we may be asked to make a bargain. From what I have said it is evident that in my view the responsibility which we may be asked to undertake is so heavy, and its potentialities so grave, that it may well jeopardise the safety of our Empire. If we are to be asked to undertake such risks, surely we must know what India has to offer in return? I have discussed this question with many intelligent Indians and the only answer I have ever received is, "We have trade to offer". But a closer examination will show that such a claim simply cannot hold water. Except for those ties of race, of affection and of loyalty to the Crown, and for certain preferences of *mutual* benefit to those concerned, we get no specific trade advantages with countries merely because they are within the Empire. Trade follows certain natural channels. It is unquestionably true that it is of vital importance to us to be able to find a wide and increasing market for our goods in India. It is equally true that if India is to live, let alone develop, she must import the type of goods which we provide. It is true she can import them from countries other than ours, but I have little doubt that for a variety of reasons too detailed to specify, a large proportion of India's trade will continue to be done with England, and if there was any unwillingness on her part to do so, the existence of the sterling balances would determine matters for very many years to come. It follows, therefore, quite clearly that India has nothing whatever to offer in exchange for any help we may be asked to give in the way of defence obligations. In the foreseeable future, India cannot conceivably be anything other than a weakness and an anxiety to other members of our Commonwealth.

I think that people like you and me who have recently come to India not only with no prejudice against this country but with a passionate desire to do all we can to atone for the mistakes we have made (whilst being justly proud of our achievements) may be perhaps a little inclined to lose our judgment. We are so anxious to go more than half way to meet our Indian friends, indeed as the Americans say, "To lean over backwards," so anxious to hold out a helping hand wherever we can, that we run the risk of being perhaps a little impetuous. I would beg of you to restrain your boundless enthusiasm and, in an endeavour to do what is best for this country, not to overlook what is good for our own Commonwealth.

Yours ever,

ARCHIE NYE

283

Record of Interview between Rear-Admiral Viscount Mountbatten of Burma and Mr Chundrigar

Mountbatten Papers. Viceroy's Interview No. 107

TOP SECRET   *2 May 1947, 11.15 am–12 noon*

I gave Mr Chundrigar a brief review of my trip to the N.W.F.P. and the Punjab, and a rough outline of the plan that Lord Ismay was taking home.

Mr Chundrigar asked me whether I had formed the impression that fresh elections should be held in the N.W.F.P.

I told him that I was not prepared to give him my impressions on this point while the civil disobedience movement leading to violence was still in full swing in that Province. I said that so long as that movement continued there would in no circumstances be fresh elections, and that if the movement gathered momentum I would draft up fresh troops and fight it; that I would never yield to violence; and that if the Muslim League had not completely stopped all violence on the frontier before I left on the transfer of power, I should hand the Province over to the Congress Government.

We then discussed the partition of Bengal, at the mere proposal of which he seemed deeply distressed; since he pointed out that East Bengal could not live by itself. I told him that that was no particular concern of mine, since I was intensely opposed to partition in any case and would only grant it on the express request of the people of the Provinces themselves. I did tell him that we were going to allow a vote to be taken first on whether Bengal, if it remained united, should be independent, or go to Pakistan, or to Hindustan; and that this should give Suhrawardy a chance of forming a coalition government, granting joint electorates, and holding Bengal together.

He agreed that this was the ideal solution, but was afraid that if it were left to the Constituent Assembly representatives to vote on partition, those representatives were very few and completely in the hands of Congress, and would be bound to vote for partition. He therefore urged that a referendum on partition should be taken by all those on the electoral roll of Bengal being allowed to vote on this issue.

I told him that I would give his proposal my serious consideration, but would certainly not carry it out if it (a) unduly delayed a decision on the transfer of power, or (b) was likely to cause any rioting or bloodshed.

Mr Chundrigar then asked me why I would not let Mamdot form a ministry in the Punjab, since he had a majority in the Assembly. He called upon me to be consistent and to face up to the Sikh threat of violence in the Punjab even as I was facing up to the League threat of violence in N.W.F.P.

I denied that this was a parallel case, since the previous Unionist Ministry had been thrown out through Muslim League violence and that was why we were in Section 93 in that Province. I said I had no intention of turning over government to a one-party Ministry for the last three or four weeks before a decision was taken about the transfer of power in the Punjab; but I would not mind turning it over to a coalition ministry.

I told him that if the Sikhs made trouble it was my intention to warn them that they would have to fight the army and air force, in exactly the same way as the Muslim League would be faced with the army and air force if they made any further trouble. I told him that I was, above everything else, determined to have law and order in this country, and that I was going to make aggression completely unprofitable. Not only would I put down any further violence by violence; I would bring down the full might of the Air force, Armoured Corps and all modern instruments of war against the aggressors, and would not hesitate to impose proscriptive bombing against their property; since the first requirement was peace, and if I could not have it by cooperation, then I would have it by making it completely disastrous for anyone who broke the peace.

284

Record of Interview between Rear-Admiral Viscount Mountbatten of Burma and Mr O. P. Ramaswami Reddiar

Mountbatten Papers. Viceroy's Interview No. 108

TOP SECRET   *2 May 1947, 12 noon–12.45 pm*

He brought with him his Secretary, and we had a general discussion on the problems of the transfer of power. I gave him a very rough outline of my scheme, stressing that my aim was still the Cabinet Mission plan.

He kept on insisting that the British had a responsibility to keep law and order in India, not only until June 1948, but he tried to involve me by saying that we owed responsibility to India to see that they were properly looked after in the future.

I made it quite clear that that was entirely up to Indians themselves, and that if they wished to leave the Commonwealth, which I quite understood, they were at liberty to do so and thus absolve us from any further responsibility. He explained the emotional necessity for breaking clear of the Empire after having been "slaves" for so long; and I said nobody denied them this right; in fact it seemed to me that there were strong emotional reasons why Indians would wish to leave the Commonwealth; though they would stand very materially to lose by doing so. Conversely, I thought there were strong emotional reasons why the British people would be glad to see them remain within the Commonwealth, although materially I thought they would lose by such a decision, since they would be involved in giving much more than they would get out of India's continuance in the Empire.

I pointed out that for defence purposes India would not be even a third-class power, and that it would be more of a liability than of material advantage to have them in the Commonwealth. I told him that in any case, no Britisher would ever suggest that they should join the Commonwealth. If they wanted to remain within it, then it was for them to say so.

He then reiterated his theory that the British had a moral responsibility for the future of India extending far beyond June 1948. He said that I was the only person who could bring peace between the two Indias. I told him that that was ridiculous. I said "One can introduce a couple to each other and hope for the best. But if they take a violent dislike to one another, it is no good tucking them off into bed and hoping that the honeymoon will be a great success."

This went very well with him, and he admitted the truth of the parallel.

His Secretary then chipped in with the remark that the British had become very popular during the last year, and how sorry everybody was going to be to lose them.

I replied "Yes, now that the British are going, the only thing that kept the Hindus and Muslims together is being removed; since it was a common hatred of the British that prevented you hating each other; the fact that we are going now has left you nothing but to hate each other."

The Prime Minister continued to the bitter end to harp on the responsibility of the British extending beyond June 1948, and as I really could not understand what he was leading up to, I urged that he should talk it over with Sir Archibald Nye when he saw him again.

285

Record of Interview between Rear-Admiral Viscount Mountbatten of Burma and Mr Sri Krishna Sinha

Mountbatten Papers. Viceroy's Interview No. 111

2 May 1947

After a few social remarks about Bihar and enquiries after the Governor I told him I was most distressed that he had allowed his police force to become so unreliable that they had ended by mutinying. I asked him why he had not arrested Ramanand Tewari when he first began stirring up trouble among the police. To this he replied that he had never been able to get any evidence, except a pamphlet which his Legal Department said constituted no evidence. He had given instructions that if he were caught inciting the police to mutiny he was to be arrested and, in fact, this had never come about.

2. He said his whole police force had been very corrupt and rotten, but that every effort was now being made to pull it together.

3. I told him I was glad to hear of this as he could not expect to run the Province on the Army.

4. I told him I had been distressed to hear he was starting a private army of his own. He expressed great horror at this and hotly denied any such intention. I told him I was referring to his anti-corruption force and he explained that they were a perfectly legal Government force specially raised because the police

were so untrustworthy in the case of corruption. I asked him why he had selected 297 ex-I.N.A. members out of a total of 333; why he had imported the vast majority from outside the Province and why he had armed such an undisciplined rabble. He seemed very surprised that I knew these figures and explained that they had deliberatly enlisted ex-soldiers in order to have well disciplined men.

5. I am afraid I laughed aloud at that and gave him a description of what the I.N.A. were like in Burma. I told him that when one saw an I.N.A. brigade on the Intelligence map we rated it at about the equivalent of a Japanese Company, and sometimes disregarded it altogether. I admitted that some men might have joined for high minded political reasons, but the vast majority had joined for convenience to avoid Japanese Prison Camps.

6. I said it was not surprising that they had, therefore, killed Professor Abdul Bari. Mr. Sinha said that this had come as a great shock to his Government. I asked him how he accounted for this, observing that the Governor had repeatedly warned him that this was bound to happen.

7. I advised him finally to disband his private armies, build up a strong well disciplined police force, to dispense with the aid of the regular Army as soon as possible, to take a firm line with subversive activities and generally to show he meant to govern Bihar.

8. I am afraid I gave him a bit of a lecture, but over the social atmosphere of luncheon I hope it did not appear to be too tough.

286

Record of Interview between Rear-Admiral Viscount Mountbatten of Burma and Sir C. P. Ramaswami Aiyer

Mountbatten Papers. Viceroy's Interview No. 110

2 May 1947

I saw him from 6 p.m. to 7 p.m. Sir C. P. poured out his heart about the Nehru statement at the People's States Conference[1] and I gave him the same reply as I have given to the Nawab of Bhopal.[2]

2. His main point, however, was that since the Constituent Assembly was proposing to give powers to the centre to raise income tax, death duties, etc. etc., and generally interfere with the administration of any unit which joined with the centre he had advised his Maharaja not to join up with the group centre at all. If the Cabinet Mission Plan by some miracle were still to be

[1] See No. 181, note 2.　　[2] See No. 225.

accepted Travancore would unreservedly join the Union, but if Hindustan and Pakistan were to emerge he had such close interests with both that he felt it would be wrong to join either.

3. He felt Travancore could not stand on its own legs and wished to be a member of the British Commonwealth, preferably on Dominion Status, but at all events in active alliance.

4. I gave him my complete policy of membership of the Commonwealth and told him that I was opposed to any membership that did not cover all India, though I admitted that the popular demand might pass over my head to the people of the Commonwealth.

5. He strongly advised me not to continue to "carry the baby" for Congress and the Muslim League for decisions which would be bound to be unpopular later. He urged, therefore, that elections should be carried out in all Provinces to determine their desires. I told him that this was the principle that we had been working on all along, and he was delighted to hear it.

6. Although he was a Hindu he said, categorically, that the N.W.F.P. was a Congress ramp of the worst order. The two Khan brothers were racketeers paid by Congress to try and keep a 94% Muslim Province from joining Pakistan. He hoped I was not being taken in.

7. On the other hand he said that fresh elections in Sind might reveal a different line in which the Muslim League might not be returned to power.

8. He told me he had discussed most of these things with Lord Ismay before he left, and Sir Eric Mieville was present for the latter part of the conversation.

287

Record of Interview between Rear-Admiral Viscount Mountbatten of Burma and Mr Jinnah and Mr Liaquat Ali Khan[1]

Mountbatten Papers. Viceroy's Interview No. 112

TOP SECRET   *2 May 1947*
HIS EXCELLENCY started by thanking Mr Jinnah for arranging for the Muslims to come and see him during his recent visit to the N.W.F.P., and also congratulated him on the behaviour of the huge crowd of Muslims who had gathered in Cunningham Park. His Excellency said that after consulting Dr Khan Sahib he showed himself to the crowd who gave him a great reception and then dispersed without any trouble. His Excellency said that he could not too strongly put to Mr Jinnah that the latter's object was to obtain fresh elections to the N.W.F.P. before the transfer of power. Lord Ismay had left for England

that morning to explain the plan for the transfer of power to H.M.G. and included in it, as Mr Jinnah knew as he had actually read the plan, was a clause to the effect that fresh elections in the N.W.F.P. would be held. He must repeat that if violence were to continue in the province, that paragraph referring to the elections would be amended. He felt strongly that Mr Jinnah obviously would want to get the N.W.F.P. into Pakistan, and that everything therefore was to be gained by Mr Jinnah quietly calling off the movement without any announcement. His Excellency further said that, in his view, there was a clear case for fresh elections, but that in no circumstances would he yield to violence.

MR JINNAH said that he was sorry but he felt that there was some misunderstanding. He had clearly understood that an announcement about a fresh election was not to be held up until the plan was made public, which he understood would not be at any rate until the end of the month, and it would be impossible for him to control the situation for so long. He said that he had carried out what he told His Excellency he would do before the latter's visit. There was no procession; the meeting was peaceful; and those Muslims in gaol came and had an interview with the Viceroy, and now, he said, "the position is that you ask me to tell my followers not to carry on with the agitation". What could he say in reply? HIS EXCELLENCY said that he could refer to the Gandhi/Jinnah appeal, that he could say that he had seen the Viceroy who was adamant that he would not give way to duress, and that the obvious thing to do was to wait for the plan. MR JINNAH agreed that it was quite wrong to give way to force and that violence must be stopped, but that His Excellency could not control the people nor could he. He could not understand that the question of dissolution had to be delayed until after the plan was made public. HIS EXCELLENCY replied that his conscience would not allow him to yield to force in any way, and he was in great trouble with the Congress over the attitude he was taking up regarding the N.W.F.P. He did not mind that. To Jinnah's definite question "as a result of your visit to the Frontier Province are you satisfied there is a case for immediate dissolution of the Government", His Excellency gave a categorical denial "No, definitely no; any election will take place solely on the issue of Pakistan or Hindustan". The election was merely to find out whether the province should go to Pakistan or Hindustan, that it might be necessary for the fair conduct of the election to go into Section 93, and that observers for the Muslim League and Congress might have to be appointed. MR JINNAH said that if the Khan Sahib administration was allowed to continue, the Congress would provoke conditions that would cause violence and that if he were to call off the campaign he would be reduced to dust in the eyes of his followers. He could say that the campaign must be peaceful, but he had no hesitation in saying that it would not remain peaceful.

At this moment, Mr Liaquat Ali Khan joined the meeting. HIS EXCELLENCY

¹ Sir E. Mieville was also present.

then told Mr Liaquat of the general tenor of the conversation. Mr Liaquat said that he saw no chance of the movement being called off. If the Muslim League had called it off immediately after His Excellency's visit, it would be said that the League was under British orders and that Mr Jinnah counted for nothing. This was a point which HIS EXCELLENCY said had not occurred to him before and one that carried weight with him.

HIS EXCELLENCY then suggested that the League would be well advised:

(1) to insist on their leaders in the Provinces leaving the gaols. He pointed out that some of the best brains in the League Party were in prison and were perfectly free to come out but would not do so as they felt that they were embarrassing the administration more by remaining in.

(2) that Mr Jinnah should send for the League leaders here and, whilst not insisting on their calling the movement off, should suggest that they should keep it alive by holding meetings in out of the way places, and not too big meetings at that; that processions and picketing should be barred; and that incidents should be prevented which have news value and are published in all the newspapers.

Mr Jinnah said once again that so long as the present Ministry was in power he saw no hope. It all sounded all right on paper but in practice it just would not work. HIS EXCELLENCY replied that he feared that the answer to that was that it would be necessary for him to send in troops and aeroplanes which he would be forced to do if the League were determined to make trouble. MR JINNAH said that the Congress knew perfectly well that they were finished in the N.W.F.P. They were playing the game of the last gambler's throw. Their whole idea was to keep up the quarrel and bloodshed and to force the hands of the Viceroy to say that under those circumstances he could not have an election. He said that the representatives for the N.W.F.P. were arriving tonight and he frankly did not quite know what he could say to them, but it was finally left that if Mr Jinnah wished to come and see His Excellency again and proposed to bring the leaders with him, he would communicate with me, and the Viceroy promised that he would receive them.

In the course of the conversation, the Punjab situation was brought up. HIS EXCELLENCY said in reply to both Mr Jinnah's and Mr Liaquat's question as to why the Muslim League Ministry could not be formed there, that feeling is centred at the moment on the forthcoming announcement of H.M.G. The Sikhs, he thought, meant to come to terms with Pakistan. One thing that would kill such an eventuality would be a further bloodbath. If we were to go out of Section 93, he would be doing the Muslims a bad turn as the Sikhs would fight. Indeed, it would be a gross act of betrayal to the Muslim League to form a Muslim League Government in that province at the present time. HIS EXCELLENCY finished by saying that he may well have saved the Punjab for Mr Jinnah by not allowing Mamdot to form a Ministry.

As regards Bengal, HIS EXCELLENCY pointed out that the Governor was most anxious to keep Bengal together. Eastern and Western Bengal were interdependent and partition would ruin them both. His Excellency gave a short account of what was proposed in the plan for Bengal after his discussions with the Governor.

E. M.

288

Cabinet

India and Burma Committee. I.B.(47) 20th Meeting

L/P&J/10/92: ff 91–5

Those present at this Meeting held at 10 Downing Street, S.W.1, on 2 May 1947 at 4 pm were: Mr Attlee (in the Chair), Sir Stafford Cripps, Mr Alexander, Viscount Addison, the Earl of Listowel.

Also present were: Mr A. Henderson, Sir Wilfrid Eady (Items 1 and 2), Sir David Monteath, Sir William Croft; Mr S. E. V. Luke, Mr G. M. Wilson, Mr F. F. Turnbull, Mr M. J. Clauson (Secretariat)

Minute 1

Procedure for negotiation of the Treaty relating to matters arising out of the Transfer of Power

(Previous Reference: I.B.(47) 17th Meeting, Minute 2)[1]

The Committee had before them a memorandum by the Secretary of State for India (I.B.(47 45)[2] on the procedure to be followed for the negotiation of the treaty relating to matters arising out of the transfer of power.

The Committee:—

Agreed that this question should be held over for discussion with Lord Ismay.

Minute 2

Proposed Treaty with India to provide for matters arising out of the Transfer of Power

The Committee considered a memorandum by the Secretary of State for India (I.B.(47) 42)[3] on the matters arising out of the transfer of power for which provision should be made in a treaty.

In discussion of the detailed proposals contained in the paper, the following points were made:—

[1] No. 54.   [2] No. 46.   [3] No. 45.

(a) There would be no need for a separate clause recognising the new status of India. It would be sufficient to include in the recital to the treaty a reference to the Act of Parliament providing for the transfer of power.

(b) When it was publicly announced in what manner His Majesty's Government proposed to transfer their responsibilities in India, His Majesty's Government should notify the Foreign States with which they had Treaties which could only be fulfilled by virtue of their authority in India that, in the new circumstances, they could no longer be responsible for the performance of those obligations under the Treaties which could only be fulfilled by the authorities in India. This notification should in itself be adequate protection against claims by foreign Governments on His Majesty's Government. The extent to which the Government of India would assume such international obligations would be a matter for them to decide: it would be inadvisable to include any general provision on this matter in the treaty.

(c) The Committee were informed that, during the preliminary discussions on sterling balances held recently in India, the Indian representatives had not opposed the proposal that the pensionary obligations of existing Indian authorities to British subjects under contract with the Secretary of State or the British Government should be taken over by His Majesty's Government in return for a capital payment. The rough figure which had been proposed was £250 million, allowing for interest at ½ per cent.

The Committee agreed that an arrangement on these lines should be sought in connection with the settlement of sterling balances. They considered that agreement might be sought at the same time, as a matter of convenience, for a similar capital payment in discharge of pensionary obligations for British members of the subordinate Services to whom the Secretary of State had no special contractual obligation. It should not, however, be suggested that the British Government had the same degree of responsibility in their case.

(d) The Committee accepted the proposal that provision should be made in the treaty for the maintenance of the existing conditions of service and the pensionary rights of existing members of the Secretary of State's Services. They disagreed, however, with the suggestion in I.B.(47) 42 that a provision should be sought permitting Indian members of those Services to commute their pensions 100 per cent on retirement. They recalled that, in the discussions on compensation, the Interim Government had given an assurance that existing conditions of service would be maintained. In the light of this assurance and of the decision that Indian officers should not in general receive compensation on the transfer of power, they thought that there would be no justification for putting this proposal to the Interim Government.

(e) The Committee considered that provision should be made in the treaty, and not in the Constitution, for the protection of persons having contracts with the existing governmental authorities.

(f) As regards the proposals in I.B.(47) 42 for transitional provisions in the treaty, it was agreed that there would be no objection to the temporary continuance of diplomatic and consular representation of India by officers of the British Foreign Service, but that it should be left to the Government of India to raise the point. The question whether these services should be charged for could then be considered further. As regards the provision of facilities for the withdrawal of British subjects and the British Armed Forces after the transfer of power, the Committee considered that these matters should be covered in the treaty but be negotiated separately by the proposed Military Mission.[4]

The Committee:—

Endorsed the proposals contained in I.B.(47) 42, subject to the above points.

Minute 3

Question of Nationality in relation to the proposed Treaty with India providing for matters arising out of the Transfer of Power

The Committee had before them a memorandum by the Secretary of State for India (I.B.(47) 41)[5] containing proposals about the categories of British subjects who should retain their British nationality after the transfer of power, and the categories who should be given the option of retaining British nationality or becoming Indian nationals.

THE SECRETARY OF STATE FOR INDIA said he understood that the Colonial Secretary, who was in consultation with Governors, was not yet in a position to express a view on the future status of Indians in the Colonies.

In discussion the following points were raised:—

(a) The retention of British nationality by any person born, or whose father was born, in any part of His Majesty's Dominions outside India would cover the bulk of first generation Anglo-Indians. Any first generation Anglo-Indian who had been born in India might, under Indian nationality laws, also be an Indian national and so have dual nationality. The retention of British nationality by such persons might place them, and His Majesty's Government, in an invidious position but there did not seem to be any way of compulsorily depriving a person born of a British father of his British nationality.

[4] Mr Turnbull noted on the file copy with respect to this para.: 'Doubt was expressed by P. of B. of T. whether transitional Commercial Agreement was desirable.'
[5] See No. 46, note 1.

(b) It would be embarrassing for His Majesty's Government to retain as British subjects, and thereby undertake the liability of protecting, any Indian who was domiciled or resident in any part of His Majesty's Dominions. This applied particularly to Indians domiciled or resident in South Africa. It was suggested that all such persons should, on the transfer of power, lose their British nationality unless they applied within a specified time to remain British subjects.

(c) Until it was known what the future status of Burma was to be, it was difficult to decide what nationality persons of Indian origin domiciled or resident there should have. It would, however, be highly embarrassing if a large number of Indians in an independent Burma were to ask for British nationality as this would place on His Majesty's Government the liability of protecting them against the Burmese Government and would also lead to complications with the Indian Government. If Burma remained within the Commonwealth, such Indians as became Burmese citizens would, however, be British nationals. The same considerations applied to Ceylon.

(d) His Majesty's Government had no special responsibility as regards Indians domiciled or resident in foreign countries. Such persons would, of course, be at liberty to apply for British nationality, in the same way as any other alien.

The Committee:—

(1) Agreed that persons whose status as British subjects was derived otherwise than solely from their connection with India should retain their status as British nationals.

(2) Agreed (subject to consideration of the Colonial Secretary's views)[6] that Indians whose status as British subjects was derived solely from their connection with India, and who were domiciled or resident in any part of His Majesty's Dominions other than India, Burma or Ceylon, should on the transfer of power lose their British nationality unless they applied within a specified time to become British subjects.

(3) Agreed that Indians domiciled or resident in an independent Burma or Ceylon should lose their British nationality; and that, if Burma or Ceylon remain within the British Commonwealth, the question of citizenship should be a matter of direct negotiation between the Indian Government and the Government of Burma or Ceylon.

(4) Agreed that Indians resident in any foreign country should lose their British nationality.

(5) Invited the Secretary of State for India, in consultation with the Law Officers, to draft paragraphs for inclusion in the treaty on Conclusions (1) to (4) above for submission to the Committee.

(6) Agreed that the Viceroy and the United Kingdom High Comissioner in India should be consulted on the above proposals.

Minute 4

Request by Columbia Broadcasting System for a Broadcast on British Policy towards India

THE SECRETARY OF STATE FOR INDIA informed the Committee that a request had been received from the Columbia Broadcasting System for a 15-minute broadcast by the Viceroy on British policy towards India.

The Committee agreed that it would not in any event be suitable for the Viceroy to accept this request. If such a broadcast was to be given at all, it should be given by a Minister. His Majesty's Ambassador in Washington should, however, be asked in the first place whether he considered it advisable that the request should be granted and whether the size of the probable audience would justify a broadcast by a Minister.

The Committee:—

Invited the Secretary of State for India to arrange for His Majesty's Ambassador in Washington to be consulted accordingly.[7]

[6] The Colonial Office subsequently produced a memorandum which involved some modification of the conclusions reached at this meeting of the India and Burma Committee. This memorandum was sent to the India Office in July (see letter 2281/47 of 31 July from A.B. Acheson (Colonial Office) to M.J. Clauson (India Office), L/P & J/10/95: ff 45-7); but as the subject was 'not at present a live issue' the Colonial Secretary did not propose to submit a paper to the India and Burma Committee at that stage. There seem to have been no further developments of importance before the date of the transfer of power.

[7] In tel. 2695 to Foreign Office (received 9 May), Lord Inverchapel said with reference to the outcome of this discussion that he could not recommend that a Minister should broadcast at that juncture. He was accordingly informing the C.B.S. of their decision. L/I/1/1467.

289

Cabinet

India and Burma Committee. Paper I.B.(47) 55

L/P&J/10/98: ff 19–25

LEGISLATION TO EFFECT THE TRANSFER OF POWER
NOTE BY THE SECRETARY OF STATE FOR INDIA

INDIA OFFICE, *2 May 1947*

At the meeting of the Committee held on 13th March,[1] the Prime Minister directed that the possibility of adapting the Act of 1935 into an interim measure

[1] Vol. IX, No. 529, Minute 5.

to meet the situation envisaged in the last sentence of paragraph 10 of the Statement of 20th February should be carefully examined. He also suggested that it might be possible, even in the absence of general agreement, to reach agreement on the establishment of a special *ad hoc* authority to assume control of a unified Army.

2. I attach a note by my officials in which they outline a plan for the modification of the 1935 Act in a way which, while it transfers all effective British authority, does not undertake the final partitioning of India or the partitioning of the Central subjects. The plan rests on provincial option and, if any Province opts out of the unified interim constitution, sets up a joint Council of delegates from the different parts of India for the discussion of the subjects which were earmarked by the Cabinet Mission as Union subjects together with subjects from which the finance for them is derived. The Council would proceed by agreement and not by majority vote.

3. It is obvious that arrangements of this kind could not continue for more than a comparatively short period. If by the end of this period an agreement was not reached on some method of joint administration of the minimum list of Central subjects or on the division of these subjects, the situation would have to be resolved by non-constitutional means. On the other hand, there is a chance that the stress of circumstances would produce cooperation which might develop into permanent joint arrangements. The question we have to decide is whether, in default of agreement, a transfer of power on the lines indicated in the note would be preferable to undertaking ourselves the partitioning of India and of the Central subjects in advance of the transfer of authority. It will be seen, however, that it is a basic element in this plan that either the Punjab and Bengal are divided territorially on communal lines or the composition of Provincial Legislatures is revised to bring them into proportion to the population of the Provinces.

4. I circulate this note in response to the Prime Minister's request that consideration should be given to the feasibility of a plan of this kind, and as preparatory material for discussion next week with Lord Ismay. The note is based on the assumption that agreement to partition India cannot be reached.

L.

LEGISLATION TO EFFECT THE TRANSFER OF POWER
MEMORANDUM BY THE INDIA OFFICE

2 May 1947

1. *Basic Assumptions*

(1) That a new constitution will not have been framed by a generally representative Constituent Assembly in accordance with the Mission's Plan in time for power to be transferred to new authorities under that constitution in June, 1948.

(2) That by October, 1947 there is no agreement between Congress and the Muslim League as to authorities to which power should be transferred.

(3) That in these circumstances the last paragraph of the Statement of December 6th and paragraph 10 of the Statement of February 20th require that the legislation to transfer power should make provision whereby the Muslim majority areas are not compelled to remain under an All-India Central authority.

(4) That while His Majesty's Government will provide a means whereby the partition of India can be brought about in an orderly and constitutional manner on the responsibility of Indians, His Majesty's Government will not themselves enforce partition or the division and re-allocation of the Central functions.

(5) That a transfer of power under these conditions must take place under an amended or modified version of the existing Act since otherwise there would be no constitution which has the force of law in India. Since the amended version of the Act must derive its authority from Parliament it must be based on the assumption that India remains within the Commonwealth, but it would contain within it provision for its amendment by Indian authorities, and for its repeal by Parliament at the request of Indian authorities.

2. The following is the outline of a possible method of transferring power under an amended version of the existing Act. It will require very considerable detailed examination and development, but is put forward as a proposition for consideration of its general principles.

Outline proposals for the transfer of authority

3. The main principle would be to provide for the transfer of authority under a modified version of the existing Act in which all provisions under which British authority is now exercised in India would be removed, except (a) the standard provisions relating to the position of the Crown in a Dominion, (b) provisions for the appointment by the Crown of the Governor General and Governors on advice of the relevant Indian Ministers but statutorily invested with the powers of a constitutional monarch only, (c) provision that these essential features of an interim constitution inside the Commonwealth cannot be amended except by Parliament on the request of the Indian Constituent Assembly (vide paragraph 13).

4. A Ministry responsible to the Legislature would take the place of the existing Central Executive Council and all special powers of the Governor General would be eliminated. The Governor General and the Governors of Provinces would exercise all their powers, except the recognised powers of a constitutional monarch, on the advice of Ministers. The question of the composition of the Central Legislature is considered in paragraph 11 below.

5. It is not proposed that provision should be made in the Act requiring

fixed communal proportions in the Central Executive, or a majority of votes of both major communities in the Central Legislature for matters raising a major communal issue. The reason is that His Majesty's Government would have no power to enforce such provisions. It will be for the majority party to give such assurances as they will on these matters in order to prevent Provinces from opting out of the Federal constitution.

6. The Act would be passed into law (but would not come into operation) at least two months before the date of the transfer of power, i.e. by the end of March, 1948. The day on which the Act comes into operation as a whole would be (say) 1st June, 1948, or whatever date is appointed. The Act would contain a provision that any Province is entitled to opt by resolution of the Provincial Legislative Assembly passed by majority vote not to remain within an All-India Constitution. This option would be exercisable either (a) within one month after the Act became law (April 1948) or (b) at any time after the interim constitution comes into operation. This provision would, however, necessitate the adoption of one of the alternatives referred to in paragraph 12 below.

7. The Act would provide that, if one or more Provinces exercised the option under the preceding paragraph, Executive and Legislative authority in respect of all the present central subjects would in the case of those Provinces pass from the Central Government to the Provincial executive and legislature. It would, however, become open to any two or more such Provinces to set up by agreement, in accordance with paragraph 11 below, a separate central government to which the central subjects could be allotted by them.

8. Since, however, it is not intended to effect a practical division of the more important central subjects, and in particular the "Union" subjects, before the transfer of power, means must be devised whereby this transfer shall, in respect of the latter, become notional only. It will become *constitutional* for Provinces which exercise the option to take independent action in respect of all the central subjects. When the difficulties and dangers of this course in regard to the more important central subjects are realised, there may be less desire to embark hastily upon it. It is therefore proposed that the Act should provide that, if any Province exercises the option to secede, a Council of India shall be set up.[2] This Council would be composed of *delegations* appointed by the Governments which have separate constitutional authority in respect of the central subjects. It would reach decisions by *agreement* and not by majority vote. The field of its deliberations would be the proposed Union subjects—viz. Foreign Affairs, Defence and Communications,—together with the subjects of Customs and Excise, Income Tax, Currency, and Reserve Bank. The first two of these additional subjects provide the revenue for the Union subjects (though part of the proceeds of Income Tax is distributable among the Provinces under

standing arrangements laid down by Order in Council); and the third and fourth are subjects the division of which, in addition to being retrograde, would be a slow and difficult process.

9. This Council would provide *machinery* for joint control by agreement of the matters within its purview. Effect would have to be given to its decisions within the different areas represented upon it, by Legislatures and Executives which have constitutional authority within those areas. The existing Central Departments which administer these subjects, so long as they remain undivided, would be under the joint authority of the Governments concerned acting through the Council of India. Political heads of these Departments could only be appointed by agreement in the Council, failing which they would be in the charge of permanent officials (the Commander-in-Chief in the case of Defence) acting under the directions of the Council given by agreement.

10. If the Council failed to function or to agree on a method of partitioning the central subjects the Hindu Central Government would no doubt attempt to seize control of the Army as it stands and of the administration of the other subjects within the Council's purview, and their success would no doubt to some extent depend upon the degree to which measures have been taken in the meantime to facilitate division, or to make it more difficult. Such action on the part of the Hindu Central Government, so far as it involved the exercise of authority in the Provinces which had exercised the option, or applied to that share of the Army and other central organisations which the opting Provinces might reasonably claim as theirs, would be unconstitutional and *ultra vires*: and the opting Provinces would be constitutionally entitled if they were strong enough to do so, to organise their own Defence forces, Customs, Income Tax and Currency and to conduct their own foreign relations. There would, however, be no sharing of assets or liabilities on the basis of equity but physical assets would be acquired according to their territorial location.

11. The Central Legislature might consist of either:—
(a) the existing Central Legislature,
(b) the British Indian personnel of the Constituent Assembly acting in a separate capacity (i.e. attendance at its meetings would not constitute joining the Constituent Assembly).

It would be provided that, if more than one Province opted out, a separate Central Executive and Legislature could be set up for those provinces if it were so decided by resolution of the lower chambers of the Provincial Legislatures of the Provinces in question. The Legislature would consist of the members of the main Central Legislature elected to represent those Provinces.

---

[2] The suggestion for setting up such a Council seems to have originated in a note dated 20 March 1947 by Mr Lumby (an official in the Political Department of the India Office). This note, together with notes on the subject by other India Office officials, may be found on L/P &J/10/98.

For the reasons shown in paragraph 13 alternative (b) seems much preferable.

12. The proposal for Provincial option (paragraph 6 above) raises again the difficulty, which arose over the Cripps Mission proposals, that owing to the weightage for minorities in existing Provincial legislatures, communities are not represented in proportion to their population. In particular in the Punjab and Bengal, the Muslims, although a numerical majority of the population, have not a majority in the Legislature. There are only two methods of over-coming this difficulty in the time available. These are:—

(1) to add to each Legislature sufficient additional members to enable it to reflect the population proportion of each community. As there is not time to revise constituencies and hold fresh elections the additional seats could only be filled by allocating the appropriate number of additional seats to each community and to fill them by proportional representation by the existing representatives of that community.

(2) To partition Bengal and the Punjab before the option is exercised, or to provide that the option be exercised separately by the members representing the Eastern and Western parts of those Provinces.

The first solution is artificial and in some cases would involve the addition of a substantial number of members. It would solve the problem technically in the Punjab and Bengal but would result in the large minorities in those Provinces being carried against their will into Pakistan. It would not solve the difficulties in the North West Frontier and Assam. The conclusion, therefore, is that the second alternative alone is practicable. Its adoption would be a fundamental requirement of any scheme based on Provincial option.

13. The Act would confer on the Central Legislature (or its two parts if it is divided), as well as ordinary legislative functions, authority to revise the interim constitution (subject to what has been said in paragraph 3 (c)). From this point of view it would be advantageous if the Central Legislature were composed as in (b) of paragraph 11 (i.e. of the British Indian personnel of the existing Constituent Assembly) since the functions of creating a new constitution and amending the interim constitution would then be discharged by the same persons acting in two different capacities. (One of the amendments in its competence would be to alter its own composition so as to include representatives of such States as wished to take part for the latter purpose.)

It would be provided that, if any Province or Provinces exercise the option not to remain within the interim Central Government under the Act, the representatives of those Provinces in the Constituent Assembly would become a separate Constituent Assembly authorised to make a new constitution or constitutions for those Provinces. Indian States would be able to join either Constituent Assembly.

14. The Act would provide that if the Council of India, provided for in

paragraph 8 above, came into being the Council might take such steps as it thought desirable to associate the Indian States with its work. It is not thought practicable to associate the Indian States more closely with the Interim Government proposed. The States would probably not accept the minimum list of subjects in paragraph 8 above and they are not able to put up a delegation which could speak authoritatively for, and be in a position to commit the Governments of, all the States.

290

Minutes of Viceroy's Twenty Fifth Staff Meeting, Item 3

Mountbatten Papers

TOP SECRET

Those present during discussion of Item 3 of this Meeting held at The Viceroy's House, New Delhi on 3 May 1947 at 10 am were: Rear-Admiral Viscount Mountbatten of Burma, Sir E. Mieville, Captain Brockman, Mr Christie, Mr I. D. Scott, Lieutenant-Colonel Erskine Crum

THE CHOICE BY PROVINCES OF THEIR OWN FUTURE

(a) Article in the *Hindustan Times*

HIS EXCELLENCY THE VICEROY drew attention to the principal news item on the front page of the *Hindustan Times*[1] of that day. He said that he considered the leakage of information disclosed in this article to be most serious. Mr Jinnah, in his interview the previous day, had very rightly complained that the newspaper *Hindu* had reported the plan almost completely. The *Hindustan Times* was now also working on the assumption that this plan would be the one to be adopted.

HIS EXCELLENCY THE VICEROY pointed out that the only Indian leaders who had seen the full draft of the plan were Mr Jinnah and Pandit Nehru—and they had not been allowed to retain any documents. Apart from them, the outline of the plan had been discussed with Mr Liaquat Ali Khan, Sardar Patel and Sardar Baldev Singh. The only persons who knew of it besides them were members of the staff, including Rao Bahadur Menon. It was surely inconceivable to think that there had been a leakage from a member of staff. Since nothing had appeared in the Muslim League newspapers and disclosure of the plan would probably be inimical to Muslim League interests, the field was reduced to Pandit Nehru, Sardar Patel and Sardar Baldev Singh.

HIS EXCELLENCY THE VICEROY said that he believed that Pandit Nehru

[1] See No. 291.

had discussed the outline of the plan with the Congress Working Committee. So far as he knew, however, Pandit Nehru had never contested the absolute justice of a fresh election in the North-West Frontier Province prior to the transfer of power. Sardar Patel had, however, embarrassed the situation greatly by publishing his disagreement with any proposal to dissolve the present Congress Ministry there.[2] HIS EXCELLENCY THE VICEROY said that the present evidence went to indicate that Sardar Patel was probably responsible for this leakage.

HIS EXCELLENCY THE VICEROY pointed out that this article, which he considered to be a deliberate blackmail, led to the belief that Congress feared that he was going to give a decision which was inimical to Congress interests. This must either be fear of an unfair decision which they would contest, or a fair one which they could not face up to. He pointed out that, whenever pressure of this nature was put on him from one side, he immediately and automatically swung to the opposite point of view. In such circumstances he found it particularly difficult to maintain an absolutely fair outlook.

(b) The North-West Frontier Province

HIS EXCELLENCY THE VICEROY said that, since the N.W.F.P. had become such a bone of contention, he considered that re-investigation was required of whether the present proposed procedure for deciding the future of that Province was absolutely fair.

MR SCOTT said that he believed that Congress were gradually losing power in the N.W.F.P. If an election was held immediately, they might still just be successful but the chances against this would increase as time went on. SIR ERIC MIEVILLE said that he considered that there was a lot in the point which Mr Jinnah had made[3] that Congress might themselves stir up trouble in the N.W.F.P. leading to bloodshed and violence.

HIS EXCELLENCY THE VICEROY said that he intended to warn Mr Gandhi and Pandit Nehru that he was particularly anxious to see no "agent-provocateur" work in the N.W.F.P. He would not be taken in by that. He went on to point out that the present plan envisaged a system of voting by representatives of the Constituent Assembly on a basis of one per million of the population for the purpose of simplicity and speed. He said that, although a referendum might not suit Congress, at the same time they would be able to protest less against it than against an immediate election. A referendum would get over the difficulty of stating a reason for the dissolution of the Ministry. It would be necessary to go into Section 93 before a referendum was held and a Committee of three Congress and three Muslim League Advisers might be attached to the Governor.

HIS EXCELLENCY THE VICEROY said that there was a further grave difficulty in connection with the N.W.F.P. Sir Olaf Caroe was under the gravest and most constant attack by Congress. Lord Wavell had stalled off a request by

Pandit Nehru that Sir Olaf Caroe should be asked to resign. Pandit Nehru agreed not to repeat this request to him (His Excellency) until he had had time to study the situation himself, but this request might not now be long delayed. Sardar Patel had made grave accusations against Sir Olaf Caroe. Dr Khan Sahib had accused him of "running the Muslim League" in the N.W.F.P. Incidentally, when Mr Jinnah had been told of these accusations he had been furious. HIS EXCELLENCY THE VICEROY said that he was personally convinced that Sir Olaf Caroe was completely honest but his very honesty put him in a practically impossible position. Mr Krishna Menon and others had accused not only the Governor, but all British officials in the N.W.F.P. of being pro-Muslim League.

HIS EXCELLENCY recalled that Mr Liaquat Ali Khan had said that he hoped that he would not yield to the Congress pressure to remove the present Governor. But he had warned Mr Liaquat Ali Khan of what he had told the Governor himself—that circumstances might lead to his having to call for his resignation. HIS EXCELLENCY THE VICEROY stated that he considered that whoever was responsible for turning over tribal affairs with the External Affairs Portfolio to Pandit Nehru, had caused a most embarrassing situation. It should surely have been an elementary precaution to continue to reserve this subject to the Viceroy himself. He was now put in a position, through that action, of Pandit Nehru being responsible to him for tribal affairs. Pandit Nehru had already written to Lord Wavell and threatened, by implication, his own resignation if Sir Olaf Caroe remained. Pandit Nehru was presumably at liberty now to write to him (His Excellency) and state that it was a choice between Sir Olaf Caroe and himself.

HIS EXCELLENCY THE VICEROY emphasised that, if Sir Olaf Caroe did have to resign, it would be with complete honour. He felt that Sir Olaf Caroe would have to stay on at any rate until the Province was put under Section 93 Government, as any successor before that time would not have a chance with Dr Khan Sahib. He asked whether it would be possible to appoint a high level Political Adviser with a new Governor. SIR ERIC MIEVILLE said that he considered that this would depend on whether the successor Governor had experience of the Frontier or not. HIS EXCELLENCY THE VICEROY said that in any case he considered that such an appointment would be desirable.

During further discussion of the desirability of holding a referendum in the North-West Frontier Province, it was felt that the main advantages of this course would be:—

(a) It would be a far better way of finding out the will of the people and of removing weightage than under the system at present envisaged in

² A statement by Sardar Patel on the N.W.F.P. situation appeared in the *Statesman* on 4 May 1947.
³ See No. 287.

the draft announcement whereby the decision is left in the hands of three persons;

(b) the issue (choice of joining up with Pakistan or Hindustan) would be straightforward and readily understood by the people;

(c) it would not involve a great loss of time or greatly increase administrative arrangements in view of the fact that an election was to be held anyhow.

Bengal

HIS EXCELLENCY THE VICEROY said that at his interview with Mr Chundrigar the previous day,[4] the latter had expressed the view that, if the decision on the partition of Bengal was left to the Constituent Assembly representatives, they, who were very few and completely in the hands of Congress, would be bound to vote for Partition. Mr Chundrigar had urged that a referendum on Partition should be taken by all those on the electoral roll of Bengal. Mr Chundrigar had not insisted that this would necessarily produce a different result, but had pointed out that it would be a far fairer method of ascertaining the will of the people. HIS EXCELLENCY THE VICEROY said that he had written to the Governor of Bengal asking him to telegraph his views on this suggestion.[5]

The Punjab

HIS EXCELLENCY THE VICEROY pointed out that it would be difficult to adopt a different procedure for voting on the issue of Partition of the Punjab to that adopted in Bengal. A telegram should therefore be sent to the Governor of the Punjab asking for his views on the possibility of a referendum.[6]

Sind

HIS EXCELLENCY THE VICEROY said that he considered the continual attacks by Congress on Sir Francis Mudie to be quite fantastic. If Sir Francis Mudie were to behave in the manner Congress wished, and if the Governors of overwhelmingly Congress Provinces behaved in a similar manner to their Governments, Congress would soon realise the error of their accusations. They evidently accused Sir Francis Mudie openly of having lost them Sind by a "sharp trick". Originally, he understood, 31 members of the Sind Legislative Assembly were Congressmen and the other 29 Muslim Leaguers. Then the Muslim League bought over one Congressman, making a total of 30 on each side. As neither party would then nominate a speaker, because it would have made them into a minority, the Governor had had to dissolve the Legislative Assembly.

HIS EXCELLENCY THE VICEROY:—

(i) instructed Con. Sec. to prepare for his approval a draft telegram to Lord Ismay in London concerning the suggestion that a referendum should be held in the N.W.F.P.;

(ii) invited Prin. Sec. to speak to Rao Bahadur Menon concerning the

---

suggestion of a referendum and also about the article which had appeared in the *Hindustan Times* that day;

(iii) directed Acting P.S.V. to draft for his approval a telegram to the Governor of the Punjab asking for his views on the possibility of holding a referendum in that Province.

[4] See No. 283.
[5] See No. 280.
[6] In the event Lord Mountbatten sent Sir E. Jenkins a letter; see No. 274, note 2.

291

Rear-Admiral Viscount Mountbatten of Burma to the Earl of Listowel

Telegram, Mountbatten Papers. Official Correspondence Files: Press and Publicity, Part I (b)

IMMEDIATE   NEW DELHI, *3 May 1947, 12 noon*
EN CLAIR   *Received: 3 May, 2.50 pm*

No. 235–GT. Following is front page item in *Hindustan Times* today. *Begins.* For the first time since Lord Mountbatten assumed Viceroyalty the feeling that he may not be playing fair has come among some Congressmen and Sikh leaders. The reason for this is the Viceroy's reported attitude towards the Frontier Ministry and his plan to divide the Punjab into 12 non-Muslim and 17 Muslim districts thereby dealing a blow to Sikh interests.

The Congress Working Committee has made the Frontier question a test case. It has been made clear to the Viceroy that any proposal to dismiss the Frontier Ministry and hold fresh election will make the Congress change its entire attitude towards the British Government. Apparently this development made the Viceroy talk to Mr Jinnah today for two and a half hours on the Frontier situation.

There will be a frank exchange of views on the whole situation between Gandhiji and the Viceroy tomorrow. The Congress Committee decided not to adopt any formal resolution on the political situation and adjourned until Sunday, partly because it would by then know the outcome of Gandhiji's talks with the Viceroy and partly because many Ministers would be busy tomorrow attending the Mazdoor Sangh Conference. It is said the Viceroy has not given up the idea of a round table conference.

Lord Ismay, who left for London today, has carried with him a communication[1] sent by the Congress Working Committee to the Viceroy embodying its reactions to the tentative conclusions which the Viceroy is reported to have

[1] cf. No. 267.

reached on the Indian situation. The Viceroy's conclusions are understood to be on the following lines:

(1) Both the Congress and the League consider division of India inevitable.

(2) The division will involve district-wise partition of the Punjab and Bengal and the appointment of a boundary commission. In the alternative Bengal should have a constitution on a fifty-fifty basis, the status of Bengal corresponding roughly to the position of Quebec in the Canadian constitution.

(3) Before division is carried out the M.L.A.s of the districts concerned should be given the opportunity to decide whether they would prefer to remain in the Indian Union or have a separate State for their areas.

(4) If the M.L.A.s decide in favour of partition then they will be asked to elect new representatives to a constituent assembly or constituent assemblies for their joint or separate areas on the basis of one representative for each million. The present Constituent Assembly for the Indian Union will remain intact. Only the members representing the partitioned areas will cease to be its members.

(5) If partition is to take place the N.W.F.P. should have fresh elections to decide whether its people would desire to remain in the Indian Union or join Pakistan or become an independent territory. Since there is a tug-of war in the province for political power the present Governor will be replaced by another and Section 93 administration will be set up to conduct elections.

The Congress Working Committee's reactions to the above proposals is stated to be on the following lines:

(1) The Congress would have favoured a strong united India but considers that the division of the country is the best solution in the circumstances. But the division should be absolute and complete since that alone will give the majority of the people of India the opportunity of building up a powerful State with a strong Centre.

(2) There must be partition of the Punjab and Bengal giving chance to the non-Muslim areas to join the Indian Union. Since the Punjab is the homeland of the Sikhs its partition should not rest merely on the basis of Sikh and Hindu population but also other considerations such as the need for bringing in a large number of Sikhs within one territory, the considerations of property and natural geographical boundary. As regards Bengal division of the Western districts and Calcutta from the rest of the province is clearly indicated.

(3) The method of violence used in the North-West Frontier Province, the Punjab and Assam to settle political issues must be put an end to. The Congress will resist to the utmost any attempt to force issues by methods of intimidation and violence.

(4) The Congress has no objection to a separate constituent assembly or assemblies being summoned for those areas that choose to stand out of the Indian Union but hopes that such areas will have the opportunity to decide

for themselves whether they would remain independent or form union with other parts.

(5) There is no occasion for any change in the Frontier. The last election was fought on the issue of Pakistan and the verdict having been given by the electorate the present M.L.A.s of the Frontier Assembly are competent to decide the future of the province.

The Congress Working Committee is expected to draw up a resolution embodying the points covered in the letter sent to the Viceroy. The Committee will meet for another two days and will then re-assemble about May 15 or 16. It is said that Mr Jinnah has been asked to summon his working committee about that date so that the British Government's proposals which will be ready by then may be considered by the two committees.

It is now gathered that Mr Jinnah's extremist statement of Thursday[2] was put forth after he had been informed of the tentative conclusions reached by the Viceroy. *Ends.*

[2] See Annex I to No. 276.

292

Record of Interview between Rear-Admiral Viscount Mountbatten of Burma and Mr Kiran Sankar Roy

Mountbatten Papers. Viceroy's Interview No. 113

TOP SECRET   *3 May 1947, 12.10–12.40 pm*

I informed Mr Roy that I had received a request for the partition of Bengal signed by the non-Muslim members of the Legislative Council and the Legislative Assembly.

He regretted there were only 74 signatures on it at present, because in their haste they had not been able to collect the signatures of all eligible persons, but these could be produced.

I asked him straight out if he was in favour of unity or partition for Bengal. He replied that he had always been strongly in favour of unity and he had only been driven to recommending partition by the intransigence of the Muslim League and pressure from Congress. I asked him if he had thought of the terrible consequences for Bengal as a whole. I painted a picture of the disastrous consequences to both East and West Bengal. I pointed out that though many people believed that East Bengal would fare worst they appeared to have overlooked the ease with which the jute factories could be transferred to eastern Bengal areas. He agreed that this was so, and said that he was glad of it since he himself was a resident of East Bengal. I congratulated him on his

Hindu patriotism at being prepared to see the Province destroyed to save a Hindu majority in West Bengal at the expense of the Hindus like himself living in East Bengal. He shrugged his shoulders.

I then told him what my general plan was on the partition of Bengal. I told him that the intention was that the Bengal representatives of the Constituent Assembly should first sit together and vote on what the future of Bengal should be if it remained united: whether it should opt for (a) Independence, (b) Pakistan, or (c) Hindustan.

I added that when the issue was clear as to what would happen if Bengal remained united, a further vote would be taken on whether to have partition or unity. I told him that this further vote might be either by the Bengal representatives of the Constituent Assembly, after an interval of a week or a fortnight, or by a referendum to the people of Bengal by using the electoral rolls and having separate electorates for the eastern and western districts of Bengal. By this means either half could vote themselves out of Bengal; in other words could impose partition on the whole Province.

I asked him which of these two methods he preferred. He seemed to think that the issue was now so clear before everybody that either method would give a true reflection of opinion.

I asked him what the chances of Bengal remaining united were in his opinion; and he said that unless the Muslim League were prepared to come forward with some offer to the Hindus, the chances were slim.

I asked him whether the offer of joint electorates would satisfy the Hindus, to which he replied with enormous enthusiasm: "Most certainly. If they give us that you can practically count on unity." I told him that I had already recommended Mr Suhrawardy to consider offering joint electorates, but that he was doubtful of being able to carry all his party with him. However, I pointed out that the consequences of failure to grant joint electorates would be so disastrous if partition followed that they might now prefer to make this offer.

I also told him that I hoped that Mr Suhrawardy might consider offering a form of coalition government before the announcement of H.M.G.'s decision was made on about the 20th May.

Mr Roy got more and more excited as the meeting progressed. He told me that he had intended staying in Delhi until the announcement was made, but he now wanted to have my advice as to what he ought to do. I advised him strongly to go straight back to Calcutta and see Mr Suhrawardy and then go on to Darjeeling and see the Governor. "You have not a moment to lose", I told him; upon which he got up dramatically, shook me warmly by the hand, and left the room.

293

Record of Interview between Rear-Admiral Viscount Mountbatten of Burma and Mr B. G. Kher

Mountbatten Papers. Viceroy's Interview No. 114

TOP SECRET   *3 May 1947, 12.45–1.10 pm*

I asked him what truth he considered there had been in the Muslim League charges that the Congress Government in Bombay between 1937 and 1939 repressed the Muslims. He refuted this charge heatedly, and said that the only three points that had ever been brought up were:

(a) That Muslim children in schools were obliged to sing the Hindu national song.

(b) That the Congress flag was hoisted on public buildings.

(c) That textbooks supplied by the schools had chapters on Christ, Maho- med, Buddha, etc, devoting an equal amount of space to each, and causing offence to the Muslims through the juxtaposition of Mahomed and other religious figures.

He said that the action his Ministry had taken was:

(a) To order that if even one member of a class objected to the singing of the song it was not to be sung.

(b) To direct that if anyone objected to the hoisting of the Congress flag it was not to be hoisted.

(c) As regards this point Mr Kher explained that these textbooks were issued on the authority of a Committee of which a Muslim was Chair- man, and was a matter for local authorities.

He assured me that beyond that, nothing harmful had been done to the Muslims and that they had been well treated. He said that they were also being well looked after now, and he did not think they had any genuine cause for com- plaint.

I congratulated him on having a quiet Province, and asked him to give me an account of the communal troubles that there had been.

He said that they had been relatively small in extent, and that his Govern- ment had passed a law to the effect that the opposite community was to pay for the damage to property of the other community, and this had had a most salutary effect both in reducing the damage and in encouraging the members of both communities to join together to put out fires, etc.

I told him I thought this should be a general law in all provinces, and he told me he had made this proposal to the other Provincial Premiers at their recent meeting, and that they thought it was a very good idea.

He confirmed Mr Patel's story that the previous Inspector-General of Police in Bombay had been entirely unsatisfactory, but not for the reasons given by Mr Patel, namely that he was pro-Muslim, but because he was soft-hearted and fell over backwards in trying to be fair to minorities. When finally he (Kher) was able to convince the Governor that he should go, the new I.G. had restored complete law and order in Bombay within three days, and there had been no serious trouble since.

He patted himself on the back for the way in which the B.E.S.T. strike had been settled, without their having to arrest any strikers. He said he had a very happy Government and that the relations with the Europeans were completely friendly. He attributed this largely to the leavening influence of the Parsee community, and said he would like me to visit one of the clubs in Bombay and see the friendly and free spirit that prevailed among Britishers and Indians there.

294

Record of Interview between Rear-Admiral Viscount Mountbatten of Burma and Rajkumari Amrit Kaur

Mountbatten Papers. Viceroy's Interview No. 115

TOP SECRET   *3 May 1947 (after lunch)*

She told me how very distressed Mr Gandhi had been that the highly secret information of his difference of opinion with some of the Congress leaders, over the plan he had outlined to me when I first saw him, should have leaked out to the Press. He was highly indignant at these leakages, and she knew he would be in sympathy with my indignation at the leakage and blackmail in the *Hindustan Times* today.[1]

She told me she was herself a Punjabi, and appealed to me not to agree to the partition of the Punjab.

I pointed out my position, and said that the very last thing I wanted was partition in any part of India. I asked her whether an offer of independence to the Punjab would save its unity. She felt that it might be a solution, and said she would recommend it to Mr Gandhi.

She urged me on no account to fall into the trap of making a decision on behalf of the British Government which would ultimately be regarded as a very wrong decision should it be in favour of the partition of India.

I thanked her for this advice, and told her that I had been alive to this point of view from the very beginning and that this was my policy—to base the final decision on the will of the people of India.

[1] See No. 291.

295

Record of Interview between Rear-Admiral Viscount Mountbatten of Burma and Khizar Hayat Khan Tiwana[1]

Mountbatten Papers. Viceroy's Interview No. 116; Official Correspondence Files: Punjab, Part I(b)

TOP SECRET   *3 May 1947*

HIS EXCELLENCY opened the conversation by saying that he was violently opposed to partition, but that as the leaders showed absolutely no signs of getting together it appeared to him that it was going to be inevitable. Sir Khizar said that he reluctantly agreed with His Excellency. Any vivisection of the Punjab would be disastrous and indeed it would be suicidal to split it up. He mentioned that the British should not be a party to a division which would damage all parts of the province. Once a division were announced re-unification would become almost impossible. He went on to say that if the idea of a notional line were pursued merely for the object of getting the wishes of the people as to whether they wished to remain unified or joined Hindustan or Pakistan, he feared the consequences because, he said, the line would inevitably favour one party or the other and the favoured party would cling to the advantage they had thus gained. Furthermore, people generally would never understand the idea of a notional line. Therefore, he said, it would be far better to delay obtaining the wishes of the people until a boundary commission or some such organisation had demarcated the exact line that would remain for all time. He went on to say that the Punjab for the Punjabis used to be the cry and that he was still in favour of it. If the Sikhs were not satisfied the Punjab could never be well run and the people would fear interference from a Hindu and capitalistic centre just as they would fear interference from a Pakistan centre. The financial responsibility that would fall on them if they joined either party would be so severe that it would break them and, he thought, communism would probably be the result.

HIS EXCELLENCY then asked him whether he would prefer the will of the people being obtained by a referendum or by the means laid down in the plan. He asked for time to think over this question and concluded by saying that the Sikhs were going to be adversely affected whatever happened. They owned property and had interests throughout the province and he felt that if the province were split, the Muslims should offer them joint electorates, in which event he thought there might be a union between the two, but let there be no mistake, the Sikhs would never join Pakistan.

---

[1] Sir E. Mieville was also present.

Note by Sir E. Mieville

Sir Khizar returned to see me in the afternoon and said that he had been thinking over the question His Excellency had put to him. His answer was that if it was feasible he was in favour of a referendum and suggested that the four following alternatives be put:

(1) Free Punjab, with an agreement or agreements with Hindustan and Pakistan about Defence.

(2) Punjab to join Pakistan.

(3) Punjab to join Hindustan.

(4) Punjab to be divided.

His only other comment was to reiterate that a decision to split the Punjab would mean Civil War.

296

Record of Interview between Rear-Admiral Viscount Mountbatten of Burma and Pandit G. B. Pant

Mountbatten Papers. Viceroy's Interview No. 118

TOP SECRET   *3 May 1947 (after lunch)*

I congratulated him on having a quiet Province, and said that the Governor had told me how pleased he was with the way the Ministry was working with him; which Pandit Pant entirely confirmed.

Nevertheless, he told me that the repercussions of events in the Punjab and Bihar and Bengal were beginning to make themselves felt in the U.P., and that he could not regard the situation as entirely satisfactory. They had gone out of their way in the U.P. to give the minorities more than a fair deal, but the Hindus were gradually becoming opposed to such generous treatment towards a community which was proving itself to be so brutal and violent in other Provinces.

He asked me whether I favoured partition, and I told him emphatically "No". He appealed to me then not to agree to a decision for partition. I pointed out that I could not go against the will of the people; the most I could do was to leave the choice as far as possible to the people of India, and this was the policy I was endeavouring to follow.

He regretted the fact that we were leaving in June 1948, at such short notice, and said that if two or three years ago we could have announced a date five years ahead for our departure everything could have been done in a much more orderly and smooth way and with less risk of violence on our departure.

He volunteered the statement that the feeling between the British and

Indians had never been so good, and said that this feeling had noticeably improved in the last couple of months. He felt that this was one of the few good things that had come out of the announcement. He also paid the usual flattering tribute to me, saying that I was the right man to settle the problem. I replied that I could now see how he had become the Chief Minister of the U.P.!

297

Pandit Nehru to Rear-Admiral Viscount Mountbatten of Burma

L/PO/6/119: ff 63-4

SECRET   NEW DELHI, *3 May 1947*

Dear Lord Mountbatten,

With your letter, dated 30th April,[1] you sent me various papers relating to your visit to the Frontier. Among these was an account of your meeting with the Governor of the N.W.F.P. and the four Ministers on the 28th April.

On reading through all these papers I was considerably surprised both at some statements of fact and at the general approach to various problems. I wrote to you a brief letter[2] expressing my distress. There was much in those papers to which I wanted to draw your attention. But I refrained from doing so, because, as I pointed out in my letter of the 1st May,[3] the basic question was one of approach. I should like to make it quite clear that I do not agree with several things that have been said in the course of the various interviews and the fact that I am not drawing particular attention to each matter should not be taken to mean that I agree with it.

This morning I had a trunk telephone call from Dr. Khan Sahib, the Chief Minister of the N.W.F.P. He told me that he had received the report of the meeting you had with the Ministers. He added that so far as paragraphs 15, 16 and 17 were concerned, there was obviously a grave misapprehension and they did not correctly represent what he or his colleagues had agreed to. It was not possible for me to go into any detail on the telephone, but I understood that he had sent a note on the subject to the Governor with the request that this may be forwarded to you.[4]

I need hardly repeat that this matter of the Frontier Province is not only important in itself but has far-reaching implications in the all-India context.

---

[1] No. 259.   [2] and [3] This letter has not been traced.

[4] On 4 May Lord Mountbatten acknowledged Pandit Nehru's letter. He said that he had asked Sir O. Caroe to obtain from Dr Khan Sahib what the latter considered to be the correct version of these paragraphs on receipt of which Lord Mountbatten would discuss matters with Pandit Nehru. Mountbatten Papers, Official Correspondence Files: North West Frontier Province, Part I(b).

Any special treatment of the Frontier Province in regard to elections, or the imposition of Section 93 Government, would create a very grave situation. I have already written to you[5] about the Congress Working Committee's reactions to such a proposal. I am personally convinced that those reactions are correct.

It is unfortunate that there should have been a misunderstanding in regard to what was said at your meeting with the Ministers. Sometimes wrong impressions are formed for lack of preciseness in language. It is desirable, above all, that there should be no misunderstanding of respective view-points. In this matter the Frontier Province Ministry is concerned, of course; but all of us are equally concerned, because of the wider implications involved. I trust, therefore, that nothing will be taken for granted and if there is any misapprehension it should be removed immediately.

In the course of our conversations I think I mentioned to you the result of a by-election in the Frontier, which was held about two months or so ago. I am sorry I gave you perhaps a slightly wrong impression. I have now enquired into this matter and the correct figures are as follows.

In the 1946 general election the Muslim League candidate won the seat at Mardan. The voting was as follows:

Muslim League	8354
Congress	8185
Muslim League majority	169

In the 1947 election the voting was as follows:

Muslim League	8941
Congress	8353
Muslim League majority	588

There was thus no change, though there was a slight increase in the Muslim League majority from 169 to 588. The total voting went up from 16539 to 17294. Both the candidates increased their poll, though the increase on the Muslim League side was somewhat greater. On the whole, it might be said that there was no marked change.

Yours sincerely,
JAWAHARLAL NEHRU

[5] No. 267.

298

Sir E. Jenkins (Punjab) to Rear-Admiral Viscount Mountbatten of Burma

Mountbatten Papers. Official Correspondence Files: Punjab,
Part I(b)

SECRET   GOVERNMENT HOUSE, LAHORE,
No. 668.   *3 May 1947*

Dear Lord Mountbatten,

Your Excellency may be interested in the enclosed note of an interview I had yesterday with Sardar Swaran Singh, Sardar Harbans [Harnam] Singh, and Lala Bhim Sen Sachar. Sardar Swaran Singh, as Your Excellency may remember, was Development Minister in the Punjab and is now prominent in Sikh politics. Sardar Harbans Singh is an Advocate, originally of the Rawalpindi District, and is a Member of the Constituent Assembly. Lala Bhim Sen Sachar was our Finance Minister. Characteristically the three gentlemen did not mention to me the proceedings or intentions of the Hindu and Sikh "Convention" which recently met at Delhi. They left me to see in this morning's newspapers that this "Convention" had demanded the partition of the Punjab with the Chenab as the western boundary between the two States. The non-Muslim State must, according to the "Convention", include the whole of the Ambala, Jullundur and Lahore Divisions, and one colony district from the Multan Division.

2. This partition business seems to me to be getting out of control. The present position may be stated as follows:—

(1) We could partition the Punjab (a) by force in pursuance of an award by H.M.G., or (b) amicably in pursuance of an agreement between the communities.

(2) Course (a) would require the use of a very large body of troops and is for this reason alone impracticable. It would in any case be a difficult and unpleasant course, resulting in the establishment of two Governments which would be compelled to rule by massacre.

(3) Course (b) has so far held the field, and until a few days ago it seemed that if Pakistan were conceded, Jinnah would instruct his followers to accept a reasonable partition. The attitude of the Hindus and Sikhs has never been certain, but there was a chance that if the Muslims met them half-way, they would be reasonable.

(4) The situation has been radically changed by Jinnah's public announcement[1] that Pakistan must include the whole of the Punjab (he would probably agree to the severance from the Punjab of a part at least of the Ambala Division,

[1] See Annex I to No. 276.

but this does not affect the main issue). The Hindus and Sikhs, particularly the latter, have countered with the most extravagent claims and are certainly not prepared to agree to the inclusion of the whole of the Punjab in Pakistan or to any reasonable partition. Their claim to the whole of the Lahore Division may be a bluff, but they would, I am sure, refuse to accept any boundary short of the Ravi, and they would insist on the inclusion in the non-Muslim State of a considerable colony area, possibly an entire district.

(5) It is thus clear that we are not going to succeed in course (b). There will not be an amicable partition in pursuance of an agreement between the parties, and if we are not very careful, we shall be manoeuvred into giving an award which we shall be unwilling or unable to enforce.

3. In these circumstances I think that Your Excellency should reconsider the terms of any early announcement embodying a solution of the Indian political problem. In the Punjab we are going to be faced with a complete refusal of the communities to co-operate on any basis at all. It would clearly be futile to announce a partition of the Punjab which no community would accept. The announcement would be regarded as an award which all three communities would dare us to enforce, and I have no doubt that all three communities would begin instantly to fight among themselves. We cannot get away from the basic facts—that Jinnah wants the whole of the Punjab, and that the Hindus and Sikhs will insist that he is not to have more than two-fifths of it. There can be no peaceful solution without a complete change of front by all communities, and unless Your Excellency sees some prospect of such a change, I think we must begin to consider very seriously what *ad hoc* arrangement can be made for the transfer of power. I have not been able to think of any suitable arrangement—failing communal agreement there can be no orderly representative Government here; and failing orderly representative Government there is no satisfactory successor.

Yours sincerely,

E. M. JENKINS

Enclosure to No. 298

2 May 1947

Sardar Swaran Singh, Sardar Harnam Singh and Lala Bhim Sen Sachar called on me at their request at 4.0 p.m. today. They said they had come to discuss the partition of the Punjab.

2. Sardar Harnam Singh, who did much of the talking, explained that he had just had an interview with Lord Ismay in Delhi. Lord Ismay had told him—

(1) that the Statement of 16th May 1946 was a dead letter;
(2) that Pakistan was coming; and
(3) that the partition of the Punjab was therefore inevitable.

Sardar Harnam Singh had been given to understand by Lord Ismay with reference to (3) that partition would be by Muslim majority districts and non-Muslim majority districts. The Sikhs were quite unable to accept this arrangement, and he had told Lord Ismay so. Lord Ismay had then advised him to see me.

In the first place Sardar Harnam Singh contended that the Census of 1941 was not reliable, especially for Lahore City. Sardar Harnam Singh referred to certain opinions alleged to have been expressed by the authors of the Census reports about the unreliability of the 1941 Census in the Punjab. He believed that the rationing figures in many towns proved the inaccuracy of the Census figures. In many districts and tahsils the Muslim majority was very small, and it would be grossly unfair to the Sikhs to hand over "marginal" districts, such as Gurdaspur, to the Muslims on the basis of admittedly inaccurate figures.

I replied to this that however bad the Census of 1941 might have been, it was the best evidence we had of our population and its distribution. We could not proceed upon the rationing figures which were compiled for a different purpose and had no great reputation for accuracy.

Secondly, Sardar Harnam Singh argued that though the Non-Muslim population of the Punjab was 43% of the total population, the territory allotted to the Non-Muslims on the basis contemplated by Lord Ismay was to be only 33% of the total area of the Punjab. He indicated with support from S. Swaran Singh that Muslims and Non-Muslims should in the first place be allotted areas corresponding to their respective population strengths and that there should subsequently be an exchange of population. Sardar Harnam Singh stressed the economic importance of Non-Muslims, who owned, according to him, not less than half of the agricultural land in the Punjab and not less than 70% of the urban house property and of the commercial interests in the cities and towns.

To this argument I replied that however the Punjab was divided, the population of the separated areas would be mixed. I did not believe that transfers of population on a grand scale were practicable. I doubted if historically there had been any voluntary transfer of population on the scale contemplated since the great tribal migrations which had so profoundly affected Europe and parts of Asia. Hitler's compulsory transfers usually led to death, the persons transferred being employed more or less as slaves. It seemed to me that any partition must take into account not only the strength of the two communities but their territorial distribution. Population must surely be the most important factor; I did not see how economic condition and other similar factors could count for very much. Sardar Harnam Singh must consider that the time available to us was very exceedingly short. It was not the intention of H.M.G. to force a partition on the Punjab or to make a rigid award to which no community agreed. Their problem was to find an authority or authorities to whom power could be demitted next year. The Punjabis would have to work out their own arrangements for themselves, but it was obvious that the successor authority or authorities would have to be identifiable and reasonably stable. I could not transfer my powers under Section 93 of the Government of India Act, 1935, to a boundary commission in the hope that in the course of some years two new states might emerge.

Thirdly, Sardar Harnam Singh said that partition on the lines contemplated would be grossly unfair because of the artificial character of some of the districts. For example, Narowal, a Tahsil of the Sialkot District, had once formed part of the Amritsar District and had a non-Muslim majority.

I pointed out that Narowal was in fact a Muslim majority Tahsil. It seemed to me that the more one discussed individual areas the clearer it became that one could not discard the population basis.

2. [sic] From this point I began to make the running. I said again that H.M.G.'s immediate and limited object was to find an authority or authorities to whom power could be demitted. Our discussion so far had simply brought out the extreme difficulties of any partition. My personal opinion was that partition was a hopeless solution which all communities would regret. But if the Punjabis wanted partition, they would have to agree about its principles. I suggested that we should try to narrow the issues by considering how far the communities were likely to agree.

On this the two Sardars said that there was no dispute about the Rawalpindi Division which was admittedly Muslim. In the Multan Division the Sikhs must have a colony district or at least an entire canal system. They might be prepared to take over Sheikhupura, and to relinquish all claim to colony land elsewhere on the understanding that the Muslim population of Sheikhupura would be exchanged with the Sikh population of Lyallpur and Montgomery. Alternatively, the Sikhs would like the Montgomery District.

In the East they said that there would be no dispute about the Ambala and Jullundur Divisions. I argued that I was receiving truculent telegrams from the Muslims of the Jullundur Division saying that they would never submit to a partition or to the Sikh yoke. I agreed however that these two Divisions were broadly non-Muslim country, though there was a large Muslim minority.

We then got on to the Lahore Division, and the two Sardars made it clear that this was the real *casus belli*. They argued vehemently that Gurdaspur was a non-Muslim district; that Amritsar must certainly go to the non-Muslims even under Lord Ismay's formula; that outside Lahore city the Lahore district was substantially Sikh; and that the Muslims had played a very small part in the development of Lahore city. Reverting to their colony claim, they showed a strong interest in the Montgomery district.

After a good deal of argument they said that any attempt to divide the Lahore Division would lead to an immediate explosion. The Sikhs would be deserting $1\frac{1}{3}$ million of their co-religionists, and this would be quite intolerable. Their area must include all districts with a substantial Sikh population. I rejoined that this idea was quite untenable since the Sikhs were not in a majority in a single district. They would do well to remember that the Muslims had precisely similar problems. The two new States would in fact have minority problems almost as acute as those which beset the Punjab today.

In the upshot the two Sardars and Lala Bhim Sen Sachar suggested the creation of a third State. The Muslims would get the Rawalpindi and Multan Divisions less Montgomery, and the non-Muslims would get the Jullundur and Ambala Divisions. The Lahore Division plus the Montgomery district would be a central State, governed jointly by Muslims, Hindus and Sikhs. It would be understood that this central State would ultimately be partitioned between the western and eastern States and the details would be a matter for the boundary commission.

3. I repeated that our discussion kept underlining the folly of partition. S. Swaran Singh agreed, but said that since Mr. Jinnah insisted on a sovereign Pakistan State, the Sikhs had no alternative but to demand a homeland of their own, and could get this only by partition. For the Sikhs it was a matter of life and death.

I pointed out, as I had done in passing at an earlier stage in the discussion, that all communities tended to deny to others what they claimed for themselves. I said I could not understand what benefit the Sikhs would get from domination over areas with a Muslim majority. Turning to the creation of three separate States, I said that this would evidently take a long time. I asked how the Sikhs proposed that the Punjab should be governed until the three States were set up. An Interim Government would be needed and would presumably be the successor authority. To this I received no very clear answer. I said that if all parties were agreed to partition in accordance with certain principles, it might be possible to adopt some form of zonal administration within the present constitution, but I emphasized that this involved agreement and cooperation between the important communities to such a degree that if a zonal system were possible, an ordinary Coalition Ministry would also be possible.

After some further desultory exchanges our discussion ended.

4. The two Sardars said that they hoped that nothing would be done to hand the Sikhs over to Muslim domination and oppression. I reiterated that H.M.G. could not force an award upon an unwilling Punjab. I adhered to the old-fashioned view that union was the real answer, but if the Punjabis would not have union, they must think out their own solution, and it would be for them to see what form of partition they would accept. I hoped that a real effort would be made to arrive at some agreed settlement.

5. This was an interesting talk. It illustrates the unreasonable demands of

the Sikhs, and also illustrates the extreme danger of an announcement by H.M.G. of a partition of the Punjab unless the parties have agreed in advance to the principles of such a partition. There may be something in the idea of the third Central State, ridiculous though it is. Our problem may be to tide over the few months remaining before June 1948 in any way which will prevent immediate fighting. Unless there is a considerable change in the Muslim view, fighting is inevitable and the only question is when it will break out.

E. M. JENKINS

299

Sir E. Mieville to Rear-Admiral Viscount Mountbatten of Burma

Mountbatten Papers. Official Correspondence Files: Punjab, Part I(b)

3 *May* 1947

Your Excellency,

A discussion was held this afternoon with Mr Abbott, Secretary to the Governor of the Punjab, on the subject of a referendum to electors in that Province. The following points were made.

(*a*) A referendum to electors requires a simple straightforward issue.

(*b*) Whereas in the N.W.F.P. the issue would be the simple one of joining Pakistan or Hindustan, in the Punjab the issue of Partition would first have to be decided. It would be no use putting a hypothetical question to electors.

(*c*) If the whole Punjab is asked to vote on Partition, without defining the areas, nearly all Muslims will vote against it, and nearly all Hindus and Sikhs for it.

(*d*) If the two half Provinces of the Punjab are asked to vote on Partition, according to the districtwise division adopted in the present plan, Muslims and the Rest are both likely to vote against it, because neither will like the line of demarcation. Hindus and Sikhs may boycott the referendum.

(*e*) The advantages of a referendum in the N.W.F.P. do not apply in the Punjab because

(1) there would be 29 representatives voting under our plan instead of only 3;

(2) the question would not be the same vide (*b*) above;

(3) there is not going to be an election in the Punjab in any case.

(*f*) A referendum in the Punjab would create a dangerous situation on the prevailing political atmosphere.

(*g*) Similar considerations apply in Bengal as in the Punjab.

E.M.

300

Rear-Admiral Viscount Mountbatten of Burma to Lord Ismay (via India Office)

Telegram, R/3/1/170: ff 3–4

IMPORTANT   NEW DELHI, *3 May 1947, 8.15 pm*
TOP SECRET   *Received: 3 May, 9.50 pm*

968–S. 1. We discussed at Staff Meeting today 3rd May the possibility of holding a referendum in the N.W.F.P.[1] Such a referendum would have to take place under Section 93 government and would precede a fresh election. It would of course be of the Provincial Assembly voters on the present electoral rolls.

2. The main advantages of such a referendum would appear to be:—

(*a*) It would be a far better way of finding out the will of the people and of removing weightage than under the system at present envisaged in the draft announcement whereby the decision is left in the hands of three persons;

(*b*) the issue (choice of joining up with Pakistan or Hindustan) would be straightforward and readily understood by the people;

(*c*) it would not involve a great loss of time or greatly increased administrative arrangements in view of the fact that an election is to be held anyhow.

3. If the result of the referendum was in favour of Pakistan we feel that Congress would either refuse to contest the subsequent election; or so much of Dr. Khan Sahib's support would be withdrawn that he would have little chance of winning. Even if Congress did contest the election and win, the major issue would already be decided and they would have to go ahead and join Pakistan.

4. I would be grateful for your views on this suggestion. It would not involve too much drastic changes in the draft announcement.

5. The idea of holding referenda in the two parts of Bengal and the Punjab has also arisen. I am consulting the two Governors and I shall be telegraphing later when I have their views. But it is realised that some of the advantages

---

[1] See No. 290.

enumerated in paragraph 2 above for the N.W.F.P. do not apply to Bengal and the Punjab.

6. You will have seen my telegram No. 235–GT to the Secretary of State[2] containing the principal news item on the front page of the *Hindustan Times* of today. I consider that this deliberate leakage of secret information by Congress, coupled with such blatant blackmail, indicates that Congress realise that they have a really weak case in the N.W.F.P.

7. I saw Mr. Jinnah yesterday[3] and am due to see Gandhi Sunday afternoon. Records of these interviews follow by bag.

8. I have just received from Nehru a reasoned but vehement letter[4] of protest against any election in the N.W.F.P. particularly under Section 93. There is no doubt that unless Caroe goes before any attempt is made to go into Section 93 the Congress reaction will be so violent as to be completely unmanageable. Therefore please start negotiations about Lockhart at once. (Paras. 1–7 repeated to Governor, N.W.F.P.)[5]

[2] No. 291.   [3] See No. 287.   [4] No. 297.
[5] In tel. 969–S of 3 May Lord Mountbatten asked for Sir O. Caroe's views on paras. 1–7 of the present telegram. Mountbatten Papers, Official Correspondence Files: Provinces and their Future, Part I(a).

301

The Earl of Listowel to Rear-Admiral Viscount Mountbatten of Burma

Mountbatten Papers. Letters to and from the Secretary of State

PRIVATE AND SECRET   INDIA OFFICE, *3 May 1947*
Dear Mountbatten,
Thank you for your letter of 24th April[1] and for Personal Report No. 4[2] and the records[3] of your meetings with Provincial Governors which accompanied it. I am very glad that the Personal Reports are to be circulated to all the members of the I. & B. Committee—I obtained the Prime Minister's agreement to this—as I myself find them most informative and enlightening. The Prime Minister has just invited Lord Chorley, Mr. C. P. Mayhew, M.P. and Mr. A. G. Bottomley, M.P. to join the Committee.[4] Mayhew and Bottomley were members of the U.K. Delegation for last December's Conversations with the Delegation from the Governor of Burma's Executive Council, and Bottomley subsequently attended the Panglong Conference. Chorley will, I am sure, be of great assistance to me in the House of Lords on Indian and Burma affairs. He was a member of the Parliamentary Delegation to India.

2. I read the full records of the Conference with Provincial Governors with the greatest interest and look forward to reading the report[5] of the Conference

with Residents, which you say is on its way. Records of such excellence prove the value of the additional staff which you have at your disposal. I was very glad to hear that the newcomers and the old hands had settled down so well together and that all are exhilarated rather than oppressed by the magnitude and urgency of the tasks confronting them.

3. Perhaps it is just as well that the episode over Mr. Porter's relief should have revealed Patel in his true colours so far as the employment of European officers is concerned, although episodes of this kind cannot fail to have adverse effects on service morale and efficiency. The truth of the matter is, I suppose, that the temptation to appoint an Indian for the first time as Secretary of the Home Department, even though the appointment was not the best that could be made on the merits of the case, proved too great for the first Indian holder of the Home Department portfolio. I hope that Mr. Williams, whose work as Joint Secretary of the Home Department is well-known and appreciated here, will be able to establish good working relations with Mr. Banerjee.

4. I am grateful to you for sending me an advance copy of Clow's pamphlet "The Excluded and Partially Excluded Areas of Assam",[6] which will be studied with interest here.

5. I find myself in whole-hearted agreement with the conclusion reached at the Conference of Provincial Governors to take no action on the suggestion that the Communist Party should be declared illegal. Such action would appear to be quite unwarranted, at any rate until there is much more conclusive evidence than exists at present that the Party is engaged in subversive activities that constitute a threat to Government.

6. I shall hope to let you have in my next letter some information as to the prospects of European police officers obtaining other suitable employment when they leave India. I am also investigating the question whether the Re-employment Bureau which has been established here can assist retiring British members of the Provincial Services to find suitable jobs. There has, as a matter of fact, been some interest shown recently in Parliament about the future of British members of subordinate services in India and Burma who are not entitled to proportionate pension on premature retirement, and I have already asked that the whole question of their future should be looked into.

7. In paragraphs 13 to 14 of Personal Report No. 4, you refer to the case put forward by the Sikh representatives when you interviewed them. I shall

---

[1] No. 210.   [2] No. 211.   [3] Nos 147 and 158.

[4] On 5 May Mr Attlee agreed that Mr Henderson should become a full member of the India and Burma Committee. L/PO/11/4: f 65.

[5] A copy of the Minutes of the Residents' Conference is on L/P &S/13/1831.

[6] L/P &J/7/10635.

hope to include in my next letter some comments on the Sikh complaints.

8. A speech of the kind made by Nehru at Gwalior[7] is certainly not encouraging from the point of view of a peaceful settlement of India's future. It is indeed extraordinary that a man of his stature can seriously contend that it is open to him to say publicly, in the capacity of President of the States' People's Conference, things which it is obviously quite improper for him to say as Vice-Chairman of the Executive Council. Not that ill-judged speeches are a monopoly of one side; Liaquat's published riposte to Nehru was in its way just as mischievous.

9. Auchinleck has arrived and I have already had a short talk with him. He is to see the Prime Minister on Monday morning and I hope will have an opportunity of talking to other Ministers. I have also this week had an interesting talk with Weightman.

10. It is a great relief to all of us here, as it must be to you, that the Compensation announcement has been made and I would like to congratulate you upon the extent to which you secured concessions from your Cabinet and their agreement upon the form of the announcements. The terms have, broadly speaking, been accorded a remarkably favourable reception here. The statements in Parliament prompted few Supplementary Questions and press editorial comment gives the impression that the terms are regarded as having struck just about the right balance. It is, of course, possible that, when there has been more time for detailed study of the White Paper and the Tables, the Opposition may press for a Debate. *Prima facie*, this would seem more likely to happen in the House of Lords than in the House of Commons, but it is a good sign that Hailey, who raised the Question by arrangement in the House of Lords and who received an advance copy of the White Paper did not raise any question upon it. I have heard from the Prime Minister that Simon is satisfied.

11. The case of Mahbub Ali, the Political officer of Malakhand who failed to prevent Nehru being stoned during his visit to the Frontier a few months ago, to which Caroe referred in his letter to you of 7th April, d.o. No. GH/37,[8] illustrates well the vindictiveness on the part of Ministers against which the Indian Services have to contend, and the genuineness of the need for compensation for Indians in the special categories.

[Para. 12, on the line taken by the Indian Representatives at an International Wheat Conference, omitted.]

13. I am greatly looking forward to seeing Ismay and hearing his impression of the present position in India. Your telegrams 954–S and 955–S[9] have only just arrived and there has not yet even been time to read them carefully,

but it will make all the difference having the outline of your plan in advance of Ismay's arrival, and we intend to embark upon intensive discussions next week.

Yours sincerely,

LISTOWEL

[7] See No. 181, note 2.
[8] Relevant extracts on R/3/1/93.   [9] Nos. 278 and 279.

302

Rear-Admiral Viscount Mountbatten of Burma to Lord Ismay (via India Office)

Telegram, Mountbatten Papers. Armed Forces, Indian, Vol. I, Part I

4 May 1947

5-U. Private and Personal for Ismay. Liaquat Ali told me at his interview today[1] that Brigadier Cariappa was carrying on propaganda among Indian officers at the Staff College in favour of setting up a military dictatorship when we handed over power. This has been reported to Liaquat by Naqvi, a student in the college.

2. Please contact Auchinleck and Slim and let me know whether there is any truth in this. Liaquat added that similar propaganda was going on in Delhi.

[1] Presumably the interview on 2 May (No. 287) as the draft was put up for approval on 2 May.

303

Rear-Admiral Viscount Mountbatten of Burma to Pandit Nehru

Mountbatten Papers. Official Correspondence Files: States, Relations

with, Part I(a)

4 May 1947

Dear Mr Nehru,

You will recall our conversation on the 22nd April[1] regarding the question of States joining the Constituent Assembly.

2. The Political Department have now sent instructions to all Residents on this subject. They have been told that if they are consulted, they should explain that there is no obligation on a Ruler who has accepted the Cabinet Mission plan to send representatives to the Constituent Assembly until the

[1] No. 193.

final stage, when that Assembly reassembles to frame the Union constitution. This stage has not yet been reached.

3. Also, it is likely that an announcement will be made by H.M.G. before long regarding the authorities to whom the powers of the Central Government in British India will be handed over. As soon as this announcement has been made, Rulers will be well advised to take immediate steps to consult public opinion in their States and thereafter without delay to announce whatever decision they may reach about joining the Constituent Assembly. They have been advised to this effect.

4. I think you will agree that these instructions meet the point you made with me namely, that Rulers should consult public opinion in their States before taking any decision, and that this should be done as soon as the decision about the method of transfer of power is announced. The decision of each State, after the people have been consulted, should be announced without delay.

Yours sincerely,

MOUNTBATTEN OF BURMA

304

Rear-Admiral Viscount Mountbatten of Burma to Pandit Nehru

R/1/29/3217: f 31

No. 1299/2.   *4 May 1947*

I was about to write to you to ask whether in view of your talk on April 26[1] with my Political Adviser you would still wish me to pursue the proposal made at the end of my letter No. 529/38 dated April 25, 1947,[2] that there should be an informal meeting between the three of us. But I have now received your letter of May 1[3] on the subject of the records of the Political Department, the abolition of Residencies and Political Agencies and direct correspondence between Departments of the Central Government and the Indian State authorities. In the circumstances I think that it would be a good thing to have this meeting to talk about these matters, which you did not, I gather, discuss with Corfield. I cannot arrange this in the immediate future since Corfield, as you probably know, has gone to England. But he should be back by about mid May and we might perhaps meet soon after that. In the meanwhile I have given orders that no further records are to be destroyed.

---

[1] See No. 236.   [2] No. 218.   [3] No. 266.

305

Sir E. Jenkins (Punjab) to Rear-Admiral Viscount Mountbatten of Burma

Mountbatten Papers. Official Correspondence Files: Punjab, Part I(b)

SECRET   GOVERNMENT HOUSE, LAHORE,
No. 669   *4 May 1947*

Dear Lord Mountbatten,

Many thanks for Your Excellency's letter of 3rd May.[1] My Secretary duly brought back with him a copy of the paper VCP 42 of 1st May,[2] and the draft of a telegram to myself which suggests a referendum on partition.

2. At the time of the Governors' Conference the position was briefly as follows:—

(i) His Majesty's Government still preferred arrangements on the lines of the Cabinet Mission's Statement of 16th May 1946.

(ii) If it proved quite impossible to secure the agreement of the party leaders to (i), Pakistan must be conceded, but with the exclusion from the Muslim majority provinces of any substantial non-Muslim majority areas.

(iii) In his discussions with Your Excellency Jinnah had seemed ready to accept the truncated Pakistan contemplated in (ii), and to instruct his followers to be reasonable about the inevitable partitions.

(iv) The attitude of the Hindus and Sikhs was uncertain, but should Jinnah prove reasonable, they might in the Punjab acquiesce in partition by Muslim majority and non-Muslim majority districts.

The plan set out in the paper VCP 42 of 1st May assumes, I think, the acquiescence of Jinnah and the Congress and Sikh leaders.

3. In my secret letter No. 668 of 3rd May[3] I have given reasons for holding that this assumption has already been falsified. Jinnah has publicly announced that the whole of the Punjab must be included in Pakistan; and the Hindus and Sikhs have publicly announced that the Punjab must be partitioned with the whole of the Ambala, Jullundur and Lahore Divisions and one colony district of the Multan Division included in the non-Muslim State. The views of the contending communities are thus incompatible not only with each other, but with the plan, and there is no chance whatever that the plan will be voluntarily carried out. Taking some of the details of the plan, I do not think that the two halves of the Assembly would ever meet (paragraph 7(b)). The Muslims would almost certainly boycott the proceedings, and the Hindus and Sikhs might follow suit. If meetings were held, the Muslims would boycott the elections (paragraphs 8 and 9). Finally, if we succeeded in holding

[1] See No. 274, note 2.   [2] This was the same as No. 279. Mountbatten Papers.
[3] No. 298.

the elections, I do not see what vote could be expected from representatives (paragraph 10) on a plan which one side rejects *in toto* and the other side regards as quite inadequate. The plan in fact becomes an award which nobody accepts—a dead letter unless we enforce it by the use of troops.

4. My answer to Your Excellency's question about a referendum is now clear. A referendum is in any circumstances a doubtful expedient in the Punjab, where the voters are entirely in the hands or at the mercy of the party leaders. On the particular issue of partition no question can at present be put to which the members of all communities could give an unqualified answer "Yes" or "No". The Muslims, guided by Jinnah, would answer "No" to any question; the Hindus and Sikhs—or most of them—want partition, but only on their own terms. They would reply "Yes" to the simple question "Should the Punjab be partitioned"; but they could not give an unqualified "Yes" to the boundary contemplated in the plan.

5. The possibilities before us seem to be:—

(*a*) agreement between the communities on any basis—however ridiculous—which will produce a stable successor authority. As long as Jinnah insists on absorbing the whole of the Punjab this possibility is remote. The division of the Punjab into three States on the lines indicated in the note appended to my letter of 3rd May might satisfy the non-Muslims.

(*b*) the enforcement of the plan—or of any other plan, such as the tripartite division of the Punjab—by the use of troops. This has so far been ruled out as impracticable, and the more I think of it the less I like it.

(*c*) the constitution of some *ad hoc* authority to succeed us. As I said in my letter of 3rd May, I have not been able to think of any suitable arrangement. If feeling were not so high, it might be possible to establish a provisional Government of "elder statesman" or non-party men; but this would be out of the question at present.

6. The plain fact is that no plan for the demission of power will work without the consent or at least the acquiescence of the communal and party leaders. The plan formulated is manifestly not acceptable to any of them.

Yours sincerely,

E. M. JENKINS

306

Rear-Admiral Viscount Mountbatten of Burma to Lord Ismay (via India Office)

*Telegram, Mountbatten Papers. Official Correspondence Files: Press
and Publicity, Part I(b)*

IMMEDIATE   NEW DELHI, *4 May 1947, 3 pm*
EN CLAIR   *Received: 4 May, 4.35 pm*

No. 240–GT. Following is front page item in *Hindustan Times* today Sunday.
Begins. "Wrong to Attribute motives to Viceroy" says Gandhiji. Addressing
the prayer meeting on Saturday evening, Mahatma Gandhi said that British
Cabinet had sent their best man, who was a warrior and statesman, as Viceroy.
He had come to carry out the noble decision of the British Government.
It was wholly wrong to distrust or attribute dishonest motives to him unless
he was proved to be unworthy of their confidence.

Gandhiji made an earnest appeal to all journalists to play their part at this
delicate stage. If they could not do so, it would be better for newspapers to
cease publication. Untruth was always indefensible and bad journalism did
infinite harm to the cause of the country, he said.

Gandhiji then complained bitterly of the attempted disclosures on Saturday
in a leading newspaper of Delhi purporting to divine what were the intentions
of the Viceroy and the decisions of the Congress Working Committee.[1]
He expressed the opinion that to act in such a manner was to lower the standards of journalism. Having been a journalist of many years' standing himself,
he could speak with authority of what the traditions of good journalism should
be. Whatever was in the Viceroy's heart was his business to disclose. Whatever
decisions were taken by the Congress Working Committee were for its
President or Secretary to give to the Press. It was hitting below the belt for
newspapers to take such titbits as they picked up from here there and everywhere and dish them up for the purpose of creating sensation. This misled
the public and harmed the cause. It was wrong to follow the bad example
of some foreign newspapers.

Indian journalists should not imitate bad manners for the sake of increasing
sales or getting notoriety for scoops. Wisdom and honour dictated that
everyone should imitate or take from others only that which was good and
worthwhile. *Ends.*

[1] See No. 291.

307

Rear-Admiral Viscount Mountbatten of Burma to Lord Ismay (via India Office)

Telegram, R/3/1/151: f 15

MOST IMMEDIATE   NEW DELHI, *4 May 1947, 4.20 pm*

TOP SECRET   *Received: 4 May, 3.15 pm*

No. 982–S. My 235–GT of 3rd May.[1] I am repeating to you in my 240–GT of 4th May[2] the castigation which Gandhi has delivered to his son and which has been published in the Sunday edition of the *Hindustan Times*.

2. My 968–S of 3rd May.[3] In the meantime it has become clear that there are no legal grounds for going into Section 93 in the Frontier Province in that Caroe can hardly say that the Government cannot be carried on with the existing administration.

3. If I force a dissolution on the present government and do go into Section 93 I have clear indications that Congress will fight to the end and I may well reach an impasse in other provinces.

4. I intend, however, to stick to my intention of obtaining the views of the people of the Frontier Province on Pakistan or Hindustan and it seems probable that Congress will back me in holding a referendum. The referendum will probably have to be organised by me and run by specially selected officers who will be independent of the Government but will work in with the officials. I am having this followed up.

5. I am seeing Gandhi at 1600 today Sunday and Jinnah at 1730 and will telegraph further after these interviews.

[1] No. 291.   [2] No. 306.   [3] No. 300.

308

Sir Walter Monckton to Rear-Admiral Viscount Mountbatten of Burma

Mountbatten Papers. Official Correspondence Files:
Hyderabad, Part I(a)

SECRET   LAKE VIEW HOUSE, HYDERABAD, DECCAN,

4 May 1947

Your Excellency,

1. Yesterday, 3rd May, Your Excellency directed me to prepare a note on the subject of a discussion which you had with Mr Krishna Menon and my-self during the afternoon.

2. Your Excellency made it clear that you wanted a Memorandum upon the constitutional, legal questions involved but that it was the political implications of the discussions which seemed to you vital matters.

3. It is manifest that one of the problems which has to be determined is the future relationship of the Indian Union or Unions with H.M.G. in the United Kingdom and with the association of free nations which comprise what is commonly known as the British Commonwealth of Nations. There are considerations which may well make it mutually advantageous that India should not completely sever the ties which connect her to that association. There are, for instance, two points which you mentioned: (a) the fact that without such association it would be extremely difficult, if not impossible, for the new Indian Union to retain the services of the most valuable officers now serving in the Indian Army, holding His Majesty's Commission, and (b) the demand which it might be politically difficult, if not impracticable, to resist from the Muslim League and other minorities not to be driven out of the British Commonwealth.

4. The principal difficulty in the way of keeping the association is the resolution of the Constituent Assembly proposing the establishment of an independent sovereign Republic, and though this may perhaps be treated as an expression of ultimate aspiration rather than an assertion of an immediate constitutional status, it would be politically difficult to find a solution which was expressly inconsistent with that aspiration.

5. It is, therefore, necessary to find a solution which does not compel retention of the King-Emperor as head of the Indian Union. On the other hand, if no allegiance in any sense is owed by citizens of the Indian Union to the Crown, it is difficult to see how the continuance of an association can be sufficiently real to permit officers holding His Majesty's Commission to continue to serve in the Army of the Indian Union or to provide a politically sufficient answer to the claim of Pakistan, and perhaps some of the Princes, to remain within the British Dominions.

6. His Majesty the King is regarded now in constitutional theory, as I think, not as the head of the British Commonwealth of Nations but as the King separately of the United Kingdom, Canada, South Africa etc., and King Emperor of India. The suggestion which was discussed with you was whether it was possible to retain the link between the Indian Union and the association by developing the idea of a "common citizenship" so as to provide that a citizen of the Indian Union would owe allegiance first of all to his own State and further to His Majesty as head of the association. There are difficulties in the way of this solution: (a) It would be necessary for such an arrangement to be reciprocal and it is not easy to say in what sense a citizen of the United Kingdom would owe allegiance, while in India, to the Indian Union. (b)

With whom would the common citizenship subsist? It is not probable that Dominions such as Australia and South Africa would be willing to admit citizens of the Indian Union to common citizenship with them. Can the community of citizenship be confined to common citizenship with the United Kingdom and, if so, is this sufficient for the purpose of attracting allegiance to His Majesty the King as Head of the association? (c) When one passes from the field of relationships between the component units in the association which now makes up the British Commonwealth to relationships between the British Commonwealth or units of it with foreign countries, further difficulties may be encountered. For example, would the treaty arrangements, which would be made by the Indian Union be made separately and without the use of His Majesty's name? The reality of such difficulties has been seen in the case of Eire.

7. Even this cursory review, necessarily made at short notice and without access to books, is enough to show that the idea of common citizenship and the allegiance which might be derived therefrom cannot be lightly accepted. The utmost that can be said is that it contains the germ of an idea which I suggest ought to be more fully considered. I return to what Your Excellency said about the importance which should be attached to political considerations in comparison and contrast with points of constitutional law. If I understood your view aright, you thought that the essential fact was that if there should be a will to continue the association in order to obtain or retain mutual political advantages, every possible way of giving effect to that will by satisfactory constitutional means ought to be examined. I can only say that I think the suggestion which Mr Krishna Menon made is worthy of ample consideration.[1]

WALTER MONCKTON

[1] On 9 May Sir E. Mieville acknowledged this letter on Lord Mountbatten's behalf as directed at that day's Staff Meeting (No. 366).

309

Record of Interview between Rear-Admiral Viscount Mountbatten of Burma and Mr Gandhi

Mountbatten Papers. Viceroy's Interview No. 120

TOP SECRET   *4 May 1947, 4–5.30 pm*

I thanked him for the strong and courageous statement he made rebuking the Press in general, and his own in particular, for their uncalled for attack on me.[1]

He said that he thought that the Press in India was very immature and had only just been released from censorship and did not realise the harm they were doing by the methods they adopted.

I outlined the plan which Lord Ismay had taken to London and asked Mr. Gandhi if he agreed that the method I was proposing to adopt, whereby the people of India would decide how they wished power to be transferred, was not a good one. He replied that he did not agree that we were leaving the people of India a free choice since we were practically imposing partition on them.

I then asked him what his plan was and he returned to his original idea and reiterated that if I believed in it firmly I could put it through.

In fact, he finally invited me to turn over power either to the Muslim League or, if they would not take it, to Congress for the whole of India, and give them immediate Dominion Status and then remain as Governor General for thirteen months and then leave them to their own devices. When I pointed out that this would lead to a civil war and a blood bath, he replied "not if Mr. Jinnah means what he has signed with me".

I told him Jinnah signed in good faith when he thought I was going to give a fair decision and that I did not for one moment suppose the Muslims would not immediately go to war if I attempted to betray them in this manner. In any case, I pointed out that H.M.G. would never allow me to hand over a colossal minority like the Muslims into the power of Congress and I much regretted therefore that his plan was not acceptable. I did, however, say I would report it to London.

¹ See No. 306.

310

Record of Interview between Rear-Admiral Viscount Mountbatten of Burma and Mr Jinnah and Mr Liaquat Ali Khan[1]

Mountbatten Papers. Viceroy's Interview No. 119

4 May 1947

HIS EXCELLENCY said that he had been into the question of applying Section 93 to the N.W.F.P. but that he had found many difficulties in the way. He had, therefore, hit upon another plan which was to set up his own machinery and hold a referendum in the Province on the simple issue of Hindustan or Pakistan. This would have the added advantage of getting rid of all weightage. He went on to say that he had just seen Mr Gandhi and had put to him the proposition that the right to hold meetings with free speech could not be denied, but that processions and picketing should be disallowed. If there was any shooting on the site where the meeting was being held, this could

¹ Sir E. Mieville was also present.

be attributable to the Party in opposition to the one that was holding the meeting. To this, Mr Gandhi had agreed.

HIS EXCELLENCY went on to talk about the "Direct Action" Campaign. He thought that the very name was an unfortunate one, in that the world at large took it to mean that it was a Campaign in which arms would be used and it contrasted badly in name with the Congress "Non-Violence Civil Disobedience" Campaign.

MR JINNAH said that the Viceroy might be correct in what he said, but in actual fact the Congress Non-Violence Campaign, whenever it was put into force, resulted in terrible bloodshed. He agreed with the Viceroy who had previously suggested that it would be a good idea to make known once again that although a resolution of Direct Action had been passed by the Muslim League the campaign had never been launched. He also agreed with another suggestion that the Viceroy had put to him that, in order to make clear to the world what the Direct Action Campaign meant and that it had never actually been launched, it would be a good plan to call the European Correspondents together and explain fully the position to them.

MR JINNAH went on to say that he had received a deputation of six of his followers released on parole from the Frontier.

They had explained to him that if they came out of gaol as they were entitled to do as a result of the Viceroy's intervention with the Khan Sahib it would mean:

(a) They would be accused of having done so under the Viceroy's orders; and

(b) It would be very difficult to explain to their people why they had come out and would destroy their prestige.

And so, MR JINNAH went on, after careful consideration he wished to say that he was quite ready to make a statement to the effect that he would suspend his Campaign on the Frontier unreservedly and that he would call for a truce. Some twenty to thirty of his leading men would come out of gaol to explain to his followers why this action had been decided upon and that there was to be no unlawful activity of any kind until after His Excellency's announcement of his plan. All this would be done provided that he could add that he had good reason to believe that His Excellency had recommended to H.M.G. that a referendum would be held in the N.W.F.P. to decide whether the people of that province were in favour of Hindustan and [or] Pakistan. It must also be understood that Congress would agree that there was no victimization and that it would be an honourable truce. He quite appreciated that H.M.G. might over-rule His Excellency's recommendation, but that would not affect the immediate issue.

HIS EXCELLENCY then said that supposing there were a referendum and it went in favour of the Muslims, he presumed that the Congress Government would resign, but if they carried on, he would expect the Pakistan Constituent Assembly to pass a Resolution asking for fresh Elections. He did not propose to twist the law so as to go into Section 93. He asked whether the Muslim League were sure that they wanted the N.W.F.P. It cost the present Government 3½ Crores a year to keep the Tribes quiet.

MR JINNAH replied that after the Viceroy's announcement had been made, he proposed to go to the Frontier himself to have a straight talk with the Tribes, and he thought that as a result he would not have to pay them anything or at any rate he felt sure that he would be able to cut the figure of 3½ Crores very considerably. He would come to some arrangement with them.

HIS EXCELLENCY then summed up and said that:

(1) Sir Eric Mieville would draft two statements—one on the lines that Mr Jinnah wanted, as mentioned above, and the other of a weaker character, which His Excellency would hold up his sleeve and only use if it were not possible to get the first one accepted by the Prime Minister, which His Excellency promised he would do his utmost to achieve.

(2) The statement would be shown to Pandit Nehru by His Excellency, who explained that if he could get Congress agreement to it, his hands would be immeasurably strengthened. (Note: All the way through the conversation His Excellency had stressed how very touchy the Congress were about the Frontier and how their attitude was stiffening every day.)

(3) No mention was to be made in either statement to a General Election to follow on the Referendum. (Note: This had been put forward with much heat by both Mr Jinnah and Mr Liaquat late in the conversation. It was, they said, a natural corollary to a referendum, if the referendum was in favour of Pakistan. His Excellency had agreed with their argument but pointed out that any mention of a general election would finish any chance he had of obtaining the concurrence of Congress agreement to the Statement.)

Finally, HIS EXCELLENCY touched on the PUNJAB, about which he said he was very worried as he knew that the Sikhs were in a truculent frame of mind. This view was confirmed by talk he had had with The Maharaja of Patiala on the previous evening.[2] His Excellency thought it would be a good thing if Mr Jinnah would see the Maharaja and have a talk with him. MR JINNAH said he would be quite ready to do so and it was left that Sir Eric Mieville should get into touch with H.H. of Patiala and make the suggestion to him.[3]

---

[2] See No. 354, paras. 22–5.

[3] Subsequently, on 14 May, Lord Mountbatten invited the Maharaja of Patiala to dinner and on 18 May Patiala sent a letter to Lord Mountbatten reporting the 'long talks' he had had with Mr Jinnah adding that it had been his 'constant endeavour to bring about an agreement between the political parties in the country and I was glad to have this opportunity of making a further effort in that direction.' Mountbatten Papers, Official Correspondence Files: Transfer of Power, Part III(a). Patiala's letter is summarised in No. 492.

311

Sir F. Burrows (Bengal) to Rear-Admiral Viscount Mountbatten of Burma

Telegram, Mountbatten Papers. Official Correspondence Files: Bengal,
Partition of, Part I(a)

IMPORTANT   *4 May 1947, 6.55 pm*
CONFIDENTIAL   *Received: 5 May, 8 am*

No. 113–C.   Your personal letter No. 592/92 of May 2nd.[1] I am afraid idea
of using threat of transfer of jute factories to East Bengal would not have
desired effect. Exact statistics are not readily available but following are
approximately correct. Of about 100 jute mills in Bengal *all* are in Calcutta
industrial area. About a dozen are entirely Indian owned and it is estimated
that probably 75% of capital of rest is in Indian hands, with Hindus vastly
predominating. Only four or five are sterling companies. In the circumstances
no one would believe that there was any chance of an industry in which Hindus
are so heavily interested and one which involves 65,000 looms and one and
a quarter million spindles and which employs 300,000 workers, who would
have to be housed, being transferred to Eastern Bengal where both coal
(on which about half the mills depend for power) and electricity on appropriate scale are entirely lacking. Surely fact that jute mainly grown in East
Bengal and industry is firmly planted on Hooghly-side is best argument
against partition? As regards a general election in Bengal to ascertain views
of electorate on partition, I should first of all explain that while I think my
Ministers would favour a plebiscite or referendum if conducted in three
separate compartments (Muslims, Caste Hindus and Schedule Caste) they
would strongly resent a dissolution and a general election as they were elected
only a year ago on "Pakistan" issue and there is nothing to indicate that they
have lost the confidence of their supporters on this issue which of course
envisages an undivided Bengal. This has a bearing on (a) of your questions
which however I shall answer last.

   3. Answer to other questions are as follows. (b) It is feasible to hold a general
election on this issue but a plebiscite or referendum though not contemplated
by 1935 Act would probably be more acceptable to all and would certainly
be more expeditious and stage of primary elections for seats reserved for
Scheduled Castes would be eliminated, compartmental voting would be
desirable as it is probable voters on Muslim and Scheduled Caste electoral
rolls are, proportionately to population figures, much fewer than Caste
Hindu voters. (c) In present state of communal feeling there would certainly
be rioting though it is difficult to estimate its incidence. In many areas, and
more particularly in East Bengal, communities who were in a majority

locally would do its utmost to prevent potential voters of other way of thinking recording their votes and this would generally lead to *communal* rioting. (*d*) Absolute minimum time for a general election would probably be four months from start to finish, with further delay if polling were seriously held up by widespread rioting. A referendum would require much the same preparation but would take a month less by elimination of primary elections. It is however for physical reasons extremely difficult to conduct polling for an election or a referendum in East Bengal between June and middle of November on account of so much of the countryside being under water which hampers communications in some areas and makes nearly impossible satisfactory arrangement of polling stations. A small or patchy poll would be criticised as inconclusive. (*e*) With a partially illiterate electorate it would be necessary to confine referendum to one specific issue admitting of a plain "yes" or "no" reply: conditional supplementary questions should [*sic* ?not] be included. This means that it would have to be expressly stated to which side in partition each area in Province would be allotted—in other words H.M.G. would still have to make a conditional award as regards plan of partition contemplated. (*a*) I do not consider it desirable to hold a general election. A plebiscite however could be held if delay involved is not a bar. Incidentally in my disscussion with Suhrawardy yesterday in regard to a coalition government (which I again strongly pressed on him) I stated explicitly that time would not allow of a plebiscite as I understood this to be position when I left Delhi.

¹ No. 280.

312

Rear-Admiral Viscount Mountbatten of Burma to Lord Ismay (via India Office)

Telegram, R/3/1/151: ff 16–17

IMMEDIATE   *4 May 1947, 11 pm*
TOP SECRET   *Received: 5 May, 12.30 am*

984–S.   My 982–S of 4th May.¹ Gandhi does not agree with my plan because he does not wish to see India partitioned.² He called upon me to turn the whole of India over either to the League or to Congress on the basis of immediate Dominion Status and to remain as Governor General till June 1948, to see fair play until then and then withdraw.

2. I told him how shocked I was that a man of peace could suggest a course which he must know could only end in civil war but I promised to report his plan to London.

¹ No. 307.   ² See No. 309.

3. I induced Gandhi to remain to shake hands with Jinnah and suggested that they should try and arrange a meeting. They met quite affably but as usual both talked inaudibly so I could not overhear what they were saying.

4. Jinnah and Liaquat came from 1730 to 2000.[3] Jinnah said that he was quite prepared to issue a statement suspending unreservedly his present campaign on the Frontier provided that he could issue a statement to the effect that he had grounds for believing that I had made a recommendation to H.M.G. that a referendum would be held in the N.W.F.P. to decide whether the people wanted Pakistan or Hindustan.

5. I am having a statement prepared which will be shown to him tomorrow Monday. I then propose to show it to Nehru, and if I can get the latter's approval I am going to ask you to approach the Prime Minister.

6. He fully realized that H.M.G. might not endorse my recommendation but nevertheless he would be quite satisfied if he could issue something on the above lines.

7. I do feel that if we can get agreement there is every chance of quietening down the electric situation on the Frontier of which you are only too well aware.

8. Caroe has stated that he considers referendum under my personal control a feasible but difficult proposition. On the other hand it is clear to me that if I persist in any attempt to go into Section 93 or even to hold elections in the face of the violent opposition from Congress a very difficult situation will be created.

[3] See No. 310.

313

Extract from letter of Mr Horace Alexander[1]

Public Record Office. CAB 127/109

NEW DELHI, 5 *May 1947*

..."I want to get across certain things while Ismay is in London, very urgent for those who may be preparing statements or speeches.
First, don't be too worried about Gandhi's Reuter statement.[2] Quite frankly, I think he confuses the inviolable human unity of India with things like political frontiers. But it's all right. He knows he has failed to convince his Congress colleagues, and he returns sorrowful to his heroic work in Bihar—turning his back gladly on the unrealities of Delhi.

Secondly, let the *word* partition be avoided at all costs. Division is a word that does not arouse the same passions, though for practical purposes it means the same.

Third, there must be no hanky-panky about the N.W.F.P.

---

[1] It is inferred from another paper on CAB 127/109 that this letter was addressed to Miss Agatha Harrison who sent on an extract to Sir S. Cripps.

[2] In answer to a question on 5 May 1947 from Reuter's correspondent in Delhi, Mr Gandhi replied he had always said, and said even then, that the communal division of India was not inevitable and would not solve the communal problem.

314

Minutes of Viceroy's Twenty Sixth Staff Meeting, Item 3

Mountbatten Papers

TOP SECRET

Those present during discussion of Item 3 of this Meeting held at The Viceroy's House, New Delhi on 5 May 1947 at 10 am were: Rear-Admiral Viscount Mountbatten of Burma, Sir E. Mieville, Captain Brockman, Mr Christie, Mr I. D. Scott, Lieutenant-Colonel Erskine Crum

THE CHOICE BY PROVINCES OF THEIR OWN FUTURE

HIS EXCELLENCY drew particular attention to the records of the interviews which he had had the previous day with Mr Gandhi and Mr Jinnah.[1] He had already sent a telegram[2] to Lord Ismay concerning these interviews.

HIS EXCELLENCY THE VICEROY said that, since Lord Ismay had left for London, a number of difficulties inherent in the draft plan which he had taken had arisen. He said that he had felt all along that Lord Ismay's departure was premature. However, the difficulties would have to be faced and Lord Ismay would have to be informed of them.

The meeting then considered a telegram[3] from the Governor of the N.W.F.P. containing his support for the suggestion that a referendum should be held in that Province. HIS EXCELLENCY THE VICEROY said that Lord Ismay should be informed of Sir Olaf Caroe's views.

The Meeting next considered a telegram[4] from the Governor of Bengal. His views were that a referendum could be held in that Province but he cited several disadvantages to such a course. After discussion, HIS EXCELLENCY THE VICEROY said that Lord Ismay should be informed that a referendum in Bengal was not recommended.

---

[1] See Nos. 309 and 310.   [2] No. 312.

[3] CA–68 of 4 May. R/3/1/151: f 14.   [4] No. 311.

HIS EXCELLENCY THE VICEROY said that he had been "attacked" at the Garden Party on 3rd May by two Scheduled Caste representatives to the Constituent Assembly from Bengal, who had warned him against Mr Mandal who they thought had been misleading him. They had stated that the Scheduled Castes on no account wanted separation from the Caste Hindus and were determined not to be left under the "brutal suppression and domination" of the Muslims. They firmly demanded partition and claimed that they did represent the views of the Scheduled Castes in Bengal. He had asked them what would happen to the Scheduled Castes in Eastern Bengal. They had replied that they themselves lived in Eastern Bengal but did not intend to stay there, and they had suggested that all the seven million Scheduled Castes in East Bengal should be moved to West Bengal. They had confirmed the atrocities in Noakhali. HIS EXCELLENCY THE VICEROY said that this conversation should be repeated by telegram to the Governor of Bengal.

The Meeting then considered two letters[5] from the Governor of the Punjab. From these it was clear that Sir Evan Jenkins was opposed to a referendum in that Province. Sir Evan Jenkins also raised objections to the plan envisaged in the Draft Announcement. These objections were mainly based on the grounds that the acquiescence of Mr Jinnah and the Congress and Sikh leaders was assumed, whereas it was, in Sir Evan Jenkins' view, unlikely that they would acquiesce in it.

HIS EXCELLENCY THE VICEROY gave his opinion that this was not in fact the case. Mr Jinnah's public announcement[6] that the whole of the Punjab must be included in Pakistan might well be pure manoeuvre; and he did not personally feel, from what Mr Jinnah had said in interviews, that Mr Jinnah would in the end absolutely refuse to acquiesce in the partition of the Punjab. Furthermore, the Congress Working Committee had virtually accepted the outline of the plan. The Sikhs presented a considerable difficulty as the partition would divide them into two fairly equal halves; but the Maharaja of Patiala had agreed that there was no alternative but for him (His Excellency) to make a notional partition—although he had been very gloomy about the probable results.[7] If the Sikhs wanted to improve their position they could only do so by negotiation.

MR CHRISTIE stated that Rao Bahadur Menon had advocated the desirability of having an alternative plan, for instance that prepared by Sir B. N. Rau,[8] ready in secret in case there was violent opposition from the Indian leaders to the plan contained in the Draft Announcement. HIS EXCELLENCY THE VICEROY pointed out that Sir Evan Jenkins had already declared Sir B. N. Rau's plan to be unworkable.

MR SCOTT said that another possible solution might be to appoint as advisers to the Governor, under Section 93 Government, one representative of each community, and eventually to hand over power to them or to a joint admin-

istration of which they would form the nucleus. HIS EXCELLENCY THE
VICEROY said that this idea savoured of handing over the Province to civil
war.

HIS EXCELLENCY THE VICEROY

   (i) instructed Con. Sec to prepare for his approval a draft telegram to the
Governor of Bengal concerning the conversation which he had had
at the Garden Party on 5th May with two representatives to the Constituent Assembly of the Scheduled Castes in Bengal;[9]

  (ii) instructed Con. Sec. to prepare for his approval a draft telegram to
Lord Ismay in London, containing the views of the Governors of the
N.W.F.P., Bengal and the Punjab on the proposal to hold a referendum
in those Provinces.

 (iii) invited Prin. Sec. to attempt to obtain from Mr Jinnah the latter's
real views on the partition of Provinces, and whether he was likely
to accept the plan in the Draft Announcement; and again to point
out to Mr Jinnah the great advantages he would reap from acceptance of
the Cabinet Mission's plan;

 (iv) directed D.P.S.V. to arrange for the Governor of the Punjab to come
and see him (His Excellency) at Simla;

  (v) directed D.P.S.V. to have prepared for him a map of the Punjab,
showing the line of notional partition, the Sikhs' demands (so far as
they were known) and the compromise solution suggested by the
Maharaja of Patiala.

---

[5] Nos. 298 and 305.   [6] Annex I to No. 276.
[7] cf No. 354, paras. 22–5.   [8] See No. 262, note 2.
[9] In the event Lord Mountbatten sent Sir F. Burrows a letter on this subject (No. 592/92 of 6 May
1947). Mountbatten Papers, Official Correspondence Files: Bengal, Partition of, Part I(b).

315

Rear-Admiral Viscount Mountbatten of Burma to Sardar Baldev Singh

R/3/1/178: f 49

No. 592/90.   *5 May 1947*

Dear Sardar Baldev Singh,

Thank you for your letter of the 1st May,[1] about a possible division of the
Punjab.

2. I should like to make it quite clear that the notional division which is being
adopted in the first instance will be solely in order to create two assemblies for
voting purposes on the broad question of partition or unity. It will in no way

---

[1] No. 269.

prejudice the subsequent work of the Boundary Commission which will have to be set up, in order to demarcate the actual limits of the two parts of the Punjab.

3. You will realise that it is not possible for me, either in equity or morally, to adopt any other criterion for this immediate purpose than demarcation by Muslim majority and non-Muslim majority areas.

4. Arrangements which I am hoping to embody in my plan will at no stage prevent the Punjab from deciding to frame a united constitution if the representatives of the people so desire; nor will they in any way prevent mutual agreed readjustment of frontiers if they decide to separate.

5. Finally, I have adopted your suggestion of leaving it open to East Punjab to negotiate with either Hindustan or Pakistan to decide which Constituent Assembly they will join.

Yours sincerely,
MOUNTBATTEN OF BURMA

316

Record of Interview between Rear-Admiral Viscount Mountbatten of Burma and Mr Ghazanfar Ali Khan

Mountbatten Papers. Viceroy's Interview No. 122

TOP SECRET   *5 May 1947, 12 noon–12.35 pm*

He said he had had a satisfactory interview with Her Excellency on health matters, and had no departmental matters to raise with me.

I therefore concentrated on talking about the Punjab which is his home. I explained to him at great length the idea of notional partition for voting purposes. He had to ask me to repeat the scheme four times and I am not absolutely certain that he understood it when he left, although he said he did.

I asked him if he had considered whether there should be a referendum or whether a vote of the representatives of the Constituent Assembly would do.

He was against a referendum as it would take too long, was liable to start rioting, and would not be likely to give a different answer to that of the representatives of the Constituent Assembly, which he favoured but only provided that it was quite clearly laid down that the representatives of the Constituent Assembly had to be readjusted to represent the districts in notional partition, since he pointed out that a number of them did not even belong to the Punjab.

I promised to follow this up.

We then discussed the fact that notional partition or almost any form of partition agreed upon for the Punjab would cut the Sikhs almost exactly into halves—18 lakhs on the one side: 20 lakhs on the other;—and that the Sikhs had now put in a demand to go up to the river Ravi and even up to the Chenab.

Mr Ghazanfar Ali agreed that partition would be a great tragedy for the Sikhs, and that there might be difficulty in imposing such a partition against their will; though he pointed out that they made tremendous threats twelve years ago, at the time of the communal award, that they would die to the last man, whereas in fact they did not die even to the first man.

I pointed out, however, that if Mr Ghazanfar Ali was against the partition of the Punjab (and he reaffirmed that he was ardently against it), then the best service he could do towards a united Punjab would be to seek out Giani Kartar Singh and discuss the matter with him now while he could still take the credit of having done so *before* H.M.G.'s decision was announced.

He told me that Giani Kartar Singh was an old friend; but that ever since the trouble they had not seen each other and indeed he (the Giani) had been saying terrible things. He agreed, however, that it was up to himself to make the first move, and he promised to go away and get into touch with Giani Kartar Singh as soon as he could and write and let me know how it went.

317

Rear-Admiral Viscount Mountbatten of Burma to Lord Ismay (via India Office)
Telegram, R/3/1/151: ff 22–3

MOST IMMEDIATE   NEW DELHI, *5 May 1947, 2.30 pm*
TOP SECRET   *Received: 5 May, 2.55 pm*

No. 987–S. 1. Further to my 968–S of 3rd May[1] and 982–S of 4th May.[2] Views of Governor of North-West Frontier Province on proposal for referendum in that Province have now been received.[3] In general he greatly favours plan. He mentions following difficulties, which, however, we both feel can be overcome:—

(a) machinery. It would be hard to find enough outside officials without calling on N.W.F.P. resources;

(b) modification of law. It might be necessary to promulgate special ordinance.

(c) Result in favour of Pakistan would have to be followed by election which owing to weightage or other reasons might, though improbably,

[1] No. 300.   [2] No. 307.
[3] These were sent in tel. CA–68 of 4 May. R/3/1/151: f 14.

return Congress to power. It would have to be made clear that on the main issue result of referendum was final.

2. In view of this I am strongly in favour of a referendum in the N.W.F.P., organised by me and run by specially selected officers. I have now sent for Nehru to discuss this at 15.30 today, Monday;[4] I will telegraph again after I have seen him.[5]

3. The Views of the Governor of Bengal on a referendum have also been received.[6] He states:—

(a) A referendum would certainly lead to rioting though it is difficult to estimate its incidence.

(b) A referendum would take about three months. It would be extremely difficult to hold one in East Bengal between June and the middle of November on account of so much of the countryside being under water which hampers communications in some areas and makes nearly impossible the satisfactory arrangement of polling stations.

(c) With the partially illiterate electorate it would be necessary to confine referendum to one specific issue permitting of a plain "Yes" or "No" reply. Conditional supplementary questions should not be included. This means that it would have to be expressly stated to which side in Partition each area in Province would be allotted—in other words H.M.G. would still have to make a conditional award as regards plan of partition contemplated.

4. I feel that the probability of rioting and the time factor are over-riding disadvantages. Furthermore, it is most unlikely that a referendum would produce any different result to the method contemplated in the Draft Announcement. Despite all the Muslim Leaders say, we feel that they are extremely optimistic in counting on any large number of Scheduled Caste votes. I am therefore opposed to the holding of a referendum in Bengal.

5. I also asked the Governor of the Punjab for his views on a referendum. He has given his views against a referendum in the Punjab and against the plan which is envisaged in the draft announcement.[7] We are examining these views most urgently and our conclusions will follow in a later telegram, but in the meanwhile you should be careful at the I.B. Committee Meeting tonight not to commit yourself to the plan for the Punjab as contained in the draft announcement.

[4] See No. 318, note 1.
[5] Para. 1 (beginning at the second sentence) and para. 2 of the present telegram were repeated by Lord Mountbatten to Sir O. Caroe in tel. 989-S of 5 May. Mountbatten Papers, Official Correspondence Files: Provinces and their future, Part I(a).
[6] No. 311.
[7] See Nos. 298 and 305.

318

*Record of Interview between Rear-Admiral Viscount Mountbatten of Burma
and Pandit Nehru (Extract)[1]*

Mountbatten Papers. Viceroy's Interview No. 129

TOP SECRET   *5 May 1947, 3.30–5.30 pm*

I next went with Pandit Nehru through Sardar Patel's letter of the 26th
April,[2] on the interpretation of H.M.G.'s statement of the 6th December. I
pointed out that the Cabinet Mission plan still held the field so far as H.M.G.
were concerned, and that I proposed to make one more attempt to get it
accepted at the meeting with the leaders. I therefore thought it would be well
to clear up the point as to whether Congress really did accept H.M.G.'s
statement of the 6th December and were prepared to abide by it or not.

Pandit Nehru replied that of course the Congress accepted the statement,
but if they were to be asked whether they were going to force Assam and the
Sikhs to abide by it they would have to admit that they were in no position
to force any Province or section of a Province to comply with all the terms
against their will and interest. All Congress could do was to advise them to the
best of their ability and try to persuade them to abide by the statement. "In
other words", he said, "the League must be realistic and must realise that if
they attempt to cheat or repress any non-Muslim community within Groups
B and C, they are bound to have trouble as a matter of normal human reaction".

I admitted that this was a sensible point of view, but said that it was not
likely to make acceptance of the Cabinet Mission plan easier for Mr. Jinnah.

[1] The heading of this document in Mountbatten Papers includes the following sentence: 'For part
of this interview Sir Eric Mieville was present and he has kept a separate record of the discussion
which took place during that part.' This separate record has not been traced but it evidently covered
discussion on the proposed referendum in the N.W.F.P.; see No. 317, para. 2.

[2] No. 226.

319

*Record of Interview between Rear-Admiral Viscount Mountbatten of Burma
and Sardar K. M. Panikkar (Extract)*

Mountbatten Papers. Viceroy's Interview No. 130

TOP SECRET   *5 May 1947, 5.30–6.40 pm*

He next explained the position which his Maharaja had taken up, on his
advice, as Leader of the group of States that had decided to join the Constituent

Assembly last month. He pointed out that it was less a question of trying to get in well with Congress than of the absolute need to stand in well with their own people and make them feel that they had a voice in affairs. He pointed out that the States could not possibly stand by themselves and that a strong Centre was absolutely essential for the States. He deprecated the weak Centre set out in the Cabinet Mission Plan, and he positively welcomed Pakistan, since it would enable a really strong Centre to be formed at Delhi, which the inclusion of Muslim majority Provinces would have rendered impossible. He was sure that Mr. Jinnah intended to set up an equally strong Centre for Pakistan, and that the two could keep in treaty relation with each other, so that the over-all defence problem could be looked after just as well as under the Cabinet Mission plan.

So far from considering the plan I was working on inferior to the Cabinet Mission plan, he said it was greatly superior and for the greater good of India in the long run. For, he pointed out, if the Pakistan States eventually joined up with the rest of the Union of India they could only do so by accepting the very strong Centre at Delhi without which India could not survive.

He then told me that he was one of the very few Indians who had made a study of strategical defence, and that this was simply not understood by any of the leaders except Sardar Patel, who was so worried by the situation now that he had told Sardar Panikkar in confidence that he was determined to try and get a really good settlement with the British while the present Congress Government was still in power, since he feared that they might be replaced by people who did not understand defence and who would not realise the import- of a good settlement with the British.

I reminded Sardar Panikkar that any settlement that failed to include India in some shape or form within the British Commonwealth or to have some arrangement for association with the Crown sufficiently strong to enable British officers to continue serving in India without resigning their King's Commissions, would be no good to India. I pointed out that unless they could have British Commissioned officers continuing to serve in India as servants of the Indian Government, and unless all the secrets of modern equipment were at the disposal of India, then a treaty would only be half the value, since we would be making arrangements with an India so weak as to be of little help; and India would be getting no help from us except promises of assistance in time of war.

I ended up by saying "You can't have your cake and eat it". He said that I had put the case more clearly to him than he had previously had it put, and that he would take an early opportunity of talking to Sardar Patel. I said "I hope you will not mention my views to him since I am not prepared to discuss this matter with any member of Congress unless they raise it first." He said he entirely understood the position.

320

Cabinet

India and Burma Committee. I.B.(47)21st Meeting

L/P&J/10/79: ff 405–9

Those present at this Meeting held at 10 Downing Street, S.W.1, on 5 May 1947 at 5 pm were Mr Attlee (in the Chair), Mr Hugh Dalton, Sir Stafford Cripps, Mr Alexander, Viscount Addison, the Earl of Listowel, Lord Chorley, Mr A. G. Bottomley

Also present were: Mr A. Henderson, Sir David Monteath, Lord Ismay, Sir William Croft, Mr Abell; Sir Norman Brook, Mr S. E. V. Luke, Mr G. M. Wilson, Mr F. F. Turnbull (Secretariat)

The Transfer of Power in India

The Committee had before them telegrams from the Viceroy to the Secretary of State for India (Nos. 954–S and 955–S of 1st May)[1] containing proposals on the procedure for determining the authority or authorities to which power should be demitted in India.

LORD ISMAY said that the Viceroy had found that communal feeling in India was far more bitter than he had expected: it had become an obsession with both Hindus and Moslems and had been much intensified by the statement of 20th February. Since his arrival, the Viceroy had made every effort to persuade the Indian political leaders to accept the Cabinet Mission's plan. Mr. Jinnah had, however, shown himself inflexibly opposed to acceptance, and the Viceroy had reached the conclusion that the prospects of agreement were negligible. The proposals set out in his telegram No. 955–S were therefore designed to place the responsibility for dividing India conspicuously on the Indians themselves. He had discussed it with Pandit Nehru, Mr. Jinnah, Mr. Patel, Liaquat Ali Khan, and Baldev Singh, who had at least acquiesced in it. Congress, indeed, seemed to be reconciled to some form of partition. The plan had, however, leaked in the papers, and the political parties were now trying to stir up opposition to it.

Lord Ismay said that the Viceroy's plan might have to be modified in certain respects in view of developments since it had been drawn up. The Governor of Bengal was anxious that that Province should have the opportunity of electing for independence and thus remaining unified, and Mr. Jinnah had agreed to this course. The Governor had been consulted about the possibility of holding a referendum but had advised against this course on account of the practical difficulties involved:[2] in any case it could only produce the same result as the plan proposed by the Viceroy. The Governor of the Punjab had

---

[1] Nos. 278 and 279.   [2] See No. 311.

also advised against the holding of a referendum,[3] and, according to a tele-gram[4] just received, was no longer in favour of the Viceroy's plan for that Province. Congress had no objection to an election being held in the North West Frontier Province, provided that this was not conceded under threat of violence. On further investigation, the Viceroy had reached the conclusion that there were at present no legal grounds for resort to Section 93 in the Province; Congress would greatly resent such action. He was, therefore, now suggesting a referendum instead of an election, and thought that this course might secure Congress support.

The Viceroy hoped to meet Indian leaders, not later than 20th May, with the object of bringing matters to a head. He wished to make them admit openly that there was no possibility of securing agreement on a unified India; he would then place before them the plan set out in his telegram No. 955–S. The Viceroy did not propose to allow any alterations of substance to be made unless both sides asked for them, but he would be ready to meet the parties on points of detail. He would tell them that the plan was to be announced both in London and India within 24 hours. If the announcement was not made very shortly after the presentation of the plan to the leaders leakage was inevitable.

Lord Ismay said that the Viceroy was most anxious that a decision on his proposal should be taken without delay. It was essential that a very early announcement should be made of the conclusions reached by His Majesty's Government on the matters which were generally known to have been referred to them.

THE PRIME MINISTER informed the Committee that Field Marshal Auchinleck had told him that morning that the situation in India was dangerous, and had strongly emphasised the necessity for an early decision.

As regards procedure, the Committee thought that, in spite of the risk of leakage, it would be advisable to allow the Indian political leaders 48 hours for consideration of the proposed statement. The lesser period suggested by the Viceroy would not afford them adequate time to reach agreement on any modifications of the plan.

In considering the terms of the draft statement contained in the Viceroy's Telegram No. 955–S, the Committee made the following points—

(a) *Paragraph 4.* The first sentence should be modified to avoid any sug-gestion that the plan had been prepared without reference to the will of the Indian people. Greater emphasis should also be laid on the fact that the plan would not involve any final demarcation of the boundaries of those provinces which have special minority problems. The Com-mittee were informed that, in those provinces where it was proposed that the Legislative Assembly should sit in two parts, the basis for division would be the administrative district; the boundaries of these districts did not in all cases coincide with those of the Parliamentary Constituencies. The plan involved, therefore, only a form of notional partition; where partition was decided upon, subsequent adjustment of boundaries would be unavoidable. This was not a responsibility which, in present conditions, the Government of India could assume. It should be made clear that these boundaries would be retained for the purpose of demitting power unless modifications were agreed upon between the local authorities of the areas concerned.

(b) *Paragraph 7.* The Committee noted that no indication was given in this paragraph of the action to be taken by the various bodies mentioned under the procedure proposed. As regards the suggestion that a plebiscite might be held in the N.W.F.P., the Committee thought that adoption of this procedure could only result in substantial delay; if the result was a vote in favour of amalgamation with Pakistan, a general election would be unavoidable, since only after an election could new representatives to the Constituent Assembly be elected. The Committee considered that, in any event, the unavoidable delay involved in an election in this Province should not be allowed to retard the progress of the plan in the other Provinces. It should be possible to provide for representatives of the Provinces to take part in the proceedings of a Constituent Assembly at a later stage.

(c) *Paragraph 9.* The Committee thought that it would be advisable to increase the numbers of the representatives to be elected by the bodies set out in paragraph 8. In their view, the numbers proposed were in many cases too small to afford adequate representation of the views of the people of the areas concerned. They recognised that the figures proposed in the draft were put forward on the basis adopted by the Cabinet Mission for the Constituent Assembly. In their view, however, there would be no objection to increasing the numbers for the immediate purpose of the present plan; if in any instance a decision was subsequently taken to take part in the existing Constituent Assembly it would then be necessary to revert to the basis of representation for that Assembly. It was agreed, therefore, that representation should be on the basis of 1 for every 250,000 of the population, instead of 1 for every million.

(d) *Paragraph 10.* The Committee were informed that careful consideration had been given to the question whether the division of a Province should be decided by majority vote or by a two/thirds vote; they saw no reason to differ from the recommendation that a majority vote should decide the issue.

(e) *Paragraph 11.* The Committee considered that, in view of the limited membership of some of the bodies set up to make the decision on

3 See No. 305.   4 No. 317.

partition, it would be inadvisable also to give them the right to form the Constituent Assemblies for independent areas. While they should have the right to decide whether to stand out independently, separate arrangements should be made for the setting up of Constituent Assemblies for independent areas.

(f) *Paragraph 17.* The Committee thought that careful consideration should be given to the wording of this paragraph; there were other "matters of common concern" in addition to defence, of which account must be taken. In general, however, the Committee emphasised that His Majesty's Government could not assume responsibility for the division of the Central subjects; that must be a matter for the Indian leaders themselves.

(g) The Committee were informed that measures to meet the situation which might arise in Bengal and the Punjab when the proposed announcement was made public were under consideration by the Commander-in-Chief. There was a possibility that the announcement might provoke widespread disorders in both Provinces; against this, failure by His Majesty's Government to take the initiative at this stage would undoubtedly have a disastrous effect on public order.

The Committee—

(1) Invited the Secretary of State for India to circulate a re-draft of the proposed statement contained in the Viceroy's Telegram No. 955–S for consideration by the Committee on 7th May.

(2) Invited the Secretary of State for Dominion Affairs to inform the Dominion Governments in general terms of the Viceroy's proposals.

321

Rear-Admiral Viscount Mountbatten of Burma to Lord Ismay (via India Office)

Telegram, Mountbatten Papers. Official Correspondence Files:
Punjab, Part I(b)

MOST IMMEDIATE   NEW DELHI, *5 May 1947, 10 pm*
TOP SECRET   *Received: 5 May, 10.15 pm*

No. 992–S. Jenkins' reply on the subject of referendum[1] is that it would be in any circumstances a doubtful expedient in the Punjab where voters are entirely in the hands of party leaders. Referendum could not be on simple issue of adherence to Pakistan or Hindustan as in N.W.F.P., but would have to be based on partition, on which no question can at present be framed to which members of all communities could answer an unqualified "Yes" or "No".

2. In regard to partition, Jenkins considers the situation since the Governors'

Conference has been radically altered by Jinnah's public announcement that Pakistan must include the whole of the Punjab. He feels that there is no chance that the plan in V.C.P.42[2] will be voluntarily carried out and that all parties are likely to boycott the proceedings.

3. I feel that Jenkins' arguments are based on false premises. In the first place I think that Jinnah's announcement,[3] was intended merely as a counter-blast to the article in the *Hindustan Times* which I repeated in my telegram No. 235–GT of 3rd May.[4] Certainly in recent conversations which Mieville and I have had with Jinnah he did not appear seriously to contest the need for partition but seemed even grateful for 17 districts of the Punjab.

4. Congress had accepted the principle of Partition as you will have seen from Nehru's letter of 1st May,[5] which has been forwarded to you by bag.

5. Patiala also accepted by implication the principle of notional partition, but he was gloomy about the hardening of the Sikhs' demands since notional partition puts two million Sikhs' into Hindustan and 1,800,000 into Pakistan.

6. Notional partition will probably cause difficulty in that it will not be understood by majority of people in the Province as merely being an instrument whereby the will of the people can be ascertained, and it will, therefore, be important to make it clear that a Boundary Commission is to be set up to settle the final partition. I think that this point can best be brought out in my broadcast rather than embodied in the Plan.

7. It is clear to me that I cannot recommend notional partition on any basis other than communal majorities in the district, and that so long as risk of open conflict remains the Punjab must remain under section 93. Only alternative, therefore, to award by H.M.G. on basis of partition as in our Plan is settlement by negotiation between the communities and this is what we must aim for. Opportunity for this might be afforded by appointing Section 93 advisers, one from each community, and development from that into some form of Regional administration as contemplated in B. N. Rau's plan,[6] first by advisers and as soon as possible by Coalition Government.

8. But I do not think this need be embodied in the Plan at the present stage, which, as far as the Punjab is concerned may go forward for H.M.G.'s decision in the form in which it now is in V.C.P.42.

9. Jenkins is coming to Simla later in the week and I will discuss the position further with him.[7]

Repeated to Governor of the Punjab.

[1] See No. 305.   [2] This was the same as No. 279. Mountbatten Papers.
[3] Annex I to No. 276.   [4] No. 291.   [5] No. 267.   [6] See No. 262, note 2.
[7] In tel. 993 of 5 May Lord Mountbatten thanked Sir E. Jenkins for Nos. 298 and 305 and explained his reactions to them as in para. 3 of the above telegram. Mountbatten Papers, Official Correspondence files: Punjab, Part I(b).

322

Sir E. Mieville to Rear-Admiral Viscount Mountbatten of Burma

R/3/1/151: ff 31-2

TOP SECRET   *undated*
No. 1446

Your Excellency.

I had an unsatisfactory talk with Mr. Jinnah this morning.[1] He flatly turned down the two drafts[2] on the grounds that there was no mention that the referendum would be held under your agency and that there was also no mention of an election. I went over the grounds once more on the lines that you took last night but he was unshaken. He said that the people on the Frontier were not particularly intelligent and unless it were made clear that an election would follow the referendum they would not be satisfied. He therefore felt that it would be best for him to issue a statement on his own responsibility, but assured me that he would not do so until he heard further from you. He added that so much of the plan had now leaked in the Congress press and was known to so many people that it was being freely and openly discussed, that he felt you would raise no objection to what he proposed to say. The gist of his statement would be as follows:—

"He had reason to believe that Your Excellency had recommended to H.M.G. a referendum in the N.W.F.P. This could only be done by the Viceroy through his own agency and he hoped that H.M.G. would accept the recommendation. If, as a result of the referendum, the people voted in favour of Pakistan, in his judgment elections were inevitable and must be held and would give an opportunity to the people to choose their representatives. A new Ministry would be formed to carry out the verdict given by the people. In these circumstances, he most earnestly appealed to the members of the Muslim League to remain strictly peaceful and not allow the movement to take a communal turn, whatever the provocation might be from the other side. He would not advise them to call off the movement, but he again repeated that they should remain strictly peaceful, and as far as possible not give a case to the other side to use violence or force which he had already denounced in unequivocal terms. They must remember that the All-India Muslim League had only changed its policy as it was bound to pursue according to its constitution strictly constitutional methods, but it had never up to now decided to resort to Direct Action. The resolution made it clear that they would launch the movement as and when necessary. Even if they were forced to resort to such extreme measures it had never been contemplated that they would use violence or force. It was quite obvious that people without arms would be ill-advised if they were to resort to violence and force against the organised power of the Government."

I then asked him whether under any conditions he would agree to accept the Cabinet Mission Plan. He replied "Under no conditions whatsoever", and then trotted out the old slogan of accepting a portion of the Sind desert rather than the Plan. I warned him that in all probability the fact that the Cabinet Mission Plan had been turned down would probably fall entirely on his shoulders, although I was not in a position to say under what conditions the Congress could accept it. He was unmoved.

I finally mentioned the PUNJAB and told him that I had seen Sikhs and Hindus from that Province who one and all had complained to me that in the 17 districts that were going to him all the rich, arable and fertile land would be his. He laughed and said that that was not his fault! This reinforced my belief that he is quite ready to accept the division of the Punjab in spite of his recent statement[3] to the contrary in the Press.[4]

E. C. MIEVILLE

[1] It is evident from No. 327 that this talk took place on 5 May 1947.
[2] See No. 310; the drafts are not on the file.
[3] Annex I to No. 276.
[4] On 6 May Captain Brockman sent copies of Nos 310 and 322 to the Secretary to the Governor of the N.W.F.P. R/3/1/151: f 30.

323

Lord Ismay to Rear-Admiral Viscount Mountbatten of Burma (via India Office)

Telegram, R/3/1/151: f 25

IMMEDIATE
PRIVATE
SECRET

5 May 1947, 11.30 pm
Received: 6 May, 7.30 am

No. 51. We have just finished Cabinet Committee meeting.[1] Reception of general principles of plan was favourable. I explained background and Committee appreciated need for very urgent decision. I reserved your position about the Punjab and explained that you were considering a referendum in N.W.F.P.

2. It was decided to refer back the plan for a redraft by officials. The points that attracted comments were as follows:

(i) The presentation wants improvement to make the procedure quite clear.

(ii) The number of representatives who will act as Constituent Assemblies

[1] See No. 320.

for Provinces and half Provinces should be multiplied by 4 or 5 to get larger bodies to consider these vital decisions.

(iii) There should be provision for reducing again the number of representatives if any Province joins existing Constituent Assembly or another group Constituent Assembly.

(iv) In any case if a Province stands out independent it will need a larger Constituent Assembly.

(v) There must be provision for adjustment of boundaries by a Boundary Commission.

3. Officials of India Office will consider a revised draft with Abell and me tomorrow and re-draft will come up to Cabinet Committee on Wednesday evening. We hope for full Cabinet decision before end of week.

4. I am not happy about the immediate necessity for referendum in N.W.F.P. Will it not be difficult to refuse to follow this precedent in Punjab and Bengal where difficulties stated by Governor are formidable? In addition there may be a difficulty owing to the minorities having relatively more votes than Muslims because of their greater wealth.

5. I am consulting experts here about Section 93. There is some doubt whether it need be ruled out on constitutional grounds.[2]

[2] Noting by India Office officials on this point may be seen on L/P &J/10/79: ff 390–5. The balance of opinion was that there were no legal grounds for going into Section 93 for the purpose of conducting an election.

324

Record of Interview between Rear-Admiral Viscount Mountbatten of Burma and Sardar Baldev Singh (Extract)

Mountbatten Papers. Viceroy's Interview No. 133

TOP SECRET   *6 May 1947, 12 noon–12.30 pm*

I explained to him that the idea of notional partition in the Punjab—17 districts to the Muslims and 12 to the non-Muslims—was based entirely on the majority of populations in the districts. He expressed the greatest regret at my decision, since he felt that the notional partition might not be understood, and that it would be thought that it was a permanent partition; and further, in the Gurdaspur district, where there was only one per cent in favour of the Muslims, and in part of Lahore district on a population basis alone, large areas should be given to the Sikhs and Hindus.

Finally I warned him that if the Sikhs did make serious trouble or tried to start a communal war, I should crush them with all the power at my command, and would instruct him as Defence Member to turn out the Army and the Air Force to fight them.

325

Rear-Admiral Viscount Mountbatten of Burma to Pandit Nehru

R/3/1/170: f 11

No. 1450.   *6 May 1947*
Dear Mr Nehru,

You will remember after Dr Khan Sahib's visit to Delhi I told you what I intended to do about Sir Olaf Caroe,[1] and Ismay has had instructions[2] to follow this up with the Secretary of State in London. I am not, however, prepared to yield to duress and unless and until this whole agitation dies down I shall take no further action in this matter any more than in the case of Dr Khan Sahib.

Yours sincerely,
MOUNTBATTEN OF BURMA

[1] No record of this conversation has been traced.   [2] See No. 300.

326

Rear-Admiral Viscount Mountbatten of Burma to Lord Ismay (via India Office)

Telegram, R/3/1/151: f 27

IMMEDIATE   NEW DELHI, *6 May 1947, 3 pm*
SECRET   *Received: 6 May, 4.55 pm*
998–S. Delighted to note from your telegram No. 51 of 5th May[1] that things are going so quickly and so favourably.

2. With reference to your para. 2, sub-para. 2. V.P. Menon opposed my suggestion that figures be multiplied by ten on the grounds that:—

(*a*) it would be a departure from the Cabinet Mission system which we are sticking to in the Hindustan Provinces, and (*b*) in Bengal, for example, it would result in 600 representatives being chosen by 225 members of the Provincial Legislative Assembly. But if only multiplied by four and reduced afterwards this may not be so objectionable. Matter is being further investigated.

3. Your para. 2, sub-para. 5. It is agreed that Boundary Commission is of utmost importance, more especially as notional partition is not generally understood among the public. It is important that this should be made crystal clear in the announcement as Sikhs are very worried indeed about notional boundary line.

[1] No. 323.

4. Your para. 4. I am absolutely convinced that we must have a referendum in the N.W.F.P. run by myself. Caroe and all of us now consider this feasible.[2] Nehru has accepted this in view of my assurance that I do not intend to dissolve the Ministry or go into Section 93. See my telegram to Secretary of State about very awkward situation which has arisen with Jinnah about this (telegram No. 999–S).[3]

5. Your telegram No. 50 of May 5th.[4] Agree that you shall leave London 14th May which is the day I return from Simla.

6. Is it safe to invite Leaders and States' Negotiating Committee to meet me on 22nd May?[5]

[2] In tel. 5827 of 7 May Mr Abell asked Captain Brockman what question would be put to the electorate in the N.W.F.P. referendum. Mr Abell believed that Lord Ismay was likely to be asked about this point at that evening's India Committee meeting (No. 341). In tel. 17–S.C. of 7 May, Captain Brockman replied that the question would be 'Do you wish to join Pakistan or Hindustan?' He added that 'referendum will not take place until it is clear that there will be partition and until the choice before the electorate is quite clear.' R/3/1/151: ff 34–5.

[3] No. 327.   [4] Not traced.

[5] Lord Ismay replied in tel. 5834 of 7 May suggesting that Lord Mountbatten should wait until he had reported the result of the India Committee meeting before issuing invitations. Lord Mountbatten agreed in tel. 30–S.C. of 8 May. Mountbatten Papers, Official Correspondence files: Transfer of Power, Part II(a).

327

Rear-Admiral Viscount Mountbatten of Burma to Lord Ismay (via India Office)

Telegram, R/3/1/151: ff 28–9

IMMEDIATE   NEW DELHI, *6 May 1947, 3 pm*
SECRET   *Received: 6 May, 5 pm*

999–S. My telegram 984–S[1] of May 4th, paras 4 to 8.

Mieville took draft round to Jinnah yesterday[2] but he refused to accept it on the ground that no mention was made of a General Election which I had made clear in my interview with him on Sunday[3] that I would *not* include in any circumstances and the following letter which I addressed to him this morning will show you the position. *Begins:*—Mieville has told me the result of his conversation with you this morning, and I must express to you my disappointment. He said that you had turned down the draft statements that he had put before you on the ground that no mention was made of an election. I thought that I had made it quite clear to you and Mr. Liaquat Ali Khan last night that any question of the use of the word "election" would rule out any chance of the statement being accepted by Pandit Nehru whose agreement as I told you I was anxious to obtain in order to present the case for your

MAY 1947
635

statement as strongly as I could to the Prime Minister and with the best hope of success. Mieville further showed me the rough draft of the statement which you told him you would like to issue on your own responsibility. I can only say to you that any statement that would imply that a decision has been reached would cause me the gravest embarrassment. H.M.G. would, I feel sure, resent it and I should be forced immediately to telegraph to London explaining the full facts of the case. As you know, conversations are now taking place in London and, much as you dislike it, you must realise that the Cabinet Mission plan still holds the field. Only if this is finally disposed of at my official meeting with the leaders on Ismay's return will a decision be taken that India should be given the chance of partition. I hope, however, that in any case you will make your statement against the use of violence and explain the position about Direct Action and that you will be able to convince your people on the Frontier of the folly of further violence and disturbance. *Ends.* Mieville took the letter round but was unable to shake him and he now says that he will issue a statement on his own responsibility calling on his people to resort to peaceful methods and saying that he has good reason to believe a referendum will be held and that *in his opinion* a general election must follow if the referendum goes in favour of Pakistan.

I have shown the letter to Nehru and in agreement with him I propose that when the statement is issued to let it be known through my Press Attaché, without of course my name appearing at all, that no final decisions have been reached and that the whole matter is at present *sub judice* in London.

¹ No. 312.   ² See No. 322.   ³ See No. 310.

328

Rear-Admiral Viscount Mountbatten of Burma to Lord Ismay (via India Office)

Telegram, R/3/1/170: f 10

IMMEDIATE   NEW DELHI, *6 May 1947, 3 pm*
SECRET   *Received: 6 May, 7.55 pm*

1000–S. An agitation has broken out in the Hindu Press calling for Caroe's resignation. It has gone so far that an "Anti Caroe" day has been announced even in Delhi. I have discussed the matter with Nehru and told him that I am put in a very difficult position as, obviously, whatever my feelings in the matter may be, I am not prepared to yield to force, and so long as the agitation continues I would not think of suggesting a change of Governor in the

N.W.F.P.[1] I pointed out the analogy of the Muslim League desiring to get rid of the Khan Sahib Govermennt.

2. Nehru entirely saw the point and promised to do what he could to help.

3. Nevertheless I still consider Caroe must be replaced as soon as possible after excitement has died down and still wish you to clear Lockhart with Secretary of State and Auchinleck leaving date of change entirely in my hands.

[1] See No. 325; no record of Lord Mountbatten's conversation with Pandit Nehru has been traced.

329

Lord Ismay to Rear-Admiral Viscount Mountbatten of Burma (via India Office)

Telegram, R/3/1/170: f 9

IMMEDIATE   *6 May 1947, 11.55 am*
SECRET   *Received: 7 May, 4 am*

No. 5773. Reference your 968–S[1] paragraph No. 8.

Submit that you should send official telegram about replacement of Caroe by Lockhart to Secretary of State giving date of relief, reasons etc. I will then follow it up this end.

2. Please let me know whether you have already squared Auchinleck.

[1] No. 300.

330

Lord Ismay to Rear-Admiral Viscount Mountbatten of Burma (via India Office)

Telegram, R/3/1/151: f 33

IMMEDIATE   *6 May 1947, 5.41 pm*
SECRET   *Received: 7 May, 6.30 am*

No. 5800. We have spent whole morning re-drafting announcement and are having another go at it this afternoon. Substance remains same but we think you will find presentation considerably improved in the light of very helpful comments of Cabinet Committee.

2. Abell and I fully agree about inadvisability of referendum in Bengal and Punjab. As regards referendum in N.W.F.P. we await your further instructions; but you ought to know that Cabinet Committee yesterday were very doubtful about it because it might lead to further delay since if referendum

was in favour of Pakistan it would have to be followed by a general election.

3. Leader in *Times* today was helpful but leader in *Daily Telegraph* somewhat the reverse.

4. We entirely agree that Jenkins' objections to plan are based on false (gr.om)s [?premises] (see your 992–S).[1] I made it clear to Cabinet Committee yesterday that there were risks in any plan but that there was a certainty of trouble if decision was long delayed.

Repeated to Simla.

[1] No. 321.

331

Cabinet

India and Burma Committee. Paper I.B.(47)56

L/P&J/10/79: ff 375–6, 378–84, 386

INDIAN POLICY
NOTE BY THE SECRETARY OF STATE FOR INDIA
INDIA OFFICE, 6 May 1947

I circulate for discussion at the meeting of the Committee on 7th May, a revised draft of the proposed announcement of policy.[1] This has been prepared by Lord Ismay and officials in the light of the discussion at the meeting of the Committee on 5th May.[2]

L.

SECRET

DRAFT ANNOUNCEMENT
(Revised by officials 6.5.47)

I. INTRODUCTION

1. On 20th February 1947 His Majesty's Government announced their intention of transferring power in British India to Indian hands by June 1948. They are determined to do their utmost to ensure that this transfer is effected in accordance with the wishes of the Indian people themselves, and that it is orderly and peaceful.

[1] Lord Ismay telegraphed the text of this draft to Lord Mountbatten in tel. 5848 of 7 May, 2.20 p.m. Mountbatten Papers, Official Correspondence Files: Transfer of Power, Part II(a). L/P&J/10/79 contains the text of another, unnumbered revision of the draft announcement prepared on 6 May (ff 410–15). Other revisions of the statement prior to the version telegraphed to Lord Mountbatten on 9 May (No. 379) are also on L/P&J/10/79.
[2] No. 320.

2. If it were possible to transfer power to a single authority, the process would be comparatively simple. H.E. the Viceroy has, however, reported that the leaders of the main political parties have been unable to reach agreement on any form of unified Government. Arrangements must therefore be made to ensure that power can be transferred by the due date to more than one authority.

3. This involves constitutional, administrative, financial and defence problems of formidable variety and bewildering complexity. It is therefore essential that the successor authorities should be determined at the earliest possible moment and that they should prepare themselves to receive power by the due date. The arrangements to this end, upon which His Majesty's Government have decided, are set out below.

4. His Majesty's Government are satisfied that the procedure laid down will ensure a sufficiently accurate indication of the wishes of the people of India to enable the successor authorities to be equitably determined. They reiterate that their sole purpose is to ensure a peaceful and orderly transfer of power, and that there is no intention of attempting to frame the ultimate Constitution of India, which is a matter entirely for Indians themselves to determine. It will be seen that there is nothing in these arrangements to preclude negotiations at any stage for a united India.

II. THE ISSUES TO BE DECIDED

5. His Majesty's Government have decided that the best way of achieving their purpose is to enable the different parts of India to decide, through elected representatives, whether:—

(A) to collaborate with the existing Constituent Assembly.

(B) to group together in one or more new Constituent Assemblies.

(C) to stand out individually and set up Constituent Assemblies of their own.

6. These decisions cannot be taken by Provincial Legislative Assemblies by majority vote. In the first place the composition of these Assemblies is weighted in favour of minorities and therefore does not correctly reflect the different elements in the population. Secondly, in certain Provinces the minority elements are so large and compact that a decision by the majority of the Provincial Legislative Assembly would result in unwilling parts of the country being coerced into a constitution unacceptable to them.

7. The dissimilarity of conditions in the different parts of India makes it impossible for the necessary decisions to be taken by the same procedure in all Provinces, and accordingly the arrangements will be as follows.

III. MADRAS, BOMBAY, UNITED PROVINCES, BIHAR, CENTRAL PROVINCES, ORISSA, DELHI, AJMER MERWARA AND COORG

8. The representatives of these Provinces in the existing Constituent Assembly will be asked to confirm that it is the wish of their Provinces to remain in the existing Constituent Assembly

IV. OTHER PROVINCES

Preliminary Arrangements

A. Bengal, Punjab and Assam

9. The Provincial Legislative Assemblies in these Provinces will each be asked to meet in two parts as indicated below, for the purpose of electing new Constituent Assembly representatives. This is necessary because the existing representatives were elected for each Province as a whole, and cannot, therefore, be divided into separate bodies representing parts of the Province.

(i) In Bengal, the Legislative Assembly (excluding the European members) will be asked to sit in two parts, one representing Moslem majority Districts and the other the rest of the Province.

(ii) In the Punjab, the Legislative Assembly (excluding the European members) will be divided, as in Bengal, into two parts representing Moslem majority Districts and other Districts respectively.

(iii) In Assam, the Legislative Assembly (excluding the European members) will be asked to sit in two parts one consisting of members elected from territorial constituencies included in Sylhet District, and the other of members elected from the remainder of the Province.

In determining the population of Districts the 1941 census figures will be taken as authoritative.

B. North-West Frontier Province.

10. The position in the North West Frontier Province is peculiar, and the issue whether the Province will or will not continue to be represented in the existing Constituent Assembly is one on which a new and clear mandate from the electorate is required. A general election

referendum to the electors

will therefore be held as soon as possible.

Further Procedure

11. The Legislative Assembly of Sind (excluding European members), the newly elected Legislative Assembly of North West Frontier Province, and two parts of the Legislative Assemblies of Bengal, the Punjab and Assam will elect representatives on the principle laid down in the Cabinet Mission's statement of 16th May 1946. But in order to provide an adequate number

of representatives, especially from the smaller areas, 1 per 250,000 of the population, instead of 1 per million, will be elected.

12. On that basis the numbers to be elected will be:

Province	General	Muslims	Sikhs	Total
West Punjab	11	49	7	67
East Punjab	22	15	8	45
West Bengal	60	17	—	77
East Bengal	49	115	—	164
Assam less Sylhet	22	6	—	28
Sylhet District	5	8	—	13
Sind	5	13	—	18
N.W.F.P.	1	11	—	12
				433 [*sic* ?424]

13. (*a*) The representatives, so elected, of the two parts of Bengal and of the Punjab, sitting separately, will be empowered to decide whether or not their Provinces should be divided. A majority vote of either body in favour of partition will decide the issue.

(*b*) The Governor may, however, if he considers that the state of opinion warrants it, convene a preliminary joint meeting of representatives of both halves of Bengal or of the Punjab to consider whether, if the two parts of the Province subsequently agree to remain united, the Province as a whole will enter a joint Constituent Assembly with other Provinces or be independent.

(*c*) As soon as a decision under (*a*) above has been reached, the Provinces or half Provinces of the Punjab and Bengal will decide, on behalf of areas which they represent, which of the three options stated in paragraph 5 above they prefer.

14. If, as a result of these decisions, Bengal is partitioned the representatives of Sylhet will forthwith sit separately, as prescribed in paragraph 9(iii), and decide whether:
(*a*) Sylhet will remain part of Assam, or
(*b*) Sylhet will join the same Constituent Assembly as East Bengal.

15. The representatives of Assam (with or without Sylhet), depending on decision in paragraph No. 14 above, and of Sind and the North West Frontier Province, will decide, on behalf of areas which they respectively represent, which of the three options in paragraph 5 above they prefer.

16. If the decision, in any case, is to join the existing Constituent Assembly it will be necessary to hold a fresh election of representatives on the same scale of one per million of the population as was prescribed by the Cabinet

Mission. By this scale the number of representatives to which each area is entitled is as follows:—

Province	General	Muslims	Sikhs	Total
West Punjab	3	12	2	17
East Punjab	6	4	2	12
West Bengal	15	4	—	19
East Bengal	12	29	—	41
Assam less Sylhet	6	1	—	7
Sylhet District	1	2	—	3
Sind	1	3	—	4
North West Frontier Province	—	3	—	3

Procedure for British Baluchistan

17. In British Baluchistan the members of the Shahi jirga (other than those members who are nominated as Sardars of Kalat State), and non-official members of Quetta Municipality, will meet to decide the issues in paragraph 5 above. The meeting will also elect a representative to attend the Constituent Assembly selected.

V. NECESSITY FOR SPEED

18. In order that the successor authority or authorities may have as much time as possible to prepare themselves to receive power it is essential that all the above processes should be completed without undue delay, and independently as far as is practicable within the conditions of this plan.

VI. FUNCTIONS OF CONSTITUENT ASSEMBLY

19. As soon as the Constituent Assembly or Assemblies have been constituted they will proceed in whatever way they deem appropriate to frame Constitutions for their respective territories.

20. The administrative consequences of the partition of India will be numerous and complicated. Negotiations will have to be initiated as soon as possible:—

(a) between the representatives of the prospective successor authorities about vital matters such as defence, finance and communications as well as all the other subjects now dealt with by the Central Government.

(b) between the different successor authorities and His Majesty's Government in regard to matters arising out of the transfer of power.

(c) In the case of provinces that may be partitioned as to the division of assets and liabilities, the police and other services, the High Courts, provincial institutions etc.

21. It is essential therefore that the various Constituent Assemblies should set up without delay the necessary machinery for consultation and negotiation.

22. It will be necessary for the respective Constituent Assemblies to con-

stitute before June 1948 provisional authorities to which power can be transferred if the new constitution for the area concerned will not then be ready
to be brought into operation.

VII. DELIMITATION OF BOUNDARIES

23. For the immediate purposes described above, boundaries must for
practical reasons be fixed by a strict application of the population criterion,
district by district, as laid down in paragraph 9. But it is evident that for the
purpose of a lasting settlement in any province in which partition may occur
a more exact adjustment of boundary questions will be needed and, as soon
as a decision involving partition has been taken for any Province, a Boundary
Commission should be set up by arrangement between those concerned.

VIII. THE TRIBES OF THE NORTH WEST FRONTIER

24. As soon as successor authorities have been determined fresh agreements
with the tribes of the North West Frontier of India will require to be negotiated.

IX. THE STATES

25. His Majesty's Government wish to make it clear that decisions announced above relate only to British India and that their policy towards
Indian States remains unchanged. When paramountcy lapses all rights surrendered by the States to paramount power will return to the States. They are
free to arrange by negotiation with those parts of British India to which
power will be demitted whatever measure of association they consider to be
in the best interests of their people. Some may confirm their wish to proceed
with framing a constitution in the existing Constituent Assembly. Some may
wish to join any other Constituent Assembly that may be established. Others
may decide to stand out independently, either singly or jointly, as is open
to the Provinces. But, whatever their decision, all will require to arrange with
successor governments alternative machinery for the future regulation of
matters of common concern.[3]

X. FURTHER ANNOUNCEMENTS BY THE GOVERNOR-GENERAL

26. The Governor-General will from time to time make such further
announcements as may be necessary, in regard to procedure or any other
matter, for carrying out above arrangements.

[3] An amendment slip attached here contained a revised last sentence of para. 25 which included a
reference to the need for 'new agreements, especially in the economic and financial sphere,' on the
lines contemplated in para. 4 of the *Memorandum on States' Treaties and Paramountcy* (Vol. VII, No.
262). It also suggested the reversal of the order of paras. 24 and 25, and verbal amendments to
para. 24. L/P &J/10/79: f 385.

332

Sir E. Jenkins (Punjab) to Rear-Admiral Viscount Mountbatten of Burma

Mountbatten Papers. Official Correspondence Files:
Punjab, Part I(b)

SECRET   GOVERNMENT HOUSE, LAHORE, 7 *May 1947*
No 671
Dear Lord Mountbatten,
Many thanks for Your Excellency's letter of 5th May.[1] Baldev Singh's letter, on which you ask for my comments, raises two points—

(*a*) that if the Punjab is partitioned, the non-Muslim or eastern zone should include, in addition to the Ambala and Jullundur Divisions, the Gurdaspur, Amritsar and Lahore districts; and

(*b*) that if a zonal scheme is adopted pending the completion of the physical partition, the non-Muslim or eastern zone should include the whole of the Ambala, Jullundur and Lahore Divisions, or at least the territory mentioned in (*a*) above.

Baldev Singh, like other Sikhs, seems quite unable to understand that the Sikhs are not the only people to be considered. They have no absolute majority of their own in any district, and the new State they contemplate is not really a Sikh State at all, but a non-Muslim State. It is all very well to say that we must "exclude from Muslim area as large a percentage of the Sikh population as possible"; but we cannot, in order to achieve this purpose, bring into the non-Muslim State a large number of unwilling Muslims. Baldev Singh's demands are rather less extreme than those of Tara Singh, Kartar Singh and some others; but if they are pressed, they will make the Muslim resistance to partition seem perfectly reasonable. Partition is justifiable only as a means of reconciling irreconcilable people; it will destroy the work of a century and ruin the Punjab. If the Sikhs insist upon it, they must be content with a reasonable share and cannot be allowed to bring Muslim majority districts under non-Muslim domination. As I said in a recent letter, one of the difficulties in the present situation is that each community denies to the rest the rights which it claims for itself.

2. I hope that the Government of India will find it possible to undertake the riot insurance scheme. I am sure that it is necessary if trade, particularly in foodgrains, is to be maintained.

3. I wrote too soon about the compensation scales for the Services. The

---

[1] In this letter Lord Mountbatten thanked Sir E. Jenkins for Nos. 262 and 263 and asked for his comments on No. 269.

officers of the Indian Police are gravely dissatisfied with them, and I am writing separately to Your Excellency about this.[2]

Yours sincerely,

E. M. JENKINS

[2] Sir E. Jenkins did this in a letter of 8 May 1947. Mountbatten Papers, Official Correspondence Files: Compensation for Members of the Services, Part II(b).

333

Sardar Baldev Singh to Rear-Admiral Viscount Mountbatten of Burma

Mountbatten Papers. Official Correspondence Files: Punjab, Part I(b)

I BHAGWAN DAS ROAD, NEW DELHI,
7 May 1947

My dear Lord Mountbatten,

Many thanks for your letter No. 592/90[1] after receipt of which I had an opportunity of discussing the partition of the Punjab during my interview with Your Excellency yesterday.[2] I must frankly say that I am considerably upset at the tentative proposals as explained and set out in your letter.

2. I have very carefully considered the proposed "notional division" and am very definitely of the opinion that a declaration on this basis is bound to create an impression on public mind that this will more or less be the final partition of the Punjab. It will stiffen the attitude of the Muslim League and make it almost impossible to realign the areas differently at a later stage. In fact, it is bound to influence the Boundary Commission as well.

3. As I explained to you personally, there does not seem to be any justification to include Gurdaspur in the Western Zone at any stage. The difference in populations is a mere fraction even if the Census figures are taken as they stand. Its inclusion in the Western Zone will cut at the root of the entire economy and communications of the district which is vitally dependent on Amritsar and will isolate the predominantly non-Muslim area of Kangra etc. It will therefore be quite unjust to separate it from the Eastern Zone even in the "notional division". What I am anxious for is that nothing should be done to prejudice the Boundary Commission or create an impression that the "notional division" was more or less the final partition of the Punjab. This could be best avoided by dividing the members of the Punjab Legislature of the two districts of Gurdaspur and Lahore, and the representatives they elect to decide partition, equally among the Eastern and Western Zones. If this suggestion of mine is accepted, it will prevent the final issue being prejudiced. I hope you will kindly give this suggestion your careful consideration.

4. The necessity for partition of the Punjab has arisen on account of the Sikh demand in particular. The Cabinet Mission went very carefully into this question as they were impressed by the Sikh case. Considerable sympathy was also expressed in both Houses of Parliament in our behalf and we were assured that H.M.G. would do us justice. This is clear from the correspondence which passed between the Members of the Cabinet Mission and Sikh leaders. I will not like to take your time by relevant quotations, but I will say that when Master Tara Singh and I met the members of the Cabinet Mission and Lord Wavell, they assured us that Sikh claim will not in any event be ignored.[3] The Viceroy was instructed accordingly to get in touch with the leaders of the political parties to see that Sikh claims were met. On my pointing out that Lord Wavell may not be here, Lord Pethick-Lawrence said that the question of Lord Wavell remaining here hardly mattered because the meeting of Sikh case was a matter of policy that had been settled by H.M.G. He added that in pursuance of this policy they would instruct the Viceroy to give special attention to the demands of Sikhs. In view of all this, we are entitled to expect that the promises made to us are now fulfilled.

5. May I repeat that the main reason for the partition of the Punjab is to satisfy the Sikh demand. It follows from this that in any scheme for partition, special regard should be paid to the interests of the community and this can only be done, first, by making sure that the plan of "notional division" does not prejudice the final partition; and, secondly, by making a definite reference in the terms of reference to the Boundary Commision that while partitioning the Punjab the two areas are to be so demarcated as to leave as small a number of the Sikhs as possible in Pakistan. I will add that now that you are seized of all the facts and particularly the undisguised aggressive and terrorist attitude of the Muslim League, it is the Sikhs who must in equity and morally be delivered from the future domination of Muslims. It would indeed be unjust if your plans, interim or long term, were to abandon large sections of my community to the risks of bestiality and terrorism, such as you yourself have witnessed and may well recur in future.

6. After the announcement of the "notional division" of the Punjab, two Interim Ministries are likely to be set up on zonal basis. The Muslim League will obviously insist that the "notional division" should be the basis of two zones. This, I must point out, will be most unjust to the Minorities in the Western Zone. It will, in any event, jeopardise completely the work of the Boundary Commission for the simple reason that the Muslim League, which will inevitably dominate this zone, will prevent fairplay and make it impossible for any part of it to be re-assigned to the Eastern Zone. For the purpose of the formation of Ministries, therefore, the Eastern Zone must include in addition

[1] No. 315.   [2] See No. 324.   [3] cf. Vol. VII, No. 463.

to the Divisions of Ambala and Jullundur, the three Districts of Gurdaspur, Amritsar and Lahore in the Division of Lahore for the interim period. The Headquarters of both the zonal Ministries should be at Lahore.

7. I was glad to learn from you that Mr. Jinnah was now anxious to settle with the Sikhs. I have had a number of opportunities to discuss matters with him. He has expressed the same sentiments to me as well. He, however, does not mean business and is not prepared to come to terms with us unless he can first rope the Sikhs in his Pakistan under Muslim domination. This shall not be. The Sikhs will in no circumstances agree to any discussion with Mr. Jinnah on the basis of being included in Pakistan. The stage has now come for the parting of ways and if he wants his sovereign state and H.M.G. are disposed to concede his claim, the Sikhs must be left out of it. It is for this reason I insist that in any short or long term plan in the case of our home province, every care should be taken to ensure that the Sikhs are not involved in Pakistan as a community.

8. May I draw your attention to an extremely enlightening editorial of the *Tribune* published this week which deals with Mr. Jinnah's claim to a share of the territory of India on the basis of his own arguments. The analysis supports our case of the partition of the Punjab and is a complete answer to Mr. Jinnah in every respect. I enclose a cutting[4] for ready reference.

9. I shall be grateful if Your Excellency will very kindly convey to H.M.G. the views expressed by me on the partition of the Punjab in my recent letters[5] as well as this.

Yours sincerely,
BALDEV SINGH

[4] Not printed.   [5] Nos. 240 and 269.

334

Sir E. Jenkins to the Nawab of Mamdot

R/3/1/177: ff 19-20

7 May 1947

My dear Khan Sahib,
Thank you for your letter of 28th April.[1] I am very glad to set out in writing the views I expressed to you during our talk on that date.

2. The essential points in your letters of 24th[2] and 28th April, some of which you amplified during our talk, are, I believe as follows:

(1) that my invitation to you of 3rd March to assist me in forming a Ministry still stands;

(2) that you have the support of 91 Members of the Punjab Legislative Assembly, including 84 Muslims, 4 Scheduled Caste Members and 3 Christians; or in other words an assured majority of 7 in a House of 175;

(3) that much as you regret the unwillingness of the Hindus and Sikhs to co-operate with you, and willing as you are to continue your efforts to secure their co-operation, their "unreasonable refusal. . . . . .to co-operate cannot be permitted to stand permanently in the way of the functioning of normal constitutional and democratic methods"; and

(4) that you should be permitted to form a Ministry immediately and to prove your majority at a very early meeting of the Assembly.

I deal with these points in order in the next paragraph.

3. (1). We did not discuss directly the question whether my invitation to you to assist me in forming a Ministry still subsists. It is clear that before the proclamation under Section 93 of the Government of India Act, 1935, can be revoked I must be satisfied that it is once more possible to carry on the Government of the Punjab in accordance with the provisions of that Act, and I concentrated on this aspect of the situation.

(2). I noted your claim to the support of 91 Members of the Punjab Legislative Assembly, but observed that some of these Members might not have decided finally to support you. From recent statements in the Press it appears that the party allegiance of some at least of the Members representing the smaller minorities is doubtful.

(3). and (4). These appeared to me to be the most important points in our discussion. Your argument, if I understood it correctly, was that since you had a parliamentary majority, you had a right to take office, and were confident of your capacity to carry on the Government of the Punjab in accordance with the provisions of the Government of India Act, 1935. I did not admit your claim to a majority, but said that in my judgement a communal Ministry—whether Muslim or non-Muslim—would find it quite impossible to maintain itself in present conditions. I reminded you that constitutional Government by a Ministry must be conducted in accordance with certain principles; and that when any large section of the population denies the validity of those principles, the position of a Ministry becomes impossible. The Muslim League agitation of January and February was unquestionably directed at the removal of the Coalition Ministry by "direct action"; at the time the Coalition Ministry had a parliamentary majority larger than that which you now claim, and the whole basis of the agitation was that no Ministry, whatever its parliamentary majority, should remain in office if it fails to represent any large section of the population. The Ministry you proposed would in fact exclude all the Hindus and Sikhs, and I did not see how the

---

¹ No. 261, Enclosure 2.   ² No. 261, Enclosure 1.

Hindus and Sikhs could be expected to respect principles which the Muslims had themselves discarded. In short, I felt that until there was some easing of the communal tension, and some prospect of agreement between Muslims, Hindus and Sikhs, the formation of a Ministry would be both dangerous and unwise. I understood that the discussions now in progress in New Delhi might be expected to produce definite results in the near future; and it seemed to me most important that we should do nothing here to prejudice all-India agreement. If the Congress and the Muslim League, and, for the Punjab, the Sikhs, could arrive at some agreement about the future of India, we might well have a fresh starting point in the Punjab. My conclusion thus was that no Ministry should be formed immediately, but that we should review the situation as soon as the all-India position was clear.

Yours sincerely,

E. M. JENKINS

335

Mr Abbott to Captain Brockman

R/3/1/89: f 196

SECRET   GOVERNMENT HOUSE, LAHORE,
No. G.S. 261   *7 May 1947*
Dear Brockman,

His Excellency the Governor asks me to write to you and say that he saw the Nawab of Mamdot this morning. H.E. the Governor referred to His Excellency the Viceroy, with his letter No. 664 of the 30th April 1947,[1] the draft of the reply[2] which he proposed to give to Mamdot, and H.E. the Viceroy's approval to this draft, with two minor alterations, was conveyed by Scott on the telephone. It was not possible for H.E. the Governor to see Mamdot earlier, as he was away on his country estate.

2. I am to add that Mamdot's only comments on H.E. the Governor's letter were:—

(*a*) that paragraph 3(2) was unfair; and

(*b*) that the expected announcement by H.M.G., so far from providing a "fresh starting point", would make matters worse.

On (*a*) His Excellency said that the letter was intended to summarize the views he expressed at their interview on 28th April. His Excellency still thought that the attitude of Christian Members of the Legislative Assembly (such as Singha) and of the Anglo-Indian, Gibbon, was very doubtful.

3. Mamdot was subdued and very gloomy. He said he saw no prospect at

all of a settlement. It was quite impossible for the Muslim League to break away and try to set up an "Independent Punjab" or anything of that kind. His Excellency replied that it would be a terrible thing if we drifted into chaos, but since the Muslims on the one hand wanted unity and Pakistan, and the Hindus and Sikhs on the other abominated Pakistan and wanted partition, and neither side would give way, we were already in great danger. Administration was getting more and more difficult; even with a stable Government the loss of most of our senior British officers would be a serious blow; without a stable Government the services would disintegrate. Mamdot said he did not understand the attitude of the British officers. His Excellency replied that most of them had regarded the Punjabi Muslims as very fine fellows, and had been shocked by the events in the Rawalpindi Division. Many of them would have stayed to serve a non-communal Ministry in a united Punjab; but they did not want to get involved in a communal war. H.E. would do his best, but it was difficult to answer those who wished to go.

4. In accordance with His Excellency the Viceroy's intructions, H.E. the Governor told Mamdot that His Excellency would be glad to see him in Delhi if he so desired.

Yours sincerely,

S. E. ABBOTT

¹ No. 261.   ² See No. 334.

336

Note by Sir E. Jenkins[1]

Mountbatten Papers. Official Correspondence Files: Punjab, Part I(b)

7 May 1947

Sardar Ujjal Singh and Giani Kartar Singh saw me at their request at 4 p.m. today.

2. After the usual compliments, S. Ujjal Singh said that the Sikhs understood that the Cabinet Mission's scheme of 16th May 1946 was dead. I replied that I hoped this was not so, and asked whether the Sikhs were really unwilling to accept this plan. Both S. Ujjal Singh and Giani Kartar Singh said, without much conviction, that if the Sikhs were given the right of communal veto, they might consider it; but they were certainly not going to be included in a separate Pakistan.

They then came to their real point, which was that if H.M.G.'s announcement defined even a provisional boundary, it would be unfair to one com-

---

[1] Sir E. Jenkins caused a copy of this note to be sent to the Viceroy's Private Office. Mountbatten Papers, Official Correspondence Files: Punjab, Part I(b).

munity or the other. If, as they understood, a provisional boundary based on Muslim and non-Muslim majority districts was contemplated, the eastern or non-Muslim State would be exceedingly poor—far worse off agriculturally and otherwise than the western or Muslim State. Such a boundary would ignore the economic claims of the non-Muslims, and particularly the Sikhs. I wrangled a little with S. Ujjal Singh at this stage and got him to admit that he really did not like the idea of partition.

The Giani then broke in and said that there was no solution except a partition. He thought that it should be based on population strengths—in other words that the communities should receive shares in proportion to their population strength with some consideration for economic conditions (ownership of land, urban immovable property, and so on). The whole idea would be to exchange populations so that the two States were really Muslim and non-Muslim and so that everybody had a fair chance. Obviously this result could not be achieved if we started with a provisional boundary line which any Boundary Commission would consider more or less binding upon it. The best arrangement would be to acknowledge the Rawalpindi Division and the Multan Division less Lyallpur and Montgomery as Muslim country; and the Ambala Division and the Jullundur Division as non-Muslim country. The central area thus left, consisting of the Lahore Division plus the Lyallpur and Montgomery districts, would be treated as a joint area, and the Boundary Commission would be instructed to lay down a boundary through this area in such a way as to give the Muslim and non-Muslim populations a reasonable start on the exchange of populations being affected.

3. I pointed out that this would be a very considerable transaction—in round figures the Muslim Government would in the end have to get rid of about $2\frac{1}{2}$ million non-Muslims and the non-Muslim Government would have to get rid of rather over 3 million Muslims.

Giani Kartar Singh then said that the Sikhs would accept an independent Punjab in which they could be given adequate safeguards, but they could not possibly agree to absorption in Pakistan.

We then discussed in some detail many of the difficulties of partition. For example, a part of the Gurdaspur district and a part of the Lahore district are socially and economically one with the Tarn Taran and Amritsar Tahsils of the Amritsar district; yet it is difficult on any population basis to get these areas into one State. Giani Kartar Singh made the rather interesting suggestion that if a plebiscite were held in Gurdaspur, the non-Muslims would win, as the Muslim village servants in Sikh villages would vote with their Sikh masters.

I ended the interview by saying that personally I could see no future for partition; that I could not force any kind of partition on the Punjab; that since it took an average Revenue Assistant about two years to partition a couple of hundred acres of land, I did not see how the Punjabis were going to partition the entire Province within any measurable time; and that the zonal scheme, which would have to be adopted for the interim period in the light of Giani Kartar Singh's proposals, would be as difficult to work as a coalition. I very much doubted if the Muslims would look at a partition of the kind proposed. In fact I directed myself to making my two visitors think a little more clearly about the difficulties ahead of them.

4. The interview indicated that the Sikhs are worried, but feel committed to partition. They obviously do not want any provisional boundary defined in H.M.G.'s announcement, and would prefer some sort of no man's land left in the central Punjab within which the Commission would have a free hand. I made it clear throughout that it was not H.M.G.'s intention to impose a solution upon the Punjab; the immediate and limited aim was to find an authority or authorities to which power could be transferred.

E.M.J.

337

Sir F. Burrows (Bengal) to Rear-Admiral Viscount Mountbatten of Burma

*Mountbatten Papers. Official Correspondence Files: Bengal,
Partition of, Part I(b)*

GOVERNMENT HOUSE, DARJEELING,

Dear Lord Mountbatten,   *7 May 1947*

Your mention of your talk with Jinnah and Liaquat Ali Khan in the last paragraph of your letter No. 592/92 of the 2nd May[1] and your telegram of the 4th May[2] about your talk with Kiran Sankar Roy made most interesting reading.

2. Following on my return from Delhi, I saw Suhrawardy the next day, 3rd May, and discussed with him again the question of a coalition government in Bengal. At the outset I mentioned to him that he seemed to have made a hit with the Viceroy. This pleased him very much and I hoped that by setting out to put him in good humour I might get something concrete out of him in respect of the formation of a coalition government. It is evident that he had taken no active steps whatever on my previous suggestion, though he must have been thinking over it from what he proceeded to tell me.

3. A coalition, formed now, must, he said, be a firm partnership based on the continued integrity of Bengal. For the formation of a coalition he must make terms with the Hindus in Bengal and come to arrangements with them,

[1] No. 280.
[2] In this telegram Lord Mountbatten sent Sir F. Burrows the text of No. 292. Mountbatten Papers, Official Correspondence Files: Bengal, Partition of, Part I(b).

before the announcement by H.M.G., to form a coalition *after* the announcement, unless Jinnah allows the formation of a coalition now. He undertook to initiate steps immediately on these lines and informed me he was seeing Sarat Bose on the matter that afternoon.

4. You will recall our discussion in conference last Thursday morning about this matter of trying to get Suhrawardy to form a coalition in Bengal without delay.[3] I did not feel at liberty on Saturday to show him the whole of my hand in respect of the tentative plan which Ismay has taken to London. I did, however, inform him, in answer to a point made by him, that there could be no question of holding a plebiscite in Bengal. (This I understood to be the position when I left Delhi). Suhrawardy reacted rather peevishly to this and said, among other things, that he would have to send a telegram to Attlee and that it meant there would be a fiat by H.M.G. on the partition question, as he claimed that the intermediate castes of West Bengal, by which I took him to mean some of the less depressed Scheduled Castes like the Mahisya, were against partition, and that the sitting Scheduled Caste members (those in West Bengal were all returned unopposed on the Congress ticket) do not reflect the feelings of their community. I implied that in my opinion the elected representatives are in fact in a position to reflect the views of the Caste Hindus, the Scheduled Castes and the Muslims.

Yours sincerely,

F. J. BURROWS

[3] See No. 264.

338

Cabinet

India and Burma Committee. Paper I.B.(47)57

L/P&J/10/79: ff 367–71

INDIAN POLICY
NOTE BY SECRETARY

CABINET OFFICE, *7 May 1947*

As instructed, I circulate for consideration by the Committee at their meeting on 8th May, a private letter from Sardar Baldev Singh on the implications of any scheme for the division of the Punjab.[1]

S. E. V. LUKE

Secretary

Enclosure to No. 338

Many thanks for your letter of the 10th. I should have replied earlier but my older boy, Surjit, has been laid up with a very serious attack of typhoid and of course this has been a cause of considerable anxiety and preoccupied most of my time.

Thank you for your very interesting suggestions. Matters here have moved rapidly and in the context of grave happenings in the Punjab and bitterness that has been created, it has been impossible for any of us to think in terms of any collaboration with the Muslim League, in its present temper. Everyone seems now to have come to the conclusion that division of the Punjab— limiting myself only to our own Province—is the only way out now.

You well know the Sikh view point in this connection. Our peculiar position in the Punjab made us realise sometime ago that it was impossible for us to agree to any communal domination. In the scheme of Pakistan as before us now, we can remain in the Punjab only at the peril of our existence. Though others failed to see how the League was drifting away, we realised their separatist tendencies more than a year ago. You will remember the Memorandum[2] we presented to the British Cabinet Mission. In it we made our position clear that the Sikhs will in no circumstances agree to remain in Pakistan area and that if Pakistan area was to be conceded, the Punjab must be divided. You will remember that the Cabinet Mission held that if the League's various claims for a sovereign State were to be conceded, no one could in justice deny the non-Muslims' claim for the division of the Punjab.

We were hoping against hope that the League would see reason. I for one, as you know, have tried my best to find some way of settling with them in order that India's unity may not be impaired. We have all failed. The boycott of the Constituent Assembly by the Muslim League and now the terrible onslaught on Sikhs and Hindus by fanatical Muslims have sealed the possibility of any settlement. We each must go our own way. I doubt if you in England have had a correct picture of what has happened in the Punjab. Even the press here was prevented, for obvious reasons, from publishing the details of gruesome happenings. Men, women and children have been mercilessly murdered; thousands have had to flee for their lives leaving their homesteads and possessions behind. The tragic part of the story is that the League leaders, from Mr. Jinnah downwards have not yet been able to realise that all this is the result of wild and reckless speeches made by topmost Muslim League leaders provoking blood lust, praising tyrants and adventurers and making light of the abominable atrocities of the past and indeed of recent

[1] The Cabinet Office are unable to establish the addressee of Sardar Baldev Singh's letter. Probably it was addressed to Major Short who passed it on to Sir S. Cripps and may be the previous letter referred to in No. 356.

[2] Not traced.

times. Mr. Jinnah has lately come out with some sort of a peace appeal. This
was done at the instance of the Viceroy. Several days have gone by and yet
predatory tribal mobs continue to operate in the Frontier. So serious is the
situation there that Lord Mountbatten has had to go to the Frontier personally.
We do not know [how] things will shape. The point of interest is that nothing
has come from the side of the League to show that its leaders are willing
genuinely to resile from their aggressive communalism or to give up the
dream of an Islamic State.

Coming now to the specific issue of the division of the Punjab, we have
after much thought arrived at some conclusions. I need hardly say that it is
impossible to reconcile ourselves to any scheme based on communal majority
in contiguous districts. This, as you know, was examined and rejected by the
British Cabinet Mission itself, among other reasons, on the ground that it
would divide the Sikh community into two. The alternatives are—

(a) to take the basis of landed property into account held respectively by
non-Muslims and Muslims in the Punjab as a whole

(b) to take the basis of the population strength of non-Muslims and Muslims
respectively according to the latest available statistics.

As regards (a) the position is simple. Non-Muslims, including Sikhs of
course, own well over 50 per cent of the landed property in the province.
The question was examined by the Punjab Government in 1931 by analysing
the incidence of land revenue paid by each community. It was then found that
of the total revenue of over Rs. 43,813,977 non-Muslims paid Rs. 21,844,913.
Taking also into account the fact that non-Muslims own well over 80
per cent of the urban property, their share of the total immovable property as
I have said is well over 50 per cent.

In this connection, I might say that because principally of this, namely that
non-Muslims pay half the total revenue of the province, the share in administrative posts of non-Muslims and Muslims was fixed on 50-50 basis some
years ago. The composition of the Punjab Cabinet was also fixed on this
basis. Taking all these factors into consideration, we claim that out of the
some 99,000 square miles of the Province, non-Muslims should get half
or say 50,000 square miles.

The enclosed copies of statements[3] issued by Mr. Jinnah recently show that
Mr. Jinnah has already accepted the principle of transfer of population. Knowing as you do, Indian conditions, such transfers would be impossible from one
province to the other; but if they are arranged within a province itself such
as the Punjab, there would be little difficulty. If the province is divided on the
basis of land holdings, there would be the least possible economic or financial
complications. The economy of the Punjab is almost wholly agricultural and
it would be but just to divide the Province on the basis of the total land holdings and separate non-Muslims from Muslims on that basis.

Another alternative is to divide the Province on the basis of population. According to the Census of 1941, non-Muslims form about 44 per cent of the population in the Punjab as a whole. These statistics have been challenged by authoritative writers in the Punjab from time to time, especially as during winter months, when the Census Operations take place, a large influx of labour takes place into the Punjab from both Kashmir and Frontier Province. These immigrants are almost hundred per cent Muslims and have gone to pad the Muslim enumeration. If the division thus takes place on the basis of population, I claim that 44 per cent of the total area of the Province must be set apart and ear-marked for non-Muslims.

In any event, I think the non-Muslims have a preponderatingly better claim on the three Divisions of Ambala, Jullundur and Lahore. The total area of these three Divisions is nearly 46,000 square miles and the population 17,352,044 Of these non-Muslims are 9,956,508, the Sikhs being 3,004,707. If we get these three Divisions we will have less than half the total area. Some 80 per cent of the total Sikh population of the Province including Nankana Sahib, the birth place of the Founder of Sikh religion, will go to this territory thus solving the Sikh problem materially—and also satisfying the concern of the British Cabinet Mission about Sikhs not being divided into half and half as under the other scheme. In this area the total revenue is Rs. 24,228,998. Of this Rs. 14,634,704 is paid by non-Muslims, the Sikhs alone paying Rs. 8,365,969. Thus both on the basis of population and revenue, these three divisions constitute a predominantly non-Muslim area.

If the division takes place on the basis as in the para. imediately above, its total area will be less than half by about 4000 square miles. This latter should be made good by inclusion in the non-Muslim area of either the District of Lyallpur or of Montgomery. Both of these districts are in the colony areas. You know very well the part played by Sikhs in developing Punjab colonies. Sir Edward Maclagan had this to say about us—

"No colony could have better material, for Ludhiana, Jullundur and Amritsar represent the flower of Indian agriculture. They are the home of Jat Sikhs who have been described as the most desirable of Colonists. . . .In his new environment, (Colony Area) the Jat Sikh has reached a point of development probably beyond anything else of the kind in India. In less than a generation, he has made the wilderness blossom like the rose. It is as if the energy of the virgin soil of the Bar has passed into his veins and made him almost part of the forces of nature which he has conquered".

My scheme therefore is that on whatever basis Punjab is divided and in order to ensure that as big a majority of the Sikh population as possible is taken out, we should get the three Divisions namely Ambala, Jullundur and Lahore plus either Lyallpur or Montgomery district.

[2] Not circulated with the Cabinet Paper; but cf. Annex 1 to No. 276.

I do share your views about the large-heartedness of Lord Mountbatten. He has an engaging and understanding mind. Very shortly he will have conveyed his impressions about the Indian situation to His Majesty's Government. I am writing these lines to you to enable you to take an intelligent interest in any discussions on this subject your end with the firm hope that you will do your best to help us and your other numerous friends in India to arrive at a fair and workable solution.

Please overlook the length of this letter. I have in this résumé given you our case as we see it to the best of my ability. We want no injury to anyone but it would undoubtedly look like pandering to brute force and aggression if in arriving at a decision on the division of the Punjab the Muslim League were to get away with not only a larger portion than is its due but to succeed in cutting my community into halves. Everything we have in this world is within the borders of the Punjab. It is our Homeland. Its present economy and affluence is to a very large measure due to Sikh vigour and enterprise. You know all this and more, and now that the time of decision has arrived, you must do all you can to see that we get justice.

Needless it is for me to say that if this is done in a genuine and helpful spirit, we look forward to the end of this desultory chapter in the history of our dear country and to the establishment of most friendly relations with your Government and people.

With kind regards,

Yours sincerly,
BALDEV SINGH

339

Minutes of Viceroy's Twenty Seventh Staff Meeting

Mountbatten Papers

TOP SECRET

Those present at this Meeting held at Viceregal Lodge, Simla on 7 May 1947 at 4.15 pm were: Rear-Admiral Viscount Mountbatten of Burma, Sir E. Mieville, Captain Brockman, Mr I. D. Scott, Rao Bahadur V. P. Menon, Mr Campbell-Johnson, Lieutenant-Colonel Erskine Crum

Item 1

AN ALTERNATIVE PLAN

SIR ERIC MIEVILLE explained that, at a meeting of the staff that afternoon, Rao Bahadur Menon had put forward the view that it was more than possible that Mr Jinnah would not accept the plan in the Draft Announcement. He had therefore suggested that it would be desirable to have another plan ready, so that Mr Jinnah could be given a clear choice of alternatives.

HIS EXCELLENCY THE VICEROY said that he had always borne the possibility of a rejection by Mr Jinnah in mind. However, Mr Jinnah had given no indication of any such intention. At all the interviews which he had had with Mr Jinnah and Mr Liaquat Ali Khan, he had watched them carefully for any sign that they intended to reject the plan. They had given no such sign. Every test which he had applied had led him to the belief that they intended to accept the plan. If Mr Jinnah really intended to spring a last-moment surprise by rejecting it, he could not have played his part better towards making that surprise complete. Surely Mr Jinnah's only reason for rejection would be that he would hope, by continuing to bargain, to obtain more than the truncated Pakistan at present offered him. Mr Jinnah's real aim was to keep the British in India—and he might think that, if he rejected the plan, he would make it more difficult for the British to go, by continuing his efforts without end to obtain a more favourable award.

HIS EXCELLENCY THE VICEROY pointed out that the only other possible reason for a last-minute rejection by Mr Jinnah would be a sudden realisation that Pakistan was not practicable. When faced with the full horrors of a truncated Pakistan, he might conceivably try to get out of it. But this was most unlikely. Mr Suhrawardy had told him (His Excellency) that Mr Jinnah had said that he would agree to an independent Bengal[1]—so presumably the latter would be quite satisfied with the North-Western Pakistan alone. HIS EXCELLENCY THE VICEROY said that he had asked Mr K. S. Roy for his comments on an independent Bengal: and Mr K.S. Roy had declared himself in favour of it so long as certain safeguards were guaranteed.[2]

RAO BAHADUR MENON said that, from information which he had received, he believed that the conditions for which Mr K. S. Roy would ask would be impossible for Mr Suhrawardy to accept. He went on to point out the ways in which Mr Jinnah could boycott the present plan if he decided not to accept it. He would direct his followers not to attend the divided halves of the Legislative Assembly in the Punjab and Bengal, and not to elect representatives to vote on the future of the Provinces and sit in the Constituent Assemblies. In RAO BAHADUR MENON'S opinion there was little doubt but that the Muslim League would obey their President's orders in this respect.

HIS EXCELLENCY THE VICEROY pointed out that it would always be open to him, in such circumstances, to go ahead with the plan and allow the Congress minority to supply the voters and form the Constituent Assemblies and Ministries in the Provinces or half-Provinces in which the Muslim League boycotted the proceedings. Such a course would prove to Mr Jinnah that two

[1] See No. 227.   [2] See No. 292.

could play at his game. But it would lead to endless massacre, and would be altogether out of accord with H.M.G.'s intention of handing over India in accordance with the will of the people. Therefore it would seem best to have ready an alternative plan which would involve the demission of power under the present Constitution. Such a plan would not, in the last resort, require the agreement of the Indian leaders. Provincial subjects would be demitted to existing Provincial Governments and Central subjects to the existing Central Government. His present intention was to confront Mr Jinnah with this alternative the day before the proposed meeting with Indian leaders. He felt that such a clear choice would make Mr Jinnah far more likely to accept the plan in the Draft Announcement.

MR SCOTT put forward the view that, if Mr Jinnah even then refused to accept the plan in the Draft Announcement, his word should not be taken as final. The two alternatives should be put before the Muslim League Working Committee in the full glare of world publicity. He gave his opinion that demission of power under the existing Constitution would not wholly favour Congress. The Muslim League would presumably be in power in Bengal and the Punjab, and, because of the importance and bargaining power of these two Provinces, relations between them and the Congress Centre would soon find their own level and the two parties would have to come together.

HIS EXCELLENCY THE VICEROY:

> instructed Con. Sec. to draft, for consideration at the Staff Meeting the following day, a telegram to the Secretary of State, concerning this alternative plan.

Item 2

THE RETENTION OF INDIA WITHIN THE COMMONWEALTH

HIS EXCELLENCY THE VICEROY said that, if the alternative plan to demit power under the existing Constitution finally came to be selected, it might be possible to put it into effect together with some form of Dominion status before June 1948. He felt that, in any case, it would be most highly desirable to give India Dominion status or its equivalent at least six months before that date. Any such grant, however, would have to include provision that the British Army in India, so long as units remained, would be under the direct control of the Governor General.

HIS EXCELLENCY THE VICEROY emphasized that he felt that there would be world-wide criticism of the British if they withdrew from India completely before June 1948, and left the country, as was bound to happen in such circumstances, in a mess.

During further discussion, RAO BAHADUR MENON made the following points:

(*a*) Sir Chandulal Trivedi had had a talk with Sardar Patel on the subject of India remaining in the Commonwealth. It was his (Rao Bahadur Menon's) opinion that, if the Viceroy approached Sardar Patel on this subject, he would get a positive reply. Pandit Nehru would say the same.

(*b*) Sir Chandulal Trivedi had suggested that His Majesty should drop the word "Emperor" from his title of "King-Emperor", and become simply "King of India". It was the associations with the term "Empire" to which so many Indians objected.

In this connection, HIS EXCELLENCY THE VICEROY pointed out that it was the substance of the future relationship and not words, which mattered. He felt that any reference to "Empire" or "Dominion" would be unfortunate. Perhaps some such phrase as "A member of the British Commonwealth (or Association) of Free Nations" might be applied to India. Furthermore, any grant of Dominion status or its equivalent should not be described as such, but as the transfer of power.

(*c*) Congress's main objects in hoping for a continued link for a number of years would be largely in order to obtain assistance in the solution of tribal problems and in connection with relationship with the States. Congress's resolution[3] calling for a sovereign independent republic could easily be ignored.

(*d*) In 1943–4 Indian opinion, with no clear goal before it, had swung towards America. But this had been reversed as a result of a trade mission to America. As soon as Congress had come into power, the Cabinet had expressed their preferences for purchasing certain goods in the order Great Britain, Canada, the U.S.A. and Switzerland.

(*e*) It would be constitutionally possible for a British Governor-General to have a dual responsibility towards two separate parts of India. He might also be an unifying link with the States.

(*f*) He did not believe that the difficulties of setting up the administrative machinery of Pakistan within 6 months were insuperable. There was already a Secretariat at Lahore, and the Government offices at Simla might also be handed over temporarily to Pakistan. Communications between Simla and Western Pakistan would, however, have to go through Eastern Punjab.

HIS EXCELLENCY THE VICEROY:

invited the Reforms Commissioner to prepare a paper setting out clearly the procedure whereby a form of Dominion status could be granted to India by January 1948, on the alternative assumptions that

(*a*) the plan in the Draft Announcement would be accepted and

(*b*) the alternative plan would come into operation.

[3] Vol. IX, No. 190.

340

Master Tara Singh, Sardar Baldev Singh and Sardar Swaran Singh to the Earl of Listowel[1]

Telegram, L/P&J/7/12252: ff 13–16

LAHORE, *7 May 1947*
Received: 8 May

After brutal happenings in Western Punjab no Sikh or Hindu's honour, life or property safe under Muslim domination in existing Punjab. Therefore division of Punjab alone can provide safety and homeland for Sikhs who ruled Punjab before British and whose historical and economic position entitles them to special consideration. The proposal to make only twelve eastern districts as homeland for Sikhs and Punjab Hindus causing consternation. This division unfair and unjust as these districts compromise only thirty five per cent area as against fifty per cent property and forty three per cent population of Sikhs and Hindus of Punjab. This proposal heaviest blow to Sikhs as it carves already small community into two halves and deprives them of entire canal colony areas developed mainly through their efforts and enterprise. Proposed Eastern Province has extremely low disproportionate share of provincial assets providing no scope for exchange of population and property. The proposal mutilates whole system of upper Bari Doab canal. We demand division of Punjab along river Chenab with provision for exchange of population and property. Thus alone can integrity and solidarity of Sikhs and their holdings be preserved and equitable distribution of provincial assets assured. Any interim arrangement inconsistent with this demand extremely prejudicial to Sikhs and will be resisted. We remind Britain of its repeated pledges to the Sikhs. Now is the time to redeem them.

MASTER TARA SINGH, BALDEV SINGH, SWARAN SINGH

[1] Cables in similar terms were sent to a number of people including Mr Attlee, Sir S. Cripps and Mr Woodrow Wyatt. The latter sent a copy to Lord Listowel remarking that he thought 'the Sikhs are going to be an exceedingly difficult proposition in any partition plan.' On 9 May Sir P. Patrick noted on the telegram that 'the protest is premature but significant'. On 14 May Lord Listowel acknowledged Mr Wyatt's letter and his Private Secretary sent an acknowledgement of the cable to Sardar Baldev Singh. L/P&J/7/12252: ff 2–3, 9, 12.

341

Cabinet

India and Burma Committee. I.B.(47)22nd Meeting

L/P&J/10/79: ff 372–4

Those present at this Meeting held at 10 Downing Street, S.W.1, on 7 May 1947 at 5.30 pm were: Mr Attlee, Mr Hugh Dalton, Sir S. Cripps, the Earl of Listowel, Mr A. G. Bottomley, Mr A. Henderson, Lord Chorley.

Also present were: Sir David Monteath, Lord Ismay, Sir William Croft, Mr Abell; Sir Norman Brook, Mr S. E. V. Luke, Mr G. M. Wilson, Mr F. F. Turnbull (Secretariat)

Minute 1

Compensation terms for Members of the Indian Services appointed by the Secretary of State and for Officers of the Indian Fighting Services
(Previous Reference: I.B.(47) 19th Conclusions, Minute 3)[1]

THE SECRETARY OF STATE FOR INDIA informed the Committee that the Viceroy had reported that the recent announcement of compensation terms had been very well received by the members of the Services; Lord Mountbatten had asked that an expression of his gratitude should be conveyed to His Majesty's Government for their decision on this question.

Minute 2
The Transfer of Power in India
(Previous Reference: I.B.(47) 21st Meeting)[2]

The Committee had before them a memorandum by the Secretary of State for India (I.B.(47) 56)[3] covering a revised draft of the announcement on the transfer of power in India.

The Committee discussed and agreed a number of amendments to the revised draft.

In discussion the following points were raised:—

(a) As regards the North West Frontier Province, Mr. Jinnah had informed the Viceroy that he would be satisfied with a referendum in the Province provided that, in the event of the referendum resulting in a vote in favour of Pakistan, it was followed by a General Election. The Viceroy was about to discuss the matter with Pandit Nehru, and it was thought that the Viceroy should be informed that His Majesty's Government saw no objection to a referendum being held.

---

[1] R/30/1/10: ff 69–70.   [2] No. 320.   [3] No. 331.

(b) The Committee were informed that Mr. Jinnah had raised the question whether Pakistan could remain within the British Commonwealth whatever the decision taken by the remainder of India. They felt that it would be premature to reach any conclusion on this point until a later stage, but they thought that the fact that this question might arise should be brought to the attention of Dominion Governments.

The Committee:—

(1) Invited the Secretary of State for India to circulate, for consideration at the next meeting of the Committee, a re-draft of the proposed announcement, embodying the amendments agreed in discussion.

(2) Invited Lord Ismay to inform the Viceroy that no objection was seen to a referendum being held in the North West Frontier Province.

(3) Invited Lord Ismay to obtain the views of the Viceroy, and of the Governors of Bengal and Assam, on the question whether the provisions in regard to the partition of Assam should not be the same as those for Bengal and the Punjab.

(4) Invited Lord Ismay to inform the Viceroy that no objection was seen to his proposal that the Indian Leaders should be invited to meet him on 22nd May.

342

Rear-Admiral Viscount Mountbatten of Burma to Lord Ismay (via India Office)

Telegram, R/3/1/170: f 12

IMMEDIATE   SIMLA, 7 May 1947, 9 pm
SECRET

No. 16–S.C. Your telegram No. 5773 May 5th.[1] I cannot send official telegram about replacement of Caroe by Lockhart to Secretary of State at this stage because, as I told you in my telegram of May 6th,[2] there is an anti-Caroe agitation going on and until this is stopped I am not prepared to make any change. I have quite made up my mind, however, that the change must come and I would therefore be grateful if you would warn the Secretary of State that I shall be approaching him at the appropriate time and I should be glad if you would obtain his agreement to Lockhart on an unofficial basis. The trouble, as you know, is that Caroe does not get on with Nehru who is Member for External Affairs and thus is in charge of the tribal areas. You also know all about his difficulties with Khan Sahib.

What I am not quite clear about in my own mind is on what grounds the announcement of his being succeeded should be framed. It would perhaps be preferable to invite him to resign. If he does not agree to this, we could put his removal down to ill-health which indeed in a way is true as he is obviously suffering from strain and is very tired.

I approached Auchinleck before he left for London and he agreed to let me have Lockhart, but please confirm this.[3]

[1] No. 329.   [2] No. 328.

[3] In tel. 5913 of 8 May Lord Ismay told Lord Mountbatten that he was discussing the question of General Lockhart with Field Marshal Auchinleck and thereafter would inform Lord Listowel of what was afoot and obtain his agreement on an unofficial basis. Lord Ismay agreed 'that best solution would be for Caroe to resign on grounds of ill-health'. R/3/1/170: f 15.

343

Rear-Admiral Viscount Mountbatten of Burma to Sir O. Caroe
(North-West Frontier Province)

Telegram, R/3/1/170: f 13

IMMEDIATE   7 May 1947, 10.30 pm
SECRET

No. 19–S.C. There has been a considerable anti-Caroe press agitation in the Delhi Congress newspapers recently, culminating in the demand for an anti-Caroe Day.[1]

2. I thought you would like to know that I wrote to protest strongly to Nehru at once; he expressed his regrets immediately and said that he would do all he could to stop these attacks.[2]

[1] In tel. 242–GT of 5 May Lord Mountbatten sent Lord Listowel the text of a lengthy statement on the N.W.F.P. situation by Acharya Jugal Kishore, General Secretary of Congress, and Diwan Chaman Lal. Lord Mountbatten said that the two men were stated to have gone to survey the Frontier and make a first hand report at Pandit Nehru's request. Their statement had appeared in all Delhi newspapers that day under such headlines as 'N.W.F.P. Governor must be recalled'. R/3/1/170: ff 5–8.

[2] In tel. CA–72 of 8 May Sir O. Caroe said he was grateful for Lord Mountbatten's telegram and noted that 'Lahore Congress Press gives me even more advertisement'. He reported that when he showed the telegram to Dr Khan Sahib 'he professed ignorance and surprise, and said he never read any paper but the Statesman!' Ibid: f 14.

344

Lord Ismay to Rear-Admiral Viscount Mountbatten of Burma (via India Office)

Telegram, L/PO/6/125: f 86

MOST IMMEDIATE

7 May 1947, 11.10 pm
Received: 8 May, 5 am

No. 5889. Point was raised in Cabinet Committee today as to whether Sylhet should be given the option of joining Bengal, even if Bengal wishes to be united and independent. At present the option given (see paragraph 12 in V.C.P.42)[1] is only that of joining East Bengal, if Bengal is partitioned. It was thought logical and reasonable that the option should be unconditional, but it was pointed out that this might reduce chance of united Bengal.

2. Secondly, view was strongly expressed that the same principle should be applied to Assam as to the Punjab and Bengal, and Assam should have the right of excluding Sylhet. If Bengal would not take in Sylhet, it might become a separate administration.[2]

3. Cabinet Committee would be grateful for your views.

4. Governors are requested to reply to Viceroy, repeated Secretary of State.

Repeated to Governors of Bengal and Assam.

[1] This was the same as No. 279.
[2] Lord Mountbatten replied in tel. 24–S.C. of 8 May that he considered the principle enunciated in this paragraph correct but that Sylhet as a separate administration might not be a practical proposition. In tel. 32–S.C. of 9 May he stated that, in modification of tel. 24–S.C., he supported the views expressed by the Governor of Bengal in No. 347. Mountbatten Papers, Official Correspondence Files: Provinces and their future, Part I(a).

345

Minutes of Viceroy's Twenty Eighth Staff Meeting, Item 2 (Extract)

Mountbatten Papers

TOP SECRET

Those present during discussion of Item 2 of this Meeting held at Viceregal Lodge, Simla on 8 May 1947 at 9.30 am were: Rear-Admiral Viscount Mountbatten of Burma, Sir E. Mieville, Captain Brockman, Mr I. D. Scott, Rao Bahadur V. P. Menon, Mr Campbell-Johnson, Lieutenant-Colonel Erskine Crum

AN ALTERNATIVE PLAN

HIS EXCELLENCY THE VICEROY said that he intended to reserve judgement on the tactics he would use for making it known to Mr Jinnah that this alternative[1] was the only one which he could hope for. His original idea had been so to inform Mr Jinnah the night before the meeting with the five Indian leaders; but it might be better policy not to bring it up until and unless Mr Jinnah signified at that meeting his rejection of the plan in the Draft Announcement. HIS EXCELLENCY THE VICEROY said that he might well in such circumstances broadcast to the world the facts of the choice before the Muslim League—or alternatively a communiqué might be issued from the Viceroy's House.

HIS EXCELLENCY THE VICEROY

invited Prin. Sec. further to consider what were the best tactics for threatening Mr Jinnah with the alternative plan; and to put forward recommendations.

[1] i.e. the alternative plan given in No. 346, para. 2; see also No. 339, Item 1, and No. 351.

346

Rear-Admiral Viscount Mountbatten of Burma to Lord Ismay (via India Office)

Telegram, L/PO/6/125: f 83

MOST IMMEDIATE   SIMLA, *8 May 1947, 11.35 am*
                                                    Received: 8 May, 9.40 am

No. 20–S.C. There is always the chance that Jinnah may spring a surprise by rejecting plan at last moment, although so far there have been clear indications that he will accept it.

2. It would be out of the question to carry on with plan in such circumstances and should contingency arise I therefore intend to tell Jinnah that only alternative open is for H.M. Government to demit power on the basis of existing Government of India Act with modifications as necessary.

3. This is the only alternative which it is in the power of H.M. Government to impose without agreement of Indian leaders, but will probably prove much less acceptable to Jinnah. Personally I do not think this situation is likely to arise, but I feel it will be as well to have our plans laid. Please tell H.M. Government of my intentions at next Cabinet meeting.

4. Full details and background follow in my immediately succeeding telegram.[1]

[1] No. 351.

347

Sir F. Burrows (Bengal) to Rear-Admiral Viscount Mountbatten of Burma

Telegram, Mountbatten Papers. Official Correspondence Files:
Bengal, Partition of, Part 1(b)

IMMEDIATE   *8 May 1947, 12.45 pm*
SECRET

112–S. Addressed Viceroy repeated Secretary of State and Governor, Assam.
Secretary of State's telegram 5889[1] from Ismay. I have not seen VCP 42:[2]
latest paper I have seen is VCP 38.[3]

2. I do not think possibility of inclusion of Sylhet would materially affect
chances of retaining a united Bengal if parties were otherwise willing. I
would suggest therefore (if this is not already provided for) that Sylhet should
vote only after all voting in Bengal is finished. Sylhet would then have complete picture before taking its own side. As suggested below, Sylhet's option,
if in favour of joining united Bengal or East Bengal, should be subject to
agreement from Bengal side. Subject to this I would agree that Sylhet should
enjoy option of voting to join either united or separate East Bengal.

3. I would agree that if there is no insuperable objection to the possibility of
Sylhet's being left to form separate administration, transfer of Sylhet from
Assam to united or partitioned Bengal should be subject to agreement from
Bengal side. I would add that I anticipate no difficulty from Bengal side in
including Sylhet.[4]

[1] No. 344.   [2] This was the same as No. 279.   [3] No. 260.
[4] Sir A. Hydari's reply to No. 344 was sent in tel. 702–C of 8 May. He agreed that the option given
to Sylhet should be unconditional and said that Assam should have the right of excluding Sylhet
though it was uncertain whether Assam would wish to exercise it. He added that economically
Sylhet could not form a separate administration. Mountbatten Papers, Official Correspondence
Files: Provinces and their Future, Part I(a).

348

Mr Gandhi to Rear-Admiral Viscount Mountbatten of Burma

Mountbatten Papers. Official Correspondence Files: Transfer of Power, Part II(a)

ON THE TRAIN TO PATNA,
8 May 1947

Dear Friend,

It strikes me that I should summarise what I said and wanted to say and left unfinished for want of time, at our last Sunday's meeting.[1]

I

Whatever may be said to the contrary, it would be a blunder of first magnitude for the British to be party in any way whatsoever to the division of India. If it has to come, let it come after the British withdrawal, as a result of understanding between the parties or an armed conflict which according to Qaid e Azam Jinnah is taboo. Protection of minorities can be guaranteed by establishing a court of arbitration in the event of difference of opinion among contending parties.

2. Meantime the Interim Government should be composed either of Congressmen or those whose names the Congress chooses or of Muslim League men or those whom the League chooses. The dual control of today lacking team work and team spirit is harmful for the country. The parties exhaust themselves in the effort to retain their seats and to placate you. Want of team spirit demoralises the Government and imperils the integrity of the services so essential for good and efficient government.

3. Referendum at this stage in the Frontier (or any province for that matter) is a dangerous thing in itself. You have to deal with the material that faces you. In any case nothing should or can be done over Dr Khan Sahib's head as Premier. Note that this paragraph is relevant only if division is at all to be countenanced.

4. I feel sure that partition of the Punjab and Bengal is wrong in every case and a needless irritant for the League. This as well as all innovations can come after the British withdrawal not before, except always for mutual agreement. Whilst the British power is functioning in India, it must be held principally responsible for the preservation of peace in the country. That machine seems to be cracking under the existing strain which is caused by the raising of various hopes that cannot or must not be fulfilled. These have no place during the remaining thirteen months. This period can be most profit-

[1] See No. 354, para. 2.

ably shortened if the minds of all were focussed on the sole task of withdrawal. You and you alone can do it to the exclusion of all other activity so far as the British occupation is concerned.

5. Your task as undisputed master of naval warfare, great as it was, was nothing compared to what you are called to do now. The singlemindedness and clarity that gave you success are much more required in this work.

6. If you are not to leave a legacy of chaos behind, you have to make your choice and leave the government of the whole of India including the States to one party. The Constituent Assembly has to provide for the governance even of that part of India which is not represented by the Muslim League or some States.

7. Non-partition of the Punjab and Bengal does not mean that the minorities in these Provinces are to be neglected. In both the Provinces they are large and powerful enough to arrest and demand attention. If the popular Governments cannot placate them the Governors should during the interregnum actively interfere.

8. The intransmissibility of paramountcy is a vicious doctrine, if it means that they can become sovereign and a menace for Independent India. All the power wherever exercised by the British in India must automatically descend to the successor. Thus the people of the States become as much part of Independent India as the people of British India. The present Princes are puppets created or tolerated for the upkeep and prestige of the British power. The unchecked powers exercised by them over their people is probably the worst blot on the British Crown. The Princes under the new regime can exercise only such powers as trustees can and as can be given to them by the Constituent Assembly. It follows that they cannot maintain private armies or arms factories. Such ability and statescraft as they possess must be at the disposal of the Republic and must be used for the good of their people and the people as a whole. I have merely stated what should be done with the States. It is not for me to show in this letter how this can be done.

9. Similarly difficult but not so baffling is the question of the Civil Service. Its members should be taught from now to accommodate themselves to the new regime. They may not be partisans taking sides. The slightest trace of communalism among them should be severely dealt with. The English element in it should know that they owe loyalty to the new regime rather than to the old and therefore to Great Britain. The habit of regarding themselves as rulers and therefore superiors must give place to the spirit of true service of the people.

II

10. I had a very pleasant two hours and three quarters with Qaid e Azam Jinnah on Tuesday last. We talked about the joint statement on nonviolence.

He was agreeably emphatic over his belief in nonviolence. He has reiterated it in the Press Statement[2] which was drafted by him.

11. We did talk about Pakistan cum partition. I told him that my opposition to Pakistan persisted as before and suggested that in view of his declaration of faith in nonviolence he should try to convert his opponents by reasoning with them and not by show of force. He was, however, quite firm that the question of Pakistan was not open to discussion. Logically, for a believer in nonviolence, nothing, not even the existence of God could be outside its scope.

Rajkumari Amrit Kaur saw the first eight paragraphs, the purport of which she was to give to Pandit Nehru with whom I was to send you this letter. But I could not finish it in New Delhi. I finished it on the train.

I hope you and Her Excellency are enjoying your hard earned rest.[3]

Yours sincerely,
M. K. GANDHI

[2] See Appendix to No. 354.
[3] Lord Mountbatten acknowledged this letter on 11 May as follows: 'Thank you for your letter of the 8th and for the advice you were kind enough to send me, which I appreciated receiving.' Mountbatten Papers, Official Correspondence Files: Transfer of Power, Part II(a).

349

Sardar Patel to Rear-Admiral Viscount Mountbatten of Burma

Mountbatten Papers. Official Correspondence Files:
Bihar, Situation In

NEW DELHI, *8 May 1947*

My dear Lord Mountbatten,
Please refer to your letter No. 1440 dated the 27th April 1947[1] and my reply thereto of the 28th April 1947[2] regarding the law and order position in Bihar.

2. I have had discussions on this question with the Bihar Premier and have impressed on him the need for maintaining strict discipline and good morale in his police force. He has promised to make every effort to this end and I have no doubt that he will fulfil his promise. I have also told him that in this task he will have my full support and you can assure the Governor that I shall not spare myself in supporting the Prime Minister in such action as he considers necessary to achieve this object.

3. The Governor has also referred to the part the Socialists are taking in fomenting trouble among the rank and file of the police. This question is

[1] No. 239.　　[2] Not traced.

engaging the attention of the Congress Working Committee and you can rest assured that they will take appropriate action.

4. Regarding the anti-smuggling force, I understand from the Premier that the Government have decided to disarm it.

5. As regards the appointment of a commission to enquire into the Bihar riots, I agree with the Governor and yourself that this step would be most inadvisable. I have exerted my influence to the extent I could to dissuade Gandhiji from pursuing this matter further, but the difficulty is created by the insistent demand of the League leaders, both inside and outside the Province. Suhrawardy has written and spoken to Gandhiji on this subject and Mr Jinnah, during his last interview with Gandhiji, also referred to this matter. In the circumstances, the best course may lie in delays and that I understand the Prime Minister is doing.

6. The Governor has been good enough to refer to my support to the Prime Minister in a strong line against the prominent members of the Congress Socialist Party and other individuals and measures undermining the discipline of the police force in the Province. You must know full well how anxious I am to exert myself to the utmost of my capacity to maintain peace and security in India. I hope you will convey to the Governor the pledge of my firm support to his Prime Minister in achieving this in the Province of Bihar.[3]

Yours sincerely,

VALLABHBHAI PATEL

---

[3] Lord Mountbatten acknowledged this letter on 13 May stating that he would convey Sardar Patel's message to the Governor. The same day he sent the Governor a copy of the letter remarking, in reference to para. 4, that he would be interested to know if the anti-smuggling force was disarmed by the Government. Mountbatten Papers, Official Correspondence Files: Bihar, Situation In.

350

Minutes of Viceroy's Tenth Miscellaneous Meeting

Mountbatten Papers

TOP SECRET

Those present at this Meeting held at Viceregal Lodge, Simla on 8 May 1947 at 3.15 pm were: Rear-Admiral Viscount Mountbatten of Burma, Pandit Nehru, Sir E. Mieville, Captain Brockman, Rao Bahadur V.P. Menon, Lieutenant-Colonel Erskine Crum

NOTE:—His Excellency the Viceroy was not present for the first fifteen minutes of this meeting. The discussion of the various items was intertwined. The point at which His Excellency entered the discussion in Items 1 and 2 is therefore shown. He was present for the remainder.

Item 1
THE NORTH-WEST FRONTIER PROVINCE

PANDIT NEHRU said that he feared that, if the N.W.F.P. were dealt with under a separate procedure (as was envisaged in the present Plan), enormous complications would ensue. Whatever was done in the N.W.F.P. should be "in the all-India context". It was essential to know definitely which way the N.W.F.P. wanted to go. But the same principles should apply throughout India. Elections had been held only a year ago on the very issue which was now being questioned. Possibly there would be new elections soon (i.e. after the new Constitution had been decided) all over India. A still further referendum or election in the N.W.F.P. was likely to lead to odd results. Unless they were completely necessary, they should be avoided. A referendum in the N.W.F.P. would result in demands for referenda from hundreds of places in India.

RAO BAHADUR MENON pointed out that, under the present plan, Bengal and the Punjab were to be given the option of partition and then of which Constituent Assembly they would join. This latter choice would surely apply "in the all-India context" also to the N.W.F.P.

PANDIT NEHRU stated that representatives of the N.W.F.P. were present in the existing Constituent Assembly. Why should that position be altered? He then gave further details of a plan which he considered better than the plan contained in the Draft Announcement. This is recorded separately in Item 2 below. His point that Provinces should not be given the right to secede until after the principles of the Constitution had been prepared applied, *inter alia*, to the N.W.F.P. RAO BAHADUR MENON made it clear that the delay involved in this plan would be unacceptable.

PANDIT NEHRU said that there was a fundamental difference of opinion as to what was right in the N.W.F.P. The Governor thought that, unless there was an election or referendum, there would be major trouble. The Provincial Government, on the other hand, was quite clear that an election or referendum, except "in the all-India context", would cause trouble

At this point His Excellency the Viceroy entered.

PANDIT NEHRU said that there had already been a flare-up in the N.W.F.P. It would be risky now to do anything to cause a bigger one. He did not consider that Mr Jinnah's latest appeal[1] was a call for non-violence at all. The whole emphasis in that appeal was, in his opinion, on the continuation of the present movement. He was sure that the effect would be that the movement

[1] See Appendix to No. 354.

would carry on. It could not be carried on peacefully. However, PANDIT
NEHRU declared, this movement was collapsing.

HIS EXCELLENCY THE VICEROY said that he had pointed out to Mr.
Jinnah, who was convinced that a referendum in the N.W.F.P. would result
in his favour, the folly of continuing destruction there. Mr. Jinnah had, he
believed, seen the force of this argument.

PANDIT NEHRU stated that, in the last two months, 200,000 Hindus and
Sikhs had migrated from the N.W.F.P. to Northern Punjab. This affected the
population of the Province. The migration was continuing daily. The Hindus
and Sikhs were the economic background of the N.W.F.P. Without them,
the whole economic structure there would collapse.

SIR ERIC MIEVILLE said that he did not fully grasp the point made by
PANDIT NEHRU that the procedure at present envisaged did not link up the
N.W.F.P. to the "all-India context".

PANDIT NEHRU's reply was that the point which he had made was that there
should be such a link-up. He reiterated his opinion that there was more likely
to be trouble in the N.W.F.P. if a referendum was held than if it was not.
HIS EXCELLENCY THE VICEROY pointed out that this was not the Governor's
opinion. And, quite apart from taking the Governor's opinion, the very
fact that there was a divergence of opinion rendered a referendum all the
more necessary. Such a referendum would, of course, be run from an outside
authority.

PANDIT NEHRU said that it was not easy for the Congress High Command
to issue orders on this subject. Their picture was that the Governor and many
of the officials were opposed to Congress, and were trying to bring about a
set of circumstances to the disadvantage of Congress.

PANDIT NEHRU said that he was intellectually in favour of a referendum.
But it would be better if it could be held in a calmer atmospere.

HIS EXCELLENCY THE VICEROY pointed out that, the longer such a referendum would be postponed and the present situation was allowed to drag
on, the worse feelings would become. A referendum would quickly settle
matters one way or the other. Pandit Nehru's advice, he pointed out, had
always been to act quickly. Surely the only way to find out whether the
Governor or the Provincial Government was right was to hold a referendum.

PANDIT NEHRU said that he agreed that a referendum would settle matters—
but only if held in a peaceful atmosphere with a clear understanding on the
part of the voters of the issues.

HIS EXCELLENCY THE VICEROY said that he fully accepted that a clear
choice of the issues involved was essential; he was also trying to obtain a
peaceful atmosphere—but the longer we waited, the worse conditions would
become.

PANDIT NEHRU said that he supposed that the Viceroy had to rely on the Governor's advice: he himself did not, at all.

HIS EXCELLENCY THE VICEROY reiterated that the only way to find out who was right was to hold a referendum.

PANDIT NEHRU gave his opinion that, if the "whole psychological background, terrors and suspicions" were upset, there would be more trouble than at present.

HIS EXCELLENCY THE VICEROY pointed out that, from the conversation so far, it was clear that the only disagreement was not whether to hold a referendum, but when. PANDIT NEHRU agreed.

HIS EXCELLENCY THE VICEROY went on to say that the date of the referendum was clearly linked up with the date of the transfer of power. Within reason, it was up to Pandit Nehru to suggest a date. But he (His Excellency) was going to have some difficulty in putting over the idea of an early transfer of power to H.M.G.—who would never agree to it if the position of the N.W.F.P. was not decided.

As a result of this discussion, two telegrams were sent to Lord Ismay in London. The first[2] contained a general description of the conversation and a recommendation that H.M.G. should insist on a referendum; the second[3] contained a draft which was dictated to Rao Bahadur Menon by Pandit Nehru after the meeting.

Item 2
PANDIT NEHRU'S PLAN

PANDIT NEHRU gave the outline of a plan which he considered preferable to the plan contained in the Draft Announcement. He called his plan "The Cabinet Mission's plan with modifications", and explained that it was on the following lines:—

1. Power should be demitted to the Central Government in June 1947.

2. The Central Government should then be responsible to either the Constituent Assembly or the Central Legislative Assembly. He would prefer the former but realised that the latter might be easier.

3. Any suggestion that Pakistan should be created straight away should be ruled out.

4. Provinces should be given the option, as in the Cabinet Mission's Plan, of forming groups.

5. This option would later be extended to freedom to leave the Union of India altogether; but this stage would not be reached until after the principles of a new Constititution had been worked out. This would take about three months.

[2] No. 358.   [3] No. 359.

6. At, but not before, this stage the question of the partition of the Provinces would arise.

RAO BAHADUR MENON drew attention to the unacceptable waste of time involved in this scheme. It would be the end of September before the question of the secession or partition of Provinces arose. Only eight months would then be left for all the detailed work which would be required on these subjects.

SIR ERIC MIEVILLE asked whether the Muslim League would ever enter the Constituent Assembly. PANDIT NEHRU replied that he had no doubt that they would if power was demitted to a Central Government responsible to the Constituent Assembly. It was possible that inter-party co-operation therein would break down—but that contingency was possible at any time.

PANDIT NEHRU gave his opinion that, once the principle of partition was recognized anywhere, there would be no limit. Mr. Jinnah was saying that there should be a Muslim enclave in every province in India. If the burden of decision, on the other hand, was cast on the Interim Government, they would have to face realities.

SIR ERIC MIEVILLE asked what Mr. Jinnah was, in Pandit Nehru's opinion, likely to do if power was demitted to the Central Government. Would he order the Muslim League representatives in the Central Government to resign? PANDIT NEHRU said that he was quite certain that Mr. Jinnah would do no such thing. The Muslim League had entered the present Government at all costs, and at all costs they would remain.

At this point HIS EXCELLENCY THE VICEROY entered.

HIS EXCELLENCY THE VICEROY said that he considered it essential to meet Pandit Nehru's views as far as possible. A telegram[4] should be sent to London expressing the hope that sufficient emphasis would be laid in the plan in the Draft Announcement on the "Union of India". Provinces adhering to the existing Constituent Assembly should be referred to as "constituting the Union of India"; and those which did not should be referred to as "contracting out of the Union".

HIS EXCELLENCY THE VICEROY said that, at the same time, it was necessary for him to emphasize that H.M.G. were most unlikely to consent to power being transferred to any organisation in which Congress had a permanent majority, until those parts of India which did not wish to join the Union had been separated. The only way in which power could be transferred quickly was by first allowing those Provinces which so wished to contract out of the Union. Whatever the validity of his reasons, Mr. Jinnah did not trust Congress. And it was his (His Excellency's) instructions to try to see fair play in the transfer.

Item 3
THE EARLY TRANSFER OF POWER

PANDIT NEHRU declared that he could say with some assurance that the Congress-majority part of India would be able to take over power almost immediately. He could not, of course, answer for the Pakistan provinces.

HIS EXCELLENCY THE VICEROY stated his earnest desire that power should be transferred quickly.

RAO BAHADUR MENON said that it would be possible, if Pakistan was not ready to receive power as soon as the Union of India, for His Excellency to continue to act as Viceroy for Pakistan and as a constitutional Governor-General for the Union. If Pakistan was not properly constituted by June, 1948, full power could then be demitted to an executive appointed by their Constituent Assembly.

Item 4
SYLHET

PANDIT NEHRU gave his opinion that the voting on the future of Sylhet was likely to be close. There was a fairly large proportion of Muslims in Sylhet who did not want to join up with Bengal.

Item 5
THE MEETING WITH THE FIVE INDIAN LEADERS

PANDIT NEHRU gave his opinion that three days would be an ample period for full consultation with the Congress Working Committee between the opening of the meeting with the five Indian leaders and the issue of the announcement containing the plan.

This opinion was later reported to London by telegram.[5]

[4] No. 357.
[5] In tel. 23–S.C. of 8 May to Lord Ismay. Mountbatten Papers, Official Correspondence Files: Transfer of Power, Part II(a).

351

Rear-Admiral Viscount Mountbatten of Burma to Lord Ismay (via India Office)

Telegram, L/PO/6/125: ff 81–2

MOST IMMEDIATE

SIMLA, 8 *May 1947, 3.45 pm*
Received: 8 May, 5.5 pm

No. 21–S.C. In continuation of my telegram No. 20–S.C. of May 8th.[1] In recent conversations which Mieville and I have had with Jinnah, the latter did not appear seriously to contest the idea of a truncated Pakistan. In fact, the

[1] No. 346.

general impression which Jinnah has given me throughout and which I think you will confirm that he gave you before you left was that he did not intend to reject the plan contained in draft announcement. In my interviews with Jinnah and Liaquat Ali Khan I have always watched them carefully for any indication of an intention to reject the plan and I have never seen such an indication. In fact every test which I have applied has passed off successfully and led me to believe that they are likely to accept the plan. If Jinnah intends to spring a surprise on me by rejecting the plan at the last moment he could not have played his part better towards making this surprise complete.

2. I am of the opinion that the statement issued by Jinnah to the press on April 30th[2] opposing partition of the provinces was only a counterblast to extreme Hindu and Sikh demands; but it would be unwise to bank on this asssumption. I have purposely refrained from asking him outright whether he would accept a truncated or "motheaten" (as he calls it) Pakistan because I have felt that he would certainly have said "No" in mistaken belief or hope that I would go further and recommend to H.M.G. the full Pakistan that he desires. Therefore we must still guard against the contingency. I know full well that Jinnah is a hard bargainer. The possibility that he has intentionally been "leading me up the garden path" has got to be catered for.

3. Clearly Jinnah's only reason for rejection of the plan would be that he would hope thereby to get more than the truncated Pakistan at present offered. He would hope to continue negotiations endlessly, always withhold (?ing his) agreement, at the last moment, from any other plan put up, hoping (as is his avowed intention) that such tactics would result in compelling the British to (? act) as arbitrators beyond June 1948 so as to ensure that he gets a long term settlement to the greatest possible advantage of the Moslem League.

4. He could make the plan unworkable in a (? similar) way to that by which he has made the Cabinet Mission plan unworkable—by ordering his followers not to attend the Legislative Assemblies in the Punjab and Bengal, and refusing to nominate representatives to the Constituent Assemblies. I have little doubt that his followers would obey his order to boycott the proceedings.

5. In that event, it would be out of the question to carry on with the plan. I feel sure that I must have an alternative plan against this contingency. It must be such an alternative as can be imposed if necessary without agreement from the Indian leaders.

6. In my opinion and I hope that H.M.G. will agree, the alternative must be to demit power on the basis of the existing Government of India Act, with modifications as necessary, i.e., to demit provincial subjects to the existing Provincial Governments and Central subjects to the existing Central Government.

7. I realise that this would lay open the possibility of Congress withdrawing their support of the present plan in favour of alternative, which might be thought, at first (? sight), to be preferable to them. But I am (? not) sure that it is. Bengal and Punjab would, under alternative plan, be governed by Moslem League Ministries. Despite the advantages which Congress would gain from domination of central subjects, they would quickly have to come to terms with those two powerful provinces which would retain very considerable bargaining powers.

² Annex I to No. 276.

352

Mr Attlee to Mr Mackenzie King, Mr Chifley, Mr Fraser and Field Marshal Smuts (via British High Commissioners in Canada, Australia, New Zealand and South Africa)

Telegram, L/P&J/10/79: ff 315–16

IMMEDIATE   DOMINIONS OFFICE, *8 May 1947, 4.25 pm*
TOP SECRET AND PERSONAL

D. No. 439. My telegram D. No. 361 of 10th April, paragraph 1.¹ India. Following from Prime Minister for Prime Minister. *Begins.*

1. During six weeks since he assumed Office Viceroy, Lord Mountbatten, has been having daily meetings with all political leaders and with many rulers and Dewans of Indian States. He has conferred with all Governors and residents, had opportunity of meeting several Provincial Premiers and during the last few days has paid a visit to North West Frontier Province. He has throughout made every effort to persuade Indian political leaders to accept unreservedly Cabinet Mission's plan of 16th May, 1946, urging that this provides the best arrangement that can be devised to meet interests of all communities of India. Communal feeling in India was however far more bitter than he expected; it appears indeed to have become an obsession with both Hindus and Moslems.

2. Mr. Jinnah has shown himself inflexibly opposed to acceptance of Cabinet plan which would secure unified India and Viceroy's discussions have not given any indication of any other plan which would preserve this unity and at same time be acceptable to leaders of Congress and Muslim League.

3. Viceroy has therefore reached conclusion that prospects of agreement

¹ This tel. gave details of Lord Mountbatten's discussions since assuming office and of the communal situation in India.
L/P&J/10/103.

on a unified India are negligible and that only alternative is partition, and that in view of rapid and grave deterioration that is taking place in communal relations in so many Provinces, need for earliest possible decision cannot be exaggerated. He has, therefore, drawn up, in discussion with Pandit Nehru, Mr. Jinnah, Mr. Patel, Liaquat Ali Khan and Baldev Singh, proposals which form the basis of those outlined in my immediately following telegram.[2] Viceroy's proposals had at least the acquiescence of the leaders mentioned, though in public statement of 1st May[3] Mr. Jinnah has strongly protested against any partitioning of Bengal and the Punjab.

4. Essence of proposals is to make it apparent to Indian people, and to the world, that United Kingdom Government are allowing as far as possible the Indians themselves to choose how they would wish United Kingdom Government to transfer power. Each province will have right to decide whether it will work in present Constituent Assembly; or whether it wishes to set up a new Constituent Assembly to frame a separate constitution jointly with other areas or independently. In case of Punjab, Bengal, and Assam proposals provide machinery to allow the two parts of these Provinces themselves to decide this question separately.

5. Viceroy's suggestion is that he should meet Indian leaders not later than 20th May with object of bringing matters to a head and of making them admit openly, if that is still the case, that there is no possibility of securing agreement to a unified India. When that stage is reached he would place before them plan summarised in my immediately following telegram on basis that no alterations of substance would be made unless both sides asked for them, though he would be ready to negotiate amendments on points of detail. Plan would be submitted in form of announcement which would be made both in United Kingdom and India say 48 hours after it had been submitted to the meeting.

6. He felt this speed essential since some leakage had already occurred and further leakage was inevitable as soon as plan had been submitted to leaders on 20th May.

7. Viceroy's plan has received in last two days preliminary consideration by Ministers, in which they have had assistance of presence of Lord Ismay who had flown from India for purpose. Consideration continues and form of proposed announcement is still subject to modification. Meantime I feel that you should have earliest indication of conclusions reached by Viceroy and of general nature of proposals which we are examining in order to deal with situation as soon as it is finally confirmed that a unified India cannot be achieved and if you have any comments or suggestions to make I should be glad to have them as soon as possible. Gravity of communal situation makes earliest decision essential and I will inform you as soon as possible of con-

clusions reached. If conference is to take place on 20th May Viceroy would like to issue preliminary invitation by 10th May.

8. I need not emphasise high degree of secrecy attaching to this and to my immediately following telegram. *Ends.*

[2] Tel. D. No. 440 of 8 May containing a summary of the Viceroy's proposed announcement is on L/P &J/10/79: ff 317–19.
[3] See Annex I to No. 276.

353

Rear-Admiral Viscount Mountbatten of Burma to the Earl of Listowel

Mountbatten Papers. Letters to and from the Secretary of State

PRIVATE AND TOP SECRET   *8 May 1947*
Dear Secretary of State,
I am afraid this will be a shorter letter than usual as I am at Simla and have no letter of yours to answer.

2. Last week[1] I referred to the passing over of Mr Williams, the Joint Secretary Home Department, by the Home Member, Patel, in favour of Mr Banerji, his own nominee, and I added that after my protest Patel proposed to appoint Williams as Secretary of the Information and Broadcasting Department. I am glad to say that Patel has now acceded to my request and agreed to release Williams to become Secretary to the Governor-General (Public) in succession to Mr Godbole, who was leaving in any case. Mr Williams is particularly well suited for this appointment as there will be a number of questions arising in regard to the Secretary of State's Services during the next few months, with which he has been dealing in the past in the Home Department. I am arranging for him to join at once as this appointment has been vacant for the past week.

3. Patel has also been creating difficulties in regard to the Chief Commissioner of Delhi, Mr Christie, who is an Englishman. It is an open secret that Patel has wished for some months past to replace him by an Indian, but his appointment is on the Viceroy's patronage list and my predecessor refused to give way. Recently Patel has trumped up two charges against the Chief Commissioner, which came to me with recommendations that he should be called upon to resign.

4. I saw Patel and asked him point blank whether he wished that the Chief Commissioner should be replaced by an Indian; I told him that if he wished to get rid of Mr Christie he should do so by coming to ask me outright for

[1] No. 275.

his relief and not to attempt to accomplish it by underhand methods. Patel somewhat surprisingly said that he was content for the Chief Commissioner to stay on provided he changed his ways, but I am sure that there will only be friction if Mr Christie stays. I have therefore written privately to the latter telling him that I think I shall have to agree to Patel's wishes and have an Indian as Chief Commissioner; but I have made it clear to him that I should have no wish that he should leave his appointment immediately and that nothing will be done until he has told me when he would like to leave. I am sure he should be treated with every consideration because, in my opinion, he has done his job efficiently and fearlessly.

5. In paragraph 7 of your letter of the 18th April,[2] you mention a letter from the Resident at Hyderabad about the steps to be taken on the death of the present Nizam, and said that you thought that I might encounter difficulties with the Central Government if I considered it necessary to despatch troops to Hyderabad to support the State Forces at such a time. Since you wrote, I understand that the Political Department has sent you a copy of a letter to the Resident at Hyderabad, dated 29th April,[3] which shows that the possibility that difficulties may arise with the Interim Government over attempts to discharge our treaty obligations with the States is being borne in mind.

6. I saw Major General Lyne just before I left for Simla and he reported to me the very satisfactory talks that he and the Indian representatives had had with the Maharajah of Nepal at Khatmandu. It looks as if with care the negotiations will be satisfactory and Gurkha troops will be provided for both the British and Indian armies, but I have impressed on Lyne the desirability of handling this matter with the very greatest care as the position is not yet completely cut and dried.

7. Clow completed his five year period as Governor of Assam on the 4th May and Sir Akbar Hydari took over the next day. I shall be sorry to lose Clow as although I have not been out here long, I saw enough of his work during the South East Asia campaign to appreciate him at his true worth. He leaves for England shortly and I hope you will take the opportunity of having a talk with him about the position in Assam.

8. Ismay has reported to me that the initial reception of my plan by the India and Burma Committee was very favourable[4] and I am so glad that this was so. I am awaiting further news from home with some eagerness.

MOUNTBATTEN OF BURMA

---

[2] No. 176 from Lord Pethick-Lawrence.   [3] Not traced.   [4] See No. 323.

354

Viceroy's Personal Report No. 6

L/PO/6/123: ff 90–9

TOP SECRET   *8 May 1947*

My interviews with Indian leaders continued at a lessening tempo during the past week, but I have seen many Provincial Premiers and Dewans of the Indian States who were in Delhi for the meeting of the Constituent Assembly. In addition I gave a garden party on Saturday the 3rd May for all the representatives of the Constituent Assembly which was extremely well attended and at which I had the opportunity of talking to a great number of the members.

2. Gandhi came to see me on Sunday afternoon at 4 p.m. on his return from Bihar and I explained to him in broad outline the plan which Ismay had taken home.[1] His comment was that it was quite wrong of the British to take any steps to facilitate the partition of India and he returned again to his original plan to demit power either to the League or to Congress to run India as a whole. He added that I could stay until June 1948 as Constitutional Governor General, or quit India immediately and leave them to run it. In reply I reminded him that he had been unable to obtain the support of any of the Congress leaders to such a plan.

3. When he left at 5.30 p.m. Jinnah was due to meet me.[2] I therefore purposely asked Gandhi to wait until Jinnah came in and urged him to arrange a meeting. This was the first meeting between these two for the last three years, but as they spoke quite inaudibly to each other I was unable to hear what was said in the few moments conversation that they had. I did however suggest that they should meet again as soon as possible, and I was gratified on arrival at Simla on the evening of Tuesday 6th May, to hear that Gandhi had gone to Jinnah's house for a meeting at 5 p.m. on that day. I do not expect that anything conclusive will emerge from this meeting, but I have just heard that a communiqué has been issued stating that they have discussed the possible partition of India, on which of course they held entirely opposite views; they also re-affirmed the pact which they had signed recently. The *Hindustan Times* in the leading article to-day, 8th May, states that the reiteration of this pact is of great value in the present political context.

4. Recently there was a clash between the Assam Rifles and the Muslim National Guards at Mankachar and firing was also opened in Sylhet to repel an attack on the Police Station. As agreement was reached between Bardoloi (the Congress Chief Minister of Assam) and Saadullah (leader of the Muslim League in Assam) for calling off the civil disobedience movement and for an

[1] See No. 309.   [2] See No. 310.

enquiry into the alleged breaches of agreement in respect of eviction. Unfortunately, this agreement failed to secure the approval of the majority of the local Muslim League Committee of action; the reasons given for rejection were the Police firings mentioned above, and also the arrest of a member of the Committee, but the Governor thinks that some members of the Committee did not want a settlement on the terms suggested. Clow fears that there is almost certain to be some deterioration of the situation in Assam. Hydari has now taken over from him.

5. I had a long letter last week from Dow[3] about the state of law and order in Bihar. It was an extremely frank letter dealing with the unsatisfactory state of the Bihar Police Force and the added anxiety of the existence of the Anti-Corruption Force to which I referred in my Personal Report No. 4.[4] Dow suggested that it was not a suitable letter for me to show to Patel, but as I felt we now understand each other pretty well, as the result of last week's verbal encounters, I thought by far the best thing was to let him have a copy of this letter and to see just what the situation is in the Province.[5] Dow's Chief Minister was in Delhi for the Constituent Assembly meeting last week and I had him to luncheon.[6] I am afraid I gave him a bit of a lecture about the whole situation in Bihar, but over the social atmosphere of lunch I do not think it appeared to be too tough.

6. There has been increased trouble in Delhi recently and a great number of cases of stabbing. Curfews have been imposed in various districts and there has been much dislocation of business and trade which had been commented on in the local press. Perhaps this and public opinion will result in improvement of the situation.

7. During the last week I have continued my efforts unremittingly to stop the Muslim League campaign from assuming dangerous proportions in the N.W.F.P. Already they have destroyed millions of rupees worth of property in Dera Ismail Khan, Bannu and Tank, etc., and laid up bitter hatred by massacres, forcible conversions and horrible atrocities. On the plea of self defence Abdul Ghaffar Khan inaugurated on 4th May a new formation of militia carrying pistols and wearing red uniforms with black embellishments and berets. There is no legal cover for this force but it is probable that the firearms are licensed by the Provincial Government. I am taking up the whole question of these private armies—which affects other provinces—with the Cabinet.

8. Meanwhile the Greenshirts (Muslim League Guards) are also arming surreptitiously, and the movement has gained such momentum on the Frontier that Jinnah himself tells me he now cannot stop it except by an announcement that they have won their campaign.

9. Jinnah has been pressing me all along to let him announce that I would

order fresh elections in the near future and go into Section 93. At my meetings with Jinnah this week I made it clear that any election would merely be in the event of the Cabinet Mission plan breaking down and Pakistan coming into being and that the issue would be to decide whether the N.W.F.P. was to go to Pakistan or Hindustan; and that any question of going into Section 93 would be related only towards the holding of fair elections in view of the allegations of Congress irregularities at the last election.

10. He then asked me outright "Do you not consider that the present agitation of the Muslim League has clearly proved that the Government has lost the confidence of the electorate and should be dissolved?" To this I returned a categorical and emphatic negative. It was indeed lucky I did so, for the next day the *Hindustan Times* launched an attack on me[7] on the grounds that I had recommended fresh elections under Section 93 in the plan sent home with Ismay, and also for recommending an unfair division of the Punjab.

11. In passing I would point out that whatever security precautions may be taken in the Viceroy's House to prevent the leakage of information there is no doubt that Congress leaders have no hesitation in passing information to the press if they think it helps.

12. Fortunately the leaders of Congress were not long in rallying to my defence. Gandhi himself castigated the *Hindustan Times* in no uncertain terms at his prayer meeting,[8] and at his behest his Secretary, Rajkumari Amrit Kaur, issued a written statement denouncing the leader in the *Hindustan Times*. As the editor of this paper is Devadas Gandi, the Mahatma's own son, the situation was not without humour, though it subsequently transpired that Devadas was away on tour. I received commiseration and apologies from all sorts of people including Nehru and Mr. Birla, who finances the paper; and in fact this attack, I think, has strengthened my position.

13. In the meanwhile, however, Congress leaders have made it clear to me that if I were to yield to force by dissolving the N.W.F.P. Ministry and going into Section 93, not only would this be wrong morally and legally but it would shake the confidence of Congress in my impartiality, and might well invite violence in other parts of India leading to further attempts to overthrow legally constituted and popularly elected Governments.

14. Fortunately I was able to say that I had categorically refused to admit Jinnah's claim that the Frontier Government should be dissolved on the grounds that it had lost popular confidence, and I was able to negotiate with Congress the idea of substituting a referendum for a re-election, on the simple issue 'Pakistan or Hindustan' without putting the Government out of power. To ensure that such a referendum would be fairly conducted, it will, of course,

3 No. 206.   4 No. 211.   5 See No. 239.   6 See No. 285.
7 See No. 291.   8 See No. 306.

be necessary for the organisation running it to be controlled by me, and this Nehru has accepted. Caroe has reported that this is a feasible though difficult proposition and I have asked him to let me have his proposals for running it.

15. When I sent for Jinnah to tell him my decision on the referendum,[9] he was at first upset, but when I pointed out that the referendum would abolish the heavy weightage (12 seats in 50) which the Hindu-Sikh minority have had in the N.W.F.P., he began to prefer the referendum to an election.

16. I told him that since I was telegraphing my recommendation for a referendum to London, I considered he should now call off his campaign in the N.W.F.P. and order the 5,000 prisoners, who had been nominally released at my request, to leave the jail. Meanwhile I had arranged for the principal leaders in jail to be given parole and flown down to see Jinnah (for I had been unable to persuade Jinnah to fly up to see them). He told me that even if he gave orders to call off the campaign, and even if these League leaders passed on the order to call it off, they would be unable to stop the forward surge of the movement, and further violence was inevitable. He, therefore, wished permission to make a statement to the effect that he knew that I had recommended a referendum, and that if it was favourable to the formation of Pakistan this must be followed up by a fresh election, since they could not have a Congress government in Pakistan.

17. I was in favour of Jinnah making a statement, provided it was a clear call to stop all violence in the N.W.F.P. I told him that the position about the Muslim League's policy of direct action was widely misunderstood, and that he owed it to his party to point out that direct action had never been implemented as a policy. I told him that I was in favour of his making a statement of this sort provided he did not mention elections.

18. Mieville and I tried to work out a formula which did not refer to elections and which was fairly harmless; but the following day, when Mieville took it round to Jinnah, he dug in his toes and said that he reserved the right to make any statement he wished; for if Congress could leak about my plan so could he.[10] I, therefore, consulted Nehru and sent a letter of protest to Jinnah[11] pointing out that, since the question was *sub judice* in London, it would not only be improper of him to hint at the outcome, but might be prejudicial to his interests if it proved to be wrong. Nehru saw the letter and agreed with it.

19. There is no doubt that my letter bore fruit, for, although Jinnah told Mieville when he brought it round that he reserved the right to make the statement in any form he wished, he promised that it would not be embarrassing to me. I consider that he has done his best to keep this promise, and the statement which he issued (a copy of which I attach) may well have the desired effect of holding the Frontier stable until His Majesty's Government's decision is announced.

20. Nehru who, as Member for External Affairs, deals with the Governor of the N.W.F.P. on tribal matters raised the question of the removal of Sir Olaf Caroe with me some six weeks ago, and I asked him to give me two months before he raised it again, and explained the position to Caroe. Meanwhile the Congress agitation against Caroe has been growing to such a pitch that newspapers have been clamouring for his withdrawal, and there is even talk of organising a "Caroe must go" Day. On hearing this I wrote at once to protest to Nehru,[12] who came round to see me immediately; and said he would do everything in his power to quell this campaign which had grown up in spite of and not because of any direction from the Congress High Command, and was based entirely on the fact that the Congress party in the N.W.F.P. were convinced that Caroe was hand in glove with the Muslim League. Personally I consider Caroe to be an honourable public servant, who is doing his duty in a very difficult situation. But it may prove unfair to ask him to continue in face of such difficulties, and he fully understands the position, which will be re-considered later.

21. I am still rather unhappy about the tribes beyond the boundary of the N.W.F.P. They are behaving quite normally at present, but there is an air of expectancy and I am afraid that they are keenly watching for any situation which will open for them the door for loot. For instance the Mahsuds and Bhittanis started making for Tank till they got a knock and saw that nothing was doing yet without a fight. Representatives of some of the sections of the Mahsud tribe then started off for Bannu, where they hoped for better luck, but fortunately they were intercepted by the Political Agent and the Scouts. I hear the tribes in Baluchistan at the back of Quetta are also restive and looking forward to loot in the Sind. There is no doubt, as I said last week,[13] that the Frontier is the most tricky area in the country at present, and it will need very careful handling and great good fortune if we are to get through without any further trouble.

22. In connection with the article in the *Hindustan Times* referred to in paragraph 10 above that I was recommending an unfair division of the Punjab, the Maharaja of Patiala came round to see me last week, and told me that the Sikh leaders were perturbed because I was ruining the idea of "Sikhistan" since the partition lines I was reputed to have chosen would divide the Sikhs, with two million of them in the East Punjab and one million eight hundred thousand in the West Punjab.

23. I made it very clear to the Maharaja that I was only making a notional partition for purposes of voting, and that if partition were decided upon by vote, then a boundary commission would have to be set up composed of

all interested parties, to try and arrive at a sensible boundary. I told him the origin of the partition request, which was that Congress wished me to take steps to ensure that no areas in which there is a non-Muslim majority should be put into Pakistan. I pointed out that there were only 12 out of 29 districts in which there was a non-Muslim majority. I drew his attention to the fact that there was not one single district in which the Sikhs had an over-all major-ity, and that in no case did any of the 17 districts proposed for West Punjab have even a Hindu/Sikh majority.

24. Patiala (and the next day Baldev Singh)[14] appealed to me to make the partition line on the basis of Sikh landed property, Sikh sacred buildings and Sikh interests. I told him that world opinion would undoubtedly be against any attempt to put Muslim majority populations of the West Punjab under Sikh/Hindu/Congress domination merely on ownership of land and religious grounds.

25. Patiala was rather worried, for, he said, "In that case I greatly fear the Sikhs will fight". I replied "If they do, Maharaja Sahib, they will have to fight the Central Government; for I and my Government are determined to put down any attempts at communal war with a ruthless iron hand; they will be opposed not only by tanks and armoured cars and artillery, but they will be bombed and machine-gunned from the air. You can tell your Sikhs that if they start a war they will not be fighting the Muslim League, but the whole might of the armed forces". The Maharaja was visibly shaken and pro-mised to report this to the Sikh leaders.[15]

26. The next day in Cabinet, I raised the question of further aggression by Muslims, Sikhs or Hindus in any part of India. I asked if the Cabinet would support me to the hilt in putting down the first signs of communal war with overwhelming force, and if they agreed that we should also bomb and machine gun them from the air, and thus prove conclusively that com-munal war was not going to pay. This proposed policy was acclaimed with real enthusiasm by the Congress and Muslim League members alike, and when I looked across at the Defence Member, Baldev Singh, and said "Are you with me in this policy", he replied "Most emphatically Yes".

27. I am quite certain that unless the communal war which is now being built up is stopped in the first round, the whole of the north of India may flare up. I have told Jenkins and his acting General Officer Commanding, Major General Bruce, and Lieutenant General Sir Arthur Smith, the acting Commander in Chief, to prepare plans for moving in additional forces into the Punjab along the disputed territory between the Ravi and the Sutlej, in good time before the announcment of the voting on partition; I have also warned them to stand by on the North West Frontier; and have given Burrows the same warning for Bengal.

28. I sincerely hope that His Majesty's Government will support me should this eventuality arise. But I feel that if we can blot out 10,000 fanatics in the first round we may stop four hundred million people from being involved in war. In any case it will not be the British Viceroy doing this, but the whole of the Interim Coalition Government of India. It is in fact where there has been failure to curb movements of violence by sufficiently strong and quick use of armed force that massacres have spread.

29. As I forecast in paragraph 26 [? 25] of my Personal Report No. 4,[16] the Chancellor of the Chamber of Princes (the Nawab of Bhopal) asked for an interview last week,[17] to ask my advice how the Princes should act under Nehru's threat of treating them as hostile if they did not immediately join the Constituent Assembly. I told him of my discussions with Nehru and explained that I pointed out to him that the Cabinet Mission had laid down that States should not send representatives to the Constituent Assembly until the third phase, which had not yet been reached. I added that when the political decision on the future of India had been taken it would be best in my opinion if he and the other princes consulted their peoples in regard to their relations with the successor authorities in British India and thereafter announced their intentions as quickly as possible.

30. I reported in paragraph 31 of my Personal Report No. 4. an incident which took place with Patel. It is not without interest that at the next meeting at which he was present he announced that he was going to write to Provincial Governments asking that officers of the Secretary of State's Services who intended to stay on in India should make up their minds within a month. I looked across at him and he immediately corrected himself with "Of course, with Your Excellency's prior permission".

31. The Nawab of Bhopal and the Maharaja of Bikaner (the latter through his Chief Minister, Sardar Pannikar) have both raised with me the question of the re-equipment and re-arming of their States Forces. They are asking for modern rifles, Bren gun carriers and so on, largely for internal security. I have sent interim replies to them to say that the matter is being looked into.

32. During her four day visit to the N.W.F.P. and the Punjab my wife visited nine hospitals, seven refugee centres varying in numbers accommodated from a small unit of forty to Wah Camp of 8,700 and four areas devastated by communal disturbances. The itinerary included Peshawar, Rawalpindi, Kahuta, Wah, Dera Ismail Khan, Tank, Amritsar and Lahore.

[14] See No. 324; the conversation with Sardar Baldev Singh took place two days after that with the Maharaja of Patiala.

[15] Lord Mountbatten sent a summary of his talk with the Maharaja of Patiala on 4 May to Lord Ismay in tel. 976–S of the same date. Mountbatten Papers, Official Correspondence Files: Punjab, Part I(b).

[16] No. 211.   [17] See No. 225.

33. At the Refugee Centres my wife spoke with some hundreds of the refugees and in hospitals she met Hindu, Sikh and Muslim patients who had been victims of the riots and were still undergoing treatment. She was given harrowing descriptions of atrocities that had been committed and of damage to property. In the areas visited the larger proportion of victims were Hindus and Sikhs but Muslims and Muslim property also had suffered in the mob disturbances.

34. Having previously heard statements that there had been cases of the police showing partiality to one or other community in the restoration and maintenance of order after the riots my wife particularly enquired into this but no concrete evidence could be produced to substantiate these vague complaints and it appeared that no action had been taken by the police which had not been justified in the prevailing circumstances. Further, the police and military deserve considerable praise for their action and behaviour under the very trying and dangerous conditions of the communal rioting.

35. In regard to the refugee centres (apart from Wah at which amenities are quite good as this was previously an Army hutted camp) the present accommodation is unsuitable for more than the purpose of temporary shelter. The buildings are all that are available, but the inevitable conditions of overcrowding, the refugees' ignorance of hygiene accompanied by lack of facilities such as adequate drainage, water, soap and clean clothing, and their lack of occupation, entail risks that are apt to result in epidemics and disturbances among the refugees as well as further degeneration of morale. Superhuman efforts have obviously been made by the civil, military and police authorities to meet the emergency and their action during and after the riots and in setting up the centres has done much to prevent further loss of life. The possible partition of the Punjab, the future of the N.W.F.P. and other factors of this nature, however, would seem to make it well nigh impossible for the authorities either to advise or plan at present for the future of these unfortunate people.

36. This four-day tour, during which my wife covered 1,500 miles by air and long distances by car and jeep as well as on foot, and the description she has given me of it, has given both of us some idea of the magnitude of the devastation caused by recent riots and the appalling loss of life and property, as well as the ghastly injuries sustained. No words can describe the moral and physical suffering of the unfortunate victims and the present seeming hopelessness of their future.

37. I have moved to Simla for a week with my staff and Nehru arrived to day, Thursday 8th May, to stay as my guest for four days.

Appendix to No. 354

JINNAH'S STATEMENT OF 7th MAY, 1947

"I have had the opportunity of discussing with Frontier League leaders the situation in the N.W.F.P. and the developments that have taken place recently. The League movement in the Frontier was started because the people, and especially the Muslim Leaguers and the League Organisation in the Province, were sought to be crushed by the Khan Sahib Ministry by fair means or foul ever since the Ministry was formed. The victimization, persecutions, suppression and oppression on the part of the Government knew no limits. Every vestige of civil liberties had ceased to exist. Ordinances, Frontier crime regulations, Section 144 and other repressive provisions of the law were being freely and ruthlessly used to deprive the people of their rights of political expression and criticism of the Ministry. These were the conditions prevailing in the Province when the top ranking leaders of the Muslim League were arrested for asserting their rights of civil liberties, and the resentment caused among the people assumed the character of mass civil disobedience. It is absolutely false, and a complete misrepresentation of the facts, that the All India Muslim League ever decided to resort to direct action.

2. The Bombay resolution of the 29th July, 1946,[18] he continued, merely indicated a change of policy. By it we declared that we would no longer be restricted to constitutional methods which had been scrupulously followed by the All Muslim League up to that time. The Congress creed, on the other hand, not only permitted them to resort to unlawful means, but it was the very essence of the organisation, and they were free to resort to mass civil disobedience at any time they considered proper for the achievement of their objectives through coercive methods. This 'Sword of Damocles', he said, was kept continually hanging over the Muslims and the British Government, and the Congress has repeatedly launched movements and used the weapons of mass civil disobedience since 1921 on various occasions, creating grave situations in the country. The last time they decided to launch the movement was in 1942, and we all know with what disastrous consequences. The attitude of the Congress towards perpetrators of acts of violence in connection with movements launched by it is evident from what the Congress Ministries have been doing since their return to power. In their Provinces acts of violence committed during the 1942 movement have been hailed by the Congress leaders as acts of heroism and patriotism.

3. As against this policy and record of the Congress the Muslim League, by its resolution of the 29th July, only made it clear that it was now free to launch a movement of mass civil disobedience as and when it was thought nesessary. It was in this sense that the phrase 'direct action' was used. It is

18 Vol. VIII, No. 86.

quite obvious that the meaning of 'direct action' which is attributed to us maliciously, namely that it is based on the principle of force, violence and bloodshed, is without any foundation and is absolutely untrue. 'Direct action' means social pressure, strike or revolt, constituting moral pressure upon the authority in power to redress our grievances and meet our demands.

4. The present movement in the North-West Frontier Province developed because the situation had become intolerable, and the Ministry could not be allowed to continue its ruthless policy of crushing the Muslims and the Muslim League Organisation. The entire public has lost its confidence in this Ministry and there is Province-wide demand for the application of Section 93, and fresh elections. Dr Khan Sahib and his co-Ministers were challenged to seek the verdict of the people, which they, in their extreme obstinacy, still refuse to do. From all the information that is available to me and I have gone through this matter most carefully, I cannot disagree with the facts as they exist, and as a result of the situation created by the Frontier Ministry thousands of the people have been arrested, sentenced to various terms of imprisonment and detained and clapped into jails under the Frontier Crime Regulations. The only honourable course for Dr Khan Sahib and his co-Ministers is to resign and seek fresh election.

5. I note that the Frontier Government subsequently issued a communiqué on the 19th April[19] in which *inter alia* they said 'The Government have, for their part, decided unconditionally to release, as soon as conditions permit, all political prisoners who are not charged with offences of violence; and the Government have no intention of interfering with the freedom of expression of political opinion or with peaceful meetings, but they must impress on all in the Province that processions and picketing have in the past proved an incitement to acts of lawlessness, and that they cannot be permitted until normal conditions return'. But the root cause still remains. I had hoped that better counsels would prevail and I do still hope that the situation will be examined dispassionately, and in its true perspective, by those concerned.

6. The Provincial Muslim League, he continued, has on the 1st May (before the Frontier leaders came to Delhi to meet me), after full consideration, come to the conclusion that the steps so far proposed by the Frontier Government in no way met the demands of the Muslim League, and were, therefore, not acceptable to the League. They, therefore, decided not to call off the movement. The Frontier leaders could not also agree to their being released, for they had not gone to the jails merely to be released. I sympathise with them and I am unable to disagree with them in the decisions that they have taken.

7. Nevertheless, we must recognise that the question of the Frontier, in all its aspects, is now before His Majesty's Government, and Lord Ismay

is in the U.K. now, and, in my opinion, it is a question of a few weeks when decisions concerning the whole of India are likely to be announced. It is quite obvious that the people of the N.W.F.P. must be given a chance to express their verdict, and the root cause of popular resentment must be eliminated. There is not the slightest doubt what the verdict will be, and the present Ministry cannot possibly thereafter continue. Therefore, as I have always said, let us hope for the best and be prepared for the worst.

8. In these circumstances I most earnestly appeal to every Muslim, especially the Leaguer, to do all in their power to remain peaceful. Without any reservation I say that on our side there should be no resort to violence or force, and we must bear up with fortitude and show tolerance, despite the gravest provocations. We should not depart from the strictly peaceful path which we are determined to follow. In no circumstances, he continued, should the Movement be allowed to take a communal turn. Our fight is not against the Hindus or Sikhs. We are fighting for a true verdict of the people of the Province, to be obtained by fair and free methods. It is against all canons of morality and civilisation, and the teachings of Islam, that we should harm the weak. On the contrary it is the duty of every Muslim to protect the minorities, in spite of whatever provocation there may be. I know it can be said that it takes two to keep peace, but on our side I say keep peace at any cost, and to the other side I may say 'don't provoke and keep peace'. I pray to God that during the few weeks that are now ahead of us, pending the final announcement, both sides will do their best and save people from destruction of life and property. When the final announcement has been made it will be entirely for us, and we will be free to decide as to what course of action we should adopt".

[19] See No. 179.

355

Cabinet

India and Burma Committee. I.B.(47)23rd Meeting

L/P&J/10/79: ff 333–5

Those present at this Meeting held in the Prime Minister's Room, House of Commons on 8 May 1947 at 5.30 pm were: Mr Attlee (in the Chair), Sir S. Cripps, Mr Alexander, the Earl of Listowel, Mr A. Henderson, Lord Chorley
Also present were: Sir David Monteath, Lord Ismay, Sir William Croft, Mr Abell; Sir Norman Brook, Mr G.M. Wilson, Mr F. F. Turnbull (Secretariat)

The Transfer of Power in India
(Previous Reference: I.B.(47) 22nd Meeting, Minute 2)[1]

The Committee had before them a note by the Secretary (I.B.(47) 59)[2] covering a revised draft of the proposed announcement on the transfer of power in India. The Secretary handed round copies of a further draft (unnumbered)[3] incorporating certain changes of drafting and arrangement which had been suggested by members of the Committee since I.B.(47) 59 was circulated. The Committee considered this unnumbered draft, paragraph by paragraph, and further amendments were suggested and approved.

The Committee invited Lord Ismay to ascertain the views of the Viceroy, and of the Governors of the Provinces concerned, on

(i) the proposed terms of the question to be put in the referendum in the North-West Frontier Province and

(ii) the proposed statement regarding the appointment of Boundary Commissions to determine the boundaries of Provinces which were to be divided under the scheme.

Other points raised in the Committee's discussion were as follows:—

(a) At their meeting on 7th May the Committee had authorised Lord Ismay to inform the Viceroy that he might invite the Indian leaders to meet him on 22nd May to discuss the proposed scheme. It was pointed out, however, that if the Viceroy did not begin these discussions until 22nd May and if the Indian leaders were to be allowed time in which to suggest modifications in the scheme before it was announced, it would be impossible for the announcement to be made in this country before Parliament adjourned for the Whitsuntide Recess on 23rd May. In these circumstances it was agreed that the Viceroy should be authorised to begin his discussions with Indian leaders on 17th May, with a view to an announcement in Parliament being made not later than 22nd May. If the discussions in India were prolonged in circumstances which suggested a real prospect of agreement between the Parties, there would be no objection to postponing a final announcement in this country until after the Whitsuntide Recess.

(b) The Committee had some further discussion on the possibility that Pakistan might ask to remain within the Commonwealth even though the remainder of India became independent. The Committee agreed that, if this possibility were mentioned in Parliament and the Government were asked to state what their attitude would be in that event, the right course would be to decline to express any opinion at this stage on the ground that this was a hypothetical situation which had not yet arisen.

The Committee:—

(1) Instructed the Secretary to prepare a revised draft of the proposed announcement embodying the amendments which had been approved in the Committee's discussion.

(2) Invited Lord Ismay to ascertain the views of the Viceroy, and of the Governors concerned, on the statements to be included in the announcement regarding the referendum in the North-West Frontier Province and the appointment of Boundary Commissions.

(3) Agreed that the Prime Minister, in consultation with the Secretary of State for India, should settle the final form of the draft announcement in the light of the Viceroy's replies on the points put to him about the position of Sylhet, the options exercisable by the Indian States, the referendum in the North-West Frontier Province and the appointment of Boundary Commissions.

(4) Took note that the Prime Minister would submit the Committee's recommendations, together with the final draft of the proposed announcement, to the Cabinet for consideration at their meeting on 13th May.

[1] No. 341. [2] L/P &J/10/79: ff 360–6. [3] Ibid: ff 348–53.

356

Major Short to Sir S. Cripps[1]

Public Record Office. CAB 127/150

8 May 1947

My very dear Sir,

Baldev has written again. Attached.

Para 1 is of no import. He wants to buy a controlling share in the C[ivil] & M[ilitary] Gazette, and me to persuade Kipling's daughter to sell same—and she won't!

[1] This letter and its Enclosures appear to have been sent to Mr Attlee; see No. 386.

But the rest, and the fact he has written again and so soon, makes me feel the Sikh is beginning to *feel* neglected—I don't doubt unjustly. But *if* he is, then I don't doubt he is due to go off with the worst bang we've yet had, and entangle all, and most of all us, with the shambles. Of course it is for Congress and the League to remove this feeling of neglect. But *they* only can if the Sikh feels *we* are urging them to remove it, *and are keeping the Sikh in the swim of what's afoot.*

However, that is a matter of opinion. What is a matter of fact is that Baldev says he agrees with the views of Sant Singh. Considering Baldev's hold over the Sikhs (proved by recent events, or they'd not have been so quiet); and that Sant is the wisest, sanest, and most moderate of any Sikh known to me, it may be useful to you now to know what those views are. They are in the airmail letter, also here attached. I have marginally marked the guts of it.

Please may I have both back?

W.

Enclosure 1 to No. 356[2]

Sardar Baldev Singh to Major Short

1 BHAGWAN DAS ROAD, NEW DELHI, *1 May 1947*

My dear Bill,

I have written another letter some days ago. I hope you have received it by now. I now make a firm offer of anything up to Rs. 150/– per share for Mrs. Bambridge's shares. I hope with this limit you will now be able to negotiate with her. Kindly let me know the result of your negotiations by cable as early as possible.

I hope the letter that I wrote to you the other day was clear. Things are moving fast here. Whether any settlement will be possible, I do not know. What I am concerned at present with is the future of my community. You will remember the assurance the Members of the Cabinet Mission and everybody else gave us of a fair deal for Sikhs. This is the time for the assurance to be fulfilled. In fact it is now or never. I hope therefore that you will do your best and persuade your friends to leave no stone unturned to help us.

Sant is here and I agree with what he writes, as the minimum that Sikhs can be expected to accept. Needless to say that it will also help people of my way of thinking who are so keen on building up cordial relations between England and India.

There is not the least doubt in my mind that some British officials here who still live in the past are doing a tremendous lot of harm to the future relations between our countries. They belong to the old diehard school and are doing their best to put the Labour Government in a very awkward position. I told you this when I was in London. Subsequent events have proved what I then said.

It is high time that the Labour Government were made aware of this unfortunate element in India, for not until the officials co-operate fully in the new policy, will worthwhile results be reaped. Anyway it is clear that these diehards must be ignored and put in their place when final decisions are being framed.

I depend on you to give us the best support you can.

Yours sincerely,
BALDEV SINGH

Enclosure 2 to No. 356

Sardar Sant Singh to Major Short

NABHA, PUNJAB, INDIA,
26 April 1947

My Dear Friend,
Many thanks for your two letters. As ever I pay homage to your deep love of humanity, intense zeal and unbounded enthusiasms. But like every airflier, one has to spend most of his time on the ground and amongst those who know little or nothing of flying. So let us talk of the ground. Facts are: For 27 years or more religious democracy has been preached and practised senselessly by the rulers and the ruled. Under the stress of circumstances mostly created by the two Great Wars the rulers perforce leaned more and more towards religious minorities. Alterable political majorities and minorities elsewhere in democratic countries have been grafted here on religion, thus losing all chance for conversion of political thought and opinion and thereby a majority into a minority. I believe every Englishman in the political field knows this fact. But instead of starting this country anew he sent the first consignment in the shape of Communal award and then the declaration "Indians should frame their own Constitution" knowing too well that the gulf was wider than the Atlantic ocean. My friend, I believe in Transmigration and Karma and you in Action and Reaction. In my conception, it is impossible to escape from Reaction—except through prayer in matters spiritual and through happening in matters secular. It was for this very reason that I readily answered Pakistan and Khalistan last year and not because these were good for those who asked for them and for our friends of the Commonwealth.

So much for the diagnosis. Now the village Hakim's prescription.

Division and Partition be accepted in principle. If 562 states can exist on the map there is room for 15 instead of 11 Provinces. Boundary Commissions to be set up later. Let Muslims and Non-Muslims including or excluding Sikhs sit in their own Constitituent Assemblies. The Sikhs may have their own C.A. if they

---

² This Enclosure is not on CAB 127/150 and a copy of it has been supplied to the Editors by Mrs Short.

so choose. Let these bodies prepare paper Constitutions. It will be interesting to see how each C.A. handles such questions as Defence, F.A., Communications, Finance, Planning and above all the problem of Minorities and Franchise. Each C.A. to produce this paper Constitution within six months with or without the help of others and then it should appoint a negotiation body to resolve the points of difference in 15 days. Amended Constitutions should be put to a referendum to the different Communities both in the majority and minority Provinces. If 25% of the majority Community votes against and 66% of the minority Community do not accept the draft Constitution, it should be considered lost. The ballot to be secret under U.N.O. All this to be completed by February 48. Some such step will bring the vainglorious Leaders on the practical plane while their past Commitments to their followers will be redeemed and their personal egoism satisfied.

I have written to Mr Moon and hope to keep it up.

Weather is warming up here. Communal tension is indescribably intense and I will not be able to get away to the hills this season.

With kindest regards to you all,

Yours sincerely,
SANT SINGH

357

Rear-Admiral Viscount Mountbatten of Burma to Lord Ismay (via India Office)

Telegram, Mountbatten Papers. Official Correspondence Files: Plans, Alternative, (for transfer of power), Part (1)

MOST IMMEDIATE   SIMLA, *8 May 1947, 9 pm*
TOP SECRET   *Received: 8 May, 8.30 pm*

No. 25–S.C. I have spent most of today Thursday in conference with Nehru.[1] He raised certain important points of which gist is dealt with in this telegram.

2. He hopes that in the wording of the plan sufficient emphasis will be laid on "Union of India," which was core of the Cabinet Mission plan. To this end he suggests and I agree that Provinces adhering to the existing Constituent Assembly should be referred to as "constituting the Union of India"; and that Provinces which go with Jinnah or become independant should be referred to as "Provinces contracting out of the Union of India".

3. I welcome the significance of dropping title "Republic of India" and therefore support this suggestion, which please put forward to the Cabinet.

[1] See No. 350.

358

Rear-Admiral Viscount Mountbatten of Burma to Lord Ismay (via India Office)

Telegram, R/3/1/153: ff 1–2

MOST IMMEDIATE   SIMLA, *8 May 1947, 8.30 pm*
TOP SECRET   *Received: 8 May, 10.35 pm*

No. 26–S.C. 1. Reference my immediately preceding telegram. The next point discussed with Nehru was in connection with the proposal to hold a referendum in the NWFP.

2. Although he still accepted the need for ascertaining the will of the people in the NWFP before the transfer of power, he had been very disturbed by a meeting held with the NWFP Provincial Government representatives, Abdul Ghaffar Khan and Congress leaders (including Gandhi) in Delhi recently.

3. The Provincial Government's view was that even a referendum held now would be yielding to force and would upset the delicately balanced equilibrium in the Frontier resulting in grave disorders. Nehru supported this view to me, which presumably means that Congress High Command would connive at such disorders. Nehru therefore wanted the referendum or even election not to take place until the Constituent Assembly had drafted at any rate the essentials of a Constitution. It was made clear to him that this would involve an entirely inacceptable delay.

4. I pointed out that Caroe had stated that unless an announcement was included in the plan that an election or referendum would be held in the near future he foresaw a real flare-up throughout the Province.

5. Nehru then asked me whether I was prepared to take the word of a man who is notoriously anti-Congress against the Provincial Government's word; to which I replied that quite apart from accepting the view of the Governor the mere fact that there was a divergence of opinion rendered a referendum all the more urgent.

6. You will see from a following telegram that Congress want power to be transferred on a dominion basis as soon as possible. I was fortunately able to use this point by saying that it would be out of the question to put this into effect until the allegiance of the NWFP had been determined.

7. I therefore recommend that H.M.G. should insist on a referendum in the NWFP run by the Governor General as soon as the whole picture for the rest of India has emerged, so that a clear issue may be put before the voters; and that a statement to this effect should form part of the plan.

8. I have left V.P. Menon with Nehru to try and draft something to which he will agree.

359

Rear-Admiral Viscount Mountbatten of Burma to Lord Ismay (via India Office)

Telegram, Mountbatten Papers. Official Correspondence Files:
Provinces and their future, Part I(a)

MOST IMMEDIATE   SIMLA, *8 May 1947, 8.30 pm*
TOP SECRET   *Received: 8 May, 11.15 pm*
No. 27–S.C. Reference last paragraph of my immediately preceding telegram.[1]
V. P. Menon has just come in with the following draft which was dictated
to him by Nehru as a result of our meeting.[2]

Begins: NWFP occupies a special position. H.M.G. are committed by their
statement of February 20th to part with power in India by June 1948. It is
their desire however to hand over power in as large a measure as possible
at as early a date as practicable. If the Constituent Assembly had been fully
representative of the whole of India there would have been no difficulty in
handing over power to it. But as is known while it represents a very large
part of India it does not fully represent certain provinces. H.M.G. have made
it clear before, and this has been accepted by Indian leaders, that there should
be no compulsion in forcing a Constitution on unwilling parts. It becomes
therefore necessary to find out definitely what parts of India are willing to
accept the authority of the Constituent Assembly. Those parts that are represented in the Constituent Assembly at present may be presumed to accept
that authority. This presumption does not arise in regard to Bengal, Punjab
and Sind. A procedure will have to be evolved to find out the decision of
Bengal and Punjab as a whole, or in parts, in regard to joining an Indian
Union. If as a result of this the decision is that the Punjab as a whole, or in
part, does not wish to adhere to the Union, then the NWFP will be placed
in a peculiar position, and it will become necessary for the people of the province to decide, in view of the new situation that would arise, whether they
wish to join the Union of India or not. In such a contingency it is proposed
to hold a referendum on this specific issue in the NWFP. The referendum will
be with the concurrence of the Provincial Government and under the supervision of the Governor General. As soon as decisions have been arrived at
by the provinces concerned on this issue, power will be transferred in accordance with them. *Ends.*

[1] No. 358. [2] See No. 350.

360

Rear-Admiral Viscount Mountbatten of Burma to Lord Ismay (via India Office)

Telegram, R/3/1/153: f 3

MOST IMMEDIATE   SIMLA, *8 May 1947, 9 pm*
SECRET   *Received: 8 May, 11.40 pm*

No. 28–S.C. Reference paragraph 6 of my telegram No. 26–S.C.[1]
I would like you to distribute copies of V.C.P. 40[2] to the Cabinet Committee and inform them that Patel and Nehru have now themselves indicated through V.P. Menon a desire for a form of early Dominion Status (but under a more suitable name) at least until a new Constitution has been fully framed which is unlikely to be for some considerable time after June 1948.

2. We shall spend the week end working out details with Nehru and obtaining Patel's concurrence. A further telegram will be sent to you on Sunday.

3. If this comes off it will not only produce a sporting chance of the main Union of India remaining indefinitely in the Commonwealth; but will also get over the difficulty of Jinnah having already indicated Pakistan's insistence on not being kicked out of the Empire. It will also largely solve the problem of those Indian States which refuse to join a Constituent Assembly.

4. I know that at the time that you and Abell left it did not seem that this scheme could be pulled off but the situation has been completely changed by Patel and Nehru coming forward themselves. This is the greatest opportunity ever offered to the Empire and we must not let administrative or other difficulties stand in the way. I rely on you both to give this your full backing.[3]

[1] No. 358.   [2] No. 273.
[3] In tel. 31–S.C. of 9 May Lord Mountbatten said that as he had not yet discussed this subject with Pandit Nehru or Sardar Patel himself he felt it would be better to await first hand confirmation of their position before taking action with the Cabinet. R/3/1/153: f 4.

361

Lord Ismay to Rear-Admiral Viscount Mountbatten of Burma (via India Office)

Telegram, L/PO/6/125: f69

IMMEDIATE   *9 May 1947, 5 am*
5959. Cabinet Committee cleared draft this evening[1] subject to consultation with you about Paragraphs 9 and 22 (see my separate telegrams of today's date)[2] and to agreement of final wording with Prime Minister. Full Cabinet will consider announcement on Tuesday morning.

[1] See No. 355.   [2] Nos. 362–365.

2. There is a snag about the dates. Parliament rises for Whitsuntide recess on 23rd May and does not sit again till 3rd June.

3. Cabinet Committee suggested that the meeting with the Big Five might start on the 17th May and the date of the announcement be left open provided it is made not later than the 22nd May. Otherwise it will mean delaying announcement till 3rd or 4th June. The result of the Cabinet Meeting will be telegraphed on the 13th. I hope to get back by the 16th. Do you accept this programme?[3]

4. Revised text of whole announcement will follow tomorrow.[4]

5. It was agreed by the Committee that the terms of the broadcast should be cleared with the Secretary of State and the Prime Minister and this will be done.

6. Consideration of your telegram No. 20–S.C.[5] about the action to be taken if Jinnah rejects the plan was postponed as your immediately succeeding telegram[6] had not arrived.

[3] Lord Mountbatten replied in tel. 35–S.C. of 9 May accepting this programme. L/PO/6/125: 62.
[4] See No. 379.   [5] No. 346.   [6] No. 351.

362

Lord Ismay to Rear-Admiral Viscount Mountbatten of Burma (via India Office)

Telegram, L/PO/6/125: f 68

IMMEDIATE   *9 May 1947, 4 am*
                                           Received: 9 May, 12 noon

5961. My telegram No. 5965[1] gives text of Paragraph 22 of the Announcement as redrafted. Cabinet Committee would be grateful for your comments.[2]

2. Paragraph 8 referred to in telegram No. 5965 indicates that the division is into non-Muslim majority districts and Muslim majority districts.

3. The options mentioned are whether to join Pakistan or Hindustan or to remain indpendent.

4. Will Governors please repeat reply to Viceroy.[3]

Repeated to Governors of Bengal, Assam, Punjab.

[1] No. 363.
[2] Lord Mountbatten replied in tel. 42–S.C. of 10 May that he had seen the comments of the Governors of Bengal and the Punjab (see note 3 below and No. 374) and that he agreed with the revised paragraphs except that he considered the penultimate sentence should read: 'terms of reference of which will be settled in consultation with those concerned'. Mountbatten Papers, Official Correspondence Files: Provinces and their future, Part I(a).
[3] Sir F. Burrows replied in tel. 113–S of 9 May that he thought such an addition would be a distinct improvement. Sir A. Hydari suggested in tel. 703–C of 10 May that Sylhet should vote after the Bengal voting had been completed. If Sylhet elected to join Bengal the transfer should be conditional on small territorial adjustments to secure Assam's communications with Cachar. L/PO/6/125 and Mountbatten Papers, Official Correspondence Files: Provinces and their future, Part I(a). For Sir E. Jenkins's reply see No. 374.

363

Lord Ismay to Rear-Admiral Viscount Mountbatten of Burma (via India Office)

Telegram, L/PO/6/125: f 67

IMMEDIATE   *9 May 1947, 2 am*
                                               Received: 9 May, 9.30 am

5965. My telegram No. 5961. Following is text of Paragraph 22. *Begins.*

For the purpose of exercising the options described above, Provinces must for practical reasons be divided according to administrative districts, as laid down in Paragraph 8. But it is evident that for the purposes of a definite partition of any Province a more detailed investigation of boundary questions will be needed and, as soon as a decision involving partition has been taken for any Province, a Boundary Commission should be set up, the membership and terms of reference of which will be settled by agreement between those concerned. Until the report of a Boundary Commission has been adopted by both parts of a Province, the provisional boundaries indicated in the Appendix will remain in force. *Ends.*

Repeated to Governors of Bengal, Assam, Punjab.

364

Lord Ismay to Rear-Admiral Viscount Mountbatten of Burma (via India Office)

Telegram, L/PO/6/125: f 66

IMMEDIATE   *9 May 1947, 7.10 am*
                                                  Received 9 May, 3 pm

No. 5969. 1. Paragraph 9 of Draft Announcement now reads as in my telegram No. 5971.[1] Cabinet Committee considered this evening whether the question should be as stated in Brockman's telegram[2] "Do you wish to join Pakistan or Hindustan." It was suggested that it might be better to frame the question "Do you support the Congress or the Muslim League" but the point was put that this would make it impossible to refuse a General Election.

2. Options (b) and (c) referred to in paragraph 9 are whether to join a Pakistan Group or remain independent.

3. Is the draft acceptable to you?

[1] No. 365.   [2] See No. 326, note 2.

4. Governor to repeat reply to Viceroy please.[3]

Repeated to Governor of North-West Frontier Province.

[3] Sir O.Caroe replied in tel. CA–74 of 9 May. He said he felt the draft in No. 365 'should meet the case' but warned that the phrase 'as soon as possible' must be elastic since 'under present rules preparation of new electoral rolls this year (viz. 1947) is mandatory. Preparation of new rolls might take as much as 6 months.'

    However Sir O.Caroe felt it might be possible to amend the rules to provide that, as a special case, the referendum be held on the existing rolls as revised for the 1946 election. L/PO/6/125:f73.

365

Lord Ismay to Rear-Admiral Viscount Mountbatten of Burma (via India Office)

Telegram, L/PO/6/125: f 65

IMMEDIATE   *9 May 1947, 4.15 am*
Received: 9 May, 3 pm

No. 5971. My telegram No. 5969.[1]

Following is text of Paragraph 9. *Begins.* The position in the North-West Frontier Province is exceptional and the issue whether the people of the Province are or are not in favour of the partition of British India is one on which a clear decision by the electorate is required. A referendum to the electors will, therefore, be held on this question as soon as possible; and if this shows that a majority of those voting favours the partition of British India a general election will be held and new representatives appointed by the new Legislature to choose between options (b) and (c) in Paragraph 4 above. *Ends.*

Repeated to Governor of North-West Frontier Province.

[1] No. 364.

366

Minutes of Viceroy's Twenty Ninth Staff Meeting, Item 5

Mountbatten Papers

TOP SECRET

Those present during discussion of Item 5 of this Meeting held at Viceregal Lodge, Simla on 9 May 1947 at 10 am were: Rear-Admiral Viscount Mountbatten of Burma, Sir E. Mieville, Captain Brockman, Mr I. D. Scott, Rao Bahadur Menon (present for part of the Item only), Mr Campbell-Johnson, Lieutenant-Colonel Erskine Crum

THE RETENTION OF INDIA WITHIN THE COMMONWEALTH

(a) *The Date*

HIS EXCELLENCY THE VICEROY said that he considered it most desirable that, if Dominion status was to be granted to India before June 1948, the grant should take place during 1947.

(b) British Forces

HIS EXCELLENCY THE VICEROY said that, if India was granted Dominion status in 1947, it would clearly be desirable for all British forces to leave the country as soon as possible. There was likely, however, to be an interim period before all could be withdrawn. In this interim period the Governor-General would have to be given special powers in relation to the employment of British troops; furthermore, provision would have to be made that they could not be employed without the agreement of both major Indian parties.

(c) Indian Forces

HIS EXCELLENCY THE VICEROY said that Mr Krishna Menon had told him that Congress would never agree, if India was given early Dominion status, to the splitting of the Army. Mr Krishna Menon had put forward the view that, if Pakistan wanted an Army, it would have to be built up from nothing. Muslims would be released from the Union of India Army for this purpose.

MR SCOTT said that he presumed that Mr Krishna Menon's object in these remarks was that Congress should have G.H.Q. and the command organisation handed over to them complete.

(d) The advantages likely to accrue to the United Kingdom from the retention of India within the Commonwealth.

SIR ERIC MIEVILLE gave his view that the advantages which India would gain from staying in the Commonwealth were obvious enough; the advantages which would accrue to the United Kingdom were not so obvious. It was possible that India would only remain in for a period of, say, three years, until the new Constitution was framed. Then there might be general elections and a Socialist or Communist Government might come into power in India and go out of the Commonwealth. The telegram[1] which had been despatched the previous day referred to "a sporting chance" of the Union of India remaining indefinitely in the Commonwealth; but would H.M.G. be prepared to take "a sporting chance"?

HIS EXCELLENCY THE VICEROY said that in his opinion the solid advantages which the United Kingdom would gain were as follows:

(i) An early transfer of power would gain her tremendous credit.

(ii) Such a transfer would involve the termination of the present responsibilities.

(iii) A request by India to remain in the Commonwealth would enhance British prestige enormously in the eyes of the world. This factor alone was of overriding importance.

(iv) Such a request would be of the greatest advantage to the prestige of the present British Government in the eyes of the country.

[1] No. 360.

(v) From the point of view of Empire defence an India within the Commonwealth filled in the whole framework of world strategy; a neutral India
would leave a gap which would complicate the problem enormously; an
hostile India would mean that Australia and New Zealand were virtually
cut off.

HIS EXCELLENCY THE VICEROY also gave his view that, even after three
years, the Indian armed forces would not be fully nationalized and would still
require British officers.

(e) *Ways and means of attaining the object*

HIS EXCELLENCY THE VICEROY said that he fully realised the difficulties
involved in transferring power on a Dominion status basis in 1947. He had no
doubt, though, that these difficulties could be overcome, in the same way that
apparently insurmountable difficulties had been overcome during the war.
One of the main difficulties was doubtless the setting-up of administrative
machinery to run Pakistan, and constitutional machinery to receive power
there. But there were, without question, ways of mitigating these difficulties.

(f) *Pandit Nehru*

RAO BAHADUR MENON gave an account of a conversation which he had
just had with Pandit Nehru on this subject, and undertook to commit Pandit
Nehru's views to paper.

(g) *Mr Jinnah*

MR SCOTT said that he considered it possible that Mr Jinnah, if told of
Pandit Nehru's and Sardar Patel's latest reactions, might give up his idea of a
completely separate Pakistan. MR SCOTT said that he felt that, if Mr Jinnah was
told how things were going, he might well start to think on different lines.

RAO BAHADUR MENON felt that, if Mr Jinnah was told at the present time,
he might publish a statement which would wreck negotiations.

HIS EXCELLENCY THE VICEROY stated that he would be prepared to take
Mr Jinnah's word of honour on this.

(h) *Sir Walter Monckton*

HIS EXCELLENCY THE VICEROY:

invited Prin. Sec to acknowledge Sir Walter Monckton's letter[2] on this
subject.

(j) *Sardar Patel*

HIS EXCELLENCY THE VICEROY said that he was considering the desirability of Sir Eric Mieville and Rao Bahadur Menon going down to Delhi to
seek Sardar Patel's views at first hand.

(k) *Sir Maurice Gwyer*

HIS EXCELLENCY THE VICEROY said that he would also consider the
desirability of Sir Eric Mieville and Rao Bahadur Menon consulting Sir
Maurice Gwyer, who was a great constitutional expert.

(l) Further steps

HIS EXCELLENCY THE VICEROY said that the advantage of taking immediate action in this matter was that Lord Ismay and Mr Abell were in London and would be able to explain it to H.M.G. However, he felt that, at the present stage, any steps they took should be purely exploratory, in order to find out the reactions of H.M.G. The next telegram to Lord Ismay on the subject should list the difficulties and the proposed solutions.

² No. 308.

367

Sir H. Shawcross to Sir S. Cripps

Public Record Office. CAB 127/109

ROYAL COURTS OF JUSTICE, LONDON,
9 May 1947

Dear Stafford,

Thank you for letting me see the letter to Ismay about India.¹ I return it to you herewith.

1. Since the Statute of Westminster, the British Commonwealth of Nations has, in effect, been a somewhat loosely knit organisation of virtually autonomous States, owing a common allegiance to the Crown, and its characteristic is perhaps that it is a voluntary association depending on the agreement of the different Dominions. I think it is clear that the nature of the association can only be altered by the free consent of its members, and that the introduction of a new member whose status differed from that of the others could only properly be done with the concurrence of the other Dominions. Subject to this point, which I have no doubt you have very much in mind, I am in complete agreement with the notes which you endorsed on the letter to Ismay.

2. I have no doubt that some form of association in the British Commonwealth of Nations would be of advantage both to the British and to India, and that the term "Dominion status", which is in itself misleading and often objected to by the other Dominions, ought in itself to provide no obstacle. Dominion status really means virtual autonomy, subject to the allegiance to a common Crown, but it is widely regarded as meaning that the country concerned is subject to outside domination.

3. I should have thought that we need not attach too much importance to the use which has been made of the word "republican". Indeed, even if there turned out to be some insuperable difficulty which prevented the Indians

¹ See Enclosure.

accepting any kind of formal relationship to the Crown, I am not certain that that would in itself completely dispose of the possibility of some new form of association which linked them up with the British Commonwealth.

4. The relationship with the Crown is obviously going to be one of the great difficulties, and the Eire model will hardly do, since I apprehend that the Indians would not be prepared to accept a constitution which depended in some measure on a British Statute, under which members of their legislature were required to take an oath of allegiance, but I should have thought that we could improvise some arrangement which would enable India to owe some sort of allegiance to the Crown as the head of the Commonwealth. Indeed, the Statute of Westminster itself refers to the Crown as the symbol of the association.

5. Common citizenship should present no difficulty, except that it is a matter in which the other Dominions would obviously be concerned, while legally there should be nothing to prevent our agreeing whatever arrangement we chose with India. I imagine we should not think it expedient to do this without securing the concurrence of the other Dominions, and agreeing similar arrangements with them. I do not know how far the present conference on nationality will have considered this matter.

I understand that you merely wanted an informal confirmation that I agreed with your view.

Yours sincerely,
HARTLEY SHAWCROSS

Enclosure to No. 367

Sir W. Monckton to Lord Ismay

2 May 1947

My dear Pug,

I think Nehru will talk to me this weekend on the following lines:

We agree   1. "Dominion Status" stinks in Indian nostrils. But some form of association with the British family of nations might have advantages for India and the British.

Yes   2. So long as India is recognised as an independent sovereign state, the word "republican" in the offending resolution could perhaps be ignored and certainly not repeated. This resolution has no constitutional effect. As an expression of a political aspiration can it be conveniently forgotten?

Vide Eire
We can
improvise
almost any-
thing by way
of compromise!!

3. The King is King of the U.K. and separately of the individual Dominions etc. Is it possible to superimpose on this the conception of him as the recognised King or head of the family of the British Commonwealth? and for the Indian sovereign state to be associated with the family and Commonwealth and in some way to owe allegiance to H.M. as King of the whole but not of India as a unit?

This too is
possible
but see
decision of
C'wealth
Conference on
this.

4. Can there be a "common citizenship" between U.K. and the Indian Union so that an Indian in the U.K. is recognised as a U.K. citizen and vice versa?

I should be grateful for guidance on all this from Stafford or, if he thinks fit, the Law Office[r]s. Please assure S. that my lips are entirely sealed on all these matters. I only want to help Dicky if I can.

Yours ever,
WALTER

368

Lord Addison to Mr Attlee

L/P&J/10/79: f 299

9 May 1947

At the last two meetings of the India Committee, reference was made to the desirability of informing the Dominion Governments of the possibility arising from Mr Jinnah's recent conversations with the Viceroy that a separate Pakistan would wish to remain within the Commonwealth whatever might be the decision of Hindustan.

I agree of course that we ought to let the Dominion Governments know as soon as we can of this possibility. But I am sure that it would be very desirable at the same time to give them some indication of the complicated problems to which such a request would give rise, and if possible some indication of our preliminary views on the matter. I would therefore propose, subject to your approval, that as a first step my Department and the India Office should get together and prepare an objective statement of the political and other considerations involved. I think we should let the Dominions know of Jinnah's suggestion and then say that we will send them the material of our "objective statement" when it has been prepared.

My view is that we should seriously hesitate before saying anything to Jinnah that would indicate objection to their remaining within the Commonwealth.[1]

[1] Mr Attlee acknowledged this minute on 10 May. He agreed that they should take the views of the Dominions on the position which would arise in the event of a section of India desiring to remain in the Commonwealth. He proposed to discuss the matter at the next meeting of the India and Burma Committee and hoped Lord Addison would be able to be present. L/P&J/10/79: f 299.

369

Mr Rowan to Mr Attlee

Public Record Office. PREM 8/565

SECRET   9 May 1947
Prime Minister.

I must confess that I am worried at the view that if questions are raised about Pakistan remaining within the Commonwealth the answer should be to decline to express any opinion at this stage on the ground that this is a hypothetical situation which has not yet arisen.[1]

The Viceroy in his last report[2] said that he had told Jinnah that if one part of India remained within the Commonwealth and civil war broke out with the other part of India the British would be in an impossible position. He says he warned Jinnah to prepare himself for a refusal.

The Viceroy has therefore gone a good long way before any consultation with the Government at home or with the Dominion Governments has taken place. In a recent minute[3] Brook said that he understood Lord Addison was doubtful about raising this issue with Dominion Governments at the present stage. The Viceroy in his last report said that he felt certain that Congress should be given no inkling about H.M.G.'s attitude to a request of this kind by Jinnah "since the main hope of bringing them back into the fold lies in the fact that this is the obvious solution for them over the difficulty of Pakistan". I do not really understand what this passage means. It is in paragraph 41.

There are two aspects on which I am not happy.

(*a*) One cannot tell what pressure would develop about this point once the announcement had been made. It is at any rate conceivable that it may be great. The Dominion Governments are always complaining of lack of, or shortage of, consultation. I should have therefore thought that there was every reason to put the problem before them at the earliest possible moment, and I cannot see what disadvantage such a course has.

(*b*) It seems to me to be a pretty formidable thing for H.M.G. to say that an application from Pakistan to remain within the Empire is a hypothetical question and to decline to express *any* opinion. On the broad front such a statement would hardly encourage other Moslem countries to look to us for leadership and help, and on the narrow Indian front it would create an additional element of uncertainty. The least I should have thought one could say on such an occasion would be that there would have to be very strong and convincing reasons before the Government would turn down a request of this kind to remain within the Commonwealth.   T.L.R.

I wrote this before Lord Addison's minute[4] below arrived; as I have said the sooner we get the point to the Dominions the better. And his last paragraph is noteworthy.

[1] See No. 355.   [2] See No. 276, paras. 39–41.
[3] Not traced.   [4] No. 368.

370

Lieutenant-General Sir A. Nye (Madras) to Rear-Admiral Viscount Mountbatten of Burma (Extract)

L/P&J/5/210: f 25

SECRET   OOTACAMUND, *9 May 1947*
No. 6/1947

2. There has been for some time a demand in this part of the world for an independent Andhra Province, but I understand that in recent years it has been less insistent. With approaching freedom, however, there seems to be, at least in this part of the world, an increasing tendency towards a rather intense form of nationalism, and in recent months there has been a demand not only for an Andhra Province but also for a Tamil one and for separate Kerala and Karnataka Provinces also. So strong has this feeling become that the Ministry felt that they could not ignore it and the other day the Legislative Assembly passed a resolution recommending to the Constituent Assembly that the Madras Province should be divided into these four parts. The only people who opposed this resolution were the Moslems who treated the subject matter somewhat flippantly and put in their own demand for a Moplahstan, and finally staged a "walk-out" when the resolution was put to the vote. I have a feeling that the really responsible politicians in the Province do not in their hearts subscribe to this resolution but they have not the courage to tell the enthusiasts for partition how unwise their proposals are.

371

The Earl of Listowel to Rear-Admiral Viscount Mountbatten of Burma

Mountbatten Papers. Letters to and from the Secretary of State

PRIVATE   INDIA OFFICE, *9 May 1947*

Dear Mountbatten,

Thank you for your letter of 1st May[1] covering Personal Report No. 5[2] which provided a most useful background to the visit of Ismay and his party. They arrived safely last Sunday afternoon and I think I may say that we have been making steady progress ever since with our consideration of your plan. There is certainly no disposition whatever here to question the need for an early decision as to the plan we are going to adopt for transferring power in June 1948 and the announcement of it. Apart from our consideration of the plan, I have had most valuable talks with Ismay and Abell and Ismay has also seen the Prime Minister.

2. I took the opportunity provided by a meeting of the India and Burma Committee yesterday to thank the Committee on your behalf for their help in arriving at a satisfactory conclusion to the discussions on compensation for the Services.

3. Nawab Mir Nawaz Jung, to whom reference was made in paragraph 7 of your letter, has now arrived in London and has lost no time in trying to build up his position as "Agent-General" for Hyderabad in the manner that was expected of him. He has arranged a banquet at the Dorchester in honour of the Nizam's birthday and has sent invitations to other Cabinet Ministers besides myself. I thought it right (and I understand that Corfield, who has been consulted, concurs) to have it indicated to the Nawab that the nature of his post of Trade Commissioner is not such as to justify the public entertainment of Cabinet Ministers. It is clearly most undesirable to give him any undue encouragement.

4. I am hoping to have a good talk with Corfield tomorrow[3] about States' matters, on the basis of the minutes of the Residents' Conference[4] which I have just received and am reading with great interest.

[Paras. 5–10, on the re-employment of members of the Indian Services; and paras. 11–12, on the British Council's proposals for their work in India, omitted.]

13. I said in my last letter[5] that I hoped to let you have my comments on your interview with the Sikhs described in paragraphs 13 and 14 of your Personal Report No. 4.[6]

14. I suppose the basic fact of the situation is that the Sikhs have an exag-

gerated idea of their proper status in the future set-up. No doubt this is due partly to their historical position as the rulers of the Punjab, partly to the rather flattering treatment they have received from us as one of the great martial races of India, and partly to the fact that they consider that they have contributed out of proportion to their numbers to the economic wealth of the Punjab. On the other hand, they are a community numbering only some 6 millions out of nearly 400 millions and in the Punjab itself they number only 4 millions among 28 millions. On any democratic basis, therefore, they must definitely be regarded as a minority (and not even as a "major" minority). Owing to the fact that in no single district of the Punjab do they constitute a majority of the population, it is out of the question to meet their claims by setting up a separate Sikh State.

15. I understand that during the Cabinet Mission these considerations were put to the Sikhs in answer to their case but evidently it has all been like water off a duck's back. It was pointed out to the Sikhs, I am told, that even minimum Pakistan would include 1½ million Sikhs and that therefore the alternatives for them were to be all together in Pakistan or divided between Pakistan and Hindustan. They were asked to say which they preferred. Their reply was that if there were Pakistan there must be Sikhistan. In short, they refused to face the facts. The Mission's plan had the great advantage from the Sikh point of view that the Sikhs would all remain within the Punjab (except those in the States). One would have thought that the right thing for the Sikhs to have done would have been to throw their weight into getting the Cabinet Mission's plan adopted and to that end to make terms with the Muslim League as to their position in Section B. There was, in fact, some skirmishing between the Sikhs and the League but it never came to anything. It may be that Jinnah adopted an unduly frigid attitude, but no doubt the Sikhs also asked for far too much. The Sikhs then clamoured to be given the same right as the Muslim and Genreal communities in the Union Constituent Assembly, i.e. a majority of Sikh votes should be required for any decision on a major communal issue. The Mission naturally felt unable to accede to this demand. It would have given four Sikh voters a veto on any question of this kind. The Sikhs also asked for the same right within Section B. This could not be conceded without conceding it also to the two major communities in all three Sections and it would have raised a demand for a similar right from the Depressed Classes.

16. I had not heard before of the Sikh contention that they were ruled out of voting on a major communal issue in the Union Constituent Assembly by the wording of paragraph 19(vii) of the Statement of May 16th. I do not think this

[1] No. 275.   [2] No. 276.
[3] See No. 376; the talk in fact took place the same day as this letter was sent.
[4] See L/P &S/13/1831.
[5] No. 301, para. 7.   [6] No. 211.

is a correct reading of that paragraph. The position, of course, is that decisions of the Union Constituent Assembly are by majority vote except where paragraph 19(vii) applies, in which case the majority must contain a majority of each of the major communities. But since on a population basis the Sikhs are entitled to four votes only, it has to be recognised that it is almost inconceivable that the Sikh votes could actually sway a decision of the Assembly.

17. There is no doubt that the Sikhs are a very dangerous element in the situation. Under your proposals they will be divided and I do not think that any subsequent adjustment of boundaries can possibly begin to satisfy the claims they put forward. I understand from Ismay that they are asking that the Lahore Division be kept out of the partition you propose pending a Boundary Commission at which Sikh claims would be considered. But Sikh claims are based not on population but on such factors as the economic position of the Sikhs in certain parts of the Punjab and religious sentiment applying to certain areas where there are Sikh shrines. Unless the Boundary Commission were told to give weight to these factors it could not do more than make marginal adjustments in the boundaries where the division by districts has included in the Muslim or Hindu areas small parts of districts in which Hindus or Sikhs or Muslims were in the majority. But if you are satisfied that a Boundary Commission, with terms of reference such as will help to keep the Sikhs quiet until the transfer of power, can be set up without provoking the hostility of the two major communities, I shall be very ready to support your view to my colleagues.

18. What the situation really calls for is a settlement between the Muslims and the Sikhs. Their interests are not necessarily irreconcilable and indeed have a good deal in common, as appears from the fact that they have worked together for many years under the Unionist party system in the Punjab. In this way the Sikhs would avoid being split up (which is their major interest) and the Muslims would get a larger and more viable Pakistan. But I fear the recent bloodletting has done much to destroy any chance of this, anyway for the present.

19. I understand from Leo Amery that he has already sent you a copy of his proposals for a "United Commonwealth of India".[7] These proposals, which, of course, have much in common with Jinnah's ideas as to the relationship of Pakistan with Hindustan, are interesting and not without some value but their practicability clearly depends to a very great extent on whether the major parties are capable of that degree of mutual trust and respect that underlies the relations between the United Kingdom and the present Dominions. No doubt, if there were full and real acceptance of partition by Congress, such relations could be established and made to work well, but if Congress only accept Pakistan in order to convince the Muslims that it is impracticable, and to force them ultimately into Federation, they could hardly do so.

20. One further point is perhaps worth mentioning. Amery's reference to "the definite solution which they" (i.e. H.M.G.) "as arbiters, are compelled to impose" seems to imply an over-estimation of the part which H.M.G. can, or indeed should, play in framing the shape of the future India. It would be impossible to impose the partition of India against the wishes of both major communities.

21. I was very glad to hear that you had decided to go to Simla for a short break. The intensive negotiations you have been conducting ever since your arrival in India, in addition to the innumerable interviews you must have had to grant on assuming the office of Viceroy, must have put a tremendous strain upon you and some degree of relaxation before the next and perhaps even more intense phase of negotiations is obviously most desirable for you.

Yours sincerely,

LISTOWEL

[7] In this note Mr Amery propounded a solution of the Indian problem along similar lines to the association evolved in the British Commonwealth. Attached to Mr Amery's note was the rough draft of a declaration which might be made. The preamble of this Declaration read: 'The Nations and States of India, in no way subordinate one to another in any of their external or internal relations, hereby resolve to remain freely associated and to co-operate actively in all matters concerning their common welfare as members of a united Indian Commonwealth.' L/PO/6/119: ff 20–6.

372

Rear-Admiral Viscount Mountbatten of Burma to the Earl of Listowel

Telegram, R/3/1/142: f 103

SECRET   *9 May 1947, 5.30 pm*

No. 33-PC. Your predecessor's letter March 31st.[1] BERAR.

2. Nehru's reaction to renewed approach by Rau has not (repeat not) been favourable. In my view further attempts to initiate negotiations have no chance of success until decision about demission of authority in British India has been announced and forum for discussion of problem has become clearer.

3. I am advised that basis of agreement suggested would be wholly unacceptable to Nizam.

(*a*) Responsibility for honouring terms of Berar Agreement during interim period rests exclusively with Crown. If Crown, with object of ensuring fulfilment of this responsibility, makes special arrangements with Interim Government this can hardly be regarded as concession in favour of Nizam.

(*b*) (i) merely recognises rights which Nizam already unquestionably possesses.

[1] No. 39.

(*b*) (ii) Hyderabad have so far been able to make their own arrangements for imports from overseas and expect little difficulty in this respect in future. Moreover, Hyderabad would require that any concession made by them formed part of agreement with an authority assured of being able to carry out its own side of the bargain.

4. Proposal more likely to be acceptable to Hyderabad would be one whereby they secured outlet to sea in return for relinquishing claim to effective control of Berar administration, though it is doubtful whether the Nizam would yet accept such a compromise. I feel, however, that terms of bargain must be left for negotiation between parties principally concerned and that our efforts should be limited to bringing parties together as soon as forum is clear.

5. No doubt you will be discussing this question with Corfield.[2]

[2] Lord Listowel replied in tel. 6221 of 15 May that he had discussed this matter with Corfield and felt 'bound to accept conclusion in last sentence of para. 4 of your telegram'. R/3/1/142: f 102.

373

Viceroy's Staff Meetings

Uncirculated Record of Discussion No. 12

Mountbatten Papers

Lord Mountbatten gave, at a Staff Meeting (otherwise unrecorded) on 9 May 1947, the following account of an interview with Pandit Nehru

He first raised the question of the appointment of ambassadors, governors, etc. I told him that he should not continue to make these appointments, as was at present being done, on an *ad hoc* basis; but should make out a full list of the posts to be filled and the names of those to be appointed. He agreed to do this. We also agreed that he should now go ahead with appointing representatives to foreign countries without consulting the Muslim League; Pakistan, when formed, could either appoint their own, share his, or share the British representatives.

I asked him what he thought of the plan for transferring power on a Dominion status basis in 1947. I pointed out that it was entirely up to him whether or not he wanted to go ahead with this plan; the advantages were almost entirely on his side. He said that he was most interested in the plan, but pointed out that he could not rush his supporters on any suggestion of long-term Dominion status. Everything depended on the interim period and the way the British behaved.

He thought that V. P. Menon had the time [timing] of this scheme absolutely wrong. In Nehru's opinion the Constitution would be finished by September; the new Government would be ready to take office by October; elections (unless a new electoral roll was required) would be held by then too; and the whole process would be over by the end of the year. Therefore, in his opinion, there was no question of the interim period lasting beyond June 1948.

In view of the fact that he thought that it was such a simple problem, and as his views on the time-factor were so very different to Menon's I decided to have a meeting with them both the following day.

374

Sir E. Jenkins (Punjab) to Lord Ismay (via India Office)

Telegram, L/PO/6/125: ff 71–2

IMMEDIATE   LAHORE, *9 May 1947, 8.10 pm*
                                                    Received: 9 May, 9.30 pm

No. 87-G. Your telegrams Nos. 5961[1] and 59 (?65)[2] May 9th. For Ismay from Governor of Punjab. Detailed comment is impossible because I do not know (A) whether options are exercisable by electorate, separate sections of legislature (?or) (?representatives) elected by (?separate) sections of legislature as in original plan and (B) provisional boundary to be included in appendix.

In the Punjab transfer of power can be made only in one of following three ways. First. An agreement between communities as to successor authority or authorities. Agreement need not be absolute but must have public support of Moslem League and Congress and of Sikh leaders. Second. In pursuance of award by H.M.G. which we are prepared to enforce. Third. By appointment of *ad hoc* successor authority which would in fact mean abandonment of the Punjab.

3. There is in my judgment now no hope of agreement on these or any other partition proposals. Whatever Jinnah may say in private he has declared publicly for united Punjab as part of Pakistan and Sikhs are making extravagant claims which may be modified but will not be abandoned. Announcement even in terms now contemplated will be treated as an award under which we shall be expected to enforce provisional boundary and to procure appointment of Boundary Commission. If as I suppose provisional boundary runs between Moslem and non-Moslem majority districts it will satisfy nobody and H.M.G. will have to choose between cancelling announcement or using force on a large scale for an indefinite period. We may rapidly find ourselves driven to third method which would be (?positive) disaster.

[1] No. 362.   [2] No. 363.

4. Assuming that announcement is made in terms now contemplated I would expect boycott of all proceedings by Moslems and Sikhs and partly by Hindus also. Moslems would not want (?any) partition and Sikhs would not be satisfied with provisional boundary based on Moslem and non-Moslem majority districts. Hindus would probably follow Sikhs.

5. Punjab situation is explosive and at the moment I can see no credible way out. But I am quite sure that we must avoid an announcement (? on which) there is no agreement. Much will depend on Viceroy's final discussion with leaders. I hope to give my views to Viceroy in greater detail on Sunday May 11th.

Repeated to Viceroy and P.S.V., New Delhi.

375

Remarks by Sardar Patel[1]

L/P&J/10/79: f 248

SARDAR PATEL SAYS BRITISH SHOULD TRANSFER POWER IMMEDIATELY

Sardar Patel, Home Member in the Interim Government, in an interview with the Associated Press of America at New Delhi on May 9th, declared that the current British policy of "remaining neutral, but holding power is a way of propagating civil war," and asserted that India's political impasse would be broken at once if power were transferred to the Central Government "as it now stands," and with "the Viceroy standing out." The functioning of India's Interim Government as a dominion government "with the Viceroy standing out", he added, would have two immediate results.

"Firstly, there would be peace in the country within a week. Those who commit acts of violence do so because they feel there is no strong central power to check them. With dominion functions, the central Government would form a strong centre and would have the necessary power to put down disorder.

"Secondly, lacking interference by a third party to whom either side could appeal, Congress and the Muslim League would settle their differences at once. If there were conflicts in the Cabinet on any question, the majority would rule."

Sardar Patel characterised the present situation in India as serious and said one of the grave problems was of the private armies now being raised and equipped. As an alternative in the event that the British decided that India must be divided, Sardar Patel suggested that power should be transferred to the Constituent Assemblies, saying that the Muslim League already has a separate

Constituent Assembly in the members elected to the Assembly they have consistently boycotted.

"The other way is much easier," he added, "transfer power to the Central Government, let the Viceroy stand out and not interfere. Then you have a strong centre which would be capable of dealing with the problems facing the country, particularly in such places as the Punjab and the North-West Frontier Province. Immediately there would be peace in the country."

Sardar Patel reiterated that Congress stood by the Statement of May 16th "*in toto*" and "in spite of its weaknesses." Congress would like to have a strong centre. Apart from external troubles, it was absolutely essential that there should be a strong army, and for defence a strong central government.

"The Congress position has always been that it will not coerce any group or area which does not want to remain. At the same time, it will not be coerced by any group or community. Therefore if the Muslim League insists it wants separation, then Congress will not compel them to remain by force. But it will result in dividing Bengal and the Punjab." Otherwise coercion would come in. Non-Muslims would be forced into Pakistan and there would be civil war.

Sardar Patel remarked: "It is a dangerous game which Mr Jinnah is playing." He said except for the League's temporary acceptance of the Cabinet Mission's plan, Mr Jinnah's position has remained the same. "We asked him to refer the question to the United Nations Organisation; he said 'No'. We asked him to arbitrate; he said 'No'."

[1] This report, sent to the India Office by the G. of I., Information and Broadcasting Dept, was circulated to the India and Burma Committee under the reference IBN(47)15 of 15 May 1947.

376

Note of Discussion on Retraction of Paramountcy with Sir C. Corfield at the India Office on 9 May 1947[1]

L/P&S/13/1831: ff 52–7

Those present were: the Earl of Listowel, Sir C. Corfield, Mr Henderson, Sir D. Monteath, Sir P. Patrick, Mr Clauson

1. *Introductory Statement.*

Sir C. Corfield, on the Secretary of State's invitation, made a general statement on the present position. He pointed out that the Cabinet Mission's Statement of May 12th, on States' Treaties and Paramountcy[2] (Cmd. 6835),

[1] This note was circulated to the India and Burma Committee under the reference I.B.(47)77 of 21 May 1947. L/P &S/13/1831: f 51.
[2] Vol. VII, No. 262.

was originally drafted with the prospect of partition in mind, and that its terms still held good. In particular, it was up to States to negotiate with British India for the future regulation of matters of common concern. The States had hitherto made little or no progress in this direction because they had been waiting to know to whom power would be demitted in British India. But there seemed every reason to hope that the new draft statement by His Majety's Government would give them the guidance they required.

2. *Retraction of Paramountcy.*

Sir C. Corfield explained the Crown Representative's present policy of withdrawing first Political Agents and then Residents, leaving by about March 1948 no more than a nucleus at Political Department headquarters. *It was agreed* that this procedure was right and in accordance with paragraphs 11 and 12 of the Statement of February 20th; progressive retraction *before* June 1948 would provide the best hope of avoiding a vacuum after complete British withdrawal.

3. *Pandit Nehru's attitude.*

Sir C. Corfield made it clear that Pandit Nehru disliked this procedure of retraction, and argued that since the structure of paramountcy was built up between the States and the Governor-General in Council, the Successor Indian Government(s) should inherit the whole nexus of agreements with the States.

It was agreed (a) that this argument was fallacious. The agreements were between *the Crown* and the States. Up to the 1935 Act, the Crown used the G.G. in C. as agent. That Act created the Crown Representative as the Crown's agent. The Government of British India did not come into the picture:

(b) that Pandit Nehru was in fact anxious for His Majesty's Government to do what they have categorically refused to do, viz. transfer paramountcy to a successor government:

(c) that in any case there could be no question of legislating to transfer the Crown Representative's powers to a successor government. Legislation would do no more than abolish the Crown Representative, and his abolition would automatically result in the voiding of paramountcy and of any agreements between the Crown and States. New arrangements would have to be made between the new parties.

The Secretary of State pointed out that it would be necessary, and in the interests of all concerned, that arrangements in regard e.g. to Posts, Telegraphs, Railways, etc. should exist between the States and the rest of India. Sir C. Corfield said there was no reason to suppose that the States would wish to cut themselves off. The difficulty so far had been that they did not know with whom to negotiate. The new Statement should make that clear.

4. The meeting then turned to consideration of the nine questions in the Annexure, and *agreed that*:

(1) there *might* be a failure of adequate information about States during the retraction period. But the withdrawal policy would not be implemented rigidly and if necessary special emissaries could be sent to obtain information in a particular State (e.g. if parliamentary interest in it were aroused).

(2) the compulsion of events was now much more potent than the advice of political officers in causing Rulers to co-operate with their subjects in such a way as to avoid civil commotion. If a serious situation arose in a State during the interim period, demanding intervention, a detachment of the Crown Representative's Police (a highly efficient and well-armed central force) could be despatched rapidly and could probably deal with the situation.

(3) if a Ruler, during the interim period, *asked* that paramountcy should cease before June 1948, the case could be considered and it might be so arranged by agreement. Otherwise, paramountcy would continue in being till the date of transfer and then lapse.

(4) the new Statement by His Majesty's Government should provide material for advice to Rulers as to the course they should adopt for negotiating the regulation of matters of common concern—viz. either through a Constituent Assembly if they join one, or else direct with adjacent territories.

(5) States who decline to join any Constituent Assembly should be assisted only to the extent that the Crown Representative should do his best to provide a *forum* for negotiation on matters of common concern with the relevant Indian authority.

(6) The Chamber of Princes was already split, and the best thing would be for it to be wound up (perhaps in the autumn), at its own request. Its continued existence was bound to cause embarrassment to all concerned and it had no statutory basis. (It was established by Royal Proclamation).

(7) Tributes and other cash payments by States (about Rs. 70 lakhs) would automatically lapse with paramountcy, but they might be taken into account when negotiations on fiscal questions took place between the States and successor authorities. They would probably in future have to be related to services rendered. It was possible that for a short time after the Crown Representative ceased to exist the U.K. High Commissioner might have to act as a depository agency.

(8) The U.K. High Commissioner might possibly have to be left with some residual functions on the disappearance of the Crown Representative. If so he would act as intermediary between His Majesty's Government and States, not between States and the Successor Government(s). He might have to have some expert staff for the purpose. As regards *accounting* staff, arrangements were already being made to attach an

Accounts Section to the Central Government for receipts and disbursements in connection with States.

(9) The Central Government, and its successor(s), would be well-advised to comply with any legitimate demands from States for arms and equipment for purposes of internal security. (Sir Conrad Corfield mentioned that in fact the present War Minister's attitude in this matter was satisfactory). But difficulty would arise over the definition of "legitimate." At present the Crown Representative decided what was legitimate and this decision was normally accepted by the Central Government. In future it was hoped to have an Indian States Forces co-ordinating branch of G.H.Q., India, and this might provide adequate *machinery* for provision of arms, equipment, administrative assistance, etc. But what was to happen if the Central Government in fact failed to meet the legitimate demands of States on political grounds? Sir C. Corfield emphasised that this was a problem which might have to be faced during the interim period. It was agreed (*a*) that direct export of arms by His Majesty's Government to States was most undesirable, (*b*) that on the other hand, the paramount power had an obligation to the States in this matter until paramountcy lapsed. It was agreed that any difficulty of this kind would have to be faced when it arose.

5. *Berar.*

Consideration was given to a suggestion made by Lord Pethick-Lawrence to the Viceroy that an effort should be made to promote a compromise between the Interim Government and Hyderabad over Berar.[3] Lord Pethick-Lawrence had suggested that the terms of such a compromise might be put forward for Pandit Nehru's consideration and that he should be urged to propose them to Hyderabad if he agreed.

Sir C. Corfield explained that such a procedure would inevitably rouse all kinds of suspicions in Pandit Nehru's mind and would have no chance of success. It was accepted by the meeting that the only thing the Crown Representative could usefully attempt to do would be to arrange a *forum* for discussion of this problem, which was becoming acute.

Annexure

(1) Do the arrangements contemplated for the intervening period provide for the Crown Representative receiving adequate information about internal developments in States?

(2) Will it still be possible for Political Officers to advise Rulers promptly so as to avoid situations arising which attract the responsibility of the Paramount Power for intervention?

(3) Is it proposed in advance of the transfer of power to negotiate with or

announce formally to Rulers the termination of any existing formal undertakings by the Crown to States, or are these to lapse *sub silentio*?

(4) What advice as to their course of action is to be given to Rulers who seek it, in modification of that contained in the last two sentences and footnote of paragraph 5 of the Cabinet Mission's Memorandum of 12th May 1946, in the event of a new statement by H.M.G. recognising some degree of partition of India?

(5) In particular, what is to be said to the States, (such as Hyderabad and Travancore) who have openly declared their intention to be independent of an Indian Union or Unions, and desire to negotiate a special relationship with the U.K. after the transfer of power?

(6) What is to be the policy towards the Chamber of Princes since the rejection by certain important States of the Chancellor's advice about waiting for the Constituent Assembly to become fully representative, and their accession thereto?

(7) Does the proposed "standstill" agreement between States and the Centre on economic matters pending the negotiation of new economic and fiscal arrangements cover the continued payment of cash contributions by States now due to the Crown?

(8) To what extent is it proposed that the U.K.H.C. should act as an intermediary between the States and the Successor Governments in matters that remain unadjusted between them on the transfer of power? Is it proposed that any nucleus of the staff of the Political Department should be temporarily attached to the U.K.H.C. to assist him in executing such functions? (It is understood that Sir Conrad had contemplated an accounting staff being taken over by the successor Government).

(9) What is contemplated to be the future of Indian States Forces now accepted for embodiment with the Crown's Forces in India? How is it anticipated that States will in future obtain the requisite arms and ammunition for their Forces and Police? (It is understood that Sir C. Corfield has received some assurances from Sardar Baldev Singh about this).

[3] See No. 39.

377

Lord Ismay to Rear-Admiral Viscount Mountbatten of Burma (via India Office)

Telegram, L/PO/6/125: f 63

IMMEDIATE   *9 May 1947, 7.40 pm*
                                                        Received: 10 May, 6 am

6037. Your 25–S.C. of 8th May.[1] Union of India.

I will put this to the Cabinet Committee on Monday but meanwhile you should know of the following comments made in meeting today with officials of India Office and Cabinet Secretariat.

2. The meeting saw considerable danger in adopting this title for the Hindu Provinces. The inference would be that those not joining the existing Constituent Assembly were rebels. Secondly, there is at present no Union but only a Constituent Assembly representing in the main the Provinces of Section A. Thirdly doubt was thrown on the validity of the argument from the Cabinet Mission Plan since the Cabinet Mission Plan is admittedly dead.

[1] No. 357.

378

Lord Ismay to Rear-Admiral Viscount Mountbatten of Burma (via India Office)

Telegram, R/3/1/151: f 45

IMMEDIATE   *9 May 1947, 10.47 pm*
SECRET   *Received: 10 May, 6 am*

No. 6036. Your 26 and 27–S.C.[1] about N.W.F.P. referendum crossed my telegrams 5969 and 5971.[2] I suggest text in latter broadly meets Nehru's points and that we could not possibly include whole of his draft. We can however amend para. No. 9 so that second half will read as follows "A referendum to electors will therefore be held on this question under supervision of Governor-General and at a time to be determined by him. If this shows that majority of those voting favours partition of British India a general election will be held and representatives will be appointed by new legislature to choose between options (*b*) and (*c*) in para. No. 4 above."

2. I suggest we should not mention concurrence of Provincial Government. I understand this has not yet been obtained and if referendum was made subject to concurrence of Government there might be difficulty later in securing their

agreement while in any case Jinnah would be highly suspicious of their intentions.

3. There will be Cabinet Committee meeting on Monday. Please telegraph whether you accept this redraft.

¹ Nos. 358 and 359.   ² Nos. 364 and 365.

379

Lord Ismay to Rear-Admiral Viscount Mountbatten of Burma (via India Office)

Telegram, Mountbatten Papers. Official Correspondence Files: Transfer of Power, Part II(a)

IMMEDIATE   *9 May 1947, 11.4 pm*
TOP SECRET   *Received: 10 May, 7.30 am*

No. 6043. Following is text of draft announcement as revised by Cabinet Committee up to May 8th. Amendment of Para. No. 12 and 13 in the light of your views is still to be made and final decision not yet taken on bracketed portion of para 23. Para No. 8 also still under consideration.

Text begins. I Introduction.

1. On 20th February 1947 H.M.G. announced their intention of transferring power in British India to Indian hands by June 1948. It is their desire that this transfer should be made in accordance with the wishes of Indian people themselves. They had hoped it would be possible to transfer power to Governments within a single Indian Union. H. E. the Viceroy has however reported that leaders of main political parties in India have been unable to reach agreement on any form of unified Government. H.M.G. have therefore decided in accordance with para 10 of their statement of 20th February 1947 that arrangements must now be made to ensure that power can be transferred by due date to more than one authority.

2. This will involve constitutional, administrative, financial and defence problems of great complexity for successor authorities. It is therefore essential that it should be determined at earliest possible moment who successor authorities will be so that they may prepare themselves to deal with these matters and to take over power by due date. After full consultation with political leaders in India H.M.G. have decided to adopt for this purpose plan set out in para 4 to 18 below.

3. The sole purpose of H.M.G.'s procedure is to ascertain wishes of people of India as to their future and to enable power to be transferred with least possible dislocation. H.M.G. have no intention of attempting to frame ultimate constitution of India which is a matter entirely for Indians

themselves. Nor is there anything in this plan to preclude negotiations between communities for an United India.

II. The issues to be decided.

4. H.M.G. are satisfied that best practicable procedure in time available is to enable different parts of India to decide through representatives chosen for purpose whether their constitutions shall be framed:
(a) in collaboration with existing constituent assembly,
(b) jointly with other parts of India or
(c) separately.

5. These decisions cannot be taken by existing Provincial Legislative Assemblies. The composition of these assemblies is weighted to give special protection to minorities and does not therefore correctly reflect true balance of different elements in population. Moreover in some provinces where there are large and compact minority elements a decision by Provincial Legislative Assemblies might have result that large areas would be brought against their will under constitution unacceptable to them. The procedure will therefore be as follows.

III. Madras, Bombay, United Provinces. Bihar, Central Provinces, Orissa, Delhi, Ajmer Merwara and Coorg.

6. The representatives of these provinces in existing constituent assembly will be asked to confirm that it is the wish of their provinces to remain in existing Constituent Assembly.

IV. Other Provinces. Preliminary Arrangements.
A. Bengal, Punjab and Assam.

7. In these Provinces existing Constituent Assembly representatives cannot take necessary decisions because they were elected for each Province as a whole and cannot therefore be divided into separate bodies representing parts of a Province. The P.L.A.s in these Provinces will therefore each be asked to meet in two parts (excluding European members) as indicated below.
(I) In Bengal the Legislative Assembly will be asked to sit in two parts one representing Moslem majority districts and other the rest of Province.
(II) In the Punjab the Legislative Assembly will be similarly divided.
(III) In Assam the Legislative Assembly will be asked to sit in two parts one consisting of members elected from territorial constituencies included in Sylhet district and other members elected from remainder of Province.
In determining population of districts 1941 Census figures will be taken as authoritative. The Moslem majority districts are set out in appendix.[1]

B. N.W.F.P.

8. The position in N.W.F.P. is exceptional and issue whether people of

Province are or not in favour of partition of British India is one on which a clear decision by electorate is required. A referendum to electors will therefore be held on this question as soon as possible and if this shows that a majority of those voting favour partition of British India a general election will be held and new representatives will be appointed by new Legislature to choose between options (b) and (c) in para No 4 above.

Further Procedure.

9. The Legislative Assembly of Sind (excluding European members) the two parts of Legislative Assembly of Bengal, the Punjab and Assam and, if referendum referred to in preceding para is followed by a general election in N.W.F.P., the Legislative Assembly of that Province will elect representatives by method laid down in Cabinet Mission's Statement of May 16th 1946. But in order to provide an adequate number of representatives especially from smaller areas one representative will be elected for every 250,000 of population instead of one for every million.

10. On this basis numbers to be elected will be:
(Read in five columns)

Province	General	Moslems	Sikhs	Total
Assam less Sylhet	22	6	Nil	28
Sylhet District	5	8	Nil	13
West Bengal	60	17	Nil	77
East Bengal	49	115	Nil	164
N.W.F.P.	1	11	Nil	12
West Punjab	11	49	7	67
East Punjab	22	15	8	45
Sind	5	13	Nil	18

11. (a) The representatives so elected of the two parts of Bengal and of Punjab sitting separately will be empowered to vote whether or not their Provinces should be divided. If a simple majority of either body vote in favour of partition the division will take place.

Provided that a preliminary joint meeting of representatives of both parts of Bengal or of Punjab may be held to consider whether in the event of two parts of Province subsequently agreeing to remain united, the whole Province will enter a joint Constituent Assembly with other Provinces or remain separate.

(b) As soon as a decision under (a) above has been reached representatives of Bengal and the Punjab (if they decide against division) or of the parts of those provinces (if they decide in favour of division) will decide on behalf of areas which they represent which of the three options in para. 4 above they choose.

12. If as a result of these decisions it is decided to partition Bengal the representatives of Sylhet will forthwith sit separately as prescribed in para. 7(iii) and

[1] The text of the Appendix was not included in the telegram; see Appendix to No. 476.

decide whether (*a*) Sylhet will remain part of Assam or (*b*) Sylhet will join the same Constituent Assembly as East Bengal.

13. Representatives of Assam (with or without Sylhet depending on decision on para. 12 above) will decide by a simple majority vote which of the three options in para. 4 above they choose.

14. If referendum in the N.W.F.P. shows that a majority of those voting favours partition of British India the representatives of the Province elected under para. 9 and para. 10 after the new provincial elections have been (held) will decide which of the options (*b*) and (*c*) in para. 4 above they choose.

Sind and Baluchistan.

15. The representatives of Sind will decide by a simple majority vote which of the three options in para. 4 above they choose.

16. In British Baluchistan the members of Shahi Jirga (other than those members who are nominated as Sardars of Kalat State) and non-official members of the Quetta municipality will meet to decide which of the three options in para. 4 above they choose. The meeting will also elect a representative to attend the Constituent Assembly selected.

17. The Representatives chosen under para. 9 and para. 10 will represent their respective Provinces or parts of Provinces in the Constituent Assembly to which their area adheres: provided that in any existing Province which decides to remain independent Provincial Legislature shall decide how new Constitution shall be framed.

18. Where it is decided that any Province or part of a Province will join existing Constituent Assembly it will be necessary to hold a fresh election of representatives on the same scale of one representative for every million of population as was prescribed by Cabinet Mission. By this scale number of representatives to which each area would be entitled is as follows:—

Province	General	Moslem	Sikhs	Total
Assam less Sylhet	6	1	nil	7
Sylhet District	1	2	nil	3
West Bengal	15	4	nil	19
East Bengal	12	29	nil	41
N.W.F.P.	nil	3	nil	3
West Punjab	3	12	2	17
East Punjab	6	4	2	12
Sind	1	3	nil	4

V. Necessity for speed.

19. In order that the successor authorities may have time to adapt themselves to take over power it is important that all the above processes should be

completed as quickly as possible. To avoid delay the different Provinces or parts of Provinces will proceed independently as far as is practicable within the conditions of this plan. As soon as constitution-framing bodies have been set up they will proceed to frame constitutions for their respective territories. It will be necessary for them to constitute before June 1948 provisional authorities to which power can be transferred.

VI Relations of Successor Authorities with H.M.G. and with one another.[2]

20. Negotiations will have to initiated as soon as possible on administrative consequences of any partition that may have been decided upon.

(a) between the representatives of prospective successor authorities about all subjects now dealt with by the Central Government including Defence, Finance and Communications.

(b) Between different successor authorities and H.M.G. for treaties in regard to matters arising out of the transfer of power.

(c) in the case of Provinces that may be partitioned as to administration of all provincial subjects such as the division of assets and liabilities, the police and other services, the High Courts, provincial institutions, irrigation etc.

The necessary machinery for consultation and negotiation for these purposes will have to be set up without delay.

VII. Delimitation of Boundaries.

21. For the purpose of exercising options described above provinces must for practical reasons be divided according to administrative districts as laid down in para. 7. But it is evident that for the purposes of a definitive partition of any province a more detailed investigation of the boundary questions will be needed and as soon as a decision involving partition has been taken for any province a Boundary Commission should be set up the membership and terms of reference of which will be settled by agreement between those concerned. Until the report of a Boundary Commission has been adopted by both parts of a province the provisional boundaries indicated in appendix will remain in force.

VIII. The tribes of the N. W. Frontier.

22. Fresh agreements with tribes of the N.W. Frontier of India will have to be (gr. omtd. negotiate?)ed by appropriate successor authorities.

IX. The States.

23. H.M.G. wish to make it clear that the decisions announced above relate only to British India and that their policy towards Indian States remains unchanged. When paramountcy lapses all rights surrendered by States to para-

[2] This heading, which is omitted from the decipher, has been taken from the copy of the draft announcement on the India Office file. L/P & J/10/79: ff 325-332.

mount power will return to States. They are free to arrange by negotiation with those parts of British India to which power will be demitted whatever measure of association they consider to be in best interests of their people. [Some may confirm their wish to proceed with framing a constitution in existing Constituent Assembly. Some may wish to join any other Constituent Assembly that may be established. Some may wish to stand out independently either singly or jointly as is open to provinces.][3] But whatever their decision all will require to enter upon negotiations for new agreements especially in economic and financial sphere on the line contemplated in para. 4 of Cabinet Mission's Memorandum on States' Treaties and Paramountcy of 12th May 1946[4] (C.M.D.6358 item B) and to set up as early as possible alternative machinery for regulation of matters of common concern on the line contemplated in para. 5 of that memorandum.

X. Further announcements by Governor General.

24. The Governor General will from time to time make such further announcements as may be necessary in regard to procedure or any other matter for carrying out above arrangements.[5]

[3] For square brackets see Ismay's remarks in first para. of telegram. The passage enclosed in brackets is included in the telegram but the brackets themselves are omitted. Their position has been determined from the copy of the draft announcement on the India Office file. *Ibid.*
[4] Vol. VII, No. 262.
[5] A further revision of this statement was made by officials and circulated as I.B.(47)65 of 10 May 1947. L/P &J/10/79: ff 208–14. However this revision was not of effective importance as it was never considered by the India Committee nor telegraphed to the Viceroy.

380

Rear-Admiral Viscount Mountbatten of Burma to Lord Ismay (via India Office)

Telegram, R/3/1/151: f 49

IMMEDIATE SIMLA, *10 May 1947, 1.45 am*
SECRET *Received: 10 May, 6.10 am*

No. 36–S.C. Your 5969 of May 9th.[1] I assume that you have definitely turned down the referendum in the NWFP on the question of support for the Congress or the Muslim League. I could not possibly agree to this and it will be difficult enough to persuade Congress to agree to the question "Do you wish to join the Union of India or Pakistan".

2. The text of your 5971 of May 9th[2] not repeated to Caroe is either incomprehensible or impracticable. Again I could not possibly agree. I do not consider that the Frontier Province should be given the option of remaining independent since obviously it could not possibly stand by itself. Your draft

in your 5971 of May 9th is the first indication that there was any question of such a suggestion.

3. One reason for holding a referendum in the NWFP and not doing so in the Punjab and Bengal is that the question in that Province is a simple choice between the Union of India and Pakistan, whereas the other two Provinces have the further choice of declaring for independence, which is a practicable proposition for each.

4. Another important reason is that the Legislative Assembly of the Frontier as at present constituted would vote for joining the Union of India, whereas Jinnah maintains that the referendum will be in favour of Pakistan; and Caroe considers there is sufficient doubt to necessitate a referendum, but only on the simple choice indicated.

5. I will telegraph you shortly a redraft of paragraph 9 which I hope will meet Nehru's wishes as reported in my telegram 27–S.C. of May 8th.[3]

Repeated to Governor of the N.W.F.P.

[1] No. 364.
[2] No. 365 which appears, in fact, to have been repeated to Sir O. Caroe. This telegram was deciphered with reasonable accuracy in Simla.   [3] No. 359.

381

Minutes of Viceroy's Thirtieth Staff Meeting, Item 1

Mountbatten Papers

TOP SECRET

Those present at this Meeting held at Viceregal Lodge, Simla on 10 May 1947 at 10 am were: Rear-Admiral Viscount Mountbatten of Burma, Sir E. Mieville, Captain Brockman, Mr I. D. Scott, Rao Bahadur V. P. Menon, Lieutenant-Colonel Erskine Crum

THE RETENTION OF INDIA WITHIN THE COMMONWEALTH

HIS EXCELLENCY THE VICEROY said that he had had a talk that morning with Mr Krishna Menon on this subject. Mr Krishna Menon had pointed out that it was he who had first suggested the early transfer of power to India on a Dominion status basis. Mr Krishna Menon had also stated that one of the advantages in such a plan which most attracted Pandit Nehru was the latter's belief that he (His Excellency) would be able greatly to influence the States. Mr Krishna Menon had said that the main difficulty was that, even if Pandit Nehru and Sardar Patel agreed to the scheme, the rest of the Congress Party would have to be persuaded accordingly. Congress always watched carefully a possible split of their Left Wing. If the Left Wing accused the present leaders of having sold themselves to Great Britain, those leaders would be finished.

RAO BAHADUR MENON pointed out that the main argument which the Indian leaders would be able to put forward to their Left Wing was that Domion status was only an interim arrangement. He went on to say that Sardar Patel had already put out a statement[1] requesting an early grant of Dominion status. He had talked on the telephone the previous evening to Sardar Patel, who had put forward the theory that Pandit Nehru was finding great difficulty in admitting to His Excellency that he wanted Dominion status because it would take a long time to produce a Constitution. Sardar Patel thought, in fact, that Pandit Nehru was "covering up".

There was then a discussion of what line His Excellency the Viceroy should take at the subsequent meeting that morning with Pandit Nehru. It was agreed that Defence constituted the biggest problem. MR SCOTT suggested that a Council should be formed with overriding powers on questions of Defence, consisting of His Excellency, one Hindu, one Muslim and one Sikh. In such a Council, His Excellency could have a double vote. HIS EXCELLENCY THE VICEROY said that he considered that this would be undesirable; the Council would far better consist of himself and one representative each from the Union of India and Pakistan, each member exercising an equal vote.

HIS EXCELLENCY THE VICEROY reiterated the view that the British Army would have to be under his absolute control until it could be phased out. British officers in the Indian Army could be retained longer than was at present intended. The Indianisation programme could go much more slowly. The period during which compensation would be paid to these officers could be extended until their services were no longer required. He added that he considered that the Royal Air Force components ought to stay attached to the R.I.A.F.

MR SCOTT suggested that efforts should be made in due course to persuade Jai Prakash Narain round to the point of view at present held by Pandit Nehru and Sardar Patel. RAO BAHADUR MENON said that he was very much opposed to Jai Prakash Narain being brought into consultation. In any case he had recently been arrested in Hyderabad and might find himself in prison there for two years.

HIS EXCELLENCY THE VICEROY said that he intended to see Sardar Patel on the question of the early grant of Dominion status as soon as he returned to Delhi. He did not intend to raise the matter with Mr Jinnah until after the announcement of the Plan.

[1] No. 375.

382

Minutes of Viceroy's Eleventh Miscellaneous Meeting

Mountbatten Papers

TOP SECRET

Those present at this Meeting held at Viceregal Lodge, Simla on 10 May 1947 at 11 am were: Rear-Admiral Viscount Mountbatten of Burma, Pandit Nehru, Sir E. Mieville, Rao Bahadur V. P. Menon, Lieutenant-Colonel Erskine Crum

Item 1

THE EARLY TRANSFER OF POWER ON A DOMINION STATUS BASIS

HIS EXCELLENCY THE VICEROY explained that Rao Bahadur Menon had been working on a scheme for the early transfer of power on a Dominion status basis long before he (His Excellency) arrived in India. He said that he would like to give Rao Bahadur Menon an opportunity of explaining the outline of this scheme to himself and Pandit Nehru together.

RAO BAHADUR MENON said that he had mentioned the scheme to Pandit Nehru the day before; and also about four months previously to Sardar Patel. Both had appeared extremely anxious for the early transfer of power. Sardar Patel had the previous day issued a statement[1] advocating that power should be transferred as soon as possible on a Dominion status basis. The scheme[2] which he had prepared made arrangements for this in the alternative events of there being an united India and of there being two separate States—the Union of India and Pakistan.

RAO BAHADUR MENON explained that the Instrument under which the transfer would take place would be the 1935 Government of India Act with suitable modifications. The modifications which he envisaged were broadly as follows:—

(a) The Secretary of State, the India Office, and the special powers of the Governor-General and the Governors would disappear.

(b) The Constituent Assembly would assume many of the responsibilities of the present Central Legislative Assembly.

(c) There would be a Constitutional Governor-General of either United India or of the two States.

(d) Governors would be appointed by the Governor-General on the recommendation of the Central Authority or Authorities.

(e) In the event of partition, there would be a joint council to deal with matters of common concern between the two states; but there would be no interference by either State in the affairs of the other.

[1] No. 375.   [2] See Appendix to No. 222; also No. 273.

(*f*) The preamble to the Act which would put these arrangements into force would contain reference to the Constituent Assembly and to the fact that these were interim arrangements until the new Constitution had been framed. This might not be finished until after June, 1948.

(*g*) The word "Emperor" would have to be dropped from the title "King Emperor". It would be revoked in an Order in Council by His Majesty.

HIS EXCELLENCY THE VICEROY pointed out that at present June, 1948 was the latest possible date for the transfer of power. Under this scheme the transfer of power would take place much earlier. He considered that there should be a distinct target for the end of the interim period proposed under the scheme and had in mind that this target might be the completion of the framing of the Constitution and the holding of new elections thereunder.

HIS EXCELLENCY THE VICEROY said that, whereas it seemed to him that it would be a fairly easy matter, so long as H.M.G. agreed, to transfer power at a very early date on a Dominion status basis to the Union of India, there would be no authorities for some time in Pakistan to whom to transfer. He asked whether it would be possible for a Constitutional Governor-General of the Union of India to continue to exercise the special responsibilities of the Viceroy in Pakistan. RAO BAHADUR MENON said that he considered that this would be possible constitutionally. He pointed out that it might take eight or nine months for Pakistan to set up an Executive.

PANDIT NEHRU said that he considered it very desirable that there should be a transfer of power as soon as possible on a Dominion status basis. Congress had made a proposal to this effect at the beginning of the war. He would show His Excellency the statement which had been made. The proposal had been repeated since. The basic reason for wanting an early transfer of power, apart from the desire of the Indians to control their own affairs, was that any developments in India would not otherwise take place properly. The present system of frequent references to H.M.G. produce the psychology of always looking elsewhere for decisions; of continual bidding by the different parties; of a lack of reality; and of an absence of self-reliance. At present there were continual references to the British Cabinet, who were doubtless trying to do the fair thing but who could not be in full possession of the psychological background in India. Their mental processes were, in his opinion, inclined to be too legal-istic and logical.

PANDIT NEHRU said that the only real difficulty in his opinion was the possibility of India being divided and Pakistan coming into existence. The normal course would have been for the Government of India Act to have continued subject to modifications and for any Dominion Government formed in India to continue to function for the whole of India. But it was now clear that facilities would have to be given for any part of India which did not wish to remain within the Union to separate. He considered that the Cabinet

Mission Plan should be adhered to subject to the major variation that Provinces should be given the option to opt out of the Union. He considered that Provinces should be given an opportunity to see the new Constitution before given the chance of separation. It was in his opinion wrong to put the process of partition first. The proper thing would be that this choice should come when the broad outlines of the future Constitution were decided. According to precedent and practice that would be the more correct procedure. It was very difficult for the normal voter to decide the issue of Partition first except on an emotional basis.

PANDIT NEHRU said that he did not think that the process of granting Dominion status to one part of India before the other would give rise to any great complications. He supposed that this was theoretically possible. He presumed that as soon as a suitable authority had been set up in Pakistan power would be handed over. He also agreed with the point made by Rao Bahadur Menon that on the Joint Council there should be no interference by either State in the affairs of the other.

PANDIT NEHRU said that he did not, however, agree with Rao Bahadur Menon's estimate of the period involved. He had no doubt that the broad features of the Constitution of the Union of India would be prepared by July. The details would take another month or so to fill in, but it would be possible to proceed on the broad features, and electoral machinery could begin to function. It would take at the most six months or a year before the elections were held. Once power had been transferred it was up to the Government of the Union of India to arrange for all consequences of the transfer. The length of the interim period would depend on what arrangements were made. It might be felt desirable and more convenient not to put a final end to the interim period by June, 1948. But from the psychological point of view it was very dangerous at the present time to hint that the period might be prolonged thereafter. He considered that the interim period might well in fact come to an end when the elections were held, but it would be dangerous to say so at the present stage.

HIS EXCELLENCY THE VICEROY said that he did not consider that the target for the end of the interim period should in any way be connected with June, 1948. That had originally been the target date for transfer of power; and it was hoped to bring the transfer forward by almost a year.

PANDIT NEHRU gave his view that if the end of the interim period and the further decisions which would then be required were connected with specific contingencies, suspicion would be created. He considered that the end of the interim period should rather be connected with further arrangements in regard to Indo-British relations. Then the issue would be dealt with on the background of the future. He did not feel that this should be compromised by limitations.

HIS EXCELLENCY THE VICEROY reiterated his view that the end of the interim period should be connected with some specific event. Possibly, if the new elections were not a suitable event, reconsideration or ratification by the newly elected Government might be. He pointed out that one of the main advantages accruing to India would be the retention of British officers. It was essential to have a new target date to work for by which they would be phased out.

PANDIT NEHRU said that he did not oppose His Excellency's viewpoint fundamentally, but to say that the date of June, 1948 had been scrapped would certainly create suspicion.

HIS EXCELLENCY THE VICEROY pointed out that the Governor General would also have to have a specific date towards which to work. He added that if the target date related to reconsideration of Indo-British relations alone there might be considerable agitation for such reconsideration to take place immediately. He had in mind the name of Jai Prakash Narain in connection with such agitation.

PANDIT NEHRU said that he also of course wished to avoid such agitation but felt that it would be more likely to be directed against the idea that Congress leaders had consented to a semi-permanent form of Dominion status. He went on to say that Jai Prakash Narain had been behaving in a very irresponsible manner recently, but he was an intelligent and honest man. He, Pandit Nehru, had no doubt that Jai Prakash Narain would play an important part in India in the future. He thought that he could bring Jai Prakash Narain round to accepting a certain line of action but it would be essential for the latter to be able to see matters developing and to have faith in the development. He must see no opportunities for domination or exploitation. Once, however, the new Dominion status began to function a new atmosphere might well be created.

HIS EXCELLENCY THE VICEROY said that he agreed with Pandit Nehru but felt that his own object would be better served by indicating the end of the interim phase. If Jai Prakash Narain was suspicious of Pandit Nehru's motives, this suspicion might be allayed after a definite date of termination was laid down.

PANDIT NEHRU gave his opinion that the possibility of Pakistan being set up and the position of the Indian States as separate entities might produce an element of confusion and disruption. It would be of the greatest importance to maintain the closest relations between Pakistan and the Union of India and with the States. HIS EXCELLENCY THE VICEROY said that it might be possible that a Governor General might be able to help with these problems. If, however, the States thought that the period of Dominion status was to be indefinite they would on account of their dilatory methods never make up their minds.

PANDIT NEHRU said that he saw the force of His Excellency's arguments and was ready to agree that it might be desirable that the target date of termination of the interim period should be linked up with the formation of a new

Government after elections. He went on to explain that, over the last many years, there had been a tremendous sentiment in India in favour of complete independence. The words "Dominion status" were likely to irritate because of past associations—although in theory it could be shown that Dominion status was equivalent to complete independence. Such fine points were not, however, considered or understood by the majority of the people. He was afraid that such phraseology might mean to many the continuation of indirect domination. He himself was most anxious, apart from sentimental reasons, to have the closest possible relations with the British Commonwealth, but he was not clear himself what form these relations would take. He thought and hoped that it would be possible for the relations to continue without the offending phraseology. He did not intend to talk about "Dominion status" openly because of the many suspicions. He wanted to prepare the ground. The world was changing and the problem must be looked at in that context.

PANDIT NEHRU pointed out that under any form of Dominion status India would always have the power to leave the Commonwealth when she wished. HIS EXCELLENCY THE VICEROY agreed with this and pointed out that this fact should be emphasised as well as the target for the termination.

HIS EXCELLENCY THE VICEROY then raised the question of Defence and the partition of the Army. He said that he was convinced that it was quite impossible both to nationalise and partition the Army by June, 1948. So far as the Royal Indian Navy and the Royal Indian Air Force were concerned, they could in such circumstances be written off. The Army could barely stand nationalisation alone. If it was also divided it would be killed stone dead. However, it could be kept as a going concern of some sort if the rate of nationalisation was slowed up and if partition was carried out gradually and on a planned basis. He suggested that while this process was going on there should be a Defence Council consisting of himself and the Defence Ministers of the two parts of India. He would be Chairman but his vote would be equal to either of the others.

HIS EXCELLENCY THE VICEROY said that he considered the British forces would have to remain under his command until they could be withdrawn which would be as soon as possible. With this PANDIT NEHRU agreed.

HIS EXCELLENCY THE VICEROY suggested that the R.A.F. components in India should be transferred on loan to the R.I.A.F. He said that he visualised that the Defence Headquarters at present in Delhi would also have to be split. Pending that, they would be under the Defence Council.

PANDIT NEHRU said that it seemed to him that the question of the partition of the Armed forces should not even be considered until a definite decision had been made on what parts of India were going to break away. It was impossible to work out a plan at present. It was not a question of dividing Hindus and Muslims but of dividing on a territorial basis. Once a definite picture of the future set-up had arisen, the question of whether to divide or not could again be considered. Even if there was insistence on the partition of India he felt that the Army should continue to function as a whole. Those who came from the territory of the Provinces which had seceded would then go out. The Army would during this period function in regard to Pakistan by the latter's agreement. He thought that it would be possible to have a Defence Council but asked who would look after the Army as a whole.

HIS EXCELLENCY THE VICEROY said that there could be a joint Defence Headquarters. He quoted the example of the Austro-Hungarian Empire before the 1914–18 war. The armies of Austria and Hungary had been separate but there had been a Defence Headquarters consisting of representatives of both according to their strength. It was an international organisation of which the Emperor had been head. He pointed out that it was no good imagining that in a Defence Headquarters in Delhi controlling both Armies, the officers would come from the Union of India alone. With this PANDIT NEHRU agreed.

Item 2
"THE UNION OF INDIA"

HIS EXCELLENCY THE VICEROY informed Pandit Nehru that he had sent a telegram[3] to Lord Ismay in London expressing the hope that sufficient emphasis would be laid in the plan in the draft announcement on "The Union of India". He had suggested that Provinces adhering to the present Constituent Assembly should be referred to as "constituting the Union of India"; and that those which did not should be referred to as "contracting out of the Union".

HIS EXCELLENCY THE VICEROY said that Lord Ismay's reply[4] had been to the effect that this suggestion had not met with support at a meeting of officials of the India Office and the Cabinet Secretariat. They had felt that such phraseology would make those provinces which did not adhere to the existing Constituent Assembly be looked upon as "rebels".

PANDIT NEHRU said that he did not understand this reference to "rebels". It did not appear to him to be the correct approach.

HIS EXCELLENCY THE VICEROY—
invited Prin. Sec. to draft, for his approval, a telegram to Lord Ismay expressing the hope that he would continue to press for emphasis on the "The Union of India".

Item 3
CALCUTTA

PANDIT NEHRU made reference to the statement issued a few days previously by Mr. Suhrawardy.[5] He gave his opinion that this statement was in the main sweet and reasonable containing as it did an appeal not to split Bengal. Towards the end of the statement, however, there was a clear hint that if Calcutta was taken away from Eastern Bengal there would be not much to take. PANDIT NEHRU expressed the view that it was possible that the Muslims would sack and destroy Calcutta rather than see it separated from East Bengal. He felt that there was likely to be trouble in Calcutta as soon as the announcement was made. He suggested the possibility of such trouble having the backing of the present Provincial Government. The problem was not the same as in the Punjab where the disturbances were likely to be caused by two groups fighting one another. In Calcutta disturbances were more likely to take the form of deliberate destruction.

HIS EXCELLENCY THE VICEROY said that he would raise this point with the Governor of Bengal and ask for an assurance that he had sufficient troops to deal with likely disturbances.

HIS EXCELLENCY THE VICEROY:—

instructed Con. Sec. to draft for his approval a telegram to the Governor of Bengal quoting Pandit Nehru's expressed opinions and asking whether he had enough troops to deal with probable disturbances and what line he proposed to take if the Provincial Government appeared to be backing such disturbances.

Item 4

A FUTURE TIME TABLE

HIS EXCELLENCY THE VICEROY—

invited Prin. Sec. to arrange for the staff to prepare an outline time table of events for the period beginning with the issue of the Announcement.

³ No. 357.   ⁴ No. 377.
⁵ In a lengthy statement issued on 7 May, Mr Suhrawardy attacked the agitation for the partition of Bengal and commended his proposal for the establishment of a united and sovereign Bengal. He also reiterated his invitation to Hindu and Muslim leaders to sit down together at a conference to give concrete form to their hopes and aims. With respect to Calcutta Mr Suhrawardy said:
'I have merely stressed what is well recognised, that the cry for partition of Bengal is nothing but an attempt to get the rich prize of Calcutta and thus deprive Muslims of trade and commerce . . . [But] if Calcutta becomes a bone of contention what will remain of it? . . . Without peace and security the city will be next to nothing . . . .'

383

Rear-Admiral Viscount Mountbatten of Burma to Pandit Nehru

*Mountbatten Papers. Official Correspondence Files: Round
Table Conference, Indian Political Leaders, etc., Issue of
Invitations to*

No. 1446(2)   10 *May 1947*

Dear Mr Nehru,

I have spent very many hours during the last month in talking over the problems which confront us with the leaders of opinion in India, and you yourself have been good enough to spare me a great deal of your time.

Convinced as I am that an announcement ought to be made at the earliest possible moment as to how H.M.G. propose to transfer authority to Indian hands by June 1948, I am most reluctant to postpone a decision on this matter for even a day longer than is necessary.

I have now reached certain conclusions, with which I have reason to believe H.M.G. will agree. I should like to have a final talk about these conclusions before they are announced and I am therefore inviting the following in addition to yourself, to meet me round the table in Delhi at 10.30 a.m. on 17th May.

> Sardar Patel
> Mr Jinnah
> Mr Liaquat Ali Khan and
> Sardar Baldev Singh.

I earnestly trust that you may see your way to accepting this invitation.[1]

Yours sincerely,
MOUNTBATTEN OF BURMA

[1] Similar letters were sent to Sardar Patel, Mr Jinnah, Mr Liaquat Ali Khan and Sardar Baldev Singh. Lord Mountbatten informed the members of the States' Negotiating Committee of these invitations the same day and hoped that they would be able to be present in Delhi for a few days from 17 May and would meet him in The Viceroy's House at 3 pm on that day. Mountbatten Papers, Official Correspondence Files: Round Table Conference, Indian Political Leaders, etc., Issue of Invitations to.

384

Rear-Admiral Viscount Mountbatten of Burma to Pandit Nehru

Telegram, R/3/1/151: f 47

No. 1446(3)   *10 May 1947*

I have read through the amendments[1] which Dr. Khan Sahib proposes to the minutes[2] of the meeting which I held with him and his Ministers last week at Peshawar which you handed to me earlier in the week at Delhi. I have also received a copy of these amendments from Caroe.

2. As you know, I am no longer of the view that it is necessary to go into Section 93 in the Frontier Province, or that fresh elections should be held now. I am, therefore, asking Caroe to explain to Dr. Khan Sahib that there is now no question of this procedure being adopted; and that instead I had recommended to H.M.G. that there should be, at a suitable date when the partition of India was clearer, a referendum on the electoral roll, which will be conducted by an organisation under my control.

3. I will tell Caroe to tell Dr. Khan Sahib that you are in general agreement with this procedure. I am sure that it is the fairest and best way of achieving the object, namely of making sure that decision whether the N.W.F.P. goes to Pakistan or Hindustan is in accordance with the will of the people.

4. In the circumstances I feel that no detailed discussion of Dr. Khan Sahib's amendments is now required.

MOUNTBATTEN OF BURMA

[1] Not traced. cf No. 297.   [2] Enclosure to No. 259.

385

Pandit Nehru to Rear-Admiral Viscount Mountbatten of Burma

R/3/1/151: ff 50-1

SECRET   SIMLA, *10 May 1947*

Dear Lord Mountbatten,

Thank you for your two letters dated 10th May[1] which I have just received. As suggested by you, I am trying to get a meeting of the Congress Working Committee convened for the 16th or 17th May in Delhi. I have telephoned to Sardar Patel to this effect and I hope he will make the necessary arrangements Gandhiji and Dr. Khan Sahib are also being invited.

[1] Nos. 383 and 384.

2. I am myself anxious that there should be no avoidable delay in coming to decisions and giving effect to them. I am anxious, however, that in our hurry a wrong step might not be taken which might lead to greater delay. I have been giving a great deal of thought to what you have told me and I find that my mind is not at all clear about the various possible developments. Apart from the original proposals which were put forward somewhat vaguely, there are now other suggestions in addition which introduce a great deal of complexity to the problems we have to face. Each step acts and reacts on the other and we have to consider carefully what the final outcome might be. I confess that I do not see much light and many things trouble me.

3. I shall not go into these matters in this letter because I hope to have a further talk with you. But I am anxious to avoid any misunderstanding. I find from one of your letters that you have asked Caroe to tell Dr. Khan Sahib that I am in general agreement with the procedure suggested, namely a referendum. Now this is the one thing on which there is very strong opinion among my colleagues not only of the Working Committee but also of Dr. Khan Sahib's Government, and I was specifically asked to inform you of their strong opposition to this. I myself greatly fear that any referendum, before the situation is much clearer and other final decisions have been taken, may lead to grave consequences. In any event such a referendum can only be held with the full concurrence of the Frontier Government. As I have told you, I am in agreement with the idea that the will of the people of the Frontier Province should be consulted before final decisions in regard to the position of the Province are taken. But it is very important when this is done and in what context.

4. You will have seen Gandhiji's reactions[2] and an interview that Sardar Patel gave yesterday.[3] I have no doubt that the former should be given due weight, though in regard to some details it does not fit in with the general Congress viewpoint. Sardar Patel's interview is a clear expression of the Congress viewpoint.

5. What I fear is that if the new proposals are not generally agreed to and are a marked departure from the position which flowed from the Cabinet Mission's Scheme, they will result in producing a very great deal of uncertainty in the public mind. This will be unfortunate from every point of view. The Cabinet Mission's Scheme at least produced some certainty. If it cannot be applied *in toto*, it might be varied to suit the exigencies of the situation. Another landmark which brought some certainty was the declaration of February 20th. If anything happens to shake that feeling of certainty, there will be complete instability in the country. The new proposals, therefore, should fit in as far as possible, subject to necessary variations, with the position as it has been thus far.

Yours sincerely,

[2] See No. 348.   [3] See No. 375.   JAWAHARLAL NEHRU

386

Sir S. Cripps to Mr Attlee

Public Record Office. CAB 127/150

BOARD OF TRADE, MILLBANK, S.W.I,
10 May 1947

My dear Prime Minister,
As you know I have been and am very worried about the Punjab part of our plan. I send you in confidence Billy Short's latest letter and enclosures.[1] May I have them back when you have digested them.

I think we have gone a long way to meet Sant Singh's point of view which is apparently also Baldev's but we must remember that the Sikhs can bust this arrangement as well as Jinnah! If we were to adopt Dickie's last alternative and hand over the Punjab to the Muslims that would mean immediate civil war. We must in the last resort divide out the Sikhs somehow or we shall never get through.

Yours,
STAFFORD

[1] The reference appears to be No. 356.

387

Mr Attlee to General Hollis

L/PO/6/119: f 35

10 May 1947

Prime Minister's Personal Minute: Serial No. D. 1/47

General Hollis.
I should like the Chiefs of Staff in their discussion with General Ismay to consider the position in the event of (a) Western India, (b) Bengal or (c) one of the States with a sea-board such as Travancore desiring to remain in the Commonwealth when the rest of India decides to go out. I should like to have their appreciation from the military point of view.

C.R.A.

388

Cabinet

India and Burma Committee. Paper I.B.(47)62

L/P&J/10/79: ff 289–92

TRANSFER OF POWER IN INDIA
MEMORANDUM BY THE SECRETARY OF STATE FOR INDIA

INDIA OFFICE, *10 May 1947*

The Viceroy has requested that the attached note[1] summarising proposals for the transfer of power in India drawn up by Mr. V. P. Menon, his Reforms Commissioner, should be brought to the notice of the Committee.

2. This plan is designed to follow upon a partition of India resulting from the Viceroy's proposals which the Committee have been considering. Under it both parts of India would have Dominion status. There would be a Consultative Committee for Foreign Affairs, Defence and Communications with equal representation of the two parts of India and a single Governor-General.

3. These proposals have a marked similarity to those circulated with my memorandum I.B.(47)55.[2] Under the proposals drawn up in the India Office the option of the different areas to secede from the Union of India was exercisable just before or after the transfer of power. The present proposals assume that partition has been agreed upon and on that basis propose a transfer of power substantially earlier than June, 1948, but to two Provisional Governments within the Empire responsible to two Constituent Assemblies.

4. There are certain obscurities in Mr. Menon's plan. It is not entirely clear that there would be a complete constitutional partition of all subjects of administration. This seems to be intended because it is stated that the decisions of the Joint Consultative Council would be implemented by the two Governments. Nor is it quite clear how the decisions of the Joint Council would be taken, whether by agreement or by majority vote.

5. These are, however, minor points. The plan as a whole seems to have much to commend it, if the agreement of both parties could be obtained. If both parts of India remain within the Commonwealth the difficulty discussed at the last meeting of the Committee[3] which would result from a claim by Pakistan that it should not be ejected from the Empire would be avoided. The proposal to advance to full self-government prior to June, 1948, might commend this plan to Congress.

L.

---

[1] This was the same as the note in No. 273.   [2] No. 289.   [3] No. 355.

389

Cabinet

India and Burma Committee. Paper I.B.(47)63

L/P&J/10/79: ff 242–3

VICEROY'S PROPOSALS FOR DEALING WITH MR JINNAH IF HE REFUSES
COOPERATION IN THE NEW CONSTITUTIONAL PLAN
MEMORANDUM BY THE SECRETARY OF STATE FOR INDIA

INDIA OFFICE, *10 May 1947*

I circulate herewith telegram No. 21–S.C.[1] from the Viceroy to Lord Ismay,
together with the Viceroy's preceding telegram[2] which was available at the
meeting of the Committee on 8th May.[3] The Viceroy asks for H.M.G.'s
authority to warn Mr. Jinnah, if he refuses to cooperate with the new plan, that
the alternative must be "to demit power on the basis of the existing Government
of India Act with modifications as necessary, i.e. to demit Provincial subjects to
existing Provincial Governments and Central subjects to the existing Central
Government."

2. The Viceroy takes the view that it would be out of the question to carry
on with the plan of enabling Provinces to opt for their own division if Mr.
Jinnah turns against it. This seems questionable. Jinnah's opposition will not
prevent the other parties from operating the plan. The Hindu parts of Provinces
could still elect representatives and decide through them to remain in the
existing Constituent Assembly. In that event the Muslim areas would be left
by themselves, whether they have opted or not; and they would only injure
their own interests if they refused to accept authority for the administration of
their own areas. A referendum could still be held in the North-West Frontier
Province, since, even if the Muslim League did not vote, the decision could be
held to go against them if the Congress polled more than half the electorate.
There appears, therefore, to be a strong case for putting out this plan and
taking the chance of non-cooperation by the Muslim League.

3. The Viceroy could not make the threat to Mr. Jinnah proposed in paragraph 6 unless we were prepared to implement it. The suggestion that Provincial subjects should be made over to existing Provincial Governments,
however, does not face the fact that there is in the Punjab no Ministerial
Government and that the whole crux of the present situation is the impracticability of responsible Government in the Punjab as at present existing. The
best advice that we have is that to put into power over the whole Province a
Muslim League administration in which the Sikhs and Hindus are not repre-

---

[1] No. 351.   [2] **No. 346.**   [3] No. 355.

sented would lead to civil war; and it is this that necessitates partition. There would surely be no possibility of avoiding civil war if power were transferred to a Muslim League Government in open conflict with a Hindu-dominated Central Government.

4. Further, the proposal to hand over the Central subjects (whether or not that is intended to include ultimate Central control of law and order in time of emergency) to the existing Central Government means handing over control of all these subjects, including the Army, to the Congress. It would be inconsistent with H.M.G.'s declared policy which is that on our departure large areas of the country should not be coerced under a constitution which they do not accept. It would also be inconsistent with the basic principles underlying the new plan which will become public at the proposed Conference. The plan amounts to an admission by H.M.G. that the Sikh and Hindu minorities in the Punjab and Bengal are entitled to exercise a separate option.

5. While in the first six paragraphs of telegram No. 21–S.C. the Viceroy proceeds on the assumption that the threat which he proposes to make to Jinnah would bring him to heel, he argues in paragraph 7 that what is suggested might not after all be wholly advantageous to the Congress. Whatever view one takes about the validity of this argument, it certainly suggests that it is an open question whether the proposed threat to Jinnah would have the effect intended, and that he might with some reason think that the Muslim League were strong enough in the Punjab and Bengal to secure control of the whole of these Provinces and shake loose from the Hindu Centre.

6. For these reasons I suggest that it is not desirable that the Viceroy should make this threat to Jinnah but that he should rather indicate to him that the plan is capable of being operated without his cooperation, and that if the Muslim League do not set up authorities to assume control of the areas which do not choose to remain in the existing Constituent Assembly they will have to improvise such arrangements as they can on our departure.

L.

390

Cabinet

India and Burma Committee. Paper I.B.(47)64

L/P&J/10/79: f 215

REQUEST BY PANDIT NEHRU AS TO THE FORM OF THE STATEMENT
OF POLICY

MEMORANDUM BY THE SECRETARY OF STATE FOR INDIA

INDIA OFFICE, *10 May 1947*

I circulate herewith, for consideration by the Committee, the Viceroy's telegram 25/S.C.[1] which he asks should be considered by the Cabinet.

2. I do not think that we can go further than we have done in the draft
Statement to meet Pandit Nehru's point. In paragraph 1 of the draft we say
that we had hoped to transfer power to Governments within a single Union
and thereafter we refer to option by the different areas whether to adhere to the
existing Constituent Assembly or otherwise. This is not only strictly correct,
because an Indian Union does not yet exist, but also reasonable because we can
hardly be expected to recognise the parts of India which adhere to the existing
Constituent Assembly as a "Union of India" at any rate until it is known how
large the areas are which choose not to adhere.

3. The existing Constituent Assembly has resolved to declare India a
sovereign republic and to prepare a Union Constitution on that assumption. It
seems very unlikely, therefore, that Pandit Nehru's proposal implies any
modification of the intention that the Union of India should have a republican
constitution.

L.

[1] No. 357.

391

Sir D. Monteath to Sir N. Brook

L/P&J/10/122: f 15

SECRET   INDIA OFFICE, *10 May 1947*

My dear Brook,

With reference to our conversation yesterday about the possibility of modifying the forms of the Commonwealth relationship to enable India (or parts of
India), Burma and other parts of the Empire now developing towards Dominion status to remain in the Commonwealth, I enclose copies of minutes of two

meetings[1] we have had on this subject and of a draft Cabinet paper[2] which formed the "agenda" for the second meeting. It was decided not to put in the paper in the form of the draft, but to pursue the matter rather from the angle of what minimum assurances of co-operation—recorded in some form of written instrument—would be required to justify us in regarding India or any other territory as "remaining within the Commonwealth".

Subsequent examination has, however, shown the difficulties of this procedure. In the first place the constitutions evolved by these territories might be such as to prejudge the issue to an irremediable degree—and that in either direction. A more substantial point is that India would certainly not give any written assurances such as the Dominions do not give.

The essential question really is whether the territories in question have the necessary common interests with the rest of the Commonwealth to make them in the long run valuable constituents of it or whether, while in time of adversity they would tend either to fall away altogether or, if not that, would fail to be a source of positive assistance, in time of prosperity they—and particularly India—would not be a constant source of discord in the existing Commonwealth owing to the divergence of their interests and outlook from those of the original Dominions.

Yours sincerely,

D. T. MONTEATH

[1] See Vol. IX, No. 522 for the second of these meetings. A note on the first meeting, between representatives of the India and Dominions Offices on 27 February 1947, is on L/P &J/10/122 at ff 41–2.
[2] Vol. IX, Enclosure to No. 338.

392

Lord Ismay to Rear-Admiral Viscount Mountbatten of Burma (via India Office)

Telegram, L/PO/6/125: f 59

IMMEDIATE   INDIA OFFICE, *10 May 1947, 11.40 am*
SECRET   *Received: 10 May, 10 pm*

No. 6046. Your No. 28–S.C. dated 8th May.[1] Dominion Status.

Abell and I entirely agree that opportunity is golden. As the result of discussions we have had with Cabinet Secretariat Norman Brook will discuss with Dominions Office and put up to Prime Minister a memorandum suggesting immediate high-level enquiry into possibility of devising a looser form of membership of the Commonwealth which will enable us to bring in new members without losing the old.

2. Your telegram will not be circulated till you give the word.

[1] No. 360.

393

Rear-Admiral Viscount Mountbatten of Burma to Sir F. Burrows (Bengal)

Telegram, Mountbatten Papers. Official Correspondence Files:
Bengal, Partition of, Part I(b)

IMMEDIATE   *10 May 1947, 4 pm*
TOP SECRET

No. 39–S.C. 1. Nehru, who is staying with me, has read into Suhrawardy's recent statement[1] a threat that the Muslims will do their best to sack Calcutta rather than let it be handed over to the Hindus after the partition of Bengal, and that the present Provincial Government will back disorders to that end.

2. Nehru thinks that a dangerous time will be reached directly after the issue of the announcement. My own hope is that Suhrawardy will at that time redouble his efforts to placate and secure the cooperation of the Hindus in order to achieve his object of an independent united Bengal.

3. I would have thought that the really dangerous moment would come after (and if) the issue of partition has been decided by the voters.

4. I would be grateful for:
(*a*) Your opinion as to which is the most dangerous moment.
(*b*) Your assurance that you have sufficient troops to deal with probable disturbances.
(*c*) An indication of what line you would take if the Provincial Government appeared to be supporting such disturbances.

See No. 382, note 5.

394

Lord Ismay to Rear-Admiral Viscount Mountbatten of Burma (via India Office)

Telegram, L/P&J/10/79: f 297

IMMEDIATE   INDIA OFFICE, *10 May 1947, 2.25 pm*
                                              Received: 11 May, 4 am

No. 6069. Your 36–S.C.[1] about N.W.F.P. Referendum.

2. I think you should know our programme. We have Cabinet Committee on Monday afternoon at which we hope to get draft announcement finalised including paragraphs on
(*a*) referendum in N.W.F.P.
(*b*) Sylhet.

[1] No. 380.

Your telegram about Union of India will also be considered. There is to be full Cabinet on Tuesday morning to approve announcement. We leave on Wednesday morning.

3. We await redraft of paragraph about referendum and will put it to I.B. Committee. Reference your paragraph 2 however the N.W.F.P. had the choice of standing out independently even in the original plan we brought home (see your telegram 954–S of 1st May[2] paragraph 13). So did the half provinces of the Punjab and Bengal. The Cabinet Committee's view has been that there must be a free choice if the scheme is to be consistent and defensible in Parliament. As you know they want to give even Sylhet the choice.

4. Reference telegram 87–G[3] from the Governor of the Punjab repeated to you. I take it you maintain attitude expressed in your No. 992–S dated 5th May[4] and I may inform Cabinet Committee that you are sure Jenkins must be overruled.

5. Your 35–SC dated 9th May.[5] I am delighted that you can accept revised programme and will inform Cabinet Committee. Have advised Auchinleck that he should return Delhi not later than 18th.

6. Longing to get back to be with you in critical days that lie ahead.

[2] The reference is to tel. 955–S of 1 May; i.e. No. 279.
[3] No. 374.   [4] No. 321.   [5] See No. 361, note 3.

395

Rear-Admiral Viscount Mountbatten of Burma to Lord Ismay (via India Office)

Telegram, L/PO/6/125: f 58

IMMEDIATE   SIMLA, *10 May, 7.45 pm*
                                              Received: 10 May, 9.30 pm

No. 40–S.C. Following has just been received from Gandhi which repeats what he has put forward to me from time to time and will I fear be line he will take up during approaching meeting, for which he is coming to Delhi. *Begins.*

1. There shall be no division of India until after British have left i.e. it is for Congress and League to settle question and not for British to impose anything.

2. The protection of minorities in interim period shall be guaranteed by establishing a Court of Arbitration.

3. The Interim Government should be composed either of Congress and persons of their choice or Leaguers and persons of their choice. The present lack of team spirit is deplorable and is having an adverse effect in every department of life.

4. A referendum in the Frontier at this stage would be a dangerous step. Nothing must be done over Doctor Khan Sahib's head.

5. The partition of Punjab and Bengal is, in my opinion, wrong. Apart from being no solution of trouble it would constitute a needless irritant to Moslem League. All this should be left to be done or not done until after British have left.

6. So long as British power remains in India, it must be responsible for maintaining peace. The machine is cracking under present strain caused by raising various hopes. Minds should be concentrated on withdrawal of British power only. "You and you alone can focus attention of all other activity so far as British occupation is concerned."

7. The task now before you is a much greater one than any naval duties or undertakings you have had to face before. Single mindedness and courage of a high degree are required.

8. If you want not to leave a legacy of chaos in the land, you must make your choice and make over power of whole country including States to one party.

9. The Constituent Assembly shall (?provide) a constitution for all parts represented therein—i.e. excluding League and such States as have not yet joined it.

10. The non-partition of the Punjab and Bengal may not mean neglect of powers and vocal minorities there who are quite capable of arresting attention. If Local Government fails to placate them, the Interim Government must interfere during the interregnum.

11. The intransmissibility of paramountcy (? is a) vicious doctrine if it means that the States become sovereign and a menace to India. British power automatically descends to their successor. Therefore, the States are as much part of India as the people of what is to-day called British India. Princes are puppets. The unchecked power used by them must go. They can only act as trustees and exercise such powers as are given them by Constituent Assembly. *Ends.*

396

Rear-Admiral Viscount Mountbatten of Burma to Lord Ismay (via India Office)

Telegram, Mountbatten Papers. Official Correspondence Files:
Transfer of Power, Part II (a)

IMMEDIATE   SIMLA, *10 May 1947, 9 pm*
TOP SECRET   *Received: 11 May, 8.25 am*
No. 44–S.C. Further to my 35–S.C. of 9th May.[1]

1. The following is the time-table to which I intend to work in the meeting with the five Indian Leaders and the issue of the announcement. Please obtain Cabinet's approval.

2. 1030 I.S.T. Saturday 17th May. Meeting begins (whether or not you have returned). I make final effort for acceptance of Cabinet Mission's plan. I then make statement on lines of my immediately succeeding telegram. I then hand out copies of the plan, in absolute confidence, stressing the need for secrecy, and ask Indian leaders to return at same time following day.

3. I keep back Jinnah at end of session. I give him a warning that, if he does not accept the plan, the only alternative, which has been approved by H.M.G., is one which I am sure he will not like. I tell him that, if his Working Committee looks like passing a resolution rejecting the present plan, he should come back to me that night and I will then tell him full details of the alternative (see my 20–S.C. and 21–S.C. of 8th May).[2] I do not tell Congress of this alternative.

4. In the afternoon of 17th May, I see members of what was the States' Negotiating Committee, read out plan to them, and only give copy to Bhopal if asked.

5. If Jinnah turns up that night, I give him full and imposing details of the alternative.

6. The meeting continues at 10.30 I.S.T. Sunday 18th May. I tell the meeting that I have assumed that they and their working Committee have accepted the general principles of the plan, and enquire whether they wish to put forward any detailed observations.

7. (I shall assume that Congress will agree—see para. 4 of my telegram 922–S of 5th May).[3] If Jinnah reports that his Working Committee has not agreed to the principle of the plan, and it is obvious that I cannot move him from this position, I give outline of the alternative plan, meeting breaks up, and I report results to H.M.G.

8. If Jinnah agrees to principle, we go through plan paragraph by para-

graph. Meeting continues, if necessary through lunch, dinner and night, until all that they want to say has been said.

9. I telegraph their observations on the plan to H.M.G. with my own comments and recommendations.

10. H.M.G. consider these on Monday, 19th May and send me their decision to reach me by Tuesday morning, 20th May.

11. On receipt of their telegram, and provided there are no difficulties, I summon leaders for 1700 I.S.T., Tuesday 20th May, tell them H.M.G.'s decision on their observations, and acquaint them of any approved alterations in the plan.

12. Announcement in Parliament 1600 D.B.S.T. Tuesday, 20th May.

13. Simultaneous release of plan in India at 1930 I.S.T. Tuesday 20th May. I broadcast on All-India Radio one hour later at 2030 I.S.T. Plan broadcast immediately afterwards. Speeches by Jinnah and Nehru (if I can persuade them and if they have accepted the plan) and Auchinleck follow.

14. I realise that it may not be possible to make the announcement on Tuesday May 20th as your telegram may necessitate further consultation with me, but I want to work to this timetable so that we still have 48 hours in hand before it is absolutely necessary for announcement to be made in Parliament. I am, however, quite convinced that no opportunity should be given to party leaders for further comments, as, otherwise, we shall enter into unending arguments.

[1] See No. 361, note 3.   [2] Nos. 346 and 351.   [3] No. 321.

397

Rear-Admiral Viscount Mountbatten of Burma to Lord Ismay (via India Office)

Telegram, Mountbatten Papers. Official Correspondence Files:
Transfer of Power, Part II(a)

IMMEDIATE   SIMLA, *11 May 1947, 9 pm*
SECRET   *Received: 11 May, 12.50 am*

No. 45–S.C. Reference my immediately preceding telegram.

Following is outline of statement which I would make on first day of meeting with Indian leaders.

1. Since Cabinet Mission Plan has not proved acceptable, and the two major Indian parties have not agreed between themselves on any other plan, it is clear that the Indian people, through their elected representatives in the Provinces, must be given the opportunity to decide on their own future.

2. I have already discussed this principle with you all individually, and you have all agreed that it is right.

3. When I first arrived as Viceroy, with the mission of transferring power, it was thought that the beginning of 1948 would be early enough for the necessary legislation to be passed in Parliament. But you have all, in our individual discussions, impressed upon me and convinced me of the need for speed. In consequence, I and my staff have been working night and day to achieve a quick and right decision.

4. I have produced the plan which I am about to read out to you and which H.M.G. have approved. It embodies, as far as possible, all the suggestions which you have put forward to me in our individual conversations.

5. This plan was taken by Lord Ismay to London a fortnight ago. It has been closely examined by the Cabinet of H.M.G., which gave it absolute priority over all other matters of state, and approved it in quicker time than an issue of this importance has ever before been dealt with. Lord Ismay arrived back with H.M.G.'s final approval a few hours ago.

6. When so much trouble has been taken not to lose a single day, it is essential that the plan should be announced as early as possible; and in any case, since Parliament rises for the Whitsuntide recess on the 23rd May, the announcement must be made by not later than the 22nd May.

7. I wish to make it clear that this plan is, and will remain, even after it has been announced, open to amendment on any points on which both parties agree.

8. If there are any points of detail, other than those which we have already discussed in the course of the past few weeks, which any of you would like to have amended, I shall, of course, put forward your suggestions to H.M.G. I shall require these suggestions at our meeting tomorrow morning, which will be the only opportunity for you to propose amendments before the plan is announced.

9. I have asked you to bring your Working Committees to Delhi so that they can:
(1) be informed of the plan at once.
(2) give a lead to the country.
(3) if they so desire, discuss together and propose agreed amendments.

10. If all parties will publicly support this plan it will be the quickest way to end the present communal tension and bloodshed. I am glad that my Cabinet has unanimously agreed to support me in the strongest possible measures necessary to put down any further violence.

398

Rear-Admiral Viscount Mountbatten of Burma to Lord Ismay (via India Office)

Telegram, R/3/1/153: f 5

IMMEDIATE   SIMLA, *10 May 1947, 10 pm*
TOP SECRET   *Received: 11 May, 12.50 am*

No. 43–S.C. Your telegram No. 6038 of 9th May.[1]

1. Despite the views expressed by the officials of India Office and Cabinet Secretariat I am glad to note that you will put before the Cabinet the contents of my telegram 25–S.C. of 8th May.[2]

2. I cannot possibly agree that those not joining Union of India should be looked upon as rebels. Jinnah has often remarked to me what a small portion of India truncated Pakistan represents.

3. I attach utmost importance to para 3 of my 25 S.C. especially in view of negotiations referred to in my 28 S.C. of 8th May.[3]

[1] This refers to tel. 6037 of 9 May; i.e. No. 377.
[2] No. 357.   [3] No. 360.

399

Rear-Admiral Viscount Mountbatten of Burma to Lord Ismay (via India Office)

Telegram, Mountbatten Papers. Official Correspondence Files:
Provinces and their Future, Part I(a)

IMMEDIATE   SIMLA, *10 May 1947, 10.30 pm*
TOP SECRET   *Received: 11 May, 8.30 am*

No. 47–S.C. 1. In my telegram 36–S.C. of May 10th[1] I said that your draft in your 5971 of May 9th[2] was the first indication that there was any suggestion that the NWFP should be given the option of standing out by itself.

2. I realise by reference to VCP–42[3] that this was not the case and I apologise. Under the general election and subsequent procedure envisaged in VCP–42 we did give this choice. But I now think that it was wrong and moreover that it can easily be avoided.

3. The referendum should be on the simple choice of whether to join Pakistan or Hindustan (though not in these words) and I do not consider that representatives should thereafter be elected by Legislature to make the further

[1] No. 380.   [2] No. 365.   [3] This was the same as the text of No. 279.

choice between options (*b*) and (*c*). Nor could I agree, in view of my under-taking to Nehru, that in the present announcement a general election should even be mentioned. If the vote went for Pakistan an election would obviously follow.

4. I have received your 6036 of May 9th[4] and agree that we should not mention concurrence of Provincial Government. But I am in favour of in-cluding "in consultation with Provincial Government" as this will make draft far more acceptable to Congress.

5. I further agree that we could not possibly include whole of Nehru's draft; but on the other hand I cannot agree with yours since the Partition of India[5] is not the issue for the NWFP.

6. My immediately following telegram[6] contains redraft of para. 8 of your 6043 of May 9th[7] and other amendments.

7. It is only since you left that Congress have made an issue of the NWFP elections. I shall have great difficulty in getting my own draft accepted and no hope of getting yours accepted.

[4] No. 378.
[5] 'since the Partition of India' deciphered as 'since Pakistan (?or) India'.
[6] Not printed; see No. 415 for the amendments of substance proposed by Lord Mountbatten.
[7] No. 379.

400

Rear-Admiral Viscount Mountbatten of Burma to Lord Ismay (via India Office)

Telegram, L/PO/6/125: f 57

IMMEDIATE   SIMLA, *10 May 1947, 11.55 pm*
Received: 11 May, 7.30 am

No. 41–S.C. My 40–S.C.[1] was despatched as a result of receiving a draft of Mr. Gandhi's letter written by Rajkumari Amrit Kaur. I have since received full (?original) letter from Gandhi and following three additional paragraphs should be added.

Begins. Similarly difficult but not so baffling is the question of Civil Service. Its members should be taught from (?how) to accommodate themselves to new regime. They may not be partisans taking sides. The slightest trace of communalism among (?them) should be severely dealt with. The English element in it should know that they owe loyalty to new regime rather than to old and therefore to Great Britain. The habit of regarding themselves as (?ruler)s and therefore superiors must give place to spirit of true service of the people.

I had a very pleasant two hours and three quarters with Qaid e Azam Jinnah on Tuesday last. We talked about joint statement on non-violence. He was agreeably emphatic over his belief in non-violence. He has reiterated it in press statement[2] which was drafted by him.

We did talk about Pakistan cum partition. I told him that any [?my] opposition to Pakistan persisted as before and suggested that in view of his declaration of faith in non-violence he should try to convert his opponents by reasoning with them and not by show of force. He was however quite firm that question of Pakistan (?was not) open to discussion. Logically, for a believer in non-violence, nothing, not even the existence of God could be outside its scope. *Ends.*

[1] No. 395.   [2] Appendix to No. 354.

401

Lord Ismay to Rear-Admiral Viscount Mountbatten of Burma (via India Office)

Telegram, Mountbatten Papers. Official Correspondence Files:
Armed Forces, Indian, Volume I, Part I

PRIVATE AND PERSONAL
SECRET

10 May 1947, 8.44 pm
Received: 11 May, 9 am

No. 6071. Your 5-U of 4th May.[1]

1. Auchinleck knows nothing about this business and I have not yet had reply from Slim who has been at Camberley all the week.

2. On the other hand report is evidently true because Cariappa came to see me yesterday and volunteered the amazing suggestion that Indian Army with either Nehru or Jinnah as Commander-in-Chief should take over power when we left in June 1948. I at once said that proposal was not only wholly impracticable but highly dangerous, that throughout history the rule of an Army had always proved tyrannical and incompetent and that Army must always be servants and not masters. I added that Indian Army by remaining united and refusing to take sides could wield a tremendous influence for good in disturbed days that lie ahead but that they must always be subservient to civil power. I concluded by begging him to put idea right out of his mind and never to mention it again even in the strictest secrecy.

3. It is hard to know whether Cariappa in putting forward this idea was ingenuous and ignorant or ingenuous [?disingenuous] and dangerous.

[1] No. 302.

402

Pandit Nehru to Rear-Admiral Viscount Mountbatten of Burma

*Mountbatten Papers. Official Correspondence Files: Transfer of Power,
Procedure for determining authorities to which power is to be
demitted, Part (2)*

PERSONAL AND SECRET　　　　VICEREGAL LODGE, SIMLA, *11 May 1947*

Dear Lord Mountbatten,

You were good enough to speak to me frankly and in a very friendly manner last night and to give me an opportunity to see the tentative proposals. I need hardly tell you how much I appreciate your confidence in me or that I am convinced of your earnest desire to help India to achieve her freedom as early as possible. It has been a privilege to get to know you better and I hope that our understanding of each other will be helpful to both and to the wider causes we have at heart.

I read the draft proposals you gave me with the care they deserved and with every desire to absorb them and accept them in so far as I could. But with all the goodwill in the world I reacted to them very strongly. Indeed they produced a devastating effect upon me. The relatively simple proposals that we had previously discussed now appeared, in the garb that H.M.G. had provided for them, in an entirely new context which gave them an ominous meaning. The whole approach was completely different from what ours had been and the picture of India that emerged frightened me. In fact much that we had done so far was undermined and the Cabinet Mission's scheme and subsequent developments were set aside, and an entirely new picture presented —a picture of fragmentation and conflict and disorder, and, unhappily also, of a worsening of relations between India and Britain. That, I am wholly convinced, was not and is not your intention; nor can I believe that this is H.M.G.'s intention. But H.M.G. seems to function in an ivory tower of their own isolated from realities in India. They proceed apparently on certain assumptions which have little relevance and ignore the basic factors of the situation in India.

If my reactions were so powerful, you can well imagine what my colleagues and others will think and feel. I think it will be a disaster if something is done now which will dam up the river of progressively friendly relations between Britain and India and reverse its current.

I have written rather hastily a note on the tentative proposals. This is necessarily rather crude as I am in a hurry to let you know how I feel about it all. I tried to make the note brief but it lengthened itself. As soon as it is ready I shall send it to you. Meanwhile I am sending this letter to you to give you some indication of how upset I have been by these proposals which, I am convinced, will be resented and bitterly disliked all over the country.

Yours sincerely,
JAWAHARLAL NEHRU

403

Minutes of Viceroy's Twelfth Miscellaneous Meeting

Mountbatten Papers

TOP SECRET

Those present at this Meeting held at Viceregal Lodge, Simla on 11 May 1947 at 11.30 am were: Rear-Admiral Viscount Mountbatten of Burma, Sir E. Jenkins, Sir E. Mieville, Lieutenant-Colonel Erskine Crum

Item 1

The choice by Provinces of their own future

SIR EVAN JENKINS reiterated the views which he had expressed two days previously in a telegram[1] to the Secretary of State. He gave his opinion that if, under the alternative plan, power was handed over to the existing Interim Government, there would be a civil war, with fighting starting at once in the Punjab. He emphasized that he could see no real solution for the Punjab— there was a curious fatalistic feeling about. It would be out of the question to keep a Muslim Ministry in power there. The Sikhs and the Hindus intended to fight.

HIS EXCELLENCY THE VICEROY said that he had received a most disturbing letter[2] that morning from Pandit Nehru, who reacted very strongly against the draft announcement of the present plan, which he had shown him the previous night. SIR EVAN JENKINS said that he considered that Pandit Nehru was reacting to the pressure of Hindu opinion to which all the Congress leaders were very sensitive. They were all, after all, no more than revolutionary agitators in different ways.

SIR EVAN JENKINS stressed that any notional partition, for voting purposes, of the Punjab would be taken by all Indian parties as an award. This was typical of the usual Indian attitude. He considered that it would be preferable to get a boundary commission working first, before the announcement of a notional partition—if the different communities could be forced to set up such a commission.

SIR EVAN JENKINS stated that he would be in favour of any plan to which all the Indian leaders agreed. He added that the suggestion that he should

[1] No. 374.   [2] No. 402.

take on three advisers, under Section 93 Government, one from each major community, was impracticable, as it would be impossible to persuade them to serve. The Muslim particularly would be committing political suicide.

HIS EXCELLENCY THE VICEROY asked SIR EVAN JENKINS what he would intend to do if the plan in the draft announcement was accepted by all Indian parties.

SIR EVAN JENKINS stated that if the leaders of all parties agreed to carry out this plan loyally, he would summon all the Punjab party leaders and try to induce them to form a Coalition Government. Alternatively, separate Governments would have to be formed on a zonal basis, but this would be much more complicated. He emphasised that if the Plan in the draft announcement was agreed to by the Indian leaders, and partition of the Punjab resulted, it would be a great disaster for the Punjab.

Item 3
The Nawab of Mamdot

HIS EXCELLENCY THE VICEROY asked SIR EVAN JENKINS why the Nawab of Mamdot had asked to be allowed to form a Ministry in the Punjab.

SIR EVAN JENKINS explained that the Nawab of Mamdot was a very stupid man. He was under the influence of some younger men, who were in a fanatical mood. They evidently thought that if the Muslim League could take power, they would be able to withdraw the proceedings which were being taken against Muslims and to use the Police force, which was 70% Muslim, to suppress the Sikhs. SIR EVAN JENKINS added that he had not seen the Nawab of Mamdot since he had left for Delhi to see Mr Jinnah.

Item 5
Precautionary arrangements for the Partition Announcement

SIR EVAN JENKINS said that, as a result of a meeting which he had had with Major General Bruce, who had later seen Lieut. General Sir Arthur Smith, it had been arranged, subject to Field Marshal Auchinleck's approval, to move 4 Indian Division less one Brigade from Poona to the Partition area in the Punjab before the announcement. He gave his opinion that this force should be adequate to suppress serious disturbances.

HIS EXCELLENCY THE VICEROY said that he agreed to this step.

404

Minutes of Viceroy's Thirteenth Miscellaneous Meeting

Mountbatten Papers

TOP SECRET

Those present at this Meeting held at Viceregal Lodge, Simla on 11 May 1947 at 2.15 pm were: Rear-Admiral Viscount Mountbatten of Burma, Sir E. Jenkins, Pandit Nehru, Sir E. Mieville, Captain Brockman, Lieutenant-Colonel Erskine Crum

Item 1
The Punjab

HIS EXCELLENCY THE VICEROY recalled that Mr Jinnah had originally claimed the whole of the Punjab in which there was a slight overall Muslim majority for Pakistan. Sikhs had then started a demand for partition and Congress had agreed to support this demand. As he understood it, this support was based on the principle that no districts in which non-Muslims predominated should go to Pakistan. PANDIT NEHRU agreed that this was the rough basis of Congress's support.

HIS EXCELLENCY THE VICEROY emphasised that it would be necessary to work on the basis of Muslim and non-Muslim districts for notional partition for voting purposes. But this would not prejudice the subsequent work of a Boundary Commission. The greatest snag as he saw it was in connection with the Sikhs' vested interests. But it would be very difficult to define demarcation on these grounds. Nevertheless the Sikhs were prepared for war and it seemed that whatever was done, short of deliberately putting Muslim majority areas under Sikh control, the latter would fight. The problem was how to make a partition acceptable to all parties.

PANDIT NEHRU said that when Congress referred to the partition of the Punjab, they had not gone into the question in any great detail. They agreed that the rough line of demarcation must be between Muslim and non-Muslim majority areas. They agreed that landed property was not on a basis which could be proceeded upon, but there were Sikh shrines in some of the predominantly Muslim areas. This point should also be borne in mind.

SIR EVAN JENKINS said that it would be very difficult to take this point into consideration when deciding on boundaries. He agreed that there were a number of Sikh shrines in Western Punjab, but pointed out that the real Sikh Holy Land was in Amritsar, which would in any case fall to the Sikhs. HIS EXCELLENCY THE VICEROY said that the Boundary Commission could be instructed to take Sikh religious interests into consideration.

PANDIT NEHRU then raised the case of the Gurdaspur district, where the population was almost exactly divided between Muslims and non-Muslims.

He asked whether it would not be possible to divide this district, even for the purposes of a notional partition. SIR EVAN JENKINS said that he did not consider that this would be possible. The Muslims were fairly equally mixed throughout the district. Nevertheless he foresaw that both Gurdaspur and Lahore districts might well be divided by the Boundary Commission.

PANDIT NEHRU said that another possibility would be that Hindu and Sikh representatives from Gurdaspur could vote with the representatives of Eastern Punjab and the Muslims with those of Western Punjab.

HIS EXCELLENCY THE VICEROY said that he was in favour of making some such gesture to the Sikhs. Perhaps a clause could be included in the Draft Announcement to the effect that any districts where the population was so evenly divided that there was less than 1% difference in the number of Muslims and non-Muslims—for example in Gurdaspur—the representatives should be divided for voting purposes as suggested by Pandit Nehru. SIR EVAN JENKINS said that he would agree to such a suggestion so long as the general plan was accepted by the party leaders.

HIS EXCELLENCY THE VICEROY explained to Pandit Nehru that orders had been given for one Division less one Brigade to move from Poona to the partition area of the Punjab in time to be in position before the announcement was made. He said that he considered this step to be sad but necessary. PANDIT NEHRU indicated assent with this latter remark.

PANDIT NEHRU asked Sir Evan Jenkins whether he had any information that arms were being smuggled into the Punjab from abroad. SIR EVAN JENKINS stated that he knew of no reports of arms coming in from foreign countries. However, a certain amount had been brought in from the Frontier: and the authorities were searching freely. PANDIT NEHRU explained that he had received information from London concerning the buying of arms from the Continent and Iraq. He asked whether Sir Evan Jenkins considered that any Indian States were playing a part in this buying of arms. SIR EVAN JENKINS replied that they were not doing so officially at any rate.

PANDIT NEHRU asked Sir Evan Jenkins whether he thought that, if it was sufficiently realised by the Muslim League that the grant of Pakistan was dependent upon the partition of the Punjab, they would react against Pakistan. SIR EVAN JENKINS replied that there might be a split of a kind in the ranks of the Muslim League but he did not know how deep this would go.

HIS EXCELLENCY THE VICEROY asked whether it was considered that there was any hope of organising transfers of population on a large scale. SIR EVAN JENKINS replied that he thought not.

HIS EXCELLENCY THE VICEROY decided to pursue the suggestion that there should be a special voting procedure in Provinces [? Districts], for example Gurdaspur, where the population was almost equally divided between Muslims and non-Muslims.

Item 2
Pandit Nehru's Plan

HIS EXCELLENCY THE VICEROY explained that he had spoken to Pandit Nehru before the meeting concerning the possible rejection of the Plan in the Draft Announcement. He had told Pandit Nehru that if the Muslim League did not accept it, the alternative to be put before them would be the demission of power to an united India on a Dominion status basis, and on the understanding that there would be safeguards which would allow Mr Jinnah to form his Pakistan later. HIS EXCELLENCY THE VICEROY stated that Pandit Nehru had told him that Congress would prefer this alternative plan. But he (His Excellency) very much doubted that H.M.G. would allow him to impose it if Mr Jinnah accepted the plan in the Draft Announcement. The Muslims would feel that they would be out-voted on every count. The great attraction to him was that it would enable the Indians to settle their own problems among themselves. But he was bound to ensure that the Muslim League were given at least a fair chance. Mr Jinnah was reportedly saying that he did not trust Congress but he (His Excellency) felt that the Congress leaders would be much more inclined to make concessions themselves in order to avoid war than to see him make them.

PANDIT NEHRU agreed with this last point. He said that it was only human nature that it should be so. He pointed out that giving in to Mr Jinnah in the past had not led to agreement but to further demands. The alternatives were settlement and conflict. So far there had not been an element of compulsion one way or the other. If the Indian leaders were left to deal with each other without outside interference, there would be a strong compulsion to come to terms.

HIS EXCELLENCY THE VICEROY said that Pandit Nehru had stated that if power was demitted to the Interim Government on a Dominion status basis, Congress would publicly announce safeguards for the Muslim League. Assistance would be given to those areas who did not want to stay in the Union of India to get out. Assistance would be given towards the setting up of Pakistan if this was wanted. But these safeguards were based on Congress's stated word. Mr Jinnah would surely not accept this.

PANDIT NEHRU said that he believed that once these safeguards were publicly announced, it would be physically impossible to go against them.

Item 3
Timetable of events

HIS EXCELLENCY THE VICEROY said that Pandit Nehru had also stressed to him that the present proposed timetable was too much of a rush.

The postponement of the present programme, whereby the Announcement would be made on 22nd May at the latest, was then discussed, and it was decided to postpone the meeting with Indian leaders until 2nd June.

SIR EVAN JENKINS declared himself in favour of this postponement. He said that any wrong step at the present stage would stimulate fighting in the Punjab; and postponement would not mean that the different parties would get any better organised than they were at the moment for fighting.

SIR ERIC MIEVILLE also agreed with the postponement.

PANDIT NEHRU said that he thought the Congress Working Committee should meet some days earlier than the Viceroy's meeting of the five Indian leaders so as to consider the principles of the Plan. HIS EXCELLENCY THE VICEROY told Pandit Nehru that he did not consider that this would be desirable.

405

Minutes of Viceroy's Fourteenth Miscellaneous Meeting

Mountbatten Papers

TOP SECRET

Those present at this meeting held at Viceregal Lodge, Simla on 11 May 1947 at 4 pm were: Rear-Admiral Viscount Mountbatten of Burma, Pandit Nehru, Rao Bahadur V. P. Menon, Sir E. Mieville, Captain Brockman, Lieutenant-Colonel Erskine Crum

Item 1
Choice by Provinces of their own future

HIS EXCELLENCY THE VICEROY said that he had that morning received a letter[1] from Pandit Nehru containing very considerable objections to the Plan as contained in the Draft Announcement, a copy of which he had shown to Pandit Nehru the previous night. He explained that he had been under the impression that there had been a large measure of agreement by both sides to this Plan. Mr. Jinnah had never actually accepted it but had implied acceptance. The views of Pandit Nehru and Sardar Patel, Mr. Jinnah and Mr. Liaquat Ali Khan had been obtained at a series of meetings[2] with the Viceroy, Lord Ismay, Sir Eric Mieville and Mr. Abell. Sir Eric Mieville had then taken the draft of the Plan round to Pandit Nehru and to Mr. Jinnah.[3] The present draft did not differ in essentials from that.

PANDIT NEHRU claimed that the draft which Sir Eric Mieville had shown him had been rough; that it had dealt mainly with the Partition of Bengal and the Punjab; and that it had consisted of only one-and-a-half pages. He stated that he had at that time criticised certain parts of the draft, particularly in connection with Baluchistan and the N.W.F.P.

SIR ERIC MIEVILLE agreed with this latter point; but he made it absolutely clear that the draft which he had shown Pandit Nehru was the full draft of the whole Plan.

HIS EXCELLENCY THE VICEROY went on to say that, after Pandit Nehru and Mr. Jinnah had seen the draft announcement, Lord Ismay had gone to London with instructions to say that nothing had been agreed to in writing by the Indian leaders, but that the draft represented in his (His Excellency's) considered opinion what the leaders had implied that they would accept. Therefore, he had been extremely surprised at receiving Pandit Nehru's letter that morning.

PANDIT NEHRU said that, as well as the letter, he had written a long note[4] reasserting his immediate reactions. He handed this note to the Viceroy. He explained that he had to speak for his colleagues and the Congress Organisation. The main point which he had mentioned in this note was that the whole background of the draft announcement was very different from what he had imagined. He had thought that Provinces were going to be asked to express their wishes on a slight variation of the Cabinet Mission's Plan. This would start on the basis of a Union of India, including the States. In the Cabinet Mission's Plan reference had been made to Provinces being able to opt out from one group to another at a later stage. Congress had now stated the principle of "no compulsion" and agreed any Province which wished to could opt out of the Union completely. But in the present draft of the announcement the conception was not so much of a Union of India but of a large number of successor States to which theoretically power would be transferred, and which would then join one group or another. This was a fundamental departure from the basis of the Cabinet Mission's Plan. The approach was different, and this became even more evident in regard to the States. Although what was said was not basically different to what had been said before, the emphasis was such that it became almost an invitation to the States to keep out and await future developments. His reading of the draft announcement led him to think that it would encourage people to realise that India was being balkanised. The procedure appeared to be first separation, then a request to join up again. The previous process had been the opposite —first request for unity and then the option to secede.

PANDIT NEHRU went on to say that in the Plan in the draft announcement the Cabinet Mission's plan was being completely thrown away; and there was an extension in some parts of what had been said in H.M.G.'s statement of the 20th February. He gave his opinion that this process of throwing away what had been previously said should be carried out as little as possible. It gave rise to the idea that there was nothing final in H.M.G.'s announcements

[1] No. 402.   [2] See Nos. 190, 194, 203 and 216.
[3] See Nos. 256 and 257.   [4] No. 406.

and that H.M.G. always changed their minds under pressure. It encouraged chaotic tendencies. The Cabinet Mission's Plan had brought about a certain definiteness; the statement of February 20th had been more definite and had been well received. This present Plan would upset everything and produce the idea that there were no assurances of what was going to happen. The Constituent Assembly was referred to in it in a manner which was likely to reduce its importance in the scheme of things.

The States

HIS EXCELLENCY THE VICEROY said that he agreed that nothing should be done to encourage States to stand out independently, but there were some which were geographically and ethnically almost bound to throw in their lot with Pakistan. The only new element which he was trying to introduce was that a few could, if they so wished, go into Pakistan.

PANDIT NEHRU said that the people of almost every State had openly declared in favour of joining the Union of India. He asked what would happen if Hyderabad wanted to join Pakistan. RAO BAHADUR MENON pointed out that it would produce a very similar situation to Kashmir joining the present Constituent Assembly.

Bengal

HIS EXCELLENCY THE VICEROY then asked Pandit Nehru for his views on the procedure whereby Bengal would be given a chance of remaining united and independent. He pointed out that, on the basis of application of the same principle, the chance of independence was, in the present draft, being given to other Provinces also.

PANDIT NEHRU said that it was obvious that the division of Bengal was harmful from many points of view, but exactly the same argument applied to the cutting off of Bengal from India. Calcutta was the port for the whole of Northern India; if Bengal was independent Calcutta would wither away.

PANDIT NEHRU went on to say that he considered that there had been quite enough rioting in Bengal without the suggestion that the Province should be partitioned; however Congress had been forced to recommend partition. He personally hoped that the conception of Partition would recede. He would be willing to consider special arrangements with Bengal and the Punjab but the feeling of the people in Western Bengal was an important factor. The situation in Bengal had become intolerable for them. There was not likely to be more than one per cent of non-Muslims who would agree to independence; Calcutta had been half ruined in the last six months.

Baluchistan

PANDIT NEHRU then referred to the proposed arrangements in the draft announcement for ascertaining the will of the people of Baluchistan. He said that he considered it amazing that one man, elected by a number of semi-feudal chiefs, should decide the fate of the Province. He considered that

Baluchistan should not be asked to make a choice until the picture in the rest of India was clear. There were only 300,000 inhabitants of Baluchistan, and a plebiscite might be organised.

HIS EXCELLENCY THE VICEROY emphasised that if an early transfer of power were to take place it would be out of the question to leave the fate of any parts of India undecided.

PANDIT NEHRU said he agreed that the question must be decided before any final decision was made; some method or other would have to be devised, but the future of Baluchistan raised many strategic problems. The way at present envisaged was a very casual way of dealing with an important Frontier area. Baluchistan's decision was bound to be influenced by the decision in the N.W.F.P. He said that he could not himself suggest an immediate answer as to the best method of finding out the will of the people in Baluchistan, and proposed that Sir B. N. Rau should be consulted.

The N.W.F.P.

HIS EXCELLENCY THE VICEROY asked Pandit Nehru whether he agreed to the present wording on the procedure for the N.W.F.P. PANDIT NEHRU asked when the proposed referendum there was likely to occur. RAO BAHADUR MENON replied that the other processes on which it was dependent would probably be complete within two months; but PANDIT NEHRU himself said that he thought they could be finished in June.

HIS EXCELLENCY THE VICEROY said that he was sure that if no referendum was held there would be a civil war in the N.W.F.P. PANDIT NEHRU said that he agreed that there should be a referendum before the demission of power.

The reframing of the draft announcement

PANDIT NEHRU then gave an outline of how he considered the Plan should be reframed in order to make it more acceptable to Congress. He argued that the Cabinet Mission's Plan was not dead except to those who had rejected it. The Constituent Assembly was functioning except for a few Provinces, the majority of whose elected representatives had not taken their seats and which could, therefore, be considered not to have adhered to it. It was these Provinces which must now be given an opportunity of choosing what to do. They were Sind; the Punjab and Bengal, where there was a demand for Partition; and the District of Sylhet, which was predominantly Muslim. He again mentioned the question of the non-Muslim area in Sind.

HIS EXCELLENCY THE VICEROY asked Pandit Nehru whether, if he could get the draft announcement reframed along the lines he wanted, he and the Congress Working Committee would agree to it. PANDIT NEHRU replied that he wanted to help the Viceroy, but "things that emerged from London were so peculiar". He suggested that instead of vague and general talk there should be something more definite.

HIS EXCELLENCY THE VICEROY asked whether Pandit Nehru could see any objection to the use of the word "Pakistan". PANDIT NEHRU replied that this was a colloquial word which had no meaning; even the Muslim League had not used it in resolutions.

Item 2
The early transfer of power on a Dominion Status basis

PANDIT NEHRU asked whether, when an early transfer of power on a Dominion Status basis was referred to, it was intended that complete power should be transferred. What was intended in connection with the Army?

HIS EXCELLENCY THE VICEROY said that the British Army would be withdrawn as quickly as possible. With this principle PANDIT NEHRU agreed.

HIS EXCELLENCY THE VICEROY said that, since a new sovereign state was to be set up, from the territories of which about thirty per cent of the present Army came, there would have to be an interim period during which the Armed Forces would be run by a Defence Council.

PANDIT NEHRU said that the proportion was rather less than thirty per cent. He agreed that there should be a joint Defence Council, but gave his opinion that it should be concerned with two matters only—the process of division and measures to ensure that the Army was not unfairly used by either side. He felt that the scope of the Defence Council should definitely be limited to these two subjects; otherwise the whole development and organisation of the Army would be compromised.

406

Note by Pandit Nehru

Mountbatten Papers. Official Correspondence Files: Transfer of Power,
Procedure for determining authorities to which power is to be demitted,
Part (2)

TOP SECRET   SIMLA, *11 May 1947*

I have very carefully considered, in the short time at my disposal, the papers shown to me. They are of such far-reaching implication that it is difficult for me to deal with the subject adequately, and in any event a full consultation with my colleagues would be necessary. But as time is limited and any delay in a clear expression of opinion might lead to further steps being taken which may have grave consequences, I am giving below my immediate reactions.

2. Although I have had no opportunity of consulting my colleagues, I am quite clear that my reactions will be shared by them probably in a stronger

measure. The first consideration of the papers produced a devastating effect upon me. The picture presented by the proposals was an ominous one and the whole approach to them appeared to me to be dangerous. Not only do they menace India but also they endanger the future relation between Britain and India. Instead of producing any sense of certainty, security and stability, they would encourage disruptive tendencies everywhere and chaos and weakness. They would particularly endanger important strategic areas.

3. It is stated in the proposals that they have taken shape after full consultation with political leaders in India. That might lead people to think that they have the consent of those leaders. This would be completely wrong in so far as all leaders are concerned except possibly the Muslim League leaders. In our consultations we had proceeded on the present basis of the Cabinet Mission's plan and the Statement of February 20th. Owing to stress of circumstances we had agreed to vary this basis to a certain extent, but the general approach continued to be the same. This variation consisted in the acceptance of the fact that certain Muslim majority areas might go out of the Union if they so willed. The Union was still the basic factor. In the new proposals the whole approach has been changed completely and is at total variance with our own approach in the course of recent talks. The proposals start with the rejection of an Indian Union as the successor to power and invite the claims of large numbers of succession States who are permitted to unite if they so wish in two or more States.

4. I have no doubt whatever that the announcement of this new policy and proposals by H.M.G. would provoke wide and deep resentment all over the country and no responsible leader of Indian opinion outside the Muslim League would be able to persuade the country to accept or even to acquiesce in them. It seems to me, therefore, essential that H.M.G. should be left in no doubt as to the total unacceptability of and opposition to both these proposals and the approach made in them, and also to the consequences which are bound to follow if H.M.G. were to persist in them.

5. Hitherto all British proposals and indeed all discussions have been basically on a United India, the inroads into such unity being confined either (a) to weakening the Centre and giving some sort of Group autonomy or (b) to giving the freedom to certain areas, which are demonstrably against joining the Union, to create themselves into separate States. The Cabinet Mission considered every aspect of a totally divided India and rejected it. Those considerations remain unchanged and indeed the disorder and violence of recent months add further weight to those considerations.

6. It must be remembered that the British Cabinet plan was accepted by all in India with the sole exception of the Muslim League and even the League had not at all times rejected it. Even today the League is prepared and continues

to reap such advantages as it obtained for itself by joining the Interim Government on the basis of acceptance of the plan. The throwing overboard not only of the plan but all its basic conceptions namely the all-India Union and provincial independence to the utmost within that Union appears to be totally at the instance of one party alone in India. The Muslim League vetoes the plan and H.M.G., therefore, throw it overboard. This step can only confirm the conviction widely held that no plan of H.M.G. can be accepted or proceeded with in the hope that H.M.G. will hold to it.

7. The present proposals virtually scrap the Constituent Assembly which includes all elements excepting the Muslim League, and deprive the Constituent Assembly of its essential character and reduce it to a body for preparing a scheme for the Union which these proposals negative.

8. This involves a complete going back by H.M.G. on its previous decisions in that (a) it throws overboard the Cabinet plan or at any rate its basic conception, (b) it violates its repeated pledge that it will not permit one party to exercise a veto, (c) it scraps all that has been done under its own scheme and by arrangements made by the Governor-General himself to implement it.

9. It appears to me that the inevitable and obvious consequences of the proposals and the approach in them are (a) to invite the Balkanisation of India, (b) to provoke certain civil conflict and to add to violence and disorder, (c) to a further breakdown of the central authority which alone can prevent the chaos that is growing, (d) to demoralise the army, the police, and the Central Services.

10. The proposal that each of the successor States is to conclude independent treaties, presumably with H.M.G. also, which follows if the all-India Union is rejected as a basis and sovereignty reverts to the Provinces, is likely to create many "Ulsters" in India. This will be so considered by the people and deeply resented. The consequences of such resentment will be to add to the suspicions that exist and to create an almost unbridgeable gulf between National India and the British people in the future. The "Ulsters" will be looked upon as so many British bases on Indian soil, possibly having British garrisons.

11. The approach to the Princes may be logical and consistent with the unfortunate position in respect of paramountcy. It shows, however, an obvious shift of emphasis and is a definite invitation to at least the major States to remain independent Kingdoms, presumably as feudatories or allies of Britain. Also it is a definite incitement to them to play off Pakistan against the rest of India. This new emphasis will let loose in the States those forces which our moderate counsels and the hopes of their being part of an Indian Union are keeping somewhat in check. People's organisations everywhere demand union. The Rulers may resist them and will be encouraged to do so by this

new emphasis in the proposals. In the States themselves there may well be civil war.

12. The proposals in respect of the Indian States also reverse the approach in the Cabinet plan wherein it is obviously indicated that the all-India Union is a Union of States as well, though their union under one Centre must be by voluntary accession. Machinery for this was provided in the Negotiating Committee.

13. The acquiescence on our side to the split up of certain areas, which are predominantly League in their loyalty, was in no wise an acquiescence in throwing overboard the all-India basis of future settlement. It was only a stretching of the Cabinet plan to make opting out operable now and an adhesion to our oft-repeated policy that we do not wish to coerce any part of India. Further the partition of Provinces to which we agreed also was for the same reasons, and we hold that such partition is consistent with an all-India Union of both separated parts with the retention of separate identities. If so desired by these parts they could go out of the Union.

14. It follows, therefore, and this has to be emphasised as H.M.G. appears to imply that we have acquiesced in a rejection of the Cabinet plan and in making the Union a later step by self-determination. We have not agreed to anything of the kind and any step that we have taken, often against our will and against the presence [? pressure] of national feeling in India, is to accept more and more completely the Cabinet plan which provides for the basic all-India Union.

15. It is difficult to go into the details of the proposals in the time available and within the compass of a note. But I might mention that the proposal about the so-called self-determination about Baluchistan seems to me to be preposterous. It leaves the future of that Province to one man chosen by a group of Sardars and nominated persons who obviously represent a vested semi-feudal element. Baluchistan has an importance also as a strategic frontier of India and its future cannot be dealt with in this partial and casual manner.

16. If Assam has to surrender a part to Bengal, and we are not opposed to this if the people concerned so wish, it stands to reason that some such procedure is equally applicable to parts of Sind.

17. The proposals about the N.W.F.P. in various forms have been repeatedly discussed by us and I have pointed out to you our strong objection to anything which places a premium on violence and may well invite civil war. We have agreed that the Frontier Province, like other areas, should be given full opportunity to express its own opinion about the future. But this must be done at the proper time and in the proper context in common with other parts of India. Otherwise that assessment of opinion itself may be defeated

apart from other consequences. In effect the present proposal implies a decision by H.M.G. that the Province must reverse or at least be given an opportunity to reverse its present decision which is to remain in the Constituent Assembly. The sole reason for this appears to be the violence and rapine carried out recently in the Province by adherents of the Muslim League or others. That violence has not stopped despite Mr. Jinnah's appeal. This may mean that the violent elements are not in control of the League or that the League leaders are not anxious to stop them. The proposal about the Frontier spot-lights the Province and proceeds on the assumption that extra-constitutional violence can declare null and void previous and recent decisions arrived at by constitutional procedure.

18. In regard to the treaties with the Tribes of the Frontier, these are presumably with the Government of India. We recognise the independence of the Tribes and their freedom to make treaties as they like. But even in the case of a properly constituted State on the frontiers of a country and integral to its defence and territorial integrity, the alliance of such a State with another party is recognised as being the concern of the given State with which it has been associated. In the present case this would be India. To give public assurance to the Tribes that they can have treaties with whomsoever they like is to invite them to profit by internal difficulties in India and also to create a situation on the Indian frontier which menaces India as well as neighbouring areas in Asia. The Tribal and Frontier Areas have been maintained by the expenditure of vast amounts of money from all-India because of strategic and other reasons. Further, if the N.W.F.P. remains with the Union, an alliance between the Tribal Areas and another State will create grave difficulties for the N.W.F.P. and India as a whole.

19. H.M.G. wishes to declare that the sole purpose of the procedure indicated in the proposals is to ascertain the wishes of the people of India and to transfer power with the least possible dislocation. These purposes will not be advanced or even achieved by the proposals. As I have indicated above, the proposals will encourage chaos and disorder and the belief that violence pays will prevent any proper assessment of opinion. Before the people choose they must have a proper picture as to what they are to choose. Two or three vague proposals without this clear background will produce confusion and may share the character of merely demagogic appeals. The transfer of power, instead of being made without dislocation, will be obstructed by violence, by a mass of complications, and by the weakness of the Central Government and its organs.

20. If there is to be any genuine assessment of opinion, the only practicable way is for two constitutions, two appeals and two prospects to be placed before the people. This means that (a) the Constituent Assembly must proceed

with the constitution-making on the basis of an all-India Union with full freedom for Provinces and effective guarantees for all, (b) equally the League can prepare its own schemes and present its own proposals on an equal level, (c) the two constitutions may be presented to all the Provinces of India on a plebiscite basis on such terms as are agreed upon.

21. Until these decisions are made, the Government of India must remain as one. In view of impending British withdrawal, the Coalition forming the Central Government must be a Cabinet with joint responsibility based upon full Dominion autonomy. It may be made clear that the Central Government will not take any steps to prejudice self-determination or subsequent partition and such other guarantees as are necessary may also be given so as to assure the League in regard to certain agreed matters. It may, for instance, be stated that in regard to certain questions they should not be decided by a mere majority in the Cabinet. Some machinery for adjudication in regard to these questions can be set up.

22. This has become a very long note hastily prepared and yet it has not dealt fully with all the aspects of the problem. As I have said above, the fullest consideration by all concerned is necessary before any commitments can be made. It is obvious that there can be no imposed solutions of our problems and any attempt to do so will lead to further difficulty. Whatever the views of my colleagues might be in regard to various details of the proposals, I have no doubt that their main reaction will be as I have indicated above. That is that they cannot accept these proposals and they are not prepared to acquiesce in the throwing overboard of the basic all-India Union or to accept the theory of Provinces being initially independent successor States.[1]

JAWAHARLAL NEHRU

[1] The text of this note was circulated to the India and Burma Committee under the reference I.B. (47)69 of 16 May 1947. L/P &J/10/79: ff 234–40.

407

Rear-Admiral Viscount Mountbatten of Burma to Mr Attlee (via India Office)

Telegram, Mountbatten Papers. Official Correspondence Files:
Transfer of Power, Part II (a)

MOST IMMEDIATE   SIMLA, *11 May 1947, 4.30 pm*
SECRET   *Received: 11 May, 3.30 pm*

No. 53–S.C. Please pass following immediately to Prime Minister from Viceroy.

(*Begins*). Although I felt we could meet accelerated time table to enable statement to be made before Whitsuntide recess, on going into this personally with Nehru and Governor Punjab am convinced it is not feasible although my original time table could just have been managed.

2. Have therefore had to telegraph to leaders and States Negotiating Committees postponing invitations to Monday June 2nd. I am so sorry about this especially after the splendid way the Cabinet Committee have worked to meet earlier date.

3. Am giving as reason for postponement Parliamentary recess.

4. Unless I hear to the contrary will inform press to this effect tomorrow Monday 14.00 D.B.S.T. (*Ends*).

India Office please give copy of this telegram to Ismay.

408

Sir F. Burrows (Bengal) to Rear-Admiral Viscount Mountbatten of Burma

Telegram, Mountbatten Papers. Official Correspondence Files: Bengal, Partition of, Part I(b)

IMPORTANT							*11 May 1947, 4.50 pm*
TOP SECRET						*Received: 12 May, 2 am*

No. 117–S. Your Top Secret telegram 39–S.C. dated 10th May.[1] I assume reference is to statement appearing in Calcutta press of 8th May.[2] In case you have not seen full text of this statement I am arranging for text to be posted to PSV direct from Calcutta.[3] The passage about Calcutta must not be divorced from context of statement as a whole which I consider a most statesmanlike utterance. I hope (though with less confidence than I should wish) that Suhrawardy was speaking with backing of his party. I cannot subscribe to Nehru's interpretation that anything in statement constitutes a threat to promote disorders in Calcutta. It seems to me to be only a realistic facing up to obvious probabilities. I have never concealed my opinion, which I still hold, that if as a result of partition of Bengal new province of East Bengal is deprived of share of resources of Calcutta it will become a battleground after our departure and that even before our departure the prospect will exacerbate feeling to breaking point. As we both, I believe, recognised when we discussed this matter last week in Delhi, the probability of trouble both in East Bengal and in Calcutta itself may have to be faced in the interests of a settlement elsewhere and over a greater part of India. But as regards Suhrawardy, his present approach to whole problem seems to me to be both sound and conciliatory and I do not for a moment believe that passage in question was intended as an indication of any intention on his part or part of his Ministry to sack Calcutta rather than let it be allocated peacefully to West Bengal. If, as I have suggested in my immediately preceding telegram No. 116–S of today,[4] you can see Suhrawardy on Wednesday, you will no doubt satisfy yourself as to his intentions.

2. As regards paras 2 and 3 of your telegram, I agree (subject to my reply to question in your para 4 (a)) with view you have expressed in para 3.

3. As regards your para 4 (a) much will turn on terms of statement to be issued on behalf of H.M.G. and of Jinnah's reactions to it but in view of probability that provisions for partition of Bengal will be of a permissive character I am inclined to agree that most dangerous period will come if and when a decision to partition Bengal is taken.

4. Your para 4 (b). I have sufficient troops, if I am allowed to utilize maximum fire-power to augment numbers, to deal with any situation likely to arise in Calcutta. I have not sufficient troops for firepower to deal with widespread rising in East Bengal nor can I visualize possibility of a sufficiency of troops to deal with such a situation there. I have repeatedly made clear my view that in the event of a serious movement by Muslims of Bengal I cannot hold East Bengal outside (temporarily) the towns of Dacca and Chittagong. In this connection I would invite a reference to relevant passages of a memorandum on situation in Bengal which I forwarded to you in triplicate in last week of March,[5] particularly two concluding sentences of section headed "Law and Order during interim period" and to the whole of section entitled "Various possibilities".

5. Your para 4 (c). In such circumstances, I should be forced to arrest my Ministers and go into Section 93 for a day or two with a view to forming a minority government to administer the Province.

[1] No. 393.

[2] See No. 382, note 5.

[3] The text of the statement, as reported in the *Statesman* of 8 May, was forwarded by Sir F. Burrows' Private Office on 12 May. Mountbatten Papers, Official Correspondence Files: Bengal, Partition of, Part I(*b*).

[4] In this telegram Sir F. Burrows reported a conversation he had had with Mr Suhrawardy that morning from which he gathered that the Chief Minister's negotiations with political leaders had made some progress. Suhrawardy had said he felt there was a great possibility of an agreed solution in Bengal and was telegraphing the Viceroy to ask for a meeting on Wednesday, 14 May. Sir F. Burrows hoped that Lord Mountbatten would be able to see him. *Ibid.*

[5] Under cover of a letter dated 26/27 March 1947. *Ibid*, Part I(*a*).

409

Rear-Admiral Mountbatten of Burma to Lord Ismay (via India Office)

Telegram, R/3/1/153: ff 7–9

IMMEDIATE
TOP SECRET

SIMLA, *11 May 1947, 9 pm*
Received: 12 May, 6.20 am

No. 54–S.C. Further to my 28–S.C. of 8th May.[1]

1. I had a long and satisfactory meeting with Nehru, Mieville and V. P. Menon yesterday[2] (the minutes are being sent to you) on the possibility of an early transfer of power on a dominion status basis.

2. I want you, before you leave London, to explain the way my mind is working, as outlined in this telegram, to H.M.G. and to find out what their reactions are. I would like you to obtain H.M.G.'s general approval to the line which I am taking. You must make them realise that speed is the essence of the contract. Without speed, we will miss the opportunity. I have just received your 6046 of 10th May[3] with which I am delighted.

3. *Date.*

I am convinced that, in order to have the best chance of obtaining our long-term object, the grant of Dominion Status must take place during 1947.

4. *Advantages.*

The advantages which would accrue to India through an early transfer of power and remaining within the Commonwealth are obvious enough. I consider that the main advantages which the United Kingdom would gain are briefly:—

(*a*) the terrific world-wide enhancement of British prestige and the enhancement of the prestige of the present Government.

(*b*) the completion of the framework of world strategy from the point of view of Empire defence.

(*c*) the early termination of present responsibilities, especially in the field of law and order, which was stressed by Patel in his statement to the press on Friday. See my next telegram.[4]

(*d*) A further strengthening of Indo-British relations which have enormously improved since the statement of 20th February.

5. *Modification to Government of India Act.*

The instrument under which the transfer of power would take place would be the 1935 Act with certain modifications. For instance, the Secretary of State, the India Office, and the special powers of the Governor-General and the Governors would disappear. One constitutional Governor-General could serve both parts of India. Governors would be appointed by him on the recommendation of the Central Executives.

6. *Difficulties.*

There are difficulties which have got to be met. The main ones are

(*a*) Defence and

(*b*) The complications resulting from the partition of India.

7. *Defence.*

(*a*) British Forces.

I consider that the British Army should be phased out as soon as possible after the transfer of power. Until this process is completed, I should have to be given special powers in relation to the employment of British troops. The elements of the RAF at present planned to remain in India should do so, being transferred on loan to the RIAF.

(*b*) *Indian Forces.*

(*i*) The process of nationalisation of the Army would be slowed down. The period of compensation for British officers would be extended until such time as they can be released under a new plan.

(*ii*) If partition of the Army is insisted upon, the process would take place in an orderly manner under a planned programme.

(*iii*) During the interim period there would be a Defence Council consisting of myself as Chairman and one representative each from the Union of India and Pakistan.

(*iv*) Defence Headquarters would also eventually be split. Until this process was complete it would be under the Defence Council.

8. *Complications resulting from partition.*

It is obvious that the Union of India will be ready to receive power before Pakistan. It may take 6–8 months for the latter to set up an executive for this purpose. I am, however, assured that the former need not wait upon the latter, and that I could be Constitutional Governor-General of the Union and my existing powers could remain meanwhile for Pakistan.

9. *Nomenclature.*

(*a*) It is apparent that the words "Dominion status" have an unfortunate association here. I would be grateful for any bring [? bright] ideas you may come across to get over this difficulty.

(*b*) The word "Emperor" would have to be dropped from His Majesty's present designation of "King-Emperor".

10. *Further steps.*

I intend to see Patel about all this as soon as I get back to Delhi. I will not talk to Jinnah about it until after the announcement of the plan; and, although his reactions to anything are always quite unpredictable, he has already hinted

---

¹ No. 360.   ² See No. 382.   ³ No. 392.

⁴ In tel. 55-S.C. of 12 May Lord Mountbatten sent Lord Ismay an extract of Sardar Patel's statement consisting of the last sentence of para. 1 and paras. 2 and 3 of No. 375. R/3/1/153: f 10.

strongly that Pakistan will wish to remain within the Commonwealth and therefore I do not anticipate any trouble as far as he is concerned.

11. Please circulate copies of this telegram and VCP 40[5] to Cabinet Committee. You may use my 28–S.C. of 8th May as you think fit.

[5] No. 273.

410

Rear-Admiral Viscount Mountbatten of Burma to Lord Ismay (via India Office)

Telegram, Mountbatten Papers. Official Correspondence Files:
Transfer of Power, Part II(a)

IMMEDIATE   SIMLA, *11 May 1947, 9.30 pm*
SECRET   *Received: 12 May, 6.20 am*

No. 56–S.C. Background to my telegram 53–S.C.[1] is as follows.

1. Although Nehru had been consulted by us in the preparation of the plan and had given his general agreement to the version contained in VCP 42[2] which Mieville showed him,[3] I had an absolute hunch that the redraft from London might not be accepted by Congress.

2. Accordingly last night, having made real friends with Nehru during his stay here, I asked him whether he would look at the London draft, as an act of friendship and on the understanding that he would not utilise his prior knowledge or mention to his colleagues that he had seen it. He readily gave this undertaking and took the draft to bed. Next morning I received a letter[4] from him in his own handwriting the text of which is in my immediately following telegram.[5]

3. You can imagine the bombshell this has been. It coincided with Jenkins' arrival to confirm his telegram No. 87–G of 10th May.[6]

4. Jenkins pointed out[7] that an additional Infantry division less one brigade would require to be moved into the partition area of the Punjab, to arrive at least five days before the announcement. This would be virtually impossible to achieve if the announcement was on the 22nd May.

5. Jenkins went on to say that unless the principal party leaders wholeheartedly agreed with the partition plan and publicly announced their agreement, large scale riots would be inevitable, probably culminating in civil war.

6. Since Nehru made it abundantly clear that the plan in its present form would never be agreed to by Congress, and since he now said it would require ample time after the plan had been handed to leaders for the Congress Working

Committee to consider even a revised version of the plan, it became obvious that the accelerated date could not be adhered to.

7. I should like you to remain in London to help with the redrafting of the plan and to pilot through my proposals on dominion status.

8. Please tell Auchinleck.

¹ No. 407.   ² This was the same as No. 279.
³ See No. 257.   ⁴ No. 402.
⁵ Tel. 57–S.C. of 11 May, which forwarded the text of No. 402, is in Mountbatten Papers, Official Correspondence Files: Transfer of Power, Part II(a).
⁶ No. 374.   ⁷ See No. 403.

411

Statement made by Mr Jinnah at New Delhi on 11 May 1947

R/3/1/153: ff 23–5

My attention has been drawn to an interview given by Mr. Patel to the A.P.A.[1] His solution comes to this: that all power should be immediately transferred to the Central Government as it now stands and strong Central Government will then be able to maintain peace in the country; and the Viceroy and every other authority under the present constitution should stand out and the Government of India Act of 1935 should cease to function. And then Mr. Patel says, if there will be any conflict in the Cabinet over any question, the Congress brute majority will rule both in the Cabinet and the present existing legislature. Then he will proceed with the existing administrative machinery, which is to be handed over to him throughout the country, with the Police and the armed forces including the British troops, to put down everybody in the country and crush particularly the 100 million Mussalmans. This is his prescription and way of keeping peace.

I note that he has now developed a sudden affection for "Dominion Status" and "Dominion functions". I wonder what has happened to the recent Resolutions passed by the Congress at its Sessions only a few months ago and the sister body, which the rump Constituent Assembly has now become, which is run by the Congress authoritative caucus, where they passed Resolutions solemnly deciding that India shall be an independent sovereign republic.[2] The Muslim League will never agree to such a monstrous proposal as the one put forward by Mr. Patel, to restore peace, which is only a dream of his.

Then he says that in case the British decided upon the division of India, power should be transferred to the Central Government and let the Viceroy stand out and not interfere, and he will have a strong Centre capable of dealing

¹ See No. 375.   ² See Vol. IX, No. 190.

with the problems facing the country. This makes neither sense nor logic. If the British decide that India must be divided and it follows that the armed forces must be divided and power transferred to the divided parts, then the Central Government must be dissolved and all power should be transferred to the two Constituent Assemblies formed and representing Pakistan and Hindustan. Mr. Patel says the Congress has always proclaimed that it will not coerce any group or area which does not want to live with Hindustan, but what is the use of saying the Congress has proclaimed it will not coerce any group or area and all the time threatening those who want to separate with all sorts of consequences and obstructing and making it more and more difficult for them to separate in a friendly way.

It is quite obvious that Mr. Patel and the Congress say that they will not compel any group or area to remain in Hindustan or use force but they are [? act] just the contrary. Why not agree? But now a new stunt has been started: that if you want division they will accept it, but we are told that it will result in the division of the Punjab and Bengal. This is another sinister move and he threatens that if non-Muslims are forced into Pakistan there will be civil war. Mr. Patel cannot see that the demand for the division of India is based on the fundamental principle that we already have our national homelands, where we want to establish a national State. It is based entirely on a different principle as I have recently pointed out in a Statement of mine,[3] whereas this new Congress stunt—the partition of Bengal and the Punjab— is started on the ground that the non-Muslim minorities there will not receive fair treatment from the Government of these provinces because the Muslims will be in a majority. The same argument applies with much greater force with regard to the Muslims and non-Caste Hindus in Hindu majority pro- vinces, especially because the Muslims form a much smaller minority than the Hindus in Punjab and Bengal. This must lead to the fragmentation of several provinces—and this cannot be supported morally—and it is absolutely des- tructive—because it will lead to seriously breaking up the provinces economi- cally; splitting up the Hindus and Sikhs and politically not only dangerous for the present but more so in the future.

The next point Mr. Patel referred to was that division of India would be difficult to carry out by June 1948 and he visualized, perhaps, years to effect the division especially the army and emphasizes that the division of the army would cause delay. It is difficult for me to believe that His Majesty's Govern- ment has fixed the deadline of June 1948 at random. The issue of division of India has been before us since 1940 and the question of the division of defence was discussed threadbare with the Cabinet Delegation in March last year and for months before their departure. Since then the alternative of division of India has received the closest attention of His Majesty's Government and the army authorities. And when the White Paper of 20th February contemplated one of the alternatives that power is to be transferred to the provinces, surely they could not have overlooked the question of defence. Transfer of power without division of the armed forces is meaningless. Besides, I see myself no difficulty in dividing the armed forces for Pakistan and Hindustan.

Lastly, Mr. Patel wants to make out that he is all saint of reasonableness and that I am the devil. He says "we asked him to refer the question to U.N.O. He says no," and "We asked him to arbitrate, he again says no." Either Mr. Patel has not got a good memory or he deliberately wants to mislead the people in India and abroad. Last August Mr. Patel accused me of what he called intransigent attitude on my part and in reply I pointed out that the demand of Pakistan was based on the right of self-determination, which is the birthright of Mussalmans and it is not and cannot be a justiciable issue. Any intelligent man would understand that the right of self-determination is an inalienable right of a nation and the recognition of the sovereignty of the people of that nation by a democratic process and it cannot be made the subject of vote of two nations Hindus and Muslims and such a process if adopted, the result is a foregone conclusion because there is a brute Hindu majority of 3 to 1. Nor can it be made subject of arbitration by any other authority. Mr. Patel knows it but he is repeating this song to confuse people here and abroad by misrepresentation.[4]

[3] See Annex I to No. 276.
[4] This full text of Mr Jinnah's statement was sent to Mr Abell by his private secretary on 14 May 1947. On 13 May Lord Mountbatten had sent Lord Ismay in tel. 75–S.C. the text of the statement as it had appeared in that day's papers. R/3/1/153: ff 22, 18–20.

412

Rear-Admiral Viscount Mountbatten of Burma to Lord Ismay (via India Office)

Telegram, Mountbatten Papers. Official Correspondence Files:
Transfer of Power, Part II(a)

IMMEDIATE   SIMLA, *11 May 1947, 11.40 pm*
TOP SECRET   *Received: 11 May, 11.20 pm*
No. 60–S.C. Further to my 57–S.C.[1]

1. I will telegraph as soon as possible the outline of how the draft announcement should be amended in order to meet the points raised by Nehru today. This will mean a very considerable recast both in principle and detail. I doubt whether I will be able to let you have this in time for the Cabinet Committee meeting on afternoon of Monday 12th May.

[1] See No. 410, note 5.

2. I can only hope, though after today I can be sure of nothing, that Congress will accept the plan when thus redrafted. But in case they do not, I feel that I should have a further alternative to threaten them with, in the same way as I have one to threaten Jinnah with (see my 20 and 21–S.C. of 8th).[2] Something on the lines of demission of power including Central Subjects to the Provinces is in my mind. I will telegraph further on this also.

[2] Nos. 346 and 351.

413

Sir E. Mieville to Lord Ismay (via India Office)

Telegram, R/3/1/153: f 11

IMMEDIATE   SIMLA, *12 May 1947, 12 noon*[1]
TOP SECRET

No. 61–S.C. Strictly private for Ismay from Mieville.

We are naturally a bit rattled by Nehru's *volte face* yesterday and can only be thankful that we did not wait until meeting of leaders to find out his attitude. I cannot help thinking that his party must have got at him. The Viceroy is now wondering more and more whether we ought not to work on the lines of trying to demit power on Dominion Status basis at an early date with Jinnah being given adequate safeguards in the interim period. What do you think?

[1] Though timed at 12 noon on 12 May this telegram would probably have been drafted before the beginning of the Viceroy's Staff Meeting that morning at 11.30 am (see No. 414).

414

Minutes of Viceroy's Thirty First Staff Meeting

Mountbatten Papers.

TOP SECRET

Those present at this Meeting held at Viceregal Lodge, Simla on 12 May 1947 at 11.30 am were: Rear-Admiral Viscount Mountbatten of Burma, Sir E. Mieville, Captain Brockman, Mr I. D. Scott, Rao Bahadur V. P. Menon, Mr Campbell-Johnson, Lieutenant-Colonel Erskine Crum

Item 1

THE CHOICE BY PROVINCES OF THEIR OWN FUTURE

HIS EXCELLENCY THE VICEROY said that whereas all the Indian parties seemed to have reasonable faith in the honesty and straightforwardness of himself and his staff, there appeared to be a unanimous phobia amongst them about any document issuing from London, in which they expected and looked for, crookedness and catches. Therefore, reframing of the Draft Announcement in a way to make it acceptable to Congress would have to be done by his own staff in India.

The Punjab

MR SCOTT said that he was very much opposed to the separate procedure which had been suggested by the meeting the previous day for Gurdaspur. He felt that any departure from the principle of clearly defining the notional boundary between Muslim and non-Muslim majority areas would lead to a spate of demands for other departures.

HIS EXCELLENCY THE VICEROY said that he did not intend to incorporate the suggestion for Gurdaspur made the previous day. Instead the Boundary Commission would be instructed to arrange for the handover from one side to the other of any area within border districts where there was clearly a majority of the opposite community.

Bengal

After discussion, HIS EXCELLENCY THE VICEROY decided that the plan should be redrafted on the basis of no option for independence being given to Bengal or any other Province. It would, he pointed out, always be possible to reconsider this decision at any time if there was an united request for independence.

Baluchistan

HIS EXCELLENCY THE VICEROY:

directed D.P.S.V. to draft for his approval a letter to Pandit Nehru asking for proposals on how to ascertain the will of the people of Baluchistan.

The Name of the Plan in the Draft Announcement

HIS EXCELLENCY THE VICEROY:

decided that this plan would in future be known by the name "Plan WE", as under it we (the British) would be responsible for carrying out the various processes.

Item 2

PANDIT NEHRU'S PLAN

HIS EXCELLENCY THE VICEROY said that he had the previous evening further discussed with Pandit Nehru the plan which he had put forward for the early demission of power to the Interim Government on a Dominion status basis. This plan was really very similar to the alternative plan with which he had previously decided to threaten Mr Jinnah if the latter did not accept Plan WE.

HIS EXCELLENCY THE VICEROY said that it was apparent that control of the Army was going to be the most difficult issue in the transfer of power on a Dominion status basis. It was apparent that it was Congress's idea that they should have almost full control of the Army except on very limited subjects, for which the Joint Defence Council would be in control.

HIS EXCELLENCY THE VICEROY said that Pandit Nehru had emphasised to him his belief that it would not be possible for either himself (His Excellency) or the British as a whole, to devise an acceptable solution for India. Furthermore, if the British did give a decision and it was regarded (as it almost certainly would be regarded) as an award, and if bloodshed followed, not only would the British have to take the blame but also Indo-British relations would deteriorate. Pandit Nehru had expressed the view that the Indians should take the blame. Pandit Nehru had reiterated that he would be prepared to afford all manner of safeguards and assurances to the Muslim League if power was handed over to the present Interim Government. He had also agreed that it would be possible to proceed with the proposal for a referendum in the N.W.F.P. and for Boundary Commissions.

HIS EXCELLENCY THE VICEROY said that he considered that this plan would be far more acceptable to Mr Jinnah if all preparations including, for example, choice of capitals, were made before it was put up to him. Simla might be loaned to Pakistan as the seat of Government as a temporary measure. Lahore might become, with the existing machinery, the seat of the Western Punjab Provincial Government. Eastern Punjab might be amalgamated temporarily with the United Provinces. The Government of Western Bengal would presumably be at Calcutta. Dacca and Chittagong were possibilities for the capital of Eastern Bengal.

SIR ERIC MIEVILLE and MR SCOTT both stated that they did not think that there was any prospect of Mr Jinnah preferring this plan to Plan WE.

HIS EXCELLENCY THE VICEROY:

(i) decided that this plan should be called "Plan THEY" as it would be the Indians who would be responsible for carrying it through;

(ii) invited Prin. Sec. to arrange for the staff to prepare a telegram, in due course, to Lord Ismay on this plan and to draft Heads of Agreement on the various safeguards which would have to be agreed between Pandit Nehru and Mr Jinnah before it was put into operation.

415

Cabinet

India and Burma Committee. Paper I.B.(47)66

L/P&J/10/79: ff 197–200

VICEROY'S SUGGESTED AMENDMENTS TO DRAFT STATEMENT

MEMORANDUM BY THE SECRETARY OF STATE FOR INDIA

INDIA OFFICE, *12 May 1947*

The Viceroy has seen the text of the draft announcement as revised on the 8th May and has suggested a number of amendments.[1] Some of these are small drafting points which can be made but there are three amendments and amendments consequential to them which I think the Committee should consider.

A. *The North-West Frontier Province.*

1. The Viceroy proposes to substitute for paragraph 8 of the text annexed to I.B.(47)65[2] the following:—

"8. The position in the North-West Frontier Province is exceptional and, after other Provinces have decided the issues put before them, the electorate in the North-West Frontier Province will be asked to choose which group of Provinces they wish to join. For this purpose, a referendum to electors will be held under the aegis of the Governor-General and in consultation with the Provincial Government."

The Viceroy's reasons for this re-draft are:—

(i) He considers that the N.W.F.P. should not be given the option of becoming an independent Province. It is substantially in deficit and therefore incapable of independent existence. The grant of independence to the N.W.F.P. might also encourage irredentist ideas in Afghanistan.

(ii) The Viceroy does not wish any reference made to an election being held if the referendum is in favour of Pakistan.

Consequential upon this amendment the Viceroy deletes the relevant passage in paragraph 9 and paragraph 13

2. This raises a considerable point of principle. The basis of the Statement as at present drafted is that the areas in question have self-determination. Sylhet is also probably incapable of separate economic survival, but the Committee's view at a previous meeting was that the same principles should apply to Sylhet as the other areas. Paragraph 15 also gives to Baluchistan the option

---

[1] See tel. 48—S. C. of 11 May. Mountbatten Papers, Official Correspondence Files: Provinces and their future, Part I(b).

[2] See No. 379 and its note 4.

to remain independent. If the option to remain independent is withdrawn from the North-West Frontier Province it ought also to be withdrawn from Baluchistan and Sylhet. Baluchistan will then have to go with the N.W.F.P. Sylhet could then only opt to go with Assam or with Eastern Bengal. But Assam could not have the right to exclude Sylhet unless Eastern Bengal would take it in. Theoretically, under the Statement as drafted the two parts of the Punjab and Bengal can remain independent though this is unlikely to happen. I should have preferred to apply the same principle throughout as the Committee had hitherto contemplated, but it may be felt that we must defer to the Viceroy's strong view at the cost of illogicality.

3. If so, I have the following comments on the Viceroy's redraft:—

(a) I think it should be transferred to come immediately before the existing paragraph 14, firstly because the referendum cannot take place until the other processes described in paragraphs 9–12 have taken place and, secondly, because the reference in the Viceroy's draft to choosing which group of Provinces they wish to join comes as a surprise to the reader in its present position.

(b) The Viceroy's redraft makes no provision for the election of new representatives by the N.W.F.P., who could represent it in a new Constituent Assembly if it shows for Pakistan. This is because he does not wish to mention new elections. I suggest that this might be met by adding to paragraph 17 the following:—

"If the North-West Frontier Province adheres to any new Constituent Assembly, new representatives will require to be elected on the basis of one for every $\frac{1}{4}$ million of the population. The number to be elected will be:—

Muslims	General	Total
11	1	12"

B. The Viceroy proposes an amendment of paragraph 11 as in the annexure. I prefer the existing draft but should be prepared to accept the Viceroy's redraft.

C. Paragraph 21. The Viceroy proposes to omit "by agreement between those concerned" at the end of the second sentence and to substitute "in consultation with those concerned".

This is important because it makes H.M.G. responsible for setting up a Boundary Commission in the absence of agreement on membership and terms of reference. Both of these may be highly controversial. I should be reluctant to be committed in advance to arbitrating upon them. An alternative would be to omit this part of the sentence and say only that a Boundary Commission should be set up.

4. I draw attention also to the revised text of the first four lines of paragraph

18 in I.B.(47)65.[3] This is to meet the point that only parts of Provinces require to re-elect Constituent Assembly representatives. It follows that Sind and N.W.F.P. should be deleted from the Table in paragraph 18 and this will be done. L.

Annexure to No. 415
VICEROY'S REDRAFT

11. (A). The representatives so elected of the two parts of Bengal and of the Punjab sitting separately will be empowered to vote whether or not their Provinces should be divided. If a simple majority of either body votes in favour of partition the division will take place.

(B) However, before the vote in 11 (A) is taken, it is desirable that representatives should clearly know the alternative to partition. Therefore, if there is a demand for it, a preliminary joint meeting of representatives of both parts of Bengal will be held. At this meeting, the representatives will be asked whether in the event of the two parts of the Province subsequently agreeing to remain united, the whole Province should remain independent or enter a Constituent Assembly with other Provinces; and, in the latter event, which Constituent Assembly. A similar opportunity will be made available to the Punjab.

(C) If, as a result of the above procedure, a decision in favour of partition is reached in Bengal and/or the Punjab the representatives of parts of the Province or Provinces affected will decide on behalf of areas which they represent, which of the three options in paragraph No. 4 they choose.

[3] Para. 18 of I.B.(47)65 was the same as para. 18 of No. 379 except that the first sentence had been amended to read:

'Where it is decided that a Province will collaborate with the existing Constituent Assembly, the representatives originally elected to that Constituent Assembly will continue to serve. Where the decision is that part of a Province will join the existing Constituent Assembly it will be necessary to hold a fresh election of representatives on the same scale of one representative for every million of the population as was prescribed by the Cabinet Mission.'

L/P &J/10/79: f 205.

416

Chiefs of Staff Committee. C.O.S. (47) 62nd Meeting

L/WS/1/1030: ff 5–12

Those present at this meeting held on 12 May 1947 at 11.30 am were: Marshal of the Royal Air Force Lord Tedder (in the Chair), Admiral Sir John H. D. Cunningham, Field Marshal Viscount Montgomery of Alamein, Lieutenant-General Sir Leslie C. Hollis
Also present were: Mr Alexander, Lord Ismay, Major-General R. E. Laycock

India—Partition Proposals
J.P. (47) 65 Final[1]
(Previous Reference: C.O.S. (47) 61st Meeting, Minute 7)[2]

THE COMMITTEE had before them a report[3] by the Joint Planning Staff attaching an Aide-Mémoire for use by the Chiefs of Staff in their discussion with Lord Ismay and as a possible basis for any advice they might decide to submit to the Cabinet; and a minute by the Secretary covering a minute from the Prime Minister[4] asking for their appreciation, from the military point of view, on the position in the event of (a) Western India, (b) Bengal or (c) one of the States with a seaboard such as Travancore desiring to remain in the Commonwealth when the rest of India decides to go out.

LORD ISMAY said he had been asked by the Cabinet to give the Chiefs of Staff a résumé of the political background which had led to the formulation of the new plan now under discussion by His Majesty's Government together with an explanation of the Viceroy's proposals and a forecast of what might follow their adoption.

Political Background
The general position was that communal feeling dominated and influenced the whole attitude and outlook of both Moslems and Hindus. It was far worse than he had imagined, and was much more serious than at the time of the Cabinet Mission's visit to India. The outlook of the leading politicians was entirely coloured by race hatred to such an extent that no logic or reasoning could influence them either to co-operation between themselves or to work out the plans necessary to the hand-over of power from Britain to India.

On assuming office, the Viceroy had held a series of talks with the political leaders to determine what chances there were of bringing the Moslems and Hindus together to work out a plan for a unified India. The Viceroy had found that no chance of achieving this object existed, and he had been forced to abandon the Cabinet Mission plan and to put forward his alternative proposals for the hand-over of power.

The plan had been prepared under threatening circumstances. The situation was such that if no announcement was made in the very near future, outlining the British proposals for the hand-over of power, there was almost certain to be a civil war. On the other hand, though the main features of the plan had been discussed privately with the leading political figures, who had indicated a certain measure of concurrence in it, it may not avoid the risk of disorders, particularly in the States of Bengal and the Punjab. There was however, no likelihood of a "joint" plan evolved by the various parties in India. The issue was a case of certain civil war in the absence of a plan, and the risk of disorders arising from opposition to the plan now proposed.

Viceroy's Proposals

The present plan contemplated Pakistan. It did not order or decree that there should be a Pakistan, but left the composition and extent of Pakistan to be settled by the Indians themselves. The two main difficulties were the position of the States of Bengal and the Punjab. The difficulty about the latter in holding an election as to whether the Punjab should be under Pakistan or Hindustan was in the first place the position of the Sikhs, and secondly in the event of a division of the Province such matters as the division of the irrigation system. In Bengal, Calcutta would no doubt remain with the Hindus, but East Bengal would be placed in a difficult position, if the main port was separated from its natural hinterland. A further difficulty was the position of the North West frontier States, where the population consisted of 97% Moslems, at present administered by a Congress Ministry. It was clear in this case that the tribes would not have Hindu domination, and were threatening violence if election facilities were not given them to determine whether they should choose to remain allied with Hindustan or Pakistan. It was the intention to have this election, but authority to do so could not be given at the present stage, under the threat of blackmail.

Forecast of Future Events

It was not possible to say into what number of independent States India would be divided on transfer of power. This would depend upon the results of the proposed elections, and upon the attitude of some of the Indian States, which at present remained uncertain. The main division would be—

(a) Pakistan comprising Sind, Baluchistan, North West Frontier Province,

[1] See note 3 below.
[2] At this meeting, held on 7 May 1947, Sir Leslie Hollis said he understood major decisions on the future of India were likely to be taken at the Cabinet meeting on 12 May. He suggested that the Chiefs of Staff would wish to meet Lord Ismay before this meeting and it was agreed that the Joint Planning Staff should note which points in their opinion required military observations or advice and should prepare an *aide mémoire* for use at a meeting with Lord Ismay on 12 May. L/WS/1/1030: f 26.
[3] *Ibid:* ff 15–19.   [4] No. 387.

the Western Punjab and Assam, with possibly a part of Bengal.

(b) Hindustan.

It was feasible that Jinnah, after the announcement of the plan, might well announce Moslem application to remain within the Commonwealth. A number of the Princes might do similarly. On the other hand, Hindustan might well stick to the declared intention of Congress to be a free Sovereign State, although there were signs that some Congress leaders had doubts of their ability to continue without some British advisers and administrators. The strategic issue which would have to be faced by the Chiefs of Staff was therefore the effect of all Succession States remaining, at least temporarily, in the Commonwealth, and secondly, the effect of Pakistan applying for inclusion in the Commonwealth while Hindustan remained out. The Viceroy and all his advisers in India had adopted a completely non-committal attitude towards the political leaders in India on this question, since to indicate that we should be favourably disposed to those who wished to remain within the Commonwealth, would be to open ourselves to strong criticism that we never intended to leave India and that we were pursuing a policy of dividing India and ensuring that we remained.

In answer to a question from the Chief of the Air Staff about the position of the Indian Army, LORD ISMAY said that Jinnah was completely opposed to continuing the present Indian Army as a unified force of all races. He would insist on its division, and would create a Moslem Army of their own. It was thus necessary to start planning the division of the Indian Army. This was being done under the direction of the Commander-in-Chief, and in consultation with both Moslems and Hindus. No division would, however, take place before the hand-over of power to the Indians.

LORD TEDDER said the Moslems would possess no Air Force after a division of the present Indian Air Force which was composed of 80% Hindus. The provision of an efficient Air Force and Air Base facilities in N.W. India was most important.

THE MINISTER OF DEFENCE said, that in the announcement of December 6th, His Majesty's Government had stated that they would not be a party to forcing the Indians as a whole, or in any section, to remain within the Commonwealth. The plan of the Cabinet Mission had been to hand over power if possible to a united India. After a series of exhaustive talks, the Viceroy had advised that such a solution was impossible. His Majesty's Government were therefore now examining what form partition should take. As he saw it, any opposition that would come from the Moslems, would be on the grounds that the present plan did not grant them the whole of their wishes in the form of the original Pakistan. The Hindus might accept the new plan, providing the future of the disputed provinces in India, i.e. Bengal and the Punjab, were settled by electoral means, and partitioned into those areas which wished to remain with Pakistan or Hindustan.

He noted that from a recent telegram,[5] the Hindus were agreeable to using the term "The Union of India" instead of "The Republic of India" as describing the areas administered by Congress. The intention of the new plan was to hand over power to a Central Government, giving power to the Provinces of electing to remain outside the authority of this Central Government and to determine whether they should become independent, part of a Pakistan system of government, and whether they should remain within or outside the Commonwealth.

LORD ISMAY said that the term "Union of India" as opposed to the "Republic of India" had much to commend it. On the other hand, it did imply by inference, that States remaining outside the Union of India might be regarded as rebels. If its adoption by Congress displayed this motive, it ought to be treated with careful consideration before we acquiesced.

THE MINISTER OF DEFENCE asked the Chiefs of Staff for their views on the strategic implications of the issue put to them by the Prime Minister, namely, if Succession States or one such as Travancore desired to remain within the Commonwealth when the rest of India decided to go out. In this connection, he referred to a memorandum[6] by the Secretary of State for India, containing a plan designed to follow upon a partition of India resulting from the Viceroy's proposals. It was a method of transferring power to successor authorities in India which would result in a form of transitional Constitution analogous to that of a Dominion.

The object would be to transfer power immediately, and at the same time to preserve the constitutional leadership and arbitral position of the Governor-General, and to introduce a measure of gradualness and continuity during the process of transfer. The transitional Dominion status would continue until and unless brought to an end by the terms of Treaties to be concluded by Great Britain on the one hand and the Successor Governments in India on the other.

The plan had certain advantages in that it would remove the main causes of communal and political bitterness, and by lessening the urgency for framing new Constitutions and creating new administrative machinery, would increase the likelihood that this would prove to be workable and sound. It would also, by providing an opportunity for joint consultation on matters of general interest, create conditions favourable to an ultimate union of all the Indias. Dominion status, if it worked well, might also prove to be acceptable as a permanent arrangement.

LORD TEDDER said that in his opinion, the most clearly desirable position from the strategic point of view, was that all Succession States remained in

[5] No. 357.
[6] No. 388 which circulated the note in No. 273.

the British Commonwealth. The continued co-operation of India in Common-wealth Defence would add greatly to our strength. The position whereby some States remained in and some elected to go out of the Commonwealth did not alter the principle that we required certain strategic facilities in India. No matter how small these facilities ultimately were, some were better than none, and if any one, or several, or all States elected to remain within the Commonwealth, he did not see how we could be placed in the position of ejecting them, particularly in the case of the Moslem States, where a refusal to allow them to remain within the Commonwealth would have repercussions throughout the entire Middle East.

SIR JOHN CUNNINGHAM entirely agreed, and said that apart from the moral and sentimental arguments, that it would be invidious to refuse the application of people who had been loyal to the Commonwealth for many years to remain in, the results of such a refusal would extend throughout the whole Moslem world, and our relations with all the peoples following this creed would be shattered to the detriment of our strategic position in the Middle East, North Africa and India. As he saw it, the immediate position was whether the United Kingdom could place itself in a position as encouraging single or several States to remain within the Commonwealth and whether or not we had the forces to guarantee their defence from external aggression from Hindustan States.

THE MINISTER OF DEFENCE said that when His Majesty's Government had decided to pursue the policy recommended by the Cabinet Mission last year, they had done so because the alternative was to decide to stay in India for a period of between 15 and 20 years, in the course of which they might have had to adopt repressive measures involving the use of a number of divisions. It would have been impossible to provide these divisions, and the alternative adopted by His Majesty's Government had been to hand over to a unified India by a certain date. The internal political position in the Congress Party was that extremist elements had always declared that Britain would not leave India of her own accord, and that the only way to get her to do so would be by a revolution of the people. From the political point of view, therefore, the objections to admitting a claim by Mr. Jinnah or others wishing to stay within the Commonwealth, was that we opened ourselves to the charge that this was an example of British bad faith; that the British had never really had any intention of leaving India, and that in order to obtain their requirements, they had manoeuvred the country into partition. Moreover, His Majesty's Government had previously given a pledge that we should not remain in India to defend one community or minority against the other, though this pledge had been given under the provision that we should be handing over power to a unified Indian authority.

LORD MONTGOMERY said that from the broad aspect of Commonwealth strategy, it would be a tremendous asset if Pakistan, particularly the North West, remained within the Commonwealth. The bases, airfields and ports in North West India would be invaluable to Commonwealth defence. Moreover, our presence would make for better civil administration, since British advisers, both civil and military, would ensure the efficiency of the Province, and might well attract Hindu States into adopting a similar relationship with the Commonwealth. In addition we should be in a much stronger position to support the integrity of Afghanistan. In his opinion, there were strong arguments in favour of Pakistan remaining within the Commonwealth, and the sooner this happened the better.

LORD ISMAY said that on the other hand the danger must be acknowledged that we might become involved in a war between Hindustan and Pakistan, and incur the permanent hostility of Hindustan. The Viceroy was convinced that it would be disastrous to allow only, for example, Pakistan to remain in, and thus back up one part of India against the other. Whilst he (the Viceroy) personally was much in favour of British India as a whole being permitted to remain in the Commonwealth, he was opposed to a system of alliance, as it would not enable the British by their presence to help India in the way they best could. The Viceroy had therefore adopted a neutral attitude on the whole question of applications from States to be admitted to the British Commonwealth. However, if Pakistan was accepted in the British Commonwealth, though Hindustan would be loud in denunciation of our bad faith at first, they would not, in his opinion, be permanently hostile to the British Commonwealth, or seek to ally themselves with any other great power.

THE CHIEFS OF STAFF agreed, and said that there was even a slight chance that in these circumstances Hindustan might think that it was to their advantage to associate themselves with the Commonwealth. Even though the acceptance of Pakistan into the Commonwealth involved a commitment either in support against Hindustan or in maintaining stability on the frontier, the danger and extent of the commitment would be small, particularly in the latter case where the frontier position might well become more settled, since the relations between the tribes and Pakistan would be easier.

The Chiefs of Staff agreed in further discussion that their views should be submitted to the Prime Minister in reply to his minute on the following lines.

From the strategic point of view there were overwhelming arguments in favour of Western Pakistan remaining within the Commonwealth, namely, that we should obtain important strategic facilities, the port of Karachi, air bases and the support of Moslem manpower in the future; be able to ensure the continued integrity of Afghanistan; and be able to increase our prestige and improve our position throughout the Moslem world. Whilst the acceptance of Pakistan only into the Commonwealth would involve a commitment for its support against Hindustan, the danger would be small, and it was doubtful if Pakistan or any state would ask for more than the assistance of British Officers in executive and advisory positions.

Our presence in Pakistan might have a stabilising effect on India as a whole, and the position in the frontier might well become more settled. There was therefore everything to gain by admitting Western Pakistan into the Commonwealth. A refusal of an application to this end would amount to ejecting loyal people from the British Commonwealth, and would probably lose us all chances of ever getting strategic facilities anywhere in India, and at the same time shatter our reputation in the rest of the Moslem world. From the military point of view, such results would be catastrophic.

In a greater or lesser degree, the same arguments applied to admitting Bengal or Travancore into the Commonwealth. Though neither of these States by themselves offered the same positive strategic advantages as North West India, the results of a refusal to include them in the Commonwealth were much the same. The most likely case was that all three of the areas, and perhaps other Indian States in addition, would apply for inclusion in the Commonwealth, and not one only. In these circustances, the military advantages of admitting them would be even greater than in the case of Western Pakistan alone.

The Chiefs of Staff therefore most emphatically believe that there were great military advantages in accepting a claim from any or all of the areas wishing to remain within the Commonwealth, and grave military disadvantages in refusing such an application.[7]

THE COMMITTEE:

(a) Took note of the statement from Lord Ismay of the political background to the Viceroy's proposals for the hand-over of power in India.

(b) Instructed the Secretary to submit their views as outlined in discussion in the form of a minute to the Prime Minister.[8]

[7] Sir D. Monteath remarked on these minutes: 'The acceptance of Pakistan as a Dominion in the Commonwealth is interpreted as meaning "our continued presence" there. But does it?' Mr Turnbull added: 'And does it mean their cooperation in Defence matters?' L/PO/6/120: f 46.

[8] Sir Leslie Hollis did this in a minute dated 12 May. L/WS/1/1030: ff 13–14.

417

The Earl of Listowel to Mr Attlee

L/PO/8/45: ff 52–4

INDIA OFFICE, *12 May 1947*
Secretary of State's Minute: Serial No. 71/47

Prime Minister.

Lord Ismay has shown me the two telegrams[1] from the Viceroy (which I attach) which indicate clearly enough that though Lord Mountbatten is determined to take no action in the matter which by its timing could be construed as a surrender to political pressure, he no longer has confidence in Sir Olaf Caroe as a Governor fully competent to hold the situation in the North West Frontier Province and feels that he must be replaced at the suitable juncture.

Sir Olaf has, quite undeservedly I am sure, become suspect of being a definite sympathiser with the Moslem League: this I am convinced is a totally unfair suspicion: but in his position as both Governor of a Province which has a Congress (albeit mainly Moslem) Ministry and Agent to the Governor-General for the Tribal areas on the Frontier and in this regard subordinate to Nehru, the Member for External Affairs, this unjust belief undermines the reputation for impartiality on which his ability to control the extremely difficult situation must so much depend. I am told that Sir Olaf, though a man of great intellectual capacity, is highly strung and is prone to suffer these aspersions on his impartiality less easily than a man of more equable temperament.

In the light of these considerations I find it impossible to resist the Viceroy's desire to make a change when the suitable moment arrives: and, with your approval, I propose to inform him that I concur in his intention.

As to the manner of achieving it I would propose to suggest to him that he induce Sir Olaf to ask permission of the King to lay down his office, on the medical consideration that he is over-strained and needs relief from his responsibilities, as soon as the Viceroy finds it possible to recommend the grant of such permission.

To succeed Sir Olaf Lord Mountbatten recommends the selection of Lieutenant-General Sir R.M.M. Lockhart, now General Officer Commanding in Chief, Southern Army. He, you will remember, was Principal Staff Officer in the India Office in the early days of the War. He has, as a soldier, long Indian experience and a profound knowledge of the North West Frontier, and, personally, the temperament required. He handled the situation in Bombay

---

[1] Nos. 328 and 342.

at the time of the Royal Indian Navy Mutiny with great ability. The Commander in Chief is prepared to make him available when required provided that, as seems to me only fair to Sir Rob Lockhart and other senior officers in the Indian Army, he remains on the active list but supernumerary to establishment, and so eligible for promotion which is due later in the year.

If you approve the selection of General Lockhart I propose to set out the whole situation to Sir A. Lascelles as soon as possible and obtain His Majesty's provisional approval of the arrangements in view.[2]

LISTOWEL

[2] On 29 May Mr Harris noted that Lord Listowel had spoken on this subject with Lord Mountbatten at Northolt that day. Lord Mountbatten 'informed him that he had discussed the matter with the Prime Minister and it had been agreed between them that no action should be taken at any rate until after the referendum due to be held in the N.W.F.P.' L/PO/8/45: f 51.

418

Sir N. Brook to Mr Attlee

Public Record Office. CAB 21/1803

12 May 1947

Prime Minister.

The attached telegram[1] from the Viceroy confirms the feeling which has been growing on me in recent weeks that we ought to be giving serious and urgent consideration to the possibility of finding some form of association other than the existing "Dominion status" in which independent States can maintain the British connection.

This is not merely a question for India alone. Eire is already in an anomalous position, as an independent Republic within the Commonwealth. South Africa was chafing at Dominion status before the war and may do so again, particularly when she is no longer guided by Field Marshal Smuts. And even Smuts dislikes the terms "Dominions" and "Commonwealth" and prefers nowadays to speak of "the British group". India and Burma have both been promised "independence within the Commonwealth"; and now Ceylon is asking for it too.

It looks as though we might have a chance of keeping both Indias within the Commonwealth if we could devise some form of association of independent peoples other than "Dominions". And it seems to me anomalous that Sir Walter Monckton should be directing himself to this problem in India on behalf of Nehru[2] while no sustained effort is being made at home, so far as I am aware, to find a solution on behalf of His Majesty's Government.

I recognise that there are arguments of policy which tend the other way.

But surely we should at least consider whether the true balance of advantage may not lie on the side of a larger though looser association rather than a smaller but more compact Commonwealth of "Dominions" and "Colonies". And enquiry might disclose some new basis of association which would make it unnecessary to choose between those alternatives. We may well fail in the attempt to find a new basis which would hold the whole of our existing group together; but it seems to be wrong to allow the opportunity to go by default.

If this problem is to be examined, how is it to be tackled? If it were referred to the Departmental lawyers, it would get bogged down and even if a solution were found it would probably come too late. The advice of Department-al officials and lawyers will, of course, be required; but the impulse must come from someone with imagination as well as a certain familiarity with constitutional questions. We should want someone of the quality of R. Coupland, or, among the younger men, possibly someone like H.V. Hodson. I mention these names merely to indicate the *type* of man I have in mind: the final choice would require much more thought than I have given it.[3]

You might also wish to appoint a small number of Ministers—e.g. the Secretary of State for Dominion Affairs and the Minister of Defence with yourself in the Chair—to consider questions of major policy and to give guidance to a suitable team of experts.

If you agreed that some such enquiry should be put in hand, I would give further thought to the method and submit more definite proposals. But before those details were further considered, you would doubtless wish to speak of this to the Secretary of State for Dominion Affairs.

NORMAN BROOK

[1] No. 360.   [2] See Nos. 272, Item 1 and 308.
[3] In a subsequent minute, dated 15 May, Sir N. Brook suggested that Professor W. K. Hancock and Miss Margery Perham might also be able to contribute ideas as outside experts. P.R.O. CAB 21/1803.

419

Rear-Admiral Viscount Mountbatten of Burma to Lord Ismay (via India Office)

Telegram, Mountbatten Papers. Official Correspondence Files: Transfer of Power, Part II(a)

IMMEDIATE   SIMLA, *12 May 1947, 4.40 pm*
SECRET   *Received: 12 May, 5 pm*

No. 62–S.C. Reference my 56–S.C. of 11th May.[1]

1. You will have gathered the general tone of Nehru's objections from his letter[2] contained in my 57–S.C. of 11th May. I am also sending you by air-

[1] No. 410.   [2] No. 402.

mail a copy of the note[3] referred to therein. His whole attitude is based on an elaboration of the point about the Union of India to which I referred in my 25–S.C. of 8th May[4] and 43–S.C. of 10th May.[5]

2. His basic argument, with which it is very difficult to disagree, is that the Cabinet Mission's plan is not dead except in a way to the Muslim League; that the Constituent Assembly is functioning except for a few Provinces, and that the Muslim League has joined the Interim Government on the basis of the Cabinet Mission's plan.

3. I asked him whether, if I could get the draft announcement reframed along the lines he wanted, he and the Congress Working Committee would agree to it. He replied "I want to help you, but things that emerge from London are so peculiar". He stressed that a draft known to be mine would be the far more likely to be accepted by all parties.

4. I am, therefore, going to redraft the whole statement myself and will let you have it as soon as possible.

[3] No. 406.   [4] No. 357.   [5] No. 398.

420

Mr Nicholls to Mr Attlee

L/PO/6/120: ff 44–5

TOP SECRET   THE OFFICE OF THE HIGH COMMISSIONER FOR THE
Ref: P.S. 13/1   UNION OF SOUTH AFRICA IN LONDON, *12 May 1947*
My dear Prime Minister.

INDIA

General Smuts has asked me to convey the following message to you with reference to the Dominion Secretary's telegram to Dominion Governments D. No. 439.[1]

"I am obliged for your full statement of the present position in India and for your invitation for comments and suggestions. The programme for partition seems carefully thought out and calls for no comment. But the issues now arising appear so far-reaching and ominous that I take the liberty to suggest another line of thought for your consideration.

When Britain was invited to quit India and acquiesced, it was on the assumption that the invitation came from India as a whole and not from a partitioned, much-divided India. Similarly, Indians may never have contemplated such an invitation if they had foreseen that India would cease to be one, would be partitioned into two or more Indias, and if *both* (?) had considered the consequences for them or their part of India. Nehru's reported statement[2] that

States not joining the present Constituent Assembly would be considered hostile gives point to their misgivings.

For Indians an entirely new situation has been created by the latest developments, and minorities may well ask for an opportunity to reconsider their position. Britain on her part again may well pause before voluntarily quitting India with a prospect before it of partition, chaos, and possibly civil war. Her record in India is so magnificent a chapter of British and World history that it should not end in such a disaster without searching consideration of possible alternatives. Britain still has a duty to India's dumb millions who look to her for justice, as well as to the minorities who may be driven to despair. Quitting India under such conditions never was contemplated and would be an inglorious ending.

It is true that with Britain's announced policy a change now might expose her to charges of duplicity and of breaking faith, but the situation now emerging is essentially an entirely new one, which calls for careful reconsideration of the whole position. Some *locus poenitentiae*, some loophole of escape from a dreadful unforeseen fate might well be left a partitioned India, and especially its minorities, who may become the victims of a catastrophic calamity.

All I can suggest under these circumstances is that the dissenting communities should have the choice, not only of independence and partition, but also of remaining, if they wish, under the British Raj. It is possible that Indian States and minorities, even perhaps the Muslims themselves, exposed to the threat of Hindu domination, may opt for continuance of the British connection. Let it be a free choice all round and not merely to the Hindu majority. The choice in the elections then would be threefold—for joining the Constituent Assembly, for independence of it, and for remaining under the British Raj in terms of the India Act. The proposed scheme may be re-shaped accordingly. Britain may thus retain a solid footing in India, which even apart from the human and economic aspects, would be of far-reaching importance strategically and for the eventual defence of India itself as a whole, should the necessity arise".[3]

I have sent a copy of this letter to the Dominions Secretary.

Yours sincerely,

G. HEATON NICHOLLS

[1] No. 352.

[2] See No. 181, note 2.

[3] The text of Field Marshal Smuts' letter was circulated to the India and Burma Committee under the reference I.B.(47)68 of 13 May 1947.

421

Lord Ismay to Sir E. Mieville (via India Office)

Telegram, R/3/1/153: f 14

IMMEDIATE   *12 May 1947, 10.50 pm*
TOP SECRET   *Received: 13 May, 8 am*

6144. Strictly private for Mieville from Ismay. Your 61–S.C.[1] I do not wonder
that you are rattled by Nehru's *volte face*. So are we.

2. I am all in favour of early dominion status *provided* both sides get a
square deal. But telegrams suggest Congress leaders have got impression that
immediate dominion status for Interim Government might be alternative
to partition plan and that they would then be given a free hand as advocated
in Patel's statement to the Press on 9th May.[2] I do not see how dominion status
without successful partition is possible in present circumstances or what
adequate safeguards for Jinnah to which you refer could be.

[1] No. 413.   [2] No. 375.

422

Lord Ismay to Rear-Admiral Viscount Mountbatten of Burma (via India Office)

Telegram, R/3/1/153: ff 12–13

IMMEDIATE   *12 May 1947, 11.55 pm*
SECRET   *Received: 13 May, 10 am*

No. 6142. Your 60–S.C. 12th May.[1]
Tomorrow's meetings of Cabinet and Cabinet Committee have been postponed pending receipt of your radical revision of draft statement. I have put
off my departure for India.

2. Your telegram 56–S.C. and 57–S.C.[2] came as a bombshell. We have
told Cabinet Committee that Nehru was in general agreement with plan
I brought home and Cabinet have made no changes of substance therein.
Ministers therefore will not understand Nehru's reference to "entirely new
picture".

3. I anxiously await your new proposals and will do my damndest to pilot
them through. Meanwhile the following are preliminary thoughts.

4. I feel that there must be some misunderstanding on the part of Congress
as to scope of your proposals for early Dominion Status. For instance Nehru's
complete rejection of plan we brought home seems to suggest that he believes
there is some alternative plan which would be a substitute for partition.

This is not the case since both Menon's plan[3] and plan in your 54–S.C.[4] proceed on the basis of successful partition and cannot be put into effect until that is achieved.

In para. 4(c) of your 54–S.C. you quote Patel's statement of which you give an extract in 55–S.C.[5] Patel himself seems to have forgotten about partition and on that wants the existing Interim Government to be given a free hand even in the Provincial field. This would be contrary to assurances by H.M.G. and is not I imagine what you contemplate.

5. In order to answer questions in Cabinet Committee I should like to be clear also on the following points. If Hindustan receives Dominion Status before Pakistan will you have any powers other than those which you exercise as Chairman of Defence Council? Would you have any powers in relation to Foreign Affairs and Finance for instance? If you have none it might be impossible to ensure a just partition of resources of Government of India since constitutionally you would have to accept everything proposed by Hindustan Government. If on the other hand you have power to ensure a fair deal for Muslim areas would that not amount to a veto and restore practically same position as at present while making Dominion Status rather a mockery?

6. I think the point will be taken here that though Dominion Status should be given to both parts of India as soon as possible it is difficult to abrogate Viceroy's powers in either part before June 1948 unless basis of a partition both of territory and of Central subjects has been made.

7. One other query in order to equip me to put your point of view to Cabinet Committee. In beginning of para. 7 you say that British army should be phased out as soon as possible after transfer of power. Present intention is that all British forces should be withdrawn immediately after transfer of power. Do you in your opinion mean that you would withdraw all British troops as soon as Hindustan alone has achieved Dominion Status? I think the Cabinet Committee will show considerable interest in this point.

[1] No. 412.   [2] See No. 410 and its note 5.   [3] See No. 273.
[4] No. 409.   [5] See No. 409, note 4.

423

Pandit Nehru to Rear-Admiral Viscount Mountbatten of Burma

Mountbatten Papers. Official Correspondence Files: Round Table Conference, Indian Political Leaders, etc, Issue of Invitations to

17 YORK ROAD, NEW DELHI, *13 May 1947*

May I suggest to you that in any conferences to which party leaders are invited, the President of the Congress should also be invited? He represents the Congress formally and officially. Others may be prominent Congressmen, but they have other capacities also and cannot be said to represent Congress formally. If the Congress President is not invited on such occasions, certain misapprehensions arise in the public mind and needless difficulties are created.[1]

Yours sincerely,
JAWAHARLAL NEHRU

[1] Mr Scott minuted on this letter: 'There is something in this; but others would be amazed.'

424

Draft Telegram from Rear-Admiral Viscount Mountbatten of Burma to Lord Ismay[1]

Mountbatten Papers. Official Correspondence Files: Transfer of Power, Part II(b)

?*13 May 1947*

1. Reference Paragraph 4 of my 62–S.C. of 12th May.[2] The redrafting of the announcement is going well and I hope to let you have it by . . . . . .

2. This plan, although its whole object is to leave the decision to the Indian people themselves, will, I am getting more and more certain, be looked upon as an award of H.M.G. Even though I get the agreement of the Indian leaders to it, it will be considered as an imposition of the British, who will get the blame for any subsequent bloodshed with a consequent worsening of the Indo-British relations. I am going to call the plan in the draft announcement "Plan WE", because it is we who will be responsible for putting it into action and for the consequences.

3. The alternative is to make the Indians really and blatantly responsible for their own future. I would call this "Plan THEY".

4. "Plan THEY" is steadily taking shape. It is a mixture of:—

(*a*) The alternative with which I said I intended to threaten Jinnah (see my 20–S.C. and 21–S.C. of 8th May).[3]

(*b*) Gandhi's opinion (see my 40–S.C. and 41–S.C. of 10th May).[4]

(*c*) My Dominion status proposals (see my 28–S.C. of 8th May and 54–S.C. of 11th May).[5]

(*d*) Suggestions which have been put forward during the last few days by Pandit Nehru, who does not believe that it is possible for me or the British as a whole to devise a peaceful solution for India.

and (*e*) Plan "WE".

5. It would mean the early demission of power on the basis of the 1935 Act with dominion status to the Interim Central Government and to existing Provincial Governments and the construction of Pakistan on dominion status thereafter.

6. It would involve as a *sine qua non* the public declaration by Congress of a number of safeguards for the Muslim League. These would include undertakings:—

(*a*) to give every facility and assistance to those areas which wished to secede from the Union of India not only to go but to set themselves up independently,

(*b*) to assist with the splitting of the armed forces and not to interfere with the use of the armed forces in the seceding areas. (This is going to be by far the most difficult one to define and to get agreement over),

(*c*) to co-operate in such procedure, for example a referendum in the N.W.F.P. and the setting-up of boundary commissions, as was necessary to ascertain the will of the people and to demarcate the areas which wished to leave. In fact the whole procedure in Plan "WE" might be handed over to the Indians to carry out themselves,

(*d*) not to use the Congress majority in the Interim Government against the Muslim League.

7. Nehru is most convincingly genuine about these safeguards. He has said time and again that, once they were announced, Congress could not conceivably disregard them; if they did, there would be the most extreme repercussions not only on world public opinion but also on India. And he honestly says that the Congress leaders would be ready to give far more away to the League if left to themselves than if under British pressure.

8. The crux is, of course, to get this across Jinnah. He has never given any indication that he would be ready to trust Congress for one moment. But if I can get him and Nehru together I might be able to convince him. In any case, "Plan THEY" remains the only alternative if Jinnah does not accept "Plan WE". He can have his choice. I would not, even if Congress preferred it, allow them to have "Plan THEY" if Jinnah accepted "Plan WE".

[1] This telegram was not sent.   [2] No. 419.   [3] Nos. 346 and 351.
[4] Nos. 395 and 400.   [5] Nos. 360 and 409.

425

Mr Abbott to Master Tara Singh[1]

R/3/1/176: f 156

13 May 1947

I am desired to say that in His Excellency's opinion the time has now come for party leaders to take a more definite line in purely law and order matters, particularly in Amritsar. With this object in view, and with no intention of discussing high political matters, His Excellency desires me to ask if you would be good enough to call and see him tomorrow (May 14th) at Government House at 3.30 p.m. His Excellency is also despatching a similar invitation to the Nawab of Mamdot to see him with some colleague of his choice during the same afternoon. If after discussion with His Excellency the suggestion is acceptable, a joint discussion with the other party leaders and His Excellency could be arranged. I would be glad of an answer by the bearer of this letter.

Yours sincerely,

S. E. ABBOTT

[1] A letter in the same terms was sent to Giani Kartar Singh. Mr Abbott also wrote in similar terms to the Nawab of Mamdot except that it was left to the latter to decide whom to bring with him should he wish to be accompanied by a colleague. The Nawab of Mamdot accepted the invitation by phone. On 14 May Mr Abbott wrote to him again to inform him that, since it had proved impossible to contact Giani Kartar Singh and since Master Tara Singh was unable to come owing to a previous engagement (See No. 426), the proposal would have to be deferred for the time being. R/3/1/176: ff 155, 161.

426

Master Tara Singh to Mr Abbott

R/3/1/176: ff 157a–159

AMRITSAR, *13 May 1947*

Dear Mr Abbott,

Thanks for your letter of today received just now (at 8–0 P.M.).[1] I am sorry I am engaged for tomorrow and must leave for Delhi early in the morning in order to be in time to keep my programme of important business.

I am sorry I am missing this opportunity of placing before His Excellency personally my view point, and expressing my feelings. I may mention here that in these days I keep my programme secret for I know that Muslim League is keenly watching my movements evidently for some mischievous object.

They are controlling telephone system of Amritsar and Lahore—if not of other stations also—and the telephone operators immediately phone to the Muslim League office the time and direction of my going out as soon as they learn. So as a precautionary measure, I try to keep the time and direction of my going out secret. So when I return from Delhi, I shall suddenly come to Lahore and take any chance of seeing His Excellency. But it is risky for me to give out time of my coming to Lahore previously.

I may say also that I shall not be a party to any hypocritical statement like that issued recently by Mahatma Gandhi and Mr Jinnah with the bitter result known to the world. I do not like to see a single innocent person murdered and shall do my utmost to prevent such murders whenever I find the Sikhs as aggressors. But so far the Sikhs have been aggressors nowhere. As regards the renewal of the trouble at Amritsar, I may say that I received information beforehand that the Muslim League had decided to intimidate the Sikhs at Amritsar and had decided upon a certain plan. How can I then sit down round a table with the persons who are not sincere now even. None of the Muslim League Leaders unequivocally condemned the unprecedented atrocities, barbarities and murders committed by their followers in the Western Punjab. I hold them responsible for the butchery and heinous atrocities committed upon my innocent sisters, brothers and children. They are even now helping, encouraging and defending the arrested ruffians in the Western Punjab. I do not believe in their sincerity. So I shall not lick the hand besmeared with the blood of my innocent children, sisters and brothers.

The peace of Amritsar is in the hands of the Muslim Leaguers and the Government officials. The Muslim Leaguers have planned to intimidate us and have attacked us. The Government has given the control of the situation in the hands of the Muslim officials. The European Officers are only misled by the Muslim officials who alone are near to them. I believe the Government can control the situation without the co-operation of the Muslim League or anybody else. But if the Government continues its present policy towards the Muslims of Amritsar nobody else will be able to do anything.

I may repeat that I shall come to see His Excellency as soon as possible with the object of being useful in His Excellency's efforts to re-establish peace; but I shall join no Conference with the Muslim Leaguers held for the purpose of anything, even establishing peace, for I have not the least faith in their sincerity.[2]

Yours sincerely,
TARA SINGH

[1] No. 425.
[2] On 15 May a copy of this letter and of No. 425 were sent to the Viceroy. R/3/1/176: f 161

427

Cabinet

India and Burma Committee. Paper I.B.(47)67

L/P&J/10/79: ff 230–2

TRANSFER OF POWER IN INDIA
NOTE BY THE SECRETARY
OFFICES OF THE CABINET, S.W.I, *13 May 1947*

At the request of Lord Ismay, I circulate to the Committee herewith, a note by the Viceroy's Political Adviser (Sir Conrad Corfield) upon the States' aspect of the proposals submitted by Mr. V. P. Menon, Reforms Commissioner, already circulated under cover of I.B.(47) 62.[1]

S. E. V. LUKE

NOTE BY SIR CONRAD CORFIELD[2]

Mr. V. P. Menon's proposals[3] for the transfer of power in India make no mention of the Indian States.

2. The Cabinet Mission's memorandum of the 12th May 1946[4] contemplated a fully-self-governing Government or Governments in British India within the British Commonwealth by agreement in India. Mr. Menon's note contemplates the establishment of transitional Dominion Status for the Successor Governments in British India by act of Parliament, until a new constitution is ready.

3. If the Crown retains its connection with British India for the period between the enactment of this legislation and the inauguration of the new constitution, many States will demand that during this period their connection with the Crown should not be terminated. But it is not practicable to retain paramountcy when British India has been made fully self-governing. The Crown's connection with an Indian State during the interim period between Dominion Status and a new Constitution would therefore have to be a new connection.

4. It would be grotesque to abolish their existing relationship with the Crown and to set up a new relationship for this interim period, since the relationship under the new constitution would set up another system in due course. Moreover, the agency for such a relationship could only be either through the High Commissioner, or by direct appointment, both of which methods would engender grave suspicion in India, and might well prejudice the chance of building up any unified government or governments in India.

5. The States can hardly be told that the Crown contemplates retaining its connection with British India for this period, but severing its connection with the States except through British India. Moreover, some States (e.g. Travan-

core) would refuse to accept an indirect connection with the Crown. It would therefore be open to such States, as soon as British India has been made self-governing, when paramountcy must lapse, to enter into negotiations with other foreign powers. Before a new constitution could be framed, parts of India might thus set up relations, which would endanger the dominion status of British India.

6. If therefore the solution contemplated in Mr. Menon's note is to be pursued, it would be essential to provide for the States to be represented in the Joint Council for regulating matters of common concern. If this Council could be set up before Dominion Status is granted, the Governor General would still be Crown Representative. Acting in both capacities the transition could be facilitated.

7. It is possible that some States may decline to be represented on this Council. But the choice would be theirs. They would not have been omitted by His Majesty's Government. And in any case this choice would be open to them from the date of the full transfer of power or the framing of the new Constitution. The Crown need not contemplate any new relationship with an individual non-acceding State until the new Constitution is framed, if provision is made for that State to share in the framing and implementation of policy in regard to matters of common concern, especially External Affairs and Defence. And if a State presses for such a new relationship, it would be legitimate for the Crown to decline to discuss the question until a new constitution has been framed and to use its influence with foreign governments to postpone any negotiations with the latter until that stage. It may be hoped that foreign governments would not wish to encourage the balkanisation of India.

[1] No. 388.
[2] Lord Ismay telegraphed the text of this note to Lord Mountbatten in tel. 6207 of 14 May, remarking that Sir C. Corfield would be 'attending the Cabinet Committee meeting tomorrow and will speak on his note without committing you. I think it advisable that problem from States' point of view should be appreciated.' R/3/1/136: ff 138–140.
[3] See No. 273.   [4] Vol. VII, No. 262.

428

Draft Telegram from Mr Attlee to Rear-Admiral Viscount Mountbatten of Burma[1]

L/PO/6/125: f 39

13 May 1947, 5 pm[2]

53. Following from Prime Minister.

I am very worried about the developments of the last two days as set out in your telegrams to Ismay Nos. 56–S.C., 57–S.C., 60–S.C., and 62–S.C.[3]

2. We were under the impression that Nehru had more or less accepted the plan that you sent home. All that we have done is to try to clarify the presentation of the case. We have made no alterations in substance, except as regards the referendum in the NWFP, which was included at your suggestion to meet Nehru's objection to a General Election. I cannot, therefore, understand what Nehru means by saying that H.M.G. "seem to function in an ivory tower of their own, isolated from realities in India", and that the "things that emerge from London are so peculiar".

3. Cabinet Committee is meeting tomorrow to consider Menon plan and the general position. It is difficult for us here to evaluate the position. I think that it would be advisable for Ismay to return to India at once in order to inform you of the views of the Government and to know your mind on recent developments. It will be desirable for him or even yourself to return here to report, but on that point I shall be glad to have your mind.

[1] This telegram was not sent. Although some phrases may suggest that the document was personally drafted by Mr Attlee, there is no positive evidence to confirm that this was so. The file copy is a top copy and carries the endorsement 'suspended'. No other copy has been traced either in the India Office Records or the Public Record Office.
[2] Time of receipt in India Office Telegraph Branch. L/S &G/3/28.
[3] See Nos. 410, 410, note 5, 412 and 419.

429

Rear-Admiral Viscount Mountbatten of Burma to Lord Ismay (via India Office)

Telegram, Mountbatten Papers. Official Correspondence Files: Transfer of Power, Part II(a)

IMMEDIATE   SIMLA, *13 May 1947, 8.35 pm*
TOP SECRET   *Received: 14 May, 2.30 am*
65–S.C. Reference my telegram No. 62–S.C. of 12th May.[1]

1. My immediately succeeding telegram contains revised draft announcement.

2. In order to avoid any further bombshells, I propose now to see Jinnah and then Nehru again privately to clear the draft as far as possible with them.

3. I leave it to you whether or not to circulate this to Cabinet Committee now, in view of possible subsequent changes. You will note that there is no reference to Dominion status in this draft. I am dealing with this in a separate telegram.

4. I have following comments to offer in explanation of changes incorporated in this draft.

(a) Introduction has been recast with a view to trying to meet viewpoints both of Congress and League. We should avoid saying as has been done in Cabinet Committee draft that arrangements must be made for transfer of power to more than one authority. Our procedure is intended to find out if such a step really proves to be necessary.

(b) I have omitted para. 5 of Cabinet Committee's draft. See (c) below.

(c) The issues as you will see from para 4 of my draft are limited to joining existing Constituent Assembly or joining together in a new Constituent Assembly. I have omitted choice to Provinces for standing out independently. In principle if choice is given to one Province we cannot deny it to others. If it is desire of all parties in a particular Province to stand alone we shall not be able to prevent them, but I do not now like the idea of H.M.G. giving them that choice. One of Nehru's main criticims was that we were encouraging the Balkanisation of India. I am seeing Suhrawardy on Wednesday, May 14, and will tell him that I cannot make provision in the plan for Bengal remaining independent; but that there is nothing in the plan to prevent the Bengal Legislative Assembly passing a resolution for independence which I would treat on its merits.

(d) In deference to Nehru I have omitted giving any choice to Madras, Bombay, etc. now represented in Constituent Assembly.

(e) I have omitted all provision for election of representatives on one to quarter million ratio. This will lead to absurd results particularly in Bengal where 225 members between them will have to elect 241 representatives. This principle was devised mainly for the N.W.F.P. where there is considerable weightage for minorities. Since we propose to hold referendum in that Province we can safely go back to original plan whereby members of Legislative Assemblies take the decisions. In Sylhet this will produce 19 Muslim votes as against 12 General which is more advantageous to Muslims than 8:5 under Cabinet Committee draft.

(f) I have revised the para. relating to the N.W.F.P. which as it now stands will be more acceptable to Nehru.

(g) Nehru took very strong exception to the proposed procedure for

[1] No. 419.

ascertaining the wishes of British Baluchistan. I am in consultation with the External Affairs Department for devising a more democratic procedure, and hope to be able to include this in the final announcement.

(*h*) You will see from para. 13 of my draft that we have made no arrangements for fresh elections to the Constituent Assembly in Sind and the N.W.F.P. This may not be acceptable to Jinnah but I shall point out that once he has his Pakistan he can do what he likes about his Constituent Assembly.

(*i*) Nehru agrees to principle of paragraph 18 but seems to think that to give such public assurances to tribes would be dangerous. I think we must keep it in.

(*j*) Nehru intensely dislikes the para. in the Cabinet Committee's draft relating to States. He feels that as drafted it will encourage disruptive tendencies with which I agree. We must preserve the position of the States but at the same time we cannot avoid giving a lead to the Princes.

430

Rear-Admiral Viscount Mountbatten of Burma to Lord Ismay (via India Office)

Telegram, Mountbatten Papers. Official Correspondence Files:
Transfer of Power, Part II(a)

IMMEDIATE   SIMLA, *13 May 1947, 7.45 pm*
TOP SECRET   *Received: 14 May, 2.20 am*
No. 66–S.C. Reference my 62–S.C. of 12/5.[1] Following is revised draft announcement.[2] *Begins.*

I INTRODUCTION

1. On Feb. 20th 1947, H.M.G. announced their intention of transferring power in British India to Indian hands by June 1948. H.M.G. had hoped it would be possible for the major parties to co-operate on the basis of the Cabinet Mission's Plan of May 16th, 1946, and evolve for India a constitution acceptable to all concerned. This hope has not in the event been fulfilled; nor have the political parties in India been able to reach agreement on any alternative plan of their own.

2. The majority of the representatives of the Provinces of Madras, Bombay, the United Provinces, Bihar, Central Provinces & Berar, Assam, Orissa and the North-West Frontier Province, and the representatives of Delhi, Ajmer-Merwara and Coorg have already made progress in the task of evolving a new Constitution. On the other hand the Muslim League Party, including in it a majority of the representatives of Bengal, the Punjab and Sind as also the representative of British Baluchistan, has decided not to participate in the Constituent Assembly.

3. It has always been the desire of H.M.G. that power should be transferred in accordance with the wishes of the Indian people themselves. This task would have been greatly facilitated if there had been agreement among the Indian political parties. In the absence of such an agreement, the task of devising a method by which the wishes of the Indian people can be ascertained has devolved on H.M.G. After full consultation and in agreement with political leaders in India, H.M.G. have decided to adopt for this purpose the plan set out below. H.M.G. wish to make it clear that they have no intention of attempting to frame any ultimate Constitution for India; this is a matter for the Indians themselves. Nor is there anything in this plan to preclude negotiations between communities for an united India.

II THE ISSUES TO BE DECIDED

4. It is not the intention of H.M.G. to interrupt the work of the existing Constituent Assembly in so far as it relates to those Provinces a majority of whose representatives are already participating (subject to the provisions of paragraphs 10 and 12 [? 11 and 13] below); and H.M.G. trust that, as a consequence of this announcement, the Muslim League representatives of those Provinces will now take their due share in its labours. At the same time, it is clear that any Constitution framed by this Assembly cannot apply to those parts of the country which are unwilling to accept it. H.M.G. are satisfied that the procedure outlined below embodies the best practical method of ascertaining the wishes of the people of such areas on the issue whether their Constitution is to be framed

(a) in the existing Constituent Assembly;

or

(b) in a new and separate Constituent Assembly consisting of the representatives of those areas which decide not to participate in the existing Constituent Assembly.

When this has been done, it will be possible to determine the authority to whom power should be transferred.

III BENGAL AND THE PUNJAB

5. The Provincial Legislative Assemblies of Bengal and the Punjab (excluding the European members) will therefore each be asked to meet in two parts, one representing the Muslim majority districts and the other the rest of the Province. For the purpose of determining the population of districts, the 1941 census figures will be taken as authoritative. The Muslim majority districts in these two Provinces are set out in the Appendix[3] to this Announcement.

---

[1] No. 419.
[2] This text of the draft announcement was circulated to the Viceroy's Staff under the reference V.C.P. 47 of 14 May.
[3] The text of the Appendix was not included in the telegram; see Appendix to No. 476.

6. The members of the two parts of each Legislative Assembly sitting separately will be empowered to vote whether or not the Province should be partitioned. If a simple majority of either part decides in favour of partition, division will take place and arrangements will be made accordingly.

7. Before such a vote takes place, however, it is desirable that the representatives of each Province should clearly know what would be the alternative to Partition. Therefore, if there is a demand for it, a preliminary joint meeting of all members of each Legislative Assembly (other than Europeans) should be held at which a decision should be taken as to which of the alternatives in para. 4 above is to be adopted for the Province as a whole, if it should eventually be decided that the Province should not be partitioned.

8. In the event of partition being decided upon, each part of the Legislative Assembly will, on behalf of the areas they represent, decide which of the alternatives in para. 4 above to adopt.

9. For the purpose of deciding on the issue of Partition, Bengal and the Punjab Provinces will be divided according to administrative districts as laid down in the appendix. But it is evident that for the purposes of a definitive partition of these provinces a more detailed investigation of boundary questions will be needed and as soon as a decision involving partition has been taken for either province a Boundary Commission will be set up, the membership and terms of reference of which will be settled in consultation with those concerned. Until the report of a Boundary Commission has been adopted by both parts of either province, the provisional boundaries indicated in the Appendix will be used.

IV SIND

10. The Legislative Assembly of Sind (excluding the European members) will at a special meeting also take its own decision on the alternatives in para. 4 above.

V N.W.F.P.

11. The position of the N.W.F.P. is exceptional. Two of the three representatives of this province are already participating in the existing Constituent Assembly. But it is clear, in view of its geographical situation, and other considerations, that if the whole or any part of the Punjab decides not to join the existing Constituent Assembly, it will be necessary to give the N.W.F.P. an opportunity to reconsider its position. Accordingly, in such an event, a referendum will be made to the electors of the present Legislative Assembly in the N.W.F.P. to choose which of the alternatives mentioned in para. 4 above they wish to adopt. The referendum will be held under the aegis of the Governor-General and in consultation with the Provincial Government.

VI BRITISH BALUCHISTAN

12. British Baluchistan has elected a member but he has not taken his seat in the existing Constituent Assembly. In view of its geographical situation, this Province will also be given an opportunity to reconsider its position and to choose which of the alternatives in para. 4 above to adopt. H. E. the Governor-General is examining how this can most appropriately be done.

VII ASSAM

13. Though Assam is predominantly a non-Muslim Province, the district of Sylhet which is contiguous to Bengal is predominantly Muslim. There has been a demand that in the event of the partition of Bengal, Sylhet should be amalgamated with the Muslim part of Bengal. Accordingly, if it is decided that Bengal should be partitioned, those members of the Assam Legislative Assembly who represent the territorial constituencies included in the Sylhet district will hold a meeting and decide whether the district of Sylhet should continue to form part of the Assam Province or should be amalgamated with the new Province of East Bengal, if that Province agrees. The rest of the Assam Province will in any case continue to participate in the proceedings of the existing Constituent Assembly.

VIII REPRESENTATION IN CONSTITUENT ASSEMBLIES

14. If it is decided that Bengal and the Punjab should be partitioned, it will be necessary to hold fresh elections to choose their representatives on the scale of one for every million of population according to the principle contained in the Cabinet Mission's Plan of May 16 1946. Similar elections will also have to be held for Sylhet in the event of its being decided that this district should form part of East Bengal. The number of representatives to which each area would be entitled is as follows:—

Province	General	Muslims	Sikhs	Total
Sylhet District	1	2	Nil	3
West Bengal	15	4	Nil	19
East Bengal	12	29	Nil	41
West Punjab	3	12	2	17
East Punjab	6	4	2	12

15. These representatives will either join the existing Constituent Assembly or form the new Constituent Assembly according to the mandate given to them by the areas concerned.

IX TRANSFER OF POWER

16. The Constituent Assembly (or Assemblies) will also constitute Provisional Authorities to whom power can be transferred.

X ADMINISTRATIVE MATTERS

17. Negotiations will have to be initiated as soon as possible on administrative consequences of any partition that may have been decided upon.

(*a*) Between the representatives of the prospective successor authorities about all subjects now dealt with by the Central Government including Defence, Finance and Communications.

(*b*) Between different successor authorities and H.M.G. for treaties in regard to matters arising out of the transfer of power.

(*c*) In the case of Provinces that may be partitioned as to administration of all provincial subjects such as the division of assets and liabilities, the police and other services, the High Courts, provincial institutions, etc.

XI THE TRIBES OF THE NORTH WEST FRONTIER

18. Agreements with tribes of the N.W. Frontier of India will have to be negotiated by appropriate successor authorities.

XII THE STATES

19. H.M.G. wish to make it clear that the decisions announced above relate only to British India and that their policy towards Indian States remains unchanged. Some of the States are already participating in the deliberations of the existing Constituent Assembly. H.M.G. hope that all the others will join either the existing Constituent Assembly or the new Constituent Assembly.

XIII NECESSITY FOR SPEED

20. In order that the successor authorities may have time to prepare themselves to take over power, it is important that all the above processes should be completed as quickly as possible. To avoid delay, the different Provinces or parts of Provinces will proceed independently as far as practicable within the conditions of this Plan. The existing Constituent Assembly and the new Constituent Assembly will proceed to frame Constitutions for their respective territories: they will of course be free to frame their own rules.

XIV FURTHER ANNOUNCEMENTS BY GOVERNOR-GENERAL

21. H.E. the Governor-General will from time to time make such further announcements as may be necessary in regard to procedure or any other matters for carrying out the above arrangements.

431

Lord Ismay to Rear-Admiral Viscount Mountbatten of Burma (via India Office)

Telegram, R/3/1/153: f 21

IMMEDIATE   *13 May 1947, 6.55 pm*
SECRET   *Received: 14 May, 4 am*

6185. Ministers here feel much in the dark about your proposed version of announcement and I am unable to enlighten their darkness as I have been out of touch with important developments that have taken place since I left. I have had long talks with Prime Minister and Secretary of State and former is cabling you the suggestion that I should return at once in order to get up to date. I much hope that you will agree to this as both Abell and I feel that we must get into your mind again before we can be of any use to you here. I am therefore making plans for Corfield, Abell and myself to leave on Thursday 15th in anticipation of your approval.[1] I can easily return after 2 or 3 days with you if you so wish.

2. We are having a meeting of Cabinet Committee tomorrow evening. It is clearly no use trying to finalise the announcement in view of your re-draft which is awaited here. But we can at least get Ministers' views on the following points:—

(a) the V. P. Menon plan.

(b) the title "Union of India" (Your telegram 25–S.C. of May 8th).[2]

(c) your proposals for dealing with Jinnah if he refuses to co-operate. (your telegram 21–S.C. of May 8th).[3]

(d) the scheme in your 54–S.C.[4] provided that I receive your answer to my 6142[5] in time.

---

[1] In tel 78–S.C. of 14 May Lord Mountbatten replied that he quite agreed with this proposal. However as he felt a link in London was essential during the present negotiations, he proposed to send Sir E. Mieville home immediately after Lord Ismay reached India. Mountbatten Papers, Official Correspondence Files: Transfer of Power, Procedure for determining authorities to which power is to be demitted, Part (2).

[2] No. 357.   [3] No. 351.   [4] No. 409.   [5] No. 422.

432

Rear-Admiral Viscount Mountbatten of Burma to Lord Ismay (via India Office)

Telegram, R/3/1/153: ff 16–17

IMMEDIATE   SIMLA, *13 May 1947*
TOP SECRET   *Received: 14 May, 2.30 am*

No. 74–S.C. Your telegram No. 6131 of May 12th.[1]

There is no doubt that the situation here is hardening. I am repeating to you the statement issued by Jinnah in today's papers[2] in reply to Patel's demand (vide my telegram No. 55–S.C. of May 11th)[3] for transfer of power on Dominion Status basis to the existing Government. He has also reiterated his demand against the partition of the Punjab and Bengal. As I told you in my telegram this morning,[4] I intend to see Jinnah on my return to Delhi tomorrow. I propose to use all my persuasive powers to induce him to accept the revised draft announcement. Thereafter, I propose to induce Nehru also to accept it. I do not see how Nehru could stand out if Jinnah is prepared to accept. Once the announcement is cleared out of the way, I propose [to] reopen the question of Dominion Status with the leaders. I propose to tell Jinnah that the time factor precludes me from fully implementing the partition plan. For instance, the material for deciding the issues connected with the assets and liabilities between the Centre and the Provinces, and the Provinces *inter se*, may not be easily available. It is also possible that the Boundary Commission may not be ready with their recommendations. It is therefore in his own interest that he should remain in the existing Central Government and the Muslim League's representatives there would be a guarantee that their interests would not be jeopardised. I should explain to him that this is merely a temporary measure until the Pakistan Government is ready to assume their responsibilities. If he agrees to this line of argument, I will take him further and ask him for his view whether he sees any objection to H.M.G. parting with power to the Central Government on a Dominion Status basis. If he reacts adversely to this suggestion, I propose to tell him that once the partition issue is decided, the Congress demand for parting with power in Hindustan will be irresistible. I therefore would ask him if he sees any objection to our parting with power to the Pakistan Constituent Assembly as soon as it is set up, and in the same way to Hindustan. This again would be on the basis of Dominion Status, but I will make one reservation, that, pending some arrangement for joint services I would insist that the existing services should continue in both Hindustan and Pakistan, which may be limited to a period of, say, three or four months.

When I know Jinnah's mind, I will then tackle Nehru and Patel. After Nehru's bombshell I intend to be very careful to get prior agreement of Jinnah and Nehru to the draft announcement and similarly to get their approval to any proposals which I may wish to put to H.M.G. about Dominion Status for India as a whole or Hindustan and Pakistan. I therefore suggest that until a clear picture emanates, I do not answer your questions in detail.

We also must reckon on the possibility that Jinnah may reject the announcement and may insist on Province-wise Pakistan without division. If he is adamant, I must be able to tell him that it would be impossible for H.M.G. to concede this demand and if he has no alternative acceptable solution to offer, I will tell him that the only thing for me to do is to recommend to H.M.G. to part with power under the Government of India (1935) Act to the existing Central Government, which would in all probability be the end of his Pakistan. I do not feel in my mind that Jinnah would be able to face up to this position, but we must have a second string to our bow. I would like you, therefore, to consult the Cabinet Committee and let me know whether H.M.G. have any objection to my proposed action, and will in fact definitely support this alternative, for without this threat we shall never get a publicly agreed solution. And if these tactics fail the threat must be put into effect as the only workable solution left us.[5]

[1] This reference appears to be incorrect. Tel. 6142 of 12 May (No. 422) was probably intended.
[2] See No. 411 and its note 4.
[3] See No. 409, note 4.
[4] No. 429.
[5] Lord Ismay replied in tel. 6233 of 14 May that he had discussed the matter with the Secretary of State but that the India Committee would not meet soon enough to enable their view on the action proposed by Lord Mountbatten to be transmitted in time for the latter's meeting with Mr Jinnah. Lord Ismay therefore suggested that the meeting should be postponed until he had reported further. Mountbatten Papers, Official Correspondence Files: Transfer of Power, Part II(b).

433

Mr Hoyer Millar to Mr Donaldson

L/P&S/12/1081: f 34

SECRET   FOREIGN OFFICE, 14 May 1947
Z 4192/3046/36
Dear Donaldson,
You will recall that we exchanged correspondence late in 1945 regarding a suggestion that the Nizam of Hyderabad might try to purchase Portuguese Goa or some part of it.[1]

Six weeks ago Sir Alexander Roger who, as you may know, is the leading figure in the two British Public Utility Companies in Portugal and has im-

[1] See L/P&S/12/1081: ff 38-9.

portant contacts among the Portuguese authorities, told me before leaving for Lisbon that the idea was again in the air. The Hyderabad authorities, with whom Sir Alexander also has contacts, had suggested that he might use a suitable opportunity to take up the question with the Portuguese Government.

I have now heard from Stirling our Chargé d'Affaires at Lisbon that Sir Alexander Roger has in fact conveyed to the Portuguese Government a proposal from the Nizam of Hyderabad to connect the Hyderabad railways with the Mormugao railway. The Nizam, according to information received by Stirling, does not wish to be entirely dependent for an outlet to the sea on the railways of what is now British India, when British control is finally removed. Stirling understands that Dr. Salazar has shown an interest in the proposal and has asked the Ministry for Foreign Affairs to prepare the draft of an agreement which he is now considering. The draft provides that Hyderabad should guarantee to send 1,000,000 tons of freight a year over the Portuguese railway. This traffic would enjoy free-port facilities in Mormugao, subject to the payment of dues sufficient to reimburse to the Portuguese Government the money they would have to spend on improving the railway and harbour.

Stirling has asked whether we would see any objection to the Embassy supporting with the Portuguese authorities any British firms who might be interested in obtaining contracts for the railway and harbour works, should anything come of the proposal. We for our part see no reason why the Embassy should withhold support from any British firm which might request it in connexion with this scheme. I should be glad to know whether you have any views on this particular point or on the scheme as a whole.

Incidentally, it is difficult to see from the map how the Hyderabad railways could be connected with the Mormugao railway without crossing some territory of British India, but I suppose what the Nizam is anxious to see is the development and expansion of the port facilities at Goa so that Hyderabad would then not be entirely dependent on a harbour in British India.[2]

Yours sincerely,

W. N. HOGG

for

F. R. HOYER MILLAR

[2] Mr Donaldson replied on 30 May after the draft letter had been shown to Lord Mountbatten. He explained that H.M.G.'s position was a delicate one. On the one hand Ministers were unlikely to want to be associated with any project which might be seen as encouraging the balkanisation of India. On the other it might become increasingly difficult to maintain a completely negative attitude to Hyderabad's desire to stand out as an independent State. He therefore felt it desirable for H.M.G. to maintain an attitude of detachment for as long as possible. Accordingly it would not be proper for the Embassy to take any diplomatic action to promote the interests of British firms in connection with the railway and harbour works. L/P &S/12/1081: f 33.

434

Mr Turnbull to Mr Harris

L/PO/11/3 Part 2: f 185

14 May 1947

I am afraid I have not had time yet to attempt to work out a time-table for the Indian Bill.[1] It is, however, obvious that there are so many uncertainties as to the character of the Bill and as to when it may be required that no such estimate could be of much value at this stage.

The Secretary of State will no doubt warn the Committee that it is possible that we might require a Bill on India before Christmas, but I should add that personally I see difficulty in getting a Bill ready by 1st November unless we know *for certain* what its form is to be by the beginning of August. If it is a Bill modifying the existing Act and providing under it for transfer to two pro-visional Governments for Hindustan and Pakistan as Dominions, I should say that two months for drafting and another month for approval of the Bill by the Viceroy and Cabinet would be the minimum if it is to be anything like a decent job. If it were a Bill repealing the Government of India Act and pro-viding for India to go out of the Commonwealth forthwith the time required would I think be rather less, provided consequential action could be taken by Order in Council.

The Parliamentary time required, of course, depends on how contentious the Bill is and that in turn depends on whether there is acquiescence by both Indian parties or not. I am no judge but I should have thought that any Bill not based on Indian agreement would be fought at every stage and that, even if it were based on such agreement, it might be fought pretty hard particularly if, as seems probable, no proper division of the Central subjects has been carried out administratively before power is transferred to the two parts of India.

I agree with Mr Morley[2] that it will be convenient to have the Nationality and Citizenship Bill proceeding in the same session, but from the Indian point of view it would be awkward if it is introduced in October unless we have before then reached agreement with the Indians or at any rate had discussions with them on the question of nationality, and sufficiently before then for the results to be taken into account in the drafting of the Bill. It might be suggested to the Cabinet that this Bill should not be introduced and proceeded with any length of time before the India Bill is introduced. No doubt in the case of

[1] Mr Turnbull was commenting on a circular from the Future Legislation Committee enquiring what minor Bills Ministers wished to propose for inclusion in the 1947–48 legislative programme. On 19 May Mr Harris informed the Committee that, so far as could be forseen, all matters relating to India requiring legislation in the 1947/48 Session would be covered by the contemplated major Bill. L/PO/11/3: Part 2: ff 191, 183, 181.

[2] A note by Mr Morley giving the Burma Office view on the circular is also on the file.

Burma minor amendments would suffice to meet what is required. In the case of India it may be very inconvenient to have a discussion in Parliament on the question of the nationality division between India and the U.K. before the India Bill has been laid and also possibly before the matter has been fully discussed with the Indians.

F. F. TURNBULL

435

Mr Rowan to Mr Attlee

Public Record Office. PREM 8/541, part 10

PRIVATE   14 May 1947
P.M.

I understand that the plan may now be for a Minister to go out to India so as to settle matters there with full powers and the minimum of reference home.

The S/S for India is perhaps too new to go himself; the Min[ister] of Defence is tied up on the Bill[1]; the President of the B[oard of] T[rade] is, I assume, free to go.

I venture to suggest however that you should go. This is one of the biggest things from India and the Commonwealth's point of view; and your leadership would count for everything. You have the L[ord] P[resident][2] and ? F[oreign] S[ecretary][3] both back—and this gesture would I feel fire the imagination of the world. If you pulled it off, it would be a master stroke. If you did not, your personal endeavours would earn respect. Of course you could take another Minister with you if you wished—but your presence there—if any Minister goes—is I feel essential.[4]

T.L.R.

[1] The Defence Conscription Bill.
[2] Mr Morrison had been recuperating in the South of France from thrombosis of the leg.
[3] In April and early May Mr Bevin had visited the U.S.S.R. and Poland.
[4] There is no reply by Mr Attlee on the file.

436

Mr Attlee to Mr Morrison, Mr Bevin, Sir S. Cripps, Mr Alexander, Lord Jowitt, Lord Addison and Mr Creech Jones

Public Record Office. CAB 21/1803

14 May 1947

Prime Minister's Personal Minute: Serial No. M.221/47

The progress of events in recent years in various parts of the British Commonwealth and Empire appear to me to call for a review of the existing status and inter-relationship of its constituent entities.[1] Theoretically there is a broad division between the self governing states Great Britain and the Dominions on the one side and the Colonial Empire on the other, the former group having their equality of status defined by the Statute of Westminster. This Dominion status is regarded as the final stage of evolution already reached by some and to be reached ultimately by others of the constituent parts of the Empire. In fact, however, this pattern has already been broken. Eire is in an anomalous position as an independent republic. The Dominions, notably South Africa and Canada, dislike the term "Dominion status". India, which only twenty years ago clamoured for Dominion status, now demands independence. Ceylon and Burma both ask for independence either within or without the Commonwealth. It is, I think clear that, while there is strong evidence of the reluctance of many leaders of political opinion in the Asiatic countries to leave the Commonwealth, the phrase if not the content of "Dominion status" is not now attractive.

2. Further, Dominion status produces some curious anomalies. Thus, the Dominions, which are now fully recognised on the international stage as Sovereign States with Ambassadors in foreign capitals, are represented in Britain by High Commissioners who rank after the representatives of Liberia or Guatemala, although India is now seeking to send an Ambassador to China.

3. There is, therefore, need for reconsideration of the present position. The critical position in India, Burma and Ceylon makes this an urgent need. There is no time for a lengthy examination by constitutional lawyers. What is required is a political decision. This needs to be taken here by the Cabinet with a view to seeking the opinion of the Dominions and if possible getting a decision without the lengthy formalities of an Imperial Conference.

4. What I think is required is the finding of a formula which will enable the greatest number of independent units to adhere to the Commonwealth without excessive uniformity in their internal constitutions or in their relation-

---

[1] See No. 418 which evidently caused Mr Attlee's minute to be written.

ship to Great Britain, the Commonwealth and one another. Some such phrase for instance as "The Associated States of the Commonwealth" might provide an umbrella under which a number of independent States might be brought together—Britain, Eire, the existing Dominions, Rhodesia, India (whether single or multiple), Burma and Ceylon. Other colonies and dependencies such as Malta and Gibraltar which for military reasons cannot have exactly the same degree of freedom as a Dominion might also be brought in.

5. I think that the problem should be considered first by a small Committee of Ministers who should be assisted by a few experts. It might be useful to bring in someone of the type of R. Coupland as the matter is really rather outside the range of departmental officials, though their expert advice will be required.

6. I should be glad if you would give this matter your consideration with a view to an early meeting to discuss the broad principle involved.[2]

C.R.A.

[2] In the event discussion of this minute by Ministers did not take place until 9 June 1947 (GEN. 186/ 2nd Meeting). The minutes of this meeting will be printed in Vol. XI.

437

Cabinet

India and Burma Committee. I.B.(47)24th Meeting

L/P&J/10/79: ff 260–2

Those present at this Meeting held at 10 Downing Street, S.W.1, on 14 May 1947 at 5.30 pm were: Mr Attlee (in the Chair), Mr Hugh Dalton, Sir Stafford Cripps, Mr Alexander, Viscount Addison, the Earl of Listowel, Mr A. G. Bottomley, Mr Arthur Henderson, Lord Chorley

Also present were: Lord Ismay; Sir Norman Brook, Mr S.E.V. Luke (Secretariat)

Transfer of Power in India
(Previous Reference: I.B.(47)23rd Meeting)[1]

The Committee had before them telegrams from the Viceroy (Nos. 65, 66, 74 and 75 S.C.)[2] about the arrangements proposed for determining the successor authorities to which power would be transferred in India, including a revised draft of the proposed announcement of policy.

THE PRIME MINISTER said that there appeared to have been a substantial change in the attitude of the Indian leaders as a result of the conversations which the Viceroy had been holding during the past few days. In particular, the raising at this stage of the possibility of early attainment of Dominion status by India, or by part of India, seemed to have produced a radical change in the situation. In these circumstances he doubted whether it would be profitable for the Committee to consider in detail the Viceroy's revised draft of the proposed announcement about the determination of the successor authorities. He thought that, in the first instance, Ministers must seek from the Viceroy further explanations of his latest views and intentions and of the present attitude of the Indian leaders.

The Committee expressed their agreement with this view.

A general discussion followed, in the course of which the following points were made:—

(a) The original proposals envisaging Dominion status, which had been circulated with I.B.(47) 62,[3] had been designed to follow upon a partition of India. It seemed likely, however, that Pandit Nehru had seen the advantages from the point of view of Congress of securing that the present Interim Government of India should attain at an earlier stage the position of a Dominion Government in relation to the whole of India. It was the view of the Committee that, unless all the political parties in India were willing to adopt the Cabinet Mission Plan and to collaborate in a Constituent Assembly for the whole of India, a plan for partition in India must precede decisions determining the status of India or parts of India within the Commonwealth.

(b) THE PARLIAMENTARY UNDER-SECRETARY OF STATE FOR INDIA said that, if the Viceroy intended to make a further effort to secure agreement on the Cabinet Mission Plan, he ought, in fairness to the Muslim League to press Congress to state whether they were prepared to accept that Plan without qualification. The Muslim League had based their refusal to enter the Constituent Assembly on the ground that the Congress statement of 5th[6th] January[4] implied that their acceptance of the Plan was subject to reservation and, if a final attempt was now to be made to secure agreement on the Plan, the Congress position ought to be fully elucidated.

(c) THE PARLIAMENTARY UNDER-SECRETARY OF STATE FOR INDIA expressed agreement with the Viceroy's view that the revised plan contained in his telegram No. 66–S.C. of 13th May could only be put into effect if it was acceptable to the Muslim League.

(d) The suggestion was made that it might be announced that power would be demitted to the Constituent Assembly in respect of the Provinces represented by that body; but that, as regards the remaining Provinces, the existing constitutional arrangements would continue until agreement could be reached on the demission of power. It was thought that a statement to this effect, while it might be acceptable to the Muslim League, would be criticised by Congress as indicating that the British Government had not been sincere in their determination to transfer power in I ndia byJune, 1948. An arrangement on these

[1] No. 355.   [2] See Nos. 429, 430, 432 and 411, note 4.
[3] No. 388.   [4] Vol. IX, No. 253.

lines might, in the event, be practicable but it should not be forecast in any statement of policy.

The Committee:—

(1) Agreed to resume consideration of the revised plan contained in the Viceroy's telegram No. 66–S.C. of 13th May when the present views and intentions of the Viceroy had been further elucidated.

(2) Invited the Secretary of State for India to arrange for officials to consider, in the light of the Viceroy's revised proposals, what plan for the transfer of power would be likely to result in the least disorder and bloodshed, in the event of a settlement having to be enforced.

438

Lord Ismay to Rear-Admiral Viscount Mountbatten of Burma (via India Office)

Telegram, Mountbatten Papers. Official Correspondence Files:
Visits and Tours

MOST IMMEDIATE   *14 May 1947, 8.40 pm*
SECRET   *Received: 15 May, 3.30 am*
PRIVATE

6299. Prime Minister, Sir Stafford Cripps, Mr Alexander and Secretary of State for India met this afternoon before Cabinet Committee meeting. I was only official present.

2. Ministers were unanimous that situation was now so confused that it was essential either

(*a*) that a Minister or Ministers should proceed to India to discuss situation at first hand with you or alternatively

(*b*) that you should be asked to fly home.

3. I strongly advised against any Ministers proceeding to India and took it on myself to say that you would be opposed to it. Prime Minister therefore decided to ask you to come here yourself. I much hope this is alternative you would prefer and I am terribly sorry that I have been unable to save you this journey.

4. In case you should decide to come the position as regards time factor and transport is as follows.

(*a*) The Prime Minister would like you here as soon as possible. He hopes to complete discussions with you by Saturday May 24th. I imagine that it would also suit you to get back to India well before meeting on June 2nd.

(*b*) Prime Minister has told Abell and myself to stand by until we get your reply. This means that York cannot leave England until Friday the 16th whatever your answer may be.

(c) A good deal of time would be saved if you started in Dakota and if York picked you up at some place en route. Prime Minister suggested that I should come out to meet you and I will of course gladly do so if you wish. On the other hand we are working fairly hard on official level on various problems that have arisen out of your more recent telegrams and Abell and I might be more useful if we stayed here.

5. Will you let me know as soon as you have decided on your plans whether you wish York to start on Friday and if so to what destination. Also whether you would like me and/or Abell to come in her.

439

Mr Attlee to Rear-Admiral Viscount Mountbatten of Burma (via India Office)

Telegram, L/PO/8/15: f 54

MOST IMMEDIATE   *14 May 1947, 9.20 pm*
PRIVATE AND PERSONAL

54. In view of the many changes and developments since Ismay came here, I feel it is impossible to decide the very important issues raised in your latest messages by exchange of telegrams. I therefore consider that if you judge it possible in existing conditions, you should return here for consultation in order to come to the final conclusions before your meeting on June 2nd.

2. Pending your reply am retaining Ismay and Abell here. They might meet you in the York at say Habbaniyah on Saturday, the 17th, but these details can be fixed later in accordance with your wishes.

3. The sort of announcement that we would make is given in my immediately following telegram.

440

Mr Attlee to Rear-Admiral Viscount Mountbatten of Burma (via India Office)

Telegram, L/PO/8/15: ff 55-6

MOST IMMEDIATE   *14 May 1947, 9.15 pm*
PRIVATE AND PERSONAL

55. My immediately preceding telegram.
Following is draft announcement:
Begins. During the past ten days His Majesty's Government have been giving the most earnest consideration to the proposals for the transfer of power that

have been submitted to them by His Excellency the Viceroy. They find themselves in general agreement with these proposals, but in view of the importance of these arrangements to the future of India, the British Commonwealth of Nations and the whole world, His Majesty's Government feel that they should have final discussions with the Viceroy before the announcement is made.

They have therefore invited the Viscount Mountbatten to come to England on a short visit as soon as convenient.[1] *Ends.*

[1] In tels. 6310 and 6311 of 15 May Mr Harris informed Captain Brockman that issue of the announcement at 3.30 pm that day was agreed subject to the amendment of the last para. to read: 'They have therefore invited the Viscount Mountbatten to come to England on a short visit as soon as possible so as to enable him to return by 2nd June'. L/PO/8/15: f 38.

441

Minutes of Viceroy's Thirty Second Staff Meeting, Item 1

Mountbatten Papers

TOP SECRET

Those present at this Meeting held in His Excellency's Study, The Viceroy's House, New Delhi on 15 May 1947 at 9 am were: Rear-Admiral Viscount Mountbatten of Burma, Sir Eric Mieville, Captain Brockman, Rao Bahadur V.P. Menon, Mr Campbell-Johnson, Lieutenant-Colonel Erskine Crum

HIS EXCELLENCY'S VISIT TO LONDON

HIS EXCELLENCY THE VICEROY said that he had that morning received a telegram[1] from the Prime Minister, asking that he should return to London for consultation. Another telegram[2] from Lord Ismay said that the alternative suggestion had been made that a Minister or Ministers should proceed to India to discuss the situation at first hand with the Viceroy.

HIS EXCELLENCY THE VICEROY said that he could not agree that a Minister should come to India at the present stage, with the possible exception of Lord Listowel.

After discussion, HIS EXCELLENCY THE VICEROY said that he was convinced that it would [be] desirable for him to go to London as soon as the present vital negotiations with Indian leaders on the revised Draft Announcement[3] permitted, and that arrangements should be made accordingly. His departure would also depend on the time it took his York aircraft to get back to Delhi, but he hope to leave on either Sunday May 18th or Monday, May 19th.

He agreed to the terms of a Press Announcement as suggested in another telegram[4] from the Prime Minister and further agreed with the suggestion[5] that Sir John Colville, subject to His Majesty's formal approval, should be appointed Acting Governor General. He wished it to be suggested that Sir G.S. Bajpai should act as Governor of Bombay.

HIS EXCELLENCY THE VICEROY said that he wished his negotiations with Indian leaders to be speeded up as far as possible. To this end, he was seeing Mr Jinnah at 5.30 p.m. that day and wished it to be arranged that he should see Sardar Patel at 4 p.m. and Pandit Nehru at 9.30 p.m.

Arrangements to put these decisions into effect were then made, and telegrams were despatched.[6]

[1] No. 439.   [2] No. 438.   [3] See No. 430.   [4] No. 440.
[5] See tel. 56 of 14 May from Lord Listowel to Lord Mountbatten L/PO/8/15: ff 52-3.
[6] In tel. 1032-S of 15 May Lord Mountbatten informed Mr Attlee that he would come home as soon as his present vital negotiations with Indian leaders permitted. He would probably be able to reach London on 19 or 20 May and wished to be back in Delhi by 30 May at the latest. Lord Mountbatten similarly informed Lord Ismay of his decision to return home in tel. 1030-S of the same date. He said that all of his advisers should remain in London. L/PO/8/15: ff 42, 44.

442

Record of Interview between Rear-Admiral Viscount Mountbatten of Burma and Mr Liaquat Ali Khan

Mountbatten Papers. Viceroy's Interview No. 135

TOP SECRET   *15 May 1947, 11 am—12.30 pm*

I began by announcing my intention to fly home.

Mr Liaquat Ali Khan heaved a sigh of relief and said "That is the only solution. I knew you would have to go. When I met Muslim editors yesterday they informed me that they were certain that the reason for the postponement of the meeting of leaders was to enable you to go home."

I then asked him whether the Muslim League was going to accept partition of the Punjab and Bengal, to which he replied: "We shall never agree to it, but you may make us bow to the inevitable". I told him it was essential that, if it did become inevitable, all parties should give their public agreement to avoid bloodshed, and that I proposed to raise this with Mr Jinnah.

I then read over to him the revised plan[1] paragraph by paragraph. He had comments on certain paragraphs, and I sent for D.P.S.V. to arrange for him to make a note of these comments. I let Liaquat Ali take the copy away, explaining it was my personal copy and I relied on him to show it to nobody at all, though he could discuss it with Mr Jinnah.

[1] See No. 430.

I asked him if he would like to accompany Mr Jinnah who was coming to see me at 5.30 this evening. He said that he thought it would be better if I saw him alone.

I discussed with him the whole question of dominion status for Pakistan and Hindustan under one Governor-General, and found that he was surprisingly receptive to this idea.

I told him that his Private Secretary was accused by the D.I.B. of being the cause of the leak about the Financial delegation going home. He expressed great surprise at this. He said that Mr Mumtaz Hassan had been Sir Jeremy Raisman's Private Secretary who had thought very highly of him. He promised to speak to him.

He agreed with me that the question of the Economy Committee should not be taken in Cabinet for the present, at any rate until after the meeting of the 2nd June.

443

Note by Mr Scott

Mountbatten Papers. Official Correspondence Files: Plans, Alternative (For transfer of power), Part (2)

15 May 1947

I discussed with Mr Liaquat Ali the points which he raised with H.E. this morning arising out of the Draft Announcement.[1]

2. *Paragraph 9. Boundaries.* Liaquat Ali made two points about this:

(1) that the last sentence of the paragraph, which states that the provisional boundaries according to the notional partition would remain until the report of the Boundary Commission had been adopted by both parts of the Punjab (or Bengal), should be altered. He wished that there should be a Boundary Commission, with a British Chairman, and that the recommendation of the Commission should be put into effect by H.M.G;

(2) he wished the terms of reference of this Boundary Commission to be such as would enable parts of a district even down to a village to be linked with adjoining Muslim majority (or non-Muslim majority, as the case may be) areas. The effect of this would be that Amritsar town was isolated like an island in West Punjab. I said to him that this was unreasonable and unlikely to be acceptable to H.M.G.

Liaquat Ali said he would discuss with Mr Jinnah this question of Boundary Commissions and speak to H.E. further on the matter.

3. *Paragraph 12. Baluchistan.* We discussed Liaquat Ali's proposal for a

plebiscite, but when I explained the vast distances and complete lack of local govenment officials in villages he eventually agreed that any form of democratic vote would satisfy the Muslims, as they were confident of winning Baluchistan.

3A. *Paragraph 13. Assam.* Liaquat Ali Khan wished that the plan should be consistent about contiguous majority areas; and in the case of Assam he pointed out that there were two districts adjoining Sylhet in which Muslims were in a majority over a considerable part of each. Provision should therefore be made in setting up the Boundary Commission for the inclusion of such parts of these two districts in Eastern Pakistan along with Sylhet.

4. *Paragraph 20. States.* Liaquat Ali made the same point that he had made to H.E., namely, that H.M.G. should not change their previous policy as laid down in the Cabinet Mission's Plan, by which it would have been possible for individual States to stand out from the Indian Union and be completely independent. After discussion, he agreed however that the present wording of paragraph 19 could remain.

5. I got the definite impression that Liaquat Ali himself has come to accept as inevitable the division of the Punjab and Bengal, and would not himself make trouble over this: I went so far as to throw a fly over him by asking if he would like Simla for the Pakistan capital, but he said that as it was in the Eastern Punjab it would be no use to them.

6. I think there is something in what he says about the terms of reference of the Boundary Commission, though these terms would have to be such as would prevent Amritsar, for instance, from being isolated from the rest of the Eastern Punjab. It would probably be possible for the Boundary Commission's terms of reference to be such as would enable contiguous tahsils (generally about a quarter of a district), or even "circles" (generally about one-twentieth of a district), to be attached to neighbouring majority areas. The provisions in respect to Assam might be modified to this extent.

I. D. SCOTT

[1] See No. 430.

444

Record of Interview between Rear-Admiral Viscount Mountbatten of Burma and Mr Bhabha

Mountbatten Papers. Viceroy's Interview No. 136

TOP SECRET   *15 May 1947, 12.30–1 pm*

I congratulated Mr. Bhabha on his efforts behind the scenes, which I presumed had helped in persuading Mr. Patel to make the statement which he had about dominion status.[1] Mr. Bhabha smiled and said that he had indeed worked hard on this, and was very glad to see that the Congress leaders were at last taking a realistic view. He added "But I feel that you are making a mistake in dealing so much with the idealistic dreamers instead of realist men of action". I said "Do you mean I should deal with Vallabhbhai Patel instead of Pandit Nehru?". He left it at that by saying that I could take it any way I liked; but it appeared perfectly clear to me that this was exactly what he meant.

Finally, he said that he was quite certain that any responsible people in India who had looked at the problem recently would be bound to take dominion status as the only solution; he went on to say that he felt convinced that if we could make a success of the first six months of dominion status, no part of India would ever dream of leaving the Commonwealth.

He was delighted to hear I was going home, and said that when he was in Bombay everybody said "Why doesn't the Viceroy go home; no-one else can ever settle this".

[1] See No. 375.

445

Record of Interview between Rear-Admiral Viscount Mountbatten of Burma and Lieutenant-General Sir A. Smith (Extract)

Mountbatten Papers. Viceroy's Interview No. 137

TOP SECRET   *15 May 1947, 1.00–1.30 pm*

I told him that the date by which I wished the additional Infantry Division to be in position in the Punjab was the 4th June, though the final statement might not be made until a few days later. I told him that I had the unanimous approval of the Cabinet, including that of Maulana Azad obtained subsequently in Simla, to the putting down of the first sign of communal warfare with the utmost rigour. I wished him to issue the necessary orders to this effect, and I said I particularly wished to have tanks, armoured cars, and aircraft used so that the poorly armed insurgent armies would feel that their resistance was futile since they were being mown down without even a chance of killing any of the regular armed forces. General Smith said he understood, and that he would take the necessary steps if the occasion arose.[1]

He then asked me if I would try and speed up the Ordinance to give special powers to the armed forces which the Governor of Bengal had asked for on the basis of the one in force in the Punjab. He also urged that this should be extended to cover all Provinces and that it should be in force by the 4th June. I promised to take this up with the Home Member.

He informed me that Dr Evatt the Australian Foreign Minister had instructed the Australian High Commissioner (General Mackay) to see Pandit Nehru and urge him to retain India within the Commonwealth, or at the very least establish special relations with Australia in view of their common defence problems; to which Nehru had reacted very favourably and was likely to arrange a meeting to discuss defence and cultural problems of common interest later in the summer. This was news to me.

I gave General Smith an insight into the dual dominion status plan for Pakistan and Hindustan, and urged him to do everything in his power to retain as many British officers as possible and to slow up any steps laid down before the dominion status question had been seriously considered. He said he was already doing this, but it would now mean not filling all the shipping space allotted to the armed forces, and he asked my authority to treat this new aspect as more important than that of filling up shipping berths.

I authorised him to treat the matter in this way, and told him to speak to J.P.S.V. about it.

He told me that he noticed that the Defence Member, whenever he discussed any long distance problem, invariably gave a ruling on the basis that British officers would continue to be available after June 1948.

[1] See No. 468, note 2.

446

Mr Suhrawardy to Sir E. Mieville

Mountbatten Papers. Official Correspondence Files: Bengal,
Partition of, Part I(b)

CAMP—6 CANNING ROAD, NEW DELHI,
15 May 1947

Dear Sir Eric,

I must confess that although on some points the situation is clearer to me than it was before the interview with His Excellency[1] there are some other points on which I am more confused than ever. I shall be grateful if you could clarify them.

I hardly think it necessary for me to reiterate that it will be a most colossal mistake to partition Bengal. If, however, the mistake has to be committed, then I would like to be clear on what steps His Excellency proposes to take. Please correct me where I am wrong, even on the basis of present knowledge.

[1] See also No. 462; the interview between Lord Mountbatten and Mr Suhrawardy took place on 14 May 1947.

I am told that in the first instance a decision of the Legislature as it exists today will be taken on the question whether Bengal should go with Group A or B or be an independent state. I suppose I could carry the resolution regarding Group B or independence by a majority. But what would be the difference in essence? If I were to carry the independence resolution, would that mean that there will be no further steps at partition? This is the first question.

If, however, steps will be taken for partition, then of course there is no point in my carrying the independence resolution; we shall carry the resolution for Group B.

As regards partition I understand that there will be a preliminary notional partition on the basis of districts of the Burdwan division plus Calcutta plus Khulna and 24-Parganas. The present representatives in the Legislature of these areas will decide whether they desire partition of Bengal or not. Here we may take it for granted that the decision will be in favour of partition and Group A as the Muslim voting will be very slight compared to the Hindu voting, and the Scheduled Caste and the Mahisya voice will not be heard.

After this is decided I understand that there will be a Boundary Commission that will demarcate contiguous areas. In the result probably the whole of Khulna and a large portion of 24-Parganas will go into the Muslim zone. If you see the Thana map prepared by me you will see why I say so.

These two notionally partitioned Legislatures will, I take it, elect representatives to the Constituent Assemblies which they wish to join. The Western Bengal Legislature will certainly vote for A and the Eastern Bengal Legislature will certainly vote for B and elect representatives accordingly. At no point of time will there be a plebiscite or a referendum or an attempt to find out the opinion of the people of the various areas or of even the existing voters.

The two Constituent Assemblies will draft constitutions of their own groups and provinces. There seems to be no *point* of time at which an agreement can be arrived at to keep Bengal together on an agreed plan. After the provinces are set up an agreement might possibly be arrived at later on, but neither section is likely to give in if Bengal as a unit is expected to join either Group A or Group B. A United Bengal may come into being through a Confederation, or an agreed settlement between Groups A and B.

As to the possibility of an agreement meanwhile, it appears to be remote. The Hindus want to browbeat me to accept a Socialist Republic. This demand cannot be made if it is decided to keep Bengal as one and allow Bengal to frame its own constitution. If I reject this, *as indeed I must*, Mr Sarat Bose walks out, and Mr Kiran Sankar Roy is too weak to fight the Hindu Mahasabha which has captured the imagination of the Hindus on the score of partition.

Keeping in view all these factors I think it will be distinctly unfair to partition Bengal and drive Muslim Bengal to the verge of ruin. How Muslim Bengal will react in terms of violence I do not know. I hope there will be no outbreak for as long as there is life there is hope. But I must emphatically declare that it will be criminally unfair if Calcutta is taken out of Muslim zone, which comes very near it. On one side it touches the subdivision of Baraset, where the Muslims are in a majority. There is no natural dividing line either other than the River Hooghly between the Hindu zone and the Muslim zone and this leaves Calcutta in the Muslim zone. In Calcutta and the industrial areas the Hindu majority is largely due to influx of foreign Hindu labour which it would not be fair to count. Calcutta will long remain a bone of contention and I would earnestly request His Excellency to consider that if Calcutta cannot be given to the Muslim zone it should not also be given to the Hindu zone, and Calcutta and the industrial areas round about it should be made into a free international zone.

Yours sincerely,

SUHRAWARDY

P.S. I cannot understand how power can be transferred to the Constituent Assemblies before the Boundary Commission has demarcated the two Bengals and before we know which parts of Bengal will be represented in which Assembly.

447

Cabinet C.M.(47)47th Conclusions, Minute 6

R/3/1/10: ff 122–3

Those present at this Meeting held at 10 Downing Street, S.W.1. on 15 May 1947 at 11 am were: Mr Attlee (in the Chair), Mr Herbert Morrison, Mr Ernest Bevin, Mr Arthur Greenwood, Mr Hugh Dalton, Sir Stafford Cripps, Mr Alexander, Viscount Jowitt, Mr J. Chuter Ede, Viscount Addision, Mr J. Westwood, Mr A. Creech Jones, the Earl of Listowel, Mr G. A. Isaacs, Mr Aneurin Bevan, Mr T. Williams, Lord Inman

    Also present during discussion of Item 6 was: Mr John Strachey

INDIA
Constitutional Position
(Previous Reference: C.M.(47)23rd Conclusions, Minute 1)[1]

6. THE PRIME MINISTER informed the Cabinet that the India and Burma Committee had for some days past been considering proposals submitted by the Viceroy for determining successor authorities to whom power could be transferred in India. The Committee had had the advantage of conferring with the Viceroy's principal advisers, who had come to London for the purpose; but since they left India the Viceroy had been continuing his conversations with

[1] Vol. IX, No. 421.

Indian leaders and the Committee had reached the conclusion that, before final decisions were taken, it would be expedient that the Viceroy should come to London himself to give Ministers his latest appreciation of the position. He had therefore been asked to come to London on a short visit as soon as possible, so that he might be able to return to India by the date (2nd June) on which he had undertaken to place definite proposals before the Indian leaders.

The Prime Minister read to the Cabinet the draft of an announcement, which was to be issued that afternoon regarding the Viceroy's visit.

The Cabinet—

Took note of the Prime Minister's statement and of the terms of the announcement which was to be made later that day.

448

Sir F. Burrows (Bengal) to Rear-Admiral Viscount Mountbatten of Burma

Telegram, Mountbatten Papers. Official Correspondence Files:
Bengal, Partition of, Part I(b)

IMPORTANT   *15 May 1947, 2.45 pm*
SECRET   *Received: 16 May, 9.30 am*

118–S. I believe you were giving an interview to Suhrawardy yesterday:[1] no doubt he informed you fully regarding progress of his negotiation for a sovereign, independent but United Bengal. As you know I myself feel strongly that formation of a coalition government now (which will probably have to be on some such basis as is contemplated by Suhrawardy, Kiran Sankar Roy and Sarat Bose), offers best prospects of a peaceful transfer of power in Bengal. Indeed if Cabinet plan of May 1946 is not accepted I should regard this as only hope for peaceful transition.

2. While I realise that negotiations must be conducted primarily between party leaders, I should like to be in a position to help if and when help is required. To do this I must be prepared to some extent to show my hand and this obviously may involve giving my blessings to principle of an independent Bengal. The tentative Suhrawardy-Sarat Bose-Kiran Sankar Roy agreement contemplates recognition of an independent Bengal with a right, after it has been set up, to link itself with any authority then existing in India or of course to stand aloof.

3. A danger I foresee is that if agreement should be reached by Congress and Moslem League in Bengal on these lines, the provincial parties concerned may wish to proceed on these lines in preference to Cabinet plan for a Union of India. This would raise a difficult problem and I feel that in any case my support

to present tentative arrangement should be without prejudice to possibility of acceptance of Cabinet's Union of India plan. I should however like your guidance whether, always without prejudice to chances of that Cabinet plan being accepted, I should promote a proposal involving an independent Bengal.

4. I am doubtful if Suhrawardy and Congressmen with whom he is treating will get agreement among themselves and with their parties here in Bengal and with their All India leaders in time to place an agreed plan before you for incorporation in scheme approved for presentation to Indian leaders on 2nd June; but if they bring this off and their proposal is acceptable to H.M.G. it would seem to involve alterations in 2nd June scheme so far as references to Bengal are concerned.

¹ See No. 462 and its note 2.

449

Lord Ismay to Rear-Admiral Viscount Mountbatten of Burma

Mountbatten Papers. Official Correspondence Files: Transfer of Power, Part II(b)

TOP SECRET AND PERSONAL   INDIA OFFICE, *15 May 1947*
My dear Viceroy,
I have spoken to Eric on the telephone this morning and the York is leaving for Delhi almost at once. This must therefore be a very hastily dictated attempt to put you in the picture this end in a few sentences.

The whole of the Cabinet Committee, individually and collectively, have been very helpful, and in spite of their other pre-occupations, have given our problems first priority. As you will have seen from their re-draft¹ of the announcement, they had no objections to raise on points of substance. Indeed, they felt that it was the only solution possible.

I told them about the V. P. Menon Plan, and indeed circulated it as a Cabinet Committee paper.² It was being examined in all its aspects and possibilities when the spate of telegrams, which resulted from your Simla talks, began to pour in.

A meeting was called to consider these telegrams last night and everyone felt that the situation was changing so fast and had become so confused that it could no longer be handled by the exchange of telegrams.³ Accordingly, they decided that either a Minister should fly out to you, or that you should be asked to fly home. I felt sure that I was voicing your opinion when I said that the former alternative would be neither effective nor acceptable to you. The

¹ See No. 379.   ² See No. 388.   ³ See also No. 438.

Prime Minister therefore at once sent off his telegram[4] asking you to come home, and I am intensely relieved that you have decided to do so.

After the despatch of this invitation, Ministers had a general talk about your more recent telegrams. The principal points that emerged are set out (not very lucidly I fear) in the attached minutes,[5] which I would like to supplement as follows:

(1) The Committee did not like the idea of reducing the number of choices from three to two, i.e. they felt that they were pledged to give the Provinces the option of remaining independent of either Hindustan or Pakistan, if they so desired. This was particularly applicable to the case of Bengal.

(2) Ministers felt that the question of the possibility of the early attainment of Dominion status by India or parts of India was one which should not have been raised until after the principle of partition had been accepted: in other words, until after the announcement, in more or less its original form, had been made. They regarded this question, in fact, as the second stage of the negotiations, and not as an alternative plan. Lord Addison made the point that, in any case, there would have to be full consultation with the Dominions before any decision on this point could be announced.

(3) The Ministers said that, so far as they could judge from your telegrams, the action that you proposed to take if Jinnah was intransigent would be a breach of the pledges that they had given to Parliament about safeguarding minorities.

It will be grand to have you here and I now feel confident again that all will be well.

Yours,
PUG

[4] No. 439.
[5] Lord Ismay evidently sent a copy of No. 437.

450

Sir E. Jenkins (Punjab) to Rear-Admiral Viscount Mountbatten of Burma
(Extract)

R/3/1/178: f 103

SECRET   GOVERNMENT HOUSE, LAHORE, 15 May 1947
No. 675

4. I have written to Your Excellency separately about Mamdot's renewed demand for the formation of a Ministry.[1] He is undoubtedly acting under instructions from Jinnah, and I find the party attitude a little hard to understand. It is in fact intelligible only on the assumption that Mamdot and his

followers believe that if they came into power, they could seize and hold the Punjab by force.

5. The partition of the Punjab has been discussed at great length and with great acrimony in the Press. The Muslims are strongly opposed to partition and are unlikely to change their view except under instructions from Jinnah. The Hindus and Sikhs say that partition is inevitable and, as I have already reported, demand the Chenab as the western boundary. I have seen the notes of the discussions in Simla on 11th May[2] and feel that they do not bring out strongly enough my view that any announcement of a partition without the public agreement and support of the League, Congress and Sikh leaders will do no good at all and will land us in a most difficult position. The distinction between an announcement demanding action by the communities and an award will not be understood, and we may slip very easily into what will be regarded as an award without the means or the intention of enforcing it. Having been manoeuvred into this position, we may slip a stage further into the abandonment of the Punjab to chaos. Khizar, who has seen me several times lately, still has faint hopes of a united and independent Punjab, and there are signs that the Muslim League, though officially dissatisfied with the very woolly statement he recently issued,[3] might welcome him as a link between them and the other communities. The hope of a settlement is very faint indeed, since the Muslim League leaders have no sense at all, and Tara Singh is almost hysterical.

[1] On 14 May Sir E. Jenkins sent Lord Mountbatten a copy of a lengthy letter of the same date from the Nawab of Mamdot asking to be allowed to prove his majority in the Punjab Assembly or to be permitted to form a Ministry. Sir E. Jenkins provided the Viceroy with a commentary on the letter and enclosed the draft of the reply he intended to send. In this draft Jenkins said he was 'convinced that it would be a grave mistake to form a Ministry of the kind you contemplate at the present juncture. As I said in my letter of 7 May [No. 334], it is most important that we should do nothing here to prejudice all-India agreement, and it will be best to review the situation as soon as the all-India position is clear.'

In tel. 1077-S of 18 May Lord Mountbatten indicated he would prefer a reply on slightly different lines. Accordingly in his letter to Mamdot of 19 May, Jenkins added a passage saying it was hoped that after the Viceroy's meeting with the Indian leaders early in June 'a statement will be issued which may make it possible to review the Punjab situation.' R/3/1/89: ff 197–204; R/3/1/177: ff 31,34.

[2] See Nos. 403 and 404.

[3] In his statement of 11 May 1947, Malik Khizar Hyat Khan reiterated that:

'I made way for the Muslim League to come to an understanding with other parties in the Punjab and to form a Government. I had pointed out then that the risks involved in adopting any other course were too obvious to be stressed.

For the peace and prosperity of my Province I would welcome an agreement between the parties, and I am still hoping that this much desired agreement will come about. For the formation of a Ministry the Muslim League party has my support and that of my Muslim colleagues.' R/3/1/177: f 30.

451

Viceroy's Personal Report No. 7

L/PO/6/123: ff 101–5

TOP SECRET   *15 May 1947*

I spent the past week at Simla. I was feeling tired and thought I could get a rest; but the pressure of events and the number of Staff Meetings and interviews I had to have kept me nearly as busy as I was in Delhi. After the heat of the plains the atmosphere in the hills is delightful, and I have come back feeling fighting fit. I asked Nehru to come as my guest, as I thought he was nearing a breakdown from overwork; and he spent four days with us. We have made real friends with him and whatever else happens I feel this friendship is sincere and will last.

2. I was greatly impressed at the speed with which Cabinet dealt with the plan which Ismay brought home, and felt every confidence in the way the matter was being handled in London. The new draft appeared to be better than ours, and when it arrived I held a Staff Meeting to discuss the final procedure. I had a distinct "hunch" that I ought to take advantage of my new-found friendship with Nehru to ask his personal opinion of the new draft. But at the Staff Meeting the general opinion was against this, since it would be departing from our agreed procedure that all five leaders should see the final version together since they had all agreed with the provisional version in Delhi. However, experience in S.E.A.C. has taught me that if I have a "hunch", it is best to follow it; so I took Nehru aside just before he was going to bed and gave him a copy to take up to read, on the understanding that he was going to advise me merely as a friend of the likely reception it would have on the 17th May.

3. The next day when I was in the middle of a meeting with the Governor of the Punjab, Nehru sent me a letter,[1] which came as a bombshell. I telegraphed this at once to London, and attach a copy of the letter to this Report for record purposes. The rest of that day was spent in trying to find out exactly what Nehru's objections were. Finally, it became distressingly clear that the mere fact that the plan had been redrafted in London had not only roused his own suspicions but would, in his opinion, make the plan less likely of acceptance at the Delhi meeting. This was my main reason for deciding to redraft the plan in Simla.

4. Since writing the above I have received the Prime Minister's telegram[2] requesting me to come home for consultations, and I shall spend the next few days endeavouring to secure the agreement of the Party leaders to the revised draft of the plan, and discussing certain aspects of Dominion Status.

[Paras. 5–10, giving an account of Lord Mountbatten's interview with Mr Suhrawardy and Mr Fazlul Rahman (see No. 462), omitted.]

11. To turn to the general situation the same unsettled atmosphere continues over the country. You will have seen from Caroe's telegrams that agitation continues in the Frontier Province and that disturbances continue, in particular in the areas around Peshawar, Dera Ismail Khan and Bannu.

12. Caroe raised with me during the past week the position of the League prisoners in the jails and asked for my directions under Section 54 of the Government of India Act whether force should be used to expel them. I informed him that the use of collective force for the expulsion of prisoners was to be avoided at all costs. Instead I suggested, and Nehru agreed, that the Frontier Government should issue a clear warning that after a specified time limit prisoners who had not taken advantage of the amnesty would be re-imprisoned, the prison gates would be closed and from that time onwards all applications for release would be considered separately, although prisoners naturally would be encouraged to leave the prison.

13. I also suggested to Caroe that the Frontier Government might consider withdrawing at the same time any special facilities now available to prisoners, and also consider transferring any prisoners who misbehaved to some other Province by arrangement with the Government concerned. Caroe's preliminary report is that political prisoners in Peshawar jail have accepted deprivation of privileges in default of going out under amnesty, but demur to withdrawal of charpoys as being a common amenity.

14. While I was in the Frontier Province recently the Afridis raised with me the question of a lump sum payment being paid in recognition of their special services during the war. I have since discussed the matter with Nehru who has informed me that the Finance Department have accepted this proposal in principle but he personally was against the disbursement of this money in actual cash, and preferred the Governor's suggestion that it should be spent on scholarships and on setting up an Afridi Hostel at the Islamia College, Peshawar and giving scholarships. I have asked Nehru to consult the Afridis about this.

15. The Afridis also raised with me the matter of the five thousand rupees fine which had been levied on them after their attack on Nehru during his visit to the Khyber last autumn. I agreed with Nehru that the fine should not be remitted, and he, in his turn has agreed to their alternative suggestion that the money should be sent for the relief of the Muslims in Bihar. The money is, therefore, being placed at the disposal of the Governor of Bihar for spending in such a manner as he considers best for the purpose, and Caroe is informing the Afridis accordingly.

[1] No. 402.   [2] No. 439.

16. There has been a recurrence of trouble in Amritsar, and a twenty-four hour curfew had to be imposed on the 10th May on the City south of the railway line, following disturbances extending over two days, resulting in fourteen killed and fourteen injured. The District Magistrate has imposed a fine on the locality in which the incidents occurred at the rate of Rs 20. per adult member residing in the area, in order to provide immediate compensation to the survivors of the deceased. I understand that the number of people living in this area is about nine thousand.

17. Calcutta is also in a rather unsettled state, and Gandhi has gone down there for a fortnight before he returns to Bihar. There were rumours of an anti-partition day to be called by the Muslims on the 10th May and of an Indian Mutiny day being promoted in retaliation by the Hindu Mahasabha on the same day, but in point of fact nothing came of either. Even Nehru was infected by these alarmist rumours, and read into a recent statement by Suhrawardy a threat that the Muslims would do their best to sack Calcutta rather than let it be handed over to the Hindus after the partition of Bengal, and that the present Provincial Government would back disorders to that end.[3] In point of fact the whole of Suhrawardy's speech was a most statesmanlike utterance, emphasising the desirability of the unity of Bengal, together with a realistic facing up to the probable disorders which would occur if, as a result of the partition of Bengal, the new Province of East Bengal was deprived of its share of the resources of Calcutta. These incidents, unimportant in themselves, do show the state of jumpiness with which almost everyone in this country is affected at present.

18. I think it is of interest to report that during the month 27th March to the 27th April, 4,518 civilian passengers left India in nine ships (our original allotment for April was less than 1,000 berths). Of the five ships which sailed in April only one had any empty berths (totalling 19). This was due to the last minute rejection of eight passengers on medical grounds by the ship's doctor, and the remaining eleven passengers were taken ill too late to fill their places before the ship sailed.

19. I realise it is of course unavoidable but it is nevertheless most unfortunate that the Chancellor of the Exchequer's speech about the scaling down of the sterling balances should have impinged on the Indian political arena at this moment.[4] The newspapers have been taking a pretty strong line about this, and say that all the goodwill which has recently been established between British and Indians may be impaired by this attempt to cheat them of their just dues. I am very glad that the Indian Sterling Balances Delegation have put off their trip until mid-June, for if they had been sitting in London either before or worse still, during my meeting with the leaders, this would have produced an extremely bad atmosphere.

20. I gave in my last report[5] details of my wife's visit to the refugee camps in the Punjab. I am glad to report that as a result of her visit full-time health clinics are being organised in each refugee centre. The idea is that each clinic should be in charge of a local medical practitioner and it is hoped that the refugees themselves will take the most active part in this important work. There is unlimited scope for their activity once they can be persuaded to take an interest in themsleves. All clinics will be under the general supervision of the Civil Surgeon who will co-ordinate their activities, wherever necessary, and arrange medical supplies, etc. My wife has spent to-day, Thursday the 15th May, visiting refugee camps in the Multan area, which she was forced to omit from her tour a fortnight ago owing to dust storms preventing her aircraft from landing.

[3] See No. 382 and its note 5.
[4] On 13 May 1947 Mr Dalton answered a question from Mr Crosthwaite–Eyre seeking an assurance that 'the rights to present counter claims against sterling balances held by India have now been exercised or, if not, that British representatives will be instructed to present and press such claims . . .' Mr Dalton replied that in the forthcoming sterling balances discussions, all relevant considerations would be borne in mind but he did not think it useful to bind himself by a declaration on the matter in advance of these discussions. See *Parl. Debs.* 5th ser., H. of C., vol. 437, cols. 1285–6.
[5] No. 354, paras. 32–35.

452

Dominions Office to the Governments of Canada, Australia, New Zealand and South Africa

Telegram, L/P&J/10/79: f 255

IMMEDIATE *15 May 1947, 8.45 pm*
TOP SECRET AND PERSONAL
D. No. 452. My telegram D. No. 448 of 12th May.[1] India.

We have been giving continued close consideration to proposals outlined in my telegram D.No. 440 of 8th May,[2] particularly in light of further discussions which Viceroy has been holding in India. These discussions, and especially certain comments made by Pandit Nehru, suggest that, while main outline of plan would remain, considerable modifications of detail may be desirable before document is finally placed by Viceroy before the Indian leaders at the meeting arranged for the 2nd of June.

2. It is also now necessary to settle what further steps in connection with

[1] Dominions Office tel. D. No. 448 of 12 May to Dominion Governments referred to No. 352, paras. 5–7, and explained that the proposed meeting with Indian leaders had now been arranged to take place on 2 June. L/PO/6/120: f 38.
[2] See No. 352, note 2.

transfer of power may be needed over period between issue of that announce-ment and coming into effect of new Indian Constitution or Constititutions to be drawn up by Constituent Assembly or Assemblies. In this connection suggestion recently made by Mr. Jinnah to Viceroy that a separate State of Pakistan might wish to remain within British Commonwealth whatever decision were reached by Hindustan requires careful consideration.

3. In these circumstances it was decided that United Kingdom Government should have personal consultations in London with Viceroy before reaching final conclusions on form of announcement and other matters which may arise at his meeting on 2nd June. We therefore telegraphed to Lord Mount-batten last night asking whether it would be practicable for him to pay short visit to London at very early date.[3] He replied today in affirmative[4] and my immediately following code telegram contains text of announcement which was accordingly released to Press here this afternoon.[5]

[3] No. 439.
[4] See No. 441, note 6.
[5] Tel. D. No. 453 contained the text of the communiqué in No. 440 with the amendment given in note 1 to that document.

453

Captain Brockman to Mr Harris

L/PO/8/15: f 6

MOST IMMEDIATE   NEW DELHI, *15 May 1947, 7.30 pm*
                                              Received: 15 May, 4.45 pm

1038–S. Your 6223 May 15th.[1]

His Excellency is very glad to hear that Corfield's visit has been so useful. He wishes Corfield to remain in United Kingdom until he arrives.

[1] In this telegram Mr Harris said Sir C. Corfield had discussed the contraction of paramountcy and other important questions such as Berar with Lord Listowel and Mr Henderson. He felt the visit had been most timely and helpful. L/PO/8/15: f 5.

454

Minutes of Viceroy's Thirty Third Staff Meeting, Item 7

Mountbatten Papers

TOP SECRET

Those present for Item 7 of this Meeting held at The Viceroy's House, New Delhi on 16 May 1947 at 10 am were: Rear-Admiral Viscount Mountbatten of Burma, Sir Eric Mieville, Captain Brockman, Mr I. D. Scott, Rao Bahadur V. P. Menon, Mr Campbell-Johnson, Lieutenant-Colonel Erskine Crum

HEADS OF AGREEMENT

Attached as Annex "A" to these Minutes is a draft "Heads of Agreement" which was prepared by Rao Bahadur Menon and to which it was hoped to obtain the signatures of the Indian leaders.

HIS EXCELLENCY THE VICEROY said that, at his meeting the previous day, Mr Jinnah and Mr Liaquat Ali Khan[1] had refused to sign this document. They had appeared absolutely to accept the Plan but had not been willing to state their agreement in writing. Pandit Nehru had pointed out to him that Mr Jinnah's success in life arose from never agreeing to anything. The Congress leaders had pointed out that they were making great concessions in order to get a final decision. HIS EXCELLENCY THE VICEROY said that the crux of the matter appeared to be the form of the letter which Mr Jinnah was going to write. He was going to discuss that with him that afternoon. He then dictated a draft[2] of the form which he considered that this letter should take.

RAO BAHADUR MENON said that he had seen Pandit Nehru and Sardar Patel that morning. The Maharaja of Patiala was lunching with Sardar Patel that day. Pandit Nehru and Sardar Patel had accepted the position in respect of the "Heads of Agreement", but they had pointed out that there would be trouble if the Muslim League rejected the Plan, or accepted it only as an interim arrangement. They had stressed that this must be the Muslim League's last territorial demand. It would satisfy Congress if Mr Jinnah accepted the announcement and used his good offices to put it into effect.

HIS EXCELLENCY THE VICEROY said that he had already cautiously tried out threatening Mr Jinnah that, unless he met requirements adequately, power would be demitted to the Interim Government on a Dominion status basis. Mr Jinnah had taken this very calmly and said that he could not stop such a step in any event. HIS EXCELLENCY THE VICEROY said that this abnormal reaction, which was typical of Mr Jinnah, was rather disturbing. If Mr Jinnah saw himself betrayed, he might derive great satisfaction by going down to

[1] No record of this interview has been traced.
[2] See No. 455.

history as a martyr for his cause, butchered by the British on the Congress altar. HIS EXCELLENCY THE VICEROY said that he would probably not face up Mr Jinnah finally to the alternative until after the first day of the meeting with the Indian leaders.

HIS EXCELLENCY THE VICEROY said that he had seen the Maharaja of Patiala and the Raja of Faridkot the previous day. He gave an account of this interview, which is recorded separately.[3]

HIS EXCELLENCY THE VICEROY
invited Prin. Sec. to keep in close touch with the Maharaja of Patiala during his absence in London.

Annex to No. 454

Heads of Agreement

(1) We agree to the acceptance of the draft announcement (attached) to be made by the Governor-General on behalf of H.M.G., and after it has been made we agree to recommend its ratification by the organisations which we represent.

(2) In view of the need for stabilising the political situation in the country we strongly press H.M.G. for early transfer of power on a Dominion Status basis as an interim arrangement. This transfer should take effect as soon as the final decision is known according to the procedure laid down in the draft announcement.

(3) The basis of such transfer of power should be the Govt. of India Act, 1935, with modifications.

(4) In the event of the decision being taken that there should be one Central authority in India, power should be transferred to the existing Central Government.

(5) In the event of the decision being that there should be two sovereign States in India instead of one, the Executive of each area should be responsible to its respective Constituent Assembly.

(6) The Governor-General should be common to both the States. We suggest that the present Governor-General should be re-appointed.

(7) The Governors of the Provinces should be appointed on the recommendation of the respective Central Governments.

(8) When the new Act comes into operation, the Armed Forces in India should be divided between the two States. The units will be allocated according to the territorial basis of recruitment and will be under the control of the respective Governments. In the case of mixed units, the distribution should be entrusted to a Committee consisting of Field-Marshal Sir Claude Auchinleck and the Chiefs of the General Staff of the two States under the super-

vision of a Council consisting of the Governor-General and the two Defence Ministers. This Council will automatically cease to exist as soon as the process of division is completed.

³ This separate record has not been traced.

455

Lieutenant-Colonel Erskine Crum to Sir E. Mieville

Mountbatten Papers. Official Correspondence Files: Plans, Alternative (For transfer of power), Part 2

16 May 1947

Prin. Sec.

At the Staff Meeting this morning, H.E. dictated the following draft which he thought might serve as a basis for Mr Jinnah's letter. It is very rough and just as he dictated it.

"Although you cannot expect me to agree to the Partition of the Punjab and Bengal, for the reasons which I have made public, if H.M.G. rule that this is a matter which must be decided by the Provinces themselves, I give you my personal assurances that I shall accept this rule and use my best endeavours to get the Muslim League to accept it peacefully. You have asked me for an assurance that I will not allow any propaganda or activities on the part of any Muslims under my control which would tend to stir up communal strife in any part of India. My reply is that I will gladly give this assurance on the understanding that a reciprocal assurance is given by Congress."

456

Pandit Nehru to Rear-Admiral Viscount Mountbatten of Burma

Mountbatten Papers. Official Correspondence Files: Transfer of Power, Part II(b)

SECRET AND PERSONAL 17 YORK ROAD, NEW DELHI,
16 May 1947

Dear Lord Mountbatten,

I am trying to arrange for Krishna Menon to leave for London as soon as possible. I understand that there is a BOAC plane going tomorrow. I do not know yet whether accommodation in this plane will be available or not.

Krishna Menon could consult our High Commissioner in London as well as the Secretary of State for India in regard to his proposal for some kind of an Ambassador for various countries in Europe with his Headquarters in London. These discussions will enable him to present a more detailed and worked-out scheme which can be considered by the Cabinet here.

2. I have read the draft you gave me. There are some changes that I should like to suggest to you when we meet. Some of these changes are in the nature of re-drafting with a variation of approach or emphasis. There is one matter, however, which has not so far been mentioned between us but which seems to me is deserving of clarification. It is really consequential to what is proposed to be done.

3. This relates to Clause 7 of Paragraph 19 of the Cabinet Mission's plan of May 16, 1946. This Clause 7 states that any resolution in the Union Constituent Assembly raising any major communal issue shall require a majority of the representatives present and voting of each of the two major communities. This Clause had some meaning in the old context of the Union Constituent Assembly comprising all the Provinces. But if there is to be a partition and some Provinces or parts of Provinces go out, then the clause ceases to have significance. Of course there will be every provision for the protection of minority rights in the constitution. The Constituent Assembly has already considered and passed many of these provisions. Apart from this, the procedure should be ordinary democratic procedure and it should not be open to a very small number of persons to hold up the proceedings of the Constituent Assembly on what may be considered a major communal issue. As I have said above, there is no point in this clause after some kind of a partition has been made. I am not trying to get out of any part of the Cabinet Mission's scheme. I wish to point out merely a necessary consequence of the other changes proposed.

4. There is one other small matter. In Sylhet I think there should be some provision for a referendum at some stage or other. This would be fair to all parties concerned and in view of the major change involved and the balance of population there, it would be desirable to have a final verdict from the people concerned.

5. As previously pointed out, a small change would be necessary in regard to a predominantly Hindu Rajput area in Sind.

6. I take it that decisions in regard to Sylhet and Baluchistan would be taken after the main decisions in Bengal and Punjab have been taken. They would partly be influenced by the latter decisions.

Yours sincerely,
JAWAHARLAL NEHRU

Krishna Menon will be leaving tomorrow noon by BOAC and reaching London on Monday morning at 7 a.m.

457

*Record of Interview between Rear-Admiral Viscount Mountbatten of Burma
and Sardar Baldev Singh*

Mountbatten Papers. Viceroy's Interview No. 138

TOP SECRET   *16 May 1947, 11.30 am–12.15 pm*

I gave Sardar Baldev Singh a copy of the present draft of the Plan, with the request that he should show it to nobody else and that he would bring it back in person at 11 o'clock tomorrow morning together with a letter expressing the greatest measure of agreement or acceptance he felt justified in putting in a letter.

He was very anxious that there should be a paragraph saying that H.M.G. had at least considered the Sikh community. I invited him to draft a proposed paragraph and said I would consider its inclusion.

I explained to him very carefully that great consideration had been given by myself and my staff, together with the Governor of the Punjab, and Pandit Nehru, as to what could be done about the Sikhs. I explained to him exactly why we could not depart from the simple formula put up by the Congress; viz that no non-Muslim majority areas should be included in Pakistan.

He said that he saw that point, but still regretted that we could not make an exception in favour of the Sikhs for all the various reasons that he had put in his previous letters.

He said that there might be regret and even resentment at this decision so far as the Sikh community was concerned, but he gave an assurance that they would not be so foolhardy as to try and fight about it.

I told him that I was indeed glad to hear this, since he as Defence Member knew very well that the Cabinet had unanimously passed a resolution to the effect that any attempt at communal warfare should be immediately put down with the utmost rigour.

I informed him that I had mentioned this resolution to Lieutenant-General Smith, and had invited him to discuss it with the Defence Member.

I called upon Sardar Baldev Singh to arrange for the full implementation of this policy so far as it lay within his power. I was leaving instructions with Sir Eric Mieville to ensure that the necessary orders were passed to those concerned.

Sardar Baldev Singh once more assured me that he was fully in sympathy with this policy and was convinced that only the most drastic action, by tanks, armoured cars, artillery and aircraft, could stop the spread of communal warfare once it started.

458

Note by Mr Scott

*Mountbatten Papers. Official Correspondence Files: Transfer of Power,
Part II(b)*

16 May 1947

I had 45 minutes discussion with Jinnah and Liaquat Ali and succeeded in arguing them out of their proposal about constituencies.

2. They finally agreed that their desires would be met by including in the announcement the major term of reference of the Boundary Commission in the following words:

"The Boundary Commission will be instructed to demarcate the boundaries of the two parts of the Punjab on the basis of ascertaining the contiguous majority areas of Muslims and non–Muslims down to girdawar circles.

"Similar arrangements will be made for Bengal and Assam."

3. This is the lowest practicable area, including probably on an average at least 30 villages, which could be allotted to one side or the other.

I. D. SCOTT

P.S. Neither Jinnah nor Liaquat Ali had heard of girdawar circles.

459

Rear–Admiral Viscount Mountbatten of Burma to Pandit Nehru

*Mountbatten Papers. Official Correspondence Files: Transfer of Power,
Part II(b)*

SECRET AND PERSONAL   NEW DELHI, *16 May 1947*
No. 1446
Dear Mr Nehru
Thank you so much for your letter of the 16th May[1] and for your comments on the draft. I note that you have some changes in the phrasing to suggest when we next meet.

2. With regard to your paragraph 3 about Clause 7 of paragraph 19 of the Cabinet Mission's plan of the 16th May 1946, I think that the point you mention is covered by the last sentence of paragraph 20 of the draft paper,[2] in which you will see it is stated that the existing Constituent Assembly and the new Constituent Assembly will be free to frame their own rules.

3. I will look into the point you mention about a referendum for Sylhet,

but, of course, this may prove to be unnecessary in the light of the decision which Bengal may take. I agree, of course, that decisions in regard to Sylhet and Baluchistan, like the Frontier Province, will have to be taken after the main decisions in Bengal and the Punjab have been reached.

4. I remember the point you raise about the predominantly Hindu area in the Sind, and the possibility of its transfer to Jodhpur. I do not think, however, that this is a matter for mentioning in the main statement, since it would open the way for Muslim League claims in other parts, which they have hinted at. However, we can discuss this.

5. Thank you for telling me of Krishna Menon's movements.

Yours sincerely,
MOUNTBATTEN OF BURMA

¹ No. 456.   ² See No. 430.

460

Rear-Admiral Viscount Mountbatten of Burma to Sardar Patel

R/3/1/130: ff 223–4

No. 592/58   *16 May 1947*

Dear Sardar Patel,

Thank you for your letter of the 1st May,¹ about the Cabinet Mission plan, which I delayed answering until I had gone into the matter while at Simla.

2. It has always been clear that the Cabinet Mission plan provided that the representatives of certain provinces should sit together in sections; and that those sections, operating by a simple majority vote, should have two main tasks:

  (i) to frame constitutions of provinces comprising the sections; and

  (ii) to decide whether or not to set up a group government under a group constitution.

3. Provinces would acquire the right to opt out of a group (if the section decided to set one up) only after the first elections held under the new constitution, which had been framed by the section. There was never any question of the constitution being referred in the first instance to existing legislative assemblies for approval.

4. There always was inherent in this plan the risk that a provincial constitution might be rigged by the majority in a section; in the case of Assam, there undoubtedly has been a fear on the part of the present Assam ministry that a constitution devised for Assam by section C would be such as would in effect

¹ No. 268.

put them out of office. The answer to this is that they must trust the majority in section C not to abuse its powers, in the same way as that majority in section C would have to trust the Congress majority in the Union Assembly not to abuse its power in regard to the federal subjects, etc.

5. The matter is of course most important from the point of view of both the major parties; and if only the position could be fully accepted and appreciated, there would still be a chance that the Cabinet Mission plan could be made effective.

Yours sincerely,
[MOUNTBATTEN OF BURMA]

461

Rear-Admiral Viscount Mountbatten of Burma to Pandit Nehru

R/3/1/155: f 2

No. 1040/4   *16 May 1947*

Dear Pandit Nehru,

When we were discussing things in Simla, you raised with me the question of Baluchistan, and how its voice could most appropriately be heard, and in this connection I have noted your view expressed in External Affairs Department letter D.O. No. 673/S of 7th May, to Sir Geoffrey Prior.[1]

2. I shall be grateful if you would suggest to me some alternative scheme which could be used instead of the Shahi Jirga; which I should be quite prepared to consider. You will, I am sure, realise that it is not possible suddenly to alter the tribal system under which most of Baluchistan functions, and that therefore any alternative proposal must take account of that fact. Secondly, the only considerable town in Baluchistan is Quetta, which is inhabited almost entirely by non-Baluchis, and in fact in its present form, is a result of British rule in India. It would therefore be undesirable that it should have any kind of deciding voice in the future of Baluchistan, although it must, of course, be represented.

3. In any case, External Affairs Department's recommendation, which I have approved, that A.G.G. Baluchistan should come to Delhi for discussions might be of great value if we get him here as soon as possible.[2]

Yours sincerely,
MOUNTBATTEN OF BURMA

[1] Not traced.

[2] Pandit Nehru acknowledged Lord Mountbatten's letter on 17 May saying that he realised the difficulties of consulting the people of Baluchistan regarding their future. After consultation with the A.G.G. Baluchistan and others, the External Affairs Department would make such suggestions as appeared feasible. Mountbatten Papers, Official Correspondence Files: Transfer of Power, Procedure for determining authorities to which power is to be demitted, Part (2).

462

Rear-Admiral Viscount Mountbatten of Burma to Sir F. Burrows (Bengal)

Mountbatten Papers. Letters to and from Provincial Governors:
Bengal

No. 40/3.   *16 May 1947*

Thank you for your letter of the 6th May.[1] I am so glad to hear that you have made such good progress in Darjeeling and that you feel able to return to Calcutta on Monday next.

2. Many thanks for your suggestion about Indian Governors. I also have been thinking along the same lines and when the political decision about transfer of power has been taken I am sure we shall have to start replacing the British Governors.

3. On my return from Simla on the 14th May I had a long talk with Suhrawardy and his Minister for Land and Land Revenue.[2] Suhrawardy told me that, as a result of our previous conversation[3] and the one that I had had with K. S. Roy,[4] they had been having discussions about retaining the unity of Bengal. He added that Sarat Chandra Bose had also joined in the conversation.

4. He said that they had made good progress and on the whole he was hopeful as to the result. He did not mention to me, however, that the document which Bose and Roy had handed to him, but of which I fortunately had already procured a copy myself, contained in its opening clause the words that "Bengal was to be a Socialist Republic".

5. I tackled him about this and told him that obviously if the term "Socialist Republic" were to be adopted now it would debar their entry into the British Commonwealth, whatever the rest of India might decide to do, and that if they wished to turn to any big power, the only one that I could think of if they insisted on calling it a "Socialist Republic" would be the Union of Soviet Socialist Republics. I went on to say that surely if they wished to be independent, it would be quite enough for them to call themselves "Bengal" and, if necessary, describe themselves as a "Free State". When they had formed

---

[1] In this letter Sir F. Burrows thanked Lord Mountbatten for his kindness and hospitality while he was in Delhi. He also explained why he favoured the idea of replacing, prior to June 1948, all Provincial British Governors by non-party Indians. Mountbatten Papers, Letters to and from Provincial Governors: Bengal.

[2] See also No. 446. No full record of Lord Mountbatten's interview of 14 May with Mr Suhrawardy appears in the Mountbatten Papers, Interviews series. The series does contain (No. 134) an addendum on the interview which was to be added to a note it was intended Sir E. Mieville would prepare. In the event Sir E. Mieville does not appear to have made the note. The addendum covers discussion on the Bihar riots.

[3] See No. 227.   [4] See No. 292.

their Constitution they could call themselves anything they liked, but it was silly to prejudge the issue at this stage. I drew Suhrawardy's attention to the recent statement by Patel on Dominion Status,[5] and suggested to him that until the situation was cleared up it seemed to me the greatest mistake possible for them to call themselves a Socialist Republic.

6. I went on to tell him that in the most recent correspondence with H.M.G. the suggestion was that provinces or parts of provinces not in A Group were going to be given the option of voting for Hindustan or Pakistan and not the option of remaining independent, but if, of course, the Bengal Legislative Assembly were to pass a resolution asking for independence and give it to you, I knew that you would pass it on to me with your recommendations and that I should judge the case in the light of what you said.

7. I finally told him that if an agreement were to be reached by the Hindus and Muslims in Bengal on a coalition Government basis, I would urge the leaders of the Congress and Muslim League High Commands to accept it, and knew that Gandhi would help. If this were done by the 2nd June I would do my utmost to obtain the agreement of the leaders that the final announcement should contain no reference to the partition of Bengal.

8. I warned him that Nehru was not in favour of an independent Bengal unless closely linked to Hindustan, as he felt that a partition now would anyhow bring East Bengal in to Hindustan in a few years.

9. Suhrawardy finished by referring once again to the question that, if the words "Socialist Republic" were cut out and Bengal asked to remain within the British Commonwealth, whether I would be prepared to support such a proposal. I told him that my position remained the same, that in no circumstances would I recommend to H.M.G. that Bengal should be allowed to come into the Commonwealth unless the bulk of India were to make a similar request.

10. I beg of you to use all your influence on Suhrawardy, Bose and Roy not to use the phrase "Socialist Republic" or anything like it until the Constituent Assembly has met later on, because, as I said in paragraph 5, it would be the greatest mistake, in the light of Patel's recent statement on Dominion Status, for Bengal to declare itself a Socialist Republic until the situation has been cleared up, and until it can be definitely seen whether the Indian Union is going to remain within the British Empire, which now seems to be a likely eventuality.

11. I have just been recalled to England for discussions and am leaving on Sunday or Monday. Colville will be taking my place as Viceroy for the ten day period I expect to be away.

[5] See No. 375.

463

Viceroy's Conference Paper V.C.P. 49

L/PO/6/121: ff 266–70

MUSLIM LEAGUE COMMENTS ON THE DRAFT ANNOUNCEMENT

TOP SECRET   THE VICEROY'S HOUSE, NEW DELHI, *17 May 1947*

Attached is a copy of a note from Mr Jinnah containing his views on the Draft Announcement.[1] This was received in the very early morning of Saturday, 17th May, 1947.[2]

V. F. ERSKINE CRUM
Conference Secretary

I have examined the copy of the "Draft Announcement" furnished to me by you a couple of days ago. As you are pressed for time and you wanted me to give you my suggestions, I have, under high pressure, complied with your wishes, especially, as I was given to understand, that you are leaving on Sunday morning.

I INTRODUCTION

1) With regard to paragraph 1, I wish to state that the Muslim League has finally and definitely decided that they cannot accept the Cabinet Mission's Plan of May 16, 1946.

2) Paragraph 2 is, as far as I can ascertain, substantially correct and, in view of what I have stated in paragraph 1, it is immaterial.

3) With regard to paragraph 3, so far as I know, there is no agreement and His Majesty's Government through you as their representative are proceeding to transfer power in accordance with the White Paper of 20th February, 1947. As regards the statement "nor is there anything in this Plan to preclude negotiations between communities for an united India", the Muslim League has already decided that India must be divided and Pakistan should be established.

II THE ISSUES TO BE DECIDED

4) I cannot agree that the present existing Constituent Assembly should be allowed to continue. Because, in my opinion, it is *ab initio* invalid, but I agree that two independent Constituent Assemblies should be established, one for Pakistan and the other for Hindustan; and all power and authority should be transferred to the Pakistan and Hindustan Constituent Assemblies.

---

[1] See No. 430.

[2] The text of Mr Jinnah's note was circulated to the India and Burma Committee under the reference I.B.(47)73 of 20 May 1947. L/PO/6/121: ff 225–36.

III BENGAL AND THE PUNJAB

5) The Muslim League cannot agree to the partition of Bengal and the Punjab. It cannot be justified historically, economically, geographically, politically or morally. These provinces have built up their respective lives for nearly a century, administratively, economically and politically, and the only ground which is put forward for the partition is that the areas where the Hindus and Sikhs are in a majority should be separated from the rest of the provinces, on the ground that the Caste Hindus and Sikhs don't want to be under a government in which the Muslims will be in a majority.

The same can be urged by the Muslims and others that they don't want to be under a Government in which the Caste Hindus are in a majority and therefore other provinces should also be partitioned. It may be noted that there will be nearly 25 million of Mussalmans under the Hindu Government in Hindustan and millions of other communities such as the Scheduled Castes, the Christians, Adibasis and Tribes. The principle underlying the demand for establishment of Pakistan and Hindustan is totally different and I have already sent my Statement to you which I issued on the 30th of April,[3] copy of which has also been sent to the Prime Minister. The Muslim League therefore cannot agree to the partition of Bengal and the Punjab and I do hope that His Majesty's Government, when they examine this demand will not accept it and that you and His Majesty's Government will both, in the name of justice and fair play, not submit yourselves to this clamour. For it will be sowing the seeds of future serious trouble and the results will be disastrous for the life of these two provinces and all the communities concerned.

In this connection I may draw your fullest consideration and earnestly press upon you that if you take this decision—which in my opinion will be a fateful one—Calcutta should not be torn away from the Eastern Bengal. It has been the heart of Bengal and the Province has developed and grown round this capital of Bengal which was for decades the capital of India before Delhi was established as capital. Merely because the majority of the Caste Hindu vocal section desires Bengal to be partitioned—for in Western Bengal there are 34% Muslims, and out of the remaining 66% the Scheduled Castes are 63% and Caste Hindus 37%, which is less than one third of the total population of the Western Bengal. I have every reason to believe that the Scheduled Castes are strongly opposed to the partition of Bengal because they rightly say that they will be divided into two parts, one at the mercy of the Caste Hindus in Western Bengal and the other at the mercy of the Muslims in Eastern Bengal. They dread the Caste Hindus and it is well known that they have suffered economical and social tyranny at the hands of the Hindus for which there is no parallel in the world. But if, unfortunately, partition is decided upon and Eastern Bengal is deprived of its only port of Calcutta which has developed its present position, in no case should it be allowed to go with the Western Bengal, otherwise it will follow as a corollary that Western Bengal will go into Hindustan and His Majesty's Government will be making the present of one great port to Hindustan. In any event, if worst comes to worst, Calcutta should be made a free port.

Paragraphs 6, 7 and 8) These paragraphs relate more to procedure on the assumption that the issue of partition is decided upon and that these two provinces of Bengal and the Punjab should be cut up into two. I cannot say that the procedure laid down is satisfactory. The one governing principle which has been accepted by you is that the real will of the people of the part that wants to separate should be ascertained and the inhabitants of that part must be given every facility to give their verdict freely and fairly and this can only be done in a satisfactory manner by a plebiscite or a referendum, no doubt on the basis of 1941 census. I may point out that having regard to the Communal Award, which was modified by the Poona Pact in tragic circumstances, the Scheduled Castes have been completely left at the mercy of the Caste Hindus in the Electorates. Besides, owing to the well known fact that the Scheduled Castes are socially and economically so weak that even in the present electorates their number does not reflect the real strength of the population. Illiteracy and poverty are rampant amongst them and they are not qualified to come on the electoral rolls having regard to the present standard of franchise which is laid down. Therefore, great danger lies in a decision being taken on the question of separation of the Western Bengal from Eastern Bengal without any effective voice of the Scheduled Castes being secured.

9) With regard to paragraph 9 and taking paragraph 5 along with it, Punjab and Bengal provinces will be divided according to administrative districts as laid down in the Appendix, and paragraph 9 says, "for the purpose of deciding the issue of partition, Bengal and the Punjab provinces will be divided according to administrative districts as laid down in the appendix". These appendices have not been furnished to me along with the "Draft Announcement" and this is not a satisfactory position and will convey a totally wrong impression to the public. I, however, note that paragraph 9 proceeds on to say that "for the purpose of a definitive partition of these provinces a more detailed investigation of boundary question will be needed [and] as soon as the decision involving partition has been taken for either province a Boundary Commission will be set up, the membership and terms of reference of which which will be settled in consultation with those concerned. Until the report of a Boundary Commission has been put into effect, the provisional boundaries indicated in the Appendix will be used". I have already said that I have not got the appendix but if the object is to ascertain contiguous majority areas of Muslims and non-Muslims, I would press upon you to lay down clearly that: the Boundary Commission will be instructed to demarcate the boundaries of

3 Annex I to No. 276.

the two parts of the Punjab on the basis of ascertaining contiguous majority areas of Muslims and non-Muslims down to Girdawar circles, and that similar arrangement will be made in the case of Bengal.

V N.W.F.P.

With regard to the paragraph 11, I cannot agree that there should be any consultation with the provincial Government. Besides there is no indication as to what will be the position of the provincial Government and the present Ministry in the N.W.F.P., if the referendum results in the verdict that N.W.F.P. wants to join the Pakistan Constituent Assembly, because after the verdict in favour of Pakistan, the present Ministry cannot be allowed to carry on the administration of the Province.

VI BRITISH BALUCHISTAN

12) I may point out that about 90% of the population of British Baluchistan is Muslim and even the present elected member of the Constituent Assembly under the Cabinet Delegation scheme from British Baluchistan is a Muslim Leaguer and has not taken his seat in the existing Constituent Assembly.

If, however, a fresh representative were to be chosen then some truly representative democratic machinery which will ensure free and fair expression of the views of the people, should be set up for the purpose.

VII ASSAM

Assam is neither a Muslim province nor a Hindu province. The district of Sylhet and the areas adjoining the district and contiguous to Bengal are predominantly Muslim. In the event of partition of Bengal, Sylhet District and other Muslim majority areas of Assam contiguous to Bengal should be amalgamated to the Eastern Bengal. Here again we want to get a true verdict, free and fair, of the inhabitants of those areas. I am not in a position to say whether the procedure that you have laid down will secure the object and it requires further examination. I may also point out here that it is difficult for me to understand how the rest of the Assam province will in any case continue to participate in the existing Constituent Assembly, or a new Hindustan Constituent Assembly.

I would further like to add that in case Bengal is partitioned those areas of the Purnea district in Bihar which are contiguous to Eastern Bengal and have a Muslim majority should be amalgamated with Eastern Bengal.

15) It is not quite clear to me when it is stated that these representatives (which are stated in paragraph 14) "will either join the existing Constituent Assembly or form a new Constituent Assembly according to the mandate given to them by the areas concerned". For up to this state in your proposals there are only two constituent Assemblies contemplated.

IX TRANSFER OF POWER

16) With regard to paragraph 16, all power including Defence, Foreign Affairs, Finance and Communications and all other matters which are now dealt with by the Central Government or His Majesty's Government, should be transferred to the Constituent Assemblies of Pakistan and Hindustan.

XI THE TRIBES OF THE NORTH WEST FRONTIER

18) It is not clear as to who will be the appropriate successor authorities to negotiate with the tribes of the N.W.F.P. of India. It must be made clear and in my opinion it can only be the Pakistan Constituent Assembly.

464

Viceroy's Conference Paper V.C.P. 50

L/PO/6/121: ff 262–5

CONGRESS COMMENTS ON THE DRAFT ANNOUNCEMENT

TOP SECRET   THE VICEROY'S HOUSE, NEW DELHI, *17 May 1947*

Attached is a copy of a note from Pandit Nehru containing his views on the Draft Announcement.[1] This was received on the afternoon of Friday, 16th May, 1947.[2]

V. F. ERSKINE CRUM
Conference Secretary

NOTE

SECRET   NEW DELHI, *16 May 1947*

1. The Congress fully accepted the Cabinet Mission's Scheme of May 16, 1946, and has since acted in accordance with its provisions. We stand by the Scheme still and we think that this should continue to be the basis of any change in the future. The Interim Government itself is an outcome of this Scheme.

2. While the Cabinet Mission's Scheme of May 16th has been functioning and been acted upon, it is true that the Muslim League has kept away from it. For the sake of a settlement with the League we are prepared to accept variations of the Cabinet Mission's Scheme though it must be understood that fundamentally that Scheme continues to function.

3. It is in this context that we have considered the plan which H.M.G. propose to put forward. This plan, as we understand it, is a continuation of the

[1] See No. 430.
[2] The text of Pandit Nehru's note was circulated to the India and Burma Committee under the reference I.B.(47)73 of 20 May 1947. L/PO/6/121: ff 225–36.

Cabinet Mission's Scheme with suitable variations to fit in with the existing situation and in order to bring about an abiding settlement. We accept this plan generally but our acceptance is strictly subject to the other parties agreeing to it as a final settlement and that no further claims are put forward.

4. In the event of the Muslim League not agreeing to this plan, we must adhere strictly to the Cabinet Mission's Scheme of May 16, 1946, under which the Interim Government was formed. In this Interim Government there is no place for those who finally reject the Cabinet Mission's Scheme.

5. In accepting generally the plan which H.M.G. propose to put forward, we should like to point out that in the event of the various partitions mentioned in that plan taking place, it follows that the clause in the Cabinet Mission's Scheme in paragraph 19 dealing with major communal matters has no further significance.

6. We would like the following variations made in the draft of the plan. These do not affect the essential nature and purpose of the plan.

(a) Paragraph 1 should read as follows "On February 20, 1947, H.M.G. announced their intention of transferring power in British India to Indian hands by June 1948. H.M.G. had hoped that it would be possible for the major parties to cooperate in working out of the Cabinet Mission's Scheme of May 16, 1946, and evolve for India a constitution acceptable to all concerned. This hope has not yet been fulfilled. H.M.G. are, therefore, faced with the task of making further efforts to implement their intention of transferring power including such variations of the Scheme of May 16th and the adjustments consequent to them as would enable the major parties to cooperate in a peaceful transfer of power."

(b) Paragraph 3. The reference to agreement with political leaders would be justified if there is a final settlement and all parties agree.

(c) Paragraph 4 should run thus: "It is not the intention of H.M.G. to interrupt the work of the existing Constituent Assembly, and H.M.G. trust that, as a consequence of this announcement, the Muslim League representatives of those Provinces a majority of whose representatives are already participating in it, will now take their due share in its labours." The rest of the paragraph will remain as drafted.

(d) Paragraph 7 is by no means clear. We do not object to it, but as drafted it may create all manner of difficulties.

(e) Paragraph 9. Who will decide the composition of the Boundary Commission? It should be stated quite clearly that the Boundary Commission will have to take into consideration many other factors also apart from the nature of the population.

(f) Paragraph 11. As stated in this paragraph, the referendum will be held in consultation with the Provincial Government. We cannot answer for the

Provincial Government or commit it, but we are prepared to request them to agree to this procedure.

(*g*) Paragraph 13. There is a reference to the contiguous Muslim majority areas of Districts adjoining Sylhet. This reference seems to be unnecessary. The Boundary Commission will certainly have to take such matters into consideration not only in Assam but also in Sind.

(*h*) Paragraph 16. This seems to be unnecessary here. We do not object to the idea underlying it, but it will be for us to consider later what is the best form of giving effect to it.

(*i*) Paragraph 19. We suggest that only the first three lines of this paragraph should remain and the rest[3] should be deleted; further that the following addition be made after "Indian States" in the 3rd line: "as stated in the Cabinet Mission's Scheme of May 16, 1946".

(*j*) Paragraph 20. In line 8 after "new Constituent Assembly" add "if formed".

7. We have not seen the appendix giving the list of districts. As we have pointed out previously, the position of the Sikhs in the Punjab is a very difficult one under the scheme and every effort should be made to ease the situation for them. A suggestion was made and apparently accepted that in Gurdaspur District and others similarly situated the Hindu and Sikh representatives should go to the Eastern Punjab group and the Muslim representatives should go to Western Punjab. This may not be very logical, but it approaches somewhat a juster solution. It would be desirable to say something in the course of the document that the Boundary Commission should give due weight to all the factors and considerations advanced by various groups before coming to a decision; further that the notional division is entirely temporary for a particular purpose and no more.

8. There is no mention in the document of the Chittagong Hill areas which are predominantly Hindu and Buddhist. These are Excluded Areas lying to the east of East Bengal. They have nothing in common with Chittagong District or with East Bengal. They will naturally line up with some of the Hindu States to the north of them and possibly with Assam.

9. No mention is also made of other territories like the Andaman Islands. These also will naturally go with the Union of India.

JAWAHARLAL NEHRU

---

[3] i.e. the second sentence.

465

Viceroy's Conference Paper V.C.P. 51

Mountbatten Papers

REVISED DRAFT ANNOUNCEMENT[1]

TOP SECRET   THE VICEROY'S HOUSE, NEW DELHI, *17 May 1947*

Attached is a copy of the Draft Announcement as revised in the light of the Muslim League and Congress comments. (See V.C.P. 49 and V.C.P. 50).[2]

This copy was taken round to the Leaders on the morning of Saturday 17th May.

V. F. ERSKINE CRUM

Conference Secretary

DRAFT ANNOUNCEMENT

I INTRODUCTION

1. [This para. is the same as in No. 430 except that the second sentence reads: 'H.M.G. had hoped that it would be possible for the major parties to co-operate in the working-out of the Cabinet Mission's Plan of May 16th, 1946, and evolve for India a constitution acceptable to all concerned.']

2. [Same as in No. 430.]

3. [Same as in No. 430 except that, in the sentence beginning 'After full consultation and in agreement with political leaders in India . . .', the words 'and in agreement' have been deleted.]

II THE ISSUES TO BE DECIDED

4. With the exception of the provisions made hereafter for Bengal, the Punjab, Assam, Sind, the North-West Frontier Province and British Baluchistan, it is not the intention of H.M.G. to interrupt the work of the existing Constituent Assembly. H.M.G. trust that, as a consequence of this announcement, the Muslim League representatives of those Provinces a majority of whose representatives are already participating in it will now take their due share in its labours. [This para. then continues as in No. 430.]

III BENGAL AND THE PUNJAB

5. [Same as in No. 430.]

6. [Same as in No. 430.]

7. Before such a vote takes place, however, it is desirable that the representatives of each Province should clearly know which Constituent Assembly the Province as a whole would join, if they decided to remain united. Therefore, if there is a demand for it, a preliminary joint meeting of all members of each Legislative Assembly (other than Europeans) will be held at which a decision on this issue will be taken.

8. [Same as in No. 430.]

9. For the immediate purpose of deciding on the issue of Partition, the members of the Legislative Assemblies of Bengal and the Punjab will sit in two parts according to Muslim majority districts (as laid down in the appendix)[3] and non-Muslim majority districts. This is only a preliminary step of a purely temporary nature, as it is evident that for the purposes of a definitive partition of these provinces a detailed investigation of boundary questions will be needed; and, as soon as a decision involving partition has been taken for either province, a Boundary Commission will be set up by the Governor-General, the membership and terms of reference of which will be settled in consultation with those concerned. It will be instructed to demarcate the boundaries of the two parts of the Punjab on the basis of ascertaining the contiguous majority areas of Muslims and non-Muslims, down to girdawar circles. It will also be instructed to take into account other factors. Similar instructions will be given to the Bengal Boundary Commission. Until the report of a Boundary Commission has been put into effect, the provisional boundaries indicated in the Appendix will be used.

IV SIND

10. [Same as in No. 430.]

V N.W.F.P.

11. [Same as in No. 430.]

VI BRITISH BALUCHISTAN

12. [Same as in No. 430.]

VII ASSAM

13. Though Assam is predominantly a non-Muslim Province, the district of Sylhet which is contiguous to Bengal is predominantly Muslim. There has been a demand that, in the event of the partition of Bengal, Sylhet should be amalgamated with the Muslim part of Bengal. Accordingly, if it is decided that Bengal should be partitioned, a referendum will be held in Sylhet district under the aegis of the Governor-General and in consultation with the Assam Provincial Government to decide whether the district of Sylhet should continue to form part of the Assam Province or should be amalgamated with the new Province of Eastern Bengal, if that Province agrees. If the referendum results in favour of amalgamation with Eastern Bengal, a Boundary Commission with terms of reference similar to those for the Punjab and Bengal will be set up to demarcate the Muslim majority areas of Sylhet district and

---

[1] Those parts of this paper that are similar to the preceding draft in V.C.P. 47 (see No. 430, note 2) have not been reprinted here, but all differences between the two drafts have been indicated.

[2] Nos. 463 and 464.

[3] The text of the Appendix was not circulated with this Paper; see Appendix to No. 476.

contiguous Muslim majority areas of adjoining districts, which will then be transferred to Eastern Bengal. The rest of the Assam Province will in any case continue to participate in the proceedings of the existing Constituent Assembly.

VIII REPRESENTATION IN CONSTITUENT ASSEMBLIES

14. [Same as in No. 430.]

15. [Same as in No. 430.]

IX THE SIKHS

16. H.M.G. have given long and careful consideration to the position of the Sikhs. The partition of the Punjab, if it takes place as a result of the decisions of Legislative Assembly members, will have the effect of dividing the Sikhs almost equally between the Muslim and non-Muslim areas. As the Sikhs constitute only 13% of the population of the Punjab and are not in a majority in even one district, it has proved impossible to provide a separate State for them. The only way the Sikhs could be kept together would be to avoid the partition of the Punjab.

X ADMINISTRATIVE MATTERS

17. Negotiations will have to be initiated as soon as possible on administrative consequences of any partition that may have been decided upon:
   (a) Between the representatives of the prospective successor authorities about all subjects now dealt with by the Central Government including Defence, Finance and Communications.
   (b) Between different successor authorities and H.M.G. for treaties in regard to matters arising out of the transfer of power.
   (c) In the case of Provinces that may be partitioned as to administration of all provincial subjects such as the division of assets and liabilities, the police and other services, the High Courts, provincial institutions, etc.

XI THE TRIBES OF THE NORTH WEST FRONTIER

18. [Same as in No. 430.]

XII THE STATES

19. H.M.G. wish to make it clear that the decisions announced above relate only to British India and that their policy towards Indian States remains unchanged.

XIII NECESSITY FOR SPEED

20. [Same as in No. 430 except that the parenthesis '(if formed)' has been inserted after the words 'new Constituent Assembly'.]

XIV FURTHER ANNOUNCEMENTS BY GOVERNOR-GENERAL

21. [Same as in No. 430.]

466

Viceroy's Conference Paper V.C.P. 52

Mountbatten Papers

PROPOSALS FOR TRANSFER OF POWER DURING THE INTERIM PERIOD

TOP SECRET   THE VICEROY'S HOUSE, NEW DELHI, *17 May 1947*

Attached is a list prepared by the Reforms Commissioner of points which the Indian Leaders were to be asked, on the morning of Saturday 17th May, to include in letters to be addressed to the Viceroy for the latter to take to London.

V. F. ERSKINE CRUM
Conference Secretary

PROPOSALS FOR TRANSFER OF POWER DURING THE INTERIM PERIOD

(1) In the event of the decision being taken as a result of the procedure announced by H.M.G. that there should be one Central Government in India, power should be transferred to the existing Constituent Assembly on a Dominion Status basis.

(2) In the event of the decision being that there should be two sovereign States in India instead of one, the Executive of each part should take over power in responsibility to its respective Constituent Assembly, again on a Dominion Status basis.

(3) The transfer of power in both the cases should be on the basis of the Govt. of India Act, 1935, with modifications to conform to the Dominion Status position.

(4) The Governor-General should be common to both the States.

(5) When the Dominion Constitution comes into operation, the Armed Forces in India should be divided between the two States. The units of these Forces will be allocated according to the territorial basis of their recruitment and will be under the control of the respective Governments. In the case of mixed units, the separation and re-distribution should be entrusted to a Committee consisting of the Commander-in-Chief and the Chiefs of the General Staff of the two States under the supervision of a Council consisting of the Governor-General and the two Defence Ministers. This Council will cease to exist as soon as its work is completed.

(6) Pending the passing of necessary legislation by Parliament which should be enacted as soon as practicable, to adjust India's position to that of a Dominion, the Interim Government at the Centre should by convention

be treated as a Dominion Government subject to the Governor-General exercising his over-riding powers to safeguard the legitimate interest of the minorities.

467

Rear-Admiral Viscount Mountbatten of Burma to Pandit Nehru

Mountbatten Papers: Official Correspondence Files: Round Table Conference, Indian Political Leaders, etc, Issue of Invitations to

No. 1446/2.   *17 May 1947*

Dear Pandit Nehru,

Thank you for your letter of the 13th May.[1] While I appreciate your point about the President of Congress representing the Party formally and officially I am afraid I do not feel able to accede to your suggestion that he should be invited to the conference I am holding on the 2nd June.

2. I am anxious, as you know, to keep our meeting as small as practicable and it is for this reason that I confined all the talks since I have been out here with yourself, Sardar Patel, Mr Jinnah, Mr Liaquat Ali Khan and Sardar Baldev Singh. I recognise, however, the importance of the President of Congress being brought fully into the picture, particularly in view of the fact that it will rest on him to steer the proposals through your Working Committee. What I propose to do, therefore, is to see him separately on the same day, but apart from my main meeting with the five leaders I have mentioned above, and to go through the paper with him.

3. I think this will meet your point and will also obviate the difficulty, with which I am sure I should be faced, of a request from Mr Jinnah for a further representative of the Muslim League to be included in order to balance the numbers, should I invite Mr Kripalani to be present.

Yours sincerely,

MOUNTBATTEN OF BURMA

[1] No. 423.

468

Rear-Admiral Viscount Mountbatten of Burma to Sir E. Jenkins (Punjab)

R/3/1/178: ff 55–6

No. 40/5.   THE VICEROY'S HOUSE, NEW DELHI, *17 May 1947*

My dear Jenkins,

Thank you for your letter of May 15th.[1] I sympathise greatly with you in the difficult days which you are having; and I am afraid that there is not likely to be any end to them until this announcement is out; and only then if I succeed in getting the agreement of the leaders to it. I am working very hard at this, and have hopes of succeeding before I leave for London. I fully agree with the strong measures you are taking, such as the prohibition of the Jor Mela and the action against *Dawn's* correspondent. The collective fine on Rawalpindi district should have a sobering effect.

2. I have spoken very strongly to Baldev Singh about the way in which Tara Singh has refused to cooperate with you and Muslim leaders in trying to control disturbances, but he says that it is because Tara Singh has had his life threatened by the Muslims that he cannot agree to meet them. Baldev, Patiala and Faridkot have also promised to do all they can to keep the Sikhs peaceful.

3. I have got the Cabinet's approval to the use of maximum force at the earliest possible moment (including air bombing if necessary) if there should be any outbreaks of violence;[2] and I shall support you up to the hilt in whatever measures you consider it necessary to take in this direction, as it is vital that the very first attempt at communal war should be utterly and ruthlessly crushed.

4. I hope to be away for less than ten days, and intend to stick to my programme of meeting the leaders on June 2nd. The points at issue in regard to the

---

[1] No. 450.

[2] Following this Cabinet meeting on 6 May 1947, the minutes of which record only that any outbreak of violence 'should be put down with a firm hand', a telegram was sent on 23 May on Baldev Singh's instructions to the Army Commander, Rawalpindi, authorising departure from the existing minimum force principle applicable to military action in support of the civil power. This telegram was almost immediately cancelled, but it was stated in a further telegram that consideration was being given to the amendment of the law so as to allow use of more than minimum force; and Mountbatten from London signified his approval of this.

The principle of minimum force, laid down in sub-section 2 of Section 130 of the Code of Criminal Procedure, had been emphatically reaffirmed in 1920 after General Dyer's flagrant departure from it at Jallianwala Bagh, Amritsar, in April 1919. To tear up this principle was now felt to be impossible and Governors were informed in a letter of 5 June 'that the long-standing principle of using the minimum force . . . must be maintained'. R/3/1/90: ff 63, 66–7; Mountbatten Papers, Minutes of Indian Cabinet Meetings, Case No. 129/28/47; *Ibid.*, Official Correspondence Files: Punjab, Situation in, Part I(b), and Pakistan and India, Plan of Action in event of Clashes etc.

announcement are now few and none of them is vital. I do not however delude myself that even if we get agreement now it will mean plain sailing hereafter.

With best wishes,

Yours sincerely,

MOUNTBATTEN OF BURMA

469

Sardar Baldev Singh to Rear-Admiral Viscount Mountbatten of Burma

Mountbatten Papers. Official Correspondence Files: Transfer of Power, Part II(b)

I BHAGWAN DAS ROAD, NEW DELHI, 17 May 1947

My dear Lord Mountbatten,

You very kindly showed me the draft Announcement yesterday.[1] I have now received the amended draft.[2] As I pointed out to you the first draft was quite unsatisfactory from Sikh point of view. The amended draft, if anything, is worse, because the relevant changes have obviously been made to meet the wishes of the Muslim League and ignore all I have represented on behalf of my community.

2. For instance, to say, as the amended draft does in paragraph 9 that the Boundary Commission "will be instructed to demarcate the boundaries of the two parts of the Punjab on the basis of ascertaining the contiguous majority areas of Muslims and non-Muslims, down to Girdawar circles", while leaving the "other factors" in the next sentence undefined, is wholly one-sided. I cannot accept this unless the phrase "down to Girdawar Circles" is omitted altogether. The next sentence should read:

"It will also be instructed to take into account other factors such as the property holdings of and land revenue paid by non-Muslims"

3. Then again, the chapter under heading "IX—The Sikhs" serves no useful purpose whatever as it stands. It should read as follows:

"H.M.G. have given long and careful consideration to the position of the Sikhs. The partition of the Punjab if it takes place as a result of the decision of the Legislative Assembly members will have the effect of dividing the Sikhs between Muslim and non-Muslim areas but as the necessity of partition has arisen mainly on account of Sikh demand and as it is impossible to devise a scheme under which the entire Sikh community can be brought into one province, care should be taken by the Boundary Commission to ensure that as large a percentage as possible of the Sikh population in the Province is left in the Eastern Punjab".

I would very strongly urge that the paragraph in the amended draft should read as I have suggested above. In any event the paragraph as it stands in the amended draft must be omitted.

4. I would again emphasise what I have stated in my earlier letters that nothing should be done in the preliminary stages of partition to prejudice the work of the proposed Boundary Commission as you yourself have agreed in your letter No. 592/90 received by me on the 5th instant.[3] To ensure this I would suggest that the basis of the formation of interim Ministries in the partitioned Punjab, as contemplated in para 17 of the amended draft should be as proposed in my letter dated the 7th May[4] and that the Eastern Punjab should consist of the two divisions of Ambala and Jullundur plus the three districts of Lahore, Amritsar and Gurdaspur in the Lahore Division. I am convinced that only by adopting this procedure for the interim period will the work of the Boundary Commission proceed satisfactorily in the interests of all parties concerned.

Yours sincerely,
BALDEV SINGH

[1] See No. 430.   [2] See No. 465.   [3] No. 315.   [4] No. 333.

470

Sir E. Mieville to Mr Suhrawardy

Mountbatten Papers. Official Correspondence Files: Bengal, Partition of, Part I(b)

PRIVATE AND CONFIDENTIAL   *17 May 1947*

Dear Mr Suhrawardy,

Thank you for your letter of the 15th May.[1] I quite understand that there must still be some confusion in your mind. I will try to answer your queries one by one so far as I am able, but you will, of course, realise that the Plan is not necessarily in its final form yet.

I feel that His Excellency would only consider a resolution of the Legislature for independence if it was subscribed to by a majority of the members of each party.

The partition vote would take place in any case. The object of the prior vote for ascertaining the likely future of the Province, if united, would only be to clarify the issue before the partition vote is taken, and give a better chance for unity.

[1] No. 446.

It is intended that the preliminary notional partition for voting purposes should be strictly on the basis of predominantly Muslim and predominantly non-Muslim districts. If the vote was in favour of partition, a Boundary Commission would sit to iron out the details. I am sure that you will agree that it is impossible to work on any other basis for the purely notional partition.

It is not intended that there should be a plebiscite or a referendum in Bengal.

I fully agree that even if Bengal was partitioned to begin with there would be nothing to prevent it from being united again on an agreed settlement.

There is no question of power being transferred to Constituent Assemblies before it is known which parts of Bengal will be represented in which Assembly.

I think that this covers your specific queries. I trust that you will regard any answers in the greatest confidence. I think that the other points of view put forward in your letter are already known to His Excellency.

E. C. MIEVILLE

471

Viceroy's Conference Paper V.C.P. 53

L/PO/6/121: ff 257–61

CONGRESS COMMENTS ON THE REVISED DRAFT ANNOUNCEMENT

TOP SECRET   THE VICEROY'S HOUSE, NEW DELHI, *17 May 1947*

Attached is a copy of further comments by Pandit Nehru on the revised Draft Announcement. This was received on the afternoon of Saturday 17th April [May], 1947.[1]

V. F. ERSKINE CRUM
Conference Secretary

SECRET AND PERSONAL   17 YORK ROAD, NEW DELHI,
17 May 1947

Dear Lord Mountbatten,

V. P. Menon has shown me the latest draft announcement[2] as well as draft proposals for the transfer of power during the interim period.[3] I have made certain comments to him in regard to them. I repeat these points below so that they may be before you in writing for facility of reference.

Draft Announcement

Paragraph 1. There has been some improvement. But I must say that I dislike the last sentence. There is no point in it and it is somewhat of an irritant. As a matter of fact, there has been an agreement between the Congress and H.M.G.

on the basis of the Plan of May 16th as well as their declaration of December 6, 1946. It might be said that all parties in India have accepted and agreed to this with the exception of the Muslim League. To go on laying stress on political parties being unable to reach an agreement is neither fair nor completely correct. In any event, it is not a very tactful approach to the problem. I still think that the changes I suggested[4] in paragraph 1 would improve it.

Paragraph 4. There has been a considerable change in this for the worse. Yesterday we were told that our suggestions had been accepted. Instead of that the whole structure of the sentence at the beginning has been changed laying emphasis on the exception rather than the rule. That exception has been dealt with separately later on in the document and there is no need to emphasise it right at the beginning of the paragraph. This emphasis leads to a wrong approach to the problem. It must be remembered that the Constituent Assembly has been functioning on the basis of an agreement with H.M.G. and in accordance with their plan of May 16, 1946. That is the basic theme. In view, however, of certain developments, it is proposed to make certain changes which are enumerated later on. Those changes apply ultimately only to the areas deliberately choosing to opt out of the purview of the Constituent Assembly. I suggest, therefore, that the wording I had recommended in my note yesterday for paragraph 4 should be kept. The present wording is not even in conformity with the original draft.

Paragraph 7. I fear that there is still lack of clarity. But I do not press this point any more as I have no objection to the intention behind this paragraph.

Paragraph 9. In this a reference is made to the demarcation of boundaries of the two parts of the Punjab on the basis of Girdawar circles. I do not know what these circles are. But I am told that our Sikh friends do not approve of this provision.

Paragraph 13. I notice the changes made. As there is a reference in this paragraph to "contiguous Muslim majority areas" and district [*sic* ? of districts] adjoining Sylhet, I do not see any logic how the same principle might not be borne in mind regarding that part of Sind which adjoins Kutch and Jodphur. This is the Thar Pakar area which is largely desert, but which contains one town Umarkot. The area is big enough in the map, but is very sparsely populated. I realise the difficulties you pointed out yesterday and I have no wish to press for any addition to the document in regard to this matter. But I hope that you will bear this in mind so that when final changes have to be made this matter should also be considered.

Paragraph 14[?16]. End-relating to the Sikhs. This is an addition. I think it is desirable that special reference be made to the Sikhs. But whether this

---

[1] The text of Pandit Nehru's letter was circulated to the India and Burma Committee under the reference I.B.(47)73 of 20 May 1947. L/PO/6/121: ff 225-36.

[2] See No. 465.   [3] See No 466.   [4] See No. 464.

paragraph will please them I rather doubt. The last sentence is not wholly correct. It is, of course, impossible to keep any group together 100 per cent. in a scheme of partition. But it must be possible to meet many of the Sikh demands by certain variations of the boundary line. As the paragraph stands, I think it will serve no useful purpose and had better be omitted.

All of us sympathise very greatly with the Sikhs and would like to help them as much as possible in their predicament. But I do not feel competent, in a matter affecting them intimately, to say anything on their behalf or to commit them.

Subject to the remarks I have above, I am prepared to agree to the draft announcement. My remarks do not relate to any basic provision in the announcement but rather to the wording of it. Naturally my general acceptance to this draft and the proposals contained therein can only be, at this stage, a personal acceptance. I shall place the matter before the Congress Working Committee when they meet, and urge them to accept these basic provisions.

May I, however, make it clear again, as I have done previously on several occasions, that this acceptance is bound up with the acceptance of others also. That is to say, if there is a settlement on this basis, we accept these proposals for the sake of the settlement. If there is no clear settlement then there is no point in our accepting these proposals and in that event we revert to the Cabinet Mission's Plan of May 16, 1946.

That Plan is, in fact, a kind of an agreement between H.M.G. and all others in India except the Muslim League. We would have liked that Plan to remain in its entirety. But with a view to a complete settlement of all claims and to the establishment of peaceful conditions, we are prepared to agree to a variation of the Plan as suggested in the draft announcement. A real settlement and an abandonment of further claims is an essential part of the scheme. Without this the proposals fall.

Proposals for transfer of Power
during the Interim Period

It is essential that there should be a transfer of power by convention or agreement simultaneously with these proposals. The present position is an intolerable one when there is no real responsibility anywhere and the situation deteriorates rapidly. If the proposals in the draft announcement are agreed to, then no further apprehension should remain in the minds of the Muslim League about any abuse of power or authority against them. In order, however, to remove any lingering apprehension, it may be said that the Governor-General will retain this over-riding power to safeguard the legitimate interests of minorities.

While we shall welcome any Parliamentary legislation for the interim period, this is really a matter for H.M.G. to consider as how best to give effect to the transfer of power. What we are more interested in is the immediate transfer by convention so that the present situation might be dealt with adequately and adjustments made immediately to fit in with the future.

In the draft proposals for the transfer of power it should be remembered, first of all, that these are for the interim period only and do not, in any way, take away from the announcement of February 20, 1947. The future set up will necessarily be determined by the authorities functioning in India or by the Constituent Assembly. The principle thing we are aiming at now is not only to create suitable conditions in India which will fit in with the interim period, but also to create a psychological atmosphere of friendship between India and England which will enable us to decide in a co-operative manner about our future relations.

Reference is made in these proposals to the transfer of power being on the basis of the Government of India Act 1935. It is inevitable that we should proceed on the basis of the existing structure subject to changes necessitated by the transfer of power. But the Government of India Act is a very complicated structure and some provisions of it may come in our way. It is to be clearly understood that power to change this Act during this interim period will vest with the authority in India. Naturally we will not desire to make changes for a brief period but the power should be there in case of need.

I do not know what Parliamentary legislation might be passed by H.M.G. Without knowing its provisions fully it is obvious that we cannot commit ourselves to it as none of us are parties to it.

I accept generally the draft proposals for the transfer of power subject to the clarification given above. In Paragraph 5 I should like to add at the end "or till other arrangements are made". This is merely to guard against the prolongation of the period contemplated in the paragraph.

We agree to the proposal that during this interim period the Governor-General should be common to both the States, if there are to be two States. For our part we shall be happy if you could continue in this office and help us with your advice and experience.

There is one important matter which so far has not been discussed, but which cannot be ignored. There should be some clause in our agreement to the effect that neither the Union nor the parts of India outside the Union forming a separate State, shall be entitled to permit bases, extra territorial rights, or other infringements of the sovereignty of their territories by any outside State or power. Some such agreement must be made between the two States in India for their mutual protection.[5]

We have discussed various schemes and proposals which involve a partition

---

[5] In a letter dated 18 May Captain Brockman asked Pandit Nehru if he would have any objection to paras. 13–19 of this letter being sent to Mr Jinnah. Pandit Nehru agreed to the request and the relevant extracts were sent to Mr Jinnah the same day. Mountbatten Papers, Official Correspondence Files: Transfer of Power, Part III(a).

of India. With great regret and in considerable agony of spirit we have agreed
to these proposals because we earnestly desire a peaceful settlement of our
problems and the least compulsion on any group or area. As you know we
have stood for a united India and we have worked for it for the greater part of
our lives. The partition proposed is not of our seeking. Our part in this proposed partition is only this that if there is to be a partition according to the will
of the people, there should also logically be a partition of certain provinces. We
have further agreed to certain territorial adjustments because H.M.G. has
apparently decided to hand over power only to a divided India. Because of our
anxiety to have power handed over and because of our belief that the present
situation urgently demands this, we are prepared to agree to the proposals
made on behalf of H.M.G. But we would greatly prefer to stand for a united
India as well as to continue to abide fully by the Cabinet Statement of May
16th. If there is no real settlement on the basis of the proposals now made and
no handing over of power in accordance with them, then inevitably we stand
for a united India and the Cabinet Statement of May 16th.

May I say how grateful I am for all the trouble you have taken in this matter.
It is largely because of your personality and our faith in your sincere goodwill
for India, that we have proceeded so far. I earnestly trust that we shall see
some (?) light soon and put an end to the horrors that are disfiguring India.

I have consulted Sardar Patel and this letter generally represents his views
also.

Yours sincerely,
JAWAHARLAL NEHRU

472

*Record of Interview between Rear-Admiral Viscount Mountbatten of Burma
and Pandit Nehru and Sardar Patel*[1]

Mountbatten Papers. Viceroy's Interview No. 139

TOP SECRET   *17 May 1947, 4.30 pm*

HIS EXCELLENCY THE VICEROY asked Pandit Nehru whether Congress
accepted the December 6th statement. PANDIT NEHRU categorically assured
His Excellency that Congress had accepted the Statement. HIS EXCELLENCY
THE VICEROY said that his request was with reference to a telegram[2] which he
(His Excellency) had received from Lord Ismay.

Then HIS EXCELLENCY THE VICEROY took Pandit Nehru through the
paragraphs of the Announcement.[3] He accepted the changes proposed. With

[1] Sir E. Mieville and Mr V. P. Menon were also present; the latter dictated this record.
[2] It is uncertain which telegram is referred to here.
[3] It is unclear whether Lord Mountbatten was considering No. 465 with Pandit Nehru or a further
amended version of it.

reference to Paragraph 13 of the Announcement, PANDIT NEHRU did not press his point concerning the Hindu areas in Sind. HIS EXCELLENCY THE VICE-ROY mentioned in this connection that Mr Jinnah had demanded the portion of Purnea District should go to Bengal. Questions of this kind should be referred to the Boundary Commission if there is a demand for amalgamation with one area or the other.

HIS EXCELLENCY THE VICEROY then showed Pandit Nehru the latest amendment to the proposals for transfer of power.[4] There was considerable discussion on this question. The important aspect which Pandit Nehru stressed very vehemently was that, once the Announcement was made, the Interim Government should be treated by Convention as a Dominion Government. HIS EXCELLENCY THE VICEROY said that he saw considerable difficulty in acceding to this request, but he was prepared, on his own part, to give the Government as much freedom as they wanted in the day-to-day administration. PANDIT NEHRU said that if the Interim Government was to be treated as a Dominion Government, it would have a great psychological effect. He was prepared to give the Governor-General over-riding powers both in respect of the protection of minorities and also on any matter affecting the separation of the Pakistan area. When these two principles were conceded, PANDIT NEHRU saw no reason why the Interim Government should not be treated by Convention as a Dominion Government. He said the present state of affairs was intolerable and he would be ready to resign if his request was not conceded. HIS EXCELLENCY THE VICEROY put forward two suggestions to meet Congress's point of view. One was that there should be Muslim members working in the Congress Departments and vice versa. This was not acceptable to both Pandit Nehru and Sardar Patel. The second alternative was that, immediately after 2nd June, the Muslim League should be asked to form a separate Government of their own, which would administer the Pakistan areas, and common matters should be discussed by both wings of Government. In the earlier part of the discussion, HIS EXCELLENCY THE VICEROY mentioned the position of Calcutta in the event of partition and of the possibility of an agreement between the two Governments of Eastern Bengal and Western Bengal as regards the jute trade. SARDAR PATEL was very strongly opposed to treating Calcutta as a free port, and His Excellency did not press his point further.

HIS EXCELLENCY THE VICEROY promised to put forward Pandit Nehru's point of view to H.M.G., and he further promised to devise some means by which Congress would be given a free hand so far as administration of Hindustan was concerned.

[4] Evidently an amended version of No. 466: see No. 482, para. 1.

473

*Record of Interview between Rear-Admiral Viscount Mountbatten of Burma
and Mr Jinnah and Mr Liaquat Ali Khan*[1]

Mountbatten Papers. Viceroy's Interview No. 140

TOP SECRET   *17 May 1947, 6 pm*

Certain minor amendments to the Draft Announcement were suggested by
Mr Jinnah and Mr Liaquat Ali Khan. HIS EXCELLENCY THE VICEROY said
that these amendments should be referred to the Congress Leaders for their
agreement.

MR LIAQUAT ALI KHAN stated that Purnea used to be a part of Bengal.
HIS EXCELLENCY THE VICEROY said that he could not, at the present stage,
tie himself down to any definite decision on the future of Purnea. He asked
Sir Eric Mieville to go into the question and to report to him by telegram.[2]
He also said that he would raise with H.M.G. the principle as to whether any
transfers of areas between British India and Indian States should be considered.
MR JINNAH gave his opinion that all transfers of territory should be confined to
British India.

MR JINNAH and MR LIAQUAT ALI KHAN had no further comments to
make on the Draft Announcement. It was agreed that Sir Eric Mieville should
send the finally revised copies the following day to the Indian Leaders.

HIS EXCELLENCY THE VICEROY said that he intended to recommend to
H.M.G. that the transfer of power in India should take place as soon as possible
—preferably by 1st October. He had informed the Prime Minister of Mr
Jinnah's expressed desire that Pakistan should remain within the British
Commonwealth. Congress had now put forward a similar request. He intended
to go ahead and pass both requests to H.M.G. The question which now required clarification was whether Mr Jinnah would prefer Pakistan to have its
own Governor-General or to share a common Governor-General with
Hindustan. He asked for Mr Jinnah's personal views.

MR JINNAH said that he could not commit himself on this subject straight
away; but he had been giving some thought to it and he felt that it would be
better to have two Governors-General. Also there should, in his opinion, be a
Representative of the Crown to be responsible for the division of assets as
between the two States. MR JINNAH said that he was extremely keen that His
Excellency should fill this post. He said that he had complete faith in His
Excellency, all of whose awards would be binding on him. He vehemently and
repeatedly declared his desire that His Excellency should stay on in India.

HIS EXCELLENCY THE VICEROY said that he was very honoured by Mr
Jinnah's remarks. However, he could not consider taking on a post such as Mr

Jinnah had suggested nor could he think of anybody else who would wish to do so. It would be an impossible position if the so-called "Arbitrator" was junior in rank to the Governors-General who would be the King's representatives.

MR LIAQUAT ALI KHAN asked how, if the two States wanted separate Governors-General, it was proposed that all assets would be divided by 1st October. HIS EXCELLENCY THE VICEROY replied that in this case the two Governors-General themselves would form an arbitration board. He went on to say that he was under extreme pressure from Congress who had stated that they would not continue in the Interim Government unless they were granted Dominion status immediately after the announcement. He felt that he might be able to hold the situation for a time but certainly not until the end of the year.

After further discussion, HIS EXCELLENCY THE VICEROY suggested that Mr Jinnah should send him a letter the following Monday (19th May) giving a full description of his suggestion of a supreme arbitrator and two Governors-General. However, he wished it to be quite clear that he would reserve his personal position unless it was clearly stated by Mr Jinnah in this letter that, if his scheme was found by H.M.G. to be impraticable, he would accept, as a less desirable alternative and as an interim measure, the appointment of a common Governor-General between the two States.

MR JINNAH at first expressed himself violently opposed to this suggestion but eventually, after prolonged discussion, he said that he would think it over. He pointed out that, if H.M.G. decided, contrary to his own opinion, that his suggestion was unworkable, there would be no reason for him not to accept an alternative.

MR LIAQUAT ALI KHAN said that he quite clearly realised the point which His Excellency the Viceroy wished Mr Jinnah to include in his letter.

It was agreed that Mr Jinnah should give this letter to Sir Eric Mieville on Monday morning, the 19th May; and that a copy of it would be sent to Congress. HIS EXCELLENCY THE VICEROY pointed out that, besides requiring the approval of H.M.G., Mr Jinnah's suggestion would also require agreement by Congress.

MR LIAQUAT ALI KHAN stated that the name of the Muslim State to be set up would definitely be Pakistan. MR JINNAH explained the derivation of the word Pakistan—P for Punjab; A for Afghan, (i.e. Pathan or N.W.F.P.); K for Kashmir; I for nothing because this letter was not in the word in Urdu; S for Sind and TAN for the last syllable for Baluchistan.

¹ Sir E. Mieville and Lieutenant-Colonel Erskine Crum were also present; the latter dictated this record.

² In tel. 1116–S of 22 May Sir E. Mieville reported to Lord Mountbatten that he had consulted Sir H. Dow on this matter who advised that 'if Bengal is divided it would probably be in best interests of Muslim majority areas of Purnea that they should be included in Muslim Bengal. There will no doubt be reactions from my Ministers and Hindu public.' R/3/1/167: f 5.

MR LIAQUAT ALI KHAN said that the literal meaning for Pakistan was "pure land".

NOTE: All the Muslim League amendments to the Draft Announcement were later accepted by Congress with the exception of one to Paragraph 18.[3] His Excellency decided later that evening that this proposal of the Muslim League would not be accepted.

[3] See No. 463.

474

Sir O. Caroe (North-West Frontier Province) to Rear-Admiral Viscount Mountbatten of Burma

Mountbatten Papers. Official Correspondence Files: Private Armies, Formation of a Territorial Army in India

TOP SECRET   PESHAWAR, *17 May 1947*
D.O. No. G.H. 57.

Dear Lord Mountbatten,

Your Excellency will remember that on the second day of the Governors' Conference the question of private armies was discussed and we were invited to keep you informed and to put forward ideas about their abolition.[1] It was also stated that you had decided to raise the question at the coming Conference with the leaders. During your visit to Peshawar I told you that my Ministry were pressing me to have a Home Guard, and also to distribute official rifles to this Guard. I resisted this, for I was quite sure at the time that they intended to use the rifles for distribution to Red Shirts, and this has now been proved.

2. While I was away in Delhi some official police rifles were issued in one District, namely Peshawar, and these have all gone to Red Shirts, who are parading them about and form armed guards when the Congress leaders go to meetings. Dr. Khan Sahib always pretends that Red Shirts are unarmed, but it is false, and entirely reliable sources confirm that the great majority of Red Shirts, particularly in the Charsadda area of Peshawar District, are very well armed indeed with .303 rifles from the Kohat Pass, most of them unlicensed. They have even been seen armed in Peshawar Cant[onmen]t.

3. On top of that we have this new formation of "Young Pathans". Dr. Khan Sahib again when I raised the matter tried to pretend, even in Council, that he knew nothing about it, but it is now confirmed by open announcement by Abdul Ghaffar Khan that this party has been raised with his blessing to form bodyguards and to "resist aggression" as a sort of counter to the League movement. The chief organiser is Abdul Ghaffar Khan's son, Abdul Ghani, the

M.L.A. (Central). I have already reported this move by telegram and it is dangerous. There is already a counter movement by the League to set up their own armed organisation. We have reached the strange position whereby the Government of the day has two armed organisations: one a sort of *corps é'élite* (its S.S.) which is acknowledged to be armed and another, the Red Shirts (its S.A.) who are known to be widely armed. In some cases the weapons may be licensed, and I am afraid it is the case that my Premier issues licenses to his own supporters with no discretion whatever in hundreds. There are cases also of unlicensed arms, for which only permits are given. The arms themselves can be got from the Kohat Pass factories, which are working overtime. It seems to me that if a responsible Government adopts measures of this kind, we are driven to think seriously once more how far it will be possible to leave it in office. How are we to hold any form of election or referendum with private armies going up and down the country? The logical course would no doubt be to declare at any rate the "Young Pathans" an unlawful association under the Criminal Law Amendment Act, but that would have to be done by the Provincial Government itself. (I suppose it is conceivable that I could take action myself in exercise of my special responsibility, but even that is a *reductio ad absurdum*.)

4. A certain amount of this may be regarded as a war of nerves, and a demonstration to set off the League meetings in Peshawar at the end of April. But it will be noticed that it all follows on the rather obscure threat uttered by Qazi Attaullah at the meeting of Ministers which Your Excellency saw in Peshawar on April 28th[2]—a threat which was repeated in the Ministry's comments on the minutes of that meeting.

Yours sincerely,

OLAF CAROE

[1] See No. 158.
[2] See Enclosure to No. 259 for the minutes of this meeting. The minutes do not record Qazi Attaullah's threat.

475

Cabinet

India and Burma Committee. Paper I.B.(47)71

L/P&J/10/79: ff 178–96

DRAFT STATEMENT OF POLICY
MEMORANDUM BY THE SECRETARY OF STATE FOR INDIA

INDIA OFFICE, *17 May 1947*

I circulate for consideration on the Viceroy's arrival a revised version of the Viceroy's revised draft communicated in telegram 66–S.C.[1] which, subject to further consideration on one major point, might I think be an acceptable compromise between the Viceroy's draft and that previously approved by the Committee. This revise is contained in Annex I. The Viceroy's own text is contained in Annex II.

2. The main differences between the Viceroy's draft and that previously considered by the Committee are:—

(i) A general change of presentation, to meet Pandit Nehru's views, which presents the existing Constituent Assembly as fulfilling the Cabinet Mission's plan and any new Constituent Assembly as a group of dissentient elements.

(ii) The removal of the proposal that the decisions should be taken by representatives elected by Legislative Assemblies or parts of Legislative Assemblies on the basis proposed in the Cabinet Mission's plan.

(iii) The choices under paragraph 4 are limited to two: adherence to the existing Constituent Assembly or to a new and separate one. The option to remain independent which was originally included has been dropped.

3. The Committee wished to know whether it would be consistent with the position taken in our previous Statements and in Government speeches in Parliament to refuse to Provinces the right to remain independent. I attach in Annex III the more important extracts from speeches bearing on this question. Under the Cripps Offer any Province had the right to opt out of the constitution made by the Constituent Assembly for the whole of India and thereafter to have a new constitution of its own with the same full status as the Indian Union (which was to be a Dominion). Between 1942 and the entry into office of the present Government it was several times reiterated that the main principles of the Cripps Offer stood as the settled policy of the Crown and Parliament. After the present Government came into office the Prime Minister in his statement of the 19th September, 1945, said that "the broad intention of British policy towards India contained in the declaration of 1942 . . . . . . stands in all its fullness and purpose" and at that time emphasis was laid on ascertaining the views of new Provincial Legislatures as to whether the Cripps Offer was

acceptable as it stood or whether some alternative or modified scheme would be preferable. Thereafter, the Cabinet Mission's plan took the field as the Government's policy and Provincial option fell out of the picture. We are, I think, bound, now that the Cabinet Mission's scheme is virtually abandoned, to adhere to the broad principles of the Cripps Offer. My colleagues may feel that this does not completely rule out limitation to the two alternatives as proposed by the Viceroy. But there are strong practical arguments for giving the third option of remaining united and framing its own constitution certainly to Bengal and probably also to the Punjab. I set these out in the next paragraph.

4. (a) The arguments for giving an option to remain united to Bengal are:—

(i) With or without Sylhet, Bengal is large enough to form an independent State.

(ii) In any event Bengal, if it does not adhere to Hindustan, will be in effect a separate State even though politically linked with North-Western Pakistan. To give the option in this case does not therefore open us to a charge of balkanisation.

(iii) Partition would be most damaging to the inhabitants of Bengal owing to the economic consequences of separating a large part of the hinterland from Calcutta.

(b) The arguments for giving a similar option to the Punjab are:—

(i) There is no other solution than a united Punjab for the Sikh problem. If the two parts of the Punjab have only two alternatives—Hindustan and Pakistan—partition becomes a certainty.

(ii) If the Punjab has an option to remain united and frame its own constitution, the Sikhs are more likely to be won over to this solution than if the constitution is framed in a Pakistan Constituent Assembly with a great preponderance of Muslim League voters.

5. The difficulties of giving such an additional option to the Punjab and Bengal alone are:—

(a) That if it is exercised, the Pakistan Constituent Assembly would contain only Sind and perhaps the North-West Frontier. Thus the result is almost the same as giving a separate option to remain independent to each area except Sylhet.

(b) That if the Punjab is given the right to frame its own constitution (which seems essential if there is to be any chance of a Muslim/Sikh settlement in the Punjab) Sind and the North-West Frontier must presumably be given the same right.

It would be possible to give the third option to Bengal only for the reasons stated under 4(a) above. It is, however, not possible to give this option to the Punjab as a whole without giving it also to Sind and the North-West Frontier.

[1] No. 430.

So far as the Punjab is concerned, therefore, the alternatives are between denying to the Punjab the chance of remaining united and thus greatly weakening what remaining chance there is of a satisfactory solution of the Sikh problem, and giving the third option to all the areas which under the plan have a separate right to choose. I think that the advantage of providing greater scope for negotiation between the parties in the Punjab is a consideration of major importance. It weighs substantially in the scales against Nehru's objections to giving an appearance of balkanisation. I should therefore be in favour of giving the third option to all the areas which have a right of choice. This has the advantage of being in conformity with the Cripps Offer and consistent with the right of self-determination. There seems no reason to suppose that in actual fact small areas such as half Provinces or the North-West Frontier would stand out for independence.

6. The revised draft in Annex I follows the Viceroy's text in regard to this main issue which must clearly be fully discussed with him. It has, however, been modified on certain other points and the modifications are shown underlined or sidelined in the text. I draw particular attention to the following points:—

(i) An amendment of the introduction and paragraph 4.

As the existing Constituent Assembly is not fully representative it is radically different from that proposed by the Cabinet Mission. The Viceroy's draft seems to go too far in the direction of accepting the existing Constituent Assembly as an implementation of the Cabinet Mission's plan. The amendments are designed to modify this tendency without emphasising the inevitability of partition.

(ii) The Viceroy's omission of provision for the election of representatives to take the necessary decisions appears to me to be acceptable. Now that the North-West Frontier is to decide by referendum, the Legislative Assembly representatives, who under the scheme will take the decisions, will in each case contain a majority of representatives of the majority of the population which they represent. In some cases the majority will be larger than it ought to be on a strict population basis owing to the weightage in the Legislature as a whole for minorities. (For example, the Sikhs will be over-represented in the Western Punjab). But this does not appear to matter in the circumstances envisaged.

(iii) New paragraph 6 contains the modified provisions for a third option for Bengal and the Punjab which I suggest above.[2]

(iv) Paragraph 11. The phrase "in consultation with the Provincial Government" in the Viceroy's version greatly weakens the effect of stating that the referendum will be under the aegis of the Governor-General. The amended version seems preferable.

(v) Paragraph 12. The possible methods of securing representation in the Constituent Assembly for Baluchistan were exhaustively considered during the Cabinet Mission and the election by the Shahi jirga and non-official members of the Quetta Municipality was found to be the only available course. I think that we should adhere to this method unless some better method can be found before the announcement is made.

(vi) Paragraph 19. I feel that it would be much better to revert to the Viceroy's original text as shown in the revised draft. It should be borne in mind that the two new Constituent Assemblies may frame much more centralised constitutions for their areas than the Union constitution under the Cabinet Mission's plan and that consequently it will be much more difficult for the States to cooperate in these Constituent Assemblies. I do not think therefore that we should give any impression of pressing the States to enter these Constituent Assemblies at any rate at this stage.

L.

Annex I to No. 475

AMENDED VERSION OF THE VICEROY'S REVISED STATEMENT[3]
I INTRODUCTION

1. [This para. is the same as in No. 430 except that the second sentence reads: 'H.M.G. had hoped that it would be possible for the major parties to co-operate on the basis of the Cabinet Mission's plan of 16th May 1946, and evolve *a Constitution for a Union of India which would be*[4] acceptable to all concerned.']
[paragraph 2 of Viceroy's draft omitted]

2. [3][5] [Same as in No. 430. In the sentence 'After full consultation and in agreement with political leaders in India, H.M.G. have decided to adopt for this purpose the plan set out below', the words 'and in agreement with' are in square brackets and a footnote states: 'the inclusion of these words will depend on whether it is decided that this statement should be made *only* if there is agreement to it.']

II THE ISSUES TO BE DECIDED

3.[4] It is not the intention of H.M.G. to interrupt the work of the existing Constituent Assembly in so far as it relates to those Provinces a majority of whose representatives are already participating (subject to provisions of paragraphs 10 and 12 below); *but* it is clear that any constitution framed by this Assembly cannot apply to those parts of the country which are unwilling to accept it. H.M.G. are satisfied that the procedure outlined below embodies the

---

[2] It would appear that the amendment described here was overlooked when Annex I was drafted as its para. 6 is precisely the same as the corresponding para. in Lord Mountbatten's telegram (No. 430).

[3] Paragraphs containing only minor verbal differences from the draft in No. 430 have not been reprinted here, but all important differences between the two drafts have been indicated.

[4] The words in italics are underlined in the original, indicating where amendments to the draft in No. 430 had been made.

[5] Numbers in square brackets indicate numbers of equivalent paragraphs of No. 430.

best practical method of ascertaining the wishes of the people of such areas on the issue of whether their constitution is to be framed (*a*) in existing Constituent Assembly; or (*b*) in a new and separate Constituent Assembly consisting of representatives of those areas which decide not to participate in existing Constituent Assembly. *When the wishes of the people as between these alternatives are known the basis on which power will have to be transferred will become clear.*

III BENGAL AND PUNJAB

4. [5]
5. [6]
6. [7]   } [Same as in No. 430.]
7. [8]

8. [9] [Same as in No. 430 except that the second sentence states that the terms of reference of the Boundary Commission will be settled 'by agreement between those concerned' instead of 'in consultation with'.]

IV SIND

9. [10] [Same as in No. 430.]

V NORTH WEST FRONTIER PROVINCE

10. [11] [Same as in No. 430 except that the last sentence reads:
'*The referendum will be held under the control of the Governor-General*'.]
[The remaining paragraphs contain only minor verbal differences from the draft in No. 430 except for para. 18.[19] which reads:]

XII THE STATES

18.[19] His Majesty's Government wish to make it clear that the decisions announced above relate only to British India and that their policy towards Indian States remains unchanged. When paramountcy lapses all rights surrendered by the States to the paramount power will return to the States. They are free to arrange, by negotiation with those parts of British India to which power will be demitted, whatever measure of association they consider to be in the best interests of their people. Whatever their decision, all will require to enter upon negotiations for new agreements, especially in the economic and financial sphere, on the lines contemplated in paragraph 4 of the Cabinet Mission's Memorandum on States' Treaties and Paramountcy of the 12th May, 1946 (Cmd. 6358, Item B) and to set up, as early as possible, alternative machinery for the regulation of matters of common concern on the lines contemplated in paragraph 5 of that memorandum.

Annex II to No. 475
VICEROY'S REVISED DRAFT
[*There follows the text of No. 430.*]

Annex III to No. 475.

EXTRACT FROM GOVERNMENT STATEMENTS AND
SPEECHES IN PARLIAMENT

1. The Prime Minister (Mr. Churchill) House of Commons, 10th September, 1942. *Hansard*: Vol. 383 Col. 302.:

"The broad principles of the declaration made by His Majesty's Government which form the basis of the Mission of the Lord Privy Seal to India must be taken as representing the settled policy of the British Crown and Parliament. These principles stand in their full scope and integrity."

Further statements to this effect were made on several subsequent occasions by the Secretary of State (Mr. Amery) during the Coalition and Caretaker Governments.

2. Broadcast by the Prime Minister (Mr. Attlee), September 19th, 1945.:

[The Cripps Offer] "was unfortunately not accepted by the leaders of the Indian political parties; the Government is, however, acting in accordance with its spirit and intention.

  ★   ★   ★   ★

The broad definition of British policy towards India contained in the Declaration of 1942, which had the support of all parties in this country, stands in all its fullness and purpose."

3. The Prime Minister, House of Commons, 15th March, 1946. *Hansard*, Col. 1424.

"We are very mindful of the rights of minorities and minorities should be able to live free from fear. On the other hand we cannot allow a minority to place a veto on the advance of the majority".

4. Cabinet Mission's Statement of 16th May (Cmd. 6821), paragraphs 11 and 12:

"We are therefore unable to advise the British Government that the power which at present resides in British hands should be handed over to two entirely different sovereign States.

12. This decision does not, however, blind us to the very real Muslim apprehensions that their culture and political and social life might become submerged in a purely unitary India in which the Hindus with their greatly superior numbers must be a dominating element".

5. Statement of H.M.G. on December 6th, 1946:

"Should a constitution come to be formed by a Constituent Assembly in which a large section of the Indian population had not been represented, His Majesty's Government could not, of course, contemplate—as the

Congress have stated they would not contemplate—forcing such a constitution upon any unwilling parts of the country."

6. Sir Stafford Cripps, House of Commons, 12th December, 1946, *Hansard,*
Col. 1354: (with reference to No. 5 above):

"This is perhaps a statement of the obvious, that if the Muslim League
cannot be persuaded to come into the Constituent Assembly then the parts of
the country where they are in a majority cannot be held to be bound by the
results."

7. Sir Stafford Cripps, House of Commons, 5th March, 1947, *Hansard,*
Col. 508:

"We shall certainly of course do all in our power to encourage the formation
of such a Government as put forward by the Cabinet Mission and in accordance
with the procedure which they suggested. But if this proves impossible of
realisation and there is no such Central Government in being or in prospect
when the time comes for us to take a decision, then we shall be forced to choose
in the light of existing circumstances at the time of our decision the most
appropriate Government or Governments to which to hand over power.
We have said in our Statement that it might be the then existing Provincial
Governments as suggested in the Offer of 1942 or [it] might be some form
of combined Government for parts of India depending on what seems best
and most helpful for the future of India.

★   ★   ★   ★

In our Statement of 6th December we stressed the fact that if a large section
of the Indian population had not been represented in the Constituent Assembly
we could not accept the forcing of unwilling Provinces into a united Indian
Government if in the making of the constitution they had not been fully
represented. To that principle we adhere; and if it should eventuate that a
large group of Provinces but not all agree upon a form of constitution then it
may be necessary to hand over separately [in] the areas which have not been
fully represented in the Constituent Assembly."

476

Viceroy's Conference Paper V.C.P. 54

R/3/1/150: ff 1–9

REVISED DRAFT ANNOUNCEMENT

TOP SECRET   THE VICEROY'S HOUSE, NEW DELHI, *17 May 1947*

Attached is a copy of the Revised Draft Announcement as taken by His Excellency the Viceroy to London.[1]

V. F. ERSKINE CRUM
Conference Secretary

DRAFT ANNOUNCEMENT

I INTRODUCTION

1. On February 20th 1947, H.M.G. announced their intention of transferring power in British India to Indian hands by June 1948. H.M.G. had hoped that it would be possible for the major parties to co-operate in the working-out of the Cabinet Mission's Plan of May 16th 1946, and evolve for India a constitution acceptable to all concerned. This hope has not been fulfilled.

2. The majority of the representatives of the Provinces of Madras, Bombay, the United Provinces, Bihar, Central Provinces and Berar, Assam, Orissa and the North-West Frontier Province, and the representatives of Delhi, Ajmer-Merwara and Coorg have already made progress in the task of evolving a new Constitution. On the other hand, the Muslim League Party, including in it a majority of the representatives of Bengal, the Punjab and Sind as also the representative of British Baluchistan, has decided not to participate in the Constituent Assembly.

3. It has always been the desire of H.M.G. that power should be transferred in accordance with the wishes of the Indian people themselves. This task would have been greatly facilitated if there had been agreement among the Indian political parties. In the absence of such an agreement, the task of devising a method by which the wishes of the Indian people can be ascertained has devolved on H.M.G. After full consultation with political leaders in India, H.M.G. have decided to adopt for this purpose the plan set out below. H.M.G. wish to make it clear that they have no intention of attempting to frame any ultimate Constitution for India; this is a matter for the Indians themselves. Nor is there anything in this plan to preclude negotiations between communities for an united India.

[1] On 20 May Sir E. Mieville (on Lord Mountbatten's instructions) sent copies of this revised draft announcement to Pandit Nehru, Mr Jinnah, Mr Liaquat Ali Khan and Sardar Baldev Singh. Pandit Nehru was sent a second copy of the announcement which was to be handed to Sardar Patel. Mountbatten Papers. Official Correspondence Files: Transfer of Power, Part III(*a*).

II THE ISSUES TO BE DECIDED

4. It is not the intention of H.M.G. to interrupt the work of the existing Constituent Assembly. Now that provision is made for certain provinces specified below, H.M.G. trust that, as a consequence of this announcement, the Muslim League representatives of those Provinces a majority of whose representatives are already participating in it will now take their due share in its labours. At the same time, it is clear that any Constitution framed by this Assembly cannot apply to those parts of the country which are unwilling to accept it. H.M.G. are satisfied that the procedure outlined below embodies the best practical method of ascertaining the wishes of the people of such areas on the issue whether their Constitution is to be framed:—

(*a*) in the existing Constituent Assembly;

or

(*b*) in a new and separate Constituent Assembly consisting of the representatives of those areas which decide not to participate in the existing Constituent Assembly.

When this has been done, it will be possible to determine the authority to whom power should be transferred.

III BENGAL AND THE PUNJAB

5. The Provincial Legislative Assemblies of Bengal and the Punjab (excluding the European members) will therefore each be asked to meet in two parts, one representing the Muslim majority districts and the other the rest of the Province. For the purpose of determining the population of districts, the 1941 census figures will be taken as authoritative. The Muslim majority districts in these two Provinces are set out in the Appendix to this Announcement.

6. The members of the two parts of each Legislative Assembly sitting separately will be empowered to vote whether or not the Province should be partitioned. If a simple majority of either part decides in favour of partition, division will take place and arrangements will be made accordingly.

7. Before such a vote takes place, however, it is desirable that the representatives of each Province should clearly know which Constituent Assembly the Province as a whole would join, if they decided to remain united. Therefore, if there is a demand for it, by any member of the Legislative Assembly, a preliminary joint meeting of all members of each Legislative Assembly (other than Europeans) will be held at which a decision on this issue will be taken.

8. In the event of partition being decided upon, each part of the Legislative Assembly will, on behalf of the areas they represent, decide which of the alternatives in para. 4 above to adopt.

9. For the immediate purpose of deciding on the issue of Partition, the members of the Legislative Assemblies of Bengal and the Punjab will sit in

two parts according to Muslim majority districts (as laid down in the appendix) and non-Muslim majority districts. This is only a preliminary step of a purely temporary nature as it is evident that for the purposes of a definitive partition of these provinces a detailed investigation of boundary questions will be needed; and, as soon as a decision involving partition has been taken for either province, a Boundary Commission will be set up by the Governor-General, the membership and terms of reference of which will be settled in consultation with those concerned. It will be instructed to demarcate the boundaries of the two parts of the Punjab on the basis of ascertaining the contiguous majority areas of Muslims and non-Muslims. It will also be instructed to take into account other factors. Similar instructions will be given to the Bengal Boundary Commission. Until the report of a Boundary Commission has been put into effect, the provisional boundaries indicated in the Appendix will be used.

IV SIND

10. The Legislative Assembly of Sind (excluding the European members) will at a special meeting also take its own decision on the alternatives in para. 4 above.

V N.W.F.P.

11. The position of the N.W.F.P. is exceptional. Two of the three representatives of this province are already participating in the existing Constituent Assembly. But it is clear, in view of its geographical situation, and other considerations, that if the whole or any part of the Punjab decides not to join the existing Constituent Assembly, it will be necessary to give the N.W.F.P. an opportunity to reconsider its position. Accordingly, in such an event, a referendum will be made to the electors of the present Legislative Assembly in the N.W.F.P. to choose which of the alternatives mentioned in para. 4 above they wish to adopt. The referendum will be held under the aegis of the Governor-General and in consultation with the Provincial Government.

VI BRITISH BALUCHISTAN

12. British Baluchistan has elected a member but he had not taken his seat in the existing Constituent Assembly. In view of its geographical situation, this Province will also be given an opportunity to reconsider its position and to choose which of the alternatives in para. 4 above to adopt. H.E. the Governor-General is examining how this can most appropriately be done.

VII ASSAM

13. Though Assam is predominantly a non-Muslim Province, the district of Sylhet which is contiguous to Bengal is predominantly Muslim. There has been a demand that, in the event of the partition of Bengal, Sylhet should be amalgamated with the Muslim part of Bengal. Accordingly, if it is decided that Bengal should be partitioned, a referendum will he held in Sylhet district under

the aegis of the Governor-General and in consultation with the Assam Provincial Government to decide whether the district of Sylhet should continue to form part of the Assam Province or should be amalgamated with the new Province of Eastern Bengal, if that Province agrees. If the referendum results in favour of amalgamation with Eastern Bengal, a Boundary Commission with terms of reference similar to those for the Punjab and Bengal will be set up to demarcate the Muslim majority areas of Sylhet district and contiguous Muslim majority areas of adjoining districts, which will then be transferred to Eastern Bengal. The rest of the Assam Province will in any case continue to participate in the proceedings of the existing Constituent Assembly.

VIII REPRESENTATION IN CONSTITUENT ASSEMBLIES

14. If it is decided that Bengal and the Punjab should be partitioned, it will be necessary to hold fresh elections to choose their representatives on the scale of one for every million of population according to the principle contained in the Cabinet Mission's Plan of May 16 1946. Similar elections will also have to be held for Sylhet in the event of its being decided that this district should form part of East Bengal. The number of representatives to which each area would be entitled is as follows:—

Province	General	Muslims	Sikhs	Total
Sylhet District	1	2	Nil	3
West Bengal	15	4	Nil	19
East Bengal	12	29	Nil	41
West Punjab	3	12	2	17
East Punjab	6	4	2	12

15. These representatives will either join the existing Constituent Assembly or form the new Constituent Assembly according to the mandate given to them by the areas concerned.

IX ADMINISTRATIVE MATTERS

16. Negotiations will have to be initiated as soon as possible on administrative consequences of any partition that may have been decided upon:—

(a) Between the representatives of the prospective successor authorities about all subjects now dealt with by the Central Government including Defence, Finance and Communications.

(b) Between different successor authorities and H.M.G. for treaties in regard to matters arising out of the transfer of power.

(c) In the case of Provinces that may be partitioned as to administration of all provincial subjects such as the division of assets and liabilities, the police and other services, the High Courts, provincial institutions, etc.

X THE TRIBES OF THE NORTH-WEST FRONTIER

17. Agreements with tribes of the N.W. Frontier of India will have to be negotiated by the appropriate successor authority.

XI THE STATES

18. H.M.G. wish to make it clear that the decisions announced above relate only to British India and that their policy towards Indian States remains unchanged.

XII NECESSITY FOR SPEED

19. In order that the successor authorities may have time to prepare themselves to take over power, it is important that all the above processes should be completed as quickly as possible. To avoid delay, the different Provinces or parts of Provinces will proceed independently as far as practicable within the conditions of this Plan, the existing Constituent Assembly and the new Constituent Assembly (if formed) will proceed to frame Constitutions for their respective territories: they will of course be free to frame their own rules.

XIII FURTHER ANNOUNCEMENTS BY GOVERNOR-GENERAL

20. H.E. the Governor-General will from time to time make such further announcements as may be necessary in regard to procedure or any other matters for carrying out the above arangements.

Appendix to No. 476

Muslim majority districts of Punjab and Bengal according to 1941 census.

1. *The Punjab.*

Lahore Division. Gujranwala, Gurdaspur, Lahore, Sheikhupura, Sialkot.

Rawalpindi Division. Attock, Gujrat, Jhelum, Mianwali, Rawalpindi, Shahpur.

Multan Division. Dera Ghazi Khan, Jhang, Lyallpur, Montgomery, Multan, Muzaffargarh.

2. *Bengal. Chittagong Division.* Chittagong, Noakhali, Tippera.

Dacca Division. Bakarganj, Dacca, Faridpur, Mymensingh.

Presidency Division. Jessore, Murshidabad, Nadia.

Rajshahi Division. Bogra, Dinajpur, Malda, Pabna, Rajshahi, Rangpur.

477

Viceroy's Conference Paper V.C.P. 55

L/P&J/10/79: ff 217–19

PROPOSALS FOR TRANSFER OF POWER DURING THE INTERIM
PERIOD ON THE BASIS OF TWO INDEPENDENT
STATES

TOP SECRET   THE VICEROY'S HOUSE, NEW DELHI, *17 May 1947*
Reference V.C.P. 52.[1] Attached are further alternative proposals for the transfer
of power during the interim period on the basis of two independent states.[2]

V. F. ERSKINE CRUM
Conference Secretary

Alternative 'A'

PROPOSALS FOR TRANSFER OF POWER DURING THE INTERIM
PERIOD ON THE BASIS OF TWO INDEPENDENT STATES

(1) In the event of a decision being taken in accordance with the procedure
laid down in H.M.G.'s announcement that there should be two independent States in India instead of one, the Executive of each State should
take over power in responsibility to its Constituent Assembly on a Dominion Status basis. The Government of India Act, 1935, may be suitably
amended for the purpose.

(2) If the States desire it, there will be one common Constitutional Governor-
General for the two States. He will also act as Arbitrator in matters of
common concern between the two States, if the Governments of the two
States agree that he should do so.

(3) When the Dominion Constitution comes into operation, the Armed
Forces in India should be divided between the two States. The units of
these Forces will be allocated according to the territorial basis of their
recruitment and will be under the control of the respective Governments.
In the case of mixed units, the separation and re-distribution should be
decided by the Governor-General and the two Defence Ministers in such a
manner as would be equitable, fair and proper.

Alternative 'B'

PROPOSALS FOR TRANSFER OF POWER DURING THE INTERIM
PERIOD ON THE BASIS OF TWO INDEPENDENT STATES

(1) In the event of a decision being taken in accordance with the procedure
laid down in H.M.G.'s announcement that there should be two independent States in India instead of one, the Executive of each State should

take over power in responsibility to its Constituent Assembly on a Dominion Status basis. The Government of India Act, 1935, may be suitably amended for the purpose.

(2) There will be a separate Governor-General for each State.

(3) When the Dominion Constitution comes into operation, the Armed Forces in India should be divided between the two States. The units of these Forces will be allocated according to the territorial basis of their recruitment and will be under the control of the respective Governments. In the case of mixed units, the separation and re-distribution should be decided by agreement between the two Governments.

[1] No. 466.
[2] Alternatives 'A' and 'B' in this Paper were circulated to the India and Burma Committee under the reference I.B.(47) 75 of 21 May 1947. L/PO/6/121: ff 177, 179–80.

478

Rear-Admiral Viscount Mountbatten of Burma to Sir F. Burrows (Bengal)

Telegram, Mountbatten Papers. Official Correspondence Files
Bengal, Partition of, Part I(b)

IMPORTANT   *18 May 1947, 11.50 am*
SECRET

No. 1075–S. Your telegram 118–S of the 15th May 1947.[1]

2. You will receive shortly my letter 40/3 of the 16th May[2] about my talk with Suhrawardy, which I think answers the points you made.

3. My talks with Nehru at Simla led me to believe that it is extremely unlikely that the Congress High Command will accept an independent Bengal or allow their followers to support such a proposal, as their view is that Bengal has no future except in Hindustan; but I do not mean by this that I should wish Suhrawardy to abandon his efforts for unity.

[1] No. 448.   [2] No. 462.

479

Rear-Admiral Viscount Mountbatten of Burma to Sir E. Mieville
(via Governor of Sind)

Telegram, R/3/1/136: f 154

IMMEDIATE   *18 May 1947, 5.28 pm*
SECRET   *Received: 18 May, 7 pm*

No. 76–C. Following for Mieville from Mountbatten.

Ask Sir B. N. Rau to let you have a copy of his secret paper "The Next Step"[1] written on 31st March 1947.

2. Ask Corfield for his comments on para. No. 8 of Rau's note. It was this and the following points that I wanted to discuss with him. But if I receive a really adequate brief by telegram on the whole question of the relationship which States would occupy in relation to VCP No. 55,[2] proposal A, I may not require Corfield to return to London.

3. I presume Political Department must be wound up by date of transfer of power and if there is a partition then the respective governments will immediately take on direct dealings with States which join their Constituent Assembly. Nehru will never agree to a continuation of Political Dept.

4. If any States choose independence exactly how can they be dealt with under VCP 55 A without arousing ill feeling with Congress or encouraging independence?

5. What would be the effect of VCP 55 A on VCP 54[3] para. 17? Could existing agreements with tribes be extended for interim period if all parties agreed?

6. VCP 54 para. 12. When do you think you can telegraph proposed procedure? See Nehru's recent letter to me on this subject.[4]

---

[1] This would appear to refer to Sir B. N. Rau's scheme for an interim or provisional constitution which is summarised in No. 262, note 2. (The copy of Sir B. N. Rau's note on the file is without a title.) In para. 8 of the note Rau argued that under his scheme the treaties between the Crown and the States would not lapse 'except perhaps as to paramountcy' and the functions of the Crown arising out of them would continue. The only difference would be 'that instead of being discharged as at present on the advice of a Political Adviser outside the Central Government, they may have to be discharged on the advice of a responsible Minister of the Central Government.' Mountbatten Papers, Official Correspondence Files: Transfer of Power, Part I(a).

[2] No. 477.

[3] No. 476.

[4] See No. 461, note 2.

480

Sir C. Corfield to Lord Ismay (via India Office)

Telegram, Mountbatten Papers. Official Correspondence Files:
Transfer of Power, Procedure for determining authorities to
which power is to be demitted, Part (2)

IMPORTANT   NEW DELHI, *18 May 1947, 6 pm*
CONFIDENTIAL
PERSONAL

No. 1078–P. Mieville tells me that His Excellency is very upset that I should not have seen him after my return and before his departure. I had no idea of course that His Excellency was not fully aware that I was returning with your concurrence. I presumed His Excellency would send for me if required though as you know I was not in on Cabinet discussions and had no background to communicate. Moreover Abell had confirmed that there was nothing I could usefully communicate. There was no urgency about informing His Excellency of my separate talks with Secretary of State and His Excellency was occupied with British Indian political leaders. In fact I tried to contact Mieville without success, but Staff were aware of my return and had informed Political Department. Kindly explain to His Excellency.[1]

[1] Lord Ismay replied in tel. 6555 of 20 May. He said he had explained the position to Lord Mountbatten and emphasised that he had agreed to Sir C. Corfield's return not knowing that Dominion Status question was going to be an immediate issue. Apparently Lord Ismay's telegram to Lord Mountbatten to this effect had never reached him. R/3/1/150: f 35.

481

Captain Brockman to Pandit Nehru

Mountbatten Papers. Official Correspondence Files: Transfer of
Power, Part III(a)

19 May 1947

Dear Mr Nehru,
As you know, Sir Eric Mieville is in touch with Mr Jinnah about the proposals for the transfer of power during the interim period. I attach a copy of the alternative proposals, A and B,[1] and Sir Eric would be very glad if you would confirm that either in their present form are acceptable to you. He understood you to affirm to this effect at the meeting which you had with H.E. at 4.30 p.m. on Saturday, 17th May.

Yours sincerely,

[1] See No. 477.   R. V. BROCKMAN

482

Pandit Nehru to Captain Brockman

Mountbatten Papers. Official Correspondence Files: Transfer of Power,
Part III(a)

SECRET   *19 May 1947*

I have received your letter of the 19th May[1] enclosing two draft proposals[2] for the transfer of power during the interim period marked "A" and "B". So far as I can make out, "A" is identical with the draft given to me on the evening of the 17th May with the exception of the deletion of paragraph 4. This draft was in supersession of a previous draft[3] given to me that day which was different in many particulars. The first clause of the original draft referred to the possibility of there being one Central Government in India. The last clause (6) referred to the adjustment of India's position to that of a Dominion by convention pending the passing of necessary legislation by Parliament. In the course of our talks with the Viceroy in the afternoon of May 17th[4] we pointed out the necessity of retaining both these clauses which had been omitted in the subsequent draft. Ultimately it was decided that clause 1 should be included; otherwise it would appear that there was no possibility of the people concerned deciding in favour of a United India. Whatever the chances of partition, it was improper to take it for granted that there will be a partition when people are asked to vote on the issue.

2. As to clause 6, we pointed out that we attach the greatest importance to this. We did not press for it to be included in the draft if this was supposed to create fresh difficulties at the last moment. But we made it perfectly clear that this was very important and H.M.G. should know our views in the matter. If some such action was not taken, very great difficulties would arise.

3. In regard to the two drafts "A" and "B" that you have sent me, the main difference appears to be that in one there is a common constitutional Governor-General for the two States and in the other there is a separate Governor-General for each State. The other changes are consequential on this. We have already stated in my letter to Lord Mountbatten dated May 17th,[5] paragraph 18, that in our opinion the Governor-General should be common to both the States if there are to be two States. Further, I added that we should be happy if Lord Mountbatten could continue in this office for the interim period.

4. We prefer, therefore, draft "A" to "B". But if, for any reason, one of the States wants to have a separate Governor-General for this period, we have no insuperable objection to it.

5. May I draw your attention to what I have said in my letter to the Viceroy

dated May 17th in regard to the proposals for transfer of power during the interim period? Also I should like to make it clear that all these proposals do not affect in any way H.M.G.'s announcement of February 20th, 1947.[6]

[1] No. 481. [2] See No. 477. [3] See No. 466.
[4] No. 472. [5] See No. 471.
[6] Sir E. Mieville sent Lord Mountbatten the text of this letter in tel. 1096–S of 20 May 1947. R/3/1/150: ff 40–1.

483

Note by Sir E. Jenkins

R/3/1/176: ff 167–9

19 May 1947

Master Tara Singh came to see me at his request between 4 and 5 p.m. today. I asked him if any agreement had been reached between the parties at Delhi before H.E. the Viceroy left for London. Master Tara Singh (who has just returned from Delhi) did not answer my question directly. He simply said that there could be no solution since neither the Muslims nor the Sikhs in the Punjab would submit to communal domination. He intimated that in Pakistan the Muslims would massacre all the Sikhs and Hindus and that in the other part of the Punjab the Sikhs and Hindus would massacre all the Muslims. I observed that this seemed to me a completely hopeless idea.

I then asked Master Tara Singh about the present disturbances in Lahore and Amritsar. He said that the Police actively helped the Muslim League. When I pulled him up he mentioned one incident during the first riot in Amritsar when he himself had seen boys breaking into a shop in the Hall Bazar with two armed policemen watching them. He thought the D.I.G., C.I.D., had witnessed this incident. He had got no satisfaction out of the Kotwal or out of Sardar Ujagar Singh of the C.I.D. It was only when he spoke to Mr. Savage that anything was done. In the circumstances he could hold out no hope whatever of the leaders influencing their communities. The only possible remedy was for Government to take really strong action. At present Government were much too weak—he mentioned the Daimganj case in which seven non-Muslims were murdered within a short distance of the Police Station and in broad daylight. He said that the Muslim League agitation had shaken the whole administration and not merely the Coalition Ministry. Like others who discussed questions of law and order, he was not at all clear as to what he wanted done. His only clear statements were that he did not trust the Police and that the political leaders could not help at all. I told him that in my view politicians like himself were responsible for stimulating the lack of confidence in the Police. He replied that this was true—he did not trust the Police himself and advised others not to trust them.

We then turned to the probable consequences of H.E. the Viceroy's talks with the leaders. Master Tara Singh asked me to help the Sikhs over the partition of the Punjab. I said that this matter would now be decided by H.M.G., but I did not see how the non-Muslims could possibly get more than the Ambala and Jullundur Divisions, the Amritsar district and perhaps parts of the Gurdaspur and Lahore districts. I said that it was most important that we should not have trouble—the Sikhs had committed two outrages in the last 48 hours at Rajgarh and Rasulpura, and if they insisted on taking revenge for the Rawalpindi affair, the Muslims would in their turn take revenge and there would be no end to the chain of massacres. Master Tara Singh said that he did not intend to take revenge for Rawalpindi now, but he could never be friendly with the Muslims again, and after the British went he would, if necessary, see that the Muslims were dealt with. The Muslim League leaders had never troubled even to condemn the atrocities committed in the Rawalpindi Division, and he could not possibly have anything to do with them. What was wanted was a temporary settlement under which the communities would agree to stop fighting and the Sikhs would get almost immediately an area to which non-Muslims could be transferred. I said that the transfer of population would be a gigantic task. To this Master Tara Singh replied that he would limit the compulsory transfer to property owners. Persons not owning property could do what they liked. I said that the final boundary would necessarily take some time to determine. Master Tara Singh remarked darkly that the Boundary Commission might never report at all since he felt that the Punjab might drift into chaos.

2. Master Tara Singh was quite amiable, but incoherent and obstinate as usual. Before he left I drew attention to the violence of some of his statements and asked him to do his best to keep his community quiet. It is lamentable that at this juncture the affairs of the Punjab should be so largely in the hands of this eccentric old man.

3. G. S. might send a copy of this interview note to P.S.V. for H.E. the Viceroy's information.

E. M. J.

484

Mr Harris to Sir A. Lascelles

L/P&S/12/3100: f 216

INDIA OFFICE, *19 May 1947*

My dear Lascelles,

I enclose a formal submission seeking The King's approval for the establishment of an Indian Diplomatic Mission in Nepal to be headed by an Ambassador accredited, in respect of India, to the King (Maharajadhiraja) of Nepal.[1] This follows a request from the Government of Nepal for an exchange of diplomatic missions with India "at the highest possible level" which the Government of India are anxious to meet.

His Majesty is already represented at Katmandu by a Minister Plenipotentiary, and the establishment of a separate Indian Embassy, if The King approves the present submission, will entail a change in His Majesty's representation, in respect of the United Kingdom, which will be considered by the Foreign Office in due course.

Discussions have recently been taking place with the Indian and Nepalese Governments regarding the future recruitment of Gurkhas both in the Indian Army and in His Majesty's Forces. The chief Indian representative at the discussions held in Katmandu was Sir Girja Bajpai, recently Indian Agent-General in Washington, and it is as a result of this visit that the Government of India have learnt that His Highness the Maharaja is anxious that the mission should be at Ambassadorial level, in order to broaden and strengthen relations between India and Nepal.

This step follows the precedents established by the approval recently given for the exchange of diplomatic missions between India on the one hand and the United States of America, China, the Union of Soviet Socialist Republics, France, the Netherlands and Siam on the other.

I am assuming that, as you wrote in your letter from Balmoral to Lord Pethick-Lawrence on 21st September last[2] concerning the Indian diplomatic missions in the United States of America, and in China, if The King approves the present submission, His Majesty's approval may be taken as covering the consequential action in regard to the reception by the Governor-General in New Delhi of the accredited Ambassador from Nepal.

I am sending copies of this letter to the Private Secretaries at the Foreign Office and Dominions Office.

Yours sincerely,

R. M. J. HARRIS

[1] H. M. King George VI approved the submission. L/P &S/12/3100: f 212.
[2] L/P &S/12/2639: f 129.

485

Cabinet

India and Burma Committee. I.B.(47)25th Meeting

L/P&J/10/79: ff 142–8

Those present at this Meeting held at 10 Downing Street, S.W.1, on 19 May 1947 at 5.30 pm were: Mr Attlee (in the Chair), Sir S. Cripps, Mr Alexander, Viscount Addison, the Earl of Listowel, Mr C. P. Mayhew, Mr A. G. Bottomley, Mr. A. Henderson, Lord Chorley

Also present were: Rear-Admiral Viscount Mountbatten of Burma, Sir David Monteath, Lord Ismay, Lieutenant-Colonel Erskine Crum; Sir Norman Brook, Mr S. E. V. Luke, Mr G. M. Wilson, Mr F. F. Turnbull (Secretariat)

The transfer of Power in India
(Previous Reference: I.B.(47)24th Meeting)[1]

At the Prime Minister's request, VISCOUNT MOUNTBATTEN informed the Committee of the latest developments in his discussions with Indian political leaders on his proposals for arranging for the transfer of power in India. The task of finding a solution would have been less difficult if he had been able to persuade Mr. Jinnah to meet the Congress leaders in discussion. As it was, he had had to ascertain, in separate discussions, the minimum demands of each side. It had become clear that the Muslim League would resort to arms if Pakistan in some form were not conceded. In the face of this threat, the Congress leaders had modified their former attitude; indeed, they were now inclined to feel that it would be to their advantage to be relieved of responsibility for the Provinces that would form Pakistan, while at the same time they were confident that those Provinces would ultimately have to seek re-union with the remainder of India. These consultations had enabled him to put forward the proposals contained in his telegram No. 65–S.C.,[2] in a form acceptable to both Congress and the Muslim League. The revised draft statement prepared by the Cabinet Committee, while involving no departure from the spirit of his original proposals, had proved unacceptable to Pandit Nehru for the reasons set out in the letter circulated under I.B.(47) 69.[3] His main criticism was that the draft statement obscured the position of the Constituent Assembly as the body established to give effect to the Cabinet Mission plan and merely treated it as a convenient body for the preparation of a constitution for one part of India. His second main criticism was that the plan would result in the Balkanisation of India. The Viceroy had, therefore, prepared a third draft statement, which had been accepted generally by the political leaders in India. He thought that this draft represented the maximum degree of agreement that could be secured.

Copies of this draft (subsequently circulated as I.B.(47) 74)[4] were handed to the Committee, together with three further papers (subsequently circulated as I.B.(47) 73)[5] embodying the comments of Congress and the Muslim League on the earlier revised draft contained in the Viceroy's telegram No. 66–S.C. A further paper (subsequently circulated as I.B.(47) 76)[6] was also handed to the Committee, summarising the suggestions made in these communications which had not been embodied in the further revised draft under I.B.(47) 74.

Viscount Mountbatten said that, within the past week, there had been a further development of major importance. He reminded the Committee that the Constituent Assembly, under the inspiration of Congress, had passed a resolution declaring that India would in due course become an independent republic. On his arrival in India the Congress leaders had repeatedly emphasised that the establishment of an independent republic was their objective. On the other hand, Mr. Jinnah and a number of the Princes had expressed a wish for Dominion status; and a similar proposal had been made on behalf of Bengal by the Prime Minister of that Province. The Viceroy had encouraged none of the Indian leaders to suppose that His Majesty's Government would be prepared to agree to a part or parts of India remaining within the Commonwealth, if the greater part had become independent. He had pointed out to Mr. Jinnah the disadvantages to His Majesty's Government of such a development. Mr. Jinnah had threatened to appeal over his head to the people of the Commonwealth and had argued that no part of the Commonwealth could be forcibly excluded against its will. This threat had had a disturbing effect on the Congress leaders; they had begun to feel that an independent Hindustan might be at some disadvantage with Pakistan still part of the British Commonwealth. In these circumstances it had been proposed to him by certain Congress leaders that His Majesty's Government should announce, simultaneously with the plan for the transfer of power, their intention to grant Dominion status to India (or, in the event of partition, to both parts in India) as soon as possible in 1947. These leaders were confident that it would be possible for them to persuade Congress to accept Dominion status provided they could say that, by this means, the actual transfer of power would be secured substantially earlier than June, 1948. It would, moreover, be necessary for them, in order to secure the assent of their party, to stress the fact that under the Statute of Westminster a Dominion could secede from the Commonwealth whenever it wished. They had, however, assured the Viceroy that in their view there would ultimately be no wish to secede from the Commonwealth once Domin-

---

[1] No. 437.   [2] No. 429.

[3] This circulated No. 406. L/P &J/10/79: ff 234–40.

[4] I.B.(47)74 circulated the draft attached to No. 476 (without its Appendix) but incorporated the amendments to paras. 4 and 15 of the draft which were agreed at the present meeting. *Ibid:* ff 158–65.

[5] This circulated the communications attached to Nos. 463, 464 and 471. L/PO/6/121: ff 225–36.

[6] No. 491.

ion status had been accepted. Copies of a paper (subsequently circulated as I.B.(47) 75)[7] were laid before the Committee by the Viceroy, who said that, of the alternative Plans 'A' and 'B' outlined therein, the Congress leaders had accepted 'A', but would probably be prepared to concede 'B'. Mr. Jinnah proposed to submit a further proposal but would be prepared, if this was unacceptable to His Majesty's Government, to acquiesce in Plan 'B'.

Viscount Mountbatten said that he would wish very shortly to put proposals to the Committee regarding the arrangements to be made for the conduct of the Interim Government during the period between the announcement to be made on 2nd June and the actual conclusion of the arrangements for partition. This raised most difficult issues on which he would wish for a decision by Ministers.

The Committee then considered the draft statement circulated by the Viceroy (I.B.(47) 74). The Viceroy made the following points in discussion:—

Paragraph 4

(a) The words "or authorities" should be inserted after the word "authority" in the last line.

(b) Neither Congress nor the Muslim League favoured the grant to Provinces, or parts of Provinces, of the option to remain independent, since this suggested that India might be "Balkanised" and might also encourage the Princes to adopt a separatist policy.

Paragraph 6

(c) All parties were agreed that the Legislative Assemblies, and not specially elected representatives, should take the necessary decisions.

Paragraph 7

(d) This paragraph applied only to Bengal, as nothing could now save the Punjab from partition. If the Sikhs had come to an agreement with the Muslims and had then asked Congress to agree to the Punjab remaining united, this might have been acceptable to Congress: as it was the Sikhs had insisted on partition in order to ensure that at any rate half of their numbers would not come under Muslim rule. The Governor of the Punjab did not think it would be possible to enforce partition without bloodshed as the Sikhs were determined to fight. Some of their leaders had promised to appeal to their people to avoid violence, but troops were being moved into the Province as a precautionary measure. The only hope of suppressing communal warfare was to deal with it promptly and ruthlessly with whatever force was necessary, including tanks and aircraft. The Viceroy had secured the unanimous approval of his Cabinet, including Baldev Singh, to this course; if it became necessary, full publicity would be given to it throughout India and it would be made clear that this action was taken with the authority of the Interim Government.

As regards Bengal, the Governor was anxious that the Province should not be partitioned; Mr. Suhrawardy thought that it might be kept united on the basis of joint electorates and a Coalition Government. Mr. Jinnah considered that, with its Muslim majority, an independent Bengal would be a sort of subsidiary Pakistan and was therefore prepared to agree to Mr. Suhrawardy's plan. Congress might also agree, but only on condition that Bengal did not form part of Pakistan and that special arrangements, which were unlikely to be acceptable to the Muslims, were made with the Central Government of Hindustan. They were opposed to Mr. Jinnah's proposal that Calcutta should become a free city as they believed that, without Calcutta, Eastern Bengal might well, within two or three years, rejoin the western part of the Province. The Viceroy had informed the parties that, if, before 2nd June, they were able to reach some agreement between themselves as to the future of the Province, he would embody such an agreement in the statement.

This was the only paragraph in the statement which had not yet been agreed. Both parties accepted the idea underlying it, but it was not very happily phrased and the Viceroy hoped it would be possible to redraft it before his return to India, in a form which would satisfy all parties.

Paragraph 9

(e) There was a danger that Indians might think that the provisional demarcation, adopted for the purpose of deciding on the issue of partition, would become permanent. In fact the final boundaries would, on a population basis, be different from those arrived at on the basis of majority districts. The draft therefore emphasised that this procedure was only temporary and that boundary commissions would be appointed. The Viceroy would be prepared to consider, on his return to India, the substitution of "final" or "ultimate" for "definitive" in the seventh line.

Paragraph 11—North West Frontier Province

(f) As a result of the intensive campaign carried out by the Muslim League, the situation in the Province was very explosive. The League wanted to prove that the present government had no longer a mandate to remain in power but, in the Viceroy's opinion, they had failed to show this. The present paragraph, which had been drafted by Pandit Nehru, had been accepted by Mr. Jinnah because a referendum avoided the weightage which was enjoyed by the Hindus and Sikhs in the Legislative Assembly.

Paragraph 12

(g) The Viceroy had suggested, as a means of ascertaining the wishes of British Baluchistan, that a commission composed of one Congress and one Muslim League representative with a British Chairman should

---

[7] This circulated, together with a note by the Viceroy, the alternative drafts attached to No. 477. L/PO/6/121: ff 177–80.

consult each Jirga; Pandit Nehru and Mr. Jinnah had agreed to this proposal and a new sentence would be added to the draft.

Paragraph 13

(*h*) The Viceroy explained that it would not be possible for Sylhet to join Bengal if Bengal should become independent. The only chance of Congress agreeing to an independent Bengal was on the basis of joint electorates and a Coalition Government. If Sylhet were subsequently added to the Province, it would throw the communal position out of balance and the agreement would be overthrown.

Paragraph 15

(*i*) It was agreed that this paragraph should be amended to read:—

"According to the Mandate given to them by the areas concerned, the representatives of the various areas will join either the existing Constituent Assembly or the new Constituent Assembly."

Paragraph 18

(*j*) The Viceroy said that the Congress leaders had suggested the omission of the paragraph in the earlier draft about the States. Mr. Jinnah preferred that it should be included but did not feel strongly about it. According to Congress, their negotiations with the States were proceeding satisfactorily, and they did not want anything said which might complicate them.

The Committee then considered the Viceroy's proposal that an immediate announcement should be made of the intention to grant Dominion status to India forthwith in accordance with the proposals set out in I.B.(47) 75.

In discussion VISCOUNT MOUNTBATTEN made the following further points:—

(*k*) The Congress leaders would not be successful in securing the agreement of their supporters to acceptance of Dominion status unless it could be shown that this would enable power to be transferred substantially earlier than June, 1948, viz., well before the end of 1947.

(*l*) The difficulties likely to be encountered in administering the Government of India between the announcement of 2nd June and the effective establishment of the two successor authorities rendered it advisable to make this transition period as short as possible.

(*m*) The Congress leaders were prepared to accept allegiance to the Crown on the understanding that the words "Emperor of India" would no longer be included in the King's title.

(*n*) The plan for the early grant of Dominion status would involve the division of the Armed Forces in India between the two States. The Viceroy proposed, while in England, to discuss the details of this proposal with Field Marshal Auchinleck. The problems involved were of immense complexity. The present position was that about 30% of the

Armed Forces was Muslim; the remainder were Hindus and Sikhs. Division would have to be made on a territorial, and not a communal, basis. The new plan would necessitate a reversal of the existing policy of progressive nationalisation: and the difficulties of division would be greatly eased if the greater part of the 6,000 British officers, with whom we should have dispensed by June, 1948, under the nationalisation policy, could be retained during the process of division. The compensation terms would have to be re-examined in order to encourage these officers to remain.

THE PRIME MINISTER said that there might be serious practical difficulties involved in the enactment of legislation to amend the Government of India Act to enable Dominion status to be granted to the two parts of India within the time desired by the Viceroy. Legislation for this purpose could not be enacted in the time envisaged without the co-operation of the Opposition leaders with whom the matter should be discussed immediately. The Lord Chancellor and the Law Officers should be invited to consider urgently the possibility of enacting legislation within the time desired. They should also consider whether action might be taken in advance of legislation, and validated by subsequent legislation.

The Committee—

(1) Took note that the Prime Minister would inform the Opposition leaders of the proposals for the transfer of power and the grant of Dominion status to India, and would seek their co-operation in securing the rapid passage of legislation for this purpose.

(2) Invited the Lord Chancellor and the Law Officers to consider the possibility of enacting legislation for the amendment of the Government of India Act, 1935 in order to enable Dominion status to be granted to the two parts of India during 1947, or, alternatively, whether action could be taken in advance of the necessary legislation.

486

Sir E. Mieville to Rear-Admiral Viscount Mountbatten of Burma (via India Office)

Telegram, R/3/1/150: ff 30 –2

IMPORTANT   NEW DELHI, *19 May 1947, 9.30 pm*
SECRET   *Received: 20 May, 10.15 am*

No. 1086–S. Your telegram May 18th despatched from Karachi.[1]

1. Paragraphs 2, 3 and 4. Corfield considers paragraph 8 of Rau's note misleading and requests reference to his note[2] despatched from London on V. P. Menon's proposals for transitional dominion status. Cabinet Mission's Memo.

[1] No. 479.   [2] See No. 427.

of 12th May, 1946, which continues to be operative document embodying H.M.G.'s policy and which will remain unchanged, makes it clear that paramountcy must lapse as soon as British India becomes fully self-governing whether in one or more parts. All rights surrendered by States to the Crown must then revert to States. The Crown itself cannot continue to exercise paramountcy rights when no longer in a position to fulfil paramountcy obligations, nor can these rights be inherited by fully self-governing dominion of British India, merely because British India retains link with Crown. If a responsible Minister of a Dominion Government were to be given control of the relations of the Crown with Indian States it would mean that His Majesty's Government had transferred paramountcy. Even if these relations were confined to coordinating functions as opposed to paramountcy functions proper (and a clear dividing line would be almost impossible to draw), the States could not be forced to deal with such a Minister without laying H.M.G. open to accusation of breach of faith.

For interim period between Dominion Status and new constitution, States who are represented in a Constituent Assembly might agree to conduct their relations with British India through Minister in the Executive Council elected by that Assembly, if their own nominee was appointed. But some States would not agree, certainly at present, and alternative arrangements for them would be required. These arrangements during interim period (and subsequently under the new Constitution if a State decided to remain independent) should be by direct dealings with appropriate departments of dominion status governments if allegations are not to be made that paramountcy is in practice being transferred. Such direct dealings with the Interim Government Departments have already started.

Political Department must be wound up by date of transfer of power, which date would be earlier than June 1948 if dominion status were granted before then, since this status makes British India fully self-governing. The *constitutional* position of States represented in the Constituent Assembly and of those not represented would be the same, until any new Constitution framed has been accepted by a State, though their attitude to the dominion status governments might be different. Direct dealings with the latter governments are necessary for all States owing to disappearance of the Political Department. The machinery only might vary by agreement.

Congress dispute validity of policy embodied in Memo. of 12th May and will only be content if paramountcy is in fact transferred. But if States, arising out of cooperation within the Constituent Assembly, were prepared to accept Minister (for coordinating functions distinguished so far as possible from paramountcy functions) in whose election they had deciding voice, Congress would have established a new relationship through a new machinery by agreement. If they can secure this, no element of paramountcy would have been transferred by the Crown. We should however have to be entirely neutral over procuring such an arrangement, and must be prepared to assist in negotiating other direct arrangements if any States so desire.

2. I have discussed your para. 5 with political officers here and the problem as I see it is:

(*a*) whether payments to the tribes would be guaranteed for this standstill period.

(*b*) whether the tribes would be satisfied with their link with the Crown through a "dominion status" Pakistan (on the assumption that the referendum in the N.W.F.P. goes in favour of Pakistan) sufficiently to preserve the *status quo*.

As regards (*a*) they could perhaps be satisfied by both successor governments who would have to agree on this point during discussions regarding the division of Central Revenues. Until there were new agreements, the G.G. could presumably hold these governments to their undertakings.

As regards (*b*), it is possible that the constitutional link with the Crown would be deemed adequate by the tribes provided actions based on the advice of Ministers led to no interference with existing practice. Such interference might however be inevitable if only from the substitution of Indian for British personnel in posts dealing with tribal areas.

3. Your para. 6. I have asked Nehru to expedite any procedure he can suggest. I understand that the A.G.G. will be here on the 24th and I doubt whether we shall get any proposals until he has had discussion with Nehru, who leaves for Mussoorie tomorrow morning.

487

Sir F. Burrows (Bengal) to the Earl of Listowel and Rear-Admiral Viscount Mountbatten of Burma

Telegram, L/P&J/10/79: ff 141

IMMEDIATE   CALCUTTA, *19 May 1947, 10.20 pm*
Received: 19 May, 5.25 am

No. 124–S. Addressed Secretary of State for information and for favour of communication to Lord Mountbatten: repeated Viceroy. My immediately succeeding telegram No. 125–C gives text of a memorandum from Suhrawardy to Kiran Sankar Roy of points on which (I understand) there is agreement between these two. It is useful as indicating trend of discussions and it is satisfactory to be able to record that there is agreement in which Sarat Bose joins to drop proposed name "Socialist Republic of Bengal" in favour of "Free State of Bengal".

2. I have, however, been impressed by urgency[1] of an immediate agreement if we are to avoid reference to possibility of partition of Bengal in proposals to be laid before Indian Leaders on June 2nd (*vide* paragraph No. 7 of Viceroy's letter to me No. 40/3 of May 16th)[2] and I have therefore discussed with Suhrawardy and Kiran Sankar Roy separately today a new approach, namely, that their present attempts to settle the broad outlines of future constitution of Bengal and its links, if any, with rest of India as basis of a coalition should be reversed[3] and that immediate steps (? should be) taken to form a coalition for Bengal *now*, before content and text of Viceroy's paper of (? June 2nd) are irrevocably settled, leaving these matters to be thrashed out in coalition without further (corrupt group) Bengal Constituent Assembly later.[4] I said I believed that when faced with formation of such a coalition in Bengal neither high command could repudiate it and that there were advantages in setting out to frame a constitution for free state of Bengal untrammelled by conditions such as those set out in Sarat Bose's list of points. My chief minister agreed and said he thought he could persuade his party and Jinnah to accept this solution. Kiran Sankar Roy also gave me his personal but very cordial agreement both as regards this line of action and to proposition that nothing else would avert bloodshed now or at all events after we go. Kiran Sankar Roy is meeting representatives of his party and Sarat Bose this evening and will put the matter (corrupt group)[5] them. Suhrawardy has made it plain to me that success of proposal, from his point of view, depends entirely on his ability to assure his party that formation of a coalition *now* will avert any reference to partition of Bengal in statement of June 2nd.

3. As result of my talks today I have great hopes of forming a Coalition Ministry. If this can be assured in time I hope it will be possible for H.M. Government
   (i) to omit any reference in statement to be made on June 2nd to possibility that Bengal may be partitioned and
   (ii) to omit any reference to ultimate (? status) or constitutional connections of future Bengal, tacitly leaving these to Bengal Constituent Assembly which Coalition Cabinet will get elected.

4. Viceroy in his letter to me No. 40/3 of May 14th [16th] has remarked that "Bengal is going to be a difficult case to fit into the new plan." I hope that solution on lines described above may be assistance but in any case I advocate it on its own merit and as a means, perhaps the only means, of averting grave disorders in Bengal. I am not aware of form the statement of June 2nd may now take but if reference to Bengal could be restricted to something on the following lines, it would meet wishes of leaders I have consulted (corrupt group)

(? avert)[6] immediate risks of a conflagration. Formula I suggest is "In Bengal where two major parties have recently agreed (? together) to form a Coalition Ministry a separate Constituent Assembly will be elected to (? draft) the future constitution."

[1] Mountbatten Papers have 'urgency of arriving at immediate agreement'. Official Correspondence Files: Bengal, Partition of.
[2] No. 462.
[3] Mountbatten Papers have 'reserved'.
[4] In Mountbatten Papers this sentence ends '. . . leaving these matters to be thrashed out in Coalition Cabinet and by Bengal Constituent Assembly later'.
[5] 'to' in Mountbatten Papers.
[6] 'and avert' in Mountbatten Papers.

488

Sir F. Burrows (Bengal) to the Earl of Listowel and Rear-Admiral Viscount Mountbatten of Burma

Telegram, L/P&J/10/79: f 140

IMPORTANT   CALCUTTA, *19 May 1947, 10.20 pm*
                                         Received: 20 May, 5.50 am

No. 125–C. Addressed to Secretary of State for information and favour of communication to Lord Mountbatten: repeated to Viceroy. Following is text of memorandum referred to in paragraph No. 1 of my immediately preceding telegram No. 124. *Begins:*

1. Bengal to be a free independent State. The Free State of Bengal will decide its relations with rest of India.

2. It is agreed that constitution of Bengal will provide for elections to Bengal Legislature on the basis of joint electorate with reservation of seats proportionate to population among Hindus and Moslems. (The seats as between Hindus and Scheduled Castes will be distributed among them in order to give to Scheduled Castes their existing proportion). The constituencies will be multiple constituencies and votes will be distributive and not cumulative. A candidate who gets majority of votes of his own community cast during elections and 25% of votes of other communities so cast will be declared elected. If no candidate satisfies these conditions, that candidate who gets largest number of votes of his own community will be elected. The franchise should be as wide as possible and should ultimately be adult franchise. In the case of women the franchise would be restricted on property qualification basis as at present for next 10 years.

3. On announcement that proposal of Free State of Bengal has been accepted

and that Bengal will not be partitioned, the present Bengal Ministry will be dissolved and a new Ministry brought into being consisting of an equal number of Moslems and Hindus (including Scheduled Caste Hindus) but excluding the Chief Minister. In this Ministry the Chief Minister will be a Moslem and Home Minister *a Hindu.*

4. Pending the final emergence of a Legislature and a Ministry under new constitution the Hindus (including the Scheduled Caste Hindus) and Moslems will have an equal share in Services including Military and Police. The Services will be manned by Bengalis.

5. A Constituent Assembly composed of 30 persons, 16 Moslems and 14 Hindus, will be elected by the Moslem and non-Moslem members of Legislature or by Moslem League and Congress respectively. Power will be transferred to this Constituent Assembly on or before June 1948. Alternatively the persons already elected to the Constituent Assembly from Bengal Legislature will form the Constituent Assembly of Free State of Bengal. *Ends.*

489

Sir E. Mieville to Rear-Admiral Viscount Mountbatten of Burma (via India Office)

Telegram, R/3/1/150: f 33

IMMEDIATE   NEW DELHI, *19 May 1947, 10.30 pm*
SECRET   *Received: 19 May, 11.55 pm*

No. 1091–S. I have at eight o'clock this evening received the promised letter from Jinnah[1] which is most unsatisfactory and which finishes with the following paragraph.

"I have, however, generally discussed this matter (i.e. Dominion Status) with His Excellency and he knows what my views are. And after the announcement is made on the 2nd of June, the subject matter of these drafts,[2] in my opinion, can be then taken up in the light of the announcement by His Majesty's Government. Perhaps then we might be able to pursue His Excellency's idea of getting an agreement on the principles underlying these drafts, in clear terms."

I am seeing Liaquat tonight and Jinnah tomorrow morning and will do my best with them and telegraph you again.

[1] Mr Jinnah's letter has not been traced.
[2] See No. 477.

490

*Sir E. Mieville to Rear-Admiral Viscount Mountbatten
of Burma (via India Office)*

Telegram, R/3/1/150: ff 37–8

MOST IMMEDIATE   NEW DELHI, *20 May 1947, 12.30 pm*

SECRET   *Received: 20 May, 10.15 am*

No. 1093–S. My telegram No. 1091–S of May 19th.[1]

I had two hours with Liaquat after dinner last night and told him how very disappointed I was with Jinnah's letter which I had not even thought worth while telegraphing to you. I reminded him that Jinnah had promised to send me in his letter details of the scheme he had put before you[2] of a supreme arbitrator of rank and status over and above the Governors General of the two Dominions, and that if the constitutional legal experts at home regarded his scheme as impracticable he would accept as a less desirable alternative and as an interim measure the appointment of one Governor General for the two Dominions with powers to act as arbitrator in matters of common concern. I reminded him that the Congress had already asked for you to be their Governor General. I went on to say that to my surprise Jinnah had not mentioned either of the above two proposals in his letter which merely contained a lot of criticisms of the extracts of Nehru's comments on the proposed transfer of power during the interim period which you had read out to him and a copy of which I had sent to him on Sunday afternoon (viz. from the words "while we shall welcome" to the words "for their mutual protection" see pages 2 and 3 of V.C.P. 53).[3] I knew that you would be extremely angry and I therefore hoped that he (Liaquat) would be able to help me to put things right.

2. Liaquat was quite frank and told me that he had helped Jinnah with the letter. The point was, he said, that Nehru's comments were based on a previous draft and not on those contained in V.C.P. 55[4] and before Jinnah committed himself in any way he wanted to have Nehru's comments on one or both of the alternatives in V.C.P. 55. If Jinnah could see those comments, he would make his own which could be shown to Congress and he would also develop his scheme of a supreme arbitrator, but he was unhappy at the stress which Nehru had made in his letter to you on the interim period. In Jinnah's opinion, this meant until June 1948 (I here pointed out that if power were transferred at an earlier date then June 1948 would have no significance). He went on to say that you had always said that Dominion Status could not be given to one part of India without the other, but so far as he could see that very position

---

[1] No. 489.   [2] See No. 473.
[3] See No. 471 and its note 5.   [4] No. 477.

would arise in June 1948. Congress would then, in his opinion, withdraw from the Commonwealth and he would wish to remain in it. Surely H.M.G. would want some guarantee that Congress would remain in for at least a term of years before granting them Dominion Status. He further could not understand what the interim period meant. If Dominion Status were granted to both states, say by October, there was no interim period *so far as H.M.G. were concerned.* There would merely be an interim period as between Hindustan and Pakistan until the division of assets and liabilities was settled. Again, what did Nehru mean by "immediate transfer by convention"—see V.C.P. 53, page 3. There was no mention of this in either of the drafts in V.C.P. 55. Nehru further stated that "power to change the Government of India (1935) Act during this interim period will rest with the authority in India". What authority, he wanted to know.

3. Liaquat finished up by saying that Jinnah and he had no objection to the principles contained in the draft proposals in V.C.P. 55 and that there would be no objection as far as Jinnah and himself were concerned and that there could be no question of any lowering of your position if you agree to stay on.

4. In the meantime, Brockman sent round to Nehru the two proposals contained in V.C.P. 55 and Nehru promised to let us have his comments thereon this morning. I am therefore not going to see Jinnah until I receive these.

491

Cabinet

India and Burma Committee. Paper I.B.(47)76

L/P&J/10/79: ff 149–54

SUMMARY OF SUGGESTIONS RECEIVED
FROM MR JINNAH AND PANDIT NEHRU

NOTE BY THE SECRETARY

CABINET OFFICE, S.W.1, *20 May 1947*

I circulate a note summarising those suggestions contained in the communications from Mr Jinnah and Pandit Nehru[1] circulated under I.B.(47)73 to which effect has not been given in the revised draft circulated as I.B.(47)74.[2] This note was handed to the Committee at their meeting on 19th May, 1947.

S. E. V. LUKE
Secretary

SUGGESTIONS RECEIVED AND NOT EMBODIED IN THE PRESENT
DRAFT BUT WHICH WILL BE SUBMITTED FOR THE CONSIDERATION
OF HIS MAJESTY'S GOVERNMENT

The sense of other suggestions has been acted on

Congress Proposals	*Muslim League Proposals*	*Viceroy's Remarks*
That Paragraph 1 should be amended to read " . . . His Majesty's Government had hoped that it would be possible for the major parties to co-operate in working out of the Cabinet Mission's Scheme of 16th May, 1946, and evolve for India a constitution acceptable to all concerned. This hope has not yet been fulfilled. His Majesty's Government are, therefore, faced with the task of making further efforts to implement their intention of transferring power including such variations of the Scheme of 16th May and the adjustments con-sequent to them as would enable the major parties to co-operate in a peaceful transfer of power".		Part of this amendment has been accepted.

¹ See Nos. 463, 464 and 471.
² See No. 485, note 4.

Congress Proposals	*Muslim League Proposals*	*Viceroy's Remarks*
That Paragraph 4 should read:— "It is not the intention of His Majesty's Government to interrupt the work of the existing Constituent Assembly, and His Majesty's Government trust that, as a consequence of this announcement, the Muslim League representatives of those Provinces a majority of whose representatives are already participating in it, will now take their due share in its labours . . ."	"I cannot agree that the present existing Constituent Assembly should be allowed to continue. Because, in my opinion, it is *ab initio* invalid, but I agree that two independent Constituent Assemblies should be established, one for Pakistan and the other for Hindustan; and all power and authority should be transferred to the Pakistan and Hindustan Constituent Assemblies".	Sense of Congress amendment has been accepted. Muslim League demand for abolition of present Constituent Assembly refused in view of their agreement for two Constituent Assemblies.

Paragraph 5.

"The Muslim League cannot agree to the partition of Bengal and the Punjab. It cannot be justified historically, economically, geographically, politically or morally. These provinces have built up their respective lives for nearly a century, administratively, economically and politically, and the only ground which is put forward for the partition is that the areas where the Hindus and Sikhs are in a majority should be separated from the rest of the provinces, on the ground that the Caste Hindus and Sikhs don't want to be under a government in which the Muslims will be in a majority.

The same can be urged by the Muslims and others that they don't want to be under a Government in which the Caste Hindus are in a majority and therefore

Congress   *Muslim League*   *Viceroy's Remarks*
Proposals   *Proposals*

other provinces should also be
partitioned. It may be noted that
there will be nearly 25 million of
Mussalmans under the Hindu Government in Hindustan and millions of
other communities such as the
Schedules Castes, the Christians,
Adibasis and Tribes. The principle
underlying the demand for establishment
of Pakistan and Hindustan is
totally different and I have already
sent my Statement to you which I
issued on the 30th of April,[3] copy
of which has also been sent to the
Prime Minister. The Muslim League,
therefore cannot agree to the
partition of Bengal and the Punjab
and I do hope that His Majesty's
Government, when they examine this
demand will not accept it and that
you and His Majesty's Government
will both, in the name of justice
and fairplay, not submit yourselves
to this clamour. For it will be
sowing the seeds of future serious
trouble and the results will be
disastrous for the life of these two
provinces and all the communities
concerned.

In this connection I may draw your
fullest consideration and earnestly
press upon you that if you take this
decision—which in my opinion will
be a fateful one—Calcutta should
not be torn away from the Eastern
Bengal. It has been the heart of
Bengal and the Province has
developed and grown round this
capital of Bengal which was for

[3] Annex I to No. 276.

Congress Proposals	Muslim League Proposals	Viceroy's Remarks
	decades the capital of India before Delhi was established as capital. Merely because the majority of the Caste Hindu vocal section desires Bengal to be partitioned—for in Western Bengal there are 34% Muslims, and out of the remaining 66% the Scheduled Castes are 63% and Caste Hindus 37%, which is less than one third of the total population of the Western Bengal. I have every reason to believe that the Scheduled Castes are strongly opposed to the partition of Bengal because they rightly say that they will be divided into two parts, one at the mercy of the Caste Hindus in Western Bengal and the other at the mercy of the Muslims in Eastern Bengal. They dread the Caste Hindus and it is well known that they have suffered economical and social tyranny at the hands of the Hindus for which there is no parallel in the world. But, if, unfortunately, partition is decided upon and Eastern Bengal is deprived of its only port of Calcutta which has developed its present position, in no case should it be allowed to go with the Western Bengal, otherwise it will follow as a corollary that Western Bengal will go into Hindustan and His Majesty's Government will be making the present of one great port to Hindustan. In any event, if worst comes to worst, Calcutta should be made a free port."	

Congress Proposals	Muslim League Proposals	Viceroy's Remarks

Paragraphs 6, 7 and 8

"These paragraphs relate more to procedure on the assumption that the issue of partition is decided upon and that these two provinces of Bengal and the Punjab should be cut up into two. I cannot say that the procedure laid down is satisfactory. The one governing principle which has been accepted by you is that the real will of the people of the part that wants to separate should be ascertained and the inhabitants of that part must be given every facility to give their verdict freely and fairly and this can only be done in a satisfactory manner by a plebiscite or a referendum, no doubt on the basis of 1941 census. I may point out that having regard to the Communal Award, which was modified by the Poona Pact in tragic circumstances, the Scheduled Castes have been completely left at the mercy of the Caste Hindus in the Electorates. Besides, owing to the well known fact that the Scheduled Castes are socially and economically so weak that even in the present electorates their number does not reflect the real strength of the population. Illiteracy and poverty are rampant amongst them and they are not qualified to come on the electoral rolls having regard to the present standard of franchise which is laid down. Therefore, great danger lies in a decision being taken on the question of separation

The Governor of Bengal raised with me the possibility of Bengal remaining united and becoming an independent state in close relations with rest of India. I have informed him that if the Bengal Constituent Assembly come to any prior agreement about the conditions in which they will remain united and if he informs me of this agreement before the 2nd June, a special paragraph on the future of Bengal may be inserted in His Majesty's Government's announcement by general agreement of the meeting with the leaders, which is being held at Delhi on the 2nd June. The views of the Governors of Bengal and the

Congress Proposals	Muslim League Proposals	Viceroy's Remarks
	of the Western Bengal from Eastern Bengal without any effective voice of the Scheduled Castes being secured."	Punjab are being sought.

THE VIEWS OF THE GOVERNORS OF BENGAL AND THE PUNJAB ABOUT THE POSSIBILITY OF HOLDING A REFERENDUM IN EACH PROVINCE

Bengal

Absolute minimum time for a referendum would be three months from start to finish with further delay if polling was seriously held up by widespread rioting. It is, however, for physical reasons extremely difficult to conduct polling for a referendum in East Bengal between June and the middle of November, on account of so much of the countryside being under water.

(Governor of Bengal's telegram 113–C of the 4th May.)[4]

Punjab

A referendum is in any circumstances a doubtful expedient in the Punjab, where the voters are entirely in the hands or at the mercy of the party leaders. On the particular issue of partition no question can at present be put to which the members of all communities could give an unqualified answer "Yes" or "No". The Muslims, guided by Jinnah, would answer "No" to any question; the Hindus and Sikhs—or most of them—want partition, but only on their own terms. They would reply "Yes" to the simple question "Should the Punjab be partitioned"; but they could not give an unqualified "Yes" to the boundary contemplated in the plan.

(Governor of Punjab's letter No. 669 of 4th May, 1947[5] substance of which was communicated to C.V.S. in Viceroy's telegram 992–S of 5th May)[6]

[4] No. 311.   [5] No. 305.   [6] No. 321.

492

*Sir E. Mieville to Rear-Admiral Viscount Mountbatten
of Burma (via India Office)*

*Telegram, Mountbatten Papers. Official Correspondence Files:
Punjab, Part II(a)*

IMPORTANT   NEW DELHI, *20 May 1947, 3.30 pm*
SECRET   *Received: 20 May, 6.30 pm*

1094–S. Patiala sent a staff officer this morning with a letter[1] for me enclosing one for you which he asked me to open in the event of your having already left Delhi. The following is a summary of the letter, the full context of which I will send by air mail tomorrow.

(*a*) He says he had long talks with Jinnah and tried to make him realise the disastrous consequences of his demand for a division of India but he found Jinnah uncompromising and adamant.

(*b*) The Sikhs consider division of the Punjab essential and any division of the Province which does not take into consideration the rights of the Sikh community in respect of their landed property, other assets, their holy shrines and does not secure for the major part of the Sikh community a national home is likely to provoke stiff opposition.

(*c*) It will be most unfair to both Sikhs and Hindus if the division of the Punjab is made merely on the basis of the incidence of population by ignoring all other factors such as the relative share of the various communities in the national assets, their relative contribution to the prosperity of the province and the desirability of making the divided units self-contained.

(*d*) The feelings amongst the Sikh community undoubtedly continue to be tense and there is a complaint that some of the authorities in the Punjab have openly followed a pro-Muslim policy. He will maintain close contacts with the Sikh opinion and will do his best to avert trouble so far as the Sikhs are concerned. In the meantime, it will be helpful if effective measures are taken in the Punjab to remove the suspicion that the balance has been tilted against the minorities because of the partisanship of some of the Civil and Policy [? Police] employees of the Punjab Govt.

(*e*) Should it be found necessary to transfer power to a divided India, he hopes that you and H.M.G. will give due consideration to the legitimate rights of the Sikh community and will arrange for a division of the Punjab on a basis which will be fair and just to the Sikhs.

[1] See No. 310, note 3.

493

Sir E. Mieville to Rear-Admiral Viscount Mountbatten of Burma (via India Office)

Telegram R/3/1/150: f 42

IMMEDIATE   NEW DELHI, *20 May 1947, 7.30 pm*

No. 1103–S. My telegram 1096–S of May 20th.[1]

I have seen Jinnah and have left with him the full text of Nehru's letter of May 17th (V.C.P. 53)[2] and of May 19th[3] repeated to you in telegram under reference. He has promised to let me have a note by tomorrow (Wednesday) evening if possible, or at any rate by 11 a.m. on Thursday. This was the best I could get out of him. He told me that he thought we were going too fast and that he could not commit the members of Pakistan Constituent Assembly.

At the end of our talk he took my arm and said "I am not speaking as a Partisan, but I beg you to tell Lord Mountbatten once again that he will be making a grave mistake if he agrees to the partition of Bengal and the Punjab". I promised him I would pass on to you his message.

[1] See No. 482, note 6.   [2] No. 471.   [3] No. 482.

494

Cabinet

India and Burma Committee. I.B.(47)26th Meeting

L/P&J/10/79: ff 125–32

Those present at this Meeting held at 10 Downing Street, S.W.1, on 20 May 1947 at 4.15 pm were: Mr Attlee (in the Chair), Sir S. Cripps, Mr Alexander, the Earl of Listowel, Mr C. P. Mayhew, Mr A. G. Bottomley, Mr Arthur Henderson, Lord Chorley

Also present were: Viscount Jowitt, Rear-Admiral Viscount Mountbatten of Burma, Sir David Monteath, Lord Ismay, Lieutenant-Colonel Erskine Crum, Mr J. Rowlatt; Sir Norman Brook, Mr S. E. V. Luke, Mr G. M. Wilson, Mr F. F. Turnbull (Secretariat)

Minute 1

The Transfer of Power in India

(Previous reference: I.B.(47)25th Meeting)[1]

The Committee further considered the revised draft (I.B.(47) 74)[2] of the announcement regarding the arrangements to be made for the transfer of power in India, which had been laid before them by the Viceroy at their previous meeting.

In addition to the amendments agreed at their previous meeting (I.B.(47) 25th Meeting), the Committee agreed that paragraph 7 should be redrafted to read as follows:—

"Before the question as to the partition is decided it is desirable that the representatives of each part should know in advance which constituent assembly the Province as a whole would join in the event of the two parts subsequently deciding to remain united. Therefore if any member of either Legislative Assembly so demands there shall be held a meeting of all members of the Legislative Assembly (other than Europeans) at which a decision will be taken on the issue as to which constituent assembly the Province as a whole would join if it were decided by the two parts to remain united."

It was also agreed that paragraph 15 should be redrafted to read as follows:—

"In accordance with the mandates given to them, the representatives of the various areas will either join the existing Constituent Assembly or form the new Constituent Assembly."

The Committee:—

Approved in principle the draft announcement annexed to I.B. (47) 74, on the understanding that the Viceroy would endeavour to secure the agreement of the Indian leaders to the amendments to paragraphs 4, 7, 12 and 15 agreed by the Committee at their meetings on 19th and 20th May, but that if they preferred the original text it should be adhered to.

Minute 2

Proposals for the Transfer of Power on the basis of Dominion Status

VISCOUNT MOUNTBATTEN emphasised that any announcement on this matter must make it clear that power would be transferred not later than the early autumn of 1947 instead of in June 1948; and that the Governor-General and any British officer who remained in India did so at the request of the Indians themselves. It would take about two months to withdraw British forces and this process should begin as soon as power was transferred. The only European members of the Defence Services to remain would be such army and naval officers as the Indians themselves required and as might volunteer to continue to serve, and any essential units that the British Government was prepared to let India have on loan.

The Viceroy said that, according to information which he had just received,[3] it appeared that Mr. Jinnah was still not prepared to commit himself in writing on the question of Dominion status for both parts of India. He had made it clear to a number of people that he wanted Dominion status for Pakistan, and that he wanted him (the Viceroy) to remain as Governor-General after June,

---

[1] No. 485.   [2] See No. 485, note 4.   [3] See Nos. 489 and 490.

1948, so as to act as an arbitrator in the division of Central functions, etc. Pandit Nehru had agreed in writing (I.B. (47) 73)[4] to a constitutional Governor-General acting as arbitrator in matters of common concern between the two independent States. It now seemed that Mr. Jinnah was unwilling to pursue the subject at all until after the announcement had been made on 2nd June. The Viceroy thought that Mr. Jinnah's objections to a common Governor-General for both States were:—

(i) that he would be resident in Delhi; and

(ii) that, when he (the Viceroy) left, Congress would attempt to secure one of their own nominees for the post.

What Mr. Jinnah really wanted was that Pakistan should have Dominion status and that Hindustan should leave the Commonwealth. The Viceroy thought that both parties should be offered Dominion status before the end of 1947 and, if they did not agree to this, both should become independent. He wanted clear guidance from the Committee on this point, and their full support in taking this line if Mr. Jinnah proved to be recalcitrant.

The Viceroy informed the Committee that the Governor of Bengal was apparently meeting with success in his efforts to secure that Bengal should remain united, and that it might therefore be possible to remove all reference to Bengal from the statement. If Bengal were to become independent, however, this would presumably involve the establishment of a third Dominion, with all the further complications which that would involve; several of the larger States might also wish to become separate Dominions.

THE LORD CHANCELLOR said that he had considered, at a meeting that morning, what legislation would be necessary in order to transfer power at the earliest possible date to two independent states on a basis of Dominion status. The difficulty was to unscramble the existing unitary Services, assets and liabilities of the existing Central Government and to reallocate them to the two successor states quickly and at the same time to provide for the day to day administration of these common services temporarily pending such reallocation. He suggested that the Bill should have a series of recitals, on the model of the Statute of Westminster, making clear that the object was to transfer power from British to Indian hands. Provision should then be made:—

(i) for the division of British India into two States, each having its own Parliament and Executive, with complete power to pass laws insofar as its own territory was concerned;

(ii) for each State to have its own Governor-General;

(iii) for the continuation of existing laws, including the Government of India Act, until altered;

(iv) for the establishment of a number of Functional Boards for the different Central subjects of administration, with some controlling board on the lines of a General Purposes Committee to organise their work, whose task it should be to continue and ultimately divide the common services, obligations, etc. Power would be given to the Governor-General of each State, after consultation with his Executive, to pass Orders-in-Council giving effect to the recommendations;

(v) for the provincial constitutions to remain in being *ad interim*;

(vi) enabling the Constituent Assemblies to amend or repeal the Government of India Act in respect of their own respective territories;

(vii) giving the United Kingdom Government power to repeal or adapt provisions in the Government of India Act which have effect in this country.

The most difficult problem was to provide for the continuance of the common services such as the Army, transport, posts and telegraphs, etc., until each State had made its own arrangements. The division of functions, and the division of assets and liabilities, including the whole question of finance, presented problems of the utmost complexity which could only be settled either by agreement between the two parties, or by somebody acting as arbitrator between them. There must be no suggestion of any kind of central Parliament or Government, and it was for this reason that Functional Boards, which should be purely technical and executive bodies, were suggested in the scheme. Their only purpose would be to divide the existing services and to administer them in the meantime.

In discussion of the scheme outlined by the Lord Chancellor the following points were raised:—

(a) The Government of India Act, 1935, would form part of the constitution of both States, each of whom would be free to alter or amend it insofar as its own territory was concerned. As and when any part of it ceased to be applicable in India as a result of legislation passed by either of the Indian Parliaments, the necessary amendments would also be made by the United Kingdom Parliament. The Act would thus be in a similar position to the British North America Act.

(b) As soon as Dominion status was granted to British India, paramountcy would come to an end. The States would then become fully independent and would be free to negotiate new agreements if they thought it desirable to do so. There should, however, be no continuity between paramountcy and the new agreements, and the United Kingdom Government could not accept responsibility for the conduct of relations between the new Dominion Governments and the States.

(c) THE VICEROY said that only a British arbitrator could adjudicate between the two independent States. He should have the assistance of some kind of tribunal—composed perhaps of one judge, and one Minister from both Pakistan and Hindustan—to present the issues to him in a form which would enable him to give his decision and the reasons for it. If no arbitrator were appointed there would be complete deadlock between the two States, which would result in considerable advantage for Hindustan, and it was therefore a concession on the part of Pandit Nehru to have agreed to the proposal. It was important that the arbitrator should be appointed by Indians, and not by the British Government. The Bill might therefore say that it was within the competence of the two Governments to nominate an arbitrator if they wished to do so.

(d) THE PRIME MINISTER thought that the Functional Boards might be called "Joint Delegations" on the analogy of the practice in the Austro-Hungarian Empire, and that it might be worth while considering how that system had worked.[5]

(e) To write the Functional Boards or Joint Delegations into the Act of Parliament might make the system too rigid and might not give sufficient latitude for dealing with some of the problems that were likely to arise. It might, therefore, be better merely to set up two Governments and create the rest of the machinery, as it became necessary, by Orders-in-Council on the advice of the Indians themselves.

(f) The right to secede from the Commonwealth should be specifically mentioned in the Bill.

(g) It was agreed that a British constitutional lawyer should be attached to the Viceroy's staff.

(h) It was thought that the Dominion Governments would welcome the proposal that power should be transferred in India on the basis of the grant of Dominion status to the two successor States.

(i) MR. ROWLATT said that, provided that everything went smoothly and provided that it was simple and non-controversial, the necessary Bill could probably be prepared within six weeks of a firm decision as to what was required.

(j) It was agreed that there should be no question of consulting Indian leaders on the form of the United Kingdom legislation.

Minute 3
Future of the present Interim Government

VISCOUNT MOUNTBATTEN raised the question of the arrangements to be made for the conduct of the Interim Government during the period between the decision to partition India and the enactment of legislation in the United Kingdom providing for the transfer of power to two states on the basis of Dominion status. Both Pandit Nehru and Sardar Patel had told him that, unless Congress could be given full control over the Hindustan area during this period, Congress Ministers would feel bound to resign from the Interim Government. There was no doubt that the Congress Ministers were becoming increasingly dissatisfied with the working of the Interim Government. They believed that their agreement to the participation of the Muslim League in the Interim Government had been obtained on the understanding that the League would in return participate in the deliberations of the Constituent Assembly; they were now convinced that the League's sole purpose in entering the Interim Government had been to prevent it from working effectively. The Interim Government had, perhaps, worked more successfully than Congress would admit, but there was little doubt that both parties had shown themselves primarily concerned to forward their own interests. The best arrangement would, of course, be for the Interim Government to continue while provisional governments were established for Hindustan and Pakistan and for its functions to be gradually transferred, either to the new Governments or to the suggested Functional Boards. There was no prospect, however, that the Congress leaders would agree to this procedure or could secure the support of their party for it. In these circumstances, there appeared to be two possible courses to follow—

(a) Once the decision to partition had been taken, two Cabinets might be formed in Delhi with complete responsibility for Hindustan and Pakistan affairs respectively. These Cabinets would meet jointly under the Viceroy for consideration of central matters of common interest to both areas. This arrangement would, of course, involve the duplication of each of the existing Ministries.

(b) The existing form of the Interim Government might be maintained, but each Minister would have a deputy, representative of the opposite party, who would understudy him.

The Viceroy said that he would wish to have the advice of Ministers whether interim arrangements on these lines could be adopted, and, if necessary, enforced, without need for amendment of the Government of India Act, 1935.

The Committee thought that arrangements of the kind at (a) above could be adopted by convention, but that such action would have to be validated in subsequent legislation.

The Committee:—

Invited the Secretary of State for India to arrange for officials to prepare, in the light of the Committee's discussion and in consultation with the Reforms Commissioner of the Government of India, detailed proposals for interim arrangements for the administration of the Government of India during the period between the decision to partition and the enactment of United Kingdom legislation to provide for the transfer of power.

Minute 4

Mr Jinnah's request for a referendum in Bengal and the Punjab

VISCOUNT MOUNTBATTEN referred to the request made by Mr. Jinnah

---

5 On 23 May Lord Listowel circulated (I.B.(47)83) a note prepared by India Office officials describing the system of Joint Delegations under the Dual Monarchy. L/PO/6/121: ff 142–4.

in his note of 17th May[6] (Annex A to I.B. (47) 73) that a referendum should be held in Bengal and the Punjab to determine whether or not these Provinces should be partitioned. The Viceroy had not felt able to accept this proposal which would, in his view, achieve no useful purpose and would merely result in delay. He had, however, promised Mr. Jinnah that the matter would be submitted for consideration by Ministers.

The Committee:—

Agreed that Mr. Jinnah should be informed that his proposal for a referendum in Bengal and the Punjab was not acceptable to His Majesty's Government.

Minute 5
Request for Boundary Adjustments

VISCOUNT MOUNTBATTEN informed the Committee that three important proposals for boundary adjustments had been made by the Indian leaders. In his note of 17th May (Annex A to I.B. (47) 73) Mr. Jinnah had proposed that, if Bengal was partitioned, those areas of the Purnea district in Bihar contiguous to Eastern Bengal should be amalgamated with it; Pandit Nehru had suggested that a small part of Sind should be transferred to Jodhpur State; and Sardar Patel had suggested that part of Kutch State should be transferred to the Bombay Presidency. Acceptance of these requests would open the door to innumerable demands of the same kind; they also raised the principle whether part of British India might be transferred to an Indian State.

The Committee thought that these were not matters on which decisions should be taken at this stage. Any boundary adjustments of this type should be a matter for settlement after the transfer of power, either by agreement between the parties concerned or under decisions by the appropriate Boundary Commissions.

[6] See No. 463.

495

Mr Abell to Sir E. Mieville (via India Office)

Telegram, L/PO/6/121: ff 160–1

IMMEDIATE   *20 May 1947, 6.45 pm*
                                              Received: 21 May, 7.30 am

No. 6580. Viceroy has considered Corfield's views as stated in telegram No. 1086 dated 19 May.[1]

2. His view at present is that if British India becomes two dominions with two Governors-General the States must be told that their relations with the

Crown will have to be through one or other of the Governors-General.

3. But there can be no direct relations between the Crown and independent Indian States because such relations would cause the disintegration of India.

4. Economic and administrative agreements should be renewed with the new Governments. This would seem to be harmless. There would be no question of Paramountcy being inherited.

5. Everything possible would have to be done to discourage direct relations of States with foreign powers; and probably the pressure of H.M.G. and the British Indian Authorities, plus the fear of agitation, would be effective.

6. Has Corfield any further comments?

¹ No. 486.

496

Rear-Admiral Viscount Mountbatten of Burma to Sir E. Mieville
(via India Office)

Telegram, R/3/1/153: f 40

IMMEDIATE   *21 May 1947, 11.44 am*
SECRET   *Received: 21 May, 5.30 pm*

No. 6591. Your 1093–S of 20th May.¹ I have discussed Jinnah's somersault with Staff and with Cabinet Committee, and we do not take it too seriously, especially after receiving account of your talk with Liaquat. I congratulate you on the way you have handled this tricky business.

2. Cabinet decided categorically that if both parts of India became Dominions and one part e.g. Hindustan, subsequently seceded, there would be no question of ejecting the other part e.g. Pakistan if it wished to remain.²

¹ No. 490.
² A decision to this effect is not recorded in the Minutes of the Cabinet India & Burma Committee. However, such a view may have been expressed during its discussions: see No. 527, para. 6.

497

Sir E. Mieville to Rear-Admiral Viscount Mountbatten of Burma
(via India Office)

Telegram, R/3/1/150: ff 46–7

IMMEDIATE   NEW DELHI, *21 May 1947, 5 pm*
SECRET   *Received: 21 May, 7.20 pm*

No. 1107–S. I have received this afternoon following letter from Baldev Singh.

Begins. I have seen the revised draft announcement enclosed with your letter of 20th May[1] and regret to point out that the Sikh point of view has not been fully met even now. I would particularly draw your attention to the following 4 points:

(1) It must be recognised that if India is to be divided, then the partition of the Punjab has to be effected to meet principally the demand of the Sikhs who, being one of the three major communities, are determined as a community not to be included in a Muslim dominated or Pakistan territory.

(2) In order that the work of the Boundary Commission may not be prejudiced or obstructed "the notional division" of the Punjab must include in addition to the 12 enumerated districts, the two districts of Gurdaspur and Lahore as well.

(3) For the same reason, when interim zonal ministries are formed the territory of the Eastern Punjab must include in addition to the two Divisions of Ambala and Jullundur, the three districts of Lahore Division as well, namely, Gurdaspur, Amritsar and Lahore.

(4) Para. 7. of the Draft Announcement is not clear. It seems to imply that on a demand from even a Single Member of the Punjab Legislature, who may be a Muslim, the entire Legislative Assembly will meet and decide—

(*a*) whether Punjab is to remain united, and

(*b*) which Constituent Assembly the Province would join as a whole.

Under this procedure as the wording of this para. stands, the Muslims who are in an absolute majority in the Legislature will force non-Muslims both to remain united and to join the proposed separate Constituent Assembly contemplated in para. 4(*b*) of the Announcement. This amounts to giving a veto to the Muslim majority in the Legislature. Para. 7 must therefore be redrafted and state clearly that this joint meeting of the Legislative Assembly as a whole can in no event prejudice the non-Muslim case for the partition of the Punjab whether India is divided or remains united and further that no vote in such a meeting shall compel the Eastern non-Muslim Punjab to form part of the separate Muslim dominated Constituent Assembly.

I would request you to communicate the above to H.E. in London immediately to clarify the ambiguity as in (4) above and in order that a complete picture is before His Majesty's Government when it is considering the final decision. *Ends.*

I have written to him and explained the position regarding para. 7 of the draft announcement.[2]

[1] See No. 476, note 1.

[2] In tel. 1122–S of 22 May Sir E. Mieville repeated to Mr Abell a passage taken from a further letter he had received from Sardar Baldev Singh which emphasised the need to re-draft para. 7. R/3/1/150: f 59.

In tel. 6731 of 23 May Lord Mountbatten informed Sir E. Mieville that para. 7 had been re-drafted to meet Sardar Baldev Singh's point. He added that as he was unable to obtain complete agreement between the Congress and League leaders on the wording of the paragraph about the Sikhs, he had followed Baldev Singh's own proposal of omitting it. He intended to put in as friendly a reference as possible to the Sikhs in his broadcast statement. *Ibid: f* 61.

498

Sir E. Mieville to Mr Abell (via India Office)

Telegram, R/3/1/150: ff 48–9

IMMEDIATE NEW DELHI, *21 May 1947, 7.25 pm*
TOP SECRET *Received: 21 May, 8.20 pm*

No. 1109–S. Your telegram No. 6580 of 20th May.[1] Following are Corfield's comments.

Begins. Your para. 2. Offer can be made to States of establishing new relations with the Crown through a Governor General in British India: but they cannot be forced to accept this arrangement. If they wish, they could refuse.

Your para. 3. If they were told that, in case of refusal, direct relations would not be considered, there would be nothing except the force of public opinion to prevent them negotiating with a foreign government.

Your para. 4. Negotiations for new agreements in the economic and financial sphere with new governments could be arranged, and to cover period of negotiations States would probably agree to a standstill period during which existing agreements continued *mutatis mutandis.* States could of course decline to include in standstill arrangements agreements which they now consider adverse to their interests, and there would be no paramountcy to bring them into line with all-India interests.

Your para. 5. I am not entirely confident that these influences would be effective but they would certainly be powerful.

On the general issue I must point out that the Crown Representative must

[1] No. 495.

disappear in both areas, if each Governor General is to be wholly constitutional. A Crown Representative could perhaps continue in an area (e.g. Pakistan) over which the Governor General retained certain powers until these lapsed. Political Department would have to drop all paramountcy functions on creation of full self-governing British Indian units, and as there would then be no Crown Representative the Department could only operate under the authority of the constitutional Governor-General. Even if its functions were limited to coordination only, such a transfer would be interpreted by States as a breach of promise, though this accusation could be mitigated if it was made clear that the Department would only continue for the minimum period required to set up alternative machinery and that no paramountcy functions whatsoever would be exercised by it in future. *Ends.*

499

Sir F. Burrows (Bengal) to the Earl of Listowel and Rear-Admiral Viscount Mountbatten of Burma

Telegram, L/PO/6/121: f 164

IMMEDIATE   CALCUTTA, *21 May 1947, 7.30 pm*
                                             Received: 21 May, 7 pm

128–S. Addressed to Secretary of State for information and for favour of communication to Lord Mountbatten; repeated to Viceroy. Reference my telegram No. 124–S dated May 19th, 1947.[1] Suhrawardy today confirms that there is agreement between himself and Kiran Sankar Roy to form a coalition in Bengal on terms practically identical with those given in my telegram No. 125–C of May 19th[2] and that Sarat Chandra Bose is not opposed. Neither leader has yet put the proposition to his party but Suhrawardy is confident he can carry his party with him: he had a satisfactory discussion with Chairman of the party, Maulana Akram Khan, today. Kiran on the other hand is putting the proposition to his All-India leaders first, firmly advocating acceptance.

2. Both have told me frankly that they consider this proposition offers the only chance of averting grave disturbances in Bengal and that is also my view. I believe there is a good chance that we shall bring this off but time factor is causing me anxiety. In view of the importance of the issue and of the chance offered that by this means we may avert disaster of communal disturbances in Bengal, I hope it may be possible for H.M.G. to keep the door open till the last moment for a settlement on these lines, if necessary by approving the June 2nd scheme in alternative so far as Bengal is concerned.

3. Kiran is flying to Mussoorie to meet Congress High Command tomorrow

(Thursday). It would immensely strengthen his hand and Suhrawardy's with their respective high commands if I can assure them that a solution on the lines suggested would obviate reference in "June 2nd" statement to possibility of partitioning Bengal.[3]

[1] No. 487.   [2] No. 488.

[3] In tel. 129 of 22 May Mr Tyson informed Mr Abell that, on receipt of No. 476 this tel. had been scrutinized again, and he was not sure if the phrase 'if necessary . . . is concerned' clearly conveyed the Governor's suggestion that the Cabinet should approve the two alternative drafts, as adoption of the Governor's proposal would involve many consequential amendments to No. 476. Mountbatten Papers, Official Correspondence Files: Bengal, Partition of, Part I(b).

500

Sir E. Jenkins to Sir J. Colville

Telegram, R/3/1/90: ff 52–3

IMMEDIATE   21 May 1947, 8 pm
CONFIDENTIAL   Received: 21 May, 10 pm

No. 100–G. Addressed Viceroy repeated Secretary of State. I reviewed Lahore situation this morning with civil officials concerned.[1] Muslims seem determined to burn Hindus and Sikhs out of greater Lahore and are concentrating on incendiarism. Hindus and Sikhs are retaliating in kind but are concentrating mainly on acquisition of arms with a view to personal vengeance.

2. We have so far employed maximum available strength of police with up to 3 companies of troops. With this strength we are not really in control of situation since buildings are fired by individuals using incendiary missiles of various kinds. Large parts of walled city can be traversed on roof tops and for several days few buildings in walled city have been freed [fired] at ground level. Some fires have been started almost under noses of police and it has been impossible to see or trace offenders. Roof spotting system is in operation but is not entirely effective. Similarly though stabbing cases are fewer we are not really in a position to prevent them.

3. Control of fires is very difficult since streets and lanes in walled city are exceedingly narrow and water supply is inadequate. Some streets are already blocked with rubble and though most fires have been controlled nearly all are still smouldering.

4. We are endeavouring to acquire more trailer pumps and are gradually organising public on ARP lines but we are unlikely to succeed without great increase in strength of police or troops. Police are not available and in view of

[1] Telegraphic reports on the Lahore situation may be found on R/3/1/90. In these it was reported that between 17–19 May 30 persons had been killed and 51 injured.

present situation and probable developments in June I consider in addition to troops of 4th Indian Division already arranged we need at as early a date as possible complete brigade for greater Lahore area alone. Police are already tired and patrolling is less effective than it was a few days ago. Troops now asked for would enable us to intensify patrolling. This may not be final answer but without intensified patrolling no answer is likely to be found.

5. I have discussed with Commander Lahore Area who is making such local arrangements as he can though all available troops are very fully employed. He will discuss further arrangements with Army Commander tomorrow.[2]

[2] In tel. 102–C of 22 May to Sir J. Colville, Sir E. Jenkins reported that the Army Commander had informed Commander, Lahore Area that no troops could be allotted to the Punjab from Northern or other Commands in addition to those already arranged. The Governor said they would do all they could with the resources available, but if, as was highly probable, there was widespread trouble in June, the control of the greater Lahore area would be a most serious problem. *Ibid* f 57.

501

Sardar Patel to Sir J. Colville

R/3/1/90: f 55

CAMP: "BIRLA HOUSE", MUSSOORIE,
21 May 1947

Dear Sir John Colville,

I have been receiving some letters and telegrams from Lahore regarding the serious situation in the city. Arson and stabbings on a large scale have been taking place, and therefore it seems the situation has not been brought under control. In fact, the latest telegram[1] from the Governor of the Punjab seems to indicate that the general population, and even top-ranking leaders, are reconciled to the inevitability of the continuance of trouble. I feel that, particularly at the present juncture, the continuance of such a state of affairs is fraught with dangerous potentialities. I had some correspondence with Lord Wavell just before he left for England, in which I suggested to him the desirability of imposing Martial Law in the affected areas of the Punjab. He then replied that he felt that a middle course should first be followed. And the result was the enactment of two Ordinances to arm the Executive and the Military with special powers to deal with the disturbances. It seems that these special powers are not proving effective, and a suggestion has been received that the city should be placed under Martial Law. None can appreciate better than the ordinary civilian the difficulties and handicaps of a Martial Law regime, but at the same time it is of the utmost importance these days that a disturbed situation is brought under control with the least possible delay and with the minimum possible waste of time and life. At a Cabinet Meeting, Lord Mountbatten gave the assurance that in future such disturbances would be put down with an iron hand.

In these circumstances, I would request you to consider once again, in consultation with the Governor of the Punjab, the suggestion which has been made to me by responsible leaders of the Punjab that the worst affected areas of the city should be placed under the Military.[2]

Yours sincerely,

VALLABHBHAI PATEL

[1] This appears to refer to Sir E. Jenkins' tel. 97–G of 19 May 1947. R/3/1/90: f 49.

[2] In tel. 1 of 26 May to Sir J. Colville, Sardar Patel said he had just seen No. 500 from which it was clear that the police were unable to control the Lahore situation and even military aid was not proving adequate. The consequences of the disturbances might not be confined to the Punjab and he felt the telegram fully vindicated his view that the affected areas in Lahore should be placed under military régime. R/3/1/90: f 79.

502

Remarks by Mr Jinnah on Pakistan made in an Interview with Reuters on 21 May 1947[1]

L/P&J/10/79: f 119

Mr. M. A. Jinnah, President of the Moslem League, called for an alliance between Pakistan (Moslem India) and Hindustan (Hindu India) here today.

Interviewed, as the British Cabinet was putting into final form its plans for transferring power to either a united or a divided India, Mr. Jinnah explained what a separate State of Pakistan, demanded by the Moslem League, would mean to India and the rest of the world.

Other points made by Mr. Jinnah were: Firstly, the Moslem League will demand a corridor through Hindustan to connect the two groups of Pakistan Provinces in North-Western and North-Eastern India. Secondly, the League will "fight every inch" against the partition of Bengal and the Punjab. Thirdly, a "really beneficial" relationship can be established between Pakistan and Britain. Fourthly, relations between Pakistan and Hindustan should be "friendly and reciprocal." Fifthly, the government of Pakistan would be "popular and representative." Sixthly, Pakistan would seek membership of the United Nations.

Mr. Jinnah said: "All the armed forces must be divided completely. I

[1] The text of this Interview was circulated to the India and Burma Committee on 22 May 1947 under the reference IBN(47)16. L/P &J/10/79: f 118.

envisage an alliance, pact or treaty between Pakistan and Hindustan in the mutual interest of both and against any aggressive outsider."

Asked if he favoured a federation of Pakistan States even if there is to be a partition of the Punjab and Bengal, Mr. Jinnah answered: "The new clamour for a partition that has been started by a vocal section of Hindus in Bengal and by Sikhs in particular in the Punjab will have disastrous results if these two Provinces are partitioned, and the Sikhs in the Punjab will be the greatest sufferers. Caste Hindus will suffer most in Western Bengal and Eastern Punjab.

"The basis of central administration of Pakistan, and that of the units to be set up, will be decided no doubt by a Pakistan Constituent Assembly. But a government of Pakistan can only be a popular, representative and democratic form of government. Its Parliament, and the Cabinet responsible to the Parliament, will both be finally responsible to the electorate, and the people in general, without any distinction of caste, creed or sect.

"As regards our attitude towards the Indian States, I make it clear once more that the policy of the Muslim League has been, and is, not to interfere with the Indian States with regard to their internal affairs.

"The foreign policy of Pakistan can only be for peace and friendly relations with all other nations and we shall certainly play our part in the membership of the United Nations."

Asked what his views were in regard to protection of the minorities in Pakistan territories, Mr. Jinnah answered: "There is only one answer—the minorities must be protected and safeguarded. The minorities in Pakistan will be the citizens of Pakistan and enjoy all the rights, privileges and obligations of citizenship without any distinction of caste, creed or sect, and I have no doubt in my mind that they will be treated justly and fairly.

"The government will run the administration and control legislative measures by its Parliament and the collective conscience of Parliament itself will be a guarantee that the minorities need not have any apprehensions of any injustice being done to them."

503

Cabinet

India and Burma Committee. Paper I.B.(47)78

L/P&J/10/79: ff 116–17

PROCEDURE IN REGARD TO THE PROPOSED STATEMENT OF POLICY
NOTE BY THE SECRETARY OF STATE FOR INDIA

INDIA OFFICE, *21 May 1947*

I circulate herewith, for the consideration of the Committee, a note which I have received from the Viceroy on the subject of the procedure to be followed in regard to the proposed Statement of Policy.

L.

NOTE BY THE VICEROY

The India and Burma Committee have now approved the draft announcement on the subject of the arrangements for the transfer of power, and I think that they would wish to know the procedure that I propose to adopt in regard to it.

2. At the Conference which commences on 2nd June, I shall pass round copies of this announcement and tell the Indian leaders:—
   (i) That it has the approval of His Majesty's Government, and
   (ii) that I do not propose to accept any amendments on points of substance, unless they are agreed by all parties. In that event, I should be prepared to submit them to His Majesty's Government for their consideration.
   (iii) I shall report the latest position about Bengal and, if both parties agree to the proposals for partition being taken out of the announcement, this will be done.

3. If, as I hope, all parties accept the arrangements set out in the announcement I shall inform the meeting that I intend to broadcast before the announcement and invite Mr. Jinnah and Pandit Nehru to broadcast after I have finished, and call on their followers to co-operate in implementing the arrangements.

4. There is, however, the possibility that one or both of the parties may not accept the announcement. Congress have, indeed, accepted it in writing, but they have emphasised that their acceptance is strictly subject to the other parties agreeing to it as a final settlement, and that no further claims are put forward. They added that, in the event of the Muslim League not agreeing to the plan, they (Congress) must adhere strictly to the Cabinet Mission plan of 16th May 1946.

5. We must be prepared for a situation of this kind, and I should be grateful for the guidance of the Committee as to the line that I should take.

504

Cabinet

India and Burma Committee. Paper I.B.(47)79

L/P&J/10/79: ff 110–13

GRANT OF DOMINION STATUS
NOTE BY THE SECRETARY OF STATE FOR INDIA

INDIA OFFICE, *21 May 1947*

I circulate herewith, for the consideration of the Committee, a note which I have received from the Viceroy on the subject of the grant of dominion status to two separate governments in India.

L.

NOTE BY THE VICEROY

The Cabinet Committee agreed in principle to the proposal that legislation should be prepared with the object of handing over power on a date in 1947 to two separate Governments in India each with dominion status. The legislation will include necessary amendments to the Government of India Act so that for the time being each of the new governments would operate on the basis of that Act.

2. The first step is to get the agreement of the leaders. I think the proposal for two separate dominions should be put to them as soon as I have cleared the draft announcement out of the way. If they agree, we can include as Part II of the announcement something on the lines of Draft A attached.

3. Congress have agreed already to the proposal but Jinnah has not committed the League. If it is impossible to get Jinnah's agreement at once, Part II of the announcement could be on the lines of Draft B attached.

DRAFT A

If as the result of the options which are to be exercised under this announcement the decision is in favour of the partition of India, His Majesty's Government in the United Kingdom after consultation with the Dominion Governments, are prepared to transfer power this year to two separate States each having dominion status, and to introduce the necessary legislation in the present session. The major political parties have indicated that they would welcome such action. This is an interim arrangement which will not prejudice the nature of the final constitutions that may be framed by the respective Constituent Assemblies.

DRAFT B

The Congress leaders have urged that if, as a result of the options which are to be exercised under the announcement, the decision is in favour of the partition of India, there should be a transfer of power this year to a separate government with dominion status for those territories which are to have their constitution framed in the existing Constituent Assembly. His Majesty's Government in the United Kingdom, after consultation with the Dominion Governments, are prepared to accept this proposal and will introduce the necessary legislation in the present session of Parliament.

The Muslim League, on the other hand, have not made up their mind on this question so far as the Muslim majority territories are concerned, in the event of a separate state being formed for those territories. His Majesty's Government consider that in the present political situation of India an early transfer of power is highly desirable. If the Muslim League, therefore, accept the offer to be associated with the Commonwealth as an autonomous state with Dominion Status, they are most welcome to do so. But on the other hand, if such a decision is not taken at a very early date His Majesty's Government propose, simultaneously with the transfer of power to the Dominion comprising the Hindu majority territories, to transfer power to an independent Government outside the Commonwealth for the Muslim majority areas.

505

Cabinet

India and Burma Committee. Paper I.B.(47)80[1]

L/P&J/10/79: ff 114–15

TRANSFER OF POWER

MEMORANDUM BY THE SECRETARY OF STATE FOR INDIA

INDIA OFFICE, *21 May 1947*

The Committee have now approved the Viceroy's Draft Statement announcing the arrangements whereby a partition of India can take place. I think that we

---

[1] On 21 May Mr Turnbull submitted a draft of this Memorandum to Sir W. Croft, Sir D. Monteath and Lord Listowel's Private Secretary. (The draft itself is not on the file.)

In his covering minute, which contained arguments similar to those in the Memorandum, Mr Turnbull explained that he had not had time to investigate how far all the points raised by Pandit Nehru and Mr Jinnah had been met. He felt, however, 'there are certain important reservations by both sides which have not been fully brought to the Committee's notice. The flood of papers has been such that I doubt if Ministers have had time to read them all with deliberation.' L/PO/6/121: f 167.

ought to consider with great care how the proposed offer of Dominion status to the two parts of India will be linked with the announcement in regard to partition.

2. I invite the particular attention of the Committee to the letter from Pandit Nehru to the Viceroy dated 17th [16th] May[2] and the letter from Mr. Jinnah to the Viceroy of the same date[3] contained in I.B. (47) 73. Pandit Nehru says that the acceptance of the partition plan by Congress "is strictly subject to the other parties agreeing to it as a final settlement and that no further claims are put forward.

"In the event of the Muslim League not agreeing to this plan we must adhere closely to the Cabinet Mission's scheme of May 16th, 1946 under which the Interim Government was formed. In this Government there is no place for those who finally reject the Cabinet Mission's scheme."

Mr. Jinnah records disagreement with the proposed Statement on a number of important points. But in particular he says. "The Muslim League cannot agree to the partition of Bengal and the Punjab". In the later paragraphs of his letter Mr. Jinnah appears to accept the fact that partition of these Provinces will take place and I have no doubt that the Viceroy is right that the Muslim League will in fact acquiesce in and operate this scheme.

3. It seems to me, however, virtually certain that the Muslim League will not accept the Statement otherwise than with the kind of reservations which they made in their original acceptance of the Cabinet Mission's plan, i.e. they will say that in their view the partition of the Punjab and Bengal is unjustifiable, that the whole of these Provinces form part of the Muslim homelands, and that they accept the limited Pakistan granted to them with the intention of securing the rest. This might be no more than a demonstration of words to save face but it would enable the Congress to say that the Statement has not been accepted without reservation and therefore that they themselves do not accept it.

4. The point I wish to make to the Committee is this. If we attach to the Statement about partition or issue simultaneously with it a further Statement about the grant of full power under Dominion forms to the whole of India or the two parts of India if it is divided, and if subsequently the Congress resile from the partition plan on the ground that it has not been fully accepted by the League, we may well find ourselves in a most awkward situation. We shall have offered to transfer full power to the whole of India or parts of India, as the case may be, on the assumption that partition would come about by agreement. If it does not come about by agreement the Congress will claim the implementation of the Cabinet Mission's plan by which they mean the recognition of a united India and the grant of immediate Dominion Status to the Interim Government with the Muslim League members removed

from it. The Muslim League will say that they have been promised partition and have accepted it though naturally protesting against the limited area allotted to them and have also been offered Dominion Status in those areas. The League will have a good case for saying that His Majesty's Government are bound to see that the Muslim League get the area which His Majesty's Government have promised them and also a fair share of the Central assets and apparatus.

5. I think, therefore, that the Committee should consider with great care the timing of the announcement about Dominion status and the transfer of power in 1947. I suggest that it is desirable not to make such a Statement until after partition has been proposed, and *accepted by both sides*.

6. I would add that the form of the Statement about Dominion Status may depend very much on the situation which results from the Statement about partition. If, as now seems possible, Bengal were to decide to remain united and to demand to be independent, the Punjab might conceivably do likewise and have to be allowed independence. It is possible that N.W.F.P. may opt for adherence to the existing Constituent Assembly. With these uncertainties in the situation I feel great doubt whether we should commit ourselves in advance to recognising two or more States in India as Dominions. Could we really regard Sind alone or Sind and Eastern [*sic*] Punjab as a Dominion?

L.

² No. 464.   ³ No. 463.

506

Note by Mr Abell

L/P&J/10/98: ff 5–6

21 May 1947

I understand that Part 3 of H.E.'s plan is that there should be a convention by which the Government of India is treated as a Dominion Government except that the Viceroy will retain special powers in regard to:

(*a*) the protection of minorities, and

(*b*) matters affecting the partition.

2. So far as the Congress is concerned, their major objective at the moment is to secure such a convention. The effect would be that Nehru would become Prime Minister and the Muslim League would either have to climb down or accept his leadership. The Cabinet would ordinarily meet in the absence of the Viceroy and the Viceroy would have to intervene specially in order

to secure a chance of considering matters which might affect his special powers. The Congress would give a great deal of publicity to the new convention and would claim to be treated exactly as a dominion government. If the Viceroy did intervene, it would be made to look as though he was going back on his word.

3. This would, I think, lead either to an abandonment of all attempts to secure a just partition and protection of the minorities, or to perpetual friction with the Congress which would be worse than the friction there is now. In any case it might well lead to the Muslim League going out of the Interim Government, which would greatly increase the difficulty of keeping the country quiet, and also make the partition a much more complicated matter.

4. Apart from these practical difficulties in India, however, there is the position of H.M.G. to consider. H.M.G. could not hide the convention from Parliament and they would have to admit that they had authorised the Viceroy to give up all attempt to fulfil his special responsibilities under the Government of India Act

(a) For the essential interests of India, including its security and the use of British troops.
(b) For the protection of the States; and
(c) For the protection of the Services.

5. I do not see how H.M.G. could sustain this position in Parliament. They would have surely to increase the special responsibilities so as to give the Viceroy control over British troops and also the power to protect British personnel in the Indian armed forces. They would also have to retain the special responsibility to protect the States, unless they were to allow paramountcy to lapse now. Thirdly, they would have to wind up the Secy. of State's Services now instead of in June 1948, and let everyone go with compensation.

6. When the Cabinet Misssion was in India there was an exhaustive examination of the extent to which the Viceroy could get rid of his special responsibilities, because the feeling then was that the Government of India should be given the maximum possible powers. Although it is obviously desirable now to go to the limit in increasing the prestige of the Interim Government, that limit has already been reached and it seems that the only possible way to go further is by getting partition finished and the two dominion governments set up. Only then can the Viceroy be rid of his unwelcome responsibilities.

7. I hope this note is enough to show that it is essential that there should be a clear proposal in writing before H.M.G., and a clear decision reached before the Viceroy goes back to India.

G.E.B.A.

507

Mr Harris to Mr Turnbull[1]

L/PO/6/124: ff 61–6

21 May 1947

Mr Turnbull.

The Viceroy yesterday gave the Secretary of State the attached copy of the revised draft of the broadcast statement which he wishes to make on the occasion of the announcement of H.M.G.'s policy. I understand that he has also given a copy of the revised draft to the Prime Minister. The Viceroy is anxious to record the broadcast in London before he returns to India and he would therefore be glad to have the draft approved by, say, Tuesday next at the latest.

I should be very grateful if you would examine the draft and consider whether any amendments ought to be suggested by this Office. It will be necessary for the S/S to minute the Prime Minister.

R.M.J.H.

DRAFT OF BROADCAST BY H.E. THE VICEROY

TOP SECRET

[Paras. 1–4, containing only minor verbal differences from Annex II to No. 276, omitted.]

5. My first course, in all my discussions, was therefore to urge the political leaders to accept the Cabinet Mission plan of 16th May 1946 unreservedly. In my opinion the plan—to which the majority of the Provinces have adhered, sending their representatives to the Constituent Assembly—provides the best arrangement that can be devised to meet the interests of all the communities of India. To my great regret it has been impossible to obtain the agreement of both the two main parties either on the Cabinet Mission plan, or on any other plan that would preserve the unity of India. But there can be no question of coercing any important areas in which one community has a majority, to live against their will under the general direction of a Government in which another community has a majority; and the only alternative to coercion is partition.

6. But when the representatives of one community demanded the partition of India, the representatives of another community used the same arguments for demanding the partition of those Provinces which contain large minorities. I am opposed to the partition of Provinces, just as I am to the partition of India herself, and for the same basic reasons; and I did not feel that I could recommend that His Majesty's Government should take upon themselves

[1] Copies of this Minute were sent to Sir W. Croft, Sir D. Monteath and Mr Henderson.

the responsibility of deciding on the partition either of India or of any of her Provinces. I therefore recommended to His Majesty's Government that this decision should rest with the people of India; and the statement that will shortly be read out explains how the people of India are to decide for themselves whether there is to be a unified India, or whether India is to be divided into separate and fully independent states. I reluctantly had to abandon the idea of an overall referendum, which is an unwieldy and lengthy process; and the next approach seemed to me the use of the legislature of the Provinces; for these are the elected representatives of the people, and I considered this the fairest compromise between an overall referendum and merely taking the views of the leaders and their working committees. The responsibility is therefore being placed firmly on the Provinces themselves to decide, with referendums only in special cases.

7. The plan may not be perfect; but like all plans, its success will depend on the spirit of goodwill with which it is put into execution. I have discussed it very fully with the leaders; and I now appeal to them and to all the people of India to accept the decision of the Provinces, and to make this settlement work. I have always felt that once the principle of the transfer of power was definitely stated, the sooner this could be put into effect the better. But although it was urgent that Indians themselves should feel it was their right and their duty to assume complete responsibility, it seemed to me that it would be impracticable and unfair to remove every British officer and official from the key positions they now hold, before Indians who would be taking over had had time to shoulder their new responsibilities effectively. On the other hand, if the British retained power until this process had been completed, this would be asking Indians to behave as though total responsibility were theirs, while at the same time limiting them psychologically by the knowledge that this was not yet the case.

8. This dilemma has been solved. The solution emerged when both the Congress and the Muslim League leaders agreed to Dominion Status on a temporary basis as early as possible: separately if two independent States are decided upon by the Provinces. I should like to make it quite clear that under the terms of the Westminster Statute any Dominion, being independent and voluntarily in full partnership with the other free and independent Dominions, can on its own initiative secede from the Commonwealth at any time it so chooses. There is therefore nothing final or binding in this decision.

9. But the way is now open to an arrangement by which power can be transferred many months earlier than the most optimistic of us thought possible; and it will now be possible for the British to offer their services in the interim period for as long as these are required. and for as long as Indians

may wish to remain in full partnership with the other Dominions of the Commonwealth.

10. The statement which His Majesty's Government have authorised me make on their behalf will now be read to you. You will notice that no new decision has been taken about the States, whose position remains as before; but should India in fact be partitioned by the decision of her own people, there would be a second Constituent Assembly to which the States could choose to go.

11. If the transfer of power is to be effected in a peaceful and orderly manner, every single one of us must bend all his efforts to the task. There is no time for bickering, much less for the continuation in any shape or form of the disorders and lawlessness of the past few months. I was shocked on my return here to find the great deterioration in communal relations that had taken place since my last visit to India less than a year before. So much bitterness, mistrust and hatred appear to have grown up in this short time; and this has been the greatest single disappointing factor that has confronted me. But the inspiring appeal of Mr Gandhi and Mr Jinnah has raised fresh hopes in the hearts of all men and women of goodwill.

12. I promise you that, whichever way the decision of the Indian people may go, I and all my British colleagues who may be asked to remain will do everything in our power to implement what the Provinces decide. I am confident that every man and woman of goodwill in India will do the same.

508

Mr Krishna Menon to Rear-Admiral Viscount Mountbatten of Burma

Mountbatten Papers. Official Correspondence Files: Transfer of Power, Part III(b)

AS FROM: INDIA HOUSE, ALDWYCH, LONDON,

PERSONAL   *21 May 1947*

My dear Lord Mountbatten,

I have now (since I saw you this morning) a letter from Panditji. It was unfortunate that it did not come to hand before I saw you. He refers in it to the possibility of seeing you again that night (the 17th May).

The letter to me deals with the question of immediate Dominion Status and his talks with you on the subject. I do not know whether this matter *now* appears in the draft. However, I should point out that the transfer of power as under Dominion Status is integral to finding a solution. Congress will not find it possible to agree to any arrangement which leaves this matter unsettled and prevents the Central front functioning even moderately well. I do not think they will agree to the plan of Deputy Ministers.[1] I have already said to you that they would agree to any reasonable proposals, including (1) your veto on specified matters, (2) undertakings not to do anything contrary to the partition agreements (if reached), (3) agreement to refer to a body constituted by agreement (such as two judges and an umpire) to decide whether any issue comes under the reserved matters, and so on.

I rather think that it is felt there that you have not quite appreciated the strength of the opinion held in this matter. As I am anxious that there should be no misunderstanding, I am writing to you even though I have seen you this morning! If Mr Jinnah wants a total separation, and that straight away, and if we agree to it for the sake of peace and dismember our country, we want to be rid of him, so far as the affairs of what is left to us of our country are concerned. I feel sure you will appreciate this, and also that it is not a matter of detail, but is fundamental.

I am always available, through India House, or through my personal secretary at Temple Bar 6426 or 6427.

With kind regards,
Yours sincerely,
KRISHNA

I will set my mind to work on what you told me and I hope you will [give] consideration to the important matters of extra–territoriality I mentioned. There is also the question of the composition and functions of the Boundary Commissions. Once partition is unhappily decided Pakistan has its states, which are provinces, the transfer of central authority, which is limited, is in the same category as the partition of the armed forces, assets and liabilities. I should also have remembered to mention that the question of the settlement on Sterling balances with U.K. should be subject to a standstill arrangement and be part of the overall settlement with H.M.G. and not one by Liaquat as at present. I believe this matter will also be before you when you return!

V.K.K.

[1] See No. 494, Minute 3.

509

Rear-Admiral Viscount Mountbatten of Burma to Sir F. Burrows (Bengal)
(via India Office)

Telegram, L/PO/6/121: f 163

IMMEDIATE   *21 May 1947, 8.40 pm*
TOP SECRET AND PERSONAL

No. 6641. Your 124-S and 125-S.[1] Delighted to hear that scheme for unifying Bengal going so well.

2. Will submit both your telegrams to the Cabinet and obtain their covering approval to changing the present reference to Bengal to read as proposed by you in your 124-S.

3. This will be subject to Congress and League leaders approving this substitution of wording at the meeting on 2nd June.

4. For your very secret information *not* to be communicated to any one else at present, position about dominion status is now as follows. Nehru and Patel have indicated that if Hindustan is offered dominion status during 1947 they will accept it. Mr Jinnah has repeatedly told Ismay, Mieville and myself he wants dominion status for Pakistan and I have now informed him that in view of Hindustan acceptance he will be able to get dominion status for Pakistan.

5. On being told this he has become cautious and has said that this is subject of course to the Pakistan Government asking for it. But he has often made it clear that he does not think Pakistan could not [*sic*] stand outside the Commonwealth and I believe this to be the case.

6. I believe that if Suhrawardy were to renew his request for dominion status for Bengal at this moment it might make Congress leaders chary of agreeing to a united Bengal since they would feel that it would lessen the chances of Bengal coming into the Union at a later date if they had independent dominion status.

Repeated to Sir J. Colville.

[1] Nos. 487 and 488.

510

Mr Abbott to Captain Brockman

R/3/1/145: ff 5-6

SECRET   GOVERNMENT HOUSE, LAHORE,
                                                21 May 1947

Dear Brockman,

H.E. desires me to forward the enclosed copy (prepared by myself) of a secret intelligence report sent up today. H.E. considers that this report is of some interest in view of the recent activities of Faridkot and Nabha personnel in the Punjab (these activities have been separately reported in "Q" cypher telegrams).[1]

Yours sincerely,

S. E. ABBOTT

Enclosure to No. 510

Information collected from several sources says that the Sikhs are determined on an offensive against Muslims where they are in a majority in the area which the Sikhs are demanding, and against the Muslims in the Punjab Police. The details of the plans the Sikh leaders have made are being kept secret, but there is some reason to think that attacks on Muslim villages are contemplated, and on police stations, and that communications will be interrupted. At first the action was planned for some time between the 15th and 25th May, but it has been postponed to the last week of May or the first week of June. Sikh organisation has not yet been completed, but the Sikh leaders are doing all they can to make progress and their Sikh followers are being encouraged to expect something big in the near future.

Hindu big business is stated to be backing the Sikhs. Most of the Sikh states and some others are also involved. Patiala is said to have agreed to supply arms and ammunition as well as explosives. He is supposed to have sent some of his soldiers, armed and in mufti, already to Amritsar. Faridkot held back but gave way on being promised Ferozepore district. Nabha is not in the business himself but his Dewan is and some of the Nabha Sirdars. Alwar, Dholpur, Bikaner and Bharatpur have all promised arms and ammunition. Kapurthala has given money and shelter to Sikh refugees but is not prepared to go further at the moment.

---

[1] Captain Brockman replied to Mr Abbott on 23 May as follows: 'H.E. saw Sardar Baldev Singh on the afternoon of the 22nd May and took the opportunity of informing him that he had been receiving disturbing reports of Sikh preparations for direct action in the Punjab. The Defence Member said that these preparations were due to nervousness and a desire to safeguard their own position, and that they would cease as soon as the Army showed up in strength. I repeat this to you for what it is worth.' R/3/1/145: f 12.

511

Captain Brockman to Sir J. Colville

R/3/1/145: f 8

22 May 1947

I have just received the attached letter[1] from the Governor's Secretary, Punjab, and I think you will wish to read it before you see Sardar Baldev Singh.

2. This Intelligence Report is ungraded and at first sight it does appear to be a little exaggerated, although there have been several reports in the past that the Sikhs are preparing for action. But Sardar Baldev Singh in his interview with Viscount Mountbatten on the 16th May,[2] said that the Sikh community would not be so foolhardy as to try and fight if the decision for partition of the Punjab was not in their favour.

3. In his interview with Viscount Mountbatten on the 3rd May[3] the Maharajah of Patiala was categorically warned of the intention to use the utmost force against anyone indulging in violence when the announcement was made. Viscount Mountbatten told me afterwards that in his opinion the Maharajah of Patiala was considerably shaken by this news, and I am therefore surprised to see in this Report that he is said to have agreed to supply arms and ammunition as well as explosives, and that he has already sent some of his troops to Amritsar in plain clothes.

4. You will also see from paragraph (b) [(d)] of Mieville's telegram No. 1094 of the 20th May[4] that the Maharajah has stated that he will maintain close contacts with Sikh opinion and will do his best to avoid trouble as far as the Sikhs are concerned.

5. I suggest that this report need not be shown to Sardar Baldev Singh, although you might well tell him that you have had disturbing reports of Sikh preparations for direct action in the Punjab. I think a copy of this report might go privately to the Commander in Chief to see whether it could be confirmed from Military Intelligence.

---

[1] No. 510.   [2] See No. 457.   [3] See No. 354, para. 25.   [4] No. 492.

512

Sir O. Caroe (North-West Frontier Province) to Sir J. Colville
(Extract)

L/P&J/5/224: f 45

CONFIDENTIAL   GOVERNOR'S CAMP, PARACHINAR,
No. GH–58   *22 May 1947*

2. The interesting local development in the political field is that my Ministry and Abdul Ghaffar Khan have started propaganda on a theme which I advised them to take up some months ago: that of a Pathan national Province under a coalition if possible, and making its own alliances as may suit it. When I put it to them then they professed what amounted to fury at the mere suggestion. There is a good deal in the theme itself, and the appeal is a far more constructive one than that of Islam in danger. The switch-over has probably come too late, but to my mind it is a strength, and not a weakness, that Pathanistan cannot subsist financially or otherwise on its own legs. The weakness is that the Pathans have hitherto been too divided among themselves to set up a stable State, and where they have ruled they have ruled as conquerors of alien populations. They themselves had always been in a state of anarchy right through history until we came and put them in order. (Afghanistan is not really a Pathan State at all).

513

Record of Interview between Rear-Admiral Viscount Mountbatten of Burma and Mr Churchill

Mountbatten Papers. Viceroy's Interview No. 141

22 May 1947

After my meeting with Mr Churchill and the Opposition leaders (Mr Eden, Lord Salisbury and Sir John Anderson),[1] I received a telephone message from Mr Churchill that the Opposition had agreed that they would facilitate legislation on the basis of this discussion. They now wished to discuss the matter further with me.

I therefore went round and saw Mr Churchill in bed. He handed me a copy of the letter that he had written to the Prime Minister, which is attached, and was extremely pleasant about what had been achieved in India in a short while. But he was extremely vitriolic about my predecessor.

He said that he hoped to get Indian matters dealt with on a bi-party basis. If I could achieve Dominion status for both Hindustan and Pakistan, the whole country would be behind us, and the Conservative Party would help to rush the legislation through.

He then asked me if I foresaw any difficulties, particularly with Mr Gandhi. I told him that Mr Gandhi was unpredictable, but that I doubted whether he would create any difficulties which could not be dealt with by Patel and Nehru.

He asked me whether I had received a letter from Nehru accepting Dominion status if power was transferred this year.[2] I replied in the affirmative and added that I had given a copy to the Prime Minister. I pointed out that I had been unable to obtain a similar written assurance from Mr Jinnah. Mr Churchill expressed great surprise: "By God", he said, "he is the one man who cannot do without British help". I pointed out that Mr Jinnah's methods of procedure could not be predicted by logic, and I told him that I must have a definite line of action to pursue in the event of his refusing to make up his mind about Dominion status. I told him that I proposed to inform Mr Jinnah that in that case we could go ahead with the transfer of power this year on a Dominion status basis for Hindustan, with an option for Dominion status to be taken up at any time by Pakistan. He told me that the Conservative Party might not agree to the passing of legislation under those terms, and that he might, in fact, have to oppose this. I then asked him if he would advise me how I should proceed if Jinnah was intransigent.

He thought about this for a long time and finally said: "To begin with you must threaten. Take away all British officers. Give them military units without British officers. Make it clear to them how impossible it would be to run Pakistan without British help".

I agreed to try and follow some such policy, but said that we could not escape the fact that ultimately I must be authorised not only to threaten, but also to implement the threat of a transfer of power without Dominion status. I pointed out that if I could not do this, Jinnah might hold out indefinitely, and that we might then lose both Hindustan and Pakistan.

This shook Mr Churchill and he asked me to obtain the Prime Minister's approval to my seeing Mr Anthony Eden, Sir John Anderson, Mr Harold Macmillan and Lord Simon in the near future, and to discuss this very point.

I told him that Mr Godfrey Nicholson wanted to see me and he told me on no account to see him. He added that he was "a very unsound Conservative with sentimental ideas about India", and he advised me to reply that if he wished to see me, then he should apply through the Prime Minister's Private Secretary.

[1] No record of this meeting has been traced.
[2] See No. 471.

Finally, he asked me to advise the Prime Minister to tell the other Dominions what was going on, so that they could get in touch with the prospective Indian Dominions and possibly help them to come in on a reasonable basis.

He authorised me to give Mr Jinnah the following message: "This is a matter of life and death for Pakistan, if you do not accept this offer with both hands."

Finally he suggested that if I were appointed Governor General of Hindustan and Governor General of Pakistan, I might adopt the title "Moderator", which at one time had been suggested by the late President Roosevelt, instead of the title "Viceroy".

Enclosure to No. 513

Mr Churchill to Mr Attlee

SECRET   HOUSE OF COMMONS, *21 May 1947*
My dear Prime Minister,
I have now had an opportunity of consulting my colleagues upon the terms of a possible settlement in India which you and the Viceroy put before us last night.

As a result I am in a position to assure you that if those terms are made good, so that there is an effective acceptance of Dominion status for the several parts of a divided India, the Conservative Party will agree to facilitate the passage this Session of the legislation necessary to confer Dominion status upon such several parts of India.[3]

Believe me,
Yours sincerely,
WINSTON S. CHURCHILL

[3] Mr Attlee replied on 21 May in his own hand as follows: 'My dear Churchill, I am much obliged to you for your letter indicating the attitude you and your colleagues would be prepared to adopt in the event of the settlement described to you by the Viceroy being accepted and of legislation being required this Session. Yours sincerely, C.R.A.' R/30/1/10: f 126.

514

Sir E. Mieville to Mr Abell (via India Office)

Telegram, R/3/1/150: ff 55-7

MOST IMMEDIATE   NEW DELHI, *22 May 1947, 1 pm*
SECRET   *Received: 22 May, 1 pm*
No. 1115–S. My telegram 1103–S of May 20th.[1] Following is text of note delivered to me from Jinnah this morning.

Begins. Sir Eric Mieville personally handed over to me what purports to be the full text of Pandit Jawaharlal Nehru's letter dated 17th of May 1947[2] addressed to His Excellency Lord Mountbatten; and also what purports to be a copy of Pandit Nehru's letter of the 19th May[3] addressed to Captain Brockman.

I have carefully gone through them and I find that in the letter of 17th May the Congress acceptance is subject to more conditions and clarifications than it appeared from the extracts of his letter that were furnished to me[4] and with which I had to deal in my note forwarded to Sir Eric Mieville on 19th May.[5]

In this letter, paragraph 2, Pandit Nehru refers to clause 6 of the draft[6] that was furnished to him; and he, once more, emphasises that he attaches more importance to it. Further, he adds that, "if some such action was not taken very great difficulties will arise," meaning thereby that clause 6 should be maintained.

Dealing with Drafts A and B[7] he concludes by referring to his letter of the 17th May and says "May I draw your attention to what I have said in my letter of 17th May, with regard to the proposals for the transfer of power during the interim period". Thereby he goes back to the draft consisting of 6 clauses, whereas we are only concerned with drafts marked A and B.

He then goes on to say "also I should like to make it clear that all these proposals do not affect in any way His Majesty's Government's announcement of 20th February 1947".

There is a complete lack of clarity and it is confusion worse confounded and I am unable really to follow this. The drafts A and B are quite clear; and a simple answer could have been given categorically and clearly, instead of what appears in these two letters. And from his reference emphatically made that these proposals A and B do not affect in any way His Majesty's Government's announcement of February 20th, I infer that these proposals will cease to operate after June 1948 and that they are meant only for this interim period.

This again takes to the central point round which these two letters revolve, namely that the present interim Government should function as a Dominion Government by convention, whereas the Draft proposals A and B make no such provision, but on the contrary clearly postulate that the present interim Government must be dissolved.

I am afraid I am therefore unable to deal with Drafts A and B as the arrangement was that I was to give my comments on these proposals after the Congress had clearly accepted either of the two Drafts A and B, which they have not done.

[1] No. 493.   [2] See No. 471.   [3] No. 482.   [4] See No. 471, note 5.
[5] This note has not been traced; see however Nos. 489 and 490.   [6] See No. 466.   [7] See No. 477.

The Muslim League will never agree to any change in the position, functions, or powers of the present Interim Government either by convention or otherwise, but that it must be dissolved as soon as two Constituent Assemblies are formed; and all power should be transferred to them immediately as it was originally laid down in paragraph 16 of the Draft Announcement.

I may add that His Excellency Lord Mountbatten's efforts will secure full justice to the 100 millions of Mussalmans. I am not in the habit of flattering any one, but I must say that throughout our discussions and examination of the various points, I was impressed by the high sense of integrity, fair play and impartiality on his part and, therefore, I feel that Lord Mountbatten will succeed in his great mission.

And finally with reference to the revised Draft Announcement furnished to me on the 20th May,[8] I find, among others, that with regard to Bengal and the Punjab no change has been made in spite of my very strong objections to the partition of Bengal and the Punjab embodied in my note of 17th May.[9] I can only reiterate all that I have said in that with regard to the partition of Bengal and the Punjab and I adhere to the views expressed therein. 21st May, 1947. *Ends.*

I am sending a copy of this note to Nehru for his confidential information. I told Jinnah when I saw him that I would do this in view of the fact that I had given him a copy of Nehru's two letters for his confidential information.

I am merely acknowledging receipt of the note to Jinnah. If Viceroy wishes me to take any further action please let me know.

[8] See No. 476, note 1.   [9] See No. 463.

515

Dr Evatt to Dominions Office

Telegram, L/P&J/10/79: f 70

TOP SECRET

22 May 1947, 5.30 pm
Received: 22 May, 3.20 pm

No. 123. Your telegrams D.No. 439 and D.No. 440 of 8th May[1] and D.No. 452 of 15th May[2] informing us of negotiations regarding India.

Developments so far do not call for any special comment by us. Having in mind constitutional question involved in necessity for concurrence of Dominions in any alteration of the Royal title, and any statement on future of India, Ceylon, Burma, South East Asia generally, it should be considered whether Dominions like Australia should not take a more effective part in discussions.

2. As was stated at Prime Ministers Conference 1946, and by Minister for External Affairs in House, we consider every endeavour should be made to persuade India to retain association with the British Commonwealth, and believe that we may be in a position to assist in securing this great objective.

[1] See No. 352 and its note 2.   [2] No. 452.

516

Cabinet Paper C.P.(47)158

L/PO/6/121: ff 148–57

INDIAN POLICY
MEMORANDUM BY THE PRIME MINISTER
10 DOWNING STREET, S.W.I, *22 May 1947*

The India and Burma Committee has had a series of discussions, first with Lord Ismay (Chief Adviser to the Viceroy) and later with the Viceroy himself.

2. Lord Mountbatten's instructions[1] were to do his utmost to secure general acceptance of the Cabinet Mission's plan. If this proved impossible he was to report by the 1st October on the steps which he considered should be taken for the handing over of power in June, 1948.

3. Since his arrival in India Lord Mountbatten has had a prolonged series of conversations with the leaders of Congress and of the Muslim League and has also conferred with representatives of the Sikhs. His conversations have convinced him that there is no prospect of acceptance of the Cabinet Mission's plan or of a Union of India on any other basis. He is also convinced that a very early announcement of His Majesty's Government's intentions as to the manner in which power will be transferred in 1948 is essential if widespread and uncontrollable communal disturbances, especially in the North-West Frontier Province and the Punjab, are to be avoided. The India and Burma Committee are fully satisfied that this diagnosis is correct and that further initiative on our part is essential.

4. The Viceroy has convened for 2nd June a small Conference consisting of leaders of the Congress, the Muslim League and the Sikhs at which he will make a final effort to get a compromise on the basis of the Cabinet Mission's plan. If, as he expects, he fails to do so, he proposes to lay before the Conference the text of a Statement by His Majesty's Government. He will inform the Conference that he is prepared to consider any modifications of it which the Conference may agree to propose to him within a short but stated period.

[1] See Vol. IX, Enclosure to No. 543.

The proposed text of this announcement, as approved by the India and Burma Committee in consultation with the Viceroy, is contained in the annex to this memorandum.

5. The Statement announces:—
  (i) that the attempt to secure a Union of the whole of India on the basis of the Cabinet Mission's proposals must now be abandoned;
  (ii) that arrangements must therefore be made whereby power can be transferred to more than one authority;
  (iii) a procedure whereby the different parts of India can choose through elected representatives whether their future constitutions shall be framed by the existing Constituent Assembly or in a new Constituent Assembly composed of representatives of those areas that hold aloof from the main body;
  (iv) provisions for setting up such new Constituent Assembly for the areas that opt for separation action.

6. The main purpose of the procedure proposed is to thrust upon Indians the responsibility of deciding whether or not India shall be divided and in what way. The elaborate nature of the procedure is unfortunately made unavoidable by the complex conditions existing in India, if a reasonably equitable expression of Indian opinion in the areas in question is to be obtained. The probable result will be that in the North-West Sind, Western Punjab, and possibly also the North-West Frontier Province will stand out from the existing Constituent Assembly. In the North-East there is some possibility of Bengal remaining united, but if this does not happen Eastern Bengal, and the one predominantly Muslim district of Assam are likely also to stand out.

7. The Viceroy in his conversations with the party leaders has revealed to them the main outlines of his proposals and is satisfied that they will be accepted by Congress. Mr Jinnah acquiesced in them in private conversation although in a subsequent public statement[2] he has protested against any proposal to partition Bengal and the Punjab. The Viceroy thinks, however, that the Muslim League is likely to co-operate in working the procedure proposed.

8. The India and Burma Committee are satisfied that these proposals are the best available in the circumstances and recommend that the Viceroy be authorised to proceed accordingly.

C.R.A.

Annex I to No. 516

DRAFT ANNOUNCEMENT

[*There follows the draft attached to No. 476 (without its Appendix), incorporating amendments to paras. 4 and 15 agreed in No. 485.*]

Annex II to No. 516

Certain minor modifications of the draft Announcement contained in Annex I have been agreed by the India and Burma Committee in consultation with the Viceroy. Lord Mountbatten will endeavour to secure the agreement of the Indian leaders to these changes. If, however, they should prefer the original text, the Committee thought that it should be adhered to.

The amendments proposed are as follows:—

Paragraph 7 should be redrafted to read:—

"Before the question as to the partition is decided it is desirable that the representatives of each part should know in advance which constituent assembly the Province as a whole would join in the event of the two parts subsequently deciding to remain united. Therefore if any member of either Legislative Assembly so demands there should be held a meeting of all members of the Legislative Assembly (other than Europeans) at which a decision will be taken on the issue as to which constituent assembly the Province as a whole would join if it were decided by the two parts to remain united."

Paragraph 9: The word "final" should be substituted for the word "definitive" in the second sentence.

Paragraph 12: Pandit Nehru and Mr. Jinnah have agreed to a suggestion by the Viceroy that, as a means of ascertaining the wishes of British Baluchistan, a Commission composed of one Congress and one Muslim League representative with a British Chairman should consult each Jirga. A reference to this procedure should be made in an additional sentence in this paragraph.

Paragraph 15 should be redrafted to read:—

"In accordance with the mandates given to them, the representatives of the various areas will either join the existing Constituent Assembly or form the new Constituent Assembly."

² See No. 502.

517

Cabinet

India and Burma Committee. I.B.(47) 27th Meeting

L/P&J/10/79: ff 71–8

Those present at this Meeting held at 10 Downing Street, S.W.1, on 22 May 1947 at 4.45 pm were: Mr Attlee (in the Chair), Sir S. Cripps, Mr Alexander, Viscount Addison, the Earl of Listowel, Mr C. P. Mayhew, Mr A. G. Bottomley, Mr A. Henderson, Lord Chorley

Also present were: Rear–Admiral Viscount Mountbatten of Burma, Sir David Monteath, Lord Ismay, Lieutenant–Colonel Erskine Crum; Sir Norman Brook, Mr S. E. V. Luke, Mr G. M. Wilson, Mr F. F. Turnbull (Secretariat)

Minute 1
Discussion with the Opposition Leaders

THE PRIME MINISTER said that he had informed the Leaders of both the Conservative and Liberal Parties of the proposals, which had been under consideration by the Committee, for the transfer of power in India and the grant of Dominion status to the resulting Successor States. They had both assured him that they would facilitate the passage of any legislation that might be necessary.

Minute 2
The Transfer of Power in India
(Previous Reference: I.B.(47) 26th Meeting, Minute 1)[1]

The Committee considered a note by the Secretary of State for India (I.B. (47) 78)[2] covering a note by the Viceroy on the procedure to be followed in connection with the announcement on the procedure for the transfer of power in India, which the Committee had approved in principle at their last meeting.

VISCOUNT MOUNTBATTEN said that, at the conference with the Indian leaders arranged for 2nd June, he proposed to hand copies of the announcement to them and to inform them—

(i) that it had the approval of His Majesty's Government;
(ii) that he did not propose to accept any amendments of points of substance, unless they were agreed by all parties, in which case he would be prepared to submit their views to His Majesty's Government for their consideration;
(iii) of the latest position in regard to Bengal; if an agreement had been reached between both Bengal leaders and if both parties agreed to it, the part of the announcement relating to Bengal could be deleted.

Later on the same day he would see the States' Negotiating Committee. The Indian leaders would wish to consult their Working Committees, and the Viceroy thought that they should be given 24 hours to do this. He would then inform His Majesty's Government of the result of these discussions, and he hoped that it would be possible to make the announcement public immediately. He proposed to broadcast a statement immediately before publication of the announcement and to invite Pandit Nehru and Mr. Jinnah to broadcast an appeal to their Parties to co-operate in the implementation of the scheme.

It was pointed out that the announcement should be made in both Houses of Parliament and subsequently issued as a White Paper, with simultaneous publication in India. Parliament would not reassemble, after the Whitsun Recess, until 3rd June, and this would have to be taken into consideration in connection with the arrangements for the Viceroy's discussions with the Indian leaders.

The Viceroy said that his prospects of securing agreement and a quick decision would be much enhanced if he could be given discretion to settle, without reference to London, points of minor importance that might arise during the discussions, provided that he did not depart from the general policy of His Majesty's Government. Experience had shown how difficult it was to reach finality when it was necessary to refer questions to London for a decision; while they were under consideration, the Indian leaders would change their minds and the opportunity of a decision would be lost. As an example, the Viceroy drew the Committee's attention to Mr. Jinnah's interview[3] with Reuter's correspondent, in the course of which he had said that the Muslim League would fight against the partition of Bengal and the Punjab and would demand a corridor to link the Eastern and Western parts of Pakistan. This was, no doubt, an attempt to blackmail His Majesty's Government; the risk was that Mr. Jinnah, by making such public announcements, would so far prejudice his position that he would be unable to return to the position which he had taken in his discussions with the Viceroy.

The Committee considered that full discretion should be given to the Viceroy in the handling of his discussions with the Indian leaders at the proposed conference. They thought that it would be inadvisable to allow as long a period as that proposed by the Viceroy for consideration of the announcement by the Indian political leaders and their Working Committees; the result would certainly be that the substance of the announcement would appear in the Indian Press. In their view, the announcement should be published on the same day on which it had been handed to the leaders; in view of the difference of time between India and the United Kingdom, it would be possible for the Viceroy to inform the Secretary of State by telegram of any

[1] No. 494.   [2] No. 503.   [3] No. 502.

amendments to the draft announcement to which he had agreed, in time for their incorporation in the announcement to be made in the Houses of Parliament.

It was agreed that the Prime Minister should make a broadcast statement to this country on the day of the announcement. This should not, however, be a major broadcast covering the same points as the Viceroy, but a short introductory broadcast immediately preceding the relaying of the Viceroy's Indian broadcast. They did not consider that it would be advisable for the Prime Minister to broadcast a statement to India; the Viceroy might include in his own broadcast a message both from The King and from His Majesty's Government.

The Committee then considered what policy should be followed in the event of either party refusing to accept the scheme for the transfer of power set out in the proposed announcement.

VISCOUNT MOUNTBATTEN said that, in that event, a decision would have to be made between four possible courses. Power might be handed over to the Interim Government: power might be transferred to the Provinces: the scheme contained in the announcement might be imposed as an Award: or the whole question might be referred to the United Nations. The Congress leaders would no doubt ask for the adoption of the first of these courses. They would argue that they had accepted the Cabinet Mission plan and that the arrangements proposed in the announcement were no more than a modification of it, under which the Provinces could opt out of the Union immediately instead of in ten years' time. The refusal of the Muslim League to accept the scheme would therefore be regarded by the Congress leaders as justification for strict adherence to the Cabinet Mission plan and for the immediate handing over of power to the Interim Government. But he did not think that Congress could be regarded as having accepted the Mission's plan, and, in fact, transfer of power to the Interim Government would be neither advisable nor practicable. In his view, the only possible course would be to carry through the scheme contained in the announcement, whatever attitude the Muslim League might adopt. The view of the Governor of the Punjab was that any attempt to impose partition of that Province would involve bloodshed, but no solution could now be found which would not result in some disorder. He did not, however, believe that Mr. Jinnah would ultimately prove completely recalcitrant, though it seemed doubtful whether he could be brought to agree to accept any plan as a final settlement. The greatest danger was that the Muslim League would adhere to their demands for full Pakistan as the inalienable right of Muslims, but at the same time acquiesce in and operate the plan. The Congress had undertaken to accept only if other parties accepted the plan as a final settlement. The adoption of such an attitude by the League might therefore lead to the withdrawal of Congress support for the plan.

The Committee shared the Viceroy's view that there could now be no question of attempting to carry out the Cabinet Mission's plan; the only course was to adhere to the plan contained in the proposed announcement, even if one of the parties should refuse to accept it. They thought that Mr. Jinnah might be persuaded to adopt a more reasonable attitude if it could be indicated to him that the consequence of refusal would be a settlement less favourable, from his point of view, than that contained in the announcement. For instance, it could be pointed out to him that the proposals in their present form were very unfavourable to the Sikhs and that, if the Muslim League refused to accept the scheme, it would be necessary to arrange for the partition of the Punjab on a basis which would be substantially less favourable to the Muslims. He might also be reminded that, if the Muslim League boycotted the scheme, the only result would be that the Congress Party would have an effective start in building up a strong and well organised Hindustan. If, on the other hand, Congress threatened to withdraw their agreement, it could be pointed out to them that the decision was a final one on the part of His Majesty's Government, and they could be asked whether they themselves accepted partition as a final and permanent solution.

Minute 3
Proposals for the Transfer of Power on the basis of
Dominion Status
(Previous Reference: I.B.(47)26th Meeting, Minute 2)[4]

The Committee had before them a memorandum by the Secretary of State for India (I.B.(47) 79)[5] covering two drafts by the Viceroy of the statement which might be made on the subject of the grant of Dominion status to two separate Governments in India.

In discussion the following points were made:—

(a) THE SECRETARY OF STATE FOR INDIA said that to transfer power to an independent government outside the Commonwealth for the Muslim majority areas, in the event of the Muslim League refusing to accept His Majesty's Government's proposal, would make it impossible to set up the Joint Functional Boards which had been suggested, since no legislation enacted by the British Parliament would have effect in an independent Pakistan. He therefore suggested that the announcement should say that Dominion status would in any event be conferred on both parts of India, but that either side would be free to secede subsequently if it wished to do so. The Committee agreed with this suggestion, and the Secretary of State said that in these circumstances, the difficulties foreseen in his paper (I.B.(47) 80)[6] would not arise.

(b) The Committee thought that the announcement should make it clear

[4] No. 494.　　[5] No. 504.　　[6] No. 505.

that, while June 1948 was the earliest date by which power could be transferred to independent States outside the Commonwealth, power could be transferred on the basis of Dominion status before the end of 1947. The offer to transfer power on this basis was therefore made in order to meet the desire that it should take place at the earliest possible date.

(c) THE SECRETARY OF STATE FOR DOMINION AFFAIRS said that the Dominion Governments would take the strongest exception to any mention in the United Kingdom legislation of a right to secede from the Commonwealth (I.B.(47) 26th Meeting, Minute 2 (f)). No mention of such a right was contained in the Statute of Westminster; the Dominion Governments regarded it as implicit in the conception of their status under that Act; and they would feel that the specific mention of the right in relation to India derogated from their own status. The Committee agreed that the right to secede should not be specifically referred to in the proposed legislation. It was suggested that, in his broadcast, the Viceroy might use the formula which had been approved on this point by His Majesty's Government for use by the Cripps Mission in 1942.[7]

The Committee:—
> Invited the Secretary of State for India, in consultation with the Viceroy, to circulate for consideration by the Committee at their next meeting, a revised draft statement on the grant of Dominion status.

Minute 4
Future of the India Office

VISCOUNT MOUNTBATTEN said that the Indian leaders would expect that on the transfer of power on the basis of Dominion status the relations of the United Kingdom with India would cease to be handled by the India Office. They would like this function to be undertaken by a Department under the direct supervision of the Prime Minister himself. If this was not possible, they would be content that relations with India should be the responsibility of the Dominions Office. He thought that it would be helpful if he could say something in his broadcast to the effect that on the transfer of power the special functions of the India Office would lapse.

The Committee:—
> Invited the Viceroy to include in his broadcast a passage to the effect that, on the transfer of power to two independent states, the special functions previously performed by the India Office would lapse and that new machinery was under consideration for handling the future relations of the United Kingdom with India.

Minute 5
Indian Officers at the Imperial Defence College and Joint
Staff College

VISCOUNT MOUNTBATTEN said that the Indians had been hurt by the refusal of facilities for their nationals to attend courses at the Imperial Defence College and Joint Staff College. He thought this refusal had been very effective at the time, but he hoped that the offer of facilities would be renewed as soon as the announcement about Dominion status had been made.

The Committee:—

(1) Considered that, on the grant of Dominion status to the two Successor States in India, the offer of facilities for Indian officers to attend courses at the Imperial Defence College and the Joint Staff College should be renewed.

(2) Invited the Minister of Defence to make the necessary arrangements in consultation with the Chiefs of Staff.

Minute 6
Relations between His Majesty's Government and the Indian
States after the Transfer of Power

VISCOUNT MOUNTBATTEN informed the Committee that there were signs that certain States, particularly Travancore, might ask for Dominion status. Travancore had the strongest claim, as, although it was a small State, it had its own port and could be a viable unit. Whenever the point had been raised with him, he had said that he did not see how any Indian State could be accepted as a Member of the Commonwealth unless the rest of India was also in the Commonwealth. On his return to India, he would be expected to say something, on the authority of His Majesty's Government, to the Negotiating Committee of the Chamber of Princes and to the Prime Minister of Travancore. He handed to Members of the Committee a note (subsequently circulated as I.B.(47) 82)[8] suggesting the line on which such a communication might be made. He emphasised that the Princes placed a high value on their relationship with the Crown and on such matters as the grant of decoration[s]; he had told Pandit Nehru that any concession that would be made on such points would be a small price to pay for securing the full co-operation of the States.

The Committee agreed that paramountcy could not be inherited by either of the two new Governments in British India, and therefore saw considerable difficulty in allowing the Princes to maintain contact with the Crown through the constitutional Governor-General of one of the Dominions, as he would only be able to act on the advice of his Ministers. It was suggested that the Princes might retain the right of access to the King for a period of, say, ten

[7] See No. 530.   [8] No. 523.

years and that the position thereafter should be left as vague as possible.
The Committee:—

> Invited the Secretary of State for India, in consultation with the Viceroy
> to revise the statement contained in the Annex to I.B.(47) 82 in the light
> of their discussion and to circulate a further draft for consideration by the
> Committee at their next meeting.

Minute 7
Future of the present Interim Government
(Previous Reference: I.B.(47) 26th Meeting, Minute 3)[9]

VISCOUNT MOUNTBATTEN reminded the Committee of the demand made
by Congress for the grant of full control over the Hindustan area as soon as
a decision had been taken to partition India. A note prepared in the India
Office (subsequently circulated as I.B.(47) 81)[10] exercised [? elaborated] three
proposals which had been made for:—

(i) the formation forthwith by Convention of two Cabinets;
(ii) the appointment of Parliamentary Under-Secretaries to each existing
Ministry, of the opposite party from the existing Minister; and
(iii) a Convention that the Governor-General would not use his Statutory
Power of over-ruling his Council except in regard to matters which
affected the rights and interests of minorities and which prejudiced
the partition of India or the future interests of either part.

The Viceroy said that for the reasons given in this paper none of these
solutions seemed satisfactory. He was convinced, however, that Congress
would resign from the interim Government if nothing was done to meet
their demands.

In discussion, it was the view of the Committee that the only solution was
to make an immediate start with the actual division of India as soon as a decision
for partition was taken, and to establish separate Ministries in anticipation
of complete partition. It was in any case important for Muslims to gain
experience of government, as otherwise they would be incapable of administering Pakistan without assistance.

THE VICEROY said that he understood that the President of the Board of
Trade would shortly be seeing Mr. Krishna Menon and that it would be use-
ful if he could discuss the situation with him.
The Committee:—

> Invited the President of the Board of Trade to discuss with Mr. Krishna
> Menon what arrangements could be made for the conduct of the Interim
> Government during the period between the decision to partition India
> and the actual transfer of power.

[9] No. 494.   [10] L/PO/6/112: ff 79–83.

518

Lord Addison to Mr Attlee

R/30/1/10: ff 134–7

DOMINIONS OFFICE, *23 May 1947*

Prime Minister.

Since our talk this morning about the inclusion in our proposed India announcement of the words "after consultation with the Dominion Governments", I have discussed the matter with my advisers here who have represented very strongly as follows:—

"It is impossible to take the line that there has in fact been consultation with the Dominion Governments in the sense which the above phrase would convey. We have kept the Dominions informed from time to time of developments and we have on occasion (as at present) asked the Prime Ministers to let us have any observations if they wished. (Actually, the only such observations received were somewhat critical ones from General Smuts[1] and inconclusive ones from Dr. Evatt[2]). Consultation in the proper sense implies that the subject is one in which the Dominion Governments are directly concerned and are prepared to accept responsibility for a share in the decision taken. This is emphatically not so in the present case, and they would be the first to disclaim any such responsibility. As a matter of fact, Dr. Evatt has just suggested (see telegram attached)[3] that the Commonwealth Governments "should take a more effective part in the discussions". This has not actually been found possible, and it is a view which Canada and South Africa at any rate would not accept. It is only necessary to refer to Mr Mackenzie King's position to realise this. For us to suggest that the Dominion Governments had been consulted (with the implication that they had agreed) would at once lead to questions in the Dominion Parliaments as to the extent of their responsibility, and it is clear that they would be bound to disclaim their concern.

It could only create friction if we attempted to persuade the Prime Ministers beforehand by a personal telegram to agree to our bringing them in in this way. Mr Mackenzie King, for his part, would say that such a proposition ought not to be put to him personally, as only the Canadian Cabinet could take decisions affecting Canada.

The above are not mere hypotheses, since it will be remembered that a precisely similar question came up during the Prime Ministers' meeting in May last year over the question of Egypt. See minutes of 14th Meeting

[1] Probably a reference to No. 420; see also Vol. IX, No. 409.
[2] Probably a reference to No. 515.   [3] No. 515.

of Prime Ministers (P.M.M. (46) 14th Meeting). On that occasion, Field
Marshal Smuts spoke as follows:—

> "The Dominion Ministers were certainly informed of what was in
> mind, but he did not think it would be right to say that they were con-
> sulted in such a way as to associate them with the decision. The decision
> was clearly that of the United Kingdom Government",

and again

> "He did not think it right that United Kingdom Ministers should
> be pressed to state in the House of Commons the views expressed by
> Dominion Governments in such consultations as this. That was hardly
> fair to those Governments. They had no means of joining in the
> debate themselves and anything said in the House of Commons might
> place them in an uncomfortable position in their own countries. He
> was in fact sure to be cross-examined in his own Parliament on the
> attitude he had adopted to the United Kingdom's proposal".

As a result, Mr Attlee made a statement in Parliament of which the following
is an extract:—

> "It is our practice and our duty as members of the British Com-
> monwealth to keep other members of the Commonwealth fully and
> continuously informed of all matters which we are called upon to
> decide, but which may affect Commonwealth interests. The object is to
> give them an opportunity of expressing their views in confidence, if
> they so desire. These views are taken fully into account, but the
> decision must be ours and the other Governments are not asked, and
> would not wish, to share the responsibility for it. Dominion Govern-
> ments follow the same practice".

This case is conclusive as to the resentment which would be aroused if we
now attempted to bring in the Dominions into an announcement in the
manner suggested".

I fully appreciate how helpful it would be to us if we could have quoted the
Dominions as concurring in our decision in this matter, but in view of the
above considerations I am clear that it would be most unwise to proceed with
the idea. A better course would be for you to tell the Dominion Prime Ministers (at the right stage) that when our announcement comes out it would
be very helpful to us if they then felt able to indicate publicly that their attitude
was favourable. But we cannot, of course, be sure that they (or at any rate
all of them) would be prepared to do so.[4]

ADDISON

[4] Later on 23 May Mr Attlee minuted: 'I agree'.

519

Note by Mr Symon[1]

L/S&G/7/1253: f 272

23 May 1947

At a predominantly Muslim party last evening I was able to have a long talk with Mr. Abdur Rab Nishtar, Member in charge of Communications, and a number of his Muslim friends.

Everyone assumed the creation of a separate Pakistan state. Mr. Nishtar made the following points during our conversation:—

1. Pakistan would be a permanent independent state with no possibility of a future union with Hindustan.

2. The Muslim League will continue to press for a Pakistan based on undivided provinces, but if a truncated Pakistan is forced on the League, they will accept it. He said, however, that this would always be a source of trouble.

3. The future capital of Pakistan is likely to be Rawalpindi.

4. Pakistan must maintain close future relations with Great Britain. They will probably wish to retain the services of British officers, both in the army and civilian life, for at least 15 years.

5. He visualised Pakistan as a sovereign independent State which might well remain in the Commonwealth if this is compatible with "independent sovereignty."

6. There will have to be agency agreements with Hindustan in respect of a number of subjects, e.g. communications.

7. He visualised a separate High Commissioner or Ambassador for Pakistan.

A. C. B. SYMON

[1] Copies of this note were forwarded by Sir T. Shone to Sir N. Brook on 28 May 1947.

520

Record, by Mr Henderson, of Conversation with Mr Krishna Menon on 23 May 1947

L/P&J/10/79: ff 67–9

In the course of a conversation here this morning Mr Krishna Menon made the following points:—

1. The Congress Party leaders were prepared to accept a modified scheme of partition as the basis of a peaceful settlement of the Indian constitutional

problem. He stressed, however, the necessity for it being a final settlement and indicated that an attempt would be made to secure from Mr Jinnah a statement that he would not continue to make further claims in respect of Muslim populations in other parts of India.

2. He was most emphatic in expressing the view that even so the basis of any settlement must be that the partition would take the form of certain areas "splitting off" from the Indian Union and should not be the division of India as such into two separate entities, Hindustan and Pakistan. He said that the Congress leaders would regard this as fundamental. In other words their view is that as the Congress Party have accepted the Cabinet Mission's plan and set up their Constituent Assembly under the plan for the purpose of establishing a constitution for the Union of India, anything that is done to meet the demands of the Muslim League must not abrogate this position.

3. He expressed the view that in the event of agreement being reached as to partition, the present Interim Government should be replaced by two Cabinets, one for what he called the Indian Union and the other for Pakistan. He stressed the view that the Congress Government of the Indian Union would seek to be regarded as the direct successors of the present Government of India in the international sphere. In other words, that they would seek to regard themselves as the India which is now a member of the United Nations. Pakistan, he said, could make its own application for membership of the United Nations, although no doubt the Government of the Union of India would do what it could to further any such application. They would take the same view with regard to diplomatic respresentation as at present. He said that the two Governments could exchange Ministers and that joint Boards could be set up to deal with matters of Finance, Defence, etc.

4. He indicated that for the time being Dominion status would certainly be acceptable to Congress India; but was doubtful whether they would wish to remain a Dominion indefinitely. His view was that some arrangement should be worked out which would provide for common citizenship for the Union of India and the United Kingdom, but that the Union of India should be a sovereign country with its officers owning allegiance to it and not to The King direct. He thought, however, that they would accept a nexus with the United Kingdom whereby The King would be the head of both countries, as well as, of course, the Dominions as at present. He was rather vague at this point, but I gained the impression that those for whom he speaks are desperately anxious to maintain the closest possible nexus with the United Kingdom. He rather plaintively stated that they would be hard pressed by their own followers as having sold out to the British, and that their task in putting over the proposals would be far from easy.

5. With regard to sterling balances he expressed the view that Indian public

opinion would not in any circumstances agree to their being scaled down. He thought, however, that an agreement could be reached on the basis of funding the balances, with interest being paid, say, at the rate of one half per cent. In the event of division of India any claim by Pakistan of a share of the balances will be met by the Congress Government, but certainly not on a fifty fifty basis.

A. HENDERSON
23rd May 1947

521

Cabinet C.M.(47)50th Conclusions

R/30/1/10: ff 129–33

Those present at this Meeting held at 10 Downing Street, S.W.1, on 23 May 1947 at 11 am were: Mr Attlee (in the Chair), Mr Herbert Morrison, Mr Arthur Greenwood, Mr Hugh Dalton, Sir S. Cripps, Mr Alexander, Mr J. Chuter Ede, Viscount Addison, Mr A. Creech Jones, the Earl of Listowel, Mr G. A. Isaacs, Mr E. Shinwell, Mr T. Williams, Mr George Tomlinson, Lord Inman
  Also present was: Mr John Strachey

INDIA
Constitutional Position
(Previous Reference: C.M.(47)47th Conclusions, Minute 6)[1]

The Cabinet had before them a memorandum by the Prime Minister (C.P. (47) 158)[2] covering the draft of an announcement to be made by His Majesty's Government on the arrangements proposed for the transfer of power in India.

THE PRIME MINISTER gave the Cabinet a general account of the recent political developments in India and the results of the discussions which the India and Burma Committee had had with the Viceroy.

The refusal of the Muslim League to participate in the work of the Constituent Assembly had destroyed any possibility that the Cabinet Mission plan could be successfully put into effect. The League had, indeed, entered the Interim Government, but the failure of both Parties to co-operate within that Government made it improbable that it could continue to hold together for much longer. The extensive discussions which Lord Mountbatten had had with the various political leaders since his arrival in India had convinced him that there was no prospect of a Union of India either on the basis of the Cabinet Mission's plan or on any other basis, and further that, unless a very early announcement was made of the method by which His Majesty's Government

[1] No. 447.   [2] No. 516.

intended to transfer power, widespread communal disturbances would be inevitable. All the Indian Parties were now convinced that, in view of the recalcitrant attitude of the Muslim League, some form of partition was unavoidable. But the Congress view was that, if partition was to be conceded, it was a necessary corollary that there should also be a division of Bengal and the Punjab.

The Viceroy had convened a conference of Indian leaders for 2nd June, at which he would make a final effort to secure agreement on the basis of the Cabinet Mission's plan. If, as he expected, he failed to do so, he intended to lay before the Conference the text of an announcement by His Majesty's Government, which was contained in the Annex to C.P. (47) 158. The plan outlined in that document had already been discussed with the Indian leaders, and represented the maximum degree of common agreement that was ever likely to be achieved. The announcement stated that His Majesty's Government had reached the conclusion that the attempt to secure a Union of the whole of India on the basis of the Cabinet Mission's proposals must now be abandoned, and that arrangements must therefore be made whereby power could be transferred to more than one authority. It then proceeded to set out a detailed plan under which the different parts of India could choose, through elected representatives, whether their future Constitutions should be framed by the existing Constituent Assembly or by a new Constituent Assembly composed of representatives from those areas which held aloof from the main body; and it provided for the establishment of a new Constituent Assembly for the areas which opted for separation. The probable result of the plan would be that, in the North-West of India, Sind, the Western Punjab and possibly also the North-West Frontier would stand out from the existing Constituent Assembly. In the North-East there were good hopes that Bengal might decide to remain united on the basis of a coalition Government elected on a joint electorate. If, however, that did not happen, Eastern Bengal and the one predominantly Muslim district of Assam were likely also to stand out.

The Prime Minister drew attention to the difficulties and dangers necessarily inherent in any scheme of partition. The situation in many parts of India was already highly inflammable. In the Punjab, in particular, the proposed announcement was likely in the Governor's view to provoke serious disorder and bloodshed. The application of the plan to that Province would involve the division of the Sikh community in fairly even proportions between the two successor States, though their position might to some extent be eased by the Boundary Commission, which would establish the final boundary. Partition would also involve highly complex administrative problems, such as the division between the successor States of the Indian Army and such subjects as finance, trade and industry, which were at present the responsibility of the Central Government. But, whatever the practical difficulties involved, there appeared to be no alternative to partition. Unfortunately, there was now reason to fear that the Muslim League might after all decide to oppose the plan. In that event, the best course would be to impose it as an award by His Majesty's Government. It seemed unlikely that the attitude of the Congress leaders to the plan would similarly change. If it did, a more difficult position would arise and the whole plan would then have to be reconsidered. During the past fortnight, however, there had been a further development of major importance which put the whole matter in a different light. While Mr. Jinnah had always claimed that Pakistan would wish to remain within the British Commonwealth, it had been the policy of the Congress Party that India should be a sovereign independent republic and they had secured a resolution to that effect in the Constituent Assembly. The prospect that one part of India would wish to remain within the Commonwealth when the other had become an independent republic had always involved issues of great complexity. It now appeared, however, that some of the Congress leaders had become increasingly apprehensive about the difficulties which the grant of immediate independence would involve, and a most significant approach to the Viceroy had been made by Pandit Nehru and Sardar Patel, who had suggested that in the event of partition Hindu India should be granted Dominion status, at any rate as a temporary measure. They had explained that they would hope to secure the agreement of their supporters to this course by arguing that acceptance of Dominion status would enable power to be transferred to Indian hands at a date substantially earlier than June 1948, and that once she had attained Dominion status Hindu India would be free to secede at any time from the Commonwealth.

This was a most important development, and the India and Burma Committee had felt that full advantage should be taken of it. If Dominion status were conferred on the two successor States as part of the plan for the transfer of power, this would greatly ease the difficulties inherent in partition. For example, both the Indian Parties wished to retain the services of European officers of the Indian Army to assist in carrying out the division of the army between the new States and building up effective military organisations on a fresh basis: this would not be possible if the successor States had become independent republics. More important, it was reasonable to suppose that the Indian Parties, in the light of practical experience of the advantages of Dominion status, would be slow to exercise their right to secede at a later stage. India's decision would also, no doubt, be closely watched by Burma, who would shortly have to choose between independence and Dominion status; and Ceylon would also be greatly influenced by the line taken by India on this question. But it must be remembered that the proposal made by the Congress leaders was that Dominion status should be granted and power transferred as early as possible in 1947. Moreover, after the proposed announcement had been made, the interim Government would become increasingly ineffective; and it was essential for practical reasons that the interim period between the announcement and the actual transfer of power on the basis of Dominion status should be reduced to a minimum. It would, therefore, be essential to enact, before the end of the present Session, legislation amending the Government of India Act, 1935. The purpose of this legislation would be to confer Dominion status on the States emerging from the plan for the partition of India and to provide the necessary machinery enabling the new Constitutions to be established and the division of powers to be gradually completed.

The grant of Dominion status to the successor States would, of course, mean that the India Office should cease to be responsible for the handling of United Kingdom relations with India: this was a point on which the Indian leaders were emphatic. The alternative arrangements needed further consideration, but it seemed possible that the best solution might be to expand the Dominions Office into a Department for Commonwealth Relations responsible for handling our relations, not only with the existing Dominions, but also with India and Burma and subsequently with Ceylon and any other territories which might attain a position of "independence within the Commonwealth."

In discussion the following points were raised:—

(a) When these Constitutional changes in the status of India took effect, it would be necessary that The King should divest himself of the title "Emperor of India." He would become King of those parts of India which attained Dominion status. His Majesty had already mentioned this point to the Prime Minister.

(b) This possible change in the status of India also emphasised the need for some further review of the existing relations between the various parts of the British Commonwealth. Though it might prove possible and appropriate that parts of India should attain the status prescribed for Dominions by the Statute of Westminster, there were other parts of His Majesty's Dominions for which some different form of "independence within the Commonwealth" might be more appropriate. THE PRIME MINISTER said that he was taking steps to set in hand a comprehensive review of the constitutional relations between the various parts of the British Commonwealth.

(c) How would India's attainment of Dominion status affect the position of Indians in South Africa? The Cabinet were informed that these people, though Indians by race, were mostly South African citizens by nationality; and their national status would not be affected by India's achieving self-Government as a Dominion. The political difficulties which had arisen over the position of these Indians would at least be no greater if India became a Dominion than if she became a foreign country.

(d) THE LORD PRESIDENT said that, in view of the congestion of the Parliamentary timetable, there would be no hope of passing a Government of India Bill before Parliament adjourned in the summer unless this legislation had the full support of the Opposition. THE PRIME MINISTER said that he had received a firm assurance in writing[3] from the leader of the Opposition that this support would be forthcoming if the proposals of His Majesty's Government proved generally acceptable to the leaders of the Indian Parties.

(e) THE PRIME MINISTER said that communal feeling in India was now intense and it was possible that serious disorders might break out in the Punjab and certain other Provinces at any time after the announcement of the plan for partitioning India. It was the Viceroy's considered view that the only hope of checking widespread communal warfare was to suppress the first signs of it promptly and ruthlessly, using for this purpose all the force required, including tanks and aircraft, and giving full publicity throughout India to the action taken and the reasons for it. In this view the Viceroy had the unanimous support of his Interim Government. It was important that he should also be assured that this policy had the support of His Majesty's Government.

The Cabinet agreed that the policy which the Viceroy proposed to follow in this matter should have their full support.

(f) THE PRIME MINISTER explained the arrangements which were being made for the publication of the proposed statement of policy. It was expected that the Viceroy would be ready to publish the announcement in India on the evening of Tuesday, 3rd June; and any last-minute changes in the text would be telegraphed to London so as to enable a simultaneous announcement to be made in both Houses of Parliament. The Viceroy also proposed to broadcast, later that evening, a message to the people of India. It was hoped that he would record this in London before returning to India, so that it might be broadcast simultaneously in this country. The Prime Minister's broadcast would then take the form of an introductory statement by way of preface to the Viceroy's broadcast.

The Cabinet endorsed the plan outlined in C.P.(47) 158 for determining the successor authorities to which power should be transferred in India. They welcomed the further proposals which had been explained by the Prime Minister for the early attainment of Dominion status by the various parts of a partitioned India. They expressed their warm appreciation of the outstanding service rendered by the Viceroy, and by the Prime Minister and his colleagues on the India and Burma Committee, in evolving these new proposals for further constitutional development in India. If this scheme could be carried through successfully, it would be a notable landmark in the development of the British Commonwealth.

THE PRIME MINISTER, in summing up the discussion, paid tribute to the remarkable skill and initiative which the Viceroy had shown in his conduct

[3] Enclosure to No. 513.

of these difficult negotiations with the Indian leaders. It was essential that, in the concluding stages of the negotiations, the Viceroy should be given a large measure of discretion to amend the details of the plan, without prior consultation with His Majesty's Government, so long as he kept within the limits of the broad policy which had now been approved by the Cabinet.

The Cabinet—

(1) Approved in principle the draft announcement annexed to C.P. (47) 158 regarding the procedure for determining the successor authorities to whom power would be transferred in India; and agreed that this should be adopted by the Viceroy as a basis for his final discussions with Indian leaders on 2nd and 3rd June.

(2) Took note with approval of the proposals outlined by the Prime Minister for the early attainment of Dominion status by the various parts of a partitioned India;

(3) Agreed that, in the concluding stages of his negotiations with the Indian leaders, the Viceroy should have a large measure of discretion to amend the details of this plan provided he kept within the broad limits of the policy approved by the Cabinet;

(4) Agreed that His Majesty's Government should give full support to the policy which the Viceroy proposed to follow, with the agreement of his Interim Government, in using whatever force might be necessary to check the first signs of any widespread outbreak of communal warfare in India after the announcement of the proposals for Partition.

522

Pandit Nehru to Sir J. Colville

R/3/1/90: ff 59–61

SECRET AND PERSONAL   MUSSOORIE.
AS AT: 17 YORK ROAD,
NEW DELHI, *23 May 1947*

Dear Sir John,

During my very short stay here I have been increasingly distressed by news from the Punjab, especially Lahore. Parts of the old walled city of Lahore are being gradually reduced to ashes and there appears to be a complete lack of control of the situation. Reports of those killed by police firing or wounded or arrested and searches made in houses indicate an extreme partiality on the part of the police. It is extraordinary how the administration, in so far as Lahore is concerned, is hardly functioning as it should. I realise fully the difficulties and the strain caused by these occurrences. At the same time it seems to me obvious that if this kind of thing continues, it will spread with great rapidity in other parts of the Punjab also. If the situation in Lahore cannot be controlled, it is still less likely that a wider conflagration will be controlled. The present police authorities are apparently totally unable to control it and reports reach me from impartial sources that no very serious attempt has been made to meet the situation. Whether these reports are correct or not, I cannot say. But the fact that such a serious situation could continue for days and weeks is bad enough. I would earnestly request you to consider what other and further steps should be taken in this matter. The only other step that suggests itself is the effective use of the army in the city of Lahore with freedom to act as they think proper to deal with the situation.

2. I realise that during your brief tenure of the Viceroyalty you will hesitate to take any new step. Perhaps Lord Mountbatten might be consulted by cable or otherwise.

3. Reports from Calcutta are also disturbing. Many of these reports are often exaggerated and alarmist. Nevertheless it is safer to take every precaution for a possible contingency. I have received a letter from a Muslim friend, whom I consider impartial and balanced, from Calcutta. I enclose a copy of this letter for your information.

4. I hope to return to Delhi on Monday morning.[1]

Yours sincerely,
JAWAHARLAL NEHRU

Enclosure to No. 522

COPY OF A LETTER DATED 21 MAY 1947 TO JAWAHARLAL
NEHRU FROM A MUSLIM FRIEND IN CALCUTTA

"An intensive whispering campaign has been started here that an all-out "Battle for Calcutta" will begin immediately after the June 2 conference. There are reports current (especially in my part[2] of the city, which has now become a virtual Pakistan) that preparations are being made to make this the "bloodiest battle in India's history", with no holds barred, not even "bacteriological warfare".

I am taking the liberty of conveying this information to you, for what it may be worth, in the hope that your Government may find it possible to immediately investigate the position and initiate such preventive measures as may be deemed necessary.

To a lay mind it would seem the most effective measure would probably be to have the army stand by, ready to take complete control of the city at a moment's notice, if need be. To leave the matter to the local authorities, with

[1] Sir J. Colville replied to Pandit Nehru on 26 May along similar lines to his letter to Sardar Patel of 24 May (No. 531). R/3/1/90: f 80.
[2] [Note in original:] Park Circus (Calcutta).

all their past record of gross incompetence and unabashed partisanship, might be simply disastrous.

I hope you will forgive my presuming to make this personal appeal".

523

Cabinet

India and Burma Committee. Paper I.B.(47)82

L/PO/6/121: ff 145–6

RELATIONS BETWEEN HIS MAJESTY'S GOVERNMENT AND
THE INDIAN STATES AFTER THE TRANSFER OF POWER
NOTE BY THE SECRETARY

CABINET OFFICE, S.W.I, *23 May 1947*

I circulate a note by the Viceroy which was handed to the Committee at their meeting on 22 May 1947.[1]

S.E.V. LUKE
Secretary

NOTE BY THE VICEROY

The question has been raised of what will happen about the Indian States if British India becomes two separate Dominions. The States may say that it is unreasonable to cut off the constitutional connection with them when such a connection is retained with both parts of British India. They may wish to remain in direct relationship with the Crown, though perhaps getting rid of such features of paramountcy as they dislike.

2. If we admit that the Indian States or even some of them can be admitted as separate Dominions into the Commonwealth we shall be charged with disintegrating India and the Congress is likely to withdraw its application for Dominion Status.

3. The solution seems to be to take the line that we cannot accept as members of the Commonwealth any of the Indian States unless they first associate themselves with one of the two Dominions of British India. In that case their relations with the Crown could be through one of the Governors-General. Fresh agreements would have to be negotiated with the British Indian Government to replace the agreements with the Crown, or the old ones could be renewed by consent. In any case paramountcy would not be inherited by either of the two new Governments in British India.

[1] No. 517.

524

Captain Brockman to Lord Ismay[1]

R/3/1/150: f 60

23 May 1947

I presume telegram referred to in the last sentence of your 6555 of 20th May[2] is your 6306[3] of the 15th May, which you will note was seen and initialled by H.E.

2. With reference to my marginal note[4] on the latter telegram please see also my 1038–S of the 15th May[5] giving H.E.'s wishes that Corfield should remain in the U.K.

3. H.E. was aware that Corfield might be returning, but he hoped that my "most immediate" telegram would arrive in time to stop his departure.[6]

R. V. BROCKMAN

[1] This minute was prepared for Lord Ismay on his return to India.
[2] See No. 480, note 1 last sentence.
[3] In this telegram Lord Ismay had reported that 'Corfield has done his stuff' and that he (Ismay) had told him to return. Mountbatten Papers, Official Correspondence Files: Transfer of Power, Procedure for determining Authorities to which Power is to be demitted, Part (2).
[4] Captain Brockman's marginal note read: 'This has crossed mine to Harris saying Corfield was to stay.'
[5] No. 453.
[6] Lord Ismay minuted 'noted' on 1 June.

525

Rear-Admiral Viscount Mountbatten of Burma to Sir F. Burrows (Bengal)
(via India Office)

Telegram, Mountbatten Papers. Official Correspondence Files:
Bengal, Partition of, Part I(b)

IMMEDIATE   *23 May 1947, 1 pm*
SECRET

6732. Your 128–S, para. 3.[1]

1. Cabinet Committee have agreed that I should have authority to re-cast statement so far as Bengal is concerned in the light of circumstances prevailing on June 2nd.

2. I cannot repeat not commit myself to specific wording at present.
  Repeated to Sir J. Colville.

[1] No. 499.

526

Rear-Admiral Viscount Mountbatten of Burma to Sir E. Mieville (via India Office)

Telegram, R/3/1/150: ff 63–4

IMMEDIATE   *23 May 1947, 3.58 pm*
SECRET   *Received: 23 May, 11.30 pm*

No. 6735. Your 1115-S.[1]
You will appreciate that I cannot enter into intricacies of arguments between Jinnah and Nehru on their respective letters and I realise that precise alternatives, A and B given in VCP 55[2] may require some re-phrasing before H.M.G. can give me authority to go ahead on them.

2. It seems to me that Mr. Jinnah may be under some misapprehension about common Governor General. It is not and never has been intention that there should be a single common appointment. From very beginning there were to be 2 entirely separate appointments: a Governor General of Hindustan nominated by Hindustan Government and a Governor-General of Pakistan nominated by Pakistan Government. He would have the distinct titles of "Governor General [of] Hindustan" and "Governor General of Pakistan" and would not have combined title.

3. If the same man is chosen voluntarily by both Hindustan and Pakistan Governments then it follows that the two governments could confer on him the right to act as an arbitrator or, better, Chairman of an arbitral tribunal in the event of a dispute about partition of assets and liabilities etc.

4. Jinnah has always asked me to endeavour to arrange for continuation of a British arbitrator until all partition is complete.

5. Now that Congress leaders have accepted idea in para. 3 in principle Mr. Jinnah has a unique chance of achieving a British arbitrator for interim period.

6. By Prime Minister's direction constitution experts are looking into Jinnah's proposals for a supreme "stake-holder and arbitrator" to be superimposed over the two Governors General but preliminary investigation is not very hopeful. In particular Mr. Jinnah has prejudiced this investigation by his failure to send me promised particulars of what he has in mind. We probably know enough however to enable investigation to be completed before I come back.

[1] No. 514.   [2] No. 477.

527

Mr Attlee to Mr Mackenzie King, Mr Chifley, Mr Fraser and Field Marshal Smuts

Telegram, L/PO/6/121: ff 96–8

IMMEDIATE   DOMINIONS OFFICE, *23 May 1947, 9.35 pm*
TOP SECRET AND PERSONAL

D.No. 469. My telegrams Nos. D. 439 and D.440 of 8th May.[1] India.
Following from Prime Minister for Prime Minister. *Begins.*
Consideration of the Viceroy's plan has proceeded both in London and in India. A revised draft announcement has been prepared by Viceroy after further detailed consultation with Indian leaders. He reports that it has been substantially accepted by them and that it represents maximum degree of agreement that can be secured. Acceptance by Congress leaders is, however, subject to unreserved acceptance by Muslim League. The revised text is contained in my immediately following telegram.[2] Viceroy has come to London in order to discuss it with Ministers before Conference with Indian leaders fixed for 2nd June.

2. Viceroy has reported that within past week there has been a further development of major importance. It will be remembered that in January the Constituent Assembly, under the inspiration of Congress, passed a resolution declaring resolve to proclaim India an Independent Sovereign Republic. Congress leaders have repeatedly emphasised to Viceroy that establishment of Independent Republic was their objective. On the other hand, Mr. Jinnah has repeatedly expressed wish that Pakistan should have Dominion status. Certain States which at present are expressing intention of remaining independent also wish to remain in Commonwealth and similar proposal has been made on behalf of Bengal by Prime Minister of that Province who is advocating that Bengal should remain united and independent. Viceroy has given Indian leaders no encouragement to suppose that United Kingdom and other Commonwealth Governments would be prepared to agree to a part or parts of India remaining within the Commonwealth if the greater part had become a separate foreign State. Mr. Jinnah thereupon threatened to appeal over Viceroy's head to the "people of the Commonwealth" and argued that no part of the Commonwealth could be forcibly extruded against its will. This attitude on his part which became known had a disturbing effect on Congress leaders who seem to have begun to feel that an independent Hindustan might be at some disadvantage if Pakistan succeeded in remaining

[1] See No. 352 and its note 2.
[2] Not printed.

part of the British Commonwealth. In these circumstances certain Congress leaders proposed to Viceroy strictly privately that United Kingdom Government should announce, simultaneously with announcement to be made on 2nd June, intention to grant Dominion status to India, (or in the event of partition, to both parts of India) as soon as possible and in any event in 1947. These leaders were confident that it would be possible for them to persuade Congress to accept Dominion status provided they could say that by doing so actual transfer of power would be secured substantially earlier than June, 1948, but would have no hope of doing so otherwise. They said that though, in order to secure assent of their party, they would have publicly to stress fact that it is inherent in Dominion status that Dominion can secede from Commonwealth whenever it wishes, in their view Hindustan would not ultimately leave the Commonwealth, once Dominion status had been accepted.

3. This most unexpected development opens up new possibility of whole of India, although divided into two or possibly three independent states, remaining in the Commonwealth after the effective transfer of power has taken place. Though at outset the constitution of the two (or three) parts would be transitional, prospect of parts of British India remaining in Commonwealth when their new and permanent constitutions come into operation would be considerably enhanced and example set by India would be likely to influence Burma, and probably later other parts of the Empire to remain in the Commonwealth. Consequently we are considering as a matter of great urgency whether legislation could be passed before August to enable the transfer of power to be made this year on the basis proposed.

4. Partition of India raises most formidable problems of administrative and constitutional character. Our conception of the manner in which transfer of power could be effected is as follows:—

Legislation would provide that British India would become two independent States. Provincial Governments such as now exist but modified to such extent as may result from the process of partition would remain in being but two provisional executives appointed by and responsible to the Constituent Assemblies for the respective areas would be set up in place of existing unified Central Government. Existing Indian laws and Government of India Act, 1935, so far as not repealed, would remain in force but would be amendable in respect of each of the new States by the Constituent Assembly for that State or by Legislatures subsequently set up by them. Joint delegations of representatives of each State would be set up charged with division of existing central administrative machinery, including Armed Forces, and of assets and liabilities, but also with carrying them on on a unitary basis in the meantime. There would be a similar joint Commission for co-ordination of the foregoing specialist Commissions. Governors-General for each State would be appointed on advice of provisional executives though at outset these posts might be held by Lord Mountbatten. In the provinces Indian Governors would be appointed on advice, and all control from Whitehall would cease.

5. Congress leaders have said that they are willing to accept the Crown but would wish title Emperor of India to be deleted from Royal Title.

6. We fully appreciate that above raises issues of first importance for all members of the Commonwealth. We should be glad of an early expression of your views on the question of grant of Dominion status to parts of India separately. In our view recognition of Pakistan as a Dominion, while remainder of India became a separate State would have been a difficult proposition which we should have had to consider most carefully in all its aspects. But if whole of India, even though in the form of two or possibly three Dominions (if Bengal becomes separate State), is ready to remain in Commonwealth such a decision should, in our view, be welcomed. No doubt if one part of India later left the Commonwealth we should have to accept the position that the others could remain in the Commonwealth, but we should not then be open to charge of having favoured one of the contending parties against the other.

7. I must emphasise the need for extreme secrecy on this matter because if it became known that Congress leaders had privately encouraged this idea, the possibility of their being able to bring their party round to it would be serious[ly] jeopardised. *Ends.*

528

Mr Attlee to Field Marshal Smuts

Telegram, L/PO/6/121: f 138

IMMEDIATE   DOMINIONS OFFICE, *23 May 1947, 9.50 pm*
TOP SECRET AND PERSONAL

No. 44. Following from Prime Minister for Prime Minister. *Begins.*
I am very grateful to you for your message[1] which your High Commissioner has conveyed to me on the question of India.

Let me say first of all that I and my colleagues have very much in mind the dangers of civil war in India and the importance to be attached to making every effort to avoid a situation in which the termination of British rule in India is the prelude to strife on an immense scale. The difficulty is that matters have now gone so far that we can scarcely draw back and even if we attempted

[1] No. 420.

to do so, it is probable that we should be faced with a very serious situation. But as you will see from my separate message[2] the prospects of an agreed solution in a reasonably satisfactory form are not unhopeful, and I am sure you will agree that we should make every effort to impress on all parties in India the absolute necessity in their own interests of the adoption of some compromise plan of this nature. *Ends.*

[2] No. 527.

529

The Earl of Listowel to Mr Attlee

L/PO/6/124: ff 56–9

SECRET   INDIA OFFICE, *23 May 1947*
Secretary of State's Minute: Serial No. 74/47

Prime Minister.

The Viceroy has sent me a copy of his broadcast for comments.[1] I understand he has sent a copy to you also.

I attach below the amendments which I suggest should be made to it. I draw particular attention to the amendment on page 3, paragraph 8, about Dominion Status. I think the alteration I propose fully makes the point which the Viceroy naturally wants included, without running any risk of trouble with the Dominions. The Secretary of State for the Dominions agreed to the Viceroy's words but it seems to me that the arguments he used against statutory provision for secession are also valid against the Viceroy's draft.

LISTOWEL

P.S. I have sent a copy of this minute to the Dominions Secretary[2]

SUGGESTED AMENDMENTS TO H.E. THE VICEROY'S BROADCAST STATEMENT

Paragraph 4,[3] line 2—for "unified India" substitute "Union of India". Lines 5 and 6—delete "have been welded together into an entity that enjoys" and substitute "enjoyed".

Page 2, paragraph 5, second sentence—read "In my opinion that plan provides best arrangement that can be devised" etc.

(All Provinces have some representatives in the Constituent Assembly. The plan was not based on the adherence of Provinces. Once the representatives were elected by Provincial Legislatures they were members and entitled to attend irrespective of the views of the Provincial Government).

Page 2, line 11—"any important areas" substitute "any large areas".

Paragraph 6, third sentence—for "the people of India" in both places substitute "Indians".

(The point here is (*a*) the population of the States are part of the people of India and are not concerned with these decisions, (*b*) it is the representatives of the people in the respective areas who take the decisions and not the people as a whole).

Paragraph 6, fourth sentence—for "of an overall referendum" read "of a referendum in each area".

(An overall referendum implies a referendum to the whole of British India voting as one which could hardly be contemplated as a method of deciding these issues.)

For "Legislature of the Provinces" substitute "Legislative Assemblies of".

Page 3, paragraph 6, last line—read "with a referendum only in one special case".

Page 3, paragraph 8, third sentence—read "I should like to make it quite clear that it is still open to the Constituent Assemblies to decide subsequently whether or not the part of India for which they are responsible will remain in the British Commonwealth. In the words of the Prime Minister: 'The British Commonwealth and Empire is not bound together by chains of external compulsion. It is a free association of free peoples.' There is therefore nothing final or binding in this decision."

(It was pointed out in the India Committee[4] that the Statute of Westminster does not provide for secession. Lord Addison thought that this passage in the Viceroy's broadcast was all right but I understand that on the official level[5] the Dominions Office had previously expressed the opinion that it would be much better to use words which applied only to India. Their point is that we should not encourage in any way the idea that a Dominion has the right of secession. India is a special case in that it is now being given independence and therefore can choose freely whether or not to become a Member of the Commonwealth. I would urge that it is much best to adhere to what you said in the House of Commons in March 1946, which is quite categorical as regards India, than to make a new statement which refers to the Dominions as well as India.)

[1] See No. 507.
[2] Later on 23 May Mr Cumming-Bruce informed Mr Harris that Lord Addison had seen Lord Listowel's suggested amendment of paragraph 8 and entirely agreed with the proposed terms of the amendment. L/PO/6/124: f 55.
[3] See Annex II to No. 276.
[4] See No. 517, Minute 3.
[5] The official concerned was Sir J. Stephenson who was reported as being 'very alarmed' by the original draft with its implication of 'a general right of Dominions as such to go out'. Turnbull to Harris, Minute, 23 May 1947. L/PO/6/124: f 60.

Page 4, paragraph 9, line 7—for "Dominions" substitute "Nations".
(This is to include the United Kingdom).
Page 4, paragraph 11, lines 6 and 7—read "when I came out as Viceroy I was shocked to find" etc.
(This might otherwise be read as referring to the Viceroy's return from his present visit to the U.K.).

530

Mr Turnbull to Mr Brown[1]

L/PO/6/124: f 54

SECRET   INDIA OFFICE, *24 May 1947*

Dear Brown,

At the Cabinet India and Burma Committee on the 22nd May[2] there was discussion about the question of the right of Dominions to secede from the Commonwealth. The President said that in 1942 in connection with the Cripps Offer the matter had been gone into in great detail with expert legal advice and that a formula had been agreed which he could use to explain the position to the Indian leaders. It was suggested that this formula should be given to the Viceroy for his guidance at the present time.

I have made a close search of all the minutes of the India Committee and the Cabinet and all the papers submitted to them for a formula of this kind and I cannot find it. Nor have I personally, though I was in the whole thing, any recollection of any document being drawn up on this subject. I know there were discussions in the India Committee but apart from the actual words in the Cripps Offer itself I do not think there is a formula.[3] The line Sir Stafford took at a Press Conference[4] was that Dominions could of course in fact secede from the Empire at any time. They have not, however, a constitutional right to do so.

Could you please ask the President and let me know as soon as possible, and certainly by Tuesday, whether he has any more precise recollection as to the connection in which he had this formula? He may be under the impression that something was included in a set of instructions which he will remember was prepared by the India Committee to be given to him but which the Cabinet subsequently decided should not be given to him formally. I have looked at this but it does not contain anything on the point in question.

The first drafts of the Cripps Offer contained a statement that the Union of India would have the same status as the Dominions and would be "free to remain in or separate itself from the British Commonwealth". This was subsequently deleted and the final text said that the Union would be a Dominion within the Commonwealth but that the Treaty which would be a condition of the transfer of power would not impose any restriction on the power of India to decide in the future its relationship to the other members of the Commonwealth.

We are suggesting here to the Viceroy that the best line for him to take is that the Prime Minister's Statement of the 15th March still stands. He then made it quite clear that if India remained in the Commonwealth it must be by her own free will. If, on the other hand, she elected for independence she had a right to do so. This seems to say all that is necessary. The Dominions Office see considerable objection from the Domions point of view to any admission that there is any constitutional right of Dominions to secede. They draw a distinction between this and the right of India before or upon becoming an independent State to choose whether or not to do so within the Commonwealth.[5]

Yours sincerely,

F. F. TURNBULL

[1] Private Secretary to Sir S. Cripps.
[2] See No. 517, Minute 3(c).
[3] For reports of discussions at the India Committee see Vol I, Nos. 191, 194 and 223; for related papers see Vol I, Nos. 190, 193, 195–6, 208 and 231. The Editors have themselves traced no formula over and above the sentences in the Draft Declaration (see Vol I, No. 456, para. 2(c)) and while it seems clear from the papers referred to above that a fuller exposition than appears in those sentences was initially contemplated, the possibility was apparently later discarded.
[4] cf. Vol. I, No. 440, p 537.
[5] No reply to this letter has been traced.

531

Sir J. Colville to Sardar Patel

R/3/1/90: f 70

No. 133/14

24 May 1947

Dear Sardar Patel,

Thank you for your letter of the 21st May,[1] which I have just received. Since you wrote the situation in Lahore has improved to some extent, and a telegram I received from the Governor this morning reports that the City is relatively quiet.

2. I have been disturbed since I have been here about the situation in Lahore and Amritsar and have been in close touch with the Governor daily. In a telegram[2] I received two days ago Sir Evan Jenkins told me that he would like,

[1] No. 501. [2] No. 500.

at as earlier [sic] date as possible, a complete Brigade for the Lahore area alone, in addition to troops already allocated.

3. I had a talk with Baldev Singh about this request, and, after consultation with the Deputy Commander-in-Chief, it has with regret been found impossible to meet it. As you know, the 4th Division is already well on its way up to the Punjab. The reserve of troops available in India is low and the Deputy Commander-in-Chief feels, and I agree with him, that it would be unwise to dissipate our reserves at the present time as it is by no means certain yet that H.M.G.'s forthcoming announcement may not be followed by further disorders.

4. The Deputy Commander-in-Chief, with the approval of Sardar Baldev Singh, is, therefore, sending a telegram to the Army Commander today, pointing out that very wide powers are given to the military by the Punjab Disturbed Areas (Special Powers of Armed Forces) Ordinance, 1947, and that if these powers are properly used they should be adequate for any purpose which the authorities may require.

5. I am getting into touch with the Governor of the Punjab again today, Saturday, but I am sure that he feels that the powers available to him are adequate, and that with the arrival of the extra troops in the immediate future the position should improve. I do not think that martial law which has many grave disadvantages, is at present necessary, as I feel that the wide powers of the Ordinance which I have quoted above should be sufficient.

Yours sincerely,

JOHN COLVILLE

532

Mr Attlee to Rear-Admiral Viscount Mountbatten of Burma

Mountbatten Papers. Demi-Official Correspondence Files: Attlee

SECRET   10 DOWNING STREET, *24 May 1947*

My dear Dickie,

I am not very happy about the wording of your broadcast.[1] It should, I think, be as much as possible your own statement in your own words, but at present it seems to me to be rather involved and not easily to be understood by the ordinary man.

I do not know the extent of your listening public in India and you will know their mentality better than I can, but your broadcast seems to me to be suited to the Indian intelligentsia rather than the common people. I do not know what the Moslems and the Sikhs will make of it.

I think it might be well to use more concrete expressions and to explain the procedure in more detail even if it involves speaking at greater length. You will no doubt have heard that the Cabinet accepted[2] the report[3] of the Committee which I submitted to it on Friday.

I hope you are getting some rest.

Yours ever,
CLEM

[1] See No. 507.   [2] No. 521.   [3] No. 516.

533

Cabinet

India and Burma Committee. Paper I.B.(47)84

L/P&J/10/79: ff 64-5

RELATIONS BETWEEN HIS MAJESTY'S GOVERNMENT AND THE INDIAN STATES AFTER THE TRANSFER OF POWER

NOTE BY THE SECRETARY OF STATE FOR INDIA

INDIA OFFICE, *24 May 1947*

At their meeting of 22nd May,[1] the Committee invited me, in consultation with the Viceroy, to revise the Statement contained in the Annex to I.B.(47) 82[2] in the light of the Committee's discussion of it and to circulate a further draft for consideration by the Committee before the next meeting. I now circulate a revised draft Statement prepared by my officials in consultation with the Viceroy's Staff.

L.

REVISED DRAFT STATEMENT

The question has been raised what will happen about the Indian States if British India becomes two or more separate Dominions. Our present relation with them is based on the British Crown's paramountcy in all India. This paramountcy will cease to exist when the two or more Dominions are set up. The Dominion Governments composed of elements of British India will in fact be paramount in their own territories. Paramountcy over the States will not pass to them: the States will regain their independence. Fresh agreements will have to be negotiated or existing agreements renewed between them and the successor Governments. Meanwhile standstill agreements will be required.

2. Our prime object should be to facilitate the exclusive association of the

[1] No. 517, Minute 6.   [2] No. 523.

States with one of the new Dominions. (A number of States have in fact already joined the existing Constituent Assembly). To the extent that they are so associated, they will enter into a new relationship with the Crown through the Governor-General, similar to that of the other constituent parts of the Dominion (except perhaps that the Rulers could if they wished maintain personal relations of a courtesy nature with the Sovereign himself, through the medium of the Governor-General as the King's representative).

3. But some States or groups of States may say that they have no wish to join a Dominion, and that it is unreasonable to cut off the Crown's relations with them when the rest of India is remaining in the Commonwealth.

4. If we admit *at this stage* that we will be prepared to maintain separate relationship with States or groups of States which do not join a Dominion, we shall be charged with disintegrating India and the Congress is likely to withdraw its application for Dominion status. On the other hand, should any State eventually not enter into relationship with a Dominion we should in fact be forced to consider a separate relationship with it.

5. The best solution seems to be to take the line (basing ourselves on paragraph 5 of the Statement of May 12th 1946 (Cmd. 6385)[3] that we hope the States will join one of the new Dominions, and thereby be able to re-establish relations with the Crown in whatever form the Dominion constitution may take; but that we cannot contemplate accepting them as members of the Commonwealth otherwise than in association with a Dominion.

[3] Vol. VII, No. 262.

534

Cabinet

India and Burma Committee. PaperI.B.(47)85 (Revised)

L/P&J/10/79: ff 60–2

DOMINION STATUS IN INDIA
MEMORANDUM BY THE SECRETARY OF STATE FOR INDIA

INDIA OFFICE, *24 May 1947*

The India and Burma Committee at its meeting on 22nd May[1] approved my suggestion that, in substitution for the two alternative drafts suggested by the Viceroy for dealing with the question of Dominion Status for the successor authorities resulting from partition (*vide* I.B.(47)79),[2] it would be preferable to have one paragraph suitable to all eventualities on the score that any objection by the Muslim League to the conferment of Dominion Status on Pakistan should be met by the reply that that must be the basis on which legislation should be framed though it would be open, in the nature of the case, to Pakistan to contract out of Dominion Status subsequently if it wished.

2. I now circulate a revised draft—prepared by my officials in consultation with the Viceroy's staff—and offer the following comments upon it for consideration by the Committee:—

(*a*) I have used in the second sentence the words "it is His Majesty's Government's intention to introduce" as being the most suitable words to meet the contingency that owing to events over which His Majesty's Government have no control their purpose may be frustrated.

It was accepted by my officials that in order to emphasise the imminence of the transfer of power it would be psychologically valuable to say in this sentence that legislation would be introduced "during the current Session". Though this is certainly the intention, the possibility has to be borne in mind that any serious delay over the exercise of the options in India may defeat the intention. If 16 days are allowed for convening the legislatures concerned in the option and a week is allowed for a decision, it is estimated that the options may be fully exercised by 1st July. The Bill could then be put into final (or semi-final) form with a view to introduction about the 7th July. This is on the assumption that all goes well; but even so the result of the referendum in the North West Frontier Province cannot be known until about the end of July; so that the Bill would have to be in a semi-final form with provision for the North West Frontier Province according to the way the referendum goes. There is also the possibility of lengthy negotiations in Bengal and the Punjab before the option can be exercised there.

For these reasons it seems desirable in the second sentence to use words which would leave it open to His Majesty's Government to explain, if necessary, the frustration of their intention by the dilatory action in India.

(*b*) The last 13 words of the second sentence have been adopted for the dual purpose of avoiding the assumption that partition is inevitable and of covering the case of Bengal, whichever way the decision there may go. (The Viceroy's staff are arranging for the provisional inclusion in the draft Statement of a paragraph to cover the contingency that if Bengal has settled its own affairs in advance it will, in the event that the rest of India is partitioned, become an independent State).

(*c*) As regards the last sentence of the attached draft, it is arguable that the right to go out of the Commonwealth should be clearly stated to be available only after June 1948; on the other hand, this might provoke immediate agitation to secede as soon as that becomes permissible. It seems desirable, therefore, to use a general word such as "subsequently".

L.

---

¹ No. 517, Minute 3.   ² No. 504.

ALTERNATIVE TO VICEROY'S DRAFTS CIRCULATED WITH
I.B.(47)79

The major political parties have repeatedly emphasised their desire that there should be the earliest possible transfer of power in India. It is His Majesty's Government's intention to introduce legislation during the current Session for the transfer of power this year on a Dominion Status basis to such successor authorities as come into being as a result of this announcement. This will be an interim arrangement without prejudice to the right of Indian Constituent Assemblies to decide subsequently whether or not the part of India in respect of which they have authority will remain within the British Commonwealth.

535

Sir J. Colville to Sir E. Jenkins (Punjab)

Telegram, R/3/1/90: f 69

IMMEDIATE   NEW DELHI, *24 May 1947, 9.20 pm*
SECRET

1155–S. Your telegram No. 100–G of the 21st May.[1]

2. I am glad to see that the position in Lahore is improving. I had a talk with Baldev Singh two days ago about further reinforcements. I regret that after investigation with the Deputy Commander-in-Chief it has been reluctantly decided that a brigade, additional to the troops of the Fourth Division now moving into the Punjab, cannot be spared from the small reserve of troops which is being held available to meet disorders which may, for example, occur after H.M.G.'s announcement next month. I hope, however that, with the arrival of the Fourth Division the position will improve from your point of view.

3. At a meeting which Baldev Singh held this morning, at which P.S.V. was also present, it was felt that the Punjab Disturbed Areas (Special Powers of Armed Forces) Ordinance, 1947, conferred sufficient powers on the military to meet the present situation in the Punjab. I should be glad if you would confirm that this is so, and whether you consider you have sufficient powers at present to handle the situation.

4. I had a letter[2] from Patel this morning, suggesting that the Punjab should be placed under martial law, but I am replying[3] that I do not think this is necessary at present, as the powers under the above Ordinance, if used to the full, should be sufficient at the present time.

[1] No. 500.   [2] No. 501.   [3] No. 531.

536

Sir E. Jenkins (Punjab) to Sir J. Colville

Telegram, R/3/1/90: f 77

IMMEDIATE   *25 May 1947, 4.20 pm*
SECRET   *Received: 25 May, 8.30 pm*

106–G. Your telegram 1155–S of May 24th.[1] Existing powers are adequate. Difficulty of handling situation is due to facts (*a*) that communal hostility is now universal and (*b*) that stabbings and fires are usually work of individuals and not of crowds. Police and troops get few targets and offenders frequently escape.

2. On martial law Patel is probably echoing constantly reiterated opinion of Punjab Hindus. Under present constitution martial law can I understand be imposed only by military commander who would usually decline to impose it unless his troops were in danger or civil authorities had ceased to function. In view of extensive emergency powers already taken and of fact that civil authorities are functioning normally everywhere imposition of martial law would mean in effect simply the substitution of G.O.C. in C., Northern Command or Lahore Area Commander for Governor. Martial law is therefore unlikely to affect situation materially.

[1] No. 535.

537

Mr Abbott to Captain Brockman

R/3/1/90: ff 84–7

SECRET   GOVERNMENT HOUSE, LAHORE,
D.O. No. G.S. 306   *26 May 1947*

My dear Brockman,

As desired by H.E. the Governor I forward herewith, for the information of H.E. the Viceroy, copies of notes recorded by him after interviews yesterday with the Hon'ble Mr Liaqat Ali Khan and today with the Hon'ble S. Baldev Singh.

Yours sincerely,

S. E. ABBOTT

Enclosure 1 to No. 537 (Extract)

Mr. Liaqat Ali Khan saw me at 12 noon today at his request. We talked until 1.30 p.m.

2. On the general situation he said that the Muslim League did not accept certain particulars in the announcement proposed by H.M.G. When I asked what these particulars were, he replied that the League would not agree to the partition of Bengal or the Punjab.

3. I said that in that case the outlook was not promising. The Muslims wanted the whole of the Punjab; the Sikhs would yield only about 2/5ths of it to them; and the Hindus would follow the Congress leaders. There was a "civil war" atmosphere in the Punjab now and all communities were fatalistic and hysterical. How did Mr. Liaqat Ali Khan suggest that the situation should be handled?

4. Mr. Liaqat Ali Khan said that the Muslims felt aggrieved—they were not the aggressors, but the present administration in the Punjab was bitterly hostile to them. Only two of the Magistrates employed in Lahore City were Muslims; and a relatively small number of the Police officers so employed were Muslims. British officers were rough and discourteous in their dealings with Muslim non-officials. I replied that I had to go on facts and not on party propaganda. The official figures for deaths caused by the disturbances since March 4th were, on 23rd May, 3410. I believed the correct figure (including Rawalpindi deaths not yet registered) to be about 3600. Of this total probably not more than 600 were Muslims. Similarly the loss of property was probably Rs 10 to Rs 15 crores, and less than 5 per cent of this was probably Muslim property. It was difficult for me to hold that the Muslims were not the aggressors—even in the renewed Lahore rioting their deaths were less than one-third of the total number of deaths recorded. I did my best to preserve communal balance in posting Magistrates, and I had no doubt that I.G। Police did the same in posting Police officers. As regards British officers, I was sure they were being fair; but many of them had been gravely shocked, and I thought the League leaders didn't realise how horrible the Rawalpindi massacre seemed to any impartial person.

5. Resuming his argument Mr. Liaqat Ali Khan said that we ought to get much tougher with the Sikhs. They had had, and missed, their chance of forming a Ministry with the League in the spring of 1946, and could not be permitted to dictate indefinitely. I said that the Muslim League must try to understand the Sikh view—the Sikhs, unreasonable and difficult as they were, had a real grievance. The League had never apologized for the Rawalpindi massacre and the continued burning in Lahore and Amritsar were making a reconciliation impossible. The Sikhs now felt, and with reason, that they would

not be safe in a Muslim State. I believed partition to be a disaster for the Punjab, but if we were to avoid it, all parties must be prepared to make sacrifices. It was no solution to say that the Sikhs were headstrong and unreasonable—three months ago this criticism was justified, but now the Sikhs had a good deal of reason on their side, though in ten years' time the present disputes might, and probably would, seem entirely futile. How would Mr. Liaqat Ali Khan solve the problem?

6. Mr. Liaqat Ali Khan replied that there would be trouble anyhow, and that the right solution was the one which would cause least trouble. Personally he thought that whatever decision H.M.G. announced should be enforced with the utmost firmness. (Rather an odd suggestion in view of the League's rejection of partition). I pointed out that H.M.G. and the British element in the services did not want to get involved in a communal civil war, and he replied that we could not evade our responsibility. There would be civil war, and we could not possibly walk out.

Enclosure 2 to No. 537 (Extract)

The Hon'ble Sardar Baldev Singh saw me at the Secretariat at 11 a.m. today at his request.

2. He took a very gloomy view of the general situation. He said that he did not think Jinnah would agree to the partition plan, and that if Jinnah ran out, the Congress would also decline to support the plan. So far as the Sikhs were concerned, he thought they would be satisfied by a passage in the last draft he had seen which laid down that the Boundary Commission should, in fixing a boundary, take into account population "and other relevant factors". He admitted that the Boundary Commission would have to be appointed by "the parties", or in other words by the leaders of the Muslim, Hindu and Sikh communities, and that the terms of reference to the Commission (which would presumably also have to be drafted by "the parties") would have to be considerably more specific. Broadly his view was that the Sikhs would accept the announcement; that the Muslim League would reject it; and that the Congress, though they might accept it initially, would withdraw their acceptance if the Muslim League proved recalcitrant.

538

Mr Nicholls to Mr Attlee

L/P&J/10/79: f 95

IMMEDIATE AND TOP SECRET   OFFICE OF THE HIGH COMMISSIONER
FOR THE UNION OF SOUTH AFRICA,
26 May 1947

My dear Prime Minister,
    Future of India
General Smuts has asked me to convey the following to you urgently:—

"Your 44[1] and Circular telegram D. No. 469.[2] My original suggestion[3] that any part of India should have the option to vote for Dominion status at the coming referendum was satisfactorily met by the new proposal whereunder Dominion status is conferred on India as a whole or in two or three parts by Act of Parliament to be passed in 1947. Should India adopt partition there is the added advantage in this that one part will thereafter hesitate to secede from Dominion status so long as the other part or parts continue to maintain it. It is obvious, for instance, that Hindustan as an independent Republic will be seriously prejudiced if Pakistan has the influence and prestige of the British Commonwealth behind it. The result may therefore well be that secession may be indefinitely postponed and the whole of India remain within the British connection. Indeed as the situation may now develop it may even be to the advantage of the Commonwealth if India is partitioned and one part acts as a check on the other part or parts against secession.

The actual partition and separation of Indian assets, services and responsibilities will be a task of immense difficulty, but it will be one of India's own making and one which she could only carry out with the active assistance of British experience and statesmanship. Britain will thus remain as the arbiter of India's destiny and the moderating influence in her racial troubles and problems. It will continue to render India great service and remain indispensable in her affairs and a vital force in India's internal peace and welfare. This does not look like quitting and latest development is therefore a promising and welcome turn of events".

Yours sincerely,
G. HEATON NICHOLLS

[1] No. 528.   [2] No. 527.   [3] See No. 420.

539

Mr Fraser to Mr Attlee

Telegram, L/P&J/10/79: ff 92–3

IMMEDIATE   *26 May 1947, 6.23 pm*
TOP SECRET AND PERSONAL   *Received: 26 May, 12.45 pm*

No. 106. For Prime Minister from Prime Minister.

I note with very great interest the encouraging developments referred to in your message D. 469.[1]

I trust most earnestly that the Congress Leaders will have the conviction and the courage to proceed along the lines they have indicated in their private declarations to the Viceroy. I agree that under these new circumstances that solution you have in mind, namely, the grant of Dominion Status to parts of India separately, should be explored to the utmost. For my own part I would willingly seek the support of my Cabinet colleagues for the new proposal and I hope that it will prove acceptable to the three sections of India you mention.

The contingency of one or more Indian States remaining in the Commonwealth while the others withdraw, may raise some practical problems which call for examination. While I would prefer that India as a whole should be admitted, alternatively I would be in favour of accepting the inclusion of any part but would like to have further information and comments of the United Kingdom authorities upon the various important issues involved.

I fear that some of the Indian Leaders may very well seek to misrepresent the motives lying behind the United Kingdom Government's advocacy of the new plan. It is presumed therefore that the announcement regarding the admission of Indian States to Dominion Status will be so couched as to counteract or preclude any charge that this represents any retraction from the previous offer of independence but rather that the Indian States at their own request are being offered the privileges of full membership of the British Commonwealth.

It is fully realized that the admission of Indian States to Dominion Status both imposes obligations on their part towards the other members of the British Commonwealth and correspondingly involves obligations on the part of the other British Commonwealth members. These will undoubtedly require careful study in the light of political strategic economic and social considerations.

In order to avoid any future misunderstanding it should be made clear at this stage that it is regarded as fundamental in New Zealand that we retain complete control over the composition of our population. By accepting India as a full member of the Commonwealth we do not include amongst our

[1] No. 527.

obligations that of giving favoured treatment in regard to immigration. Nor do we regard this question as constituting any reservation on our part or that of the other Dominions to the admission of India within the Commonwealth. The opportunity to bring India in should in my opinion be welcomed. Just as it was felt in the past in almost every significant development of British Commonwealth relations that risks were being taken so on this occasion I hope that we are likely to be justified in our faith that the Commonwealth has the capacity to grow into a free association of self-governing peoples of diverse colours and races—all maintaining their unique characteristics and all contributing according to their capacities towards the welfare and advancement of the whole.

540

Sir E. Mieville to Rear-Admiral Viscount Mountbatten of Burma

Telegram, R/3/1/150: ff 70–2

IMMEDIATE   NEW DELHI, 26 May 1947, 7 pm
SECRET   Received: 26 May, 9.20 pm

No. 1165–S. My telegram No. 1115–S of May 22,[1] penultimate paragraph.

I have today received a long letter from Nehru containing his reactions to Jinnah's two notes. Following are salient extracts. *Begins.* It is clear that Mr. Jinnah's notes and the attitude he has taken up in them make a vital difference to the talks we have had so far with the Viceroy.

In effect we had accepted the revised draft announcement as well as the other proposals. But we had made it clear that there was no point in our accepting them unless they were the basis of a settlement and no further claims would be put forward. If the Muslim League did not accept the very structure of those proposals, then there could be no settlement on that basis and the proposals fell through. We were not prepared to have a one sided acceptance of them.

Mr. Jinnah's note of the 19th May[2] is chiefly an argument for being unable to say anything definite without seeing the full text of my letters[3] addressed to the Viceroy. His note of the 22nd May[4] is an argumentative criticism of various things said. It is clear, however, from what Mr. Jinnah says that he does not accept the very basis of the proposals with regard to the partition of Bengal and the Punjab. In the course of a press interview[5] he has gone much further and stated that he will resist any such partition. He has also added a demand for a corridor from the North-West to the North-East.

In view of the attitude taken up by Mr. Jinnah, we cannot give a one-sided agreement to any proposal which does not lead to a full settlement. I have tried to make this perfectly clear in my previous letters and I wish to emphasise this again so that there might be no doubt in regard to it.

The consequence of Mr. Jinnah's rejection of the main proposals in the draft announcement is that we must necessarily fall back upon the Cabinet Mission's Scheme of May 16, 1946. We have adhered to this and have been functioning in accordance with this in the Constituent Assembly and otherwise.

Mr. Jinnah's notes are confused and lack clarity, except for the fact that he seems to object to most things. In regard to one matter, however, that is our desire that the Interim Government should be immediately treated by convention as a Dominion Government subject to the Viceroy's over-riding authority in regard to the protection of minority interests, Mr. Jinnah has expressed strong disagreement. This has nothing to do with the draft announcement. But, as we have stated previously, it is a vital matter for us. The present position has given rise to an enormous amount of trouble. I do not see how it can possibly be carried on in future even for a brief period, more especially when other changes are envisaged. We attach the greatest importance to this and I really do not see why Mr. Jinnah or the Muslim League should object to it when their particular interests are safeguarded and kept under the Viceroy.

Mr. Jinnah further says that he is unable to understand what is meant by my stating that any Act of the British Parliament conferring Dominion Status on India during the Interim period may be varied by the authority in India. I thought that Dominion Status necessarily carried this right; otherwise it is not Dominion Status.

During the past few years it has been our repeated experience that Mr. Jinnah does not commit himself to anything and does not like coming to a settlement. He accepts what he gets and goes on asking for more. We have arrived at a stage when this kind of thing will do good to nobody, and we are not prepared to have one-sided commitments in future.

I am anxious that there should be no misunderstanding about our attitude in the Viceroy's mind or in the mind of H.M.G. I would, therefore, request you to inform the Viceroy and H.M.G. immediately of our strong feelings on this subject and our reaction to Mr. Jinnah's notes. *Ends.*

Personally, I feel that Nehru is stressing too much Jinnah's recent effusions to the Press about a corridor and the question of the partition of Bengal and Punjab. I do not believe Jinnah's attitude has changed since you last saw him and my belief is strengthened by the fact that Colville had a long talk with Jinnah when the latter came to lunch here today and he formed the opinion that Jinnah was absolutely determined on the principle of Pakistan but gave the impression as being prepared to negotiate on details and unlikely to throw away the chance of getting a limited Pakistan in an attempt to get the whole.

[1] No. 514.
[2] This note has not been traced; see however Nos. 489 and 490.
[3] See Nos. 464 and 471; also No. 482 addressed to Captain Brockman.
[4] See No. 514.   [5] See No. 502.

541

Pandit Nehru to Sir J. Colville

R/3/136: f 162

No. F.14(1)–PS/47.   NEW DELHI, *26 May 1947*

Dear Sir John,

[Paras. 1 and 2, on the appointment of the Superintendent of the Hyderabad Railway Police, omitted.]

May I also write to you about a matter to which I have already drawn Lord Mountbatten's attention?[1] This relates to various steps being taken by the Political Department to wind up Residencies and Agencies in the States and to direct the States to correspond directly with various Departments of the Government of India. To take any such step without consultation with the Government of India seems to me highly improper and even unconstitutional. The Residents and Agents undoubtedly represent the Crown Representative in the States. At the same time they are the channel for the Government of India also to function in the States in regard to many common matters and to that extent they also represent the Government of India. To put an end to a well established machinery without any reference to the Government of India which is concerned with it, seems to me a very extraordinary procedure. On the merits such a proposal would lead to chaotic conditions in the relationship of the States with the Government of India. Whatever the future set-up might be, it is obvious that there must be a machinery and a proper channel for constant communication between the Government of India and the States, even for the purpose of setting up a new relationship. To put an end to existing machinery in a hurry and without consultation can only mean that there is a desire to hinder in every way the development of any new arrangements between the States and the Government of India.

I should like to repeat what I have said previously that we consider these activities of the Political Department objectionable, harmful and discourteous to the Government of India.

I do not know what steps were taken in regard to this matter when I wrote to Lord Mountbatten about it some weeks ago. Owing to the pressure of other events I did not like to remind him on it, but I gather that nothing has been done so far to stop this process of disintegration. I would beg of you to have this matter put up in the Cabinet so that the Government of India might consider it and express its opinion in regard to it.

The Political Department has long been considered as being opposed to

Indian progress and unity and it will be unfortunate if anything is done to substantiate this general impression.[2]

Yours sincerely,

JAWAHARLAL NEHRU

[1] See No. 266.

[2] Sir J. Colville acknowledged this letter on 30 May. He said he thought Pandit Nehru would agree that Cabinet consideration of the programme for the retraction of paramountcy must await Lord Mountbatten's return. Sir J. Colville knew that Lord Mountbatten wished to discuss the subject with both Pandit Nehru and Sir C. Corfield. R/3/1/136: f 190.

In a letter to Pandit Nehru of 27 May, Sir C. Corfield said he was very glad to learn of the suggestion that the question of contraction of paramountcy should be brought up in Cabinet. He felt sure this would lead to the removal of a number of misunderstandings. *Ibid*: f 179.

542

Sir J. Colville to the Earl of Listowel

Mountbatten Papers. Letters to and from the Secretary of State

26 May 1947

My dear Secretary of State,

Although Mountbatten's absence is a short one I thought I should reply to your weekly letter dated 9th May,[1] which he did not have time to deal with before his departure and at the same time give you a rough picture of the situation in the country during the past week.

[Para. 2, on future careers for Police and Provincial Service Officers; and para. 3, on the line taken by Indian representatives at a Wheat Conference, omitted.]

4. The position in the Punjab has been very disturbing during the last week, particularly at Lahore and Amritsar and I have been keeping in close touch with what has been going on. You have, I think, seen all the situation telegrams, which have been repeated to you, and in particular Jenkins' telegram No. 100–G of the 21st May[2] in which he asked for a complete brigade as soon as possible for Lahore alone. I have been into this fully with Baldev Singh and the Deputy Commander in Chief and with reluctance it has been decided that it would be unwise to call on the small reserves now available in India, until we see whether any more disturbances arise as a result of His Majesty's Government's announcement early in June. The 4th Division is now well on its way up from the south to the Punjab and when it arrives the situation will be healthier. There has been some improvement in Lahore according to latest telegrams, but feeling is running high. I have asked Jenkins[3] whether there is

[1] No. 371.   [2] No. 500.   [3] See No. 535.

anything further he requires and whether the powers now available to him and the Army under the Punjab Disturbed Areas (Special Powers of Armed Forces) Ordinance 1947, are sufficient.

5. I have had letters[4] from Nehru and Patel, who are recessing in Mussoorie for a week, expressing concern at the situation in Lahore and suggesting martial law. There are grave disadvantages attaching to this and I have told them[5] that with the arrival of the 4th Division, and with the special powers I have referred to above, the situation should show improvement.

6. Both the Faridkot State Forces and Nabha State Forces have been concerned in incidents in Lahore and these two Rajahs have been informed, through the Resident Punjab States, that they are to send neither vehicles nor armed personnel into the Punjab in future without the specific permission of the Punjab Government.

7. I have also had an Intelligence Report from Jenkins[6] giving details of preparations which the Sikhs are said to be making for an offensive against the Muslims, and which it is stated will take place in the last week of this month or in the first week of June. Besides the Rajahs of Faridkot and Nabha, the Maharajah of Patiala is stated to be implicated and also the Maharajahs of Alwar, Dholpur, Bikaner, Bharatpur and Kapurthala. I discussed this with Baldev Singh at an interview with him a couple of days ago and his view was that although there might be preparations taking place, they were not intended offensively but were in self defence and were a sign of nervousness which would, he thought, disappear when the extra troops arrived in the Punjab. I hope he is correct and I hope too that the Intelligence Report, which was ungraded, may prove to be exaggerated.

[Paras. 8–9, on the N.W.F.P. situation and an outbreak in Peshawar Jail; para. 10, saying there was an uneasy quiet in the rest of the country though stabbings continued in Calcutta, Bombay and Delhi; and para. 11, on proposals for the revision of the Governors' Allowances and Privileges Order, omitted.]

[4] Nos. 501 and 522.   [5] See No. 531.   [6] See No. 510.

543

Cabinet

India and Burma Committee. Paper I.B.(47)86

L/P&J/10/79: ff 52-7

THE INDIA BILL

NOTE BY THE SECRETARY OF STATE FOR INDIA

INDIA OFFICE, *26 May 1947*

I circulate for consideration on Wednesday a note by officials on certain points which have arisen in connection with the proposed Bill on which decisions are required.

L.

INDIA OFFICE NOTE

In the course of discussions with Parliamentary Counsel about the drafting of the India Bill the following important points have come to light on which decisions of principle are required. Other points will probably arise later which also will have to be referred to Ministers:—

1. *The Andaman and Nicobar Islands.* Are these to be included by the Act in Hindustan or are they to go with Bengal?

The Andaman Islands are a Chief Commissioner's Province and are therefore administered by the Central Government. The Indian population of the Andamans is composed largely of ex-convicts and their descendants from all parts of India (and to a small extent from Burma). The economic communications of the Andaman Islands are primarily with Bengal through Calcutta. If Calcutta were in Hindustan it would seem clear that the Andamans should go to Hindustan. If there were an independent Bengal a decision is needed whether the Andamans should go with Bengal or with Hindustan.

The Chiefs-of-Staff have raised the question whether, in the course of the transfer of power in India, it cannot be arranged for the Andamans to come under the British Government because of their strategic importance as a potential naval and air base. It is true that we are now contemplating the transfer of power on the basis of Dominion Status as an interim measure. If, however, the Act of Parliament transfers the Andamans to one of the Indian Dominions, and that Dominion were later to secede from the Commonwealth, they could only be recovered by negotiation, nine points of the law being already in Indian possession.

[Para. 2, on Sterling Pensions and Sterling Debt, omitted.]

3. *Powers of Central Governments over Provincial Governments.*

It is assumed that the legislation should provide for the removal of all the special responsibilities of Provincial Governors and that Governors of Provinces will become constitutional heads of State acting on the advice of Ministries in all matters except the prerogative functions constitutionally proper to such appointments. Under Section 126 of the existing Act it is provided that the executive authority of every Province shall be so exercised as not to impede or prejudice the exercise of the executive authority of the Central Government which is empowered to give directions to a Province so far as necessary for that purpose. This power will devolve on the two Provisional Central Governments for Hindustan and Pakistan. The Section, however, further provides that the Governor-General in his discretion may issue orders to the Governor of a Province to secure that such directions are given proper effect and that the Governor-General in his discretion may "at any time issue orders to the Governor of a Province as to the manner in which the executive authority thereof is to be exercised for the purpose of preventing any grave menace to the peace and tranquillity of India or any part thereof". These important powers had effect by virtue of the Governor's special responsibilities, one of which was to secure the due execution of orders issued by the Governor-General in his discretion. If, therefore, the Governor's special responsibilities are deleted, these powers of the Governor-General lapse unless provision is made that the Central Governments have power to issue orders to Provincial Governments in the same sense. The question requiring decision is whether the legislation should provide for this or not. Without such provision the Centre in each part of India will have no power of control over Provincial Governments in matters of law and order, except where a Proclamation of Emergency is in operation whereby the Governor-General has declared that the security of Hindustan or Pakistan is threatened by war.

There is a special consideration in this connection in regard to the North West Frontier Province. Is the Pakistan Government to have no power to issue orders to the North West Frontier Province Government as to what action is to be taken in the event of a threat to security through a tribal incursion? At present this is provided for through the provisions above referred to, including the Governor's special responsibility coupled with the special passage in the Instrument of Instructions to the Governor of the North West Frontier Province. In this particular instance it would seem essential that the "Central" Government which conducts relations with the tribal areas should have special powers in regard to measures necessary to be taken within a Province to deal with tribal disturbances.

Apart from this consideration it would seem desirable to let the powers lapse and make Provinces autonomous in regard to internal security subject to the fact that the Constituent Assemblies will be vested with power to amend the existing provisions of the Act which remained in force in such a matter.

[Para. 4, on the position of Bengal if it became an independent Free State, omitted.]

544

Mr Chifley to Mr Attlee

Telegram, L/P&J/10/79: f 94

IMMEDIATE
TOP SECRET

27 May 1947, 3.25 pm
Received: 27 May, 11 am

No. 129. Addressed Secretary of State for Dominion Affairs No. 129, repeated
to Wellington No. 134.

Following for the Prime Minister from the Prime Minister.

Your D. No. 469 and D. No. 470.[1]

1. The developments in India in relation to possible declaration of Dominion
status covering separable portions of India are, as pointed out in paragraph 6 of
your D. No. 469, of great significance to Australia. Development has an
important bearing on your Ceylon proposal mentioned in your D. No. 441
and D. No. 428.[2]

2. On several occasions it has been stated on behalf of the Australian Government by Dr. Evatt that Australia is anxious that India should remain a member
of the British Commonwealth of Nations. Through our High Commissioner
in India, we have put this view as strongly as possible before Indian leaders of
varying political opinions. We adhere to this attitude on the grounds of past
association and future need for friendship and security, pointing out that the
Dominions interest in the retention of India in the Commonwealth is en-
trenched by the declaration contained in the preamble to the Statute of Westminster; which requires the consent of all the Dominions to any change in
Royal titles.

3. If Dominion status is feasible in relation to portions of India, it is more
feasible in the cases of Ceylon and Burma, and perhaps other areas in South East
Asia. We feel strongly that the future interest and security of Australia are
intimately bound up with the solution of all these regional problems.

4. In message sent to you through the High Commissioner at London, we
shall reiterate our desire to have British Commonwealth consultations in
Australia as soon as practicable relating to the settlement with Japan and in
these consultations it would of course be necessary for India to be suitably
represented. It should be possible to broaden these proposed discussions here so
as to cover common interests in South-East Asia as well as the Pacific.

[1] See No. 527 and its note 2.   [2] Not traced.

545

Cabinet

India and Burma Committee. Paper I.B.(47)87

L/P&J/10/79: ff 48–51

INTERIM GOVERNMENT IN INDIA
MEMORANDUM BY THE PRESIDENT OF THE BOARD OF TRADE
CABINET OFFICE, S. W. I, *27 May 1947*

I circulate herewith, for consideration by the Committee at their Meeting on 28th May, 1947, some suggestions regarding the procedure to be followed in setting up the Interim Government in India.

R. S. C.

INTERIM GOVERNMENT IN INDIA

The assumptions upon which these suggestions are put forward are as follows:
  (i) The agreed statement as to Partition will be made on 3rd June.
  (ii) The process of decision as to division will be substantially complete by or before 1st August.
  (iii) An Act will be passed by the British Parliament by the end of the present session in August.
Under these circumstances the following procedure is suggested.
  (*a*) Immediately on making the statement under (i) above the Viceroy will ask for the resignation of all the existing members of the Executive, but will ask those who are willing to carry on with their jobs until he notified them that their resignation has been accepted.
  (*b*) At the same time he will ask Pandit Nehru and Mr Jinnah to set about the formation of two Governments, one for India and one for Pakistan so as to be ready with the names for submission to him when called upon.
  (*c*) In the meanwhile the Government of India will be carried on as at present, though preliminary and tentative arrangements will be worked out by officials as to the splitting of the administrative services as and when the time arrives.
  (*d*) As soon as it has become apparent that there are to be two or more states formed (i.e. India, Bengal and Pakistan) the resignations of the existing Executive will be accepted and two Executives—or duplicate Executives—will be set up, one for India, the other for Pakistan.
  (*e*) If Bengal decides to hive off as an independent state the central Government Functions will be handed over (by convention) to the Provincial Government.

(f) At the same time a joint delegation will be set up of representatives of the divided parts (India, Pakistan and Bengal) under the Chairmanship of the Viceroy consisting of one Hindu and one Sikh from India, two Muslims from Pakistan and one Muslim and one Hindu from Bengal which will fulfil the following functions:

    (i) To carry on the administration of all central services until they can be divided;

    (ii) To make arrangements for the Division of the administration of all central subjects.

(g) The joint delegation will be a policy deciding body acting jointly for all purposes and no individual will be responsible for any particular branch of the administration. The administration will be carried on by the existing officers until division takes place. The Joint delegation will set up sub-delegations upon the same pattern to carry out the division of the various functions now performed by the Government of India as a whole. These sub-delegations will deal separately with the following subject matters:

    (i) Administrative services and police;

    (ii) Finance assets and revenue;

    (iii) Armed Forces;

    (iv) Customs and Tariffs;

    (v) Food;

    (vi) Communications;

    (vii) Irrigation;

    (viii) Other matters.

(h) Both in the Joint delegation and in the sub-delegations the delegates shall have rank as Ambassadors or other diplomatic rank and shall be deemed to represent independent states. They shall be subject to recall by their Governments at any time but shall be authorised as plenipotentiaries to arrive at binding decisions which will be accepted by all the Governments concerned.

(i) Any matter which is not decided unanimously by the sub-delegations shall be referred to the Joint delegation for decision. In the event of there not being unanimity amongst the members of the Joint delegation, the matter shall be referred to the arbitral Tribunal under (k) hereof.

(j) The Joint delegation may decide to delegate their executive functions under (f)(i) above to any of the sub-delegations (e.g. communications).

(k) There shall be appointed by each of the three Governments an arbitrator of high judicial standing and the arbitrators shall by agreement select an Umpire (not being the Viceroy) who shall together with the arbitrators form the arbitral Tribunal mentioned in (i) above. Decisions in the arbitral Tribunal shall be by majority vote provided that in the event of an equality of votes the Umpire shall have a second or casting vote.

(*l*) All three Governments will agree to accept the decision of the arbitral Tribunal as final and binding upon them, and will incorporate such decisions in the Treaties regulating the division.

(*m*) At any time by agreement between the governments the sub-delegations may be turned into permanent commissions for the purpose of administering combined services.

(*n*) Until the completion of the work of the Joint delegation the Viceroy shall remain the Governor-General of each of the separate areas, though a Deputy Governor-General may also be appointed for any of the areas of the Government as recommended.

(*o*) The Viceroy may at any time if he so considers it advisable call a meeting of any two or more of the Executives under his Chairmanship to discuss matters relating to the progress of division on the maintenance and or administration of common services.

(*p*) As soon as the legislation mentioned under (iii) above comes into force, separate Governments will be set up under it, responsible to the Constituent Assemblies or in Bengal to the legislative assembly, but the Joint delegation and the sub-delegations shall continue to function by agreement between the Governments until they have completed their task.

(*q*) The Boundaries arranged for the purpose of arriving at a decision as to partition of the Punjab shall not be considered as in any way binding upon the Governments eventually concerned as to the actual boundaries to be laid down between the two countries.

(*r*) There shall be set up forthwith a Boundary commission whose function it shall be to determine the boundaries between India and Pakistan.

(*s*) The Boundary Commission shall consist of six members and an independent Chairman. The six members shall be appointed as follows:

  by the Muslim League, two from Western Punjab and one from Eastern Punjab;
  by the Sikhs, one from Western Punjab and one from Eastern Punjab;
  by the Congress, one from Eastern Punjab.

The Chairman shall be chosen by agreement of all the members or failing agreement shall be nominated by the Viceroy after consultation with the three communities.

(*t*) The Boundary Commission may, by agreement, divide up into sub-commissions or may, by agreement, appoint fact-finding sub-commissions, provided that all final decisions are made by the Boundary Commission itself.

(*u*) The decisions of the Boundary Commission shall be taken by a majority vote, provided that in the event of an equality of votes the Chairman shall have an extra or casting vote.

(*v*) In the event of any decision being carried only by the Chairman's vote or by his casting vote, it shall be open to the minority to appeal to the United Nations Organisation or the Hague Tribunal (if they or either of them are willing to accept such appeal) to hear and decide the point in issue.

(*w*) If the United Nations Organisation and the Hague Tribunal both refuse to consider such appeal then the minority may appeal to the Arbitral Tribunal under paragraph (*k*) hereof but there shall for such purpose be added to the said Tribunal one person appointed by the Muslim League and one person appointed by the Sikhs.

(*x*) The decision under (*v*) or (*w*) or in the event of there being no appeal, the decision under (*u*) shall be accepted by both parties as final and binding upon them and shall be incorporated in a binding Treaty between them.

(*y*) If any other questions of boundaries arise the Viceroy shall set up a Boundary Commission to deal with any and all such questions on the lines above set out for the Punjab but with suitable adjustments and variations according to the territories and communities concerned, and the final decisions shall be equally accepted as final and binding upon the parties.

546

Cabinet

India and Burma Committee. Paper I.B.(47)88

L/P&J/10/79: ff 40–3

INTERIM GOVERNMENT OF INDIA
MEMORANDUM BY THE SECRETARY OF STATE FOR INDIA

INDIA OFFICE, *27 May 1947*

I circulate a note by my officials commenting on the President of the Board of Trade's memorandum I.B.(47)87.[1] I commend to my colleagues the variant of the plan, put forward in paragraphs 4 and 5 [?3 and 4] of this note. It is designed to avoid action which is clearly contrary to the Act.

L.

NOTE BY THE INDIA OFFICE

1. (*d*) and (*e*) are unconstitutional since the 9th Schedule provides that there shall be one Executive Council for the whole of India deciding by majority vote, and the functions of the Provincial Government of Bengal and the

[1] No. 545.

Central Government are clearly laid down in the Act. (*f*), (*g*) and (*h*) and subsequent provisions in regard to the Joint Delegation are an admirable description of the sort of machinery that is required, (though the list of functions in (*g*) lacks some important items and, in mentioning Police and Irrigation, trenches on Provincial functions), but the question is whether such machinery could be set up prior to the passage of legislation. Even if it is felt that *vis-à-vis* Parliament it is possible to take such drastic steps in advance of a second reading of approval of the proposed Bill, there remains the question whether the Acts of the two Central authorities for Hindustan and Pakistan would not be challenged in the Courts and found invalid. The Central Legislature will remain in being, unless abolished, empowered to make laws for the whole of India. It is difficult to see how it could be deprived of this power, or legislation passed by anyone else become enforceable in the Courts as valid legislation without amendment of the Act. But retrospective provision could no doubt be made to cover this point in the Bill. Assuming that it is certain that the Bill will be got through quickly and not kept over until the autumn, this might not greatly matter.

2. It is also a substantial difficulty in these proposals that two separate Governments for two parts of a Province can only be set up constitutionally either by Act of Parliament or by Order-in-Council under Section 290 of the Act which requires Parliamentary approval. Until one of these processes has been gone through the administration of the Punjab cannot be finally divided and the Punjab Government would have to give effect to the decisions of two different Governments at the Centre in two different parts of its area of administration. It is not clear whether it is contemplated that under (*g*) of the President of the Board of Trade's memorandum it is proposed that the Central Joint Delegation should deal with the partition of Provinces. The reference to the partitioning of Police Forces rather suggests this. It would seem, however, much more appropriate for the Governor of the Province concerned to set up a similar joint delegation for Provincial partition purposes. It would be advantageous if such partition had gone some way before separate Executives for Pakistan and Hindustan are set up.

3. As an alternative to setting up two new Executive Councils it is suggested that the existing Council might be dissolved and a new one appointed composed as proposed for the Joint Delegation under (*f*) of Sir Stafford Cripps' paper. This would then divide into two Committees which by mutual agreement would each take decisions on all matters relating only to the affairs of the respective areas. Although these decisions would be rubber-stamped by the Council as a whole it would be a part of the understanding that they were not disputed except when they prejudiced or affected the interests of the other part or parts of India. It is suggested that a Pakistan and possibly a Bengal Secre-

tariat should be set up which would gradually be enlarged into a nucleus of Central administration for these two areas. Orders of the Government of India in regard to Pakistan and Hindustan matters would issue respectively from the Pakistan Secretariat and the existing Secretariat. The Pakistan Secretariat would be given all papers and records relating to matters which affect Pakistan only and all joint matters. All matters put up to the Hindustan or Pakistan Committee would be brought to the notice of the other Committee which would thus have an opportunity of stating a case to the Governor-General that the matters under discussion affect their interests. Such matters and matters which are obviously joint matters would be discussed by the Council as a whole which at a later stage would be the Joint Delegation. It would be part of the agreement that in the existing phase the Council would proceed by agreement.

4. If the Congress can be brought to agree it would be very desirable that the new members of Council should not be political heads of departments, i.e. should not be "Ministers" responsible for executive action by a particular department, but that the permanent Civil Service heads of departments and the Commander-in-Chief should act in responsibility to the Council as a whole or, in appropriate cases, its two Committees.

5. The arrangement suggested in paragraphs 3 and 4 would seem capable of gradual development. Thus, in the case of Defence, so soon as practicable a separate General Headquarters for the Pakistan and Hindustan forces could be set up and, as soon as maintenance arrangements can be made, the troops obviously belonging to Pakistan and Hindustan respectively can be placed under the control of these two Headquarters which would be responsible to the Commander-in-Chief who would be responsible to the Pakistan or Hindustan Committee of the Council. For some time there will be mixed troops under the Commander-in-Chief in process of being sorted out, in regard to which the Commander-in-Chief will be responsible first to the Council as a whole and later, after legislation has been passed, to a Joint Delegation or a Sub-Committee of it consisting of the same personnel as have composed the Executive Council.

6. The essential feature of this variant of Sir Stafford Cripps' plan is that—(i) It preserves the legal position under the Act whereby the Central Government is the Executive Council headed by the Governor-General; and (ii) It does not set up two unconstitutional Executives for Pakistan and Hindustan or purport to transfer by "convention" Central functions to the Provincial Government of Bengal. This can be done as soon as the Act is through and, assuming that it will be through early in August, a period of two months under a first transitional phase of the above kind might work quite well, and greatly shorten any period between the passing of the Act and its coming into operation.

7. The disadvantage is that the Executives for Hindustan and Pakistan get no practice before taking over full responsibility. A way out of this might be to make the Executive Council double the size proposed by Sir Stafford Cripps for the Joint Delegation, i.e. 12, and to reduce that number by half on the dissolution of the Central Government and the coming into effect of the Joint Delegation as such. The other half of the Executive Council will then be available for membership of the Executive Council.

8. As regards the residue of Sir Stafford Cripps' proposals, attention is drawn to the following small points:—

(i)—(b) [?(p)]. If the Legislative Assembly in Bengal is to be the Constituent Assembly, presumably the Europeans should not be permitted to vote when it acts in that capacity.

(ii)—Paragraph (s). An alternative to the Chairman of the Boundary Commission being chosen by the Viceroy failing agreement would be for him to be chosen by the umpire provided for under (k). This would avoid involving the Governor-General in a very controversial decision.

547

Cabinet

India and Burma Committee. Paper I.B.(47)89

L/P&J/10/79: ff 35–9

DIVISION OF THE ARMED FORCES OF INDIA
NOTE BY THE SECRETARY OF STATE FOR INDIA

INDIA OFFICE, *27 May 1947*

I circulate herewith a note prepared by the Commander-in-Chief in India, at the invitation of His Excellency the Viceroy, on the division of the armed forces of India between Pakistan and Hindustan for consideration at tomorrow's meeting of the Committee.

L.

DIVISION OF THE ARMED FORCES OF INDIA BETWEEN "PAKISTAN" AND "HINDUSTAN"
NOTE BY COMMANDER-IN-CHIEF IN INDIA. 27TH MAY, 1947

Assumption

That India is divided into two self-governing member States of the British Commonwealth with, at any rate, in the first instance a common Governor General and that British Officers will be required to continue to serve in the Armed Forces of these two States for some time to come.

(NOTE. In this paper the term Hindu is used throughout to include Sikhs and Gurkhas)

1. Administratively, the division of the existing Indian Navy, Indian Army and Indian Air Force into separate "Pakistan" and "Hindustan" Forces, must be a most complicated and delicate operation in any circumstances.

2. It is not merely a matter of saying Muslims to the left, Hindus to the right. In all three Forces there are many officers and men whose homes are in parts of India which must inevitably come under the rule of the opposite community or party. In dividing the forces, each such case will have to be decided individually as no officer or man could be compelled to serve a government of which he does not approve. In many cases no such decision will be possible until the boundaries between the two States have been definitely and finally fixed.

3. In the Navy and the Air Force there are no "Muslim" units or "Hindu" units. All classes and creeds are inextricably mixed in all units, occupations, trades and establishments and the complete breaking down and rebuilding of all units and establishments will be necessary before separate new and efficient forces can be made out of the existing "all-India" forces. Moreover, the installations necessary for the maintenance of new separate forces will have to be created in each State where they do not now exist.

4. In the Army there are certain fighting units (Battalions and regiments) which consist, so far as the rank and file are concerned, wholly of Hindus or wholly of Muslims, but this does not apply to their officers. British, Muslim, and all other classes of Indian Officers are completely mixed throughout the Army without any regard to their race or religion, so that even units which are composed of men of one class only, could not be transferred as such to one State or the other until the Indian Officers of the Army have been completely reshuffled.

The administrative units and installations of the Army, on which it depends entirely for its continued existence, such as Ordnance, Supply, Pay and Medical units, are completely "non-Class" that is they are manned without regard to race, religion or creed similarly to the Navy and Air Force. It would be quite impossible to divide these units as they stand to-day between the new armies of the two States. They, like the Navy and the Air Force, must be gradually broken down and rebuilt. The process must be gradual and centrally controlled, otherwise the Army will cease to be fed, paid, clothed, moved or medically attended and will cease to exist as an organised force.

The sorting and re-allocation of personal records, documents, pay and pension claims, recruiting areas, training depots etc. will in itself be a tremendous labour and must take a long time.

5. The object of this brief outline of what would be entailed by the division of the Armed Forces of India to enable them to serve two separate autonomous States is to show that this cannot be done in a moment and that the process

must be centrally controlled until it is completed, unless there is to be a complete administrative breakdown and a consequent disintegration of the Armed Forces.

6. It cannot be too strongly stressed that the continuance of central control of the general administration of the Armed Forces is essential until the process of dismemberment is complete and the new administrative machinery necessary to serve the separate forces of each of the new States has been set up.

7. If the services of British officers are to be retained in the Armed Forces of the two new States, it will be essential to ensure:—

(a) That these officers retain their present position and privileges as regular officers serving under the Crown.

(b) That the pay, pensions and future prospects of these officers are guaranteed from the outset by His Majesty's Government.

(c) That during the process of dismemberment of the Indian Forces discussed in the foregoing paragraphs, and until the setting up of the separate forces for "Pakistan" and "Hindustan" is complete, these officers shall be under the central control of the Commander-in-Chief in India who will be responsible for them to the Governor General and through him to His Majesty's Government in the United Kingdom.

8. The Commander-in-Chief must be free to post and employ all British officers serving in the Indian Armed Forces as he thinks fit and all such officers must know that their interests will be safeguarded by him acting under the Governor General and His Majesty's Government.

Any other system is bound to create suspicion, dissatisfaction non co-operation and eventual confusion.

9. British regular officers of the Indian Armed Forces cannot be compelled to serve on under Indian Governments with Dominion status. They must be given the option of serving on or of availing themselves of the compensatory terms which have already been published. If they do volunteer to serve on they must retain the right to receive at some future date when their services are no longer required, the compensatory terms already laid down by His Majesty's Government, or they must be allowed to take the compensation already due to them and then accept new terms of service.

10. In any event, it will be necessary to transfer such officers as volunteer to serve under the new conditions, to the Royal Navy or the British Army and then to "lend" them to the forces of the new States. It must be realized that in their present disillusioned and disappointed state of mind, many British regular officers of the Royal Indian Navy or the Indian Navy [? Army] are not in a mood to volunteer for further service in India, thinking as they do, that they will not receive fair treatment from the future rulers of that country. Moreover they know that the retention of British officers in the Indian Armed Forces must

give rise to dissatisfaction and jealousy in the minds of the senior Indian officers of those Forces, who have been recently led to expect that they will soon replace the British officers even in the highest appointments.

It will be essential, therefore, so to form the terms of service as to induce the British officers to volunteer to serve on. As already mentioned, they cannot be compelled to remain against their will and, in any event, to attempt this would defeat the end in view.

These new terms should be announced with the least possible delay once the decision to divide India has been made public.

11. In no circumstances must these British officers be placed in a position in which they can be ordered by an Indian Dominion Government to take action repugnant to their code of behaviour as officers or to their allegiance to the King. It is for this reason that central control must be retained over them until the separation process is complete and the Armed Forces of the two new States can stand on their own feet.

12. During the process of separation of the Forces, it will be necessary to suspend the proposed programme of "Nationalisation" of the officer cadres of the three Forces, that is the substitution by June 1948 of all British by Indian officers from the Commander-in-Chief in India downwards. The two processes cannot proceed concurrently without grave risk of a complete administrative breakdown, owing to the extreme youth and inexperience of the great bulk of the available Indian officers. This fact must be accepted by the Indian leaders and explained by them to the public and to the Indian officers of the Forces.

13. Central control of the Forces during partition could be ensured by a Joint Defence Council comprising the Governor General (in the chair), the Commander-in-Chief in India and representative Ministers of the "Pakistan" and "Hindustan" Governments. Naval Headquarters, General Headquarters and Air Force Headquarters and the Military Finance organisation must be kept in being at Delhi until the separation is complete.

Conclusions

14. The administrative difficulties inherent in dividing the rank and file of the Armed Forces between Pakistan and Hindustan are apparent. These difficulties are no less pronounced in the action of dividing the Officers between the two States.

The retention of the voluntary services of British Officers in the Forces of the new States must be contingent on the willingness of His Majesty's Government in the United Kingdom to safeguard their position as officers of the British Regular Army and to guaranteee their pay, pensions and any compensation to which they may be entitled under the announcements already made. This should be the subject of immediate examination and very early announcement.

The vital considerations which must not be overlooked are the need for a centrally controlled military administration while the process of division is taking place and the time required to carry out the operation, which might well be two or three years.

Failure to realise and provide for these fundamental requirements can only result in a breakdown of what must in any case be a delicate operation.

During the process of division India will be virtually undefended.

548

The Nizam of Hyderabad to Rear-Admiral Viscount Mountbatten of Burma

Telegram, L/PO/6/125: f 14

27 May 1947

Unnumbered. In continuation of my telegram to Your Excellency dated 24th May[1] I sincerely trust you will support my request before the British Cabinet for the Membership of the Commonwealth Nation for Hyderabad and also my making some kind of Treaty with the British Government after their handing over power in June 1948. For after enjoying the proud title of Faithful Ally of British Government for years I would not like to sever my connection with the British Crown. As times are critical and in view of what the political situation is in India just now it [is] my opinion this is the best course for Senior States to adopt in order to protect their interests and dynasty against the inimical odds who are bent to destroy them. Therefore protection of British is absolutely necessary for them who are the staunch supporters of the British Popa[2] in India by their unfaltering devotion and loyal[ty] to the British Crown. I trust Your Excellency will forgive my giving you trouble since you are very busy with important problems in England.[3]

[1] A copy of this telegram is on R/3/1/136: ff 157–9.
[2] Apparently 'Power' was intended.
[3] Lord Mountbatten replied in a telegram dated 28 May as follows: 'I am grateful for Your Exalted Highness' cables of 24th and 27th May and am placing latter before H.M.G. When I meet States' Negotiating Committee shortly, I will inform your Representative about attitude of H.M.G.' Mountbatten Papers, Official Correspondence Files: States, relations with, Part I(a).

549

Sir E. Jenkins (Punjab) to Sir J. Colville

Telegram, R/3/1/90: f 94

IMMEDIATE   *27 May 1947, 11 pm*
CONFIDENTIAL   *Received: 28 May, 4 am*

No. 109–G. Addressed Viceroy repeated Secretary of State and Governors of U.P., Sind and N.W.F.P.

Lahore situation unchanged. One person injured and 3 fires since yesterday reported. Two of fires abortive.

2. Amritsar casualties one dead two injured with two fires. Attack by Muslims on train near suburban station narrowly averted.

3. Another Muslim village attacked and burnt in Gurgaon. Elsewhere tension remains high. Troops had to fire on May 25th on riotous crowd at Chiniot Jhang District. Incidents reported from Lyallpur and elsewhere. Intelligence reports suggest that we must expect large scale disturbances after June announcement particularly in Jullundur, Amritsar, Lahore, Sheikhupura, Lyallpur and Montgomery.

550

Note by Sir O. Sargent of his Interview with the Duke of Palmella[1]
on 27 May 1947 (Extract)

L/P&S/12/1081: f 30

Incidentally, the Ambassador said that his Government had been approached indirectly by the Government of Hyderabad first with an offer [?request] to sell the colony of Goa, which had been turned down, and secondly, with a proposal to give Hyderabad special railways and shipping facilities in the port of Goa. The Ambassador asked me whether I thought that they would be well advised to respond to this approach at the present moment. To which I said that inasmuch as the first interest of Portugal must be to establish friendly relations with the Congress Government of India whose territory surrounded Goa on three sides, it seemed unwise to antagonise them by entering into commitments with Hyderabad which the Congress Government might dislike and resent. Besides, it was too early at present to know what the future

---

[1] Portuguese Ambassador in London.

relations between the Congress Government of India and Hyderabad were going to be, and the Portuguese Government would lose nothing by playing for time before entering into any dealings with Hyderabad.

O. SARGENT

551

Mr Krishna Menon to Sir S. Cripps

Public Record Office. CAB 127/109

STRICTLY PERSONAL   AS FROM: INDIA HOUSE, ALDWYCH,
TOP SECRET   LONDON, W.C.2, *27 May 1947*

My dear Sir Stafford,

I enclose the notes of our talk on the stages of transfer of power between now and the passage of the contemplated parliamentary legislation. There are perhaps gaps in these notes and some points may require explanation, though I rather think that we went over them in essentials. I have shown the notes to Lord Mountbatten, who had also discussed this matter with me previously. He will no doubt tell you what he thinks of these suggestions.

I am coming to Margate[1] tomorrow morning, as early as possible, and returning in the afternoon. As I told you, I want to see Mr. Bevin; if I return without doing this, it would create misunderstandings, which in the present situation I want to do my best to avoid! Perhaps if you have not left by the time I arrive, I shall be able to see you. I will try.

The other two matters we talked about are, I hope, also engaging your attention. If I can be of any assistance, I shall be glad to be available, both here and in the next few weeks in India. Perhaps we may go over this again when we meet at Margate or here.

I was glad to be able to see Lady Cripps, even if it was only for a short time.

Kind regards,
Yours sincerely,
KRISHNA

Enclosure to No. 551

Notes by Mr Krishna Menon

CONFIDENTIAL

ASSUMING PARTITION IS AGREED ON

Stage 1.

  I. Statement of H.M.G. on June 3rd.

 II. (*a*) Members of the Interim Government hand in their resignations and the Governor General asks them to carry on their administration while at the same time permitting those who want to leave the Government forthwith to do so.

(b) The administration will function as a Cabinet with joint responsibility, and majority decisions will prevail subject to the Governor General's veto on agreed safeguards if any such decision is contrary to the statement of June 3rd in regard to Pakistan.

(c) Each side is asked to proceed with the formation of Governments for the two respective States, so that they may be in readiness immediately Stage 2 is reached. (Until that stage is actually reached, the group governments will be only shadow cabinets of the two future States.)

(d) Time limit at which Stage 1 expires (not later than July 4th).

Stage 2. June 4th to . . . . (not later than July 4th).

I. Partition. Ascertainment of wishes of the people as in statement of June 3rd.

II. Setting up of separation machinery as follows:—

(i) A Central "Separation Commission" consisting of the representative of the Pakistan State to the Government of India and that of the Government of India to the Pakistan State (as they will be when Stage 3 emerges not later than July 4th. All three [sic] have votes) presided over by the Governor General.

> (a) The functions of this Committee are strictly confined to the problem of effecting separation.
>
> (b) It is not a joint government of the two States.
>
> (c) The Central Separation Committee may sit with any of the functional committees (or boards) described below to deal with matters relevant to those committees.
>
> (d) The procedure of the Central Committee shall be decided by itself on the basis of agreement reached between the Governments of the two States.
>
> (e) The Central Committee shall refer to the Tribunal named in (iii) below all matters on which it requires an advisory opinion, adjudication or investigation of relevant facts and legal issues, or such other matters as appropriately fall within the competence of a tribunal of a judicial character.

(ii)

(a) Functional Committees or Boards in respect of the following main items of separation:

(1) Armed Forces.

---

[1] The Labour Party Annual Conference met at Margate from 26 to 30 May 1947.

(2) Boundaries Commission or Commissions.

(3) Finance, assets and liabilities.

(4) Migration and repatriation.

(5) Communications including irrigation.

(6) Food.

(*b*) It is suggested that decisions and awards of the above Boards should be by way of "advice" to the Central Separation Committee, which in theory makes such decisions or awards, by accepting the advice or obtaining their modification.

(*c*) Time limits may have to be placed on the work of the Committees by the Central Separation Committee, and these time limits need not be the same in regard to all Committees.

(*d*) Composition and size of the Committees should correspond to the general basis of agreement, but would have to vary in respect of each problem.

(iii) An Inter-State Tribunal composed as follows:—

one person nominated by India and one person nominated by Pakistan, with an umpire agreed upon by the two.

It is suggested that a panel of two should be set up by each side, from which the choice of one can be made by the Governor General or by agreement.

Note. This Tribunal is an independent body and not subordinate to the Central Separation Committee or the functional boards. It will decide on disputes referred to it by the Central Separation Committee, to which all disputes will be taken initially by the functional boards. The award of the Tribunal shall be final.

Stage 3.

Period between partition (on July 4th) and passing of parliamentary legislation.

(1) In this period the government of the two States would, for the purposes of the law of the constitution, be carried on by the Governor General functioning through two Cabinets (or Committees).

(2) In practice, the Governor General would treat the Indian Government as a Dominion government, and remain as constitutional head, subject only to such reservations or veto to which the Indian Government agrees as part of the settlement.

(3) How the Pakistan Government desires to be treated is a matter for the League, but the Governor General shall not be put in a position, in his relation to that Government, which makes it impossible for him to function as a truly constitutional head of the Government of India in the spirit of the agreement reached.

Stage 4.

This period begins on the day the contemplated parliamentary legislation receives the assent of the King.

Note. Some provision would be required in this legislation which enables each of the Dominions (States) to change their boundaries, obtain the accession of states and territories and also enter into union with each other.

552

Sir E. Mieville to Mr Abell (via India Office)

Telegram, R/3/1/150: f 86

IMMEDIATE　　　　　　　　　　　　　　　　　　*28 May 1947, 1.20 pm*
SECRET

No. 1186–S. Your telegram No. 6859 of May 27th, paragraph 2.[1] In the course of a talk I had with Nehru last night, I asked him how he viewed the discussions now going on about an independent Bengal. He reacted strongly and said there was no chance of the Hindus there agreeing to put themselves under permanent Muslim domination which was what the proposed agreement really amounted to. He did not, however, rule out the possibility of the whole of Bengal joining up with Hindustan.

[1] In para. 2 of this telegram Mr Abell explained that the text of the draft announcement was still subject to alteration in the event of an agreement about Bengal. He also gave the latest draft of the additional section on Dominion Status. R/3/1/150: f 82.

553

Cabinet

India and Burma Committee. I.B.(47)28th Meeting

L/P&J/10/79: ff 20–30

Those present at this Meeting held at 10 Downing Street, S.W.1, on 28 May 1947 at 11 am were: Mr Attlee (in the Chair), Sir S. Cripps, Mr Alexander, the Earl of Listowel, Viscount Addison, Mr C. P. Mayhew, Mr A. G. Bottomley, Mr A. Henderson, Lord Chorley

Also present were: Rear-Admiral Viscount Mountbatten of Burma, Field Marshal Sir C. Auchinleck, Sir D. Monteath, Lord Ismay, Lieutenant-Colonel Erskine Crum; Sir N. Brook, Mr S. E. V. Luke, Mr G. M. Wilson, Mr F. F. Turnbull (Secretariat)

Minute 1
The Transfer of Power in India
(Previous Reference: I.B.(47)27th Meeting, Minute 2)[1]

VISCOUNT MOUNTBATTEN drew attention to the acting Viceroy's telegram

[1] No. 517.

No. 1165–S of 26th May[2] which contained a summary of a letter from Pandit Nehru commenting on Mr. Jinnah's attitude towards the proposals under consideration for the transfer of power. Pandit Nehru argued that his acquiescence in a scheme involving the partition of India had been conditional on the acceptance by the Muslim League of the scheme as a final settlement. In his view, however, Mr. Jinnah had made it clear, in his notes of the 19th[3] and 22nd May[4] and in his interview[5] with Reuter's correspondent, that no such agreement from the League had been forthcoming; he had indeed stated definitely that he could not accept partition of Bengal or the Punjab, and he had put forward a demand for a corridor to link the eastern and western parts of Pakistan. In these circumstances, Pandit Nehru's view was that the proposals set out in the draft announcement should now be abandoned; that the Cabinet Mission's plan should be imposed as a settlement; and that the Interim Government should be immediately treated by convention as a Dominion Government subject to the Viceroy's overriding authority in regard to the protection of minority interests.

It was the general view of the Committee that there could be no question of attempting to impose the Cabinet Mission plan as a final settlement; it had been no part of that plan to force unwilling parts of India under the control of the Central Government. For the same reason, it would be neither practicable nor justifiable to grant Dominion status to the Interim Government. In the Committee's view, if either or both of the Parties should now decline to accept the proposed scheme for the transfer of power, there would be no alternative to its enforcement as an award by His Majesty's Government, on the basis of the grant of Dominion status to the two successor States. As suggested at their previous meeting (I.B.(47) 27th Meeting, Minute 2), if Mr. Jinnah should prove intransigeant, he might be induced to adopt a more reasonable attitude by the suggestion that the consequence of refusal would be a provisional definition of boundaries in the Punjab which would be less favourable from his point of view.

Minute 2
The future of Bengal

VISCOUNT MOUNTBATTEN drew the Committee's attention to the report in the *News Chronicle* of 27th May[6] of an interview given by Pandit Nehru, in the course of which he had said that Congress could agree to Bengal remaining united only if it remained in the Union of India. This statement would no doubt receive the widest publicity in India, and was an example of the tendency of the Indian leaders to make public statements from which they could not subsequently withdraw. The Viceroy was afraid that, in view of this development, the prospects of saving the unity of Bengal and securing its establishment as a third Dominion in India had been gravely prejudiced; indeed, he thought that, if Pandit Nehru had completely committed himself, the only means by which the partition of Bengal could be avoided would be by Mr. Jinnah's abandonment of his claim to the Province for Pakistan and by its acceptance of a position, similar to that of an Indian State, of quasi-independence in close relationship with one or other of the Dominion Governments. If it proved impossible to avoid the partition of the Province, the future of Eastern Bengal would present very difficult problems, since it was clearly not a viable unit. This area might possibly submit a claim for recognition as a separate Dominion in order to secure the assistance and backing of His Majesty's Government.

The Committee agreed that, in the event of the partition of Bengal, Dominion status could not be granted to Eastern Bengal alone; it would have to unite with one or other of the Indian Dominions.

Minute 3
The Transfer of Power on the basis of Dominion Status
(Previous Reference: I.B.(47)27th Meeting, Minute 3)[7]

The Committee had before them a memorandum by the Secretary of State for India (I.B.(47) 85)[8] covering a revised draft of the statement regarding the grant of Dominion status to be included in the Viceroy's forthcoming announcement on the transfer of power in India.

After discussion, it was agreed that the statement should be amended to read as follows:—

'X' "The major political parties have repeatedly emphasised their desire that there should be the earliest possible transfer of power in India. With this desire His Majesty's Government are in full sympathy, and they are willing to anticipate the date of June, 1948, for the handing over of power by the setting up of an independent Indian Government or Governments at an even earlier date. Accordingly, as the most expeditious, and indeed the only practicable, way of meeting this desire His Majesty's Government propose to introduce legislation during the current session for the transfer of power this year on a Dominion status basis to such successor authorities as come into being as a result of this announcement. This will be without prejudice to the right of Indian Constituent Assemblies to decide in due course whether or not the part of India in respect of which they have authority will remain within the British Commonwealth".[9]

VISCOUNT MOUNTBATTEN asked for authority, after discussion with the Indian leaders, to substitute the words 'one or two successor authorities" for the words "such successor authorities" with a view to lessening any appre-

[2] No. 540.   [3] This note has not been traced; see however No. 489.
[4] See No. 514.   [5] No. 502.   [6] See No. 560, Enclosure (iii).
[7] No. 517.   [8] No. 534.
[9] The text of this amendment was telegraphed to India in tel. 6935 of 29 May. L/P &J/10/80: ff 69–70.

hensions that might exist that India was to be split up into a large number of separate parts. This would, of course, depend on what decision was taken about the future of Bengal.

THE SECRETARY OF STATE FOR DOMINION AFFAIRS reported that the Prime Ministers of Australia,[10] New Zealand[11] and South Africa[12] had welcomed the proposal that power should be transferred to two Successor States in India on the basis of the grant of Dominion status. He proposed to tell them that they would be kept informed of further developments, and to suggest to them that it would be helpful if, after the Viceroy's announcement had been made, they would give public expression to their approval of the scheme.

The Committee agreed with this suggestion, provided that nothing was said which might give the impression that the two independent States had agreed to remain permanently within the British Commonwealth.

The Committee:—

(1) Invited the Viceroy to include in his forthcoming announcement, under the heading "Immediate Transfer of Power", the passage at 'X' above, subject to any amendment that might be made in accordance with Conclusion (2) below.

(2) Authorised the Viceroy to settle, in the light of developments in regard to Bengal, the final form of wording for the phrase "to such successor authorities as come into being as a result of this announcement".

(3) Invited the Secretary of State for Dominion Affairs to inform the Dominion Prime Ministers that it would be helpful if, after the Viceroy's announcement, they would give public expression to their approval of the plan, but without in any way giving the impression that the two independent States had agreed to remain permanently within the British Commonwealth.

Minute 4
Relations between His Majesty's Government and the Indian States after the Transfer of Power
(Previous Reference: I.B.(47)27th Meeting, Minute 6)[13]

The Committee had before them a note by the Secretary of State for India (I.B.(47) 84)[14] covering a draft statement for use by the Viceroy in his forthcoming discussions with the Indian States Negotiating Committee.

The Committee:—

Approved the revised draft statement annexed to I.B.(47) 84.

Minute 5
The India Bill

The Committee had before them a note by the Secretary of State for India

(I.B.(47) 86)[15] covering a memorandum prepared in the India Office raising certain points for decision in connection with the drafting of the Bill to provide for the transfer of power in India.

(a) *The Andaman and Nicobar Islands*

VISCOUNT MOUNTBATTEN said that the Congress leaders were clearly concerned about the future of these islands. Pandit Nehru had referred to the point in paragraph 9 of his letter of 16th May[16] (Annex B to I.B.(47) 73); Sardar Patel had informed him that the Congress Party had under consideration a large-scale plan for forest development. They certainly regarded the islands as part of British India, and would no doubt take their stand on the fact that they were a Chief Commissioner's Province under the Government of India Act, 1935.

THE PRESIDENT OF THE BOARD OF TRADE said that Mr. Krishna Menon had hinted, in conversation with him, that the Congress leaders might be prepared to take into account the disposal of the islands in the discussions for the settlement of the Indian sterling balances.

THE MINISTER OF DEFENCE said that these islands were of vital importance in the scheme of Commonwealth defence as an essential link in our air communications with the Far East.

The Committee considered that nothing should be done in the legislation or said to the Indian leaders to suggest that His Majesty's Government accepted the view that the Andaman and Nicobar Islands could be regarded as an organic part of British India. In their view, the position of these islands was comparable to that of the Settlement of Aden, administrative responsibility for which was in 1936, by Order-in-Council under the Government of India Act, 1935, taken from the Government of India and vested, as for a Colony, in His Majesty's Government.[17] It was not desirable that the Viceroy should take the initiative in raising this matter with the Indian leaders; if, however, they should raise it with him, he should indicate that these were the views of His Majesty's Government on the subject.

(b) *Sterling Pensions and Sterling Debt*

The Committee were disposed to consider that His Majesty's Government would have to assume statutory liability for the discharge of the sterling pensions of officers of the Secretary of State's and the Defence Services, and of other persons appointed by His Majesty's Government to posts in connection with Indian affairs. Provision for this would, no doubt, have to be made in the proposed Bill, but it would be essential to avoid any commitment at this stage in the United Kingdom legislation which would prejudice the Committee's

---

[10] No. 544.   [11] No. 539.   [12] No. 538.   [13] No. 517.
[14] No. 533.   [15] No. 543.   [16] See No. 464.
[17] On 29 May the Cabinet Office issued an amendment slip which substituted this sentence as printed here for the one originally contained in this Minute.

earlier decision that every effort should be made to secure, in connection with the sterling balances' negotiations, a settlement whereby a capital sum would be transferred to His Majesty's Government sufficient to discharge these obligations.

(c) *Power of Central Governments over Provincial Governments*

VISCOUNT MOUNTBATTEN pointed out that the leaders of both the Indian political parties would wish to secure powers for the Central Governments which would enable them to maintain close control over the Provincial Governments. One of the arguments which had weighed with the Congress leaders in acquiescing in the establishment of Pakistan had been the prospect that this would enable the Central Government to be granted more effective powers of control over the Provinces. The Congress leaders would certainly not wish to see any weakening of the existing powers possessed by the Central Government.

It was pointed out that the existing position would be radically affected by the establishment of the two successor States on a basis of Dominion status. Both the Governor-General and the Provincial Governors would thereafter have to exercise the powers hitherto reserved to them alone on the advice of their Ministers; there was, therefore, the possibility that a Provincial Governor might, on the advice of his Ministers, refuse to accept the directions of the Governor-General. How could this position be met?

The Committee considered that, in the United Kingdom legislation, it would not be possible to do more than make it clear that the Governor-General would exercise his discretionary functions on advice. The question of the future relationship between the Central Governments and the Provincial Governments was a matter which should be discussed by the Viceroy with the Indian leaders.

(d) *Bengal*

In view of the developments to which the Viceroy had drawn attention, as recorded under Item 1 above, the Committee thought that there was now no prospect that agreement could be reached for the grant of independence to Bengal as a separate Dominion. If its unity could be preserved by its association with one or other of the Indian Dominions on a basis comparable with that of the Indian States, it would be necessary to consider the establishment of a special interim regime pending the division of central subjects and the establishment of the new relationship.

(e) *Date for Transfer of Power*

The Committee considered that provision should be made in the proposed Bill for the Act to come into force not later than a specified date, the exact date to be fixed subsequently by an Order in Council.

(f) *Titles of Successor States*

VISCOUNT MOUNTBATTEN said that it was virtually certain that the Congress

Party would decide that Hindu India should, after the transfer of power, be called either "India" or the "Union of India"; Muslim India would be known as "Pakistan". He would ascertain the decision of the political leaders on the matter as soon as possible in order that acceptable titles could be included in the United Kingdom Bill.

Minute 6
Lease of Bases, etc. by Successor States

VISCOUNT MOUNTBATTEN drew the Committee's attention to the paragraph in Pandit Nehru's letter of 17th May[18] (Annex C to I.B.(47) 73) which read as follows:—

"There should be some clause in our agreement to the effect that neither the Union nor the parts of India outside the Union forming a separate State shall be entitled to permit bases, extra territorial rights, or other infringements of the sovereignty of their territories by any outside State or power. Some such agreement must be made between the two States in India for their mutual protection."

The Viceroy said that this was a matter to which the Congress leaders attached great importance and on which they would undoubtedly expect His Majesty's Government to use their good offices with the Muslim League. Pandit Nehru had made it clear in conversation that his fear was that Pakistan might be driven, by economic necessity, into making extensive concessions for the grant of bases and other defence facilities to a foreign power. An agreement on the lines suggested by Pandit Nehru would, of course, preclude both the British Commonwealth from securing any defence facilities in India and the possibility of any part of India entering into a scheme of Regional Defence, but the power that Pandit Nehru undoubtedly had in mind was the United States.

In discussion, it was pointed out that it would be well within the recognised powers of a Dominion Government to grant bases and other similar facilities to a foreign power; there was a precedent in the facilities granted by the Canadian Government to the United States. On the other hand, the close geographical contiguity of the two Indian Dominions rendered it highly desirable that agreement should be reached on this issue. His Majesty's Government were in a good position to influence the attitude of the Muslim League towards the question in view of the extensive facilities and assistance in defence matters which Pakistan would no doubt expect to secure from them so long as it remained within the British Commonwealth.

The Committee:—

Agreed that His Majesty's Government should assist in promoting an agreement that neither India nor Pakistan would lease bases, etc to any

[18] See No. 471.

power outside the British Commonwealth otherwise than in pursuance of a scheme of Regional Defence approved by the United Nations.

Minute 7
The future of the present Interim Government
(Previous Reference: I.B.(47)27th Meeting, Minute 7)[19]

The Committee had before them a memorandum by the President of the Board of Trade (I.B.(47) 87)[20] containing proposals regarding the government of India between 3rd June and the transfer of power. A memorandum by the Secretary of State for India (I.B.(47) 88)[21] containing comments by the India Office on the suggestions made in I.B.(47) 87 was also considered.

VISCOUNT MOUNTBATTEN said that it was only possible to solve this problem as a result of detailed negotiations in Delhi with the leaders of the major political parties. He was not wholly satisfied with the schemes that had been proposed by the President of the Board of Trade and the Secretary of State for India. There were points in both of them that were of great value and in particular he was attracted by the alternative in paragraph 3 of the India Office paper. He thought that the best course would be for him to discuss the matter with the Indian leaders in the light of the views which had been expressed, and to report to His Majesty's Government on his negotiations.

The Committee:—

Invited the Viceroy to discuss the future of the Interim Government with the Indian leaders, and to keep them informed of the progress of his discussions.

Minute 8
The division of the Armed Forces of India

The Committee had before them a memorandum by the Secretary of State for India (I.B.(47) 89)[22] covering a note prepared by the Commander-in-Chief in India on the division of the Armed Forces of India.

FIELD MARSHAL AUCHINLECK emphasised two points:—

(i) that the continuance of central control of the general administration of the Armed Forces was essential until the process of division was complete and the necessary machinery had been established in the new Dominions;

(ii) that British officers, who held their commissions from the King, could not be required to serve a Dominion Government except with their consent. Such officers as were necessary for effecting the division of the Armed Forces of India and were willing to undertake such sevice, should therefore be transferred to the British Army or the Royal Navy, and their services thereafter lent to the Indian Governments.

The Committee agreed that those British officers of the Indian Armed Forces who were prepared to serve the new Indian Dominion Governments, and whose services were required for this purpose, would have to be transferred to the British Service for the duration of their service in India. Provision would also have to be made to safeguard the position of British officers who might be asked by the Indian Dominion Governments concerned to take action repugnant to their code of behaviour as officers or to their allegiance to the King: their rights of compensation on retirement should be preserved to cover the contingency of compulsory retirement as a result of such a situation.

In discussion, the following points were raised:—

(a) The Treasury wished to be fully consulted about any proposal to guarantee the pay, pensions and future prospects of British officers whose services were retained in the Armed Forces of the two new States.

(b) It was pointed out that each of the Governments in India would wish to be assured that it had control over the Armed Forces in its area and that they could move troops as they wished. This desire would be met, provided the Armed Forces continued to be centrally controlled until their division was complete, by the Commanders-in-Chief for Pakistan and India making appropriate requests or recommendations to the Supreme Commander-in-Chief for the whole of India, who would not interfere in such cases any more than he did at present in the case of requests made to him by District Commanders.

(c) It was suggested that an Official Committee, under the Chairmanship of Sir Henry Wilson Smith, and representative of the Ministry of Defence, Service Departments, the India Office and the Treasury, and including a representative from Field Marshal Auchinleck's staff, should consider, subject to the decision of the Committee recorded above, and make recommendations on the matter raised in the note by the Commander-in-Chief, India.

The Committee:—

Invited the Minister of Defence to set up a Committee under the Chairmanship of Sir Henry Wilson Smith, with representatives of the Ministry of Defence, Admiralty, War Office, Air Ministry, India Office and Treasury, and including a representative of the Commander-in-Chief, India, to examine and, subject to the decisions of the Committee recorded above, make recommendations upon the points raised in the note by the Commander-in-Chief in India annexed to I.B.(47) 89, and such other matters as might arise from the continued service of British officers in the Armed Forces of two independent States in India.[23]

[19] No. 517.   [20] No. 545.   [21] No. 546.   [22] No. 547.

[23] The Minutes of this Committee, the first meeting of which was held on 5 June 1947, will be found on L/WS/1/1115.

Minute 9
The British Army in India

VISCOUNT MOUNTBATTEN said that a decision would have to be taken, in the light of the policy now agreed upon, about the withdrawal of the British Army from India. In his view, there would be every advantage in withdrawing it as soon as practicable after the enactment of the legislation providing for the transfer of power on the basis of the grant of Dominion status to the two successor States. In so far as immediate and complete withdrawal might not be found practicable or desirable, British Army units could remain in India only with the agreement of the new Governments, and for the express purpose of the defence of India and not for the maintenance of internal security. In that event, however, it would have to be made clear that the control of the British Army during such time would remain in our hands and would not pass to the new Governments. It would be advisable to discuss this question with the Indian leaders as soon as possible. A decision to withdraw the British Army would no doubt focus attention on the position of the British community in India. The only indication which he had so far received of disquiet among the British community had come from the Governor of Bengal, who had reported that the British in Calcutta were very nervous about their future security.

THE PARLIAMENTARY UNDER-SECRETARY OF STATE FOR INDIA pointed out that the arrangements for the evacuation of British subjects from India ought to be re-examined in the light of recent developments.

THE PRIME MINISTER said that the matters raised by the Viceroy should be considered in the first instance by the Chiefs of Staff.

The Committee:—

Decided to resume consideration of this question after the views of the Chiefs of Staff had been obtained.[24]

Minute 10
Request for British Cruiser for the Indian Navy

VISCOUNT MOUNTBATTEN said that the Interim Government was very anxious to obtain a British cruiser for service with the Indian Navy. It was, in his view, essential to the efficiency of the Indian Navy that this request should be met; this would have the further advantage that the Indian Navy would for many years be dependent on the British Navy for active help in maintaining in service a naval unit of this size. He thought that it might be possible for a British cruiser to be loaned to the Indian Navy under arrangements similar to those recently made with the Norwegian Government.

THE PRIME MINISTER said that this was a matter which should be considered in the first instance by the Chiefs of Staff.

The Committee:—
> Invited the Chiefs of Staff to consider the request made by the Interim Government of India that a British cruiser should be made available to the Indian Navy.

24 Further documents on this subject will be printed in Vol. XI.

554

Sir F. Burrows (Bengal) to Rear-Admiral Viscount Mountbatten of Burma[1]

Mountbatten Papers. Official Correspondence Files: Bengal, Partition of,
Part I(b)

SECRET 　　　　　　　　　　　　　GOVERNMENT HOUSE, CALCUTTA,
28 May 1947

Dear Lord Mountbatten,

You will believe me when I say that I was both relieved and delighted to receive your telegram of the 23rd May[2] informing me that H.M.G. had agreed to your having authority to recast the forthcoming statement, so far as Bengal is concerned, in the light of the circumstances prevailing on the 2nd June. It is primarily to bring you up to date as regards Coalition prospects in Bengal, as far as I can do so, that I am now writing. I say "as far as I can do so" because both Suhrawardy and Kiran Shankar Roy have left for Delhi to take the matter up with their respective High Commands and the final decision "to coalesce or not to coalesce" will now be taken there. I can therefore only give you the position as it was this week end when they left Calcutta for Delhi and my own estimate of the prospects. Suhrawardy proposes to seek an interview with you on your return at which to give you the final result of his efforts there. Should Kiran Shankar Roy also ask to see you and be given an interview it would help you to complete the picture.

I should perhaps recall that there have been latterly two sets of negotiations proceeding concurrently,—those between Suhrawardy, with some of his followers, and Kiran Shankar Roy and Sarat Bose for the formulation of certain points of agreement as the basis of a future Coalition Government and of a separate constituent assembly formed under its aegis to draft a constitution for the sovereign independent "Free State of Bengal". The other set of negotiations to which, so far as I know, only Suhrawardy and Kiran Shankar Roy are parties, was inaugurated at my suggestion and directed to

---

1 Mr Tyson transmitted this letter to Captain Brockman on 28th May explaining that it was intended to give Lord Mountbatten up to date information about coalition prospects in Bengal. Mountbatten Papers, Official Correspondence Files: Bengal, Partition of, Part I(b).
2 No. 525.

the formation of a Coalition Government here and now without any binding commitment as to the future constitutional or "international" set up of the Province. The two sets of negotiations are not mutually antagonistic in any way but rather complementary. I felt that while some progress was undoubtedly being made in the long term negotiations, these had already been in progress since the New Year and finality was not likely to be attained before the critical date of June 2nd. It was common ground between the three of us that the object of those negotiations would almost certainly be defeated if it once became known for certain that H.M.G. had decided to link the possibility of partition in BENGAL with any decision to partition India, and we therefore decided to try to secure the immediate setting up [of] a Coalition without any definite commitments but obviously on the basis of a tacit recognition of the ground already covered towards agreement in the discussions to which Sarat Bose and a wider circle on both sides have been parties. Suhrawardy and Roy were both impelled to my proposal for a short cut by their conviction that only by getting a Coalition set up in time to avert reference in the state-ment of June 2nd to the possibility of partitioning Bengal could we hope to escape a holocaust in Bengal. The discussions in which Sarat Bose has figured are still proceeding and have been the subject of a good deal of discussion in the Press,—not all of it unfavourable. Documents purporting to be heads of agreement actually reached between the three protagonists have been shown to me from time to time,—I telegraphed a recent edition to you in my No. 125-C of the 19th May,[3] and while I cannot say that finality has been reached even by the principals to the discussion, there is probably enough agreement to justify the formation of a Coalition on that basis now if the High Commands would agree. It is true that the formula has not been put to or accepted by either Party's Working Committee in Bengal and that the newspapers controlled, on the one side, by the Mahasabha (which is pressing for partition) and, on the other, by the faction which is critical of Suhrawardy on personal grounds, are strongly critical both of the main idea of an inde-pendent but united Bengal and of some of the details (e.g. joint electorates). But I know for a fact that some of the "rebels" in Suhrawardy's camp have approached Kiran Shankar Roy with almost identical proposals as the basis of a future coalition if only he will deal with them rather than with Suhrawardy: and Suhrawardy claims to have talked over the hitherto hostile Chairman of the Muslim League Party in Bengal, Maulana Akram Khan. Suhrawardy has considerable support among his personal followers and I believe him when he says that, if Congress will "play", he is confident he could bring his Party up to support his move for a united and independent Bengal, as they all want at all costs to avoid partition. He is not, however, prepared to burn his boats unless he can be assured that Kiran Shankar Roy will be able and willing to bring the Bengal Congress in, with or without the approval of his own High

Command. Roy for his part has gone so far as to tell me and others that he will resign his position as leader of the Congress Assembly Party in Bengal if the High Command will not listen to him, as he is not prepared to take responsibility for the bloodshed that will ensue; but I must confess I share Suhrawardy's apprehension that, if Nehru and Patel prove adamant, Roy is not the man to move them and Bengal will be sacrificed on the altar of Nehru's All-India outlook.

The plan to form a Coalition without firm conditions and, if necessary, in the faces of the respective High Commands has not matured and I doubt if it will do so now as the Provincial parties have not been approached. Though Suhrawardy and Roy might get together in Delhi, I doubt if they would defy their respective High Commands without more definite assurance of the support of their parties here. But if the High Commands would agree to a Coalition of this kind at once,—either without conditions or on the Suhrawardy-Roy-Bose formula,—I am confident that both Suhrawardy and Roy could put it over down here: Gandhi is on the side of avoiding partition and there has been some sign, this last week, of a revulsion of feeling among the Hindus (especially of East Bengal) against partition if it can be avoided. Short of the Cabinet Plan of May 1946, partition can only be avoided by maintaining, for the time being at all events, a right to stay out of either Hindustan or Pakistan. The reason for this in a nutshell is that the Hindus of Bengal are determined not to surrender their ideal of a link with a Hindu centre (and the protection they think that would afford to a Hindu minority) unless they can be guaranteed that they will not be forced under a Pakistan centre and, lacking that guarantee, they demand partition: the Muslims, on the other hand, while not so adamant about joining a North Western Pakistan, are determined not to come under a Hindu-controlled centre. To be independent, for the time being, of either Hindustan or Pakistan is the only platform on which they can unite. And a united Bengal ought to be a viable proposition in peace time, however defenceless it might prove in war. It is something to which we could hand over power with a clear conscience that it represented the greatest measure of agreement of the population and I believe it would offer the best chance now remaining of a peaceful hand over. The alternative of partition is politically and economically a deplorable prospect, especially for Eastern Bengal, but as I cannot be sure that Suhrawardy and Roy will bring off Coalition to avert it, I must now deal with this possibility.

All our information—and there is plenty of it—goes to show that if as a result of the discussions beginning on the 2nd June it appears that partition is being forced on Bengal or that the Hindus can have partition for the asking, the Muslims will refuse to take it lying down and will adopt every form of resistance, in the course of which much blood will be shed and much property

3 No. 488.

devastated, especially in Calcutta, the loss of any interest in which will be the greatest blow, financially and in prestige, to the Muslims of Eastern India. In the Province generally there is a feeling of pessimism and almost of resignation to the prospect of renewed communal strife on an unprecedented scale and in some parts the wildest ideas are current regarding the preparedness of the rival community to launch a planned campaign of violence the moment the signal is given. Calcutta is particularly "jittery",—I enclose a copy of a document[4] which Kiran Shankar Roy handed to me on Saturday with the comment, merely, that it was handed to him by a Muslim. I have had this checked up by our Intelligence and have reason to believe that this particular document represents merely a collection by the Congress Party of the rumours prevalent (among Hindus and Muslims alike) in Calcutta and that most of the assertions of fact in it are palpably false: but that exaggerated rumours of this sort are being freely circulated and given ready credence by both sides is undeniable. Other panicky reports that have recently come to notice in Calcutta are that the 2nd June (earlier dates have already been mentioned but discarded when nothing eventuated) will be marked by a planned attack by the Muslims on Hindu life and property in Calcutta and elsewhere: that the prospects of peace are so gloomy that a four-day continuous curfew covering the 2nd June is in contemplation: that the Ministry will be dismissed and rule u/s 93 inaugurated with a view to maintaining law and order for a period round about the 2nd June: (curiously enough Suhrawardy when he saw me just before leaving for Delhi on Monday quite unexpectedly and inconsequentially asked me at what date I proposed to dissolve the Ministry and go into Section 93): and, finally, that simultaneously with the forthcoming announcement martial law will be enforced. There is no doubt that both sides are preparing for trouble,—though preparations are not on the scale suggested in Kiran Shankar Roy's paper—and that both sides have bombs and firearms and other weapons to an extent hitherto not experienced in communal disturbances in Bengal. But to my mind most dangerous of all is this mentality that a struggle is inevitable, that "the other side" are only waiting for a signal to begin it and that one must therefore be on one's guard night and day for the outbreak of the trouble. In such an atmosphere the smallest incident occurring round what the public regard as the critical date (June 2nd) may cause people to say "This is it" and may start the widest conflagration.

In this superheated and explosive atmosphere I deemed it necessary to give a broadcast last night[5] (copy enclosed) with a view to steadying public opinion. Certain leaders also have of themselves circulated a statement[6] appealing for calm (enclosure 3): copies of this were widely dropped over Calcutta from the air yesterday. We are, of course, taking all possible precautions, unobtrusively and without provocation, to be prepared for an outburst should there be one following on publicity being given to transactions at

Delhi on and after the 2nd June. But what I really have in mind in acquainting you with this aspect of the position down here is to give you material (which I believe Suhrawardy and Kiran Shankar Roy will confirm and reinforce) for impressing on the All-India leaders of both sides the danger of the position in Bengal,—the danger of widespread communal strife, followed almost immediately, as it inevitably would be in present circumstances, by a complete breakdown of our feeding arrangements for Calcutta and the deficit pockets of the Province (largely in East Bengal). A serious outbreak of communal strife at this moment might well cost us more lives by famine in the next few months than the rioting itself. If, therefore, and this is the point I am leading up to, division of India becomes inevitable and with it the opportunity to the Hindus to partition Bengal, it is in my opinion of supreme importance that if that is by any means an agreed decision or even a decision acquiesced in by the All-India leaders, these (and from my point of view especially Jinnah) should, if it is humanly possible, be got to the microphone at the earliest possible moment to say that all should acquiesce in the decisions taken at Delhi and to appeal in the strongest possible terms for their peaceful implementation. Though the response in Calcutta, so far, to the Gandhi-Jinnah appeal to abjure violent means has not been conspicuously favourable in practice, I believe that a strong indication by Jinnah (if he can be got to give it) that the decision is accepted by him as the best that can be got and as worthy of acceptance and working out, for what it is worth, in peace and amity, would have a most steadying effect on Muslims down here and, incidentally, on Hindu apprehensions.[7]

Yours sincerely,

F. J. BURROWS

[4] Not printed.   [5] and [6] Not printed.
[7] Lord Mountbatten replied to this letter in tel. 1237-S of 1 June which will be printed in Vol. XI.

555

Mr Attlee to Field Marshal Smuts

Telegram, L/PO/6/121: f 94

TOP SECRET AND PERSONAL   DOMINIONS OFFICE, *28 May 1947,*
6.40 pm

No. 45. My telegram D. No. 469 of 23rd May,[1] India. Following from Prime Minister for Prime Minister. *Begins.*

Many thanks for your message[2] sent through your High Commissioner in

[1] No. 527.   [2] See No. 538.

reply to my telegrams about India. I am delighted to find that your views about latest developments coincide so closely with our own.

In my message of 23rd May, I mentioned the suggestion that an announcement should be made of the intention to grant Dominion status to India (or in the event of partition to both parts of India) as soon as possible. We have been considering the terms of a statement to be made on these lines and my immediately following telegram contains the text of what we consider that the Viceroy should say as a concluding part[3] of the draft announcement already telegraphed to you in telegram D. No. 470.

We will keep you informed as to developments, but if following upon the Viceroy's discussions with Indian leaders a statement is made as now proposed on 2nd June by Viceroy, it would be very helpful if you felt able to indicate publicly that your attitude was favourable to the proposal. It would of course be important that any such statement should not suggest that India has taken a *final* decision to remain within the Commonwealth cf. last sentence of draft in my immediately following telegram. I should be grateful if you would consider this. I am sending a similar message to the other three Prime Ministers.[4] *Ends*.

³ See No. 553, Minute 3.
⁴ See L/PO/6/121 for the telegrams to Mr Mackenzie King, Mr Chifley and Mr Fraser.

556

Sir C. Corfield to Sir E. Mieville

Mountbatten Papers. Official Correspondence Files:
Political Situation in India and Constitutional Position
of Viceroy, Part 3

TOP SECRET   NEW DELHI, *29 May 1947*
My dear Eric,
I enclose herewith a note on the subject which we discussed the other evening. I think you agreed that it would be best if this question could be laid before His Excellency the Viceroy's Staff Conference at the next suitable opportunity.

Yours sincerely,
CONRAD CORFIELD

Enclosure to No. 556
SECRET
The principles and policy governing the Crown's future relations with Indian States are laid down in the Cabinet Mission's Memorandum of 12th May, 1946.[1] This Memorandum provided categorically for the lapse of para-

mountcy, and recognised the consequential freedom of States to decide their own future. To avoid the vacuum that would otherwise occur on the lapse of paramountcy it was realised that it would be necessary for the Crown Representative, the Political Department, Residencies and Political Agencies to fade out gradually before the final transfer of power. Only in this way would it be possible for alternative machinery to be built up providing a new nexus of relations between States and British India.

2. At the Residents' Conference held in December 1946 the general lines on which paramountcy should be retracted were discussed. The Secretary of State in a telegram of the 5th March[2] entirely agreed with the approach to the relaxation of paramountcy on the lines contemplated at this Conference, adding that the question appeared to him to have been tackled in a businesslike and realistic fashion.

3. It was at that time anticipated that there would be a period of years during which the machinery of paramountcy could be retracted, but after the announcement of the 20th February, retraction required to be greatly accelerated.

4. Shortly after this announcement I prepared a handing-over note[3] for Lord Wavell, which he passed on to his successor. In the concluding paragraph of that note I stated as follows:—

"The Central Government of British India is anxious to inherit paramountcy and considers that in any case some form of paramountcy will have to be established after we go. For this purpose they would like to obtain control of the Political Department now. The only policy fair to States is therefore to close down the Political Department as soon as practicable, and to arrange for direct contact with each Central Government department concerned on the subjects of common concern with which that Department deals."

5. In V.C.P. 11 dated the 29th March[4] I submitted a note regarding the alternative machinery which would carry out the duties now performed by the Political Department as that Department contracts. This note was considered at the Viceroy's Staff Conference on the 31st March,[5] and it was recorded that His Excellency approved the note with the addition of a few words.

6. Subsequently the Residents' Conference, which was summoned again in April,[6] examined in detail the steps which would be required to ensure retraction of paramountcy with the least possible confusion. The minutes of this

[1] Vol. VII, No. 262.   [2] Vol. IX, No. 489.
[3] Mountbatten Papers, Official Correspondence Files: Political Situation in India and Constitutional Position of Viceroy, Part 2.
[4] This circulated Enclosure to No. 25.   [5] No. 34, Item 6.
[6] Minutes of this Conference are on L/P &S/13/1831.
37*

Conference were submitted to His Excellency, and a copy was forwarded to the Secretary of State.

7. In pursuance of His Excellency's instructions I went home early this month to discuss these minutes with the Secretary of State. The discussion took place on the 9th May 1947, and a note of the discussion[7] recorded by the India Office has, I understand, been forwarded to the Viceroy. This note accorded the Secretary of State's approval of the programme contained in the minutes of the Residents' Conference held in April, over the opening of which His Excellency presided.

8. Under the Letters Patent constituting the office of the Crown Representative, the Secretary of State exercises a special control over the Crown Representative. The corresponding control over the Governor-General has been considerably relaxed: and in the telegram of the 5th March 1947 referred to above, the Secretary of State agreed that the Crown Representative should have maximum discretion in carrying out the policy of relaxation with a view to the greatest possible devolution by the end of 1947, but avoiding any step which would prejudice the future unity of India in regard to defence and communications.

9. The attitude of the Central Government towards this policy and its programme has recently become apparent, especially in the following cases:—
Gilgit. In spite of the concurrence of Defence Department, Pandit Jawaharlal Nehru attempted to delay the question of cancelling the Gilgit Lease on the ground that there was no particular urgency and action could be postponed till 1948. This objection was overruled.
Abu. Sardar Vallabhbhai Patel has protested against the retrocession of jurisdiction over Abu, which is an integral part of Sirohi State, and has suggested that it might be taken over by the Central Government. He has, I understand, been told that this would be entirely contrary to the policy accepted by His Majesty's Government.
Bangalore and Secunderabad. After detailed inter-departmental discussions proposals were made for regional negotiations between representatives of the Central Government and the States concerned, assisted by Political Officers, in order to make arrangements for retroceding jurisdiction on terms which would be acceptable to the State, would protect all-India interests and could continue until new permanent arrangements had been made. Sardar Baldev Singh has declined to proceed with these negotiations for the time being.
Railways. After careful inter-departmental discussion certain proposals have been put forward for similar negotiations regarding retrocession of jurisdiction over railways in Indian States. After considering these proposals for two months the Home Department have suggested that 'an

effort should be made to retain—even during the post-paramountcy future—exactly the same control, rights and privileges which all Departments of the Central Government are now able to exercise by virtue of these lands vesting in the Crown Representative. Pandit Jawaharlal Nehru has also protested against the suggestion of the Resident at Hyderabad for an interim arrangement which would help to obviate chaotic conditions on the automatic reversion of jurisdiction over the Hyderabad Railways after the lapse of paramountcy.

Direct correspondence with the Central Government.

Objection was taken in certain quarters of the Central Government to the arrangements proposed for direct correspondence, in a limited sphere, between the Departments and States. As a result, however, of a recent Secretaries' Conference presided over by the Cabinet Secretary, it has been agreed that the proposals of the Political Department should be implemented. Pandit Nehru has since characterised these arrangements as 'objectionable, harmful and discourteous'.[8]

10. As a result of more recent proposals regarding the establishment of transitional dominion status, the urgency of the programme for the contraction of paramountcy has vastly increased. It seems now that it will be almost impossible for alternative machinery to be established in time, even if there is the fullest cooperation from the Central Government and from the States, but the Political Department are trying their best to set in train alternative arrangements. If however they are blocked any longer, the task will be quite impossible, and the chaotic conditions which will result may well lead to the Balkanisation of India.

11. It seems necessary therefore that the programme should be discussed with the Central Government so that their co-operation can be secured if possible, but so that in any case they may appreciate the reasons for the policy and programme accepted by the Secretary of State.

12. The letter of the Prime Minister to His Excellency dated [18] March '47,[9] contains the following sentence:—

'You will also aid and assist the States in coming to fair and just arrangements with the leaders of British India as to their future relationships.'

I am not sure to what extent this sentence refers to the interim relationships which must be set up before the parties come to an agreement amongst themselves; but in any case it seems clear that, if we do not make arrangements to return to States, in advance of the lapse of paramountcy, the rights surrendered to the paramount power, the Central Government or Governments will be in a position to bring unfair pressure to bear on them, and the Crown Representative can then be justifiably accused of a gross breach of faith.

[7] No. 376.   [8] See No. 541.   [9] Vol. IX, Enclosure to No. 543.

Moreover, the States will become more and more antagonistic to the successor Government or Governments of British India, and will be less likely to accept even standstill arrangements for preserving some measure of economic and administrative integration, until new relationships have been established.

557

The Earl of Listowel to Mr Attlee

L/PO/6/124: ff 18–19

INDIA OFFICE, *30 May 1947*

Secretary of State's Minute: Serial No. 79/47

Prime Minister.

I feel bound to draw your attention to one passage in the recorded text of the Viceroy's broadcast[1] (a copy of which, I understand, is available to you) namely, the words "to which the representatives of the majority of the Provinces have in fact adhered" in lines 4 to 5 of paragraph 5[2] on page 2. This passage will almost certainly be taken by Congress as justifying their claim that His Majesty's Government acknowledge that the Congress accept the Cabinet Mission's plan and have been operating it. I do not think that, in fact, the Viceroy holds that this is the case or intended anything in his broadcast to give that impression. I think it is important that Congress should be given no ground for claiming that His Majesty's Government have acknowledged them as having genuinely accepted the Cabinet Mission's plan, because that would greatly strengthen their position if and when they say that Jinnah will not accept the Viceroy's proposal as a final settlement and that therefore the Mission's plan must be carried through and full power be transferred to the Interim Government whether the Muslims are in it or not. I feel, therefore, that the Viceroy should be asked whether he would be willing to omit the words in question. It has been confirmed from the B.B.C. that, from a technical point of view, it would be practicable for the words to be omitted from the recorded broadcast and, if you agree, I will telegraph to the Viceroy on the matter.

You will remember that I suggested in my Minute No. 74/47[3] that the corresponding words in the draft of the broadcast should be omitted. Unfortunately, I did not see the final text until after it had been recorded.[4]

LISTOWEL

[1] The complete text of the Viceroy's broadcast, made on 3 June 1947, will be printed in Vol. XI. See No. 507 in this Volume for an early draft; also Nos. 529 and 532. In a minute dated 29 May, Mr Harris stated that it had proved difficult to keep track of the Viceroy's draft broadcast after submission of No. 529. He had been informed that the draft was the subject of direct exchanges between the Viceroy and the Prime Minister. In the end, the final text was decided upon only just in time for it to be recorded by the B.B.C. at the time arranged on 28 May. He had therefore received a copy only after it had been recorded. Harris to Turnbull, 29 May 1947. L/PO/6/124: f 46.

[2] The first two sentences of para. 5, as recorded by Lord Mountbatten on 28 May, had read: 'My first course, in all my discussions, was therefore to urge the political leaders to accept unreservedly the Cabinet Mission plan of 16th May 1946. In my opinion that plan, to which the representatives of the majority of the Provinces have in fact adhered, provides the best arrangement that can be devised to meet the interests of all the communities of India.' R/3/1/150: f 136.

[3] No. 529.

[4] On 31 May Mr Attlee noted on Lord Listowel's minute: 'I agree that this point should be put to the Viceroy'. Lord Listowel did this in tel. 65 of the same date, using similar arguments to those in his minute. Lord Mountbatten replied in tel. 1249–S of 1 June (which will be printed in Vol. XI) agreeing to the omission of the clause in question. L/PO/6/124: ff 12–15.

558

Mr Liaquat Ali Khan to Rear-Admiral Viscount Mountbatten of Burma

R/3/1/90: ff 114–15

IMMEDIATE   NEW DELHI, *30 May 1947*
SECRET

No. 40–P.S.F.R./47

Dear Lord Mountbatten,

Allow me to extend to you a hearty welcome on your return to New Delhi. I wish that I could spare you from our tale of woe for at least some time after your arduous journey. The problem of saving millions of lives in Gurgaon district and, I believe, the adjoining territory in the U.P. has, however, become so imperative that I feel compelled to draw your attention to it immediately.

My colleague, the Hon'ble Mr. Ghazanfar Ali Khan, has been making representations about the situation in Gurgaon district (only about 40 to 50 miles from Delhi) to Sir John Colville during your absence. The situation has, however, been rapidly worsening since trouble started there on Saturday night last. Arson, looting and killing has been going on unchecked over a wide area and the trouble has spread to several parts of the district. Judging from the reports which are being received almost hour after hour from the afflicted areas, it appears that very big mobs, numbering sometimes 20,000 to 30,000 carrying 303 rifles and other modern as well as crude weapons, besiege one village of Muslims after another and destroy it, killing as many as cannot escape and looting whatever can be easily removed.

The military has been patrolling part of this area; but either because of inadequate strength or for some other reason, has almost entirely failed to check this one sided war of the majority upon the minority community in this area. There are persistent complaints that troops from Alwar and Bharatpur States which are posted at various points near the borders of the Gurgaon district move in the district territory in plain clothes or even in uniforms, carrying modern firearms, and take a hand in rioting.

Almost every hour some village is being sacked and destroyed. The situation calls for immediate action. If possible, more military (of a mixed composition) should be sent into this area. Even the use of cavalry and para-troops may be considered. I suggest that, if it be not too inconvenient to you, an aerial survey of the area by yourself will be most useful and will probably have a salutary effect on the situation.

Before this there was serious trouble in Lahore. There also men from certain Sikh States, who had in their possession arms belonging to the States and who in certain instances wore uniforms, were found to have been helping rioters. From such reports as have reached us, it appears that they were treated with undue leniency. The situation in Lahore seems, however, to have quietened down now. The most imperative problem now is that of Gurgaon and adjoining parts of the U.P. I do hope that with your drive and well known capacity for bold decisions and action, we shall save this area from impending disaster.[1]

Yours sincerely,
LIAQUAT ALI KHAN

---

[1] Lord Mountbatten replied on 31 May. He said he had been distressed to hear from Sir J. Colville of the serious nature of the disturbances in Gurgaon. Sir J. Colville had assured him that everything possible was being done with the troops available to deal with the situation, both in Gurgaon and other parts of the Punjab. He (Mountbatten) was going to Gurgaon himself the next day to see whether anything further could be done. However, 'we are very thin on the ground with troops all over India, considering the number of disturbances with which we have to contend.' R/3/1/90: f 120.

559

Note by Mr Abell

R/3/1/150: ff 173-4

30 May 1947

The Interim Government

I have been thinking about the old problem of the status of the Interim Government and have discussed it this morning with Mr Menon.

2. The demand for dominion status now has been turned down by H.M.G.[1] This is the demand that the Congress have been pressing.

3. Various proposals have been put forward by way of palliatives.

4. Krishna Menon's suggestion[2] was that the Muslim League members should be deprived of their portfolios which should be distributed among the other members. The League members would remain in the Cabinet but be Ministers without Portfolio and come in only (*a*) on Cabinet meetings, and (*b*) on Cabinet Committee meetings, especially meetings of the Partition Committee. Their sole function would be to deal with the separating of the Pakistan administration from the rest.

The Congress demand that the League should be prevented from sabotaging the Government of India is reasonable, but to deprive the League members of their portfolios would be likely to lead to their resignations and this would make everything much more difficult.

5. Sir B.N. Rau's plan was to have two regional Ministries, one for Hindustan and one for Pakistan. This is impracticable until the administration has been divided up. Finance, for instance, is administered for India as a whole on an All-India Budget. Any expenditure on Pakistan affects Hindustan too and *vice versa*. Even if one could say at once that so much % of the revenue is available for expenditure on Hindustan and so much on Pakistan there would still be only a very few matters for decision which would concern *only* Hindustan or *only* Pakistan. Practically everything would have to go to *both* Ministries or both Finance Members. Thus the regional ministries could not really work as such immediately. The Congress have rejected the proposal for regional ministries, and would no doubt reject the alternative in paragraph 3 of the India Office note which was to the same effect.

6. Sir S. Cripps' proposal[3] involved a committee rule instead of a Government, and would be quite inacceptable to Congress.

7. A compromise which occurs to me is as follows. There would be (as already planned) a partition committee of the Cabinet with the Viceroy as

---

[1] See No. 553, Minute 1.   [2] cf. No. 551.   [3] See No. 545.

Chairman and equal numbers of Leaguers and non-Leaguers as members. The two halves of this committee would be the embryo ministries of Pakistan and Hindustan, though no doubt smaller in size than the full-fledged ministries.

The Committee as a whole would decide the many policy questions about partition which will arise. It would direct the work of the official steering committee (to consist of 3 or 4 experienced secretaries) and through that committee control the departmental teams working on partition.

It would also function in two halves for the following purpose. There would be a rule of business that if any matter of importance came up for decision in the Department of a Muslim League Member and if that matter concerned *exclusively* or *mainly* Hindustan, it would be necessary for the Member in charge to obtain the concurrence of the Hindustan half of the Partition Committee. Similarly if a matter came up for decision in a department controlled by a Hindustan Member, and concerned exclusively or mainly Pakistan, the concurrence of the Pakistan half of the Partition Committee would be required. The responsibility to see that the necessary concurrence was obtained would rest on the Secretary in each Department, and three of the four Secretaries in League departments are British.

This I admit would be a clumsy device, and it would mean that important Government business in the League Departments would be disposed of very slowly during this short period, but it has the following merits.

(1) There would be a single Member in effective charge of each Department, and routine work could go on unhampered.
(2) The League Members would not be deprived of their portfolios.
(3) The Congress would have the degree of control in the League departments to which they are entitled.
(4) The Hindustan Ministers would not be seriously hampered in the administration of their own departments.
(5) The rule would be the same for both parties.

8. I do not suggest that the plan above should be offered to the Congress at once. It would be better to leave things as they are if possible, to concentrate on the very complex work of partition and not to worry too much about the anomalies of the Interim Government for the next month or two.

9. Mr Menon thinks he may be able to persuade the Congress not to press the point. But if they do, we could have this up our sleeves as a possible compromise. The League will not like it but they are unlikely to resign on the issue.

G. E. B. ABELL

560

India and Burma Committee. Paper IBN(47)17

L/P&J/10/79: ff 14–16, 31b–34

SELECTION OF CABLED NEWS AND PRESS REPORTS
FROM INDIA AND BURMA

INDIA OFFICE AND BURMA OFFICE, *30 May 1947*

(i) Mr. Gandhi—The British "can only get off our backs."
(ii) Congress President on division of India.
(iii) Pandit Nehru's interview in *News Chronicle*, 27.5.47.[1]

Circulated by direction of the Secretary of State for India and Burma.

Enclosure (i) to No. 560

"BRITAIN SHOULD WITHDRAW EVEN FROM CHAOS"

Mr Gandhi's Views

I. AND B. DEPARTMENT,
NEW DELHI, *27 May 1947*

Mr. Gandhi, in his address after prayers in New Delhi on May 26th, urged "every patriot, and certainly the British power, to out-face the worst violence and leave India, as it can be left, under the Cabinet Mission document of May 16th."

Mr Gandhi said it was not for the British to give India liberty. "They can only get off our backs. That they are under a promise to do. But for keeping it and giving it shape, we have to look to ourselves." He added: "In my opinion we are unable to think coherently whilst British Power is still functioning in India. Its function is not to change the map of India. All it has to do is to withdraw and leave India, if possible, carrying on in an orderly manner, but withdraw in any case on or before the promised date, maybe even in chaos.

"But there is an additional reason why no vital change in the shape of Hindustan, with or without partition, is possible in the present state of the country. There is the joint statement issued by the Quaid-e-Azam (Mr. Jinnah) and me. It enunciates the sound principle that there should be no violence employed in pursuit of a political aim. If in the teeth of that document the country continues on a mad career of violence of the worst kind, and the British power is weak enough to submit to it in the vain hope that after the mad thirst is quenched things will run smooth, it would have left a bloody legacy for which not only India but the whole world will blame her."

Mr. Gandhi observed: "Today, in the presence of British power, we are only demoralised by an orgy of blood, arson and worse. After it is withdrawn,

[1] The record of this interview actually circulated under this reference was a shortened version. The full text, circulated the next day under reference I.B.(47)91, has been preferred here.

let me hope we shall have the wisdom to think coherently and keep India one or split it into two parts or more. But if we are bent even then on fighting, I am sure we will not be so demoralised as we are today, though admittedly all violence carries with it some amount of demoralisation. I shall hope against hope that a free India will not give the world an additional object-lesson in violence with which it is already sick almost unto death."

Enclosure (ii) to No. 560

CONGRESS PRESIDENT ON DIVISION OF INDIA

I. AND B. DEPARTMENT,
NEW DELHI, *28 May 1947*

The Congress President, Acharya Kripalani, after the termination of his visit to the Punjab, in an interview with A.P.I. in New Delhi on May 28th said one immediate upshot of the disturbances was that the demand for the partition of the Punjab had become insistent. He said Congress was not happy over the prospect of any kind of division of the country, and a united India continued to be its objective and ideal. That is why Congress had agreed to the State Paper of May 16th despite its shortcomings. "To ask us again to accept the Cabinet Mission's proposals would have no meaning because we have already, not only accepted the document of May 16th, but also the December 6th interpretation given to it by His Majesty's Government. Even today we adhere to that position and it is on that basis that the Constituent Assembly is functioning. This position of ours has been well understood and recognised by His Majesty's Government.

If, despite all this, the country must be divided at the bidding of the Muslim League—division which would do good to nobody—responsibility for such a division of the country must rest primarily with the League and then with the British Government. And if partition must come, the division must be fair. Under no circumstance will Congress allow the inclusion of non-Muslim areas in so-called Pakistan."

Mr. Kripalani said: "We also do not want this division to be carried out by the British Government. Even today the British Government can divest itself of all power and responsibility and allow the Interim Government to function as a Dominion Government, the Viceroy occupying the position of constitutional head. It should then be for the free Government to decide whether India shall be partitioned or not, and if partitioned, on what principle partition is to be effected."

Emphasising that the powers of the Interim Government should immediately be enhanced he said: "Even apart from the question of partition, it is necessary that the Interim Government should have the power that rests with the Viceroy to interfere in provincial affairs if internal security is threatened. I believe if responsibility for internal security is thrown on the Interim Government there is every possibility of stabilising peace in the Provinces and stopping communal rioting."

The division of India, if it must come, can be carried out democratically and peacefully, the Congress President concluded.

Enclosure (iii) to No. 560²

Extract from *News Chronicle* dated 27.5.47

CONGRESS WILL ACCEPT OUR INDIA PLANS

IF SETTLEMENT IS FINAL

From Norman Cliff,

Mussoorie, Monday

When the Viceroy, at the opening of the Delhi Conference next Monday, asks the Indian leaders to say finally whether they are prepared to operate the Cabinet Mission plan of last year for a united India, the Congress reply will be an unqualified "Yes."

Should the Moslem League refuse, Congress will not oppose the British Government's proposed variations of the plan, on condition that a final settlement can be assured.

This is made clear in an exclusive interview Pandit Jawaharlal Nehru, vice-president of the Interim Government, has given me after closely studying the Viceroy's amended plan of procedure in consultation with Sardar Patel, Home Minister, who will be the other Congress representative at the Conference.

Following are questions I put to Pandit Nehru and his replies:

What will be your response to a final appeal by the British Government and the Viceroy to all Indian parties to give the Cabinet Mission plan a trial?

Congress has not only accepted the plan fully, but has acted up to it. So also have all the other groups with the single exception of the Moslem League. Congress still wishes to adhere to the plan, but is prepared to vary it somewhat if there can be a full settlement on that basis. If there can be no settlement there is no particular point in varying the plan.

VARIATIONS

Do you approve the variations of the plan as suggested as a possible alternative by the Viceroy?

It would not be proper for me to express an opinion on the Viceroy's proposals, but the variation of the Cabinet Mission plan envisaged was the right and opportunity to particular areas to opt out of a Union of India if they so desire, provided no area is forcibly taken out against its will. This inevitably involved partition of the Punjab and Bengal. Afterwards those parts which opted out in this manner could deal directly with a Union of India in regard to future relations and common subjects.

² See note 1.

But all this could be done only on the basis of a full settlement with no further claims left over to be agitated for and above all a cessation of violence and direct action movements. If there is no settlement then we continue with the Cabinet Mission's plan.

PARTITION

Division of the Punjab and of Bengal being a condition of Congress concurrence in any proposals involving partition, would Congress still concur if the present movements for unity within these two provinces succeeded on the basis of their independence or any other basis?

The independence of Bengal really means in present circumstances the dominance of the Moslem League in Bengal. It means practically the whole of Bengal going into the Pakistan area, although those interested may not say so.

We can agree to Bengal remaining united only if it remains in the Union. As a matter of fact, there is an overwhelming feeling in Western Bengal and in Eastern Punjab to separate from Eastern Bengal and Western Punjab.

REFERENDUM

Would you regard a referendum based on the present limited franchise as a fair method of testing the wishes of the masses in those areas on this issue?

Their opinion may be tested by a referendum, but any kind of test would be a general test applied to other places as well. The present franchise is roughly 20 per cent of the possible electorate.

There is no doubt that on this issue, whether the test were made under the franchise as at present or under a wider franchise, the verdict would be for partition of these areas if the whole provinces do not go into the Union.

GANDHI

Are you hopeful of persuading Mahatma Gandhi—who has expressed opposition to any division of India—to acquiesce in any proposal that involves partition?

Gandhiji has held the opinion strongly that any arrangement for division of India or of provinces should not take place through British agency. If the people of the areas concerned desire division there will be nothing to stop them.

May we assume that Gandhi would naturally accept the popular verdict?

A few years ago he actually suggested to Mr Jinnah a scheme for people to be consulted on such an issue. His main point is that anything of the kind should be done by mutual consent, and not by imposition by the British Government. Mutual consent involves a settlement. Imposition involves carrying on the dispute.

I entirely agree with Gandhiji's approach to this problem, and I think there will be no final settlement until the people of India are left entirely to their own resources and have themselves to shoulder this responsibility.

BRITAIN

In the event of partition, is there a possibility of Hindustan choosing to remain associated with the British Commonwealth, at least for a limited period?

There is no doubt that the Union of India is going to be a Republic, as the Constituent Assembly has declared. At the same time there is a strong desire among many people in India to have very close relations with the British Commonwealth. What form these relations might take it is difficult to say now.

Obviously a very great deal will depend on what happens during the next few months, or the next year, and the reactions to what happens in the public mind.

BASES

Would any attempt by the British Government to secure bases or other privilege of that kind in any part of India adversely affect the prospect of future relations?

Obviously if there is any special treatment of any part of India by the British Government this will react adversely on relations with the rest. If any portion of India ultimately does not form part of the Union there should be an agreement between it and the Union not to allow any outside Power to have bases or extra-territorial rights.

DEFENCE

Assuming that any division of India would involve a division of forces, do you envisage the formation of a Joint Defence Council?

The immediate issue in India is to have firm authority and a centre which can act with one mind so as to stop the violence that is going on. If any division takes place it will be fatal to weaken the central authority for the area which it controls.

If in case of division the Army also has to be divided it cannot be controlled by some kind of dyarchical system that would make it useless at a time of emergency such as the present.

CORRIDOR

Pandit Nehru emphasised that Congress was willing to accept much that it disliked if agreement and peace in India could be achieved.

He is of opinion that even if division becomes inevitable it will not be of long duration, and if agreement could be secured the danger of civil disorder would be removed. He dismisses Mr Jinnah's demand for a corridor connecting the Eastern and Western zones of Pakistan as fantastic and absurd.

Glossary

ADIBASIS Tribal people originating in central India.

AFRIDIS A PATHAN tribe.

AHOMS Shan tribe from which Assam takes its name.

AJIT Unconquerable.

AKALI *Lit.*: Worshipper of the eternal one. Particularly strict devotee of the SIKH faith. In modern usage, a member of the extreme Sikh nationalist party.

AKHAND HINDUSTAN Indivisible India, a slogan used by militant Hindus in opposition to the Muslim League's demand for Pakistan.

ANGAMIS A NAGA tribe.

ANJUMAN E WATAN *Lit.*: Association of the country; a Muslim organisation in Baluchistan.

AOS A NAGA tribe.

BAISAKH The first month of the luni-solar year of the Hindus (April–May).

BANIA Hindu trader or shopkeeper, often also a moneylender.

BAR Upland between rivers in the Punjab.

BHITTANIS A PATHAN tribe.

CASTE HINDU A Hindu not belonging to the SCHEDULED CASTES, ie not an Untouchable.

CHARPOY The common Indian bedstead.

CRORE 100 lakhs or ten million.

DAL Organisation, association.

DARBAR (DURBAR) Court; ceremonial assembly; government of a Princely State.

DAURS A PATHAN tribe.

GHALLUGHARA Massacre, holocaust.

GIANI (GYANI) Title of respect accorded to one learned in the Sikh religion and scriptures.

GIRDAWAR CIRCLE The area assigned to a revenue official known as a Girdawar.

GOONDA Hooligan.

GURKHA Ruling race of Nepal.

GURMUKHI The script in which the Punjabi language is usually written; reputed to have been invented by Guru Nanak (*see* SIKH); used particularly by the Sikhs.

GURU Spiritual adviser, religious preceptor; for Sikh Gurus *see* SIKH.

HAKIM Doctor, physician.

HUR *Lit.*: free man. Member of a group of guerrillas or bandits with a quasi-religious background operating in Sind under the leadership of the Pir Pagaro.

INDIAN NATIONAL ARMY (I.N.A.) Of about 70,000 men of the Indian Army. who became Japanese prisoners of war, some 20,000 defected and joined the I.N.A. commanded from late 1943 by Subhas Chandra Bose.

JAGIR An assignment of land revenue; sometimes conditional on the maintenance of troops, or other service.

JAGIRDAR Holder of a Jagir.

JAMIAT-UL-ULEMA *Lit.*: association of learned men. Pro-Congress Muslim organisation.

JAT The great agricultural tribe of north-west India found in the Punjab, western United Provinces and Rajputana and comprising people of Muslim, Hindu and Sikh faiths.

JATHA Company, party, organised band of people proceeding somewhere for the purpose of political demonstration.

JATHEDAR Leader of a JATHA.

JI *Lit.*: life, soul. As a suffix to a name denotes affectionate respect.

JIRGA A Council of elders.

JOR MELA Annual fair (Mela) or gathering to commemorate the martyrdom in 1606 of Guru Arjan, the fifth GURU.

KARMA Fate, destiny as the consequence of acts.

KESHA Long, unshorn hair of Sikhs.

KHALISTAN The name given to a projected Sikh State; also referred to as Sikhistan.

KHALSA *Lit.*: pure; word used by Sikhs to denote their community.

KHASSADAR Member of a loose irregular body of police who operated in the Tribal Area of the N.-W.F.P., choosing their own officers and finding their own rifles.

KI JAI Victory (Jai) of.

KIRPAN Sikh dagger, a Sikh religious emblem.

KOTWAL The chief police-station in a city.

KULLAGHORIS A PATHAN tribe.

LAKH 100,000.

LAMBARDAR Headman of a village.

MAHASABHA *Lit.*: Great Assembly. Hindu Mahasabha: a political party based on militant Hinduism.

MAHISYA One of the SCHEDULED CASTES of Bengal.

MAHSUDS A PATHAN tribe.

MALIK A Muslim title inferior to Khan and Amir. Chief man of one of the kinship groups into which PATHAN tribes are divided.

MARWARI Strictly a native of Marwar in Rajputana; often settled elsewhere in India; usually a banker or merchant; loosely used for trader, synonymously with BANIA.

MAULANA *Lit.*: our Master; title of respect accorded to Muslim judges, heads of religious orders and persons of great learning.

MAULVI Judge or Doctor of Law. Title of respect often given to learned Muslims.

MAZDOOR SANGH Worker Party.

MOHALLA A quarter or area of a town.

MORCHA *Lit.*: a ditch, entrenchment, sometimes used in the sense of a defensive battle position.

NAGAS A group of hill tribes in Assam and Burma.

NAWAB Originally a Governor under the Moghul Empire; thence a title of rank conferred on Muslim nobles.

NAWABZADA Son of a Nawab.

NIHANG SIKHS A militant Sikh sect.

PANTH A path, way of life, sect, religious order, used particularly of the Sikh Community.

PANTHIC BOARD Board representative of the Panth (Sikh Community).

PANTHIC PARTY (SIKH) Formed spring 1946 in Punjab Assembly to resist idea of Pakistan.

PARDHAN Head (of community).

PATHAN Generic name given to Pushtu-speaking peoples inhabiting North-West Frontier of India and Afghanistan.

PHULKIAN STATES The States of Patiala, Jind and Nabha whose rulers were all descended from a common ancestor, Phul.

POTHOHAR (POTHAR) Area near Rawalpindi.

QAID–E–AZAM The Supreme Ruler.

RASHTRIYA SWAYAM SEWAK SANGH (R.S.S.S.) National Volunteer Service Association. The para-military arm of militant Hindu nationalism.

RED SHIRTS Congress volunteer movement of N.W.F.P. started by Khan Abdul Ghaffar Khan.

SALMANIS A PATHAN tribe.

SARDAR (SIRDAR) *Lit.*: a chief, leader. Title borne by all Sikhs, also by some Hindus and Muslims.

SCHEDULED CASTES or Depressed Classes. At the lower end of the scale of castes; considered to cause pollution by touch.

SHAHI JIRGA Royal JIRGA; a principal Council of Elders.

SHIA (SHIAH) *Lit.*: party, sect. The name given by other Muslims to those who believe that Ali, cousin and son-in-law of the Prophet, was his rightful successor.

SHINWARIS A PATHAN tribe.

SHIROMANI AKALI DAL Central Akali Organisation.

SHIROMANI RIASTI AKALI DAL Central State Akali Organisation.

SHRI (SRI) Sanskrit term used by Hindus to denote 'Mr.'.

SIKH *Lit.*: disciple. Follower of Guru Nanak (1469–1538), the first of the line of ten Gurus (religious preceptors) who formulated the Sikh faith and welded the Sikhs into an independent community.

TENTH GURU Guru Gobind Singh (*see* Index of Persons).

TUMANDAR Chief of a tribe.

WAZIRS A PATHAN tribe.

INDEX OF PERSONS
WITH BIOGRAPHICAL NOTES

FOR THE PERIOD 22 MARCH–30 MAY 1947

The extensive correspondence of the Secretary of State (Lord Pethick-Lawrence and Lord Listowel) and the Viceroy (Lord Mountbatten), whether written or telegraphed, can be readily followed in the Summary of Documents at the beginning of the Volume and for that reason it is not listed again in this Index.

Neither previous nor subsequent changes in office are listed unless they have an immediate relevance to the contents of this Volume. A list giving the names of principal holders of office in this period is to be found on pages xxxiii–xxxv.

The references are to Document Numbers

CROSTHWAITE-EYRE, Colonel Oliver Eyre, M.P. (Con.) for New Forest and Christchurch Division of Hampshire from 1945 451

CUMMING-BRUCE, Francis Edward Hovell-Thurlow, Principal Private Secretary to the Secretary of State for Dominion Affairs 529

CUNNINGHAM, Sir George, I.C.S., Governor of North-West Frontier Province 1937–46 171

CUNNINGHAM, Admiral Sir John Henry Dacres, First Sea Lord and Chief of the Naval Staff 1946–8 416

CURRIE, Colonel Douglas Hendrie, Military Secretary to the Viceroy from 1944 24, 29, 33–4

CURZON OF KEDLESTON, Marquess (George Nathaniel Curzon 1859–1925), Viceroy 1899–1905 as Baron Curzon of Kedleston 205

DALTON, Hugh, M.P. (Lab.) for Bishop Auckland Division of Durham; Chancellor of the Exchequer from 1945 54, 144, 193, 320, 341, 437, 447, 451, 521

DAULTANA, Mian Mumtaz Muhammad Khan, General Secretary of the Punjab Muslim League; Member, Punjab Legislative Assembly 32, 40, 263

DAWN, EDITOR OF see ALTAF HUSAIN

de la FARGUE, Lieutenant-Colonel Dudley Gordon Heriot, Chief Secretary to the Govt of the North-West Frontier Province from 1944 122, 162

DEPUTY COMMANDER-IN-CHIEF, INDIA see SMITH

DEPUTY INSPECTOR-GENERAL OF POLICE, C.I.D., PUNJAB see JENKIN

DEPUTY INSPECTOR-GENERAL OF POLICE, RAWALPINDI RANGE, PUNJAB see SCOTT, J. A.

DEPUTY LEADER OF MUSLIM LEAGUE IN LEGISLATIVE ASSEMBLY see YAMIN KHAN

DEPUTY PRIVATE SECRETARY TO THE VICEROY see SCOTT, I. D.

DEVELOPMENT MINISTER, PUNJAB see SWARAN SINGH

DEWAS JUNIOR, Maharaja of 44

DHOLPUR, Maharaj-Rana of 44, 187–8, 510, 542

DISTRICT (DEPUTY) COMMISSIONER, PESHAWAR see SHAH

DISTRICT MAGISTRATE, AMRITSAR see FRASER, J. D.

DISTRICT MAGISTRATE, BENARES see SINCLAIR–DAY

DONALDSON, Eion Pelly, Assistant Secretary, External Dept, India Office from 1945 82, 213, 433

DOW, Sir Hugh, I.C.S., Governor of Sind 1941–6; Governor of Bihar 1946–7 17, 42, 49, 51, 53, 81, 98, 108, 136, 147, 158, 168–9, 206, 211, 220, 239, 253, 349, 354, 451, 473

DUNDAS, Ambrose Dundas Flux, I.C.S., Secretary, Govt of India, War Dept 1946–7; on special duty Foreign and Political Dept 1936 213

DUNGARPUR, Maharawal of 44

DYER, Brigadier-General Reginald Edward Harry, Indian Army (retd 1920); commanded troops of 45th Infantry Brigade at Amritsar, 13 April 1919 468

EADY, Sir Wilfrid Griffin, Joint Second Secretary, H.M. Treasury from 1942 288

EDE, James Chuter, M.P. (Lab.) for Mitcham Division of Surrey 1923, for South Shields 1929–31 and from 1935; Home Secretary from 1945 144, 447, 521

EDEN, Robert Anthony (later 1st Earl of Avon), M.P. (Con.) for Warwick and Leamington; Secretary of State for Foreign Affairs 1940–5 513

ELLIOTT, Colonel James Gordon, Indian Army; Deputy Secretary (Mil.), Defence Committee, India 1947–8 215

ERSKINE CRUM, Lieutenant-Colonel Vernon Forbes, Conference Secretary to Viceroy from March 1947 14, 20, 24,

JENKINS (cont.):

for violent agitation against Muslims 109; his discussion with Kartar Singh on 10 April 1947 115; expresses pessimistic views on partition of the Punjab 141, 147, 263, 274, 298, 305, 314, 321, 330, 332, 374, 403, 410, 450, 485; at Governors' Conference 147, 158; on attitude of the Services in the Punjab 147, 160; his impartiality challenged by Liaquat 148; on steps required to give effect to partition of the Punjab 156; his reply to Liaquat's strictures 160, 178; sets out dangers of a purely Muslim Ministry in the Punjab 212; his discussion with Abell on Punjab situation on 26 April 1947 235; objects to proposal that he and Mountbatten should jointly interview Mamdot 244; his meetings and correspondence with Mamdot on formation of a Ministry 248, 261, 276, 334–5, 450 n.; comments on proposal to form regional Ministries 262; reports Sikh preparations for an offensive 263; and proposal for referendum in the Punjab 274 n., 290, 300, 305, 314, 317, 320–1, 323, 491; comments on Baldev Singh's partition demands 332; records views on partition expressed by Ujjal Singh and Kartar Singh 336; on problems of partitioning the Punjab 404; attempts joint discussion with party leaders 425; interview with Master Tara Singh on 19 May 1947 483; reports on incendiarism in Lahore 500; his need for complete Brigade for Lahore area alone 500, 531, 535, 542; on martial law 536; his notes on interviews with Liaquat and Baldev Singh on 25 and 26 May 1947 537; also 26, 59, 67, 161, 169, 173, 208, 216, 229, 240, 264, 354, 362–3, 394, 407, 451, 457, 468, 501

JIND, Maharaja of 109, 173

JINNAH, Miss Fatima 108, 207, 211, 276

JINNAH, Mahomed Ali, President, All-India Muslim League 1916, 1920 and from 1934; called Qaid-i-Azam (the Great Leader); Nehru's opinion of 11;

Liaquat's remarks on 12; Matthai's remarks on 15; Azad's remarks on 27; and question of Pakistan remaining in the Commonwealth 28–9, 119, 165, 225, 229, 232, 276, 360, 368–9, 409, 416, 452, 473, 485, 509, 521, 527; and coalition Cabinet in Bengal 30, 174, 487; and Gandhi's scheme 47, 53, 55, 66, 75–7, 79, 83, 85, 96, 129, 131, 155, 165; his interviews with Mountbatten 84, 92, 101, 105, 116, 229, 287, 310, 473; his possible inclusion in Interim Government 87, 96, 105, 110, 119, 121, 132, 139, 147, 165, 181; firmly opposed to reversion to Cabinet Mission Plan 92, 101, 116, 119, 131, 165, 174, 194, 216, 220, 229, 264, 276, 318, 320, 322, 352, 463; his insistence on splitting the Defence Forces 92, 101, 105, 161, 276 Annex, 411, 416, 502; and joint appeal with Gandhi for truce to violence 96, 101, 116, 124–5, 131–2, 136, 151–3, 158, 165, 167–8, 171, 176, 179, 182, 191, 210–11, 220, 287, 348, 400, 426, 507, 554, 560; Mountbatten on his personality 119, 165, 264; and a truncated Pakistan 147, 149, 158, 165, 181, 211, 214, 243, 276, 305, 351, 540; his meeting with Shone 159; and transfer of population 173, 240, 276, 338; and elections in N.W.F.P. 203, 259, 287, 322, 327, 351, 429; and League leaders held as prisoners in Peshawar 209, 238, 276, 287, 351; and formation of League Ministry in Punjab 212, 229, 244, 287, 450; his statement of 24 April on N.W.F.P. 214 App.; agreeable to a united Bengal remaining independent and not joining Pakistan 227–9, 242, 320, 485; and draft announcement 231, 256; informed of results of Mountbatten's visit to N.W.F.P. 265; his Press statement of 1 May 1947 demanding complete Pakistan 274, 276 Annex, 305, 314, 321–2, 351; unwillingness to accept partition of Bengal and Punjab 276, 463, 491, 502, 505, 514, 540, 553; and referendum in N.W.F.P. 310, 312, 322, 326–7, 341, 350, 354, 378, 380, 463, 480, 485; has meetings with

KNIGHT, Sir Henry Foley, I.C.S., Adviser to the Governor of Bombay 1939–46; Acting Governor of Bombay March–June 1945; Acting Governor of Madras Feb.–May 1946; Acting Governor of Burma June–Aug. 1946; Acting Governor of Assam Sept.–Dec. 1946 134

KRIPALANI (KIRPALANI), Acharya J. B., General Secretary, Indian National Congress 1934–46; President, Indian National Congress from Oct. 1946 53, 112, 124–5, 131, 136–7, 140, 165, 168, 423, 467, 560

KRIPALANI, Suchetadevi, wife of Acharya J. B. Kirpalani 112, 165

KRISHNAMACHARI, Sir Vangal Thiruven-katachari, Diwan of Baroda 1927–44; Prime Minister of Jaipur from 1946 68, 117, 146, 236

KUNZRU, Pandit Hirday Nath, Member, Council of State; President, Servants of India Society from 1936; presided over National Liberal Federation 1934 138

LAITHWAITE, Sir (John) Gilbert, Private Secretary to the Viceroy 1936–43; Assistant Under-Secretary of State, India Office 1943; an Under-Secretary (Civil) of the War Cabinet 1944–5; Deputy Under-Secretary of State for Burma 1945–7 19

LASCELLES, Sir Alan Frederick, Private Secretary to the King from 1943 417, 484

LASCELLES, Captain John F., Personal Assistant to Lord Ismay 141

LAYCOCK, Major-General Robert Edward, Chief of Combined Operations 1943–7 416

LENIN, name assumed by Vladimir Ilyich Ulyanov (1870–1924), leader of the Bolshevik revolution 64

LIAQUAT (LIAQAT) ALI KHAN, Nawab-zada, General Secretary, All-India Muslim League from 1936; Deputy Leader of Muslim League Party in the Indian Legislative Assembly from 1940; Member, Interim Govt (Finance) from 26 Oct. 1946; interviews with Mountbatten 12, 65, 126, 178, 287, 310, 442, 473; his budget proposals 15, 30, 59, 204; and sterling balances 46, 193, 275, 508; and I.N.A. 50, 52, 60, 62, 69, 108; and compensation for Services 59; and appointments committee 65, 95–6, 100, 126, 145; his correspondence with Mountbatten about division of the Armed Forces 94, 101, 106, 126, 135, 138, 164, 220; his desire that Pakistan should be a dominion 126, 161, 190, 249; writes to Mountbatten about Punjab situation 148, 160; his paper on partition of Armed Forces 161, 211, 215, 221, 276; and elections in N.W.F.P. 162, 171, 185, 203, 209, 211, 310, 327; discusses Punjab situation with Mountbatten 178, 287; and situation in N.W.F.P. 190–1, 287; and Scheduled Castes in Bengal 190, 264; asks Mountbatten to allow Muslims to carry swords 211; his talk on 29 April 1947 with Mieville about Bengal and Punjab 249, 276; outline of partition plan discussed with 290, 320, 352, 405; and referendum in N.W.F.P. 310, 312; invited to meeting of leaders on 17 May 1947 383; comments on revised plan 443; unwilling to sign draft Heads of Agreement 454; his talk with Mieville on 19 May 1947 490; his interview with Jenkins on Punjab situation 537; writes to Mountbatten about situation in Gurgaon district 558; also 9, 11, 29, 54, 74, 125, 129, 139, 150, 163, 165, 177, 181, 192, 200, 205, 214, 216, 248, 280, 290, 301–2, 337, 339, 351, 458, 467, 476, 489, 496

LINLITHGOW, 2nd Marquess of (Victor Alexander John Hope), Viceroy and Governor-General of India 1936–43 21, 75, 209

LISTOWEL, 5th Earl of (William Francis Hare), Parliamentary Under-Secretary of State for India and Burma 1944–5; Postmaster-General 1945–7; Secretary of State for India and Burma from 23 April 1947. *See note at head of this Index.* 19, 30, 54, 157, 166

PATEL (*cont.*):
ance by Muslim League 454; and proposals for transfer of power in interim period 472, 494; suggests declaration of martial law in Punjab 501, 531, 535–6, 542; and Andaman Islands 553; protests against retrocession of jurisdiction over Abu 556; *also* 18, 29–30, 46, 68, 75–6, 84, 139, 164–5, 181, 204, 236, 247, 276, 293, 319, 366, 385, 441, 467, 471, 476, 513, 522, 554, 560

PATIALA, Maharaja of, Pro-Chancellor of the Chamber of Princes from March 1946 9–10, 68, 109, 158, 165, 173, 184, 211, 310, 314, 321, 354, 454, 468, 492, 510–11, 542

PATNA, Maharaja of 44

PATRICK, Sir Paul Joseph, Assistant Under-Secretary of State, India Office from 1941 107, 340, 376

PERHAM, Miss Margery, Director, Institute of Colonial Studies, Oxford 1945–8 418

PERSONAL SECRETARY TO THE VICEROY *see* BROCKMAN

PETHICK-LAWRENCE, 1st Baron *cr.* 1945 (Frederick William Pethick-Lawrence), Secretary of State for India and Burma 1945–7; Member of Cabinet Mission. *See note at head of this Index.* 333, 376

POLITICAL ADVISER TO THE CROWN REPRESENTATIVE *see* CORFIELD

POLITICAL AGENT (BANNU) NORTH WAZIRISTAN *see* MURRAY

POLITICAL SECRETARY TO THE CROWN REPRESENTATIVE *see* GRIFFIN

PORTER, Alfred Ernest, I.C.S., Secretary, Govt of India, Home Dept 1945–7 206, 209–10, 301

PRASAD, Dr Rajendra, President, Indian National Congress 1934 and 1939; Member, Working Committee, Indian National Congress; Member, Interim Govt (Agriculture and Food) from 2 Sept. 1946; President of the Constituent Assembly 22, 111, 194, 204, 276

PRESIDENT OF THE ALL-INDIA HINDU MAHASABHA *see* MOOKERJI

PRESIDENT OF THE INDIAN NATIONAL CONGRESS *see* KRIPALANI, A. J. B.

PRESS ADVISER *see* CAMPBELL-JOHNSON

PRIME MINISTER OF AFGHANISTAN *see* SHAH MAHMUD

PRIME MINISTER OF NEPAL *see* PADMA SHAMSHERE

PRINCIPAL INFORMATION OFFICER, GOVT OF INDIA *see* IENGAR, A.S.

PRIOR, Lieutenant-Colonel Sir Charles Geoffrey, Indian Political Service, Political Resident, Persian Gulf 1939–46; A.G.G. Baluchistan 1946–7 257, 461, 486

PRITAM SINGH GUJRAN, Sardar, Member of the Akali Dal Working Committee 1947 109

PRIVATE SECRETARY TO THE PRIME MINISTER *see* ROWAN

PRIVATE SECRETARY TO THE SECRETARY OF STATE FOR INDIA *see* HARRIS

PRIVATE SECRETARY TO THE VICEROY *see* ABELL *and* BROCKMAN

QUEEN, H.M.The (Elizabeth, wife of George VI) 124

RAIKUT, Prasanna Deb, M.L.A., Bengal 251

RAISMAN, Sir (Abraham) Jeremy, I.C.S., Finance Member, Viceroy's Executive Council 1939–45 442

RAJAGOPALACHARI (–RIA, –RIAR and the abbreviation RAJAJI), Chakravarti; Prime Minister of Madras 1937–9; resigned from the Working Committee, Indian National Congress April 1942; Member, Interim Govt for Industries and Supplies from 2 Sept. 1946, for Education and Arts from 26 Oct. 1946 and for Industries and Supplies from 13 Jan. 1947 75, 121, 276

RAMPUR, Nawab of 188

RANCE, Major-General Sir Hubert Elvin, Director of Civil Affairs, Burma 1945–6; Governor of Burma 1946–8 144

INDEX OF SUBJECTS

The references are to Document Numbers